ANNUAL REVIEW OF PSYCHOLOGY

ANNUAL REVIEW OF PSYCHOLOGY

MARK R. ROSENZWEIG, *Editor*
University of California, Berkeley

LYMAN W. PORTER, *Editor*
University of California, Irvine

VOLUME 30

1979

ANNUAL REVIEWS INC.   4139 EL CAMINO WAY   PALO ALTO, CALIFORNIA 94306

COPYRIGHT © 1979 BY ANNUAL REVIEWS INC., PALO ALTO, CALIFORNIA, USA. ALL RIGHTS RESERVED. The appearance of the code at the bottom of the first page of an article in this serial indicates the copyright owner's consent that copies of the article may be made for personal or internal use, or for the personal or internal use of specific clients. This consent is given on the condition, however, that the copier pay the stated per-copy fee of $1.00 per article through the Copyright Clearance Center, Inc. (P. O. Box 765, Schenectady, NY 12301) for copying beyond that permitted by Sections 107 or 108 of the US Copyright Law. The per-copy fee of $1.00 per article also applies to the copying, under the stated conditions, of articles published in any Annual Review serial before January 1, 1978. Individual readers, and nonprofit libraries acting for them, are permitted to make a single copy of an article without charge for use in research or teaching. This consent does not extend to other kinds of copying, such as copying for general distribution, for advertising or promotional purposes, for creating new collective works, or for resale.

REPRINTS   The conspicuous number aligned in the margin with the title of each article in this volume is a key for use in ordering reprints. Available reprints are priced at the uniform rate of $1.00 each postpaid. The minimum acceptable reprint order is 5 reprints and/or $5.00 prepaid. A quantity discount is available.

International Standard Serial Number: 0066-4308
International Standard Book Number: 0-8243-0230-3
Library of Congress Catalog Card Number: 50-13143

Annual Reviews Inc. and the Editors of its publications assume no responsibility for the statements expressed by the contributors to this Review.

PRINTED AND BOUND IN THE UNITED STATES OF AMERICA

PREFACE

This thirtieth volume of the *Annual Review of Psychology* appears in 1979, the year that many consider to be the centenary of psychology's emergence as a separate discipline. We are honored to mark the occasion with a prefatory chapter by Jean Piaget. Dr. Piaget's chapter also initiates a new feature in the *Annual Review of Psychology*: succeeding volumes in this series will continue to include prefatory chapters by distinguished senior psychologists.

The second chapter also departs from our usual list of topics. It is a consideration by Conrad Mueller of the sense in which this is psychology's centennial year and, more generally, of the origins of scientific psychology.

Further emphasis on the long-term development of psychology was achieved in this volume by inviting more chapters than usual from senior psychologists who bring to their reviews the perspective of long involvement with a field of research. We regret that three chapters planned do not appear; the chapters on "Electrophysiology and Behavior" and "Multidimensional Scaling" are now scheduled for Volume 31.

After five years on the Editorial Committee, Conrad Mueller now ends his service, to the regret of his fellow members. Throughout his term, Connie not only demonstrated wide knowledge of the field and insistence on the highest of standards for reviewing, but he was also particularly instrumental in planning this thirtieth volume. We welcome Richard L. Solomon as a new member of the Committee.

M. R. R.

L. W. P.

SOME RELATED ARTICLES IN OTHER *ANNUAL REVIEWS*

From the *Annual Review of Anthropology,* Volume 7 (1978):

Cognition as a Residual Category in Anthropology, Laboratory of Comparative Human Cognition

Apes and Language, Jane H. Hill

The Social Organization of Behavior: Interactional Approaches, R. P. McDermott and David R. Roth

Context in Child Language, Deborah Keller-Cohen

From the *Annual Review of Sociology,* Volume 4 (1978):

Achievement Ambitions, Kenneth I. Spenner

Theories of Social Conflict, Anthony Oberschall

Business and Society, Ivar Berg

Human Spatial Behavior, Mark Baldassare

The Comparative Sociology of Organizations, Cornelis J. Lammers

Social Experiments, Henry W. Riecken

From the *Annual Review of Neuroscience,* Volume 2 (1979):

The Metamorphosis of a Psychobiologist, Seymour S. Kety

The Development of Behavior in Human Infants, Premature and Newborn, Peter H. Wolff and Richard Ferber

The Biology of Affective Disorders, Edward J. Sachar and Miron Baron

Visual Areas of the Mammalian Cerebral Cortex, David C. Van Essen

The Brain as a Target for Steroid Hormone Action, Bruce S. McEwen, Paula G. Davis, Bruce Parsons, and Donald W. Pfaff

From the *Annual Review of Medicine,* Volume 29 (1978):

Control of the Onset of Puberty, Robert M. Boyar

Informed Consent, George J. Annas

Genetic Transmission of Schizophrenia, Dennis K. Kinney and Steven Matthysse

Anorexia Nervosa: Recent Investigations, Katherine A. Halmi

From the *Annual Review of Physiology,* Volume 41 (1979):

Hibernation: Neural Aspects, E. Craig Heller

Avian Orientation and Navigation, William Keeton

Posterior Parietal Cortex: Relations of Unit Activity to Sensorimotor Function, Ian Darian-Smith, Kenneth Johnson, and Anthony Goodwin

Annual Review of Psychology
Volume 30, 1979

CONTENTS

RELATIONS BETWEEN PSYCHOLOGY AND OTHER SCIENCES,
  Jean Piaget   1
SOME ORIGINS OF PSYCHOLOGY AS SCIENCE, *Conrad G. Mueller*   9
AUDITORY PSYCHOPHYSICS, *Constantine Trahiotis and Donald E.*
  Robinson   31
HUMAN MEMORY, *Fergus I. M. Craik*   63
PSYCHOLOGICAL DEVELOPMENT: EARLY EXPERIENCE,
  J. McVicker Hunt   103
WHAT'S CULTURAL ABOUT CROSS-CULTURAL COGNITIVE
  PSYCHOLOGY?, *Laboratory of Comparative Human Cognition*   145
PREVENTION: THE CLINICAL PSYCHOLOGIST, *Lois Barclay*
  Murphy and Colin Frank   173
THE BIOLOGY OF MOTIVATION, *Sebastian P. Grossman*   209
ORGANIZATIONAL BEHAVIOR, *Terence R. Mitchell*   243
NEURAL MECHANISMS AND BEHAVIORAL ASPECTS OF TASTE,
  C. Pfaffmann, M. Frank, and R. Norgren   283
CONCEPTS OF MOTOR ORGANIZATION, *F. A. Miles and E. V.*
  Evarts   327
INFORMATION PROCESSING MODELS OF COGNITION, *Herbert A.*
  Simon   363
SOCIAL AND CULTURAL INFLUENCES ON PSYCHOPATHOLOGY,
  John S. Strauss   397
THE PSYCHOLOGY OF GROUP PROCESSES, *Alvin Zander*   417
SMALL GROUP METHODS OF PERSONAL CHANGE, *John J.*
  Hartman   453
PERSONNEL SELECTION AND CLASSIFICATION SYSTEMS, *Marvin*
  D. Dunnette and Walter C. Borman   477
FACIAL EXPRESSIONS OF EMOTION, *Paul Ekman and Harriet*
  Oster   527
COUNSELING PSYCHOLOGY, *John D. Krumboltz, Jane F.*
  Becker-Haven, and Kent F. Burnett   555
INDIVIDUAL DIFFERENCES IN COGNITIVE ABILITIES, *John B.*
  Carroll and Scott E. Maxwell   603
INDEXES
  Author Index   641
  Subject Index   663
  Cumulative Index of Contributing Authors, Volumes 26 to 30   688
  Cumulative Index of Chapter Titles, Volumes 26 to 30   690
CHAPTERS PLANNED FOR VOLUME 31 (1980)   694

Jean Piaget

Ann. Rev. Psychol. 1979. 30:1–8
Copyright © 1979 by Annual Reviews Inc. All rights reserved

RELATIONS BETWEEN PSYCHOLOGY AND OTHER SCIENCES

❖300

Jean Piaget

Centre International d'Epistémologie Génétique, Université de Genève, CH-1211 Geneva, Switzerland

CONTENTS

PSYCHOLOGY AND BIOLOGY 1
PSYCHOLOGY AND LOGICO-MATHEMATICAL DISCIPLINES 2
PSYCHOLOGY AND HUMAN SCIENCES 4
    Linguistics 4
    Economics 5
    Sociology 5
PSYCHOLOGY AND CYBERNETICS 6
PSYCHOLOGY AND PHYSICS 7

Psychology occupies a key position in the family of sciences in that it depends upon each of the others, to different degrees, and in turn it illuminates them all in distinct ways.

PSYCHOLOGY AND BIOLOGY

In the relations between psychology and biology these two-way exchanges are particularly striking. It might seem that psychology was completely subordinated to such sciences of organic life as physiology, studies of epigenesis and genetics (extending to analysis of the genome). But we now know well that there is much feedback from behavior to details of organization of the brain and nervous system (see among others the research of Rosenzweig, Krech and Bennett; this and related work is reviewed in the

1

0066-4308/79/0201-0001$01.00

chapter by Hunt in this volume). Psychosomatic medicine shows the existence of even more extensive interactions. Ethology is a branch of both psychology and general biology. As to heredity, it is not clear that its mechanisms are exactly the same for transmission of purely morphological characteristics (a color, the form of a particular organ, etc) or for the formation of general organs that condition behavior (locomotion, etc). We know now that behavior is not simply a result of evolution but is one of the factors that govern evolution. I have in fact written a small book—rather speculative, it is true—to argue that behavior actually is the main driving force behind evolution. It therefore seems probable that the better one knows these connections, the greater will be the influence of causal explanations from psychology on the interpretation of the central mechanisms that biology studies. In turn it seems evident to me that if contemporary psychologists had more knowledge of biology, there would be fewer partisans of pure behaviorism, and Skinner's "black box" would be furnished with more fruitful hypotheses.

PSYCHOLOGY AND LOGICO-MATHEMATICAL DISCIPLINES

While psychology thus seems to depend on biology and also reciprocally to illuminate some parts of biology, it might at first seem that no direct relation links our modest science, which is so young (begun scarcely more than a century ago) and still weak in substance, to the imposing mass of the logico-mathematical disciplines which are so rich and solid. At the most one might say that the psychologist seeks to be as logical as possible in his reasoning and that he borrows some formulas from the theory of probability when he does his statistics. In a word, compared to mathematics, psychology seems like a youngster and scarcely related to the mature giant of the logico-mathematical disciplines which dates from the origins of our scientific civilization (from Greece and the Orient) and which enjoys complete autonomy. It is, for example, inconceivable that a mathematician would consult a psychologist to see whether a new theorem that seems to have been proved is truly valid as to its intrinsic content.

Nevertheless, when one studies the psychogenesis of structures of the intellect, as we have attempted to do in children, one perceives the startling fact of an undeniable convergence between them and the most general structures that the mathematicians are creating. For example, the structuralist school of Bourbaki, to cite living authors, has attempted to reduce the ensemble of presently known mathematical structures to elementary and universal forms which they call "mother-structures" and from which all others can be derived by differentiations or combinations. The three "mother-structures" are the following: (*a*) the algebraic structures with their reversible operations, (*b*) the structures of order, and (*c*) the topological structures (regions, boundaries, etc). Now it happens that before hearing of the work of the Bourbaki school, we had found that the earliest structures achieved by the infant (in the sense of what he can do and not what he thinks or says, which come much later) are these: (*a*) elementary operations dealing with classes and their nesting (union and exclusion), that is, algebraic structures in the sense defined just above; (*b*) ordinal structures that govern relations, for example, in the elementary construction of seriations; and (*c*) topological structures based on regions, enclosures, and boundaries, etc.

This convergence between the abstract structures created by mathematicians and the elementary and very concrete structures formulated by the infant thus shows that the former, as theoretic as are the considerations that governed their construction, are nevertheless "natural" structures in the same sense that we speak of "natural numbers" for the integers 1, 2, 3, 4 ... that each youngster discovers by combining algebraic structures with those of "orders." These "natural" structures thus have roots that go much deeper than those considered in the thematic thinking of scientific mathematics. It follows from this evidence that the roots of mathematics are to be sought in the spontaneous cognitive activity of the human subject, even one who is young and innocent of any scientific thought.

Since such a subject and his cognitive activity constitute the specific concern of psychology from the psychogenetic viewpoint, it is not an exaggeration to say that it is up to psychology to explain to us the formation of elementary mathematics and that, in this sense, if one is not a Platonist or dominated by an a priori philosophy such as that of Kant, there is a linkage, not of course between higher mathematics and the psychogenesis of early behavior, but between the source of logico-mathematical structures and the constructive activities of the subject who is studied by developmental psychology. This is true in the case of the "correspondences" or "morphisms" studied theoretically by McLane and Eilenberg following the Bourbaki school and their elementary forms that the child of 7 to 12 also constructs. (The correspondences employed by Cantor were already known to children well before this great mathematician promoted this concept to the rank of a theoretical instrument.)

What we have just stated demonstrates that the source of mathematics is certainly not psychology but rather the *person* that psychology studies. On the other hand, the *epistemology* of mathematics needs psychology and is based largely on it. Now the epistemology of mathematics is a part of mathematics known by the name of theory of foundations, and this necessarily combines logical considerations with those furnished by the study of psychogenesis. In this sense, psychology plays an indispensible role in the initial or metamathematical sectors of the logico-mathematical disciplines.

There is a fundamental problem of mathematical epistemology to whose solution psychology makes an indispensable contribution. This is the basic question of why mathematics fits so well with physical reality. This is a problem on the biological level concerning adaptation of the organism to the environment, but it is even more profoundly a psychological question since it deals with the possibilities of adaptation of the intellect itself. We find only a single reasonable response to this difficult question. This is that the subject who can be considered to be the creator of logic and of mathematics is also and at the same time one material object among others. He is a physical object not only in terms of his organism but just as much in terms of the physical actions that he exerts on objects (grouping, ordering, etc). Consequently, when he constructs logico-mathematical operations, he does so by extending the material actions that he executes as a physical organism. In a word, the agreement between mathematics and physical reality is accomplished within the physiological organism or by its instrumentality and not only by means of the poor and scanty empirical verifications furnished by its initial actions. So here is a further proof that if mathematics is not derived from psychology, its source is in the activities of the individual who is a physical entity in the form of an organism already highly adapted and intrinsically structured and made known through psychology.

PSYCHOLOGY AND HUMAN SCIENCES

Linguistics

Relations between psychology and human sciences should be simpler than those considered above, but actually they are rather complex because here they are no longer links but rather intersections. To start with linguistics, we know that earlier linguists of the generation of de Saussure did not want to have anything to do with psychology, believing that language as a social institution forced itself on all individuals regardless of their personal characteristics. It took the "Cartesian linguistics" of Chomsky to make people see that intelligence is not subordinated to language but that the inverse is true. But the psychology of Chomsky and his school remains rather impoverished; instead of placing language among the self-regulatory mechanisms where all the cognitive processes belong, he called upon a "fixed innate core," as if it would simplify the problem by throwing it back to biology. Actually, deriving language from sensorimotor intelligence raises many very interesting questions and ones to which it is already possible to offer answers that can be tested experimentally. In any case, the existence of psycholinguistics and especially its psychogenetic forms is a pledge of collaboration that is full of promise.

Economics

Relations between psychology and economic sciences also show partial collaboration and once more in the form of intersections rather than links. Let us limit ourselves to two examples, both of which are rather instructive. The first is impressive in furnishing a method in common and one that can also be stated mathematically; this is the invention by Morgenstern and von Neumann of "game theory," which makes it possible to calculate the strategies best adapted to optimalizing successes in competitions between opponents. Shortly after it was inaugurated in the economic domain, this method was tried out on certain psychological problems; here it showed itself useful even in questions far removed from economic conflicts, such as interpretations of perceptual phenomena. In general one can consider the following as contestants in a game: on the one hand the occurrence of psychological and even physical events (that is, the succession of phenomena as objects of study), and on the other hand the observer who tries to anticipate them and to explain the reasons for his successes and failures.

Another point of convergence between psychology and economics comes this time not from a method of calculation with its decision tables but from attempts to extract a general theory of action. Under the name of "praxeology," certain authors (Kotarbinski and others) have tried to analyze the general conditions that permit effective action. While some economists have criticized this theory as too general or too abstract to be used in economics, others have claimed that this is the basis needed for all economic analyses. It is certain that if these concepts attain the necessary level of precision (and this is still debated), they will be of great interest to psychologists. Since we have sought to find in action the source of all cognition, we will be particularly interested in the success of this enterprise.

We will not consider in this paper the possible influences of Marxist economics on psychological research, because that would take us too far afield and especially because we would be confronted with the problem of carefully disentangling the not inconsequential role of ideologies from what is fertile in all dialectical methods. But since this problem is much more general than the relations between psychology and economics, it would not be prudent to go into it here.

Sociology

If the connections and conflicts between psychology and linguistics or economics are a matter of course, one might suppose that this would be true *a fortiori* between psychology and sociology. It is extraordinary that the latter relations have remained up to now much poorer than the former ones, an exception being the work of the eminent intellect Talcott Parsons. This poverty is certainly due to the sterile disputes aimed at determining to what extent the action and thought of people are based on social factors and to what extent they are due to individual initiative. Now since every person is socialized, even the most solitary of researchers, and since every society is formed of individuals who have nervous systems that are not due to social life, along with the continuous functioning that the nervous systems afford, it should be clear that the real problems lie on a different plane. An approach is suggested in the cognitive domain where we see in the history of science the impressive number of cases of simultaneous but independent discoveries—Newton and Leibniz in the case of the calculus, Darwin and Wallace for evolution through natural selection, and so forth. In such cases it seems that the Zeitgeist functions as a sort of common regulatory system acting at a level that transcends both the social and the individual. The nature of this influence deserves to be analyzed further, but this is not the place for me to attempt to do so.

PSYCHOLOGY AND CYBERNETICS

To return to verifiable hypotheses, let us now consider relations between psychology and the still young but highly promising discipline of cybernetics. This is essentially a theory of teleonomic models that deal, for one thing, with relations of means to ends, for another, with regulatory modulations (positive and negative feedbacks, as exemplified in the chapter by Miles and Evarts in this volume), and generally with the acquisition and transmission of information. As such, cybernetics pertains to all biological and psychological processes as soon as they go beyond simple direct causation. While cybernetic models can be relatively simple when they deal with circumscribed cases of regulation, they become complicated when they reach autoregulatory systems (regulation of regulation) and when they take up problems not yet entirely resolved of the origins and especially the modification of programs. The more complicated are the phenomena to be explained, the more the relations between psychology and cybernetics become interchanges and mutual enrichment. For one thing, cybernetic models afford explanations in domains where earlier thinkers saw only two types of solutions that are now out of date. One was an excessively simple reduction to pure mechanism, in imitation of physics, thus eliminating all purposive or goal-seeking aspects; the other was an equally unfounded vitalism calling, as did Driesch, on "entelechies" or other imaginary metaphysical entities. Cybernetics has thus enriched biology and psychology with new models that make possible interpretations based on equilibria that improve, that is, moving to higher level equilibria and not just returning to the starting point. On the other hand, biology and psychology often supply cybernetics with factual examples that call for more and more complex models of self-organizing systems which can then be studied by simulations (see, for example, the discussion of information processing and of "artificial intelligence" in Simon's chapter in this volume); this affords an enriching stimulation to cybernetic theorists.

PSYCHOLOGY AND PHYSICS

This leads us at last to examine relations between psychology and physics, the domain where at a glance it seems that relations are the most impoverished. But we should start by noting a profound statement made at the start of this century by the great physicist Charles Eugene Guye (the first investigator to have verified experimentally a relativistic prediction of Einstein). Guye maintained that physics is not yet a truly general science since it remains artificially limited to the study of inert matter; he claimed that a complete physics would also study living beings and especially thinking ones. His hopes with regard to living beings are being realized since we now have both biophysics and biochemistry. With regard to the physics of thought we still know nothing. Guye hypothesized that thought might occur through subatomic physical reactions; this is clearly a daring hypothesis but perhaps not impossible.

While awaiting a possible physics of thought, we can point out two kinds of help that psychologists can furnish to physicists and, indeed, to all scientists. The first is to emphasize that what we call an observation is never a pure observation because it always and everywhere implies an interpretation which constitutes a necessary frame of reference, either implicit or inferred. To say, for example, that an object occupies a particular location requires a set of spatial references. To say that it bumps into another object requires certain preconceived ideas about the nature of the collision. When microphysics teaches us that a phenomenon always depends on the reactions of the observer as well as on the object observed, that is true at all levels, and we can note further that the more closely the observer approaches the object, the more the object seems to retreat by becoming more complicated and by raising new problems. This in no way excludes progress in conquest of the object, but it occurs through successive approximations and is never completely achieved; there is always a limit in the mathematical sense. This is not philosophical idealism because the object exists before it is known and it conserves its properties independently of us while it is being explored by experimentation. But the exploration cannot be reduced to a pure "reading" of observables; there is always a contribution of the observer who interprets what he sees, even if he is not aware of interpreting. Nor is this a theory of Kantian noumena, because the apparent object of intuition keeps changing into new phenomena as it is studied experimentally.

A further service that psychology can render to other sciences is to supply a theory of causal explanation. Establishing a law is not an explanation but only the simple generalization of observations without supplying the reason behind them. This is still true when a particular law is subsumed under a more general law; the latter still remains classificatory and alien to reasons. Explanation, on the contrary, implies the construction of a model and elaboration of the model by operations available to the investigator. But he can use these operations in two ways. The first consists simply of applying them as tools of description or measurement; in this case the researcher does not go beyond the reading of observations and still does not attain an explanation. Explanation begins only when the operations are not simply applied but are "attributed" to objects in the sense that these then become "operators" and this permits one to understand how they interact. The clearest and most common example of this is that of the structure of a group when this is attributed to an organized set of phenomena and when their transformations and interactions are taken as the expression of a group located or projected into reality. Thus current microphysics continually uses an ensemble of groups and operators that are attributed to objects and that explain their varied behaviors. The models are constructed by means of operations of the investigator but the models consist in finding these operations at the heart of the phenomena that are to be understood. So that we are no longer simply describing observables but attaining the reasons for the laws in considering constructions that are both objective and outside of ourselves but that we can understand thanks to their analogy with our logico-mathematical structures. A group is, in fact, a system of transformations, and if we project it into the real world we can therefore penetrate to the causal transformations of the world.

Ann. Rev. Psychol. 1979. 30:9–29
Copyright © 1979 by Annual Reviews Inc. All rights reserved

SOME ORIGINS OF PSYCHOLOGY AS SCIENCE

❖301

Conrad G. Mueller

Center for Neural Sciences, Indiana University, Bloomington, Indiana 47401

CONTENTS

THE NOMINAL BEGINNING 9
AN INTERPRETATION OF THIS BEGINNING 12
SOME EVENTS 25 YEARS LATER 14
A SUGGESTED HISTORICAL MODEL 15
FIFTY YEARS OF SYSTEMATIC DEBATE 17
A SEARCH OF PSYCHOLOGY'S PAST 23

THE NOMINAL BEGINNING

This year, 1979, marks the 100th anniversary of the consensual beginning of psychology as a distinctive scientific discipline. It seems appropriate to describe and discuss briefly the when, where, and who of those nominal beginnings, and to examine some of the intellectual linkages between those events and some present psychological activities and interests.

It is customary to acknowledge explicitly that the search for the "when" of an event such as the beginning of a discipline, as with the beginning of the decline and fall of the Roman Empire, is uncomfortably arbitrary. As one attempts to decide which one of several persons, or which one of several dates, seems most appropriate to mark a "beginning," it becomes clear that what we gain by such an exercise is found less in the understanding of the "when, where, and who," but more in an appreciation of "what" was begun. As we make the many arbitrary decisions necessary for eliminating candidates we are, in fact, discovering what parts of psychology were available at a given time, and how well and in what manner these parts were articulated.

9

The search for the date for a beginning quickly pushes to the forefront the prior question of who was involved in this beginning. Historical search has, by consensus, been narrowed to one main line of intellectual inquiry; then the search rather quickly reduces to three or four candidates. The short list of final entries usually includes Fechner, Helmholtz, Wundt, and James. Fechner remains on this list primarily for his major work in psychology, *The Elements of Psychophysics,* published in 1860, but also for his many other contributions to the philosophy of mind and the theory of measurement, including applications to esthetics. Helmholtz remains on the list because he is the best scientist on any list we might generate, long or short, but more specifically because of his major contributions to the psychology and physiology of hearing and vision. Examples of these contributions are seen in the three volumes of the *Handbook of Physiological Optics,* published over the decade of 1856–1866, and the volume on hearing which appeared in 1863. James remains on the list at this late screening primarily because he forces us to ask how much of the modern flavor of psychology we demand. James was concerned with many topics that occupy current psychologists but that were not treated by the other three possible founders. His *Principles of Psychology* did not appear until 1890, but he had begun teaching topics in psychology at Harvard in the middle 1870s. Wundt is on the list because of a prodigious amount of work he did beginning around 1862 in the area he called physiological psychology. The book that had a major influence on the emergence of psychology as a science was his *Principles of Physiological Psychology* which appeared in 1873–1874 and went through six editions in approximately four decades. His writings are extensive in terms of breadth of subject matter as well as magnitude of output. Wundt wrote on topics that ranged from ethics and logic to animal psychology, physiological psychology, and the natural history of man.

Of the four men listed, James would probably be the first to be deleted on grounds of temporal priority. The other three men were doing something in this developing area when James was deciding that such work should be done. Perhaps this priority is shown most clearly by James himself in a letter he wrote while in Europe in 1867.

> It seems to me that perhaps the time has come for psychology to begin to be a science —some measurements have already been made in the region lying between the physical changes in the nerves and the appearance of consciousness . . ., and more may come of it. Helmholtz and a man named Wundt at Heidelberg are working at it. (5).

Helmholtz would probably be dropped from the list next, primarily because he was too busy doing good science to devote much effort to starting a new "discipline." Fechner poses the most difficult final choice because of the priority of his *Elements of Psychophysics* and the fact that he is widely regarded as having exerted an important influence on subsequent measurement and quantitative developments in psychology, notably on the work of Ebbinghaus and later the work of Binet. Some historians of psychology, such as Pillsbury, trace the beginnings jointly to Fechner and Wundt and may be interpreted as giving priority to Fechner. Pillsbury's view is that "Wundt may be said to share with Fechner the honor of founding experimental psychology" (21).

Nevertheless, the consensus is that Wundt should be viewed as the most convincing candidate for "founder" for two major reasons. The first reason is a matter of judged intent; Wundt specifically stated that he intended to mark out psychology as a new science. This can be seen clearly in his preface to the first edition of *Principles of Physiological Psychology* in 1873:

> The work which I here present to the public is an attempt to mark out a new domain of science. I am well aware that the question may be raised, whether the time is yet ripe for such an undertaking. The new discipline rests upon anatomical and physiological foundations which, in certain respects, are themselves very far from solid; while the experimental treatment of psychological problems must be pronounced, from every point of view, to be still at its first beginnings. At the same time the best means of discovering the blanks that our ignorance has left in the subject matter of a developing science is, as we all know, to take a general survey of its present status (28).

This is what Wundt did in the early editions of his *Physiological Psychology*.

The second reason for selecting Wundt derives from the manner in which he and his laboratory were viewed by other scholars. Beginning around 1880 his Leipzig laboratory became the place to go if one was interested in psychology as a science. Within the next 15 years the list of Americans who spent time in the laboratory is impressive. The publication of the first psychological journal, begun in 1881, was associated with this research activity; this was a journal devoted to reporting psychological research in action. The founding of this journal is counted by some historians as a third reason for honoring Wundt as the founder of psychology.

Having decided that Wundt is the preferred candidate, the selection of a date to mark the beginning of experimental psychology becomes more directed. If we take seriously the multiple-criterion argument we used in selecting Wundt, certain dates that might have been plausible on other grounds are eliminated. If the reasons Wundt was chosen are to be based on the joint facts that he articulated that psychology was a science and outlined some of its properties, that he had a functional laboratory which served as more than a demonstration room housing a few items of equipment, and that this laboratory was perceived by others as a place where they could work, then events that satisfy only one of these criteria cannot be used. We have quoted the statement of intent with a dateline of 1873; with the criterion of intent and belief alone, this date could be used. Yet, using only that criterion, we could find passages in his earlier (1862) *Contributions to the Theory of Sense Perception* that would have been almost as convincing. With the intent established by 1873, the date of choice must now involve a judgment of when the laboratory became functional. There is some difference of opinion on this point; yet the differences are not great, and it is not clear that all of the dates suggested are meant to refer to when the laboratory became functional, as opposed to when Wundt went to Leipzig and had some space assigned (1875). Statements by three students of Wundt cover the range of dates offered, 1875 (Scripture), 1878 (Titchener), and 1879 (Cattell). Although it is not good historical technique, one is tempted to let Wundt decide the issue, unless his version seems to be in gross violation of other "facts." Boring (6) quotes Wundt as writing of this period in the following way: ". . . there grew up in the autumn of 1879 some independent research which made use of this space for experimental work." Thus, with Wundt's help we can suggest the when (1879), the where (Leipzig), and the who (Wundt).

AN INTERPRETATION OF THIS BEGINNING

We have picked Wundt, Wundt has picked 1879, and most psychologists are willing to accept these choices as an appropriate solution to the question of what marks the beginning of psychology as science. This acquiescence to the judgment of psychology's historians is very likely to be accompanied by two other observations. The first is that if we ask most psychologists what Wundt did experimentally, or what he represented theoretically or systematically, we find that answers are surprisingly brief. The reply is likely to include some statement about introspection as an experimental method, perhaps a brief reference to a theory of feeling. From some psychologists there may be a few additional comments about attention or apperception; in some of these cases, if the comments start to get detailed, we will usually find that the respondent is talking about Titchener rather than Wundt. Perhaps this observation should not be surprising because there is a second observation. If we inform the respondent of some of the detailed discussions of Wundt's work as it appears in history textbooks, he or she is very likely to feel that the work does not bear importantly on the kind of work and theory that characterizes the last 50 years. For example, for most psychologists, limiting the experimental method to controlled introspection seems to restrict the new science unduly and to lead to a definition of the subject matter of psychology that leaves most of the interesting questions outside of the "new domain of science."

In Wundt's defense the point can be justly made, and it has been made recently by Blumenthal (2), that Wundt has been incompletely treated in most psychology-history textbooks. Setting aside, for the present purposes, Wundt's contributions in the areas of logic and ethics, and restricting ourselves to his writings on psychology, it is clear that his work falls into two broad categories. The first is his work on experimental psychology (as he defines it), the second is his work on *Völkerpsychologie*. The second aspect of his contribution is frequently not even mentioned in history textbooks, and rarely is it discussed in a systematic way. In some cases this treatment may be considered a matter of benign neglect, but a failure to comment on this half of Wundt's work frequently leads to a misinterpretation of what he considered the subject matter of psychology to be. For example, one recent textbook (24) states that "For Wundt, 'psychology,' 'experimental psychology,' and 'physiological psychology' were three terms for the same subject." This gives the reader an incorrect impression of Wundt's views. For Wundt "objective psychology," and "experimental psychology" can both be included under psychology, but the first two terms do not deal with the same subject matters because of the methods that must be used. For Wundt psychology includes many topics that *cannot* be studied by the experimental method, but can be studied objectively. Wundt is so explicit about this issue that it seems puzzling that any systematic treatment of his works would fail to emphasize this point. For example, in his preface to the fifth edition of *Principles of Physiological Psychology,* after describing some of the properties of experimental method he states ". . . fortunately for the science, there are other sources of objective psychological knowledge, which become accessible at the very point where the experimental method fails us." He then briefly describes what *Völkerpsychologie* is, and then says, "The results of ethnic psychology constitute, at the same time, our chief source of information regarding the general psychology of the complex mental processes. In this way, experimental psychology and ethnic psychology form the two principal departments of scientific psychology at large" (28).[1]

Boring's account (3) of Wundt's work is perhaps symptomatic of this unbalanced treatment. In writing a 700 page volume dedicated to Wundt, he devoted less than ten lines to this second aspect of Wundt's work. "The new century brought him the leisure to return to the unfulfilled task, outlined in the *Beiträge* of 1862, the writing of *Völkerpsychologie,* the natural history of man, which only, Wundt thought, could give the scientific answer to the problem of the higher mental processes." That is the extent of the substantive treatment of what Wundt thought was one of the "two principal

[1]Thousands of words have been written about the appropriate translation of the term *Völkerpsychologie;* it probably should be left in the original German to avoid incorrect images of the subject matter. The actual material that is discussed can be used to define the subject matter.

departments" of scientific psychology. Murphy (18), although also very brief in his coverage, seems more receptive to the nature of the work and provides more information as to its substance.

To folk psychology Wundt devoted some of his best energies (1904–1914). Believing that "cultural products," as well as introspective reports, are a legitimate subject matter for psychology, he undertook a systematic psychological interpretation of the data of anthropology and history. His studies on the psychological interpretation of language are perhaps his best-known contributions. He emphasized the interpenetration of psychical and physiological factors in linguistic structure, protesting against that naive psychologism to which phonetics was a mere incident and, with equal explicitness, against that merely philological approach which had sought to explain all linguistic change in terms of the laws of vocal utterance.

Nonetheless, it is important to emphasize that, even with all of the possible amendments to the historical treatment of Wundt, it is still the case that our hypothetical respondent who feels that the Wundtian beginning does not significantly anticipate psychology as it has been for the last 50 years would still be correct. This conclusion is not altered by the fact that no other single individual's work at that time can be viewed as anticipating the subsequent developments more accurately. It is to this problem that we must now turn.

SOME EVENTS 25 YEARS LATER

At the outset the point was made that while the date, the man, and the place per se are not key factors in the understanding of our origins, the search could help us understand what was begun and the manner in which it was articulated. What can we say about "what" was begun? There is general agreement on several conclusions: 1. a functional laboratory devoted to experimental research in psychology was begun; 2. a psychological journal was begun; and 3. a way of thinking about psychology was begun. This way of thinking stated that psychology was a science. Allowing for the previous discussion about Wundt's system to the effect that it included methods other than his experimental method, the fact is that Wundt's work (and his impact) in the first quarter-century of psychology's history, are limited to the experimental phase of his program; it was this method and its related subject matter that were begun in this period. Even accepting that Wundt would eventually write *Völkerpsychologie* (and he does anticipate this work in 1862), it is fair to say that one cannot anticipate from Wundt's work the kind of explosion of ideas and research that engulfed psychology at the end of its first quarter-century. This is not meant as a criticism of Wundt as, I hope, will be clear in a moment. It does say something important about the origins of modern psychology.

Let us select the year 1904 as an anchor date, the end of the first quarter-century of psychology's history. Let us open up a window in time, say 4 years, on each side of that date, and look at the diversity of published works that signal what forces were acting to define psychology. Choosing just a few authors representative of the diversity of ideas related to psychology, we have such works as Adler's *Study of Organic Inferiority* (1907); Baldwin's *Development and Evolution* (1902); Binet's *Suggestability* (1900) and *Experimental Study of Intelligence* (1903); Claraparede's *Psychology of the Child* (1905); Freud's *Interpretation of Dreams* (1900), *Psychopathology of Everyday Life* (1901), and *Three Essays on the Theory of Sexuality* (1905); Hall's *Adolescence* (1904); Hobhouse's *Mind in Evolution* (1901); Jennings's *The Behavior of Lower Organisms* (1906); Jung's *The Psychology of Dementia Praecox* (1907); Loeb's *Forced Movements, Tropisms and Animal Conduct* (1908); McDougall's *Social Psychology* (1908); Morgan's *Animal Behavior* (1900); Sherrington's *Integrative Action of the Nervous System* (1906); Thorndike's *Educational Psychology* (1903) and *The Measurement of Twins* (1905); and Washburn's *The Animal Mind* (1908).

Such a list could easily be tripled, and this is only a list of books. Many other events of equal or greater importance could be listed. Pavlov had just begun his work on conditioning; the first dissertation to use the term "conditioned reflex" appeared in 1903. Pearson, the outstanding statistician, published several papers on the inheritance of mental characteristics in man. Spearman published a factor analysis of intelligence. Obviously none of these works occurred in an intellectual vacuum; for each we could trace an historical path. The point is that in writing the history of this limited number of works, we would be taken to names, ideas, and experiments that are not encountered in the path to Wundt and, through him, to 1904. Not only does the historic path through Wundt not anticipate these events, there is no other particular vantage point in 1879, no other person's work at that time, that would have permitted the forecasting of all of these events. Any interpretation of psychology's origins must deal with this rapid emergence of thinking and research on psychological matters around the turn of the century.

A SUGGESTED HISTORICAL MODEL

What kind of historical model should we use? The common textbook model suggests that experimental psychology as science started with Wundt and that this tradition brought scientific psychology to the turn of the century. By this time criticism had grown from a number of quarters, including some of Wundt's students. At about this time the main features of Wundt's views, with modifications, were systematically articulated by Titchener and he became the focal point for the beginning of a second quarter of a century of debate over the nature, scope, and methods of psychology. Everyone agrees that "other influences" coming from different lines of research played an important role in this debate. This second quarter-century is the period of the so-called "schools" or "systems." If the historian goes beyond that period, the position adopted will range between two main models. One model says that the schools are modified by the debate of the first two decades of the twentieth century; some schools may drop out, but the others continue to exert influence in modified form to the present. The other model says that the schools gradually disappear, or are absorbed, and what emerges is what is euphemistically called the mainstream of psychology. Let us look at two examples of views of the postschool era.

> Although . . . most of the factionalism and intense controversy has diminished, the effect of these questions of the Age of Schools upon the science still remains despite the apparent lack of concern by contemporary psychologists. Thus the events and issues of the Age of Schools are not simply a matter of cultural heritage, but when seen in historical perspective, emerge as valid, ongoing concerns for the field (13).

> We have seen how the various systems of psychological thought came into being, prospered for a time, and then, with the exception of psychoanalysis, were absorbed by the mainstream of contemporary psychology. We also saw that each movement grew strong through opposition to another system. When there was no longer any need for strong and vociferous protest, the schools, as such, died a gradual death. Yet each of these protests died a successful death because it made substantial contributions to psychological thought. Thus, each was a fruitful protest—each accomplished its mission (25).

I should like to propose a different kind of model for the history of psychology. This model has two components. It acknowledges that Wundt established the first experimental psychology laboratory and the first psychological journal, and that this laboratory became one important fountainhead for research in psychology. It credits Wundt with institutionalizing psychology as a discipline. It suggests that Wundt, the tradition that he established, and the tradition from which he came, represent only one path leading from the seventeenth century, when the era of modern science began, to the twentieth century when psychology as science took on its modern form. There were many other paths of science from the seventeenth to the twentieth century that had psychological questions as a major part of their concern. It cannot be assumed that the path through Wundt was the most important path and it is probably not fruitful at this state to try to establish the relative importance of the different paths of intellectual inquiry. Each path branched many times and, in so doing, partially intertwined with other influences; the interdependence of these paths is obvious, yet very difficult to assess. Along each of these paths any one of many individuals *could* have declared and implemented the notion of psychology as an experimental science. While others could have, Wundt did. That is the event and the man that we commemorate in 1979. The event and the man serve as a token or a symbol that, in some nontrivial sense, things were happening in the second half of the nineteenth century that were going to produce a sharp change in thinking. It was the acceleration in the acquisition of information and ideas along each of these paths of inquiry, and the relevance of much of the information and many of the ideas to the formulation of what psychology was all about, that led to the conceptual explosions around the turn of the century.

The second component of the suggested model is that, as we examine each of the quarter-centuries since the first, i.e. since 1904, there is no discernible long-term systematic direction that has emerged following these explosions. There is no agreed-upon systematic mainstream. Psychology has been searching and sampling a variety of directions, trying different ways of talking about its subject matter, but no systematic view can be said to have become dominant for more than a couple of decades. This position may seem unduly pessimistic. This is not to say that there has been no scientific progress. Quite the contrary; the advances in information and understanding about the *specific questions of science,* for example, the day-to-day research concerns that relate to problems of human or animal learning, physiological mechanisms of hunger and thirst, and interpretations of group decision-making processes, have been great indeed. It is only when psychology tries to articulate what the science is all about that it encounters difficulty. Most psychologists feel the need to think along systematic lines, to put their research in some broader context. It is when psychology attempts to do this with some unity that the situation shows itself as being analogous to Truesdell's description of physicists and the laws of thermodynamics, "Every physicist knows exactly what the first and second law mean, but . . . no two physicists agree about them" (22, p. 22).

FIFTY YEARS OF SYSTEMATIC DEBATE

Even a brief examination of the periods that follow the turn of the century shows clear signs of the search for a unified way of thinking about the nature of psychology. The quarter-century from 1904 to 1929 was a period in which the scope and method of research in psychology were intensely debated. The "systematic" (as opposed to the "school") aspects of this period have probably been overdrawn; many of the diverse positions were too vague, too fluid and short-lasting to qualify as systematic positions. Nevertheless, it was an important period precisely because relatively dogmatic positions were adopted which provided targets for debate; such debate held the promise of laying a foundation for the kind of critical analysis that would be required by the science at a later stage. Histories of this period paint the distinctions among the various "psychologies" much more clearly than they appear in the original, but that may be because our descriptions tend to focus on the "leader" rather than on the large number of scientists actually doing research. Boring said of these leaders, "Psychologically the attitude of these men tends to be dynamic and positive; they are quick to attack or to defend, they are possessed of a productive intolerance . . ." (4).

There can be no doubt that the controversy was intense; but the battles were less often between organized, united camps, and they were more often hand-to-hand fights on a shifting terrain and with mixed objectives. Consider structuralism, for example. It probably arose from a footnote in the writings of William James. It became a "system" rubric on the basis of an article by Titchener on the postulates of a structural psychology in 1898. That analogy with the morphological and physiological areas of biology etched into history a distinction that was the basis of much discussion, but was a very small part of the actual area of disagreement. Within 20 years Titchener had decided that ". . . 'functional' and 'structural,' as qualifications of 'psychology,' are now obsolete terms" (26). By the time Murchison began to capture the diversities of early twentieth century psychology in his volumes on the *Psychologies,* Madison Bentley, whose task it was to cover structural psychology, wrote in *Psychologies of 1925* "If we ask today who represents the psychology of 'structure,' I doubt whether we shall find anyone to acknowledge that his own brand is of that kind; though the epithet will often be accompanied by a gesture of indication toward a fellow-psychologist." Later in that same chapter Bentley wrote as if structuralism was already of another time. "We can hardly expect, therefore, to recover the structural point of view of that time unless we consider the counter doctrine of function against which it contended" (1). Five years later in the *Psychologies of 1930,* Nafe, a student of Titchener's, also wrote of structuralism as belonging to another generation.

> Many of the logical and metaphysical questions so important to another generation of psychologists have faded, unanswered, from the picture, and the present generation, impatient of such matters, prefers the risk of untenable positions and temporary confusions to the certainty of time lost in attempts to take positions upon question of fact before the facts are known . . . With the shift of emphasis from systematic considerations to experimentally observed facts, the distinctions between schools of psychology have tended to disappear. . . . (19).

Similar comments could be made about the functionalist view. In *Psychologies of 1930* the reviewer of functionalism says, "There is no functional psychology; rather there are many functional psychologies." That chapter was written by Harvey Carr of the "Chicago" school (within the functionalism school), and he provides an excellent example of the lack of specificity of the "systems" that were extant when he says ". . . we shall use the term functionalism to refer to the American empirical movement that rebelled against the proposed limitations of the structural or existential school of Titchener . . ." (10).

The number of psychologies represented in *Psychologies of 1925* was six; by the time of the *Psychologies of 1930* this number had grown to eleven. The sign that perhaps the science was beginning to mature by the early 1930s is seen not only in the quote from Nafe concerning the shift to experimental emphasis, but also by the fact that Murchison chose *not* to continue this series with a volume of *Psychologies of 1935*. Instead, in 1934 Murchison edited the *Handbook of General Experimental Psychology,* which still stands as a monument to science in action.

In America the third quarter of psychology's century, 1929–1954, was a period of self-consciousness about psychology as science and a period of concern about the nature of science. This was also a period in which systematic issues were hotly debated. It was a period that was ushered in by wide discussion of Bridgman's book *The Logic of Modern Physics,* and a concern about the impact of Operationism on the use of psychological concepts. Bridgman's book had a much greater impact on psychologists than on physicists; as someone said of this period, psychologists mistook a footnote in the philosophy of science for a philosophy of science. But the change in the third quarter far transcended that particular influence. The period was one of a search for an appropriate model or metaphor for psychology. Psychology was still puzzling over what kind of science it was, and it needed some guidelines to pull itself away from the disappointing fruits of the arguments of the "schools." This period of search for a scientific model began at a time when philosophy of science was itself in a kind of euphoric period. Bertrand Russell, Alfred North Whitehead, and Ludwig Wittgenstein were dominant figures in philosophy, and the prevailing mood was that "the empirical content of science could be expressed in the formulae of classical mathematics, and would therefore be arranged ultimately in a closed system of axioms . . ." (9). The goal then would be ". . . to establish a system of axioms from which all the phenomena of nature could be derived" (9). The proof that not even algebra could be represented in the manner being prescribed for science was not appreciated soon enough to save some of the energies expended in the early part of this period by psychologists.

Psychology's third quarter-century was a period that produced a book entitled *A Dynamic Theory of Personality* (15) that devoted the first 42 pages to a discussion of the differences between Aristotelian and Galilean modes of thought in psychology. It was a period that produced the volume by Hull et al on *The Mathematicodeductive Theory of Rote Learning* (12), in which some 18 postulates and 86 definitions were generated with the net effect of accounting for the serial position curve in verbal learning and a few related phenomena. It was a period of topological diagrams of an individual's "life space," and vector diagrams of the dynamic forces acting on (or in) the organism.

In spite of the uncertain advances along systematic lines, this was a period of rapid growth of solid scientific research in many different areas. While there may have been an overly optimistic view of the fruits of mathematization and postulational procedures, it was a period in which the foundations for such techniques as factor analysis, test theory, scaling, etc were broadly expanded. In areas such as physiological and sensory psychology, human and animal learning, and social and abnormal psychology, the empirical bases of psychology as science were made as firm in that period as they have ever been. This period established psychology as a provable science, not just an "in-principle" science.

Yet, at the systematic level, this period also ended in disenchantment. The plan to solve psychology's systematic differences by being quantitative, precise, and explicit, the plan to formulate issues in such a way that they would be testable against alternative formulations did not succeed in any general way. Formulations that could be solved to many decimal places included terms that could not be contained. The broad programmatic formulations were still found to be remarkably immune to disproof. To borrow a metaphor from Medawar used in another context, "A lava flow of *ad hoc* explanation pours over and around all difficulties, leaving only a few smoothly rounded prominences to mark where they might have lain" (17).

There are two reasons for thinking that the changes in emphasis and direction that we have seen in the last 75 years cannot be viewed as a permanent progressive development, a systematic mainstream. The first reason is the nature of the rhetoric of change. The words that were used when (and after) these changes took place are not the words of scientific advance; they are more characteristic of the words of moral victory. For example, one very prominent cognitive psychologist, in commenting on the approximately three decades following the demise of the introspective method, referred to them as "thirty arid years" (20). Another psychologist summarized some of the changes in personality theory in this 75 year period under the title *The Death and Rebirth of Psychology* (23). Such phrases offer a sign of the apocalyptic view of some of these changes of viewpoint. Compare the phrase "thirty arid years" to the manner in which Max Born, the great quantum physicist, handled the changeover from Bohr's atomic model to quantum mechanical theory. Born had been asked to give a series of lectures at MIT just after the appearance of Heisenberg's first paper on the new quantum theory and after Born had written a paper with Heisenberg giving the problem a new mathematical framework.

Though the results contained in this third paper left no doubt in my mind as to the superiority of the new methods to the old, I could not bring myself (in beginning the lecture series) to plunge directly into the new quantum mechanics. To do this would not only be to deny to Bohr's great achievement its due need of credit, but even more to deprive the reader of the natural and marvelous development of an idea (7).

It is this notion of a cumulative building on previous achievements that seems to be lacking in our systematic debates. We seem to be unable to generate the kind of attitude expressed by Brett in discussing Wundt's contributions: "But no generous student of history would care to emphasize this change of mood as a disparagement of the life-work of Wundt. Progress is itself a kind of critic; but it does not despise the things it must discard" (8).

The second consideration that leads me to view recent changes more as exploration rather than advance is the transferability of attitudes from one period to another with frequent reversals back to earlier periods. Consider the following statements:

The inclusion of subjective experiences in the world of reality knowable by the scientist (for us now defined as wanting to know all of reality, not just the shared, public portions of it) breeds two consequences at least. One is the obvious differentiation between the immediacy of experiential knowledge and the distance of what I have called "spectator knowledge" (16).

In other words, whatever all men inevitably mean by the word I (the empirical *ego* of philosophy), whenever they say I think, or feel, or intend this or that; and whatever they understand others to mean by using similar language—thus much and no more, we propose at first to include under the term "mind" (14).

Is the first a part of the debate in the Wundt-Titchener era? Is the second from a discussion of self- or ego-psychology? The answer is no on both counts. The first is a 1967 expression of intent and interest from humanistic psychology; the second is a quote from Ladd's *Elements of Physiological Psychology* (1887), published over 90 years ago.

When we look at the changes that have taken place in each of the quarter-centuries since 1904, we do not find that they have been brought about by any crucial or provocative set of experiments, nor do we find any strikingly new or different set of ideas or theoretical developments that demanded the change. There are, in each case, new ideas and new experiments, but they did not cause the change in emphasis, they arose to fill a vacuum. The changes seem to have taken place when some particular effort or emphasis or strategy had run its course. One is reminded of the passage from T. S. Eliot:

So here I am . . . Twenty years largely wasted/ Trying to use words, and every attempt/ Is a wholly new start, and a different kind of failure/ Because one has only learnt to get the better of words/ For the thing one no longer has to say, or the ways in which/ One is no longer disposed to say it. And so each adventure is a new beginning, a raid on the inarticulate/ With shabby equipment always deteriorating . . . (11).

Reference was made earlier to the fact that one author had characterized the years from approximately 1930–1960 as "thirty arid years." In my opinion any objective analysis of the twentieth century will view that period as establishing psychology as a science in a sense that was not true in any other period. Yet the difference of opinion is important. The basis for that acrid view was that during that period it was relatively uncommon to encounter the use of the term "mind." The adjective mental was frequently used, but only in some areas of the psychological literature. It was a period that placed great emphasis on methodology and definition, with a resulting emphasis on behavior (although, it must be emphasized, not necessarily behaviorism in the "school" sense of that term). By the 1970s the wave of rejection of that third quarter and the return to an earlier mode of thinking had grown to the point that a popular textbook dealing with the psychobiology of sensory coding stated that psychology "is a science whose proper content is the set of the inner awareness . . ." A few pages later we find that

> . . . it is to the behavior of others that we must turn for our experimental data. This methodological twist often obscures the fact that the behavior is not the subject matter of the psychological sciences, but is rather only an approach to the real content, which is represented by such symbolic terms as consciousness, awareness, thought . . . (27).

It is clear that, for this author, conceding the methodological position of the behaviorist did not mean that the subject matter of the science had changed. Perhaps there is a little ambiguity with terms such as "subject matter" and "real content," but the passage raises an interesting problem. It is a problem similar to one encountered during the intense debate over operational definition of terms. The point being made is that the kinds of measurements one makes do not define a discipline. There are thousands of scientists whose laboratory measurements have the dimensions of voltage, current, or impedance. These scientists may be physicists, chemists, neurophysiologists, physiological psychologists, or members of any one of a number of other disciplines. Similarly, there are thousands of scientists studying behavior; zoologists, psychologists, anthropologists, linguists, sociologists, and economists are representatives of just a few disciplines. While measuring instruments may in some important sense define the "subject matter," a discipline is defined by the questions that it asks. That topic, the questions that psychologists ask, must be the focal point in any attempt to resolve systematic differences.

In trying to understand the systematic differences that have persisted within psychology for the past 75 years, perhaps the most important step we could take would be to search through our past and try to outline explicitly what kinds of questions were being asked. In particular, what questions were brought to the twentieth century along the many paths of scientific inquiry. Therein may lie a solution to the systematic deadlock that has existed in psychology. It may not be a solution in the sense that some view will "win." It may be a solution in the sense that there might be some agreement on what questions are empirically solvable, at least in principle. Stated differently, we may be able to agree on what problems are matters for science and what parts of our disagreements are matters for metaphysics. There could be no more fitting goal in commemorating Wundt, and the discipline he institutionalized, than to ask what parts of the psychological endeavor are science and what parts, by the nature of the rules of evidence and decision making, are more correctly placed in philosophy. While we think of Wundt as setting up a new domain of science, we must also remember that Wundt, for most of his tenure at Leipzig, was against separating psychology from philosophy within the university.

A SEARCH OF PSYCHOLOGY'S PAST

I would like to suggest that the hope psychology has for clarifying the nature of its differences in systematic viewpoint will depend on its ability to look back at the lines of inquiry that come into the twentieth century and to ask what questions were being asked.

I have been deliberately unspecific with respect to labeling the various paths of scientific inquiry that had a bearing on the development of psychology as science. This has been for good reason; any such partitioning of past research and theory into major paths is itself a theoretical statement about what the key questions are. I have also tried, perhaps to the point of being repetitious, to use the term "past" rather than the term "history." The reason for this stems directly from the nature of history. The search of our past that is being suggested here is not the same as a suggestion that we go back and read history. Psychology's systematic problems are not problems for history, they are problems for science, and it is important to recognize that the goals of history and the goals of science do not always coincide. A history is a story, and the writing of history is the telling of a story. There are many different ways of writing history, but in very few of them is the vocabulary and the syntax that of science. The kinds of questions asked, the rules of evidence, the guidelines for the presentation of evidence, the question of what constitutes an explanation, all of these are subject to different interpretations in these two domains of scholarship.

The suggestion is, therefore, that as we search the past in an attempt to identify the questions that might be a source of the systematic deadlock, we execute this search as scientists, not as historians. This implies that we should also temporarily suspend many of the views of our heritage that come from existing histories of our past. Many of our historical accounts have been heavily influenced by the partitioning of problems and approaches into the rubrics of the "schools" of the early twentieth century. In many cases the histories were guided by the way in which a few psychologists of the first two decades of this century saw the influences acting on them. We have already seen the selective role that this kind of thinking can play when we examined the partial representation of Wundt's work. Historians, looking through the eyes of the "schools" could find no place for a *Völkerpsychologie* so it was ignored. In a similar vein Boring, in the Preface to his *History of Experimental Psychology* in 1929, could find no ancestors of behaviorism, while Esper (3) could write a *History of Psychology* years later with a strong behaviorist emphasis in which most of the analysis was based on the writings of the Greek philosophers.

As we search the past we will encounter ideas, events, and people. As historians we would have the freedom to select any one of these as the basis for constructing a story. As scientists looking for some resolution of systematic differences our interest will, of necessity, be on ideas. Yet we must strike a delicate balance between the ideas expressed and the empirical work that was being done in the context of those ideas. It is frequently easy to emphasize what a few individuals said about a few topics, and to forget to ask what difference these ideas made in what many other individuals did. After all, the number of distinctly different ideas that have been generated about "psychological" matters is very limited. What has tended to change over time are the different ways of asking specific questions related to these ideas and devising procedures for answering those specific questions. What we should be interested in is the manner in which, and the extent to which, the form and the content of the questions have been influenced by empirical observations, by experiments.

Questions will be encountered at two levels. The first level will involve what will be called short-term questions, i.e. those questions that directed individual experiments, or sets of experiments, perhaps individual programs of research. A few representative lines of inquiry can be listed. All of these lines had their roots partly in philosophy as did all branches of science at some stage. One line of inquiry came jointly from physics and from biology, but mostly from the former. This line of questions dealt with sensations and images. It included such investigators as Newton, Young, Müller, Fechner, Helmholtz, and Wundt. This line was to have widespread influence on all quantitative analyses in psychology.

A second line comes primarily from biology. It deals with questions of the localization of psychological functions. It has two main branches of research. One of these branches deals with questions of reflexive as opposed to voluntary functions. It would include the works of such men as Bell and Magendie, Sechenov, Sherrington, and Pavlov. The second branch would be the more traditional one of localization of function, and would include the names of such workers as Willis, Whytt, Gall, Fritsch and Hitzig, Hughlings Jackson, Goltz, Munk, and others. This branch would include the clinical literature on brain damage and psychological function.

A third line would have an inclusive label such as sociomedical. It would include such workers as Pinel, Charcot, Janet, and Freud; it would also include men such as Binet and Ebbinghaus, both of whom worked on mental testing in an applied setting. This branch would obviously overlap with a neurophysiological research line, as in the case of both Pinel and Freud, who had done physiological research in addition to the work for which they are most widely known. It would also contain the major lines of research in medical psychology with which all of these names (except Ebbinghaus) are associated.

A final line of inquiry comes jointly from chemistry and biology; it is linked to philosophy through its views on materialism. The early forms of this line of inquiry dealt with vitalism but found expression in attempts to reduce all living functions to physiochemical analysis. By the late nineteenth century this found clear representation in analyses of behavior of intact organisms in the work of men such as Loeb and Jennings.

The above outline provides one example of the kind of delineation that one would encounter if the emphasis is on specific experimental questions. The list includes paths of research that would provide the background for such areas as sensation, perception, learning, personality, and abnormal psychology. There is no doubt that this specific list blurs some areas and misses others. It could be extended to include other areas, and it could be elaborated to describe in detail more specific research questions. It is offered as an example of the first level of ideas that could be examined. While there could be extended discussion about the details of such an outline of questions, it is not likely that there would be intractable parts. Because each entry in such an outline is relatively closely tied to a research area and because a given experiment or the work of a given person could appear in several lines of inquiry, each line of questions can be established without regard to other lines even though they may turn out to be highly related. No intransigent problems are likely to arise as long as one avoids questions of the relative importance of the various lines of inquiry. It would be at that point that one would uncover systematic differences.

There is a second level at which questions have been asked. If one looks back at the history of science, one can trace at least three lines of inquiry, three sets of questions whose articulation was becoming provocative by the turn of the century. The answers to each of these sets of questions were to have a profound influence on the way individuals viewed the problems of psychology. These questions concern (a) the nature of mind, (b) the nature of man, and (c) man's place in nature. These sets of questions are highly related, yet they are clearly distinct. Each category has a long background both in philosophy and in science. All of the different scientific paths to modern psychology dealt in key ways with one or more of these questions. By the first decade of the twentieth century it was clear that how one dealt with these questions had a direct bearing on what psychology was to become as a science and whether psychology would lie exclusively within the cloak of science. Every psychological system was to acquire, at least implicitly, some position with respect to these three issues. Yet each system could place a different weighting on each of these lines of inquiry.

Under the rubric of the nature of mind are questions of sensations, images, feelings, ideas, thinking. Historically the study of mind has been tied to the concept of consciousness. The problems center around how to characterize the things that happen and/or the things we do when we are conscious. One must delineate what kinds of questions about mind are permissible. Is the link with consciousness a necessary one? Do we have to define consciousness or is it taken as obvious, therefore as given? If some procedure is to be specified for its recognition, does that procedure depend on the phenomena of learning? Does it require language? Should we limit our conceptualization to the adjectival forms, i.e. restrict our terms to mental and/or conscious? What other questions can we ask? Can we ask where it is located, what it does, how it works? Is controlled introspection an acceptable experimental procedure for studying it? If it is not, then in what ways are the mind (or consciousness and awareness) when defined by the "methodological twist" of behavior different from the mind that is so palpably a subject of everyday discourse?

Under the heading of the nature of man we encounter a set of questions that goes back to the Greeks on the philosophic issues and has had several distinct lines of scientific inquiry since the seventeenth century. The rational, the passionate, and the vegetative souls of the Greek philosophers have had their parallels in the scientific study of man and other animals in several areas of biology as well as in psychology. The questions involve the concepts of volition and choice, notions of voluntary behavior and its relation to reflexive and instinctive behavior. Views along the dimension of determinism and "freedom of choice" are diverse and are found along many of the paths of scientific inquiry. Three quarter-centuries of research have accumulated since the publication of Sherrington's *Integrative Action of the Nervous System* and since the work of Jennings and Loeb on the behavior of "lower organisms." Key theoretical and experimental advances have been made in our understanding of these areas of research, yet labels such as reflexive behavior, instinctive behavior, and voluntary behavior retain an emotional component. They take on positive or negative properties depending on one's point of view and the context in which they are used.

The set of questions raised under the heading of man's place in nature also extends back to antiquity. It involves the concept of the Chain of Being that began with Plato and was articulated by Aristotle. We tend to associate the phrase with Thomas Huxley and his exposition of Darwin and the implication of his work, but the issue has two distinct histories. On the one hand, there is the tradition in philosophy dealing with the continuity of forms of life, and the relation to the views of a Supreme Being. On the other hand, there is the tradition in science dealing with fossils, body structures, speciation, and other matters that are associated with the names of Darwin, Lyell, Cuvier, Huxley, and others. These are two different traditions that are frequently not distinguished.

Psychology has been assigned, or has assumed, the task of attending to aspects of the mind and of conduct. When it decided to become a science it assumed an additional responsibility. It had to restrict the way it studied, explained, and talked about these topics. The three lines of inquiry just outlined conspired to make this task difficult. Each possessed face validity as having some bearing on the question of how to define psychology. The answers to each set of questions had clear implications for some of the questions in the other lines of inquiry. One difficulty was that the rules for evaluating the relative importance of the evidence for the different kinds of questions were not clear.

What emerges from a detailed examination of some of the questions just outlined is the view that many of the arguments between and among the "schools" were never joined because they involved different levels of discourse and were based on different assumptions. In looking back at the systematic discussions of the past, it seems necessary to distinguish between (a) what they were arguing about and (b) the basis on which each was arguing. For example, a behaviorist could adopt a certain view of the nature of man on the basis of a specified line of research. This might lead him to a view of mind that would be difficult to change by evidence restricted to the study of mind alone. Similarly, the introspectionist could adopt a certain view of mind on the basis of specific lines of research, and this view might be relatively immune to data and theory coming from a different set of questions and experiments.

Such considerations suggest an important strategy in cases of important differences in systematic views. For each position the question should be raised regarding what kind of evidence would be required in order to produce a change in view. Such an exchange could lead to the articulation of which of the several origins of psychology is playing the dominant role.

If it is not possible to delineate the kinds of evidence that would lead to a change in position, the primary question then must turn to one of whether the discussion is in the domain of science.

This leads to a final comment on psychology's heritage as a science. It has been suggested that Wundt institutionalized psychology as a discipline. There is no way, and no need, to subtract from that accomplishment. His emphasis on controlled observations and "objectivity" was an attempt to separate psychology from philosophy, although he was against a formal administrative separation at the university. We have also suggested that Wundt's way of thinking about psychology, and the thinking of those that followed in his tradition, did not contain the essential ingredients that could have generated twentieth century psychology. One sense in which this is true is paradoxical. Regardless of the level at which we review the past, whether it is at the empirical level, close to the areas of research of present interest, or whether the review selects the research that skirts the edges of metaphysics, as with some of the questions just outlined, one encounters one compelling observation. It is this: as we examine the many lines of thinking that come from, for example, the study of sensation by Helmholtz, the research on human learning by Ebbinghaus, the developments in mental testing by Binet, the work on localization of psychological function by such men as Fritsch and Hitzig, Ferrier, Hughlings Jackson, and others, the analysis of animal behavior by individuals such as Loeb, Jennings, Lloyd Morgan, and Pavlov, one is struck by the fact that all are characterized by experimental or observational procedures that are still acceptable as bona fide scientific procedure. The one line of inquiry that specified, and was based on, an "experimental" procedure that is not judged acceptable as a method of scientific investigation at the present time is the line established by Wundt. The paradox is that psychology has selected as the founder of its science a man whose line of inquiry brought with it no acceptable experimental method. The Wundtian and related traditions brought to the twentieth century some interesting psychological questions; yet they brought no method for demonstrating whether the questions were for science or philosophy. The other lines of inquiry were to furnish psychology with the method to become a science. Any eventual resolution of the relative importance of psychology's origins will have to evaluate the implications of this paradox.

Literature Cited

1. Bentley, M. 1926. Psychologies called "structural:" Historical derivation. In *Psychologies of 1925*, ed. C. Murchison, pp. 383–412. Worcester: Clark. 412 pp.
2. Blumenthal, A. L. 1975. A reappraisal of Wilhelm Wundt. *Am. Psychol.* 30:1081–88
3. Boring, E. G. 1929. *A History of Experimental Psychology.* New York: Century. 699 pp.
4. Boring, E. G. 1930. Psychology for eclectics. In *Psychologies of 1930*, ed. C. Murchison, pp. 115–27. Worcester: Clark. 497 pp.
5. Boring, E. G. 1950. The influence of evolutionary theory upon American psychological thought. In *Evolutionary Thought in America*, ed. S. Pearsons, pp. 268–99. New Haven: Yale. 462 pp.
6. Boring, E. G. 1965. On the subjectivity of important historical dates: Leipzig 1879. *J. Hist. Behav. Sci.* 1:5–9
7. Born, M. 1970. *Problems of Atomic Dynamics.* Cambridge: MIT. 200 pp.
8. Brett, G. S. 1921. *A History of Psychology*, Vol. 3. New York: Macmillan. 322 pp.
9. Bronowski, J. 1974. Humanism and the growth of knowledge. In *The Philosophy of Karl Popper*, ed. P. A. Schilpp, pp. 606–31. LaSalle: Open Court. 670 pp.
10. Carr, H. 1930. Functionalism. See Ref. 4, pp. 59–78
11. Eliot, T. S. 1945. *Four Quartets.* London: Faber & Faber. 44 pp.
12. Hull, C. L., Hovland, C. I., Ross, R. T., Hall, M., Perkins, D. T., Fitch, F. B. 1940. *Mathematicodeductive Theory of Rote Learning: A Study in Scientific Methodology.* New Haven: Yale. 343 pp.
13. Krantz, D. L., ed. 1969. *Schools of Psy-*

chology: *A Symposium.* New York: Appleton-Century-Crofts. 134 pp.
14. Ladd, G. T. 1897. *Elements of Physiological Psychology.* New York: Scribner's. 708 pp.
15. Lewin, K. 1935. *A Dynamic Theory of Personality.* New York: McGraw-Hill. 286 pp.
16. Maslow, A. H. 1969. *The Psychology of Science.* Chicago: Regnery. 168 pp.
17. Medawar, P. 1973. *The Hope of Progress.* Garden City: Anchor. 145 pp.
18. Murphy, G. 1930. *An Historical Introduction to Modern Psychology.* New York: Harcourt, Brace. 470 pp. 2nd ed.
19. Nafe, J. P. 1930. Structural psychology. See Ref. 4, pp. 128–40
20. Neisser, U. 1972. A paradigm shift in psychology. *Science* 176:628–30
21. Pillsbury, W. B. 1929. *The History of Psychology.* New York: Norton. 326 pp.
22. Popper, K. R. 1974. Autobiography. See Ref. 9, pp. 3–181
23. Progoff, I. 1956. *The Death & Rebirth of Psychology.* New York: McGraw-Hill. 275 pp.
24. Robinson, D. N. 1976. *An Intellectual History of Psychology.* New York: Macmillan. 434 pp.
25. Schultz, D. 1975. *A History of Modern Psychology.* New York: Academic. 395 pp. 2nd ed.
26. Titchener, E. B. 1921. Functional psychology and the psychology of act: I. *Am. J. Psychol.* 32:519–42
27. Uttal, W. R. 1973. *The Psychobiology of Sensory Coding.* New York: Harper & Row. 679 pp.
28. Wundt, W. 1948. *Principles of Physiological Psychology.* In *Readings in the History of Psychology*, ed. W. Dennis, pp. 248–54. New York: Appleton-Century-Crofts. 587 pp.

Ann. Rev. Psychol. 1979. 30:31–61

AUDITORY PSYCHOPHYSICS   ♦302

Constantine Trahiotis

Department of Psychology and Department of Speech and Hearing Science, University of Illinois, Champaign, Illinois 61820

Donald E. Robinson[1]

Department of Psychology, Indiana University, Bloomington, Indiana 47401

CONTENTS

INTRODUCTION 31
TEXTBOOKS 32
PITCH PERCEPTION 36
NONLINEAR EFFECTS 39
INTENSITY PERCEPTION 41
BINAURAL HEARING 45
    External Ear Transformations 45
    Localization 46
    Lateralization 48
    Masking 51
    Pitch 54
SUMMARY AND COMMENTS 55

INTRODUCTION

Our thoughts about how we would cover the material in auditory psychophysics were dominated by several considerations. We wished to include some representative portions of the primary literature which have not been

[1]Preparation of this chapter was supported in part by research grant BNS 77-17308 from the National Science Foundation. We are grateful to William Rabinowitz and Robert Gilkey for their suggestions and criticisms. Thanks also to Harriet Rairdon and Sheryl Mobley for their assistance in the final production of the manuscript. A special acknowledgment is due DNE and LAJ, who having traveled this road before, failed to warn us of the hazards. We also wish to thank our respective wives who tolerated both our presence and our absence while this manuscript was being prepared.

0066-4308/79/0201-0031$01.00

included in the *Annual Review of Psychology* for the last 4 years. We also desired to discuss in some detail the several textbooks that have appeared during this period. At the same time, we wanted to convey to our readers our impressions of those areas that contain either important new data or important theoretical formulations which will influence future research. We also wished to provide a document that would be useful to neophytes in the area as well as to professionals who wish to increase their knowledge in areas ancillary to their own.

Since our space, time, and abilities are limited, the pursuit of these goals necessitated a severe restriction on the number of areas that could be covered. We chose to focus upon the areas of the literature concerning pitch perception, auditory nonlinearities, intensity perception, and binaural hearing. We also chose to include discussions of several review papers and textbooks that not only bring together many of the classical data and theories, but also provide impetus for current research. We end these introductory remarks with two comments. First, we have omitted recent research concerning the phenomena of monaural masking including behavioral tuning curves, pulsation thresholds, modulation transfer functions, temporal acuity, nonsimultaneous masking, and critical bands. We also have omitted reference to many experiments that utilize auditory information to study phenomena which we consider appropriate for reviews which focus on cognitive or information processing models. Second, we are aware that our attempt to blend tutorial and expository writing styles may detract from the usefulness of the review. We are hopeful, however, that our inclusion of historical information will be beneficial and outweigh any shortcomings due to style.

TEXTBOOKS

Those who teach courses in sensory processes, sensation and perception, and hearing science are no longer forced to rely on outdated textbooks and original articles when attempting to provide their students with basic knowledge in audition. In contrast, the current problem will be to decide which of several books is best suited for the course. The following review of new textbooks may help those who are faced with this pleasant task.

In *Fundamentals of Hearing, An Introduction,* Yost & Nielsen (180) have provided a valuable textbook for teaching at the undergraduate level. The treatment of the physics of sound is adequate if not challenging. The chapters dealing with auditory anatomy and physiology are excellent and beautifully illustrated with photomicrographs provided by Ivan Hunter-Duvar and his colleagues. Of the four chapters devoted to anatomy and physiology, the weakest is that dealing with the central auditory nervous system. The chapter is brief and the content is not explicitly related to the preceding chapters dealing with the cochlea and eighth nerve nor to those that follow dealing with psychoacoustics. The six chapters devoted to psychoacoustics are generally well written and the coverage is adequate for a first course. In discussing classical psychophysics and signal detection theory, the authors, apparently intentionally, avoid any reference to the theoretical issues that once enlivened the journals. In fact, a kind of atheoretical bias pervades the book. Although there are ample reasons to omit current theoretical positions from an introductory text, such an omission may make it difficult for students to appreciate or to understand the motivation and excitement which provide impetus for current research in hearing. The authors have, however, managed to touch on most of the issues that have been prominent in psychoacoustics in recent years and the basic data are provided in numerous figures and tables. At the end of the chapters are provided "supplements" that include additional information, elaboration of ideas discussed in the chapters, and suggested additional readings. Also provided are four appendices which expand the text material dealing with sinusoids, logarithms, anatomy and histology, and physiology.

A second important contribution, in the form of a textbook, is *Bases of Hearing* by Durrant & Lovrinic (35). Some portions of this book are written at a more advanced level than the comparable portions of the Yost-Nielsen text. In particular, the chapters treating Physical Concepts, Acoustics, and Measurement of Sound, along with four appendices on related topics, will probably challenge the knowledge of mathematics and physics of the average undergraduate in psychology or speech and hearing. These chapters are remarkably broad in coverage and lucid in presentation. The chapters devoted to the anatomy and physiology of the auditory system provide an excellent picture of our current knowledge at a general, introductory level. Unfortunately, the weakest part of the book is that dealing with psychoacoustics. The authors have attempted to survey psychoacoustics in one 25-page chapter. There is no treatment of psychophysical methods and no mention of modern approaches to psychophysical theory. Not only is the chapter limited in its scope, but when topics are mentioned, few data are provided.

The recently revised version of Roederer's *Introduction to Physics and Psychophysics of Music* (138) merits mention because of its thorough treatment of the generation and processing of complex acoustic waveforms. While we agree with the author that the book should neither be classified nor evaluated as a textbook of audition, the book does contain several sections which will be of value to those interested in the modern literature of pitch perception. The clear and extensive treatment of the physics of complex sounds and the detailed examination of the Goldstein (48), Wightman (173), and Terhardt (156) models of pitch perception should nicely complement the material presented by Yost and Nielsen and by Durrant and Lovrinic.

Perhaps the most difficult new text to read and to evaluate is *Introduction to the Psychology of Hearing* by B. C. J. Moore (109). Moore simply does not introduce the reader to some subset of audition in a coherent and general fashion. Instead he provides extensive and detailed discussions of classic and modern theories as well as data against the background of heavy doses of criticism, constraints, and interpretations based on his extensive knowledge of the modern primary literature. This book is probably best suited for students who have been introduced to the basic knowledge in audition and are ready to cope with the complexities and ambiguities which abound when one confronts general statements with the wealth of available empirical data. Graduate students or professionals who wish to examine progress in several areas of audition may find the book valuable. Certainly the extensive treatment of the modern primary literature will provide the reader with extremely useful references to material not likely to be covered in general textbooks in the near future.

A more sophisticated and technical coverage of audition is provided in Green's *An Introduction to Hearing* (54), which is addressed to advanced undergraduate and graduate students who will profit from Green's ability to blend classic ideas and data with the modern literature. This text will be very useful in graduate courses taught by psychologists, engineers, and hearing scientists whose students possess some background in college level mathematics. Green's treatment of most topics is written to help the student grasp and understand the major issues under discussion. Perhaps more importantly, Green's discussions provide the student with a coherent framework which should foster evaluation and integration of supplementary material from the primary literature. Students may need background or supplementary material when attempting to understand those chapters concerning the anatomy of the auditory system, middle and inner ear mechanics, and the particular nonlinearity called the "cubic difference tone." Most teachers will also probably wish to supplement the material on pitch perception which is an excellent overview of the problems and questions in the area rather than an explication of current theories and data. We feel that the strongest portions of the book are the chapters on frequency analysis and electrical activity emanating from the cochlea and eighth nerve. Those familiar with Green's prior text and other extensive contributions may be disappointed to find that Green never mentions Signal Detection Theory, does not discuss psychophysical methods, and does not discuss the many experiments and models developed in the context of Signal Detection Theory. This lack is most noticeable with regard to monaural masking and models of ideal detectors, energy detection, envelope processing, etc. Setting aside our judgments concerning the depth of treatment given certain topics, we believe that Green's book is an excellent graduate level text.

Although a thorough treatment of recent contributions concerning Signal Detection Theory is beyond the scope of this review, Egan's scholarly treatise on the formal aspects of Receiver Operating Characteristic (ROC) analysis deserves mention (36). This ambitious work treats in considerable detail ROCs based on several different pairs of probability distributions. Egan's great strength resides in his ability to explore and to communicate clearly and lucidly the implications of various assumptions concerning the nature of information provided observers in various tasks. This has resulted in a graduate level text which should mesh well with other sources and be a worthy supplement to Green's *Introduction to Hearing* in courses which stress the use of mathematical models based on decision theory.

Those who wish to learn about selected topics in audition will be well served by the recent publication of several books, review articles, and collections of original research reports which focus on restricted substantive problems (40, 69, 85–87, 139, 147, 155, 157, 165). Of particular note is the *Festschrift* honoring Hallowell Davis (72). This volume, edited by S. Hirsh and her colleagues at The Central Institute for the Deaf, is a tribute not only to Davis but to the many scientists whose work has been encouraged by that institution.

It should be noted that, against a background of several decades of research in hearing devoted to developing an understanding of the encoding properties and mechanisms of the auditory system, an interesting shift in emphasis appears to be evident in the recent literature. While researchers continue to perform experiments which provide more detailed information about encoding, the major thrust of modern models resides in postulated manners of decoding or extracting the information that has been transformed peripherally. Thus, questions concerning the perception of pitch, for example, are now directed toward attempts to describe how various stimuli may be processed in a manner that leaves pitch invariant rather than directed toward decisions about whether pitch is determined by means of temporal or spatial codes.

We now turn our attention to the literature concerning pitch perception, auditory nonlinearities, intensity perception, and binaural hearing. We will attempt to provide the reader with an appreciation of the relevant historical issues and make an effort to integrate information in the recent primary literature with the data and theoretical statements which appear in the aforementioned books.

PITCH PERCEPTION

Many investigators concerned with pitch perception have sought to answer a deceptively simple question: Does pitch perception depend upon the spectral composition of the stimulus rather than on the temporal features of the physical waveform? It is clear that attempts to answer this question have provided the bulk of the literature dealing with pitch. The previous *Annual Review* chapter on auditory psychophysics (124) included a thorough discussion of pitch perception, and there have been relatively few new empirical findings published in the interim. This lack does not mean that progress has not been made regarding our understanding of pitch. Perhaps the most important developments are attempts to synthesize and unify knowledge in the area. These trends are evident in numerous symposium proceedings and in papers, book chapters, and monographs (27, 40, 53, 126, 147, 192). Much of this synthesis is embodied in the development of several recent mathematical models dealing with pitch perception (10, 27, 48, 87). Further, although not within the scope of this review, recent contributions concerning the possible physiological correlates of frequency analysis also reflect a growing sophistication in the understanding of pitch perception (e.g. 40, 192).

Another expression of the trend toward synthesis and order in the area is the appearance of detailed articles which discuss data and theories not only in a historical context, but in terms of the general store of knowledge concerning the auditory system. Plomp's review (124) includes Békésy's statement to the effect that extant theories of hearing were essentially theories of pitch. Perhaps it is now equally true that theories of pitch have evolved to the point where they now subsume or include the major theoretical formulations that were spawned by research in monaural and binaural masking. In this light, it is interesting to note that modern theories of pitch assume that input waveforms are processed by a contiguous series of filters or critical bands and that the processed information is subjected to some centrally located further processing that is related to autocorrelation, cross-correlation or to some version of the operations described in Durlach's equilization and cancellation model of binaural detection (32).

These viewpoints are indicated in de Boer's chapter in *The Handbook of Sensory Physiology* (27), which is an excellent critical review and synthesis of historical issues, empirical data, and theories dealing with pitch perception. As de Boer points out, his chapter is "... more a textbook on the psychophysics of pitch than a review of recent research" (p. 481).

de Boer begins with a brief statement of some mathematical considerations emphasizing the importance of linear and nonlinear transformations and Fourier analysis. The historical discussion which follows emphasizes the well-known criticisms of Helmholtz's theoretical conceptions based on Seebeck's observations that the pitch of a complex sound is not determined by the fundamental Fourier component. Rather, the pitch of the complex appeared to be determined by periodicities in the temporal waveform. Seebecks' observations and Fletcher's discussion of the "missing fundamental" are discussed as antecedents to the series of papers written by Schouten which emphasized that a number of harmonically related spectral components could produce one pitch sensation which Schouten termed the "residue." This led to several approaches that attempted to account for pitch judgments strictly on the basis of periodicities occurring in the envelope or in the fine structure of the stimulus complex. Attention then turns to Ritsma's experiments that indicated that the residue pitch had an *existence* region (i.e. was heard only when the three component stimuli were not spaced too far apart and were confined to the frequency region below 5000 Hz) This observation led directly to the concept of *dominance* which essentially is a statement that the lower frequency components associated with the existence region dominate the pitch perception of stimuli that contain a large number of components. The critical aspect of these observations is that pitch appears to be determined by *spectrally resolved* components rather than by the unresolved partials as proposed by Schouten's residue theory. Spectral components produced by the observer's nonlinear processing of the stimulus are discussed both in general terms and in the context of the contribution of nonlinearities (particularly the cubic difference tone) to residue pitch. Further discussion emphasizes experiments that support the spectral nature of the basis for pitch. One of the most important of these is a demonstration by Houtsma & Goldstein (74) that a residue-like pitch can be obtained with dichotic stimuli. Such evidence has led theorists away from temporally based notions, such as Schouten's, and toward those that are insensitive to the fine structure of the complex stimulus. Goldstein's (48) and Wightman's (173) recent models of pitch extraction assume a central processor that extracts pitch on the basis of spectral information which could be provided to it via either a spatial or temporal code. de Boer gives proper emphasis to important new data concerning monotic and dichotic repetition pitch. We will include a discussion of these and related phenomena in our section on binaural hearing.

Many of these issues are also discussed in an excellent recent monograph written by an investigator who has heavily influenced the development of current notions of pitch perception. Plomp's *Aspects of Tone Sensation* (125) is a lucid description of the perception of steady-state tones. In addition to a thorough treatment of the pitch of complex tones, Plomp has written a general discussion of the ear as a frequency analyzer which includes a treatment of pulsation thresholds and lateral suppression phenomena. Of direct relevance to the study of pitch are Plomp's chapters on combination tones, beats of mistuned consonances, roughness and tonal dissonance, and the timbre of complex tones. Following a thorough review, Plomp concludes, in accord with de Boer, that pitch is determined on a spectral basis. Anyone wishing to understand pitch perception will certainly profit from studying these two scholarly works. Less extensive treatments of pitch perception may be found in Green (53) and Wightman & Green (174), but see Goldstein (49) for a contrasting position.

de Boer, Plomp, Goldstein, Green, and Wightman all apparently agree that there is a strong spectral basis for the perception of pitch. This is not to say that there are no dissenters. For example, Moore (110) has shown that under certain circumstances the phase relations among components of a complex may affect the pitch of the residue. This result is difficult to reconcile with models of pitch that are heavily dependent upon spectral cues. While we know that phase effects on pitch are related to interactions of the physical components and aural nonlinearities as well as to the interactions occurring between nonlinearities, we are not certain that we can preclude the possibility that the resulting envelope and fine structure cues are irrelevant (16–18, 91, 92).

One must also contend with the study of Burns & Viemeister (12) which showed that observers could recognize melodies and musical intervals produced by amplitude modulation of wide band noise. This ability is restricted to a range of modulation rates between 50 Hz and about 800 Hz. These results are apparently not compatible with models of pitch perception that neglect the time domain.

Other challenges for spectrally based models may be found in Moore's contention that a strong pitch sensation may be obtained even though none of the various components are separately audible (107). Another possible difficulty for these models is van den Brink's observation that the pitch of complex tones may be determined by the *pitches* of the components rather than the spectral compositions of the complex waveform (159). A great deal of additional information regarding pitch may be found in collections of papers edited by Zwicker & Terhardt (192) and Evans & Wilson (40). The latter contains an article by de Boer (28) which suggests that the modern models of pitch perception may be unified within a single mathematical framework.

Further evidence on the processing of spectral cues can be found in several articles which focus upon the auditory system's ability to resolve differences in frequency. Feth (41) and Feth & O'Malley (42) indicate that observers process instantaneous frequency differences which arise when two sinusoids differing in amplitude and frequency are presented simultaneously. These findings extend the observations reported much earlier by

Jeffress (77) and underline the importance of the short-term power spectrum. Wier et al (172) report that frequency difference limens are a rather unique function of frequency and are little affected by changes in sensation level above 20 dB.

Jesteadt & Sims (81) and Wier et al (171) provide information concerning the variance in measures of frequency discrimination attributable to the psychophysical methods used to gather the data.

Moore (108) finds that frequency difference limens are not simply related to the size of the critical bandwidth, thus supporting the contention of Evans (39) that the mechanisms underlying frequency resolution may be different from those mediating frequency discrimination.

The creative study of Green et al (55) is an example of how data interpreted in terms of pitch may sometimes be explained in terms of frequency discrimination. They show that the stimulus conditions used by Pumphrey & Gold (128) to argue for extremely high-Q (narrow band) auditory filters can be described spectrally in such a way that high-Q filters are not necessary to explain the behavioral data.

NONLINEAR EFFECTS

Since Helmholtz, it has been known that the auditory system is nonlinear. However, the effects of these nonlinearities were assumed to be significant only at relatively high intensities. Typically, distortion was described by a polynominal transformation in which the coefficients of the higher order terms were thought to be relatively small. Further, it was generally believed that the source of the nonlinearities was associated with the middle ear.

We now know that this view is incomplete and that, in particular, the cubic difference tone $2f_1-f_2$ is evident at low levels of the primary tones, displays rates of growth not expected from a polynomial expression, and is critically dependent upon the frequency separation of the primary tones. Goldstein (46) has emphasized that these results suggest an *essential* nonlinearity originating within the cochlea. Historical and empirical considerations of these issues will be found in Plomp (125) and de Boer (27).

Erdreich (38) confirms that the growth of $2f_1-f_2$ is a linear, approximately unity slope function of the intensity level of the two equal level primaries. He also reports that the combination tone $2f_1+f_2$ grows at a rate of between 2 and 3 dB for each decibel increase in the level of the primaries. However, Hall (64) and Weber & Mellert (168) have shown that the growth and phase characteristics of $2f_1-f_2$ can be very complicated functions of the level and the frequencies of the primaries even when the primaries are equally intense. Zurek & Leshowitz (188) come to a similar conclusion based upon data obtained in a discrimination experiment.

In a second paper, Zurek & Leshowitz (189) extend Goldstein's (47) suggestion that combination tones behave as though they were spectral components present in the stimulus. These authors find that combination tone stimuli interact binaurally in a manner similar to externally generated tones.

Most of the estimates of the magnitude of distortion products have been made by noting the amount of a physical tone needed to cancel the subjective tone. Smoorenburg (154) argues that measures of the level of the combination tones made with a cancellation procedure may be too large because the cancellation tone may be subjected to lateral suppression. He finds that measures of the distortion products obtained with the pulsation-threshold technique may be up to 20 dB smaller than those measured with cancellation methods.

The desire to learn more about the peripheral mechanisms responsible for combination tones led to the neurophysiological investigations which were reported by Goldstein & Kiang (50) and Goldstein (47). These authors found that a single unit in the eighth nerve may respond to the presence of the cubic difference tone even when the two primaries fail to elicit a response in that unit. They also found that the neural response to the cubic difference tone could be cancelled by an external tone of proper level and phase. Interestingly, the neural data indicated the possibility that the cancellation tone was being suppressed by the primary tones. These results mesh well with the psychophysical data of Smoorenburg discussed previously.

One might conclude from these observations that the cubic difference tone propagates down the cochlea in the same manner as an externally applied tone. Several experiments reported by Dallos and his colleagues (23, 24) indicate that the distortion products found in the cochlear microphonic are not subject to simultaneous cancellation in all regions of the cochlea. These data imply that the cubic difference tone probably does not propagate apically as a traveling wave. This observation is consistent with the data of Wilson & Johnstone (176) obtained from the guinea pig. Wilson and Johnstone used a capacitive probe technique to measure basilar membrane displacement and found that responses were highly linear with input level and only a small amount of distortion at $2f_1$-f_2 was present. On the other hand, Rhode and his colleagues (133, 134, 137) find that the basilar membrane response measured with the Mössbauer technique is nonlinearly related to the input level. de Boer (27) points out that the type of nonlinearity observed by Rhode could be the basis of the generation of the cubic difference tone; but only at input levels greater than those required to produce the distortion measured in psychophysical experiments. In fact, Rhode (133) failed to find evidence for the cubic difference tone for primary levels as high as 120 dB SPL. Rhode concludes that there is no evidence in measures of the mechanical disturbances in the cochlea which would indicate that the distortion products propagate in the form of a traveling wave. The resolution of these apparent discrepancies may entail a great deal of effort. These studies diverge greatly in the techniques used to monitor the physiological response; and it should be remembered that no two of these techniques have been used to measure responses in the same cochlear location in one species. We can agree with Plomp's (125) conclusion that the nature of the origin of distortion products is an open question. We can also agree with de Boer's (27) conclusions that the site of origin of the distortion products is totally unknown, that there is an essential nonlinearity, and that this nonlinearity is probably responsible for, or related to, other nonlinear phenomena.

Several recent papers concerning the neural correlates of peripherally generated nonlinearities may be found in (2, 14, 25, 26, 57, 123). Many of these considerations have been included in models that attempt to explore the origin and functional role of auditory nonlinearities (31, 45, 63, 65, 88, 114, 146–148).

INTENSITY PERCEPTION

Our ability to process auditory information based on the intensity of the stimulus continues to be studied in two somewhat diverse manners. While some investigators measure and model our ability to resolve intensity differences, others emphasize relations obtained in experiments that require observers to judge, scale, or rate the loudness of the acoustic input.

Many current studies of the resolution of intensity differences are addressed to the factors or conditions which are responsible for the "near-miss" to Weber's law. The term near-miss was used by McGill & Goldberg (104), who noted that the magnitude of the intensity difference limen decreased with increases in the level of the standard stimulus. They found that the slope of the line relating ΔI to I was about 0.9 and offered a Poisson-based counting model to account for the data. Viemeister (161) demonstrated that Weber's law adequately described the data when observers discriminated between pulsed sinusoids in the presence of high-pass and band-reject noise. Viemeister interpreted these data as indicating that the near-miss to Weber's law is obtained when observers use intensity information provided by aural harmonics. This line of reasoning led to the Penner et al (120) investigation of intensity discrimination for pulsed sinusoids at various test frequencies up to 12 kHz. These authors, along with Jesteadt et al (83), obtained data conforming to the near-miss over a large range of frequencies and suggested that Viemeister's arguments about the utilization of aural harmonics should have led to data conforming to Weber's law at the highest frequencies where the aural harmonic was thought to be inaudible. Our interpretation of their argument places the origin of the nonlinearity in the middle ear. We believe their data do not necessarily negate the possibility of aural harmonics produced at a more central region such as the cochlea.

Moore & Raab (111) were able to obtain data conforming to Weber's law for pure tones presented in band-reject noise. High-pass noise, on the other hand, resulted in a masking function with a slope value between 0.9 and 1.0. These authors also show that a narrow-band noise masker one octave above the 1 kHz pulsed sinusoid was sufficient to remove the near-miss to Weber's law. Moore & Raab emphasize the import of information in masking noise at frequencies below the frequency of the signals to be discriminated. A second study by Moore & Raab (112) investigated the intensity discrimination of wideband noise bursts presented either alone or in the presence of continuous band-reject noise. They found that observers were only slightly less sensitive at high intensity levels than would be predicted by Weber's law. Viemeister's (162) similar experiment employing pulsed, band-reject noise indicates that Weber's law holds over at least an 80 dB range for intensity discrimination of bursts of noise. Both of these studies contain thoughtful discussions of the data and their relations to what is known about the neural coding of intensity by the peripheral auditory system. The principal theoretical difficulty is to account for the large intensity range for which Weber's law obtains in terms of what is known about firing rates in single neural units. These units are known to produce increases in spike rates proportional to the intensity of the stimulus for only a relatively small intensity range above their thresholds. Further increases in stimulus intensity do not produce an increase in the rate of response, a condition called *saturation* (2, 141). One might postulate that the way the system encodes intensity information over a large range includes the contribution of information from fibers whose characteristic frequencies are higher than those which respond to the stimuli at low levels. Thus, intensity would be coded by the neural information in a large subset of auditory fibers. The band-reject noise used in these behavioral experiments was intended to drive the off-frequency tuned fibers to saturation so that the dynamic range of a restricted set of neural units could be investigated. While these considerations are fairly straightforward, we agree with each of the author's discussions which indicate that the behavioral experiments may not provide strong tests of these notions. We arrive at this conclusion by noting that (*a*) the auditory system may encode intensity in terms of temporal patterns that do not show saturation, (*b*) the spike rates produced by broadband stimuli may be effected by complicated lateral suppression mechanisms (140, 142), and (c) we do not know the degree to which the pertinent neural data obtained in cats and monkeys reflect the properties of the human auditory system. These experiments may be relevant to Zwicker's model (190) which deals with idealized patterns of excitation that are a nonlinear function of stimulus amplitude. It should be stressed that Moore and Viemeister appear to disagree about the importance of such "off frequency" listening implied in the Zwicker model when discussing their respective experiments.

Those readers who have sufficient mathematical background will appreciate the Raab & Goldberg (129) study of intensity discrimination which used reproducible noise as a stimulus. The authors present several sets of important data some of which indicate that (1.) Weber's law holds for reproducible noises, (2.) observers are more sensitive to changes in intensity of reproducible noise than they are to changes in intensity in random noise, (3.) intensity discrimination improves as stimulus duration is increased from 10 to 100 msec, and (4.) discrimination is unaffected by rather large changes in stimulus bandwidth. This paper includes an excellent discussion of psychophysical models of intensity discrimination and emphasizes the importance of "internal noise" to models which attempt to account for Weber's law in experiments that utilize deterministic signals.

Schacknow & Raab (143) investigated the effects of signal-bandwidth and masker-bandwidth on noise intensity discrimination. Their data indicate that when signal and masker are of the same bandwidth, discrimination is independent of bandwidth and that mode of masker presentation (pulsed vs continuous) had no effect. On the other hand, when the signal bandwidth was less than that of the masker, discriminability improved with increases in signal bandwidth. This effect was increased when the masker was gated. The authors develop an interesting modification of Green's energy detection model (52) to account for these data.

Luce & Green (97) have attempted to use data obtained from studies of auditory nerve fibers to develop two models to account for both intensity and frequency discrimination: a counting model and a timing model. They conclude that, based on the available data, the timing model can be rejected while the counting model cannot. However, according to Luce & Green (98), Colburn has pointed out a mathematical error which makes it doubtful that either of the two models can be rejected as a basis for explaining intensity or frequency discrimination.

Summaries of numerous data relevant to intensity discrimination may be found in Schacknow & Raab (143) for noise stimuli, and in Rabinowitz et al (131) for pure tone stimuli. The latter paper summarizes many data collected for 1000 Hz signals and uses an interesting measure by which data obtained from several paradigms may be compared. The authors' Figure 2 nicely demonstrates the stimulus regions for which Weber's law does and does not hold.

Resnick & Feth (132) investigated the discriminability of pairs of clicks as a function of absolute level of the pair and of the intensity difference of members of the pair. They found that the discriminability of time-reversed click pairs was a complicated function of the time between members of the pair, pointing to the importance of forward and backward masking effects in this type of paradigm. Jesteadt & Bilger (80) measured intensity and frequency discrimination in single-interval, two-interval forced-choice and same-different experiments. They also evaluated how behavior was affected by changes in the level of the standard in the two-interval tasks. Performance was degraded in those conditions employing variable standards, and rather strong response biases were found for the conditions in which the standard was varied over a 40 dB range. Many of the data confirmed the importance of memory factors in experiments dealing with intensity and frequency resolution. Moray & Fitter (113) also find that memory factors may play a role in intensity discrimination. Their data indicate that observers were more efficient in detecting intensity increments when the interstimulus interval was 400 msec, and that discriminability decreased as the time between signals was increased. Small (153) investigated observers' abilities to detect the direction of changes in signals containing monotonically changing intensity levels. He found that observers often displayed a bias for stating that the stimuli were growing louder. Jesteadt & Wier (82) found that intensity and frequency discrimination limens are smaller for diotic than for monotic conditions. This article also contains a discussion of the greater resolution obtained when frequency discrimination is measured with the method of adjustment, a finding in accord with data reported earlier by Wier et al (171). Watson and his colleagues (166) have also commented on the efficacy of the method of adjustment in experiments which require that observers discriminate small frequency differences in a tone embedded in a temporal pattern composed of several different frequencies.

Lippman et al (96) report that the accuracy of identification of absolute intensity values was essentially independent of the payoff matrix. Their data resemble those collected in classical signal detection experiments in that the criteria adopted by the subjects were less extreme than those required for optimal payoff. A very detailed examination of intensity discriminations in a roving level paradigm was performed by Berliner et al (7). This paper, taken in conjunction with those reported above and the recently published papers of Luce et al (99) and Weber et al (167), illustrates the trend toward experiments and models which are directed toward an understanding of the cognitive factors that may mediate performance in experiments utilizing simple signal configurations. An application of the most recent version of the Durlach & Braida model of intensity resolution (33) is found in Lim et al (95). The results indicate that the theory can be fairly successful in relating measures of intensity discrimination to judgments of loudness. It will be interesting to continue to monitor the use of these various models to see if they are applied to the data of other studies concerned with loudness judgments. For example, Elmasian & Galambos (37), Zwislocki & Sokolich (194), and Zwislocki et al (193) present a host of data which indicate that the loudness of a stimulus may be affected by the intensity of a preceding stimulus.

Those readers who wish to integrate the relations of loudness judgments to the neurophysiological data bearing on saturation phenomena will profit from the discussions presented by Hellman & Hellman (68). They develop a model which indicates that an extended dynamic range of neural activity can be obtained if information from neural units is processed in a multiplicative manner rather than being summed. In this fashion, the loudness can be a function of neural activity over a very large range of stimulus intensities. Howes (75) presents a model that relates loudness functions to the number of active neural elements and their discharge rates.

Scharf (144) has also investigated the loudness of two acoustic events and finds that loudness summation is dependent upon the temporal and frequency differences of the two stimuli and is relatively independent of the real or apparent locus of the sound source. These data and those presented by Zwicker (191) indicate how the spectral nature of sounds affects loudness judgments. Zwicker presents an interesting electronic model of loudness judgments for amplitude and frequency modulated signals. He notes that such signals are judged to be of different loudness than steady state tones of the same sound pressure level.

BINAURAL HEARING

The relatively large number of recent papers in this area fall into five more or less distinct categories. While some theoretical papers may be germane to the data presented in more than one category, no one theory encompasses the data available across all five areas. Consequently, we will discuss the theories in greater detail within the context of the data that appear to be most directly relevant to each theory and note in passing how some of the theories may be useful in other areas.

External Ear Transformations

Shaw's (151) recent review of the functional properties of the external ear contains a wealth of information concerning interaural intensity and temporal disparities which serve as cues to the localization of sound. This paper also provides data which indicate that sound pressure levels measured at frequencies above 5 kHz are highly dependent on the angle of elevation of the sound source. The data from 12 different experiments bearing on the sound pressure level transformations caused by the head and external ear due to the position of the source in the horizontal plane are summarized by Shaw (152). He also provides measures of the frequency dependence of the resulting interaural level differences. Abbagnara et al (1) provide further data on diffraction effects and interaural time delays that corroborate the data reviewed by Shaw. A recent paper by Searle et al (149) provides extensive binaural measurements of the transfer function from the free field sound source to a point in the external ear canal. These authors find systematic changes in the frequency response and in interaural disparities as a function of angle of elevation of the source. They indicate that these spectral cues are large enough to be of value when one attempts to locate the position of a source in a psychophysical experiment. Mehrgardt & Mellert (105) make use of an impulse response technique to obtain a transfer function from the free field to the entrance to the ear canal. They show that the amplitude of the transfer function is a function of source positions in the medial sagittal and horizontal planes. This relatively quick and interesting technique shows reasonably good agreement with the data summarized by Shaw (152).

Localization

The data concerning the spectral transformation provided by the head and external ear suggest physical cues that could be utilized by the listener to locate sounds either monaurally or binaurally. Although it is clear that these spectral cues may be used binaurally, Hebrank & Wright (66) highlight data which indicate that observers can easily learn to locate sounds in the median plane with one ear. This observation, coupled with the finding that rapid changes in the high-frequency portion of the spectrum produce similar degradations of monaural and binaural localization performance, led them to conclude that localization in the median plane is primarily monaurally based. Hebrank & Wright (67) found that observers' judgments of the position of sounds originating in the median plane depend upon spectral peaks and valleys in the higher frequency regions of the spectrum. They related their observer's localization responses to spectral cues which result from the filtering properties of the pinna (as measured in artificial ears). They observed that judgments of elevation in the frontal quadrant seem to be associated with the change in the position of a deep spectral notch in the region of 5 kHz to 11 kHz. Bloom (11) measured elevation-dependent changes in absolute sensitivity to narrow bands of noise and from those measurements was able to derive the transfer function of the pinna.

The resulting function agrees well with data discussed previously in that they display spectral notches which vary as a function of source elevation. Butler & Belendiuk (14) adopted the techniques used by Searle et al (149) and, by means of insert microphones, recorded waveforms in the ear canals of their observers. The stimuli were broadband noise bursts presented at several elevations in the medial saggital plane. They then played back these recorded sounds through headphones and had observers judge the stimuli with regard to localization. They found, in agreement with Hebrank & Wright (67), that the responses were a function of the position of a spectral notch occurring above 5 kHz. The spectral cues were shown to be highly individualistic by a rather ingenious but simple manipulation. Observers were presented, through headphones, the sounds that were recorded in the ear canals of one another. Interestingly, an observer who was very poor at performing the task with information provided by his own external ear was quite capable of utilizing cues provided by the external ear of another person. The observation that none of the other observers could perform well with sounds recorded in this particular observer's ear canal was linked to the extreme variance in the depth of the spectral notch recorded in this observer's meatus.

The monaural localization of sounds in the horizontal plane appears to require a very broad stimulus spectrum which contains high frequencies (15). The strong response biases which were correlated with stimulus bandwidth were further studied by Belendiuk & Butler (5). These authors found that sounds appear to emanate from different locations depending upon the center frequency and bandwidth of the stimulus. Observers are found to be quite accurate when localizing sounds that contain information in the region above 4 kHz, an observation previously reported by Belendiuk & Butler (4). Butler (13) discusses some of the issues in a review paper which is historically oriented. Jeffress (78) treats these issues and others related to sound localization in another chapter within the same volume.

Searle et al (150) provide a quantitative model of localization which describes how observers may utilize six separate physical cues. Further, the model is not restricted to stimuli located within the median or horizontal planes. The results from 40 different localization experiments, for which the model provides a reasonably good fit, are summarized in a useful table. We are particularly impressed by the finding that the interaural pinna-cue is relatively more important than the monaural pinna-cue, an implication which has not previously been emphasized. The degree to which localization accuracy depends upon the total angle spanned by the sound sources is another variable which these authors bring to our attention. We feel that this paper is a particularly important contribution because it not only provides a vehicle for describing and understanding the empirical data, but also makes quite clear the need for further data concerning the localization of sound sources outside of the horizontal and vertical planes.

A mathematical analysis of the possible use of head movements in the localization of sounds is provided by Lambert (90). The ability to quantify and control real head movements may make the formulations presented in this paper difficult to evaluate.

Lateralization

The ability of investigators to control independently temporal and intensity aspects of binaural stimuli has no doubt been responsible for the great number of papers which have been published in this area over the last several decades. This body of research has provided a general understanding of the utilization of available binaural cues. The major thrust of many current efforts appears to entail a more or less parametric evaluation of the salience of available cues as well as measurement of the capacity of observers to utilize those cues in various contexts. Mills' (106) observation that people were able to discriminate smaller changes in the position of a sound source away from midline as compared to changes in position near the aural axis provided interesting data, the interpretation of which was clarified in experiments with headphones. Because such changes in location inherently produce nonlinear changes in the amount of interaural temporal disparity, one could interpret the data as either indicating that the sensitivity of the observer was attributable to a greater amount of the physical cue or to a greater sensitivity of the observer to stimuli presented near the midline. Yost (177) used earphones to investigate interaural phase discrimination as a function of interaural phase difference. His data clearly indicate that observers are indeed more sensitive to changes in phase for stimuli lateralized near the midline. Yost et al (183) compare lateralization performance measured with four psychophysical procedures. They conclude that lateralization judgments based on phase or temporal information may depend on different subjective cues across single and double-interval tasks. While observers appear to use image position as a cue in single-interval tasks, they appear to use changes in image position in the double-interval tasks.

Hafter & De Maio (61) found that interaural temporal thresholds for low-pass clicks were somewhat smaller for small values of interaural delay than for delay values that approached the maximal delay available for natural sounds. Their data are closely comparable to the data collected by Mills. These data and those provided by Yost (177) should be compared while keeping in mind the ambiguous image judgments that occur for interaural phase differences between 90° and 180°. Hafter et al (62) evaluated their observers' abilities to resolve interaural intensity differences with click stimuli. Their primary independent variable was the initial interaural level difference. They found that sensitivity is quite constant over a 24 dB range of interaural disparity. This paper contains a thoughtful discussion of the need to preclude the possibility that observers use monaural intensity cues in this type of experiment. Domnitz & Colburn (30) confirm these observations and include conditions in which interaural level and interaural temporal thresholds were measured as a function of combinations of both cues. Their stimuli were 500 Hz tones, and they found that interaural amplitude thresholds are a symmetric function of interaural temporal difference across interaural level differences. On the other hand, interaural temporal difference thresholds depended upon whether the intensity and temporal cues were in opposition.

Yost et al (182) used a left-right judgment procedure to investigate the interaural level differences that produce acoustic images judged to be in the same location as are images produced by interaural temporal differences. The data confirm the findings of several earlier experiments.

The fact that tones with interaural level differences favoring one ear may be judged to have a midline locus when simultaneous interaural temporal differences favor the opposite ear has been known for some time. These data have traditionally been interpreted to mean that time and intensity "trade." An excellent paper by Hafter & Carrier (60) made it clear that stimuli which are composed of both cues in a manner which would place acoustic images in the midline are discriminable from diotic stimuli. This finding seriously questions the utility of models which treat interaural intensity cues by transforming them into a temporally coded dimension. In essence, a strong interpretation of the data would lead one to conclude that so-called time-intensity-trade data are merely recipes for combinations of tones which would be judged to be in some particular intracranial locus. Interpretations of many of the data obtained in experiments concerned with time-intensity trading are exceedingly tenuous because of the known multiple images that may be produced by the stimuli. Further, it has recently been shown that the function relating the interaural intensity difference required to offset an interaural temporal difference depends strongly on the variable (time or intensity) under the control of the subject (187). Kappauf & Trahiotis (84) have interpreted the data of Young and Levine in terms of judgmental response biases. They note that such biases are apparently present in the data of several other studies (e.g. 30, 170).

Domnitz & Colburn (30) present a position-based model to account for data obtained in interaural discrimination experiments as well as those obtained in experiments which utilize an acoustic pointer to locate the position of the image produced by a dichotic input. Considering the variability inherent in data which are obtained using pure tones with large interaural temporal differences, the model appears to provide a qualitatively good fit to both position-matching and discrimination data.

The phrases "rotating tones" and "binaural beats" have each been used to describe the subjective impressions that occur when two tones, close together in frequency, are presented, each to one ear. Some authors have distinguished between the subjective effects of movement and of loudness fluctuations when applying these terms. Perrott & Musicant (122) indicate that rotating tones having one image were heard for small values of interaural frequency difference, and binaural beats were heard at larger frequency differences which also produced two images (one image at each ear).

Most of the experiments discussed previously that have manipulated interaural temporal differences have done so in a manner such that only the fine structure of the waveform is delayed; i.e. no onset or offset temporal cues were available. Perrott & Baars (121) report that temporal disparities at stimulus onset and offset are more easily detected for short than for long duration noise bursts and that temporal differences provided at offset are less detectable than temporal differences at onset. Interestingly, their observers reported only one image for the longer duration signals and stated that a "separate" transient cue allowed them to discriminate between the stimuli in these conditions. Yost (179) reported that the lateralization of tones with onset, ongoing, and offset temporal differences depends on low-frequency information. While it is probably true that observers can use such cues to lateralize the stimuli for the shorter durations, the same-different paradigm used in this experiment does not allow one to be certain that the observers were in fact making their decisions on the basis of lateralized images. It is also not clear that there would be large amounts of low-frequency spectral information available in the 1 sec, 4050 Hz signals that were discriminable on the basis of temporal differences. Perhaps the subjective reports of Perrott and Baars' observers may suggest an explanation for the extremely good performance found with long duration, high-frequency signals.

Scharf et al (145) have made use of onset temporal differences and interaural frequency differences to estimate the width of the "critical band" effective in lateralization. They report that when the interaural frequency difference is less than a critical band the threshold interaural temporal difference is independent of interaural frequency difference. The critical bandwidths obtained for signal frequencies over the range of 110 Hz to 6000 Hz are reported as being in good agreement with critical bandwidths measured monaurally. Other types of data have been used to argue that the bandwidths measured binaurally are larger than those measured monaurally (e.g. 93). Perhaps these data are relevant to the model proposed by Colburn (19) which requires that only a limited frequency region in each ear can provide information which is processed or compared centrally. Thus, the binaural system could be construed to be sensitive to interaural temporal differences because of the transient response of particular neural units. In this light, Scharf's data may be thought of as indicating the width of the bands of frequencies that can interact centrally.

Several recent studies have investigated the lateralization and discrimination of high-frequency signals having relatively slowly time-varying envelopes (70, 71, 103, 116). These studies indicate that observers can use temporal disparities in the envelope to extract useful binaural cues. McFadden & Moffitt (101) and Nuetzel & Hafter (116) found that the discriminability of interaural, time-varying envelope differences improves as a function of stimulus duration. McFadden and Moffitt clearly indicate that the improvement in performance is not due to the number of cycles of the envelope available to the observer. Nuetzel and Hafter used amplitude modulated sinusoids and showed that sensitivity to envelope information was affected by interaural differences in the carrier frequency. They also reported that observers cannot fuse the envelope information available at high carrier frequencies with a pure tone at the envelope frequency presented contralaterally. This result was reported earlier by Young & Carhart (185). Young & Carhart (186) found that observers can offset interaural temporal differences in the envelope of a high-frequency AM waveform by an appropriate interaural level difference favoring the "lagging" ear. We believe, in conjunction with McFadden & Pasanen (103), that these studies, which confirm a number of observations reported over the last two decades, should make it clear that the textbook notion that the binaural system utilizes intensity cues at high frequencies and temporal cues at low frequencies is naïve.

Nordmark (115) makes use of jittered, filtered pulse trains to generate FM stimuli which result in astonishingly small binaural temporal difference thresholds. These thresholds were found to decrease monotonically with increasing frequency. The ability to perform this task appears to require that the FM be random in time.

Altman & Viskov (3) measured velocity thresholds for binaural click trains which contain temporally increasing degrees of interaural temporal difference. They found that the velocity difference thresholds were nearly linearly related to the relative amount of velocity of the fused image.

Masking

Traditionally, experiments in binaural masking have involved broadband noise maskers and tonal signals. In recent years, however, experimenters have begun to employ a wider variety of waveforms as both signals and maskers. Green & Yost (56) and McFadden (100) provide summaries of the literature up to 1974. Green & Yost also include brief descriptions of the major models that stimulated research during that period. Two very recent and exhaustive reviews will be found in Durlach & Colburn (34) and Colburn & Durlach (21). While Durlach and Colburn summarize the available data, Colburn and Durlach explicate the several models and theories of binaural interaction. This latter review includes detailed discussions of the assumptions of each of the models, the interrelationships of the models, and judgments concerning the ability of the models to describe and to predict the empirical results.

Robinson et al (136) have investigated the detectability in homophasic and antiphasic stimulus conditions when signals and maskers were both either 250 Hz tones or broadband noise. By varying the phase angle of addition of the signals with respect to the coherent maskers, they were able to evaluate sensitivity in conditions with various degrees of interaural temporal and intensity information. They found, as had previous investigators, that the performance in the homophasic conditions was based on Weber's law. Detectability for the antiphasic conditions was only slightly dependent upon signal-masker phase angle. This paper includes a discussion of the previous literature concerned with these phenomena as well as discussions concerning the relevance of the data to models. Yost et al (181) found that two different antiphasic conditions produced different functions relating detectability to the phase angle of addition of their 500 Hz signals to maskers of the same frequency. It should be remembered that the interaural cues in the antiphasic conditions of both of these experiments are those typically employed in lateralization experiments. McFadden & Pasanen (102) performed a similar experiment utilizing 50 Hz wide noise bands at several center frequencies. They find that detectability for masker (and signal) frequencies centered at 2 kHz and 4 kHz in the antiphasic conditions is probably determined by monaural level increments rather than by interaural differences. Grantham & Robinson (51) utilized amplitude modulated sine waves as maskers in an experiment similar to those just described. They employed the carrier frequency of the masker as signal and varied the phase relation of signal and carrier in homophasic and antiphasic conditions. The results were similar to those found in tone-on-tone and noise-on-noise experiments.

The fact that binaural advantages in detection are maintained when signal and masker are presented nonsimultaneously is well established. Lakey (89) provides parametric data which confirm and extend prior investigations. Yost & Walton (184) indicate that the rank order of efficiency in detection for several interaural conditions is maintained independent of the temporal relations between signals and maskers. Berg & Yost (6), using a click as a signal, investigated forward, backward, and combined forward-backward masking for several interaural combinations of signal and noise. They emphasize the difference between the amount of masking for homophasic and antiphasic conditions when masker level was manipulated. We concur with their conclusion that detectability in the antiphasic conditions cannot be accounted for by a running-average hypothesis (135).

As was pointed out earlier, high-frequency signals having slowly time-varying envelopes have been shown to be lateralizable. Henning (71) failed to observe a release from masking when AM waveforms having a high-frequency carrier were interaurally time-delayed and used as signals in broadband noise. This result led Henning to suggest that the mechanisms responsible for release from masking may be different from those responsible for lateralization. Yost (178) attempts to argue against this interpretation by emphasizing that the noise masker used by Henning may have disrupted the temporal information required for the binaural processing of the high-frequency waveform. Yost shows that the presence of noise disrupts the lateralizability of such AM signals. While Yost interprets this outcome as indicating that "... lateralization and binaural detection of complex waveforms are not essentially different" (p. 1214), we believe that Yost's data do not resolve the issues surrounding release from masking at high frequencies.

An attempt to explain the decline in detectability with increasing signal frequency that occurs in antiphasic conditions was made by Hafter (58). He presents a theoretical argument based on his lateralization model which leads him to acknowledge the possibility that high-frequency detectability is based upon interaural temporal differences. His argument ignores the well-known increase in auditory bandwidth with increasing frequency. It is not clear what effect this consideration would have on the argument.

Recent articles (44, 73, 163, 164) dealing with lateralization and binaural detection with cats serving as observers indicate that cats are affected by many of the stimulus parameters that affect people. While many of the data indicate the similarity of man and cat, one discrepancy seems worthy of mention. Hoppe & Langford (73) and Geesa & Langford (44) found evidence that indicates that the binaural interaction of information in the cat occurs over a greater frequency region than it does in man.

Data relevant to the release from masking obtained in certain binaural experiments have been interpretable in terms of models formulated by Webster (169), Jeffress et al (79), Durlach (32), Osman (117), Hafter & Carrier (59), and Colburn (19). Each of these models accounts for many of the available data. While particular experiments have been interpreted in terms of one or more of these models, Domnitz & Colburn (29) argue that binaural detection models based on interaural amplitude and/or phase differences and those based on interaural correlation all correctly predict performance in experiments investigating tones masked by noise while the interaural parameters of tonal signals are manipulated. Thus, rejection or acceptance of these models must be based on experiments involving parameters other than interaural signal differences for tonal signals. On the other hand, it is clear that the manipulation of these other parameters will not necessarily allow a choice among models. For example, Osman et al (119) find that both Osman's and Durlach's model provide adequate fits to data reported by Wilbanks & Whitmore (175), who investigated the detectability of monaural signals as a function of signal frequency and interaural correlation of the masking noise. Pohlman & Sorkin (127) find good agreement between Osman's model and data obtained in an experiment in which pulse-train signals differing in interaural correlation were detected in interaurally phase reversed broadband noise. It remains to be seen if Domnitz and Colburn's result applies to such spectrally complex signals.

Colburn (20) has recently described how the binaural detection of low frequency tones masked by broadband noise can be fit by his neurophysiologically based model. This model utilizes the properties of firing patterns of auditory neural units as inputs to a centrally located coincidence detector. The model provides excellent fits to a variety of data. As Colburn points out the model is ". . . a quantification and elaboration of some of the ideas expressed by Jeffress" (p. 527).

The models have as yet not been applied to several experiments which employed pulsed maskers. Osman (118) provides data from several such conditions and alludes to the difficulty in accounting for these data with the well-known models.

Pitch

The models of binaural detection appear to be applicable to experiments concerning the pitch produced by dichotic presentations of broadband noise. Following the demonstration of Cramer & Huggins (22) that pitch may be produced by interaural differences in the phase spectrum of broadband noise, Fourcin (43) found that interaural temporal delays in bands of noise could elicit pitch. Bilsen & Goldstein (10) have shown that the pitch arising from dichotically delayed noise is similar to that produced when a delayed version of a noise waveform is mixed with the original and presented monaurally. The portions of this paper relevant to this discussion concern their use of the Durlach model of binaural detection to account for their data on dichotic pitch. They show that a process like that proposed by Durlach can result in a "central" spectrum. Pitch is assumed to be extracted from this spectrum as proposed by Goldstein (48). Bilsen (9) presents a thorough discussion of several combinations of dichotic stimuli which produce a pitch that is explainable on the basis of information contained in the central spectrum. Bilsen chooses to emphasize a physiological model of pitch extraction which operates on the information from the monaural channels in terms of mechanisms proposed by Jeffress (76) and Licklider (94), and formalized by Colburn (19, 20). Raatgever & Bilsen (130) extend these notions by investigating the lateralization of dichotically produced pitches. They also present data concerning binaural masking in conditions which produce dichotic pitch.

Bilsen (8) presents a simple analog circuit that transforms noise so that the interaural phase shifts studied by Cramer and Huggins can occur simultaneously over several frequency regions. Bilsen notes that this type of stimulus produces a more robust dichotic pitch. van den Brink (158) investigated monotic and dichotic pitch matches with harmonic and inharmonic tonal complexes. He also presents data which indicate the frequency region over which such signals result in a fused image. Related additional information may be found in van den Brink et al (160).

SUMMARY AND COMMENTS

The recent publication of numerous textbooks, handbooks, and collected papers will certainly benefit teachers and students who must deal with a literature that grows at an alarming rate. These books, however, sometimes fail to capture one of the striking common elements that we see in the four areas we have reviewed: the growing importance of rather sophisticated models and theories. Such theories and models play an important role in determining the directions in which research will proceed in the future, as well as providing an increased understanding of the data which will be produced. While we consider the development of these models and theories to be a vital and integral part of the science, we are concerned that, at least in some cases, the complexity of the models may be such that their usefulness is vitiated.

We hope that the reader shares our impressions that much progress has been made in the last 4 years. We have indicated several instances where knowledge concerning audition is being integrated, unified, and applied to further the understanding of fundamental phenomena. An increasing number of papers address both behavioral and physiological data. The areas of pitch perception and frequency analysis are being integrated. Models of intensity perception now deal with the problems of loudness. Auditory nonlinearities are being recognized as important influences on pitch perception. Models of binaural signal detection and lateralization are being melded with models of pitch extraction. Such efforts reveal thoughtful attempts to delineate the importance and relevance of knowledge obtained in one realm to phenomena studied in another.

Literature Cited

1. Abbagnara, L. A., Bauer, B. B., Torick, E. L. 1975. Measurements of diffraction and interaural delay of a progressive sound wave caused by the human head. II. *J. Acoust. Soc. Am.* 58:693–700
2. Abbas, P. J., Sachs, M. B. 1976. Two-tone suppression in auditory-nerve fibers: Extension of a stimulus-response relationship. *J. Acoust. Soc. Am.* 59:112–22
3. Altman, J. A., Viskov, O. V. 1977. Discrimination of perceived movement velocity for fused auditory image in dichotic stimulation. *J. Acoust. Soc. Am.* 61:816–19
4. Belendiuk, K., Butler, R. A. 1975. Monaural localization of low-pass noise bands in the horizontal plane. *J. Acoust. Soc. Am* 58:701–5
5. Belendiuk, K., Butler, R. A. 1977. Spectral cues which influence monaural localization in the horizontal plane. *Percept. Psychophys.* 22:353–58
6. Berg, K., Yost, W. A. 1976. Temporal masking of a click by noise in diotic and dichotic listening conditions. *J. Acoust. Soc. Am.* 60:173–77
7. Berliner, J. E., Durlach, N. I., Braida, L. D. 1977. Intensity perception. VII. Further data on roving-level discrimination and the resolution and bias edge effects. *J. Acoust. Soc. Am.* 61:1577–85
8. Bilsen, F. A. 1976. Pronounced binaural pitch phenomena. *J. Acoust. Soc. Am.* 59:467–68
9. Bilsen, F. A. 1977. Pitch of noise signals: evidence for a "central spectrum." *J. Acoust. Soc. Am.* 61:150–62
10. Bilsen, F. A., Goldstein, J. L. 1974. Pitch of dichotically delayed noise and its possible spectral basis. *J. Acoust. Soc. Am.* 55:292–96
11. Bloom, P. J. 1977. Determination of monaural sensitivity changes due to the pinna by the use of minimum-audible-field measurements in the lateral vertical plane. *J. Acoust. Soc. Am.* 61:820–28
12. Burns, E. M., Viemeister, N. F. 1976. Nonspectral pitch. *J. Acoust. Soc. Am.* 60:863–69
13. Butler, R. A. 1975. The influence of the external and middle ear on auditory discriminations. See Ref. 86, pp. 247–60
14. Butler, R. A., Belendiuk, K. 1977. Spectral cues utilized in the location of sound in the median saggital plane. *J. Acoust. Soc. Am.* 61:1264–69
15. Butler, R. A., Planert, N. 1976. The influence of stimulus bandwidth on localization of sound in space. *Percept. Psychophys.* 19:103–8

16. Buunen, T. J. F. 1975. Two hypotheses on monaural phase effects. *Acustica* 34:98–105
17. Buunen, T. J. F., Bilsen, F. A. 1974. Subjective phase effects and combination tones. See Ref. 192, pp. 344–52
18. Buunen, T. J. F., Festen, J. M., Bilsen, F. A., van den Brink, G. 1974. Phase effects in a three-component signal. *J. Acoust. Soc. Am.* 55:297–304
19. Colburn, H. S. 1973. Theory of binaural interaction based on auditory nerve data. I. General strategy and preliminary results on interaural discrimination. *J. Acoust. Soc. Am.* 54:1458–70
20. Colburn, H. S. 1977. Theory of binaural interaction based on auditory-nerve data. II. Detection of tones in noise. *J. Acoust. Soc. Am.* 61:525–33
21. Colburn, H. S., Durlach, N. I. 1978. Models of binaural interaction. In *The Handbook of Perception*, Vol. 4, ed. E. C. Carterette, M. P. Friedman. New York: Academic. In press
22. Cramer, E. M., Huggins, W. H. 1958. Creation of pitch through binaural interaction. *J. Acoust. Soc. Am.* 30:413–17
23. Dallos, P. 1973. *The Auditory Periphery: Biophysics and Physiology.* New York: Academic. 548 pp.
24. Dallos, P. 1974. Combination tones in cochlear microphonic potentials. See Ref. 192, pp. 218–26
25. Dallos, P., Cheatham, M. A. 1977. Analog of two-tone suppression in whole nerve responses. *J. Acoust. Soc. Am.* 62:1048–51
26. de Boer, E. 1975. Synthetic whole-nerve action potentials for the cat. *J. Acoust. Soc. Am.* 58:1030–45
27. de Boer, E. 1976. On the residue and auditory pitch perception. See Ref. 87, pp. 479–83
28. de Boer, E. 1977. Pitch theories unified. See Ref. 40, pp. 323–34
29. Domnitz, R. H., Colburn, H. S. 1976. Analysis of binaural detection models for dependence on interaural target parameters. *J. Acoust. Soc. Am.* 59:591–601
30. Domnitz, R. H., Colburn, H. S. 1977. Lateral position and interaural discrimination. *J. Acoust. Soc. Am.* 61:1586–98
31. Duifhuis, H. 1976. Cochlear nonlinearity and second filter: Possible mechanisms and implications. *J. Acoust. Soc. Am.* 59:408–23
32. Durlach, N. I. 1963. Equalization and cancellation theory of binaural masking

level differences. *J. Acoust. Soc. Am.* 35:1206–13

33. Durlach, N. I., Braida, L. D. 1969. Intensity perception. I. Preliminary theory of intensity resolution. *J. Acoust. Soc. Am.* 46:372–83

34. Durlach, N. I., Colburn, H. S. 1978. Binaural phenomena. See Ref. 21

35. Durrant, J. D., Lovrinic, J. H. 1977. *Bases of Hearing Science.* Baltimore: Williams & Wilkins. 185 pp.

36. Egan, J. P. 1975. *Signal Detection Theory and ROC Analysis.* New York: Academic. 277 pp.

37. Elmasian, R., Galambos, R. 1975. Loudness enhancement: monaural, binaural and dichotic. *J. Acoust. Soc. Am.* 58:229–35

38. Erdreich, J. 1977. Intermodulation product pair $2f_l \pm f_h$: Masking and growth. *J. Acoust. Soc. Am.* 62:1252–55

39. Evans, E. F. 1976. Temporary sensorineural hearing losses and 8th nerve changes. See Ref. 69, pp. 199–23

40. Evans, E. F., Wilson, J. P., eds. 1977. *Psychophysics and Physiology of Hearing.* London: Academic. 525 pp.

41. Feth, L. L. 1974. Frequency discrimination of complex periodic tones. *Percept. Psychophys.* 15:375–78

42. Feth, L. L., O'Malley, H. 1977. Two-tone auditory spectral resolution. *J. Acoust. Soc. Am.* 62:940–47

43. Fourcin, A. J. 1970. Central pitch and auditory lateralization. See Ref. 126, pp. 319–26

44. Geesa, B. H., Langford, T. L. 1976. Binaural interaction in cat and man. II. Interaural noise correlation and signal detection. *J. Acoust. Soc. Am.* 59: 1195–96

45. Geisler, C. D. 1976. Mathematical models of the mechanics of the inner ear. See Ref. 87, pp. 390–415

46. Goldstein, J. L. 1967. Auditory nonlinearity. *J. Acoust. Soc. Am.* 41:676–89

47. Goldstein, J. L. 1970. Aural combination tones. See Ref. 126, pp. 230–45

48. Goldstein, J. L. 1973. An optimum processor theory for the central formation of the pitch of complex tones. *J. Acoust. Soc. Am.* 54:1496–1516

49. Goldstein, J. L. 1974. Letter to the editor. *Am. Sci.* 62:519–21

50. Goldstein, J. L., Kiang, N. Y. S. 1968. Neural correlates of the aural combination tone $2f_1-f_2$. *Proc. I.E.E.E.* 56: 981–92

51. Grantham, D. W., Robinson, D. E. 1977. Role of dynamic cues in monaural and binaural signal detection. *J. Acoust. Soc. Am.* 61:542–51

52. Green, D. M. 1960. Auditory detection of a noise signal. *J. Acoust. Soc. Am.* 32:121–31

53. Green, D. M. 1975. Pitch perception. See Ref. 157, pp. 147–55

54. Green, D. M. 1976. *An Introduction to Hearing.* Hillsdale, NJ: Erlbaum. 353 pp.

55. Green, D. M., Wier, C. C., Wightman, F. L. 1975. Gold and Pumphrey revisited, again. *J. Acoust. Soc. Am.* 57: 935–53

56. Green, D. M., Yost, W. A. 1975. Binaural analysis. See Ref. 86, pp. 461–80

57. Greenwood, D. D., Merzenich, M. M., Roth, G. L. 1976. Some preliminary observations between two-tone suppression and combination-tone driving in the antereoventral cochlear nucleus of the cat. *J. Acoust. Soc. Am.* 59:607–33

58. Hafter, E. R. 1977. Lateralization models and the role of time-intensity tradings in binaural masking: Can the data be explained by a time-only hypothesis? *J. Acoust. Soc. Am.* 62:633–35

59. Hafter, E. R., Carrier, S. C. 1970. Masking-level differences obtained with a pulsed tonal masker. *J. Acoust. Soc. Am.* 47:1041–47

60. Hafter, E. R., Carrier, S. C. 1972. Binaural interaction in low-frequency stimuli: The inability to trade time and intensity completely. *J. Acoust. Soc. Am.* 51:1852–62

61. Hafter, E. R., De Maio, J. 1975. Difference thresholds for interaural delay. *J. Acoust. Soc. Am.* 57:181–87

62. Hafter, E. R., Dye, R. H., Nuetzel, J. M., Aronow, H. 1977. Difference thresholds for interaural intensity. *J. Acoust. Soc. Am.* 61:829–34

63. Hall, J. L. 1974. Two-tone distortion products in a nonlinear model of the basilar membrane. *J. Acoust. Soc. Am.* 56:1818–28

64. Hall, J. L. 1975. Nonmonotonic behavior of distortion product $2f_1-f_2$: Psychophysical observations. *J. Acoust. Soc. Am.* 58:1046–50

65. Hall, J. L. 1977. Spatial differentiation as an auditory "second filter": Assessment on a nonlinear model of the basilar membrane. *J. Acoust. Soc. Am.* 61: 520–24

66. Hebrank, J., Wright, D. 1974. Are two ears necessary for localization of sound sources on the median plane? *J. Acoust. Soc. Am.* 56:935–38

67. Hebrank, J., Wright, D. 1974. Spectral cues used in the localization of sound sources on the median plane. *J. Acoust. Soc. Am.* 56:1829–34

68. Hellman, W. S., Hellman, R. P. 1975. Relation of the loudness function to the intensity characteristic of the ear. *J. Acoust. Soc. Am.* 57:188–92
69. Henderson, D., Hamernik, R. P., Dosanjh, D. S., Mills, J. H. 1976. *Effects of Noise on Hearing.* New York: Raven. 565 pp.
70. Henning, G. B. 1974. Detectability of interaural delay in high-frequency complex waveforms. *J. Acoust. Soc. Am.* 55:84–91
71. Henning, G. B. 1974. Lateralization and the binaural masking-level difference. *J. Acoust. Soc. Am.* 55:1259–62
72. Hirsh, S. K., Eldredge, D. H., Hirsh, I. J., Silverman, S. R., eds. 1976. *Hearing and Davis.* St. Louis: Washington Univ. Press. 476 pp.
73. Hoppe, S. A., Langford, T. L. 1974. Binaural interaction in cat and man. I. Signal detection and noise cross correlation. *J. Acoust. Soc. Am.* 55:1263–65
74. Houtsma, A. J. M., Goldstein, J. L. 1972. The central origin of the pitch of complex tones: evidence from musical interval recognition. *J. Acoust. Soc. Am.* 51:520–29
75. Howes, W. L. 1974. Loudness function derived from data on electrical discharge rates in auditory nerve fibers. *Acustica* 30:247–59
76. Jeffress, L. A. 1948. A place theory of sound localization. *J. Comp. Physiol. Psychol.* 41:35–39
77. Jeffress, L. A. 1968. Beating sinusoids and pitch changes. *J. Acoust. Soc. Am.* 43:1464
78. Jeffress, L. A. 1975. Localization of sound. See Ref. 86, pp. 449–59
79. Jeffress, L. A., Blodgett, H. C., Sandel, T. T., Wood, C. L. III. 1956. Masking of tonal signals. *J. Acoust. Soc. Am.* 28:416–26
80. Jesteadt, W., Bilger, R. C. 1974. Intensity and frequency discrimination in one- and two-interval paradigms. *J. Acoust. Soc. Am.* 55:1266–76
81. Jesteadt, W., Sims, S. L. 1975. Decision processes in frequency discrimination. *J. Acoust. Soc. Am.* 57:1161–68
82. Jesteadt, W., Wier, C. C. 1977. Comparison of monaural and binaural discrimination of intensity and frequency. *J. Acoust. Soc. Am.* 61:1599–1603
83. Jesteadt, W., Wier, C. C., Green, D. M. 1977. Intensity discrimination as a function of frequency and sensation level. *J. Acoust. Soc. Am.* 61:169–77
84. Kappauf, W. E., Trahiotis, C. 1978. A regression interpretation of differences in time-intensity trading ratios obtained in laterality studies using the method of adjustment. *J. Acoust. Soc. Am.* In press
85. Kiedel, W. D., Neff, W. D. eds. 1974. *Handbook of Sensory Physiology,* Vol. V/1. New York: Springer-Verlag. 704 pp.
86. Kiedel, W. D., Neff, W. D., eds. 1975. *Handbook of Sensory Physiology,* Vol V/2. New York: Springer-Verlag. 526 pp.
87. Kiedel, W. D., Neff, W. D., eds. 1976. *Handbook of Sensory Physiology,* Vol. V/3. New York: Springer-Verlag. 811 pp.
88. Kim, D. O., Molnar, C. E. 1975. Cochlear mechanics: Measurement and models. See Ref. 157, pp. 57–68
89. Lakey, J. R. 1976. Temporal masking-level differences: The effect of mask duration. *J. Acoust. Soc. Am.* 59:1434–42
90. Lambert, R. M. 1974. Dynamic theory of sound-source localization. *J. Acoust. Soc. Am.* 56:165–71
91. Lamoré, P. J. J. 1975. Perception of two tone octave complexes. *Acustica.* 34: 1–14
92. Lamoré, P. J. J. 1977. Pitch and masked threshold in octave complexes in relation to interaction phenomena in two-tone stimuli in general. *Acustica* 37: 249–57
93. Langford, T. L., Jeffress, L. A. 1964. Effect of noise cross-correlation on binaural signal detection. *J. Acoust. Soc. Am.* 36:1455–58
94. Licklider, J. C. R. 1959. Three auditory theories. In *Psychology: A Study of Science,* ed. S. Koch, 1:41–144. New York: McGraw-Hill. 710 pp.
95. Lim, J. S., Rabinowitz, W. M., Braida, L. D., Durlach, N. I. 1977. Intensity perception. VIII. Loudness comparisons between different types of stimuli. *J. Acoust. Soc. Am.* 62:1256–67
96. Lippman, R. P., Braida, L. D., Durlach, N. I. 1976. Intensity perception. V. Effect of payoff matrix on absolute identification. *J. Acoust Soc. Am.* 59:129–34
97. Luce, R. D., Green, D. M. 1974. Neural coding and psychophysical discrimination data. *J. Acoust. Soc. Am.* 56(2): 1554–64
98. Luce, R. D., Green, D. M. 1975. Erratum: Neural coding and psychophysical discrimination. *J. Acoust. Soc. Am.* 57(2):1552
99. Luce, R. D., Green, D. M., Weber, D. L. 1976. Attention bands in absolute identification. *Percept. Psychophys.* 20: 49–54
100. McFadden, D. 1975. Masking and the

binaural system. See Ref. 157, pp. 137–46

101. McFadden, D., Moffit, C. M. 1977. Acoustic integration for lateralization at high frequencies. *J. Acoust. Soc. Am.* 61:1604–8

102. McFadden, D., Pasanen, E. G. 1974. High-frequency masking-level differences with narrow-band noise signals. *J. Acoust. Soc. Am.* 56:1226–30

103. McFadden, D., Pasanen, E. G. 1976. Lateralization at high frequencies based on interaural time differences. *J. Acoust. Soc. Am.* 59:634–39

104. McGill, W. J., Goldberg, J. P. 1968. A study of the near-miss involving Weber's law and pure-tone intensity discrimination. *Percept. Psychophys.* 4: 105–9

105. Mehrgardt, S., Mellert, V. 1977. Transformation characteristics of the external human ear. *J. Acoust. Soc. Am.* 61:1567–76

106. Mills, A. W. 1958. On the minimum audible angle. *J. Acoust. Soc. Am.* 30:237–46

107. Moore, B. C. J. 1973. Some experiments relating to the perception of complex tones. *Q. J. Exp. Psychol.* 25:451–75

108. Moore, B. C. J. 1974. Relation between the critical bandwidth and the frequency-difference limen. *J. Acoust. Soc. Am.* 55:359

109. Moore, B. C. J. 1977. *Introduction to the Psychology of Hearing.* Baltimore: University Park. 311 pp.

110. Moore, B. C. J. 1977. Effects of relative phase of the components on the pitch of three-component complex tones. See Ref. 40, pp. 349–58

111. Moore, B. C. J., Raab, D. H. 1974. Pure-tone discrimination: some experiments relating to the "near miss" to Weber's law. *J. Acoust. Soc. Am.* 55:1049–54

112. Moore, B. C. J., Raab, D. H. 1975. Intensity discrimination for noise bursts in the presence of a continuous band-stop background: effects of level, width of the bandstop, and duration. *J. Acoust. Soc. Am.* 57:400–5

113. Moray, N., Fitter, M. J. 1974. Intensity discrimination in a rapid sequence of tone bursts. *J. Acoust. Soc. Am.* 56:1577–84

114. Nilsson, H. G., Moller, A. R. 1977. Linear and nonlinear models of the basilar membrane motion. *Biol. Cybern.* 27: 107–12

115. Nordmark, J. O. 1976. Binaural time discrimination. *J. Acoust. Soc. Am.* 60:870–80

116. Nuetzel, J. M., Hafter, E. R. 1976. Lateralization of complex waveforms: Effects of fine structure, amplitude, and duration. *J. Acoust. Soc. Am.* 60: 1339–46

117. Osman, E. 1971. A correlation model of binaural masking level differences. *J. Acoust. Soc. Am.* 50:1494–1511

118. Osman, E. 1975. Signal-noise duration, psychophysical procedure, interaural configuration, and the psychometric function. *J. Acoust. Soc. Am.* 58:243–48

119. Osman, E., Tzuo, H., Tzuo, P. L. 1975. Theoretical analysis of detection of monaural signals as a function of interaural noise correlation and signal frequency. *J. Acoust. Soc. Am.* 57:939–42

120. Penner, M. J., Leshowitz, B., Cudahy, E., Ricard, G. 1974. Intensity discrimination of pulsed sinusoids of various frequencies. *Percept. Psychophys.* 15: 568–70

121. Perrott, D. R., Baars, B. J. 1974. Detection of interaural onset and offset disparities. *J. Acoust. Soc. Am.* 55:1290–92

122. Perrott, D. R., Musicant, A. D. 1977. Rotating tones and binaural beats. *J. Acoust. Soc. Am.* 61:1288–92

123. Pfeiffer, R. R., Molnar, C. E., Cox, J. R. Jr. 1974. The representation of tones and combination tones in spike discharge patterns of single cochlear nerve fibers. See Ref. 192, pp. 323–31

124. Plomp, R. 1975. Auditory psychophysics. *Ann. Rev. Psychol.* 26:207–32

125. Plomp, R. 1976. *Aspects of Tone Sensation.* London: Academic. 167 pp.

126. Plomp, R., Smoorenburg, G. F. 1970. *Frequency Analysis and Periodicity Detection in Hearing.* Leiden: Sijthoff. 482 pp.

127. Pohlmann, L. D., Sorkin, R. D. 1974. Binaural masking level differences for pulse train signals of differing interaural correlation. *J. Acoust. Soc. Am.* 55: 1293–98

128. Pumphrey, R. J., Gold, T. 1948. Phase memory of the ear: a proof of the resonance hypothesis. *Nature* 161:640

129. Raab, D. H., Goldberg, I. A. 1975. Auditory intensity discrimination with bursts of reproducible noise. *J. Acoust. Soc. Am.* 57:437–47

130. Raatgever, J., Bilsen, F. A. 1977. Lateralization and dichotic pitch as a result of spectral pattern recognition. See Ref. 40, pp. 443–53

131. Rabinowitz, W. M., Lim, J. S., Braida, L. D., Durlach, N. I. 1976. Intensity perception. VI. Summary of recent data on deviations from Weber's law for

1000-Hz tone pulses. *J. Acoust. Soc. Am.* 59:1506–9

132. Resnick, S. B., Feth, L. L. 1975. Discriminability of time-reversed click pairs: intensity effects. *J. Acoust. Soc. Am.* 57(2):1493–99

133. Rhode, W. S. 1977. Some observations on two-tone interaction measured with the Mössbauer effect. See Ref. 40, pp. 27–38

134. Rhode, W. S., Robles, L. 1974. Evidence from Mössbauer experiments for nonlinear vibration in the cochlea. *J. Acoust. Soc. Am.* 55:588–96

135. Robinson, C. E., Pollack, I. 1973. Interaction between forward and backward masking: a measure of the integrating period of the auditory system. *J. Acoust. Soc. Am.* 53:1313–17

136. Robinson, D. E., Langford, T. L., Yost, W. A. 1974. Masking of tones by tones and of noise by noise. *Percept. Psychophys.* 15:159–67

137. Robles, L., Rhode, W. S., Geisler, C. D. 1976. Transient response of the basilar membrane measured in squirrel monkeys using the Mössbauer effect. *J. Acoust. Soc. Am.* 59:926–39

138. Roederer, J. G. 1975. *Introduction to the Physics and Psychophysics of Music.* New York: Springer-Verlag. 200 pp. 2nd ed.

139. Ruben, R. J., Elberling, C., Salomon, G., eds. 1976. *Electrocochleography.* Baltimore: University Park. 506 pp.

140. Ruggero, M. A. 1973. Response to tone of auditory fibers in the squirrel monkey. *J. Neurophysiol.* 36:569–87

141. Sachs, M. B., Abbas, P. J. 1974. Rate versus level functions for auditory-nerve fibers in cats: tone-burst stimuli. *J. Acoust. Soc. Am.* 56:1835–47

142. Sachs, M. B., Kiang, N. Y. S. 1968. Two-tone inhibition in auditory-nerve fibers. *J. Acoust. Soc. Am.* 43:1120–28

143. Schacknow, P. N., Raab, D. 1976. Noise-intensity discrimination: effects of bandwidth conditions and mode of masker presentation. *J. Acoust. Soc. Am.* 60:893–905

144. Scharf, B. 1974. Loudness summation between tones from two loudspeakers. *J. Acoust. Soc. Am.* 56:589–93

145. Scharf, B., Florentine, M., Meiselman, C. H. 1976. Critical band in auditory lateralization. *Sens. Processess* 1:109–26

146. Schroeder, M. R. 1975. Amplitude behavior of the cubic difference tone. *J. Acoust. Soc. Am.* 58:728–32

147. Schroeder, M. R. 1975. Models of hearing. *Proc. I.E.E.E.* 63:1332–50

148. Schroeder, M. R., Hall, J. L. 1974. Model for mechanical to neural transduction in the auditory receptor. *J. Acoust. Soc. Am.* 55:1055–60

149. Searle, C. L., Braida, L. D., Cuddy, D. R., Davis, M. F. 1975. Binaural pinna disparity: another localization cue. *J. Acoust. Soc. Am.* 57:448–55

150. Searle, C. L., Braida, L. D., Davis, M. F., Colburn, H. S. 1976. Model for auditory localization. *J. Acoust. Soc. Am.* 60:1164–75

151. Shaw, E. A. G. 1974. The external ear. See Ref. 85, pp. 455–90

152. Shaw, E. A. G. 1974. Transformation of sound pressure level from the free field to the eardrum in the horizontal plane. *J. Acoust. Soc. Am.* 56:1848–61

153. Small, A. M. Jr. 1977. Loudness perception of monotonically changing sound pressure. *J. Acoust. Soc. Am.* 61:1293–97

154. Smoorenburg, G. F. 1974. On the mechanisms of combination tone generation and lateral inhibition in hearing. See Ref. 192, pp. 332–42

155. Stevens, S. S. 1975. *Psychophysics.* New York: Wiley. 329 pp.

156. Terhardt, E. 1974. Pitch, consonance and harmony. *J. Acoust. Soc. Am.* 55:1061–69

157. Tower, D. B., ed. 1975. *The Nervous System, Vol. 3: Human Communications and Its Disorders.* New York: Raven. 564 pp.

158. van den Brink, G. 1974. Monotic and dichotic pitch matchings with complex sounds. See Ref. 192, pp. 178–88

159. van den Brink, G. 1975. The relation between binaural diplacusis for pure tones and for complex sounds under normal conditions and with induced monaural pitch shift. *Acustica* 32:159–65

160. van den Brink, G., Sintnicolaas, K., van Stam, W. S. 1976. Dichotic pitch fusion. *J. Acoust. Soc. Am.* 59:1471–76

161. Viemeister, N. F. 1972. Intensity discrimination of pulsed sinusoids: The effects of filtered noise. *J. Acoust. Soc. Am.* 51:1265–69

162. Viemeister, N. F. 1974. Intensity discrimination of noise in the presence of band-reject noise. *J. Acoust. Soc. Am.* 56:1594–1600

163. Wakeford, O. S., Robinson, D. E. 1974. Lateralization of tonal stimuli by the cat. *J. Acoust. Soc. Am.* 55:649–52

164. Wakeford, O. S., Robinson, D. E. 1974. Detection of binaurally masked tones by the cat. *J. Acoust. Soc. Am.* 56:952–56

165. Watson, C. S. 1973. Psychophysics. In *Handbook of General Psychology*, ed. B. B. Wohlman, pp. 275–306. Englewood Cliffs, NJ: Prentice-Hall. 1006 pp.

166. Watson, C. S., Kelley, W. J., Wroton, H. W. 1976. Factors in the discrimination of tonal patterns. II. Selective attention and learning under various levels of stimulus uncertainty. *J. Acoust. Soc. Am.* 60:1176–86

167. Weber, D. L., Green, D. M., Luce, R. D. 1977. Effects of practice and distribution of auditory signals on absolute identification. *Percept. Psychophys.* 22:223–31

168. Weber, R., Mellert, V. 1975. On the nonmonotonic behavior of cubic distortion products in the human ear. *J. Acoust. Soc. Am.* 57:207–14

169. Webster, F. A. 1951. Influence of interaural phase on masked thresholds. I. The role of interaural time-deviation. *J. Acoust. Soc. Am.* 23:72–78

170. Whitworth, R. H., Jeffress, L. A. 1961. Time vs. intensity in the localization of tones. *J. Acoust. Soc. Am.* 33:925–29

171. Wier, C. C., Jesteadt, W., Green, D. M. 1976. A comparison of method-of-adjustment and forced-choice procedures in auditory frequency discrimination. *Percept. Psychophys.* 19:75–79

172. Wier, C. C., Jesteadt, W., Green, D. M. 1977. Frequency discrimination as a function of frequency and sensation level. *J. Acoust. Soc. Am.* 61:178–84

173. Wightman, F. L. 1973. The pattern-transformation model of pitch. *J. Acoust. Soc. Am.* 54:407–16

174. Wightman, F. L., Green, D. M. 1974. The perception of pitch. *Am. Sci.* 62:208–15

175. Wilbanks, W. A., Whitmore, J. K. 1968. Detection of monaural signals as a function of interaural noise correlation and signal frequency. *J. Acoust. Soc. Am.* 43:785–97

176. Wilson, J. P., Johnstone, J. R. 1975. Basilar membrane and middle-ear vibration in guinea pig measured by capacitive probe. *J. Acoust. Soc. Am.* 57:705–23

177. Yost, W. A. 1974. Discriminations of interaural phase differences. *J. Acoust. Soc. Am.* 55:1299–1303

178. Yost, W. A. 1975. Comments on "Lateralization and the binaural masking-level difference" (see Ref. 71). *J. Acoust. Soc. Am.* 57:1214–15

179. Yost, W. A. 1977. Lateralization of pulsed sinusoids based on interaural onset, ongoing, and offset temporal differences. *J. Acoust. Soc. Am.* 61:190–94

180. Yost, W. A., Nielsen, D. W. 1977. *Fundamentals of Hearing: An Introduction.* New York: Holt. 240 pp.

181. Yost, W. A., Nielsen, D. W., Tanis, D. C., Bergert, B. 1974. Tone-on-tone binaural masking with an antiphasic masker. *Percept. Psychophys.* 15:233–37

182. Yost, W. A., Tanis, D. C., Nielsen, D. W., Bergert, B. 1975. Interaural time vs. interaural intensity in a lateralization paradigm. *Percept. Psychophys.* 18:433–40

183. Yost, W. A., Turner, R., Bergert, B. 1974. Comparison among four psychophysical procedures used in lateralization. *Percept. Psychophys.* 15:483–87

184. Yost, W. A., Walton, J. 1977. Hierarchy of masking-level differences obtained for temporal masking. *J. Acoust. Soc. Am.* 61:1376–78

185. Young, L. L., Carhart, R. 1973. The lateralization of the residue for preselected interaural phase disparities. *J. Acoust. Soc. Am.* 54:310 (Abstr.)

186. Young, L. L., Carhart, R. 1974. Time-intensity trading functions for pure tones and a high-frequency AM signal. *J. Acoust. Soc. Am.* 56:605–9

187. Young, L. L. Jr., Levine, J. 1977. Time-intensity trades revisited. *J. Acoust. Soc. Am.* 61:607–9

188. Zurek, P. M., Leshowitz, B. H. 1976. Measurement of the combination tone stimuli f_2-f_1 and $2f_1-f_2$. *J. Acoust. Soc. Am.* 60:155–68

189. Zurek, P. M., Leshowitz, B. H. 1976. Interaural phase discrimination for combination tone stimuli. *J. Acoust. Soc. Am.* 60:169–72

190. Zwicker, E. 1970. Masking and psychological excitation as consequences of the ear's frequency analysis. See Ref. 126, pp. 376–96

191. Zwicker, E. 1977. Procedure for calculating loudness of temporally variable sounds. *J. Acoust. Soc. Am.* 62:675–82

192. Zwicker, E., Terhardt, E., eds. 1974. *Facts and Models in Hearing.* New York: Springer-Verlag. 360 pp.

193. Zwislocki, J. J., Ketkar, I., Cannon, M. W., Nodar, R. H. 1974. Loudness enhancement and summation in pairs of short tone bursts. *Percept. Psychophys.* 16:91–95

194. Zwislocki, J. J., Sokolich, W. G. 1974. On loudness enhancement of a tone burst by a preceding tone burst. *Percept. Psychophys.* 16:87–90

Ann. Rev. Psychol. 1979. 30:63–102
Copyright © 1979 by Annual Reviews Inc. All rights reserved

HUMAN MEMORY ❖303

Fergus I. M. Craik

Department of Psychology, University of Toronto, Toronto, Ontario, Canada

CONTENTS

INTRODUCTION 63
SENSORY AND REPRESENTATIONAL MEMORY 66
  Iconic Memory 67
  Auditory Memory 68
  Words and Gestures 69
  Memory for Pictures and Words 70
  Faces and Scenes 71
  Memory for Chess Positions 72
  Overview of Sensory Memory 73
SHORT-TERM RETENTION 73
  Theoretical Developments 73
  Characteristics of Primary Memory 75
  Release from Proactive Inhibition 76
  Recency 77
ENCODING PROCESSES 77
  Levels of Processing 77
  Alternatives to Levels 79
  Rehearsal and Repetition 81
RETRIEVAL PROCESSES 84
  Gaining Access to the Trace 85
  Encoding Specificity 87
  Recall and Recognition 88
MEMORY FOR SENTENCES, STORIES, AND DISCOURSE 91
  Memory for Sentences and Paragraphs 92
  Memory for Stories 93
FUTURE DIRECTIONS 95

INTRODUCTION

The literature on human memory has been reviewed relatively recently in this series, and so the present article is necessarily brief and highly selective. The articles and books reviewed were published predominantly between January 1976 and April 1978, although some earlier references are included

63

0066-4308/79/0201-0063$01.00

to illustrate trends and developments. The review deals exclusively with memory for episodic events—thus, work that focuses on problems of learning and on the structure of knowledge (semantic memory) is not covered except where such studies are helpful in understanding memory for events. Studies on scanning (for example, those using Sternberg's short-term reaction-time paradigm) are also excluded, as are most experiments in which response time is the principal measure used, largely because they are concerned with rather different issues from the bulk of experiments reviewed here. The chapter emphasizes experimental work taking an information processing or cognitive view of memory, and there is a further bias toward work that exhibits some freshness of approach to method and theory.

What general trends are apparent in the field? It is clear that memory researchers are still people who dearly love a good paradigm. However, there is a definite move toward descriptive studies that focus on phenomena and away from "experiments on experiments." Together with this more descriptive approach there is a trend to using a much broader sample of materials and situations; thus, within the domain of verbal memory, researchers are studying sentences, stories, and conversations, and there is a growing tendency to explore nonverbal memory for materials such as pictures, faces, environmental sounds, smells, sign language, and motor movements. It seems that, belatedly, the field is working through its natural history phase. This greater concern for a broader data base and for the potential applications of knowledge about memory is surely to be welcomed, both from the point of view that our work may be of some benefit to society, and also in that our theories must benefit from the greater range of materials and situations used.

In verbal memory there is a parallel trend away from the Ebbinghaus tradition of dissection and analysis of the components of memory, toward the Bartlett approach of wholistic description of larger units (10, pp. 3–15). In fact, in a sort of Gold Rush of Verbal Learning, investigators are increasingly turning from the humdrum study of nonsense syllables and word lists to the more exciting exploration of sentences, paragraphs, and stories. This Race for the Novel (the ultimate achievement—a free recall study of *War and Peace?*) is to be welcomed from considerations of greater realism and breadth, although there is also a danger of forgetting that general principles of memory can be demonstrated with simple as well as with complex materials.

A further trend, related to the current emphasis on complex materials, is the growing popularity of the schema as a theoretical explanatory device (6, 114, 124). Schemas are coherent conceptual frameworks, built up on the basis of experience, which allows interpretation and comprehension of novel events. When a schema is involved in comprehension, the explicitly presented stimuli are fitted into the schema that selects them, but in addition, further words or ideas are "instantiated" to permit fuller comprehension to occur. As far as memory is concerned, schemas come into play both during encoding and during reconstructive retrieval. If memory reflects those mental operations that take place at input, then plausible inferences, invoked during comprehension, should be falsely recognized and should function as effective retrieval cues for the explicitly presented material. The first of these results was found by Thorndyke (124) and the second by R. C. Anderson et al (6). Some ingenious studies are presented by Anderson & Pichert (5) to show how the invocation of a new schema can lead to remembering of "forgotten" information; the experiments and their implications are described later in the chapter.

The notion of the schema, although still rather vaguely defined, occupies a central position in cognitive psychology at present. As such, it serves to emphasize the necessary interrelations among perception, attention, comprehension, memory, and action. The past few years have seen some breakdown of barriers between workers in artificial intelligence and those in experimental psychology. A further development is the growth of shared interests between cognitive and social psychologists, as illustrated, for example, by the work of Schank & Abelson (118). As yet, mainstream memory theory has not been greatly affected by these movements, but recent important publications (2, 6, 95, 114) seem likely to influence theoretical and empirical work in this direction. Rogers, Kuiper & Kirker (110) reported an interesting result that may promote common interests between memory and personality theorists. Rogers et al carried out a levels-of-processing experiment in which they replicated the finding that a semantic orienting task (judging adjective pairs for synonymity) was associated with higher retention levels than a structural or a phonemic task; however, a further orienting task—in which the subject decided whether the adjective described himself—was associated with the highest retention levels of all. The authors attributed this result to the notion that the "self" is a particularly well-organized schema and is thus ideally suited for encoding and remembering information. Further exploration of this paradigm may yield important clues to remembering in other situations.

Another recent trend, perhaps attributable to the liberating influence of social and personality theorists, is a growth in the use of jocular labels for findings and whimsical titles for articles. Thus, in the former category, as well as the "tip-of-the-tongue phenomenon" (10), we now have the "tip-of-the-nose state" (73) the "flashbulb effect" (27) and the "soap opera effect" (97). In the latter category the clear winner is J. M. Mandler with her articles on story grammars: "A Code in the Node" (78) and "Remembrance of Things Parsed" (79). We look forward to Dr. Mandler's forthcoming articles on interference effects in verbal memory ("When Words Collide"), on memory for natural environments ("Recall of the Wild"), and a review article in French on dichotic listening ("Double Entendre").

To conclude this overview of the field, some recent books will be mentioned. J. R. Anderson (2) published a major theoretical statement of his views on memory and cognition; to some extent this work amends and revises the ideas set forth in the HAM model of Anderson and Bower (see 10). A number of textbooks and reviews were published during 1976 and 1977. Two advanced texts providing excellent coverage and evaluation of the field were written by Baddeley (10) and Crowder (34). Whereas both are first-class additions to the literature, they provide an interesting contrast in approaches: Baddeley's book is free-wheeling and somewhat eclectic; as well as setting current ideas and experiments in verbal memory in their historical context, he devotes some space to neuropsychology, effects of arousal, various types of nonverbal memory, mnemonic systems, and individual differences. The book is given cohesion by a functionalist viewpoint stressing the importance of coding, retrieval, and the central role of working memory in an information-processing framework. Crowder's book deals more narrowly with a number of issues that have been central to American theories of learning and memory during this century. He considers the effects of repetition, the nature of organization, problems of serial order, and the evolution of interference theory in an impressive and scholarly way. The bulk of the book evaluates recent work in the cognitive and information-processing paradigms; these current concerns are given an added perspective by being viewed against a background of classical work. Finally, M. W. Eysenck (44) has written a book with the very commendable aim of integrating work on individual differences (arousal, anxiety, extraversion, aging, and intelligence) with recent views on memory. This is a messy area at present, but one that is clearly of great importance. Eysenck's book may well accelerate the growing interest in individual differences in cognition.

The remainder of the chapter deals with specific issues and results in some selected areas.

SENSORY AND REPRESENTATIONAL MEMORY

By "sensory" I mean the kinds of information generally studied under the headings of iconic and echoic memory systems, and their counterparts in other sense modalities; by "representational" I mean longer-lasting nonverbal information for voices, sounds, pictures, patterns, orthography, signs, faces and so on. It has become increasingly clear over the last few years (69) that surface information such as orthography, voice, and the actual words used to convey a message, are not to be thought of as a package which is "unwrapped" by sensory analyzers, the semantic gist extracted, and the package then thrown away. At the very least, the medium modulates the message and remains part of its encoded representation. The theoretical implications of this view are discussed after the evidence is reviewed. This point, among others, is covered in a useful review of sensory memory by Crowder (35).

Iconic Memory

Two novel suggestions regarding iconic memory are described in this section. The first, by Sakitt (117), is that the icon is predominantly a retinal phenomenon mediated by rod vision. This argument is made on the basis of obtaining normal partial-report results from a subject with no cone system. In addition, Sakitt showed that the icon was similar to the rod system in terms of spectral sensitivity. Sakitt's view that the icon is essentially an after-image has not gone unchallenged. Banks & Barber (15) have demonstrated typical partial-report results using colored letters against a background that scotopically yielded the same shade of grey as the letters. Under such conditions, the rod system would be unable to distinguish the letters from the background, thus presumably the cone system was used. Banks and Barber suggested that iconic memory, like normal vision, obtains most information from rods in dim light and cones in bright light—that is, both systems are involved. A further article by Meyer & Maguire (86) also expressed doubts about Sakitt's conclusions. Meyer and Maguire showed subjects visual gratings of different spatial frequency; the gratings were switched on and off, with an on-time of 50 msec and a variable off-time that the subject adjusted until the pattern appeared continuously present. This value of off-time indicated iconic persistence. The authors found that iconic persistence increased from about 300 to 450 msec as spatial frequency increased; since a purely rod-mediated system would be indifferent to spatial frequency, the authors argue that their result points to a more central locus of iconic memory and is incompatible with Sakitt's view.

The second interesting suggestion in this area is by Di Lollo (40), who proposed that iconic memory can more properly be regarded as an ongoing feature-extraction process than as the decaying contents of a sensory store. He based his arguments on some ingenious experiments using a 5 X 5 dot matrix with one dot missing. Thus, on each trial, 24 dots were presented and the subject's task was to indicate the location of the missing dot, which changed randomly from trial to trial. The display was presented as two randomly chosen blocks of 12 dots, always separated by 10 msec. The first block was exposed for durations ranging from 10 to 200 msec, and Di Lollo found that *increasing* durations of the first block led to more errors in locating the missing dot. This result is difficult for the view that iconic memory bridges the gap between the first and second blocks since, if anything, longer first-block times should strengthen the icon and prolong its duration. Di Lollo argues instead that "iconic memory" represents continued processing of the input; once sufficient information has been extracted from the display, iconic memory ceases. Thus with long first-block exposures, all the required information has been extracted by the time the stimulus exposure terminates, and no iconic persistence is found. The identification of iconic memory with an active process of feature extraction is an appealing one; in addition, the finding that longer stimuli show less persistence has previously been demonstrated by Haber in vision and by Efron in audition (10, pp. 189 and 238). Finally, it is interesting to note that Meyer & Maguire (86) found longer iconic persistence for visual gratings of higher spatial frequencies; these gratings were harder to see, thus plausibly the necessity to extract further visual information lengthens the duration of the icon.

Auditory Memory

Traditional studies of echoic memory (10, 34) have recently been augmented by experiments on longer-term retention of voices and other sounds. In the former category, several studies of the suffix effect have been reported. This effect appears when a string of auditorily presented letters or digits is presented for recall in their original order; the recency effect is greatly reduced when the string is followed by a further speech sound that need not be recalled. Foreit (48) used this technique with sequences of tones, and found that a tone suffix depressed recall of the last tone. Rowe & Rowe (111) conducted a similar study using sequences of either short environmental sounds or their verbal labels (e.g. siren, bell, whip); the suffix used was either of the same type as the string to be recalled or of the other type (e.g. sounds followed by a verbal suffix). The investigators found that the suffix effect was obtained only when the string and suffix were of the same type. On the basis of these and many previous experiments it is tempting to attribute the suffix phenomenon simply to the degree of physical discriminability of the terminal item from the suffix. To the extent that the suffix differs from the previous string in modality of presentation, ear of arrival, speaker's voice, and so on, the detrimental effect of the suffix is reduced. Temporal similarity may be an exception to this general rule, however, as Morton (88) has shown that for a string presented at a 1 sec rate, a suffix presented out of rhythm (0.5 sec after the last item) was as disruptive as a suffix presented in rhythm. On the basis of his results, Morton concluded that the suffix may have two effects; some passive masking, and a second effect that interferes with the encoding of the terminal item. It seems equally plausible to attribute the second effect to a failure of discriminability, however, and a consequent difficulty in retrieval. The discriminability hypothesis was advanced by Darwin and Baddeley and is discussed by Baddeley in his recent book (10, p. 250).

Geiselman & Glenny (51) carried out an ingenious experiment on longer-term retention of voice information. Subjects were first familiarized with the voices of a male and a female speaker; then word pairs were presented visually with instructions to the subjects to say the words to themselves either in the male voice, the female voice, or in their own voice. In the recognition test, the words were presented auditorily by the male or the female speaker. A strong interaction was found such that recognition was superior in cases where the test voice matched the voice mimicked by the subject at encoding. The same interaction was found, though at a lower absolute level, when the test words were presented by *different* male and female speakers. The authors argued against any kind of "literal copy" theory, on the grounds that the male or female voice was never presented explicitly at input; but it is surely the match of internal representations that is crucial, however these representations are formed. A further possibility advanced by the authors is that the semantic sense of encoded words is modified by the sex of the presenting speaker—thus subjects may store "male" or "female" senses of words and this information may facilitate recognition. The finding that the *same* male or female speakers at presentation and test were superior to *different* male or female speakers does suggest a specific role for voice information however. Recognition level may depend both on physical features and on linguistic information.

Words and Gestures

Siple, Fischer & Bellugi (121) examined interrelations between memory for words and the form in which they were presented. The medium studied here was American Sign Language (ASL). One experiment demonstrated good retention of the form in which a word was presented (visually or by sign). An extremely interesting difference emerged between deaf subjects (who knew ASL) and hearing subjects (who did not) in their liability to choose gesturally related signs as false alarms in a recognition test; the hearing subjects did make such errors whereas the deaf subjects did not. The authors suggested that if the gesture is meaningful, the resulting code is predominantly semantic, whereas if the sign has no semantic reference for a subject, he necessarily encodes it in terms of the gesture alone, and is thus liable to falsely recognize similar signs in the later retention test. Siple et al concluded that both gestural and semantic aspects of the stimuli are stored.

Memory for Pictures and Words

Pictures are better retained than their verbal labels in many paradigms (98) and much recent work has attempted to find out why. The dominant theoretical notion in the area has been Paivio's dual-coding theory, which ascribes the superior retention of pictures to their greater likelihood of inducing both an imaginal code and a verbal code. Paivio (98) reviewed evidence relating to his theory and to other possible accounts of the effect. Of these alternatives, a levels-of-processing view that pictures induce a "deeper" encoding does not seem helpful in the absence of an independent index of depth. Further, D'Agostino, O'Neill & Paivio (36) have shown that the higher levels of retention associated with semantic relative to phonemic orienting tasks is restricted to concrete words and is not found with either pictures (which are well recalled after both tasks) or abstract words (which are poorly recalled after both tasks). The authors' interpretation is that dual coding occurs relatively automatically for pictures, whereas only verbal coding is possible for abstract words. In the case of concrete words, the phonemic orienting task induces a verbal code only, whereas the semantic task gives rise to both verbal and imaginal codes, thereby making concrete words like pictorial stimuli. However, the assumption that verbal labeling of pictures occurs with high probability is challenged by the results of D. L. Nelson and his colleagues discussed in the next two paragraphs.

The most viable alternative to the dual-coding account of picture superiority, and one that appears to be gaining ground, is the simple suggestion that pictures induce a richer, more detailed representation in memory, and this in turn makes them more distinctive at the time of retrieval (93, 104). Whether the richer encoding induced by pictures is specifically "visual" in character or whether both words and pictures are encoded in a common abstract propositional form is still a moot point. It is clear that verbal and pictorial information can influence each other, presumably through some abstract form of representation (75, 102), but that does not rule out the possibility that each type of stimulus is also represented by modality-specific codes at shallower levels of analysis.

Paivio's theory is one which involves different types and levels of representation, and it would seem relatively easy to modify his view from the notion that "the critical factor is the number of codes activated by the orienting task" (36, p. 253) to the idea that performance depends on the distinctiveness of the multilevel representation. This latter view is advocated by D. L. Nelson (93) in the context of his sensory-semantic model. He reviews convincing evidence showing that pictures do not automatically induce encoding of their labels (thereby contradicting the dual-encoding view) and that words are retained better than pictures if the words are phonemically distinctive and the pictures are visually confusable. As several researchers have pointed out (39, 93, 98), there are strong indications of convergence among dual-coding, levels of processing, and sensory-semantic ideas—a common theoretical position may emerge from the current debate.

Faces and Scenes

As part of the movement toward studying more "ecologically valid" materials, several experiments have been reported on memory for faces and complex scenes. In the former category, Patterson & Baddeley (99) have shown that initial judgments of personality (for example, rating the depicted person on scales of nice-nasty, intelligent-dull) were associated with higher levels of subsequent recognition than were judgments of physical characteristics (e.g. small-large nose). The difference in recognition was small but quite reliable, and the authors suggested that the personality ratings may direct subjects' attention to the face as a whole. They also reported some initial work of practical importance on the relative effectiveness of various types of disguise.

Some of the growing experimental work on memory for scenes also has implications for giving testimony in court. Loftus, Miller & Burns (75) showed subjects a series of slides of an automobile accident; between presentation of the slides and a recognition test for a critical slide, the subjects were exposed to verbal information that was either consistent, misleading, or irrelevant to the scenes viewed. The authors found that the misleading information was incorporated into the memory for the events and gave rise to later recognition errors; further, the misleading information had greater impact if presented just before the retention test rather than just after initial viewing of the slides. As with Pezdek's (102) work, this result demonstrates the integration of verbal and pictorial information in memory.

An imaginative study by Kraft & Jenkins (72) examined recognition memory for orientation. Subjects saw slides of a meaningful sequence (e.g. a person taking a box from a shed to a car) but the slides were presented either in a consistent orientation so that subjects could infer the sequence easily, or they were not. Later recognition of orientation depended critically on the subjects' ability to form the meaningful story—this is shown by the fact that subjects who had constructed meaningful stories were able to infer the correct orientation of new slides from the sequence (that is, slides not presented initially). Clearly, memory here did not depend on a literal copy, but on the formation of some higher-order construct.

The concept of schemas has been used explicitly by J. M. Mandler in her recent work on memory for pictures. In one typical study, Mandler & Ritchey (80) asked what people remember from a picture over the long term and whether different kinds of information are lost at different rates. They examined memory for 1. inventory information—a simple listing of the objects in the picture, 2. ability to describe the objects, 3. relative spatial location of the objects, and 4. overall composition of the picture. The authors tested recognition performance over 4 months by changing various aspects of presented pictures; they also explored the effects of organization on recognition—that is, whether the picture conformed to real-life rules. They found that degree of organization enhanced the retention of inventory information and spatial relations, but not of object descriptions or picture composition; also the first two types of information were well retained over 4 months whereas the latter two were not. Mandler and Ritchey concluded that scene schemas contain an inventory of objects and their relative spatial positions, but not object descriptions or details of overall picture composition.

Memory for Chess Positions

The concept of schema might again be applied to the perception and retention of complex meaningful patterns, especially where meaningfulness is a function of lengthy practice and expertise. Experiments carried out by de Groot (10, pp. 271–73) showed that chess masters were able to place 90% of the chess pieces correctly after one 5-sec exposure to a game position; under the same conditions weak players could reproduce only 40% of the position. With random board settings, however, chess masters were little better than the weak players. Later Chase & Simon replicated de Groot's findings and suggested that the chess masters' advantage arose from their ability to hold larger "chunks" in short-term memory. It seems very plausible that the experts should be able to deal with the pieces as large meaningful configurations, but it now seems that the advantage is in long-term, not short-term memory. Charness (30) found that 30 sec of interpolated activity reduced memory for chess positions by only 6%; despite the small loss in accuracy, subjects took much longer to reproduce the position after interpolated activity—apparently the memory had to be reconstructed in some sense, it was not held in a fragile, easily accessible form. Charness's conclusion that the masters' advantage does not reside in short-term memory was strengthened by Frey & Adesman (49). They found that expert chess players could remember almost the same proportion of pieces from two positions as from one position. Frey and Adesman conclude that strong players process information rapidly to an abstract deep level of meaning; they discover more semantic relations among pieces and chunks. Presumably "schema-based" organization and rules allow the chess masters to perceive, store, and reconstruct the positions with relative ease.

Overview of Sensory Memory

In summary, much recent evidence points to the probability that the memory record of an event contains several qualitatively different kinds of information. Different input modalities can communicate and influence each other through common, abstract codes but the trace also contains modality-specific information. Contrary to the general belief of some years ago, "surface" or "representational" information can persist in memory for long periods of time. A dramatic example of surface information enhancing performance after a lengthy interval was reported by Kolers (69); he gave subjects extensive practice at reading pages of text printed in a geometrically inverted typography. When subjects were retested it was found that pages presented for the second time (after a 15 month interval) were read faster than pages presented for the first time. Kolers argues that this finding reveals memory for the specific pattern-analyzing operations involved in reading a particular page. He discounts the more likely possibility that subjects retained something of the semantic context of reread pages and that this general knowledge of the subject matter facilitated the difficult reading task, but to my mind the reasons for rejecting this alternative possibility are not overwhelming. Whatever the final judgment on this demonstration, there can be little doubt that Kolers' recent arguments (70) for a greater role in memory processes for surface information are gradually becoming accepted.

SHORT-TERM RETENTION

Theoretical Developments

Two major theoretical lines are being actively developed in short-term memory research: First, the notion of working memory (10, Chap. 8) and second, the formulation of attention and short-term storage proposed by Shiffrin & Schneider (120).

The concept of working memory developed from earlier characterizations of the short-term store [perhaps especially the rehearsal buffer notion of Atkinson & Shiffrin (8)]; the stress is on an executive processor of limited capacity that plays a central role in most if not all nonautomatic cognitive functioning. The central processor's efficiency is enhanced by auxiliary systems such as an articulatory rehearsal loop that can retain short verbal sequences with a minimal expenditure of capacity. Recent work (58) has explored the functioning of the working memory system in a variety of cognitive tasks; also, Baddeley (12) has suggested ways in which working memory is involved in reading. For beginning readers, the articulatory loop is used to store sounds already decoded, thereby freeing the central processor for further decoding, blending, and testing hypotheses about identification and meaning. In Baddeley and Hitch's view, memory span is largely mediated by the articulatory loop, therefore findings that dyslexic children have impaired digit span (12) provide good evidence that such children have a defective articulatory loop and that this deficit underlies their poor performance, in part at least. Baddeley stresses that fluent readers probably do not use the articulatory loop, except when verbatim retention is required or when the rate of input exceeds the rate of semantic processing.

Further evidence suggesting that short-term retention is mediated by several mechanisms was provided by Perfetti & Goldman (100). They found that performance on a probe digit task bore no relation to reading ability, whereas performance on a continuous story task did; thus, it seems that only certain types of short-term memory ability affect reading comprehension. Apparently short-term memory is not "one thing" but is an aggregate of mechanisms and skilled processes.

The second major theoretical contribution to the area of short-term retention was made by Shiffrin & Schneider (120). Their theory incorporates ideas on attention, memory, and perceptual learning. With regard to memory, the central notion is the short-term store (STS), whose principal function is the active control of thinking, problem-solving, and general memory processes—in this respect, STS is equivalent to working memory and to Atkinson and Shiffrin's rehearsal buffer. Rather than being a separate structure, however, Shiffrin and Schneider's STS is an activated subset of the permanent, long-term store (LTS). At input all features of incoming stimuli are analyzed and are represented as active elements in LTS; thus, there are no attentional limitations on the input, but attentional processes select important information for maintenance, decision, or transfer to LTS. Unattended information is lost very rapidly, the rate of loss being dependent on the level at which information has been analyzed, on interference from similar encodings in LTS, and on background context changes between encoding and test (119, pp. 217–18). "Transfer to LTS" in this model is the formation of new associations in LTS. Shiffrin goes on to show how a small set of limitations in a single system can account in a satisfactory way for a large number of phenomena.

The one point that strikes me as being somewhat unreasonable in an otherwise impressive model is the notion of "full" automatic analysis of all inputs followed by almost immediate forgetting of most encodings. To someone who, like myself, has just read a very large number of articles in a comparatively short time, the notion of a system with a voracious, attention-free input, followed by forgetting, sometimes within "tens of milliseconds" (119, p. 217) has an undeniable intuitive appeal; but, apart from the difficulty of distinguishing empirically between no encoding and encoding followed immediately by forgetting, there are two additional points giving rise to doubts. The first is the lack of biological economy involved in analyzing all inputs, however peripheral, and the second is the implicit assumption that there is only one way to analyze a complex stimulus array — all we know about ambiguity and set denies this latter possibility. If set operates *after* initial registration, presumably *all possible interpretations* of the input complex must be computed, and this is difficult to accept.

Characteristics of Primary Memory

Murdock (90) has again stressed the usefulness of distinguishing between item and order information in short-term serial memory. He showed that recall of items is enhanced when the items are drawn from the same category, but that recall of order is poorer in categorized than in noncategorized lists. In recognition memory, categorization again helps item information but has no effect on order information. Lee & Estes (74) also distinguished between item and order information; further, they were able to separate position and order in a sequence by embedding the letters to be remembered among distractor digits. They showed that under primary memory conditions, memory for order is derived from memory for position.

Another current issue in primary memory research is whether items are forgotten when attention is diverted to a second task. Roediger, Knight & Kantowitz (108) examined this problem by having subjects retain five words while performing an easy or a difficult perceptual-motor task. Task difficulty had no effect on retention. The authors speculated that the two tasks drew upon separate pools of capacity; thus retention of verbal items in primary memory may not demand the same type of attention that is utilized to perform nonverbal tasks. The functional independence of at least two primary memory systems was also postulated, with supporting evidence, by Peterson, Rawlings & Cohen (101). They found that rehearsal in visual-spatial memory could proceed concurrently with verbal rehearsal—total memory capacity is apparently additive among various subsystems. This notion of several active memory systems accords with previous formulations of special-purpose processors, each with its own attentional capacity (1). Further developments of this line of theorizing are awaited with interest.

What processes underlie performance on a memory span task? Watkins (131) suggested that word span reflects components from both secondary and primary memory; he concluded that the initial few items in the span are drawn from secondary memory since only these items are sensitive to word frequency effects. Martin (82) found that digit span performance across subjects correlated with neither the primary memory nor the secondary memory components of free recall. She concluded that digit span may predict ability to remember temporal sequences but not item information. However, she speculated that word span (as opposed to digit span) might predict aspects of free recall performance because word span places more emphasis on memory for items. Martin also suggested that word span would be a better diagnostic index of memory dysfunction since it taps memory for both item and order information.

Release from Proactive Inhibition

Many investigators are converging on the view that the detrimental effects on recall caused by prior items (proactive inhibition) is attributable to a loss of distinctiveness or discriminability in the current items. It follows from this view that in the "release from PI" paradigm, performance on the trial involving a shift in encoding should depend on the degree of discriminability between the present and preceding items. In line with this expectation, Wickens, Dalezman & Eggemeier (134) showed neatly that the amount of release obtained after a series of fruit names depended on the number of features shared by the preceding fruit names and the critical words; progressively greater amounts of release were found for names of vegetables, flowers, meats, and professions. O'Neill, Sutcliffe & Tulving (96) demonstrated that two factors are necessary for release to occur—a distinctive encoding must be formed and the appropriate retrieval cue must be present. This conclusion points up the oversimplification involved in attempts to attribute the release from PI effect to one of encoding, storage, or retrieval (107). A discriminable encoding must be formed at input (aided for example by the type of material or type of encoding induced), the discriminability must persist in storage and be tapped by appropriate retrieval information.

An interesting and provocative result was reported by Gardiner et al (50). In a standard release from PI paradigm, they used a switch in print color as the release manipulation, and found that color gave good release (95%) with consonant trigrams as the to-be-remembered items, but *no* release when word triads were used. This result is important as it implies that the release from PI paradigm cannot be used as a means to index the absolute salience of various encoding dimensions. First, the degree of release reflects the *relative* discriminability of "critical" from "proactive" encodings, and second, the salience of a particular dimension apparently depends on its context—thus, speculatively, the Gardiner et al result shows that color forms a relatively important part of the encoding of meaningless letter strings but is relatively unimportant when meaningful material is used (see also 121).

Recency

The concept of recency and its underlying causes was examined in an impressive paper by Baddeley & Hitch (13). They rejected the commonly held view that recency (in most laboratory paradigms using verbal materials) is attributable to output from a phonemically encoded short-term store. First, recency was obtained under incidental learning conditions, even after a 30 sec unfilled interval—in this situation there is no need for subjects to switch to a phonemic code or to consciously maintain the items over an interval. Second, articulatory suppression techniques have very little detrimental effect. Third, recency effects are easily demonstrated in long-term memory also—think of the last few movies you saw or the last occasions when you ate in a restaurant. Baddeley and Hitch proposed a common mechanism for all examples of recency in terms of the strategic utilization of ordinal retrieval cues; by this view time is less important than number of similar intervening events. As the authors pointed out, their ideas are not yet worked out in final detail, but their suggestion of a common underlying mechanism is an important lead to follow.

ENCODING PROCESSES

Levels of Processing

Many studies published during the last two years examined memory from the point of view of the depth, elaborateness, or extensiveness of the encoding induced at input; the experiments often utilized orienting tasks in the incidental learning paradigm popularized by Jenkins and his associates (34, pp. 15–16). Some of these studies have explicitly adopted the levels-of-processing viewpoint of Craik & Lockhart (32), and others have suggested alternative frameworks for describing their results. The two major trends have been the collection of further useful data on processing approaches to memory, and second, a growing number of criticisms of the levels-of-processing framework.

Only a brief selection can be given of interesting new work. Arbuckle & Katz (7) suggested that different orienting tasks may not induce qualitatively different memory codes but that, for example, a nonsemantic orienting task may simply yield a weaker semantic trace. This possibility seems unlikely, however, given the demonstrations of encoding specificity by Tulving and his colleagues, who have shown that the effectiveness of a particular type of retrieval cue is strongly dependent on the type of encoding induced at input. Semantic cues are maximally effective following semantic encoding, for example (128). In addition, two experiments have shown that subjects tend to choose acoustically related distractors in a recognition test following an acoustic orienting task and semantically related distractors following a semantic orienting task (31, 38). The results of further experiments discussed later (85, 87) also give good support to the notion that differences in encoding processes yield correlated differences in the resulting memory traces. All these findings strongly support the notion of qualitatively different codes. However, the codes so induced are probably not exclusively either acoustic or semantic; it seems rather that the orienting task biases the encoding in a certain way (31, 103).

Goldman & Pellegrino (55) asked the interesting question of how multiple encodings of an item affect later recognition and recall. They concluded that traces are "additive" to some extent. They also found an interaction between repetition and level of encoding, in that repetitions of deeper-level encodings were more beneficial for later retention [but see (29, 94)]. Goldman and Pellegrino asked whether retrieval of semantically encoded items took longer than retrieval of shallower codes, but found no relation between type of encoding and retrieval latency. It seems plausible that rich, elaborate codes support good retention, but will take more time and effort to reconstruct; however, this line of speculation is discouraged by Goldman and Pellegrino's results, and also by results obtained by Griffith (57). Griffith examined the relative attentional or processing demands of forming mnemonic mediators when supplied by the experimenter or generated by the subject. He found that subject-generated mediators required more capacity to form, were more effective as aids to recall, and were associated with *less* attentional demands at retrieval. It seems that processing effort, like processing time, is not related to depth or type of encoding in any simple way. More processing effort to achieve comprehension (and provided comprehension *is* achieved) is associated with higher levels of retention (9) probably because more extensive processing is necessitated (70). But once an event is well encoded it apparently can be accessed as rapidly as (55), and with less effort than (57), a poorly encoded trace. Undoubtedly familiarity and expertise enter the picture (21) and it seems likely that the relative degrees of integration and elaboration (77) are important also. That is, a well-integrated trace is plausibly less effortful to retrieve than is an elaborate but loosely organized encoding [e.g. the retrieval of novel chess positions by good players (30)].

A levels-of-processing approach to memory for sentences and prose has been taken by several authors (41, 81). Dooling & Christiaansen (41) demonstrated the multilevel nature of memory for prose by showing that surface detail was lost relatively rapidly, whereas higher-level ("deeper") codes were more durable. They also found that context affected the memorability of a particular code, however, and used this result to argue against a constant, rigid, processing hierarchy. The levels-of-processing viewpoint was adopted for studies of pictorial encoding by D. L. Nelson and his colleagues, though in more recent work (93), Nelson has stressed the greater differentiation of pictorial codes.

In other experiments on encoding processes, Johnson-Laird, Gibbs & de Mowbray (62) showed that not all aspects of a word's meaning are encoded during semantic processing. A similar conclusion was reached by Mathews (84). The studies demonstrated that retention was a function both of semantic processing and the congruence of words to a descriptive category. Postman & Kruesi (103) did not argue against the notion that input processes heavily influence the encoding and thus retention level, but pointed out that if the importance of the memory task is stressed, subjects can carry out more beneficial encoding operations than they would do under an incidental learning set.

Alternatives to Levels

Some researchers have endorsed the general pattern of findings grouped under the levels-of-processing heading, but have pointed out alternative ways of describing the data. For example, Glanzer & Koppenaal (53) argued that because encoding manipulations of the semantic/nonsemantic type affect secondary memory but not primary memory (10, Chap. 6), there was not much to choose between the levels-of-processing formulation and a two-stage theory. However, the point of most levels-of-processing studies has been to gain a fuller understanding of processes operating in secondary memory, not to deny the usefulness of the distinction between primary and secondary memory (32, p. 676). As Glanzer and Koppenaal remark, the work on levels of processing extends rather than replaces a stage analysis.

Whereas Paivio and his colleagues have usually stressed the additivity of verbal and imaginal codes in their accounts of differences in memory (98), they have recently argued that "Dual coding can explain the depth-of-processing results—in terms of the degree of representational, referential, and associative processing demanded by the particular orienting tasks" (36, p. 253). In those terms, there does indeed seem to be little difference between the formulations; it seems possible that a common viewpoint, stressing both levels of processing and qualitatively different codes, could emerge. A further similar position was adopted by Anderson & Reder (4), who argued that "depth" manipulations have their effect by changing the number and the type of elaborations stored. "Deeper levels of processing" by this view are those types of encoding that allow a greater variety of elaborate codes to be formed.

Bellezza, Richards & Geiselman (18) contrasted the concepts of depth and organization. They pointed out that "depth" refers to the types of encoding performed on a single item, whereas "organization" refers to further interitem processing. The view propounded by Bellezza et al is that deep, semantic processing is necessary for good recall, but it is not sufficient; interitem organization is also necessary. In a second article, Bellezza, Cheesman & Reddy (17) distinguished between two types of further processing once an item has been comprehended semantically; one type is elaboration—semantic enrichment of the single item—and the second is organization. They showed that organization (linking the words together in a coherent story) did enhance recall substantially but that elaboration of each word separately (generating sentences or defining the word) had little beneficial effect. By minimizing the role of single-item elaboration, Bellezza et al's view is apparently at odds with Anderson and Reder's position. However, the relative efficacy of elaboration and organization may depend critically on the particular tasks chosen and also on retrieval conditions; thus it seems wisest to defer judgment on this issue for the present.

Two central postulates of the levels-of-processing view are first that deeper codes are more meaningful and second that such deeper codes are more durable. Several recent papers have questioned these points and suggested an important alternative view. Morris, Bransford & Franks (87) argued that meaningfulness is not an absolute characteristic, but must be defined relative to particular goals. They also pointed out that shallow encodings may typically be poorly retained because they are tested for in an inappropriate way; if the retrieval test is appropriate for the encoding, then perhaps no one encoding type is "better" than any other. Tulving (128) also stressed the relativity of remembering, arguing from an encoding specificity standpoint. In confirmation of their views, Morris et al (87) showed that when a phonemic encoding was tested appropriately (by asking questions about rhymes at retrieval) performance levels were superior to the combination of semantic encoding and rhyme-based retrieval. Thus, semantic encoding is not necessarily superior, and phonemic encodings are quite durable. In a more direct test for surface characteristics, McDaniel et al (85) showed that subjects could recognize the typescript in which a particular word had been presented, provided that the initial orienting task stressed perceptual features also. There is no doubt that the "transfer appropriate processing" view is an important one (21); it is now clear that performance level depends on the compatibility of encoding and test. But it is also true that a semantic encoding followed by a semantic test is associated with higher retention levels than is a phonemic encoding followed by a phonemic test (87, 128). Thus, possibly there *is* something inherently "better" about semantic processing; it may typically yield a more elaborate or a more distinctive code (46, 68).

The suggestion that deeper codes are also more discriminable, and that this greater distinctiveness is the crucial factor underlying superior retention, has been made several times, notably by Klein & Saltz (68) and by Eysenck (46). Klein and Saltz showed that in a situation in which subjects were given two semantic orienting tasks to perform on the same material at input, performance levels are highest when the tasks involved uncorrelated dimensions of judgment. In their view, the uncorrelated dimensions specified the event's encoding more precisely and distinctively in "cognitive space." This approach allows for exploration of encodings *within* the semantic domain; it is complementary in many ways to Anderson's (2, 4) view that greater amounts of elaboration yield superior memory performance.

The levels-of-processing view has been criticized by a number of researchers on both theoretical and empirical grounds. T. O. Nelson (94) demonstrated that, contrary to Craik & Lockhart's (32) speculation, repetitions of an encoding at the same level were associated with an increment in retention; this issue is further discussed below. Nelson also made the strong point that since "depth" cannot at present be indexed independently from its alleged memorial consequences, the levels-of-processing view is circular, vacuous, and scientifically worthless. This point was echoed by other critics (11, 45) and is clearly a damaging one. It remains to be seen whether the heuristic value of the levels approach remains valuable in the absence of a tight, falsifiable theoretical structure. In a balanced and reasonable article, Baddeley (11) criticized a number of additional aspects; for example, in what sense are there "levels" within, say, the semantic domain? He also pointed out that in light of recent evidence, the notion of a fixed hierarchical processing sequence is most unlikely. On empirical issues Baddeley, like Nelson, made the point that maintenance processing *does* have some beneficial effects; also, that shallow codes are apparently much more durable than Craik and Lockhart supposed. There are counterarguments to some of these points (33), but this is not the place to air them. The next few years will show whether the levels-of-processing ideas will be accepted and extended, rejected, or perhaps assimilated into further theoretical formulations.

Rehearsal and Repetition

The notion of rehearsal has been clarified by recent work; the concept is becoming more complex, but the characterization of the underlying operations and their effects on retention is correspondingly more general and more adequate. One line of inquiry has stemmed from the distinction between the "maintenance" and "elaborative" properties of rehearsal (32, 135). One strong view of this distinction (32) held that maintenance rehearsal could be construed as "same-level" processing and should not lead to a facilitation of retention; only elaborative rehearsal should lead to deeper processing and thus to enhanced retention. This view has recently been successfully attacked and must now be abandoned, in its original form at least.

Experiments by T. O. Nelson (94) showed that recall and recognition were both improved by repetition of words at the same level of processing; the "same level" was achieved by requiring subjects to make either a phonemic or a semantic decision about words on each of two presentations. There seems no doubt that repetition of an event, even if it is treated in the same way on both occasions, enhances retention; this result has also been reported by several other investigators, including Chabot, Miller & Juola (29) and Goldman & Pellegrino (55). However, there appears to be a critical difference between a further explicit presentation of an event (repetition) and maintenance rehearsal (in the sense of continuous generation of the item by the subject). Further work showing relatively little effect of maintenance rehearsal is discussed below. Interestingly, Nelson showed that mass repetitions (zero lag) did enhance recall; it is unclear why two massed presentations should increase performance levels whereas one presentation maintained briefly by rehearsal does not—two discrete psychological events are apparently more beneficial for retention than one event, even if the one event is maintained over the same presentation interval. Nelson found no interaction between the "depth" of the orienting task and number of repetitions—the semantic task benefited no more than did the phonemic task from repeated presentation. This absence of an interaction between repetition and depth has been reported by some investigators (29) but not by others (55) who have found greater effects of repetition on semantic than on structural processing. The difference in findings may depend on whether subjects perform an identical orienting task on the repeated item (as in Nelson's study) or a same-level task with some changes from trial to trial (as in the Goldman and Pellegrino study). The issue of additive and multiplicative effects of repetition was discussed by Jacoby, Bartz & Evans (60).

Is it the case that repetition improves memory but maintenance rehearsal does not? Unfortunately the issue is not that simple. Dark & Loftus (37) reported a study in which 3–5 words were maintained over an unfilled retention interval of 1–20 sec; subjects expected to recall the words immediately, but on some trials the words were not tested. In an unexpected final free recall of all words, it was found that recall of untested words (thus uncontaminated by a previous retention test) did increase as a function of initial retention interval. The authors concluded that maintenance rehearsal does lead to higher recall levels. However, the words were presented at a rate (1/sec) that would not allow very adequate encoding at input, also subjects were expecting to recall them, so it is possible that subjects used the initial retention interval to carry out further processing or organizing of the presented words (60). In order to achieve minimal processing of words, Glenberg, Smith & Green (54) and Rundus (115) have used the ingenious technique of having subjects repeat one or two words continuously, ostensibly as a rehearsal-preventing activity in the Brown-Peterson paradigm; subjects are then unexpectedly tested on the words at the end of a series of trials. Using this paradigm, Rundus found that maintenance rehearsal of one word did not enhance recall, although later work (116) revealed that 60 sec of maintenance activity was associated with an increment in recall over 5 sec of maintenance. In a further experiment Rundus showed that repetition of the same word in subsequent trials *did* increment recall, whereas length of the maintenance rehearsal interval had little effect; this result neatly emphasizes the difference between repetition and maintenance. Rundus also presented evidence that subjects can maintain information at different levels of analysis; subjects either repeated a word or generated rhymes or associates to the word throughout the rehearsal interval. The results showed that semantic generation supported higher recall levels than did repetition or rhyme generations, but that the length of the rehearsal interval had relatively little effect.

Using the same paradigm, Glenberg et al (54) found that maintenance rehearsal does not improve recall performance. However, they also showed that such rehearsal is associated with an increment in subsequent recognition of the rehearsed words. This interesting result of an effect on recognition but none on recall confirms earlier observations by Woodward, Bjork & Jongeward (135). Woodward et al suggested that maintenance rehearsal (or primary processing) strengthens the word's representation in memory but does not result in the formation of associations necessary to support recall. Glenberg et al discussed various other possibilities underlying the effect. One analysis that may be helpful here is Mandler's (77) distinction between integration and elaboration; integration enhances the item's cohesiveness (intraunit organization), whereas elaboration (as the term is used by Mandler) refers to the buildup of interitem connections. Even though the units are words (which are presumably already well integrated), integrative processes may act to enhance the cohesion and distinctiveness of the word's encoded representation and thus to increment recognition. As a speculation, maintenance rehearsal may lead to increased integration and thus higher levels of recognition, but not to the further elaboration necessary to enhance recall performance. A related suggestion discussed by Crowder (34, pp. 386–87) is that maintenance rehearsal acts to strengthen the relations between the item and the local context—again, the notion is that this activity helps recognition but not recall.

Though it is clear that repeating an event does enhance its later recall and recognition, it is still unclear why repetition sometimes does and sometimes does not interact with the type of material presented or the type of operation carried out. Jacoby et al (60) suggested that repetition acts to enhance trace accessibility, whereas such factors as meaningfulness and depth of processing act to give greater coherence and integration to the trace (see also 77). Various workers have suggested that rehearsal could usefully be broken down into maintenance and elaborative components; it now seems more satisfactory to suggest a *continuum* of rehearsal operations running from the minimal processing necessary to repeat a word continuously to various types of elaborative processing involving either further enrichment of one item or associative linkage of several items. The effects of rehearsal on subsequent retention may thus depend both on its position on the maintenance-elaborative dimension and also on the qualitative nature of the information rehearsed (e.g. phonemic, semantic, imaginal). Mandler (77) has suggested that elaborative processing requires processing capacity, whereas rote repetition of an integrated unit can be accomplished relatively automatically. There is now good evidence to back up the notion that processing near the "pure maintenance" end of the continuum requires little capacity or effort, whereas greater elaboration requires greater expenditure of capacity (57, 59, 63). A final point concerns the differential effects of maintenance rehearsal on recall and recognition. A straightforward possibility is that recognition is simply a more sensitive test, and thus detects the weakly enhancing effects of maintenance rehearsal. A somewhat more interesting possibility, proposed by several workers, is that different types of processing lead to differential enhancement of recognition and recall. Thus, Mandler (77) suggested that integrative processing is associated with increments in recognition, whereas interitem organization leads to improved levels of recall.

RETRIEVAL PROCESSES

There is growing agreement that retrieval processes are quite similar to encoding processes in many respects (47, 56, 113) and may even be identical —a viewpoint that follows logically from Kolers' argument that remembering depends on repetition of the same mental operations (70). Generally it seems that retrieval cues are effective to the extent that they induce operations, or records of operations, that match the original event-as-encoded (the encoding specificity principle), although Anderson & Pichert (5) provided an interesting apparent exception to this rule. In cases where the information provided at retrieval is only a fraction of the original episode, how does the cue act to "redintegrate" the missing information? What factors set a limit to the power of retrieval? How should we conceptualize retrieval failure? What similarities and differences exist between the processes of recall and recognition? Empirical and theoretical work on these central issues is being pursued vigorously at present.

Gaining Access to the Trace

Jones (64) advanced a "fragmentation hypothesis" in which the trace is viewed as a fragment of the perceived situation and a retrieval cue is effective to the extent that it is stored in the fragment. This view of the memory trace as an integrated, "multicomponent" set of attributes is an attractive one endorsed by several recent theorists (47, 98). With regard to the redintegration problem, Jones postulated that "any attribute contained in the fragment, used as a cue, gives access to the remainder of the fragment" (64, p. 281). This account seems too all-or-none and automatic, however; it is more likely that the redintegrative power of a cue depends on the specific guidance the cue provides to reconstructive processes. This latter conclusion follows from Bower & Glass's (20) demonstration that some fragments of nonsense line drawings are much more powerful cues than other fragments as aids to recall the drawing. Fragments corresponding to structural units of the pattern made better cues, where structural unity was derived from Gestalt principles.

In an important article, Spyropoulos & Ceraso (122) also found that certain trace components made better cues than others. They suggested that a cue is effective if it acts as the identifying property of the total unit. To illustrate this principle, Spyropoulos and Ceraso had subjects sort cards on which colors and shapes were drawn; the depicted patterns were either unitary (e.g. a red triangle) or nonunitary (e.g. an outline triangle and a separate patch of red); and subjects sorted the cards either by shape or by color. In a later test of cued recall, they found that the dimension of classification was a much better cue, but only for unitary patterns. Apparently the same classification system mediates both initial categorization and later access to the trace. Redintegration depends (in part at least) on the degree of unity achieved during initial perception.

An interesting corollary to this position is that effective integration of stimulus components at input serves to insulate trace components from cues that are not part of the encoded unit. Baker & Santa (14) showed that high word associates (not presented at input) were quite effective as cues for target words encoded as members of word pairs, but that the associates were less effective as cues when the target words were encoded in meaningful sentences. The nature of the decreased accessibility of well-integrated units to normative cues is unclear; speculatively, the sentence context may lead to formation of a highly context-specific version of the encoded stimulus.

A pedagogical application may be that information should not be too well integrated with the learning situation, or decreased access in other situations will result (14).

Retrieval processes are constrained and inhibited in various lawful ways. Graesser & Mandler (56) suggested that retrieval from natural categories involves a sampling system that is limited by the span of apprehension (5 ± 1 items). Once the sample limit is reached, there is a pause while the system seeks a new point of entry into the category. The same limit on span of apprehension constrains encoding processes also.

Roediger and his associates have carried out further work on factors underlying the inhibiting effect of presenting some list items as cues for the remaining items. Roediger, Stellon & Tulving (109) showed that both extralist and intralist cues produced an inhibitory effect but that the latter effect was stronger. The effect is not attributable to the necessity of checking retrieved words against the provided cues (to see whether they need be emitted or not) because the inhibition remained when a very long retrieval interval was allowed and when subjects were permitted to recall all items, both target words and cues. The phenomenon of cueing inhibition may be one example of "cue-overload" (133). That is, just as the effectiveness of a cue declines as more items are nested under it, so the remaining effectiveness of the general list context to retrieve items from the list declines as some items are either retrieved or (as in the present case) are provided as "cues." Some support for this view was found by Roediger et al (109) and by Mueller & Watkins (89).

The reasons underlying these demonstrated limits on retrieval are far from clear at present; the number of cues provided by Roediger et al was either 16 or 32—greatly exceeding Graesser and Mandler's 5 ± 1—so a commonality between the two sets of results is hard to perceive. The findings are there, however, and they are intriguing ones.

A further puzzle is provided by the problem of how we know that we have *not* experienced a particular event. This problem was addressed by Kolers & Palef (71) and by Brown, Lewis & Monk (26). Both sets of workers rejected the notion of an exhaustive search or matching procedure. Brown et al suggested that subjects assess the "memorability" of an event presented to them for possible recognition; well-known or salient events possess a high potential for memorability, and thus such an event is rejected confidently when presented as a distractor item. In confirmation, intrusions and false alarms were found to be events of low subjective memorability. In tasks involving personal knowledge, Kolers and Palef found an inverse relation between times to make correct positive and negative decisions. Thus, when Canadian subjects were asked to decide whether or not they had visited certain cities, positive decisions were substantially faster for US cities than

by Brown (25) and by Rabinowitz, Mandler & Patterson (106). In a thoughtful analysis, Brown concluded that recognition is usually easier than recall because the presence of the target word facilitates access to stored information, but that once access is achieved, the evidence used to decide that the word was on the list (or that the event did occur) is the same in recognition and recall. Rabinowitz, Mandler and Patterson also argued the case for similar processes operating in recall and recognition; using lists of categorized words, they concluded that a "generate-recognize" strategy can play a useful auxiliary role in recall, though it may not be the way in which recall typically proceeds. They also concluded that retrieval processes operate in recognition as well as in recall; thus, a word's accessibility in recall will affect its probability of recognition. In a reply to the article by Rabinowitz et al, Broadbent & Broadbent (23) objected that their techniques of comparing recognition and recall were invalid because one test contaminated the other. The Broadbents cited their own finding that nonrecalled words are as well recognized as are *all* words in a list (the total list presumably includes some recallable words), and argued that this finding speaks against retrieval processes in recognition because nonrecalled words are harder to retrieve and thus should also be harder to recognize. One possible resolution of this contentious issue is that similar processes do indeed operate in recall and recognition (it seems necessary, for example, to postulate retrieval of encoding context during recognition) but that rather different information must be retrieved in the two cases. In recall some aspect of the context is provided, and the system must retrieve the target item; in recognition, the item is provided and the contextual aspects of the original episode must be retrieved (23, 47).

The apparently well-established findings and conclusions relating to the serial position effect in free recall (34, pp. 137–44) have been called into question by a reanalysis of serial position in terms of recency of last rehearsal, as opposed to recency of presentation. Brodie & Murdock (24) required subjects to rehearse aloud and were thus able to plot "functional" serial position curves in terms of how recently a particular item had been rehearsed. The authors found that rate of presentation affected the recency portion of such reanalyzed functional serial-position curves and thus suggested that rate affects primary memory but not secondary memory—a conclusion diametrically opposed to previous conclusions based on "nominal" (presentation order) serial-position curves. The functional serial position analysis also strongly suggests an explanation of the recency effect in terms of recency of processing, rather than in terms of coding differences. Functional serial-position curves are well described as a function of two variables, number of rehearsals and recency of processing (91). It is unclear at present how the implications of a functional serial-position analysis can be integrated with more traditional views, but there is no doubt that this represents a provocative challenge to established ways of thinking.

Hypermnesia—the rather awkwardly entitled phenomenon of improvements in remembering without further input—has occasioned some recent interest. In one interesting study, Erdelyi, Buschke & Finkelstein (43) presented 40 items as words, pictures, or riddles. In the last-named case, subjects were given a very constraining definition to ensure that they produced the same words used in other conditions. All items were presented, or generated, under intentional learning conditions, and the one input trial was followed by five successive recall attempts. Recall improved for all three types of presentation across the five attempts, but the improvement was greatest for the riddles—the "Socratic stimuli." The same phenomenon under the label of "reminiscence" was explored by Madigan (76). The findings are clearly present although the underlying causes are obscure; Madigan suggests dissipation of interference and enhanced access to appropriate cues as possible lines to pursue.

Some final points relating to recall and recognition are noted briefly. The concept of organization has not received much critical attention recently; however, two useful methodological articles have appeared and are likely to be influential. Buschke (28) described a very direct way of identifying subjective clustering by requiring subjects to write words that were remembered together on the same line of the recall sheet. Buschke proceeds to develop the ramifications and implications of the method. Sternberg & Tulving (123) reviewed various measures of subjective organization and concluded that the repetition of word pairs from trial to trial provided the best available index.

A further topic of interest at present is the phenomenon of state-dependent learning. This effect occurs when subjects learn and retrieve items in the same physiological state—for example, alcoholic intoxication—a beneficial effect on retrieval of "same state" compared with "different state" has sometimes been observed. Eich (42) reviewed 47 studies and reported the occurrence of reliable state-dependent effects in only 23 cases. However, Eich went on to make the important observation that state-dependent effects occurred quite reliably in experiments using noncued recall as the retention task (14 out of 17 cases), whereas in studies using cued recall and recognition, the effect occurred much less reliably (9 out of 30 cases). The reasons for the task differences are unclear; as a speculation, when retrieval must make extensive use of subject-initiated constructive processes (that is, noncued recall tasks), any similar features of the environment between learning and retrieval, or similarities in the way the processing system is operating, may help to guide constructive processes appropriately and thus lead to successful recall. This notion also suggests that in general, context similarities between learning and retrieval should be more beneficial to recall than to recognition.

Finally in this section, much interest has been caused by Kolers' suggestion that recognition involves repetition of analytic operations, and by his demonstrations that sentences are better recognized subsequently if they are read from inverted rather than from normal typography. Masson & Sala (83) have shown that semantic processes play a major role in Kolers' task. Requiring the subject to carry out a fuller semantic analysis of the sentence (by means of a sentence continuation task) increased recognition of originally normal sentences, yet had little effect on recognition of originally inverted sentences. Given the incidental learning task and highly practiced readers, the reading of normal text apparently results in a somewhat impoverished semantic representation. However, Masson and Sala also confirmed Kolers' findings that repetition of wording and typography enhanced recognition; they concluded that semantic and surface information processing procedures interact in the achievement of comprehension and recognition.

MEMORY FOR SENTENCES, STORIES, AND DISCOURSE

One major new force in the study of memory processes is reflected in the rapidly growing interest in the acquisition and retention of more complex and realistic verbal materials; for example, of sentences, paragraphs and short stories. The ideas and concepts used often derive from linguistics and from work on artificial intelligence as well as from a broad range of topics in cognitive psychology; this cross-fertilization of ideas, along with the inherent interest of the materials, makes the area a very exciting one at present. In the realm of story comprehension and recall in particular, a number of impressive models have been proposed to formally represent the processes involved in understanding and remembering (19, 67, 79, 113). Several ideas are common to most of the models. For example, comprehension proceeds by means of a parsing analysis of the spoken or written text into its components; these components, in turn, are represented as an organized, multilevel, deep structure, in which different levels represent different degrees of abstraction or of specificity. The structures have schema-like properties, in that past knowledge is used to infer the likely structural framework of the story and to infer missing elements—both from the explicitly presented text at input and from the residual memory trace at retrieval. Forgetting of specific surface structure occurs more rapidly than forgetting of the abstracted gist of the story; thus there is a reversion over time to the canonical or prototypical form (since gist is more heavily influenced by preexisting knowledge). The form and content of summaries is also predictable from an analysis of the higher levels of the story representation. At the present stage of the field's development many of the empirical findings would be expected on intuitive grounds, but the value of the models is that they give coherence to a collection of disparate observations and provide a rationale for understanding known results and for predicting new ones. Some representative work in the area is now briefly reviewed.

Memory for Sentences and Paragraphs

One very central point in the general area of memory for sentences and stories is that the larger units (sentences, paragraphs etc) have wholistic properties that are not predictable from a consideration of their constituents. Sentences (like Gestalt forms) have configurational properties. This point has been made by several writers including Till (126), who illustrated his argument with the demonstration that the effectiveness of a retrieval cue for a sentence was not well predicted by associative relations between the cue and individual words or phrases in the sentence. Effective cues were typically based on a probable inference from the complex sentence.

Several researchers have been interested in the relative retention of the abstract gist and the verbatim surface structure of various types of prose material. At present the general conclusion appears to be that meaning is more memorable than the actual words used to convey that meaning, but that retention of verbatim information is nonetheless surprisingly good, especially under certain circumstances. J. R. Anderson & Paulson (3) found very rapid loss of verbatim information (one intervening sentence was enough to erase it) in a sentence verification paradigm in which positive test sentences were either identical to the presented sentence or involved a voice switch (e.g. from active to passive). In this situation, apparently, comparing identical forms in primary memory confers an additional benefit to the speed of response. At the other extreme, Keenan, MacWhinney & Mayhew (65) also Kintsch & Bates (66) found good retention of verbatim information over several days, while Rubin (112) found evidence for excellent verbatim recall over a number of years! What factors contribute to such surprising findings?

In an ingenious study, Keenan et al (65) tape-recorded statements made in a research seminar and then unexpectedly tested the seminar participants for their recognition of the transcribed statements 30 hours later. Their main finding was that memory was good, both for the meaning expressed and the exact surface form used, but that the latter finding depended on the statements having high "interactional content"—that is, statements with affective overtones; wit, sarcasm, and personal criticism. Kintsch & Bates

(66) found somewhat similar results in the recognition of statements presented in a classroom lecture. In terms of the *type* of meaning retained, the authors found equivalent memory for topic and detail, and quite good memory for verbatim information, even after a 5-day retention interval. In line with the Keenan et al study, Kintsch and Bates found best memory for extraneous statements, such as jokes and announcements; subjects were particularly good at rejecting new items (that is, those not presented in the lecture). These studies raise two interesting problems: first, why exactly are emotional or personally involving materials so highly memorable (97, 110)? Second, how is it that people can so easily tell they have *not* experienced an event before (71)?

In a further study of verbatim retention, Rubin (112) investigated how much children and young adults remembered from poems and prose passages learned by rote months or years earlier. He found a very high tendency to recall the material verbatim; but this is unsurprising given the nature of the material and the subjects' task at learning. The extreme regularity of the data is impressive, however; the correlation between amount recalled and the precise words recalled was .99 in the case of Hamlet's soliloquy. Taking the various studies in this section into account, it is obvious that no simple generalization can be made concerning the retention of verbatim information; yet it seems quite possible that lawful principles can be educed from the data.

Memory for Stories

Rumelhart's (113) model for understanding and remembering stories relies heavily on schemas and on hierarchical structure. The topmost schema in the hierarchy represents the story-telling episode in general terms. This schema has various constituents (CAUSE, TRY, OUTCOME, etc) which are composed, in turn, of more specific lower-order schemas. Overall, the system of schemas forms the underlying structure of which the actual story is the surface representation. This model makes various predictions about recall. For example, assuming that retrieval involves a top-to-bottom reconstruction, loss of a higher-level schema (or node) will necessarily result in the loss of material nested below it. Also, higher nodes should be better remembered, and summaries of stories should reflect the information contained in these higher nodes. Rumelhart presented empirical work confirming the model's predictions. Gentner (52) demonstrated a further application of Rumelhart's story grammar—to the analysis of learning material from a textbook. Over several learning trials, the structure of recall changed from being dominated by serial order factors to a structure reflecting the underlying grammar as the overall meaning emerged for the subject.

J. M. Mandler (78, 79) has developed a story grammar related to Rumelhart's, but she lays more emphasis on the role of schemas at retrieval. In particular, violations of the underlying grammar and losses of detail from the memory trace will lead to recall that is nearer to the ideal story form than to the original version. She has explored these ideas in several studies with children and adults and found that children showed a *greater* reliance than adults on schema-based retrieval—that is, children's recall conformed more to the ideal canonical form. Both Rumelhart's and Mandler's work suggests the interesting notion that retrieval processes "interpret" the memory trace in a manner which is quite similar to the way in which the cognitive system interprets the stimulus array during initial perception and comprehension.

Bower (19) and Thorndyke (125) described a somewhat different grammar in which rewrite rules allow the parsing of the story into such constituents as setting, theme, plot, and resolution; further analysis decomposes each constituent into smaller units of more detailed information. Again the various propositions are structured in a hierarchical manner and again the story framework acts as a retrieval plan during the course of remembering. Thorndyke (125) reported a number of experiments using this framework; he found that the amount of plot structure given was a major determinant of recall (where "structure" was defined in terms of the Bower-Thorndyke grammar), and he also showed that whereas repetition of a plot from one story to another enhanced recall, repetition of the characters led to interference and reduced recall. Owens, Bower & Black (97) stressed the role of inference during comprehension. Given a certain predisposing "set," subjects interpreted quite bland statements in particular ways; for example, episodes concerning a visit to the doctor, attendance at a lecture, and going to a party were remembered differently by control subjects and subjects who believed that the main character in the story was pregnant by her professor-lover! In particular, experimental subjects recalled more episodes, more detail, and retained order information better than did the controls; the experimental subjects also made many more theme-relevant intrusions. This study nicely illustrates the roles of affect, interest, and personal relevance in comprehension and recall.

Kintsch and his associates (67) postulated that comprehension involves the construction of an underlying propositional "text base." For lengthy material such as stories, the base is organized into a framework—the macrostructure in Kintsch's terms. In one study he and his colleagues showed that in order to comprehend a scrambled story, the formation of a macrostructure was just as necessary; subsequent recall of scrambled and normal stories was indistinguishable, suggesting that identical macrostructures had been formed in both cases. Dooling & Christiaansen (41) also stressed the role of underlying structure in reconstructive retrieval. They found that lower-level codes in the hierarchy were forgotten more rapidly, and made the further important point that context plays a strong determining role in the construction of the hierarchical representation of an episode; thus a given event may occupy different positions in the hierarchy depending on its salience as determined by the context. The parts played by context, affect, inference, and personal preference are rightly made prominent in the various models proposed to deal with stories and discourse; equally obviously, such factors will prove difficult to pin down in a formal way and will provide an interesting challenge as the work develops.

As a final illustration in this area, an inventive study by Anderson & Pichert (5) showed how two different retrieval schemas gave rise to differences in the details recalled. Groups of subjects were given a story about a house from either a home-buyer's or a burglar's perspective; as expected, recall showed strong effects of the importance level of details relevant to the subject's particular perspective. However, subjects were then given the *other* perspective, and they proceeded to remember further information relevant to the new retrieval schema. This experiment makes the important point that information comprehended and organized from one point of view can be accessed from a quite different point of view. The crucial parts played in retrieval by preexisting general knowledge (about buying a home or about burglars, for instance), and the interactions between such general knowledge and specific episodic traces, are well illustrated by Anderson and Pichert's experiment.

FUTURE DIRECTIONS

In this final section, an attempt is made to select one or two ideas that may prove influential during the next few years of memory research.

Remembering is particularly vivid in the case of events with high emotional impact or far-reaching consequences for the person experiencing them. A good example is the memory of hearing about President Kennedy's assassination; people typically recall with great clarity the circumstances in which they heard the news. Brown & Kulick (27) described these vivid recollections as "flashbulb memories," and went on to inquire why *peripheral* detail should be as well remembered as details of the emotional event itself. They speculated that there may be some biological value connected with the keeping of an exact record of the circumstances surrounding a significant event. The phenomenon should provide a rich field for exploratory study. How necessary is the emotional component, for example? Does *any* salient event enhance encoding of contextual detail? Is context better remembered for isolated events and for primacy items in a list than for relatively neutral middle items? Clearly, the flashbulb phenomenon fits with recent notions of distinctiveness—it signals a uniquely and richly encoded event that has unique links to potential retrieval information.

An interesting theoretical schema was proposed by Norman & Bobrow (95). They argued that the output of perceptual processing may be viewed as a *description* of the stimulus array, with the description existing at various levels of analysis. Higher levels of description at input (that is, meaningful, inferential, and elaborative levels) will result in a memory record that is potentially highly discriminable at retrieval. Remembering is viewed as a process involving the reconstruction of a further description whose function is to specify the wanted information from the "data base" of memory records. The degree of ease with which the retrieval description can be constructed is referred to as the recoverability of the description. Norman and Bobrow's account of memory processes brings together a number of topics discussed in the present review; their account involves schemas and inferences, the notion that mnemonic information is represented at different levels of analysis, the ideas of distinctiveness, reconstructive remembering, and encoding specificity. An additional attractive feature is their stress on the active processes involved in the construction and reconstruction of descriptions.

The emphasis on remembering as a skilled activity, as opposed to the passive matching of features, is taken further by Bransford et al (22) and by Kolers (70). From fundamentally different viewpoints of perceptual theory (neo-Gibsonian in the case of Bransford et al and constructivist in the case of Kolers) these theorists unite in the view that remembering should be thought of as a cognitive skill rather than as the matching of the products of perception against postulated memory traces from previous perceptual experiences. The cognitive system learns by assimilating experiences; in this way the whole system is modified and becomes increasingly skilled at interpreting and differentiating new inputs. Context plays a crucial role (especially in Bransford et al's account) in modifying and setting the system to treat further events in a given way. For Kolers, remembering involves repetition of the same mental operations as those carried out on the occasion of the event's initial occurrence. These accounts, with their emphasis on memory as an activity rather than a thing, are attractive in many ways. Personally, however, I see the need to retain the notion of specific memory records to account for our ability to reconstruct details of the event's initial episodic context. Perhaps Norman and Bobrow's view, embracing the ideas of an elaborate system of memory records and the active formation of descriptions, retains the best of both worlds.

Finally, is progress being made in the field of episodic memory? To my mind the answer is clearly positive. I would go farther and claim that despite differences in terminology, emphasis, and point of view, there is now broad agreement on the general outlines of a theory of episodic remembering. This outline theory holds that past experience, in some organized form, interprets the input and infers missing information where necessary. The mental operations involved in the processes of interpretation and comprehension are either assimilated into the slightly modified cognitive system (22, 70) or leave an episodic record of the analyses performed (2, 95, 127). If the event is one that is common and probable, it will be dealt with relatively automatically by the cognitive system, and in this case (because no new information has been transmitted, if you like) the processing capacity expended is minimal and the memory record of the event correspondingly impoverished (120). Alternatively, if the task, the material or the subject's strategy induces extensive (69) or elaborate processing, a rich mnemonic record will be retained, and this distinctive trace will be highly discriminable at retrieval (46, 68). The trace is composed of analyzed features in a number of different dimensions (47, 98); the effectiveness of the various types of feature in the overall process of remembering will depend on their similarity to records of previously analyzed features and to features of further events analyzed between encoding and retrieval of the episode under consideration (46, 133). In particular, sensory or "surface" features will often be lost rapidly because of their similarity to other encoded events; but this is not necessarily true if the surface information is sufficiently distinctive (65). Finally, retrieval operations must be compatible with the original encoding operations and must in turn be elaborated sufficiently to specify the wanted trace (or operations) with precision (69, 87, 127).

Although the theoretical convergence sketched here is stated in very general terms, it seems possible that scientific understanding, like the processes of perception and comprehension themselves (92), may proceed from the global to the specific, from an overall prospect of the forest to a clearer view of the individual trees. Alternatively, comprehension may reflect the interaction of global, conceptual information with specific sensory details. If the analogy to scientific progress is drawn again, the consensus view forms a set of guiding principles that interact with specific empirical facts to yield a more adequate theory.

ACKNOWLEDGMENTS

Preparation of this chapter was made possible by a grant from the National Research Council of Canada. The chapter was written while I was on research leave at Stanford University, and I would like to thank members of the Stanford Department of Psychology for their hospitality. In particular I am very grateful to Herbert Clark, Jim Cutting, Ellen Markman, Edward Smith, and Barbara Tversky for helpful comments on an earlier draft.

Literature Cited

1. Allport, D. A., Antonis, B., Reynolds, P. 1972. On the division of attention: a disproof of the single channel hypothesis. *Q. J. Exp. Psychol.* 24:225–35
2. Anderson, J. R. 1976. *Language, Memory, and Thought.* Hillsdale, NJ: Erlbaum. 546 pp.
3. Anderson, J. R., Paulson, R. 1977. Representation and retention of verbatim information. *J. Verb. Learn. Verb. Behav.* 16:439–51
4. Anderson, J. R., Reder, L. M. 1978. An elaborative processing explanation of depth of processing. In *Levels of Processing in Human Memory,* ed. L. S. Cermak, F. I. M. Craik. Hillsdale, NJ: Erlbaum. In press
5. Anderson, R. C., Pichert, J. W. 1978. Recall of previously unrecallable information following a shift in perspective. *J. Verb. Learn. Verb. Behav.* 17:1–12
6. Anderson, R. C., Pichert, J. W., Goetz, E. T., Schallert, D. L., Stevens, K. V., Trollip, S. R. 1976. Instantiation of general terms. *J. Verb. Learn. Verb. Behav.* 15:667–79
7. Arbuckle, T. Y., Katz, W. A. 1976. Structure of memory traces following semantic and nonsemantic orientation tasks in incidental learning. *J. Exp. Psychol. Hum. Learn. Mem.* 2:362–69
8. Atkinson, R. C., Shiffrin, R. M. 1968. Human memory: a proposed system and its control processes. In *The Psychology of Learning and Motivation,* ed. K. W. Spence, J. T. Spence, 2:89–195. New York: Academic
9. Aubley, P. M., Franks, J. J. 1978. The effects of effort toward comprehension on recall. *Mem. Cognit.* 6:20–25
10. Baddeley, A. D. 1976. *The Psychology of Memory.* New York: Basic Books. 430 pp.
11. Baddeley, A. D. 1978. The trouble with levels: A re-examination of Craik and Lockhart's framework for memory research. *Psychol. Rev.* 85:139–52
12. Baddeley, A. D. 1978. Working memory and reading. In *The Proceedings of the Conference on the Processing of Visible Language,* ed. P. A. Kolers, M. E. Wrolstad, H. Bouma. In press
13. Baddeley, A. D., Hitch, G. J. 1977. Recency reexamined. In *Attention and Performance,* ed. S. Dornic, 6:647–67. Hillsdale, NJ: Erlbaum
14. Baker, L., Santa, J. L. 1977. Context, integration, and retrieval. *Mem. Cognit.* 5:308–14
15. Banks, W. P., Barber, G. 1977. Color information in iconic memory. *Psychol. Rev.* 84:536–46
16. Bartling, C. A., Thompson, C. P. 1977. Encoding specificity: Retrieval asymmetry in the recognition failure paradigm. *J. Exp. Psychol. Hum. Learn. Mem.* 3:690–700
17. Bellezza, F. S., Cheesman, F. L. II, Reddy, B. G. 1977. Organization and semantic elaboration in free recall. *J. Exp. Psychol. Hum Learn. Mem.* 3: 539–50
18. Bellezza, F. S., Richards, D. L., Geiselman, R. E. 1976. Semantic processing and organization in free recall. *Mem. Cognit.* 4:415–21
19. Bower, G. H. 1976. Experiments on story understanding and recall. *Q. J. Exp. Psychol.* 28:511–34
20. Bower, G. H., Glass, A. L. 1976. Structural units and the redintegrative power of picture fragments. *J. Exp. Psychol. Hum. Learn. Mem.* 2:456–66
21. Bransford, J. D., Franks, J. J., Morris, C. D., Stein, B. S. 1978. Some general constraints on learning and memory research. See Ref. 4
22. Bransford, J. D., McCarrell, N. S., Franks, J. J., Nitsch, K. E. 1977. Toward unexplaining memory. In *Perceiving, Acting, and Knowing.* ed. R. Shaw, J. Bransford, pp. 431–66. Hillsdale, NJ: Erlbaum
23. Broadbent, D. E., Broadbent, M. H. P. 1977. Effects of recognition on subsequent recall: Comments on "Determinants of recognition and recall: Accessibility and generation" by Rabinowitz, Mandler, & Patterson. *J. Exp. Psychol. Gen.* 106:330–35
24. Brodie, D. A., Murdock, B. B. Jr. 1977. Effect of presentation time on nominal and functional serial-position curves of free recall. *J. Verb. Learn. Verb. Behav.* 16:185–200
25. Brown, J. 1976. An analysis of recognition and recall and of problems in their comparison. In *Recall and Recognition,* ed. J. Brown, pp. 1–35. New York: Wiley
26. Brown, J., Lewis, V. J., Monk, A. F. 1977. Memorability, word frequency and negative recognition. *Q. J. Exp. Psychol.* 29:461–73
27. Brown, R., Kulick, J. 1977. Flashbulb memories. *Cognition* 5:73–99
28. Buschke, M. 1977. Two-dimensional recall: Immediate identification of clusters in episodic and semantic memory. *J. Verb. Learn. Verb. Behav.* 16:201–15

29. Chabot, R. J., Miller, T. J., Juola, J. F. 1976. The relationship between repetition and depth of processing. *Mem. Cognit.* 4:677–82

30. Charness, N. 1976. Memory for chess positions: Resistance to interference. *J. Exp. Psychol. Hum. Learn. Mem.* 2:641–53

31. Coltheart, V. 1977. Recognition errors after incidental learning as a function of different levels of processing. *J. Exp. Psychol. Hum. Learn. Mem.* 3:437–44

32. Craik, F. I. M., Lockhart, R. S. 1972. Levels of processing: A framework for memory research. *J. Verb. Learn. Verb. Behav.* 11:671–84

33. Craik, F. I. M., Lockhart, R. S. 1979. Levels of processing: A reply to our critics. In preparation

34. Crowder, R. G. 1976. *Principles of Learning and Memory.* Hillsdale, NJ: Erlbaum. 523 pp.

35. Crowder, R. G. 1978. Sensory memory systems. In *Handbook of Perception,* ed. E. C. Carterette, M. P. Friedman. New York: Academic. In press

36. D'Agostino, P. R., O'Neill, B. J., Paivio, A. 1977. Memory for pictures and words as a function of level of processing: Depth or dual coding? *Mem. Cognit.* 5:252–56

37. Dark, V. J., Loftus, G. R. 1976. The role of rehearsal in long-term memory performance. *J. Verb. Learn. Verb. Behav.* 15:479–90

38. Davies, G., Cubbage, A. 1976. Attribute coding at different levels of processing. *Q. J. Exp. Psychol.* 28:653–60

39. Dhawan, M., Pellegrino, J. W. 1977. Acoustic and semantic interference effects in words and pictures. *Mem. Cognit.* 5:340–46

40. Di Lollo, V. 1977. Temporal characteristics of iconic memory. *Nature* 267:241–43

41. Dooling, D. J., Christiaansen, R. E. 1977. Levels of encoding and retention of prose. In *The Psychology of Learning and Motivation,* ed. G. H. Bower, 11:1–39. New York: Academic

42. Eich, J. E. 1977. State-dependent retrieval of information in human episodic memory. In *Alcohol and Human Memory,* ed. I. M. Birnbaum, E. S. Parker, pp. 141–57. Hillsdale, NJ: Erlbaum

43. Erdelyi, M., Buschke, H., Finkelstein, S. 1977. Hypermnesia for Socratic stimuli: The growth of recall for an internally generated memory list abstracted from a series of riddles. *Mem. Cognit.* 5:283–86

44. Eysenck, M. W. 1977. *Human Memory: Theory, Research and Individual Differences.* Oxford: Pergamon. 366 pp.

45. Eysenck, M. W. 1978. Levels of processing: A critique. *Br. J. Psychol.* 69:157–69

46. Eysenck, M. W. 1978. Depth, elaboration, and distinctiveness. See Ref. 4

47. Flexser, A. J., Tulving, E. 1978. Retrieval independence in recognition and recall. *Psychol. Rev.* 85:153–71

48. Foreit, K. G. 1976. Short-lived auditory memory for pitch. *Percept. Psychophys.* 19:368–70

49. Frey, P. W., Adesman, P. 1976. Recall memory for visually presented chess positions. *Mem. Cognit.* 4:541–47

50. Gardiner, J. M., Klee, H., Redman, G., Ball, M. 1976. The role of stimulus material in determining release from proactive inhibition. *Q. J. Exp. Psychol.* 28:395–402

51. Geiselman, R. E., Glenny, J. 1977. Effects of imagining speakers' voices on the retention of words presented visually. *Mem. Cognit.* 5:499–504

52. Gentner, D. R. 1976. The structure and recall of narrative prose. *J. Verb. Learn. Verb. Behav.* 15:411–18

53. Glanzer, M., Koppenaal, L. 1977. The effect of encoding tasks on free recall: Stages and levels. *J. Verb. Learn. Verb. Behav.* 16:21–28

54. Glenberg, A., Smith, S. M., Green, C. 1977. Type I rehearsal: Maintenance and more. *J. Verb. Learn. Verb. Behav.* 16:339–52

55. Goldman, S. R., Pellegrino, J. W. 1977. Processing domain, encoding elaboration, and memory trace strength. *J. Verb. Learn. Verb. Behav.* 16:29–43

56. Graesser, A. II., Mandler, G. 1978. Limited processing capacity constrains the storage of unrelated sets of words and retrieval from natural categories. *J. Exp. Psychol. Hum. Learn. Mem.* 4:86–100

57. Griffith, D. 1976. The attentional demands of mnemonic control processes. *Mem. Cognit.* 4:103–8

58. Hitch, G. J., Baddeley, A. D. 1976. Verbal reasoning and working memory. *Q. J. Exp. Psychol.* 28:603–21

59. Imhoff, D. L., Horton, D. L., Weldon, L. J., Phillips, R. V. 1977. Rehearsal and processing capacity as factors in memory. *J. Exp. Psychol. Hum. Learn. Mem.* 5:551–59

60. Jacoby, L. L., Bartz, W. H., Evans, J. D. 1978. A functional approach to levels of processing. *J. Exp. Psychol. Hum. Learn. Mem.* 4:331–46

61. Jenkins, J. J. 1974. Remember that old theory of memory? Well forget it. *Am. Psychol.* 29:785–95
62. Johnson-Laird, P. N., Gibbs, G., de Mowbray, J. 1978. Meaning, amount of processing, and memory for words. *Mem. Cognit.* 6:372–75
63. Johnston, W. A., Heinz, S. P. 1976. *Attention: An integrative conceptual framework.* Presented at Ann. Meet. Psychon. Soc., St. Louis
64. Jones, G. V. 1976. A fragmentation hypothesis of memory: Cued recall of pictures and of sequential position. *J. Exp. Psychol. Gen.* 105:277–93
65. Keenan, J. M., MacWhinney, B., Mayhew, D. 1977. Pragmatics in memory: A study of natural conversation. *J. Verb. Learn. Verb. Behav.* 16:549–60
66. Kintsch, W., Bates, E. 1977. Recognition memory for statements from a classroom lecture. *J. Exp. Psychol. Hum. Learn. Mem.* 3:150–59
67. Kintsch, W., Mandel, T. S., Kozminsky, E. 1977. Summarizing scrambled stories. *Mem. Cognit.* 5:547–52
68. Klein, K., Saltz, E. 1976. Specifying the mechanisms in a levels-of-processing approach to memory. *J. Exp. Psychol. Hum. Learn. Mem.* 2:671–79
69. Kolers, P. A. 1976. Reading a year later. *J. Exp. Psychol. Hum. Learn. Mem.* 2:554–65
70. Kolers, P. A. 1978. A pattern analyzing basis of recognition. See Ref. 4
71. Kolers, P. A., Palef, S. R. 1976. Knowing not. *Mem. Cognit.* 4:553–58
72. Kraft, R. N., Jenkins, J. J. 1977. Memory for lateral orientation of slides in picture stories. *Mem. Cognit.* 5:397–403
73. Lawless, H., Engen, T. 1977. Associations to odors: Interference, mnemonics, and verbal labeling. *J. Exp. Psychol. Hum. Learn. Mem.* 3:52–59
74. Lee, C. L., Estes, W. K. 1977. Order and position in primary memory for letter strings. *J. Verb. Learn. Verb. Behav.* 16:395–418
75. Loftus, E. F., Miller, D. G., Burns, H. J. 1978. Semantic integration of verbal information into a visual memory. *J. Exp. Psychol. Hum. Learn. Mem.* 4:19–31
76. Madigan, S. A. 1976. Reminiscence and item recovery in free recall. *Mem. Cognit.* 4:233–36
77. Mandler, G. 1978. Organization and repetition: An extension of organizational principles with special reference to rote learning. In *Perspectives on Memory Research: Essays in Honor of Uppsala University's 500th Anniversary,* ed. L. G. Nilsson. Hillsdale, NJ: Erlbaum. In press
78. Mandler, J. M. 1978. A code in the node: The use of a story schema in retrieval. *Discourse Processes* 1:14–35
79. Mandler, J. M., Johnson, N. S. 1977. Remembrance of things parsed: Story structure and recall. *Cognit. Psychol.* 9:111–51
80. Mandler, J. M., Ritchey, G. H. 1977. Long-term memory for pictures. *J. Exp. Psychol. Hum. Learn. Mem.* 3:386–96
81. Marslen-Wilson, W., Tyler, L. K. 1976. Memory and levels of processing in a psycholinguistic context. *J. Exp. Psychol. Hum. Learn. Mem.* 2:112–19
82. Martin, M. 1978. Memory span as a measure of individual differences in memory capacity. *Mem. Cognit.* 6:194–98
83. Masson, M. E. J., Sala, L. S. 1978. An interactive approach to reading and recognizing sentences. *Cognit. Psychol.* 10:244–70
84. Mathews, R. C. 1977. Semantic judgments as encoding operations: The effects of attention to particular semantic categories on the usefulness of interitem relations in recall. *J. Exp. Psychol. Hum. Learn. Mem.* 3:160–73
85. McDaniel, M. A., Friedman, A., Bourne, L. E. Jr. 1978. Remembering the levels of information in words. *Mem. Cognit.* 6:156–64
86. Meyer, G. E., Maguire, W. M. 1977. Spatial frequency and the mediation of short-term visual storage. *Science* 198:524–25
87. Morris, C. D., Bransford, J. D., Franks, J. J. 1977. Levels of processing versus transfer appropriate processing. *J. Verb. Learn. Verb. Behav.* 16:519–33
88. Morton, J. 1976. Two mechanisms in the stimulus suffix effect. *Mem. Cognit.* 4:144–49
89. Mueller, C. W., Watkins, M. J. 1977. Inhibition from part-set cueing: A cue-overload interpretation. *J. Verb. Learn. Verb. Behav.* 16:699–709
90. Murdock, B. B. Jr. 1976. Item and order information in short-term serial memory. *J. Exp. Psychol. Gen.* 105:191–216
91. Murdock, B. B. Jr., Metcalfe, J. 1978. Controlled rehearsal in single-trial free recall. *J. Verb. Learn. Verb. Behav.* 17:309–24
92. Navon, D. 1977. Forest before trees: The precedence of global features in visual perception. *Cognit. Psychol.* 9:353–83

93. Nelson, D. L. 1978. Remembering pictures and words: Appearance, significance, and name. See Ref. 4
94. Nelson, T. O. 1977. Repetition and depth of processing. *J. Verb. Learn. Verb. Behav.* 16:151–71
95. Norman, D. A., Bobrow, D. G. 1977. Descriptions: A basis for memory acquisition and retrieval. *Cen. Hum. Inf. Process. Tech. Rep. 74.* 24 pp.
96. O'Neill, M. E., Sutcliffe, J. A., Tulving, E. 1976. Retrieval cues and release from proactive inhibition. *Am. J. Psychol.* 89:535–43
97. Owens, J., Bower, G. H., Black, J. B. 1978. The 'Soap Opera' effect in story recall. Submitted for publication
98. Paivio, A. 1976. Imagery in recall and recognition. See Ref. 25, pp. 103–29
99. Patterson, K. E., Baddeley, A. D. 1977. When face recognition fails. *J. Exp. Psychol. Hum. Learn. Mem.* 3:406–17
100. Perfetti, C. A., Goldman, S. R. 1976. Discourse memory and reading comprehension skill. *J. Verb. Learn. Verb. Behav.* 14:33–42
101. Peterson, L. R., Rawlings, L., Cohen, C. 1977. The internal construction of spatial patterns. See Ref. 41, pp. 245–76
102. Pezdek, K. 1977. Cross-modality semantic integration of sentence and picture memory. *J. Exp. Psychol. Hum. Learn. Mem.* 3:515–24
103. Postman, L., Kruesi, E. 1977. The influence of orienting tasks on the encoding and recall of words. *J. Verb. Learn. Verb. Behav.* 16:353–69
104. Potter, M. C., Valian, V. V., Faulconer, B. A. 1977. Representation of a sentence and its pragmatic implications: Verbal, imagistic, or abstract? *J. Verb. Learn. Verb. Behav.* 16:1–12
105. Rabinowitz, J. C., Mandler, G., Barsalou, L. W. 1977. Recognition failure: Another case of retrieval failure. *J. Verb. Learn. Verb. Behav.* 16:639–63
106. Rabinowitz, J. C., Mandler, G., Patterson, K. E. 1977. Determinants of recognition and recall: Accessibility and generation. *J. Exp. Psychol. Gen.* 106:302–29
107. Radtke, R. C., Grove, E. K. 1977. Proactive inhibition in short-term memory: availability or accessibility? *J. Exp. Psychol. Hum. Learn. Mem.* 3:78–91
108. Roediger, H. L. III, Knight, J. L. Jr., Kantowitz, B. 1977. Inferring decay in short-term memory. *Mem. Cognit.* 5:167–76
109. Roediger, H. L. III, Stellon, C. C., Tulving, E. 1977. Inhibition from part-list cues and rate of recall. *J. Exp. Psychol. Hum. Learn. Mem.* 3:174–88
110. Rogers, T. B., Kuiper, N. A., Kirker, W. S. 1977. Self-reference and the encoding of personal information. *J. Pers. Soc. Psychol.* 35:677–88
111. Rowe, E. J., Rowe, W. G. 1976. Stimulus suffix effects with speech and nonspeech sounds. *Mem. Cognit.* 4:128–31
112. Rubin, D. C. 1977. Very long-term memory for prose and verse. *J. Verb. Learn. Verb. Behav.* 16:611–21
113. Rumelhart, D. E. 1977. Understanding and summarizing brief stories. In *Basic Processes in Reading: Perception and Comprehension,* ed. D. Laberge, J. Samuels, pp. 265–304. Hillsdale, NJ: Erlbaum
114. Rumelhart, D. E., Ortony, A. 1977. The representation of knowledge in memory. In *Schooling and the Acquisition of Knowledge,* ed. R. C. Anderson, R. J. Spiro, W. E. Montague, pp. 99–136. Hillsdale, NJ: Erlbaum
115. Rundus, D. 1977. Maintenance rehearsal and single-level processing. *J. Verb. Learn. Verb. Behav.* 16:665–81
116. Rundus, D., Hekkanen, J. S., Barrett, S. E. 1978. Maintenance rehearsal, elaboration, and long term recency. Submitted for publication.
117. Sakitt, B. 1976. Iconic memory. *Psychol. Rev.* 83:257–76
118. Schank, R. C., Abelson, R. P. 1977. *Scripts, Plans, Goals and Understanding.* Hillsdale, NJ: Erlbaum. 248 pp.
119. Shiffrin, R. M. 1976. Capacity limitations in information processing, attention and memory. In *Handbook of Learning and Cognitive Processes,* ed. W. K. Estes, 4:177–236. Hillsdale, NJ: Erlbaum
120. Shiffrin, R. M., Schneider, W. 1977. Controlled and automatic human information processing: II, Perceptual learning, automatic attending, and a general theory. *Psychol. Rev.* 84:127–90
121. Siple, P., Fischer, S. D., Bellugi, U. 1977. Memory for nonsemantic attributes of American sign language signs and English words. *J. Verb. Learn. Verb. Behav.* 16:561–74
122. Spyropoulos, T., Ceraso, J. 1977. Categorized and uncategorized attributes as recall cues: The phenomenon of limited access. *Cognit. Psychol.* 9:384–402
123. Sternberg, R. J., Tulving, E. 1977. The measurement of subjective organization in free recall. *Psychol. Bull.* 84:539–56
124. Thorndyke, P. W. 1976. The role of in-

ferences in discourse comprehension. *J. Verb. Learn. Verb. Behav.* 15:437–46

125. Thorndyke, P. W. 1977. Cognitive structures in comprehension and memory of narrative discourse. *Cognit. Psychol.* 9:77–110

126. Till, R. E. 1977. Sentence memory prompted with inferential recall cues. *J. Exp. Psychol. Hum. Learn. Mem.* 3:129–41

127. Tulving, E. 1976. Ecphoric processes in recall and recognition. See Ref. 25, pp. 37–73

128. Tulving, E. 1978. Relation between encoding specificity and levels of processing. See Ref. 4

129. Tulving, E., Watkins, O. C. 1977. Recognition failure of words with a single meaning. *Mem. Cognit.* 5:513–22

130. Verbrugge, R. R., McCarrell, N. S. 1977. Metaphoric comprehension:

Studies in reminding and resembling. *Cognit. Psychol.* 9:494–533

131. Watkins, M. J. 1977. The intricacy of memory span. *Mem. Cognit.* 5:529–34

132. Watkins, M. J., Ho, E., Tulving, E. 1976. Context effects in recognition memory for faces. *J. Verb. Learn. Verb. Behav.* 15:505–17

133. Watkins, M. J., Watkins, O. C. 1976. Cue-overload theory and the method of interpolated attributes. *Bull. Psychon. Soc.* 7:289–91

134. Wickens, D. D., Dalezman, R. E., Eggemeier, F. T. 1976. Multiple encoding of word attributes in memory. *Mem. Cognit.* 4:307–10

135. Woodward, A. E. Jr., Bjork, R. A., Jongeward, R. H. Jr. 1973. Recall and recognition as a function of primary rehearsal. *J. Verb. Learn. Verb. Behav.* 12:608–17

Ann. Rev. Psychol. 1979. 30:103–43
Copyright © 1979 by Annual Reviews Inc. All rights reserved

PSYCHOLOGICAL DEVELOPMENT: EARLY EXPERIENCE[1]

❖304

J. McVicker Hunt

Department of Psychology, University of Illinois, Champaign, Illinois 61820

CONTENTS

INVESTIGATIONS INSTIGATED BY DENIAL OF IMPORTANCE TO
    EARLY EXPERIENCE 105
    Instincts as Unlearned Patterns of Behavior 105
    Predetermined Development 109
CONCEPTIONS OF EARLY EXPERIENCE FROM PSYCHOANALYSIS 112
    The Theory of Psychosexual Development 112
    The Theory of Infantile Trauma 115
INVESTIGATIONS FLOWING FROM ETHOLOGICAL CONCEPTIONS 119
    Imprinting 119
    Critical Periods 123
MATERNAL DEPRIVATION, MATERNAL ATTACHMENT, AND
    PSYCHOLOGICAL DEVELOPMENT 124
EFFECTS OF EARLY EXPERIENCE ON PROBLEM-SOLVING,
    NEUROANATOMY, AND NEUROCHEMISTRY 128
    Perceptual Versus Motor Experience 128
    Effects of Variations in Sensory Experience 129
    Effects of Complexity of Rearing Conditions 131
        Effects on problem-solving and animal intelligence 131
        Effects on neurochemistry and neuroanatomy 133
CONCLUSION 135

[1] I wish to acknowledge with gratitude the grant from the Waters Foundation which has supported the writing of this review. I wish to thank Professors Ina C. Uzgiris and William T. Greenough for excellent and helpful counsel concerning the content of the sections, respectively, on the role of experience in maternal attachment and on the effects of visual and rearing experiences on the neuroanatomy and neurochemistry of the brain. Professor Greenough's reading of the latter sections in earlier versions has done much to improve their accuracy. I wish also to thank Norma Howard of the Educational Resources Information Center for help with a computerized search of the literature on early experience, and finally, to thank Bonnie Stone for transcribing accurately and quickly the successive versions of this piece, for help with the references, and for preparing the final manuscript.

0066-4308/79/0201-0103$01.00

Although this is the first time the evidence has been reviewed in this series, the idea that early experience is of special importance for psychological development is very old. It appears in *The Republic* (Book II) and in *The Laws* where Plato had the Athenian prescribe a course of experiences beginning even before birth, but admittedly with "a want of clearness." Although it has since been embraced occasionally by philosophers who concerned themselves with education, this idea never, contrary to the claim of Clarke & Clarke (44), became educationally or socially or politically significant until after World War II. Until the second half of the eighteenth century, preformationism was the dominant conception of development. Then, despite John Locke's introduction of empiricism into epistemology in 1690 with his *Essay on Human Understanding,* such biologically oriented figures of the nineteenth century as Herbert Spencer and Francis Galton substituted predeterminism for preformationism. The special importance of early experience in modern educational philosophy has come from Rousseau's *The Origin of Inequality* in 1753 and *Emile* in 1761 through the writings of Pestalozzi, Froebel, James Simpson, Horace Mann, and others. Their influence, despite Binet's objections in 1909, was held under the domination of predeterminism (see 100, Chap. 2, 3).

After World War II, the effects of early experience attained sufficient credibility to become several streams of investigation. Even as late as 1954, the titles in the relevant reviews indicate that the total number of such investigations could hardly have been as many as 300. It is hard to determine how many such investigations were published during the next 14 years, but a computer search for the decade from 1968 through 1977 has yielded over 1500 titles—1197 titles from the data base of the *Psychological Abstracts* alone. Despite, but not because of, exploding knowledge in this domain, the pendulum of opinion favoring special significance for early experience appears to have reached its extreme and started to swing back. The failure of Project Head Start to achieve the unrealistic goals set for it (see 104) prompted Jensen (114, 115) to revisit the faith and methodology of predeterminism and to reawaken the useless controversy over the relative importance of heredity and environment. Although the idea is generally accepted by clinicians, the special importance of early experience for mental health has also been questioned (see 119), and for education, evidence dissonant with the claims of irreversibility has been reviewed (44), and for schooling, the Moores (143) have published a book under the title *Better Late Than Early.*

Since no comprehensive review has appeared since that of Thompson & Grusec (183), and since none has traced the origins of the several streams of investigation, the purpose of this review is to identify the various conceptions that have instigated the several streams of investigation and to show

how the findings have modified these conceptions and shaped our current views. Due to limitations of space, no attempt will be made to cover investigations of prenatal influences, dietary influences, genetic interactions (see 183), or education. Moreover, these limitations also require indirect referencing (indicated by the word "see" before number of the reference cited) through reasonably accessible reviews.

The several streams of investigation come from at least four main sources. The first of these has been a denial of any significant importance of early experience in behavioral development. The second major source is the work of Sigmund Freud. The third consists of the observations and theorizing of the ethologists. The fourth consists of the neuropsychological theorizing of Donald Hebb (87).

INVESTIGATIONS INSTIGATED BY DENIAL OF IMPORTANCE TO EARLY EXPERIENCE

The denials have come in two related forms. According to one, instincts constitute unlearned patterns of behavior which emerge automatically with neuromuscular maturation. According to the second, the rate of behavioral development is determined by maturation which, in turn, is fixed or predetermined by heredity.

Instincts as Unlearned Patterns of Behavior

Anyone who has observed a fledgling bird take off in flight with its first emergence from the parental nest can readily understand why, in 1873, Spalding made flying a paradigm for unlearned motor patterns. Coghill's classic studies on the behavioral development of amphibian embryos, described in his book of 1929, lent scientific authority to the view that behavioral patterns emerge automatically with neural maturation. From observing the embryonic development of chicks, Zing Yang Kuo took issue with Coghill's generalizing to organisms higher in the evolutionary scale. Nevertheless, Coghill's general principles of behavioral progression from head to tail, from trunk to peripheral limbs, and from integrated patterns to individuated reflexes were widely accepted as general for even the human species (see 100, Chap. 2).

Even so, the possibility that experience might be of importance even for instinctive patterns led both skeptics and the believers in the theory of instinct to undertake investigations in which typical experiences were subtracted or various kinds of stimulation added in order to determine if there were any effects on the organization of such patterns as pecking in newly hatched chicks, flying in newly hatched birds, or nursing in neonatal mammals. In general, subtractions of typical experience for short periods had little effect on the level of perfection achieved in the organization of such patterns or in the time required for their perfection. On the other hand, with longer periods of subtraction, animals of all investigated species failed to achieve a level of efficient organization and failed to improve in organization without adequate use or practice. Moreover, in a study by Padilla, when chicks were kept in darkness and fed artificially with a spoon for 2 weeks, the inclination to peck for food was completely lost, and the chicks would starve to death with an ample supply of grain. Padilla's report met with skepticism, but as any dairy farmer knows, a calf kept away from cows and pail-fed for 2 or 3 weeks will lose the inclination to suckle for food. Use of such feeding patterns as pecking in birds and nursing in mammals is readily lost if those patterns go unused and alternative actions become reinforced in the feeding process (see 14; 100, Chap. 3, 8; 176, 183). Presumably this process can be reversed, but this reviewer knows no reports of such research.

When this investigative strategy of subtracting typical experiences was extended to human beings, Dennis & Dennis (56) found that the restrictions of leg use in the practice of cradling by Hopi mothers failed to alter the distribution of ages for the appearance of walking. They also found that some 50 behavioral items would develop autogenously, that is, "without encouragement of instruction or reward or example," but their appearance was clearly retarded. Dennis and Dennis concluded that "maturation in and of itself seldom produces new developmental items, but maturation of structures when accompanied by self-directed activity, leads to new infant responses" (56, p. 130). When the effects of early practice on such motor skills as scissor-cutting, ladder-climbing, tower-building, and buttoning were investigated by Josephine Hilgard, Gesell and Thompson, and others, they appeared to be evanescent. Within something like a week of practice, control groups or twins attained nearly the same level of performance as trained groups or twins had achieved in the course of 12 or more weeks of practice beginning at a younger age. Thus, Gesell & Thompson (69) concluded that "training does not transcend maturation." This conclusion of evanescence, however, failed to take into account first, how low the ceiling is for such performances, and second, the fact that those children or twins who were trained did achieve these motor skills well ahead of their untrained controls. Moreover, they retained some superiority. Had they been provided with an opportunity to use their early achievements in more complex behavioral organizations, their training would be expected to have had a cumulative, hastening effect (see 100, Chap. 8; 183).

This idea of such a cumulative, hastening effect of experience presumes an epigenesis of hierarchical structures of increasingly comprehensive organization in behavioral development. It is Piaget (151, 152) who has suggested such a concept most forcefully. Yet evidence that might well have suggested just such a conception has come from investigations of the effects of early experience on such motor patterns as copulation, nest building, and mothering. These patterns traditionally have been considered to be instinctive even though they make their first appearance in or near adulthood. An extended program of investigation of the copulatory pattern by Beach (13) has shown it to be mediated, especially in male rats and dogs, by central nervous mechanisms in the development of which past experience has an essential role. Further evidence of this sort has come from studies of the development of the affectional system in primates (83). Monkeys reared in isolation, for instance, show severe defects in the copulatory pattern which Harlow also found to be greater in males than in females. Early experience has also been found to be important for the development of mothering behavior. When Riess reared female rats in cages that contained nothing that could be picked up or transported, they failed to build nests at the time of their parturition, even though appropriate materials were made available. In another study, Birch (22) found that female rats that had been made to wear rubber collars from the time of their weaning to the time of their parturition were slow to pay attention to their pups. Once they did find them and began to lick them, they proceeded to eat them. The rubber collars had prevented self-licking through which female rats learn an inhibition of the licking, chewing, and swallowing organization in the presence of the odor from the genital area, according to Birch's interpretation. Such findings suggest that even for the late-developing instincts of infrahuman animals, there is a hierarchical epigenetic sequence of behavioral structures in the development of which experience is highly important.

In human beings, both locomotion and language have been considered to be "instinctive" in the sense that they have been supposed to develop with little influence from experience. When Mary Shirley found the succession of motor patterns leading to walking in each of her 20 infant subjects showing correlations with the modal pattern which were all above +0.93 with 60% above +0.97, she concluded that "motor development . . . is little influenced by . . . fashion in child training." On the other hand, when, in 1957, the same Wayne Dennis who in 1940 had interpreted the findings of his cradling study to be evidence that experience plays little role in the development of walking, observed in a Tehran orphanage that 58% of the infants in their second year were not yet sitting up alone and that 85% in their fourth year were not yet walking, he attributed this retardation, along with scooting instead of creeping as the modal pattern, to a "lack of opportunities to learn" (55). Later, in this same orphanage, providing ten foundlings with three caretakers instead of one served to decrease the age of the onset of "standing and cruising" from a mean of 70 weeks to a mean of 41.

With the three caretakers, there was time to carry the infants about and put them into strollers. Being carried permitted the infants to use their balancing mechanisms, and the strollers invited them to put weight on their legs. This advance in the locomotor scheme came, however, without corresponding advances in any of the Uzgiris-Hunt (191) scales of psychological development, scales inspired by Piaget's observations (108). This finding illustrates the specificity of relationships between the kinds of early experience and kinds of developmental advance to be met in this review again and again.

The Chomsky and Lenneberg interpretations of language achievement are "instinctive" in nature. Both note that children typically learn the basic elements of their native tongue during the first 18 months. From this Chomsky has explicitly considered language analagous to "complex innate behavior patterns . . . studied in lower organisms" (42, footnote 48), and contended that children must come equipped with an inherent "Language Acquisition Device" (LAD). Lenneberg has acknowledged a need for an appropriate speech environment, and spoken of a "critical period" for language acquisition while arguing that language has a biological basis (122, p. 247; see also 123). Lenneberg's latter argument has in its favor the fact that no infrahuman animals manifest any tendency to babble and imitate vocally as do human infants (117). On the other hand, several species of apes do imitate gesture patterns, and they have been taught to use gestures for symbolic communication (see 67). In human infants, however, experience appears to be much more important in the acquisition of language than the writings of either Chomsky or Lenneberg would allow. Retardation in language acquisition has long been noted in children being reared in institutions (see 139, p. 584ff). At the Tehran orphanage discovered originally by Dennis, samplings of foundlings reared from shortly after birth under the customary practices of the institution were found to be without either expressive or receptive language at nearly 3 years of age. Believing that Chomsky's presumption of an innate LAD showed lack of appreciation of the epigenetic nature of language acquisition, Hunt et al (107, 108) reduced the infant-caretaker ratio and taught the caretakers how to foster vocal imitation and how to sharpen the association of phonemic patterns with experience of objects and events in order to foster semantic mastery. Consequence: the 11 foundlings in this program not only achieved the top step on the scale of vocal imitation somewhat younger on the average than did a sample of home-reared American children from predominantly professional families, but they also showed at age 2 years better skill in pronunciation and as large a vocabulary as that of a sample of foundlings at age 4 years for whom the infant-caretaker ratio had also been reduced, but whose caretakers had been allowed to do "what came naturally." Clearly experience plays a very major role in whether and how rapidly language acquisition occurs, and imitation is important in the acquisition of the phonemic repertoire.

Predetermined Development

Once Wilhelm Stern hit upon the idea of dividing mental age by chronological age to obtain the IQ, predeterminism became operationalized as the principal tool for measuring development. The IQ ratio was taken not only as a measure of an individual's past development, but also of his/her ultimate potential for competence. Consequently, the validity of IQ tests was defined longitudinally, that is, in terms of how well scores from early testings would predict those from later ones. Although Binet explicitly deplored such a view, his own use of what Clyde Coombs has termed "substitutive averaging" across several branches of development to obtain a unitary measure of "the intelligence" served to obscure both the hierarchical nature of developing abilities and the details concerning the kinds of experience that advance development along the several branches (105). The studies of the contributions of experience (usually termed environment) and heredity to individual differences in the IQ typically credited variations in home experience with less than 20% of the variance in IQ (see 116, p. 232ff). When norm-referenced testing was extended to infancy, the substitutive averages across branches became developmental ages (DA) and the ratio became a DQ. When DQs obtained during infancy failed to show appreciable correlation with IQs from testings at 18 years, and plots of sigma scores for individual children in the Berkeley growth and guidance studies showed variations that occasionally ranged over four standard deviations, it was the validity of the infant tests that were called into question despite Bayley's evidence of highly satisfactory test-retest reliabilities (see 100, p. 21). It was partly to free measurements of development from this presumption of constancy in the IQ-ratio and partly to avoid the obscuring effect of Binet's substitutive averaging across branches that Uzgiris & Hunt (191), inspired by the observations of Piaget, developed ordinal scales for what was intended to be six branches of sensorimotor development. These turned out to be seven because the rates at which gestural imitation and vocal imitation develop can vary independently according to the kinds of experience infants have (108, 109).

In recent years, very substantial gains from experience have been demonstrated in the average ages at which infants living under differing rearing conditions achieve various landmarks of psychological development. In one such study, providing infants with visual targets with dangles to invite fixation at varying distances, beginning at 5 weeks of age, made a difference of 3.4 weeks in the appearance of the blink response (74). In another such study, arranging crib conditions to elicit the reaching and touching of visual targets served to reduce the median age of achieving top-level, visually directed reaching from 145 days, for infants being reared in the same setting without such experience, to 89 days (205). In the more familiar terms of the DQ-ratio, these are advances of approximately 48 points for the blink response and 63 points for visually directed reaching. While such studies show the very considerable effect that experience can have on the average age of attaining such skills, the gains, like those of scissor-cutting, etc must inevitably be evanescent unless the living conditions of the infants are arranged to invite them to utilize their early achievements in more complex behavioral organizations.

In her marvelous observations of neuromuscular development in human infants, Myrtle McGraw noted a waxing and waning of the inclination of infants to use various motor patterns. As was the fashion in the 1930s, she attributed these to an automatic unfolding of behavior with anatomic maturation. Nevertheless, her spectacular success in teaching her trained twin, Johnny, to swim at less than half a year of age and to roller skate with skill by the time he was 16 months old demonstrated clearly a means of increasing the effects of early experience. Here the trick was to introduce an opportunity to use a sensorimotor system when the infant showed a waxing of inclination toward it. When such a system is newly elicited, it is readily subject to adaptive modifications, or what Piaget has termed *accommodation*. Thus, Johnny mastered both walking and roller skating about simultaneously. On the other hand, when McGraw attempted to teach her untrained twin, Jimmy, to skate after he had already become a well-practiced toddler, she failed because he became frightened (see discussion of fear, p. 123). Although Johnny and Jimmy proved not to be identical twins, it is nevertheless suggestive that when they were tested as 8-year-olds, the responses of the trained twin on projective tests were much more elaborate than those of the untrained twin (see 100, p. 322).

Before World War II, the observed variations in the rates of development in individual growth curves was attributed to heredity because the case histories failed to disclose the nature of any environmental factors that would account for them. In recent research, on the other hand, the strategy of correlating observational measures of various aspects of rearing conditions with later attainments and that of intervening in child-rearing practices longitudinally have both shown very substantial effects of experience on the rate of development. These newer correlational studies have related environmental conditions which control the intimate, proximal experiences of infants with levels of attainment along several branches of development. Not only have the correlations turned out to be very substantial (28, 58), but unexpected specificities of relationship between kinds of experience and kinds of development have appeared (192–194, 208, 214). Moreover, interventions in the child-rearing practices at the orphanage in Tehran, already mentioned, have advanced the mean ages at which comparable groups of foundlings have attained the top steps on the several Uzgiris-Hunt scales by 34 to 87 weeks. When these differences are transformed to variations in DQ-ratios for the various branches, they range from 34 to 80 points (108). In other parts of this research program, moreover, the mean ages at which groups of children being reared under differing conditions achieved the top step on the scale of object permanence have differed by more than 2 years, which transforms to a difference in mean DQ-ratio of the order of 90 points (110). Moreover, some of the advances in achieving top steps on these scales were quite unexpected, and they suggest the existence of unexpected kinds of specificity between the nature of the experiences and the nature of the developmental advances observed (106). This is one of the methodological advantages of measuring several branches of development simultaneously, and one which was lost by the substitutive averaging of Binet and Simon to obtain a global developmental or mental age (105). Although detailed information about such specificities is still very limited, it is precisely the kind of information required for an effective pedagogy for infancy and early childhood.

Corroborative evidence has come from the Milwaukee project (88, 89). By means of educational day care, with one trained caretaker for each infant, 20 offspring of black mothers from the poverty sector with IQs of 75 or below were enabled to obtain a mean IQ of 124 at age 66 months. This mean was 30 points above that for a control sample of offspring from comparable mothers. At 66 months, the special treatment ceased, and both groups of children became dependent on their families and the public schools for the development-fostering quality of their experience. As would be expected from the fact that homes contribute more than do schools to what is measured by tests of intelligence (113), the mean IQ of the treated group had dropped by the end of the fourth grade from 124 to 109. Nevertheless, the 30-point effect of the educational day care during the preschool years continued to be manifest in their superiority over the controls (88). In other words, to a considerable degree, plasticity can cut both ways, but early gains tend to be maintained.

Ironically, both forms of the denial of special importance for early experience in behavioral development have inspired investigations producing evidence denying the denial. Experience clearly participates in the maintenance and/or the origin of instinctive organizations. Experience clearly plays a major role in the rate of psychological development. While plasticity can cut both ways, the longer any given quality of development-fostering experience persists, the more difficult it becomes to alter its effects.

CONCEPTIONS OF EARLY EXPERIENCE FROM PSYCHOANALYSIS

Probably no one has done more than Freud to foster a belief in a special importance of early experience. Three conceptions of the special importance of early experience have come from psychoanalysis and been sources of streams of investigation: 1. the theory of psychosexual development, 2. the theory of infantile trauma, and 3. the role of mothering and the basis for attachment. This last point will be considered following a discussion of the studies inspired by the ethologists.

The Theory of Psychosexual Development

The theory of psychosexual development, presented by Freud in the second of his *Three Contributions to the Theory of Sex* published in 1905, described an epigenetic sequence of libidinal investments in the oral, anal, and phallic zones and functions. The theory was taken to imply that the experiences of infants and young children associated with feeding, toilet training, infantile masturbation, and identification with the like-sexed parent are correlated with later personality characteristics and disorders. The early attempts to verify the theory were based upon retrospective studies comparing the frequencies of various supposedly pathogenic experiences in samples of patients and nonpatients or samples of individuals with and without some personality characteristic. For a time such evidence was taken to be supportive, but critical reviews by Child (41), Orlansky (146), and Sewell (177) soon showed that the evidence concerning such alternatives as breast-feeding versus bottle-feeding, feeding on demand versus feeding on schedule, weaning early or weaning late, was highly fallible. The better controlled the study, the less likely it was to have found significant effects. Freud's own assertion that "it looks as if the desire of the child for its first form of nourishment is altogether insatiable, and as if it never got over the pain of losing the mother's breast" (63, p. 166) proved to be quite wrong. As was the case with pecking in chicks and sucking in calves, providing infants with a cup of milk to drink ahead of offering the breast or the bottle led regularly to self-weaning without evidence of frustration [Sears & Wise (176)].

Some evidence for the constellation known as *anal character* exists in correlational studies (see 12), but evidence that this derives from the management of toilet training proved to be lacking. The anal character shows considerable resemblance to the "authoritarian personality," however, and the inflexibility of adjustment involved in both tends to be associated with a past experience of impatient and punitive management of children's intentional activities. Such inflexibility also appears to be analogous to the fixitive effects of shock on learned turns by rats in a T-maze, discovered first by I. E. Farber (see 167; see also below, pp. 115–17, 121–22).

The evidence available has called into question the oedipal hypothesis that children regularly compete with parents of the same sex for the attentions and love of the parent of the opposite sex. Even from psychoanalytic evidence, Karen Horney has argued that the oedipal complex is a form of infantile neurosis. Moreover, a study by Helper (90) has suggested that the degree to which a son identifies with his father is substantially correlated with his mother's approval of the man who is her husband and his father.

Taken all together, the evidence has suggested that it is not so much the fate of these instinctual forms of pleasure striving as it is the fate of children's moment-to-moment intentions which shapes their personal characteristics. Later reviews, with somewhat different centers of focus, have tended to support these conclusions (34, 38, 212). While such findings discounted the importance of the kinds of experience which were the focus of investigators attempting to validate the theory of psychosexual development, they did not impugn Freud's general contention that early experience has special importance for development.

Although retrospective studies continue to be done (e.g. 118, 121) despite the unreliability of mothers' reports (203, 213), the main strategy of investigating what kinds of experience are important has shifted to prospective approaches. This shift began with the study of developmental retardation associated with group care in a hospital by René Spitz (181). This study was severely criticized for methodological reasons, but the prospective strategy caught on.

One form of this prospective strategy has consisted of obtaining assessments of various behavior-eliciting and controlling circumstances of infants and correlating them with measures of various characteristics of infants and young children (e.g. 29, 194, 208, 214). The second form of the prospective strategy has consisted of comparing the ages at which developmental achievements appear in children being reared under differing circumstances (33, 39, 148). A third form has consisted of manipulating the behavior-eliciting and controlling circumstances of infants over extended periods of time and determining their effects on the age at which various developmental landmarks appear (75, 89, 108).

Instruments for assessing the several kinds of circumstances which control the experiences of infants and young children have been devised by several investigators [for infants see (208, 214); for children aged 3 to 6 see (35, 45)]. Useful checklists for measuring the amount and the characteristics of the interaction between infants and their material environments have also been devised (131, 208, 214), and on the side of dependent variables there are the ordinal scales inspired by Piaget's observations (191) and the measures of some seven kinds of competence identified by White and his collaborators in preschool children (207).

It should be noted that in the process of shifting from retrospective to prospective strategies, the concern about what early experience is important for has also changed from personality to cognition and from aspects of mental health to the achievement of competencies.

These prospective investigations are modifying conceptions of what kinds of experiences are important for early development. In early infancy, tactile stimulation and body contact have shown lower correlations with various measures of infant behavior at 6 months than would be expected from the claims of such psychoanalytic observers of infants as Ribble or from the studies of monkeys reared in isolation by Harlow and his collaborators (214). Kinesthetic-vestibular stimulation, on the other hand, appears to be of genuine importance from cross-cultural evidence (2), from positive correlations with measures of object permanence (+0.44) and with persistence of efforts to secure objects out of reach (+0.57) at age 6 months (214), and from the hastening effect on the age at which sitting and standing appear (108). Perhaps the biggest change has come in the importance attributed to the distance receptors. Auditory and visual experience appear to be far more important for social responsiveness than they were ever conceived to be by psychoanalytic observers [see (195) and discussion of attachment below, pp. 127–28].

Much more important than receptor modalities per se, however, are the various intimate, proximal characteristics of infant experiences. Highly important is the temporal tie between all infant's actions and experiences he receives. The more quickly caregivers or mothers respond to behavioral indications of distress or attempts to elicit attention by their infants, the more generally responsive and active are the infants at age 6 months (214; see also 29, 58). Some investigators have been surprised to find that the infants of mothers who respond promptly to their cries and appeals for attention cry less than those of mothers who do not, and have considered the fact to be dissonant with the principle of reinforcement (16). What they neglect to note is that delay of response leads to louder crying. Few mothers fail to respond to the louder crying. Thereby they reinforce loud crying instead of more polite appeals, as Mowrer (145) pointed out long ago.

The importance of such proximate aspects of experience extend to inanimate materials. Among the very highest correlations with infant behavioral characteristics at age 6 months are measures of the responsiveness, the complexity, and the variety of the inanimate materials available to the infant (214; see also 29, 193, 194). Ordinary paper turns out to be among the most responsive of inanimate materials; it changes shape and makes crackling sounds as it is manipulated. This explains why a child receiving a present is often more interested in the wrapping than in his/her present. Such direct reinforcement from manipulative acts fosters an inclination to act upon the world and to persist in striving for intentional goals (214).

This correlational form of the prospective strategy has also uncovered the nature of some experiences that are important for their inimical effect on development. These include noisy confusion in the home (193, 194, 208), lack of regularity in daily schedules of events (29, 58, 170), overcrowding (17, 192), and physical restrictions on exploratory behavior (192, 193, 208, 211). Yet another form of inimical experience consists of maternal expectancies of achievement beyond children's capacity of adaptive modification (109).

The importance of such inimical experiences as the prevalence of noise unrelated to an infant's actions and goals has been shown first by negative correlations of the order of –0.70 with the level of the child's advancement along several branches of sensorimotor development among which vocal imitation is prominent (192, 194). Such a finding suggests that when irrelevant noise is prevalent, the inclination of infants to orient and attend to adult speech habituates. Receptor inputs to which the orienting response is weak serve poorly as either conditional stimuli or cues in learning (135). Since irrelevant noise from unresponsive adults or television is all too common in homes of the uneducated poor, it is hardly surprising that children aged 4 and 5 from families of poverty are less attentive to adult talk and do a poorer job of discriminating vocal patterns than do children from better educated families (see 102, pp. 202–14). Secondly, evidence suggesting that this inimical influence persists has come from a recent cross-lagged panel analysis (the purpose of which is to identify causal relationships) of cognitive measures for four different grade levels where a measure of listening and comprehension at grade 5 shows a very substantial correlation (+0.73) with an intellectual composite measured at grade 11 (7). Such evidence has obvious implications for training, for caretaking and parenting, and for compensatory education.

While the stream of investigation flowing from Freud's theory of psychosexual development has dimmed the significance of the kinds of experience to which Freud or those attempting to validate his theory had originally attributed importance, it has supported his general contention of special importance for early experience, and it is showing what kinds of experience are important.

The Theory of Infantile Trauma

The second large stream of investigations from psychoanalysis has its source in Freud's conception of infantile trauma as a level of excitement within the nervous system beyond the capacity of the infant to master (62, 64). Every stage of development was considered to have its own particular condition for anxiety and trauma. During infancy it was pain and/or the helplessness resulting from loss of love or care. The later consequences were conceived to be proneness to anxiety and lack of adaptability. The infant was thought to find evidence of love and care in tactile contact, especially during early infancy (25, 159, 181).

Inspired by this conception, several investigators examined the later behavioral effects of what was termed "gentling," "petting," and "handling" of rats for some 10 minutes a day for 3 weeks following their weaning at 21 days of age. At 60 days of age such animals were found to be less "emotional," more "adaptive," heavier, and less subject to stress than their littermate controls (21, 171, 199, 200). Such evidence supported the theory of infantile trauma. Evidence dissonant with the theory came first, and serendipitously, from a study by Levine and collaborators (129). Noting that rat pups are hardly infants after weaning, these investigators introduced their intervention on the second day following birth. The interventions consisted of placing pups daily on an electrified grid for 3 minutes with the current kept strong enough to keep them squealing, and placing others on the grid when it was not electrified, with a control group that remained unmolested in the maternal nest. When tested at 60 days of age, following 39 days of routine cage-rearing with food and water ad lib, the three groups failed to differ in "emotionality," and contrary to expectations, both those shocked and those placed on the unelectrified grid learned to respond to an anticipatory signal to avoid electric shock more rapidly than did those left unmolested in the maternal nest. In subsequent studies, Levine (125, 126) confirmed these findings and also found that, at 60 days of age, rats left unmolested in their nests drank substantially less water following a period without it than did rats handled or shocked during infancy. Moreover, in these later studies, both those shocked daily and those placed on the grid without shock were less "emotional," in the sense that they exhibited less defecation and more activity in a strange situation than did those left unmolested in the maternal nest. These findings quickly inspired other investigators [see (52, 57, 66, 127); for the most recent and complete review, see (183)].

For measures of precisely those kinds of behavior for which the trauma theory would predict clear differences, the nature of the preweaning experiences turned out to make essentially no difference. Rat pups left unmolested in the maternal nest regularly turned out to be more "emotional," more "timid," slower in responding to an anticipatory signal to avoid shock, less ready to drink when thirsty, and less resistant to stress than animals provided with special experience between birth and weaning. Moreover, for such measures of adult behavior, the consequences were essentially the same whether the pups were petted, shocked, handled inconsistently or roughly, put on ice, heated, or submitted to loud auditory or vibratory stimulation during the period between birth and weaning. Aversiveness is all these experiences have in common.

The age at which such aversive experiences occur is, however, very important. Such findings have occurred regularly *only* when the infantile experiences were provided between birth and weaning. When such aversive experiences came after about 30 days of age, conditional fears resulted (32, 68), and when they came between the ages of 20 and 30 days, the later effect, paradoxically, included both fears of specific cues associated with the early aversive experience and reduced fearfulness in general (133).

Such evidence can hardly be reconciled with the theory of infantile trauma, yet such a judgment is merely intuitive without the confirmation from direct measures of the levels of "excitement in the nervous system" from the various treatments. Evidence more crucially dissonant with the theory of infantile trauma came from an experiment, conducted in four replications with five litters each, showing that being shocked for 2 minutes daily during days 10 to 20 serves to halve the fixative effects of electric shock in adulthood on resistance to the extinction of T-maze training, and this effect did not occur as a consequence of either being petted or lying on an unelectrified grid during the same period before weaning (167). Thus, infantile experience with painful electric shock during the period between birth and weaning can be said with confidence to attenuate the effect of that kind of experience in adulthood.

It appears to be the rule that repeated or prolonged early experience with aversive receptor inputs attenuates the aversiveness of such inputs encountered later. Such results have appeared in rats for ethanol (20), garlic-laced food (31), a vibrating environment (111), flashing illumination (140), and the bitterness of sucrose octaacetate (196).

The existence of attenuations in the aversiveness of such experiences in animals helps, at least tentatively, to explain some puzzling human behavior. During the depression years of the 1930s, Holmes (96) found that 4-year-olds from day-care centers in New York slums, where encounters with rough and painful treatment were common, showed far less fear in a variety of fear-inducing situations than did nursery-school children from upper middle-class homes, where encounters with such rough and painful treatment could be expected to be much less common. Moreover, the rigid symptomatic patterns of psychopathic personalities appear to result from rearing conditions which contain a great deal of both punishment and interpersonal frustration (see 25). Such evidence appears to be much more consonant with Helson's (91) theory of adaptation levels and with a similar position formulated, apparently independently, by Welch (202) than with the psychoanalytic conception of infantile trauma.

On the other hand, conditioned fears do exist. Their demonstrations go back 60 years to the conditional fears of little Albert in the experiments by Watson and Raynor. Yet against accepting conditional fears as the basis for chronic anxiety deriving from early experiences of unmanageable anxiety or pain is a finding of Campbell and his associates that the retention of avoidance responses established in young rats and guinea pigs is much poorer than retention of those established when subjects of the same species are older (36). Fears conditioned early in Pavlovian fashion can, however, become a basis for adult anxieties through a process of "reinstatement" suggested by Campbell & Jaynes (37).

It was Levine who first sought a physiological mechanism for reduced aversiveness. In view of the possibility that the lesser "emotionality" of pups handled or shocked before weaning might mean that their autonomic nervous systems had been made less responsive than those of unmolested littermates, he examined adrenal responses and found less adrenal hypertrophy at 24 hours following an injection of hypertonic glucose in rats shocked before weaning than in their unmolested controls (125). Such investigators as Ader, Denenberg, and Levine have also found less elevation of plasma corticosterone from exposure to either novel or noxious stimuli in animals handled before weaning than in their littermate controls (see 183, p. 589). Under such conditions of acute stress and intense shock in adulthood, animals handled or shocked before weaning responded with larger elevations of plasma corticosterone than their unmolested littermates, but these larger initial elevations were also followed by more rapid decreases in plasma corticosterone following the termination of the shock. These findings have suggested that such aversive stimuli as shocking before weaning result in physiological responses which are more nicely adaptable to adult variations in aversive stimulation and stress (54, 128, 198).

While the details of the nature of the registration and storage of the traces of handling and aversive stimulation in early infancy continues to be a subject of controversy (6, 150, 198; see also 1, 50), it appears that the traces of such experiences must reside in the neuroendocrine system. On the other hand, as will be seen below, the traces of Pavlovian and operant conditioning along with sensorimotor patterns of learning in general must involve the microscopic architecture and the biochemistry of the cerebral cortex.

One more point from this stream of investigation is of apparent significance for the theory of drive as general arousal. While early encounters with aversive or noxious stimulation result later in an attenuation of its aversiveness or noxiousness, exactly the opposite appears to be the consequence of early experiences of intense hunger and thirst. The earliest of the studies of infantile feeding frustration focused on adult hoarding as the effect and discovered serendipitously an additional consequence in rapid eating (99, 112). Later investigators have found rapid eating to be the more consistent consequence (e.g. 137). Moreover, early encounters with high levels of thirst have also been found to cause the following effects: to prime animals with perceptual alertness for cues that lead to water (43), to motivate them to eat more quickly in a strange situation and to press a bar more rapidly for satisfaction of the need deprived in infancy (136), to learn a discrimination more rapidly for reward based on satisfaction of the deprived need (53), and to enter more quickly a place where they have been shocked but which also leads on to satisfaction of the deprived need (157). Both Freud (62) and the neobehaviorists (see 98) have treated drive as a unitary state of general arousal regardless of whether the source was a painful stimulation, a homeostatic need such as hunger or thirst, or even sex. But the experimental findings just cited indicate that the direction of later motivational effect of early experiences with painful stimulation are precisely the opposite to the effect of experience with homeostatic need; therefore, the theory of drive as generalized excitement, if anyone still believes it, is in serious need of correction.

It is somewhat ironic that a stream of investigations inspired originally by the hope of validating the concept that infant animals and human beings require tender contact lest they become prone to anxiety has produced evidence indicating rather that very early encounters with any kind of aversive stimulation attenuates the aversiveness of that stimulation later. On the other hand, the later effect may not be socially desirable. Once again, the evidence from this stream of investigations flowing from Freud's ideas has lent support to his general proposition about the special importance of early experience, but not to the kinds of experience he emphasized.

INVESTIGATIONS FLOWING FROM ETHOLOGICAL CONCEPTIONS

Ethology is a combination of naturalistic observations and the theory of instinctive behavior formulated by Karl von Frisch, Konrad Lorenz, and Nikolas Tinbergen (the first behavioral scientists to share in a Nobel Prize, 1973) and their colleagues and followers. Even though their theory aims to account for instinctive behavior, it is concerned with the perceptual aspects rather than the more traditional motor aspects (see 134, 186). The ethologists have done much to emphasize the special importance of early experience, chiefly through two important concepts: "imprinting" and "critical periods."

Imprinting

Although Spalding and various other naturalistic observers noted that precocial birds (i.e. those able to locomote at the time of hatching) will follow the first moving object they see, it was Lorenz (134) who first called this phenomenon "imprinting" (his own translation from the German word

"Prägung"). It was also Lorenz and his ethological colleagues who noted that imprinting consists: 1. of seeing and perhaps hearing an object and following it; 2. showing not only a proneness to follow an object but to approach it in preference to other objects; 3. showing a tendency to utter cries of distress as the imprinted object escapes perceptual contact and sounds of contentment as perception or actual contact is reestablished; 4. that, in the typical circumstances of nature, this process has survival value for hatchlings by guaranteeing that they become attached to the mother bird that has warmed the eggs from which they have hatched and is therefore the first object to be seen.

The investigations of the ethologists discovered that the following response and the choices dictated by imprinting are quite stable and, in some instances, so irreversible that birds of one species imprinted on the hen of another will seek to mate only with the bird of the imprinted species. They discovered also that the process is unspecific with respect to the characteristics of the imprinted object. This has permitted hatchlings of various species to become attached to and to be reared by domestic hens in bird farming (see 173, 186). It may possibly be somewhat easier for an infant bird to become imprinted to an object resembling a hen of its own species, yet so unspecific is the object that hatchlings can become imprinted to almost anything, even to a purple cube (156). Because of lack of specificity in the imprintable object, Thorpe (186, p. 254) has considered imprinting to be "an innate disposition to learn" and has extended its meaning to cover attachment to the type of environment first perceived (186, p. 117), the acquiring of song patterns for imitation by birds (see 186, p. 116), and to food preferences (31, 215). The imprinting process, with varying degrees of intensity, has been observed not only in birds, but in fishes and insects (186, p. 116–17), in such mammals as domestic lambs, goats, and dogs (see 14, 173), and the concept of imprinting has influenced ideas about the basis for the attachment of infant anthropoids and human beings to their mothers, as will be considered below.

Although Thorpe considered imprinting to be a disposition to learn, categorizations of this process in the lexicon of psychology have differed. In one of the most extensive programs of experimentation with the process, Eckhard Hess (see 92, 93) has been concerned to show how sharply it differs from such examples of associative learning as operant and classical conditioning. This issue is tangential for the story of early experience, but some of the evidence from Hess's excellent experiments may readily be reinterpreted with theoretical consequences of interest for our topic.

Although Hess has emphasized the importance the effort that hatchling birds put into their following in explaining the imprinted attachment, this interpretation has omitted several aspects of hatchling behavior which implicate primary importance of the perceptual experience. First, chicks exposed during their second day after hatching to a circular black disc or a black triangle spent most of their time near the figure to which they had been exposed when, on the next day, they were placed for 15 minutes in a choice apparatus. Here, clearly, no following was involved. In Hess's imprinting process, the sounds which emanated from the imprinting object got turned on before that object moved. They served to attract the eyes of the hatchling bird to its source. Moreover, the following itself served to keep within sight the object that was the source of the sound. Finally, in some of Hess's experiments, the object to be imprinted passed the hatchling several times before the chick actually began to follow the object.

All these items support an interpretation that it is the perceptual familiarity of the object that instigates the following. If one takes seriously Hebb's contention that interest, motivation, and even a substantial kind of pleasure reside in "a directed growth or development in cerebral organization" (87, p. 232), one can readily see a basis for the attractiveness of imprinted objects in the growth of a "cerebral organization" that permits recognitive familiarity during these repeated perceptual encounters. This is not to say that there can be no influence from the effort the hatchling puts into the following response, but any sensorimotor organization can gain stability when it has endured through effort (see 179) or even rigidity when it has endured through excitement and pain (167).

Hess has also contended that it is the maturation of the fear response which terminates the period during which imprinting can occur, but one can readily see this fear as a consequence of the recognitive familiarity developed for the imprinted object. One clear consequence of rearing chimpanzees in the dark for 16 months following their birth was an absence of the fear response to strange objects so typical of infant chimpanzees at that age. Fear does not come automatically with maturation. If one takes seriously Hebb's (86) theory that fear, although it is an unlearned response, is evoked by a perception too discrepant from what has become recognizable from past experience to be accommodated, the alternative interpretation is clear. Once hatchlings have become imprinted, they have stored a perceptual scheme of the imprinted object which gives it recognitive familiarity. At that point, strange objects might be expected, from this alternative interpretation, to evoke fear.

It was such a set of considerations that in part led to the idea of intrinsic motivation, i.e. a system of motivation inherent in information processing and action (101) with its own epigenesis in psychological development (103). This conception, in turn, suggested that human infants could be expected to show a preference, in the sense of looking longer at, for visual patterns becoming recognitively familiar from perceptual exposure before they would show the commonly noted preference for novel or unfamiliar patterns. Although the limitations for this hypothesis are still far from clear, it has empirical support from both the visual (75, 201, 204) and auditory (65) modalities.

According to the outline of the epigenesis of intrinsic motivation, an infant's interest shifts from what is perceptually and recognitively familiar in the way of perceptual information to what is novel and unfamiliar when most of the objects, persons, and places encountered have become recognizable and the infant has acquired an expectation that "things should be recognizable." Such an expectation appears to motivate his focused scrutiny of what is novel among things that have become recognizable. Similarly, interest shifts from models of actions already mastered, as the afferent feedback from them becomes fully anticipated and stale, to the novelty of new patterns (see 103). On the other hand, situations that can engage the attention but create demands beyond the individual's capacity for adaptive modification (or *accommodation,* to use Piaget's term) evoke distress. Those entirely beyond the individual's cognitive ken fail even to elicit attention; they have no more significance to the individual than "talking to a pig about Sunday." It is encounters with situations sufficiently discrepant from those already fully recognized and mastered to engage an infant's interest and to elicit adaptive modifications of which he is capable that foster his development. For caretakers, parents, and teachers, providing such situations in order to foster a child's development is a problem—the "problem of the match" (100, p. 267ff; 103).

This conception of optimal discrepancy for development shares much with Piaget's concept of a "mobile equilibrium" (153, p. 40), or "equilibration" (154). Piaget's concept, however, is limited to the cognitive aspects of the discrepancy between situational demands and past development achievements whereas this one emphasizes the emotional and motivational aspects of the individual's cognitive appreciation of such discrepancy.

This theory appears to have considerable explanatory power. As already noted, it suggests that the fear shown by chicks at about 3 days of age may be less a matter of predetermined maturation than an example of Hebbian fear following the development of recognition for the imprinted object. It also suggests a highly plausible reason why Myrtle McGraw was unable to teach her untrained twin, Jimmy, to roller skate at 22 months of age despite her earlier success with Johnny when he was first attempting to stand and toddle. Once a child has become accustomed to the perceptual feedback from such an activity as walking, the feeling of feet sliding on roller skates becomes so different from the accustomed feeling of feet that stay put on the floor that it is frightening. In the limited state of our present knowledge about fostering early development, perhaps the best solution to the "problem of the match" consists in learning to identify the behavioral signs of interest in infants and young children and choosing for their play and imitation those materials and models which both elicit their interest and promise to lead to attitudes and competencies that the culture demands.

Critical Periods

It was the ethologists who recognized that imprinting occurs in birds only during a period of brief duration following hatching. Lorenz (134) drew a parallel between this transformation in behavior and those epigenetic transformations in anatomic structure which occur during the embryonic maturation of organs. Since both imprinting and such epigenetic transformations are confined to very limited amounts of time, Lorenz called the limited time a "critical period." The existence of a critical period for imprinting in birds suggested the possibility of critical periods for other behavioral transformations and for other species including human beings.

There do indeed appear to be genuine critical periods for light experience and for experience with various patterns in the development of the visual system shortly after birth or after the eyes open (see p. 130). There also appear to be critical periods for encounters with painful stimulation if it is to reduce the aversiveness of that stimulation without also producing conditioned fears (see p. 117). Unfortunately, the dependable information we have is limited to rats. Although there are analagous phenomena in human beings, they are only analogs. In each of these cases, it appears that certain specific kinds of experience must be timed to occur while rapid maturation is underway within a functionally relevant portion of the nervous system.

Something somewhat akin to critical periods exists for the taming of wild animals, the formation of fears, and for attachment to mothers, fears, species, and environments. If pups born to wild rats are not handled regularly during the week or 10 days following the opening of their eyes and ears, they will never allow themselves to be picked up by human hands without a fight (personal observation). Lambs isolated from their mothers at birth and reared by human beings for 10 days will never become strongly gregarious members of the flock. Moreover, in dogs, there is "a period of socialization beginning at about 4 weeks after birth and continuing from 3 to 7 weeks, or until the pups become largely independent of their mothers" (174; see also 172). The periods in which the formation of such specific social attachments occurs range widely across species from a few hours in precocial birds, a few days in such ungulates as sheep, 3 or 4 weeks following the opening of the eyes and the ears in dogs or a similar period following birth in monkeys, some 5 or 6 weeks in chimpanzees, and something like 5 or 6 months in human infants. An even greater range of periods appears to exist for becoming attached to environments, and in human beings it may extend from birth to adulthood (81). Roughly speaking, the higher the species on the evolutionary scale, the longer is the period and the less resistant and reversible are such attachments. Whether the term *critical* is appropriate for such instances is highly dubious, the term *sensitive* has been suggested and appears to be more appropriate.

Related to this concept of critical periods is Epstein's hypothesis of *phrenoblysis*. In both rat pups and human children, he has found evidence of spurts of head size, and of inferred brain growth, independent of somatic growth. In human children, these spurts are reported to occur at ages 2–4, 6–8, 10–12, and 14–16 (59). Epstein has also reported evidence of spurts in the IQ which come at these same age periods (60). He suggests, therefore, that the capacity of children to learn tends to peak during such spurts of brain maturation. This suggestion has interesting implications for the so-called failure of Project Head Start and for appropriate times to attempt compensatory education (see 104).

It is impossible to generalize about critical periods across sensorimotor systems or across species for any one system. Except for the receptor systems, and most of the evidence concerns the visual system, it is doubtful that truly critical periods exist in human development. One of the major outcomes of research on the effects of early experience is the evidence of greater plasticity in early development than was ever believed. If one takes seriously Piaget's hierarchical conception of behavioral organization and the theory of an epigenesis in intrinsic motivation, every point in the process of psychological development is sensitive to experiences involving a proper degree of discrepancy between situational demands and past achievements to elicit interest and call forth adaptive modification in those past achievements. It is also clear, however, that the longer a young organism lives with experience of a given development-fostering quality, the more difficult it is to change the nature of the effect.

MATERNAL DEPRIVATION, MATERNAL ATTACHMENT, AND PSYCHOLOGICAL DEVELOPMENT

The conceptions of what aspects of tender loving care are important for early psychological development have gone through several revisions in the twentieth century (see 182). With the advent of influence from psychoanalysis in the 1930s, the emphasis shifted from the scheduling and habit training of Watson (197) to the practices suggested by the theory of psychosexual development. As these were discredited and as evidence of retarded physical, motor, and intellectual development in orphanage-reared infants came from studies in several countries, these effects were attributed to maternal deprivation. At about the same time came evidence from retrospective studies by several investigators that children and adolescents who show the rigid forms of psychopathic delinquency have had histories of infantile neglect and of being shifted from one foster home and mother to another. In 1951, John Bowlby (25) brought this information together in a highly influential review for the World Health Organization with the conclusion that depriving an infant of a continuing, one-to-one relationship with either its own mother or a permanent substitute results in retardation of physical and intellectual development and defects in emotional and social development. So convincing had been the cinemas of children in orphanages made by René Spitz, moreover, that institutional care for infants had already been outlawed in most of the United States in favor of foster-home placement.

Those neobehaviorists influenced by psychoanalysis painted a similar conceptual picture. Mothers were conceived to acquire reward value by satisfying hunger and other needs of their infants (see 175). In turn, the infants developed a dependency on their mothers that motivated their acquiring behaviors and values of the mothers and perhaps their fathers. Failure to develop such dependency was seen as a major source of later problems with discipline, uncontrolled aggressive behavior, and rigid patterns of psychopathic maladjustment [see e.g. (9)].

The findings from retrospective studies supported such a view. Since retrospective evidence had become suspect, however, the suggestive support from these retrospective studies gained considerably in credibility from the findings of prospective studies with infrahuman subjects. Monkeys reared in social isolation by Harlow and his associates during the periods when love of mothers and love of peers develop regularly failed later to show normal skills in executing either the copulatory acts of heterosexual love or the caretaking acts of maternal love (83, 84). Puppies kept in a kennel beyond 14 weeks, before transfer to a family with a child for intense socialization, typically failed to become attached to their blind owner as seeing-eye dogs (149). In yet another example, cats reared for a time shortly after their eyes opened with rats as playmates would not, as adults, kill rats even when hungry (120). A great deal of evidence on human development suggests that the experiences of the first 3 years of life are especially important for the development of close emotional relationships and what Erikson (61) has termed "trust" and "initiative." When such traits are well developed, they are prominent among those found by White (206–208) to be characteristics of children already outstanding by age 3.

On the other hand, the importance attributed to a continuous one-to-one relationship between infant and mother soon proved to be exaggerated. Much of the retardation of the first year turned out to be reversible as Skeels and Dye had discovered in 1939 and as others have confirmed (108, see also 100; 183, p. 606ff). Moreover, from the findings of a follow-up study of 60 children admitted to a tubercular hospital for extended periods before they reached age 4, Bowlby and his collaborators were forced to conclude that the importance he had attributed to an infant of having a continuous one-to-one relationship with a mother figure had been exaggerated in his WHO report (27).

The issue of what kinds of experience are important in fostering an infant's attachment to its mother or surrogate became the subject of a large stream of investigations. The findings depend to some extent upon the behavioral criteria for attachment: (a) portion of time that an infant chooses to spend in the presence of its mother, (b) the capacity of maternal presence to reduce the stress and to release exploration, (c) the amount of distress produced by separation.

What Bowlby termed the "cupboard theory"—that an infant's attachment to its mother derives from satisfying hunger through nursing—was modified by Harlow's discovery that infant monkeys reared in isolation spent 15 or 20 times as much time on the terry-cloth-covered surrogate without a nursing bottle as on a wire surrogate with a nursing bottle (26). Moreover, as those concerned with maternal attachment in the development of human infants became acquainted with the phenomenona of imprinting, they introduced further amendments to their conception of what is important for becoming attached. Bowlby, for instance, took such unlearned behaviors of human infants as crying, clinging, smiling, and sucking as analogs of instinctive following in hatchling birds (26). When it was noted that human infants aged from 6 weeks to nearly 5 months spend a major share of their time just looking at things which change or move or have edges where contrast is great, this suggested that it is "not physical, but visual contact that is the basis for human sociability" (158, p. 168), and that the infant's perceptual experience is highly important in establishing the attractiveness of the maternal figure. Such a view fits well with the theory of intrinsic motivation described above. Even though it has become more and more certain that vision and audition make important contributions to the formation of maternal attachments, the rules of imprinting in birds have been found to fail in a variety of ways to apply to the process of maternal attachment in the human species (3–5, 144, 169, 195). Moreover, it is not so much a matter of which receptor modality is important for attachment, for, in all likelihood, every modality makes its contribution. What does appear to be important for human infants is the operational nature of "tender loving care," i.e. the variations in the manner in which mothers interact with their infants (4, 16). Evidence from longitudinal studies is suggesting that what may be most important for the infant's relationship with its mother is the mutual delight that each takes in their transactions with each other (5, 15, 158).

Attachment, however, is a two-way affair which various pediatricians have termed "bonding" (30, 132). Usually the experience of pregnancy fosters an anticipatory bonding, but when the pregnancy is unwanted, it can greatly diminish the joy of a mother's interacting with and the strength of her attachment for her infant. Second, when an infant is inactive, is clumsy at nursing, and has an appearance that fails to match the expectations of the mother, the early transactions may be distressful with later consequences in both the degree and form of subsequent attachment to the infant (23, see 132). Third, the traditional hospital practice of separating the infant from mother during the first few days following birth has been found in a number of studies to interfere with the mother's later attachment to her infant (see 30). Yet a strong inclination for mothers to show special concern for their neonates in the days immediately following birth is attested by the fact that even teenage mothers from uneducated families of poverty can regularly and easily be recruited for classes in parenting if they are interviewed at the lying-in hospital on the first day or two after having given birth, but not so regularly or easily later (8). One of the survival advantages of the high degree of plasticity in human beings, and also in their mothers, is the fact that at least a considerable share of any such early damage can be made up later if mothers initially frustrated by the early unresponsiveness of their infants can be shown how to engage them in vocal games that bring smiles, laughter, and joy by repeating their infant's spontaneous vocalizations (8, 108, 124).

This recognition of mutuality in the infant-mother relationship combined with evidences of precocious neonatal capacities in perception and cognition (see 24, 82, 141) are leading to further revisions in the theoretical conception of what is more important in the infant-mother relationship. Where this relationship has been conceived chiefly as a one-sided chain of mother actions and infant reactions, the new model is one of reciprocal interaction to which such terms as "communication," "conversation," "dialogue," and "dance" are being applied (30, 132, 147, 168, 187, 188, 190). Conversational quality, albeit without either semantics or syntax, is unmistakable in the vocal games of many mother-child dyads (47) and can readily be elicited through vocal pseudo-imitation in older infants (108). Just as Myrtle McGraw used the early inclinations toward swimming of her trained twin to get him to use and perfect the scheme by the time he was 6 months old, such conversation-like behavior can be utilized very early to foster attachment and, through the attachment, many aspects of development. In typical middle-class homes, for instance, pseudo-imitation is established at an average age of about 8 weeks (189, 191), but typically comes much later in the offspring of uneducated parents of poverty and not at all in many of the children reared in understaffed orphanages (108). Cinematic records of neonatal behavior have shown that neonates, even at only 3 weeks of age, tend to *do something with their toys* which is continuing and persistent, but they show *cycles of interaction that resemble communication with their mothers* (30, 187). Since it is typically the mother who matches her behavior to that of the infant, however, this "conversation" is probably what Piaget has termed pseudo-imitation rather than genuine imitation where the infant matches the behavior of the model (see 191). Half a century ago, John B. Watson was ridiculing the idea of any influence from imitation on infant development by remarking snidely that it is mothers who imitate infants rather than the contrary. What he missed is the fact that such sequencing establishes contingencies between acts of infants and the responsive acts of their mothers which bring forth expressions of delight reminiscent of "effectance" (209) or the joys of recognitive familiarity (103). Since central processes run off faster than events, such sequencing also leads inevitably to the mutual expectancies comprising shared information or knowledge and the beginnings of the rules for social communication. Thus, the Papouseks (147) speak of such early infant-mother interaction as the basis for a "cognitive head start" (see also 130, 168). Such is the developmental plasticity in the human species, however, that infants considerably retarded during their first year for lack of reciprocal mothering can make up at least a share of that loss during their second and third years as has been shown in the Tehran study (108) and by the results obtained from the Mother-Child Home Program (124). Catching up, however, may be possible only because mothers of typical middle-class homes commonly fail to manage the phase of toddlerhood as well as they manage early infancy (see 208, Chap. 11).

EFFECTS OF EARLY EXPERIENCE ON PROBLEM-SOLVING, NEUROANATOMY, AND NEUROCHEMISTRY

It is usually difficult to locate the specific source of a new stream of investigation, but, to mix the metaphor, for this one, as Riesen (162, p. xiii) has written, "Hebb's 1949 book, *The Organization of Behavior* was the document of that launching." Hebb's neuropsychological theory, Riesen's (160) discovery that infant chimpanzees reared for their first 16 months in the dark are functionally blind, and Hebb's own finding that pet-reared rats made progressively fewer errors than cage-reared rats in learning a series of mazes set off three separate streams of investigation.

Perceptual Versus Motor Experience

Hebb's emphasis on the importance of sensory experience in the formation of "cell assemblies" in early learning flew in the face of the traditional emphasis on the motor side. McGill students investigated the issue. Studies by Hymovitch and the Forgays demonstrated the importance of cues from distant vision in maze learning. Forgus demonstrated that whether the early experience facilitates or interferes with later learning is a matter of whether or not the test situations permit use of the perceptual skills acquired early. At Cornell, the findings of Gibson and Walk tended to confirm the Forgus interpretation when rats exposed to cutouts of such geometric shapes as circles and triangles learned as adults to discriminate them in substantially fewer trials than did controls (see 70; 100, p. 87ff; 183). Evidence dissonant with Hebb's emphasis on the sensory side has come from investigations by Held and his colleagues. Kittens with only passive exposures to objects proved in tests of visually guided paw-placements to be grossly inferior to kittens allowed active, self-initiated exploration and manipulation. Thus, it appears that the relative importance of sensory versus motor aspects of interaction with the environment may be a pseudo issue. What appears to be important is the acquisition of sensorimotor organizations in which the afferent inputs from self-induced movements are essential. In human infants, this principle probably extends to the "conversation-like interaction" with adults, but the facts that they spend extended periods of time in visual exploration and show specificity in relationships between kinds of infantile experience and kinds of developmental advance suggest limitations even to such a generalization (see 70; 77, pp. 258–60; 100, pp. 91–102; 162; 183).

Effects of Variations in Sensory Experience

Roux made the speculative suggestion in 1895 that there are two phases in the maturation of the nervous system, an early one controlled by heredity, and a later one in which neural growth is a consequence of function. But Goodman ended a review of the evidence in 1932 with the conclusion that no firm support exists that sensory function or experience affects the neuroanatomical structure of the brain (see 161). The force of Goodman's conclusion was reduced when, in 1943, Hydén demonstrated that variable rotation of rabbits increased the size of cells in their vestibular nuclei. It was further reduced when ophthalmoscopic examinations unexpectedly showed alterations in the optic discs of chimpanzees reared in darkness for 16 months, when Brattgård found that ganglion cells of dark-reared rabbits showed reduction in RNA and changes in nuclear protein, and when Chow, Riesen, and Newell found degeneration in the cells of the retinae of the dark-reared chimpanzees (see 161, 162). All skepticism about early experience having an effect on central neural structures evaporated with the accumulation of demonstrations that prolonged reductions in visual experience from dark-rearing, contact occluders, the suturing of eyelids in infant mice, rats, rabbits, kittens, monkeys, and chimpanzees resulted regularly not only in defects in later visuo-motor coordinations but also in evidence of degenerative changes in the retinae, in the lateral geniculate body of the thalamus, and in the granular and supragranular layers of the visual cortex (see 71, 161). Other studies have shown loss of ganglion cells, reductions in both length and branching of the dendrites of neurons in the visual cortex, and reduction in synaptic spines on the dendrites of the large pyramidal cells of the visual cortex. The effects of deprivations of early visual experience are similar to those from surgical deafferentation, but they are less profound. The earlier the deprivation begins and the longer it lasts, the more pronounced the effects are. Moreover, only a few hours of exposure to light following either birth or the opening of the eyes serves to reduce the neuroanatomic effects of later visual deprivation (see 71). In this sense, there is a genuine critical period for visual experience with light.

The neurochemical effects of early visual deprivation have hardly been investigated enough to permit a meaningful synopsis (see 162, Chap. 3). Although the study of the effects of early visual deprivation on properties of the electrophysiological measures is recent, a massive literature has demonstrated that such effects clearly exist (see 10, 80). These include alterations in various components of the electroretinogram, which vary with species and from which recovery is typically rapid with exposure to light, and altered cell responses to visual stimuli in both the lateral geniculate nuclei (178) and the visual cortex (210) of kittens, from both of which recovery has been slow and poor. Moreover, the relationship of kind of experience to kind of physiological change can be quite specific. During early development in cats, selective exposure to horizontal, vertical, or slanted lines tones the visual cortex to respond accordingly (94, 180), and movement experience has another specific effect (49), as shown by the patterns of evoked potentials (see also 10, 80).

That deprivation of early experience in early infancy hampers neuroanatomic and neurochemical maturation as well as interferes with the development of visually controlled behavior is no longer in doubt. On the other hand, whether visual experience has any constructive effect on the fine tuning of the visual nervous system is still a matter of controversy. Finding cells in the visual cortex of kittens before eye-opening, and also in neonatal monkeys, that respond to the stimulation of both eyes led Hubel & Wiesel (97) to contend that the patterns of transneural connections which mediate normal vision come into being through genetically controlled maturation. Studies differ on the proportion of cortical cells that show such evidence of predetermined connections, with a study by Hubel & Wiesel (97) at the high extreme and one by Barlow & Pettigrew (11) at the low extreme. Thus, Barlow has pointed out that "neither an inexperienced animal nor an inexperienced neuron has been shown to have normal powers of resolution, and selectivity of disparity especially seems to require experience" (10, p. 203). Moreover, since early deprivation of vision in one eye modifies cortical organization, and since Cragg (48) found less than one percent of the synapses in the primary visual cortex already developed before eye-opening, "explaining what the other 99% do is embarrassing . . . if Hubel and Wiesel are correct" (10, p. 203). Another open question concerns whether visual experience directs the formation of synapses and is, therefore, "a creative factor in establishing the functional organization of the mammalian nervous system," as contended by Barlow (10) and by Grobstein & Chow (80), or serves rather to preserve selectively synapses from a larger number provided originally by genetically controlled maturation (see 78).

Although investigations of the effects of sensory deprivation have been concerned chiefly with the visual modality, the auditory modality has received some attention from studies by Gauron and Becker and by Thies (see 162, p. 232ff), and by Clopton & Winfield (46), as has also the somatosensory modality (see 162, p. 231ff).

Effects of Complexity of Rearing Conditions

EFFECTS ON PROBLEM-SOLVING AND ANIMAL INTELLIGENCE
Thompson and Heron followed Hebb's model of comparing the problem-solving of pet-reared and cage-reared rats with experiments on dogs. Of their 13 cage-reared pups, two encountered neither other dogs nor human beings from weaning until 8 months of age; three were restricted only by being reared in cages that allowed a view of the laboratory; the other eight lived in cages with solid walls that limited their vision. Each cage-reared pup had a littermate that was reared as a pet in a home. All 26 dogs spent 10 months in a dog pasture before testing began at 18 months of age. On the tests, only one of the cage-reared dogs made a score as high as the lowest of the pet-reared. Other investigators have obtained analogous findings with other breeds of dogs, rats, and cats (184, see also 77, 163). Parenthetically, the behavior of the isolated dogs in novel situations and in response to pain was bizarre (185). Inasmuch as the earlier studies of the effects of experience on the development of human children had lost much of their credibility because of methodological flaws, these findings from animals under conditions of better control did much to establish the credibility of the importance of early experience in the 1950s.

With primates, however, the findings on problem-solving have depended upon the kind of tests used. When the test has consisted of using a stick to obtain food out of reach, chimpanzees with early experience manipulating sticks usually solve the problem, but those without such experience seldom do [(142); for studies by Birch and Jackson, see (100)]. In tests of delayed reaction, wild-born chimpanzees with rich past experience have regularly performed with fewer errors than those laboratory reared, and for delays of 10 seconds or longer, their superiority has persisted throughout months of testing (51). At the Wisconsin laboratory, on the other hand, Harlow's group at first found that monkeys reared from birth in isolation for various periods of time learned form discriminations, discrimination reversals, and learning sets as readily as their controls (85). The absence of differences in performance on such tests, may, as Mason (138) has suggested, be a matter of controls with life histories differing too little from those of the isolates. Moreover, more recent studies by Harlow's group have shown isolates to be definitely inferior in solving more complex tasks (73). Yet two meanings of intelligence have been recognized by both Hebb (87, p. 294) and Cattell (40). One consists of ability to learn which is diminished by early brain damage (87, p. 289) and which Cattell has called "fluid intelligence." The other consists of knowledge and skills, presumably based on experiential modification of cerebral organization, which Cattell has called "crystalized intelligence." Such a distinction has some use. Perhaps heredity has more to do with the former than the latter, but it is dubious whether any observable and measurable characteristic of either animals or human beings exists without an interacting influence of both genetic constitution and functioning or experience throughout the life history.

As this stream of investigations increased in volume, the model was modified. The original contrast between pet-rearing and cage-rearing became one between an "enriched condition" (EC) and an "isolation condition" (IC). In the enriched condition, several animals were reared together in a large area provided with materials for manipulation which were changed regularly, if not daily. In the impoverished condition, animals were reared in small cages and often in isolation for various periods following weaning. Sometimes an intermediate level of complexity, termed a "social condition" (SC) has also been provided with two or three animals reared together in a laboratory cage. The effects of the isolation condition have sometimes been contrasted with those of overcrowding (see 77; 162, Chap. 7). Tests of the effect of these contrasts have included the Hebb-Williams mazes, the Lashley III maze, and reversals of such discriminations as that for visual brightness (see 77, 163; 162, Chap. 7). Although the operational definitions of these conditions have varied from investigator to investigator, rodents that have experienced the enriched condition have regularly done better on these tests than rodents reared in isolation. For some tests, early postweaning experience seems most beneficial while for others no sensitive period is evident (see 77, p. 262ff). Cats reared under such enriched conditions have made fewer errors on the Hebb-Williams mazes than cats reared in colony fashion even though the differential treatment did not begin until their 46th day. On the other hand, such special treatment as being handled daily for various periods following birth typically failed to affect the quality of performance of either rats or cats. Again there is evidence of specificity: differing kinds of early experience produce effects in differing kinds of adult behavior.

Whether these effects on maze-learning and the like are a matter of improvement in animal intelligence from the enriched condition or a matter of defect from the isolation condition is still a matter of controversy (see 19, 77). There is no question that damage exists from the isolation condition, but the limits of facilitative effects from increased complexity have hardly been fully tested by the standardized enriched condition commonly employed. Such evidence from animal studies has some relevance for the role of early experience in the cognitive development of human beings, but so far as bettering the ability to solve problems by increasing the complexity of experience is concerned, the evidence from human studies is now perhaps more solid than that from animal experiments.

EFFECTS ON NEUROCHEMISTRY AND NEUROANATOMY   A speculative possibility of functioning or experience modifying brain anatomy and chemistry existed throughout the nineteenth century and was illustrated in this century by Lashley's search for the engram. It was not, however, until an interdisciplinary team at the University of California, following a serendipitous finding, started a stream of investigations that this possibility was established as fact (see 18, 163). While seeking correlates of individual differences in learning ability among rats in brain chemistry, this group found indications that differential problem-solving experience altered enzymes involved with the neurotransmitter, acetylcholine. This finding suggested the possibility that variations in the complexity of rearing condition, such as those employed by Hebb's group at McGill, might modify this synaptic-transmitter system (see 18). Such variations in the complexity of rearing conditions (EC, SC, and IC) did modify cholinergic enzymes in littermate rats subjected to these three conditions. Furthermore, the data also contained suggestions of neuroanatomic effects. When the cortexes of rats reared under the enriched condition proved to be heavier and thicker (166) as well as showing a higher ratio of butyrylcholinesterase (ChE—a glial enzyme) to acetylcholinesterase (AChE—a neural enzyme which breaks down acetylcholine), the suggestion was confirmed. These early findings met with a great deal of skepticism, but repetitions and modifications conducted by the California group with meticulous controls, along with confirmations by other investigators, established their credibility. From this has flowed a major stream of investigations (163). The brain effects of variations in the complexity of rearing conditions also extend beyond those originally discovered by the California group. On the side of brain chemistry, complexity of rearing conditions has been found to correlate positively not only with ratios of ChE to AChE, but also with measures of total protein, total ribonucleic acid (RNA) and amounts of leucine incorporated in such subcortical brain regions as the hippocampus, amounts of glial tissue, and, on the other hand, to correlate negatively with amount of norepinephrine in the whole brain (see 77, pp. 263–64). The effect of norepinephrine appears to be limited chiefly to the isolated condition and may, therefore, be due to stress. The effects of complexity of rearing on the thickness and weight of the cortex in rats are maximal in the occipital lobe. Moreover, the size of both neurons and their nuclei as well as the density of glial cells have been found to be positively correlated with the complexity in rearing conditions (see 77, p. 265). In addition, higher frequencies of synaptic spines have been found on the basal dendrites of pyramidal neurons in the occipital cortex of rats reared in the enriched condition than in those of the isolated condition (72). Also, the numbers of third, fourth, and fifth level branches on the dendrites of pyramidal neurons in the visual cortex have been found to be several times as great for rats reared in the enriched conditions as in the social conditions, and twice as great for rats reared in the social condition as rats reared in the isolation condition (79, 95). When the branching of dendrites of pyramidal cells in other cortical regions was examined, those in which high frequency of higher level branches was most definite tended to correspond with those regions of greatest difference in weight and thickness of cortex as found by the California group. This finding suggests that these differences in weight and thickness may be a function of corresponding differences in dendritic and spine volume, glial density, and the size of neuron cell bodies (77, p. 266). Such findings also suggest that it is not merely light experience that can account for neuroanatomic effects within the visual cortex, but rather functioning in general for which vision is an extremely important modality.

Different strains of rats and even different species of rodents showed similar cerebral effects, but female rats showed smaller effects than males (163). Greenough and his collaborators have found the contribution of litters to the amount of variance in dendritic branching to be as great or greater than that from the rearing conditions, with the interation between these factors contributing sometimes more than either of the main effects (76).

The age at which animals encounter the variations in complexity of rearing conditions appears to be a factor in both the rate and amount of effect, but much less of one than was the case for early visual experience. Weight effects have been found even when the increased complexity of living conditions began as late as 285 days of age. On the other hand, it has taken longer to attain maximal effects in older animals than in younger ones (165).

That variations in experience, and especially early experience, affect both the neuroanatomy and neurochemistry of the brain as well as the organization of subsequent behavior is now quite clear. What is not at all clear, however, is how and which of these neuroanatomic and neurochemical effects in turn influence the subsequent behavior. Nevertheless, these studies of brain development and adult behavior as a function of rearing experiences of differing complexity have begun to yield information which promises better understanding. While many questions remain unanswered, Pribram (155) has put together the modifiable aspects of the brain to provide a theory of a system for coding information and for decision making. Although many of the propositions in this theory are issues for investigation rather than final answers, they promise a basis for systematizing investigations which studies of the effects of early experience on the brain have yet to attain.

CONCLUSION

Until this century, the idea that early experience is of special importance for psychological development was only an opinion held by occasional philosophers. During the first four decades of this century, it became the source of a trickle of investigations with confirmatory findings that commonly met with incredulity. After World War II, that trickle swelled into at least nine substantial streams of investigation. The evidence from these streams has been highly effective in modifying the fictitious beliefs that inspired them, and it has regularly lent support to the general idea of special importance of early experience. Yet that evidence has not yet become organized into a new over-arching synthesis, nor has the investigating become systematized by theory.

Research on the effects of early experience has produced so many specificities that it is difficult to generalize, but here are some plausible generalizations: It appears that the relative importance of experience in development increases up the evolutionary scale. The environmental circumstances of the earliest phases of development become less variable up the evolutionary scale with the advent of the environmental controls provided by shells for the eggs of birds and by the uteri of mammals. Similarly, there is a period of dependence and tutelage for the young which increases up the evolutionary scale. As this period increases, the plasticity of development increases and with it the role of experience in ontogenetic development.

The term "critical period" has become a catch word, yet in mammals nothing quite the equivalent of the brief period for imprinting in precocial birds exists, except possibly the importance of light immediately following the opening of the eyes for the development of vision. While experience is exceedingly important for the formation of the attachment of the young to their mothers with great significance for later social behavior, the periods in which this takes place appears to become increasingly longer up the evolutionary scale in parallel with the increase in that portion of the brain without direct connections with either receptors or effectors. Moreover, the effects of experience become less irreversible and more plastic, so the term "sensitive" may be more appropriate than is "critical." Even so, in human beings the preschool years, and especially the first three of them, appear to be highly important for the achievement of initiative (or roughly the opposite of learned helplessness), of trust (or readiness and skill in eliciting help from adults and others), of compassion (or readiness to appreciate the needs of and come to the aid of others), of curiosity (or the appreciation of dissonance and concern to understand it), and of various still poorly understood attainments (or learning sets) that seem to be important for the later development of competencies. Yet plasticity can cut both ways. A major share of early losses can be made up if the development-fostering quality of experience improves, and a great deal of early gain can be lost if the quality of experience depreciates. Organismic plasticity may be reduced by the tendency toward a cultural lock-step in the association of kind of experience with age. Whatever achievements are acquired early help the child to cope with later situations demanding adaptive modifications and behavioral organizations of greater complexity. Thus, the old adages apply to psychological development: "A stitch in time saves nine," and/or "An ounce of prevention is worth a pound of the cure."

A great deal of progress has been made since Plato wrote Book VII of *The Laws,* but admittedly a "want of clearness" still remains with respect to various aspects of early experience.

Literature Cited

1. Ader, R. 1975. Early experience and hormones: Emotional behavior and adrenal functions. In *Hormone Correlates of Behavior,* ed. B. C. Eleftheriou, R. L. Sprott, 1:7–33. New York: Plenum
2. Ainsworth, M. D. S. 1963. The development of infant-mother interaction among the Ganda. In *Determinants of Infant Behavior,* ed. B. M. Foss, 2:67–112. New York: Wiley
3. Ainsworth, M. D. S., Bell, S. M. V., Stayton, D. J. 1971. Individual differences in strange-situation behavior of one-year-olds. In *The Origins of Human Social Relations,* ed. H. R. Schaffer, pp. 17–52. New York: Academic
4. Ainsworth, M. D. S., Bell, S. M. V., Stayton, D. J. 1972. Individual differences in the development of some attachment behaviors. *Merrill-Palmer Q.* 18:123–43
5. Ainsworth, M. D. S., Wittig, B. A. 1969. Attachment and exploratory behavior of one-year-olds in a strange situation. In *Determinants of Infant Behaviour,* ed. B. M. Foss, 4:111–36. London: Methuen
6. Ardila, R., Rezk, M., Polanco, R., Pereira, F. 1977. Early handling, electric shock, and environmental complex-

ity: Effects on exploratory behavior, "emotionality," and body weight. *Psychol. Rec.* 2:219–24

7. Atkin, R., Bray, R., Davison, M., Herzberger, S., Humphreys, L., Selzer, U. 1977. Cross-lagged panel analysis of sixteen cognitive measures at four grade levels. *Child Dev.* 48:944–52

8. Badger, E. 1977. The infant stimulation/Mother training project. In *Infant Education: A Guide for Helping Handicapped Children in the First Three Years*, ed. B. M. Caldwell, S. J. Steadman. New York: Walker

9. Bandura, A., Walters, R. H. 1959. *Adolescent Aggression.* New York: Ronald

10. Barlow, H. B. 1975. Visual experience and cortical development. *Nature* 258:199–204

11. Barlow, H. B., Pettigrew, J. D. 1971. Lack of specificity of neurons with adaptation level in the cat retina. *J. Physiol.* 218:98–100

12. Barnes, C. A. 1952. A statistical study of the Freudian theory of levels of psychosexual development. *Genet. Psychol. Monogr.* 45:105–75

13. Beach, F. A. 1955. The descent of instinct. *Psychol. Rev.* 62:401–10

14. Beach, F. A., Jaynes, J. 1954. Effects of early experience upon the behavior of animals. *Psychol. Bull.* 51:239–63

15. Beckwith, L. 1972. Relationships between infants' social behavior and their mothers' behavior. *Child Dev.* 43:397–411

16. Bell, S. M. V., Ainsworth, M. D. S. 1972. Infant crying and maternal responsiveness. *Child Dev.* 43:1171–90

17. Belmont, L., Morolla, F. 1973. Birth order, family size and intelligence. *Science* 182:1096–1101

18. Bennett, E. L., Diamond, M. C., Krech, D., Rosenzweig, M. R. 1964. Chemical and anatomical plasticity of the brain. *Science* 146:610–19

19. Bennett, E. L., Rosenzweig, M. R., Diamond, M. C. 1970. Time courses of effects of differential experience on brain measures and behavior of rats. In *Molecular Approaches to Learning and Memory,* ed. W. L. Byrne, pp. 55–89. New York: Academic

20. Berman, R. F., Cannon, D. S. 1974. The effect of prior ethanol experience on ethanol-induced saccharin aversions. *Physiol. Behav.* 12(6):1041–44

21. Bernstein, L. A. 1952. A note on Christie's "Experimental naivete and experiential naivete." *Psychol. Bull.* 49:38–40

22. Birch, H. G. 1956. Sources of order in maternal behavior of animals. *Am. J. Orthopsychiatry* 26:279–84

23. Blehar, M. C., Lieberman, A. F., Ainsworth, M. D. S. 1977. Early face-to-face interaction and its relation to later infant-mother attachment. *Child Dev.* 48:182–94

24. Bower, T. G. R. 1974. *Development in Infancy.* New York: Freeman. 258 pp.

25. Bowlby, J. 1951. *Maternal Care and Mental Health.* Geneva: *WHO Monogr.* 2

26. Bowlby, J. 1969. *Attachment and Loss, Vol. 1: Attachment.* New York: Basic Books. 409 pp.

27. Bowlby, J., Ainsworth, M. D. S., Boston, M., Rosenbluth, D. 1956. The effects of mother-child separation: A follow study. *Br. J. Med. Psychol.* 29:211–47

28. Bradley, R. H., Caldwell, B. M. 1976. Early home environment and changes in mental test performance in children from 6 to 36 months. *J. Dev. Psychol.* 12:93–97

29. Bradley, R. H., Caldwell, B. M. 1977. Home observation for measurement of the environment: A validation study of screening efficiency. *Am. J. Ment. Defic.* 81:417–20

30. Brazelton, T. B., Tronick, E., Adamson, L., Als, H., Wise, S. 1975. Early mother-infant interaction. In *Parent-Infant Interaction,* Ciba Symp. 33. Amsterdam: Assoc. Sci. Publ.

31. Bronstein, P. W., Crockett, D. P. 1976. Exposure to the odor of food determines the eating preferences of rat pups. *Behav. Biol.* 18:387–92

32. Brookshire, K. H., Littman, R. A., Stewart, C. N. 1961. Residua of shocktrauma in the white rat: A three-factor theory. *Psychol. Monogr.* 75(10)

33. Brossard, L. M., Decarie, T. G. 1968. Comparative reinforcing effect of eight stimulations on the smiling response of infants. *J. Child Psychol. Psychiatry* 9:51–73

34. Caldwell, B. M. 1964. The effects of infant care. In *Review of Child Development Research,* ed. M. L. Hoffman, L. W. Hoffman, 1:9–87. New York: Sage

35. Caldwell, B. M. 1978. Home observation for measurement of the environment: I. Inventory and instruction manual for infants; II. Inventory and instruction manual for ages 3–6. (Mimeo available from author, Center for Early Development and Education, 814 Sherman St., Little Rock, Ark. 72303)

36. Campbell, B. A. 1967. Developmental studies of learning and motivation in infra-primate mammals. In *Early Behavior: Comparative and Developmental Approaches*, ed. H. W. Stevenson, E. H. Hess, H. L. Rheingold, Chap. 3, pp. 43–72. New York: Wiley

37. Campbell, B. A., Jaynes, J. 1966. Reinstatement. *Psychol. Rev.* 73:478–80

38. Casler, L. 1961. Maternal deprivation: A critical review of the literature. *Monogr. Soc. Res. Child Dev.* 26:1–64

39. Casler, L. 1965. The effects of extra stimulation on a group of institutionalized infants. *Genet. Psychol. Monogr.* 71:137–75

40. Cattell, R. B. 1963. Theory of fluid and crystallized intelligence: A critical experiment. *J. Educ. Psychol.* 54:1–22

41. Child, I. L. 1954. Socialization. In *Handbook of Social Psychology*, ed. G. Lindzey, Chap. 18. Cambridge, Mass: Addison-Wesley

42. Chomsky, N. 1959. Review of *Verbal Behavior* by B. F. Skinner. *Language* 35(1):26–58, footnote 48

43. Christie, R. 1952. The effect of some early experience in the latent learning of adult rats. *J. Exp. Psychol.* 43:281–88

44. Clarke, A. M., Clarke, A. D. B. 1976. *Early Experience: Myth and Evidence.* New York: Free Press

45. Clarke-Steward, K. A. 1973. Interactions between mothers and their young children: Characteristics and consequences. *Monogr. Soc. Res. Child Dev.* 38 (No. 6–7). 109 pp.

46. Clopton, B. M., Winfield, J. A. 1976. Effect of early exposure to patterned sound in unit activity in rat inferior colliculus. *J. Neurophysiol.* 39(5):1081–89

47. Condon, W. S., Sander, L. W. 1974. Speech: Interactional participation and language acquisition. *Science* 183:99–101

48. Cragg, B. G. 1975. Development of synapses in the visual system of the cat. *J. Comp. Neurol.* 160:147–66

49. Cynader, M., Chernenko, G. 1976. Abolition of direction selectivity in the visual cortex of the cat. *Science* 193:504–5

50. Daly, M. 1973. Early stimulation of rodents: A critical review of present interpretations. *Br. J. Psychol.* 64:435–60

51. Davenport, R. K., Rogers, C. M. 1968. Intellectual performance of differentially reared chimpanzees: I. Delayed response. *Am. J. Ment. Defic.* 72:674–80

52. Denenberg, V. H. 1962. The effects of early experience. In *The Behavior of Domestic Animals*, ed. E. S. E. Hafez, Chap. 6, pp. 109–38. London: Bailliere, Tindall, Cox

53. Denenberg, V. H., Naylor, J. C. 1957. The effects of early food deprivation upon adult learning. *Psychol. Rec.* 7:75–77

54. Denenberg, V. H., Zarrow, M. X. 1971. Effects of handling in infancy upon adrenocortical reactivity: Suggestions for a neuroendocrine mechanism. In *Early Childhood: The Development of Self-Regulatory Mechanisms*, ed. D. N. Welcher, D. L. Peters, pp. 40–74. New York: Academic

55. Dennis, W. 1960. Causes of retardation among institutional children: Iran. *J. Genet. Psychol.* 96:47–59

56. Dennis, W., Dennis, M. G. 1941. Infant development under conditions of restricted practice and minimum social stimulation. *Genet. Psychol. Monogr.* 23:149–55

57. Eells, J. F. 1961. Inconsistency of early handling and its effect upon emotionality in the rat. *J. Comp. Physiol. Psychol.* 54:690–93

58. Elardo, R., Bradley, R., Caldwell, B. M. 1975. The relation of infants' home environments to mental test performance from 6 to 36 months: A longitudinal analysis. *Child Dev.* 46:71–76

59. Epstein, H. T. 1974. Phrenoblysis: Special brain and mind growth periods. I. Human brain and skull development. *Dev. Psychobiol.* 7(3):207–16

60. Epstein, H. T. 1974. Phrenoblysis: Special brain and mind growth periods. II. Human mental development. *Dev. Psychobiol.* 7(3):217–24

61. Erikson, E. H. 1950. *Childhood and Society.* New York: Norton

62. Freud, S. 1915. Instincts and their vicissitudes. In *Collected Papers*, 4:60–83. London: Hogarth, 1950

63. Freud, S. 1926. *Inhibition, Symptom, and Anxiety.* Transl. H. A. Bunker, *The Problem of Anxiety.* New York: Norton, 1936.

64. Freud, S. 1933. *New Introductory Lectures on Psychoanalysis.* Transl. W. J. H. Sprott. New York: Norton. 257 pp.

65. Friedlander, B. Z. 1970. Receptive language development in infancy: Issues and problems. *Merrill-Palmer Q.* 16:7–51

66. Galbrecht, C. R., Dykman, R. A., Peters, J. E. 1960. The effect of traumatic experiences on the growth and behavior of the rat. *J. Psychol.* 50:227–51

67. Gardner, B. T., Gardner, R. A. 1974. Comparing the early utterances of child

and chimpanzee. *Minn. Symp. Child Psychol.* 8:3–23

68. Gauron, E. 1964. Infantile shock traumatization and subsequent adaptability to stress. *J. Genet. Psychol.* 104:167–78

69. Gesell, A., Thompson, H. 1929. Learning and growth in identical twin infants. *Genet. Psychol. Monogr.* 6:1–124

70. Gibson, E. J. 1969. *Principles of Perceptual Learning and Development.* New York: Appleton-Century-Crofts

71. Globus, A. 1975. Brain morphology as a function of presynaptic morphology and activity. See Ref. 162, pp. 9–91

72. Globus, A., Rosenzweig, M. R., Bennett, E. L., Diamond, M. C. 1973. Effects of differential experience on dendritic spine counts in rat cerebral cortex. *J. Comp. Physiol. Psychol.* 82:175–81

73. Gluck, J. P., Harlow, H. F., Schlitz, K. A. 1973. Differential effect of early enrichment and deprivation on learning in the rhesus monkey (Macaca mulata). *J. Comp. Physiol. Psychol.* 84:598–604

74. Greenberg, D. J., Uzgiris, I. C., Hunt, J. McV. 1968. Hastening the development of the blink-response with looking. *J. Genet. Psychol.* 113:167–76

75. Greenberg, D. J., Uzgiris, I. C., Hunt, J. McV. 1970. Attentional preference and experience: III. Visual familiarity and looking time. *J. Genet. Psychol.* 117:123–35

76. Greenough, W. T. 1975. Experiential modification of developing brain. *Am. Sci.* 63:37–46

77. Greenough, W. T. 1976. Enduring brain effects of differential experience and training. See Ref. 164, pp. 255–78

78. Greenough, W. T. 1978. Development and memory: The synaptic connection. In *Brain and Learning*, ed. T. Teyler, pp. 127–45. Stamford, Conn: Greylock

79. Greenough, W. T., Volkmar, F. R. 1973. Pattern of dendritic branching in occipital cortex of rats reared in complex environments. *Exp. Neurol.* 40:491–504

80. Grobstein, P., Chow, K. L. 1975. Receptive field development and individual experience. *Science* 190:352–58

81. Haggard, E. A. 1964. Isolation and personality. In *Personality Change*, ed. P. Worchel, D. Byrne, pp. 433–69. New York: Wiley

82. Haith, M. M., Campos, J. J. 1977. Human infancy. *Ann. Rev. Psychol.* 28:251–93

83. Harlow, H. F. 1958. The nature of love. *Am. Psychol.* 13:673–85

84. Harlow, H. F. 1971. *Learning to Love.* San Francisco: Albion

85. Harlow, H. F., Harlow, M. K., Schlitz, E. A., Mohr, D. J. 1971. The effect of early adverse and enriched environments on the learning ability of rhesus monkeys. In *Cognitive Processes of Nonhuman Primates*, ed. L. E. Jarrad, pp. 121–48. New York: Academic

86. Hebb, D. O. 1946. On the nature of fear. *Psychol. Rev.* 53:259–76

87. Hebb, D. O. 1949. *The Organization of Behavior.* New York: Wiley

88. Heber, R. 1978. Research in prevention of socio-cultural mental retardation. In *Primary Prevention of Psychopathology.* Vol. 2: *Environmental Influences*, ed. D. G. Forgays, pp. 39–62. Hanover, NH: Univ. Press of New England

89. Heber, R., Garber, H., Harrington, S., Hoffman, C., Falender, C. 1972. *Rehabilitation of Families at Risk for Mental Retardation.* Madison: Rehabil. Res. Train. Cent. Ment. Retard., Univ. Wisconsin

90. Helper, M. M. 1955. Learning theory and the self concept. *J. Abnorm. Soc. Psychol.* 51(2):184–94

91. Helson, H. 1964. *Adaptation-Level Theory.* New York: Harper & Row

92. Hess, E. H. 1959. The relationship between imprinting and motivation. *Nebr. Symp. Motiv.* 7:44–77

93. Hess, E. H. 1973. *Imprinting: Early Experience and the Developmental Psychobiology of Attachment.* New York: Van Nostrand. 472 pp.

94. Hirsch, H. V. B., Spinelli, D. N. 1970. Visual experience modifies distribution of horizontally and vertically oriented receptive fields in cats. *Science* 168:869–71

95. Holloway, R. L. 1966. Dendritic branching—Some preliminary results of training and complexity in rat visual cortex. *Brain Res.* 1:393–96

96. Holmes, F. B. 1935. An experimental study of children's fears. In *Children's Fears*, ed. A. T. Jersild, F. B. Holmes, pp. 167–296. New York: Columbia Univ. Teachers Coll.

97. Hubel, D. H., Wiesel, T. N. 1965. Receptive fields of cells in striate cortex of very young visually inexperienced kittens. *J. Neurophysiol.* 28:1041–59

98. Hull, C. L. 1943. *Principles of Behavior.* New York: Appleton-Century-Crofts

99. Hunt, J. McV. 1941. The effects of infantile feeding-frustration upon adult hoarding in the albino rat. *J. Abnorm. Soc. Psychol.* 36:338–60

100. Hunt, J. McV. 1961. *Intelligence and Experience.* New York: Ronald
101. Hunt, J. McV. 1963. Motivation inherent in information processing and action. In *Motivation and Social Interaction: The Cognitive Determinants,* ed. O. J. Harvey, pp. 35–94. New York: Ronald
102. Hunt, J. McV. 1969. *The Challenge of Incompetence and Poverty: Papers on the Role of Early Education.* Urbana: Univ. Illinois Press
103. Hunt, J. McV. 1971. Intrinsic motivation and psychological development. In *Personality Theory and Information Processing,* ed. H. M. Schroder, P. Suedfeld, Chap. 5. New York: Ronald
104. Hunt, J. McV. 1975. Reflections on a decade of early education. *J. Abnorm. Child Psychol.* 3(4):275–330
105. Hunt, J. McV. 1976. Utility of ordinal scales derived from Piaget's observations. *Merrill-Palmer Q.* 22(1):31–45
106. Hunt, J. McV. 1977. Specificity in early development and experience. Annual Mary Elaine Meyer O'Neal Award Lecture in Developmental Pediatrics. Omaha: Meyer Children's Rehabil. Inst. Univ. Nebraska Med. Cent.
107. Hunt, J. McV. 1979. Language acquisition and experience: Tehran. In preparation
108. Hunt, J. McV., Mohandessi, K., Ghodssi, M., Akiyama, M. 1976. The psychological development of orphanage-reared infants: Interventions with outcomes (Tehran). *Genet. Psychol. Monogr.* 94:177–226
109. Hunt, J. McV., Paraskevopoulos, J. 1978. Children's psychological development as a function of the inaccuracy of their mothers' knowledge of their abilities. In preparation
110. Hunt, J. McV., Paraskevopoulos, J., Schickedanz, D., Uzgiris, I. C. 1975. Variations in the mean ages of achieving object permanence under diverse conditions of rearing. In *The Exceptional Infant, Vol. 3: Assessment and Intervention,* ed. B. L. Friedlander, G. M. Sterritt, G. E. Kirk, pp. 247–62. New York: Brunner/Mazel
111. Hunt, J. McV., Quay, H. C. 1961. Early vibratory experience and the question of innate reinforcement value of vibration and other stimuli: A limitation on the discrepancy (burnt soup) principle in motivation. *Psychol. Rev.* 68:149–56
112. Hunt, J. McV., Schlosberg, H., Solomon, R. L., Stellar, E. 1947. Studies of the effects of infantile experience on adult behavior in rats: I. Effects of infantile feeding frustration on adult hoarding. *J. Comp. Physiol. Psychol.* 40:291–304
113. Jencks, C. 1972. *Inequality: A Reassessment of the Effect of Family and Schooling in America.* New York: Basic Books
114. Jensen, A. R. 1969. How much can we boost IQ and scholastic achievement? *Harv. Educ. Rev.* 39:1–123
115. Jensen, A. R. 1973. *Educability and Group Differences.* New York: Harper & Row
116. Jones, H. E. 1954. The environment and mental development. In *Manual of Child Psychology,* ed. L. Carmichael. New York: Wiley
117. Kellogg, W. N. 1968. Communication and language in the home-reared chimpanzee. *Science* 162:423–27
118. Kemper, T. D., Reichler, M. L. 1976. Father's work integration and types and frequencies of rewards and punishments administered by fathers and mothers to adolescent sons and daughters. *J. Genet. Psychol.* 129:207–19
119. Kessler, M., Albee, G. W. 1975. Primary prevention. *Ann. Rev. Psychol.* 26:557–91
120. Kuo, Z. Y. 1938. Further study on the behavior of the cat towards the rat. *J. Comp. Psychol.* 25:1–8
121. LaVoie, J. C., Looft, W. R. 1973. Parental antecedents of resistance-to-temptation behavior in adolescent males. *Merrill-Palmer Q.* 19:107–16
122. Lenneberg, E. H. 1966. The natural history of language. In *The Genesis of Language: A Psycholinguistic Approach,* ed. F. Smith, G. H. Miller, pp. 219–52. Cambridge, Mass: MIT Press
123. Lenneberg. E. H. 1967. *The Biological Basis of Language.* New York: Wiley
124. Levenstein, P. 1976. The mother-child home program. In *The Preschool in Action,* ed. M. C. Day, R. K. Parker. Boston: Allyn & Bacon. 2nd ed.
125. Levine, S. 1957. Infantile experience and resistance to physiological stress. *Science* 126:405
126. Levine, S. 1958. Noxious stimulation in infant and adult rats and consummatory behavior. *J. Comp. Physiol. Psychol.* 51:230–33
127. Levine, S. 1962. The effects of infantile experience on adult behavior. In *Experimental Foundations of Clinical Psychology,* ed. A. J. Bachrach, pp. 139–69. New York: Basic Books
128. Levine, S. 1969. An endocrine theory of infantile stimulation. In *Stimulation in Infancy,* ed. A. Ambrose, pp. 45–63. London: Academic

129. Levine, S., Chevalier, J. A., Korchin, S. J. 1956. The effects of early shock and handling on later avoidance learning. *J. Pers.* 24:475–93.
130. Lewis, M. M. 1976. *Origins of Intelligence.* New York: Plenum
131. Lewis, M. M., Goldberg, S. 1969. The acquisition and violation of expectancy: An experimental paradigm. *J. Exp. Child Psychol.* 7:70–80
132. Lewis, M. M., Rosenblum, L. A., eds. 1974. *The Effect of an Infant on its Caregiver.* New York: Wiley-Interscience
133. Lindholm, B. W. 1962. Critical periods and the effects of early shock on later emotional behavior in the white rat. *J. Comp. Physiol. Psychol.* 55:597–99
134. Lorenz, K. 1935. Der Kumpen in der Umwelt des Vögels. *J. Ornithol.* 83: 137–214; 289–413. Translated by author and republished as "The companion in the bird's world." *Auk* (1937) 54:245–73
135. Maltzman, I., Raskin, D. C. 1965. Effects of individual differences in the orienting reflex on conditioning and complex processes. *J. Exp. Res. Pers.* 1:1–16
136. Mandler, J. M. 1958. Effects of early food deprivation on adult behavior in the rat. *J. Comp. Physiol. Psychol.* 51:513–17
137. Marx, M. H. 1952. Infantile deprivation and adult behavior in the rat: Retention of increased rate of eating. *J. Comp. Physiol. Psychol.* 45:43–49
138. Mason, W. A. 1970. Information processing and experiential deprivation: A biological perspective. In *Early Experience and Visual Information Processing in Perceptual and Reading Disorders,* ed. F. A. Young, D. B. Lindsley, pp. 302–23. Washington DC: Natl. Acad. Sci.
139. McCarthy, D. 1954. Language development in children. In *Manual of Child Psychology,* ed. L. Carmichael, Chap. 9. New York: Wiley. 2nd ed.
140. Meier, G. W., Foshee, D. P., Wittrig, J. J., Peeler, D. F., Huff, F. W. 1960. Helson's residual factor versus innate S-R relations. *Psychol. Rep.* 6:61–62
141. Meltzoff, A. N., Moore, M. K. 1977. Imitation of facial and manual gestures by human neonates. *Science* 198: 75–78
142. Menzel, E. W. Jr., Davenport, R. K. Jr., Rogers, C. M. 1970. The development of tool using in wild born and restriction reared chimpanzees. *Folia Primatol.* 12: 273–83
143. Moore, R. S., Moore, D. N. 1975. *Better Late than Early.* New York: Reader's Digest Press (Distrib. E. P. Dutton)
144. Morgan, G. A., Ricciuti, H. N. 1969. Infants' responses to strangers during the first year. See Ref. 5, 4:253–72
145. Mowrer, O. H. 1938. The meaning and management of crying. *Child Study,* Jan.:1–5
146. Orlansky, H. 1949. Infant care and personality. *Psychol. Bull.* 46:1–48
147. Papousek, H., Papousek, M. 1977. Mothering and the cognitive head start. See Ref. 168, pp. 63–85
148. Paraskevopoulos, J., Hunt, J. McV. 1971. Object construction and imitation under differing conditions of rearing. *J. Genet. Psychol.* 119:301–21
149. Pfaffenberger, C. J., Scott, J. P. 1959. The relationship between delayed socialization and trainability in guide dogs. *J. Genet. Psychol.* 95:144–55
150. Pfeifer, W. D., Rotundo, R., Myers, M., Denenberg, V. H. 1976. Stimulation in infancy: Unique effects of handling. *Physiol. Behav.* 17:781–84
151. Piaget, J. 1936. *The Origins of Intelligence in Children.* Transl. Margaret Cook. New York: Int. Univ. Press. 1952
152. Piaget, J. 1945. *Play, Dreams, and Imitation in Childhood.* Transl. C. Gattegno, F. M. Hodgson. New York: Norton, 1951
153. Piaget, J. 1947. *The Psychology of Intelligence.* Transl. M. Piercy, D. E. Berlyne. Paterson, NJ: Littlefield, Adams, 1960
154. Piaget, J. 1977. *Topics in Cognitive Development, Vol. 1. Equilibration: Theory, Research, and Application,* ed. M. H. Appel, L. S. Goldberg, pp. 3–13. New York: Plenum
155. Pribram, K. H. 1971. *Languages of the Brain: Experimental Paradoxes and Principles In Neuropsychology.* Englewood Cliffs, NJ: Prentice-Hall
156. Ramsey, A. O. 1951. Familial recognition in domestic birds. *Auk* 58:57–58
157. Renner, K. E. 1966. Temporal integration: The effect of early experience. *J. Exp. Res. Pers.* 1:201–10
158. Rheingold, H. L. 1961. The effect of environmental stimulation upon social and exploratory behavior in the human infant. In *Determinants of Infant Behavior,* ed. B. M. Foss, pp. 143–71. New York: Wiley
159. Ribble, M. A. 1944. Infantile experience in relation to personality development. In *Personality and the Behavior Disorders,* ed. J. McV. Hunt, Vol. 2, Chap. 20. New York: Ronald

160. Riesen, A. H. 1947. The development of visual perception in man and chimpanzee. *Science* 106:107–8
161. Riesen, A. H. 1966. Sensory deprivation. In *Progress in Physiological Psychology,* ed. E. Stellar, J. Stellar, pp. 117–47. New York: Academic
162. Riesen, A. H. 1975. *The Developmental Neuropsychology of Sensory Deprivation.* New York: Academic
163. Rosenzweig, M. R., Bennett, E. L. 1977. Effects of environmental enrichment or impoverishment on learning and on brain values in rodents. In *Genetics, Environment and Intelligence,* ed. A. Oliverio, pp. 163–96. Amsterdam: North-Holland Biomedical
164. Rosenzweig, M. R., Bennett, E. L., eds. 1976. *Neural Mechanisms of Learning and Memory.* Cambridge, Mass: MIT Press
165. Rosenzweig, M. R., Bennett, E. L., Diamond, M. C. 1972. Chemical and anatomical plasticity of brain: Replications and extensions. In *Macromolecules and Behavior,* ed. J. Gaito, pp. 205–77. New York: Appleton-Century-Crofts. 2nd ed.
166. Rosenzweig, M. R., Krech, D., Bennett, E. L., Diamond, M. C. 1962. Effects of environmental complexity and training on brain chemistry and anatomy: A replication and extension. *J. Comp. Physiol. Psychol.* 55:429–37
167. Salama, A. A., Hunt, J. McV. 1964. "Fixation" in the rat as a function of infantile shocking, handling, and gentling. *J. Genet. Psychol.* 105:131–62
168. Schaffer, H. R., ed. 1977. *Studies in Mother-Infant Interaction.* New York: Academic
169. Schaffer, H. R., Emerson, P. E. 1964. The development of social attachments in infancy. *Monogr. Soc. Res. Child Dev.* 29(3). 77 pp.
170. Schoggen, M. F. 1967. The imprint of low-income homes on young children. In *Research, Change, and Social Responsibility: An Illustrative Model from Early Education,* ed. S. Gray, J. O. Miller. DARCEE Papers and Reports, 2(3). Nashville, Tenn: Peabody Coll. Teachers
171. Scott, J. H. 1955. Some effects at maturity of gentling, ignoring or shocking rats during infancy. *J. Abnorm. Soc. Psychol.* 51:412–14
172. Scott, J. P. 1962. Critical periods in behavioral development. *Science* 138: 949–58
173. Scott, J. P. 1968. *Early Experience and the Organization of Behavior.* Belmont, Calif: Brooks/Cole Div. Wadsworth. 177 pp.
174. Scott, J. P., Fredericson, E., Fuller, J. L. 1951. Experimental exploration of the critical period hypothesis. *Personality* 1(2):162–83
175. Sears, R. R., Maccoby, E. E., Levin, H. 1957. *Patterns of Child Rearing.* Evanston, Ill: Row, Peterson
176. Sears, R. R., Wise, G. W. 1950. Relation of cup feeding in infancy to thumbsucking and the oral drive. *Am. J. Orthopsychiatry* 20:123–38
177. Sewell, W. H. 1952. Infant training and the personality of the child. *Am. J. Soc.* 58:150–59
178. Sherman, S. M., Hoffmann, K. P., Stone, J. 1972. Loss of specific cell type from dorsal lateral geniculate nucleus in visually deprived cats. *J. Neurophysiol.* 35:532–41
179. Solomon, R. L. 1948. The influence of work on behavior. *Psychol. Bull.* 45: 1–40
180. Spinelli, D. N., Hirsch, H. V. B., Phelps, R. W., Metzler, J. 1972. Visual experience as a determinant of the response characteristics of cortical receptive fields in cats. *Exp. Brain Res.* 15:289–304
181. Spitz, R. A. 1945. Hospitalism: An inquiry into the genesis of psychiatric conditions in early childhood. *Psychoanal. Study Child* 1:53–74
182. Stendler, C. 1950. Sixty years of child training practices: Revolution in the nursery. *J. Pediatr.* 36:122–34
183. Thompson, W. R., Grusec, J. E. 1970. Studies of early experience. In *Carmichael's Manual of Child Psychology,* ed. P. H. Mussen, pp. 565–654. New York: Wiley. 3rd ed.
184. Thompson, W. R., Heron, W. 1954. The effects of restricting early experience on the problem-solving capacity of dogs. *Can. J. Psychol.* 8:17–31
185. Thompson, W. R., Heron, W. 1954. The effects of early restriction on activity in dogs. *J. Comp. Physiol. Psychol.* 47:77–82
186. Thorpe, W. H. 1956. *Learning and Instinct in Animals.* London: Methuen
187. Trevarthen, C. 1974. Conversations with a two-month-old. *New Sci.* 62: 230–35
188. Trevarthen, C. 1977. Descriptive analyses of infant communicative behavior. See Ref. 168, pp. 227–70
189. Uzgiris, I. C. 1972. Patterns of vocal and gestural imitation in infants. In *Determinants of Behavioral Development,* ed. F. J. Monks, W. W. Hartup,

J. DeWitt, pp. 467–71. New York: Academic

190. Uzgiris, I. C. 1978. The many faces of imitation in infancy. In *Fortschritte der Entwicklungspsychologie*, ed. L. Montada. Presented at Int. Seminar Dev. Psychol. Trier, West Germany, August, 1977. In press

191. Uzgiris, I. C., Hunt, J. McV. 1975. *Assessment in Infancy: Ordinal Scales of Psychological Development:* Urbana: Univ. Illinois Press

192. Wachs, T. D. 1976. Utilization of a Piagetian approach in the investigation of early-experience effects: A research strategy and some illustrative data. *Merrill-Palmer Q.* 22:11–30

193. Wachs, T. D. 1978. Relationship of infants physical environment to their Binet performance at 2.5 years. *Int. J. Behav. Dev.* In press

194. Wachs, T. D., Uzgiris, I. C., Hunt, J. McV. 1971. Cognitive development in infants of different age levels and from different environmental backgrounds: An exploratory investigation. *Merrill-Palmer Q.* 17:283–317

195. Walters, R. H., Parke, R. D. 1965. The role of the distance receptors in the development of social responsiveness. *Adv. Child Dev. Behav.* 2:59–89

196. Warren, R. P., Pfaffmann, C. 1958. Early experience and taste aversion. *J. Comp. Physiol. Psychol.* 52:263–66

197. Watson, J. B. 1928. *Psychological Care of Infant and Child.* New York: Norton

198. Weinberg, J., Levine, S. 1977. Early handling influences on behavioral and physiological responses during active avoidance. *Dev. Psychobiol.* 10:161–69

199. Weininger, O. 1953. Mortality of albino rats under stress as a function of early handling. *Can. J. Psychol.* 7:111–14

200. Weininger, O. 1956. The effects of early experience on behavior and growth characteristics. *J. Comp. Physiol. Psychol.* 49:1–9

201. Weizmann, F., Cohen, L. B., Pratt, R. J. 1971. Novelty, familiarity, and the development of infant attention. *Dev. Psychol.* 4(2):149–54

202. Welch, B. L. 1965. Psychophysiological response to the mean level of environmental stimulation: A theory of environmental integration. In *Symposium on Medical Aspects of Stress in the Military Climate*, pp. 39–99. Washington DC: GPO

203. Wenar, C., Coulter, J. B. 1962. A reliability study of developmental histories. *Child Dev.* 33:453–62

204. Wetherford, M., Cohen, L. B. 1973. Developmental changes in infant visual preferences for novelty and familiarity. *Child Dev.* 44:416–24

205. White, B. L. 1967. An experimental approach to the effects of experience on early human development. *Minn. Symp. Child Psychol.* 1:201–26

206. White, B. L. 1975. *The First Three Years of Life.* Englewood Cliffs, NJ: Prentice-Hall

207. White, B. L. 1977. Early stimulation and behavioral development. In *Genetics, Environment, and Intelligence,* ed. A. Oliverio, pp. 337–60. Elsevier, North Holland: Biomed. Press

207a. White, B. L. 1978. *Experience and Environment: Major Influences on the Development of the Child,* Vol. 2. Englewood Cliffs, NJ: Prentice-Hall

208. White, B. L., Watts, J. C. 1973. *Experience and Environment: Major Influences on the Development of the Young Child.* Englewood Cliffs, NJ: Prentice-Hall

209. White, R. W. 1959. Motivation reconsidered: The concept of competence. *Psychol. Rev.* 66:297–333

210. Wiesel, T. N., Hubel, D. H. 1963. Effects of visual deprivation on morphology and physiology of cells in the cat's lateral geniculate body. *J. Neurophysiol.* 26:978–93

211. Williams, E., Scott, J. P. 1953. The development of social behavior patterns in the mouse in relation to natural periods. *Behavior* 6:35–64

212. Yarrow, L. J. 1961. Maternal deprivation: Toward an empirical and conceptual reevaluation. *Psychol. Bull.* 58:459–90

213. Yarrow, L. J. 1963. Research in dimensions of early maternal care. *Merrill-Palmer Q.* 9:101–14

214. Yarrow, L. J., Rubenstein, J. L., Pedersen, F. A. 1975. *Infant and Environment: Early Cognitive and Motivational Development.* Washington DC: Hemisphere

215. Zahorik, D. M. 1976. The role of dietary history in the effects of novelty on taste aversions. *Bull. Psychon. Soc.* 8:285–88

Ann. Rev. Psychol. 1979. 30:145–72

WHAT'S CULTURAL ABOUT CROSS-CULTURAL COGNITIVE PSYCHOLOGY?[1]

❖305

Laboratory of Comparative Human Cognition

Center for Human Information Processing, University of California, San Diego, La Jolla, California 92093

CONTENTS

FOUR BASIC RESEARCH APPROACHES 148
COGNITIVE UNIVERSALS 148
    Logical Operations à la Piaget 148
    Categorization 153
SOCIALIZATION THEORIES 154
    Psychological Differentiation 155
    The Soviet Cultural-Historical Approach 159
"MIXED" APPROACHES: CULTURE AND MEMORY 160
ETHNOGRAPHIC PSYCHOLOGY 163
IN SUMMARY 167

The first review of cross-cultural psychology was published in the *Annual Review of Psychology* 6 years ago (81). Already swamped by the volume of material at hand, the reviewers reported that they covered only one quarter of the relevant material. Since that time a special journal devoted entirely to cross-cultural research has appeared, several summaries devoted to sub-areas of research have been published (19, 23, 34a, 46, 48, 54, 63, 77, 90), an "advances" series has been initiated (85), handbooks are in progress, and books of readings grouped around special topics abound (2, 9, 13, 62, 67).

[1]This article represents the joint labor of the following members of our laboratory: Kenneth Traupmann, Warren Simmons, Sylvia Scribner, Judy Orasanu, Louis Moll, Ray McDermott, Deborah Malamud, Helga Katz, Jan Jewson, Lois Hood, Martha Hadley, William S. Hall, Zoe Graves, Joseph A. Glick, Lenora Fulani, A. J. Franklin, Michael Cole. Preparation of this article was made possible by a grant from the Carnegie Corporation.

145

0066-4308/79/0201-0145$01.00

In mid-1978 it would be impossible to list all of the relevant articles concerning "psychology and culture" in the space allotted, let alone review them.

This flood of fact and opinion has faced us with a difficult problem of selection which we have decided to handle in the following fashion. First, we will concentrate our review in that subarea of cross-cultural research which deals with the relation between culture and intellectual processes for the combined reasons that it has received increasing attention as the decade of the 1970s has proceeded and because our firsthand knowledge of this area of research is greatest. Second, we will concentrate on research problems which have received sustained attention from more than a single researcher. Among the rare consensuses to emerge from a field where disputation and diversity abound is the idea that firm evidence in support of hypotheses requires sustained research in carefully chosen locations using series of studies that build in a logical fashion. Despite this consensus by commentators in the field, the number of research programs which fit this specification is exceedingly small [Sechrest (76), for example, noted that of 239 authors contributing to the *Journal of Cross-Cultural Psychology* in a sample of four volumes, 209 contributed only a single study].

Within this more restricted domain we would like to examine seriously the topic suggested by the title of our article: *in what sense(s) does culture enter into the formulation of problems, the identification of independent variables, the observational techniques and, hence, the dependent variables of cross-cultural, cognitive research?*

This might be considered a frivolous choice of foci. After all, it seems difficult to find fault with Brislin, Lonner & Thorndike's definition of the field: "Cross cultural psychology is the empirical study of members of various cultural groups. . . . who have had different experiences that lead to predictable and significant differences in behavior" (13, p. 5).

Any feelings of acceptance that this definition may arouse have to be tempered by two grave and generally unresolved difficulties. First, there is no agreed-upon definition of culture in *any* academic discipline that psychologists can draw on as a means of specifying what it is they mean when they speak of culture as an independent variable that can lead to predictions. Insofar as there is agreement (for example, among anthropologists to whom the psychologist typically turns as the source for a definitional warrant) those who are concerned with the study of culture emphasize the *patterning* of ideas, institutions, and artifacts produced by the group in question.

Recognition of the difficulty that such patterning poses for the psychologist is widespread in principle, but very difficult to apply in particular circumstances. We take it as symptomatic of the difficulties which this situation presents that the previous *Annual Review* chapter on Culture and Psychology pointed to lack of progress in description of our independent variables as a major gap in research activities up to that time. B. Whiting's (88) discussion of the need to "unpackage" culture as an independent variable several years later indicates clearly that the problem did not quietly disappear because it was recognized. But we must proceed carefully. One of the quandaries that mechanical unpackaging presents us with (if culture is, as anthropologists tell us, a human-produced, *patterned* set of experiences) is that we may, by unpackaging, destroy the network of relations which gave the variable its (packaged) meaning in the first place.

In our view, matters are in no better shape concerning the status of our dependent variables, the "predictable and significant differences in behavior" to which Brislin et al (13) refer.

It is our impression that cross-cultural psychologists have (implicitly at least) agreed with B. Whiting's assertion that sufficient progress has been made on the problem of identifying and measuring dependent variables to permit greater concentration on disentangling the sociocultural and biological precursors of these measures of behavioral processes. This appears to be the assumption underlying the recent work of Berry (8), Kagan and his associates (40), and many others. Here we will demur; while we strongly agree on the need for the serious study of culture as an independent variable, we will attempt to show that important ambiguities in current cross-cultural cognitive research arise precisely out of an insufficient knowledge of the behavior(s) that constitute the substance of the dependent variable. Moreover, we will want to examine for dependent variables—as we will for independent variables—the sense(s) in which the concept of culture enters into the process of identification and measurement. This is a major point of disagreement among psychologists and between psychologists and anthropologists. It arises because in order to specify cognitive *process* the psychologist must rely upon experimental manipulations (or, far more weakly, on tests and intertest correlations). But our ignorance of the multiple, systematic behaviors that give rise to the criterion behavior too often leaves us mute regarding an unambiguous interpretation of the outcome. The point is a very old one that is not restricted to cross-cultural cognitive research, but is just more acute there:

Group tests reveal the *product* of thinking, not the *processes* responsible for the product. Any notion of development expressed merely in terms of accuracy or speed in achievement seems inadequate. The true measure of development is not the degree of accuracy, but the manner in which the pupil thinks. . . . (86, p. 366).

For the anthropologist these ambiguities give rise to judgments like the following from the 1977 *Annual Review of Anthropology:*

... there seems to be little awareness that the measures used may be full of our cultural biases and therefore highly inappropriate to the task of comparing across cultures. Psychologists, I have argued, would do well to consider actively the hypothesis that their measures may be biased (25, p. 51).

While "bias" is not well specified in this passage, the article of which it is a part makes it clear that the author is pointing to many specific features of tests and experiments that are *not* a part of the psychologist's theory of the task but which, nonetheless, exert an unevaluated influence on the outcome and the conclusions which flow from it.

FOUR BASIC RESEARCH APPROACHES

At this point in our discussion we face a fundamental decision. It would be possible, following the tradition of previous reviews, to organize the discussion around major categories of cognitive behavior as they have been applied by various investigators, or we could review major areas of dispute centering on issues of tactics and methodology. However, in the discussion that led to the preparation of this manuscript, we repeatedly found ourselves caught up in arguments over method which hinged on the nature of the theoretical problem with which the investigator under scrutiny was trying to deal; in short, many issues of method are not "theory-free." Rather, they are attempts to narrow the range of plausible alternatives to the central hypothesis under investigation.

As a consequence of this experience, we have decided to organize this review as follows: We will first survey developments since 1972 with respect to four general classes of research on culture and cognition—universalistic hypotheses (such as those associated with the work of Piaget and Rosch); socialization theories (including the work of Berry/Witkin and the Soviet sociohistorical school); "mixed" approaches as exemplified in the work of Kagan/Klein, their colleagues, and Wagner; and finally functional approaches that gear their observations to specific relations between culturally organized activities and specific cognitive outcomes. In each case we will examine how researchers represent culture in the populations studied, the methods of observation, the dependent variables that are tokens of "results," and finally the conclusions that they draw from their data.

COGNITIVE UNIVERSALS

Logical Operations à la Piaget
Several of the general references given at the beginning of this review centered on Piagetian theory, or at least on the use of Piagetian tasks to compare different cultural groups.

The classical formulation of Piaget's position concerning cultural variability in cognition is given in his 1966 article (60) and summarized by Dasen (24). Four sets of factors responsible for cognitive development are listed:

1. Biological factors, which interact with the physical environment during parturition and growth.
2. "Equilibration" factors, which arise as the young organism interacts with its immediate physical environment.
3. Social factors of interpersonal coordination, which arise as child and adult exchange information and the child learns to coordinate his behavior with the activities of important others.
4. Educational and cultural transmission factors, which are culturally distinct pressures to learn about specific features of the (cultural) environment (as reflected, for example, in different classification schemes).

The standard perspective on this categorization of causal factors in development has generally been that the first three lead to predictions of universality (22, p. 4) with the burden of cultural variation falling into the fourth category. It is important to realize that when "universal" is employed as an adjective in relation to stages or levels of development in applications of the Piagetian system, it is being used in two different senses: that (a) the sequences of stages, including their structural properties and the kinds of explanations given by children at different stages, are invariant; and (b) the horizontal decalage (e.g. the order in which conservation of quality, weight, and volume are acquired) is invariant. Dasen's recent work speaks of a third kind of universal, which occurs when the quantitative level of achievement at the same age in different cultures is equivalent. In 1972 it appeared that the hypothesized universalities were rather strongly confirmed for stage sequencing, generally supported for within-stage decalages, and disconfirmed for levels of quantitative achievement. Indeed, it appeared that quantitative achievement of older subjects in some cultures threatened the hypothesis of universality in the existence of the highest level, "formal operational," stage (61).

By 1978, the situation has become considerably more complex. Whereas the empirical verifications of the sequencing of major stages seems to have remained a robust phenomenon up through the concrete operational stage (23), failures to find formal operational thinking have engendered suggestions that it is necessary first to establish the end state toward which developmental processes move in different cultures. If this step is not taken, the absence of a concrete formal-operational phase becomes a theoretical nonsequitur, which presupposes the Western scientist as the epitome of developed thinking (36).

Evidence about inconsistency in the order in which various concepts are achieved and "lags" in development for various cultural groups have met with three kinds of responses. First, there are what we shall term the "psychological method" critiques. As summarized in a number of discussions, investigators have become increasingly aware of problems arising from unfamiliarity of materials, use of standardized questioning procedures rather than flexible, clinical interviews that adhere to local norms of conversation and interaction, and inhibitions produced by the presence of foreigners, to mention some of the more prominent problems studied (12, 26, 41, 59). In some cases, performance differences between educated and noneducated populations, or between some "exotic" populations and European norms, have been reduced or eliminated through procedures that are designed to make the testing conditions as similar as possible in local terms to those that exist in the European countries from which the research methods arose. These criticisms are valid, important, and are increasingly coming to be accepted by those engaged in all cross-cultural work. However, we have to agree with Dasen (24, p. 13) that such explanations cannot account for all of the differences found in the substantial studies carried out to date, particularly in cases where performance differences between groups are uneven in ways that cannot be explained away by any simple "methodological" difficulties.

A second approach to cultural variability in response to Piagetian problems has been to apply Flavell & Wohlwill's (28) version of a competence-performance distinction to the cross-cultural Piagetian arena.

As formulated by Dasen, the extension works as follows: Flavell and Wohlwill assert that the probability of successfully completing a given task is the product of the probability that the child has acquired the operational structure and that the relevant attributes will be applied to the operational structure. Dasen adds a third factor, representing the probability that the operation called for by a given task "will in fact be called into play in a given cultural milieu" (22, p. 333). This formulation gives us performance as a multiplicative outcome of competence, task-specific, and culture-specific knowledge. The goal of cross-cultural Piagetian research then becomes to determine if cultural differences are to be attributed primarily to differences in basic competence or in either of the two "performance" parameters.

Perhaps the most significant development in comparative cognitive research of all kinds, but of Piagetian work in particular, is that a broad spectrum of researchers have explicitly or implicitly accepted some version of Dasen's model. Once performance is treated as problematic with respect to competence, this research then finds itself confronted with the task of learning more and more about local cultural conditions in order to carry out its newly recognized inferential program. This latter necessity represents the third major direction visible in recent cross-cultural Piagetian research. (As we shall see, it is a direction characteristic of the entire range of research under review).

Paradoxically, the Piagetian researchers who seek to determine specific cultural factors that influence development have to confront an absence of guidance from the European research base that generated their theoretical framework. As Greenfield cogently remarks, Piagetian researchers who would seek to specify the organism-culture interactions that enter into cognitive performance are faced with the central difficulty that ". . . although the role of organism-environment interaction is central to his constructivist theory, Piaget has never specified the nature of these interactive processes nor has he himself made them the object of empirical study . . ." (36, p. 327). Nonetheless, faced with the necessity of specifying the kinds of culturally organized experience that foster the development of particular competences, ingenious new experiments have been conducted.

A major line of research, initiated by Price-Williams, Gordon & Ramirez's (64) finding that Mexican potters' children were precocious in their conservation of clay substances, has now given rise to several replication studies which are beginning to specify the nature of the interactions necessary to stimulate construction of the conservation concept.

Adjei (1) contrasted child and adult groups of rural farmers, potters, and tradespeople. He had expected, like Price-Williams et al, to find experience-specific differences among the groups with respect to different kinds of conservation performance (potters' children excelling on weight and volume, sellers' children on numbers, etc). His expectations were only partially fulfilled, in part because performance was excellent in all groups for the number task where he had expected the sellers' children to excel. Potters' children reliably outperformed the other two groups only on the conservation of weight task. The potters themselves, however, reliably outperformed both the farmer and seller groups on all three conservation tasks where direct experience in potting is explicitly implicated.

As part of her large study, Bovet (12) also observed group differences in performance on various conservation tasks which she attributed directly to differential experience with the materials and operations involved. For example, women in her sample habitually compared the weights of two lumps of dough as a part of their baking activities and were reported to be extremely skilled in detecting differences in weight. These women often refused to make judgments about weight in the conservation task unless allowed to experiment with the materials using their own (experimentally inappropriate) method. Men never made such requests, and their responses were more easily coded according to traditional criteria. Superior performance of men in a lengthy conservation task was attributed to their greater mobility (which presumably indexed experience with such task demands).

The problems and promise of this line of research are highlighted by a recent failure to find an experience-specific effect on conservation of the kind expected from research by Price-Williams et al. Steinberg & Dunn (80) carried out a study contrasting the performance of children from two neighboring villages on conservation of weight and quantity. Women in one village were potters, those in another were not. No differences among children from the two villages were found. In seeking a reason for this failure to replicate, Steinberg and Dunn zeroed in directly on the different involvement of children in the two studies in the actual process of potting and differences in the requirements of the potting process itself. In the Price-Williams et al study, the children participated at various points in a production process which is very similar to the classic operation of conservation and repeatedly observed relevant operations even when they did not actively participate. In the Steinberg and Dunn village, the production process not only did not permit experience of invariance across transformations, but it actually provided experience of variance because the process of firing the pots transformed their size and weight. Their conclusion is important, even if its applications to the studies in question is post hoc: ". . . familiarity with the materials *per se* does not significantly facilitate performance on conservation tasks. The nature of the child's particular experience with the material may have some relevance" (80, p. 23).

This conclusion is relevant to another strain of recent Piagetian cross-cultural research which uses the competence-performance distinction to encompass findings that are otherwise difficult to incorporate into a Piagetian framework. We are referring here to that body of work made prominent by Heron (39) which has failed to find the "structure d'ensemble," or intercorrelations among tasks, supposedly calling on the same underlying operations. Heron has strongly questioned the unity of the various stages based on the lack of correlations that he has observed. A position which assumes that lack of correlation among tasks diagnostic of a particular stage arises because of differences in task and culture-specific knowledge associated with each task is one obvious strategy for retaining the notion of universal stages in the development of cognitive competence, while accounting for cultural variation at the level of performance.

Before leaving this section, one additional line of cross-cultural Piagetian work requires mention because it demonstrates the way in which culture-specific knowledge can bolster claims for cognitive universals. In each of these studies, children were tested for their comprehension of kin terms in languages where the kinship terminology and family structure vary considerably from the Genevan norm (37, 65). In each case, the sequence of comprehension—from errors based on failure to take another's perspective (egocentricism) to understanding of reciprocal relations among two others, to the understanding of reciprocity applied to oneself (reversibility)—was confirmed. Further, indigenous linguistic categories, for which rather complex componential analyses are available, failed to account for the ordering of children's responses, leaving the "universalistic stage" hypothesis without serious rival.

A puzzle about his line of work which was raised by Piaget more than half a century ago now becomes more interesting than when it was first posed. Piaget noted that only-children were no slower to acquire comprehension of kin terms than children from multichild families. When we begin to notice that successively more difficult kin relations must be probed with questions that are syntactically more and more complex (Compare: "What is the name of your sister?" with "As for your younger sister Mary, what is the name of her older brother?") we want to ask, how are kin terms used in the various societies in question? Granted that componential analysis of (say) Tzeltal kin terminology does not predict the order of understanding questions about kinship, what domains of activity *do* give rise to the differential adult terminology and child comprehension? The investigations of how other Piagetian tasks fit in with native, culturally organized "contexts of activity" which seemed so important to understanding orders of acquisition of different conservation concepts must have parallels in domains such as kinship as well.

Categorization

When the previous *Annual Review* article on cross-cultural psychology appeared, only the initial rumblings of the earthquake that was to hit psychological theories of categorization and the Whorfian linguistic relativity hypothesis were discernible. Common wisdom and some data (cf 19 Chap. 3) had it that different languages code the world differently, and that ease of codability predicts ease of information processing (for example, highly codable colors will be most easily remembered).

In 1969 Berlin & Kay (7) provided evidence that the number of basic color terms is very limited, and that despite variations in the boundaries of color categories, the focal colors are universal. In a lengthy series of studies, Rosch (69) has explored the psychological implications of the idea that for concrete objects as well as colors and other attributes (such as form) there are universal "focal instances" (in the case of attributes) or "basic level objects" (in the case of objects) which arise either from universal characteristics of the human sensory system (11) or from characteristics of objects in the real world.

Rosch's key experiment, which sets the logical pattern for all the others, was carried out among the Dani of New Guinea who have a two-term color vocabulary. Pretesting with eight focal colors (taken from Berlin and Kay's classification) showed that they were no more codable linguistically than "internominal" (nonfocal) colors. When recognition memory for these equally codable focal and nonfocal colors was tested among the Dani, recognition of the focal colors was significantly superior to that of the nonfocal colors. Exactly the same relationship held for American subjects for whom the focal colors were more easily coded. By demonstrating an invariant relation between focalness and recognition on the one hand and random variation between codability and recognition on the other, Rosch cleanly separated the effects of focalness and codability on recognition and showed the cross-cultural universality of a very important cognitive activity. Still to be dealt with are cases (79) where categorization occurs in the absence of any focal instances. Here codability may remain a powerful influence.

In addition to its inherent theoretical interest concerning the understanding of categorization, Rosch's work is one of the best illustrations in the cross-cultural psychological literature of a strategy that tests cross-cultural hypotheses in terms of the interactions between variables *within* cultures. It is the *within-culture* invariance of the relation between recognition and focality replicated *across* cultures that makes her hypothesis so robust. As Campbell and others have pointed out (14), this approach removes many of the threats to inferential validity with which "main effects" cross-cultural studies have to contend. (It is worth noting in this context that the Piagetian kin-term work is based upon exactly this logic of between-culture invariance of the within-culture difficulty of problem solving).

In subsequent work, Rosch has extended her approach to research on basic level objects and events (69, 70). Unfortunately, this work has not yet been extended to the study of categorizing in different cultures. If and when such research is done, a good deal of culture-specific knowledge will be needed by the investigator, since the particular objects and events that will be seen as basic will, according to the logic of Rosch's approach, vary. Only the relationship among "basic" and "peripheral" instances should remain constant.

SOCIALIZATION THEORIES

We labeled the work reviewed in the previous section "universalistic" because the investigators were primarily concerned with demonstrating behavioral invariance in the face of environmental (cultural) variation. Their basic presupposition was that crucial environmental factors (social interactions, experiences with physical properties of the world) are so widespread in human societies that relevant cultural variability would be minimal and located in a few, unevenly distributed institutions such as formal schooling. In the case of Rosch, the specific presupposition was that the structure of *Homo sapiens* and the real world is such that certain characteristics of categorization will vary across cultures only in the particular objects that fulfill invariant relations.

The opposite stance toward cultural variability has, explicitly or implicitly, underpinned a great deal of the remaining work in culture and cognition. The general logic of what we are terming the socialization perspective goes something like the following: The physical environment in which people live will determine the kinds of economic activities in which they engage. Their basic economic activities will require different kinds of knowledge; simply as a result of direct ecological press, the Kalahari bushman (45) and the Kpelle rice farmer (30) will have to develop different strategies for survival of the individual and the group. Even at a very rudimentary level, these activities will have to be coordinated among members of a culture in order to insure an adequate supply of food, shelter, and care of the young.

The different means of coordinating basic economic demands entail different divisions of labor which produce specialized activities between individuals within groups (the most conspicuous being sexual divisions of labor). It seems reasonable to suppose that, depending upon the environmental circumstances in which the group lives and the coordinated activities that the group has evolved to meet the demands of maintaining and propagating itself, groups will differently organize children's lives so that they will fit in with adult requirements and insure that the children can fulfill those requirements when they reach maturity (8, 45, 82, 89b).

The basic problem of the socialization theorist is to trace the ecology→ economic activity→social coordination→child-rearing paths invented and transmitted by various cultures. Standard practice uses variations among groups to tease apart the independent contributions of these different aspects of human ecology to the development of psychological processes. As Serpell points out in his thoughtful review (77), a good deal of current research within this tradition springs more or less directly from the culture and personality work that came to prominence in the 1940s and 1950s. This parallel is particularly strong in the case of those theorists who treat cognition as a reflection of a global characteristic of individuals.

Psychological Differentiation

Far and away the largest enterprise in the cross-cultural cognitive socialization tradition has been associated with the work of Berry (8), who has extended Witkin's socialization model to include ecological, biological, and "acculturative" (cultural importation) factors as well.

For several decades, Witkin and his associates have been engaged in a massive exploration of the causes of self-consistent individual differences in the way individuals adapt to their social and physical environments. A key concept in this evolving theory has been the notion of psychological differentiation, which characterizes intraindividual specialization of psychological functions and the degree of segregation of the individual from his surround. Differentiation has, in turn, been characterized in terms of underlying dimensions, particularly the dimension of field dependence–independence which shapes the way the individual responds to his environment. The focus of this review does not permit us to treat extensively the evidence based on research in the United States, but the reader may find a concise presentation of this work in Witkin's recent summary (89a), which also contains references to more extensive discussions.

The aspect of Witkin's theory which concerns us here is the way in which it derives causal hypotheses about the effect of socialization practices on cognitive development. Using the intracultural evidence as a base, cross-cultural work has sought to confirm hypotheses about the effects of different socialization practices, extend the list of practices which exist as a part of the normal, human repertoire, and relate them to broader contexts for socialization.

Berry's large study of "human ecology and cognitive style" included data from 18 cultural groups who varied in their exploitative patterns (animal husbandry-agriculture-gathering-fishing-hunting), settlement patterns, community sizes, political and social stratifications, family organizations, and patterns of child-rearing (in particular, the amount of constraint put on children with respect to social compliance and individual achievement). Finding generally high intercorrelations among these factors, Berry combined them into an ecocultural index. He also constructed an acculturation index, composed of years of schooling, involvement in the wage economy, and urbanization. These two clustered independent variables were then used to order performance on the following tasks, linked in varying degrees to Witkin's theory of psychological differentiation: the embedded figures test, Koh's blocks, Raven's matrices, Morrisby shapes, and a discrimination task (discrimination of rapidly presented geometric figures with gaps in the perimeter which have to be drawn by the subject on a piece of paper). Berry found a strong relationship between the ecocultural index (e.g. toward hunting and away from sedentary agriculture, toward autonomous child-rearing practices and away from strict socialization that fosters dependency) and performance on these tests of psychological differentiation. Less, though significantly, related to psychological differentiation was the acculturation index.

To paraphrase Berry (8, p. 200), there is a sense in which this style of work disguises a lot of internal complexities and also a sense in which it covers a lot of ground. No other cross-cultural effort studying cognition has attempted to cast such a broad theoretical net; no other effort has systematically sampled world cultures in a manner designed to test theory and *then* gone out to make the psychological test observations (as Berry has done). There can be little quarrel with the general attempt to relate behavior to larger and larger spheres of the individual's cultural and (ultimately) physical environment. There is also great plausibility in the idea that cultures which, as part of their basic adaptive strategy, vary in the activities they require of adults and children will also vary in the way their members respond to various psychological tests. But it is a very different matter to conclude that the particular theory of culture and cognition represented by this work has been confirmed by the evidence. Rather, we recommend a more cautious view: Using terminology applied broadly to cross-cultural research by Malpass, we believe that the Berry/Witkin differentiation theory is "weakly consistent" with the data because we are "for the most part unable to reject not only alternatives to the hypothesis, but also alternative interpretations of the data based on what are thought of as methodological matters" (51, p. 68).

Taking up Malpass's two impediments to theory confirmation in reverse order, we note, as does Berry himself, that the problems of method are many. The following difficulties appear paramount to us:

1. The tests of significance from which Berry's correlations take their significance require independence among samples; several of Berry's samples were clearly *not* independent, a difficulty known as Galton's problem (57). When the number of *independent* culture groups is taken to be 8 (in contrast to the number of different cultural groups sampled, which was 18), the degrees of freedom for tests of statistical significance drops to 6. Many of the reported relationships between Berry's independent variables are no longer significant if tests are restricted to the independent samples. Exactly how Galton's problem applies to the problem of predicting culture-behavior relations is an unresolved problem. Berry, recognizing the issue, feels that nonindependence of samples is only a problem when correlating cultural variables with each other. In our opinion, the same logic applies to predicting behavioral outcomes.

2. The theory implies that perceptual tests that do not require "disembedding" will be less sensitive to the cultural variations in question than tests that emphasize psychological differentiation. The discrimination task included in Berry's test battery is assumed not to involve differentiation; hence, discrimination performance would not be expected to relate to the ecocultural and acculturational indexes as highly as measures of psychological differentiation. Yet the relationship between discrimination perfor-

mance and measures of psychological differentiation was as strong as the relationship between the ecocultural index and differentiation. This finding raises the possibility that variation in differentiation scores resulted from underlying differences in visual discrimination ability rather than psychological differentiation.

3. The theory of psychological differentiation is a theory of *individual* differences. However, Berry's tests have often been at the group level. It is essential to demonstrate the independent variable-dependent variables relationship *within* cultures just as it is to demonstrate the relationship *between* cultures. This is the principle referred to as "metric" equivalence by Berry & Dasen (10, pp. 18–19). For example, while two groups of adults from different cultures may, on the average, vary in the degree of compliance they require of their children, individual children within each group can be expected to vary in the amount of compliance that is actually required of them. The burden of Berry's analysis rests upon correlations between the ecocultural index and test performance including individuals from all cultures. This procedure remains very much a between-groups comparison, although the individual appears to be the unit of analysis.

Cognizant of this problem, but limited in his ability to carry out within-culture analyses owing to limited variation in the ecocultural index within the cultures, Berry presents within-culture analyses for each group he studies relating complaint socialization self-ratings and education to cognitive performance (8, pp. 155–57). While substantial correlations between cognitive performance and education are obtained, correlations with the socialization index are variable and quite low on the average, in sharp contrast to the general picture given by the between-culture analyses.

Although these general points of method are important, they should not be viewed as special to Berry's research. In a sense, they surface clearly because the scope of the research makes it possible for us to note them.

Matters of method, narrowly defined, are not the only reason to question Berry and Witkin's conclusions. Serpell, for example, prefers a less global hypothesis, which he terms the perceptual skills hypothesis (77), to the theory of psychological differentiation as an explanation for the intercultural differences in performance on the kinds of tasks reported in Berry's monograph. In its essence, the perceptual skills approach treats as unproven the claim of organism-wide generality to performance, focusing instead on the relationship between task-specific skills required by each of the tests and particular aspects of the environment (ecocultural system would presumably be an acceptable term to Serpell) that could be expected to encourage activities that foster those skills.

One line of evidence pursued by Serpell (77) arises from analysis of intercorrelations among tasks. For example, he cites a study by Okonji in which two psychological differentiation tasks, the embedded figures test and the rod-and-frame test, were uncorrelated with presumably predictive socialization factors; the rod-and-frame test did not correlate significantly with the embedded figures test; but the embedded figures test did correlate with Raven's matrices. Serpell hypothesized that skill in dealing with pictorial stimuli may be the common skill producing the correlation between these latter two tasks.

Cole & Scribner (21) pursued a similar logic in their discussion of the interdomain consistency implied by the psychological differentiation theory. Their review of the literature led them to conclude that cross-cultural evidence for consistency of responding implied by the theory across the range of human activities, including perception, cognition, defense mechanism, etc is still lacking. This point was acknowledged by Berry & Witkin (89b, pp. 29–30), and we can expect future research to reflect the important challenge that this gap poses for the theory. Until there is evidence to the contrary, we believe that a perceptual skills interpretation of this line of research is the most parsimonious available hypothesis the data can support. Berry and Witkin would strongly disagree with this judgement, and the interested reader should consult their forthcoming publications for more positive characterizations of the relationship between their rapidly evolving theory and the data.

The Soviet Cultural-Historical Approach

It has become a basic principle of materialistic psychology that mental processes depend on active life forms in appropriate environments. Such a psychology also assumes that human action changes the environment so that human mental life is a product of continually *new* activities manifest in social practice (50, p. 29).

This quotation summarizes the basic position underlying two remarkable cross-cultural expeditions carried out in the early 1930s by Alexander Luria and his colleagues to determine if rapid changes in "appropriate environments" led to qualitative changes in the structure of human mental activity. Basing their experimental work on the general psychological position developed in collaboration with Lev Vygotsky (83), Luria sought to demonstrate that the higher forms of mental activity promoted by different cultural milieus would differ according to the leading activities demanded by the culture and made possible by the cultural tools (forms of intellectual activity) that the culture has accumulated in the course of its history.

The setting for Luria's work was the small villages and newly organized collective farms of Uzbekistan and Kirghizia in Soviet Central Asia. His major contrast groups were village women, who were particularly isolated and restricted to their villages, village men, and people who had begun to take part in collectivized agriculture. This latter group also had been instructed in basic literacy skills.

Luria hypothesized that the leading activities of the villagers would be based upon their concrete experience, organized according to what he termed graphic-functional principles. He believed that with the advent of literacy and involvement in the modern economy, more abstract-theoretical mental structures come to dominate thinking. In a combination of experimental and clinical interview tasks that is unique in the cross-cultural literature, Luria provided support for his basic proposition in the domains of color classification, classification of objects, logical reasoning, imagination, and self-analysis. Luria did not use formal, statistical techniques to demonstrate his belief that the changes he was talking about were organism-wide. However, his basic theory and the fact that he was working with a relatively small population of subjects, each of whom were administered most if not all of the tasks, suggested to him that the basic principles he was studying were characteristic of the whole person, not just their functioning on his specific tasks. In this respect, Luria's work is very much in the same spirit as Berry and Witkin's, a similarity which may stem in part from their common admiration for Werner (87).

Questions have (17) and should be raised about the interpretations which flow from Luria's observations, especially as they related to the developmental implication that nonliterate people lack abstract thought. Whatever their weaknesses, however, these studies are unique not only for their subject populations, but as an example of how the clinical method can be used creatively in cross-cultural research.

Since the publication of Luria's work, additional studies have been undertaken by Soviet psychologists which have sought to extend his observations to other peoples of the USSR. As yet, publications of this work are available only in Russian (53). A small set of earlier observations are available in English (38, 49).

"MIXED" APPROACHES: CULTURE AND MEMORY

In the discussion thus far we have reviewed two contrasting approaches to the relation between culture and cognition. The first emphasizes cognitive universals, the second cultural variability. Some investigators take an explicit middle ground between these two stances, a ground not unlike that currently occupied by Dasen's competence/performance version of Piagetian theory in certain formal respects. Research we characterize here as "mixed" uses theoretical distinctions motivated by experimental-cognitive research in the United States to support differentiation between universal and culture-specific aspects of performance on a variety of cognitive tasks.

Illustrative of this work are two independent lines of research that have attempted to establish the existence of universal processes of memory and to distinguish these from culture-specific processes. Kagan and his associates formulated their enterprise as follows:

> It is assumed that performance on tests of basic cognitive processes generally will show a linear increase with age in all cultural settings, although the rate of improvement and the age at which asymptotic functioning is reached will be a function of local cultural characteristics. Performance on tests of culturally specific functions will differ markedly in both their growth functions and asymptotes across different societies (40, p. 374).

A variety of memory tasks, differing in their specific demands, were administered to children from 6–12 years of age in two Mayan towns and Cambridge, Massachusetts. For all groups there was a regular, average increase in performance with age. But there were wide differences between the two Mayan towns and between the Guatemalan children and the Cambridge students. Performance differences were particularly marked for those tasks that explicitly required the subject to transform information in memory before responding. On these tasks the curves suggest not only that the Guatemalan children lag behind their Cambridge counterparts, but that they may be reaching a lower asymptote.

Kagan et al interpret their results as support for the notion of a universal increase in basic cognitive competence, but variation in the growth of strategic organization and rehearsal functions. Variations in strategy activation is in turn attributed to delays in the development of "executive" cognitive processes which they believe depend upon such factors as infant care practices, attitudes toward schooling, exposure to a varied environment, and other experiential factors, generally of a cultural nature.

While the interpretation of these data by Kagan et al is plausible, their evidence for universal processes of memory and their separation of performance into universal and culture-specific components has to be considered little more than a hypothesis suggested by their data, rather than a conclusion that follows from the data. The interpretive weaknesses come from three sources. First, Kagan et al lack a process theory of performance for each of their tasks, rendering separation of universal and specific contributions to performance very problematic. Second, they lack a theory relating presumed culture-specific experiences to performance. (For example, how, theoretically, is one's attitude toward schooling supposed to influence performance on a test of memory for the physical orientation of a set of dolls?) Third, their hypotheses are not framed in a way that will allow them to make intracultural tests that can be compared cross-culturally (unless one accepts the age-related increase in mean performance as such a relation). As a consequence, a variety of competing hypotheses (differential nutrition, experimenter differences, motivational differences, etc) could be trotted out to question the authors' conclusions with regard to the universality or culture-specificity of particular test performances.

Wagner's work in Morocco (84) succeeds in dealing with some, but not all, of the difficulties of the Kagan et al Guatemalan work by drawing on Atkinson and Shiffrin's general model of memory circa 1968. Wagner used this model to distinguish between cultural universals, which he located in *structural* processes of memory (e.g. size of the short-term buffer and rate of transfer between short- and long-term memory) and cultural variability in the *control* processes of memory (e.g. rehearsal, elaborated encoding of stimuli). Wagner's basic contrast groups were children of different ages living in an urban or rural environment and attending school or not. Important supplementary groups were Quaranic (Koranic) students and rug sellers, who, he hypothesized, should exhibit culture-specific control process characteristics.

Wagner's first study, replicating his own previous research in Yucatan, demonstrated educational and urban/rural differences in short-term memory for the location of pictured objects. Fine grain analysis showed that the average differences were located primarily in the primacy portion of the recall set. On the basis of the model and a great deal of collateral research in the United States, Wagner plausibly attributed these differences to the control process of rehearsal, with invariance in the "structural," recency portion of the list. Contrary to his speculation based upon observation of Quaranic education, Quaranic students behaved like their unschooled peers. In Wagner's second study, continuous recognition of rug patterns was the task assigned to his basic groups. Here the special experience of the rug sellers was of obvious interest. In this study, Wagner associated control processes with the level of acquisition (number correct) and structural processes with the forgetting rate over a period of time.

If matters had worked out neatly, Wagner would have observed group variation in overall number correct, but none in rate of forgetting. Matters did not work out neatly. Some of the expected invariance was obtained (e.g. no age effects were found), but that invariance applied to both the structural and control aspects of the task. Relevant variation was also obtained, but it was not restricted to the "control" aspect of the task and its direction was opposite to that obtained in Experiment 1 in an important way: Instead of the control processes of the urban children exceeding those of the rural children, the opposite was found. Again, Quaranic scholars performed like unschooled children. Interestingly, rug sellers forgot at a slower rate than the other Moroccan groups. Since the task involved recognition of rugs, this result was anticipated, but it occurred in the theoretically wrong aspect of the performance, forgetting, which was hypothetically a structural universal.

Despite interpretive difficulties, Wagner's study is interesting as an example of a theoretically motivated study in which tasks were chosen to permit specific tests of universal and culture-specific components of cognitive performance. The success of the rug sellers and the failure of the Quaranic scholars may have been more or less congenial to Wagner's experimental hypotheses, but in each case his inclusion of local cultural institutions provided the basis for a theoretically motivated selection of tasks and groups.

ETHNOGRAPHIC PSYCHOLOGY

At the 1935 meeting of the American Association for the Advancement of Science, Florence Goodenough addressed the anthropological section on "The measurement of mental functions in primitive groups." At one point in her address she remarked:

> Now the fact can hardly be too strongly emphasized that neither intelligence tests nor the so-called tests of personality and character are measuring devices, properly speaking. They are sampling devices. . . .

and

> . . . we must also be sure that the test items from which the total trait is to be judged are representative and valid samples of the ability in question, as it is displayed within the particular culture with which we are concerned (34, p. 5).

Thirty years later Goodnenough's wise words describe two major characteristics of a fourth approach to the study of culture and cognition which has come to be called ethnographic psychology (not to be confused with the *völkerpsychologie* that Wundt proposed almost a century ago). Motivation for this development stemmed from observations of gross discrepancies between performance by "exotic" groups on psychological tests and anthropological accounts of their everyday behavior. For example, Cole & Scribner (19, Chap. 8) reported that in an experimental communication task originally designed to assess children's ability to consider another person's information requirements, unschooled Liberian *adults* performed much like young American children. On the basis of their performance on this task alone, these adults could be labeled "egocentric." However, these same people engaged in sophisticated arguments in local courtrooms and other settings that indicated no general lack of communicative skill or insensitivity to their listeners' needs (4, 13, 16). Similarly, Gladwin (32) and Lewis (47) have described complex navigational skills of uneducated Micronesian islanders who had difficulty in solving Piagetian problems that American teenagers generally master quite easily. The magnitude of such discrepancies was sufficient to generate suspicion that the methods currently in use to investigate the cognitive skills of non-Western people are not appropriate to the inferences about culture and cognition which motivated the research in the first place.

The ethnographic approach represents a deviation from both the current goals and methods of the previously described approaches. Its primary goal is neither to locate universals in cognitive structures nor to discover generalized mental abilities which develop as a function of socialization practices that are measurable by universally applicable techniques. Rather, it seeks to explicate the relation between culturally organized activities and the development of systems of cognitive skills: cognitive universals may be demonstrated, and socialization practices certainly control the organization of activities, but a firm understanding of what people are doing, what their activities are, is the starting point of analysis (18, 20, 29, 73).

These investigators' acceptance of the proposition that psychological tests are not measuring devices has required the development of techniques that permit valid statements about the (mental) activities which subjects engage in when confronted with particular cognitive tasks. Specification of these activities has made the experiment, rather than the test, the basic tool of psychological analysis (16, 18, 71, 72, 74). The distinction between test and experiment is important here, because a great deal of cross-cultural work is based on process inferences from tests, a procedure that has helped to generate almost endless debate about item equivalence, validity, and other problems generally spoken of as methodological. Consistent with current thinking and technology in domestic versions of experimental cognitive psychology (66), researchers within the ethnographic-cognitive psychology group have relied heavily on the series of experiments to warrant inferences about psychological process. Performance in any given experimental condition is viewed as the product of complexly interacting basic processes, organized into functional systems (50, 83), the principles of which require extended experimental analysis if they are to be explicated. Variations within the series of experiments is motivated by hypotheses concerning what is required for performance on a particular task and the relation of that task to others posed in the group's experience.

There has also been a growing realization that Goodenough's comments on sampling have very broad implications for the cross-cultural enterprise. The major methodological lesson is that ethnographic analysis of cultural activities that require and promote particular cognitive skills must be carried out in close proximity with (and preferably prior to) experimental analysis of the skills in test-like situations. Otherwise, we remain critically ignorant of how the behaviors sampled in the test relate to those routinely demanded by the culture.

It should be clear from this bare description that the requirements that the ethnographic psychological enterprise lays before the practitioner are stringent indeed; she must be adept at both cognitive-psychological task analysis and cultural task analysis; she must be knowledgeable about relevant theory in both domains. Nor is such knowledge a sure foundation on which to build. The technology for the former kind of analysis is still rudimentary (31, 52, 66, 78), the latter, embryonic (3, 5, 15, 29, 35, 42, 56).

The early work in this tradition must be considered inadequate on both experimental/psychological and ethnographic grounds. Cole et al's cursory ethnography of Kpelle intellectual activities, while suggestive of interesting areas of inquiry, would have benefited from a far deeper understanding of Kpelle modes of discourse as contained, for example, in Bellman (4). Lancy's (43) studies of memory among the Kpelle suffer from a far-too-cursory ethnographic description of Kpelle remembering activities, in addition to the weakness of his tasks as measures of the presumed activities [contrast Murphy (55)]. The only way to avoid the elements of superficiality which this research has struggled with, but largely failed to overcome, is to combine experimentation and fieldwork in a multiyear, multidisciplinary effort where ethnography and psychology can interact over time to allow crucial modification of each. However, the early efforts did demonstrate important and heretofore explored connections between the activities that people ordinarily engage in and the skills they develop as reflected in psychological tasks. They also slowed, if not halted, the all-too-frequent cultural deficit interpretations of group differences in mental ability which were to be found in the comparative psychological literature.

The ethnographic-psychological approach connects up with several issues that have been widely debated in the cross-cultural psychological literature. First, the analysis of within-group variation as it relates to between-group variation is a natural result of the basic tenets of this approach (19, p. 198 ff). Group differences are not viewed as end points of analysis, particularly end points defined in terms of "amount of" or "level of" cognitive ability achieved by the cultural groups. They become instead the starting points for an investigation of within-group organizations of experience that could produce the between-group variation. Such differences are a source of hypotheses concerning both the task requirements and cultural "practice" in relation to the tasks.

Second, while experiments retain their privileged status as environments for making clear the activities that generate analyzable cognitive activities, they are not privileged as samples of culturally appropriate behavior. Quite the opposite. They are viewed as extremely problematic in the matter of their representativeness, which must be explored carefully in every instance of application. The problem of representativeness is in turn closely related to the problem of insuring that the task as conceived by the experimenter is the task as perceived by the subject. All process-oriented cognitive psychology rests on the assumption that the task-as-given and the task-as-received are equivalent. Experiments are particularly susceptible to error from this source when done comparatively, but the problem does not change in principle from that facing those who study paired-associate learning in college sophomores (20, 52).

Two independent lines of research will be described which have adopted the ethnographic psychology approach. Scribner & Cole (75) analyzed the cognitive consequences for tribal Vai adults of becoming literate in Vai or Arabic, neither of which is accomplished in Western-type schools. Vai is learned informally from a friend or relative who knows the script, while Arabic is acquired in special Koranic schools. Ethnographic information was obtained on three aspects of each literacy: 1. the acquisition process, 2. the process of reading, and 3. typical literate practices. Arabic literacy is acquired by first learning to recite passages from the Koran by what appeared to be a specialized rote memory process (the students don't understand or speak Arabic). The authors hypothesized that such practice would lead to the development of specific memory skills that would appear only if the experimental task mimicked the learning environment. To test this hypothesis, all subjects were given three different memory tasks: incremental recall in which one item was added to a list on each trial, starting with one item and building up to 16, free recall of a word list in any order, and recall of a narrative story. Arabic literates performed better than Vai literates only on the incremental memory task, which presented requirements most similar to those of the Koranic schools.

An analysis of the process of reading Vai script indicated that special requirements are posed by the script. It is a syllabary, which means that each character represents a syllable; tone (which is important in Vai) is not marked, and no word boundaries or punctuation are indicated. The reader must group the syllables together to form words, then integrate these into meaningful linguistic units. Grouping and integration skills were tested by requiring subjects to "read" and comprehend sequences of pictures and to repeat and comprehend strings of disjointed syllables or words. Vai and Arabic literates did not differ in their ability to comprehend the word strings, but Vai literates were superior on the picture reading and syllable integration tasks which mapped onto their normal reading activities.

The uses to which Vai and Arabic literacy are put vary considerably. Arabic is used strictly for purposes of reading the Koran, while Vai literacy is used for record keeping and letter writing. In letter writing, the information needs of the reader must be taken into account. Thus, it was hypothesized that those individuals with letter writing practice should be more explicit in other forms of communication as well. A board game was taught to participants in the experiment and they were required to teach it to someone else. The Vai literates not only provided more information than the Arabic literates, they also were more likely to introduce the game by a general characterization before describing specific rules, a strategy common to the form of Vai letters. In each case, outcome reflected cultural practice.

Lave (44) began with an ethnography of tailoring activities by Vai and Gola tailors in Monrovia, Liberia, followed by tests to assess transfer of tailoring and mathematical skills to problems involving familiar and unfamiliar materials. The unfamiliar problems could be solved using common tailoring algorithms. Tests of arithmetic operations and number skills were also included. Master and apprentice tailors who differed in both number of years at tailoring and formal schooling were compared.

Both formal education and tailoring experience influenced nontailoring tasks, but only years of tailoring was related to performance on tailoring-type tasks. Among the several virtues of Lave's research is the possibility of testing the theory that formal schooling leads to generalized, abstract problem-solving skills in contrast to the supposedly more restricted domain of applicability of skills learned in a nonformal situation. Clearly, the general change theory was not supported by Lave's results. On the other hand, it is interesting that proficiency in tailoring produced performance at novel tasks equivalent to that resulting from formal education. Whether the similarity in performance resulted from similar cognitive processing was not addressed by Lave, a point made by Ginsberg (31a). However, this research and that of Scribner and Cole is useful insofar as it provides a test of generalizability of culturally organized practice.

IN SUMMARY

This highly selective review has covered several lines of research that have become dominant in the study of culture and cognition during the latter half of the 1970s. It is now possible to return to the question with which we began: how is culture represented in the work we have been reviewing? In our opinion, a dispassionate answer to this question must be—superficially at best.

Cross-cultural Piagetian research began with a strong set of hypotheses regarding the order in which a variety of tasks would be mastered ontogenetically, a competence model linking these tasks to cognitive development, and a theory that posited cognitive universals because of an (unexamined) belief in universal organism-environment interactions that underpin development. Much of the early work in this tradition represented a classic example of tests being used as measures (despite the example set by Piaget). Failures to find equal performance across groups motivated a search for ways to include culture in the form of varied materials and procedures designed to equate (psychologically) relevant test factors (familiarity, for example). Only as the enterprise has encountered greater and greater difficulties have its adherents begun to look seriously at more complex features of the culture, searching for the presence or absence of culture-*specific* organism-environment interactions to explain the presence or absence of *specific* cognitive achievements. This challenge to Piagetian theory may prove the spur to crucial analyses that can enrich both the theory and our understanding of culturally organized activities (e.g. 1, 12, 33, 37).

Matters have been little better in the socialization work. On the independent variable side, ethnographic work has typically been minimal (with heavy emphasis on the Human Relations Area Files) or based on selected aspects of the culture taken out of context to permit later quantification. One of the heartening changes in this area is the increased use of theoretically motivated, *within-group* observation as a means of specifying culturally patterned activities that can be used as "measures" by procedures which maximize representativeness (68). New work using ethnographic eliciting techniques to provide the basic categories for scaling independent variables are also important (27, 58, 77a). However, as Rogoff (68) points out, even careful spot observations can succeed only if there is a *theoretical* link between the observations of everyday behaviors (or indigenous activities) and the cognitive tasks that are the dependent measures.

Recent work that combines intense ethnography with psychological research techniques in the socialization tradition makes it clear that the ethnographic-psychological approach is not incompatible with the other approaches reviewed here (6, 38a). Berland used the tools and language of cognitive differentiation theory in an extremely interesting account of the lives and socialization practices of Pakistani gypsies. But his work also contains a fine-grained description of the activities that different socialization practices require of children. For example, when we are told how young children are taught to care for, train, and act alongside of large carnival bears or to do sleight-of-hand tricks as part of a magic show, and when we are told how adults carry out this training, it becomes clear that it is these organized activities and the skills they generate, not the strictness or laxness of the socialization practices per se, that are crucial to producing increased cognitive performance.

Culture is still distressingly absent on the dependent variable side of a great deal of cross-cultural work where psychological ability tests continue to be treated as measures instead of samples. The absence of well-defined theories of the task-specific activities which give rise to the dependent variables is a central source of the ambiguity in almost all this work. Advances in this area will almost certainly depend upon cross-cultural psychologists keeping abreast of, and applying, the most advanced techniques for specifying process that the noncomparative study of cognitive processing will allow. Cases in which there is a strong theory of the task and its relation to cultural practices point the way to incorporating culture into our dependent variables.

As cultural practices become the focus of more and more cross-cultural cognitive work, greater emphasis will have to be put on developing cognitive ethnographies which go beyond cognitive anthropology's current products (42). A new concern for specifying culturally organized activities on a level which the psychologist can use is one of the major tasks confronting the study of culture and cognition in the coming decade.

Literature Cited

1. Adjei, K. 1977. Influence of specific maternal occupation and behavior on Piagetian cognitive development. See Ref. 23, pp. 227–56
2. Adler, L. L., ed. 1977. Issues in cross-cultural research. *Ann. NY Acad. Sci.* Vol. 285. 753 pp.
3. Bateson, G. 1958. *Naven.* Stanford: Stanford Univ. Press. 312 pp. 2nd ed.
4. Bellman, B. L. 1975. *Village of Curers and Assassins: On the Production of Kpelle Cosmological Categories.* The Hague: Mouton
5. Bellman, B. L., Jules-Rosette, B. 1977. *A Paradigm for Looking.* New York: Academic. 211 pp.
6. Berland, J. C. 1977. *Cultural amplifiers and psychological differentiation.* Mimeo, Northwestern Univ. 527 pp.
7. Berlin, B., Kay, P. 1969. *Basic Color Terms: Their Universality and Evolution.* Berkeley: Univ. California Press. 178 pp.
8. Berry, J. W. 1976. *Human Ecology and Cognitive Style.* New York: Sage. 242 pp.
9. Berry, J. W., Dasen, P. R., eds. 1970. *Culture and Cognition: Readings in Cross-Cultural Psychology.* New York: Harper & Row. 487 pp.
10. Berry, J. W., Dasen, P. R. 1970. Introduction: History and method in the cross-cultural study of cognition. See Ref. 9, pp. 1–22
11. Bornstein, M. 1975. The influence of visual perception on color. *Am. Anthropol.* 77:774–98
12. Bovet, M. C. 1970. Cognitive processes among illiterate children and adults. See Ref. 9, pp. 311–34
13. Brislin, R. W., Lonner, W. J., Thorndike, R. M. 1973. *Cross-Cultural Research Methods.* New York: Wiley. 351 pp.
14. Campbell, D. R. 1961. The mutual methodological relevance of anthropology and psychology. In *Psychological Anthropology,* ed. F. L. K. Hsu, pp. 333–52. Homewood, IL: Dorsey
15. Childs, C., Greenfield, P. M. 1978. Informal modes of learning and teaching: the case of Zinacanteco weaving. In *Advances in Cross-Cultural Psychology,* ed. N. Warren, 2:1–22. London: Academic. In press
16. Cole, M. 1975. An ethnographic psychology of cognition. In *Cross-Cultural Perspectives on Learning,* ed. R. W. Brislin, S. Bochner, W. Lonner. pp. 157–76. Beverly Hills: Sage. 336 pp.
17. Cole, M. 1976. Forward to *Cognitive Development,* A. R. Luria, pp. xi–xvi. Cambridge: Harvard Univ. Press. 164 pp.
18. Cole, M., Gay, J., Glick, J. A., Sharp, D. W. 1971. *The Cultural Context of Learning and Thinking.* New York: Basic Books. 304 pp.
19. Cole, M., Scribner, S. 1974. *Culture and Thought.* New York: Wiley. 227 pp.
20. Cole, M., Scribner, S. 1975. Theorizing about socialization of cognition. *Ethos* 3:250–68
21. Cole, M., Scribner, S. 1977. Developmental theories applied to cross-cultural cognitive research. *Ann. NY Acad Sci.* 285:336–76
22. Dasen, P. R. 1977. Cross-cultural cognitive development: the cultural aspects of Piaget's theory. *Ann. NY Acad. Sci.* 285:332–37
23. Dasen, P. R., ed. 1977. *Piagetian Psychology: Cross-cultural Contributions.* New York: Gardner. 379 pp.

24. Dasen, P. R. 1977. Introduction to *Piagetian Psychology.* See Ref. 23, pp. 1–25

25. Ember, C. R. 1977. Cross-cultural cognitive studies. *Ann. Rev. Anthropol.* 6:33–56

26. Feldman, C. F. 1974. *The Development of Adaptive Intelligence.* San Francisco: Jossey-Bass. 142 pp.

27. Fjellman, J. 1971. *The myth of primitive mentality: a study of semantic acquisition and modes of thought.* PhD thesis. Stanford Univ., Stanford, CA. 188 pp.

28. Flavell, J., Wohlwill, J. F. 1969. Formal and functional aspects of cognitive development. In *Studies in Cognitive Development,* ed. D. Elkind, J. H. Flavell, pp. 67–120. New York: Oxford Univ. Press. 503 pp.

29. Frake, C. O. 1962. The ethnographic study of cognitive systems. In *Anthropology and Human Behavior,* ed. T. Gladwin, W. C. Sturtevant, pp. 72–85. Washington, DC: Anthropol. Soc. Washington. 214 pp.

30. Gay, J., Cole, M. 1967. *The New Mathematics and an Old Culture.* New York: Holt, Rinehart & Winson. 100 pp.

31. Gelman, R. 1978. Cognitive development. *Ann. Rev. Psychol.* 29:297–332

31a. Ginsburg, H. 1977. Some problems in the study of schooling and cognition. *Q. Newsl. Inst. Comp. Hum. Dev.* 1:7–10

32. Gladwin, T. 1970. *East is a Big Bird.* Cambridge: Harvard Univ. Press. 241 pp.

33. Glick, J. 1975. Cognitive development in cross-cultural perspective. In *Review of Child Development Research,* ed. F. D. Horowitz, 4:595–654. Chicago: Univ. Chicago Press. 690 pp.

34. Goodenough, F. 1936. The measurement of mental functions in primitive groups. *Am. Anthropol.* 38:1–11

34a. Goodnow, J. J. 1976. The nature of intelligent behavior: questions raised by cross-cultural studies. See Ref. 66, pp. 169–88

35. Goody, J., Cole, J., Scribner, S. 1977. Writing and formal operations. *Africa* 47:289–304

36. Greenfield, P. M. 1976. Cross-cultural research and Piagetian theory: paradox and progress. In *The Developing Individual in a Changing World,* ed. K. F. Riegel, J. A. Meacham, 1:322–43. The Hague: Mouton. 409 pp.

37. Greenfield, P. M., Childs, C. P. 1977. Understanding sibling concepts: A developmental study of kin terms in Zinacantan. See Ref. 23, pp. 335–58

38. Gurova, R. G. 1978. A study of the influence of sociohistorical conditions on child development (comparative investigation, 1929 and 1966). In *Soviet Developmental Psychology,* ed. M. Cole. pp. 369–92. White Plains, NY: Sharpe. 621 pp.

38a. Harris, S. 1977. *Milingimbi Aboriginal Learning Contexts.* PhD thesis. Univ. New Mexico, Albuquerque, NM. 575 pp.

39. Heron, A., Dowel, W. 1974. The questionable unity of the concrete operations stage. *Int. J. Psychol.* 9:1–10

40. Kagan, J., Klein, R. E., Finley, G. E., Rogoff, B. 1977. A study in cognitive development. *Ann. NY Acad. Sci.* 285:374–88

41. Kamara, A. I., Easley, J. A. 1977. Is the rate of cognitive development uniform across cultures? A methodological critique with new evidence from Themne children. See Ref. 23, pp. 26–63

42. Laboratory of Comparative Human Cognition. 1978. Cognition as a residual category in anthropology. *Ann. Rev. Anthropol.* 7:51–69

43. Lancy, D. F. 1977. Studies of memory in culture. *Ann. NY Acad. Sci.* 285:297–307

44. Lave, J. 1977. Cognitive consequences of tradition apprenticeship training in West Africa. *Anthropol. Educ. Q.* 8:177–80

45. Lee, N. R., De Vore, I., eds. 1976. *Kalahari Hunter-Gatherers: Studies of the !Kung san and their Neighbors.* Cambridge: Harvard Univ. Press. 408 pp.

46. Le Vine, R. A. 1970. Cross-cultural study in child psychology. In *Carmichael's Manual of Child Psychology,* ed. P. H. Mussen, 2:559–614. New York: Wiley. 1519 pp.

47. Lewis, E. 1972. *We the Navigators.* Honolulu: Univ. Hawaii Press. 335 pp.

48. Lloyd, B. B. 1972. *Perception and Cognition: A Cross-Cultural Perspective.* Harmondsworth: Penguin

49. Luria, A. R. 1930. *Rech' i intellekt. Derevenskogo, gorodskogo i bespirizornogo rebenka.* Gosudarstvennoe izdatel'stvo RSFSR. Reprinted in *Soviet Psychology,* 1974, 13:5–6

50. Luria, A. R. 1976. *Cognitive Development.* Cambridge: Harvard Univ. Press. 164 pp.

51. Malpass, R. S. 1977. On the theoretical basis of methodology: a return to basics. See Ref. 62, pp. 64–72

52. Medin, D., Cole, M. 1975. Comparative psychology and human cognition. In

Handbook of Learning and Cognitive Processes, ed. W. K. Estes, pp. 111–50. Hillsdale: Erlbaum. 303 pp.

53. Mukanov, M. M., ed. 1975. *Developmental and Social Problems of Intellectual Activities.* Alma Ata: Kazakh Pedagogical Inst. 139 pp. (in Russian)

54. Munroe, R. L., Munroe, R. H. 1975. *Cross-Cultural Human Development.* Monterey: Brooks/Cole. 181 pp.

55. Murphy, W. P. 1976. *A semantic and logical analysis of Kpelle proverb metaphors of secrecy.* PhD thesis. Stanford Univ., Stanford, CA. 239 pp.

56. Nadel, S. F. 1937. Experiments in culture psychology. *Africa* 10:421–35

57. Naroll, R. 1973. Galton's problem. In *A Handbook of Methods in Cultural Anthropology,* ed. R. Naroll, R. Cohen, pp. 974–89. New York: Columbia Univ. Press. 1017 pp.

58. Nerlove, S. B., Roberts, J. M., Klein, R. E., Yarbrough, C., Habicht, J. P. 1974. Natural indicators of cognitive development: an observational study of rural Guatemalan children. *Ethos* 2:265–95

59. Otaala, B. 1973. *The Development of Operational Thinking in Primary School Children: An Examination of Some Aspects of Piaget's Theory among the Itseo Children in Uganda.* New York: Teachers Coll. Press. 119 pp.

60. Piaget, J. 1966. Need and significance of cross-cultural studies in genetic psychology. *Int. J. Psychol.* 1:3–13

61. Piaget, J. 1972. Intellectual evolution from adolescence to adulthood. *Hum. Dev.* 15:1–12

62. Poortinga, Y. H., ed. 1977. *Basic Problems in Cross-Cultural Psychology.* Amsterdam: Swets & Zeitlinger. 380 pp.

63. Price-Williams, D. R. 1975. *Explorations in Cross-Cultural Psychology.* San Francisco: Chandler & Sharp. 128 pp.

64. Price-Williams, D. R., Gordon, W., Ramirez, M. 1969. Skill and conservation: a study of pottery-making children. *Dev. Psychol.* 1:769

65. Price-Williams, D. R., Hammond, D. W., Edgerton, C., Walker, M. 1977. Kinship concepts among rural Hawaiian children. See Ref. 23, pp. 296–334

66. Resnick, L., ed. 1976. *The Nature of Intelligence.* Hillsdale, NJ: Erlbaum. 364 pp.

67. Riegel, K. F., Meacham, J. A., eds. 1976. *The Developing Individual in a Changing World,* Vol. 1. Chicago: Aldine. 409 pp.

68. Rogoff, B. 1978. Spot observation: an introduction and examination. *Q.*

Newsl. Inst. Comp. Hum. Dev. Vol. 2. In press

69. Rosch, E. 1977. Human categorization. In *Studies in Cross-cultural Psychology,* ed. N. Warren, 1:3–47. New York: Academic. 212 pp.

70. Rosch, E. 1978. Principles of categorization. In *Cognition and Categorization,* ed. B. Lloyd, E. Rosch. Hillsdale, NJ: Erlbaum. In press

71. Scribner, S. 1974. Developmental aspects of categorized recall in a West African society. *Cognit. Psychol.* 6:475–94

72. Scribner, S. 1974. Recall of classical syllogisms: a cross-cultural investigation of error on logical problems. In *Psychological Studies of Logic and Its Development,* ed. R. Falmagne, pp. 153–73. Hillsdale, NJ: Erlbaum

73. Scribner, S. 1976. Situating the experiment in cross-cultural research. See Ref. 67, pp. 310–21

74. Scribner, S. 1978. Modes of thinking and ways of speaking: culture and logic reconsidered. In *Discourse Production and Comprehension,* ed. R. O. Freedle. Hillsdale, NJ: Erlbaum. In press

75. Scribner, S., Cole, M. 1978. Unpackaging literacy. *Soc. Sci. Inf.* 17:19–40

76. Sechrest, L. 1977. On the dearth of theory in cross-cultural psychology: there is madness in our method. See Ref. 62, pp. 73–82

77. Serpell, R. 1976. *Culture's Influence on Behavior.* London: Methuen. 144 pp.

77a. Serpell, R. 1977. Strategies for investigating intelligence in its cultural context. *Q. Newsl. Inst. Comp. Hum. Dev.* 3:11–14

78. Siegler, R. S. 1976. Three aspects of cognitive development. *Cognit. Psychol.* 8:481–520

79. Steffre, V., Vales, V., Morley, L. 1966. Language and cognition in Yucatan: a cross-cultural replication. *J. Pers. Soc. Psychol.* 4:112–15

80. Steinberg, B. M., Dunn, L. A. 1976. Conservation competence and performance in Chiapas. *Hum. Dev.* 19:14–25

81. Triandis, H. C., Malpass, R. S., Davidson, A. R. 1973. Psychology and culture. *Ann. Rev. Psychol.* 24:355–78

82. Vayda, A. P., McCay, B. J. 1975. New directions in ecology and ecological anthropology. *Ann. Rev. Anthropol.* 4:293–306

83. Vygotsky, L. S. 1978. *Mind in Society,* ed. M. Cole, V. John-Steiner, S. Scribner, E. Souberman. Cambridge: Harvard Univ. Press

84. Wagner, D. A. 1978. Memories of Morocco: the influence of age, schooling, and environment on memory. *Cognit. Psychol.* 10:1–28

85. Warren, M. 1977. *Advances in Cross-Cultural Psychology,* Vol. 1. New York: Academic. 212 pp.

86. Werner, H. 1937. Process and achievement—a basic problem of education and developmental psychology. *Harv. Educ. Rev.* 7:353–68

87. Werner, H. 1948. *Comparative Psychology of Mental Development.* New York: Int. Univ. Press. 564 pp.

88. Whiting, B. 1976. The problem of the packaged variable. See Ref. 67, pp. 303–9

89. Witkin, H. A. 1977. Theory is cross-cultural research: its uses and risks. See Ref. 62, pp. 83–92

89a. Witkin, H. A. 1978. *Cognitive styles in personal and cultural adaptation.* Heinz Werner Lect. Ser. Worcester: Clark Univ. Press. 68 pp.

89b. Witkin, H. A., Berry, J. W. 1975. Psychological differentiation in cross-cultural perspective. *J. Cross-Cult. Psychol.* 6:4–87

90. Wober, M. 1975. *Psychology in Africa.* London: Int. African Inst. 247 pp.

Ann. Rev. Psychol. 1979. 30:173–207
Copyright © 1979 by Annual Reviews Inc. All rights reserved

PREVENTION: THE CLINICAL PSYCHOLOGIST

❖306

Lois Barclay Murphy

Academic Advisory Staff, Children's Hospital, Washington, DC

Colin Frank

Assistant Clinical Professor, George Washington University Medical School, Washington, DC

CONTENTS

INTRODUCTION 174
THE ADVOCACY ROLE OF THE PSYCHOLOGIST 174
WHAT KIND OF PREVENTION? 175
TRAINING IN PREVENTIVE ROLES 177
    Some of the Contexts in which Psychologists Practice and Prevent 180
    Innovative Prevention Efforts in the Work Setting 181
    Preventive Efforts in Crime and Delinquency 181
NATIONAL PROPOSALS 182
    Developmental Review for All Children 185
    Interdisciplinary Conferences Initiated by a Psychologist 187
LOCAL PREVENTION PROGRAMS 187
    Multiple Goals for Prevention Programs 188
    Ways of Involving Shy and Suspicious Mothers 190
    Effective Programs with High-Risk Children 190
    Prevention of Prolonged Disturbance in Children of Divorce 192
UNDERSTANDINGS BASIC TO PREVENTION PLANNING 193
    Difficult Babies Can Be Too Much for Mothers 194
    Toward Understanding Schizophrenia: A Prerequisite for Prevention 195
    What Strengths Should Prevention Efforts Support? 198
    Experimental Studies Relevant to Prevention of Aggression 199
    Ecology and Behavior 200
    Community Activity Centers as Prevention 200
    Hazards, Blinders, and Reflections 201
    Antilabelers vs Diagnosticians 202
    Cautions 203
CONCLUSION 204

0066-4308/79/0201-0173$01.00

INTRODUCTION

Clinical psychology has been undergoing serious struggles during the last 20 years, and these have resulted in changes in the direction of community involvement, consultation, and prevention instead of a rigid commitment to diagnostic testing and treatment. Gottesfeld (18) sees clinical psychologists as ill equipped for adequately meeting the new challenges since their scientific training in psychology provides little orientation to the nature and functions of the community or the kinds of community interventions that are possible. "Social psychologists know more about those matters than clinical psychologists, and anthropologists, sociologists, and social workers probably know more about them than social psychologists" (p. 290). In 1978 we find that clinical psychologists who get involved in certain prevention efforts learn by experience that differences in subculture values, child-rearing approaches, and family relationship patterns have to be considered if the programs are to be successful.

It would be redundant to retrace the paths sketched out in the superb articles by Mark Kessler & George Albee (27) in the 1975 *Annual Review of Psychology* and by E. L. Cowen (7a) in the 1973 volume, and other articles (8, 9). Both of the *Annual Review* articles have extensive bibliographies covering relevant literature up to the time of their publication. Kessler and Albee complained of the size, undisciplined nature, and vagueness of the existing maps of the field of prevention which they likened to the Okefenokee Swamp: "attractive from a distance . . . it lures the unwary into quagmires, into uncharted and impenetrable byways." As a result of the work of these and other outstanding and creative psychologists, trails have been blazed and quagmires still existing seem less threatening.

Since definitions have been discussed at length in these and other papers (15), we shall not use many pages on problems of classification of prevention efforts in terms of primary, secondary, or tertiary levels, but rather we shall focus on examples, some of which may be models of prevention which might stimulate other psychologists to explore further. We shall give some attention to research problems in the area of prevention, and to lacunae in the training of clinical psychologists for preventive work, as well as a limited sketch of what clinical psychologists across the country are now doing in this area.

THE ADVOCACY ROLE OF THE PSYCHOLOGIST

An example of a psychologist with the dedication and energy to combine training, administration, and advocacy of prevention of distorted development in children is Professor Edward Zigler, Sterling Professor of Psychology at Yale and Director of the Psychology Unit at the Child Study Center and former Director of the US Office of Child Development. In addition to these responsibilities, he writes vigorously, even passionately, about the neglect of children's needs in America (63):

> Over 30 percent of pregnant women receive no prenatal care during the first trimester of pregnancy. . . . Poor prenatal care and maternal malnutrition are major factors in the incidence of prematurity, mental retardation and other birth defects . . . the inoculation rate is down to 70 percent nationally . . . although children constitute one-third of the American population they receive only 10 percent of the funds spent in community mental health centers . . . the incidence of suicide, alcoholism and depression is rising rapidly in children under 14 . . . two thousand children die from abuse annually . . . violence against children is appallingly widespread . . . parents kick, punch, or bite as many as 1.7 million children a year and "beat up" or attack with knives or guns hundreds of thousands more.

A psychologist himself, he criticizes the tendency of psychologists and educators to maintain that a particular child-rearing technique or the latest curriculum are the keys to a child's optimal development. The state of the economy, amount of unemployment, availability of food stamps, parents' work schedules (and we can add the pattern of "relocating" and job transfers along with rigid school programs, overcrowded classes, and tired teachers) are a few other factors contributing to tension and disturbed behavior in children. With the tendency to have fewer children in the family, there is less opportunity for older children to observe younger ones and to help care for them; thus, they have little background for bringing up their own. Zigler emphasizes the need for early education for parenthood.

WHAT KIND OF PREVENTION?

In a college nursery school, teachers sent children like these to the clinical developmental psychologist: Three-year-old Gary would not go to the toilet when he needed to. When given the Minature Life toys to play with, he spent a little time exploring them, then picked up a tiny baby doll and threw it down the nearby drain. The psychologist remarked thoughtfully, "You know, Gary, sometimes little boys are afraid they will be flushed down the toilet so they stay away from it. But that couldn't really happen, could it?" After this clarification, Gary went to the toilet along with the other children.

Two-year-old Kent spent all his time either in the sandbox or trying to turn on light switches. He did not talk and did not seem to hear. (His working mother had left him in the care of a deaf nurse who kept him in a crib where his chief activity was reaching up to the light switch and turning the light off and on.) A gifted student was assigned to spend an hour a day with him—first sharing this obsession, then gradually bringing in other mechanical toys. As time went on, he began to talk and to play with other children, and his IQ in elementary school was 136. In high school, he was chairman of the Lights Committee, a thoroughly socialized integration of his infantile preoccupation.

Before commenting on these episodes of intervention, some examples of help from a Head Start group: The morning after the country's most devastating tornado swept through Topeka, demolishing apartments, houses, and uprooting trees, the teacher of the younger group in North Topeka Day Care Center was absent. North Topeka, across the river from the demolished strip where the teacher lived, had been spared. Two-year-old Annie was silent and immobile, but wetting her panties as she had not done before. The psychologist sat down next to her, quietly asking, "Are you worried, Annie?" The little girl, still silent, nodded her head anxiously. "Are you worried about your teacher?" Another silent nod. "But she is safe, and she will be back in a few days. Her house was blown down, but she is staying with her mother, and she is looking for a new house for herself. She is really all right." Annie relaxed, there was no more wetting, and she was now able to play.

Tara seemed to be a very hyperactive little 4-year-old, tearing around, shrieking and yelling the first days of Head Start. She lived with her mother in a cottage at a reformatory for boys where her mother worked and, probably tired from her strenuous job, had little time to mother her daughter. The psychologist suggested to the teacher that she might stand behind Tara, quietly holding her and talking to her—not reprimanding, just holding her attention and interest. With special attention to help in getting involved in structured activities, Tara settled into a pattern of vivid participation in games, action songs, and other types of play in the group—a leader instead of a disturber.

Now have we been talking about primary or secondary prevention (15, 28)? Insofar as the psychologist was present to nip trouble in the bud whenever it began, and to help whichever child needed help to prevent development of potential chronic disturbed behavior, or even functional retardation or mental illness, she felt that it was indeed primary prevention. Insofar as the work often involved what could be regarded as "treatment" of an emotional or behavior problem, some authorities would call it "secondary prevention." It doesn't matter what we call it. The important thing is that help was given where and when it was needed. In situations like this, the distinction is slippery. If the psychologist had confined her work to conferences with the staff, orienting them to children's feelings and needs, this would doubtless have satisfied a rigid criterion of primary prevention. But the staff learned more, faster, and more unforgettably from the modeling of help to the children. From the point of view of this psychologist, it would be unethical to take a rigid stand on the exclusive definition of primary prevention, especially in a traumatic situation like the one Annie faced.

TRAINING IN PREVENTIVE ROLES

The *Handbook of Clinical Psychology,* edited by Wolman (62), appeared in 1965 and addressed the subject of prevention in the profession of clinical psychology. Sanford's chapter, "The Prevention of Mental Illness" (48), reviewed the history, the so-called "public health model," and the values of a profession working toward the humanistic ends of freedom from, or resistance to, mental illness and the ideal of fulfilling human potentialities. His criterion for judging such preventive efforts is that the motives of the helper be examined as well as the effects on those who are helped.

Sanford also relates the activity of primary prevention to three levels: national or state, community, and the level of personal interaction. Examples of the first two would include education of parents in child-rearing practices and improving conditions for populations at risk for psychopathology. At the personal level, primary prevention would consist of face-to-face discussion as with a parent in regard to her child or in consultation with teachers. Here the psychologist must necessarily be sensitive to the culture and environment of those to be helped. To be most useful socially, the psychologist must enlarge his perspective beyond diagnosis and treatment.

In order to prepare clinicians properly for new roles, Sanford (48) notes that: "As we think of the future and of the new roles for the clinical psychologist that are emerging, the deficiencies of present training programs become apparent."

Direct service connotes working with clientele either in diagnostic or therapeutic endeavors. Even though most of the survey's respondents identified direct service, the majority of those respondents worked in institutional settings. Clinical psychologists are in a position to influence positively the quality of human interactions in those settings. Consulting also broadens the psychologist's scope so that a great deal of effort is expended outside the consulting room, working in communities. Not all of this effort can reasonably be assigned to prevention in the narrow sense that all of the survey group would say "I am working at prevention." However, there is ample evidence that psychologists are working outward in communities and spend a significant part of their time working at other than direct services and that consultation is an activity that connotes the preventive outlook that training has been pointed toward, as described above.

A more recent picture of the activities and roles of clinical psychologists may be found in Gottfredson & Dyer's (19) survey conducted by the APA in which they canvassed over 16,000 "health service providers." This term stands for those psychologists listed in the National Register of the APA and represents professionals who spend any of their time in direct services. The choices of practitioners included in the Register are based on qualifications and experience of clinical psychologists who offer their service to the public for a fee and who, by and large, are licensed/certified in the states where they practice. The survey requested information about two aspects of where clinicians work.

The first area asked about was the main employment setting. This would show the range of settings where the psychologist is employed. The related question was where the psychologist actually provides the "health services." This is to say that a psychologist working for a governmental agency full time might actually deliver service through a part-time private practice, for example. In this portion of the survey, over 30 different settings were distinguished, as contrasted with the eight settings identified in Garfield & Kurtz's review (11). It is recognized in the field that clinical psychology is exercising a spreading influence in society in the increased variety of settings into which psychologists assign themselves or are assigned.

A large proportion of the psychologists who responded said they spend nearly 50% of their time in direct service across settings. It is significant that the survey asks about "other applied" psychological activities, by which is meant program evaluation, organizational consultation, or training, for example. The mean reported amount of time spent in this kind of activity is 4.4 hours—over 10% of a 40-hour work week. "Other activities" account for an average of 1.3 hours per week, or an aggregate of 5.7 hours per week. It would appear that clinical psychologists are indeed torquing their talents and expertise into a greatly expanded area. The model we see is the clinician as a person uniquely trained to perceive and respond to human emotional problems and positioned to influence constructively the many organizations and populations served.

Besides receiving the usual education in theory and clinical practice, the need for placement in a variety of settings such as schools, criminal justice and welfare agencies, and for work in a consultative fashion with other direct providers of service, the psychologist "should be as much a diagnostician of bad situations as a diagnostician of individual pathology." Experience and expertise in psychotherapy, for example, develop the capacity to perceive others' needs and see that they are met in ways that prevent development of mental illness.

Sanford's call for new kinds of training for clinicians was echoed in the Chicago Conference on the Professional Preparation of Clinical Psychologists (24). Appearing in an advance summary of the conference proceedings in 1966 was a recognition of the need for a "social commitment" among psychologists and the need for innovative training of clinical psychologists. Beyond the demand for more and more capable clinicians, the Conference sought a response from participants to increase their concern for the need to prevent psychological problems and the need to provide a community psychology viewed as "the more effective utilization of human potential." This kind of need requires the clinical psychologist to fill "unaccustomed roles" without abandoning the "scientist-practitioner" model. At the same time, training programs were encouraged to assist students in learning to work in new, more varied, and nontraditional settings. Universities were encouraged to experiment and diversify accordingly. It was clear, however, that the American Psychological Association policymakers intended that clinical psychologists should use traditional techniques to drive a widening wedge into nontraditional territory.

Concerns among clinical psychologists for new roles and preventive activities continue to grow. These concerns were identified as part of the impetus for the convening of the Vail Conference on the Levels and Patterns of Professional Training in Psychology. Korman's summary (30) of the reasons for convening the conference began with the unhappiness of many clinicians "with the apparent lack of appropriateness of training provided by many doctoral programs, their low responsivity to social issues, and their uncritical allegiance to the traditional scientist-professional model."

The conference lent its support to programs that would follow a "basic service orientation." Programs were encouraged to bring training in line with the demands of settings where the psychologist will actually work. A need for a direct service to underserved populations as well as "a motivation to build programs that foster and maintain human competencies and prevent dysfunction or disruption" was recognized. In order to lower service costs and multiply their effectiveness, the trainees also need to learn how to foster competencies among helpers.

Certain prevention-related themes recur throughout the recommendations of the various task and interest groups. Advocacy for humans in need, and the ability to integrate the need-filling activities appropriately into culturally diverse communities, was amplified in several sets of recommendations. At-risk or underserved groups were referred to throughout the proceedings with the implicit or explicit logic of prevention: that response and service now will drastically reduce psychological problems later.

The most compelling arguments for priority attention to human needs according to the prevailing logic of prevention were the recommendations of the Interest Group on Clinical, Child, and Developmental Psychology. This group stressed the need for increased training with children and youth in clinical programs. As they stated:

The interest group also wishes to stress that preventative programs are ultimately less costly to society not only in economic terms but also, and more importantly, in terms of human resources. Thus, programs oriented around the preventative concept, such as improved day care programs, assistance in the development of parenting skills, and similar activities, should have a high priority in terms of the provision of technical assistance.

Again, the conference did not wish to abandon the scientist-practitioner model altogether, but rather to broaden its scope. The infiltration of one's clinical services into new settings, transfer of technology as in paraprofessional training, knowledge of social systems and how they can be changed must be integrated with the undiminished need for diagnostic and therapeutic expertise and a sound academic base of knowledge about human beings and the rigor to verify one's perceptions. The clinical psychologist should approach his tasks with a unique awareness of needs and vulnerabilities of his clients and the environments in which they live. His obligation is not only to remedy but to prevent, and the logic of prevention is to provide for children on a priority, but not necessarily an exclusive, basis.

Some of the Contexts in which Psychologists Practice and Prevent

It may be useful to attempt to describe the range of work settings where psychologists function and to attempt to identify the kind of activities they engage in that might properly be called prevention.

Garfield & Kurtz (11) sampled one-third of the members of the Division of Clinical Psychology of the APA in order to determine the type of activities that clinical psychologists engage in, in addition to demographic information. The respondents indicated that their "primary institutional affiliation" (with about 35% reporting) was in an institutional setting such as a hospital or community mental health clinic. Universities were the next most frequent primary employment setting with 30%, followed by 23% in private practice. Thus, close to 60% of the clinical psychologists answering the survey were primarily identified with service-providing affiliations. When asked to identify a secondary role, nearly a third of the group chose consultation.

Clinical psychologists are engaged in consultation and work with diverse populations. In the aggregate, they said they spent 41% of their time in direct service, as compared to slightly over 5% in "community consulting." Sundberg, Tyler & Taplin (56) review in greater depth the work psychologists are doing in communities and in consulting with organizations. Heller (22, 23) develops the contribution of social support and community change to psychotherapy.

Innovative Prevention Efforts in the Work Setting

Concern for employees with emotional problems has grown in recent years. The National Institute for Alcoholism and Alcohol Abuse (NIAAA) has sponsored innovative programs for "troubled employees" who have problems with alcohol consumption. Industry has availed itself of such programs, usually run with a title of "employee assistance programs," to combat the inroads of excessive absenteeism, loss of effectiveness and productivity.

Employee emotional stress is the target of a new role being carved out by psychologist Dan Dana in the US Office of Education, Washington, D.C. In discussions with personnel officials, he recognized a need to run an employee workshop on stress (personal communication). Dr. Dana's effort in providing these workshops has continuity with on-call availability to employees by himself and his co-workers. Personal counseling is carried out on a crisis basis with referral to agencies or private practitioners for long-term treatment when indicated. The most innovative part of the program is the opportunity for third party conflict resolution. This often involves a clash between employee and supervisor. The session has as its premise the resolution of conflicts before any official disciplinary action. In effect, the goal of the program is to improve the quality of face-to-face interactions where the usual relationship has deteriorated to intra- or interpersonal conflict.

Preventive Efforts in Crime and Delinquency

The problems posed by delinquent and criminal behavior to our society are too well known to warrant further exposition here. It is in this area that clinical psychologists have expanded their activities immensely in recent years. These practitioners have been able to confront and grapple with difficult problems as service-providers, occasionally misapplying techniques and concepts from the consulting room and more docile clientele. This movement has been amply documented in Brodsky's volume, *Psychologists in the Criminal Justice System* (6). This book traces how applied psychology has moved from a fairly timid and distant collaborator of criminal justice agencies to advocacy roles, many of which are clearly preventive in nature.

The kinds of activities Brodsky describes include direct assessment and treatment of psychological dysfunction among delinquent and criminal populations, in custody and under supervision in the community. Training of criminal justice personnel, consultation and program development are other kinds of activities that psychologists have begun to provide. The psychologist often becomes a "system-challenger," perceiving that "the system's" procedures for dealing with criminality may evoke the behavior that they are supposed to diminish. Accordingly, clinical psychologists have lent their expertise to prison riot prevention and crisis counseling of police or prison correctional officers, as examples.

Although psychologists have joined in improving correctional environments, they have recognized that prevention should begin at an earlier stage in the criminal justice process, or earlier in one's life before the label of offender has been inextricably applied.

The National Advisory Commission on Criminal Justice Standards and Goals in a volume called *Community Crime Prevention* (44) identifies the youth service bureau as "a coordinating agency to provide consulting services to youth." These small locally based agencies accept youths diverted from every phase of the criminal justice process as well as voluntary participation by juveniles referred by parents or schools. Colin Frank has participated in developing a consultant model within "outreach" programs for youth and in a youth service bureau.

Montgomery County, Maryland, administers youth service bureau programs via contractual relationships with private agencies such as the Mental Health Association of Montgomery County and the YMCA. As a clinician, Frank has been involved as a consultant to these programs. Consulting revolves around case presentations, listening skills, training, and community intervention. Activities range from participating in client interviews with the "outreach" workers to helping to establish rapport with school administrators and personnel.

The consultant, developing a trusting relationship and support system, could best be thought of as psychological "back-up" to the outreach worker. This support system involves introducing the workers to the needs of adolescents, especially in developmental crises, and the ways in which the youth worker needs to be available as a model, limit-setter, and reflective agent. The consultant shows the worker how he can provide the corrective need-filling experience to the adolescent. Often consulting takes the shape of helping the workers, frequently young and impressionable themselves, to sort out and cope with their personal reactions to the heavy emotional demands placed upon them. This, then, is an example of the multiplicative kind of effort described above in relation to training in preventive roles in the area of crime and delinquency.

NATIONAL PROPOSALS

The President's Commission on Mental Health included a Task Force on Prevention (57a). Six of the 12 members of this panel were psychologists. This panel saw the thrust toward prevention of mental illness as the fourth revolutionary change in society's approach to the mentally ill. Early changes began with Pinel's removal of chains binding the insane in the dungeons of Paris. Next came Freud's work illuminating continuities between the sane and the insane; and recently the development of comprehensive community mental health centers where help could be found for a wide range of human mental and emotional problems.

The effort toward prevention would seek both to prevent needless distress and psychological dysfunction and to build strengths and increase competence and coping skills. Primary prevention activities were seen as justified both by their efficacy and by the economic costs of relying on corrective measures as well as the insufficiency of resources to meet all the needs.

The Task Force states that while an understanding of etiology is necessary in order to develop adequate strategies for prevention, mental illnesses do not generally have the single etiology which has led to such dramatic results in medical prevention work in diseases such as tuberculosis, malaria, or typhoid fever. Usually mental illnesses are the outcome of multiple interacting factors and consequently need more complex strategies.

The degree of complexity can be inferred from the recognition that personality development, family relationships, social forces, and environmental stress (and, we must add, weaknesses and strengths related to genetic and physiological factors) are all involved in the development of emotional illness.

The panel saw its task as including: an operational definition of the term "prevention"; the review of various services and programs to determine which were successful; finding barriers which interfere with consumers' ability to obtain preventive services and the capacity of community institutions to provide these services; assessment of the need for prevention services and the manpower and research needs involved in providing services; reporting to the President's Commission on what works and in what settings, citing practical modes of preventive programs for use by states, local governments, community mental health centers, and other institutions.

Among the definitions offered were: "Most fundamentally, primary prevention is proactive in that it seeks to build adaptive strengths, coping resources, and health in people; not to reduce or contain already manifest deficit. Primary prevention is mass-oriented, including especially groups at high risk. . . ." (57a).

Concretely, the panel felt that strategies should be encouraged for prevention of psychoses, neuroses, and other social disorders, learning disabilities, child abuse, and other behavioral, emotional, and developmental deviations. It emphasized the need to establish priorities, to select infants and children at high risk, and develop strategies to promote optimal development in these target groups. The panel advocated the establishment of programs designed to prevent persistent destructive maladaptive behaviors, recognizing that judgments of behavior might endanger personal freedom, and that unwanted suffering and behavior endangering others rather than mere nonconformity are to be prevented.

Both physical and environmental factors have been found to contribute to disturbed behavior: for instance, the spirochete which can cause syphilis followed by general paresis, under and oversecretion of some endocrine glands, including thyroid and adrenals (but the panel did not discuss the role of stress and exhaustion in distorting the functioning of endocrine glands). Extreme combat stress contributing to emotional disturbances in soldiers and sudden losses of a spouse through death or divorce bringing on a depression were among the environmental factors seen as contributing to reversible conditions. Social-environmental stressors such as racism, "sexism," and "ageism" were considered to place the victims of prejudice at high risk for mental disorder.

The comment of the panel that our society is crisis-oriented and geared to helping people with here-and-now suffering, and also to repairing existing dysfunction, is relevant to the functioning of psychologists as well as the medical profession. Lack of funding, administrative structures, training oriented to prevention, and lack of adequate research in prevention all act as barriers to development of primary prevention efforts.

We can add here that difficulties in prediction of risk, aside from extreme stress which comes under the heading of crisis, make it hard to justify intruding on privacy. Making help available would reach some people who already felt the need for help but not those who were valiantly coping with the crisis but in ways that could lead to future problems.

The panel gave high priority to programs oriented to the very young. While medical care during the prenatal, perinatal, infant, and childhood periods and adequate, individually prescribed nutrition are obvious needs, the psychological needs cannot always be easily assessed with our present knowledge and tools. Correlations between infant intelligence tests and tests at an older age are modest indeed, and variability in scores is not completely understood although longitudinal studies have thrown some light on patterns of change in individual children (38, 55). Here, clinical psychologists adequately trained in child development could make contributions which would lead to wiser perspectives on prediction and prevention. Macfarlane et al's (36) study of changes in behavior problems from 21 months to 14 years points to the child's tendency to outgrow certain expressions of tension or anxiety, but does it throw light on the question of whether the anxiety load in general changes? There is much to learn about "outgrowing" as well as the capacity of the child to mobilize new coping resources as new situations are met and new skills are acquired and new supports experienced (34, 35).

We must note the vague way in which the terms "competence" and "coping" are often used, without clear differentiation between them or specification of behaviors to be observed in each category. Competence is generally considered to include culturally accepted and required skills, while coping refers to the capacity to deal with new challenges and to manage problem situations in ways which support, comfort, and decrease tension at least to a level which supports good functioning. While competence is likely to refer to objective behavior responses to external situations, both social and material (e.g. climbing a jungle-gym), coping challenges involve an interaction of the child's individual pattern of vulnerabilities and the external situation.

The pattern of combining a mass program with individualized assessment and help is a necessary part of the current thrust toward mainstreaming handicapped children. A couple of emotionally disturbed, blind, or deaf children in a group of children with the usual range of learning and social problems can present difficulties literally overwhelming to the teacher with good training and educational techniques but no background in special education. The result is that the handicapped children may preoccupy her attention while other children are neglected.

The US Administration for Children, Youth, and Families (formerly Office of Child Development) addresses this problem in the Head Start program by looking at the diagnostic and assessment process at the local level. The purpose is to improve training and technical assistance for assessment and planning of services for handicapped children.

Interviewers used a questionnaire developed to complete case studies of a sample of 106 handicapped children in 35 centers. These interviewers were specially trained interdisciplinary consultants from psychology, psychiatry, religion, social work, speech and hearing, pediatrics, physical and occupational therapy, nursing, nutrition, education, law, architecture, and administration. We can hope that such collaboration will help to break down the barriers that often isolate professional groups and thereby limit the potentialities of prevention efforts.

The mandate is to provide a functional assessment describing a child's functioning and areas of need—what a child can do and what areas need to be improved, in addition to a diagnosis of the category of handicapping conditions in which the child was placed. Recommendations for parents and teachers' handling of the child are also to be provided.

Developmental Review for All Children

While most prevention programs are geared to "target" groups of disadvantaged, deprived, poor, handicapped, or "at-risk" groups of infants and children, there is an emerging trend toward evaluation of the developmental needs of all children. A major proposal with this orientation is Developmental Review in the Early and Periodic Screening, Diagnosis, and Treatment Program (25). The final report of this proposal, prepared by Dorothy Huntington, integrates working papers by Allan G. Barclay, Frances D. Horowitz, Wendell Rivers, and Jane R. Mercer, psychologists, and Thomas Coleman, M. D. and Anne-Marie Foltz, M.P.H., M. Phil., along with the contributions of discussions of the February 1977 Conference on Developmental Screening and Assessment assembled by the American Association of Psychiatric Services for Children.

The report proposes a major shift in emphasis in the Early and Periodic Screening, Diagnosis, and Treatment Program (EPSDT) which became a mandated service under the Medicaid program through an amendment in 1967 to the Social Security Act, Title XIX, Section 1905(a)(4)(B). It became effective July 1, 1969, and required early and periodic screening and diagnosis of individuals eligible for Medicaid or under the age of 21 to ascertain their physical and mental defects and such health care, treatment, and other measures to correct or ameliorate defects and chronic conditions discovered.

The new emphasis is on competence—how well a child has met, and now meets, expectations of society for an individual of his/her age and sex group.

> The legislation authorizing EPSDT makes it national policy that the development of our children . . . be safeguarded so as to insure that each child reaches maturity functioning at a maximum level of development. . . . We must develop a system of health care that treats the person rather than the disease or dysfunction. . . . Any review must be oriented to the discovery of developmental strengths as well as weaknesses, not to the exclusive search to rule in or rule out pathology.

The report further emphasized that every attempt must be made to engage and utilize parents voluntarily in the entire process of continuity of care and developmental review.

> . . . Developmental review is seen as the first step in engaging children and parents in an ongoing concern with their health and well-being. We see this as a way of promoting strengths . . . of strengthening parent-child ties, and of reducing the anxiety so prevalent in our society today regarding issues in parenting and child rearing.

Similarly, emphasis was placed on the recognition and respect for ethnic, cultural, social, and linguistic differences that exist in a pluralistic nation such as the United States.

Limits to intrusion into personal and family life were implied in the limitation of the mass government-financed screening program to:

1. those measures of organic functioning and basic adaptive coping skills which enjoy a high degree of consensus within the health professions and affected communities, and

2. those behavioral factors especially associated with learning, language and speech development, motor skills and perceptual abilities.

Specific assessment of emotional and behavioral adjustment and parent/child interactions and should be left to parental initiative and sensitive clinical observation.

The report included many recommendations oriented to implementation of the program, needed safeguards, and funding of the program beyond the scope of this review. Our purpose here is to emphasize the ground-breaking nature of the proposal with its potential for systematically reversing the symptom-oriented approach to prevention and initiating instead a comprehensive longitudinal developmental assessment of the strengths and needs of the child. The intent is to outmode the pejorative and often destructive effects of diagnostic labeling, and to orient the supporting community to the positive potentialities of each child.

Interdisciplinary Conferences Initiated by a Psychologist

We want to call attention to Albee & Joffe's volume (2) presenting papers on one of the most sophisticated, deeply probing, and fruitful conferences on prevention; the papers draw from psychoanalytic, social science, educational, as well as medical and psychological professions. The scope of the conference can be illustrated by the range of topics from genetic, prenatal, and perinatal factors in primary prevention to a stimulating discussion by E. T. Vance (58) on the relation of the powerlessness often accompanying low status to failure of development of an active capacity to cope with stress. Again, Mednick & Witkin-Lanoil's report (37) on intervention techniques in children at high risk for schizophrenia deals with problems at the opposite end of the scale from those approached in T. Gordon's parent effectiveness training program (17). Reports on two subsequent conferences are forthcoming.

LOCAL PREVENTION PROGRAMS

Effective prevention efforts depend on a detailed understanding of interferences with adequate cognitive and social development and an equally detailed understanding of what families do for their well-developing children. Burton White focused on the latter and uses his findings in parent-education activities of several kinds (61). Langlois & Sawin at the University of Texas (31) are engaged in a cross-cultural comparison of early parent-infant interaction; they plan to explore relationships between early interaction patterns as well as later interactional patterns and later behavioral characteristics in the child.

On the basis of data indicating that large numbers of infants do not receive adequate health care and that this failure may be due in part to parents' unawareness of the need for early care—unawareness of available medical services, and inability to use the services—a companion project is being conducted. This project provides parents with "personal advisors" to help them utilize the health care system available and to conduct small discussion groups dealing with basic health care information for infants.

In addition, these psychologists are joining a collaborative research effort by faculty from the departments of anthropology, social work, and nutrition at the University of Texas to study problems of nutrition, physical growth, and mental development in a multiethnic sample of infants of teenage mothers. It is important to note at the same time that impressive development of children in many infant-parent education programs has been reported (16, 32). However, we do not know enough about healthy side benefits that may accrue in even a limited program.

Multiple Goals for Prevention Programs

A psychologist actively dealing with several aspects of prevention is J. E. Rolf at the University of Vermont; he has written on identification of at-risk preschool children, guidelines for prevention, the incidence of behavior disorders in the same group, etiological research on schizophrenia and the rationale for prevention, and epidemiology of, and intervention for, at-risk children. We can distinguish between clinical psychologists who are involved in prevention on a part-time basis along with teaching, diagnosis, treatment, and other activities, versus clinical psychologists whose chief focus of interest is precisely prevention in all of its aspects.

Rolf, with his collaborator, Hasazi (47), has described the Vermont Child Development Project first as an example of applied research investigating the etiology of behavior disorders in early childhood, and second, testing several early intervention procedures oriented toward primary prevention of psychopathology.

Their summary of sources and indicators of risk for young children includes five categories: 1. Presence of physical or mental disability; 2. demonstration of developmental lag; 3. current problems in social behavior; 4. "pathogenic potential" in family background; 5. pathogenic factors in physical environment (including greater exposure to physical injury, malnutrition, and/or severe illness; living within severely impoverished socioeconomic strata; acculturation within deviant subcultural neighborhoods and/or schools). As with the Langlois & Sawin studies (31), the project attempts to maximize the use of data by joining strategies for two different types of studies: epidemiological surveys in natural settings, and developmental psychology studies of group differences among preschool-aged children in natural and laboratory settings. The project also has tried to determine the base rates of behavior disorders in the preschool-aged population of the general community for comparison with the target children at varying degrees of risk. [This current baseline picture of behavior problems should be compared with those in a representative sample of children in the early '30s studied in Macfarlane's project (36; see also 34, 41).]

Prospective studies of target children with known disorders or inferred vulnerabilities were considered the best strategy for obtaining information on the development and duration of behavior pathology—information needed in order to assess the relevance of childhood antecedents to adult psychopathology. Incidentally, we need to remember Tarjan's report (57) that about two-thirds of individuals diagnosed as retarded during the developmental period lost this label during late adolescence or early adulthood.

Rolf noted that long-term prospective studies cannot be successfully completed unless one chooses a geographical area having a sufficiently representative but nonmobile population. However, we also have to note that this choice precludes the study of children in a mobile population—who are exposed to repeated separations from familiar friends, teachers, school settings, and subculture activities and mores—separations often contributing to stress for the children.

Along with the study of behavior disorders, Rolf set additional goals: to collect data on the children's success in attaining age-appropriate competence skills; to describe the development of certain target groups of vulnerable children, including those with psychotic and neurotic parents, those from severely deprived backgrounds, those with physical, mental, or temperamental handicaps as well as those with recognized serious behavior disorders; to create a system for identifying at-risk preschool children for early intervention; to develop effective and intensive therapeutic day-care intervention techniques in treating behavior disorders; and to quantify the effects of a preschool child's experience in home or day-care settings as they relate to his adaptation to public schools.

Rates of acquisition of developmental skills and rates of abandonment of behavior problems are to be compared as between subjects receiving intervention and no-treatment controls drawn from the large-scale surveys. As an example, the progress over 2 years from the age of 3 to 5 years in a therapeutic day-care center illustrates what could be accomplished with a child of emotionally disturbed parents and a father in prison. The child had almost no language at entrance and self-care and toileting skills were nonexistent. A year and a half after entrance into the day-care center, he "is performing at or close to his age level in these areas." However, speech, "prosocial" behavior, and behavior problems were highly variable, in relation to serious episodic family crises and attendance problems.

The resourcefulness of this project goes beyond the scope of this chapter to report in detail. But one question has to be raised. Rolf reports the small success in attracting parents to "formal education or therapeutic activities." Many parents are seriously disturbed themselves, and it was felt that there was no easy way to circumvent the problems that emerged.

Ways of Involving Shy and Suspicious Mothers

It happens coincidentally that Gardner and Lois Murphy were consultants to a parent-child center in Barton, Vermont, in a very deprived area. We had an opportunity to share in the social "coffees" to which parents were brought when they lacked transportation or were shy and hesitant. We saw the way in which the informal friendly atmosphere thawed out the distrustful parents. One worker, asked how she involved a particularly suspicious mother, said, "I went to visit her every week for eight months like a neighbor until she finally responded." There is no easy way, but still there are ways. Similar instances occurred in Topeka when a social worker expected shy, isolated parents in a deprived area to come to the office. "It would be a growth experience," she maintained, while getting no cooperation at all. In this case, a flexible and insightful director went to the home of the most resistant parents, stayed for a friendly visit, and after more of these visits during which the child was discussed in an appreciative, nonthreatening way, was able to move toward discussion of the child's problems and needs.

The old principle that learning proceeds fastest when the learner is ready for it and, we can add, wants it, applies not only to elementary school but to preventive work with parents. No one wants to be pushed.

Effective Programs With High-Risk Children

An outstanding program carried on by Heber (21) in Milwaukee is described in the Task Force report. This 10-year longitudinal program focused on high-risk children of mothers with IQs of 75 or less, and started right after the infant's birth. The children spent each weekday for the first 5 years of life at a day-care center, while a home teacher taught mothers how to care for their children and also taught them other everyday skills they needed to acquire.

The high-risk children at age 7 had a mean IQ of 121 vs 87 for controls—a result which reminds us of the dramatic and exciting results in the Skeels & Skodak ventures (54; see also 54a). While programs like this are expensive in the short run, in the long run they could save far more than their cost because of the expense of even poor institutions.

The effectiveness of involving mothers as well as children has been demonstrated in other studies as well; for example, the Houston program with bilingual families of Mexican background (26). This model for prevention of educational retardation is an example of thoughtful planning geared to a special subculture, the Mexican-American families, with the lowest income level, fewest years of schooling, and the most children under age 5 in the city. Educational progress was hampered by the fact that many families spoke only Spanish at home and that school teachers were inclined to give their attention to the Anglo children with adequate command of English. In addition, the Mexican-American children were brought up to be compliant and obedient, and were not oriented toward the competitive atmosphere in school. Parents did not regard their responsibilities as including education of the infant and young child, so the children arrived at school with little or no background for school learning.

Attention to language, cultural, and other factors unique to this Mexican-American group led to this program for parent education and involvement in the stimulation of the children—different from what it might have been if the program had been planned for poor white families. Since the Mexican-Americans are unusually family-centered and are bilingual, the focus was on work with the mothers, and the fathers to the extent that they could become involved. The assumption was that if the parents could be stimulated to become teachers of their children and were provided with resources to use in working with their children, their educational interest and skills would continue through the child's growing years and would support the children's experience in school.

Working successively with six cohorts of families, the program was revised as a result of experience. Certainly the thoughtfulness with which the values, needs, family life, child-rearing patterns, and relation to the community were explored before formulating the program is a model for any prevention project. The mothers were trained at home when the infants were 12 to 24 months old, and the children were in a nursery from 24 to 36 months of age. Careful formulation of goals for the development of the child in social, emotional, and cognitive areas also distinguished the program from narrowly oriented cognitive stimulation programs. Both the attitudes of the mothers toward the program and the influence of the program on the mothers were seen to be positive in the evaluation of results. Mothers became more affectionate, used affection in a more discriminating way, gave appropriate reinforcement, and communicated more verbally with the children. The children enjoyed the nursery, and over time fewer were referred for behavior problems.

Training local people as paraprofessionals to teach the mothers and work with the children kept the budget within practical limits. This has the advantage of reducing the social distance between trainers and the mothers and children—a matter often overlooked in prevention programs initiated by professional workers in the helping professions, ironically. Paraprofessionals were also used in I. J. Gordon's (16) parent-infant education program which demonstrated positive long-term effects.

Prevention of Prolonged Disturbance in Children of Divorce

One of the most carefully thought-through prevention programs we have seen is the program for preventive interventions with children of divorce carried on by Wallerstein & Kelly (59) at the Community Mental Health Center of Marin County, California. In 1970, just before the establishment of the program, the number of people applying for divorce far exceeded those applying for a marriage license, and 11.6% of the families with children were headed by a single parent. Mindful of the nationwide increase in divorce and the lack of systematic planning for help to the children not recognized as at-risk, along with the concerns of teachers, school counselors, ministers, and pediatricians about these children, Wallerstein and Kelly came to see children of divorce as a target group needing help.

Their approach was guided by the belief that normal emotional development during childhood required continuity in a relationship with two emotionally available parents. They regarded the prevention of an acute rupture in a growth-promoting parent-child relationship as the single most useful preventive measure. So they combined a therapeutic approach to the children with helping the parents to sustain their parental roles during and after the family disruption.

An average of 14.2 hours was spent with each family in the project—each parent and each child seen separately by the same clinician three to six times. In addition, one staff member visited the schools to obtain independent information directly from the child's teachers.

The project provided for longitudinal observations in further consultation within a year of the initial six-week intervention, in order to explore psychological changes in the context of changes in the family structure and relationships. A second and third intervention took place 1 year from the initial one, and 4 to 5 years after separation. Fifty-eight out of the 60 families in the initial counseling returned for both of these follow-up sessions.

An overall assessment was made of each parent in terms of the impact of the divorce. This assessment of each parent along with a comparable assessment of the child or children was the basis for planning agendas and priorities in the counseling process. Children's understanding and affective responses were explored and the extent to which the anger or depression was "burdening the developmental processes."

The importance of the project lies in its wise and flexible adaptation of psychoanalytic understanding and a range of skills to a time-limited and practical prevention project with a group of at-risk families. The description of the process of working with the children and parents and the outcomes of the prevention could inspire prevention programs with other at-risk groups where a combined group and individualized form of help is needed.

We are emphasizing the productiveness of this integration and flexibility because of the rigidity in certain quarters in adhering to a mass-only approach under the mandate for prevention. Help to school children is a case in point. While some threats such as those involved in the transition from elementary school to junior high can be diminished by group orientation to junior high school in the last weeks of sixth grade, other kinds of stress require individual help; for instance, the child who is very sensitive to noise and movement in the classroom and, by contrast, the energetic child who cannot sit still for long periods.

UNDERSTANDINGS BASIC TO PREVENTION PLANNING

Since Kessler & Albee (27a) have dealt quite thoroughly—if rather irritably —with the endless arguments between narrow organicists and narrow psychogenecists, we do not need to go into this debate in detail. Certainly in the 1940s Gardner Murphy's biosocial approach to the development of personality—an integration of contributions from the physiological, social, and psychological domains of research and theory—was both a summation and a forecast of the need for an interdisciplinary study of both normal and disturbed or deviant personality (39). By now the leaders in schizophrenia research, such as Shakow (49–52) with his more than half-century of work in the field, and Garmezy (12, 14) with many years of work on vulnerability to schizophrenia, have illuminated the interaction of congenital or neurological and social—especially familial—factors.

The concepts of predisposition and vulnerability are useful for understanding both the range of deviations regarded as abnormal and also the variations of behavior in the normal range. The Topeka study of vulnerability, coping, and growth (43) did not include neurological or neuropsychological examinations, which are made in the best of the new studies of infants and at-risk children. But it did outline a range of aspects of vulnerability which were observed to interact with each other to create difficulties for some of the children, contributing to frustrations and anxiety with related adaptational problems and difficulties in coping with them. The outcomes of the interactions of vulnerabilities with each other, with environmental stresses and supports, and with the child's own coping resources and defenses (42) depended on variations in the child's strengths at different times. Prevention efforts can gain from studies of coping patterns developed by normal children in dealing with their vulnerabilities.

It is not possible for us to review the entire range of sources of vulnerability in detail, but we can mention various temperamental characteristics, with low thresholds for irritability and anxiety (7, 20); deviant arousal patterns; autonomic lability; tendency to frequent disturbances of vegetative functioning; somatic reactions to stress; susceptibility to infections; allergies; tendency to low thresholds for loss of perceptual cognitive integration under stress as contrasted with loss of motor coordination under stress, or deterioration of speech under stress; tendency to loss of security with loss of physical contact with the supporting adult; low "sending power," limited vocal, mimetic, affective, and other expressive capacities to evoke response and help.

Along with specific areas of vulnerability, we saw effects of imbalance such as motor response, tempo more rapid than perceptual-cognitive orientation; this contributes to adaptational problems. Similarly, high perceptual intake more complex and rapid than can be integrated into action contributes to difficulty in the integration of responses to the environment. We see infants with high vocal-social responsiveness who evoke more stimulation from the environment than they can integrate, and who then burst into tears in the midst of apparent enjoyable play. Other imbalances discussed in the literature and observed by us include: drives stronger than control capacities resulting in impulsiveness; aggressive drives stronger than capacity for love, resulting in a failure to modulate aggression.

Prevention programs need to encourage alertness to everyday vulnerabilities that expose children to embarrassment, ridicule, failure in activities their peers succeed in. Depending on their goals and their energy or drive, children either become discouraged and withdrawn or make a determined effort to compensate for their deficiency. Some reactions can plant seeds of neurotic self-depreciation, self-distrust, or angry irritability and defensiveness. Some do find ways of cautiously selecting areas of potential success and adaptively avoiding what they are not well equipped to master.

Difficult Babies Can Be Too Much for Mothers

We have been concerned with patterns of characteristics of the child as an organism, interacting with demands, pressures, feelings of peers and family and others in the environment.

Another major source of vulnerability includes acquired predispositions to anxiety developed during the birth process (20) or from disturbing handling in infancy during the early period of perceptual-cognitive integration. Since traumatic birth experiences can result from such conditions as a large infant with a mother who has a small pelvis, or unusual positions of the

baby's body in delivery, we can hardly speak of the resulting vulnerabil
as purely environmentally generated. Low energy reserves, tendency to
fatigue easily, and other obscure characteristics of easily disturbed babies,
some of which have been described by Chess and her associates (7), can
make the care of the baby problematic enough so that the most experienced
mother is hard put to help the baby maintain an equilibrium. Differences
in responsiveness, vocal and affective expressiveness also influence the cues
the mother is given, and where cues are vague or nonexistent, the environment cannot always respond appropriately. It is unrealistic under such
circumstances to blame the environment as having the responsibility for
developmental problems.

It is here that clinical psychologists working with programs of infant
stimulation, prevention of retardation, or emotional disturbance can be
helpful by recognizing the contribution of the infant's unique characteristics
to the interaction with the environment, with the mother, and others in
contact with the baby.

Toward Understanding Schizophrenia: A Prerequisite for Prevention

It is intriguing to note that despite the relatively low incidence of schizophrenia, this disorder has attracted some of the best minds, with commit-
ments to the longest-term research, and with the broadest interdisciplinary
thinking in all prevention work. Since extensive reviews with comprehensive bibliographies are available, this discussion is being limited to some of
the trends in etiological studies and a few examples of prevention efforts.
The NIMH *Schizophrenia Bulletins* beginning September 1969, especially
Garmezy's reports in the Spring and Summer 1974 issues, are a major
resource.

Shakow, after more than 50 years of research, reflection, and creativity
in theory development, is a towering figure in the field. Several of his papers
are available in *Psychological Issues* (52) and a new monograph is forthcoming. Albee & Joffe's volume, *Primary Prevention of Psychopathology* (2),
contains four important reports, one by each of these investigators: McNeil
& Kaij, Erlenmeyer-Kimling, Mednick & Witkin-Lanoil, and Anthony.

There is more agreement in delineation of cognitive problems—variously
specified as association drift, attentional difficulties, set, cognitive slippage
—than there is in reports of etiological factors in the environment and
response to it. Deviant autonomic nervous system functioning, reaction-
time, EEG records, and other aspects of neuropsychological and physiological functioning as well as biochemical deficiencies are explored with varying
results in different samples. The hope is that correction of one of the latter
might improve the functioning of the patient.

While it is quite general to study a group of variables in a sample of subjects, we miss any effort to relate these functions and deficits in terms of simultaneous or immediate antecedent-consequent observations. What is the *process* in which the deviant biochemical, neurological, cognitive, social, etc variables contribute to schizophrenia? Garmezy (12) and his colleagues emphasize the high-risk potential of externalizing (antisocial) children as opposed to internalizing (anxious, somatizing) children; the former show attentional defects, marked signs of peer rejection, and lack of self-control. Reviewing 20 programs of studies of children at-risk for mental disorders, he lists a wide variety of variables—psychological, psychophysiological, biochemical. Against their broad background of reflection and experimentation with a multitude of variables important for discriminating vulnerable and invulnerable children, they have focused on competence criteria such as delay of gratification, reflection-impulsivity, foresight and planning, peer acceptance, attention and information-processing mechanisms, and vigilance. Ingenious experimental procedures confirmed differences between vulnerable and invulnerable children in contrast to the absence of difference between children of different socioeconomic groups. Sources of these deficits in vulnerable children obviously range from neurological and biochemical to learning in the broadest sense (including identification with a parent with such deficits).

In the course of his studies of children at-risk for schizophrenia—for instance, having one or both parents schizophrenic—Garmezy (12) has used the concept of vulnerability. He has also been interested in children who, though at-risk because of similar factors, appear to be invulnerable to schizophrenia. More than this, he generalizes to "invulnerable children" (13). Here we have to raise a question. In our Topeka studies, no child was totally without affective, cognitive, somatic, or other reactivity to stress. With some children, marked autonomic nervous system reactions betrayed effects of stress; with others, tensing of muscles or loss of their normal levels of motor coordination; with others, social or cognitive functioning deteriorated; with others, emotional upsets occurred without other changes. In some instances where reactivity to stress is not obvious on the surface, children may be regarded as more tough, more invulnerable that they actually are, and thus be exposed to pressures which become overwhelming. Moreover, a child's defenses which mask reactions to stress involve a high cost which limits the child's development in some areas. Thus, a child we observed to be apparently unbothered by his mother's blatant irrationality was found by teachers to be distant and distrustful of adults. Psychologists thus need to be aware of the total range of zones of vulnerability, the relation of these to different environmental pressures and the individual preventive, often supportive measures which could forestall maladaptive coping efforts. Moreover, we miss any consideration of Melanie Klein's (29) theory of the paranoid position at about four months, which Murphy hypothesizes could result from biochemical flooding of the infant's brain at the early period when perceptual differentiation and integration processes are being structured. Such flooding could occur in states of affective and autonomic upheaval in reaction to prolonged stress at a stage when reactivity is intense. Interference with differentiation and integration could reinforce anxiety which may have contributed to vulnerability to stress. Following Greenacre (20), a predisposition to anxiety may be one effect of birth difficulties. In order to test such hypotheses, we need very close observation of the at-risk infant from pregnancy through the first year; observations should include both everyday experiences and potentially traumatic events such as inoculation shots. We have seen extreme reactions lasting over hours and days to unsoothed inoculations. Other painful events and reactions to them should be studied as well, obviously in the home, the doctor's office, or clinic where the baby is treated.

Such research is even more time-consuming than longitudinal programs already under way. But if carried out on even a small group of high-risk infants (with two schizophrenic parents), the close observation of development of attention, differentiation, reactions to stress, etc might fill in a gap in current findings or help to explain some of the contradictions in results of investigations up to now.

Moreover, since problems in attention set and the like are generally found in both child and adult schizophrenia, it should be apparent that study of the development of these functions from birth, both in high-risk infants and in normal babies, is an important prerequisite for well-conceived preventive efforts.

Mednick's (37) prevention project in Mauritius is challenging in the simplicity of the intervention and the complexity of the processes potentially involved in change. Fifty-four 3-year-old children were selected on the basis of psychophysiological screening showing extremely fast ANS recovery (found in studies of schizophrenics); 32 with average speed of recovery and 14 nonresponders were also included in the experimental group, which was given a nursery school experience with warm and enthusiastic young nursery school teachers. One hundred control children matched on the skin conductance tests were identified and left undisturbed in their community.

The experimental group were described by their mothers as hiding under a table or in a closet at home; a large number of them were terribly frightened and had to be held most of the time when they first entered nursery school; they had also cried more during testing and showed more anxiety. After a time in nursery school, most of the children showed "vast" changes—playing spontaneously, greeting strangers with lively interest and curiosity. Parents describe them as having become "normal, happy children at home." Positive effects are thought to be related to any one or a combination of the following factors: the good protein-rich nursery school diet; placement in the group of other frightened children; the quality of handling by warm teachers; the special atmosphere created by the Danish experts who run the schools; separation from their home environment for part of the day; selection for this special experience. Observation of the community controls and follow-up in schools are planned.

Anthony's (3) prevention project, in common with Wallerstein & Kelly's (59) prevention work with children of divorce, has the combination of classical psychotherapy with cathartic interventions during the acute phases of parents' illness, with the addition of compensatory and corrective interventions aimed respectively at building up the child's ego resources, self-confidence, and differentiation of self, objects, and fact from fantasy. The classical intervention procedures generated greater change than did the other interventions. Anthony's analytic thinking provides much deeper insight into the children's functioning than we found in other studies.

What Strengths Should Prevention Efforts Support?

An extended inventory of vulnerabilities, innate and acquired, can be found in Murphy & Moriarty (43). But we also have to look at the balancing strengths of the individual, child or adult. Here we find wide differences in flexibility and readiness to respond to alternatives, to seek substitutes; to forgive and forget when frustrated in a personal interaction; in resilience and spontaneous recovery after hurts or illness; in the capacity to integrate healthy defense mechanisms with active coping efforts and the capactiy to think up a range of solutions for problems; determination and persistence along with a commitment to solve the problem; to structure or restructure the environment in useful ways; ability to protest unwanted stimulation, food, or activity constructively; to selectively respond to the environment in terms of what contributes to one's own well-being. Willingness to seek or accept help when one's resources are insufficient was also seen as an aspect of healthy coping in the Topeka children.

The outcome of interactions between vulnerabilities and the environment, then, will not depend solely on how benign the efforts of others in behalf of the beleaguered child or adult may be, but on how the vulnerable person uses the environment along with his or her own resources. And here it behooves the clinical psychologist who wishes to prevent escalation of problems to be perceptively aware, in interdisciplinary terms, if you like, of the complex patterns of plus and minus features on both sides, and ways of assisting efforts toward a better balance.

Experimental Studies Relevant to Prevention of Aggression

Lewin, Lippitt & White's pioneer study (33) of the effects on boys' behavior of different experimentally created social climates suggests a model for prevention of aggression. Adult leaders of boys were programmed to treat the boys autocratically in one part of the experiment and democratically in another part. The same boys who developed hostility and behaved aggressively under the autocratic treatment were cooperative and constructive and developed high morale with the democratic handling.

Sherif and his collaborators (53) carried out another classical, imaginative study of effects of group orientations at a boys' camp. Highly competitive games and contests replaced the original cooperativeness, with mounting hostility between two groups at the camp. Cooperativeness was restored between them when they engaged in competition with a different camp. But this hostility displaced onto an outside group evaporated when the two groups cooperated in a joint effort to pull a broken down food truck into camp; following this, the two groups spontaneously cooperated in preparing the food.

Less systematic because it was a serendipitous finding, Murphy (40), comparing data from her study of sympathy in preschool children with the results of Jersild and Markey's study of conflicts in the same group, found differences in both sympathy and conflicts (involving aggressive behavior) in two groups differently organized and in different ecological settings. One group of 2-year-olds within a 10-month age range played on a relatively small roof-top with limited equipment. The children, with similar wants, had to compete for use of the few tricycles, wagons, and slides available. The other group included children from 2 to 6 years of age on a much larger outdoor playground with more room for free movement. The first group fought more and showed little sympathy, while sympathetic behavior in the second group was impressive. The differences between these situations, as well as between the experimental groups described above, can be seen in terms of differences in the systems in which the children's behavior was being studied—the system of interpersonal relationships, the relation of these to the ecological setting as well as to the ideology, personalities, needs, and training of the adults involved.

Some clinical psychologists are making use of the systems approach which recognizes the need for dealing with complex interactions of multiple variables instead of looking for assumed "causes" in single variable terms as if asocial behavior were as easy to prevent as measles. The full development of systems approaches will come about when all relevant social, ecological, biological, as well as psychological findings are assimilated into integrated hypotheses and strategies for prevention.

Ecology and Behavior

A part of current ecological awareness is Barker's (4) study of effects on behavior of different environments—perhaps stemming indirectly from the concept of the therapeutic milieu. At Stanford University, a group of psychologists (Moos, Trickett, Insel) developed measures of environments in schools, work units, hospital wards, military companies, and have found relationships between the characteristics of the human environment and the behavior of people in these different settings. This work on measuring environments was continued in the correctional setting as detailed by Wenk & Frank (60). A revised instrument, the C.I.E.S., is now a standarized test to measure and help prevent potentially corrosive effects of prisons.

Other examples can be studied easily: differences between nurseries for the newborn—where much crying is generally heard—and rooming-in wards where mothers are close to their babies and crying occurs seldom and is quickly soothed; school rooms with tired, cold, authoritarian teachers in contrast to rooms where children are warmed and relaxed by caring, understanding teachers who work with them in a friendly democratic way. Qualities of support and interested involvement on the part of the adults evoke comfort and better integration, control, and both social and cognitive development in the children. This contrast was illustrated for us years ago when tense, hostile girls seen at a state training school directed by a hardbitten, punitive supervisor changed to constructive, friendly girls when a new warm-hearted supervisor turned the system around, providing appropriate activities instead of repression and rigid control.

Community Activity Centers as Prevention

Joan Erikson's book, *Activity, Recovery, and Growth*, (10) reports on a community activity program for patients at the Austen Riggs Center oriented toward recovery and rehabilitation; it contains insights and program elements equally applicable to prevention of social and personal maladjustment. In fact, Part III of this book advances a community program which could offer such activities as those developed at Riggs to any community: "A Community Activities Center could enhance community life and provide those nutritive elements which encourage optimal individual growth through personal participation and communal involvement."

She envisions a community center open to all ages with areas for a wide range of activities in which members of a community could engage spontaneously, without pressure, for the joy and companionship it would bring. Extraordinarily imaginative and rich in suggestions for ways in which a center could be developed with a small budget—with community members helping to rehabilitate an old barn, factory, or group of houses—the center reminded us of the way the North Topeka Day Care Center came into being. With minimal financing, the gift of one little house from a local realtor, help from parents who cleaned and painted inside and outside, from the Fire Department that removed debris from the yard, from interested community members who brought toys and equipment, the development of the center brought a level of morale, enthusiasm, and friendliness which the isolated poverty area had not experienced before.

We were also reminded of the "settlement houses" in New York and Chicago, with beginnings at Hull House where activity areas for crafts, cooking, sewing, woodwork, games, and gymnastics brought children and adults together. Language learning, music lessons, art classes provided opportunities for people who could not pay the usual fees for instruction but who longed to learn.

The difference between Joan Erikson's dream and the centers we have described is that her community activity center would be planned not just for the poor and deprived in lower economic groups, but for community members who, in our isolating urban and even suburban areas, have no access to creative activity opportunities and no setting in which to develop relationships with other people. The relevance to prevention and to the work of clinical psychologists is that a center for activities can promote growth, provide enrichment which strengthens the sense of self, of capacity to do and to make good things, and to find oneself in empathic relationships. If such a center were developed in conjunction with a community mental health center, or if a community activities center included a mental health unit, the psychologists could find support for their own efforts to stimulate new explorations of the potentialities of persons they undertook to help. Primary prevention, if we want to think of the activity center in that way, could go hand in hand with treatment where individual help was needed, just as it happened at Riggs.

Hazards, Blinders, and Reflections

Research problems, paradoxically, are in part a result of certain rigid habits in statistical thinking. As a result of studies of samples of children given intelligence tests over a series of years, it was concluded that since the average IQ of the group remained relatively stable, the IQ was stable for individual children and represented a measure of inherited intelligence. It was not until more clinically minded studies of groups of children were carried on by Macfarlane and her staff (35, 36), by Nancy Bayley (5) in the same Berkeley research center, and by the coping study group in Topeka that a more sophisticated picture of mental development emerged. Macfarlane (34) found that 32 percent of her sample of 150 children changed 20 or more points in IQ over 12 years. A. E. Moriarty (38) in the Topeka group found that only about 25% of the children she tested over 8 years had IQs within 10 points; while some children persistently accelerated, some others declined. And Bayley found that correlations from the youngest years to older levels were small indeed.

The internationally distinguished statistician, Radakrishna Rao (46), commented in a major conference that American statisticians often lost important information by dealing only with averages in heterogeneous groups. Averages, he pointed out, often masked contrasting trends in subgroups. In the field of intelligence testing, the error of concluding stability of IQ could have been avoided 50 years ago if statisticians had looked carefully at subgroups of children whose IQs changed in opposite directions.

Antilabelers vs Diagnosticians

The controversy between the antilabelers and those who feel diagnostic categories are indispensable is fed in part by differences in their experiences. Some clinical psychologists, social workers, and teachers have seen destructive effects and self-fulfilling prophecy consequences from labels like "retarded." They have also been impressed by their own observations of change and research data on change. In therapy, we have seen a child diagnosed as "borderline psychotic" showing no evidence deserving such a label after a few sessions. She had suffered unbearably stressful pressures from a rigid, ranting grandmother and a very seductive father. In a benign atmosphere, she was a normal, but very sensitive, child.

In other words, the antilabelers are not dreamers nor wishful thinkers; their points of view are shaped by their experiences, just as clinicians who have seen dramatic recovery with the use of pharmaceutical therapy selectively prescribed for accurately labeled disorders are basing their confidence in labels on their own data.

Experienced teachers and therapists and developmental psychologists have seen, in both natural situations and in research contexts, the capacity for change, the transitory problems, the "outgrowing" effect, the situational variations in children labeled as withdrawn, resistant, insecure, hostile, and so on. In short, they see children reacting to situations as the children experience them and responding flexibly to change.

Moreover, they observe the selective as opposed to wholesale identification processes in some children who say of an alcoholic, sick, or irrational parent, "I am not going to be like that." Some children internalize positive aspects of their parents' behavior while rejecting painful or socially undesirable or unpleasant aspects.

The concept of competence—as judged by intelligence tests, grades in school, and other judgments of social and cognitive skills—does not ordinarily take into account what Piaget & Inhelder (45) discuss as "the process of equilibrium . . . of self-regulation, that is, a series of active compensations on the part of the subject in response to external disturbances . . ." We see this process of restoring and maintenance of equilibrium as a basic aspect of coping which goes beyond culturally recognized and demanded cognitive and social skills. The capacity to distance oneself, protest, or in other ways terminate imminent threats of overstimulation, or even simply disliked sensory or other body experiences is an example often misunderstood by the adult judging the child's behavior solely in terms of his concept of respect for adult authority.

It is this aspect of coping which is particulary impressive in children like those in the Topeka sample, most of whom continued to belong in the "normal" category. By contrast we find that children vulnerable to stress —in the sense of remaining victims of, and helpless to avoid, excessive pressure—are among those at-risk, regardless of specific genetic predispositions to pathology.

Cautions

1. Statistical elegance cannot compensate for superficial observation or ethnically and socioeconomically biased data.
2. Precoded observation schedules with items drawn from previously reported work do not permit the new discoveries which await us in natural history recording.
3. Related to this is the question of limiting the study to a single variable; for example, using only verbal stimulation in infancy for comparison with later intelligence test scores. It is important to assess the total range of transactions with the environment for correlation with current and later tests.
4. Sensitive or critical phases have been discussed in age-level terms primarily, but there is much evidence for different developmental patterns. Ignoring these can result in unrealistic assumptions about the age at which a given crisis will be experienced by an individual child. "Eight-months anxiety" is experienced much earlier by some infants who differentiate mother from other adults at a younger age.
5. "One-shot" samples of data often ignore the effects of the state of the child—sleepy, hungry, tired, getting a cold—with resulting deviations from the child's typical response pattern.
6. Linear correlations are not adequate when extremes on the independent variable produce similar effects on the dependent variable. For example, both the highest amount of maternal attention and the lowest evidently contributed to functional difficulties in the baby in our study, as indicated by curvilinear correlations.

7. Ignoring the infant's responses to stress from any source results in the failure to document processes of disintegration and reintegration at an early level—processes relevant to the development of psychopathology.

CONCLUSION

In our exploration of recent work, we found some exciting examples of effective preventive efforts by clinical psychologists working with children at risk because of deprivation, meager stimulation, parental schizophrenia, or other traumas such as divorce etc. We have also reviewed some work in correctional institutions. Preventive work in medical centers initiated by physicians, nurses, or social workers has not been reviewed here although this sometimes involves clinical psychologists as well. Similarly, we did not review much preventive work in schools initiated by educators, teachers, or other school personnel.

Among the inspiring successes is the Milwaukee program by Heber (21). Children of mothers with IQs of 75 were cared for in all-day nurseries from infancy to 5 years while their mothers were helped to learn good child care. Children's IQs in the experimental group varied around a mean of 120.7 at 72 months in contrast to the control group mean of 87.2, a difference of over 30 points. The forthcoming report of the second Vermont conference includes a full account of Heber's careful planning before this destined-to-be-classical study. Impressive also is Mednick's report on Mauritius children of schizophrenic parents—children who apparently "deschizophrened" themselves (our term, not Mednick's) during time in a warm and caring nursery school.

In line with our mandate, we made no attempt to catalog an extensive bibliography; we did point to certain especially good sources such as the Vermont conferences (2) and the *Schizophrenia Bulletin* from NIMH.

Successful programs included those that sustained long-term work with children from infancy into the school years; programs that involved mothers in activity with the children (not just didactic group sessions); programs implemented by warm interested personnel who by implication gave of themselves and did not simply apply programmed techniques. In short, much of what has been successful prevention is devoted, informed, creative help to children. All children need this and it is actually provided by the best teachers when they work with groups small enough to make it possible for them to know the children as individuals.

We also reviewed concepts of vulnerability, competence, and coping seen as prerequisites to planning prevention programs. We noted the vigorous emphasis by Shakow and by Garmezy on the urgent need for prospective, that is, developmental study of both normal children and those at risk for psychopathology. Such studies, we believe, should be oriented toward the processes of disintegrative reactions, defenses against them, and children's ways of achieving an equilibrium—in other words, coping which goes deeper than typical competence skills.

Zones of vulnerability and the relation of these to the kinds of stress to which a given child is sensitive need to be studied along with the whole range of ego resources and deficits. While the last 20 years have seen a multitude of studies of aspects of cognitive functioning—in part stimulated by Piaget's work—we have had no intensive studies of infants' efforts to maintain equilibrium or the effects of intense or prolonged pain, frustration, long crying, and physiological upheaval on the processes of differentiation and integration so crucial to mental health. Nor have we had enough studies of differences in what soothes different babies and the different ways in which a mother tries to restore a baby's equilibrium.

There is still much to learn about how to prevent emotional disturbance and mental illness.

Literature Cited

1. Advisory Committee on Child Development, Assembly of Behavioral and Social Sciences, National Research Council. 1976. *Toward a National Policy for Children and Families.* Washington DC: Natl. Acad. Sci.
2. Albee, G. W., Joffe, J. M., eds. 1977. *Primary Prevention of Psychopathology.* Vol. 1, *The Issues.* Hanover, NH: Univ. Press of New England. 426 pp.
3. Anthony, E. J., Koupernik, C. 1974. *The Child in His Family: Children at a Psychiatric Risk,* Vol. 3. New York: Wiley
4. Barker, R. G. 1968. *Ecological Psychology.* Stanford, Calif: Stanford Univ. Press
5. Bayley, N. 1949. Consistency and variability in the growth of intelligence from birth to eighteen years. *J. Genet. Psychol.* 75:165–96
6. Brodsky, S. L. 1972. *Psychologists in the Criminal Justice System.* Am. Assoc. Correct. Psychol. 183 pp.
7. Chess, S., Thomas, A., Birch, H. 1959. Characteristics of the individual child's behavioral responses to the environment. *Am. J. Orthopsychiatry* 29:719–802
7a. Cowen, E. L. 1973. Social and community interventions. *Ann. Rev. Psychol.* 24:423–72
8. Cowen, E. L. 1977. Baby-steps toward primary prevention. *Am. J. Community Psychol.* 5:1–22

9. Cowen, E. L. 1977. Mental health in the schools. In *International Encyclopedia of Neurology, Psychiatry, Psychoanalysis and Psychology.* New York: Brunner-Mazel
10. Erikson, J. M. 1976. *Activity, Recovery, and Growth.* New York: Norton
11. Garfield, S. L., Kurtz, R. 1974. A survey of clinical psychologists' characteristics, activities, and orientations. *Clin. Psychol.* 28(1):7–10
12. Garmezy, N. 1971. Vulnerability research and the issue of primary prevention. *Am. J. Orthopsychiatry* 41:101–16
13. Garmezy, N. 1974. The study of competence in children at risk for severe psychopathology. See Ref. 3, pp. 77–97
14. Garmezy, N. 1977. The role of an emergent developmental psychopathology in the study of vulnerability. In *The Study of Vulnerability to Psychosis,* ed. B. Brown. Washington DC: GPO
15. Goldston, S. E. 1977. Defining primary prevention. See Ref. 2, pp. 18–23
16. Gordon, I. J. 1978. *Long-term effects of the infant-parent education program.* Presented at Ann. Meet. AAAS, Washington DC, Feb. 1978
17. Gordon, T. 1977. Parent effectiveness training: A preventive program and its delivery system. See Ref. 2, pp. 178–86
18. Gottesfeld, H. 1974. New developments in clinical psychology. *Trans. NY Acad. Sci.* 36(3):283–94

19. Gottfredson, G. D., Dyer, E. D. 1977. *Health Service Providers in Psychology: 1966.* Washington DC: APA. 68 pp.

20. Greenacre, P. 1952. *Trauma, Growth, and Personality.* New York: Norton

21. Heber, F. R. 1978. Sociocultural mental retardation: A longitudinal study. In *Primary Prevention of Psychopathology, Vol. 2, Environmental Influences,* ed. D. G. Forgays. Hanover, NH: Univ. Press New England

22. Heller, K. 1978. The effects of social support: Prevention and treatment implications. In *Maximizing Treatment Gains: Transfer Enhancement in Psychotherapy,* ed. A. P. Goldstein, F. H. Kanfer. New York: Academic

23. Heller, K., Monahan, J. 1977. *Psychology and Community Change.* Homewood, Ill: Dorsey

24. Hoch, E. L., Ross, A. C., Winder, C. L. 1966. Conference on the professional preparation of clinical psychologists: A summary. *Am. Psychol.* 21:42–51

25. Huntington, D. 1977. *Developmental review in the early and periodic screening, diagnosis and treatment program.* Rep. 1977 Conf. Am. Assoc. Psychiatr. Serv. To Child. HEW Medicaid Bur. (HCFA) 77–24537

26. Johnson, D. 1976. *Final report, Houston Parent-Child Development Center.* Dep. Psychol., Univ. Houston, Houston, Tex.

27. Kessler, M., Albee, G. W. 1975. Primary prevention. *Ann. Rev. Psychol.* 26:557–91

27a. Kessler, M., Albee, G. W. 1977. An overview of the literature of primary prevention. See Ref. 2, pp. 351–99

28. Klein, D. C., Goldston, S. E. 1977. *Primary prevention: An idea whose time has come.* Proc. Pilot Conf. Primary Prev. 1976. Rockville, Md: ADAMHA, NIMH

29. Klein, M. 1948. *Contributions to Psychoanalysis.* London: Hogarth

30. Korman, M., ed. 1976. *Levels and Patterns of Professional Training in Psychology.* Proc. Conf., Vail, Colo. Washington DC: APA. 163 pp.

31. Langlois, J., Sawin, D. 1978. *Cross-Cultural Longitudinal Investigation of Parent-Infant Interactions.* Psychol. Dep., Univ. Texas. To be published

32. Lazar, I., Hubbell, V. R., Murray, H., Rosche, M., Royce, J. 1977. *The Persistence of Preschool Effects: A long-term follow-up of fourteen infant and preschool experiments.* The Consortium on Developmental Continuity, Education Commission of the United States. In-

quire of Irving Lazar, N-135 MVR Hall, Cornell Univ., Ithaca, NY 14853

33. Lewin, K., Lippitt, R., White, R. R. 1939. Patterns of aggressive behavior in experimentally created social climates. *J. Soc. Psychol.* 10:271–99

34. Macfarlane, J. W. 1963. From infancy to adulthood. *Child. Educ.* 39:336–42

35. Macfarlane, J. W. 1971. Perspectives on personality consistency and change from the guidance study. In *The Course of Human Development,* ed. M. C. Jones, N. Bayley, J. W. Macfarlane, M. P. Honzik, pp. 410–16

36. Macfarlane, J. W., Allen, L., Honzik, M. P. 1954. A developmental study of the behavior problems of normal children between twenty-one months and fourteen years. *Univ. Calif. Publ. in Child Dev. 2.* Berkeley, Los Angeles: Univ. California Press

37. Mednick, S. A., Witkin-Lanoil, G. H. 1977. Intervention in children at high risk for schizophrenia. See Ref. 2, pp. 153–63

38. Moriarty, A. E. 1966. *Constancy and I.Q. Change: A Clinical View of Relationships Between Tested Intelligence and Personality.* Springfield, Ill: Thomas

39. Murphy, G. 1947. *Personality: A Biosocial Approach to Origins and Structure.* New York: Harper

40. Murphy, L. B. 1937. *Social Behavior and Child Personality.* New York: Columbia Univ. Press

41. Murphy, L. B. 1956. *Colin: A Normal Child. Personality in Young Children,* Vol. 2. New York: Basic Books

42. Murphy, L. B. 1970. The problem of defense and the concept of coping. See Ref. 3

43. Murphy, L. B., Moriarty, A. E. 1976. *Vulnerability, Coping and Growth: From Infancy to Adolescence.* New Haven: Yale Univ. Press

44. National Advisory Commission on Criminal Justice Standards and Goals, 1973. *Community Crime Prevention.* Washington, DC: GPO. 364 pp.

45. Piaget, J., Inhelder, B. 1969. *The Psychology of the Child.* New York: Basic Books

46. Rao, C. R. 1965. Discrimination among groups and assigning new individuals. In *The Role and Methodology of Classification in Psychiatry and Psychopathology.* Proc. 1965 Conf., Washington DC, P.H.S. Publ. No. 1584. Washington DC: GPO

47. Rolf, J. E., Hasazi, J. E. 1977. Identification of preschool children at risk and

some guidelines for primary prevention. See Ref. 2

48. Sanford, N. 1965. The prevention of mental illness. See Ref. 62, pp. 1378–1400

49. Shakow, D. 1971. Some observations on the psychology (and some fewer on the biology) of schizophrenia. *J. Nerv. Ment. Dis.* 153(5):300–16

50. Shakow, D. 1973. Some thoughts about schizophrenia research in the context of high risk studies. *Psychiatry* 36:353–65

51. Shakow, D. 1977. Segmental set, the adaptive process in schizophrenia. *Am. Psychol.* 32(2):129–39

52. Shakow, D. 1977. *Schizophrenia: Selected Papers. Psychol. Issues* 10(2), Monogr. 38. New York: Int. Univ. Press. 354 pp.

53. Sherif, M., Harvey, O. J., White, B. J., Hood, W. R., Sherif, C. W. 1961. *Intergroup Conflict and Cooperation: The Robbers Cave Experiment.* Norman: Univ. Oklahoma Inst. Group Relat.

54. Skeels, H. M., Skodak, M. 1938. Study of environmental stimulation: An orphanage preschool project. *Studies in Child Welfare,* 15(4). Des Moines: Univ. Iowa Press

54a. Skodak Crissey, M. 1977. Prevention in retrospect: Adoption follow-up. See Ref. 2, pp. 187–202

55. Sontag, L. W., Baker, C., Nelson, V. 1958. *Mental Growth and Personality Development. Soc. Res. Child Dev. Monogr.* 23(2)

56. Sundberg, N. D., Tyler, L. E., Taplin, J. R. 1973. *Clinical Psychology: Expanding Horizons,* pp. 414–69. Englewood Cliffs, NJ: Prentice-Hall. 656 pp. 2nd ed.

57. Tarjan, G. et al. 1970. Natural history of mental retardation: Some aspects of epidemiology. *Am. J. Ment. Defic.* 77(4):369–79

57a. Task Force on Prevention, G. Albee, coordinator. 1978. Report to the President's Commission on Mental Health, Vol. 4. Document No. 040-000-00393-2 from Supt. of Documents, GPO

58. Vance, E. T. 1977. A typology of risk and the disabilities of low status. See Ref. 2, pp. 207–37

59. Wallerstein, J. S., Kelly, J. B. 1978. *Children of Divorce: Preventions in Parent-Child Relationships.* To be published

60. Wenk, E., Frank, C. 1974. *Some Progress in the Measurement of Correctional Environments.* Fed. Probation Rep., US Probation Serv., pp. 76–83

61. White, B. L. 1975. *The First Three Years of Life.* Englewood Cliffs, NJ: Prentice-Hall

62. Wolman, B. B. 1965. *Handbook of Clinical Psychology.* New York: McGraw-Hill. 1596 pp.

63. Zigler, E., Hunsinger, S. 1978. Our neglected children. *Yale Alumni Mag.* 41, 6 Feb. 1978. New Haven: Yale Alumni Publ.

Ann. Rev. Psychol. 1979. 30:209–42
Copyright © 1979 by Annual Reviews Inc. All rights reserved

THE BIOLOGY
OF MOTIVATION

♦307

Sebastian P. Grossman[1]

Committee on Biopsychology, University of Chicago, Chicago, Illinois 60637

CONTENTS

INTRODUCTION 209
GENERAL STATEMENT OF ISSUES 210
BASIC SUPPORT FOR A HYPOTHALAMOCENTRIC HYPOTHESIS 213
IS THERE A LATERAL HYPOTHALAMIC FEEDING CENTER? 214
IS THERE A HYPOTHALAMIC SATIETY CENTER? 221
    Functional Questions 221
    Anatomical Questions 228
CONCLUSIONS 232

INTRODUCTION

There is little agreement among contemporary psychologists as to how one should define the elusive theoretical construct "motivation." Some view it as a generic term for a variety of psychological functions (e.g. hunger, thirst, sexual arousal, etc) which have in common only the ability to "direct" behavior toward specific goals (such as food, water, a mate, etc). Others have reduced the problem of motivation to a single overriding need to maintain the degree of activation or arousal in the central nervous system or parts thereof within optimal limits—the term "optimal" being defined somewhat differently by various proponents of this type of interpretation.

Most contemporary psychologists prefer an eclectic position that assigns important organizational functions to specific motivational mechanisms but agrees that a moderate level of general arousal is essential for the execution of complex behavior. Many also find the hypothesis appealing that some

[1]The preparation of this manuscript was supported by grant MH 26934.

0066-4308/79/0201-0209$01.00

components of the arousal system of the brain may perform gating functions for sensory input, particularly that which is relevant to currently active specific motivational states.

When one looks into the voluminous and rapidly expanding literature on the biological bases of motivational functions, several facts stand out: (a) We have, as yet, not the slightest idea what the biological substrate of the directing function might be that is the essential aspect of the definition of specific motivational states; how arousal mechanisms might organize complex behavior so as to control the level of CNS activation; or how arousal mechanisms might interact with specific motivational mechanisms so as to gate relevant sensory input. (b) There is a great deal of information about the neuroanatomy, neurophysiology, and neuropharmacology of central neural pathways believed to represent at least part of the biological substrate of various specific and nonspecific motivational influences on behavior. (c) Recent developments in the field have seriously questioned, on anatomical as well as behavioral grounds, the validity of the interpretations which have been placed on experimental observations that are critical for the contemporary conceptualization of motivational mechanisms.

Nowhere are the interpretational problems more explicit than in the recent literature on the biological bases of hunger and thirst—the two appetitive motivational states that have traditionally served psychologists as model systems for so-called primary motivational mechanisms. So as not to lose sight of the principal issues, the following discussion will focus on the conceptual problems that have arisen in this context, but it should be clear that similar questions can and indeed have been raised with respect to the biological substrate of other motivational states. Because of space limitations, I will consider peripheral (i.e. gastric, pancreatic, and hepatic) influences only when they have been related specifically to the functions of the central pathways that are the principal subject of our discussion. The reader is invited to consult several excellent recent reviews of the progress that has been made in our understanding of peripheral factors in satiety (45, 172, 217, 244) to complement and extend the present approach.

GENERAL STATEMENT OF ISSUES

A review of the extensive literature that describes the effects of electrolytic, surgical, or chemical lesions and electrical or chemical stimulation in various portions of the brain on ingestive behavior (81, 84)[2] indicates that feeding and drinking are influenced by many diverse aspects of the nervous

---

[2]Italic citation numbers identify extensive review articles on the topic which the reader should consult for further detail.

system. It is nonetheless widely believed that hunger and thirst are controlled primarily by hypothalamic mechanisms that direct the organism's behavior on the basis of humoral as well as neural information from various peripheral and central sources. This "hypothalamocentric" hypothesis has enjoyed a great deal of popularity ever since Stellar (224) first presented it nearly 25 years ago, in spite of the rapid accumulation of evidence for the importance of various extrahypothalamic structures (*81, 82, 83, 84*). Although a few voices in the wilderness were heard earlier (164), fundamental questions about the adequacy of the hypothalamocentric hypothesis have been raised only in recent years. The principal issues which have surfaced in this context are not unique to the hypothalamocentric hypothesis but concern our understanding of brain-behavior relationships in general.

One area of increasing concern has been the localization of function in the central nervous system. We have become increasingly aware of the fact that the available techniques for the experimental study of the relationship between brain function and structure in vivo cannot adequately distinguish between the functions of cellular (i.e. somal) components of the area under study and fibers of passage that originate in distant regions of the brain and may have no functional relation to the region. This problem is most obvious when one considers the effects of electrolytic lesions or electrical stimulation —procedures that have provided most of the data base for the hypothalamocentric hypothesis as well as our understanding of brain-behavior relationships in general. Various alternatives to these classic tools have been developed in recent years but the resulting technological advances have not entirely solved the basic problems. Surgical knife cuts (*85*) affect axons selectively, provided damage to major blood vessels can be avoided, but the technique cannot distinguish between the afferent and efferent connections of the area under investigation on the one hand and fibers of passage on the other. Microinjections of putative neurotransmitters or compounds that interfere with their normal synaptic action or metabolism may have selective effects on somal or dendritic components of nerve cells (*79, 133*), but the injections are often effective only when relatively high doses are used that may result in nonspecific effects on neural as well as glial tissue. Electrophysiological recordings of the activity of single neurons are capable of differentiating between somal and axonal potentials, but it has been extraordinarily difficult to relate the firing pattern of individual nerve cells to changes in the organism's energy or fluid balance on the one hand and ingestive behavior on the others.

The limitations of presently available neuroanatomical and neurophysiological techniques are especially apparent when one tries to understand the functions of structurally complex and heterogeneous parts of the brain. The lateral hypothalamus, which is traversed by numerous diffuse ascending and descending fiber systems and has no clearly demarcated cellular accumulations, is a prime example of such an area (*169*). At first glance, matters would seem to be simpler in the case of the medial hypothalamus, but the presence of well-defined nuclei (161) in this area has not contributed to our understanding of its functions because they do not appear to be related, in any obvious fashion, to the regulation of ingestive behavior.

The second major problem that has complicated the interpretation of research in this area (as well as many others) concerns the behavioral specificity of the effects of whatever experimental treatments are used to investigate the relationship of a particular brain area to motivational functions. Electrolytic as well as surgical or chemical lesions in many regions of the brain reduce or abolish food and/or water intake but the effects rarely, if ever, occur in isolation. Instead, a variety of often severe side-effects typically occur which include complex sensory, motor, and arousal dysfunctions (154, 262) that may well be responsible for some or all of the observed impairments in ingestive behavior (*137, 227*). An interpretation of hyperphagia and hyperdipsia following structural or functional lesions is similarly complicated. An animal may overeat or overdrink not only because an hypothesized satiety mechanism is impaired but also because of a variety of metabolic and/or hormonal disorders or changes in reactivity to the sensory qualities of the diet. Hyperphagia and hyperdipsia may also be the result of an increase in general activity or reactivity to environmental stimuli (151) that is reflected in feeding or drinking only because these are two of the very few behaviors an animal in a small cage can readily display.

Similar problems have been raised with respect to the effects of electrical or chemical stimulation of hypothalamic or extrahypothalamic brain structures. There is little doubt that one can elicit ingestive behavior with these techniques (*101, 162, 200*), but it is not clear at all that this reflects an activation of neural pathways specifically related to hunger or thirst. A number of investigators (14, *243*) have suggested that such stimulation may increase general activation or arousal and result in the display of any behaviors that are high on the animals' response hierarchy or happen to be appropriate to environmental variables such as the presence of food, etc.

When one considers the results of experiments that attempt to relate single nerve cell activity to ingestive behavior or hunger and thirst, various related interpretational questions arise. A number of investigators have demonstrated changes in neural activity in the hypothalamus as well as other areas of the brain when an animal is exposed to food or water (*95, 201*), engages in ingestive or food- or water-rewarded instrumental behavior (140, 176), or merely awaits the delivery of food or water in response to a conditioned signal (174). What has not been demonstrated convincingly in most of these experiments is that the observed electrophysiological changes are, in fact, specifically related to hunger or thirst rather than to increments in general arousal, the processing of sensory information, the organization of motor reactions, or perhaps the general rewarding effects of food or water (*173, 201*). Experiments involving iontophoretic application of very small quantities of solutions containing sugars or salts to cells in the hypothalamus (*150, 177, 178*) have supported the hypothesis that neurons in this area of the brain may act as gluco-receptors or osmo-receptors. However, all nerve cells use glucose and are sensitive to changes in the osmolality of their immediate environment, and it remains to be proved that the demonstrated responsiveness of certain hypothalamic cells are related to metering functions specifically related to hunger or thirst.

BASIC SUPPORT FOR A HYPOTHALAMOCENTRIC HYPOTHESIS

Attention was first focused on the hypothalamus on the basis of early experimental and clinical research which culminated in the demonstration by Brobeck and associates that electrolytic lesions in the ventromedial hypothalamus (VMH) resulted in overeating and obesity (33) whereas lesions in the adjacent dorsolateral portion of the hypothalamus produced aphagia and adipsia (9). Although the assumption did not go unquestioned (160, 164), it was generally assumed that the behavioral deficits reflected an interference with basic motivational mechanisms directly related to hunger and thirst. A hypothalamocentric hypothesis appeared plausible in spite of some early indications that lesions elsewhere in the brain affected food and water intake because the effects of hypothalamic damage appeared much more severe and persistent.

The hypothalamocentric hypothesis has received support from various sources. Feeding or drinking (159, 163) as well as food- or water-rewarded instrumental behaviors (13, 39, 159) have been elicited by electrical stimulation of lateral hypothalamic sites, microinjections of putative neurohumors or blocking agents into cannulas with tips in the hypothalamus (75, 76, 79, 133, 198), or by the transfer of a perfusate from the hypothalamus of a deprived monkey to that of a sated one (258).

That the diencephalon might contain cells that specifically monitor the body's fluid or energy metabolism is suggested by reports of (*a*) selective destruction of the VMH (and hyperphagia and obesity) after systemic injections of toxic glucose compounds such as goldthioglucose [(38); but see (51) for recent questions about this effect]; (*b*) elicitation of copious drinking after microinjections of hypertonic solutions into the anterior hypothalamus and adjacent areas of the preoptic region (12, 24, 183); (*c*) elicitation of feeding after injections of glucose or the competitive glucose analog 2-deoxy-D-glucose into the hypothalamus (17, 72); and (*d*) the demonstration of electrophysiological (EEG as well as single cell) responses in the hypothalamus to peripherally induced hyper- or hypo-glycemia (11, 177); and (*e*) more recently, changes in single unit activity to glucose, insulin, fatty acids, etc, that are applied directly (i.e. iontophoretically) to cells in the medial or lateral hypothalamus (150, 178).

IS THERE A LATERAL HYPOTHALAMIC FEEDING CENTER?

When the hypothalamocentric hypothesis was first promulgated, the available experimental evidence indicated that feeding and drinking were abolished only by lesions in the lateral hypothalamus (LH). In the subsequent 25 years, numerous reports of similar effects of lesions in diverse aspects of the brain have appeared. The principal question that concerns most investigators in the field today is why one should continue to assign a special regulatory role to the LH.

Collins's (38) report of aphagia and adipsia after tegmental lesions opened a floodgate through which the spate of research has increased in recent years. Collins's observation has been replicated by numerous investigators (64, 146, 181) and most have supported his conclusion that the observed impairments seemed related to sensory-motor dysfunctions. Zeigler & Karten (261, 262) more recently have shown that an interruption of the trigeminal projection system at several levels of the brainstem (including the diencephalon) produced aphagia (without adipsia) in the rat and pigeon. Gold's (64) observation that the mild and quite transient effects of a unilateral tegmental lesion were additive with the effects of a contralateral LH lesion suggests that a common neural mechanism may be affected by at least some of the tegmental lesions and LH damage.

Although sensory-motor dysfunctions undoubtedly contribute to the effects of many of the tegmental lesions, recent reports of feeding or drinking after electrical stimulation in the tegmentum of the rat (158, 248) and cat (22, 257) suggest that mechanisms specifically related to hunger and thirst may also be represented in this region of the brainstem.

Aphagia with or without adipsia have also been observed in rats, cats, monkeys, and other species after lesions in the frontal cortex (36, 127) and amygdala (10, 28, 56). In both cases, there is reason to believe that sensory-motor dysfunctions (28, 44, 127, 238) and perhaps nonspecific motivational impairments (10, 74) may contribute significantly to the effects of these lesions on food and water intake. In the case of amygdaloid damage, there is, in addition, evidence (44) that the effects on food and water intake reflect extra-amygdaloid (i.e. capsular and pallidal) damage [see (*84*) for a detailed review of the effects of frontal and amygdaloid lesions and stimulation on food and water intake].

The relatively meager literature on the effects of electrical or chemical stimulation in the amygdala consistently confirms the impression that this area may well be the source of inhibitory influences on ingestive behavior but does not harbor truly excitatory mechanisms (77, 86, 126, 148). In the case of the frontal cortex, matters are not as clear since several investigators have reported voracious feeding after electrical or chemical stimulation of this area (109, 148).

These observations could quite readily be incorporated into a hypothalamocentric hypothesis since the postulated regulatory center must, after all, receive inputs concerning the current state of the organism's energy and fluid balance and gain access to motor functions via efferent pathways. A number of recent experimental reports suggest, however, that some, or perhaps even all, of the effects of LH lesions might be due to incidental damage to fiber systems that are not known to synapse in the region.

Morgane (164) first suggested the potential involvement of pallifugal fibers in the LH lesion syndrome when he found that lesions in portions of the globus pallidus that give rise to the pallidofugal fiber system result in persistent aphagia and adipsia. Teitelbaum and Krantz's (cited in 232) subsequent demonstration of additive effects of contralateral LH and pallidal lesions indicates that components of the same neural system, if not in fact the same fiber system, may be involved in the two lesions.

Subsequently, Ungerstedt (240) and others (106) have demonstrated aphagia and adipsia after lesions in the substantia nigra (SN) which gives rise to the nigrostriatal projection system that completes the feedback circuit to the basal ganglia. That the effects of SN lesions might be specifically due to an interruption of this dopaminergic pathway was indicated by the fact that intranigral (54, 55, 152, 240), intrapallidal (152), and even intracerebroventricular (263, 264) injections of the neurotoxin 6-hydroxydopamine (6-OHDA) which preferentially although not exclusively destroys catecholaminergic neurons (35, 187) also resulted in aphagia and adipsia. Although this compound destroys noradrenergic (NE) neurons (which are plentiful in the LH) as well as dopaminergic (DA) cells, a selective effect on the latter appears to be responsible for its effects in ingestive behavior since: (a) pretreatments with drugs that selectively increase the destruction of DA cells produce more severe and persistent inhibitory effects on food and water intake (225, 263, 264), and (b) the 6-OHDA–induced disturbances in food and water intake are reversed by intraventricular injections of dopamine agonists such as apomorphine (142, 155).

There is at this time little doubt that an interference with the dopaminergic nigrostriatal projections can produce transient aphagia and adipsia as well as many of the persisting "regulatory" deficits [e.g. impaired feeding in response to glucoprivic challenges such as insulin or 2-deoxy-D-glucose; lost or delayed drinking to experimental treatments which result in cellular (e.g. intraperitoneal NaCl) or extracellular (e.g. subcutaneous polyethyleneglycol) dehydration] that characterize animals with LH lesions (54, 55, 152, 225, 226).

There is also little doubt that animals that have sustained extensive surgical or chemical damage to the nigrostriatal projection system display very severe sensory (152), motor (240, 242), and arousal (225, 263) disturbances that may well make it impossible for them to eat or drink during the initial post-treatment period and may make it difficult for them to respond promptly and efficiently to stressful, experimental treatments that elicit ingestive behavior in the intact animal, as Stricker & Zigmond (227) have suggested.

What is not so clear is whether one should conclude, as Stricker & Zigmond (227) suggest, that the effects of LH lesions on food and water intake are due exclusively to an interruption of the DA nigrostriatal projections and the resultant loss of arousal or endogenous activation, rather than any selective interference with neural mechanisms specifically concerned with the regulation of hunger and thirst (energy and water balance, or food and water intake).

While it is true that LH lesions deplete striatal dopamine (63, 175), the magnitude of the depletion is far below the thresholds shown to be effective in chemical depletion studies. Lateral hypothalamic lesions that deplete striatal DA by only 50–60% produce much more persistent aphagia and adipsia (and more severe regulatory deficits) than intraventricular 6-OHDA injections (complemented by pretreatments with NE uptake inhibitors) that deplete striatal DA by 95% or more. Indeed, the investigators who have been most insistent on demonstrating a relationship between the effects of LH lesions and striatal DA depletion (264) have observed that intraventricular 6-OHDA treatments do not produce significant aphagia or adipsia unless striatal DA is depleted to 10% or less of control levels.

On the other side of the same coin, there can be no doubt that LH lesions result in sensory (153, 154), motor (18), and arousal (137) impairments that may well contribute to the aphagia and adipsia syndrome as well as the persisting regulatory deficits seen after recovery of voluntary ingestive behavior. Whether these LH lesion effects are qualitively or quantitatively comparable to those seen after destruction of the substantia nigra (152, 241), globus pallidus (164), or the central DA pathways in general (225, 263, 264) remains to be established.

Some light on the problem has recently been shed by the results of a series of experiments that investigated the behavioral and biochemical effects of surgical knife cuts that interrupt some of the principal afferent and efferent connections of the basal ganglia. In the first studies of this group (88), most of the connections between the diencephalon and the basal ganglia in the rat were interrupted by a knife cut in the parasagittal plane along the medial border of the internal capsule (IC). Although this cut produced little or no direct cellular damage in the hypothalamus, the animals were aphagic and adipsic for several weeks or even months after surgery. The cuts produced transient sensory-motor dysfunctions but the parallel recovery of ingestive behavior and sensory-motor capabilities which has been described in the rat with LH lesions (137, 152, 153) was not observed. Although some animals retained persisting impairments in the acquisition and performance of complex learned behaviors (115, 117), the animals' abilities to orient promptly and efficiently to stimuli of all modalities and to perform simple motor acts such as grooming, walking, balancing on a rotorod, etc, and their general level of locomotor activity and arousal typically appeared normal within a few days after surgery, whereas the aphagia and adipsia often persisted for several months. When the regulatory capabilities of these animals were examined (89) several months after surgery, it became apparent that they displayed the full complement of persisting deficits that characterize the rat with LH lesions. The animals did not eat in response to glucoprivic challenges (insulin or 2-deoxy-D-glucose); did not drink in response to experimental treatments that result in cellular or extracellular dehydration; and did not drink when food deprived, suggesting that they remained fundamentally adipsic.

In recent extensions of this work (6, 7, 156, 157) the same basic pattern of effects has been replicated, using smaller parasagittal cuts in various locations along the lateral border of the LH. No single area has been found to be critical in these studies although the severity and persistence of the feeding or drinking-related impairments has varied considerably. In many of the animals with these smaller cuts, there were no detectable sensory, motor, or arousal dysfunction after the first day postoperatively. Monoamine assays demonstrated that these cuts depleted striatal (as well as forebrain) DA to about 20% of control values; reduced forebrain NE to about 50% of control values but left hypothalamic NE, DA, and 5-HT in the normal range. The duration of aphagia and adipsia but not the severity of any of the regulatory deficits correlated reliably with the extent of striatal and forebrain DA depletion.

These results indicate that the full complement of disorders in food and water intake regulation that is seen after LH lesions can be produced by knife cuts that (a) do not directly damage cells indigenous to the LH; (b) do not produce severe and persistent deficits in sensory-motor functions or endogenous arousal; and (c) do not deplete striatal DA as severely as the 6-OHDA (plus NE uptake inhibitor) treatments that have been shown to reproduce the LH syndrome at least to a large extent.

Several investigators (25, 47, 165) have reported that medial forebrain bundle lesions anterior or posterior to the hypothesized feeding center do not produce aphagia and adipsia (although more subtle regulatory deficits have been observed). These observations suggest that the effects of cuts along the lateral border of the hypothalamus might be due to an interruption of projections to or from neurons in the LH proper. The results of several knife-cut studies suggests, however, that fibers that ascend or descend in medial segments of the IC may be responsible for some or all of the effects of the parasagittal cuts. Albert et al (4) reported aphagia and adipsia after very large coronal cuts through posterior aspects of the LH that invaded the IC. Kent et al (118) noted long-persisting aphagia and adipsia after small cuts in the coronal plane just rostral to the substantia nigra. McDermott et al (156, 157) found aphagia and adipsia as well as most of the classic syndrome of persisting regulatory deficits (the animals did not drink in response to extra- or intracellular dehydration or eat after 2-DG but responded normally to insulin) after coronal cuts across lateral components of the MFB which invaded the IC. Although these cuts spared one of the regulatory functions that are typically abolished by LH lesions as well as by knife cuts along the lateral border of the LH, they interfered with the animals' ability to increase intake after a period of food deprivation, one of the few regulatory capabilities that are often intact after parasagittal cuts. The perhaps most interesting aspect of the results of these studies is the fact that most of the LH lesion syndrome was replicated by coronal knife cuts that depleted striatal and forebrain DA by less than 50% and produced little or no sensory-motor or arousal dysfunctions. That striatal mechanisms may nonetheless play an as yet poorly understood role in ingestive behavior is suggested by the fact that the duration of aphagia and adipsia again correlated significantly with the degree of striatal DA depletion in these studies.

The results of another group of studies which investigated the effects of knife cuts medial, dorsal, or ventral to the globus pallidus or portions of the caudate nucleus support this conclusion (5–7). Cuts between the globus pallidus (GP) and IC that interrupted most pallidal efferents as well as portions of cortical, thalamic, and nigral afferents to the basal ganglia reproduced the LH syndrome in much the same way coronal cuts across the lateral MFB had done (the animals were aphagic and adipsic for about one week and responded to none of the classic regulatory challenges except insulin). These cuts produced severe sensory-motor dysfunctions similar to those seen after large LH lesions and also resulted in major depletions of striatal dopamine.

Cuts in the horizontal plane, just below the striatum, produced periods of aphagia and adipsia that were comparable to those seen after parasagittal cuts medial to the GP or lateral to the LH but little evidence of regulatory deficits after voluntary ingestive behavior had returned. These animals increased intake after deprivation, responded normally or nearly so to insulin and 2-DG, and drank water after i.p. injections of hypertonic saline. They failed to drink water after polyethyleneglycol-induced extracellular hypovolemia but avidly consumed isotonic saline, indicating that critical components of the extracellular thirst mechanisms were functional. There was little or no evidence of sensory-motor or arousal dysfunctions in these animals. The behavioral effects of these cuts are particularly interesting when viewed in the context of their biochemical consequences—striatal DA was reduced only to 30–50% of control levels and the concentrations of other amines were normal or nearly so in all areas of the brain investigated.

Perhaps the most intriguing results of this series of experiments were obtained in animals with cuts which interrupted fibers passing between the dorsal aspects of the globus pallidus and the caudate nucleus. These cuts produced no significant effects on ad libitum food or water intake or feeding reactions to insulin or 2-DG but selectively reduced or abolished water intake during periods of food deprivation and drinking responses to cellular as well as extracellular thirst stimuli. Striatal DA (as well as 5-HT) were normal after this surgical procedure.

This pattern of behavioral and biochemical effects is very similar to that recently described after electrolytic or surgical lesions in the anterior zona incerta (ZI) or subthalamus. Lesions in this area have no effect on ad libitum food intake or feeding responses to insulin but the animals do not eat in response to 2-DG (250). Ad libitum water intake is reduced by 20–30% and drops to zero when food is withheld, suggesting that the animals drink only to satisfy prandial requirements (249). This suspicion is strengthened by the observation that even severe cellular dehydration fails to induce drinking in the absence of dry food (251). Experimental treatments such as subcutaneous injections of formalin or polyethylene glycol that result in extracellular hypovolemia increase water intake but fail to arouse the sodium appetite essential for a correction of the physiological imbalance (252). Other experimental treatments that are believed to act via extracellular thirst mechanisms (such as intracerebral injections of angiotensin or systemic administration of the β-adrenergic agent isoproterenol) do not elicit water or saline ingestion in rats with anterior ZI lesions (253). It is particularly important in the context of our discussion to emphasize that the rat with ZI lesions has no arousal difficulties, sensory-motor impairments, or, for that matter, DA depletions in the striatum or forebrain (254).

It is interesting to note here that selective impairments in reactivity to specific glucoprivic and hydrational challenges have been reported after various other brainstem lesions. A loss of response to 2-DG in animals that ate normally after insulin has been observed after knife cuts in the tegmentum both in animals that overate and in normophagic rats (90) and after lesion in the anterior hypothalamus (25). Electrolytic lesions (130) or parasagittal knife cuts (210) in medial portions of the LH have been reported to selectively impair drinking responses to extracellular stimuli whereas lateral LH lesions (130) or lateral preoptic area lesions (24) selectively reduced or abolished the response to cellular dehydration.

These observations indicate that electrolytic lesions in the subthalamic region, as well as surgical transections of some striatal connections, can produce surprisingly selective effects on feeding or drinking responses to quite specific glucoprivic or hydrational signals. It would appear that there are at least two neural systems that respond to different glucoprivic signals (insulin-induced hypoglycemia and 2-DG–induced cellular glucoprivation); distinct neural mechanisms for responses to cellular and extracellular thirst stimuli; and indeed, apparently distinct pathways for responding to a number of stimuli which have been classified as extracellular. Many of these pathways are represented in the subthalamic region just dorsal to the classic LH feeding center, and it appears plausible that the traditional LH lesion syndrome may reflect, at least in part, damage to these subthalamic mechanisms. Specific feeding and drinking-related pathways also appear to involve aspects of the striatum, and it appears possible that at least some aspects of ingestive behavior may be organized at this level of the neuraxis.

Although it is not uncommon to find little or no effect of partial striatal lesions on ad libitum food or water intake (*84*), there is considerable support for this conclusion. Aphagia and adipsia have been reported after electrolytic as well as chemical lesions in the caudate nucleus of the rat (170, 185) and cat (10), and decortication appears to leave ingestive behavior intact until the striatum is also removed (220). Some investigators (135) have suggested that the impairment may be due primarily to sensory-motor dysfunctions, but recent reports of selective regulatory impairments after caudate nucleus lesions (170, 207) indicate that pathways related to the organization of responses to specific glucoprivic or hydrational challenges may also be represented in the area. This, of course, is in excellent agreement with the selective effects of knife cuts that partially deafferent and/or de-efferent the striatum (above). That this region may play an important integrative role is further supported by reports of a selective interference with ongoing ingestive behavior during electrical stimulation of the caudate nucleus (10) and the observation by Travis and colleagues (236, 237) that 30% of the cells sampled from the GP of the monkey were inhibited, apparently quite specifically, during feeding or the execution of food-rewarded behaviors.

Just what the LH regulates has been the subject of some recent debate. The very selective effects of subthalamic lesions and striatal knife cuts on reactivity to specific glucoprivic or hydrational signals suggest that pathways that are concerned with the maintenance of the organism's energy and fluid balance are represented in this portion of the brain. The selectivity of some of the lesion effects indicates that more than the simple weight-regulating mechanism suggested by Keesey and associates (114) may be involved, but there is evidence that signals from body fat depots may be one of the inputs to the system. Rats with small LH lesions chronically maintain a lower body weight than age mate controls (190) and adjust their intake when the palatability or caloric density of the diet are changed so as to defend a proportionally lower weight than controls (29, 113). The duration of aphagia is shortened by preoperative fasting (190) and increased by postoperative force feeding (114). When force-fed enough to elevate its body weight to control levels or when starved to a level significantly below its new maintenance level, the rat with small LH lesions will adjust its intake upon cessation of the experimental dietary manipulation so that its body weight returns to the level of LH animals that had ad libitum access to food throughout the experiment (114).

IS THERE A HYPOTHALAMIC SATIETY CENTER?

Functional Questions

A number of questions have been raised concerning the role of various extrahypothalamic mechanisms in the control of satiety and, indeed, in the VMH lesion syndrome itself, as we shall see in a moment. However, the more fundamental issue that has been raised in recent years is whether a hypothalamic satiety mechanism exists at all.

The concept of a satiety center originated with the pioneers in the field who discovered that lesions in the VMH produced hyperphagia and obesity and that the increased intake occurred mainly in the form of longer and larger rather than more frequent meals (33, 34). The basic observations have been replicated by many recent investigators (16) although other abnormalities in ingestive behavior (e.g. a breakdown of the normal circadian rhythm and a modest increase in meal frequency) have also been noted (20).

The notion of a distinct inhibitory influence on hunger has proved hardy in spite of numerous experimental observations that seem incompatible with it. As soon as food intake and food-motivated instrumental behavior began to be investigated in greater detail some puzzling observations became apparent. Rats with VMH lesions overate and became obese only when a palatable (e.g. high-fat or high-sugar) diet was available, but ate less than controls when the taste or texture of the diet was made aversive, and worked less hard for food rewards in a variety of instrumental test paradigms (73, 160, 230, 231). The apparent paradox has led to a great deal of experimental interest, and we now know that rats with VMH lesions are "finicky" and apparently poorly motivated to work for food only under certain circumstances.

Some investigators (121, 122, 213) have shown that rats with VMH lesions work as hard or harder than intact controls if extensive preoperative training is given. Others (149, 188, 255) have shown that VMH rats starved to preoperative body weights or below will work as hard or harder than controls. A recent comprehensive study (122) indicates that both preoperative training and body weight are relevant determinants of the operant performance of rats with VMH lesions. The operant performance of rats with VMH lesions is also affected by deprivation. Preoperatively trained rats work about as well as controls when deprived but significantly harder when tested undeprived (119, 184, 212). An interaction between the finickiness syndrome and operant performance is suggested by studies which indicate that rats with VMH lesions work quite well for highly palatable rewards (19).

The finickiness of the VMH rat also appears to have interesting boundary conditions. When obese VMH rats are given a quinine diet they are finicky and lose weight until they reach a basal level of body weight which is similar to the weight of intact controls. They then defend that body weight by ingesting as much of the unpalatable diet as controls do (53, 57). When VMH and control animals are starved prior to surgery both readily accept an unpalatable, quinine adulterated diet until the prestarvation body weight is reattained. Apparently the VMH rat is not finicky unless its body reserves provide an adequate supply of energy.

There is, in fact, a fair amount of evidence suggesting that rats with VMH lesions do regulate body weight, albeit in a somewhat different manner than intact controls. Hoebel & Teitelbaum (102) demonstrated some years ago that rats that were made obese by prolonged insulin treatment gained little extra weight after VMH lesions. When rats who had gained a fair amount of weight after VMH lesions were further fattened by force feeding, they reduced their voluntary intake and lost weight until they had returned to the weight attained earlier during the dynamic phase of hypothalamic hyperphagia. In conjunction with the common observation that the weight (and food intake) of animals with VMH lesions tends to reach a stable plateau (the so-called static phase) (34), it is tempting to assume that the animal simply defends a new, elevated body weight, and several investigators (116, 212) have proposed theoretical models that are in accord with such an interpretation. However, there are a number of reports of animals with VMH lesions that appear to remain in the dynamic phase of excessive food intake and body weight gain (32, 34), and a recent paper describes the appearance of a second dynamic phase in a number of obese animals which had maintained stable elevated body weights during static phases lasting for several weeks or even months (123).

That rats with VMH lesions can, in fact, respond to metabolic signals that control food intake in the intact animal is further indicated by several experimental observations. Rats with VMH lesions: (a) increase their intake as much or more than controls when a *palatable* diet is calorically diluted (37, 136, 219); (b) decrease their intake after stomach preloads of fats, proteins, or carbohydrates (141, 180, 218, 234) or intraperitoneal (195, 204) or intravenous (203) infusions of nutrients; and (c) increase their food intake after insulin (52) or 2-deoxy-D-glucose (124, 125) although their response may be delayed.

There is nonetheless ample evidence that VMH lesions interfere with a number of important endocrine and metabolic functions and this might be responsible for at least part of the VMH lesion syndrome (*59, 189*).

The most conspicuous endocrine dysfunction is an increase in the level of circulating insulin and an enormously exaggerated release of insulin in the first minutes of a meal (103, 112, 145, 222). This is accompanied by an inhibition of growth hormone release that normally modulates the effects of insulin (30, 60). Because of increased gluconeogenesis (69) and consequent increase in glucose turnover, blood glucose levels are slightly elevated or within the normal range (94, 221).

Animals with VMH lesions also have high plasma lipid levels (21, 94), incorporate excessive amounts of glucose as fats, burn little fatty acids, and recruit less fat from adipose tissue than controls (62, 69, 70, 93). Increased lipogenesis has been demonstrated even after growth hormone replacement or elimination of the hyperinsulinimia (69, 70). This suggests that the disorders in fat metabolism which some investigators believe to be the critical determinants of hyperphagia as well as obesity (59) may be due only in part to hyperinsulinimia.

In the context of any discussion of the possibility of a causal relation between the endocrine and metabolic consequence of VMH lesions on the one hand and the increased food intake and/or obesity on the other, it is important to note that elevated circulating insulin levels have been recorded as soon as 24 hours after the lesion (223) and a significantly increased insulin response to a glucose challenge as early as 25 minutes after the lesion (23).

Although excessive fat deposition has been observed in normophagic or pair-fed animals with VMH lesions (96, 97, 193, 245), it is generally agreed that the obesity seen in most animals with VMH damage is primarily the result of hyperphagia (32). The principal question that has arisen in recent years is whether the exaggerated food intake reflects a primary disturbance of satiety mechanisms, as was originally believed, or one or more of the metabolic and endocrine dysfunctions that have more recently come to light.

That peripheral factors play an important role in the VMH syndrome is indicated by the observation that vagotomy reverses the hyperphagia and obesity syndrome (34, 105, 191). Since vagotomy also abolishes the hyperinsulinimia and gastric hyperacidity typical of the rat with VMH lesions (192), Powley (189) and others (105) have proposed that the reversal of the hyperphagia/obesity syndrome might be the direct result of reduced insulin release, aided perhaps by other metabolic consequences of vagotomy.

King et al (120) have recently replicated the basic observation that vagotomy reverses the hyperphagia of rats with VMH lesions, but they also demonstrated that rats permitted to recover from the debilitating effects of vagotomy (the initial consequences of that operation include anorexia and severe weight loss) *before* the placement of the VMH lesions do, in fact, overeat and become obese. The effects of the lesion were somewhat smaller than in nonvagotomized controls, indicating that endocrine and metabolic factors may play a significant role in the VMH lesion syndrome. This observation is congruent with an earlier report of hyperphagia and obesity in experimentally diabetic rats (58, 71).

How can one reconcile the apparently paradoxical findings of Powley & Opsahl (191) and King et al (120)? King et al (120) have pointed out that vagotomy severely interferes with swallowing (48) and gastric motility (105), the effect being more severe the higher the transection. It appears likely that this may be the immediate cause of the anorexia and hypodipsia as well as impaired responses to glucoprivic and hydrational challenges which have been described in vagotomized rats (27, 128, 196). If one remembers that the rat with VMH lesions is hyperreactive to sensory stimuli (151) in general and noxious stimuli (239) in particular, that it curtails its intake to control levels when its diet or water supply are aversive because of quinine adulteration (see above), and does not defend its obese weight when required to work on aversive, low density reinforcement schedules (see above), it becomes reasonable to assume that at least part of the inhibitory effects of vagotomy on the food intake of rats with VMH lesions may be related to the simple fact that feeding has acquired distinctly negative properties. The hyperphagia seen by King et al (120) in animals that had adapted to these negative components of feeding for 90 days prior to the placement of the lesion may be analogous to the hyperphagia seen in VMH lesioned animals after preoperative adaptation to unpalatable diets (214) or work requirements (121, i22).

Indeed, it seems plausible to suggest, as I have done earlier (78), that at least part of the peculiar ingestive behavior of animals with ventromedial hypothalamic lesions reflects a general hyperreactivity to the hedonic properties of sensory input, combined, it would appear, with metabolic and endocrine dysfunctions. Such an interpretation accounts readily for the overeating on palatable diets, including the disappearance of this symptom at high body weights when noxious stimuli may arise as a consequence of the animals' extreme body weight; the decreased acceptance of quinine-adulterated or otherwise unpalatable diets unless the animal is defending a very low body weight (and may be experiencing noxious hunger sensations); the decreased willingness to work on reinforcement schedules (such as FR) which are known to be particularly aversive (15, 235); and the increased sensitivity to frustrative nonreward (99). The hypothesis accounts for the effects of preoperative adaptation to unpalatable diets or work requirements and finds support in the observation that neither finickiness nor the apparently low motivational state are unique to feeding. Numerous investigators have reported that rats with VMH lesions drink little or no water when it is quinine adulterated (40, 129, 168) and it appears that this effect can be abolished by preoperative adaptation to the bitter fluid (214). Rats with electrolytic (122) or chemical (78) lesions of the VMH also work less than controls for water as well as food rewards. This effect too can be abolished by preoperative training (122).

Although these considerations deserve, in my opinion, considerably more attention than they have received in recent years, they do not, of course, account for the metabolic and endocrine dysfunctions typical of animals with VMH lesions, and their contribution to the VMH syndrome remains to be elucidated. Exogenous insulin has long been known to increase food intake (147), and many contemporary investigators (30, 59, 189, 259) believe that the hyperinsulinimia that characterizes animals with VMH lesions may be the principal cause of the hyperphagia as well as the obesity.

That insulin is essential for the excessive fat deposition and general obesity portion of the syndrome is demonstrated by a number of experimental findings: destruction of the pancreatic beta cells that secrete insulin, prior to destruction of the VMH (by pancreatectomy or alloxan or streptozotocin treatments) prevents the development of obesity (259, 260) or reduces it markedly (58, 71). When exogenous insulin is administered to these experimentally diabetic rats, overeating and obesity occur. However, the effects are typically smaller than in nondiabetic rats (58, 246, 259), and there are reports of hyperphagia or obesity in insulin-deficient animals (58,

71). These observations clearly demonstrate that rats with VMH lesions can become hyperphagic and obese when pancreatic insulin release is sharply reduced or abolished and controlled circulating insulin levels (which do not result in overeating in nonlesioned diabetic animals) are maintained by the administration of exogenous insulin. The differences in the magnitude of the hyperphagia and obesity between insulin-treated diabetic VMH rats and nondiabetic VMH animals which several studies have demonstrated indicate that the increased insulin level of the VMH animal may, under normal circumstances, contribute to the increased food intake and fat deposition.

Less clear at this time is the relationship between the increased insulin release and hyperphagia itself. In the weanling rat, VMH lesions produce hyperinsulinimia and disorders in fat metabolism but no hyperphagia (60, 61). In the adult, Powley & Opsahl (191) reported that vagatomy [which abolished the hyperinsulinimia according to Powley et al, as cited in (192)] reversed the hyperphagia of VMH lesioned rats—suggesting a causal relationship. However, the results reported by King et al (120) indicate that hyperphagia and obesity can occur in the vagotomized rat. The effects of VMH lesions were somewhat smaller than those seen in nonvagotomized controls, but this need not be due to the elimination of vagally mediated effects on insulin secretion and intermediary metabolism as King et al (120) proposed. It is plausible that the vagotomized VMH rats ate less than their nonvagotomized controls because the prelesion period of adaptation did not entirely eliminate the VMH rats' exaggerated reactivity to the presumably noxious consequences of the vagotomy (that appeared to be the only plausible explanation of the differential effects of vagotomies performed before or after the VMH lesion). Such an interpretation is supported by the common observation that preoperative adaptation ameliorates but rarely eliminates finickiness and poor performance on low-density reward schedules (121, 122, 214).

Matters are complicated by the fact that the vastly increased levels of circulating insulin that have been recorded in rats with VMH lesions are to a large extent the result rather than the initial cause of excessive food intake. Insulin levels are elevated in pair-fed animals not permitted to overeat (98, 103, 229), but the effects are relatively small. Increases in circulating insulin have been observed during the first 24–36 hours after hypothalamic lesions (223, 229), but it is clear that the magnitude of the effect increases as the animal begins to overeat and gains excess weight in the ensuing weeks (94, 223). Indeed, when rats with VMH lesions were allowed only 24 hours of ad libitum intake after the lesion, followed by 24 hours of starvation, insulin levels were normal (94). Insulin increases that persisted after 24 hours of starvation were seen only in animals permitted longer periods of excessive food intake in this study. Rats with VMH lesions typically overeat dramatically during the first 24–48 hours after surgery (16, 32), and it appears doubtful that increased levels of circulating insulin can account for this effect.

Friedman & Stricker (59) have recently proposed a physiological theory of hunger which assumes, in fact, that "an animal with VMH lesions may not increase its food intake *in order to* gain weight but because it is gaining weight." According to this interesting hypothesis the lesion results in a primary disturbance in fat metabolism (increased lipogenesis) that is only secondarily reflected in food intake. The hypothesis is based, in essence, on the observation that rats with VMH lesions incorporate more glucose as fat, use less fatty acids, and mobilize less fat from adipose tissue than controls (62, 69, 70, 93). Some of these changes can occur within a few hours after the lesion (104), but it seems very improbable that their time course could explain the eating seen within seconds after a functional lesion is made in the VMH by local injections of procaine (50, 131). According to Friedman & Stricker (59), hyperphagia is due simply to the fact that more nutrients are removed from the circulation for storage in fat deposits and the animal must increase its intake to maintain an adequate energy balance. Hyperinsulinimia plays an important role in the proposed metabolic disturbances according to this theory, but other factors such as impaired secretion of growth hormone (60) and unspecified "alterations in the neural control of glucose and fat metabolism" are also said to play a significant part in determining food intake.

More impressive than the relatively small initial increase in baseline circulating insulin levels is the effect of VMH lesions on the insulin response that occurs within the first minute after the onset of feeding (228). This presumably centrally mediated sudden insulin release is enormously exaggerated in rats with VMH lesions (145, 222, 223). Powley (189) has suggested that this exaggerated "cephalic reflex" response (which includes various other peripheral reactions, including salivary, gastrointestinal and hepatic functions) to palatable foods may set in motion major adjustments in energy metabolism that eventually cause the hyperphagia. According to this hypothesis the exaggerated cephalic reflexes "shift the animals' energy metabolism in the direction of anabolism and fat storage. A key adjustment is the excessive release of insulin, which promotes lipogenesis, glycogenesis, and consequent hypoglycemia" (189, p. 102). This interpretation is not unlike that proposed by Friedman & Stricker (59), in suggesting that the animal overeats to keep up with its disturbed metabolism. As indicated above, rats with VMH lesions are not hypoglycemic but have normal or even slightly elevated blood glucose levels (94, 98, 221), and hypoglycemia thus cannot be a significant factor in the hyperphagia or metabolic disturbances seen in the VMH rat. Powley's (189) suggestion that exaggerated cephalic reactions to food may be the cause of metabolic disturbances that secondarily increase food intake, fat deposition, and body weight nonetheless deserves further study and consideration.

Anatomical Questions

It has long been known that lesions lateral and caudal to the ventromedial nuclei of the hypothalamus produce hyperphagia and obesity as well as most, if not all, other symptoms of the classic VMH lesion syndrome (33, 73). Indeed, lesions that are confined to the nucleus tend to be ineffective (108). What has been added in recent years is extensive evidence that lesions in structures that are caudal or rostral to the hypothalamus also produce hyperphagia and hyperdipsia. These observations do not, of course, disprove the existence of a hypothalamic satiety center. They do, however, indicate that other central mechanisms may contribute to satiety in still poorly understood ways and have raised the possibility that the VMH may be mainly a funnel for feeding- or satiety-related pathways.

Numerous recent investigations (see below) have demonstrated that an interruption of the caudal connections of the hypothalamus can reproduce the effects of VMH lesions and that electrolytic, surgical, or chemical lesions in various midbrain and lower brainstem sites also produce hyperphagia, obesity, and, in many instances, hyperdipsia. Is this because these lesions interrupt caudal projections from the hypothalamic "satiety center," as Brobeck (32) suggested more than 30 years ago; because afferents and efferents to the stomach, pancreas, and liver are interrupted, as Powley's (189) "cephalic phase" hypothesis seems to suggest; or because ascending catechol- or indol-aminergic pathways somehow influence the hypothalamic satiety mechanism, as Leibowitz (133), Hoebel (101), and others believe? These essential questions have been difficult to answer because visceral afferents and efferents which originate, terminate, or pass through the hypothalamus (169, 171) and the diffuse ascending amine projections are profusely interdigitated in most areas of the brainstem were lesion effects have been reported.

Although the role of visceral afferents and efferents has recently received increased attention (59, 172, 189), there is as yet little specific evidence to relate the facilitatory effects of lower brainstem lesions on food and/or water intake to these projections. The potential role of ascending, aminergic projections, on the other hand, has been the subject of extensive study mainly because there is a substantial body of pharmacological evidence for a role of noradrenergic hypothalamic mechanisms in satiety.

It has long been known that microinjections of noradrenergic (NE) compounds and related substances into the perifornical and medial hypothalamus elicit feeding in sated rats and that NE receptor blockers produce opposite, inhibitory effects in deprived rats (75, 76, 79). Leibowitz (133) has localized this effect in the paraventricular portion of the medial hypothalamus and has described a second region in the perifornical hypothalamus were the injection of β-adrenergic compounds result in opposite, inhibitory effects on food intake. Although the earlier experiments relied on relatively large doses, more recent studies have overcome this criticism to a significant extent (133, 134, 198). Moreover, an internally consistent pattern of results (comparable results from various types of agonists, opposite effects from various types of antagonists) has indicated that the effects of these injections may indeed reflect the activation or inactivation of feeding-related catecholamine neurons. If this conclusion is accurate, one must look to the lower brainstem for the origin of these catecholaminergic pathways, and there is now a good deal of relevant experimental evidence even though the picture is not yet entirely clear and harmonious.

It has been known for some time that coronal knife cuts in the perifornical region lateral and caudal to the ventromedial nucleus (VMN) result in hyperphagia and obesity (80, 92, 156) that may be complicated by hormonal and metabolic dysfunctions (100). Similar cuts directly caudal to the VMN (92, 209) or larger cuts involving the lateral hypothalamus (182) do not reproduce these effects. These observations are significant in the present context because the ventral NE bundle which projects to most of the hypothalamus traverses the perifornical region (107, 139).

A number of investigators (1, 111, 143) have made electrolytic lesions in the perifornical, premammillary, and tegmental trajectory of this diffuse pathway and reported hyperphagia and/or weight gain. Gold (67, 111) concluded from his studies of the effectiveness of premammillary and tegmental lesions (alone or in combination with parasagittal knife cuts lateral to the VMH) that the VMH lesion syndrome was entirely the result of an interruption of the ventral NE bundle. Gold did not support this potentially important hypothesis with biochemical evidence concerning the effects of his lesions on hypothalamic NE levels or activity, and subsequent experiments have supported a much more limited conceptualization of the noradrenergic influence on food intake.

Ahlskog & Hoebel (1) have shown that hyperphagia can be obtained by intrategmental injections of the neurotoxin 6-hydroxydopamine (6-OHDA) which preferentially (but not exclusively) destroys catecholaminergic neurons (35). The effects of these injections (as well as those of electrolytic lesions in the region) are typically small and appear to be additive with VMH lesions (3). Unlike VMH lesions, their effect on feeding appears to be entirely pituitary dependent (2), a fact that is particularly significant in view of Leibowitz's (133) observation that feeding responses to intrahypothalamic injections of NE also disappear after hypophysectomy. This constellation of experimental observations has led most investigators to the conclusion that the NE input to the hypothalamus may play only a specialized function in the regulation of food intake which may be related to the complex hormonal influences on ingestive behavior (247) which have been documented in recent years.

Even this limited conclusion has been questioned by the results of a number of recent studies. Osumi et al (179) did not observe reliable changes in food or water intake after ventral bundle lesions that produced reliable depletions of hypothalamic NE [although the effect was smaller than those reported by Ahlskog et al (2, 3)]. Lorden et al (143) reported obesity after electrolytic lesions in the tegmental trajectory of the ventral NE bundle but could not reproduce the effect with local injections of 6-OHDA which produced larger depletions of hypothalamic NE than the electrolytic lesions. Grossman & Grossman (90) produced significant hyperphagia with surgical knife cuts across the tegmental trajectory of components of the ventral bundle but were unable to obtain reliable correlations between the observed increase in food intake and the extent of NE depletion from hypothalamus or forebrain (91). Redmond et al (194) have recently reported hyperphagia (as well as hyperdipsia) after electrolytic lesions in the locus coeruleus of the monkey which gives rise to the *dorsal* NE projections to the forebrain. Unfortunately, the authors did not investigate the effects of this lesion on hypothalamic NE. It is noteworthy that locus coeruleus lesions in the rat apparently do not affect food intake (8, 179).

There is a fair amount of pharmacological evidence (26) which indicates that various pharmacological treatments that increase the availability of serotonin (5-HT) or directly stimulate serotonin receptors reduce food consumption whereas treatments that inactivate or destroy serotonin receptors elicit or increase feeding. That this is due to an action on central serotonin pathways is suggested by recent reports of hyperphagia and increased growth after intraventricular injections of neurotoxins which reversibly (31) or irreversibly (46, 205) block or destroy serotonergic neurons in the brain [but see (41)]. A specific role of forebrain serotonin is suggested by the recent observation that the hyperphagia that resulted from knife cuts in the tegmentum appeared to be related to the severity of forebrain serotonin depletion (91).

In view of the consistent pharmacological literature, it is surprising to find that lesions that destroy the raphe nuclei (which give rise to the ascending serotonin projections) result in little or no effect on ad libitum food intake (42, 144, 206) and may even prevent the hyperphagia normally seen after VMH lesions (43).

This apparently paradoxical situation finds a perfect match when one considers water intake. Lesions in the raphe nuclei of the brainstem produce quite marked if transient hyperdipsia (42, 144) which does not appear to be secondary to an interference with pituitary functions (42). Yet there is nothing in the pharmacological literature that would lead one to suspect that the regulation of water intake would be affected by an interference with serotonergic pathways either centrally or peripherally (26, 31, 205). It is interesting to note that lesions in the locus coeruleus which gives rise to the dorsal NE projections to the forebrain and has been shown to be intimately connected with the nuclei of the raphe (186) have been reported to result in hyperdipsia in the rat (179, 199) and monkey (194). Electrolytic lesions (179) as well as surgical knife cuts across portions of the tegmentum (90, 91), which deplete forebrain NE severely, produce similar effects.

We thus have ample if largely circumstantial evidence for a significant influence of ascending adrenergic and serotonergic pathways on food as well as water intake, although it is clear that an interruption of these pathways does not duplicate the effects of VMH lesions. It will take a great deal of additional research to elucidate the nature and significance of this input and the specific location of the target neurons in the hypothalamus or elsewhere.

One must not forget, however, that the presently available literature also indicates that brainstem pathways which may not be catechol- or indol-aminergic may be responsible for the effects of some, and possibly all, midbrain lesions on food and water intake. In addition to the uncertainties pointed out in our discussion of the current literature on the biochemical and behavioral effects of chemical, electrolytic, or surgical lesions in the midbrain (above), there are a number of earlier reports of hyperphagia after lesions in portions of the midbrain not known to contain significant cate-chol- or indol-aminergic projections (110, 216). These lesion studies are complemented by reports of feeding after electrical stimulation of electrode sites in the central gray of cats (257), or the region of the motor nucleus of the vagus in the ram (132).

The preceding discussion clearly shows that the influence of caudal brain-stem mechanisms on the hypothesized hypothalamic satiety mechanism is as yet poorly understood. Further complications are introduced by the fact that lesions and/or stimulation of several rostral structures as well as knife cuts that transect rostral (87, 182) and rostrolateral (65, 66, 209, 211) connections of the medial hypothalamus also result in hyperphagia and hyperdipsia.

Hyperphagia, often accompanied by compensatory increases in energy loss, has been reported after lesions in a variety of structures (*81, 85*) including the entorhinal cortex (49, 202), septal area (215), and frontal cortex (197). The effects are typically small when compared to those seen after VMH damage, and it is thus tempting to view the influence of these structures as somehow secondary.

What is less readily disregarded are the often large effects of amygdala or periamygdaloid cortex lesions. Their magnitude and persistence varies with lesion placement and size, and apparently with species (86, 166, 167, 208, 233), but it is clear that they often rival the effects of VMH lesions. Morgane & Kosman (166), for instance, have reported that cats with amygdaloid-piriformcortex lesions consumed two to three times their normal food intake, displayed alternating periods of dynamic hyperphagia (when food intake is far greater than expenditure) and static hyperphagia (when intake approximates output), and eventually became grossly obese. When VMH lesions were added, food intake did not increase further but the rate of weight gain was accelerated (167). That the temporal lobe influence on food intake is indeed mediated by the same pathways that are affected by VMH lesions is indicated by the observation that the selective inhibitory effects of amygdaloid stimulation on food intake (86) are abolished by medial hypothalamic or stria terminalis lesions (256).

CONCLUSIONS

It is difficult to characterize the present state of the field because there is constant activity and constant change. The following conclusions are a tentative appraisal of the situation:

The ventromedial satiety mechanism may influence feeding, in part because it exercises important inhibitory functions with respect to the organism's hedonic response to sensory input, and in part because it exercises control over endocrine and metabolic processes that regulate energy use and storage. Catechol- and possibly also indol-aminergic projections from the lower brainstem as well as inputs from the amygdala and periamygdaloid cortex seem to influence food intake but the nature of their action is as yet poorly understood.

With respect to the excitatory feeding mechanism of the lateral hypothalamus, it is likely that neural mechanisms specifically related to the regulation of feeding and/or drinking are indeed represented in the LH or directly adjacent portions of the subthalamic region. Specific regulatory functions that initiate feeding or drinking in response to insulin-induced hypoglycemia, 2-deoxy-D-glucose–induced cellular glucoprivation, cellular dehydration, and various extracellular thirst stimuli appear to be exercised by neural mechanisms that are sufficiently distinct anatomically in some portions of the area that surgical or electrolytic lesions can produce selective impairments. Largely on the basis of this evidence and the observation of protracted aphagia and adipsia in animals that do not display persisting sensory-motor or arousal dysfunctions, I do not favor Stricker & Zigmond's (227) hypothesis that the LH syndrome is entirely the result of arousal dysfunctions. I do not disagree in any way with their conclusion that a significant disruption of the dopaminergic nigrostriatal projection system results in severe arousal deficits that may well interfere with ingestive (as well as other) behaviors or that arousal dysfunctions may contribute to the immediate, postoperative consequences of LH lesions. My reading of the complex knife cut literature leads me to believe that ingestive behavior may be organized by an interaction of hypothalamic, subthalamic, and striatal mechanisms and the latter may exercise quite selective influences on feeding and drinking behavior.

Literature Cited

1. Ahlskog, J. E., Hoebel, B. G. 1973. Overeating and obesity from damage to a noradrenergic system in the brain. *Science* 182:166–69
2. Ahlskog, J. E., Hoebel, B. G., Breisch, S. T. 1974. Hyperphagia following lesions of the noradrenergic pathway is prevented by hypophysectomy. *Fed. Proc.* 33:463 (Abstr.)
3. Ahlskog, J. E., Randall, P. K., Hoebel, B. G. 1975. Hypothalamic hyperphagia: dissociation from hyperphagia following destruction of noradrenergic neurons. *Science* 190:399–401
4. Albert, D. J., Storlien, L. H., Wood, D. J., Ehman, G. K. 1970. Further evidence for a complex system controlling feeding behavior. *Physiol. Behav.* 5:1075–82
5. Alheid, G. F. 1975. *Striatal neural connections and the lateral hypothalamic syndrome.* PhD thesis. Univ. Chicago, Chicago, Ill.
6. Alheid, G. F., Kelly, J., McDermott, L. J., Halaris, A., Grossman, S. P. 1977. Supersensitivity to norepinephrine or dopamine antagonists after knife cuts that produce aphagia and adipsia in rats. *Pharmacol. Biochem. Behav.* 6:647–57
7. Alheid, G. F., McDermott, L. J., Kelly, J., Halaris, A., Grossman, S. P. 1977. Deficits in food and water intake after knife cuts that deplete striatal DA or hypothalamic NE in rats. *Pharmacol. Biochem. Behav.* 6:273–87
8. Amaral, D. G., Foss, J. A. 1975. Locus coeruleus lesions and learning. *Science* 188:377–88
9. Anand, B. K., Brobeck, J. R. 1951. Localization of a feeding center in the hypothalamus of the rat. *Proc. Soc. Exp. Biol. Med.* 77:323–24
10. Anand, B. K., Dua, S., Chhina, G. S. 1958. Higher nervous control over food intake. *Indian J. Med. Res.* 46:277–78

11. Anand, B. K., Dua, S., Singh, B. 1961. Electrical activity of the hypothalamic "feeding centres" under the effect of changes in blood chemistry. *Electroencephalogr. Clin. Neurophysiol.* 13:54–59
12. Andersson, B. 1953. The effect of injections of hypertonic NaCl-solutions into different parts of the hypothalamus of goats. *Acta Physiol. Scand.* 28:188–201
13. Andersson, B., Wyrwicka, W. 1957. The elicitation of a drinking motor conditioned reaction by electrical stimulation of the "drinking area" of the goat. *Acta Physiol. Scand.* 41:194–98
14. Antelman, S. M., Rowland, N. E., Fisher, A. E. 1977. Stimulation bound ingestive behavior: A view from the tail. *Physiol. Behav.* 17:743–48
15. Azrin, N. H. 1961. Time-out from positive reinforcement. *Science* 133:382–83
16. Balagura, S., Devenport, L. D. 1970. Feeding patterns of normal and ventromedial hypothalamic lesioned male and female rats. *J. Comp. Physiol. Psychol.* 71:357–64
17. Balagura, S., Kanner, M. 1971. Hypothalamic sensitivity to 2-deoxy-D-glucose and glucose: effects on feeding behavior. *Physiol. Behav.* 7:977–80
18. Balagura, S., Wilcox, R. H., Coscina, D. V. 1969. The effects of diencephalic lesions on food intake and motor activity. *Physiol. Behav.* 4:629–33
19. Beatty, W. W. 1973. Influence of type of reinforcement on operant responding by rats with ventromedial lesions. *Physiol. Behav.* 10:841–46
20. Becker, E. E., Kissileff, H. R. 1974. Inhibitory controls of feeding by the ventromedial hypothalamus. *Am. J. Physiol.* 226:383–96
21. Bernardis, L. L., Schnatz, J. D. 1971. Localization in the ventromedial hypothalamic nuclei of an area affecting plasma triglyceride and cholesterol levels. *J. Neuro-Vis. Relat.* 32:90–103

22. Berntson, G. G., Hughes, H. C. 1974. Medullary mechanisms for eating and grooming behaviors in the cat. *Exp. Neurol.* 44:255–65

23. Berthoud, H. R., Jeanrenaud, B. 1977. Acute hypothalamic control of insulin secretion in the rat. *Int. Conf. Physiol. Food Fluid Intake, 6th, Paris* (Abstr.)

24. Blass, E. M., Epstein, A. N. 1971. A lateral preoptic osmosensitive zone for thirst in the rat. *J. Comp. Physiol. Psychol.* 76:378–94

25. Blass, E. M., Kraly, F. S. 1974. Medial forebrain bundle lesions: specific loss of feeding to decreased glucose utilization in rats. *J. Comp. Physiol. Psychol.* 86:679–92

26. Blundell, J. E. 1977. Is there a role for serotonin (5-hydroxytryptamine) in feeding? *Int. J. Obesity* 1:15–42

27. Booth, D. A. 1972. Model of the feeding responses to peripheral insulin, 2-deoxy-D-glucose or 3-O-methyl-glucose injections. *Physiol. Behav.* 8:1069–76

28. Box, B. M., Mogenson, G. J. 1975. Alterations in ingestive behaviors after bilateral lesions of the amygdala in the rat. *Physiol. Behav.* 15:679–88

29. Boyle, P. C., Keesey, R. E. 1975. Chronically reduced levels of body weight in LH lesioned rats maintained upon diets and drinking solutions of varying palatability. *J. Comp. Physiol. Psychol.* 88:218–23

30. Bray, G. A. 1974. Endocrine factors in the control of food intake. *Fed. Proc.* 33:1140–45

31. Breisch, S. T., Zemlan, F. P., Hoebel, B. G. 1976. Hyperphagia and obesity following serotonin depletion by intraventricular p-chlorophenylalanine. *Science* 192:382–85

32. Brobeck, J. R. 1946. Mechanisms of the development of obesity in animals with hypothalamic lesions. *Physiol. Rev.* 26:541–59

33. Brobeck, J. R., Tepperman, J., Long, C. N. H. 1943. Experimental hypothalamic hyperphagia in the albino rat. *Yale J. Biol. Med.* 15:831–53

34. Brooks, C. McC., Lambert, E. F. 1946. A study of the effect of limitation of food intake and the method of feeding on the rate of weight gain during hypothalamic obesity in the albino rat. *Am. J. Physiol.* 147:695–707

35. Butcher, L. L. 1975. Degenerative processes after punctate intracerebral administration of 6-hydroxydopamine. *J. Neural Transm.* 37:189–208

36. Butter, C. M., Snyder, D. R. 1972. Alterations in aversive and aggressive behaviors following orbitofrontal lesions in rhesus monkeys. *Acta Neurobiol. Exp.* 32:525–66

37. Carlisle, H. J., Stellar, E. 1969. Caloric regulation and food preference in normal, hyperphagic and aphagic rats. *J. Comp. Physiol. Psychol.* 69:107–14

38. Collins, E. H. 1954. Localization of an experimental hypothalamic and midbrain syndrome simulating sleep. *J. Comp. Neurol.* 100:661–97

39. Coons, E. E., Levak, M., Miller, N. E. 1965. Lateral hypothalamus: learning of food-seeking response motivated by electrical stimulation. *Science* 150:1320–21

40. Corbit, J. D. 1965. Hyperphagic hyperreactivity to adulteration of drinking water with quinine HCl. *J. Comp. Physiol. Psychol.* 60:123–24

41. Coscina, D. V. 1978. Effects of central 5,7-dihydroxytryptamine on the medial hypothalamic syndrome in rats. Serotonin neurotoxins. *Ann. NY Acad. Sci.* In press

42. Coscina, D. V., Grant, L. D., Balagura, S., Grossman, S. P. 1972. Hyperdipsia following serotonin-depleting midbrain lesions. *Nature New Biol.* 235:63–64

43. Coscina, D. V., Stancer, H. C. 1976. Selective blockade of hypothalamic hyperphagia and obesity in rats by serotonin-depleting midbrain lesions. *Science* 195:416–19

44. Dacey, D. M., Grossman, S. P. 1977. Aphagia, adipsia, and sensory-motor deficits produced by amygdala lesions: A function of extra-amygdaloid damage. *Physiol. Behav.* 19:389–98

45. David, J. D., Collins, B. J., Levine, M. M. 1976. In *Hunger: Basic Mechanisms and Clinical Implications,* ed. D. Novin, W. Wyrwicka, G. A. Bray, pp. 395–408. New York: Raven. 494 pp.

46. Diaz, J., Ellison, G., Masuoka, D. 1974. Opposed behaviour syndromes in rats with partial and more complete central serotonergic lesions made with 5,6-dihydroxytryptamine. *Psychopharmacologia* 37:67–75

47. Di Cara, L. V., Wolf, G. 1968. Bar pressing for food reinforcement after lesions of efferent pathways from lateral hypothalamus. *Exp. Neurol.* 21:231–35

48. Donald, D. E. 1952. Esophageal dysfunction in the rat after vagotomy. *Surgery* 31:251–57

49. Entingh, D. 1971. Perseverative responding and hyperphagia following entorhinal cortex lesions in cats. *J. Comp. Physiol. Psychol.* 75:50–58

50. Epstein, A. N. 1960. Reciprocal changes in feeding behavior produced by intra-hypothalamic chemical injections. *Am. J. Physiol.* 199:969–74

51. Epstein, A. N., Nicolaidis, S., Miselis, R. 1975. In *Neural Integration of Physiological Mechanisms and Behavior*, ed. G. J. Mogenson, F. R. Calaresu, pp. 148–68. Toronto: Univ. Toronto Press. 442 pp.

52. Epstein, A. N., Teitelbaum, P. 1967. Specific loss of the hypoglycemic control of feeding in recovered lateral rats. *Am. J. Physiol.* 213:1159–67

53. Ferguson, N. B. L., Keesey, R. E. 1975. Effect of a quinine-adulterated diet upon body weight maintenance in male rats with ventromedial hypothalamic lesions. *J. Comp. Physiol. Psychol.* 89: 478–88

54. Fibiger, H. C., Phillips, A. G., Clouston, R. A. 1973. Regulatory deficits after unilateral electrolytic or 6-OHDA lesions of the substantia nigra. *Am. J. Physiol.* 225:1282–87

55. Fibiger, H. C., Zis, A. P., McGeer, E. G. 1973. Feeding and drinking deficits after 6-hydroxydopamine administration in the rat: similarities to the lateral hypothalamic syndrome. *Brain Res.* 55:135–48

56. Fonberg, E. 1969. Effects of small dorsomedial amygdala lesions on food intake and acquisition of instrumental alimentary reactions in dogs. *Physiol. Behav.* 4:739–43

57. Franklin, K. B., Herberg, L. J. 1974. Ventromedial syndrome: The rats 'finickiness' results from the obesity not from the lesion. *J. Comp. Physiol. Psychol.* 87:410–14

58. Friedman, M. I. 1972. Effects of alloxan diabetes on hypothalamic hyperphagia and obesity. *Am. J. Physiol.* 222:174–78

59. Friedman, M. I., Stricker, E. M. 1976. The physiological psychology of hunger: A physiological perspective. *Psychol. Rev.* 83:409–31

60. Frohman, L. A., Bernardis, L. L. 1968. Growth hormone and insulin levels in weanling rats with ventromedial hypothalamic lesions. *Endocrinology* 82: 1125–32

61. Frohman, L. A., Bernardis, L. L., Schnatz, J. D., Burek, L. 1969. Plamsa insulin and trigliceride levels after hypothalamic lesions in weanling rats. *Am. J. Physiol.* 216:1496–1501

62. Frohman, L. A., Goldman, J. K., Bernardis, L. L. 1972. Metabolism of intravenously injected ^{14}C-glucose in weanling rats with hypothalamic obesity. *Metabolism* 21:799–805

63. Glick, S. D., Greenstein, S., Waters, D. H. 1974. Lateral hypothalamic lesions and striatal dopamine levels. *Life Sci.* 14:747–50

64. Gold, R. M. 1967. Aphagia and adipsia following unilateral and bilaterally asymmetrical lesions in rats. *Physiol. Behav.* 2:211–20

65. Gold, R. M. 1970. Hypothalamic hyperphagia produced by parasagittal knife cuts. *Physiol. Behav.* 5:23–25

66. Gold, R. M., Jones, A. P., Sawcheko, P. E., Kapatos, G. 1977. Paraventricular area: critical focus of a longitudinal neurocircuitry mediating food intake. *Physiol. Behav.* 18:1111–19

67. Gold, R. M., Quackenbush, P. M., Kapatos, G. 1972. Obesity following combination of rostrolateral to VMH cut and contralateral mammillary area lesions. *J. Comp. Physiol. Psychol.* 79:210–18

68. Goldman, J. K., Bernardis, L. L. 1975. Gluconeogenesis in weanling rats with hypothalamic obesity. *Horm. Metab. Res.* 7:148–52

69. Goldman, J. K., Schnatz, J. D., Bernardis, L. L., Frohman, L. A. 1970. Adipose tissue metabolism of weanling rats after destruction of ventromedial hypothalamic nuclei: Effect of hypophysectomy and growth hormone. *Metabolism* 19:995–1005

70. Goldman, J. K., Schnatz, J. D., Bernardis, L. L., Frohman, L. A. 1972. In vivo and in vitro metabolism in hypothalamic obesity. *Diabetologia* 8: 160–64

71. Goldman, J. K., Schnatz, J. D., Bernardis, L. L., Frohman, L. A. 1972. Effects of ventromedial hypothalamic destruction in rats with preexisting streptozotocin-induced diabetes. *Metabolism* 21: 132–36

72. Gonzales, M. F., Novin, D. 1974. Feeding induced by intracranial and intravenously administered 2-deoxy-D-glucose. *Physiol. Psychol.* 2:326–30

73. Graff, H., Stellar, E. 1962. Hyperphagia, obesity and finickiness. *J. Comp. Physiol. Psychol.* 55:418–24

74. Green, J. D., Clemente, C. D., De-Groot, J. 1957. Rhinencephalic lesions and behavior in cats. *J. Comp. Neurol.* 108:505–45

75. Grossman, S. P. 1962. Direct adrenergic and cholinergic stimulation of hypothalamic mechanisms. *Am. J. Physiol.* 202:872–82

76. Grossman, S. P. 1962. Effects of adrenergic and cholinergic blocking agents on hypothalamic mechanisms. *Am. J. Physiol.* 202:1230–36

77. Grossman, S. P. 1964. Behavioral effects of chemical stimulation of the ventral amygdala. *J. Comp. Physiol. Psychol.* 57:29–36

78. Grossman, S. P. 1966. The VMH: A center for affective reaction, satiety, or both? *Physiol. Behav.* 1:1–10

79. Grossman, S. P. 1967. In *Handbook of Physiology. Section on the Alimentary Canal,* ed. C. F. Code, pp. 287–302. Baltimore: Williams & Wilkins. 459 pp.

80. Grossman, S. P. 1971. Changes in food and water intake associated with an interruption of the anterior or posterior fiber connections of the hypothalamus. *J. Comp. Physiol. Psychol.* 75:23–31

81. Grossman, S. P. 1972. Neurophysiologic aspects: Extrahypothalamic factors in the regulation of food intake. *Adv. Psychosom. Med.* 7:49–72

82. Grossman, S. P. 1975. Role of the hypothalamus in the regulation of food and water intake. *Psychol. Rev.* 82:200–24

83. Grossman, S. P. 1976. See Ref. 45, pp. 51–60

84. Grossman, S. P. 1978. In *Handbook of Nutrition and Food,* ed. M. Rechcigl. Cleveland: CRC Press. In press

85. Grossman, S. P. 1978. In *Central Mechanisms of Anoretic Drugs,* ed. S. Garattini, R. Samanin. New York: Raven. In press

86. Grossman, S. P., Grossman, L. 1963. Food and water intake following lesions or electrical stimulation of the amygdala. *Am. J. Physiol.* 205:761–65

87. Grossman, S. P., Grossman, L. 1970. Surgical interruption of the anterior or posterior connections of the hypothalamus: Effects on aggressive and avoidance behavior. *Physiol. Behav.* 5:1313–17

88. Grossman, S. P., Grossman, L. 1971. Food and water intake in rats with parasagittal knife cuts medial and lateral to the lateral hypothalamus. *J. Comp. Physiol. Psychol.* 74:148–56

89. Grossman, S. P., Grossman, L. 1973. Persisting deficits in rats "recovered" from transections of the fibers which enter or leave the hypothalamus laterally. *J. Comp. Physiol. Psychol.* 85:515–27

90. Grossman, S. P., Grossman, L. 1977. Food and water intake in rats after transections of fibers en passage in the tegmentum. *Physiol. Behav.* 18:647–58

91. Grossman, S. P., Grossman, L., Halaris, A. 1977. Effects on hypothalamic and telencephalic NE and 5-HT of tegmental knife cuts that produce hyperphagia and hyperdipsia in the rat. *Pharmacol. Biochem. Behav.* 6:101–6

92. Grossman, S. P., Hennessy, J. W. 1976. Differential effects of coronal cuts through the posterior hypothalamus on food intake and body weight in male and female rats. *Physiol. Behav.* 17:89–102

93. Haessler, H. A., Crawford, J. D. 1967. Fatty acid composition and metabolic activity of depot fat in experimental obesity. *Am. J. Physiol.* 213:255–61

94. Hales, C. N., Kennedy, G. C. 1964. Plasma glucose, non-esterified fatty acid and insulin concentrations in hypothalamic-hyperphagic rats. *Biochem. J.* 90:620–24

95. Hamburg, M. D. 1971. Hypothalamic unit activity and eating behavior. *Am. J. Physiol.* 220:980–85

96. Han, P. W. 1967. Hypothalamic obesity in rats without hyperphagia. *Ann. NY Acad. Sci.* 30:229–43

97. Han, P. W. 1968. Energy metabolism of tube-fed hypophysectomized rats bearing hypothalamic lesions. *Am. J. Physiol.* 215:1343–50

98. Han, P. W., Frohman, L. A. 1970. Hyperinsulinemia in tube-fed hypophysectomized rats bearing hypothalamic lesions. *Am. J. Physiol.* 219:1632–36

99. Henke, P. G. 1974. Lesions in the ventromedial hypothalamus and response to frustrative nonreward. *Physiol. Behav.* 13:143–46

100. Hennessy, J. W., Grossman, S. P. 1976. Overeating and obesity produced by interruption of the caudal connections of the hypothalamus: Evidence of hormonal and metabolic disruption. *Physiol. Behav.* 17:103–10

101. Hoebel, B. G. 1976. In *Brain Stimulation Reward,* ed. A. Wauquier, E. T. Rolls, pp. 335–72. Amsterdam: North Holland. 622 pp.

102. Hoebel, B. G., Teitelbaum, P. 1966. Weight regulation by normal and hypothalamic hyperphagic rats. *J. Comp. Physiol. Psychol.* 61:189–93

103. Hustvedt, B. E., Lovo, A. 1972. Correlation between hyperinsulinemia and hyperphagia in rats with ventromedial hypothalamic lesions. *Acta Physiol. Scand.* 84:29–33

104. Hustvedt, B. E., Lovo, A. 1973. Rapid effect of ventromedial hypothalamic lesions on lipogenesis in rats. *Acta Physiol. Scand.* 87:28A–29A

105. Inoue, S., Bray, G. A. 1977. The effects of subdiaphramatic vagotomy in rats with ventromedial hypothalamic obesity. *Endocrinology* 100:108–14

106. Iversen, S. D. 1971. The effects of surgical lesions to frontal cortex and substantia nigra on amphetamine responses in rats. *Brain Res.* 31:295–311

107. Jacobowitz, D. M., Palkovits, M. 1974. Topographic atlas of catecholamine and acetylcholinesterase containing neurons in the rat brain. I. Forebrain (telencephalon and diencephalon). *J. Comp. Neurol.* 157:13–28

108. Joseph, S. A., Knigge, J. M. 1968. Effects of VMH lesions in adult and newborn guinea pigs. *Neuroendocrinology* 3:309–31

109. Kaada, B. R. 1951. Somatomotor, autonomic and electrocorticographic responses to electrical stimulation of rhinencephalic and other structures in primates, cat and dog: A study of responses from the limbic, subcallosal, orbital, insular, pyriform, and temporal cortex, hippocampus, fornix and amygdala. *Acta Physiol. Scand.* 24:Suppl. 83, pp. 1–285

110. Kaelber, W. W., Mitchell, C. L., Way, J. S. 1965. Some sensory influences on savage (affective) behavior in cats. *Am. J. Physiol.* 209:866–70

111. Kapatos, G., Gold, R. M. 1973. Evidence for ascending noradrenergic mediation of hypothalamic hyperphagia. *Pharmacol. Biochem. Behav.* 1:81–87

112. Karakash, C., Hustvedt, B. E., Lovo, A., Le Marchand, Y., Jeanrenaud, B. 1977. Consequences of ventromedial hypothalamic lesions on metabolism of perfused rat liver. *Am. J. Physiol.* 232:E286–E293

113. Keesey, R. E., Boyle, P. C. 1973. Effects of quinine adulteration upon the body weight of LH-lesioned and intact male rats. *J. Comp. Physiol. Psychol.* 84:38–46

114. Keesey, R. E., Boyle, P. C., Kemnitz, J. W., Mitchel, J. S. 1976. See Ref. 45, pp. 243–55

115. Kelly, J., Alheid, G. F., McDermott, L. J., Halaris, A., Grossman, S. P. 1977. Behavioral and biochemical effects of knife cuts that preferentially interrupt principal afferent and efferent connections of the striatum in the rat. *Pharmacol. Biochem. Behav.* 6:31–45

116. Kennedy, G. C. 1961. The central nervous regulation of caloric balance. *Proc. Nutr. Soc.* 20:58–64

117. Kent, E. W., Grossman, S. P. 1973. Elimination of learned behaviors after transection of fibers crossing the lateral border of the hypothalamus. *Physiol. Behav.* 10:953–63

118. Kent, E. W., Rezak, M., Grossman, S. P. 1973. Transection and chemical lesion of nigrostriatal pathways: A comparison of effects on learned behavior. *Proc. Soc. Neurosci.* 3:410 (Abstr.)

119. Kent, M. A., Peters, R. H. 1973. Effects of ventromedial hypothalamic lesions on hunger-motivated behavior in rats. *J. Comp. Physiol. Psychol.* 83:92–97

120. King, B. M., Carpenter, R. G., Stamoutsos, B. A., Frohman, L. A., Grossman, S. P. 1978. Hyperphagia and obesity following ventromedial hypothalamic lesions in rats with subdiaphragmatic vagotomy. *Physiol. Behav.* In press

121. King, B. M., Gaston, M. G. 1973. The effects of pretraining on the bar-pressing performance of VMH-lesioned rats. *Physiol. Behav.* 11:161–66

122. King, B. M., Gaston, M. G. i976. Factors influencing the hunger and thirst motivated behavior of hypothalamic hyperphagia rats. *Physiol. Behav.* 16:33–41

123. King, B. M., Gaston, M. G. 1977. Reappearance of dynamic hyperphagia during the static phase in medial hypothalamic lesioned rats. *Physiol. Behav.* 18:945–50

124. King, B. M., Grossman, S. P. 1977. Response to glucoprivic and hydrational challenges by normal and hypothalamic hyperphagic rats. *Physiol. Behav.* 18:463–73

125. King, B. M., Stamoutsos, B. A., Grossman, S. P. 1978. Delayed response to 2-deoxy-D-glucose in hypothalamic obese rats. *Pharmacol. Biochem. Behav.* In press

126. Koikegami, H., Fuse, S., Yokoyama, T., Watanabe, T., Watanabe, H. 1955. Contributions of the comparative anatomy of the amygdaloid nuclei of mammals with some experiments of their destruction or stimulation. *Folia Psychiatr. Neurol. Jpn.* 8:336–68

127. Kolb, B., Nonneman, A. J. 1975. Prefrontal cortex and the regulation of food intake in the rat. *J. Comp. Physiol. Psychol.* 88:806–15

128. Kraly, F. S., Gibbs, J., Smith, G. P. 1975. Disordered drinking after abdominal vagotomy in rats. *Nature* 258:226–28

129. Krasne, F. B. 1966. Decreased tolerance of hypothalamic hyperphagics to quinine in drinking water. *Psychon. Sci.* 4:313–14

130. Kucharczyk, J., Mogenson, G. J. 1975. Separate lateral hypothalamic pathways for extracellular and intracellular thirst. *Am. J. Physiol.* 228:295–301
131. Larkin, R. P. 1975. Effect of ventromedial hypothalamic procaine injections on feeding, lever pressing, and other behaviors in rats. *J. Comp. Physiol. Psychol.* 89:1100–8
132. Larsson, S. 1954. On the hypothalamic organization of the nervous mechanism regulating food intake. *Acta Physiol. Scand.* 32:Suppl. 115, pp. 1–63
133. Leibowitz, S. F. 1976. See Ref. 45, pp. 1–18
134. Leibowitz, S. F. 1978. See Ref. 85. In press
135. Levine, M. S., Schwartzbaum, J. S. 1973. Sensory-motor functions of the striatopallidal system and lateral hypothalamus and consummatory behavior in rats. *J. Comp. Physiol. Psychol.* 85:615–35
136. Levison, M. J., Frommer, G. P., Vance, W. B. 1973. Palatability and caloric density as determinants of food intake in hyperphagic and normal rats. *Physiol. Behav.* 10:455–62
137. Levitt, D. R., Teitelbaum, P. 1975. Somnolence, akinesia, and sensory activation of motivated behavior in the lateral hypothalamic syndrome. *Proc. Natl. Acad. Sci. USA* 72:2819–23
138. Liebelt, R. A., Perry, J. H. 1957. Hypothalamic lesions associated with goldthioglucose-induced obesity. *Proc. Soc. Exp. Biol. Med.* 95:774
139. Lindvall, O., Bjorklund, A. 1974. The organization of the ascending catecholamine neuron systems in the rat brain as revealed by the glyoxylic acid fluorescence method. *Acta Physiol. Scand. Suppl.* 412:1–48
140. Linseman, M. A., Olds, J. 1973. Activity changes in rat hypothalamus, preoptic area and striatum associated with Pavlovian conditioning. *J. Neurophysiol.* 36:1038–50
141. Liu, C. M., Yin, T. H. 1974. Caloric compensation to gastric loads in rats with hypothalamic hyperphagia. *Physiol. Behav.* 13:231–38
142. Ljungberg, T., Ungerstedt, U. 1976. Reinstatement of eating by dopamine agonists in aphagic dopamine denervated rats. *Physiol. Behav.* 16:277–83
143. Lorden, J., Oltmans, G. A., Margules, D. L. 1976. Central noradrenergic neurons: differential effects on body weight of electrolytic and 6-hydroxydopamine lesions in rats. *J. Comp. Physiol. Psychol.* 90:144–55
144. Lorens, S. A., Sorensen, J. P., Yunger, L. M. 1971. Behavioral and neurochemical effects of lesions in the raphé system of the rat. *J. Comp. Physiol. Psychol.* 77:48–52
145. Louis-Sylvestre, J. 1976. Preabsorptive insulin release and hypoglycemia in rats. *Am. J. Physiol.* 230:56–60
146. Lyon, M., Halpern, M., Mintz, E. 1968. The significance of the mesencephalon for coordinated feeding behavior. *Acta Neurol. Scand.* 44:323–46
147. MacKay, E. M., Callaway, J. W., Barnes, R. H. 1940. Hyperalimentation in normal animals produced by protamine insulin. *J. Nutr.* 20:59–66
148. MacLean, P. D., Delgado, J. M. R. 1953. Electrical and chemical stimulation of fronto-temporal portion of limbic system in the waking animal. *Electroencephalogr. Clin. Neurophysiol.* 5:91–100
149. Marks, H. E., Remley, N. R. 1972. The effects of type of lesion and percentage body weight loss on measures of motivated behavior in rats with hypothalamic lesions. *Behav. Biol.* 7:95–111
150. Marrazzi, M. A. 1976. See Ref. 45, pp. 171–78
151. Marshall, J. F. 1975. Increased orientation to sensory stimuli following medial hypothalamic damage in rats. *Brain Res.* 86:373–87
152. Marshall, J. F., Richardson, J. S., Teitelbaum, P. 1974. Nigrostriatal bundle damage and the lateral hypothalamic syndrome. *J. Comp. Physiol. Psychol.* 87:808–30
153. Marshall, J. F., Teitelbaum, P. 1974. Further analysis of sensory inattention following lateral hypothalamic damage in rats. *J. Comp. Physiol. Psychol.* 86:375–95
154. Marshall, J. F., Turner, B. H., Teitelbaum, P. 1971. Sensory neglect produced by lateral hypothalamic damage. *Science* 174:523–25
155. Marshall, J. F., Ungerstedt, U. 1976. Apomorphine-induced restoration of drinking to thirst challenges in 6-hydroxydopamine-treated rats. *Phsyiol. Behav.* 17:817–22
156. McDermott, L. J., Alheid, G. F., Halaris, A., Grossman, S. P. 1977. A correlational analysis of the effects of surgical transections of three components of the MFB on ingestive behavior and hypothalamic, striatal and telencephalic amine concentrations. *Pharmacol. Biochem. Behav.* 6:203–14
157. McDermott, L. J., Alheid, G. F., Kelly, J., Halaris, A., Grossman, S. P. 1977.

Regulatory deficits after surgical transections of three components of the MFB: Correlation with regional amine depletions. *Pharmacol. Biochem. Behav.* 6:397–407

158. Micco, D. J. 1974. Complex behaviors elicited by stimulation of the dorsal pontine tegmentum in rats. *Brain Res.* 75:172–76

159. Miller, N. E. 1963. Some motivational effects of electrical and chemical stimulation of the brain. *Electroencephalogr. Clin. Neurophysiol. Suppl.* 24:247–59

160. Miller, N. E., Bailey, C. J., Stevenson, J. A. F. 1950. "Decreased hunger" but increased food intake resulting from hypothalamic lesions. *Science* 112:256–59

161. Millhouse, O. E. 1973. The organization of the ventromedial hypothalamic nucleus. *Brain Res.* 55:71–87

162. Mogenson, G. J. 1973. In *The Neuropsychology of Thirst*, ed. A. E. Epstein, H, R. Kissleff, E. Stellar, pp. 119–42. Washington DC: Winston. 357 pp.

163. Mogenson, G. J., Stevenson, J. A. F. 1967. Drinking induced by electrical stimulation of the lateral hypothalamus. *Exp. Neurol.* 17:119–27

164. Morgane, P. J. 1961. Alterations in feeding and drinking behavior of rats with lesions in globi pallidi. *Am. J. Physiol.* 201:420–28

165. Morgane, P. J. 1961. Medial forebrain bundle and "feeding centers" of the hypothalamus. *J. Comp. Neurol.* 117:1–26

166. Morgane, P. J., Kosman, A. J. A. 1957. Rhinencephalic feeding center in the cat. *Am. J. Physiol.* 197:158–62

167. Morgane, P. J., Kosman, A. J. A. 1960. Relationship of the middle hypothalamus to amygdalar hyperphagia. *Am. J. Physiol.* 198:1315–18

168. Nachman, M. 1967. Hypothalamic hyperphagia, finickiness, and taste preference in rats. *Proc. Ann. Conv. Am. Psychol. Assoc., 75th, Washington DC* 2:127–28

169. Nauta, W. J. H., Haymaker, W. 1969. In *The Hypothalamus*, ed. W. Haymaker, E. Anderson, W. J. H. Nauta, pp. 130–209. Springfield, Ill: Thomas. 805 pp.

170. Neill, D. B., Linn, C. L. 1975. Deficits in consummatory responses to regulatory challenges following basal ganglia lesions in rats. *Physiol. Behav.* 14:617–24

171. Norgren, R. 1976. Taste pathways to the hypothalamus and amygdala. *J. Comp. Neurol.* 166:17–30

172. Novin, D. 1976. See Ref. 45, pp. 357–68

173. Olds, J. 1976. See Ref. 101, pp. 1–30

174. Olds, J., Mink, D., Best, P. J. 1969. Single unit patterns during anticipatory behavior. *Electroencephalogr. Clin. Neurophysiol.* 26:144–58

175. Oltmans, G. A., Harvey, J. A. 1972. LH syndrome and brain catecholamine levels after lesions of the nigrostriatal bundle. *Physiol. Behav.* 8:69–78

176. One, T., Oomura, Y., Sugimori, M., Nakamura, T., Shimizu, N., Kita, H., Ishibashi, S. 1976. See Ref. 45, pp. 159–70

177. Oomura, Y. 1973. Central mechanisms of feeding. *Adv. Biophys.* 5:65–142

178. Oomura, Y. 1976. See Ref. 45, pp. 145–58

179. Osumi, Y., Oishi, R., Fujiwara, H., Takatori, S. 1975. Hyperdipsia induced by bilateral destruction of the locus coeruleus in rats. *Brain Res.* 86:419–27

180. Panksepp, J. 1974. Hypothalamic regulation of energy balance and feeding behavior. *Fed. Proc.* 33:1150–65

181. Parker, S. W., Feldman, S. M. 1967. Effect of mesencephalic lesions on feeding behavior in rats. *Exp. Neurol.* 17:313–26

182. Paxinos, G., Bindra, D. 1972. Hypothalamic knife cuts: effects on eating, drinking, irritability, aggression, and copulation in the male rat. *J. Comp. Physiol. Psychol.* 79:219–29

183. Peck, J. W., Novin, D. 1971. Evidence that osmoreceptors mediating drinking in rabbits are in the lateral preoptic area. *J. Comp. Physiol. Psychol.* 74:134–47

184. Peters, R. H., Sensenig, L. D., Reich, M. J. 1973. Fixed-ratio performance following ventromedial hypothalamic lesions in rats. *Physiol. Psychol.* 1:136–38

185. Pettibone, D., Lytle, L. D., Scally, M. C., Meyer, E., Kaufman, N. 1977. Feeding behavior: possible involvement of non-dopaminergic striatal neurons. *Fed. Proc.* 36:394 (Abstr.)

186. Pickel, V. M., Joh, T. H., Reis, D. J. 1977. A serotonergic innervation of noradrenergic neurons in nucleus locus coeruleus: demonstration by immunochemical localization of the transmitter specific enzymes tyrosine and tryptophan hydroxylase. *Brain Res.* 131:197–214

187. Poirier, L. J., Langelier, P., Roberge, A., Boucher, R., Kitsikis, A. 1972. Non-specific histopathological changes induced by the intracerebral injection of

6-hydroxydopamine (6-Oh-DA). *J. Neurol. Sci.* 16:401–16

188. Porter, J. H., Allen, J. D., Arazie, R. 1974. Reinforcement frequency and body weight as determinants of motivated behavior in hypothalamic hyperphagic rats. *Physiol. Behav.* 13:627–32

189. Powley, T. L. 1977. The ventromedial hypothalamic syndrome, satiety, and a cephalic phase hypothesis. *Psychol. Rev.* 84:89–126

190. Powley, T. L., Keesey, R. E. 1970. Relationship of body weight to the lateral hypothalamic feeding syndrome. *J. Comp. Physiol. Psychol.* 70:25–36

191. Powley, T. L., Opsahl, C. A. 1974. Ventromedial hypothalamic obesity abolished by subdiaphragmatic vagotomy. *Am. J. Physiol.* 226:25–33

192. Powley, T. L., Opsahl, C. A. 1976. See Ref. 45, pp. 313–26

193. Rabin, B. M. 1974. Independence of food intake and obesity following ventromedial hypothalamic lesions in the rat. *Physiol. Behav.* 13:769–72

194. Redmond, D. E., Huang, Y. H., Baulu, J., Snyder, R. D., Maas, J. W. 1977. In *Anorexia Nervosa*, ed. R. A. Vigersky, pp. 81–96. New York: Raven. 496 pp.

195. Reynolds, R. W., Kimm, J. 1965. Effects of glucose on food intake in hypothalamic hyperphagic rats. *J. Comp. Physiol. Psychol.* 60:438–40

196. Rezek, M., Vanderweele, D. A., Novin, D. 1975. Stages in the recovery of feeding following vagotomy in rabbits. *Behav. Biol.* 14:75–84

197. Richter, C. P., Hawkes, C. D. 1939. Increased spontaneous activity and food intake produced in rats by removal of the frontal poles of the brain. *J. Neurol. Psychiatry* 2:231

198. Ritter, R. C., Epstein, A. N. 1975. Control of meal size by central noradrenergic action. *Proc. Natl. Acad. Sci. USA* 72:3740–43

199. Roberts, D. C. S., Price, M. T. C., Fibiger, H. C. 1976. The dorsal tegmental noradrenergic projection: An analysis of its role in maze learning. *J. Comp. Physiol. Psychol.* 90:363–72

200. Roberts, W. W. 1969. Are hypothalamic motivational mechanisms functionally and anatomically specific? *Brain Behav. Evol.* 2:317–42

201. Rolls, E. T. 1976. See Ref. 101, pp. 65–88

202. Ross, J. F., Walsh, L. L., Grossman, S. P. 1973. Some behavioral effects of entorhinal cortex lesions in the albino rat. *J. Comp. Physiol. Psychol.* 85:70–81

203. Rowland, N., Meile, M. J., Nicolaidis, S. 1975. Metering of intravenously infused nutrients in VMH lesioned rats. *Physiol. Behav.* 15:443–48

204. Russek, M., Morgane, P. J. 1963. Anorexic effect of peritoneal glucose in the hypothalamic hyperphagic. *Nature* 199:1004–5

205. Saller, C. F., Stricker, E. M. 1976. Hyperphagia and increased growth in rats after intraventricular injections of 5,7-dihydroxytryptamine. *Science* 192:385–87

206. Samanin, R., Ghezzi, D., Valzelli, L., Garattini, S. 1972. The effect of selective lesioning of brain serotonin or catecholamine containing neurons on the anoretic activity of fenfluramine and amphetamine. *Eur. J. Pharmacol.* 19:318–31

207. Schiff, B. B., Carter, D. 1977. Long-term effects of caudate nucleus lesions on body weight in the rat. *Physiol. Behav.* 18:375–79

208. Schwartzbaum, J. S. 1961. Some characteristics of amygdaloid hyperphagia in monkeys. *Am. J. Physiol.* 74:252–59

209. Sclafani, A. 1971. Neural pathways involved in the ventromedial hypothalamic lesion syndrome in the rat. *J. Comp. Physiol. Psychol.* 77:70–96

210. Sclafani, A., Berner, C. N., Maul, G. 1973. Feeding and drinking pathways between medial and lateral hypothalamus in the rat. *J. Comp. Physiol. Psychol.* 85:29–51

211. Sclafani, A., Grossman, S. P. 1969. Hyperphagia produced by knife cuts between the medial and lateral hypothalamus in the rat. *Physiol. Behav.* 4:533–38

212. Sclafani, A., Kluge, L. 1974. Food motivation and body weight levels in hypothalamic hyperphagic rats: A dual lipostatic model of hunger and appetite. *J. Comp. Physiol. Psychol.* 86:28–46

213. Singh, D. 1973. Effects of preoperative training on food-motivated behavior of hypothalamic hyperphagic rats. *J. Comp. Physiol. Psychol.* 84:47–52

214. Singh, D. 1974. Role of preoperative experience on reaction to quinine taste in hypothalamic hyperphagic rats. *J. Comp. Physiol. Psychol.* 86:674–78

215. Singh, D., Meyer, D. R. 1968. Eating and drinking by rats with lesions of the septum and the ventromedial hypothalamus. *J. Comp. Physiol. Psychol.* 65:163–66

216. Skultety, F. M., Gary, T. M. 1962. Experimental hyperphagia in cats follow-

ing destructive midbrain lesions. *Neurology* 12:394–401

217. Smith, G. P., Gibbs, J. 1976. See Ref. 45, pp. 349–56

218. Smith, M. H., Salisbury, R., Weinberg, H. 1961. The reaction of hypothalamic-hyperphagic rats to stomach preloads. *J. Comp. Physiol. Psychol.* 54:660–64

219. Smutz, E. R., Hirsch, E., Jacobs, H. L. 1975. Caloric compensation in hypothalamic obese rats. *Physiol. Behav.* 14:305–9

220. Sorenson, C. A., Ellison, G. D. 1970. Striatal organization of feeding behavior in the decorticate rat. *Exp. Neurol.* 29:162–74

221. Steffens, A. B. 1969. Blood glucose and FFA levels in relation to meal pattern in the normal rat and the ventromedial hypothalamic lesioned rat. *Physiol. Behav.* 4:215–25

222. Steffens, A. B. 1970. Plasma insulin content in relation to blood glucose level and meal pattern in the normal and hypothalamic hyperphagic rat. *Physiol. Behav.* 5:147–51

223. Steffens, A. B., Mogenson, G. J., Stevenson, J. A. F. 1972. Blood glucose, insulin, and free fatty acids after stimulation and lesions of the hypothalamus. *Am. J. Physiol.* 222:1446–52

224. Stellar, E. 1954. The physiology of motivation. *Psychol. Rev.* 61:5–22

225. Stricker, E. M., Zigmond, M. J. 1974. Effects on homeostasis of intraventricular injections of 6-hydroxydopamine in rats. *J. Comp. Physiol. Psychol.* 86:973–94

226. Stricker, E. M., Zigmond, M. J. 1975. In *Control Mechanisms of Drinking,* ed. G. Peters, J. T. Fitzsimons, pp. 55–61. Berlin: Springer. 209 pp.

227. Stricker, E. M., Zigmond, M. J. 1976. In *Progress in Psychobiology and Physiological Psychology,* ed. J. M. Sprague, A. N. Epstein, 6:121–88. New York: Academic. 226 pp.

228. Strubbe, J. H., Steffens, A. B. 1975. Rapid insulin release after ingestion of a meal in the unanesthetized rat. *Am. J. Physiol.* 229:1019–22

229. Tannenbaum, G. A., Paxinos, G., Bindra, D. 1974. Metabolic and endocrine aspects of the ventromedial hypothalamic syndrome in the rat. *J. Comp. Physiol. Psychol.* 86:404–13

230. Teitelbaum, P. 1955. Sensory control of hypothalamic hyperphagia. *J. Comp. Physiol. Psychol.* 48:156–63

231. Teitelbaum, P. 1957. Random and food directed activity in hyperphagic and normal rats. *J. Comp. Physiol. Psychol.* 50:486–90

232. Teitelbaum, P. 1967. See Ref. 79, pp. 319–35

233. Terzian, H., Ore, G. 1955. Syndrome of Klüver and Bucy reproduced in man by bilateral removal of the temporal lobes. *Neurology* 5:373–80

234. Thomas, D. W., Mayer, J. 1968. Meal taking and regulation of food intake by normal and hypothalamic hyperphagic rats. *J. Comp. Physiol. Psychol.* 66:642–53

235. Thompson, D. M. 1964. Escape from S^d associated with fixed-ratio reinforcement. *J. Exp. Anal. Behav.* 7:1–8

236. Travis, R. P. Jr., Hooten, T. F., Sparks, D. L. 1968. Single unit activity related to behavior motivated by food reward. *Physiol. Behav.* 3:309–18

237. Travis, R. P. Jr., Sparks, D. L., Hooten, T. F. 1968. Single unit responses related to sequences of food motivated behavior. *Brain Res.* 7:455–58

238. Turner, B. H. 1973. Sensorimotor syndrome produced by lesions of the amygdala and lateral hypothalamus. *J. Comp. Physiol. Psychol.* 82:37–47

239. Turner, S. G., Sechzer, J. A., Liebelt, R. A. 1967. Sensitivity to electric shock after ventromedial hypothalamic lesions. *Exp. Neurol.* 19:236–44

240. Ungerstedt, U. 1971. Adipsia and aphagia after 6-hydroxydopamine induced degeneration of the nigro-striatal dopamine system. *Acta Physiol. Scand. Suppl.* 367:95–122

241. Ungerstedt, U. 1974. In *The Neurosciences, Third Study Program,* ed. F. O. Schmitt, F. G. Worden, pp. 695–703. Cambridge, Mass: MIT Press. 809 pp.

242. Ungerstedt, U., Ljungberg, T., Steg, G. 1974. Behavioral, physiological, and neurochemical changes after 6-hydroxydopamine-induced degeneration of the nigro-striatal dopamine neurons. *Adv. Neurol.* 5:421–26

243. Valenstein, E. S. 1976. See Ref. 101, pp. 557–76

244. Vanderweele, D. A., Sanderson, J. D. 1976. See Ref. 45, pp. 383–94

245. van Putten, L. M., van Bekkum, D. W., Querido, A. 1955. Influence of hypothalamic lesions producing hyperphagia and of feeding regimens on carcass composition in the rat. *Metabolism* 4:68–74

246. Vilberg, T. R., Beatty, W. W. 1975. Behavioral changes following VMH lesions in rats with controlled insulin levels. *Pharmacol. Biochem. Behav.* 3:377–84

247. Wade, G. N. 1976. *Adv. Study Behav.* 6:201–79
248. Waldbillig, R. J. 1975. Attack, eating, drinking, and gnawing elicited by electrical stimulation of rat mesencephalon and pons. *J. Comp. Physiol. Psychol.* 89:200–12
249. Walsh, L. L., Grossman, S. P. 1973. Zona incerta lesions: Disruption of regulatory water intake. *Physiol. Behav.* 11:885–87
250. Walsh, L. L., Grossman, S. P. 1975. Loss of feeding to 2-deoxy-D-glucose but not insulin after zona incerta lesions in the rat. *Physiol. Behav.* 15:481–86
251. Walsh, L. L., Grossman, S. P. 1976. Zona incerta lesions impair osmotic but not hypovolemic thirst. *Physiol. Behav.* 16:211–15
252. Walsh, L. L., Grossman, S. P. 1977. Electrolytic lesions and knife cuts in the region of the zona incerta impair sodium appetite. *Physiol. Behav.* 18:587–96
253. Walsh, L. L., Grossman, S. P. 1978. Dissociation of responses to extracellular thirst stimuli following zona incerta lesions. *Pharmacol. Biochem. Behav.* In press
254. Walsh, L. L., Halaris, A. E., Grossman, L., Grossman, S. P. 1977. Some biochemical effects of zona incerta lesions that interfere with the regulation of water intake. *Pharmacol. Biochem. Behav.* 7:351–56
255. Wampler, R. S. 1973. Increased motivation in rats with ventromedial hypothalamic lesions. *J. Comp. Physiol. Psychol.* 84:275–85
256. White, N. M., Fisher, A. E. 1969. Relationship between amygdala and hypothalamus in the control of eating behavior. *Physiol. Behav.* 4:199–205
257. Wyrwicka, W., Doty, R. W. 1966. Feeding induced in cats by electrical stimulation of the brain stem. *Exp. Brain Res.* 1:152–60
258. Yaksh, T. L., Myers, R. D. 1972. Neurohumoral substance released from hypothalamus of the monkey during hunger and satiety. *Am. J. Physiol.* 222:503–15
259. York, D. A., Bray, G. A. 1972. Dependence of hypothalamic obesity on insulin, the pituitary and the adrenal gland. *Endocrinology* 90:885–94
260. Young, T. K., Liu, A. C. 1965. Hyperphagia, insulin and obesity. *Chin. J. Physiol.* 19:247–53
261. Zeigler, H. P., Karten, H. J. 1973. Brain mechanisms and feeding behavior in the pigeon (Columbia livia). II. Analysis of feeding behavior deficits after lesions of quinto-frontal structures. *J. Comp. Neurol.* 152:83–101
262. Zeigler, H. P., Karten, H. J. 1974. Central trigeminal structures and the lateral hypothalamic syndrome in the rat. *Science* 186:636–38
263. Zigmond, M. J., Stricker, E. M. 1972. Deficits in feeding behavior after intraventricular injections of 6-hydroxydopamine in rats. *Science* 177:1211–14
264. Zigmond, M. J., Stricker, E. M. 1973. Recovery of feeding and drinking by rats after intraventricular 6-hydroxydopamine or lateral hypothalamic lesions. *Science* 182:717–20

Ann. Rev. Psychol. 1979. 30:243–81

ORGANIZATIONAL BEHAVIOR ❖308

Terence R. Mitchell[1]

Department of Management and Organization and Department of Psychology, University of Washington, Seattle, Washington 98195

CONTENTS

FORMAT OF THE REVIEW 244
PERSONALITY AND INDIVIDUAL DIFFERENCES 245
   Main Effects 245
   Matches and Moderators 246
JOB ATTITUDES 247
   Causes of Job Satisfaction 247
   Consequences of Job Satisfaction 248
   New Directions 249
   Job Commitment 249
   Job Involvement 250
   Attributions 250
MOTIVATION 251
   Expectancy Theory 253
   Goal Setting 255
   Equity Theory 258
   Operant Conditioning 259
   Motivation: New Directions 261
LEADERSHIP 263
   The Contingency Model of Leadership Effectiveness 263
   Path-Goal Theory 264
   Other Contingency Ideas 265
   New Measures 266
   New Theories 267
   New Paradigms 268
CONCLUSIONS: PEAKS AND VALLEYS 270
   Peaks 270
   Valleys 271

[1] I would like to thank Milton Blood, Fred Fiedler, and Gary Latham for their comments on an earlier draft of this paper.

0066-4308/79/0201-0243$01.00

The field of organizational behavior is thriving and apparently prospering. It has become a distinct discipline with a focus on individual and group behavior in the organizational context. There are more texts, courses, journals, and professionals dealing with this content than ever before. On almost every criterion of growth we must be considered successful.

The substantive progress of the field, however, is somewhat more uneven. On the one hand, there are still large numbers of empirical studies with little or no theoretical orientation. These studies are hard to integrate into a coherent body of knowledge. On the other hand, at least in the fields of leadership and motivation, there are some viable and well-articulated theories. And new ones have appeared in the last few years with operant conditioning and attribution theory providing new insights and diametrically opposite philosophical orientations. Thus, the theoretical richness is substantially improved from 10 years ago.

The methodological sophistication has continued to increase. Complex statistics and complex designs are more frequent. The large correlational study with everything related to everything else seems to be disappearing. There is a greater interest in causal relationships than associational ones.

The purpose of this review is to document these additions and changes in the field of organizational behavior. In general, theoretical issues are discussed more fully than any particular study and ideas are emphasized over methods. A section at the end of the review summarizes what currently appears to be the major strong and weak points in the field.

FORMAT OF THE REVIEW

My initial intention was more ambitious and more comprehensive than what appears in this review. After going through the journals and books between 1975 and the beginning of 1978, it was clear that some topics would of necessity be emphasized and others omitted. My criteria for omission were coverage elsewhere or lack of research. Reviews of topics such as group dynamics, role theory, communication, task design, organization development, decision making, power, and politics are available in *The Handbook of Industrial and Organizational Psychology* (55), recent editions of the *Annual Review of Psychology,* or *New Directions in Organizational Behavior* (229).

The four most frequently researched areas, and ones in need of updating were personality, job attitudes, motivation, and leadership. A section on each of these topics covers (*a*) the theory and research that is a continuation of work already in the literature in 1975, (*b*) new theories and research, and (*c*) a summary and critique.

PERSONALITY AND INDIVIDUAL DIFFERENCES

The area of personality research has suffered from two rather crucial controversies over the past few years. First, Mischel (165) and others have argued that personality traits as traditionally defined have questionable validity. The major criticism is that these traits seem to have little consistency over time or place, suggesting that perhaps our notions of deepseated and permanent personalities may be incorrect [see Buss (28) for a brief review of this issue]. While some recent empirical research has challenged Mischel's assumptions (57, 207), a second criticism seems to be more widely accepted. Essentially, this second point is that even if personality traits are consistent and persistent, they control little of the variation in behavior when compared to situational variables. Studies comparing the variance controlled by these two components almost always indicate the dominance of the situation [see Sarason et al (206) for a review]. The conclusion drawn by many researchers is that since so much of the variance in our criteria is unexplained it is far more promising to study situational factors than personality variables. Much of the research on organizational behavior using personality variables reflects the above issues. In most cases the variables are seen as moderators of stronger environmental-criteria relationships. Since the review by Gough (76) only covers the literature up to 1971, we will briefly cover some of the major topics in the area.

Main Effects

Some of the research has focused on personality main effects: direct correlations between personality variables and various criteria of satisfaction, motivation, and performance. Perhaps the best articulated and researched theory has been the consistency theory suggested by Korman (127). Essentially, Korman argues that people choose an occupation, effort levels, friends, and interpersonal behaviors based upon the consistency between their perceptions of their self-esteem and the demands of a job or the expectations of their friends. For example, for people with high self-esteem, there should be consistency between (a) the characteristics of the person and his or her chosen occupation, (b) task success and satisfaction, (c) perceived similarity of others and liking for others, and (d) measured abilities and job performance. Self-esteem, we would add, is only partially defined as a personality variable; Korman also sees immediate situational factors such as task success or others' expectations as part of the definition of self-esteem. Korman's 1976 paper presents a good review of the theory and its empirical support, and Dipboye (48) and Korman (128) present a debate on some criticisms of the theory.

The two other variables that have received the most attention have been those depicting achievement orientation and locus of control. Research on the former variable (included here are a variety of measures reflecting achievement) has shown that high achievers stay on the job longer (200), perform better and respond more positively to criticism (83), and that high achievement-oriented managers are characterized by candor, openness, receptivity, the use of participation, and concern for people (91). A new behaviorally based scale for measuring need achievement (and some other needs) was recently developed and validated by Steers & Braunstein (232).

The recent research on locus of control has shown that internals have lower stress levels, cope better with stress (7, 8), and have better jobs, higher pay, and satisfaction (10, 170) than externals. Also, a study by Duffy et al (53) replicated some of these findings using a multidimensional scale of locus of control which was shown to be more valid than the traditional measure. A possible explanation of these findings is provided by an attributional analysis. More specifically, it can be argued that people who are successful attribute this success to themselves, while people who have failed report the causes of failure to be external to themselves. We will discuss this issue more fully at a later point in the paper.

Matches and Moderators

There have been an increasing number of studies that have used personality traits as moderator variables. The personality trait is treated as a factor that increases the precision or "best fit" of our situation → criterion relationships. Jacobs & Soloman (110), for example, have shown that people with high self-esteem show a stronger job satisfaction → job performance relationship than those with low self-esteem. (This is as predicted by Korman.) Other studies have investigated the moderators of the task characteristics → job satisfaction/performance relationships [see Oldham (179) or Pierce & Dunham (189) for reviews]. For example, Steers & Spencer (234) have shown that need achievement moderated the job scope-job performance relationship, and Stone et al (239) found that need achievement moderated the job scope-job satisfaction relationship. A study by O'Reilly (182) found that variables reflecting achievement (called expressive) and instrumental orientations moderated the job challenge-job satisfaction/performance relationship. Other studies (88, 181, 220) have shown that growth needs strength moderates the job enrichment → job satisfaction relationship. In general, these studies show that people who are high in achievement needs or growth needs respond more favorably (are more satisfied, perform better) when faced with enriched, challenging jobs than do people low in these needs. Research on the moderators of the goal-setting characteristics (e.g. participation, difficulty, etc) → job satisfaction/performance relationships have shown less promise. Numerous studies (1, 12, 135, 139) have generated few significant results and little consistency in interpretation.

In summary, a review of the personality research leaves one rather unsettled. The measures lack reliability and validity, the empirical results, while statistically significant, frequently lack practical significance, and, except for the work by Korman (127) and Hackman & Oldham (88), the theory is not well developed. Much of the work seems to have relegated personality variables to the role of a moderator or "fine tune" variable. However, in many cases the personality measure seems to be an attachment to the research rather than its heart. We will find throughout this review that personality traits appear as predictors of attitudes (e.g. involvement), motivation (e.g. expectancies), and leadership (e.g. behavioral styles), but the central focus of that research is usually motivation, attitudes, or leadership and not personality (that is why the above types of studies are not in this section).

This secondary role seems justified and necessary. If Mischel's arguments are correct (165), then we will be better served by continuing in the direction we are heading. Personality variables probably control only a minor percentage of variance in behavior when compared to situational factors, and there is little consistency over time or settings. Besides these theoretical reservations about personality variables there are also empirical ones. People like Blood & Mullet (24a) and others have indicated why our analyses of moderator effects are highly conservative and unlikely to produce striking effects. Thus, the methodological and theoretical limitations in the use of personality variables is likely to limit their future importance.

JOB ATTITUDES

Job attitudes continue to be a major research topic in organizational behavior. They are typically defined as positive or negative evaluations of aspects of one's work environment. Included here are evaluations of one's job in the form of satisfaction, commitment, and involvement as well as evaluations of one's self and others. Job satisfaction is the most frequently researched attitude and has been a topic of study for a long time. Two recent studies (224, 225) show a continuing decrease in satisfaction for American workers. Since satisfaction is obviously an important topic, we will cover it first.

Causes of Job Satisfaction

There are a number of recent reviews of the job satisfaction literature. James & Jones (112) review the conceptual literature relating organization structure variables to job satisfaction, while Berger & Cummings (21) provide a comprehensive review of the empirical literature. These latter authors conclude that occupational level and decentralization seem to be positively related to job satisfaction but that the relationships with span of control, organizational or subunit size, or the line/staff distinction were complex and hard to determine. Locke's (146) review covers the historical development of the job satisfaction concept, the major theoretical orientations, and a review of the empirical work on both the causes and consequences of satisfaction. He reports that the literature suggests that satisfaction is caused by challenging jobs (high autonomy, stimulation, responsibility, variety, etc), high and equitable pay, good opportunities for promotion, and good work conditions.

The most recent literature has added no new theoretical statements but has provided additional support for some of the above relationships. Adams et al (3) report positive relations between satisfaction and occupational level and also show differences across functional specialty at a given level. O'Connell & Cummings (176) report that tension increases dissatisfaction while influence increases satisfaction. Katz & Van Maanen (117) support the contention that job satisfaction is caused by job properties (e.g. independence, challenge), interaction features (leadership, feedback), and organizational policies (promotion, compensation). Using this model Van Maanen & Katz (247) show how these types of satisfaction differ over careers and across job types. Finally, Dyer & Theriault (58) report that job satisfaction was positively related to the absolute level of pay as well as some "fairness" measure of the degree to which it met expectations. There are also numerous studies where satisfaction is the dependent variable but the focus of the study is some independent variable (e.g. goal setting). These types of studies are discussed in other sections of the paper.

Consequences of Job Satisfaction

Locke's (146) review gives comprehensive coverage to the consequences of being satisfied on the job. In general, satisfied people are more satisfied with their life, have better physical and mental health, and tend to be on the job more frequently and leave the organization less frequently than those who are dissatisfied. No empirically strong or theoretically compelling relationship between satisfaction and performance is apparent.

The new studies provide continued support for these findings. London et al (150), Kavanagh & Halpern (118), and Dubin & Champoux (52) report that job satisfaction is related to general life satisfaction and the degree to which one's job is important in one's life. Organ (184) has reviewed the satisfaction/performance issue and suggests that there is evidence that satisfaction can indeed cause performance as well as the reverse (which has been more popular of late). Baird (13) shows that satisfaction was more highly related to performance in unenriched jobs than enriched ones.

The job satisfaction/absenteeism/turnover relationships have had more theoretical work and controversy. Mobley (172) has presented a model of how satisfaction can impact on turnover. Smith (223) and Ilgen & Hollenback (103) both report studies where satisfaction was negatively related to absenteeism. However, Nicholson et al (174) reviewed 29 studies and carried out one of their own and came to the conclusion that dissatisfaction had little impact on absenteeism. They suggest that an examination of "absence cultures" as well as our definitions of absenteeism might help to clear up the discrepancy between their results and much of the literature.

New Directions

A number of new methodological, practical, and theoretical approaches have appeared in the attitude literature. The methodological findings stress two things. First, the more specific the attitude measure, the more likely it is to be related to behavior (92, 109). Second, a study by Dunham et al (54) which compared a new satisfaction measure (The Index of Organizational Reactions) with the Job Descriptive Index, the Minnesota Satisfaction Questionnaire, and the Faces Scale showed acceptable convergent and discriminant validity for all four measures.

A major practical contribution was made by Mirvis & Lawler (164). They imposed a cost accounting system on their study and showed how attitudes (intrinsic motivation, satisfaction) can have an important financial impact on absenteeism, turnover, and performance. The new theoretical approaches have dealt with the issues of commitment, involvement, and attributions.

Job Commitment

The research on job commitment as a specific job attitude is relatively recent. Commitment is typically defined in terms of one's loyalty, identification, and involvement with the organization. It is seen as a binding force on individuals to carry out and adhere to organizational policies and philosophy. Extensive reviews by Salancik (203) and Steers (231) discuss the causes and consequences of commitment. In general, commitment is caused by personal characteristics (e.g. need achievement), job characteristics (e.g. responsibility), and job experience. The consequences may be a greater desire to remain in the organization and better attendance, as well as greater commitment to goals and norms. Empirical studies by Steers (231) and Marsh & Mannari (154) support the causes suggested above, and Steers (231) and Porter et al (192) support the commitment/turnover relationship. The relationship of commitment to performance is still unclear.

Job Involvement

The work on job involvement has been more extensive than that on commitment. Since the early work by Lodahl & Kejner (149), involvement has been seen as a value orientation toward work which suggests that people think a lot about their job, that their job means a lot to them in terms of their life satisfaction, and that jobs provide an indication of one's status. A recent review by Rabinowitz & Hall (197) reviews the definitions of involvement, its causes and consequences. Research over the years has shown that involvement is related to personal characteristics such as older age, internal locus of control, belief in the Protestant Ethic, and needs for growth. Job factors such as autonomy, variety, feedback, and participation in decision making are also seen as causes of involvement. A number of studies (160, 198, 201, 230) provide support for these interpretations.

The consequences of involvement seem to be high satisfaction and lower turnover (197) and more hours worked (258). Rabinowitz & Hall (197) found little consistency for the involvement/performance relationship, but Cummings & Manring (42), using a measure of alienation which included involvement, found relationships with effort, performance, and tardiness.

In summary, commitment and involvement seem to be broader in scope than job satisfaction and based more on general value orientations than satisfaction. All three concepts are influenced positively by enriched jobs and all three have as yet undetermined relationships with performance. However, it is fairly clear that committed, involved, and satisfied employees should have lower turnover and absenteeism.

Attributions

For many years it was assumed that attitudes were the antecedents and therefore the causes of behavior. However, the research and debates resulting from Festinger's dissonance theory (66) changed that interpretation. It was argued by many authors that people observe their actions and infer their attitudes from these observations (19, 20). According to this self-perception theory, when people were asked about their job satisfaction they would say "Well, I come to work all the time, I must like my job." Thus, attendance is seen as the cause of satisfaction rather than the reverse.

A further step in this type of analysis was the work of Kelley (120). Kelley argued that when we observe our behavior or someone elses, we try to fit that behavior into some general story or intuitive explanation of events. We attribute motives, intentions, and attitudes to ourselves and others based upon (a) observations of actions, and (b) our naive theories of causality which we use to interpret these actions. Ajzen (5) presents a recent summary and overview of this type of analysis.

The relevance of attributional approaches for topics such as motivation and leadership are covered in other sections of this paper. In terms of attitudes, two areas of research seem relevant. The first of these deals with our commitment or attitude about various courses of action in decision tasks, and the second concerns our evaluations of our own and others' performance.

One recent study by Staw (226) investigated the commitment issue in a decision task. He argued that when people were faced with the fact that they had made a bad choice in the past they would justify this action by reevaluating their attitude toward the alternative in a more positive light. When faced with the choice again, their commitment to the bad alternative (the one they had previously chosen) would increase rather than decrease! Using an investment decision problem, Staw (226) supports this interpretation and a later study by Staw & Fox (228) provides further support.

A related area of research focuses on evaluations of performance and some attributional biases that occur in these attitudes. There is now considerable evidence for what is called a "defensive attribution" effect. This effect occurs when people are asked to give the causes of their own or others' successes or failures. In general, what is found is that we tend to attribute our successes to internal causes (e.g. our skill or ability) and our failures to external causes (bad luck or forces out of our control). However, the failure of others is more likely to be seen as internally caused than our own failure (163, 235). These biases occur for individuals working alone or for people working in groups (208).

These sorts of biases could have a significant effect on our attitudes about performance and performance appraisal. For example, Garland & Price (74) provide data showing that prejudiced male managers attribute female managerial success to luck and an easy job while unprejudiced males attributed this success to skill and hard work. While the work on applying attribution theory to the organizational context is rather recent, what has been done seems promising.

MOTIVATION

Motivation is a popular topic. Almost 25% of the articles reviewed for this paper were concerned with motivation. This interest is also reflected by the fact that the last two *Annual Review* articles in the area of organizational behavior (129, 145) dealt almost exclusively with this topic. Since those reviews and the one by Campbell & Pritchard (35) provide thorough and insightful coverage, the present paper will limit itself to (a) an update of the empirical research and (b) a statement about new developments in the area.

There are some important theoretical distinctions about motivation that serve as guides for organizing this material. First, motivation in organizational settings can be divided into three general questions: (*a*) Why do we initiate effort on a task? (*b*) How much effort do we choose to expend? (*c*) Why do we persist in working at the task over time? The questions of initiation (arousal, activation) and choice of effort level are much more heavily researched than those of persistence, and most of the following discussion centers on those two questions.

A second useful and somewhat similar distinction pointed out by Campbell et al (34) is between process theories and content theories. The process theories are concerned with the psychological processes involved in making choices, usually about levels of effort. The content theories, on the other hand, focus on the substantive nature of those variables that influence the motivational process. These latter theories have frequently been used to address the arousal or initiation of action question. For example, given a number of rewards (e.g. pay, promotion, recognition) a process theorist might be concerned with how frequently the rewards were administered (e.g. expectancy) and in what pattern they were administered (e.g. reinforcement schedules), while a content theorist might be concerned with how important these three rewards were and the specific needs which they satisfied.

Perhaps the most interesting trend in the recent motivational literature pertains to the content/process distinction. Except for one or two minor exceptions [e.g. Mitchell & Moudgill (171)] the complete body of literature on motivation has dealt with questions of process. The work of Maslow (155) on the hierarchy of needs, Alderfer's ERG model (6), and Herzberg's dual factor model (94) have simply been absent from current research. Given the fact that these theories dominated the field in the 1950s and 1960s, it is surprising to see such a complete shift in emphasis. However, this general shift away from need-based theories has occurred in other areas of psychology (e.g. social psychology). An excellent discussion of this movement is provided by Salancik & Pfeffer (205) in their critique of need-based approaches.

Thus, we are left with a discussion of the major process theories of motivation. Three of these theories are concerned with the psychological processes that determine the choice of effort levels on a particular task. These theories are expectancy theory, goal-setting theory, and equity theory, with the first two dominating the literature. More than 75% of the motivational research was conducted on topics relevant to the expectancy or goal-setting approaches. The fourth major process theory of motivation is based on an operant analysis. The determinants of effort are seen as environmental processes rather than psychological ones. While the predictions and conclusions drawn from an operant approach are similar to those suggested by an expectancy or goal-setting analysis, the causes of the behavior are seen as very different. We will return to this distinction later in the paper.

Expectancy Theory

Expectancy theory is one of a class of theories based on the principle of expected value. This principal suggests that people make choices based on the expected payoff of the alternatives. In the organizational area it is suggested that people will choose a level of task effort that results in the greatest benefit (personal payoff) when compared to other effort levels. The value or payoff of different effort levels is determined by the assessment of (a) the probability that a particular effort level leads to various outcomes and (b) the value of the outcomes. Thus, the effort level that is seen as most likely to lead to valued outcomes is predicted to occur. The first expectancy model in the organizational area was presented by Vroom (249), and modifications by Porter & Lawler (193), Graen (77), and Lawler (140) have been suggested. Recent reviews by Lawler (140), Mitchell (167), Wahba & House (251), and Connolly (38) are available for more detailed discussions of expectancy theory.

Most expectancy studies prior to 1975 assessed the degree to which "working hard" led to good performance and the valence of good performance. This latter valence was defined in terms of the degree to which good performance led to organizational outcomes (instrumentality) and the value of these outcomes (valence). This overall score of the expected value of working hard was gathered for each subject and was correlated across subjects with some criterion of effort or performance. Due to a number of criticisms (167, 251) this correlational methodology has for the most part been dropped. Tests using this approach have either found minimal support (199) or have been found wanting in comparison to other methodologies.

One technique that has been used frequently and provided considerable support for the expectancy model has been the use of a within-subjects analysis (167). This methodology requires that expected value scores be generated for different effort levels (or decision alternatives such as the choice of an occupation), and the alternative with the highest expected value is the predicted action or level of effort. This type of analysis requires asking the subject many more questions and demands more precision in the criterion assessment than is required by the traditional across-subjects technique. However, a number of studies (39, 124, 153, 156, 180, 186) provide support for such an approach. In addition, the papers by Oldham (180),

Machinsky (153), and Kopelman (124) found that the within-subjects approach did better than the across-subjects approach in predicting performance.

Other modifications and refinements of the original expectancy methodology have been suggested. First, the study by Parker & Dyer (186) found that the reenlistment decisions of naval officers were more accurately predicted when the list of outcomes used in the analysis was small [8] rather than large [25]. Ivancevich (104) found that predictions of the performance of engineers using an expectancy approach were better when the subjects generated their own outcomes. Both studies suggest that getting a small number of important outcomes is critical for the best prediction. Too many outcomes of secondary importance simply add noise.

Some work with the criterion variables suggests that better predictions result when (a) initial criterion levels are accounted for (125) and when (b) more refined behavioral measures are used (10). Finally, both the papers by Parker & Dyer (186) and Kopelman & Thompson (125) suggest that the expected value → behavior relationship may be moderated by task characteristics (e.g. difficulty) or external pressures (family, friends).

The above research mostly pertains to methodological refinements in expectancy research. There has been some work on theoretical issues as well. One area of research has been to investigate the causes of people's expectancies: that is, to what extent are expectancies caused by specific reward contingencies, personality variables, or group or organizational characteristics? The theory would suggest that reward contingencies would be a major determinant of expectancies and instrumentalities since these variables are defined as effort-performance or performance-outcome relationships. Two studies which actually manipulated reward contingencies and assessed resultant expectancies found support for this proposition (187, 195). The Peters study was particularly impressive in that expectancies (the behavior-performance link), instrumentalities (the performance-outcome link), and valences (the value of the outcomes) were all influenced strongly in the predicted direction when performance evaluations, the distribution of rewards, and the desirability of the rewards were manipulated. Also, some work by Kopelman (122) suggests that people's expectancies are related to the "reward responsiveness" of the organization. These results provide strong support for the notion that expectancies do indeed reflect the subjects' perceptions of behavior-outcome relationships.

Some personality and organizational variables have also been shown to be related to expectancies. Oldham (180) found that people with higher self-esteem had higher expectancies, and a number of studies (143, 170, 221) report that people with an internal locus of control have higher expectancies than those with an external locus of control. These studies make sense;

people who are confident about their ability to influence the world around them see stronger relationships between what they do and the results of their actions than do people who see these outcomes occurring as a function of fate or luck.

Finally, a few investigations (111, 221, 244) have found positive relationships between leader behavior (e.g. support) and expectancies. The James et al study (111) also found that expectancies were higher in a supportive organizational climate and lower where role ambiguity existed. These results make intuitive sense and are not contradictory in any fashion with the propositions of the theory.

In summary, expectancy theory has generated considerable research and most of the results have been supportive. In general, people work hard when they think that working hard is likely to lead to desirable organizational rewards. The modifications and refinements in methodology and theory have increased our understanding of the usefulness of the theory. However, one final point should be made. Expectancy theory is based on a *normative* model. Expected value approaches argue that *if* people (*a*) knew all the alternatives, (*b*) knew all the outcomes, (*c*) knew all the action → outcome relationships, and (*d*) knew how they felt about these outcomes, that they would use a rather complex formula to come up with an estimate of the best choice of action. It is obvious that people don't have all of the above information, nor do they use a complex formula in determining their actions [see Behling et al (18) for a discussion of these issues]. Rather, expected value should be seen as a general approximation of people's behavior. It points out the factors of importance (i.e. expectancies, instrumentalities, and valences) and it suggests ways in which these variables alone and in combination influence behavior. In that perspective it has made a valuable contribution to the field.

Goal Setting

The initial statement of goal-setting theory for organizational issues was made by Locke (144). His early laboratory work prompted a number of studies, and current reviews are available by Latham & Yukl (137) and Steers & Porter (233). Essentially, the theory argues that intentions to work toward a goal are the primary motivating force of work behavior and effort on a task. It is suggested that (*a*) specific goals are better than general goals like "do your best," and (*b*) difficult goals (if accepted) will lead to greater effort than easy goals. The 1975 reviews seemed to support these propositions, and more evidence for these issues and some related topics has been generated since then.

First, a number of studies have shown that having goals results in higher performance than not having goals (105, 106, 133, 135, 136, 139, 242, 245,

257). All of these studies were either conducted in a field setting or were simulations of a work setting. Only a study by Frost & Mahoney (73) failed to unequivocally support this hypothesis. They found that having a goal on an unstructured task was helpful for performance but not on a highly structured one. Combining these recent findings with earlier studies provides very strong support for the proposition that goals increase performance.

The goal difficulty proposition has also been supported. Yukl & Latham (260) showed that difficult goals resulted in better performance than easy goals, and Campbell & Ilgen (32) found that goal difficulty increased performance when task difficulty was held constant. London & Oldham (151) also found that harder goals led to better performance, but Oldham (177) failed to find this effect. In general, however, it continues to appear that difficult goals (if accepted) will result in higher performance than easy goals.

There are some other areas of goal-setting research which are still surrounded by controversy. For example, it is still not entirely clear what the effects of participation in the goal-setting process are. A number of studies have shown that participative goal setting leads to higher satisfaction (12, 86, 230). The effects on performance are more ambiguous. Latham & Yukl (138), in a study of uneducated loggers, found that participation led to higher goals and higher performance than for a group with assigned goals. This finding was not replicated for educated loggers. Other studies (105, 106, 135, 136, 139) report no difference in performance between assigned and participative goal setting.

The question seems to be, "What, if anything, besides increasing satisfaction, does participation do?" The only finding which seems to have some support is that participation may increase the difficulty of the set goals, and if this occurs, then performance might also be higher due to a goal difficulty effect. Some support for this proposition is available. The Latham & Yukl (138) study with loggers may be interpreted this way, and a recent study by Latham et al (135) clearly shows that participation leads to more difficult goals when goal difficulty is assessed in numerical terms. However, in studies where goal difficulty is measured by questionnaires (rather than the assessment of a specific numerical goal), this finding does not appear (36, 135, 260). In the two studies where goal difficulty level was held constant (49, 136), there were either no differences in performance between the assigned and participative group or performance was better in the assigned group. These findings suggest that assigned goal setting can serve an important motivational function, especially if the assigned goals are difficult but attainable.

Another set of studies has questioned the proposition that other factors such as rewards, knowledge of results (KOR), or social pressures influence motivation only insofar as they influence goals. Studies by Terborg (242) and Latham et al (135) suggest that rewards (especially financial ones) may have an independent motivating effect on performance. Research by Tosi & Hamner (243) suggests that knowledge of results may also have an independent effect, but a study by Erez (60) seems to show that KOR has its main impact through the goal that is set. A study by White et al (257) suggests that the apprehension about being evaluated by one's supervisor and social pressure from coworkers may also increase performance independent of the goal. Combining these studies with Ivancevich's (105, 106) findings that the effects of goal setting may diminish over time suggests that perhaps goal setting combined with incentive systems, appraisals, and feedback is the best way to increase and maintain high levels of performance.

The research on the effects of goal setting on satisfaction measures is also unclear. Some studies (105, 106) showed that having goals increased job satisfaction while other studies (139, 151, 245, 257) failed to find an effect. The White et al (257) study did find, however, that satisfaction with performance was increased by having goals. This result is consistent with earlier statements by Locke. It also appears as if the way in which goals are set may influence satisfaction. Studies by Steers (230) and Arvey & Dewhirst (11) show that factors such as goal clarity, feedback, and participation increase one's job satisfaction, and in the Steers study, job involvement.

There have also been attempts to expand our understanding of the goal-setting process. One set of studies has attempted to use biographical and personality variables as moderators of the goal setting → performance/satisfaction relationships. The results from these studies are ambiguous at best. Latham & Yukl (138) found that participation in goal setting helped for uneducated workers but not for educated ones. Ivancevich & McMahon (107) found that goal clarity and feedback were positively related to performance for low education levels but not for high. Steers (230) found that the relationship between goal-setting factors (e.g. specificity, difficulty, participation, feedback) and satisfaction and involvement was higher for people with high needs for achievement, affiliation, and autonomy, but Arvey & Dewhirst (11) failed to replicate this result. A study by Yukl & Latham (260) found that high need achievers set higher goals than low need achievers in the participative goal-setting condition, but other measures of self-esteem, locus of control, and need for independence produced no significant results in the study or in the Latham & Yukl (139) study. Thus, while it seems likely that personality variables moderate the goal setting-performance relationship, little consensus has appeared as to what these relationships look like.

Finally, there have been two attempts to present an overall theoretical view of goal setting. Yukl & Latham (260) present a comprehensive model that includes factors such as participation, individual differences, goal difficulty, goal acceptance, instrumentality, and performance. They discuss the literature that generated the model and they provide some empirical support for it. Also, Hall & Hall (90) and Hall & Foster (89) describe the role of goals in an overall psychological success cycle. They suggest that goals lead to effort which increases performance and results in success. Success, in turn, is seen as increasing self-esteem and job involvement which results in higher goals. Support for this model is presented from both field and laboratory settings.

In summary, it appears rather convincingly that goals are a major source of work motivation. Goal setting was one of the most frequently tested theories in the field of organizational behavior, and a recent paper by Locke (148) suggests that most of the other major theories of motivation (e.g. expectancy theory, behavior modification) include goals in their formulation. The recent research is both large in number and frequent in its support. Two areas of research need to be pursued. First, we need to know more about the psychological processes underlying goal setting. Little is known about the role of commitment and acceptance and their relationship to goal difficulty or goal specificity. Second, more research is needed on how external factors—such as financial rewards, social pressure, and evaluation apprehension—complement, enhance, or act independently of the goal-setting process.

Equity Theory

Equity theory is one of a family of exchange-like theories that argue that motivation is essentially a social comparison process. According to Adams (4), who first presented a comprehensive summary of the theory, people assess their inputs (e.g. effort) to the work situation and their outcomes (e.g. rewards), and these factors are expressed as a ratio. This ratio is then compared to the ratios believed to be had by important coworkers. If the focal person believes that he or she has a better ratio (more outcomes than inputs compared to the other person) or a poorer ratio (less outcomes than inputs compared to the other person), then a state of inequity exists. This inequity serves as a motivational force for the individual to change his behavior (it creates tension) and return to a state of equity.

Very little research on equity theory has appeared the last few years. Only one comprehensive literature review was done (75), and it points out very well what some of the problems are. First, very little is known about how people select a "comparison other." Second, it is very hard to define inputs and outcomes. Third, there is little known about how combinations of inputs and outcomes are accomplished, and finally, it is hard to know when and how these factors change over time. Goodman's (75) paper attempts to deal with these issues and suggests a general framework for social comparison processes.

Most of the empirical work seems either to modify slightly or to challenge the basic equity notion. Middlemist & Peterson (161), for example, found that people were a little more comfortable with a condition where they had a slight competitive edge over their comparison coworker than they were with a condition of complete equity. In a similar vein, Kopelman (123) showed that a return on investment (ROI) measure of motivation was related to performance. This ROI measure reflects the difference between expected outcomes under different conditions of input and suggests that people will choose that level of effort that leads to the highest payoff for the lowest investment of effort.

Two papers by Larwood & Blackmore (131) and Larwood et al (132) show that different distribution strategies than equity are sometimes preferred. The former study showed that salaried employees preferred equality (everyone gets the same) while those under an hourly rate preferred equity. In some cases people choose a winner-take-all strategy. Finally, some work by Weick et al (253) shows that equity ratios and resolution strategies are influenced by a number of contextual factors related to culture, family orientation, and personal values (e.g. value of independence).

In summary, equity theory has not been enthusiastically pursued. While most people believe that a sense of justice is an important factor in effecting work motivation, we still do not know much about how it is defined or its actual impact on performance. It also appears that justice will to some extent be compromised by self-serving interests—people prefer a little more justice for themselves than for others. We will return to this point at the end of the motivation section.

Operant Conditioning

Operant conditioning, or behavior modification, has been with us as an approach to motivation for quite a while (222). Based on Skinner's work, these principles have been applied to the work setting (108, 157). Essentially, an operant analysis argues that most behavior is environmentally caused. The major factors that control behavior are called reinforcers. A reinforcer is simply any consequence which, when it immediately follows a response, increases the probability that the behavior will be repeated. In organizational settings a variety of reinforcers can and are used (e.g. pay, recognition, praise) and a variety of behaviors studied (e.g. effort, attendance, accidents).

There have been only a few empirical studies recently which have systematically examined operant propositions. In general, two types of studies have been done. The first simply introduces some sort of procedure described as reinforcing and compares people's behavior under those conditions with people who are not reinforced. Studies by Adam (2) and Komaki et al (121) use this type of methodology, and both studies provide support for their hypothesis that reinforcement increases performance.

The second type of study compares different types of reinforcement schedules, that is, the frequency with which a reinforcer is made contingent upon a specific response. The three types of schedules most frequently studied are the continuous (where a reinforcer is made contingent upon every incidence of the desired behavior), fixed ratio (where a reinforcer is provided on, let's say, every second or third incidence of the desired behavior), and variable ratio (where a reinforcer is provided *on the average* every second or third incidence of the behavior). The results from this type of research are highly confusing. Yukl & Latham (259) and Yukl, Latham & Purcell (261) describe results with tree planters where a continuous schedule did better than a variable ratio, but Deslauriers & Everett (46) suggest that a variable schedule did better for inducing people to ride the bus. Studies by Yukl et al (262), Berger et al (22), Pritchard et al (196), and Latham & Dossett (134) compared variable ratio to fixed ratio or continuous schedules. The findings are difficult to summarize since all four studies find somewhat different things. However, it is safe to conclude from these studies that (*a*) there is little difference in performance between the types of schedules, and (*b*) there is a big difference in performance between using a schedule and not using one.

The problems with using an operant analysis are part definitional and part methodological. In many cases the definitions of schedules and reinforcement are inconsistent across studies and with the original definitions provided by Skinner. Mawhinney's (157) paper discussed in detail some of these problems, but they do not seem to have been resolved in current studies.

The second issue is methodological. In many cases the use of reinforcement introduces other factors that are equally if not more plausible explanations of the findings. For example, the study by Adam (2) used feedback and the study by Komaki et al (121) used goals as part of its reinforcement procedures. Those studies that attempted a competitive test of theories (e.g. expectancy versus operant) found little difference between them (22, 196).

Perhaps the best review of these methodological problems is presented by Locke (147). In an examination of most of the studies using an operant procedure, Locke points out how numerous other confounding factors could cause these results. He argues quite convincingly that reinforcement most probably affects action through goals, expectations, and other cognitive processes.

And from a theoretical and applied perspective these problems are crucial. If one believes in operant conditioning and its philosophical foundation of environmental determinism, then reference to internal cognitive events is irrelevant for the prediction of behavior (168). With this belief it is easy to omit consent, participation, and the joint setting of goals in applications of operant conditioning. This type of research may increase organizational effectiveness, but it does little to increase our understanding of how and why the increase occurs. More operant studies that gather empirical data and rule out alternative interpretations are sorely needed, as well as investigations that examine how operant procedures and cognitive events jointly result in increased motivation.

Motivation: New Directions

The above four theories represent the major theoretical approaches to motivation that have dominated the field for the last 10 years. Except for a few articles on specific motivational issues [e.g. a study by Wheaton et al (256) on how ability becomes more important as task difficulty increases, and some work by Chung & Vickery (37) on the effects of performance feedback], most of the work has focused on these topics. The one major exception has been the work on the motivating effects of intrinsic and extrinsic outcomes.

There are at least two major issues that are being discussed in the literature on this topic. The first is simply a descriptive question: What do we mean by intrinsic and extrinsic and how are these terms being used in the research literature (186)? A recent paper by Broedling (27) discusses this issue in detail. She points out the conceptual distinctions between such terms as psychological states, traits, and consequences or outcomes of action. While there is some agreement that extrinsic rewards (e.g. pay) are somehow external to the person (and perhaps controlled by others) and intrinsic rewards (an interesting task) are more internal and controllable by one's self, there is still little agreement on the specific meaning and use of the terms. However, it is clear that people have different preferences for these types of outcomes (9) as a function of age, class, and job and that they influence work behavior.

The second question, and the one around which most of the controversy revolves, is whether the effects of these two types of rewards are compatible or conflicting. The argument is as follows: People work at certain levels of effort and they observe these effort levels. In order to explain their behavior they make attributions about why they are doing what they are doing [see Bem (19) or Kelley (120) for discussions of this approach]. These attributions then change people's work-related attitudes and behavior.

In some cases we are faced with a task for which there are few intrinsic and extrinsic rewards. This situation is described as the insufficient justification condition. If the person is induced to do the task, then it is predicted that the person will change his initial evaluation of its intrinsic properties —"I must find this task interesting; otherwise, why am I doing it." (Chairpersons of committees and academic departments as well as Annual Review authors may readily recognize this phenomenon.) Numerous studies have supported this hypothesis [see Staw (227) for a review].

The situation where there is oversufficient justification has been where the controversy arises. Deci (45) has shown that when people are engaged in an intrinsically interesting task, if an external reward (e.g. a financial bonus) is added, that motivation will decrease rather than increase. In this case intrinsic and extrinsic rewards are seen as competing or conflicting rather than additive. This type of finding is seemingly in direct contradiction of an operant analysis which would argue that positive reinforcers were additive (213).

A number of reviews and critiques of Deci's work have appeared (31, 175, 213), and the empirical work has left the issue unresolved. Studies by Farr (63) and Farr et al (64) have failed to support the overjustification effect. However, research by Shapira (217), Tarnage & Muchinsky (241), Pinder (190), and Pritchard et al (194) have all reported support for the hypothesis. This latter study was explicitly designed to account for earlier methodological problems in this type of research, and it generated strong support for the nonadditive effects of these types of rewards.

On the theoretical level, a recent paper by Scott & Erskine (215) suggests some ways in which the overjustification hypothesis and an operant approach can be seen as compatible. They argue that reinforcement causes arousal and that certain interpretations of multiple reinforcements could produce the "Deci" effect. Also, a paper by Blood (24) extends and elaborates the idea of self-rewarding. He defines and discusses self-rewarding and its possible uses in organizations. Thus, some theoretical refinements and extensions of the original Deci analysis are available.

In summarizing the work on motivation, we can say that the following are likely to increase performance: (a) clear, difficult goals; (b) contingent rewards; (c) fair, explicit systems of compensation and reward. However, the content of the rewards, how they are distributed, how goals are set and by whom are still issues that need further work. Papers like those by Scott & Erskine (215) and Staw (227) have attempted theoretical integrations, and research by White et al (257) or Berger et al (22) are examples of empirical studies that provide competitive tests and integrations. More of this type of work is needed.

LEADERSHIP

The area of leadership is still a major topic of research. Since Stogdill's (238) comprehensive *Handbook* (around 3000 references) there have been at least 150 new studies. Aside from motivation, leadership is the most frequently conducted area of research. Barrow (15) and Schreisheim & Kerr (209) have provided current reviews of this literature.

The content of the research seems to split into two areas. One is the pursuit of contingency notions that attempt to match certain types of leaders with specific types of settings. The work by Fiedler on his contingency model (69) and House's path-goal theory (97) are excellent examples of this research strategy. Contingency theories have dominated leadership thinking for the past 15 years and they remain the major paradigm.

However, there are some new directions in the field as well. A number of researchers have shifted their focus from the *effects* of leader behavior in certain settings to the *causes* of this behavior. The focus is on why leaders do what they do and why they are perceived as leaders. Since this material is fairly recent, we will spend relatively more time on it than on the more traditional contingency ideas which are reviewed frequently and thoroughly [e.g. Barrow (15), Stogdill (238)].

The Contingency Model of Leadership Effectiveness

Fiedler's contingency model (67) was really the first major theory to specifically propose contingency relationships in the field of leadership. The theory suggests that group performance is a joint function of the leader's motivational structure and the amount of control and influence available in the situation. The motivational structure is measured by the Least Preferred Coworker (LPC) scale, and it is used to divide people into task-motivated and interpersonally motivated categories. The amount of control or influence is seen as a combination of the leader-member relations, the structure of the task, and the power inherent in the position. Fiedler's research shows that task-motivated leaders are more effective in situations of high or low control and interpersonally motivated leaders are most effective in situations of intermediate control.

The theory has generated rather intense debate. Through the years there have been both supporting and nonsupporting research studies and supportive and critical literature reviews. Recent studies by Utecht & Heier (246) and Vecchio (248) are examples of nonsupportive empirical pieces and Fiedler's evaluation of the latter study is available (69). The recent literature review by Schriesheim & Kerr (209) is also highly critical, and Fiedler's rebuttal to their comments and their reply are all in the same book (68).

Essentially, the arguments focus on the meaning and use of the LPC measure as an indication of leadership style and the methodology used to support the model. Some recent work has provided support for Fiedler's interpretation of LPC (82), but it is beyond the scope of this paper to go into detail on these controversies.

Perhaps the most important thing to mention is that Fiedler has recently extended the model into new areas. First, he has suggested ways in which the model can predict how leadership effectiveness will change as a function of changes in the leader (e.g. experience, training) or changes in the situation [see Bons & Fiedler (25) or Fiedler (69)]. These papers give empirical support for the contingency model as a dynamic model, one that can predict current as well as future group effectiveness. The second new area is that of leadership training. Fiedler and his associates have developed a training manual called *Leader Match* (70) which teaches a leader how to (*a*) assess his or her own leadership style, (*b*) assess the amount of situational control, and (*c*) change the situation so that it matches his or her style. A paper by Leister et al (142) describes a study which validates this training procedure, and other supporting evidence is available (69). Thus, Fiedler has shown some support for his earlier contention that leadership training would be more effective if we tried to teach leaders how to change settings rather than the traditional approach of trying to change the leaders themselves.

Path-Goal Theory

The Path-Goal approach was originally proposed by Evans (61) and by House (97) and has generated considerable research since then. The most recent version of the theory argues that the role of the leader is to provide subordinates with coaching, guidance, and the rewards necessary for satisfaction and effective performance. These actions are seen as ways to influence subordinates' perceptions of the clarity of the paths to goals and the desirability of the goals themselves. The second major point is that the specific style of leadership behavior that is best suited for increasing motivation is dependent upon the situation which is comprised of (*a*) subordinate personal characteristics and (*b*) environmental pressures and task demands.

The measures of leader behavior typically are obtained from the Leader Behavior Description Questionnaire–Form XII (237) or some variant of it (211). This measure provides an estimate of two leadership styles: consideration and initiation of structure. The typical study relates these two styles to job satisfaction and performance with various personal and task factors serving as moderators. Reviews of the empirical literature are available in House & Mitchell (99) and Schriesheim & Kerr (209).

In general, the recent findings seem to suggest that consideration generally leads to higher subordinate satisfaction (113, 162) and that structuring behavior is frequently an irritant and tension producer, especially when consideration is low (162, 210). Path-goal theory predicts that consideration will be most helpful in structured situations and less helpful in unstructured ones. Studies by Downey et al (50, 51) and others [e.g. Stinson & Johnson (236)] have found some support for this notion. The theory also predicts that initiating structure will lead to greater satisfaction when the tasks are ambiguous or stressful than when they are highly structured and well laid out. Studies by Downey et al (50) and Stinson & Johnson (236) provided little support for this hypothesis, while Schriesheim & Murphy (210) found that job stress did moderate the initiating structure/job satisfaction relationship. Other task moderators have also been investigated. Johns (113) found that job scope moderated the leader behavior/satisfaction relationships, while Dessler & Valenzi (47) found no moderator effects for supervisor level. Thus, one is left with the feeling that the findings are stronger for the consideration hypotheses than the structuring hypotheses and stronger for satisfaction as a criterion than for performance.

We should point out that just as for the contingency model, there has been considerable research on Path-Goal theory that precedes our 1975 cutoff point. Most of this work is reviewed by Schriesheim & Kerr (209) or House & Mitchell (99), and in general it provides support for the underlying theoretical propositions. However, there are considerable problems with the measures used to assess leader behavior (211), the general contingency methodology (126), and some of the specific propositions generated from Path-Goal (209). Thus, while the Path-Goal approach has stimulated numerous studies, it still needs work to become a valid set of well-accepted empirical generalizations.

Other Contingency Ideas

There have also been a series of studies that use contingency ideas but do not fit into either of the theoretical orientations described above. Some of this research looks at personality variables, some at leader behavior, some at member characteristics or task characteristics. They all have one thing in common: successful leadership is contingent upon a variety of factors and what we must determine is the best match between leaders and the situation.

A few studies have focused on personality tendencies of the leaders or followers. Schuler (212) found that participative leadership was liked by people low in authoritarianism regardless of the task but that participation was liked by high authoritarian people only when the task was low in repetitiveness. Weed et al (252) found that a considerate leadership style matched with low dogmatism subordinates produced high performance, and a structuring style was best with high dogmatism subordinates. Shaw & Harkey (218) found that groups in which the leaders have ascendant tendencies did better than groups in which nonascendent people were leaders. Finally, Hunt et al (101) show that whether upper level management is authoritarian or not has an impact on what sort of leadership style at lower levels is most effective.

The studies focusing on leader behavior have shown that different types of tasks require different types of behavior (152). For example, Katz (116) found that considerate leadership was most successful when the group faced external conflict, and structuring behavior was best when there was internal interpersonal conflict. The behaviors may have differential effects as well. Keller & Szilagyi (119) report that leader-rewarding behavior shows strong positive relationships with expectancies and satisfaction and negative relationships with role conflict and ambiguity. Punitive behaviors were not related to any of the criteria except a negative relationship with role ambiguity.

Some of the work has focused on subordinates' perceptions of a number of issues. Justis (114) found that leader competency has a lower impact on performance when members are less dependent on the leader. O'Reilly & Roberts (183) show that low supervisor influence and low subordinate mobility aspirations reduce the impact of leader behavior on satisfaction and performance. Graen & Ginsburgh (81) report that low leader acceptance and low role orientation are associated with high turnover, and Murnighan & Leung (173) found that leader participation helps performance only when the task is seen as important by the subordinates.

A summary of the above studies suggests that effective leadership is a function of where the leader is in the organization, what sort of task is being performed, the personality attributes of the leader and the subordinates, and a number of factors relating to the subordinates' acceptance and dependence upon the leader. While diverse in some ways, the studies have much in common. They generally see leadership in terms of two styles (task and interpersonal), and these styles are seen as the causes of subordinate satisfaction and performance.

The critical reactions to this general paradigm for studying leadership have been numerous over the last few years. Some authors have criticized the measures in use (209, 240, 263), the methodology employed (85, 115, 126, 130), and the general theoretical orientation (33, 159, 188). New measures, theories, and paradigms have appeared and are discussed in the following sections.

New Measures

Only two new measures of leader behavior have appeared in the literature. Bass et al (16) developed a measure of leadership style using five scales: Direction, Negotiation, Consultation, Participation, and Delegation. A facet analysis by Shapira (216) provided some validity for this approach. Oldham (178) also developed a new leadership scale. It included measures of Personally Rewarding, Personally Punishing, Setting Goals, Designing Feedback Systems, Placing Personnel, and Designing Job Systems. Oldham presents data showing significant relationships between these scales and measures of effectiveness and shows also that these relationships are stronger than those found using consideration and structure as measures of leader behavior.

New Theories

Three new theoretical statements have been made which are worthy of note. While not much data exist for any one of them, they each provide a new and perhaps fruitful perspective for leadership research. First, a number of authors have suggested that operant conditioning principles could be used to understand leadership (158, 214, 219). The paper by Mawhinney & Ford (158) focuses on a reinterpretation of path-goal theory using an operant analysis. Scott (214) argues that concepts such as influence or persuasion have not helped in our understanding of leadership and that we would be better served by an analysis of observable leader behaviors that change the behavior of subordinates. Both Scott (214) and Sims (219) emphasize the idea of reinforcement and making rewards contingent upon desired behavior as the focal point for effective leadership. Sims (219) also presents data showing that positive reward behavior on the part of the leader increases subordinate performance.

A different approach has been proposed by House (98). He suggests that the term charisma, which has long been forgotten in the leadership literature, may be an important and useful concept. He describes the personal characteristics of charismatic leaders (confident, dominant, purposeful), their behavior (goal articulation, image building), and their effects on followers (devotion, unquestionning support, radical change). He argues that some leaders fit this description and that charismatic leadership is an area for further study. No empirical data have, as yet, been generated to support or refute the theory.

Finally, Fiedler has developed and tested (71) a model which is called the Multiple Screen Model to help explain the relationship between leader intelligence and task performance. Fiedler & Leister (71) argue that various interpersonal and personal factors serve as blocks or screens for the leader intelligence/group performance relationship. They present a model which suggests that this relationship is high when leaders have (*a*) high motivation, (*b*) much experience, (*c*) good leader-boss relations, and (*d*) good leader-group relations. They then provide an empirical test of the model and generate support for it. Thus, both the House (98) and Fiedler & Leister

(71) papers have reopened issues in the leadership field (e.g. charisma and intelligence) which have been neglected for a long time.

New Paradigms

Two new meta-strategies or research paradigms have appeared in the leadership field. These strategies suggest that we have been looking at leadership in the wrong way. The first of these, which we might describe as the interactionist or transactionist position, attempts to shift the focus of leadership studies. Most of the contingency oriented studies look at the effect of leadership behavior on member behavior, attitudes, and performance. The interactionist position sees the reverse causality as equally important. That is, if we want to understand leadership, we have to know the causes of the leader's behavior as well as its effects.

There are three main theoretical camps that have this emphasis. First there are some people who emphasize macro-type variables as factors that cause different leadership styles. Hunt & Osborn (100) and Osborn & Hunt (185) proposed an adaptive-reactive approach to leadership, arguing that leaders adapt their behavior to the organizational environment and react to the demands of their subordinates. Papers by Hunt et al (101) and Salancik et al (204) provide empirical support for this approach.

A second strategy has been emphasized by Graen and his associates (78, 79). Graen focuses on the role-making process and sees the leader and subordinate as agreeing over time (through the use of reciprocal reinforcement) as to the general and specific nature of their behavioral interaction. One implication of this theory is that Graen sees leadership as a dyadic exchange rather than the traditional leadership approach where it is assumed that the leader behaves in a similar fashion with all subordinates. A second implication is that leadership is seen as a developmental process, one in which change is inherent through the process of learning and socialization. Papers by Graen et al (80) and Dansereau & Dumas (44) discuss these issues in more detail, and the former paper provides some empirical evidence that the types of dyadic links that are most likely to be of high quality have (a) high latitudes of acceptance, (b) mutual support, (c) involvement, and (d) positive feelings about the leader.

Finally, work by Hollander (96) has also emphasized the leader-subordinate interaction. Calling his approach a transactional one, Hollander focuses on the exchange process between the leader and the follower. This exchange is seen as active and ongoing and as going in two directions. The leader and each subordinate develop a psychological contract and their behavior is regulated by reinforcement, expectations (role prescriptions), and negotiation.

A number of empirical studies have been done recently which investigate the personal, task, or subordinate variables that cause leader behavior. Hinton & Barrow (95) showed that leader-reward behavior was most frequently used by leaders who were responsible, confident, and enthusiastic. Studies by Barrow (14) and Herold (93) found that leaders behaved more punitively toward poor performers and were rewarding toward good performers. Fodor (72) reports that leaders are more authoritarian when faced with a disparaging and disruptive subordinate, and they rate that subordinate lower and give him less pay than subordinates who do not engage in this behavior. Finally, Greenberg & Leventhal (84) report that leaders will offer financial bonuses to poor performers to motivate them when that is the only sanction they have available. All of these studies suggest that leadership is a two-way process, and they provide support for the general theoretical positions described above.

The second and perhaps more controversial paradigmatic shift suggests that leadership is a perceptual phenomenon in the mind of the observer (33, 188). Eden & Leviatan (59) and Calder (30) have argued that people utilize what might be described as implicit leadership theories. Calder's paper presents an excellent discussion of this approach and its attributional foundations. He argues that leadership is essentially a perceptual construct. People observe the behavior of leaders and they infer the causes of these behaviors to be various internal traits or external pressures. If these causes (e.g. assertiveness or deadlines) match up with the observer's naive assumptions about what leaders should do, then the label of leadership is likely to be used to describe the person observed.

This type of analysis has two profound impacts on the field of leadership. As Calder (30) argues, leadership switches from a scientific concept that is really "out there" to a study of the social reality of observers. The meaning of the term leadership becomes a study in how the label is used, when it is used, and how one develops assumptions about the nature of leadership. This social reality will undoubtedly be related to how these observers (e.g. subordinates) behave and perform, but the level of analysis and the research process are very different.

Another important impact of this type of analysis is that it brings into question much of the work currently published on leadership. If an attributional approach has validity, then all those studies that use subordinates or observers as raters of leader behavior have questionable validity. These ratings are likely to be biased by the observer's social reality and therefore be poor indicators of how the leader "actually" behaved.

There are now a number of studies which support this interpretation. First, there is evidence that observers and group members show little agreement in their ratings of leader behavior (102, 166). Second, people at different organizational levels disagree about the leader's behavior (23, 29). Third, the personal characteristics of the raters such as their sex (29), personality (56), and similarity to the leader (255) influence their ratings. And finally, the rater's perceived performance influences the ratings of the leader's behavior (169, 202).

Some of these research studies were experimental in nature. That is, all of the raters saw exactly the same behavior. The only difference among raters was the cues they used to make these ratings (29, 169, 202). Thus, differences in ratings could only be attributed to rater differences.

In summary, research on leadership seems to be thriving. Older theories such as the Contingency Model and Path-Goal continue to be developed and new approaches have appeared as well. The interactionist and attributional positions provide a new focus for understanding the meaning of leadership and should prompt continued research and theoretical debate for years to come.

CONCLUSIONS: PEAKS AND VALLEYS

It is obvious that the above review is selective and cursory. Space limitations permit little in-depth analysis on any given topic. However, one of the consequences of engaging in such a review is that the author has the opportunity of seeing trends, omissions, strong points, and weak points within the field. The paper concludes with a discussion of these issues.

Peaks

The advancements in theory, methods, and practice have been substantial. In terms of theory there have been a number of new approaches suggested, and well-established theories continue to be developed and refined. There will continue to be a debate between operant approaches and cognitive ones, and within the cognitive area, need based and information processing types of analyses will also be competitive alternatives. This debate is healthy partly for its prompting of further research but mostly for its focus on some issues related to the philosophy of science and our underlying assumptions about the causes of behavior.

There also seems to be some (but not enough) recognition of the fact that no one theory or approach is best for all people in all settings. Our continued development of contingency-like approaches in areas such as leadership, participation (250), group dynamics (87), and decision making (17) attests to this fact. The increased use of moderator variables also reflects this trend.

Our sophistication in methodology has increased as well. Reviews of current measurement procedures (26), statistical analyses (254), and designs (41) describe this progress. In general, there is a better understanding of patch-up designs and quasi-experimental designs (62, 141). When correlational designs are used there is a greater emphasis on techniques like path analysis or cross-lagged correlations (65) as well as more complex multivariate procedures (254). Operant procedures have helped in more thorough analyses of individual behavior using base rates and reversal designs (121). In general, these new designs and analyses have provided us with a greater ability to assess the validity of causal models in field settings where previously we were confined to associational inferences. The increased use of organizational simulations has also added strength to these causal inferences.

Valleys

The picture, however, is not altogether rosy and bright. There are problems as well. While the quantity of theory has increased, there are questions about its quality. Some writers have argued that not enough attention is being paid to contextual issues in organizational behavior [e.g. see Campbell (33) on leadership or Dachler & Wilpert (43) on participation in decision making]. These writers argue, and I would concur, that our theories are often too narrow in focus. We still have little understanding or closure about the interrelationships of behavior and the organizational context.

This theoretical problem is reflected in some methodological issues as well. The construct validity of many of our theoretical terms is questionable. There is still little agreement on the specific meaning of the terms leadership, motivation, personality, participation in decision making, and so on. Yet most of the research in these areas proceeds with the assumption that we all know and agree on the meaning of these terms.

A related issue is that there seems to be little attempt to integrate or competetively test different theories. Surely some combination of equity, operant, goal setting, and expectancy principles would be a step forward. Our current research has left us with little understanding of how these factors combine, their relative importance, and the changes that occur in these contributions as a function of different people or settings. More integrative theories, competitive tests, and attention to contextual and system factors is needed.

Finally, there has been very little attention to the values and ethics of doing research in the field of organizational behavior. It is clear that both subject and experimenter values can bias both what we study and what we find. Recognition of this problem is frequent in many other areas of psychology. However, except for a paper by Connor & Becker (40), little has been written in our field.

The ethical problems of applying our knowledge in organizations has also received little coverage. Questions about confidentiality, consent to participate in research or program applications (e.g. sensitivity training), use of data, and rights to privacy are seldom addressed. There is also the potential harm of premature applications (191). As a profession we are more visible, more involved in ongoing organizations, and more concerned with applications than ever before. We will be held responsible for what we do, yet little clarification, guidance, or debate takes place on these issues.

In summary, there seems to be progress in our field. Theory and research are developing and much of what is being done is being used in practice. There is reason for controlled optimism. Yet the challenges are still there for the years ahead. We can continue to extend our knowledge and contribute to the practice of organizational behavior.

Literature Cited

1. Abdel-Halim, A. A., Rowland, K. M. 1976. Some personality determinants of the effects of participation: A further investigation. *Personnel Psychol.* 29: 41–45
2. Adam, E. 1975. Behavior modification in quality control. *Acad. Manage. J.* 18:662–79
3. Adams, E. F., Laker, D. R., Hulin, C. L. 1977. An investigation of the influence of job level and functional specialty on job attitudes and perceptions. *J. Appl. Psychol.* 62:335–43
4. Adams, J. S. 1965. Inequity in social exchange. *Adv. Exp. Soc. Psychol.* 2:267–300
5. Ajzen, I. 1977. Intuitive theories of events and the effects of base-rate information on prediction. *J. Pers. Soc. Psychol.* 35:303–14
6. Alderfer, C. P. 1972. *Existence, Relatedness and Growth: Human Needs in Organizational Settings.* New York: Free Press. 198 pp.
7. Anderson, C. R. 1977. Locus of control, coping behaviors, and performance in a stress setting: A longitudinal study. *J. Appl. Psychol.* 62:446–51
8. Anderson, C. R., Hellriegel, D., Slocum, J. W. 1977. Managerial response to environmentally induced stress. *Acad. Manage. J.* 20:260–72
9. Andrisani, P. J., Miljus, R. C. 1977. Individual differences in preferences for intrinsic versus extrinsic aspects of work. *J. Vocat. Behav.* 11:14–30

10. Andrisani, P. J., Nestel, G. 1976. Internal-external control as a contributor and outcome of work experience. *J. Appl. Psychol.* 61:156–65
11. Arvey, R. D., Dewhirst, H. D. 1976. Goal setting attributes, personality variables and job satisfaction. *J. Vocat. Behav.* 9:179–89
12. Arvey, R. D., Dewhirst, H. D., Boling, J. C. 1976. Relationships between goal clarity, participation in goal setting and personality characteristics on job satisfaction in a scientific organization. *J. Appl. Psychol.* 61:103–5
13. Baird, L. W. 1976. Relationship of performance to satisfaction in stimulating and nonstimulating jobs. *J. Appl. Psychol.* 61:721–27
14. Barrow, J. C. 1976. Worker performance and task complexity as causal determinants of leader behavior style and flexibility. *J. Appl. Psychol.* 61:433–40
15. Barrow, J. C. 1977. The variables of leadership: A review and conceptual framework. *Acad. Manage. Rev.* 2: 231–51
16. Bass, B. M., Valenzi, E. R., Farrow, D. L., Solomon, R. J. 1975. Management styles associated with organizational, task, personal and interpersonal contingencies. *J. Appl. Psychol.* 60:720–29
17. Beach, L. R., Mitchell, T. R. 1978. A contingency model for the selection of decision strategies. *Acad. Manage. Rev.* 3:439–49

18. Behling, O., Schriesheim, C., Tolliver, J. 1975. Alternatives to expectancy theories for work motivation. *Decis. Sci.* 6:449–61

19. Bem, D. J. 1967. Self-perception: The dependent variable of human performance. *Organ. Behav. Hum. Perform.* 2:105–21

20. Bem, D. J. 1972. Self-perception theory. *Adv. Exp. Soc. Psychol.* 6:2–62

21. Berger, C. J., Cummings, L. L. 1978. Organizational structure, attitudes and behaviors. In *Research in Organizational Behavior*, Vol. 1, ed. B. Staw. Greenwich, Conn: JAI Press. 400 pp.

22. Berger, C. J., Cummings, L. L., Heneman, H. G. 1975. Expectancy theory and operant conditioning predictions under variable ratio and continuous schedules of reinforcement. *Organ. Behav. Hum. Perform.* 14:227–43

23. Bernardin, H. J., Alvares, K. M. 1975. The effects of organizational level on perceptions of role conflict resolution strategies. *Organ. Behav. Hum. Perform.* 14:1–9

24. Blood, M. R. 1977. Organizational control of performing through self-rewarding. In *Managerial Control and Organizational Democracy*, ed. S. Streufert, F. E. Fiedler, B. T. King. New York: Halstead. 287 pp.

24a. Blood, M. R., Mullet, G. M. 1977. *Where have all the moderators gone? The perils of type II error.* Atlanta: Georgia Inst. Technol. Coll. Ind. Manage. Tech. Rep. #1, May

25. Bons, P. M., Fiedler, F. E. 1976. Changes in organizational leadership and the behavior of relationship and task motivated leaders. *Adm. Sci. Q.* 21:453–73

26. Bouchard, T. J. Jr. 1976. Field research methods: Interviewing, questionnaires, participant observation, systematic observation, unobtrusive measures. See Ref. 55, pp. 363–414

27. Broedling, L. A. 1977. The uses of the intrinsic-extrinsic distinction in explaining motivation and organizational behavior. *Acad. Manage. Rev.* 2:267–74

28. Buss, A. R. 1977. The trait-situation controversy and the concept of interaction. *Pers. Soc. Psychol. Bull.* 3:196–201

29. Butterfield, D. A., Bartol, K. M. 1977. Evaluators of leader behavior: A missing element in leadership theory. In *Leadership: The Cutting Edge*, ed. J. G. Hunt, L. L. Larson, pp. 167–88. Carbondale, Ill: Southern Illinois Univ. Press. 286 pp.

30. Calder, B. J. 1977. An attribution theory of leadership. See Ref. 229, pp. 179–204

31. Calder, B. J., Staw, B. M. 1975. The interaction of intrinsic and extrinsic motivation: Some methodological notes. *J. Pers. Soc. Psychol.* 31:76–80

32. Campbell, D. J., Ilgen, D. R. 1976. Additive effects of task difficulty and goal setting on subsequent task performance. *J. Appl. Psychol.* June: 319–24

33. Campbell, J. P. 1977. Comments on the cutting edge. See Ref. 29, pp. 221–33

34. Campbell, J. P., Dunnette, M. D., Lawler, E. E. III, Weick, K. E. Jr. 1970. *Managerial Behavior, Performance and Effectiveness.* New York: McGraw-Hill. 546 pp.

35. Campbell, J. P., Pritchard, R. D. 1976. Motivation theory in industrial and organizational psychology. See Ref. 55, pp. 63–130

36. Carroll, S. J. Jr., Tosi, H. L. Jr. 1970. Goal characteristics and personality factors in an MBO program. *Adm. Sci. Q.* 15:295–305

37. Chung, K. H., Vickery, W. D. 1976. Relative effectiveness and joint effects of three selected reinforcements in a repetitive task situation. *Organ. Behav. Hum. Perform.* 16:114–42

38. Connolly, T. 1976. Some conceptual and methodological issues in expectancy models of work performance motivation. *Acad. Manage. Rev.* 1:37–47

39. Connolly, T., Vines, C. V. 1977. Some expectancy type models of undergraduate college choice. *Decis. Sci.* 8:311–17

40. Connor, P. E., Becker, B. W. 1977. Value biases in organizational research. *Acad. Manage. Rev.* 2:421–30

41. Cook, T. D., Campbell, D. T. 1976. The design and conduct of quasi-experiments and time experiments in field settings. See Ref. 55, pp. 223–36

42. Cummings, T. G., Manring, S. L. 1977. The relationship between worker alienation and work related behavior. *J. Vocat. Behav.* 10:167–79

43. Dachler, H. P., Wilpert, B. 1978. Conceptual dimensions and boundaries of participation in organizations: A critical evaluation. *Adm. Sci. Q.* In press

44. Dansereau, F. Jr., Dumas, M. 1977. Pratfalls and pitfalls in drawing inferences about leader behavior in organizations. See Ref. 29, pp. 68–83

45. Deci, E. L. 1975. *Intrinsic Motivation.* New York: Plenum. 324 pp.

46. Deslauriers, B. C., Everett, P. B. 1977. Effects of intermittent and continuous

token reinforcement on bus ridership. *J. Appl. Psychol.* 62:369–75

47. Dessler, G., Valenzi, E. R. 1977. Initiation of structure and subordinate satisfaction: A path analysis test of path-goal theory. *Acad. Manage. J.* 20:251–59

48. Dipboye, R. L. 1977. A critical review of Korman's self-consistency theory of work motivation and occupational choice. *Organ. Behav. Hum. Perform.* 18:108–26

49. Dossett, D. L. 1977. *The effect of participation on performance with goal difficulty held constant.* PhD thesis. Univ. Washington, Seattle, Wash. 138 pp.

50. Downey, H. K., Sheridan, J. E., Slocum, J. W. Jr. 1975. Analysis of relationships among leader behavior, subordinate job performance and satisfaction: A path goal approach. *Acad. Manage. J.* 18:253–62

51. Downey, H. K., Sheridan, J. E., Slocum, J. W. Jr. 1976. The path-goal theory of leadership: A longitudinal analysis. *Organ. Behav. Hum. Perform.* 16:156–76

52. Dubin, R., Champoux, J. E. 1977. Central life interests and job satisfaction. *Organ. Behav. Hum. Perform.* 18: 366–77

53. Duffy, P. J., Shiflett, S., Downey, R. G. 1977. Locus of control: Dimensionality and predictability using Likert scales. *J. Appl. Psychol.* 62:214–19

54. Dunham, R. B., Smith, F. J., Blackburn, R. S. 1977. Validation of the Index of Organizational Reactions with the JDI, the MSQ and Faces Scale. *Acad. Manage. J.* 20:420–32

55. Dunnette, M. D., ed. 1976. *Handbook of Industrial and Organizational Psychology.* Chicago: Rand McNally. 1740 pp.

56. Durand, D. E., Nord, W. R. 1976. Perceived leader behavior as a function of personality characteristics of supervisors and subordinates. *Acad. Manage. J.* 19:427–37

57. Dworkin, R. H., Burke, B. W., Maher, B. A., Gottesman, I. I. 1976. A longitudinal study of the genetics of personality. *J. Pers. Soc. Psychol.* 34:510–18

58. Dyer, L., Theriault, R. 1976. The determinants of pay satisfaction. *J. Appl. Psychol.* 61:596–604

59. Eden, D., Leviatan, U. 1975. Implicit leadership theory as a determinant of the factor structure underlying supervisors behavior scales. *J. Appl. Psychol.* 60:736–41

60. Erez, M. 1977. Feedback: A necessary condition for the goal setting-performance relationship. *J. Appl. Psychol.* 62:624–27

61. Evans, M. G. 1970. The effects of supervisory behavior on the path-goal relationship. *Organ. Behav. Hum. Perform.* 5:277–98

62. Evans, M. G. 1975. Opportunistic organizational research: The role of patch-up designs. *Acad. Manage. J.* 18:98–108

63. Farr, J. L. 1976. Task characteristics, reward contingency, and intrinsic motivation. *Organ. Behav. Hum. Perform.* 16:294–307

64. Farr, J. L., Vance, R. J., McIntyre, R. M. 1977. Further examinations of the relationship between reward contingency and intrinsic motivation. *Organ. Behav. Hum. Perform.* 20:31–52

65. Feldman, J. 1975. Considerations in the use of causal-correlational techniques in applied psychology. *J. Appl. Psychol.* 60:663–70

66. Festinger, L. 1957. *A Theory of Cognitive Dissonance.* Stanford: Stanford Univ. Press. 291 pp.

67. Fiedler, F. E. 1967. *A Theory of Leadership Effectiveness.* New York: McGraw-Hill. 310 pp.

68. Fiedler, F. E. 1977. A rejoinder to Schreisheim and Kerr's premature obituary of the contingency model. See Ref. 44, pp. 45–50

69. Fiedler, F. E. 1978. The contingency model and the dynamics of the leadership process. *Adv. Exp. Soc. Psychol.,* Vol. 11

70. Fiedler, F. E., Chemers, M. M., Mahar, L. 1976. *Improving Leadership Effectiveness: The Leader Match Concept.* New York: Wiley. 219 pp.

71. Fiedler, F. E., Leister, A. F. 1977. Leader intelligence and task performance: A test of a multiple screen model. *Organ. Behav. Hum. Perform.* 20:11–14

72. Fodor, E. M. 1976. Group stress, authoritarian style of control and use of power. *J. Appl. Psychol.* 61:313–18

73. Frost, P. J., Mahoney, R. A. 1976. Goal setting and the task process I. An interactive influence on individual performance. *Organ. Behav. Hum. Perform.* 17:328–50

74. Garland, H., Price, K. H. 1977. Attitudes toward women in management and attributions for their success and failure in a managerial position. *J. Appl. Psychol.* 62:29–33

75. Goodman, P. S. 1977. Social compari-

son process in organizations. See Ref. 229, pp. 97–132

76. Gough, H. 1976. Personality and personality assessment. See Ref. 55, pp. 571–607

77. Graen, G. 1969. Instrumentality theory of work motivation: Some experimental results and suggested modifications. *J. Appl. Psychol. Monogr.* 53:1–25

78. Graen, G. 1976. Role making processes within complex organizations. See Ref. 55, pp. 1201–45

79. Graen, G., Cashman, J. F. 1975. A role making model of leadership in formal organizations: A developmental approach. In *Leadership Frontiers,* ed. J. G. Hunt, L. L. Larson, pp. 143–66. Carbondale, Ill: Southern Illinois Press. 220 pp.

80. Graen, G., Cashman, J. F., Ginsburgh, S., Schiemann, W. 1977. Effects of linking-pin quality on the quality of working life of lower participants. *Adm. Sci. Q.* September: 491–504

81. Graen, G., Ginsburgh, S. 1977. Job resignation as a function of role orientation and leader acceptance: A longitudinal investigation of organizational assimilation. *Organ. Behav. Hum. Perform.* 19:1–17

82. Green, S. G., Nebeker, D. M. 1977. The effects of situational factors and leadership style on leader behavior. *Organ. Behav. Hum. Perform.* 19:368–77

83. Greenberg, J. 1977. The protestant work ethic and reactions to negative performance evaluations on a laboratory task. *J. Appl. Psychol.* 62:682–90

84. Greenberg, J., Leventhal, G. S. 1976. Equity and the use of over-reward to motivate performance. *J. Pers. Soc. Psychol.* 34:179–90

85. Greene, C. N. 1977. Disenchantment with leadership research: Some causes, recommendations and alternative directions. See Ref. 29, pp. 57–67

86. Greller, M. M. 1975. Subordinate participation and reactions to the appraisal interview. *J. Appl. Psychol.* 60:544–49

87. Hackman, J. R. 1976. Group influences on individuals. See Ref. 55, pp. 1455–1526

88. Hackman, J. R., Oldham, G. R. 1976. Motivation through the design of work: Test of a theory. *Organ. Behav. Hum. Perform.* 16:250–79

89. Hall, D. F., Foster, L. W. 1977. A psychological success cycle and goal setting: Goals, performance and attitudes. *Acad. Manage. J.* 20:282–90

90. Hall, D. T., Hall, F. S. 1976. The relationship between goals, performance,

success, self-image, and involvement under different organizational climates. *J. Vocat. Behav.* 9:267–78

91. Hall, J. 1976. To achieve or not: The manager's choice. *Calif. Manage. Rev.* Summer: 5–18

92. Heberlein, T. A., Black, J. S. 1976. Attitudinal specificity and the prediction of behavior in a field setting. *J. Pers. Soc. Psychol.* 33:474–79

93. Herold, D. M. 1977. Two way influence processes in leader-follower dyads. *Acad. Manage. J.* 20:224–37

94. Herzberg, F., Mauser, B., Snyderman, B. 1959. *The Motivation to Work.* New York: Wiley. 157 pp.

95. Hinton, B. L., Barrow, J. C. 1976. Personality correlates of the reinforcement propensities of leaders. *Personnel Psychol.* 29:61–66

96. Hollander, E. P. 1978. *Leadership Dynamics: A Practical Guide to Effective Relationship.* New York: Free Press

97. House, R. J. 1971. A path goal theory of leadership effectiveness. *Adm. Sci. Q.* 16:321–38

98. House, R. J. 1977. A 1976 theory of charismatic leadership. See Ref. 29, pp. 189–207

99. House, R. J., Mitchell, T. R. 1974. Path goal theory of leadership. *J. Contemp. Bus.* 3:81–97

100. Hunt, J. G., Osborn, R. N. 1978. A multiple approach to leadership for managers. In *Leadership for Practitioners,* ed. J. Stinson, P. Hersey. Athens, Ohio: Center for Leadership Studies, Ohio Univ.

101. Hunt, J. G., Osborn, R. N., Larson, L. L. 1975. Upper level technical orientation and first level leadership within a noncontingency and contingency framework. *Acad. Manage. J.* 18: 476–88

102. Ilgen, D. R., Fujii, D. S. 1976. An investigation of the validity of leader behavior descriptions obtained from subordinates. *J. Appl. Psychol.* 61:642–51

103. Ilgen, D. R., Hollenback, J. H. 1977. The role of job satisfaction in absence behavior. *Organ. Behav. Hum. Perform.* 19:148–61

104. Ivancevich, J. M. 1976. Expectancy theory predictions and behaviorally anchored scales of motivation: An empirical test of engineers. *J. Vocat. Behav.* 8:59–75

105. Ivancevich, J. M. 1976. Effects of goal setting on performance and job satisfaction. *J. Appl. Psychol.* 61:605–12

106. Ivancevich, J. M. 1977. Different goal setting treatments and their effects on

performance and job satisfaction. *Acad. Manage. J.* 20:406–19

107. Ivancevich, J. M., McMahon, J. T. 1977. Education as a moderator of goal setting effectiveness. *J. Vocat. Behav.* 11:83–94

108. Jablonsky, S. F., DeVries, D. L. 1972. Operant conditioning principles extrapolated to the theory of management. *Organ. Behav. Hum. Perform.* 7:340–58

109. Jaccard, J., King, G. W., Bomazal, R. 1977. Attitudes and behavior: An analysis of specificity of attitudinal predictors. *Hum. Relat.* 30:817–24

110. Jacobs, R., Soloman, T. 1977. Strategies for enhancing the prediction of job performance from job satisfaction. *J. Appl. Psychol.* 62:417–21

111. James, L. R., Hartman, A., Stebbins, M. W., Jones, A. P. 1977. Relationships between psychological climate and a VIE model of work motivation. *Personnel Psychol.* 30:229–54

112. James, L. R., Jones, A. P. 1976. Organizational structure: A review of structural dimensions and their conceptual relationships with individual attitudes and behavior. *Organ. Behav. Hum. Perform.* 19:74–113

113. Johns, G. 1978. Task moderators of the relationship between leadership style and subordinate responses. *Acad. Manage. J.* In press

114. Justis, R. J. 1975. Leadership effectiveness: A contingency approach. *Acad. Manage. J.* 18:160–67

115. Karmel, B. 1978. Leadership: A challenge to traditional research methods and assumptions. *Acad. Manage. Rev.* In press

116. Katz, R. 1977. The influence of group conflict on leadership effectiveness. *Organ. Behav. Hum. Perform.* 20:265–86

117. Katz, R., Van Maanen, J. V. 1977. The loci of work satisfaction, job interaction and policy. *Hum. Relat.* 30:469–86

118. Kavanagh, M. J., Halpern, M. 1977. The impact of job level and sex differences on the relationship between life and job satisfaction. *Acad. Manage. J.* 20:66–73

119. Keller, R. T., Szilagyi, A. D. 1976. Employee reactions to leader reward behavior. *Acad. Manage. J.* 19:619–26

120. Kelley, H. H. 1974. The process of causal attribution. *Am. Psychol.* 28:107–28

121. Komaki, J., Waddell, W. N., Pearce, M. G. 1977. The applied behavioral analysis approach and individual employees: Improving performance in two small businesses. *Organ. Behav. Hum. Perform.* 19:337–52

122. Kopelman, R. E. 1976. Organizational control system responsiveness, expectancy theory constructs, and work motivation: Some interrelations and causal connections. *Personnel Psychol.* 29:205–20

123. Kopelman, R. E. 1977. Psychological stages of careers in engineering: An expectancy theory taxonomy. *J. Vocat. Behav.* 10:270–86

124. Kopelman, R. E. 1977. Across individual, within individual and return on effort versions of expectancy theory. *Decis. Sci.* 8:651–62

125. Kopelman, R. E., Thompson, P. H. 1976. Boundary conditions for expectancy theory predictions of work motivation and job performance. *Acad. Manage. J.* 19:237–58

126. Korman, A. K. 1973. On the development of contingency theories of leadership: Some methodological considerations and a possible alternative. *J. Appl. Psychol.* 58:384–87

127. Korman, A. K. 1976. Hypothesis of work behavior revisited and an extension. *Acad. Manage. Rev.* 1:50–63

128. Korman, A. K. 1977. An examination of Dipboye's "A critical appraisal of Korman's self-consistency theory of work motivation and occupational choice." *Organ. Behav. Hum. Perform.* 18:127–28

129. Korman, A. K. Greenhaus, J. H., Badin, I. J. 1977. Personnel attitudes and motivation. *Ann. Rev. Psychol.* 28:175–96

130. Larson, L. L., Hunt, J. G., Osborn, R. N. 1976. The great hi-hi leader behavior myth: A lesson from Occam's razor. *Acad. Manage. J.* 19:628–41

131. Larwood, L., Blackmore, J. 1977. Fair pay: Field investigations of the fair economic exchange. *Proc. Acad. Manage.* 20:81–85

132. Larwood, L., Kavanagh, M., Levine, R. 1978. Perception of fairness with three alternative economic exchanges. *Acad. Manage. J.* In press

133. Latham, G. P., Baldes, J. J. 1975. The practical significance of Locke's theory of goal setting. *J. Appl. Psychol.* 60:122–24

134. Latham, G. P., Dossett, D. L. 1978. Designing incentive plans for unionized employees: A comparison of continuous and variable ratio reinforcement. *Personnel Psychol.* In press

135. Latham, G. P., Mitchell, T. R., Dossett, D. L. 1978. The importance of partic-

ipative goal setting and anticipated rewards on goal difficulty and job performance. *J. Appl. Psychol.* In press

136. Latham, G. P., Saari, L. M. 1978. The effects of holding goal difficulty constant on assigned and participatively set goals. *Acad. Manage. J.* In press

137. Latham, G. P., Yukl, G. A. 1975. A review of research on the application of goal setting in organizations. *Acad. Manage. J.* 18:824–45

138. Latham, G. P., Yukl, G. A. 1975. Assigned versus participative goal setting with educated and uneducated wood workers. *J. Appl. Psychol.* 60:299–302

139. Latham, G. P., Yukl, G. A. 1976. Effects of assigned and participative goal setting on performance and job satisfaction. *J. Appl. Psychol.* 61:166–71

140. Lawler, E. E. III 1973. *Motivation in Work Organizations.* Belmont, Calif: Brooks/Cole. 224 pp.

141. Lawler, E. E. III 1977. Adaptive experiments: An approach to organizational behavior research. *Acad. Manage. Rev.* 2:576–85

142. Leister, A., Borden, D., Fiedler, F. E. 1977. Validation of contingency model leadership training: Leader Match. *Acad. Manage. J.* 20:464–70

143. Lied, T. R., Pritchard, R. D. 1976. Relationships between personality variables and components of the expectancy-valence model. *J. Appl. Psychol.* 61:463–67

144. Locke, E. A. 1968. Toward a theory of task motivation and incentives. *Organ. Behav. Hum. Perform.* 3:157–89

145. Locke, E. A. 1975. Personnel attitudes and motivation. *Ann. Rev. Psychol.* 26:457–80

146. Locke, E. A. 1976. The nature and causes of job satisfaction. See Ref. 55, pp. 1297–1350

147. Locke, E. A. 1977. The myths of behavior mod in organizations. *Acad. Manage. Rev.* 2:543–52

148. Locke, E. A. 1978. The ubiquity of the technique of goal setting in theories of and approaches to employee motivation. *Acad. Manage. Rev.* In press

149. Lodahl, T., Kejner, M. 1965. The definition and measurement of job involvement. *J. Appl. Psychol.* 49:24–33

150. London, M., Grandall, R., Seals, G. W. 1977. The contribution of job and leisure satisfaction to quality of life. *J. Appl. Psychol.* 62:328–34

151. London, M., Oldham, G. R. 1976. Effects of varying goal types and incentive systems on performance and satisfaction. *Acad. Manage. J.* 19:537–46

152. Lord, R. G. 1977. Function leadership behavior: Measurement and relation to social power and leadership perceptions. *Adm. Sci. Q.* 22:114–33

153. Machinsky, P. M. 1977. A comparison of within and across subjects analyses of the expectancy valence model for predicting effort. *Acad. Manage. J.* 20:154–58

154. Marsh, R. M., Mannari, H. 1977. Organizational commitment and turnover: A prediction study. *Adm. Sci. Q.* 22:57–75

155. Maslow, A. H. 1954. *Motivation and Personality.* New York: Harper. 369 pp.

156. Matsui, T., Kagawa, M., Nagamatsu, J., Ohtsuka, Y. 1977. Validity of expectancy theory as a within person behavioral choice model for sales activities. *J. Appl. Psychol.* 62:764–67

157. Mawhinney, T. C. 1975. Operant terms and concepts in the description of individual work behavior: Some problems of interpretation, application and evaluation. *J. Appl. Psychol.* 60:704–12

158. Mawhinney, T. C., Ford, J. D. 1977. The path goal theory of leader effectiveness: An operant interpretation. *Acad. Manage. Rev.* 2:398–411

159. McCall, M. W. Jr. 1976. Leadership research: Choosing gods and devils on the run. *J. Occup. Psychol.* 49:139–53

160. McKelvey, B., Sekaran, U. 1977. Toward a career-based theory of job involvement: A study of scientists and engineers. *Adm. Sci. Q.* 22:281–305

161. Middlemist, R. D., Peterson, R. B. 1976. Test of equity theory by controlling for comparison co-worker efforts. *Organ. Behav. Hum. Perform.* 15:335–54

162. Miles, R. H., Petty, M. M. 1977. Leader effectiveness in small bureaucracies. *Acad. Manage. J.* 20:238–50

163. Miller, D. T. 1976. Ego involvement and attributions for success and failure. *J. Pers. Soc. Psychol.* 34:901–6

164. Mirvis, P. H., Lawler, E. E. III. 1977. Measuring the financial impact of employee attitudes. *J. Appl. Psychol.* 62:1–8

165. Mischel, W. 1973. Toward a cognitive social learning reconceptualization of personality. *Psychol. Rev.* 80:252–83

166. Mitchell, T. R. 1970. The construct validity of three dimensions currently studied in the area of leadership research. *J. Soc. Psychol.* 80:89–94

167. Mitchell, T. R. 1974. Expectancy models of satisfaction, occupational preference and effort: A theoretical, methodological and empirical appraisal. *Psychol. Bull.* 81:1053–77

168. Mitchell, T. R. 1976. Cognitions and Skinner: Some questions about behavioral determinism. *Organ. Adm. Sci.* 6:63–72

169. Mitchell, T. R., Larson, J. R., Green, S. G. 1977. Leader behavior, situational moderators and group performance: An attributional analysis. *Organ. Behav. Hum. Perform.* 18:254–68

170. Mitchell, T. R., Smyser, C. M., Weed, S. E. 1975. Locus of control: Supervision and work satisfaction. *Acad. Manage. J.* 18:623–31

171. Mitchell, V. F., Moudgill, P. 1976. Measurement of Maslow's need hierarchy. *Organ. Behav. Hum. Perform.* 61:334–49

172. Mobley, W. H. 1977. Intermediate linkages in the relationship between job satisfaction and employee turnover. *J. Appl. Psychol.* 62:237–40

173. Murnighan, J. K., Leung, T. K. 1976. The effects of leadership involvement and the importance of the task on subordinates' performance. *Organ. Behav. Hum. Perform.* 17:299–310

174. Nicholson, N., Brown, C. A., Chadwick-Jones, J. K. 1976. Absence from work and job satisfaction. *J. Appl. Psychol.* 61:728–37

175. Notz, W. W. 1975. Work motivation and the negative effects of extrinsic rewards: A review with implications for theory and practice. *Am. Psychol.* 30:884–91

176. O'Connell, M. J., Cummings, L. L. 1976. The moderating effects of environment and structure on the satisfaction-tension-influence network. *Organ. Behav. Hum. Perform.* 17:351–66

177. Oldham, G. R. 1975. The impact of supervisory characteristics on goal acceptance. *Acad. Manage. J.* 18:461–75

178. Oldham, G. R. 1976. The motivational strategies used by supervisors: Relationships to effectiveness indicators. *Organ. Behav. Hum. Perform.* 15:66–86

179. Oldham, G. R. 1976. Job characteristics and internal motivation: The moderating effect of interpersonal and individual variables. *Hum. Relat.* 29:559–69

180. Oldham, G. R. 1976. Organizational choice and some correlates of individual expectancies. *Decis. Sci.* October: 873–84

181. Oldham, G. R., Hackman, J. R., Pearce, J. L. 1976. Conditions under which employees respond positively to enriched work. *J. Appl. Psychol.* 61:395–403

182. O'Reilly, C. A. III. 1977. Personality-job fit: Implications for individual attitudes and performance. *Organ. Behav. Hum. Perform.* 18:36–46

183. O'Reilly, C. A. III, Roberts, K. H. 1978. Consideration, initiating structure and situational moderators: Supervisor influence and subordinate mobility aspirations. *J. Appl. Psychol.* In press

184. Organ, D. W. 1977. A reappraisal and reinterpretation of the satisfaction causes performance hypothesis. *Acad. Manage. Rev.* 2:46–53

185. Osborn, R. N., Hunt, J. G. 1975. An adaptive-reactive theory of leadership: The role of macro variables in leadership research. See Ref. 79, pp. 27–44

186. Parker, D., Dyer, L. 1976. Expectancy theory as a within-person behavioral choice model: An empirical test of some conceptual and methodological refinements. *Organ. Behav. Hum. Perform.* 17:97–117

187. Peters, L. H. 1977. Cognitive models of motivation, expectancy theory and effort: An analysis and empirical test. *Organ. Behav. Hum. Perform.* 20: 129–48

188. Pfeffer, J. 1977. The ambiguity of leadership. *Acad. Manage. Rev.* 2:104–12

189. Pierce, J. L., Dunham, R. B. 1976. Task design: A literature review. *Acad. Manage. Rev.* 1:83–97

190. Pinder, C. C. 1976. Additivity versus nonadditivity of intrinsic and extrinsic incentives: Implications for work motivation, performance and attitudes. *J. Appl. Psychol.* 61:693–99

191. Pinder, C. C. 1977. Concerning the application of human motivation theories in organizational settings. *Acad. Manage. Rev.* 2:384–97

192. Porter, L. W., Crampon, W. J., Smith, F. J. 1976. Organizational commitment and managerial turnover: A longitudinal study. *Organ. Behav. Hum. Perform.* 15:87–99

193. Porter, L. W., Lawler, E. E. III 1968. *Managerial Attitudes and Performance.* Homewood, Ill: Dorsey. 209 pp.

194. Pritchard, R. D., Campbell, K. M., Campbell, D. J. 1977. Effects of extrinsic financial rewards on intrinsic motivation. *J. Appl. Psychol.* 62:9–15

195. Pritchard, R. D., De Leo, P. J., Von Bergen, C. W. Jr. 1976. A field experimental test of expectancy-valence incentive motivation techniques. *Organ. Behav. Hum. Perform.* 15:355–406

196. Pritchard, R. D., Leonard, D. W., Von Bergen, C. W. Jr., Kirk, R. J. 1976. The effects of varying schedules of reinforcement on human task performance. *Or-*

gan. Behav. Hum. Perform. 16:205–30

197. Rabinowitz, S., Hall, D. T. 1977. Organizational research on job involvement. *Psychol. Bull.* 84:265–88

198. Rabinowitz, S., Hall, D. T., Goodale, J. G. 1977. Job scope and individual differences as predictors of job involvement: Independent or interactive. *Acad. Manage. J.* 20:273–81

199. Reinharth, L., Wahba, M. A. 1976. A test of alternative models of expectancy theory. *Hum. Relat.* 29:257–72

200. Rhode, J. G., Sorensen, J. E., Lawler, E. E. III. 1976. An analysis of personal characteristics related to professional staff turnover in public accounting firms. *Decis. Sci.* 7:771–800

201. Ruh, R. A., White, J. K., Wood, R. R. 1975. Job involvement, values, personal background, participation in decision making and job attitudes. *Acad. Manage. J.* 18:300–12

202. Rush, M. C., Thomas, J. C., Lord, R. G. 1977. Implicit leadership theory: A potential threat to the internal validity of leader behavior questionnaires. *Organ. Behav. Hum. Perform.* 20:93–110

203. Salancik, G. R. 1977. Commitment and the control of organizational behavior and belief. See Ref. 229, pp. 1–54

204. Salancik, G. R., Calder, B. J., Rowland, K. M., Leblebici, H., Conway, M. 1976. Leadership as an outcome of social structure and process: A multidimensional analysis. See Ref. 79, pp. 81–102

205. Salancik, G. R., Pfeffer, J. 1977. An examination of need satisfaction models of job attitudes. *Adm. Sci. Q.* September: 427–56

206. Sarason, F. G., Smith, R. E., Diener, E. 1975. Personality research: components of variance attributable to the person and the situation. *J. Pers. Soc. Psychol.* 32:199–204

207. Schaie, K. W., Parham, I. A. 1976. Stability of adult personality traits: Fact or fable. *J. Pers. Soc. Psychol.* 34:146–58

208. Schlenker, B. R., Soraci, S. Jr., McCarthy, B. 1976. Self-esteem and group performance as determinants of egocentric perceptions in cooperative groups. *Hum. Relat.* 29:1163–76

209. Schriesheim, C. A., Kerr, S. 1977. Theories and measures of leadership: A critical appraisal of current and future directions. See Ref. 29, pp. 9–44

210. Schriesheim, C. A., Murphy, C. J. 1976. Relationships between leader behavior and subordinate satisfaction and performance: A test of some situational moderators. *J. Appl. Psychol.* 61:634–41

211. Schriesheim, C., Von Glinow, M. A. 1977. The path goal theory of leadership: A theoretical and empirical analysis. *Acad. Manage. J.* 20:398–405

212. Schuler, R. S. 1976. Participation with supervisor and subordinate authoritarianism: A path goal reconciliation. *Adm. Sci. Q.* 21:320–25

213. Scott, W. E. Jr. 1976. The effects of extrinsic rewards on intrinsic motivation. *Organ. Behav. Hum. Perform.* 15: 117–29

214. Scott, W. E. Jr. 1977. Leadership: A functional analysis. See Ref. 29, pp. 84–93

215. Scott, W. E. Jr., Erskine, J. A. 1978. The effects of variations in task design and monetary reinforcers on task behavior. *Organ. Behav. Hum. Perform.* In press

216. Shapira, Z. 1976. A facet analysis of leadership styles. *J. Appl. Psychol.* 61:136–39

217. Shapira, Z. 1976. Expectancy determinants of intrinsically motivated behavior. *J. Pers. Soc. Psychol.* 34:1235–44

218. Shaw, M. E., Harkey, B. 1976. Some effects of congruency of member characteristics and group structure upon group behavior. *J. Pers. Soc. Psychol.* 34:412–18

219. Sims, H. P. Jr. 1977. The leader as a manager of reinforcement contingencies: An empirical example and a model. See Ref. 29, pp. 121–37

220. Sims, H. P. Jr., Szilagyi, A. D. 1976. Job characteristics relationships: Individual and structural moderators. *Organ. Behav. Hum. Perform.* 17:211–30

221. Sims, H. P. Jr., Szilagyi, A. D., McKemey, D. R. 1976. Antecedents of work related expectancies. *Acad. Manage. J.* 19:547–59

222. Skinner, B. F. 1938. *The Behavior of Organisms.* New York: Appleton-Century-Crofts. 457 pp.

223. Smith, F. J. 1977. Work attitudes as predictors of attendance on a specific day. *J. Appl. Psychol.* 62:16–19

224. Smith, F. J., Roberts, K. H., Hulin, C. L. 1976. Ten year job satisfaction in a stable organization. *Acad. Manage. J.* 19:462–68

225. Smith, F. J., Scott, K. D., Hulin, C. L. 1977. Trends in job related attitudes of managerial and professional employees. *Acad. Manage. J.* 20:454–60

226. Staw, B. M. 1976. Knee-deep in the big muddy: A study of escalating commitment to a chosen course of action. *Organ. Behav. Hum. Perform.* 16:27–45

227. Staw, B. M. 1977. Motivation in organizations: Toward synthesis and redirection. See Ref. 229, pp. 54–95

228. Staw, B. M., Fox, F. V. 1977. Escalation: The determinants of commitment to a chosen course of action. *Hum. Relat.* 40:431–50

229. Staw, B. M., Salancik, G. R., ed. 1977. *New Directions in Organizational Behavior.* Chicago: St. Clair. 300 pp.

230. Steers, R. M. 1976. Factors affecting job attitudes in a goal setting environment. *Acad. Manage. J.* 19:6–16

231. Steers, R. M. 1977. Antecedents and outcomes of organizational commitment. *Adm. Sci. Q.* 22:46–56

232. Steers, R. M., Braunstein, D. N. 1976. A behaviorally-based measure of manifest needs in work settings. *J. Vocat. Behav.* 9:251–66

233. Steers, R. M., Porter, L. W. 1974. The role of task-goal attributes in employee performance. *Psychol. Bull.* 81:434–52

234. Steers, R. M., Spencer, D. G. 1977. The role of achievement motivation in job design. *J. Appl. Psychol.* 62:472–79

235. Stevens, L., Jones, E. E. 1976. Defensive attribution and the Kelley tube. *J. Pers. Soc. Psychol.* 34:809–20

236. Stinson, J. E., Johnson, T. W. 1975. The path-goal theory of leadership: A partial test and suggested refinement. *Acad. Manage. J.* 18:242–52

237. Stogdill, R. M. 1963. *Manual for the Leader Behavior Description Questionnaire—Form XII.* Columbus: Bur. Bus. Res. Ohio State Univ. 13 pp.

238. Stogdill, R. M. 1974. *Handbook of Leadership: A Survey of Theory and Research.* New York: Free Press. 613 pp.

239. Stone, E. F., Mowday, R. T., Porter, L. W. 1977. Higher order need strengths as moderators of the job scope-job satisfaction relationship. *J. Appl. Psychol.* 62:466–71

240. Szilagyi, A. D., Keller, R. T. 1976. A comparative examination of the supervisory behavior description questionnaire (SBDQ) and the revised leader behavior description questionnaire (LBDQ—Form XII). *Acad. Manage. J.* 19:642–49

241. Tarnage, J. J., Muchinsky, P. M. 1976. The effects of reward contingency and participative decision making on intrinsically and extrinsically motivating tasks. *Acad. Manage. J.* 19:482–89

242. Terborg, J. 1976. The motivational components of goal setting. *J. Appl. Psychol.* 61:613–21

243. Tosi, J. S., Hamner, W. C. 1976. Effects of performance feedback and goal setting on productivity and satisfaction in an organizational setting. *J. Appl. Psychol.* 61:48–57

244. Turney, J. R., Cohen, S. L. 1976. Influence of work content on extrinsic outcome expectancy and intrinsic pleasure predictions of work effort. *Organ. Behav. Hum. Perform.* 17:311–27

245. Umstot, D. D., Bell, C. H., Mitchell, T. R. 1976. Effects of job enrichment and task goals on satisfaction and productivity: Implications for job design. *J. Appl. Psychol.* 61:379–94

246. Utecht, R. E., Heier, W. D. 1976. The contingency model and successful military leadership. *Acad. Manage. J.* 19:606–18

247. Van Maanen, J., Katz, R. 1976. Individuals and their careers: Some temporal considerations for work satisfaction. *Personnel Psychol.* 29:601–16

248. Vecchio, R. P. 1977. An empirical examination of the validity of Fiedler's model of leadership effectiveness. *Organ. Behav. Hum. Perform.* 19:180–206

249. Vroom, V. H. 1964. *Work and Motivation.* New York: Wiley. 331 pp.

250. Vroom, V. H., Yetton, P. W. 1973. *Leadership and Decision Making.* Pittsburgh: Univ. Pittsburgh Press. 233 pp.

251. Wahba, M. A., House, R. J. 1974. Expectancy theory in work and motivation: Some logical and methodological issues. *Hum. Relat.* 27:121–47

252. Weed, S. E., Mitchell, T. R., Moffitt, W. 1976. Leadership style, subordinate personality and task type as predictors of performance and satisfaction with supervision. *J. Appl. Psychol.* 61:58–66

253. Weick, K. E., Bougon, M. C., Maruyama, G. 1976. The equity context. *Organ. Behav. Hum. Perform.* 15:32–65

254. Weiss, D. J. 1976. Multivariate procedures. See Ref. 55, pp. 327–62

255. Weiss, H. M. 1977. Subordinate imitation of supervisor behavior: The role of modeling in organizational socialization. *Organ. Behav. Hum. Perform.* 19:89–105

256. Wheaton, G. R., Eisner, E. J., Mirabella, A., Fleishman, E. A. 1976. Ability requirements as a function of changes in the characteristics of an auditory signal identification task. *J. Appl. Psychol.* 61:663–76

257. White, S., Mitchell, T. R., Bell, C. H. 1977. Goal setting, evaluation apprehension and social cues as determinants of job performance and job satisfaction in a simulated organization. *J. Appl. Psychol.* 62:665–73

258. Wienew, Y., Gechman, A. S. 1977. Commitment: A behavioral approach to job involvement. *J. Vocat. Behav.* 10:47–52

259. Yukl, G. A., Latham, G. P. 1975. Consequences of reinforcement schedules and incentive magnitudes for employee performance: Problems encountered in an industrial setting. *J. Appl. Psychol.* 60:294–98

260. Yukl, G. A., Latham, G. P. 1978. Interrelationships among employee participation, individual differences, goal difficulty, goal acceptance, instrumentality and performance. *Personnel Psychol.* In press

261. Yukl, G. A., Latham, G. P., Pursell, E. D. 1976. The effectiveness of performance incentives under continuous and variable ratio schedules of reinforcement. *Personnel Psychol.* 29:221–31

262. Yukl, G., Wexley, K. N., Seymore, J. P. 1972. Effectiveness of pay incentives under variable ratio and continuous reinforcement schedules. *J. Appl. Psychol.* 56:19–23

263. Yunker, G. W., Hunt, J. B. 1976. An empirical comparison of the Michigan Four-Factor and Ohio State LBDQ leadership scales. *Organ. Behav. Hum. Perform.* 17:45–65

Ann. Rev. Psychol. 1979. 30:283–325

NEURAL MECHANISMS AND ♦309
BEHAVIORAL ASPECTS OF TASTE[1]

C. Pfaffmann, M. Frank, and R. Norgren

The Rockefeller University, New York, NY 10021

CONTENTS

HISTORICAL PERSPECTIVES IN THE STUDY OF TASTE
(by Carl Pfaffmann) 284
Conclusions 291
Recent Compilations 291
PERIPHERAL PROCESSES 291
Sensory Electrophysiology, Coding, and Behavioral Discrimination 291
Receptor Fields and Single Papilla 299
The Sugar Receptor 301
Taste Preferences and Hedonic Processes 302
CENTRAL ANATOMY AND PHYSIOLOGY OF THE GUSTATORY
SYSTEM 305
CENTRAL INVOLVEMENT IN COMPLEX GUSTATORY PHENOMENA 312
CONCLUSIONS 317

The first section of this chapter presents an overview of earlier research on taste, drawn partly from the more than 40 years of participation in this field by the senior author. The later sections of the chapter then bring up to date certain main themes that were identified in the earlier research. Reasons are given for expecting a final resolution within the next decade of the long-standing controversy concerning the existence of a few basic taste receptors versus a multireceptorial array. Progress in research on central nervous system mechanisms of taste gives promise of further advances that will link

[1]Abbreviations used in this chapter include the following: BNST, bed nucleus of the stria terminalis; CG, coronal gyrus; CNA, central nucleus of the amygdala; CT, chorda tympani; EP, evoked potential; IC, internal capsule; LH, lateral hypothalamus; MCA, middle cerebral artery; NST, nucleus of the solitary tract; PBN, parabrachial nucleus; PS, presylvian sulcus.

0066-4308/79/0201-0283$01.00

gustatory functions even more closely to appetite, intake, preferences, and hedonic processes, and that may ultimately illuminate the physiological nature of reinforcement.

HISTORICAL PERSPECTIVES IN THE STUDY OF TASTE (by Carl Pfaffmann)

Professor E. G. Boring documented in his *History of Sensation and Perception in Psychology* (24) the early beginnings of experimental psychology within the context set by the nineteenth century German sensory physiologists. They did not particularly distinguish between physiological and psychological aspects in their work. Indeed, Hermann von Helmholtz, the giant of that era, combined in a very modern way the multidisciplinary study of physics, physiology, and psychology. He studied and wrote not only about the physics and physiology of these senses, but also on the nature of auditory and visual perception and their genesis (208, 209). The chemical senses history has had no giants of his stature, although the physiologist Zwaardemaker (224) and the psychologist Henning (87) made notable advances. The general status of classical knowledge of the chemical senses was well documented in von Skramlik's thorough and comprehensive handbook (210). To some degree, chemistry, receptor anatomy, but mostly psychophysics, were the source of information. Stimulus-response (structure-function) relations in the chemical senses did not reveal such well-ordered stimulus dimensions as wavelength of light or frequency of sound.

The study of sensory function over the years was dominated by the concept of the specific energies of nerves. The sensation perceived did not reside in the stimulus but in the nerve stimulated. Pressure against the skin was felt as touch, pressure against the eyeball was perceived as light. These principles were recognized early as shown by an example from Sir Charles Bell's writings in 1811 (11) concerning the four kinds of papillae on the tongue:

> Of these the papillae of one kind form the seat of the sense of taste; the other papillae (more numerous and smaller) resemble the extremities of the nerves in the common skin, and are the organs of touch in the tongue. When I take a sharp steel point and touch one of these papillae, I feel the sharpness. The sense of touch informs me of the shape of the instrument. When I touch a papilla of taste, I have no sensation similar to the former. I do not know that a point touches the tongue, but I am sensible of a metallic taste, and the sensation passes backward on the tongue.

Johannes Mueller's name is usually associated with this doctrine, for he named it the "Specific Energies of Nerves," and documented it in thorough detail in his great *Handbuch der Physiologie* (122). Determining the physiological mechanisms undergirding this principle has been a major focus of much of the research in sensory psychology and physiology.

A great new breakthrough in the study of all the senses came with the application of the electrophysiological methods pioneered by Lord Adrian and his colleagues. Adrian's classical works, *The Basis of Sensation* (1) and *The Physical Background of Perception* (2), and the then contemporary work of Erlanger & Gasser on the *Electrical Signs of Nervous Activity* (59) delineated the new era. Their methods provided a way for tapping in on the sense organs themselves, on their afferent nerves and ultimately on the brain centers activated by sensory stimuli. The first senses to be examined, of course, were vision, hearing, cutaneous senses, proprioception, and later the vestibular apparatus. The chemical senses, especially gustation, which is the subject of this review, were not attacked until relatively late. Adrian had initiated work on the olfactory bulb and olfactory nerves in 1950 (3). He himself never studied the gustatory apparatus. When I began my study of the afferent taste nerves of cats in Adrian's laboratory in 1937 as a doctoral student, there had been a few beginnings. Hoagland (89) had recorded in the barbel nerves of the catfish, a species richly endowed with taste buds over the external body surface. Impulses generated upon chemical stimulation are relatively small compared with the spikes generated by tactile stimulation. Pumphrey (167) recorded impulses from the frog's tongue and palate to salts and acids. Barron (7) made a similar observation in the cat, and Zotterman (223) recorded from the cat chorda tympani and lingual nerves. Taste impulses, as in the catfish, were of a relatively small size compared with those initiated by tactile stimulation. With all due modesty, I can recall that my studies in the late 1930s provided the first detailed study of the function of individual taste nerve fibers that responded to taste stimuli applied to the tongue of the cat. My first brief report, "Specific Gustatory Impulses" (155), was presented at the 1939 spring meeting of the Physiological Society in Oxford. A more detailed account appeared 2 years later (156).

The chorda tympani nerve had been exposed by appropriate surgery in an anesthetized animal, and nerve fibers teased out with dissecting needles observed under a binocular microscope. I began these studies in order to obtain objective physiological evidence relative to the four basic taste sensitivities hypothesized for man: salt, sour, bitter, and sweet. What I found complicated the situation. First of all, the cat nerve did not respond to sugar, and although it did have acid sensitive (Type H) units, which did not respond to sodium chloride or quinine, there were also salt (NaCl) sensitive units that responded both to sodium chloride and to acid (Type H + N), and a third class that responded both to quinine and acid (Type H + Q). Theoretically acidity could be coded by concomitant activity in all three types of fibers. Saltiness (NaCl) could be coded by fractional activity, i.e. discharge of (N + H) group only. Similarly, bitterness (quinine) could be coded by discharge of the (Q + H) group alone.

Thus, taste quality seemed coded not simply by the "all or nothing" activation of specific fiber groups alone, but by the pattern of activation of that group in relation to the other fibers activated. My later comparative study of gustatory nerve impulses in rat, cat, and rabbit confirmed these ideas (157). These results led to a formulation which came to be known as the *pattern theory* of taste quality discrimination in which a central decoding step was required. A similar conception was expanded in one study by Zotterman and collaborators (40) in a further detailed study of cat single units, but he did not pursue this model in subsequent publications.

At about this general period in sensory psychology and physiology, it should be remembered that the classical views were under attack. In vision, von Helmholtz (208) had postulated three basic color receptors for red, blue, and green, each with an appropriate visibility function. In hearing, he had postulated that different regions of the basilar membrane resonated, that is, were tuned to individual tonal frequencies. Thus, placed along the basilar membrane and the specific nerve fibers innervating these regions were mediators of pitch (209). In 1930 Wever & Bray (213) found that the auditory nerve as a whole seemed capable of conveying the whole audible range of frequencies which extended the rate beyond that which any one fiber was capable of following. This revitalized the so-called telephone theory of hearing, another form of afferent coding by patterned discharge. In the cutaneous domain, Joan Paul Nafe in the 1930s (125) was making a strong case for a quantitative rather than qualitative theory of feeling. Nafe said:

> It is not obviously true that all felt experiences are patterns but psychological analysis has discovered no criterion by which we may always distinguish a complex experience from a simple one. This difficulty has not appeared to be serious because it should be possible by studying the skin and its end organs to determine what types of experiences have separate mechanisms. But this study too has faltered, and after 50 years of investigation, we have no demonstrated correlation between any particular type of sensitivity and the special end organs and fibers that subserve it.

The difficulty in establishing a relationship between painful or nociceptive stimuli and a specific afferent input stood as one of the major stumbling blocks in applying a classical specific nerve energies doctrine to the skin senses.

Early observations in taste seemed to be in line with these trends. However, with increasing study, greater technical competence, and greater appreciation of the interaction between peripheral and central processes, the pendulum has swung back to some degree. Galambos & Davis's demonstration (69) of tuning curves for individual second order auditory nerve fibers showed that at the lowest threshold intensity, each unit has only one best frequency to which it responds. With increases in stimulus intensity, the range of frequencies stimulated spreads on either side. The best frequency for any particular unit is still apparent in its highest rate of neural discharge; the side band frequencies cause relatively lower neural discharges. At low frequencies (less than 100 Hz) single units have such a wide frequency response band that many believe low pitches are discriminated by their temporal pattern of discharge. Thus a dual mechanism is invoked: temporal pattern for low tones, specific nerve fibers for high tones (200).

In vision, photosensitivity of three primary receptor sensitivities now resides comfortably with opponent process mechanisms within the lower synaptic relays in the central nervous system (50, 90). The recent demonstration of specific high threshold nociceptive afferents (34) has resolved the question of afferent specificity of pain, but the complete story requires "central gating" of afferent inputs within the spinal cord and brain (114). Thus a neo-Müllerian principle seems applicable to nearly all the senses, namely, that there are specific sets of receptors and afferent nerves for different modalities and within modalities specific clusters of afferent nerves specific for the different qualities of sensation. The new view takes into account gating or inhibitory lateral interactions among receptors and similar integrative processes.

Robert Erickson and colleagues (57, 58) examined the responses of a large number of rat chorda tympani single fibers and developed a statistical analysis of the across-fiber correlations. Since the physical dimensions of taste stimuli were and even today are still unclear, he worked backward from responses of single fibers to pairs of stimuli, using the Pearson correlation coefficient to give a quantitative estimate of the degree to which any two stimuli activated any single unit within a population of units in the same way. Figure 1 gives two examples.

Table I [from Pfaffmann (162)] gives a recent compilation of such an analysis. Such a correlation matrix did not seem to fit the classical model derived from human psychophysics. The data, however, show three clusters of sensitivity as indicated by crosshatching, although Erickson has continued to maintain that obvious receptor types or clusters are not apparent. In the more recent results on gustation in our laboratory and those of others, although individual receptors appear to have a wide sensitivity, i.e. a chemical spectrum, they are classifiable into receptor types or clusters. These can be identified and designated by the chemical which causes the largest response, i.e. their best stimulus. In the early days of taste electrophysiology, these apparently more complex relationships caught our attention almost to the point of obscuring the regularities present. Von Békésy's introductory chapter in the *Annual Review of Physiology* in 1974 (207) is devoted largely to his experiences and experiments on hearing and includes a brief account of his early adventures with the chorda tympani (CT) nerve.

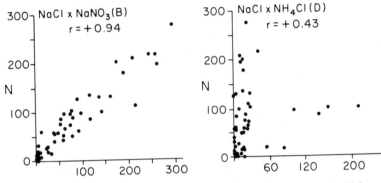

Figure 1   Two examples of cross-fiber correlation scatterplots for responses in 49 hamster single chorda tympani fibers. Each dot represents the response (in impulses in 5 sec) to two stimuli. NaCl (N) responses are plotted along both ordinates, NaNO₃ along upper left abscissa and NH₄Cl along upper right abscissa. The calculated Spearman rank-difference correlation coefficients (r) appear in the upper left of each panel. From Frank (62).

Since this nerve passes over the tympanic membrane and is easily accessible via the external meatus, his professor of physiology at Budapest thought it was suited for measuring the velocity of nerve impulse conduction in the secretion of saliva its efferent fibers elicited. Békésy was interested in the opposite transmission, that is, from the taste afferents, but since the CT subserves two functions and the distribution of the two is very different in different cats, he concluded: "The chorda tympani is thus not the best object of research."

In returning to this early interest in taste later in von Békésy's career (207a, 207b), he utilized only psychophysical approaches combined, however, with exquisite instrumentation and precise stimulus control that characterized his work in audition. That the CT and other taste nerves are complex is clear from its early history, but its complexities are yielding to analysis. Contemporary evidence increasingly supports the concept that taste is comprised of a limited number of primary receptor classes, which can be identified by prototypic stimuli to which they respond best, i.e. their best-stimulus, even though they can be activated to varying degrees by other chemically related or unrelated stimuli. The details of such broad "tuning" are just now becoming apparent.

Taste as a sensory system has other interesting properties. Curt Richter played a key role in calling attention to the role of behavior in maintaining homeostasis. In his epoch-making studies on self-selection behavior (170), he showed that organisms seem able to compensate for dietary deficiencies and to maintain a normal balanced intake. Best known is the enhanced intake of salt to compensate for dietary or physiological deficiency. Most

Table 1 Cross fiber correlations (CFC's) in rat chorda tympani[a]

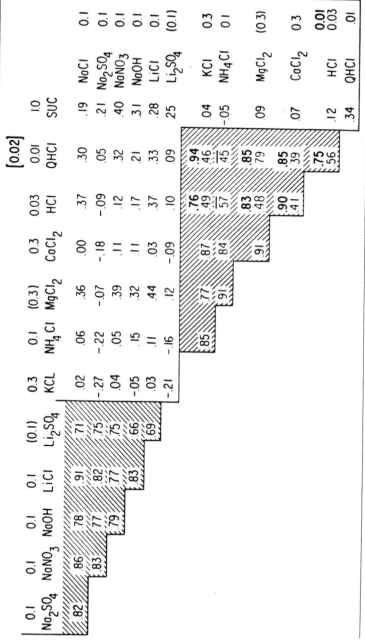

	Na_2SO_4 0.1	$NaNO_3$ 0.1	$NaOH$ 0.1	$LiCl$ 0.1	Li_2SO_4 (0.1)	KCl 0.3	NH_4Cl 0.1	$MgCl_2$ (0.3)	$CaCl_2$ 0.3	HCl 0.03	$QHCl$ 0.01 [0.02]	SUC 1.0
$NaCl$ 0.1	.82	.86	.78	.91	.71	.02	.06	.36	.00	.37	.30	.19
Na_2SO_4 0.1		.83	.77	.82	.75	-.27	-.22	-.07	-.18	-.09	.05	.21
$NaNO_3$ 0.1			.79	.77	.75	.04	.05	.39	.11	.12	.32	.40
$NaOH$ 0.1				.83	.66	-.05	.15	.32	.11	.17	.21	.31
$LiCl$ 0.1					.69	.03	.11	.44	.03	.37	.33	.28
Li_2SO_4 (0.1)						-.21	-.16	.12	-.09	.10	.09	.25
KCl 0.3							.85	.77	.87	**.76** / .49	**.94** / .46	.04
NH_4Cl 0.1								.91	.84	.57	.45	-.05
$MgCl_2$ (0.3)									**.91**	**.83** / .48	**.85** / .79	.09
$CaCl_2$ 0.3										**.90** / .41	**.85** / .39	.07
HCl 0.01 0.03											**.75** / .56	.12
$QHCl$ 0.01												.34

[a]Most values from Erickson, Doetsch & Marshall (58); Bold faced figures from M. Sato (176a).

dramatic was the description of a child with an adrenal tumor whose abnormal craving for salt was strong enough to make up for the excessive daily excretion of sodium chloride. His subsequent studies of adrenalecto-mized rats further documented how they could compensate for excessive salt excretion by their increased salt intake sufficient to maintain good health as long as salt was available. Because animals in a two-bottle prefer-ence test could detect salt solutions at lower concentrations than did normal animals, he theorized that the salt receptors had become more sensitive in salt need. John Bare and I (163) and later Marvin Nachman and I (124) tested this proposition electrophysiologically and found no evidence for an enhanced salt sensitivity of gustatory receptors. Electrophysiological thresholds for sodium chloride were not lower in the salt needy animal. Since our recordings were based on whole nerve responses, not single unit analysis, Rob Contreras, working first at Michigan State and now as a postdoctoral fellow in my laboratory, has more recently reexamined this problem and indeed has found evidence (reviewed in *Peripheral Processes* section) of a specifically reduced receptor reactivity to NaCl (42, 43).

Another class of taste stimuli with potent effects on behavior are the sugars, including artificial sweeteners. Richter (171, 172) also led the way with behavioral studies of rats by showing that a seriation in sugar prefer-ence follows this order: maltose > glucose > sucrose > fructose > galac-tose > lactose. This, however, does not correspond to the order of sweetness and only partially matches the subsequently determined electrophysiologi-cal effectiveness of these sugars for rat gustatory receptors. The current status of this problem area is also reviewed below.

The relationship of taste to appetite and intake controlling mechanisms, as distinct from discrimination, has implications as to the central nervous system (CNS) projections of taste; in particular with regard to such struc-tures as amygdala, the hypothalamus, and other regions known to control food and fluid intake. R. M. Benjamin, beginning with his work in my laboratory, has carried out with his colleagues over the years an excellent series of studies on the CNS taste pathways from medulla via the thalamus to cortex (35). The recent developments in taste neuroanatomy and central neural physiology (largely Norgren's work) reviewed here open up another projection system relative to motivationally related mechanisms of taste. The reinforcing effects of taste stimuli, and especially of the sugars, are remarkable; they can activate hundreds of bar presses on intermittent schedules of reinforcement for a brief taste of a non-nutrient sweet stimulus. Such control of behavior is reminiscent of the potency of electrical brain stimulation at certain sites (149, 150). How taste and the central neural reinforcement are related is still to be clarified.

Conclusions

Overall we can say that (*a*) taste has certain general features that it shares with other sensory systems, i.e. concern for the mechanisms of transduction, afferent coding, and organization of its neural pathways; (*b*) it has certain special features as a specific chemosensor strategically located at the entrance to the oropharyngeal orifice of the digestive tract for detecting palatability of fluids and food on the one hand, or their noxious or unpalatable characteristics on the other. These features control the consummatory reflexes which appear to provide the substrate for acceptance or rejection behavior; (*c*) taste is a specific sensory channel which arouses hedonic processes reflected not only in taste preferences and aversions, but also in the reinforcement of a variety of instrumental responses; (*d*) all these effects can be modulated by feedback from the viscera and also by learning.

Recent Compilations

Since the last *Annual Review of Psychology* (202) in which taste was reviewed, there have appeared several compilations of research on taste; for example, in the triennial volumes of the Proceedings of the International Symposium on *Olfaction and Taste* (ISOT), Volumes 3, 4, 5, and 6, (47, 105, 158, 183). *Chemical Senses 2 Taste,* edited by L. M. Beidler, appeared as part of Volume 4 of the Springer *Handbook of Sensory Physiology* in 1971 (10). Other symposium volumes which have also appeared in this period include: CIBA Foundation Symposium, *Taste and Smell in Vertebrates* in 1970 (219); another in the series *The Chemical Senses and Nutrition* in 1977 (96); and a symposium on *Taste and Development, The Genesis of Sweet Preference* in 1977 (212), sponsored by the National Institute of Dental Research (NIDR). Various aspects of taste are included in the DHEW Symposium Series on *Oral Sensation and Perception* (24a) also sponsored by NIDR. A new journal, *Chemical Senses and Flavor* (99), first appeared in January 1974 to provide a much needed outlet for research in this field. The very well prepared and most valuable *Chemoreception Abstracts* made its debut in January 1973, and is compiled quarterly by Information Retrieval, London and Washington, D.C., in association with the European Chemoreception Research Organization (ECRO).

PERIPHERAL PROCESSES

Sensory Electrophysiology, Coding, and Behavioral Discrimination

Pursuing the "across fiber pattern" mechanism as the taste quality code, Erickson and his colleagues (52, 70, 190) searched for transformations of this peripheral pattern in more central parts of the nervous system and for transformations imposed on this pattern by manipulating stimulus intensity. Each molecule with a taste, of which there are many thousands, could elicit a different pattern across neurons, and the number of taste qualities could be extended indefinitely (57a).

Wang & Bernard (211) proposed that since (*a*) thresholds (measured in logarithmic steps above the whole nerve threshold for the compound) varied for single fibers, and (*b*) individual fibers responded best to one of three stimuli (NaCl, HCl, or quinine) at all intensity steps above threshold, there were three neural channels mediating taste quality in the cat CT. Sucrose, the fourth prototypic stimulus, was not used because the cat CT does not respond to sugars.

Most taste units show an increase in response with increased molarity of an effective test stimulus (71, 103, 145, 165, 179, 211) although the rate of increase, threshold, and saturation levels vary. Generally, if a stimulus has a lower threshold, relative to the whole nerve threshold for that compound, it will elicit consistently larger responses with concentration increases compared to a compound with a higher threshold. Figure 2 illustrates concentration-response functions of two squirrel monkey CT fibers and their response profiles across the four tastes. Thus, it is reasonable that profiles

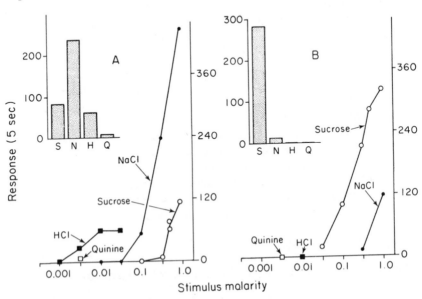

Figure 2 Squirrel monkey chorda tympani response profiles and concentration-response functions. S is 0.5 M sucrose; $N = 0.1$ M NaCl; $H = 0.01$ M HCl; and $Q = 0.003$ M quinine. From Pfaffmann et al (165).

based on single concentrations across these stimuli would be adequate in describing many fibers' relative sensitivities, as long as the test concentrations were chosen at equal steps above threshold. There are exceptions, and one has been demonstrated in three species: hamster, rat, and macaque monkey (146, 179). Responses to increasing concentrations of Na-saccharin increase and then decrease, peaking between 0.01 and 0.03 M in some units, but they show a typical concentration-response function in other units for which the threshold is higher. The first group of units are sucrose sensitive (in both rodents and monkey), but the second group of units are NaCl sensitive (in the rodents and monkey) or quinine sensitive (in the monkey). This implies that saccharin changes its prevalent taste as concentration is increased in these beasts as it does in man.

Boudreau and his colleagues (24b–28, 103, 214) have approached the classification of tongue taste units in a very different way. Recording from neural units in the geniculate ganglion in the cat, they have classified these units on the basis of conduction velocity (latency to electrical stimulation) and spontaneous response rate. Using these criteria, they have found three classes: Group I has short latencies and low spontaneous rates; Group II has middle-sized latencies and high spontaneous rates; and Group III has long latencies and low spontaneous rates. They then used a great variety of chemicals (some of which surely would be found in a cat's food) to characterize the chemical sensitivities: Group I responds primarily to malic and citric acids, O phosphorylethanolamine, butyryl choline and creatinine. Group II units were all discharged by L-proline and L-cysteine, but inhibited by L-tryptophan and L-isoleucine. Group III units were less homogeneous and seemed composed of two subgroups, one activated by nucleotides, the other only to phytic acid and butyryl choline. Among the classic basic taste stimuli, sucrose was found to be ineffective, as reported by nearly all earlier workers. Acid sensitivity seemed to correspond to Group I but not exclusively so. NaCl activated more Group II units, but would activate some units of the other two groups. Quinine normally inhibited Group II, but stimulated some Group I and Group III units. For the cat geniculate units they found the classic basic taste stimuli less adequate as marker stimuli than those enumerated above, with the possible exception of acid for Group I. They also note that single fiber studies on rat and hamster indicate an oral chemosensitivity quite different from that of the cat.

Frank (62), using midrange concentrations of the four stimuli, found three repeating patterns of sensitivity in hamster CT fibers. Although many units responded to more than one stimulus, fibers responding most to NaCl respond best to NaCl and second best to HCl; fibers most sensitive to HCl or sucrose also show typical patterns of response; but responses to quinine were small in all units. However, when all sucrose-best, NaCl-best, and HCl-best sensitive units were also tested with fructose (*F*) and ammonium chloride (*A*), it can be seen that fructose stimulates the sucrose-best units very well, while ammonium chloride stimulates HCl-best units very well (see Figure 3; dark lines connect means). In fact, with seven more test

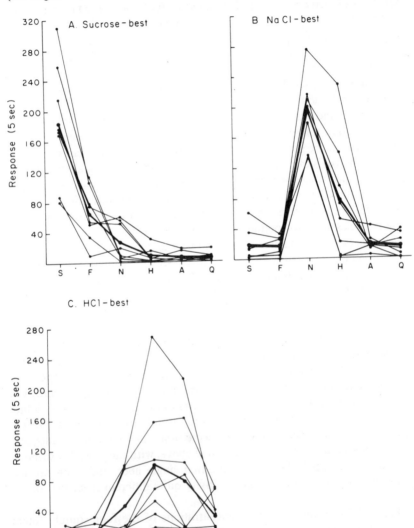

Figure 3   Hamster chorda tympani response profiles. *S* is 0.1 M sucrose; *N*, 0.03 M NaCl; *H*, 0.003 M HCl; *Q*, 0.001 M quinine hydrochloride; *F*, 0.3 M fructose; and *A*, 0.03 M NH₄Cl. Modified from Frank (62)

stimuli (citric acid, acetic acid, Na-saccharin, $NaNO_3$, KCl, $MgSO_4$, and urea) no new response pattern emerges. Saccharin stimulates the sucrose-best; $NaNO_3$, the NaCl-best, and the other five stimulate primarily the HCl-best.

When rat glossopharyngeal nerve fibers innervating the circumvallate are sampled, units highly sensitive to quinine are found, and these units also show a typical pattern (64). When the profiles of all neurons which respond best to each of the four prototypes are averaged, the mean response profiles for the sucrose-best, NaCl-best, HCl-best, and quinine-best peripheral taste neurons are described. Figure 4 depicts mean profiles for taste sensitive units from both CT (149) and glossopharyngeal nerves of the rat (64). Not only do certain response patterns occur repeatedly in one of the taste nerves of the rat, but no matter whether CT or glossopharyngeal fibers are sampled, or whether they innervate fungiform, foliate, or circumvallate papillae, sucrose-best (A), NaCl-best (B), or HCl-best (C) units have similar response profiles. The quinine-best pattern is found neither in hamster nor rat CT, but is in glossopharyngeal neurons innervating circumvallate and foliate taste buds (D). The major difference in fibers sensitive to taste innervating the three tongue areas lies then in the numbers of each of the four patterns found. For example, NaCl-best units occur most frequently in the CT and constitute about 50% of that population in rat; whereas quinine-best units occur most frequently in the glossopharyngeal branch innervating the circumvallate papilla and constitute about 40% of that population. These mean profiles show a nearly exclusive sensitivity to just one of the four stimulus prototypes (with the acid-sensitive units being the only notable exception) although concentrations of test stimuli varied, and experiments were carried out in two different laboratories. These more extensive data have further strengthened the hypothesis that four repeating patterns of sensitivity occur in mammalian tongue taste units.

These profiles, however, are mean profiles. Why do individual unit response functions show so much variation within a class? Recently Berland and colleagues (18) have shown that responses of gerbil cut glossopharyngeal nerves were drastically reduced one hour after cutting. Typically, Frank has recorded for 6 hours after cutting a nerve. Thus, there are units sampled in the first hour and in the sixth hour in the samples which may differ in absolute sensitivity; hence it is not surprising that some profiles are relatively flat. But why should some sucrose-best units respond so well to NaCl, some very little, and some not at all? Why do not all sucrose-sensitive units exhibit the same relative response to NaCl? An observation of Kruger & Boudreau (103) may be relevant. They found that cat taste units which were most sensitive to 0.05 M L-proline had consistently greater responses to 1.0 M NaCl after extensive stimulation than before. Thus, previous stimulation can increase a unit's sensitivity to NaCl. They also found that units most sensitive to acids decreased in sensitivity to pH change after extensive stimulation. Since units sampled at the beginning and end of a 6-hour experiment will have had different amounts of previous stimulation, their sensitivities would be expected to be different.

Furthermore, Ogawa and colleagues (147) report responses of eight units of rat CT to six repetitions of the four stimulus prototypes. Several of the salt-best units show increasing sensitivities to HCl and decreasing sensitivi-

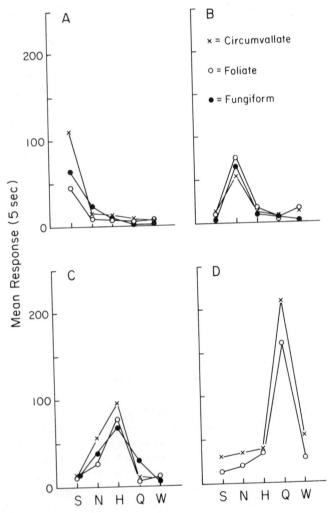

Figure 4   Rat chorda tympani and glossopharyngeal response profiles. *S* is sucrose; *N,* NaCl; *H,* HCl; and *Q,* quinine. *W* is water after water adaptation. From Nowlis & Frank (141).

ties to NaCl with repetition of stimulation. Armed with the profile variations recorded from the same unit in a relatively short period, one need not attribute the variation in profiles to systematic variations from fiber to fiber. It is equally likely that the variations are attributable to sensitivity changes within units in response to nerve cutting and extensive stimulation.

Figure 5 is a different way of plotting single unit taste data provided by Professor Sato of Tokyo. It shows 67 single unit responses to a standard single concentration of each test stimulus in a study of the macaque chorda (179). Its sense of taste resembles man's more than does the squirrel monkey's. In this plot, responses of each single unit are represented vertically in seven rows, each representing a different stimulus. In the top row, units are arranged beginning from left in order of magnitude of response to sodium chloride. In the second row, responses are arranged from the right side in approximate order of effectiveness to sucrose. In this species salt sensitivity and sugar sensitivity are relatively uncorrelated. The next row shows the magnitude of responses to HCl, which overlap significantly but not totally with sodium chloride. In the next row, those units that respond best to quinine are grouped. This seems to form a separate cluster. The responses to warming and cooling of the tongue are also shown. In this form of plot, there are at least three clusters that seem identifiable: salt, sugar and quinine, while acid shows significant overlap with the sodium chloride cluster.

The degree of sensitivity overlap among taste receptors is, as noted above, conveniently quantified by the cross-fiber correlations. Frank's evidence (63) demonstrates that the taste receptors for sugars show significant cross-fiber correlations (cfc's) only with other sweeteners; similarly quinine shows cfc's with other normally bitter stimuli, each forming more specific groups or clusters of sensitivities which do not overlap with the electrolytes. The latter show more overlapping sensitivity. Species differences (80) in how various chemical classes relate to clusters of sensory receptivity are to be expected. The dotted lines drawn across each row in Figure 5 indicate the maximum level of spontaneous discharge of any unit. Suppose that the level of spontaneous activity provides an undifferentiated background "noise." If clear taste perception requires that activity of specifically different clusters rise above this "noise" level, then the response of the sweet, bitter, and salty clusters do so. Since sodium chloride sensitivity overlaps with that to HCl, many of the same fibers, but not all, are activated by both NaCl and HCl. Each stimulus produces a different cross-fiber pattern and can be distinguished from every other by its unique across-fiber pattern. Each electrolyte that can be discriminated behaviorally may be expected to have a different cross-fiber pattern (cfp) and discrimination by the central nervous system may depend upon such differences in cfp's (160).

However, none of the data described above alone can distinguish between the labeled-line and pattern theory of taste quality coding or some combination thereof. Bernard (20) felt that even with a limited number of neuron types, which bore a simple relationship to the primary taste qualities of man (salty, sour, bitter, sweet), the cfp might be the mechanism which the

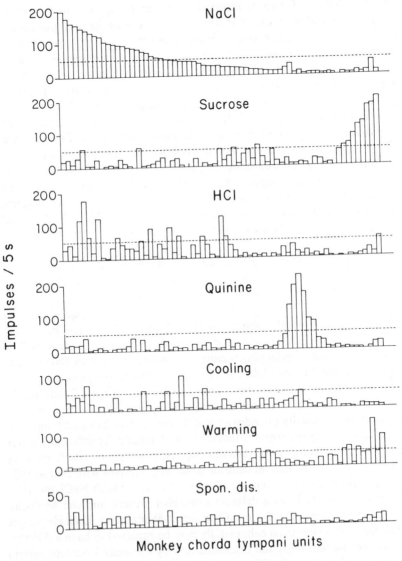

Figure 5 Plot of 67 single chorda units from macaque monkey. See text for explanation. Modified from Sato, Ogawa & Yamashita (179).

central nervous system used to discriminate between stimuli which were "close" in quality or fell within one of the quality categories, e.g. NaCl and LiCl or sucrose and glucose. The regular variation in temporal patterns of response with different stimulating chemicals (68, 117, 147) is also a possible contributor to quality discrimination. Just as in the other senses mentioned in Historical Perspectives, the final resolution in taste may be an amalgam of positions that were once thought to be irreconcilable. The determination of the code for quality necessitates a precise knowledge of the discriminatory capabilities of the organism under study.

The use of measures of generalizations of conditioned aversions in order to determine how a given species groups chemicals on the basis of their perceived quality has met with some success (141, 198). Nowlis & Frank (141) found that hamsters generalize aversions conditioned to sucrose, fructose, or Na-saccharin to sucrose; not to NaCl, HCl, or quinine. Therefore, to the hamster the former three substances taste similar to each other and not similar to the latter three. Hamsters generalize aversions to NaCl or $NaNO_3$ only to NaCl of the four test stimuli; they generalize aversion to HCl, acetic acid, or citric acid to HCl, and to a lesser extent, to quinine, not to NaCl or sucrose; and they generalize aversions to quinine or $MgSO_4$ to quinine, and to a lesser extent to HCl, not to NaCl or sucrose. These data suggest that at least some substances taste alike to hamster and man (112). However, other substances have different tastes for different species, even to the two rodent species: hamster and rat. For example, although Na-saccharin tastes similar to sucrose for man, rats, and hamsters, Na-cyclamate, sweet to man, is similar to sucrose and NaCl for hamster, but similar to only quinine for rat; and aspartame, extremely sweet to man, has only a slight taste similar to quinine for both hamster and rat.

In this review, we have made only passing reference to human psychophysical studies. This is an active field with many theoretical and practical aspects in its own right. It includes also its own versions of the debate over a few primary versus a many receptored array of sensory endings (111, 181, 182, 192).

Receptor Fields and Single Papilla

Punctate electrical stimulation has been used to map receptive fields of gustatory nerve fibers in the chorda tympani of the rat (159). Anodal electrical pulses were adjusted in intensity so that when the punctate stimulus was applied between taste papillae on the rat tongue surface, no discharge of CT taste fibers was observed, but when the electrode was moved to the top of the taste pore, there was a discharge of impulses. Anterior tongue taste buds occur individually upon the surface of the fungiform papilla in both rat and hamster, and the taste pore can be visualized in a dissecting microscope. Wang and Frank (cited in 159) found with this method that the average number of taste buds innervated by a single afferent fiber was 4.5, ranging from 1 to 9. Reactive taste buds were also tested for chemical sensitivity with a punctate stimulator. One particular fiber, examined in detail, responded best to NaCl, but also responded to HCl, but not to sucrose or quinine when the whole receptive field was flooded with the stimulus solutions. When each of the five reactive taste buds connected to the parent fiber was stimulated individually, each was found to be sensitive to both salt and acid and did not respond to either sucrose or quinine. Thus the sensitivities of this fiber to NaCl and HCl did not result from its innervation of two types of taste buds, one sensitive to NaCl and the other to HCl. This evidence, as well as Oakley's (143) that single cat CT fibers tend to show the same sensitivities in all their branches, suggests there is a matching between the taste nerve fiber and all the receptors it innervates. A fiber does not innervate receptors randomly. Further, since receptor cells appear to be at least as broadly tuned as the peripheral fibers which innervate them, the notion that afferent fiber sensitivities are a scrambling of more specific receptor cell sensitivities does not hold water.

Miller (115) examined interactions between individual papillae and their surrounding fields. The unit discharge by a single papilla fluid stimulator could be increased or inhibited by the surround depending upon the chemical applied. A similar lateral inhibition was hypothesized by Bernard (19) to account for his finding that stimulating a large tongue area was less than the sum of the single papillary responses.

Electrical stimulation of an individual taste papilla on the human tongue usually elicits only one taste quality (53), but chemical stimulation of single papilla may (in fact typically does) produce more than one quality, especially if stimulus concentrations are above threshold (9, 113). Recordings from taste receptor cells have been few because of the extreme difficulty of recording slow potentials from cells whose immediate environment needs to be bathed with stimulus solutions, many of which are electrolytes. Sato & Ozeki (180) confirmed earlier findings with microelectrodes inserted in taste buds that individual receptor cells respond to more than one of the four prototypic taste stimuli. There are some unexplained peculiarities about these recordings, the most important is the poor match in sensitivities and latencies to response between receptor cells and CT fibers. For instance, Sato and Ozeki found that most of the rat taste cells they sampled responded best to HCl (75%); whereas only relatively few CT fibers responded best to HCl (20%). More than 50% of rat CT fibers responded best to NaCl, and only 20% of the receptor cells did. The sucrose sensitivity was also greatly underrepresented in the receptor cell population. The typical receptor potential change elicited by HCl was four times greater than that elicited by the other three chemicals, when the four chemicals were presented at concentrations which elicit responses of comparable size in sensitive CT units. This mismatch in sensitivities between the receptor cells and the fibers which innervate them is difficult to interpret. One guess is that the recorded receptor cell electrical potentials are more affected by activity of the cells in their immediate environment than are the transduction processes that initiate activity in the fibers which innervate them.

The Sugar Receptor

Besides the statistical analysis of sugar-best units that imply a relatively high specificity of their actual receptors, there have been notable advances at the molecular level. A single class of sugar-best units does not rule out multiple receptor sites (sometimes called acceptors) on the taste cell membrane. To aid in this explication, we shall turn briefly to some recent findings in insect chemoreception. Morita and colleagues have recorded from single sugar chemosensory hairs of the fleshfly. Shimada et al (191) reported functional separation of two receptor sites after a 3 min treatment with parachloromercuribenzoate (PCMB). The response to D-glucose was completely depressed; the response to D-fructose was unaffected. Since these two monosaccharides joined by a glycosidic bridge make up the disaccharide sucrose, its response was partially reduced. These results confirm earlier speculations that the sugar site is made up of a gluco-pyranose and a fructo-furanose site.

Mammalian sucrose sensitivity is reduced by PCMB (10a), but such a separation of monosaccharide sensitivity, as in the fleshfly, has not been demonstrated. In a series of studies on gerbil whole CT, Jakinovich and collaborators (92–94) found data consistent with two monosaccharide sites. The disaccharide sucrose was more stimulating than any other disaccharide and than either of its constituents or other monosaccharides. The gerbil's taste system has less rigid conformational requirements than the insect so that many more sugars were stimulating. The rat CT is not as sensitive to sugars as is the gerbil or hamster CT. There are fewer sugar-sensitive units in the rat CT than in the hamster CT (65, 145). Sugar-sensitive units in the rat CT are simply hard to find, whereas they are plentiful in the hamster CT. Noma and colleagues (127, 128) have shown that the effectiveness of sugars for the hamster CT whole nerve response and for three sugar-sensitive fibers was sucrose > fructose > glucose > maltose > galactose, an order very similar to that for the rat whole nerve. The order of effectiveness of disaccharides for gerbils is like that of other mammals, including man: sucrose > maltose > lactose, and for monosaccharides, fructose > mannose > glucose > galactose. These orders are consistent with a two-site model like that in insects. Sucrose's great effectiveness would be due to its two constituents (monosaccharides glucose and fructose), both of which also stimulate in their own right. On the other hand, other details of the gerbil's response do not rule out a specific sucrose site into which the other disaccharides fit less well and into which the monosaccharides only partially fit. These molecular relations are still being examined for final delineation. In broader terms the sugars as food sources of energy occur widely in nature and in one form or another are avidly sought by many insect and vertebrate species. Sucrose is the most common soluble sugar found in plants. It is the sweetest disaccharide and its two constituents, fructose and glucose, are sweet, fructose in fact being the sweetest monosaccharide. Thus the sensory and powerful behavioral effectiveness of sugars is becoming understandable in evolutionary and molecular terms.

In contrast to these observations suggesting a commonality of the sugar-sweet receptors across species are the indications that taste modifiers and nonsugar sweeteners including the sweet-tasting proteins have different effects across species. Gymnemic acid (GA), the classic blocking agent for all sweet stimuli in man, does not block sucrose sensitivity in primates or subprimates, except in dogs and hamsters (8, 85). Besides changes in the CT response, GA also causes a deficit in hamster sucrose preferences (61). Guinea pigs, pigs, or rats are little affected (83, 85). The active principle of miracle fruit, miraculin (MIR), that adds a sweetness to acids, apparently does so only for man and old world monkeys (51, 83). In the latter cases, GA does have an effect in blocking the enhanced discharge to acid caused by MIR, i.e. presumably the added activity of the sweet receptors (86). The stimulating effect of the sweet proteins monellin and thaumatin does not occur below man or old world primates, except for a slight effect of monellin in dog (33). For these reasons Hellekant believes there are many different sugar-sensitive receptor sites which differ especially in subprimate species (82, 84). An alternative hypothesis would be that it is not the molecular sites that differ but that the membrane proteins and neighboring constituents provide steric or other molecular hindrances.

The responses of different macaque monkeys (148, 179) to sweeteners such as saccharin, dulcin, and Na-cyclamate, aspartame, and stevioside have been studied. Besides finding good responses to these electrophysiologically and behaviorally, which indicated they stimulated the sugar or sweet receptor of the monkey, Sato and colleagues (178) not only examined the responses of individual animals on both measures but measured an extractable putative sweet receptor protein from these same animals. There was a good correspondence between responsivity, electrophysiological measures, and chemical indices of the receptor protein.

Taste Preferences and Hedonic Processes

Preferences for sweet-tasting compounds have been studied in man and a variety of other species (60, 157a, 161, 171, 177, 194). The volume of a sweet solution which an animal will drink is determined both by immediate taste factors and by factors which develop upon ingestion of the solutions. With sham drinking the relative preferences for sucrose and glucose, as well as the shapes of the concentration-response functions for their preference, closely parallel the effects of these sugars on the recorded response of the whole chorda tympani nerve (194).

Other procedures for limiting intake, such as short-term preference tests and operant procedures which limit ingestion to a few sips between many bar presses in fixed or variable interval schedules, can also yield behavioral measures more related to sensory efficiency. Davis (44) presented several concentrations of sucrose, fructose, and glucose to rats for 30 sec intervals, and found the number of licks elicited was greatest for sucrose, next greatest for fructose, still less for glucose, at equimolar concentrations. This corresponds to the order of effectiveness of these three sugars in eliciting activity in rat CT (127). Davis and colleagues (45) reported that the order of effectiveness of sugars in increasing lick rates in a 3 min test period was maltose > glucose > galactose > lactose, which correspond fairly well with these sugars' order of effectiveness in stimulating activity in rat CT—glucose > maltose > galactose (127).

Richter (171) found more maltose and glucose to be consumed during 48-hour, 2-bottle perference tests than equimolar concentrations of sucrose or fructose, and attributed these differences to the assimilability of these sugars, that is, the relative efficiency with which these sugars are metabolized, and specifies how many grams of a substance per kilogram of body weight can be metabolized in unit time. Maltose and glucose are the most assimilable of the six common sugars tested by Richter, and they are also the most preferred in long exposure tests.

Davis & Levine (46) report several experiments which support their mathematical model of the control of ingestion. In this model, initial lick rate is a direct function of gustatory intensity (e.g. sugar concentration), modified by a palatability factor, whereas longer term lick rates decrease as a function of a stimulus's effectiveness in blocking absorption from the gut. Evidence is converging, then, on the notion that the hedonic value of a stimulus can indeed be viewed as a function of its input to the peripheral gustatory nervous system. Pfaffmann and colleagues (165) have shown that the relative hedonic value of two sugars for the squirrel monkey reflects their relative effectiveness in stimulating activity in sucrose-best CT fibers, rather than their relative effectiveness in stimulating activity in the CT as a whole.

The inference that animals show a preference for sugar because of the hedonic or pleasurable affect associated with the arousal of the quality of sweetness suffers from a basic logical circularity. If we say that animals prefer sugar because of a positive hedonic value, we can ascribe such an hedonic value to sugar because animals prefer it. Mook (118), in fact, prefers an information interpretation to the hedonic one, noting that if something is sweet, rats respond to it as food. While mimetic or other oro-facial responses can be photographed or videotaped as independent responses (see Central Anatomy and Physiology of the Gustatory System section for a description of work on these responses by Steiner and Grill and Norgren), it is only the human subject that can give a direct rating of hedonic value distinct from taste quality. That hedonic value is not merely a judgment of increasing taste sensation under a new guise, at least in the case of increasing concentrations of sugar or sodium chloride, is shown by the independence of the two functions for both stimuli. Psychophysical ratings of sensory intensity of either sweetness or saltiness show increasing functions from 0.03 to 2.0 M concentration, whereas ratings of magnitude of pleasantness show a break point at 0.5 M for glucose and 1 M for NaCl (120, 121, 151). Hedonic value is not simply sensory magnitude.

Interest in hedonic value as a functional property of taste was stimulated by a series of studies by Cabanac (38). He showed that ratings of pleasantness of a glucose solution were unchanged upon repeated tasting if the solution was not swallowed. When swallowed, the ratings become increasingly unpleasant. These same effects could be produced by intubating glucose solution into the stomach; intubation of control solutions of equal osmotic value did not have this effect. Other workers (56, 194) have found that not all subjects show this phenomenon, but a sufficient number do so to indicate that this is a real phenomenon. Cabanac has proposed the term alliesthesia for the internal regulation of the hedonic aspect of sensory experience distinct from the sensation itself. He has demonstrated this in olfaction and temperature sensitivity as well as gustation.

The clearly hedonic character of neonates' facial expressions when presented with sucrose versus quinine or acid solutions to which adults have no difficulty assigning an hedonic score was exemplified vividly in Steiner's important studies (193). The demonstrated control of infant feeding behavior in proportion to the degree of sweetness is further indication of the importance of this increasingly studied process (48, 49, 139, 142).

Another classic and much studied preference is that for salt; here recent findings show that preference changes induced by sodium deficiency are also accompanied by reduced discharge in peripheral taste nerve in the rat (42, 43). The changes were specific to NaCl-best units which gave a lesser frequency of discharge to the higher concentration of salt (0.1 M and greater). A small change in the whole nerve response for high concentrations of NaCl was also observed. Responses to weaker concentrations around threshold did not seem to change. In our earlier work (124, 163) the more discriminating single unit analysis was not employed. Such changes would make the normally aversive strong salts less stimulating to the salt-deprived animal (42). The role of more complex central processes, however, is indicated by the demonstration that deprivation can activate a memory of the source where salt is available (101, 102).

CENTRAL ANATOMY AND PHYSIOLOGY OF THE GUSTATORY SYSTEM

In the last major review of the central gustatory projections, which appeared 7 years ago in the *Handbook of Sensory Physiology,* Burton and Benjamin summarized the extensive evidence documenting that the first central gustatory relay occurs in the rostral pole of the nucleus of the solitary tract (NST) in the medulla (35, 79, 164). Similarly, studies with a variety of anatomical, electrophysiological, and lesion-behavioral techniques in most common, and a few not so common, laboratory species attest to the location of the thalamic gustatory relay in the most medial, parvocellular region of the ventrobasal complex (6). Terminological differences in labeling thalamic nuclei across species, and among anatomists within species, confuse the issue, but the thalamic gustatory area appears to occupy homologous areas in all species examined (138).

The medullary and thalamic taste relays have been examined electrophysiologically with both electrical activation of the relevant peripheral nerves (chorda tympani of VII and lingual of IX) and chemical stimulation of the receptor fields while recording either multi- or single neuron discharges (35, 164). Compared to adjacent trigeminal somatosensory nuclei, the subcortical gustatory areas are miniscule. In the rat, they average less than 1.0 mm on a side, and within that area many neurons sensitive to chemical stimuli also respond to either tactile or thermal stimuli applied to the tongue (66). In the cat, dog, and monkey thalamus more cells respond exclusively to sapid stimuli, and there seems to be an orderly progression of lingual sensibility with taste most medial, then thermal, and touch most lateral (13, 54, 68). A similar arrangement has been reported for the rat lingual thalamus, but gustatory stimuli can influence tactile responses (13, 22, 133).

When compared with CT fibers, central gustatory neurons exhibit no fundamental changes in response profiles. Multiple sensitivity to sapid stimuli is the rule rather than the exception. In the solitary nucleus, the most extensive analysis of single neuron response revealed an increase in overall rate of response during chemical stimulation with some diminution in the relative amplitude of the initial phasic compared to the later static activity. In addition, second order gustatory neurons appear somewhat more broadly tuned (respond more uniformly to more stimulus categories) than their CT counterparts (52). Two less extensively analyzed reports, one in rat, the other in hamster, generally support these results (107, 201). In the thalamus, extensive testing of single units responding to sapid stimuli is again confined to a single study in the rat (190), but data from at least three other species (cat, dog, and monkey) are not inconsistent with observations in the rodent (13, 54, 68). In paralyzed, unanesthetized rats the average response rate more closely resembled peripheral neurons than those in the solitary nucleus. The similarity is somewhat superficial, however, because thalamic cells seldom exhibited initial phasic responses, but the ongoing activity fluctuated considerably. Thalamic cells respond as vigorously to sucrose and quinine as to NaCl and HCl. The latter two are much more effective than the former in driving peripheral receptors innervated by CT fibers. Finally, inhibitory responses occur in the thalamus (7% of the observations); these have seldom been reported in either first or second order gustatory neurons.

Discussions of coding central gustatory information are limited to the two investigations from Erickson's laboratory just summarized. Both compare the data with CT responses obtained in the same laboratory under similar conditions in the context of across-fiber pattern theory. Although Scott & Erickson (190) state that only one cell in 40 responded to only one stimulus, similar data from peripheral nerve studies can be categorized equally well with best stimulus criteria (63). A significant number of units isolated in both the monkey and dog thalamus responded to only one or two of the stimuli employed (35, 68). In each of these investigations, the definition of a response is left unclear, and insufficient data make recategorization impossible. The utility of the best-stimulus approach in comprehending the central gustatory system awaits a parallel series of experiments conducted at different levels similar to those carried out by Erickson and his colleagues.

The analysis of gustatory sensibility within the brain has been limited in another sense as well. The only receptor field stimulated while recording central gustatory neurons has been the anterior two-thirds of the tongue innervated by the CT. Four other distinct gustatory receptive fields exist within the oral cavity of most mammals, the foliate and circumvallate papilla, and taste buds on the palate, epiglottis, and larynx. Until these fields have been examined at least to the same extent as the CT field, the analysis of the central mechanisms of taste can hardly be said to have begun.

The localization of the cortical taste representation rests primarily on evoked potential (EP) maps derived from electrically stimulating the peripheral taste nerves, and behavioral assessments of altered taste preferences after ablation of those EP zones (35). In rats, lesions confined to the thalamic gustatory relay result in degeneration filling a cortical zone previously defined as critical for maintaining normal quinine rejection thresholds (14, 138). In cats, however, a similar anatomical study indicated that only cortex buried in presylvian sulcus (PS) received projections from the thalamic taste relay (175). The evoked potential method originally placed feline taste cortex on the exposed coronal gyrus (CG), although later depth recording extended the CT projection area ventrally from CG into the lateral bank of PS (36, 41, 152). Since responses to gustatory stimuli are few and far between on CG, but reportedly frequent within PS, the effectiveness of the EP method seems questionable (41, 119). In primates, taste nerve stimulation revealed three separate EP foci on cortex, two within the primary somatosensory area on the lateral convexity, and one buried in anterior opercular insular cortex (15, 16). All three areas must be ablated before the thalamic gustatory relays shows signs of retrograde cell loss, but opercular damage alone raises bitter rejection thresholds (15, 153, 174).

Sudakov and his colleagues (195) report that 14 units isolated from the frontal opercular cortex and insula of awake behaving squirrel monkeys responded to gustatory stimuli. They all responded to more than one of the fluids (sucrose, saline, milk, and water), three with inhibition. The location of these gustatory units conforms closely with the opercular taste nerve EP zone. Besides being the only report of primate cortical gustatory neurons, this study represents one of the two investigations of activity in the central gustatory relays in awake behaving animals. The other study utilized dogs, but the unit data were combined with similar data from paralyzed rat preparations (68). More than a third of the 60 units isolated from dog and rat cortex responded to only one of the five stimuli, and another third responded to two. An additional ten cells were excited by one stimulus, and inhibited by one or more of the others. Although the data appear only in summary, they suggest that cortical gustatory neurons are more specific than their subcortical or peripheral counterparts. Analogous observations have recently been reported for olfactory neocortex in primates (197).

Cortical gustatory neurons appear not only more specific, but spatially segregated to some extent, in the order quinine, acid, salt, and sucrose sensitivity. Some discrepency exists between this and other studies, however, in that the canine gustatory cells were located on the coronal gyrus, rather than buried in the presylvian sulcus as in cats (67). In rats, the cortical taste responses were aligned dorsoventrally just posterior to the middle cerebral artery (MCA), while other methods delineated an anterior-posterior orientation which straddled MCA (14, 138, 220). The most detailed report of cortical gustatory neurons employed acute rabbit preparations, and apart from identifying some inhibitory responses, does not support earlier observations in dogs and rats (221). No spatial arrangement of sensitivity is mentioned, aside from the inference that some of the cells may have been located within the claustrum, and more cells responded to three or more stimuli than to less than three. At all levels of the central gustatory system, but particularly on cortex, the paucity of data combined with vagaries introduced by differing anesthetic conditions, differing species, and differing stimulus conditions, renders generalizations about coding or function unwise.

Unlike the somatosensory system, the cortical and thalamic gustatory representation is largely ipsilateral. The evoked potential fields of the CT and glossopharyngeal nerves are larger ipsilaterally than contralaterally in the thalamus, while the opposite is true for the lingual somatosensory nerve (22, 23, 55). The opercular taste nerve zones in primates are completely ipsilateral (15), as are the receptive fields of thalamic taste neurons in both monkey and cat (13, 54). The classic anatomical descriptions of the secondary projections from the solitary nucleus, however, maintained that the thalamopetal axons crossed as internal arcuates and ascended in conjunction with the contralateral trigeminal lemniscus (5, 72). This discrepancy led Norgren and Leonard (134–136) to reexamine the projections of NST using a combination of electrophysiological and experimental neuroanatomical techniques.

In the rat, neurons in the solitary nucleus which respond to gustatory stimuli do not project to the thalamus of either side. Instead, they terminate in the caudal parabrachial nuclei (PBN) of the pons barely 2.0 mm anterior to their origin in the rostral medulla (see Figure 6). Although this nuclear area had not previously been associated with gustatory function, neurons in PBN respond to gustatory stimuli applied to either the anterior (CT) or posterior (IX) tongue fields (see Figure 7) (137). Instilling xylocaine into the middle ear to anesthetize the CT graphically illustrates the magnitude of gustatory afferent input to these parabrachial neurons. Not only the response to sapid stimuli applied on the anterior tongue disappears, but also the "spontaneous" activity drops to near zero. Pontine gustatory neurons resemble other taste neurons recorded from the periphery, medulla, or thalamus, in that they respond to multiple stimuli, often to cold water, and the response magnitude varies directly with the spontaneous rate. A small percentage of responses are inhibitory (137, 154). As we have seen, both CT and IX receptor fields influence pontine neurons, and in some cases, the same neurons. (The palatal taste buds innervated by the greater superficial petrosal nerve could have contributed to the input attributed to the glossopharyngeal receptors.) For several units, anterior tongue stimuli inhibited activity, while posterior excited, or vice-versa (137). The generality of these complex interactions cannot be judged, since the response of central gustatory cells to posterior tongue stimulation has been tested in this one relatively small sample.

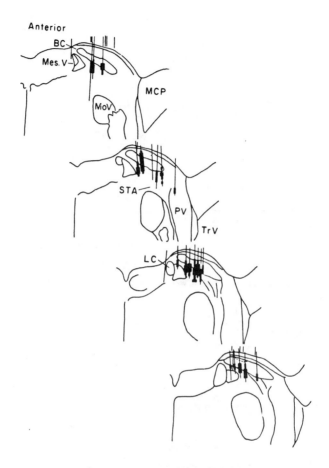

Figure 6 Location of gustatory responses recorded from six rat preparations plotted on tracings of projected sections through the dorsal pons. The sections are separated by 200 μm. Fine lines indicate the extent of the penetrations. Thin bars represent the location of responses which produced integrator deflections of less than 5 mm maximum amplitude. In general these were background responses without any unit activity. Thick bars represent responses greater than 5 mm in amplitude (40 mm maximum), and include all responses with appreciable unit activity. All stimuli were applied to the anterior tongue with a wash bottle. The largest response to any stimulus was measured, but for practical purposes this meant the response to 0.25 M NaCl. The lines above the first and last sections represent penetrations anterior or posterior to the level of the section, respectively. No gustatory responses were recorded during any of these penetrations. Abbreviations: BC, brachium conjunctivum; LC, locus coeruleus; MCP, middle cerebellar peduncle; Mes. V, mesencephalic trigeminal nucleus; MoV, trigeminal motor nucleus; PV, principal trigeminal nucleus; STA, supratrigeminal area; TrV, trigeminal tract. From Norgren & Pfaffmann (137).

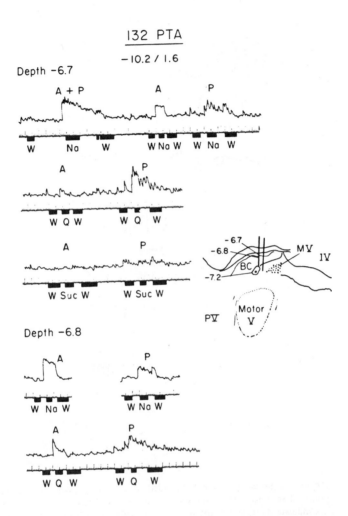

Figure 7 Integrated multiunit responses recorded from the dorsal pons while sapid stimuli flowed over the entire tongue (A + P), or the Anterior (A) and posterior (P) fields independently. At a depth of 6.7 mm the posterior quinine response was considerably larger than the anterior quinine response (second frame). One hundred μm more ventral (depth of 6.8 mm), the anterior quinine response equals or betters the posterior (fifth frame). Inset figure is a partial tracing of a projected section containing the electrode tract from which the responses were recorded. Stimulus abbreviations: *Na,* 0.25 M NaCl; *Q,* 0.003 M quinine hydrochloride; *S,* 0.5 M sucrose; *W,* distilled water. Anatomical abbreviations: BC, brachium conjunctivum; IV, fourth ventricle; Motor V, trigeminal motor nucleus; MV, mesencephalic trigeminal nucleus; PV, principal trigeminal nucleus. From Norgren & Pfaffmann (137).

Although the existence of a pontine relay in the central gustatory system has only been established in one species—the rat—data from several other species also implicate the parabrachial nuclei in gustatory function [see Norgren & Leonard (136) and Norgren (132, 134) for a review]. Neurons responding to sapid stimuli have been isolated from the parabrachial area in both hamsters and cats (21, 206). In some species primary afferents of the nerves conveying gustatory information end in or near the PBN as well as in the nucleus of the solitary tract (39, 168, 169). In fish with greatly hypertrophied gustatory apparatus, the secondary gustatory nuclei are obvious in normal material, and occupy a position in the pons analogous to the caudal PBN of rats (88, 136). In 1906 Nageotte (126) published experimental evidence from a patient who died with a tubercular lesion of nervous intermedius, the sensory branch of the facial nerve which consists primarily of axons from the CT and greater superficial petrosal nerves, indicating its central terminus extended from the rostral solitary nucleus into the dorsal pons. In other words, numerous suggestions exist for the phylogenetic generality of a pontine taste area, but the evidence is not conclusive.

In rats at least, substantial evidence from neuroanatomical (degeneration stains, orthograde transport of tritiated amino acid, and retrograde transport of horseradish peroxidase) and neurophysiological (orthodromic and antidromic activation) investigations indicate that pontine (PBN) rather than medullary (NST) gustatory neurons project to the thalamic taste relay (131, 135, 136, 144). These pontothalamic axons ascend in the central tegmental bundle, which roughly speaking includes all the ascending and descending axons in the dorsomedial reticular formation, and are largely ipsilateral, which is consistent with the electrophysiological evidence from thalamic gustatory receptive fields.

In addition to their thalamic terminations, pontine gustatory neurons contribute to an elaborate axonal system in the ventral forebrain. These axons follow the same course from the pons to the thalamus as the thalamo-petal taste axons, but turn ventrally in the caudal diencephalon, penetrate the subthalamus, lateral hypothalamus, and internal capsule (IC), and ramify extensively rostral to IC in substantia innominata (136). The anatomical evidence suggests this system may synapse in the sub- and far lateral hypothalamus, as well as substantia innominata. The presence of many fibers of passage in these areas, however, renders inferences based on anatomical evidence alone at best tenuous. Denser terminal fields with many fewer fibers of passage fill the central nucleus of the amygdala, immediately lateral to substantia innominata, and part of the bed nucleus of the stria terminalis, lateral and ventral to the septal nuclei (132). Some of the axons of this pontolimbic projection convey gustatory information, because electrical stimulation along its course or in the amygdala antidromically activates gustatory neurons in the parabrachial nuclei (131, 132). A substantial proportion of these neurons can also be invaded by thalamic stimulation indicating that the same neuron projects both to the thalamic gustatory relay and the limbic system.

Although the same gustatory information may be reaching both the thalamocortical and limbic systems, it would be imprudent to conclude similar functions for gustatory afferents in the two systems. Indeed, the smattering of electrophysiological data germane to the subject suggests that a limbic gustatory area, a concentration of neurons responding exclusively to sapid stimuli, may not exist. Neurons in the lateral hypothalamus, substantia innominata, and central nucleus of the amygdala do respond to gustatory and other intraoral stimuli, but are not concentrated in any particular area, and often respond to other, nonfood related stimuli as well (37, 129, 185). None of the data implies the units receive direct input from the pontine gustatory area. In fact, one study implicated gustatory cortex in mediating the response of posterior hypothalamic neurons to taste stimuli (97). The importance attached to the limbic system, and particularly the hypothalamus and amygdala, in the neural control of energy, fluid, and electrolyte balance, including feeding and drinking behavior, tempts speculation into the functions of this ventral gustatory pathway. The probability that the central gustatory system closely parallels the other visceral afferent systems relaying through NST could broaden the functional implications to include most of the autonomic, endocrine, and behavioral systems known to be influenced by the limbic system (132, 134).

CENTRAL INVOLVEMENT IN COMPLEX GUSTATORY PHENOMENA

Since the adequate stimuli (molecules) must be in solution, the sense of taste cannot operate in the absence of some concomitant intraoral somatosensory afferent input. Under ordinary circumstances, normal feeding or drinking behavior, this concomitant stimulation can consist of tactile, pressure, thermal, pain and olfactory activity in conjunction with proprioceptive feedback from the ingestive behavior and quite possibly responses from gastric afferents as well. The interaction of these sensations, which we call flavor, results in the palatability of foods and fluids and significantly influences the choice and amount of substances ingested in both people and animals. The neural basis for flavor, much less its influence on food intake, remains unknown, but recent evidence has provided some testable hypotheses.

The interaction of taste and temperature begins on the periphery, in that most gustatory fibers in the CT will also respond to large changes in tongue temperature (145, 176, 179). Similarly, gustatory units in the medulla, pons, and thalamus also respond to tongue thermal stimuli, and in the pons at least some neurons respond to relatively small temperature changes (2–3°C) (13, 54, 107, 137). Unlike the periphery, however, a significant, anatomically distinct population of gustatory cells in the pons and thalamus do *not* respond to temperature (13, 54, 137). Lingual tactile stimuli influence medullary, but not thalamic gustatory units (13, 54, 107). Gustatory interaction with nonlingual intraoral stimuli has yet to be reported. Intranasal chemical or irritant receptors innervated by trigeminal afferents impinge upon intraoral zones within the trigeminal nuclei and medullary units responding to sapid stimuli (204, 205). In our experience, proprioceptive activity elicited by passive jaw stretch has never altered the spontaneous rate of medullary or pontine gustatory units. At the level of the first central synapse at least four possible components of the flavor amalgam may converge on a small population of neurons in or near the NST.

Despite this convergence in the medulla, as we have seen, most evidence from the thalamus emphasizes the separation of lingual modalities even though cells with dual sensitivity do occur in border areas. In rats, the cortical lingual and gustatory representations have similar juxtaposition (14, 17, 138). In cat somatosensory face area, a small percentage of neurons that respond to lingual touch or temperature stimuli are activated by taste as well (41, 104). The buried gustatory zone of feline and primate cortex has yet to be tested for sensitivity to other intraoral stimuli. In rats, true olfactory neocortex on the dorsal bank of the rhinal sulcus abuts the overlying gustatory cortex (100, 133, 196). In fact, lateral olfactory tract stimulation elicits relatively long latency evoked potentials throughout the lingual representation on cortex (73). An analogous neocortical olfactory area exists on the posterior orbito-frontal gyrus of primates, but its relation to the nearby opercular gustatory zone cannot be established easily since the data derive from widely differing primate species (15, 197).

While the anatomical possibility for flavor interaction exists on cortex, the newly detected gustatory projections to ventral forebrain provides a basis for olfactory and taste convergence in areas traditionally implicated in the control of ingestion. Neurons with olfactory input in piriform cortex and olfactory tubercle traverse the entire length of the lateral hypothalamus (LH) (31, 32, 186, 187). Pontine gustatory neurons invade the same area, though perhaps less densely (132, 136). Both olfactory and gustatory stimuli influence LH neurons, but the different chemical modalities have not been tested on the same neurons (129, 188, 189). The classic observations of Teitelbaum (199) on the importance of palatability for eliciting ingestive behavior from LH lesioned rats imply that the hypothalamus cannot act as the sole mediator for the effects of flavor on food intake. The sensory inattention which accompanies LH lesions could diminish the capacity of food-related stimuli to support ingestion and thus contribute to the aphagia and adipsia (108–110). Highly palatable foods are required to overcome the deficit in utilizing orosensory stimuli. The aphagic and adipsic effects of trigeminal deafferentation lend support to such an interpretation (81, 91, 116, 222).

The major terminus for the ventral gustatory pathway appears to be the central nucleus of the amygdala (CNA) and perhaps the bed nucleus of the stria terminalis (BNST). Both these areas also receive olfactory input, CNA from the main olfactory bulb via the periamygdaloid cortex and BNST directly from the accessory olfactory bulb (31). In addition, some nongustatory pontine neurons which respond to intraoral stimuli also project directly to the hypothalamus and amygdala (131, 132). At present, very little data exist on the sensory characteristics of the neurons in any of these areas which could serve as a basis for the interaction of the modalities contributing to flavor. Nevertheless, an anatomical substrate for the exteroceptive sensory influence on ingestion can be documented. Its most salient feature seems to be that it extends from the medulla to both the neocortex and limbic forebrain. While we do not yet understand which, if any, of these potential areas is in fact important to the perception of flavor, its distribution across several levels of neural function is consistent with the organization of other sensory systems and could account for the relative inefficiency of focal lesions in obliterating the influence of flavor on food intake.

Discriminative ingestive responses to sapid stimuli are, in fact, organized within the caudal brainstem (midbrain, pons, and medulla) (166). Chronic decerebrate preparations have use of only these structures, and are permanently aphagic and adipsic, which obviates the use of traditional consummatory measures of preference and aversion. To circumvent this difficulty, Grill & Norgren (75) developed the taste reactivity test, in which small volumes of sapid stimuli are injected into the oral cavity, and the immediate orofacial response to the stimulus is videotaped for subsequent frame-by-frame analysis. In normal rats, taste reactivity compares favorably with preference tests in that the thresholds are quite similar and the duration of the response is a direct function of stimulus concentration. The two measures differ, however, in how they group the four standard taste stimuli. In both cases, sucrose is accepted, barring postingestive feedback, and quinine rejected. At high concentrations salt and acid are avoided in consummatory tests, but the immediate orofacial response to these chemicals mimics the response to sucrose.

The response to sucrose begins with low amplitude mouth movements followed by midline tongue protrusions then lateral tongue flicks. The first sequence always occurs in that order, but subsequent bouts of mouth movements, tongue protrusions, and lateral flicks are randomly ordered. The total response to a particular chemical is highly stereotyped within and between animals, proceeds without pause, and ends abruptly. The response to quinine begins with one or several large amplitude gapes which are followed by a stereotyped sequence of whole body movements: chin rubbing, head shaking, face washing, forelimb flailing and paw rubbing. The entire sequence has the effect of removing the stimulus fluid from the oral cavity, and in that sense, constitutes a sort of reflex aversion.

Given the same stimuli, the chronic decerebrate (forebrainless) rat behaves in a manner almost indistinguishable from neurologically normal rats (76). The threshold, form, and sequence of responses to all sapid stimuli were identical in both preparations, only the decerebrates responded somewhat more slowly. This difference may be attributable to generally lowered muscle tone (77). Normal and anencephalic human infants also exhibit virtually identical facial expressions when presented with gustatory stimuli (193). Not only do chronic decerebrate rats display normal taste reactivity, but the responses are to some extent modifiable. A food-deprived rat, either normal or decerebrate, will consume large quantities of weak sucrose solution (> 20 cc) injected intraorally. When sated (1–2 hours postgavage), however, both preparations begin to reject the same stimulus after consuming only 4–5 cc (78).

When a conditioned aversion to sucrose was established by pairing it with intraperitoneal injections of lithium chloride which produce sickness, the orofacial reaction to sucrose of normal rats so conditioned becomes indistinguishable from the response to quinine (74). As many as 12 similar pairings in chronic decerebrate rats fail to alter their basic ingestive response to sucrose (78). While the neural apparatus for the basic discriminative behavior required of food selection resides in the caudal brainstem, and even responds to the immediate effect of crude postingestive manipulations, the capacity for long-term modification of taste reactivity appears to require the forebrain. Most components necessary to express a changed stimulus-response sequence do exist in the caudal brainstem. In the normal rat, the change following lithium poisoning consists of response substitution—a behaviorally normal rejection response comes to be elicited by a stimulus which previously elicited only ingestion. The caudal brainstem generates both behavioral sequences, and even has the capacity to switch sucrose from acceptance to rejection during ongoing satiation (food in the gut). What it lacks is the ability to associate a previous stimulus with a subsequent event (malaise), or perhaps just the memory for the association over an extended period.

Similar defects have apparently been produced by focal lesions in the ventral forebrain. Rats that have recovered from lateral hypothalamic damage remember a prelesion taste-illness association, they avoid that particular stimulus but not others, though most cannot acquire a new aversion after the lesion (173, 184). Rats with bilateral amygdalar damage, on the other hand, did not retain an aversion acquired prior to the lesions, but were capable of relearning postlesion, although the postlesion learning was not normal (123). Normal rats are inherently neophobic, particularly with respect to novel gustatory or food-related stimuli. This neophobia enhances the association of learned taste aversions (95). Lesions of the amygdala disrupt neophobic responses, and the acquisition of taste aversions proceeds more slowly, as if all sapid stimuli were familiar. In addition, the amygdalar damage led to a generalized aversion to both water and sucrose after sucrose-illness pairing and depressed sodium appetite elicited by steroid injections, but did not alter the direction of preference-aversion functions for the four standard taste stimuli (123).

This constellation of symptoms parallels the deficits arising after lesions that include gustatory neocortex (98). Rats with taste cortex ablations exhibit decreased neophobia, do not retain a prelesion taste aversion, nor acquire postlesion aversions as rapidly (30, 98, 106). Gustatory neocortex damage does not change the sign of preference-aversion functions, but it does increase the magnitude of preference (intake) for sucrose and weak salt (29, 98). Amygdalar lesions, and for that matter, parabrachial nucleus lesions, also exaggerate sucrose intake (140, 172a). The major difference in gustatory function between rats with neocortical damage and those with amygdalar damage seems to be in the induction of salt appetite. As with hypothalamic damage, amygdalar lesions prevent expression of salt appetite after depletion, but neocortical ablation does not (123, 215, 217, 218). Even this difference, however, may result from differential preoperative experience. Preoperative experience eliminates the preference threshold increases associated with taste cortex lesions (12). Similarly, exposure to salt, but not salt depletion, protects most rats with thalamic lesions from deficits in sodium appetite (4, 216).

The deficits resulting from either lateral hypothalamic or amygdalar lesions are not unique to gustatory sensibility. The interpretation of the results does not emphasize gustatory sensibility per se, but rather a general inability to form associations (184) or to recognize the significance of stimuli (123). The complex of deficits detectable after limbic system lesions can easily support a variety of interpretations without overlap. Assuming the similar deficits in utilizing gustatory information observed after cortical, amygdalar, or hypothalamic lesions result from interrupting different stages of the same processes, then the latter argument seems more plausible. In rats, sodium appetite is an innate response to sodium depletion, and under laboratory conditions at least, requires no associative mechanisms (217).

Taste aversion requires not just associative mechanisms but often relatively long-term storage. An inability to recognize the significance of the malaise, however, would lead to the same behavioral outcome. The sensory inattention which accompanies both LH and amygdalar lesions, in effect, represents an inability to recognize or respond to the significance of stimuli (109, 110, 203). In either case, these interpretations serve only to conceptualize behavioral deficits, but provide little or no basis for inferring neuronal mechanisms.

The deficits resulting from lesions of gustatory cortex parallel those following amygdalar damage, but might be more specific to gustatory sensibility. Should this prove true, then gustatory neocortex, or one of the relays leading to it from the periphery, would be preferred for future investigations of the central processing of gustatory information. The ventral gustatory pathways represent a known source of afferent input to limbic areas which influence ingestive behavior. The analysis of limbic system influence on behavior has been long impeded by an inability to characterize either the afferent information available or the efferent instructions which result, and now that progress has been made in removing these impediments, further advances can be expected.

CONCLUSIONS

In conclusion we wish to make only a few brief comments. One important new terminological development has been the best-stimulus or best-stimuli characterization of the different classes or groups of gustatory afferent units. As has long been known, most single taste afferent units respond to a range of chemicals. The "best stimulus" designator or marker provides a way of bringing more order into the classification of units, especially in relation to certain specificities. For example in rats, quinine-best fibers are found almost exclusively in the glossopharyngeal nerve. The way is now clear also to examine the chemical relations among stimulating agents within each such class. In the next decade, we can effect final resolution of the controversy of a few basic taste receptors versus a multireceptored array with the study of a wider range besides the classical tastants. More stress will be laid upon analytical animal psychophysics on the same species for which electrophysiological data are obtained. The best stimulus designations of taste units may indeed turn out to be a conceptual as well as a terminological innovation.

We can expect many new developments on the CNS aspects of taste as the neural relations of the ventral taste pathway and its limbic projections are revealed. Increasingly here, as in the study of peripheral mechanisms, we can expect exciting new advances that will link gustatory function even more closely to appetite, food, and fluid intake, preferences and aversions, and hedonic processes. Insights into the control of behavior by gustatory stimuli may ultimately illuminate the physiological nature of reinforcement.

ACKNOWLEDGMENT

Prepared under support of NSF BNS 75-18067, NSF BNS 76-81408 and PHS 10150. We wish especially to thank Ms. Jean Clement for her stellar secretarial assistance that made it possible to meet the *Annual Review* deadline.

Literature Cited

1. Adrian, E. D. 1928. *The Basis of Sensation.* New York: Norton. 122 pp.
2. Adrian, E. D. 1947. *The Physical Background of Perception.* London: Oxford Univ. Press. 95 pp.
3. Adrian, E. D. 1950. The electrical activity of the mammalian olfactory bulb. *Electroencephalogr. Clin. Neurophysiol.* 2:377–88
4. Ahern, G., Landin, M. L., Wolf, G. 1978. Escape from deficits in sodium intake as a function of preoperative experience. *J. Comp. Physiol. Psychol.* In press
5. Allen, W. F. 1923. Origin and destination of the secondary visceral fibers in the guinea pig. *J. Comp. Neurol.* 35:275–310
6. Andersson, B., Jewell, P. A. 1957. Studies on the thalamic relay for taste in the goat. *J. Physiol.* 139:191–97
7. Barron, D. H. 1936. A note on the course of the proprioceptive fibers from the tongue. *Anat. Rec.* 66:11
8. Bartoshuk, L. M. 1969. Blockade of single chorda tympani fibers by K gymenmate. Reported by Pfaffmann. See Ref. 158, p. 529
9. Bealer, S. L., Smith, D. V. 1975. Multiple sensitivity to chemical stimuli in single human taste papillae. *Physiol. Behav.* 14:795–99
10. Beidler, L. M., ed. 1971. *Handbook of Sensory Physiology, Vol. 4, Chemical Senses 2 Taste.* Berlin: Springer-Verlag. 410 pp.
10a. Beidler, L. M. 1975. Transductive coupling in the gustatory system. In *Functional Linkage in Biomolecular Systems,* ed. F. O. Schmitt, D. Schneider, D. Crothers, pp. 255–62. New York: Raven. 350 pp.
11. Bell, C. 1811. Idea of a new anatomy of the brain. Facsimile. In *The Way In and The Way Out,* P. F. Cranefield, 1974, pp. 9–10. Mt. Kisco, NY: Futura
12. Benjamin, R. M. 1959. Absence of deficits in taste discrimination following cortical lesions as a function of the amount of preoperative practice. *J. Comp. Physiol. Psychol.* 52:255–58
13. Benjamin, R. M. 1963. Some thalamic and cortical mechanisms of taste. In *Olfaction and Taste,* ed. Y. Zotterman, pp. 309–29. Oxford: Pergamon. 396 pp.
14. Benjamin, R. M., Akert, K. 1959. Cortical and thalamic areas involved in taste discrimination in the albino rat. *J. Comp. Neurol.* 111:231–60
15. Benjamin, R. M., Burton, H. 1968. Projection of taste nerve afferents to anterior opercular-insular cortex in squirrel monkey (Saimiri sciureus). *Brain Res.* 7:221–31
16. Benjamin, R. M., Emmers, R., Blomquist, A. J. 1968. Projection of tongue nerve afferents to somatic sensory area I in squirrel monkey (Saimiri sciureus). *Brain Res.* 7:208–20
17. Benjamin, R. M., Pfaffmann, C. 1955. Cortical localization of taste in the albino rat. *J. Neurophysiol.* 18:56–64
18. Berland, D. W., Chu, J. S., Hosley, M. A., Jones, L. B., Kaliszewski, J. M., Lawler, W. C., Oakley, B. 1977. New approaches to the problem of the trophic function of neurons. In *Olfaction and Taste 6,* ed. J. LeMagnen, P. MacLeod, pp. 217–24. London, Washington DC: Information Retrieval. 527 pp.
19. Bernard, R. A. 1972. Antidromic inhibition: A new model of taste receptor function. In *Olfaction and Taste 4,* ed. D. Schneider, pp. 301–7. Stuttgart: Wissenschaftliche Verlagsgesellschaft MBH. 400 pp.
20. Bernard, R. A. 1975. Can taste neuron specificity coexist with multiple sen-

sitivity? In *Olfaction and Taste 5,* ed. D. A. Denton, J. P. Coghlan, pp. 11–14. New York: Academic. 460 pp.
21. Bernard, R. A., Nord, S. G. 1971. A first-order synaptic relay for taste fibers in the pontine brainstem of the cat. *Brain Res.* 30:349–56
22. Blomquist, A. J., Benjamin, R. M., Emmers, R. 1962. Distribution of thalamic units responsive to thermal, mechanical and gustatory stimulation of the tongue of the albino rat. *Fed. Proc.* 21:343
23. Blomquist, A. J., Benjamin, R. M., Emmers, R. 1962. Thalamic localization of afferents from the tongue in squirrel monkey (Saimiri sciureus). *J. Comp. Neurol.* 118:77–87
24. Boring, E. G. 1942. *Sensation and Perception in the History of Experimental Psychology.* New York: Appleton-Century. 631 pp.
24a. Bosma, J. F., ed. 1973. *Fourth Symposium on Oral Sensation and Perception:* Bethesda: DHEW Publ. No. (NIH) 73–546. 419 pp.
24b. Boudreau, J. C. 1974. Neural encoding in cat geniculate ganglion tongue units. *Chem. Senses Flavor* 1:41–51
25. Boudreau, J. C. 1976. Comparison of cat and human taste responses to amino acid solutions. *Neurosci. Abstr.* 213:151
26. Boudreau, J. C., Alev, N. 1973. Classification of chemoresponsive tongue units of the cat geniculate ganglion. *Brain Res.* 54:157–75
27. Boudreau, J. C., Anderson, W., Oravec, J. 1975. Chemical stimulus determinants of cat geniculate ganglion chemoresponsive group II unit discharge. *Chem. Senses Flavor* 1:495–517
28. Boudreau, J. C., Nelson, T. E. 1977. Chemical stimulus determinants of cat geniculate ganglion chemoresponsive group I unit discharge. *Chem. Senses Flavor* 2:353–74
29. Braun, J. J., Kiefer, S. W. 1975. Preference-aversion functions for basic taste stimuli in rats lacking gustatory neocortex. *Bull. Psychon. Soc.* 6:438–39
30. Braun, J. J., Slick, T. B., Lorden, J. F. 1972. Gustatory neocortex: Involvement in learning taste aversions. *Physiol. Behav.* 9:637–41
31. Broadwell, R. D. 1975. Olfactory relationships of the telencephalon and diencephalon in the rabbit. 1. An autoradiographic study of the efferent connections of the main and accessory olfactory bulbs. *J. Comp. Neurol.* 163(3):329–46
32. Broadwell, R. D. 1975. Olfactory relationships of the telencephalon and dien-

cephalon in the rabbit. II. An autoradiographic and horseradish peroxidase study of the efferent connections of the anterior olfactory nucleus. *J. Comp. Neurol.* 164(4):389–409
33. Brouwer, J. N., Hellekant, G., Kasahara, Y., Van Der Wel, H., Zotterman, Y. 1973. Electrophysiological study of the gustatory effects of the sweet proteins monellin and thaumatin in monkey, guinea pig and rat. *Acta Physiol. Scand.* 89:550–57
34. Burgess, P. R., Perl, E. R. 1967. Myelinated afferent fibres responding specifically to noxious stimulation of the skin. *J. Physiol.* 190:541–62
35. Burton, H., Benjamin, R. M. 1971. Central projections of the gustatory system. See Ref. 10, pp. 148–64
36. Burton, H., Earls, F. 1969. Cortical representation of the ipsilateral chorda tympani nerve in the cat. *Brain Res.* 16:520–23
37. Burton, M. J., Rolls, E. T., Mora, F. 1976. Effects of hunger on the response of neurons in the lateral hypothalamus to the sight and taste of food. *Exp. Neurol.* 51:668–77
38. Cabanac, M. 1971. Physiological role of pleasure. *Science* 173:1103–7
39. Car, A., Jean, A., Roman, C. 1975. A pontine primary relay for ascending projections of the superior laryngeal nerve. *Exp. Brain Res.* 22:197–210
40. Cohen, M. J., Hagiwara, S., Zotterman, Y. 1955. The response spectrum of taste fibers in the cat. A single fiber analysis. *Acta Physiol. Scand.* 33:316–32
41. Cohen, M. J., Landgren, S., Ström, L., Zotterman, Y. 1957. Cortical reception of touch and taste in the cat. A study of single cortical cells. *Acta Physiol. Scand.* 40: Suppl. 135, pp. 1–50
42. Contreras, R. J. 1977. Changes in gustatory nerve discharges with sodium deficiency: A single unit analysis. *Brain Res.* 121:373–78
43. Contreras, R. J., Frank, M. 1977. Gustatory nerve discharges in sodium deficient rats. See Ref. 18, p. 278
44. Davis, J. D. 1973. The effectiveness of some sugars in stimulating licking behavior in the rat. *Physiol. Behav.* 11:39–45
45. Davis, J. D., Collins, B. J., Levine, M. W. 1975. Peripheral control of meal size: Interaction of gustatory stimulation and postingestional feedback. In *Hunger: Basic Mechanisms and Clinical Implications,* ed. D. Novin, W. Wyrwicka, G. Bray, pp. 395–408, New York: Raven. 494 pp.

46. Davis, J. D., Levine, M. W. 1977. A model for the control of ingestion. *Psychol. Rev.* 84:379–412
47. Denton, D. A., Coghlan, J. P., eds. 1975. *Olfaction and Taste 5.* New York: Academic. 460 pp.
48. Desor, J. A., Maller, O., Greene, L. S. 1977. Preference for sweet in humans: infants, children, and adults. In *Taste and Development: The Genesis of Sweet Preference,* ed. J. M. Weiffenbach, pp. 161–72. Bethesda: DHEW Publ. No. (NIH) 77–1068. 435 pp.
49. Desor, J. A., Maller, O., Turner, R. 1973. Taste in acceptance of sugars by human infants. *J. Comp. Physiol. Psychol.* 84:496–501
50. DeValois, R. L. 1965. Analysis and coding of color vision in the primate visual system. In *Sensory Receptors,* pp. 567–80. Cold Spring Harbor, NY: Cold Spring Harbor Lab. Quant. Biol.
51. Diamant, H., Hellekant, G., Zotterman, Y. 1972. The effect of miraculin on the taste buds of man, monkey and rat. See Ref. 19, pp. 241–44
52. Doetsch, G. S., Erickson, R. P. 1970. Synaptic processing of taste-quality information in the nucleus tractus solitarius of the rat. *J. Neurophysiol.* 33:490–507
53. Dzendolet, E., Murphy, C. 1974. Electrical stimulation of human fungiform papillae. *Chem. Senses Flavor* 1:9–15
54. Emmers, R. 1966. Separate relays of tactile, pressure, thermal, and gustatory modalities in the cat thalamus. *Proc. Soc. Exp. Biol. Med.* 121:527–31
55. Emmers, R., Benjamin, R. M., Blomquist, A. J. 1962. Thalamic localization from the tongue in albino rats. *J. Comp. Neurol.* 118:43–48
56. Engen, T. 1977. The discrimination of glucose and water by newborn infants. See Ref. 48, pp. 143–45
57. Erickson, R. P. 1963. Sensory neural patterns and gustation. See Ref. 13, pp. 205–13
57a. Erickson, R. P. 1968. Stimulus coding in topographic and nontopographic afferent modalities: On the significance of the activity of individual sensory neurons. *Psychol. Rev.* 75:447
58. Erickson, R. P., Doetsch, G. S., Marshall, D. A. 1965. The gustatory neural response function. *J. Gen. Physiol.* 49:247–63
59. Erlanger, J., Gasser, H. S. 1937. *Electrical Signs of Nervous Activity.* Philadelphia: Univ. Pennsylvania Press. 221 pp.
60. Ernits, T., Corbit, J. D. 1973. Taste as a dipsogenic stimulus. *J. Comp. Physiol. Psychol.* 83:27–31
61. Faull, J. R., Halpern, B. P. 1971. Reduction of sucrose preference in the hamster by gymnemic acid. *Physiol. Behav.* 7:903–7
62. Frank, M. 1973. An analysis of hamster afferent taste nerve response functions. *J. Gen. Physiol.* 61:588–618
63. Frank, M. 1974. The classification of mammalian afferent taste nerve fibers. *Chem. Senses Flavor* 1:53–60
64. Frank, M. 1975. Response patterns of rat glossopharyngeal taste neurons. See Ref. 20, pp. 59–64
65. Frank, M. 1977. The distinctiveness of responses to sweet in the chorda tympani nerve. See Ref. 48, pp. 25–41
66. Frommer, G. P. 1961. Gustatory afferent responses in the thalamus. In *The Physiological and Behavioral Aspects of Taste,* ed. M. R. Kare, B. Halpern, pp. 50–65, Chicago: Univ. Chicago Press. 149 pp.
67. Funakoshi, M., Kasahara, Y., Yamamoto, T., Kawamura, Y. 1972. Taste coding and central perception. See Ref. 19, pp. 336–42
68. Funakoshi, M., Ninomiya, Y. 1977. Neural code for taste quality in the thalamus of the dog. In *Food Intake and Chemical Senses,* ed. Y. Katsuki, M. Sato, S. F. Takagi, Y. Oomura, pp. 223–32. Tokyo: Univ. Tokyo Press. 614 pp.
69. Galambos, R., Davis, H. 1943. The response of single auditory nerve fibers to acoustic stimulation. *J. Neurophysiol.* 6:39–58
70. Ganchrow, D., Erickson, R. P. 1972. Thalamocortical relations in gustation. *Brain Res.* 36:289–305
71. Ganchrow, J. R., Erickson, R. P. 1970. Neural correlates of gustatory intensity and quality. *J. Neurophysiol.* 33:768–83
72. Gerebtzoff, M. A. 1939. Les voies centrales de la sensibilité et du gout et leurs terminaisons thalamiques. *Cellule* 48: 91–146
73. Giachetti, I., MacLeod, P. 1975. Cortical neuron responses to odours in the rat. See Ref. 20, pp. 303–7
74. Grill, H. J. 1965. Sucrose as an aversive stimulus. *Neurosci. Abstr.* 1:525
75. Grill, H. J., Norgren, R. 1978. The taste reactivity test. I. Mimetic responses to gustatory stimuli in neurologically normal rats. *Brain Res.* 143:263–79
76. Grill, H. J., Norgren, R. 1978. The taste reactivity test. II. Mimetic responses to gustatory stimuli in chronic thalamic

and chronic decerebrate rats. *Brain Res.* 143:281–97

77. Grill, H. J., Norgren, R. 1978. Neurological tests and behavioral deficits in chronic thalamic and chronic decerebrate rats. *Brain Res.* 143:299–312

78. Grill, H. J., Norgren, R. 1978. Chronic decerebrate rats demonstrate satiation but not baitshyness. *Science* 201:267–69

79. Halpern, B. P., Nelson, L. M. 1965. Bulbar gustatory responses to anterior and to posterior tongue stimulation in the rat. *Am. J. Physiol.* 209:105–10

80. Harper, K. J., Kenagy, J. G., Oakley, B. 1976. Gustatory responses of two species of kangaroo rat. *Neurosci. Abstr.* #224, 157

81. Harris, R. 1978. *Trigeminal deafferentation in the rat: Dissociation of effects upon self-stimulation and stimulus bound feeding.* Presented at East Psychol. Assoc., Washington DC

82. Hellekant, G. 1975. Different types of sweet receptors in mammals. See Ref. 20, pp. 15–21

83. Hellekant, G. 1976. On the gustatory effects of gymnemic acid and miraculin in dog, pig, and rabbit. *Chem. Senses Flavor* 2:85–95

84. Hellekant, G. 1977. Effects of miraculin and gymnemic acid in the rhesus monkey (*Macaca mulatta*). See Ref. 68, pp. 201–10

85. Hellekant, G., Gopal, V. 1976. On the effects of gymnemic acid in hamster and rat. *Acta Physiol. Scand.* 98:136–42

86. Hellekant, G., Hagstrom, E. C., Kasahara, Y., Zotterman, Y. 1974. On the gustatory effects of miraculin and gymnemic acid in the monkey. *Chem. Senses Flavor* 1:137–45

87. Henning, H. 1921. Physiologie und Psychologie des Geschmacks. *Ergeb. Physiol.* 19:1–78

88. Herrick, J. C. 1905. The central gustatory paths in the brains of bony fishes. *J. Comp. Neurol. Psychol.* 15:375–456

89. Hoagland, H. 1933. Specific nerve impulses from gustatory and tactile receptors in catfish. *J. Gen. Physiol.* 16:685–93

90. Hurvich, L. M., Jameson, D. 1957. An opponent-process theory of color vision. *Psychol. Rev.* 64:384–404

91. Jacquin, M. 1978. *Trigeminal orosensory deafferentation in the rat: Effects upon a food-reinforced operant response.* Presented at East. Psychol. Assoc., Washington DC

92. Jakinovich, W. Jr. 1976. Stimulation of the gerbil's gustatory receptors by disaccharides. *Brain Res.* 110:481–90

93. Jakinovich, W. Jr. 1976. Stimulation of the gerbil's gustatory receptors by monosaccharides. *Brain Res.* 110:491–504

94. Jakinovich, W. Jr., Oakley, B. 1976. Stimulation of the gerbil's gustatory receptors by polyols. *Brain Res.* 110:505–13

95. Kalat, J. W. 1974. Taste salience depends on novelty, not concentration in taste-aversion learning in the rat. *J. Comp. Physiol. Psychol.* 86:47–50

96. Kare, M. R., Maller, O., eds. 1977. *The Chemical Senses and Nutrition.* New York: Academic. 488 pp.

97. Kawamura, Y., Kasahara, Y., Funakoshi, M. 1970. A possible brain mechanism for rejection behavior to strong salt solution. *Physiol. Behav.* 5:67–74

98. Kiefer, S., Braun, J. 1977. Absence of differential associative responses to novel and familiar taste stimuli in rats lacking gustatory neocortex. *J. Comp. Physiol. Psychol.* 91:498–507

99. Koster, E. P., Moskowitz, H. R., eds. 1974. *Chemical Senses and Flavor,* Vol. 1, No. 1

100. Krettek, J. E., Price, J. L. 1977. The cortical projections of the mediodorsal nucleus and adjacent thalamic nuclei in the rat. *J. Comp. Neurol.* 171:157–92

101. Krieckhaus, E. E. 1970. "Innate recognition" aids rats in sodium regulation. *J. Comp. Physiol. Psychol.* 73:117–22

102. Krieckhaus, E. E., Wolf, G. 1968. Acquisition of sodium by rats: Interaction of innate mechanisms and latent learning. *J. Comp. Physiol. Psychol.* 65:197–201

103. Kruger, S., Boudreau, J. C. 1972. Responses of cat geniculate ganglion tongue units to some salts and physiological buffer solutions. *Brain Res.* 47:127–45

104. Landgren, S. 1957. Convergence of tactile, thermal, and gustatory impulses on single cortical cells. *Acta Physiol. Scand.* 40:210–21

105. LeMagnen, J., MacLeod, P., eds. 1977. *Olfaction and Taste VI.* London, Washington DC: Information Retrieval. 527 pp.

106. Lorden, J. F. 1976. Effects of lesions of the gustatory neocortex on taste aversion learning in the rat. *J. Comp. Physiol. Psychol.* 90:665–79

107. Makous, W., Nord, S., Oakley, B., Pfaffmann, C. 1963. The gustatory relay in the medulla. See Ref. 13, pp. 381–93

108. Marshall, J. F., Richardson, J. S., Teitelbaum, P. 1974. Nigrostriatal bundle damage and lateral hypothalamic syn-

drome. *J. Comp. Physiol. Psychol.*
87:808–30
109. Marshall, J. F., Teitelbaum, P. 1974.
Further analysis of sensory inattention
following lateral hypothalamic damage
in rats. *J. Comp. Physiol. Psychol.*
86:375–95
110. Marshall, J. F., Turner, B. H., Teitelbaum, P. 1971. Sensory neglect produced by lateral hypothalamic damage.
Science 174:523–25
111. McBurney, D. H. 1974. Are there primary tastes for man? *Chem. Senses Flavor* 1:17–28
112. McBurney, D. H., Shick, T. R. 1971.
Taste and water taste of twenty-six
compounds for man. *Percept. Psychophys.* 10:241–52
113. McCutcheon, N. B., Saunders, J. 1972.
Human taste papilla stimulation: Stability of quality judgments over time.
Science 175:214–16
114. Melzack, R., Wall, P. D. 1965. Pain
mechanisms: A new theory. *Science*
150:971–79
115. Miller, I. J. Jr. 1971. Peripheral interactions among single papilla inputs to gustatory nerve fibers. *J. Gen. Physiol.*
57:1–25
116. Miller, M. 1978. *Trigeminal orosensory control of feeding behavior.* Presented at East. Psychol. Assoc., Washington DC
117. Mistretta, C. M. 1972. A quantitative
analysis of rat chorda tympani fiber discharge patterns. See Ref. 19, pp. 294–
300
118. Mook, D. G. 1974. Saccharin preference in the rat: Some unpalatable
findings. *Psychol. Rev.* 81:475–90
119. Morrison, A. R., Tarnecki, R. 1975.
Chemical stimulation of the cat's
tongue will affect cortical neuronal activity. See Ref. 20, pp. 247–49
120. Moskowitz, H. R. 1971. The sweetness
and pleasantness of sugars. *Am. J. Psychol.* 84:387–405
121. Moskowitz, H. R. 1977. Sensations,
measurement and pleasantness: Confes-
sions of a latent introspectionist. See
Ref. 48, pp. 282–94
122. Mueller, J. 1830. *Handbuch der Physiologie des Menschen für Vorlesungen.*
Coblenz: Hölscher. 2 vols.
123. Nachman, M., Ashe, J. H. 1974. Effects
of basolateral amygdala lesions on neophobia, learned taste aversions and
sodium appetite in rats. *J. Comp.
Physiol. Psychol.* 87:622–43
124. Nachman, M., Pfaffmann, C. 1963. Gustatory nerve discharge in normal and

sodium-deficient rats. *J. Comp. Physiol.
Psychol.* 56:1007–11
125. Nafe, J. P. 1934. The pressure, pain and
temperature senses. In *Handbook of
General Experimental Psychology,* ed.
C. Murchison, pp. 1037–87. Worcester,
Mass: Clark Univ. Press. 1125 pp.
126. Nageotte, J. 1906. The pars intermedia
or nervus intermedius of Wrisberg, and
the bulbo-pontine gustatory nucleus in
man. *Rev. Neurol. Psychiatry* 4:472–88
127. Noma, A., Goto, J., Sato, M. 1971. The
relative taste effectiveness of sugars and
sugar alcohols for the rat. *Kumamoto
Med. J.* 24:1–9
128. Noma, A., Sato, M., Tsuzuki, Y. 1974.
Taste effectiveness of anomers of sugars
and glycosides as revealed from hamster taste responses. *Comp. Biochem.
Physiol.* 48:249–62
129. Norgren, R. 1970. Gustatory responses
in the hypothalamus. *Brain Res.* 21:
63–77
130. Norgren, R. 1970. Behavioral correlates
of the thalamic taste area. *Brain Res.*
22:221–30
131. Norgren, R. 1974. Gustatory afferents
to ventral forebrain. *Brain Res.* 81:
285–95
132. Norgren, R. 1976. Taste pathways to
hypothalamus and amygdala. *J. Comp.
Neurol.* 166:17–30
133. Norgren, R. 1977. On the anatomical
substrate for flavor. In *Chemical Signals
in Vertebrates,* ed. D. Muller-Schwarze,
M. M. Mozell, pp. 515–28. New York:
Plenum. 609 pp.
134. Norgren, R. 1978. Projections from the
nucleus of the solitary tract in the rat.
Neuroscience 3:207–18
135. Norgren, R., Leonard, C. M. 1971.
Taste pathways in rat brainstem.
Science 173:1136–39
136. Norgren, R., Leonard, C. M. 1973. Ascending central gustatory pathways. *J.
Comp. Neurol.* 150:217–38
137. Norgren, R., Pfaffmann, C. 1975. The
pontine taste area in the rat. *Brain Res.*
91:99–117
138. Norgren, R., Wolf, G. 1975. Projections
of thalamic gustatory and lingual areas
in the rat. *Brain Res.* 92:123–29
139. Nowlis, G. H. 1977. From reflex to representation: Taste-elicited tongue movements in the human newborn. See Ref.
48, pp. 190–204
140. Nowlis, G. H., Braun, J. J., Norgren, R.
1977. The central gustatory system: Ingestion and rejection functions after lesions. *Abstr. 6th Int. Conf. Physiol. Food
and Fluid Intake*

141. Nowlis, G. H., Frank, M. 1977. Qualities in hamster taste: behavioral and neural evidence. See Ref. 18, pp. 241–48

142. Nowlis, G. H., Kessen, W. 1976. Human newborns differentiate differing concentrations of sucrose and glucose. *Science* 191:865–66

143. Oakley, B. 1975. Receptive fields of cat taste fibers. *Chem. Senses Flavor* 1:431–42

144. Ogawa, H., Akagi, T. 1977. Location of pontine relay neurons projecting to VPMm in the rat by means of horseradish peroxidase. See Ref. 18, p. 289

145. Ogawa, H., Sato, M., Yamashita, S. 1968. Multiple sensitivity of chorda tympani fibers of the rat and hamster to gustatory and thermal stimuli. *J. Physiol.* 199:223–40

146. Ogawa, H., Sato, M., Yamashita, S. 1969. Gustatory impulse discharges in response to saccharin in rats and hamsters. *J. Physiol.* 204:311–29

147. Ogawa, H., Sato, M., Yamashita, S. 1973. Variability in impulse discharges in rat chorda tympani fibers in response to repeated gustatory stimulations. *Physiol. Behav.* 11:469–79

148. Ogawa, H., Yamashita, S., Noma, A., Sato, M. 1972. Taste responses in the macaque monkey chorda tympani. *Physiol. Behav.* 9:325–31

149. Olds, J. 1958. Self-stimulation of the brain. *Science* 127:315–23

150. Olds, J., Milner, P. 1954. Positive reinforcement produced by electrical stimulation of septal area and other regions of rat brain. *J. Comp. Physiol. Psychol.* 47:419–27

151. Pangborn, R. M. 1970. Individual variations in effective responses to taste stimuli. *Psychon. Sci.* 21:125–26

152. Patton, H. D., Amassian, V. E. 1952. Cortical projection zone of chorda tympani nerve in cat. *J. Neurol. Psychiatry* 15:245–50

153. Patton, H. D., Ruch, T. C. 1946. The relation of the foot of the pre- and postcentral gyrus to taste in the monkey and chimpanzee. *Fed. Proc.* 5:79

154. Perrotto, R. S., Scott, T. R. 1976. Gustatory neural coding in the pons. *Brain Res.* 110:283–300

155. Pfaffmann, C. 1939. Specific gustatory impulses. *J. Physiol.* 96:41–42

156. Pfaffmann, C. 1941. Gustatory afferent impulses. *J. Cell. Comp. Physiol.* 17:243–58

157. Pfaffmann, C. 1955. Gustatory nerve impulses in rat, cat, and rabbit. *J. Neurophysiol.* 18:429–40

157a. Pfaffmann, C. 1965. De Gustibus. *Am. Psychol.* 20:21–33

158. Pfaffmann, C., ed. 1969. *Olfaction and Taste*, Vol. 3. New York: Rockefeller Univ. Press. 648 pp.

159. Pfaffmann, C. 1970. Physiological and behavioural processes of the sense of taste. In *Ciba Foundation Symposium on Taste and Smell in Vertebrates*, ed. G. E. W. Wolstenholme, J. Knight, pp. 31–50. London: Churchill. 402 pp.

160. Pfaffmann, C. 1974. Specificity of sweet receptors of the squirrel monkey. *Chem. Senses Flavor* 1:61–67

161. Pfaffmann, C. 1977. Biological and behavioral substrates of the sweet tooth. See Ref. 48, pp. 3–24

162. Pfaffmann, C. 1978. The vertebrate phylogeny of taste, neural code and integrative processes. In *Handbook of Perception*, Vol. 6, ed. E. C. Carterette, M. Friedman. New York: Academic. In press

163. Pfaffmann, C., Bare, J. K. 1950. Gustatory nerve discharges in normal and adrenalectomized rats. *J. Comp. Physiol. Psychol.* 43:320–24

164. Pfaffmann, C., Erickson, R., Frommer, G., Halpern, B. 1961. Gustatory discharges in the rat medulla and thalamus. In *Sensory Communication*, ed. W. A. Rosenblith, pp. 455–73. New York: Wiley, 844 pp.

165. Pfaffmann, C., Frank, M., Bartoshuk, L. M., Snell, T. L. 1976. Coding gustatory information in the squirrel monkey chorda tympani. In *Progress in Psychobiology and Physiological Psychology*, ed. J. M. Sprague, A. Epstein, 6:1–27. New York: Academic. 296 pp.

166. Pfaffmann, C., Norgren, R., Grill, H. J. 1977. Sensory affect and motivation. *Ann. NY Acad. Sci.* 290:18–34

167. Pumphrey, R. J. 1935. Nerve impulses from receptors in the mouth of the frog. *J. Cell. Comp. Physiol.* 6:457–67

168. Rhoton, A. L. Jr. 1968. Afferent connections of the facial nerve. *J. Comp. Neurol.* 133:89–100

169. Rhoton, A. L. Jr., O'Leary, J. L., Ferguson, J. P. 1966. The trigeminal, facial, vagal, and glossopharyngeal nerves in the monkey. *Arch. Neurol.* 14:530–40

170. Richter, C. P. 1942. Self-regulatory functions. *Harvey Lect.* 38:63–103

171. Richter, C. P. 1977. Six common sugars as tools for the study of appetite for sugar. See Ref. 48, pp. 387–98

172. Richter, C. P., Campbell, K. H. 1940. Taste thresholds and taste preferences of rats for five common sugars. *J. Nutr.* 20:31–46

172a. Rolls, B. J., Rolls, E. T. 1973. Effects of lesions in the basolateral amygdala on fluid intake in the rat. *J. Comp. Physiol. Psychol.* 83:240–47

173. Roth, S. R., Schwartz, M., Teitelbaum, P. 1973. Failure of recovered lateral hypothalamic rats to learn specific food aversions. *J. Comp. Physiol. Psychol.* 83:184–97

174. Ruch, T. C., Patton, H. 1946. The relation of the deep opercular cortex to taste. *Fed. Proc.* 5:89–90

175. Ruderman, M. I., Morrison, A. I., Hand, P. J. 1972. A solution to the problem of cerebral cortical localization of taste in the cat. *Exp. Neurol.* 37:522–37

176. Sato, M. 1963. The effect of temperature change on the response of taste receptors. See Ref. 13, pp. 151–64

176a. Sato, M. 1973. Gustatory receptor mechanisms in mammals. *Adv. Biophys.* 4:103–52

177. Sato, M., Hiji, Y., Ito, H. 1977. Taste discrimination in the monkey. See Ref. 18, pp. 233–40

178. Sato, M., Hiji, Y., Ito, H., Imoto, T., Saku, C. 1977. Properties of sweet taste receptors in macaque monkeys. See Ref. 68, pp. 187–99

179. Sato, M., Ogawa, H., Yamashita, S. 1975. Response properties of macaque monkey chorda tympani fibers. *J. Gen. Physiol.* 66:781–810

180. Sato, M., Ozeki, M. 1972. Transduction of stimuli into electrical events at the gustatory cell membrane in the rat fungiform papillae. See Ref. 19, pp. 252–58

181. Schiffman, S. S., Dakis, C. 1975. Taste of nutrients: amino acids, vitamins, and fatty acids. *Percept. Psychophys.* 17:140–46

182. Schiffman, S. S., Erickson, R. P. 1971. A psychophysical model for gustatory quality. *Physiol. Behav.* 7:617–33

183. Schneider, D., ed. 1972. *Olfaction and Taste 4.* Stuttgart: Wissenschaftliche Verlagsgesellschaft MBH. 400 pp.

184. Schwartz, M., Teitelbaum, P. 1974. Dissociation between learning and remembering in rats with lesions in the lateral hypothalamus. *J. Comp. Physiol. Psychol.* 87:384–98

185. Schwartzbaum, J. S., Morse, J. R. 1978. Taste responsivity of amygdaloid units in behaving rabbit: A methodological report. *Brain Res. Bull.* In press

186. Scott, J. W., Chafin, B. R. 1975. Origin of olfactory projections to lateral hypothalamus and nuclei gemini of the rat. *Brain Res.* 88:64–68

187. Scott, J. W., Leonard, C. M. 1971. The olfactory connections of the lateral hypothalamus in the rat, mouse, and hamster. *J. Comp. Neurol.* 141:331–44

188. Scott, J. W., Pfaffmann, C. 1967. Olfactory input to the hypothalamus: Electrophysiological evidence. *Science* 158:1592–94

189. Scott, J. W., Pfaffmann, C. 1972. Characteristics of responses of lateral hypothalamic neurons to stimulation of the olfactory system. *Brain Res.* 48:251–64

190. Scott, T. R. Jr., Erickson, R. P. 1971. Synaptic processing of taste-quality information in thalamus of the rat. *J. Neurophysiol.* 34:868–84

191. Shimada, I., Shiraishi, A., Kijima, H., Morita, H. 1974. Separation of two receptor sites in a single labellar sugar receptor of the flesh-fly by treatment with p-chloromercuribenzoate. *J. Insect Physiol.* 20:605–21

192. Smith, D. V., McBurney, D. H. 1969. Gustatory cross-adaptation: Does a single mechanism code the salty taste? *J. Exp. Psychol.* 80:101–5

193. Steiner, J. E. 1973. The gustofacial response: Observation on normal and anencephalic newborn infants. See Ref. 24a, pp. 254–78

194. Stellar, E. 1977. Sweet preference and hedonic experience. See Ref. 48, pp. 363–73

195. Sudakov, K., MacLean, P. D., Reeves, A., Marino, R. 1971. Unit study of exteroceptive inputs to claustrocortex in awake, sitting, squirrel monkey. *Brain Res.* 28:19–34

196. Switzer, R. C., Heimer, L. 1976. A direct olfactory projection to area frontalis in the opossum. *Neurosci. Abstr.* 2:164

197. Tanabe, T., Yarita, H., Iino, M., Ooshima, Y., Takagi, S. F. 1975. An olfactory projection area in orbitofrontal cortex of monkey. *J. Neurophysiol.* 38:1269–83

198. Tapper, D. N., Halpern, B. P. 1968. Taste stimuli: A behavioral categorization. *Science* 161:708–10

199. Teitelbaum, P. 1955. Sensory control of hypothalamic hyperphagia. *J. Comp. Physiol. Psychol.* 48:156–63

200. Thompson, R. F. 1967. *Foundations of Physiological Psychology.* New York: Harper & Row. 688 pp.

201. Travers, J. B., Smith, D. V. 1976. Response properties of taste neurons in the nucleus tractus solitarius of the hamster. *Neurosci. Abstr.* 2:165

202. Tucker, D., Smith, J. C. 1969. The

chemical senses. *Ann. Rev. Psychol.* 20:129–58

203. Turner, B. H. 1973. Sensorimotor syndrome produced by lesions of the amygdala and lateral hypothalamus. *J. Comp. Physiol. Psychol.* 82:37–47

204. Van Buskirk, R. L., Erickson, R. P. 1977. Odorant responses in taste neurons of rat NTS. *Brain Res.* 135:287–303

205. Van Buskirk, R. L., Erickson, R. P. 1977. Responses in the rostral medulla to electrical stimulation of an intranasal trigeminal nerve: Convergence of oral and nasal inputs. *Neurosci. Lett.* 5:321–26

206. Van Buskirk, R. L., Smith, D. V. 1977. Gustatory responsive neurons in the hamster parabrachial pons. *Neurosci. Abstr.* 3:85

207. von Békésy, G. 1974. Some biophysical experiments from fifty years ago. *Ann. Rev. Physiol.* 36:1–16

207a. von Békésy, G. 1964. Sweetness produced electrically on the tongue and its relation to taste theories. *J. Appl. Physiol.* 19:1105–13

207b. von Békésy, G. 1966. Taste theories and the chemical stimulation of single papillae. *J. Appl. Physiol.* 21:1–9

208. von Helmholtz, H. L. F. 1852. Ueber die Theorie der Zusammengesetzen farben. *Ann. Phys. Chem.* 163:45–66

209. von Helmholtz, H. L. F. 1870. *die Lehre von den Tonempfindungen.* 3rd ed.

210. von Skramlik, E. 1926. *Handbuch der Physiologie der niederen Sinne, Bd. 1, Die Physiologie des Geruchs-und Geschmacksinnes.* Leipzig: Thieme

211. Wang, M. B., Bernard, R. A. 1968. Characterization and interaction of taste responses in chorda tympani fibers of the cat. *Brain Res.* 15:567–70

212. Weiffenbach, J. M., ed. 1977. *Taste and Development, The Genesis of Sweet Preference.* Bethesda: DHEW Publ. No. (NIH) 77–1068. 435 pp.

213. Wever, E. G., Bray, C. W. 1930. Action currents in the auditory nerve in response to acoustical stimulation. *Proc. Natl. Acad. Sci.* 16:344–50

214. White, T. D., Boudreau, J. C. 1975. Taste preferences of the cat for neurophysiologically active compounds. *Physiol. Psychol.* 3:405–10

215. Wolf, G. 1964. Effect of dorsolateral hypothalamic lesions on sodium appetite elicited by desoxycorticosterone and by acute hyponatremia. *J. Comp. Physiol. Psychol.* 58:396–402

216. Wolf, G. 1968. Thalamic and tegmental mechanisms for sodium intake: anatomical and functional relations to lateral hypothalamus. *Physiol. Behav.* 3:997–1002

217. Wolf, G., Dicara, L. V., Braun, J. J. 1970. Sodium appetite in rats after neocortical ablation. *Physiol. Behav.* 5:1265–69

218. Wolf, G., Quartermain, D. 1967. Sodium chloride intake of adrenalectomized rats with lateral hypothalamic lesions. *Am. J. Physiol.* 212:113–18

219. Wolstenholme, G. E. W., Knight, J., eds. 1970. *Taste and Smell in Vertebrates.* London: Churchill. 402 pp.

220. Yamamoto, T., Kawamura, Y. 1972. Summated cerebral responses to taste stimuli in rat. *Physiol. Behav.* 9:789–93

221. Yamamoto, T., Kawamura, Y. 1975. Cortical responses to electrical and gustatory stimuli in the rabbit. *Brain Res.* 94:447–63

222. Zeigler, H., Karten, H. 1974. Central trigeminal structures and the lateral hypothalamic syndrome in the rat. *Science* 186:636–38

223. Zotterman, Y. 1935. Action potentials in the glossopharyngeal nerve and in the chorda tympani. *Scand. Arch. Physiol.* 72:73–77

224. Zwaardemaker, H. 1925. *L'odorat.* Paris: Doin. 305 pp.

Ann. Rev. Psychol. 1979. 30:327–62

CONCEPTS OF MOTOR ORGANIZATION[1]

♦310

F. A. Miles and E. V. Evarts

Laboratory of Neurophysiology, National Institute of Mental Health, Bethesda, Maryland 20014

CONTENTS

INTRODUCTION 328
Part 1. CENTRALLY PROGRAMMED MOVEMENT 328
Proprioception and Active Movement 330
Alpha-Gamma Coactivation 331
Central Driving of Sensory Relay Neurons 333
Feedback to Motor Cortex 335
Part 2. CONTROL SYSTEM MODELS AND ADAPTIVE GAIN CONTROL   337
Open-Loop Control 337
Adaptive Gain Control 338
Closed-Loop Control 342
  Steady-state errors 344
  Dynamic errors and stability... 345
  Use of damping to improve stability 345
  Use of feedforward to improve dynamic responses 345
  Use of postive feedback to reduce steady-state errors 347
  The stabilization of retinal images: A preliminary model 349
  Ocular pursuit of small moving targets (head stationary) 350
  Head turns while fixating stationary targets 350
  Combined eye-head tracking 351
Part 3. EFFERENCE COPY AND COROLLARY DISCHARGE 352
Visuomotor Coordination 352
Perceptual Stability 354
Perceptual versus Motor Localization 356
Sensations Attributable to Impulses Arising in Muscle Stretch Receptors 356
Gamma Motoneuron Discharge Viewed as Efference Copy 357

[1]The US government has the right to retain a nonexclusive, royalty-free license in and to any copyright covering this paper.

INTRODUCTION

Within the past two decades the role of CNS neurons in motor control has been studied in relation to acts ranging from elementary automatisms to volitional movements, and data have proliferated as paradigms and techniques have multiplied. This proliferation makes it increasingly important to have concepts according to which the data may be arranged, and the purpose of this review is to discuss certain of these concepts. Part 1 will deal with *reflexes* and *central programs*, concepts stemming in large part from Sherrington's studies of spinal cord organization. Many of the principles discovered in studies of the spinal cord have now been shown to operate in the cerebral motor cortex of intact primates performing manual control tasks, and Part 1 will also review evidence showing that the cerebral motor cortex (like the spinal cord) is a summing point for central programs and peripheral feedback as these interact in volitional movement.

The use of formal *Control Systems Models* in studies of motor organization was pioneered by Stark and Young in studies of eye movement, and the use of such models is becoming increasingly important. In Part 2 we will consider some of the concepts inherent in these models, discussing terms such as open-loop and closed-loop, feedback and feedforward, etc. Part 2 will also focus on the concepts of plasticity and adaptive gain control in motor systems, as exemplified by changes in the vestibulo-ocular reflex resulting from changes in visual experience.

Part 3 will discuss efference copy and corollary discharge, concepts which arose in relation to theories of sensory processing during active movement. Recordings of neuronal activity in actively moving animals now provide examples which may qualify as efference copy and corollary discharge, and part 3 will consider such data in relation to these two important concepts.

Part 1.   CENTRALLY PROGRAMMED MOVEMENT

Many of our current ideas concerning central motor programs evolved from the work of Sherrington and of Graham Brown on scratching and locomotion in deafferented spinal animals. Sherrington (92) found that within a few months following transection of the cervical spinal cord in the dog, a scratch reflex could be elicited by mechanical stimuli (e.g. tickling the skin or pulling lightly on the hair) within a large saddle-shaped region over the upper part of the body. The scratching movement consisted of a rhythmic alternate flexion and extension at the hip, knee, and ankle. Though intact afferents from the cutaneous locus eliciting the reflex were essential for this triggering, afferent input from the rhythmically moving hindlimb was not necessary. In describing the occurrence of the scratching in the deafferented limb, Sherrington (92, p. 252) stated that the movements were "executed without obvious impairment of direction or rhythm when all the afferent roots of the scratching hind-limb have been cut through." A more intense triggering cutaneous stimulus increased scratching amplitude without altering the rhythmical properties of scratching, with these rhythmical properties being instead dependent upon internal spinal cord mechanisms involving alternate excitation and inhibition of motoneurons occurring on the basis of internal spinal cord rhythm generators which continued to operate in the absence of any phasic afferent return from the rhythmically moving limb. Sherrington's work on the scratch reflex underlies our concepts of the *triggered movement* based on a *central program* involving a *spinal rhythm generator*.

Graham Brown (37) showed that rhythmical limb movements similar to those occurring with walking could occur in the deafferented spinal animal, providing evidence for the existence of spinal rhythm generators for locomotion. Of course, the existence of rhythmical scratching or walking movements in the deafferented animal was not taken by Sherrington or Graham Brown as evidence against the importance of feedback in the intact animal, and many current investigations on locomotion are aimed at clarifying the way in which afferent input interacts with central programs. A striking example of this interaction has been provided by the recent work of Forssberg et al (26), who studied responses to tactile stimuli applied to the hindlimbs at different phases of the step cycle in chronic spinal cats. When the limb was being flexed in the swing phase, a tactile stimulus applied to the dorsum of the foot enhanced flexion, leading the limb to be elevated so as to pass over the obstacle which delivered the tactile stimulus. In contrast, the same tactile stimulus applied during the extension phase resulted in a large response in the extensor muscles and none in the flexors. Thus, an identical tactile stimulus could give rise either to flexion or to extension depending on the phase of the step cycle in which the stimulus occurred.

This observation on *reflex reversal* points to the way in which centrally programmed movement can utilize afferent triggers to generate one sort of output at one phase of the program and a different output at another phase of the program. It is sometimes thought that centrally programmed movement should be independent of afferent input at the time of program readout, but these results on reflex reversal show that the central program itself contains contingency plans for a variety of different afferent inputs, each of which can generate a subroutine of the program. Such would clearly seem to be the case for the response of the hindlimb to an obstacle where the central program includes the contingency of meeting the obstacle and then stepping over it. Pearson (78) has provided additional understanding of the role of feedback in locomotion, showing that the switching of the motor program from swing to stance is triggered by a sensory input. He points out that feedback during locomotion can be thought of as having two broad functions, the first being to switch the motor programs from one phase to the next and the second being to modify the motor output within a single phase. Tactile inputs are especially important in switching, while proprioceptive feedback provides continuous control of motoneuronal discharge during movement.

Proprioception and Active Movement

Sherrington introduced the term *proprioception* in reference to inputs arising in the course of centrally driven movements when "the stimuli to the receptors are delivered by the organism *itself* ..." (93, p. 472). The term proprio (from the Latin *proprius,* meaning own) was used because Sherrington believed that the major function of proprioceptors was to provide feedback concerning the organism's *own* movements.

Muscle proprioceptors are of two types (cf 38): the Golgi tendon organ (GTO) which senses tension and the muscle spindle which senses length. The length receptors are located on specialized muscle fibers (called intrafusal fibers) innervated by gamma motoneurons (γ-MNs) which regulate receptor sensitivity. The central synaptic terminations from a given muscle spindle excite alpha motoneurons (α-MNs), sending axons back to the muscle in which the spindle is located. Thus, increased activity of spindle receptors resulting from increased muscle length will lead to activation of α-MNs innervating the lengthened muscle, and this in turn will cause muscle contraction opposing the increased muscle length.

GTOs sense tension (or force) rather than length, and their central connections lead to disynaptic inhibition of the motoneurons supplying the muscle in which the tension receptors lie. Increased muscle tension generates increased GTO activity which is fed back to motoneurons so as to reduce muscle tension. Thus, both length and tension receptors may be viewed as components in a negative feedback control system that maintains stability by resisting changes of muscle length and muscle tension.

To clarify the operation of this servo, let us first consider the case of a person seeking to maintain immobility of a steadily outstretched arm in the absence of any external disturbances. There will of course be slight unintended fluctuations in position, especially as the subject becomes fatigued. For example, there will be occasional unintended decreases of tension output in the muscles opposing the forces of gravity with consequent increases in length of these same muscles. The resulting proprioceptive input will be decreased activity in tension receptors (because muscle tension has decreased) and increased activity in length receptors (because of increased muscle length). Though these are opposite directions of change in impulse frequencies, their central effects are synergistic: the increased discharge of muscle length receptors will result in excitation of the motoneuron pool, whereas the decreased activity of the tension receptors will result in *disinhibition* of the same motoneuron pool. Note that this synergistic action of the two types of muscle receptors will occur for muscle length changes secondary to changes of tension output by the subject's own muscles, but will not occur for muscle length changes secondary to application or removal of external loads. Thus, muscle lengthening caused by application of an external load will involve increased activity of length receptors, without any decrease in activity of tension receptors. The term *active movement* is commonly used to denote the subject's *own* movements, while *passive movements* refer to externally produced displacements. In using the term proprioceptor, Sherrington called attention to the important differences in neural organization underlying active as compared to passive movements. Sherrington's idea of the special importance of muscle stretch receptors in active movement was dramatically proved by Leksell's (56) discovery of the role of the γ-MN, and the importance of active muscular contraction for the GTO was demonstrated by Houk & Henneman (43), who found that active contraction of any of the muscle fibers lying directly in series with a GTO could cause it to discharge vigorously at any length. These results led Houk & Henneman to suggest that "in the intact animal, the only important input to a tendon organ is the active force developed directly in series with it. The threshold to this input is extremely low. The contribution of passive forces to it is sufficiently small to be negligible."

Alpha-Gamma Coactivation

The way in which γ-MNs (which lead to contraction of the intrafusal fibers of the muscle spindle) participate in active movement is best understood in relation to Granit's concept of *coactivation of a-and γ-MNs* (38), whereby central programs activating α-MNs will at the same time coactivate γ-MNs. The consequences of α-γ coactivation are illustrated in Vallbo's (107) results (Figure 1), showing increased spindle afferent discharge due to γ-MN discharge during a smooth ramp finger flexion involving shortening of the muscle in which the spindle was located. The increased spindle afferent discharge due to coactivation of γ-MNs more than compensated for the decreased spindle afferent discharge due to shortening of the extrafusal muscle in parallel with the spindle. Had the γ-MN coactivation been absent, then the shortening of the extrafusal muscle occurring with the ramp movement would have "unloaded" the muscle spindle receptor, with the result that the discharge of the spindle afferent would have decreased. As muscle shortening continued, the spindle would eventually have shortened to the extent that all spindle afferent discharge would have stopped.

In the absence of continuous spindle activity which could have been modulated by fluctuating muscle length, the servo would have ceased to operate. If, however, a mechanism existed whereby a "carrier" discharge frequency of the spindle afferents could be maintained in spite of shortening of the extrafusal muscle, then fluctuations in the rate of change of length (i.e. the velocity of shortening) of the extrafusal fibers would continue to be reflected in changes of discharge frequency of the spindle afferents. These changes would in turn provide corrective servo action during movement, giving a measure of error velocity. Vallbo's (107) results (Figure 1) show that this regulatory action does indeed take place. At the onset of the ramp finger movement (just as the muscle was beginning to shorten) there was a marked increase in the discharge frequency of the spindle primary. Since the muscle was shortening (a change that would tend to decrease spindle primary discharge), Vallbo could infer that the increase of spindle afferent discharge which actually occurred must have been the result of γ-coactivation. In Figure 1 (for a finger movement of only 10°) decreases in velocity are associated with increases in the discharge frequency of the spindle afferent, while increases in velocity are associated with decreases in the discharge frequency of the spindle afferent. As a consequence of the "carrier" discharge caused by this γ-coactivation, the spindle afferent remained sensitive to minute distortions in movement velocity over the whole range of movement.

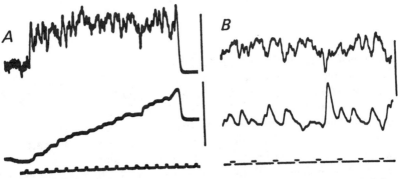

Figure 1 Response of a spindle primary ending during an isotonic contraction. *A.* Relation to joint angle. The top trace represents the impulse frequency of the single unit and the lower trace the angle at the metacarpo-phalangeal joint when the subject slowly flexed his ring finger. The events associated with the second half of this contraction are also illustrated in *B.* Calibrations: 0 and 25 imp/sec, 155° (bottom) and 145° (top). Time signal: 1 sec. *B.* Relation to the speed of joint movement. The upper trace shows the single unit impulse frequency and the lower trace the time derivative of the joint angle signal and, hence, it represents the speed of the joint movement. Calibrations: 0 and 25 imp/sec. Time signal: 1 sec. [From Vallbo (107).]

Additional information on α-γ coactivation has come from the studies of Severin and colleagues (90, 91) showing that spinal mechanisms alone can give rise to linked α-γ discharge during treadmill locomotion in spinal cats. The demonstration of this linkage involved recordings of discharge in single α- and γ-efferent fibers in relation to the phasic locomotor activity. It was found that discharge of γ-efferents reached a peak at the same time that discharge of α-efferents to the same muscle reached a peak. Severin (90) concluded that a major consequence of γ-activation accompanying α-discharge was *reinforcement* or enhancement of α-discharge.

Central Driving of Sensory Relay Neurons

Studies in spinal animals have shown that sensory relay neurons as well as γ-MNs can be driven by central inputs during active movement. An example of such driving is seen in the results of studies (4, 5, 15) on the scratch reflex in the spinal preparation. In these experiments the neural events of the scratch reflex were elicited by electrical stimulation within the spinal cord but actual scratching was prevented by curarization. Thus, the central events ordinarily accompanying the scratch reflex occurred relatively normally, but there was no actual movement. The term "fictive scratching" is used in reference to the central events of scratching without the actual movement. Recordings from individual neurons during "fictive scratching" demonstrated rhythmical discharge in sensory relay neurons within the spinal cord in the absence of any sensory input. This demonstration of central driving of sensory relay neurons was made for ventral spinocerebellar tract (VSCT) neurons which receive inputs from a variety of somesthetic receptors, including cutaneous, joint, and smaller-diameter muscle afferents. It was found that the activity of VSCT neurons during "fictive scratching" is rhythmically modulated in phase with the scratching movements. Since no afferent input could have been returning during the "fictive scratching," it follows that the rhythmical discharge of these VSCT neurons must have been set up by central connections. If we define corollary discharge as activity of sensory relay neurons driven by central inputs occurring in association with active movement, then VSCT discharge during "fictive scratching" would qualify as corollary discharge. Earlier experiments on locomotion (2, 3) had shown similar corollary discharge in VSCT cells, and taken together these results confirmed Lundberg's (59) hypothesis that ascending pathways such as VSCT might transmit central as well as peripheral feedback.

Impulses ascending to the cerebellum via VSCT have consequences for the brain as a whole: fibers from cerebellum to vestibular nuclei cause rhythmical activity of vestibulospinal neurons during fictive scratching, and vestibulospinal tract axons return to interact with spinal rhythm generators. In the intact animal, vestibulospinal neurons (driven by inputs from the labyrinth) play a role in postural stability necessary for maintenance of the upright posture, and if one were to observe discharge of vestibulospinal neurons during scratching in the intact animal, it would be assumed that the discharge was due to direct sensory inputs from the vestibular system as the animal shook. However, the occurrence of periodic modulation of activity in vestibulospinal neurons in "fictive scratching" demonstrates that vestibulospinal neurons can be modulated by rhythmical activity coming from the spinal cord via the cerebellum even without afferent input from the vestibular system. Thus, both VSCT and vestibulospinal neurons exhibit corollary discharge during centrally programmed scratching. Similar results on corollary discharge of VSCT and vestibulospinal neurons have been obtained in association with locomotion in cats with brain stem transection by Orlovsky (77), who showed that this corollary discharge of vestibulospinal neurons was eliminated by removal of the cerebellum.

Another example of corollary discharge is seen in the case of the so-called "Ia interneuron," a spinal cord element that has been shown to receive dual impingement from muscle spindle Ia afferents and from central generators active during treadmill locomotion in the spinal cat. In addition to sending monosynaptic excitatory connections to motoneurons whose axons return to the muscles from which the Ia afferents arise, Ia afferents send branches to interneurons which then inhibit the motoneurons supplying antagonists of the muscle in which the spindle lies. Thus, the consequences of Ia discharge are excitation of motoneurons supplying the muscle in which the spindle is located and inhibition of motoneurons supplying the antagonist. Both of these effects underlie the servo of which the Ia afferent fiber forms the afferent limb. Feldman & Orlovsky (23) have shown that Ia inhibitory interneurons impinged upon by Ia afferents are simultaneously driven by central programs and peripheral feedback during locomotion in spinal animals. The modulation of the Ia interneuron by central programs during locomotion was shown during "fictive locomotion," in which the central program for locomotion occurred but in which actual movement was blocked by curare or by severing the ventral roots. Ia interneurons in the spinal cord were identified by muscle stretch, and then the behavior of these Ia interneurons was studied during centrally programmed locomotion in which there was no possibility of variations of Ia input since the ventral roots had been cut. Changes in the discharge of Ia interneurons in phase with locomotion in such a preparation could only have been based on central driving, showing that during locomotion, signals coming to the Ia interneurons from central networks modulate the activity of these interneurons in the same way that they would have been modulated by the Ia input coming from the periphery. Thus, just as Ia and centrally programmed inputs to motoneurons are combined during locomotion, so too the Ia input to inhibitory interneurons is combined with a corollary discharge in these same interneurons during locomotion. The central program controlling locomotion in the spinal animal sets up a coordinated pattern of excitation and inhibition in α-MNs, γ-MNs, and Ia interneurons.

Other instances of corollary discharge have been described by Zipser & Bennett (117) for cells of the lateral line lobe during the neural command to discharge the electric organ, by Roberts & Russell (82) for neurons of lateral line efferent systems, and by Robinson & Wurtz (88) for cells of the superior colliculus in association with eye movement. Still other examples are considered in the recent review by Kennedy & Davis (51). The instances of corollary discharge which have now been considered occur when neural activity of central programs impinges upon elements that are also impinged upon by peripheral sensory inputs. The corollary discharge resulting from this "dual impingement" turns out to be a cardinal feature of centrally programmed movement: central programs modify the activity of both motoneurons and of the sensory elements that will transmit feedback during active movement. A centrally programmed movement involves coordinated control of excitability in both afferent and efferent systems.

Feedback to Motor Cortex

During active movement the spinal cord α-MN is a summing point for peripheral feedback and central programs from a number of CNS loci. To what extent is there analogous summation of peripheral feedback and central programs in cerebral motor cortex, whose pyramidal tract neurons (PTNs) descend to the spinal cord? Until recently it was commonly assumed that PTNs receive discontinuous central rather than continuous peripheral feedback during movement and that the PTN output provided a central program or command signal specifying some peripheral event. Little attention was given to the altered feedback that might have been reaching the PTN during movement until Phillips (79) proposed that the changes in PTN activity with changed loads might be the result of a mismatch between actual and intended movement. Phillips' suggestion that we view the PTN as a summing point in a transcortical servo loop allows us to interpret the increased PTN discharge with increased loads (18) not merely as a "force command" but rather in part at least as an error signal corresponding to a mismatch between intended and actual displacement.

Support for the broad features of Phillips' proposal has now been obtained in a number of studies (12, 13, 19–22, 27). According to Phillips' "transcortical servo" hypothesis, a peripheral disturbance that opposes (i.e. "mismatches") the active movement with which a PTN discharges should enhance this discharge, whereas an assisting (i.e. "matching") disturbance should reduce discharge. Put in another way, the transcortical servo hypothesis predicts that PTN activity will change in opposite directions in association with active and passive movement. Results of Conrad et al (12, 13) and of Evarts & Tanji (22) showed such opposite relations to active and passive movement in a majority of PTNs, and the additional results of Evarts & Fromm (21) confirmed this finding.

A model illustrating this concept of continuous feedback onto PTNs is illustrated in Figure 2. In this model separate lines are drawn from PTNs to α-MNs and γ-MNS. We do not yet know the extent to which α-MNs and γ-MNs are independently controlled by PTNs, but the results of Koeze, Phillips & Sheridan (53) show that there is at least a degree of independence of motor cortex control of α- as compared to γ-MNs. Phillips has proposed that the most important function of fusimotor coactivation by motor cortex in the case of the hand is to maintain the inflow of information on muscle length to the cortex and cerebellum. Thus, the motor cortex outflow itself has a major role in creating the fusimotor activation necessary for optimizing the sensitivity of the muscle spindles.

Though there is not yet anatomical evidence for separate PTNs acting on α-MNs as compared to γ-MNs, it would seem a priori desirable that such independent control exist. The γ-MN should discharge such that an op-

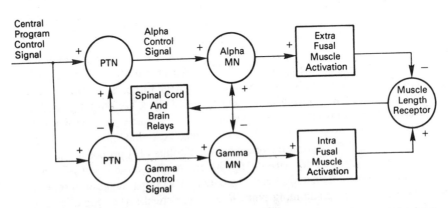

Figure 2 Pyramidal tract neurons (PTNs) are driven by central programs generated prior to volitional movement. PTN outputs coactivate alpha and gamma motoneurons (α-MNs and γ-MNs). α-MN discharge causing extrafusal muscle shortening reduces length receptor discharge, whereas γ-MN discharge causing intrafusal muscle shortening increases length receptor discharge. Length receptor discharge excites the α-MN, but within the loop as a whole the sign of the feedback is negative. Analogous negative feedback is delivered to PTNs. It has been suggested (cf 21) that increased discharge of length receptors may inhibit γ-MNs and PTNs controlling γ-MNs, an effect that would be required for closed-loop negative feedback control of these elements.

timum spindle afferent "carrier" frequency is maintained during muscular contraction—whether this contraction is intended to produce movement or fixed posture. When a central program calls for a given velocity of muscle shortening, the tendency to increased spindle afferent discharge resulting from increased γ-MN discharge should be exactly offset by the tendency to decreased spindle afferent discharge resulting from muscle shortening. In this case, any fluctuations of spindle afferent discharge would reflect distortion from the intended velocity of movement, and this fluctuation of spindle input would reduce this distortion. According to this formulation γ-MN discharge should depend on the velocity of the centrally programmed muscle shortening rather than on the tension necessary to produce the shortening, and this would call for independent pathways to α-MN and γ-MN.

Thus far the discussion of inputs to motor cortex PTNs has focused on spindle afferent inputs, but this one-sided consideration has been adopted merely for simplicity: we wished to point out an analogy between servo control in spinal cord and cerebral cortex. In actuality, there is strong reason to believe that the transcortical servo controlling limb movement involves convergent inputs from a variety of limb receptors. Anatomical studies (47, 108) have shown that the inputs to motor cortex from cortical area 2 (receiving joint inputs) are stronger than from area 3a (receiving muscle inputs). The importance of convergent inputs to motor cortex is emphasized by Wiesendanger (113), who concluded that convergence from different modalities and from different nerves is a characteristic feature for the majority of PTNs. A role for convergent inputs has also been considered by Marsden et al (63), who proposed that a cortically mediated servo response might be dependent on the interactions of muscle, cutaneous, and joint inputs.

Part 2. CONTROL SYSTEM MODELS AND ADAPTIVE GAIN CONTROL

Two types of control—open-loop and closed-loop—operate in the oculomotor system with a machine-like quality which makes this system particularly amenable to an engineering approach. The interactions between the different elements, even in a comparatively simple system, often take an unexpected turn which defies a simple intuitive or phenomenological approach, and much current work on eye movements is guided by—indeed, originates from—the control theory needs of the system.

Open-Loop Control

This is the simplest type of control in which the input, or command signal, is processed to produce motoneuron discharge and muscular contraction.

In the nervous system, with its long synaptic delays and transmission times, the major advantage of such a simple arrangement is speed. A good example of open-loop control is the vestibulo-ocular reflex (VOR), which maintains stability of the eyes, and hence the retinal image of the world, during head rotations. In this system the input is *head rotation* and the final output is a *compensatory eye rotation;* the intervening signal processing involves a transducer (the semicircular canals), brainstem pathways, and the extraocular muscles acting on the eyeball (see Figure 3). The semicircular canals act "as an integrating angular accelerometer, or in other words as an angular speedometer for the skull" (68), so that the vestibular primary afferent discharges provide the brain with frequency coded information about the head's angular velocity (25, 69). However, this "velocity" signal must be integrated (to provide a "position" signal) before passing to the oculomotor motoneurons which activate the eye muscles (85); we know from electrophysiological recordings (31, 50, 84, 89, 102) that extraocular muscle tension is increased by the recruitment and rate modulation of motoneurons and that the latter has two components: 1. a maintained discharge rate, which increases linearly with eye *position* (in the case of the VOR, derived from an integrated head velocity signal) and serves both to hold the eye in place against the elastic forces in the orbit and to offset the loss of tension which results from muscle shortening; 2. a transient discharge, which is proportional to eye *velocity* (derived directly from the vestibular head velocity signal) and is required to move the eye against the inertia and considerable viscous resistance in the orbit. Exactly how or where this integration is performed is not yet clear, though "integrated" unit discharges related to eye position have been recorded in both the reticular formation (48) and vestibular nuclei (29, 49, 70).

Adaptive Gain Control

With its virtually instantaneous inertial receptor, short central pathways, few synaptic delays, and extremely rapid plant (the extraocular muscles and eyeball), the VOR achieves the one major advantage of an open-loop control system—high speed—which is essential if retinal image stability is to be preserved during the rapid head rotations which occur in everyday life. However, there is one major problem that the system must solve: it must be appropriately calibrated so that head rotations are exactly matched by equal counter rotations of the eyes. If the compensatory eye movements are inappropriate when the head turns, then there is nothing that this particular system can do to *immediately* improve performance, and retinal image slip will result. This calibration problem is common to all open-loop control systems and is one that the brain can solve only by some long-term motor learning process, which further requires that the system be modifiable in

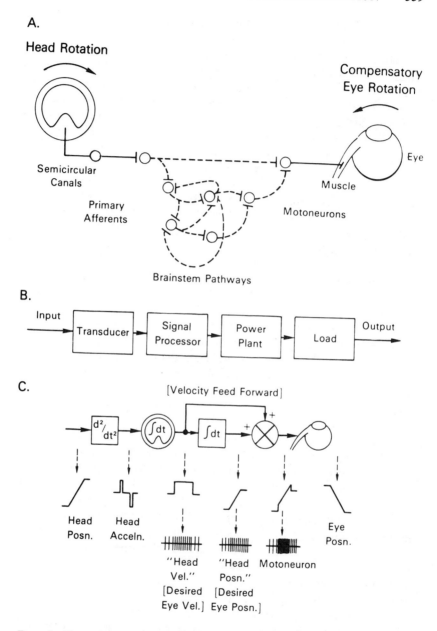

Figure 3 The vestibulo-ocular reflex (VOR) viewed as an open-loop control system. *A.* A highly simplified diagram of the anatomical arrangements. *B.* A signal flow diagram showing the basic elements in an open-loop control system. *C.* A simplified signal flow diagram of the VOR showing the major signal processing within the system.

some way. Gonshor & Melvill Jones (34, 35) fitted human subjects with dove prism spectacles that produce left-right reversal of the visual input, and observed that the *gain* of the VOR (measured as slow phase eye velocity divided by head velocity when the subject is oscillated to and fro in the dark) fell dramatically over a period of a few days and, after two or three weeks, even showed some reversal. Similar observations have since been made in cats and monkeys (66, 71, 87). That the system is subject to adaptive gain control has been further emphasized in studies using telescopic spectacles (32, 72) which can be arranged to magnify or diminish the visual input, and result in corresponding increases or decreases in the VOR gain: these changes are adaptive, always operating to minimize retinal image slip during head turns. (It is important to realize that these spectacles call *only* for a change in the eye movements coupled to head movements, i.e. the VOR, and do not require any modification in the mode of operation of the other oculomotor subsystems. The rapid *saccadic* eye movements that are used to bring the retinal image of eccentric targets onto the fovea and the *pursuit* movements required to hold them there if they move, must continue to function in exactly the same way when the world is viewed through reversing prisms or telescopic spectacles.)

Once an appropriate VOR calibration has been achieved, it would be advantageous for the system to retain it, and this requires some plasticity in the system. Such a feature would insure that the system could operate appropriately for long periods without the need for continuous recalibration: once molded into the correct form, it would tend to retain this state (plasticity) until the need arose to remold it (adaptive learning). The plastic nature of the VOR is apparent from its ability to survive many days of head immobilization or darkness, during which it receives no "visual reinforcement" (72, 87). The plastic changes that occur with spectacle experience seem to involve some gradual consolidation process which takes several days. Thus, the gain changes that occur in the first few days after wearing the spectacles are not very enduring and the gain tends to slip back to its previous level if the animal is placed in darkness or its head immobilized during this time (87; F. A. Miles & B. B. Eighmy, in preparation). Several more days of spectacle exposure are required before the "new" gain is able to survive without continued reinforcement.

Plasticity implies the existence of a *single state system* which, in the case of the VOR, means that at any given time it operates with only one gain. However, it is known that man can adopt strategies that can have a considerable immediate influence on the eye movements coupled to head rotations even in the dark (6). It seems that man has direct access to the vestibulo-ocular pathways, allowing him to override the basic reflex on those infrequent occasions when it is advantageous to do so. If one is to conceive of a fundamental reflex with an invariant gain at any given time, one must establish that no other influence is at work when that "gain" is assessed. In the case of the VOR, it is common to ask human subjects to perform mental arithmetic to ensure that they are alert during the oscillation test; gains of about 0.6 are usually reported under these conditions, yet this number can be increased to 1.0 merely by asking the subject to be on the lookout for a small stationary light that occasionally is turned on in the otherwise darkened room (6). Thus, in man it is difficult to establish the gain of the "basic" reflex. This particular experiment has not been performed on monkeys, but then no one has reported VOR gains appreciably less than 1.0 in this species (72, 76, 102), nor observed the kind of sudden changes which might imply that other influences were at work (F. A. Miles & B. B. Eighmy, in preparation), hence the idea of a single state, plastic reflex has more credence in this species.

It is not yet known how visual signals come to influence the efficacy of transmission in the vestibulo-ocular pathways, but Ito (45) has suggested that the vestibular cerebellum forms an inhibitory side loop of the VOR whose contribution can be adaptively modified and so provide a variable gain element. Marr (62) and Albus (1), working independently, had earlier followed up Brindley's suggestion that the cerebellum was involved in motor learning (7), by hypothesizing that the synapses between the parallel fibers and Purkinje cells in the cerebellar cortex were modifiable, and they invoked the climbing fiber input as the shaping influence. Precisely how the climbing fiber input would bring these changes about was not specified. In applying the Marr-Albus model, Ito suggested that the climbing fibers might convey retinal image slip information to the flocculus (a part of the vestibular cerebellum) to signal the need for a change in the efficacy of the vestibular parallel fiber input to the Purkinje output cells (see Figure 4). Ito realized that the existence of retinal image slip during head turns not only signaled the need for a change in the gain of the VOR, but indeed would provide a direct index of the error in the reflex. This model became even more plausible when it was discovered that the climbing fibers did indeed receive a visual input (61) and, furthermore, that it was directionally selective (98), an essential requirement if it was to provide useful error information.

Others have since invoked Ito's model to explain the adaptive capability of the VOR (14, 87), and a major current concern is to establish whether or not the modifiable elements are located in the vestibular cerebellum. Robinson has recently shown (87) that removal of the vestibular cerebellum in the cat results in a slight, but permanent, increase in the gain of the VOR which not even prolonged exposure to reversing prisms can modify. However, recent electrophysiological studies in awake monkeys (57, 73) indicate

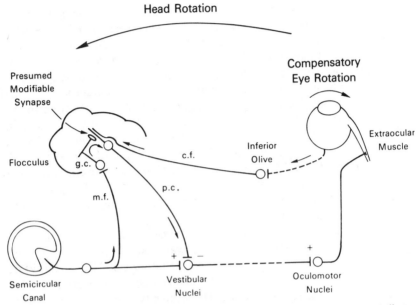

Figure 4   A simplified diagram illustrating the hypothetical role of the vestibular cerebellum (flocculus) in the long-term calibration of the vestibulo-ocular reflex (VOR). The flocculus is viewed as an inhibitory side-loop of the main vestibulo-ocular pathway, receiving a mossy fiber (m.f.)-granule cell (g.c.) primary vestibular afferent input and in turn projecting inhibition back onto the relay neurons in the vestibular nuclei through its Purkinje cell (p.c.) output. Also shown is the visually driven climbing fiber (c.f.) input from the inferior olive, an essential element in Ito's hypothetical model for long-term adaptive control of the VOR (45). Ito suggests that activity in the c.f. pathway denotes an error in the VOR and, if persistent, causes a gradual change in the efficacy of the g.c. input to the Purkinje cell which will adjust the inhibitory contribution from the flocculus until the overall VOR gain is once again appropriate.

that the flocculus, a part of the vestibular cerebellum, is much more than an appendage of the VOR and, in this species at least, is involved in other, previously unsuspected, aspects of oculomotor behavior such as visual tracking. This complicates the interpretation of the lesion experiments.

Closed-Loop Control

A major disadvantage of open-loop control is its lack of immediate error correction. Closed-loop systems deal with this problem by the use of negative feedback. In order to detect, and *immediately* compensate for, any tendency of the system to deviate from desired performance, two major additions must be made to the basic control system that was outlined in Figure 3: 1. a transducer is needed to monitor the actual performance (output) of the system, and 2. a comparator is required to compare this output with the desired one, that is, compare output and input (see Figure 5A). Ideally, the signal from the transducer constitutes a feedback signal which is proportional to the output of the whole system and, as such, indicates the extent to which the system is carrying out the instructions of the input or controller. Subtracting this feedback signal from the input signal (so-called negative feedback) leaves an error signal, which indicates the extent to which the *actual* performance falls short of the *desired*. When this error signal drives the system, power will be automatically delivered in an appropriate way whenever the output deviates from the desired level. A good example of negative feedback operation in the nervous system is the visual stabilization of the eyes by the optokinetic system (see Figure 5B). From the control standpoint, the input to this visually mediated, ocular stabilization system is movement of the retinal image, and the output is an appropriately directed eye movement tending to minimize that retinal image movement; the retina performs the functions of both the transducer and the comparator, and the visual slip signal represents the error. The system operates essentially as a velocity servo (10, 52), responding only to wide-field image motion across the retina, hence being dominated by the station-

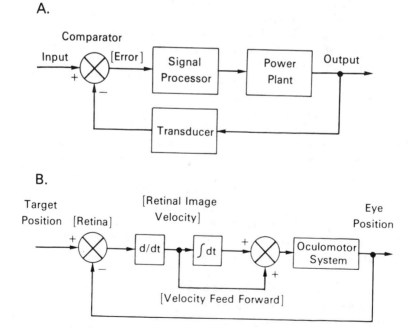

Figure 5 Visual stabilization of the eye viewed as a negative feedback system. *A.* A signal flow diagram showing the basic elements in such a system. *B.* A simplified signal flow diagram showing the major signal processing operations in the optokinetic system.

ary environmental background and working in concert with the VOR to stabilize the eye.

The accessory optic system seems to play a crucial role in mediating optokinetic responses, especially in lower vertebrates (11, 17), though there remains some question of exactly where these visual inputs enter oculomotor pathways. It is generally assumed that the visual input, like the vestibular, is velocity coded and shares the same processing needs (integration); it is therefore not unreasonable to expect that it might share the same neural circuitry. Such "economic" arguments would suggest that the visual input enters the system at the vestibular nuclei, and there is some electrophysiological evidence in support of this (41). Furthermore, the illusion of circularvection, in which movements of the visual background are mistaken for movements of the whole body (16), could be explained nicely by convergence of vestibular and optokinetic inputs at an early stage in processing. It is also not unreasonable to suppose that evolution would favor the early convergence of signals in two systems that are so clearly synergistic.

Since negative feedback systems (such as the optokinetic) automatically attempt to correct for any discrepancy between desired and actual performance, whether due to internally or externally generated disturbances, calibration of the individual elements is not nearly so critical as in the open-loop situation. Indeed, at this point the reader might well ask why the open-loop VOR is needed at all? Why can't the closed-loop optokinetic system alone maintain retinal image stability? The answer is very simple: the optokinetic system is too slow. In fact, it is an order of magnitude slower than the VOR, primarily because of a large delay in the visual pathway (67, 115). Thus, if the optokinetic system were the only means of stabilizing the image of the world on the retina, then considerable slip would have to be endured during rapid head turns. As it is, the optokinetic system is relegated to the role of a backup system, responding and further minimizing any residual retinal image slip due to imperfections in the operation of the VOR. We thus see that retinal image stability is protected by two independent and complementary systems that are mediated by two different modalities: the fast, open-loop VOR that can deal with the high velocities achieved during head turns ("coarse" control), and the slow, closed-loop optokinetic system that attends to the low velocity residual image shifts ("fine" control).

STEADY-STATE ERRORS   In assessing the performance of a control system, we are interested in the magnitude of the errors during operation, and for descriptive convenience we can consider these to be of two kinds: *steady-state* errors and *dynamic* errors. In a simple negative feedback system such as that in Figure 5, the steady-state error will be a simple function of the feedback loop gain. For example, if the loop gain in the optokinetic model were 10, then a steady-state velocity error (retinal image slip velocity) of 1°/sec would sustain an eye velocity of 10°/sec. Thus, a steady input target velocity of 11°/sec would be matched by an output eye velocity of only 10°/sec; as the target velocity increases to, say, 110°/sec, the steady-state velocity error would increase to 10°/sec. The steady-state error clearly increases progressively with the demand on the system, and its magnitude with any given input is inversely related to the loop gain. In order to minimize such errors therefore, a high loop gain is required; unfortunately, in practice this creates dynamic problems.

DYNAMIC ERRORS AND STABILITY Obviously, long loop delays such as those seen in the optokinetic system inevitably result in slow responses, and in dynamic situations the output will lag behind the input, severely restricting the useful dynamic range of the system. However, such delays can have even more deleterious consequences in a negative feedback system because they can lead to oscillation and instability: by the time the system has begun to respond to the feedback, external conditions may have changed, so that what was appropriate 100 ms ago is now inappropriate, and the feedback contribution becomes counterproductive; in practice, such a system would oscillate spontaneously. (Inertia in the load has a similarly deleterious effect on performance.) The greater the gain of the feedback loop, the more acute is this problem.

USE OF DAMPING TO IMPROVE STABILITY Unless dealt with, this stability problem would severely restrict the loop gain that could be employed in negative feedback systems and this would give rise to intolerable steady-state errors. A useful and widely employed partial solution is to introduce *damping,* which operates like viscous friction and prevents the output from achieving the high velocities where momentum builds up to produce overshoot and oscillation. In practice, damping is introduced by augmenting the negative feedback signal by an amount proportional to the velocity of the output: output-derivative, negative velocity feedback (see Figure 6A). Whether the nervous system employs this solution or not is polemical, but potentially any sensory feedback signal with a velocity component (and there are many of them) might perform such a function.

USE OF FEEDFORWARD TO IMPROVE DYNAMIC RESPONSES Unfortunately, while damping prevents unwanted oscillations, it also slows the system down further, adding to the transmission delay problems inherent in the nervous system. The problem now is to speed up the system. While the finite delays cannot be circumvented, some dynamic improvement can be effected by boosting the input signal whenever rapid changes are re-

A. Damping and Feed Forward

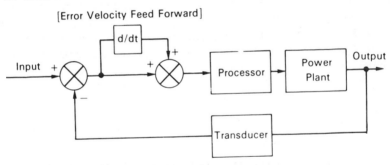

B. Error Rate Control

Figure 6 Signal flow diagrams of hypothetical negative feedback systems incorporating additional signal processing elements to improve performance. See text for explanation.

quired; this can be achieved by adding a further signal to the *input* that is proportional to its velocity: input-derivative, velocity feedforward (see Figure 6A).

Because the difference between two derivatives is equal to the derivative of the difference, it is possible to collapse the above two additions—output-derivative, negative velocity feedback and input-derivative feedforward—into one: *error-derivative velocity feedforward*, also known as error rate control (see Figure 6B). This will produce the necessary damping and at the same time boost the system when speed is essential. Velocity feedforward signals are probably common in the nervous system and are found in both open- and closed-loop systems at various stages in signal processing. The unintegrated vestibular and optokinetic velocity signals that are conveyed directly to oculomotor motoneurons are one such example, operating to improve dynamic responses (see Figures 3C & 5B).

USE OF POSITIVE FEEDBACK TO REDUCE STEADY-STATE ERRORS While velocity feedforward improves the dynamic capabilities of the system, it does not directly address the steady-state errors. The use of damping allows some increase in the loop gain, hence reducing steady-state errors, but with the long finite delays in the optokinetic system, the allowable loop gain would still be too low. What is really needed to address the problem directly is some means of effectively increasing the loop gain as the error increases without disrupting stability. It has been suggested (85) that this is achieved in the optokinetic system through an internal positive feedback loop in which a neural representation of eye velocity is fed back and summed with the error velocity signal (see Figure 7). In order for the positive feedback loop to function appropriately in the above scheme, it is essential that it have dynamic properties identical to those of the negative feedback loop, necessitating processing through some central model of the plant (81). The eye velocity signal fed back thus represents an exact copy of the efferent output, justifying its description as an "efferent copy" signal (85).

Actually this positive feedback scheme had been proposed some years earlier by Fender (24) and Young et al (116) to explain certain properties of the smooth pursuit system, another subdivision of the primate oculomotor system which is used to track small targets moving against a stationary background and hence must override the optokinetic system. These authors were attempting to devise a pursuit model which could explain man's ability to track retinal afterimages which, of course, do not move across the retina (24, 42, 114), and it will be apparent from Figure 7 that positive feedback could help to sustain tracking in such situations where there is no retinal image slip. [Because of this potential for error-free performance in some situations, the external observer might infer that such a system has predictive capabilities. However, this would be seen only with simple linear target motions and would not, for instance, explain the well-known ability of human subjects to use predictive strategies with sinusoidal target motions (104).]

Recent electrophysiological recordings have revealed that some of the Purkinje output cells in the primate vestibulo-cerebellum encode *gaze velocity* by summing together two signals—orbital eye velocity and angular head velocity (30, 58, 73). These neurons thus indicate movement of the line of sight with respect to the stationary surroundings. When tracking a moving target with the head stationary—a "pure" ocular pursuit situation

A. Positive Feedback [Plant Model Control]

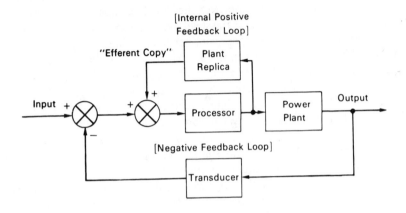

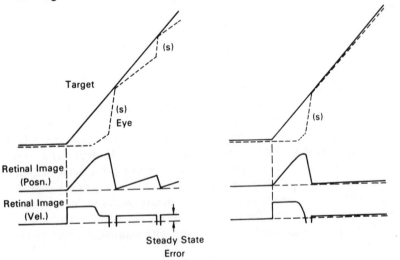

Figure 7 The use of positive feedback in negative feedback control systems to reduce steady state errors. *A.* A signal flow diagram showing the basic elements in such a system. *B* and *C.* Schematic diagrams showing how ocular pursuit of a target might be improved by internal positive feedback loops. S: saccadic eye movements.

in which head velocity is zero—these neurons emit a pure eye velocity signal which provides positive feedback support for the tracking. However, during combined eye-head tracking, which is the more usual strategy in normal behavioral circumstances, the situation is much more complicated, with visual and vestibular interactions that can be clarified only by recourse to a composite model such as that postulated in the next section.

THE STABILIZATION OF RETINAL IMAGES: A PRELIMINARY MODEL
The objective in this section is to integrate the three subsections of the oculomotor system that operate to stabilize retinal images—the VOR, the optokinetic system and the smooth pursuit system—into one model. We shall not be concerned here with the rapid saccadic eye movements which operate quite independently in a ballistic fashion to break fixation and transfer gaze to new objects of interest.

Figure 8 is a signal flow diagram of the various subsystems under consideration. We shall first consider each of the component parts of this model before proceeding to consider how they might interact in various behavioral

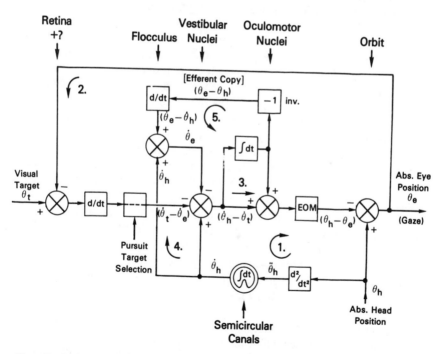

Figure 8 A tentative (simplified) signal flow model of the systems responsible for stabilizing retinal images. See text for an explanation. θ_t, θ_h and θ_e represent absolute positions of the target, head and eye, respectively.

situations. Loop 1 at the lower right in Figure 8 represents the open-loop VOR, operating to offset the effect of head movements on absolute eye position in space; note the convergent flow of the signals. Loop 2 represents the negative feedback loop of the optokinetic and smooth pursuit subsystems, in which image motion across the retina elicits eye movements that reduce that motion; note the circulating flow of signals with a net subtraction. The smooth pursuit subsystem is regarded, possibly naively, as merely a target selection option (mechanism unknown). Loop 3 introduces velocity feedforward (equivalent to desired eye velocity) to boost the dynamic response of the oculomotor output. Loop 4 represents an inhibitory side-loop of the VOR which has been postulated to provide adaptive gain control (though no details relating to the mechanism of gain adjustment are shown); another important function of this loop will emerge later. Loop 5 is a positive feedback loop which has been postulated to reduce the steady-state errors during visual tracking; again note the circulating flow of signals, but this time with a net addition. Loops 4 and 5 are known to converge in the vestibular cerebellum at least in primates, producing a neural representation of absolute eye velocity, often conveniently termed *gaze* vel.

OCULAR PURSUIT OF SMALL MOVING TARGETS (HEAD STATIONARY) The optokinetic system represents a potential inpediment to the ocular pursuit of small moving targets because it operates to oppose movement of the extensive background images. Thus, some target selection process must operate to ensure that the retinal slip input in loop 2 pertains only to the image of the moving target. Of course, the problem of optokinetic resistance during ocular pursuit does not arise until after the eyes have begun to move, hence the need for a target selection process arises only during the sustaining phase of pursuit and not the initiation. The pursuit system has a latency in excess of 100 ms (28, 83) so that when a target first starts to move, its image will traverse the retina at a velocity equal to that of the target itself. This will initiate ocular pursuit of the target (80). Once pursuit is under way, it will be sustained by the residual retinal image slip of the target and receive a further boost from the positive feedback loop (loop 4). Provided that the positive and negative feedback loops have similar transfer characteristics, then the regenerative tendencies of the former will be held in check by the latter (85).

HEAD TURNS WHILE FIXATING STATIONARY TARGETS Any turning of the head, whether self-generated or passively imposed, will activate the VOR, and in an animal like the monkey, in which the VOR gain is normally close to one, there is minimal disturbance of gaze. Because the head movement is matched by an eye movement that is almost equal in magnitude and opposite in direction, the two signals converging from loop 4 (head velocity) and 5 (eye velocity) cancel (reflecting the zero gaze velocity); the flocculus thus makes no contribution to the vestibular maintenance of ocular stability in such situations, which must be borne by loop 1. Any residual retinal image slip will be minimized by the optokinetic/pursuit system (loop 2).

COMBINED EYE-HEAD TRACKING   When pursuing a target with combined head and eye movements, all of the various subsystems are interacting, together with one which we have so far ignored—the head movement system. For the present discussions, it will suffice to assume merely that a head turn is initiated and achieves a velocity somewhat less than that of the target—the precise magnitude of the movement is of little consequence here. The ocular pursuit system, exerting its influence through the target selection process in loop 2, will be required to generate an orbital eye movement which, when summed with the head movement, will produce a gaze velocity closely matching that of the target. It might seem at first glance that the ocular pursuit system's task is rendered easier by the head movement because it is required only to make up the difference between the movements of the target and head. Unfortunately, the VOR (loop 1) will operate to generate compensatory eye movements that offset the head rotation, and the pursuit system will therefore derive no benefit from the head movement. Furthermore, when the head is moving, then of course eye movements will contribute proportionally less to the overall shift in gaze and there will be a corresponding decrease in the eye velocity signal in loop 5 which provides positive feedback support for the ocular pursuit. However, it is here where the vestibular (head velocity) input from loop 4 makes a subtle contribution, ensuring that the flocculus output continues to provide the same gaze velocity signal to support tracking, whether the head is stationary or moving. Such interactions help to explain why head movements have so little influence on tracking performance (55). Furthermore, if we assume a small delay in loop 4, then it is possible to explain why sudden interruptions of the head during combined eye-head tracking produce only a momentary disruption (10 msec or so)—too short for visual compensation to be involved in the process (55): when the head is stopped, the primary vestibular input to the vestibular nucleus (loop 1) will collapse within a millisecond or two, but the gaze velocity input signal coming from the flocculus will be sustained briefly by the continued (delayed) operation of loop 4. Thus, as the head is brought to a halt, the output from the vestibular nucleus increases so that the eyes will accelerate and reach a velocity equal to the previous gaze velocity. Assuming appropriate timing, as the head velocity signal subsequently decreases in loop 4, the eye velocity signal in loop 5 increases, so that the gaze velocity signal leaving the flocculus is maintained constant throughout the disturbance. The net result is a smooth transition from combined eye-head tracking to pure ocular pursuit.

Part 3.   EFFERENCE COPY AND COROLLARY DISCHARGE

Two related concepts—corollary discharge and efference copy—have long been important in theories of sensorimotor coordination and visual perception. Part 1 in this review has described instances of corollary discharge in sensory relay neurons during the course of centrally programmed movement after deafferentation, and Part 2 has presented control system models in which the existence of efference copy was postulated. Given the importance of these concepts, we believe it will be useful to consider their evolution and current usage.

Visuomotor Coordination

The idea of a central replica of eye movements has been invoked many times to explain various aspects of visual motor behavior (73, 75, 86, 94, 101, 103, 106, 109). Take, for example, visually guided reaching. In order to reach out and touch a seen object rapidly, without using continuous visual feedback to guide the hand (something we do quite well), it is necessary to reconstruct the target's position relative to the body. This requires that the brain sum together three signals: 1. the target's position relative to the visual axis, that is, relative to the eye, 2. the position of the eye relative to the head, 3. the position of the head relative to the body (40, 75, 86, 101) (see Figure 9). These last two pieces of information can each be derived from two possible sources—efference copy corresponding to the motor output and/or proprioceptive input—generally distinguished as "outflow" and "inflow." Setting aside for the moment the head position signal (which has received little attention experimentally), it has been assumed until very recently that extraocular proprioception makes little if any contribution to the central reconstruction of orbital eye position, and most models invoke some efference copy signal (75, 86). However, Steinbach & Smith (105) have now reported that immediately following corrective surgery, human strabismics mispoint at targets viewed with only the *normal, unoperated eye open* (i.e. with the operated eye closed). These subjects seem to be using proprioceptive inputs from the previously strabismic, nonviewing eye to reconstruct target position. Their pointing errors were less than the surgical correction, which might mean that efference copy does make some contribution or merely that the system uses proprioception from both eyes and only one has been operated on.

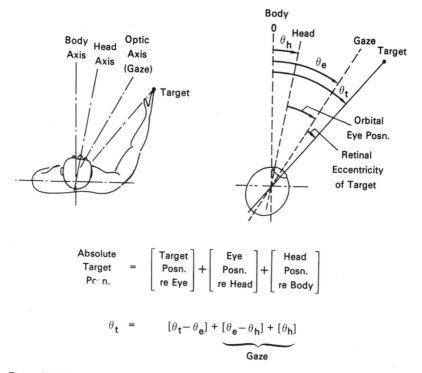

$$\theta_t = \underbrace{[\theta_t - \theta_e] + [\theta_e - \theta_h]}_{\text{Gaze}} + [\theta_h]$$

Figure 9 The neural reconstruction of target position relative to the body. See text for explanation.

The continuous circling that accompanies surgical eye rotation in fish (103) and head rotation in insects (74) is often ascribed to a corollary discharge or efference copy phenomenon (75, 103, 110, 111). The reasoning here is somewhat indirect since the circling can be explained without invoking these phenomena: rotating the eyes 180° reverses the sign of the feedback signal in the optokinetic system so that what is normally a negative feedback stabilization system becomes a positive feedback regenerative one; hence, visual signals will now reinforce, rather than oppose, eye movement, producing continuous circling. At the time that these experiments were done, this explanation was thought to be inadequate because it implied that the animal was the slave of its own optokinetic system; the animal's ability to move its eyes voluntarily during the normal course of behavior was cited as evidence that this was not so. Indeed, efference copy or corollary discharge signals were invoked as the means by which the animal could offset the visual consequences of self-generated movement (reafference) and thereby free itself of its own optokinetic system to allow a shift in gaze. Surgical rotation of the eyes was assumed to reverse this process, so that the efference copy or corollary discharge signal added to the visual input, producing circling.

We now know that voluntary shifts in fixation can be executed only by the saccadic system, which generates rapid ballistic movements whose velocities so far exceed the operating range of the optokinetic system that they do not encounter optokinetic opposition; slow, smooth eye movements cannot be initiated against a stationary featured background. Thus, voluntary shifts in gaze of the kind originally envisaged (calling for a cancellation of reafference) are not—indeed, cannot be—made, hence it is questionable whether the efference copy or corollary discharge signals, which are assumed to support circling, are even available for this purpose. For the present therefore, simple reversal of the feedback sign in the optokinetic system would seem to be an adequate explanation of circling.

Perceptual Stability

Under normal conditions, our eyes are stabilized in space (by the nonvisual VOR) so that visual information is derived from a stable sensory vantage point; in generating a spatial percept of our surroundings there seems to be an assumption of stability, which is applied to both the visual surroundings and the receptor surface—the retina—used to monitor it. When surrounded by a moving visual scene as in the usual laboratory optokinetic tests, the human subject erroneously feels that it is he that is moving and not the surroundings, particularly if a stationary fixation target is available [the illusion of circularvection (see 16)]. Similarly, when first worn, reversing prisms or telescopic spectacles have a seriously disorienting effect even when the subject is merely seated and not attempting any coordinated movement other than turning his head.

However, this receptor stability principle is frequently violated under *normal* conditions by rapid, saccadic eye movements which reposition the image of the environment on the retina, yet we do not become disoriented and do not perceive these shifts of the retinal image as movements (or displacements) of either ourselves or our surroundings. The nervous system's ability to distinguish retinal image motions due to eye movements from those due to objective movements of the visual scene was first recognized by von Helmholtz (109), and it is now generally agreed that nonvisual eye position information is required for this process. A major polemic is the origin of this oculomotor information: von Helmholtz (109) originally suggested that it derived from the "effort of will" (Willensanstrengung) or what is now termed "outflow," while James (46) and Sherrington (94) favored "inflow" signals from extraocular muscle proprioceptors.

Two lines of evidence are usually advanced in support of the "outflow" hypothesis: the first argues that if extraocular muscle proprioception were to mediate this process, then perceptual stability should be retained even during passive displacement of the eye; it is common knowledge, however, that movement and displacement are perceived when the eye is passively deflected, for example by pressing on the eyelids (109). Furthermore, if one eye is covered and then passively displaced, the subject perceives neither apparent motion of afterimages in that eye (109) nor illusory movement of the world through the uncovered eye (75, 100). Taken together, these observations seem to present a strong case against the "inflow" hypothesis, but there are two potential flaws in this evidence. The first concerns the *rate* of displacement. Although the perceived environment appears stable during rapid, saccadic eye movements, this is not true during slower saccades (as in drowsiness) nor during foveal pursuit movements (39); if while tracking a small moving target against a stationary background, the subject's attention is directed to that background, then he reports a strong sensation of movement there. A further problem might be that proprioceptive information is only "gated in" during saccadic eye movements, ruling out its appearance in any study in which saccades were not programmed; in this event, of course, it would have to be assumed that the gate is inoperative during drowsiness.

The second line of evidence generally held to support the outflow hypothesis concerns the illusory movement that is said to accompany attempts to move the paralyzed eye. Unfortunately, paralysis was incomplete in the usually cited studies (9, 54, 112), and the situation is less clear in those studies in which paralysis was complete: most maintain that no illusory displacement is seen (8, 95–97), though others claim that it is apparent but may require very strong effort to perceive it (106). It should be noted that the illusory shifts described in the latter study were "not necessarily visual" and "were difficult to describe." The illusion appears to be one of *displacement without movement,* contrasting with the illusion of *movement without displacement* experienced in the common waterfall effect. During normal saccadic eye movements we experience neither movement nor displacement of either ourselves or of our surroundings, and it is possible that the compensatory mechanisms operating in these two perceptual domains are different. Hence, observations on the one cannot be used to infer the mechanism of the other. Unfortunately, the need to distinguish between them has been realized only very recently.

Even conceding that the illusion exists, however, it is still very difficult to totally exclude extraocular proprioception from these experiments. In those studies employing retrobulbar block, only one eye was immobilized, hence movements of the other, mobile eye might provide relevant inflow information; in those studies employing systemic neuromuscular blocking agents, γ-input to the muscle spindles may still be functional since the intrafusal system is known to be less sensitive to curare than the extrafusal system (65). Thus, a potential source of inflow signals might survive in these experiments and, if the α-γ coactivation characteristically found in other skeletal muscle systems also applies to this one, then afferent discharge might emanate from the γ-input accompanying each attempted eye movement. Of course, in this event, both inflow and outflow signals would be involved.

Whatever the *source* of the eye movement information needed to distinguish self-generated from externally generated image motions, there remains the question of the *mechanism* by which it achieves this end. Perhaps the best-known idea is the "cancellation" hypothesis of von Holst & Mittelstaedt (111) in which eye movement information is used to cancel out the visual inputs generated by such eye movements (reafference). MacKay, on the other hand, argues that "from an information-engineering standpoint the need is not for the changes due to voluntary movement to be *eliminated* from the sensory input, but for them to be appropriately *evaluated* by the central mechanism responsible for the organism's 'conditional readiness' to reckon with its environment" (60, p. 308). The reader is directed to the original review article (60) for a detailed discussion.

Perceptual versus Motor Localization

It is important to distinguish between perceptual and motor indices of spatial localization. When human subjects are asked to judge the locations of targets seen only briefly during rapid saccadic eye movements (in the dark), they make large, though consistent, errors (64). The nature of these errors suggests that the perceptual adjustments associated with saccadic eye movements have only a loose temporal relationship with oculomotor events, actually commencing more than 100 ms before the onset of the eye movement and not reaching completion until several hundred milliseconds after the eye movement has ended (64). If, however, the subjects are asked to strike at such fleeting targets (e.g. with a hammer), then they can do so with considerable precision, and their accuracy approaches that achieved under optimal viewing conditions when the target is continuously visible and the eye stationary (101). Furthermore, these subjects were unaware of their remarkable performance and, indeed, were often under the impression that they were wildly inaccurate. Thus, while we may misperceive the locations of targets because of eye movements, our motor system can nonetheless be relied upon to emit appropriately directed responses.

Sensations Attributable to Impulses Arising in Muscle Stretch Receptors

Until quite recently it was commonly held that inputs from muscle afferents did not evoke any conscious sensation (9, 33, 44). Using a lever attached to a suction contact lens, Skavenski has shown that subjects could "reliably report when, and in which direction, loads were applied to their eyes in total darkness," and furthermore, that these subjects were able to maintain a given eye position during this loading, showing that "inflow information can be used for extraretinal oculomotor control" (99). The nature and functional significance of these sensations is not clear. In particular, one would like to know what, if anything, eye position sensation has to do with visuomotor coordination or perceptual stability.

Just as evidence now points to a role of extraocular muscle afferent inputs in sense of eye position, so too there is now evidence that muscle afferent inputs play a critical role in sense of limb position. Goodwin, McCloskey & Matthews (36) performed a series of experiments in which the subject positioned one limb (the "tracking limb") to provide a measure of the perceived position of the other limb whose afferent input was manipulated by muscle tendon vibration and/or selective elimination of cutaneous and joint afferent input. It was shown that tendon vibration (which excited muscle afferents) gave rise to sensations of limb movement and position shifts even when actual displacements were prevented. In studies on finger movements in subjects with hands made anesthetic by local anesthetics and/or occlusion of circulation at the wrist, it was found that subjects could detect obstruction of active movement even though the only afferent input was via muscle afferents in the forearm above the zone of anesthesia. These observations demonstrated that muscle afferents provide information as to extent of movement even when joint and cutaneous afferents are nonfunctional.

In commenting on their findings, Goodwin, McCloskey & Matthews have stated that the most intriguing questions posed by these results "relate to the mode of interaction between corollary discharges and afferent signals." Far from concluding that perceptions arising from muscle afferent inflow make it unnecessary to postulate the existence of efference copy, they point out that a contribution of muscle afferents to kinaesthesia makes it necessary to postulate the existence of efference copy, because a given muscle afferent signal has no absolute meaning in itself, but only in relation to degree of motor activity. In the past there has been a tendency to speak of the "inflow" (i.e. peripheral feedback) versus the "outflow" (i.e. efference copy) hypotheses. The above-quoted statement, however, makes it clear that the tendency to oppose these hypotheses should be abandoned.

Gamma Motoneuron Discharge Viewed as Efference Copy

While the concepts of efference copy and corollary discharge first appeared in relation to visuomotor coordination and visual perception, much of the neurophysiological data relevant to the concepts has actually come from studies at the level of the spinal cord. Corollary discharge of several classes of spinal cord neurons occurs during centrally programmed locomotion and scratching, and observations relevant to the concept of efference copy have come from work of Severin (90, 91) and of Vallbo (107) on central driving of γ-MNs. It might at first seem surprising to think of γ-MN activity as a form of efference copy, but if we use the term *efference copy* to denote activity corresponding to a motor output but occurring in a neuron which does not of itself directly give rise to movement, then γ-MN coactivation would constitute efference copy. It is generally assumed that the neuronal discharge constituting the efference copy is driven by branches of the signal line driving discharge of α-MNs, but it is not assumed that there need be a linear relation between α-MN discharge and efference copy. It is interesting to note that discharge of spindle afferents due to γ-MN coactivation has one of the consequences attributed to efference copy in relation to eye movements. In von Holst's (110) formulation, efference copy cancels sensory inputs resulting from self-generated movement. While such cancellation is hypothetical in the visual system, it is demonstrable for the muscle spindle since coactivated γ-MN discharge acts to cancel the effects of centrally programmed muscular shortening. The control process utilizing α-γ coactivation may be viewed as one in which efference copy allows spindle afferent discharge to signal the *distortion* or *error* of a centrally programmed movement. The spindles whose activity is controlled by γ-MN discharge are part of a negative feedback loop, and efference copy enables this negative feedback loop to signal distortion of movement while nullifying the intended "on target" aspects of movement.

Literature Cited

1. Albus, J. S. 1971. A theory of cerebellar cortex. *Math. Biosci.* 10:25–61
2. Arshavsky, Yu. I., Berkinblit, M. B., Fukson, O. I., Gelfand, I. M., Orlovsky, G. N. 1972. Recordings of neurones of the dorsal spinocerebellar tract during evoked locomotion. *Brain Res.* 43: 272–75
3. Arshavsky, Yu. I., Berkinblit, M. B., Fukson, O. I., Gelfand, I. M., Orlovsky, G. N. 1972. Origin of modulation in neurones of the ventral spinocerebellar tract during locomotion. *Brain Res.* 43:276–79
4. Arshavsky, Yu. I., Gelfand, I. M., Orlovsky, G. N., Pavlova, G. A. 1975. Activity of neurones of the ventral spinocerebellar tract during "fictive scratching." *Biophysics* 20:762–64
5. Arshavsky, Yu. I., Gelfand, I. M., Orlovsky, G. N., Pavlova, G. A. 1975. Origin of modulation in vestibulospinal

neurons during scratching. *Biophysics* 20:965–67
6. Barr, C. C., Schultheis, L. W., Robinson, D. A. 1976. Voluntary, nonvisual control of the human vestibulo-ocular reflex. *Acta Otolaryngol.* 81:365–75
7. Brindley, G. S. 1964. The use made by the cerebellum of the information that it receives from sense organs. *IBRO Bull.* 3(3):80 (Abstr.)
8. Brindley, G. S., Goodwin, G. M., Kulikowski, J. J., Leighton, D. 1977. Stability of vision with a paralysed eye. *J. Physiol.* 258:65P–66P
9. Brindley, G. S., Merton, P. A. 1960. The absence of position sense in the human eye. *J. Physiol.* 153:127–30
10. Collewijn, H. 1972. An analog model of the rabbit's optokinetic system. *Brain Res.* 36:71–88
11. Collewijn, H. 1975. Direction selective units in the rabbit's nucleus of the optic tract. *Brain Res.* 100:489–508

12. Conrad, B., Matsunami, K., Meyer-Lohmann, J., Wiesendanger, M., Brooks, V. B. 1974. Cortical load compensation during voluntary elbow movements. *Brain Res.* 71:507–14
13. Conrad, B., Meyer-Lohmann, J., Matsunami, K., Brooks, V. B. 1975. Precentral unit activity following torque pulse injections into elbow movements. *Brain Res.* 94:219–36
14. Davies, P., Melvill Jones, G. 1976. An adaptive neural model compatible with plastic changes induced in the human vestibulo-ocular reflex by prolonged optical reversal of vision. *Brain Res.* 103:546–50
15. Deliagina, T. G., Feldman, A. G., Gelfand, I. M., Orlovsky, G. N. 1975. On the role of central program and afferent inflow in the control of scratching movements in the cat. *Brain Res.* 100:297–313
16. Dichgans, J., Brandt, T. 1972. Visual-vestibular interaction and motion perception. In *Cerebral Control of Eye Movements and Motion Perception,* ed. J. Dichgans, E. Bizzi, pp. 327–38. Basel: Karger
17. Easter, S. S., Landreth, G. E. Northcutt, R. G. 1974. The goldfish brain and optokinetic nystagmus. *Soc. Neurosci. Abstr.,* p. 197
18. Evarts, E. V. 1968. Relation of pyramidal tract activity to force exerted during voluntary movement. *J. Neurophysiol.* 31:14–27
19. Evarts, E. V. 1973. Motor cortex reflexes associated with learned movement. *Science* 179:501–3
20. Evarts, E. V., Fromm, C. 1977. Sensory responses in motor cortex neurons during precise motor control. *Neurosci. Lett.* 5:267–72
21. Evarts, E. V., Fromm, C. 1978. The pyramidal tract neuron as summing point in a closed-loop control system in the monkey. In *Motor Control in Man: Long Loop Mechanisms,* ed. J. E. Desmedt, 4:56–69 Basel: Karger
22. Evarts, E. V., Tanji, J. 1976. Reflex and intended responses in motor cortex pyramidal tract neurons of monkey. *J. Neurophysiol.* 39:1069–80
23. Feldman, A. G., Orlovsky, G. N. 1975. Activity of interneurons mediating reciprocal Ia inhibition during locomotion. *Brain Res.* 84:181–94
24. Fender, D. H. 1962. The eye-movement control system: evolution of a model. In *Neural Theory and Modeling,* ed. R. F. Reiss, 306–24. Stanford: Stanford Univ. press. 427 pp.
25. Fernandez, C., Goldberg, J. M. 1971. Physiology of peripheral neurons innervating semicircular canals of the squirrel monkey. II. Response to sinusoidal stimulation and dynamics of peripheral vestibular system. *J. Neurophysiol.* 34:661–75
26. Forssberg, H., Grillner, S., Rossignol, S. 1977. Phasic gain control of reflexes from the dorsum of the paw during spinal locomotion. *Brain Res.* 132:121–39
27. Fromm, C., Evarts, E. V. 1977. Relation of motor cortex neurons to precisely controlled and ballistic movements. *Neurosci. Lett.* 5:259–65
28. Fuchs, A. F. 1967. Saccadic and smooth pursuit eye movements in the monkey. *J. Physiol.* 191:609–31
29. Fuchs, A. F., Kimm, J. 1975. Unit activity in vestibular nucleus of the alert monkey during horizontal angular acceleration and eye movement. *J. Neurophysiol.* 38:1140–61
30. Fuchs, A. F., Lisberger, S. G. 1975. Response of flocculus Purkinje cells during smooth pursuit eye movements. *Neurosci. Abstr.* 1:209
31. Fuchs, A. F., Lushei, E. S. 1970. Firing patterns of abducens neurons of alert monkeys in relationship to horizontal eye movement. *J. Neurophysiol.* 33:382–92
32. Gauthier, G. M., Robinson, D. A. 1975. Adaptation of the human vestibulo-ocular reflex to magnifying lenses. *Brain Res.* 92:331–35
33. Gelfan, S., Carter, S. 1967. Muscle sense in man. *Exp. Neurol.* 18:469–73
34. Gonshor, A., Melvill Jones, G. 1976. Short-term adaptive changes in the human vestibulo-ocular reflex arc. *J. Physiol.* 256:361–79
35. Gonshor, A., Melvill Jones, G. 1976. Extreme vestibulo-ocular adaptation induced by prolonged optical reversal of vision. *J. Physiol.* 256:381–414
36. Goodwin, G. M., McCloskey, D. I., Matthews, P. B. C. 1972. The contribution of muscle afferents to kinaesthesia shown by vibration induced illusions of movement and by the effects of paralysing joint afferents. *Brain* 95:705–48
37. Graham Brown, T. 1914. On the nature of the fundamental activity of the nervous centres; together with an analysis of the conditioning of rhythmic activity in progression, and a theory of the evolution of function in the nervous system. *J. Physiol.* 48:18–46
38. Granit, R. 1955. *Receptors and Sensory Perception.* New Haven: Yale. 366 pp.

39. Gregory, R. L. 1958. Eye movements and the stability of the visual world. *Nature* 182:1214–16

40. Hansen, R. M., Skavenski, A. A. 1977. Accuracy of eye position information for motor control. *Vision Res.* 17:919–26

41. Henn, V., Young, L. R., Finley, C. 1974. Vestibular nucleus units in alert monkeys are also influenced by moving visual fields. *Brain Res.* 71:144–49

42. Heywood, S., Churcher, J. H. 1971. Eye movements and the afterimage. I: Tracking the afterimage. *Vision Res.* 11:1163–68

43. Houk, J. C., Henneman, E. 1967. Responses of Golgi tendon organs to active muscle contractions of the soleus muscle of the cat. *J. Neurophysiol.* 30:466–81

44. Irvine, S. R., Ludvigh, E. J. 1936. Is ocular proprioceptive sense concerned in vision? *Arch. Ophtalmol.* 15:1037–49

45. Ito, M. 1972. Neural design of the cerebellar motor control system. *Brain Res.* 40:81–84

46. James, W. 1950. *The Principles of Psychology,* Vol. 2 (original publisher: Holt, 1890). New York: Dover

47. Jones, E. G., Wise, S. P. 1977. Size, laminar and columnar distribution of efferent cells in the sensory-motor cortex of monkeys. *J. Comp. Neurol.* 175:391–438

48. Keller, E. L. 1974. Participation of the medial pontine reticular formation in eye movement generation in monkey. *J. Neurophysiol.* 37:316–32

49. Keller, E. L., Daniels, P. D. 1975. Oculomotor related interaction of vestibular and visual stimulation in vestibular nucleus cells in alert monkey. *Exp. Neurol.* 46:187–98

50. Keller, E. L., Robinson, D. A. 1972. Abducens unit behavior in the monkey during vergence movements. *Vision Res.* 21:369–82

51. Kennedy, D., Davis, W. J. 1977. Organization of invertebrate motor systems. *Handb. Physiol.* 1:1023–87

52. Koerner, F., Schiller, P. H. 1972. The optokinetic response under open and closed loop conditions in the monkey. *Exp. Brain Res.* 14:318–330

53. Koeze, T. H., Phillips, C. G., Sheridan, J. D. 1968. Thresholds of cortical activation of muscle spindles and α-motoneurones of the baboon's hand. *J. Physiol.* 195:419–49

54. Kornmueller, A. E. 1931. Eine experimentelle Anastesie der ausseren Augenmusckeln am Menschen und ihre Auswirkungen. *J. Psychol. Neurol. Leipz.* 41:354–66

55. Lanman, J. M., Bizzi, E., Allum, J. 1976. Smooth tracking with combined eye-head movements. *Neurosci. Abstr.* 2:279

56. Leksell, L. 1945. The action potential and excitatory effects of the small ventral root fibres to skeletal muscle. *Acta Physiol. Scand.* 10: Suppl. 31. 84 pp.

57. Lisberger, S. G., Fuchs, A. F. 1974. Response of flocculus Purkinje cells to adequate vestibular stimulation in the alert monkey: fixation vs compensatory eye movements. *Brain Res.* 69:347–53

58. Lisberger, S. G., Fuchs, A. F. 1975. Response of flocculus Purkinje cells to interactions of smooth pursuit eye movements and natural vestibular rotation. *Neurosci. Abstr.* 1:208

59. Lundberg, A. 1966. Integration in the reflex pathway. In *Muscular Afferents and Motor Control,* ed. R. Granit, pp. 275–305. New York: Wiley. 466 pp.

60. MacKay, D. M. 1973. In *Central Processing of Visual Information,* ed. R. Jung, 307–31. New York: Springer

61. Maekawa, K., Simpson, J. I. 1973. Climbing fiber responses evoked in vestibulocerebellum of rabbit from visual system. *J. Neurophysiol.* 36:649–66

62. Marr, D. 1969. A theory of cerebellar cortex. *J. Physiol.* 202:437–70

63. Marsden, C. D., Merton, P. A., Morton, H. B. 1972. Servo action in human voluntary movement. *Nature* 238:140–43

64. Matin, L., Matin, E., Pearce, D. G. 1969. Visual perception of direction when voluntary saccades occur. I. Relation of visual direction of a fixation target extinguished before a saccade to a flash presented during the saccade. *Percept. Psychophys* 5:65–80

65. Matthews, P. B. C. 1964. Muscle spindles and their motor control. *Physiol. Rev.* 44:219–88

66. Melvill Jones, G., Davies, P. 1976. Adaptation of cat vestibulo-ocular reflex to 200 days of optically reversed vision. *Brain Res.* 103:551–54

67. Melvill Jones, G., Drazin, D. H. 1961. Oscillatory motion in flight. In *Human Problems of Supersonic and Hypersonic Flight,* ed. A. B. Barbour, H. E. Whittingham, pp. 134–51. Oxford: Pergamon

68. Melvill Jones, G., Gonshor, A. 1975. Goal-directed flexibility in the vestibulo-ocular reflex arc. In *Basic Mechanisms of Ocular Motility and Their Clinical Implications,* ed. G. Lennerstrand,

P. Bach-y-Rita, pp. 227–45. Oxford: Pergamon. 584 pp.

69. Melvill Jones, G., Milsum, J. 1970. Characteristics of neural transmission from the semicircular canal to the vestibular nuclei of cats. *J. Physiol.* 209:295–316

70. Miles, F. A. 1974. Single unit firing patterns in the vestibular nuclei related to voluntary eye movements and passive head movement in conscious monkeys. *Brain Res.* 71:215–24

71. Miles, F. A., Braitman, D. J., Eighmy, B. B. 1977. Vestibulo-ocular responses in the rhesus monkey following prolonged optical reversal of vision. *Neurosci. Abstr.* 3:545

72. Miles, F. A., Fuller, J. H. 1974. Adaptive plasticity in the vestibulo-ocular responses of the rhesus monkey. *Brain Res.* 80:512–16

73. Miles, F. A., Fuller, J. H. 1975. Visual tracking and the primate flocculus. *Science* 189:1000–2

74. Mittelstaedt, H. 1949. Telotaxis und Optomotorik von Eristalis bei Augeninversion. *Naturwissenschaften* 36:90–91

75. Mittelstaedt, H. 1958. The analysis of behavior in terms of control systems. In *Group Processes,* ed. B. Schaffner, pp. 45–84. Princeton: Trans. 5th Conf.

76. Morasso, P., Bizzi, E., Dichgans, J. 1973. Adjustment of saccade characteristics during head movements. *Exp. Brain Res.* 16:492–500

77. Orlovsky, G. N. 1972. Activity of vestibulospinal neurons during locomotion. *Brain Res.* 46:85–98

78. Pearson, K. 1976. The control of walking. *Sci. Am.* 235:72–86

79. Phillips, C. G. 1969. Motor apparatus of the baboon's hand. *Proc. R. Soc. London Ser. B.* 173:141–74

80. Rashbass, C. 1961. The relationship between saccadic and smooth-tracking eye movements. *J. Physiol.* 159:326–38

81. Reswick, J. B. 1956. Disturbance-control feedback—a new control concept. *Trans. Am. Soc. Mech. Eng.,* p. 153

82. Roberts, B. L., Russell, I. J. 1972. The activity of lateral-line efferent neurones in stationary and swimming dogfish. *J. Exp. Biol.* 57:435–48

83. Robinson, D. A. 1965. The mechanics of human smooth pursuit eye movement. *J. Physiol.* 180:569–91

84. Robinson, D. A. 1970. Oculomotor unit behavior in the monkey. *J. Neurophysiol.* 33:393–404

85. Robinson, D. A. 1971. Models of oculomotor neural organization. In *The Control of Eye Movements,* ed. P.

Bach-y-Rita, C. C. Collins, pp. 519–38. New York: Academic

86. Robinson, D. A. 1975. Oculomotor control signals. See Ref. 68, pp. 337–74

87. Robinson, D. A. 1976. Adaptive gain control of vestibuloocular reflex by the cerebellum. *J. Neurophysiol.* 39:954–69

88. Robinson, D. L., Wurtz, R. H. 1976. Use of an extraretinal signal by monkey superior colliculus neurons to distinguish real from self-induced stimulus movement. *J. Neurophysiol.* 39:852–70

89. Schiller, P. H. 1970. The discharge characteristics of single units in the oculomotor and abducens nuclei of the unanesthetized monkey. *Exp. Brain Res.* 10:347–62

90. Severin, F. V. 1970. The role of the gamma motor system in the activation of the extensor alpha motor neurones during controlled locomotion *Biophysics* 15:1138–45

91. Severin, F. V., Orlovsky, G. N., Shik, M. L. 1967. Work of the muscle receptors during controlled locomotion. *Biophysics* 12:575–86

92. Sherrington, C. S. 1906. *The Integrative Action of the Nervous System.* New Haven: Yale, 413 pp.

93. Sherrington, C. S. 1906. On the proprioceptive system, especially in its reflex aspect. *Brain* 29:467–82

94. Sherrington, C. S. 1918. Observations on the sensual role of the proprioceptive nerve-supply of the extrinsic ocular muscles. *Brain* 41:332–43

95. Siebeck, R. 1953. Wahrehmungsformen bei experimentellen Augenmuskellahmungen. *Dtsch. Ophthalmol. Ges. Ber.* 58:24

96. Siebeck, R. 1954. Wahrenehmungsstorung und Storungswahrnehmung bei Augenmuskellahmungen. *Albrecht von Graefes Arch. Ophthalmol.* 155:26–34

97. Siebeck, R., Frey, R. 1953. Die Wirkungen muskelerschlaffender Mittel auf die Augenmuskeln. *Anaesthesist* 2:138–41

98. Simpson, J. I., Alley, K. E. 1974. Visual climbing fiber input to rabbit vestibulocerebellum: a source of directionspecific information. *Brain. Res.* 82:302–8

99. Skavenski, A. A. 1972. Inflow as a source of extraretinal eye position information. *Vision Res.* 12:221–29

100. Skavenski, A. A., Haddad, G., Steinman, R. M. 1972. The extraretinal signal for the visual perception of direction. *Percept. Psychophys.* 11:287–90

101. Skavenski, A. A., Hansen, R. M. 1978. In *Eye Movements and the Higher Psychological Functions,* ed. J. Senders, D.

Fisher, R. Monty, pp. 15–34. New York: Erlbaum

102. Skavenski, A. A., Robinson, D. A. 1973. Role of abducens neurons in vestubuloocular reflex. J. Neurophysiol. 36:724–38

103. Sperry, R. W. 1950. Neural basis of the spontaneous optokinetic response produced by visual inversion. J. Comp. Physiol. Psychol. 43:482–89

104. Stark, L., Vossius, G., Young, L. R. 1962. Predictive control of eye tracking movements. IRE Trans. Hum. Factors Electron. 3:52–59

105. Steinbach, M. J., Smith, D. R. 1976. Effects of strabismus surgery on spatial localization. Neurosci. Abstr. 2:282

106. Stevens, J. K., Emerson, R. C., Gerstein, G. L., Kallos, T., Neufeld, G. R., Nichols, C. W., Rosenquist, A. C. 1976. Paralysis of the awake human: visual perceptions. Vision Res. 16:93–98

107. Vallbo, A. B. 1973. Muscle spindle afferent discharge from resting and contracting muscles in normal human subjects. In New Developments in Electromyography and Clinical Neurophysiology, ed. J. E. Desmedt, 3:251–62. Basel: Karger. 870 pp.

108. Vogt, B. A., Pandya, D. N. 1978. Cortico-cortical connections of somatic sensory cortex (Areas 3, 1 and 2) in the rhesus monkey. J. Comp. Neurol. 177:179–92

109. von Helmholtz, H. 1866. Handbuch der Physiologischen Optik. Leipzig: Voss. English transl. from ed. 3, 1910, J. P. C.

Southall, ed. A Treatise on Physiological Optics, Vol. 3, 1962. New York: Dover

110. von Holst, E. 1954. Relations between the central nervous system and the peripheral organs. Br. J. Anim. Behav. 2:89–94

111. Von Holst, E., Mittelstaedt, H. 1950. Das Reafferenzprinzip. Wechselwirkungen zwischen Zentralnervensystem und Peripherie, Naturwissenschaften 37:464

112. West, R. 1932. Curare in man. Proc. R. Soc. Med. 25:1107–16

113. Wiesendanger, M. 1973. Input from muscle and cutaneous nerves of the hand and forearm to neurones of the precentral gyrus of baboons and monkeys. J. Physiol. 228:203–19

114. Yasui, S., Young L. R. 1975. Eye movements during after-image tracking under sinusoidal and random vestibular stimulation. See Ref. 68, pp. 509–13

115. Young, L. R. 1962. A sampled data model for eye tracking movements. PhD thesis. Massachusetts Inst. Technol., Cambridge, Mass.

116. Young, L. R., Forster, J. D., van Houtte, N. 1968. A revised stochastic sampled data model for eye tracking movements. NASA-Univ. Conf. Manual Control, 4th, Univ. Michigan, Ann Arbor, Mich.

117. Zipser, B., Bennett, M. V. L. 1976. Interaction of electrosensory and electromotor signals in lateral line lobe of a mormyrid fish. J. Neurophysiol. 39:713–21

Ann. Rev. Psychol. 1979. 30:363–96

INFORMATION PROCESSING MODELS OF COGNITION

❖311

Herbert A. Simon[1]

Department of Psychology, Carnegie-Mellon University, Pittsburgh, Pennsylvania 15213

CONTENTS

ORIGINS OF THE INFORMATION PROCESSING APPROACH 364
PROBLEM SOLVING 366
    Strategies as Intervening Variables 367
    The Expert's Knowledge 368
    Semantically Rich Domains 369
    Production Systems 370
    Understanding Processes 371
    Protocol Analysis 372
SEMANTIC MEMORY 375
INDUCTION OF PATTERNS 378
LEARNING AND DEVELOPMENT 380
    Performance of Piagetian Tasks 381
    Language Acquisition 382
    Adaptive Production Systems 382
MOTIVATION AND EMOTION 383
THE ELEMENTARY PROCESSOR 385
    Aggregative Models 386
    Models of the Elementary Processor 386
    Flow-Diagram Models 387
    Activation of Memory 388
    Automation of Processes 388
CONCLUSION 389

This chapter will review recent progress in modeling human cognitive processes. Particular attention will be paid to the use of computer programming languages as a formalism for modeling, and to computer simulation of the behavior of the systems modeled.

[1]This research was supported by Research Grant MH-07722 from the National Institute of Mental Health.

0066-4308/79/0201-0363$01.00

Theories of human cognitive processes can be attempted at several levels: at the level of neural processes, at the level of elementary information processes (e.g. retrieval from memory, scanning down lists in memory, comparing simple symbols, etc), or at the level of higher mental processes (e.g. problem solving, concept attainment). This chapter will not deal at all with neural models, and it will focus mainly upon higher mental processes, but not without some attention to modeling the elementary processes and especially to the relations between elementary and complex processes.

Computer modeling (and, to a lesser extent, mathematical modeling) tend to encourage attention to process rather than to state functional relations between experimental conditions and outcomes. They also encourage the building of theories that extend over whole ranges of cognitive tasks and experimental settings and that handle the interactions of several cognitive mechanisms (e.g. short-term memory, attentional mechanisms, and fixation in long-term memory) rather than single mechanisms in isolation (105).

Models of cognitive processes pose, in turn, new questions of methodology; in particular, how to obtain data with sufficient temporal density to "track" a system that is operating at millisecond speeds, how to use verbal protocols (one of the best sources of relatively dense observations) as objective reproducible data, and how to compare the theoretical models with the empirical data. This chapter will take brief note of these methodological issues as well as substantive progress in information processing psychology.

ORIGINS OF THE INFORMATION PROCESSING APPROACH

Modeling of human cognition as information processing had to await the appearance of the electronic digital computer at the end of World War II. Actual computer realizations of artificial intelligence systems began to appear about 1955–56 with Selfridge and Dineen's visual pattern recognizer (46, 138) and Newell, Shaw & Simon's Logic Theorist (106). Models intended to serve as psychological theories followed soon thereafter: the General Problem Solver (GPS) (108) and EPAM (55). The ideas were first exposed to psychologists in the pages of the March 1958 issue of the *Psychological Review* (107) and at a RAND Corporation Summer Workshop that same year. [The early history of information processing psychology is treated in more detail in (109), pp. 873ff.]

The simulation models of the 1950s were offspring of the marriage between ideas that had emerged from symbolic logic and cybernetics, on the one side, and Würzburg and Gestalt psychology, on the other. From logic and cybernetics was inherited the idea that information transformation and transmission can be described in terms of the behavior of formally described symbol manipulating systems. From Würzburg and Gestalt psychology were inherited the ideas that long-term memory is an organization of directed associations (139), and that problem solving is a process of selective goal-oriented search (14, 47).

While the new computer simulation models attracted a good deal of interested attention, it was 10 years or more before they had much impact on the mainstream of experimental psychology. The idea that a "machine" could, in any meaningful sense, simulate human mental processes had to overcome initial prejudices and misconceptions about the nature both of machines and people. Analysis of thinking-aloud protocols, one of the principal methods used for comparing the behavior of the models with human behavior, was not a widely used or widely accepted technique in experimental psychology, and was (and still is) sometimes confused with the discredited method of introspection (110).

Perhaps the most important factors that impeded the diffusion of the new ideas, however, were the unfamiliarity of psychologists with computers and the unavailability on most campuses of machines and associated software (list processing programming languages) that were well adapted to cognitive simulation. The 1958 RAND Summer Workshop, mentioned earlier, and similar workshops held in 1962 and 1963, did a good deal to solve the first problem for the 50 or 60 psychologists who participated in them; but workshop members often returned to their home campuses to find their local computing facilities ill adapted to their needs. Only within the past 5 or 10 years can the second problem be said to have been solved to a reasonable degree (e.g. easy availability of LISP or SNOBOL programming languages) at more than a dozen or so universities.

In spite of these difficulties, a steady stream of research in information processing psychology, using computer models, was produced by the half dozen or so laboratories that were active in such research at any one time. (If we include research in artificial intelligence that had important implications for psychology, the active laboratories included those at the RAND Corporation, Carnegie-Mellon University, Massachusetts Institute of Technology, Yale University, the Systems Development Corporation, Stanford University, Stanford Research Institute, the University of Michigan, SUNY Buffalo, the University of North Carolina, the University of Wisconsin, and the University of California at San Diego.)

The period from about 1956 to 1972 saw the emergence of a well-developed theory of problem solving (109), theories of rote verbal learning (55), and theories of the performance of two kinds of induction tasks: concept attainment (69) and sequence extrapolation (153). A substantial beginning had been made in the construction of systems that could process natural language text (96), and initial steps had been taken toward modeling long-term semantic memory (117). A few explorations had been made of the links between cognition and emotion and motivation, psychopathology, and social behavior, but most information processing research during this period was limited to cognitive processes.

A close relation was maintained between work on cognitive simulation and research in artificial intelligence (AI). The laboratories most actively engaged in the former were also heavily involved in the latter, with some overlap of faculty and students between the two efforts. This close relation of AI with cognitive psychology is equally evident today, and is becoming institutionalized under the banner of "cognitive science."

Two books published in 1972 and 1973 provide a review of the state of knowledge and research in information processing psychology in the early 1970s, the date we shall take as the starting point for the main body of our review here. Problem solving and the information processing approach are surveyed by Newell & Simon (109). Natural language processing and the organization of semantic memory are reviewed by Anderson & Bower (9). Unfortunately, there is no equally comprehensive review of the extensive research prior to 1972 on rote verbal learning or on inductive tasks.

PROBLEM SOLVING

By 1972, the main mechanisms for solving well-structured, puzzle-like problems were fairly well understood (109, Chap. 14). Typically, the problem was conceptualized by the solver in terms of a problem space that could be searched selectively for a solution, using such heuristics as means-ends analysis. Computer programs like the General Problem Solver had been shown to exhibit many of the main features of human behavior in these kinds of problem situations.

The past 5 years have seen the extension of these basic ideas in at least five directions:

1. It has been shown that, even in relatively simple problem domains, a number of alternative, basically different strategies may be efficacious for finding solutions (62, 66, 149). Some of these strategies depend strongly on attention to perceptual clues, others upon structures of goals and subgoals held in memory, others upon the discovery of sequential patterns of correct moves. Something has been learned about the range of strategies available and the circumstances under which they are likely to be adopted, and most of the strategies that have been identified have been successfully modeled.

2. Research on the nature of expertness in chess playing and other tasks has deepened our understanding of the kinds of knowledge the expert must have and how that knowledge is stored in long-term memory (LTM) and

evoked by perceptual cues when relevant (30, 31). The storage and evocation of expert knowledge has been modeled for several tasks (17, 18, 25).

3. A good start has been made in exploring problem solving not only in chess but in other semantically rich domains (that is, domains requiring extensive knowledge for solving problems), including problem domains at the level of school subjects. Models have been constructed and tested for specific domains within physics (kinematics, statics, thermodynamics, electronics) and cost accounting (17, 18, 25, 145).

4. So-called "production systems" have been developed and tested extensively as an appropriate formalism for representing cognitive processes in problem-solving tasks (43, 104, 109).

5. The processes of understanding natural language instructions, which precede problem-solving processes, have been modeled successfully for a nontrivial set of problem-solving tasks (71).

We now proceed to review briefly these five strands of development.

Strategies as Intervening Variables

In the familiar Tower of Hanoi puzzle, the solver must move a pyramid of disks from one to another of three pegs, under the conditions that only the top disk on any peg may be moved and a larger disk may never be placed on a smaller (60, 73, 88, 149, 160). A number of strategies can be used to solve the problem that make quite different demands on the information processing system (149). It can be solved by a recursive subgoal strategy [to move k disks from A to C, move (k–1) from A to B, then the kth from A to C, then (k–1) from B to C]; a perceptual strategy (if K is the largest disk not on the target peg, and L is the largest disk that blocks a movement of K, set the goal of moving L out of the way); and a pattern-following strategy (move the disks in the order: 1 2 1 3 1 2 1 4 1 2 1 3 1 2 1 . . .); as well as a rote strategy (the exact sequence of moves is memorized).

The recursive strategy requires a whole "stack" of unrealized goals to be held in short-term memory (STM), while the others do not. The perceptual strategy requires the solver to notice the "largest blocking disk," and so on. At the same time, the recursive and perceptual strategies can both be modeled as special cases of a GPS-like means-ends analysis. Neves (102) has demonstrated the psychological reality of these strategies by showing that subjects can be trained to acquire one or the other with consequent observable differences in eye movements and latencies when they are presented with a particular intermediate situation and asked to make a move.

Although in a given problem space various subjects may use quite different problem-solving strategies, several studies of isomorphs of the missionaries-and-cannibals problem (77, 155) and of water jug problems (12) have shown that a wide range of behavior can be accounted for by simple means-ends strategies with some memory for repetition of moves but little planning or look-ahead (see also 66). It appears not to be necessary to postulate forward planning, as was suggested earlier by Greeno (65), Reed, Ernst & Banerji (119), and Thomas (161), in order to model behavior in these tasks.

The Expert's Knowledge

The bulk of the research on problem solving has been carried out with naive subjects (the ubiquitous college sophomore) on tasks that do not call for much, if any, specific subject-matter knowledge. A major exception has been research on chess, where, since the pioneering investigations of de Groot (44, 45), the decision making and problem solving of grandmasters and masters has been compared with that of lesser players. One of de Groot's important findings was that a master could reconstruct a position from a game (approximately 25 pieces) after having seen it for 5 or 10 seconds, while an ordinary player could remember the locations of only a half dozen pieces after the same exposure. An explanation of this finding has been provided, and the explanatory mechanism modeled, by Chase, Gilmartin, and Simon (30, 31, 151), and the corresponding phenomena examined for the Oriental game of Go by J. Reitman (120), and for bridge by N. Charness (personal communication).

The model, which is essentially an application of the EPAM theory of rote verbal learning (55), assumes that STM has a capacity of about seven chunks, where a chunk is any organization of information that has previously become familiar (e.g. a familiar word, a familiar configuration of pieces on a chess board). When the grandmaster looks at a chess position from a game, he recognizes it as being made up of some half dozen familiar patterns of small groups of pieces (say, three to five pieces each). Since he can hold this much information (a half dozen chunks) in STM, he is able to remember and reconstruct the position. The ordinary player, however, not having the same repertory of familiar chunks stored in LTM, encodes the position as a configuration of 25 separate pieces, but he is able to hold only about a half dozen of these in STM.

Simon & Gilmartin (151) simulated this contrast with an EPAM-like program, which had a limited STM capacity. At the outset, the system could retain information for about only a half dozen pieces in its STM. To simulate the master's performance, the program was exposed to a large number of configurations of pieces that commonly occur on the chessboard during games, and gradually stored these patterns in LTM. After this familiarization training, the program could recognize these patterns when it encountered them in a new chess position, and could encode them in STM as single symbols "pointing" to the associated information in LTM. With about 1300 familiar patterns stored in LTM, the program approximated the performance of a Class A player, but not a master. It was estimated that familiarity with some 50,000 patterns would be required to match the performance of a chess master or grandmaster.

Semantically Rich Domains

The game of chess is an example of a *semantically rich* domain, i.e. a task domain in which successful performance calls for specific knowledge as well as general problem-solving skill. Increasingly, research on problem solving (in artificial intelligence as well as psychology) has addressed itself to such domains.

The central research questions are two: (*a*) how much knowledge does an expert or professional in the domain have stored in LTM (30), and (*b*) how is that knowledge organized and accessed so that it can be brought to bear upon specific problems (39, 80, 126)? Among the domains other than chess that have received some attention are chemical engineering thermodynamics (18), mechanics (112, 145), electronics (25), cost accounting (17), business policy (17), medical diagnosis (43, 115, 141), and identification of molecules with mass spectrograph data (56).

The question of how much knowledge the expert needs can be answered by artificial intelligence studies as well as by psychological research. In order for a medical diagnosis program, for example, to perform as accurately as a physician, the program must have available to it the same knowledge of symptomology that the physician has. The most successful existing diagnosis programs are organized as *production systems* (see next section), that is, as sets of conditional actions ("If conditions X, Y, and Z hold, then do W"). We can measure the size of such a program by the number of productions it contains. MYCIN (141), which diagnoses bacterial diseases at a professional level, and INTERNIST (115), which diagnoses internal ailments, each contain several hundred productions. If we reflect that the professional knowledge of a physician deals not only with symptomology but also with treatment, including a more or less deep understanding of the biochemical and physiological mechanisms underlying medical phenomena, we might estimate that his professional knowledge is equivalent to some thousands of productions—a number not out of line with our estimate that the chess master is familiar with tens of thousands of recurring patterns in that game.

None of the psychological models simulating problem solving in semantically rich domains has reached the size of the artificial intelligence models. From the experiments with tasks in physics (18, 145), it would appear that the knowledge communicated in a typical textbook chapter can be embedded in a set of a dozen or so productions. This would lead again to the estimate that mastering a course is equivalent to acquiring a few hundred productions, and achieving professional competence in a subject like physics, acquiring some thousands or tens of thousands. All of the studies that have been carried out in different task domains provide a reasonably consistent picture of the amount of knowledge that is required for professional levels of skill.

Production Systems

An adequate theory of human cognitive processes must include a description of the *control system*—the mechanism that determines the sequence in which operations will be performed (94). Traditional computer programming languages, in which one process "calls" another through a hierarchy of routines and subroutines, appear far too rigid to simulate the flexible way in which newly appearing stimuli or new ideas recovered from long-term memory may repeatedly divert the course of human thought.

Production systems (104, 109) provide an alternative, and much more flexible, method of controlling the sequence of thought. A production system is a set of instructions called *productions*. Each production consists of two parts: a *condition* and an *action*. The basic rule of interpretation is that whenever the condition of a production is satisfied, the action of that production will be executed. Additional rules are needed to determine which production will fire when the conditions of several are satisfied simultaneously. Production systems have been widely used for several decades as computer programming formalisms.

In application to cognitive psychology, the conditions in productions are tests applied to stimuli (perceptual conditions) or to the symbols that are held in STM. Thus, the presence in STM of the symbol denoting a certain word can cause the action of recognizing that word to be executed, i.e. locating in LTM the information about it that is stored there. Similarly, a pattern of pieces on a chess board may constitute the condition for recognizing that pattern—accessing the information about it in LTM. Thus, the scheme described earlier for storing the chess master's knowledge is essentially a production system, with the EPAM discrimination net serving as an "index" to the conditions.

The condition-action pair in a production bears an obvious resemblance to the stimulus-response pair in classical S-R psychology. The idea of modeling psychological processes with production systems, proposed in the early 1970s (104, 109), has since been pursued by a number of investigators (5, 100, 104, 149). Production systems have also been used in several of the AI schemes mentioned earlier for modeling problem solving in semantically rich domains (56, 115, 141). Several production system languages have now been built specifically for cognitive simulation, incorporating specific psychological assumptions about the organization of STM and LTM (5, 21, 104).

Production systems also show great promise for modeling learning processes, for it is not hard to construct *adaptive production systems* (166) that are capable of generating new productions and adding these to the system.

Understanding Processes

Before a person can attempt to solve a problem, he must understand or assimilate a description of the problem (67). In most problem-solving research, a period of instruction and training precedes the experiment proper, so that subjects may assimilate the problem before the experimenter begins to record data on the solution process itself. If we believe the adage that "a problem well formulated is half solved," then the standard experimental procedure loses half of the interesting phenomena of problem solving— specifically, the processes of understanding.

Similarly, information processing models of the problem-solving process have generally taken as their inputs a formalized representation of the already assimilated problem whose problem space is already defined. These models also assume that an initial understanding process has previously run to completion.

During the past 5 years, progress has been made in exploring and modeling the problem assimilation process for the (usual) case where the problem is presented initially in the form of natural language instructions (70). On the empirical side, this progress has largely stemmed from experiments using problem *isomorphs* (72, 152). An isomorph of a problem is another problem whose legal moves can be mapped in a one-to-one fashion on the legal moves of the original problem. For example, number scrabble is an isomorph of the familiar game of tic-tac-toe. In number scrabble, nine tiles, numbered from 1 to 9, are placed face up between the two players. The players draw single tiles alternately, and the player who is first able to complete a triad of tiles whose numbers add to 15 wins the game. To see the isomorphism of this game with tic-tac-toe, map the tile number 5 on the center square, the remaining tiles having odd numbers on the squares along the sides, and the tiles having even numbers on the corners, in such a way that each row, column, and diagonal adds to 15.

Numerous isomorphs and homomorphs (many-one mappings of legal moves) are known for tic-tac-toe (98), for the Missionaries and Cannibals puzzle (65), and for the Tower of Hanoi puzzle (72, 152). A common way to create problem isomorphs is to clothe the rules of the problem in various "cover stories."

Empirical research on problem isomorphs has demonstrated that skill gained in solving one form of a problem will not always transfer to isomorphic forms of the same problem—the transfer often being asymmetric. [Generally there will be transfer from a harder to an easier isomorph, but little transfer on the opposite direction (65, 72).] A second important finding is that rather minor and seemingly "innocent" changes in the cover story for a problem—for example, a change from active to passive voice—can alter the time required for solution by as much as a factor of two (72). Third, it has been shown that the changes in problem difficulty are associated with changes in the problem representation that the solver assimilates from the instructions (72, 152). That is to say, certain forms of the problem instructions induce the solver to adopt one problem representation that permits him to solve the problem easily, while other forms of the instructions induce him to adopt a different representation that makes solution difficult. In the Tower of Hanoi, for example, when the solver represents the problem as requiring the transfer of objects from one locus to another it is much easier to solve than when he represents it as requiring changes in the properties of objects at various loci.

The process of assimilating problem instructions was first modeled in Bobrow's (20) STUDENT program, which was able to understand and solve algebra story problems. This program made a direct, syntactic translation from the natural language of the problem statements to the algebraic equations. STUDENT was shown to provide a good simulation of the behavior of some human subjects solving simple algebra problems, but not of other subjects who made more use of semantic information (113). The UNDERSTAND program (70, 71) models the assimilation process for puzzle-like problems like the Tower of Hanoi isomorphs, and is able to account for the way in which changes in the problem statement produce changes in the resulting problem representation. An artificial intelligence program, ISAAC (112), assimilates physics (statics) problems written in natural language, creating an intermediate, qualitative representation of the problem ("physical representation") which it then uses as an aid to constructing the appropriate algebraic equations. Detailed evidence is not yet available on the correspondence of ISAAC's physical representation to what is usually called "physical intuition," but there is a good chance that the former will cast important light on the nature of the latter (J. Larkin and J. McDermott, personal communication).

Protocol Analysis

The basic information processes that have been postulated for most of the computer simulations of problem solving are processes that take from a few hundred milliseconds to a few seconds for their execution. Verifying that processes like these are actually being executed by the problem solver is not a trivial methodological task.

Of course much of the testing of these theories, as of any scientific theories, is of an indirect nature. A theoretical model is postulated, certain observable consequences are deduced from the model, and these consequences are compared with the observed data. If a simulation model of a problem-solving task predicts the relative frequency of different moves, and if the moves are observed actually to occur with approximately those relative frequencies, then to that extent the model has received support from the data—even though there has been no direct observation of the component processes of the model. The model has been shown *sufficient* to account for these data. Neither these nor any other data could show that the model was *necessary*, that no alternative model could produce the same data.

Nevertheless, our confidence in a theoretical explanation of phenomena will be the greater the more points of contact there are between theory and empirical observations and the more detailed are the components of the theory that can be confronted directly with data. There is a great deal to be gained, therefore, in the testing of process theories if we can increase the temporal density of our data points so as to increase the number of testable predictions of the theory relative to the number of its degrees of freedom.

In problem-solving tasks, overt subject responses ("moves") generally take of the order of seconds, or even tens of seconds. Two methods have been successful for interpolating additional observations between these responses: recording eye movements and recording verbal protocols when the subject thinks aloud as he solves the problem (109). Typically, eye fixations succeed each other at intervals of a quarter second or a little longer. Likewise, a subject who is thinking aloud may emit statements at intervals of a fraction of a second to a few seconds. Eye movements tend to provide a denser stream of data than verbal utterances, but the latter, because their potential variety is limited only by the richness of natural language, tend to contain far more information. Under favorable circumstances, the two data-gathering techniques can be used simultaneously.

Just & Carpenter (79) have recently demonstrated how eye movement data can be used to test models of processing in a variety of tasks: processing rotated figures (cf 40), comparing sentences with figures, and making quantitative comparisons. The basic assumption they make in order to relate eye fixations to the theoretical processing model is that the eye fixates at each moment the referent, in the visual display, of the symbol being operated upon at that moment.

The usefulness of subjects' verbalizations as data for testing theoretical models also rests on some assumptions that have been tested to a limited extent but by no means thoroughly. The issues include these: 1. To what extent and under what circumstances can a subject produce a thinking-aloud protocol without interfering with his performance of the problem-solving task? 2. To what extent do the verbalizations provide a complete record of the basic information processes that are being executed, or any record at all? How closely does a protocol track the actual solution process?

The available evidence on these points has recently been reviewed by Ericsson (50). He concludes that thinking aloud does not interfere with, or significantly modify, task performance provided that: (a) the thinking-aloud instructions are "bland" and do not direct the subject to produce specific kinds of information, and (b) the instructions are given in such a way that the subject assigns first priority to performing the task. To inter-pret the content of the verbalizations, it should be assumed that the subject will report aloud (a) some subset of the symbolized information that is held in STM during performance of the task (e.g. the inputs and outputs to the basic processes), (b) provided that the internal encoding of this information allows it to be expressed easily in words. By the last condition we may expect fuller verbal reports when the stimuli are themselves verbal than when they are pictorial, and this appears to be the case.

Since the thinking-aloud protocols are expressed in natural language, they must be encoded before they can be compared with the trace of the simulation model to be tested. This raises the question of the objectivity and reproducibility of the coding process. An additional practical difficulty is that coding verbal protocols is an exceedingly arduous and tedious task. Some attention has been given to solving or alleviating the problems of coding objectivity and difficulty by fully or partially automating the process.

Waterman & Newell (167) constructed PAS-II, an interactive computer system for automatic protocol analysis. This system must be provided, by hand, with a formal description of the problem space in which the subject is operating as he solves the problem. Using this description, and supplied with the thinking-aloud protocol, PAS-II will encode the subject's state-ments in terms of the information they contain and the operations they imply. Inability to encode particular statements in the protocol will reveal errors in the assumptions about the subject's problem space.

Bhaskar & Simon (18) developed a less ambitious system, SAPA (Semi-automated Protocol Analyser), which also operates interactively with the coder. SAPA requires a gross model of the problem-solving process and prompts the user to encode each successive protocol segment, using the model to generate the prompting questions. When the protocol segment does not fill the category anticipated by the prompt, the coder uses a "breakout" feature in the SAPA program to encode the actual segment. Thus, SAPA reveals immediately whenever the sequence of statements in the protocol departs from the sequence predicted by the model.

High intercoder reliability can be attained with encoding systems like PAS-II and SAPA, and such systems appear also to reduce substantially the tediousness of the encoding task.

SEMANTIC MEMORY

An extremely active area in information processing psychology today is the modeling of semantic long-term memory. As long as cognitive theory and research concerned itself mainly with relatively abstract task domains, where the nature and organization of the information that the subject brought with him to the laboratory was not a central concern, only relatively sketchy models of long-term memory were required to account for the phenomena under study. Today a good deal of research is directed at understanding the ways in which large bodies of semantic information referring to complex task domains are stored in long-term memory and accessed.

A theory of LTM must account both for the organization of information stored in the memory (the "text") and for the routes by means of which information in the memory can be accessed (the "index"). [For a discussion of these two components of LTM and their relation, see (150).] Since Aristotle, the "text" of LTM has been supposed to be associative, so that sequences of items can be retrieved by searching along links that connect them. The "index," on the other hand, links LTM to the senses, permitting stored information to be accessed by *recognition* of stimulus patterns. By the former, associative, route, if a person is thinking about John, this may remind him of Mary (give him access to information about Mary), who is a friend of John. By the latter, recognition, route, sight of a picture of Mary, or of Mary herself, may give access to the same information.

Until the present decade, there was little modeling of the associative structure, the text, of LTM. An important early exception was W. Reitman's ARGUS system (121), which solved analogy problems by searching along relational links in an associative net. The theory of verbal learning, EPAM (55), mentioned earlier, incorporated a model of the recognition mechanisms of LTM (the "index") but did not need a detailed model of the associative connections within the memory. It has already been mentioned that EPAM has more recently been used successfully as one component of a model of expert knowledge (151).

In this earlier period, not much effort was devoted to modeling the processing of natural language. Although automatic translation of natural language was an early goal of artificial intelligence research, there was relatively little interaction between the machine translation projects and either traditional linguistics or psycholinguistics. (An early exception was Lindsay's SAD SAM program (96), which understood statements in Basic English about genealogies, and stored them in a semantic memory in such a way as to permit implicit relations to be inferred. Another exception was the BASEBALL program (64), a system for answering natural-language questions, which was oriented more toward AI than toward psycholinguistics.)

This situation changed rapidly with the publication of Quillian's model (117, 118) of a semantic network for storing information presented in natural language. Although the experimental evidence adduced to support the psychological validity of Quillian's memory model was relatively modest (38, 127), the general idea of representing semantic knowledge by a node-link structure caught hold as a result of his proposal. Several semantic memory models employing this node-link structure are under active development today (1, 2, 5, 9, 111, 135, 144), and some experimental work has been initiated to test their predictive power.

Two basic ideas are central to all of these systems: *node-link structures* and *schemata.* The former of these may be thought of as realizations of the directed associations of the Würzburg psychologists, while the latter are descendants, if some generations distant, of the schemata of Bartlett's *Remembering* (13).

Suppose that we consider the following abstract memory scheme (9, 109): There is a set of *symbols,* each of which is stored at a *node.* When certain familiar stimuli are presented to the system (through its visual senses, say), it *recognizes* the stimuli, i.e. it accesses the appropriate node and stores in STM a symbol designating that node. (This is the "index" or EPAM-like part of the system.) Each node in memory is connected with a number of other nodes by *links* that designate relations. Thus, the relation "superordinate" may link the "cat" node to the "animal" node, while the relation "coordinate" may link the "cat" node to the "leopard" and "tiger" nodes. These relational links are the directed associations.

By the use of the associational links, there may be stored at a node a description of the object or event designated by that node. If a node designates a type or class (e.g. "cat"), the information associated with that node may define and describe the characteristics of members of that class. Many of these characteristics, of course, are variable (not all cats are identical). We can think of these variable characteristics as "slots" that can be filled in or *instantiated* with information describing any particular member of the class. Descriptions of this kind, containing variables that can be instantiated, have been called schemata or schemas (14, 111, 130), templates (147), frames (99), and scripts (135). While these concepts are not quite synonymous (scripts, for example, are schemata describing classes of event sequences), it is worth emphasizing the basic similarities before concerning ourselves with the relatively minor, if possibly significant, distinctions.

The schemata in terms of which a semantic memory is organized may have either a topical or an episodic character (168). The nodes of topical schemata represent objects (e.g. the New York Public Library, the oak tree on my front lawn) or concepts (e.g. tree, truth, revolution). The nodes of episodic schemata represent a system of temporally and causally related events. Thus, in a topically organized memory, associated with a node for "restaurant" could be all sorts of information about restaurants: their purpose, physical layout, organization and staffing, and so on—the contents of a handbook on restaurants (111). In an episodically organized memory, the schema associated with "restaurant" could be a *script* (135), describing the typical sequences of events that occur when one enters a restaurant. There seems to be no reason, in principle, why a node-link memory should not have aspects of both topical and episodic organization—the same basic machinery will support either or both. There is, of course, a genuine *psychological* question of the extent to which human memory is actually organized in either of these ways.

Semantic memories have frequently been designed to model the way in which natural language inputs are processed and added to the memory store (57, 58, 63, 93). These memory designs may differ with respect to depth of processing, that is to say, the amount of encoding the input strings undergo before they can be stored in the node-link structure. In Quillian's initial scheme (117, 118), the processing was quite shallow; the structures stored in memory bore a close resemblance to the clauses of the original input sentences. In Schank's conceptual dependency proposal (132–134), the input strings are transformed into a small number (one or two dozen) of different types of semantic structures. From a linguistic point of view, the encoded structures may be viewed as representing the "deep structure" of the input linguistic strings, and different depths of processing correspond to different theories about the relation of linguistic deep structure to linguistic utterances. Clearly, Schank's proposal calls for deeper processing, including more semantic transformation, than does Quillian's.

Again, one can ask the associated psychological question: how is natural language actually transformed before it is stored in LTM? (5, pp. 390–406). The well-known experiments of Bransford and Franks (23, 24) demonstrated that when subjects were given tasks that required them only to retain meanings, they failed to store much of the syntactical detail of stimulus sentences. Extending the Bransford-Franks paradigm, Rosenberg & Simon (128) showed that subjects were frequently unable to remember whether they had seen a particular sentence or a simple picture having the same semantic meaning as the sentence. Similarly, bilingual subjects were frequently unable to remember whether they had seen a particular sentence in French or only its translation in English. A computer simulation model

(128) of semantic memory, making use of Schrank's conceptual dependency scheme (132), explained not only these gross findings, but much of the fine structure of the data as well (e.g. why certain sentences and not others were confused).

A model of semantic memory may be evaluated in terms of its ability to handle the range of tasks that are handled in human memory (3–8, 10, 81, 95, 97, 125, 129, 131, 156, 162, 163). Anderson (3), for example, undertakes to evaluate his ACT system by looking at human performance in such tasks as free recall, inferential thought, verbal learning, language comprehension, and the induction of rules. Schank & Abelson (135) have explored the properties of a memory organized in terms of scripts, plans, and goals by building programs for understanding stories, telling stories, and skimming stories on the basis of information stored in such a memory (see also 19, 29). Similarly, the problem-solving systems for semantically rich domains, described in a previous section, can be evaluated in terms of their ability to store in appropriate form the information needed for problem solving in their respective domains (26, 39, 48).

Node-link memories of all species have been used in these programs to produce "humanoid" behavior in a wide variety of tasks, even to handle visual imagery (15, 53, 89, 90, 101, 114, 165). Empirical data that would allow us to discriminate among the schemes in terms of their veridicality as human simulators are hard to come by. The safest conclusion at the present time is that human LTM can probably be represented as a node-link memory with an EPAM-like index, but that various alternatives are still open for the detailed structure and organization of that memory.

INDUCTION OF PATTERNS

The human ability to detect order or pattern in stimuli is an important competence that has received considerable attention from information processing psychologists. A number of different tasks, familiar from the psychological laboratory, fall under this general heading, in particular, concept attainment and extrapolating sequential patterns.

The 1960s saw the successful construction of an information processing theory that explained some of the main phenomena of concept attainment (22, 69, 169), and a theory that explained the human ability to discover the patterns in sequences of letters or numbers and to extrapolate such sequences (91, 123, 146, 153). With wide acceptance of these theories, attention during the past 5 years has turned to (a) generalizing the theories to a wider range of induction tasks and defining a unified theory that holds over that range, and (b) explaining variation in behavior as a function of task instructions and other conditions of the tasks.

In addition to concept attainment (69) and sequence extrapolation (91) tasks, analogies tasks (26, 52, 75), grammar induction tasks (5, 87, 143, 164), formula induction tasks (61, 74) and others have been studied by investigators in artificial intelligence and cognitive psychology. In substantially all of the processing schemes that have been proposed to explain human performance in these tasks, the core consists of a generate-and-test scheme that proposes successive hypotheses (concepts or patterns), and tests them against a set of instances.

Needless to say, the hypotheses are not generated completely randomly, but are functions of the instances themselves. In concept attainment experiments, the task instructions or the initial instances provide information about the potentially relevant dimensions and values that can enter into the definition of the concept, while hypothesis-generation in the sequence extrapolation task starts with a small set of primitive relations (e.g. "same" and "next") that can be detected in the stimuli and combined into more complex patterns (91). It is the feedback of information from the instances and, in the more complex tasks, the incremental generation of the full hypotheses, that enables pattern to be discovered in quite large problem spaces with a moderate amount of processing.

The various inductive tasks have been compared by Egan & Greeno (49) and by Simon & Lea (154), and the latter have shown, by constructing a formal model (General Rule Inducer), how a single processing system can account for performance in concept attainment, sequence extrapolation, and grammar induction tasks. The executive program for GRI is exhibited in Figure 1.

Simon & Lea (154) have also observed that rule-induction tasks can be interpreted as problem-solving tasks using a dual problem space instead of a simple problem space. The two components of the dual space are a space of rules and a space of instances. Induction involves a problem-solving search in the rule space (for a rule satisfying certain conditions), using information extracted from the space of instances to guide the search and

---

General Rule Inducer:

1. generate rules (→ rules);
       generate instances (→ instance);
          classify instance by rules (→ instance-class);
          test instance-class (→ test-result).
          if test-result = "correct" tally = tally + 1,
             else set tally = 0;
          if tally = criterion exit, else go to 1.

Figure 1   Executive program for the General Rule Inducer.

make it selective. Thus, concept attainment involves a search for a particular concept in the space of possible concepts, testing each candidate solution against instances, supplied by experimenter or subject, in the other space. This formulation of rule induction provides more than just a metaphor, for it makes available to the rule-induction system all of the processes used in problem solving.

Of course any proposal for a "general" theory of rule induction—or of problem solving, for that matter—must account for the fact that there are wide individual differences in behavior in these task environments, and that these differences can be enlarged further by relatively small changes in the conditions under which the tasks are performed. Individual differences can be accommodated in the processing models in at least two different ways. First, individuals may differ in the primitive predicates and relations that are available to them for forming concepts. Hunt (76) has shown how items on the Raven Progressive Matrices Test might be solved by means of two quite different kinds of methods, one using perceptual Gestalt-like predicates and relations, the other by more cognitive and analytic predicates and relations. Some test items, however, can be solved only with the analytic procedures, hence subjects using these would succeed on these items while subjects using only the others would fail. Hunt does not offer any direct empirical evidence that these two distinct procedures are, in fact, used by different groups of subjects, but he makes a plausible case for the possibility.

Even if individuals use the same basic predicates, relations, and processes, their task behavior may be quite different if they use dissimilar strategies for organizing those elements. As in the theory of problem solving, the subject's strategy becomes a crucial intervening variable between the task environment in which he works and the behavior he produces. Some strategies may be more effective than others, but effective strategies may be difficult to discover, and it must not be assumed, particularly in unfamiliar tasks, that all subjects will come equipped with the best strategies or will be able to find them during the experimental session. For example, Gregg & Simon (69) have shown that large differences in number of trials required to learn simple concepts could be produced by rather small differences in the amount of information about previous instances that subjects are able to hold in short-term memory. Recent research (68, 78, 124) has shown that rather subtle differences may be detected in the ways in which subjects encode serial patterns, partly as a function of the patterns themselves and partly as a function of individual differences.

LEARNING AND DEVELOPMENT

Most computer simulations and other large-scale models of cognitive processes have, in the past, been concerned with the performance of tasks rather than either with learning to perform them or with the development of cognitive capabilities through childhood and adolescence. In the quite recent past, initial steps have been taken to fill this gap.

The strategy of building theories of performance prior to attempting theories of learning is understandable. It is hard to construct a model of learning until there is some understanding of what is learned: what knowledge and skills are acquired, and how they are organized and represented in long-term memory. Once the memory structures of the skilled performer are somewhat understood, then it seems feasible to undertake the task of specifying processes for creating those memory structures. Whether or not this strategy has been a conscious one in the cognitive psychology of the past two decades, it does describe the actual course of events. Learning theory has not been nearly as prominent as it was in the period just before and just after World War II.

One recent direction of concern with learning has already been discussed in a previous section: the construction of programs that understand problem instructions and generate representations for new problem-solving tasks. In this section, a number of others will be considered:

1. Models of children's performance in Piagetian tasks which, while they are performance models and not learning models, constitute a first step toward building a developmental theory in information-processing terms.
2. Models of language acquisition processes and of learning in semantic networks.
3. Adaptive production systems and applications of this kind of system to specific kinds of learning tasks.

Performance of Piagetian Tasks

Piagetian theory implies that at different developmental stages the child employs different programs to perform the same tasks. A first step toward understanding the information processing that underlies stages of development would be to construct programs, in the form, say, of production systems, that would simulate these alternative processing methods. This general strategy has been followed by Klahr & Wallace (82–86), Baylor & Gascon (16) and Young (170). For example, Klahr & Wallace (86) describe production systems for quantitative comparison, quantification, class inclusion, conservation of quantity, and transitivity of quantity. For each of these tasks one would want a whole sequence of production systems, modeling the performance of children at different levels of proficiency on the same task.

The second step toward a developmental theory would be to explain how the child could move from the less advanced and sophisticated production systems for doing a given task to the more advanced. Up to the present, only some preliminaries have been accomplished toward taking this step. Klahr & Wallace (e.g. 86, p. 102 and Chap. 8) have discussed the problem in general terms, while Siegler (142) has demonstrated experimentally some attentional and perceptual differences between lower-level and higher-level programs for a balance-beam task, and has shown how training can enable children to move from the lower to the higher level. The concept of an adaptive production system, which will be discussed below, offers a promising technique for building models of this learning process, but such modeling has not yet been carried out for Piagetian tasks.

Language Acquisition

The acquisition of language is one of the most fundamental of all human learning processes. A number of attempts have been made to model the process, the most recent and the most successful being those by Anderson (5), and Siklóssy (143). For example, Siklóssy (143) assumes that most early language learning takes place in the presence of the situations denoted by the language. The child, according to this assumption, learns the meaning of "the cat drinks the milk" in the presence of a cat drinking milk. It is assumed that the child already has some way of representing the scene internally (presumably in the form of list structures), and the language learning task therefore involves mapping the components of the sentence on the components of the representation of the scene. Thus, the words "cat" and "milk" must be mapped on those two objects, respectively, and "is drinking" on the representation of the relations between them.

The learning in Siklóssy's scheme is incremental. When a scene is presented, along with a sentence describing it, if the system already understands all but one component (object name or name of relation), it can infer the meaning of the single unknown word. Thus, it gradually builds up new word meanings and new grammatical structures. While none of the existing language acquisition schemes has been shown to be adequate to handle complex scenes or sentences, they provide a promising set of ideas for the further development of models of language acquisition.

Adaptive Production Systems

An adaptive production system is a production system that is capable of building new productions and adding them to the original system. An early demonstration of the feasibility of this kind of learning system was provided by Waterman (166), who constructed an adaptive production system for learning to play the game of poker skilfully. The system utilized its experience during play to discover the conditions under which particular actions were advantageous and to form these new condition-action pairs into new productions.

Since that initial demonstration, adaptive production systems have been constructed for a number of different tasks. A recent example is a program (D. Neves, personal communication) that discovers an algorithm for solving linear algebraic equations by examining a single worked-out example of the sort that are presented in algebra textbooks. The system uses means-ends analysis like that employed in the General Problem Solver. By examining each pair of successive expressions in the example, the program finds what action has been performed to transform the algebraic equation, and detects a characteristic of the initial expression that motivated the step. Thus, for example, the transformation from $4X = 2X + 10$ to $2X = 10$ involves subtraction of $2X$ from both sides of the equation. It is motivated by the presence of a term in X on the right-hand side of the original expression. The system then creates a new production equivalent to: "Whenever there is an expression in X on the right-hand side of the equation, subtract that expression from both sides."

A worked-out example is only one of many contexts in which an adaptive production system can be made to learn successfully. The construction of such systems to explain learning phenomena is currently a very active area of investigation in cognitive simulation.

MOTIVATION AND EMOTION

Relatively little modeling has been done of motivational and emotional processes or of their interaction with cognitive processes. A major exception (35, 36, 54) is Kenneth Colby's model, PERRY, of a paranoid patient, which illustrates well the problems and possibilities in this domain. [See also (136) on modeling of social perception.]

In any computer model of cognitive processes there is, of course, at least an implicit motivational mechanism. A problem-solving program has to be "motivated" to solve problems, a pattern-discovery program, to search for pattern. However, this motivational mechanism is usually trivially embedded in the top, executive level of the program. The program is provided with a test of task completion, and continues to engage in a sequence of potentially relevant activities until the test is satisfied or a specified effort limit has been reached. The program attempts to solve the problem "because it is there." The activity is simply switched on, and the program says nothing psychologically interesting about the switching mechanism.

A central difficulty that has to be faced in modeling the interaction of motivation and emotion with cognition is that the communication codes appear to be so radically different in the affective and cognitive subsystems. Information in the cognitive system (or at least a considerable part of it) is encoded symbolically, while the signaling systems for motivation and emotion appear much more analogical and continuous. Davis & Levine (42), for example, have constructed a servomechanism model to explain the rates at which an organism ingests food as a function of palatability and cumulated amount ingested. Their model operates entirely in terms of real magnitudes and mathematical functions relating them. The problem is to specify how mechanisms of this quantitative sort could influence the course of thinking rather than simply the rate of eating.

Colby (35, 36) handles this problem in the PERRY simulation by introducing real numbers to represent the levels of affect—for example, anger, fear, and mistrust. The responses of PERRY to the statements or questions of its interlocutor depend on two factors: (a) the current levels of these affective variables, and (b) words or phrases in the communications that are associated in PERRY's memory with the cognitive content of his delusion topic, or that can be interpreted by him as personal references. Thus, the level of affect determines the sensitivity threshhold of PERRY to symbols that are capable of triggering defenses or evoking his delusions. When the threshholds are high (anger and fear are low), PERRY is capable of connected discourse of a "normal" sort; although references to personal themes on which he is sensitive (sex, personal appearance, family) or to matters related to the topic of the delusion can trigger off paranoid responses. When anger and fear are high, PERRY will usually defend himself by a verbal attack on his interlocutor (anger), or by withdrawal (fear).

The affect levels, in turn, are increased, slightly or sharply, when cues are detected in the interlocutor's speech that evoke these sensitive themes and delusions. Affect, once evoked, subsides only gradually (anger most rapidly, mistrust most slowly), even if not further cued. Thus, there is a two-way associative linkage in the model between the levels of affect, represented as numerical quantities, and the symbolic, cognitive content of long-term memory.

The theory of paranoia incorporated in PERRY is not novel; it represents, as Colby has pointed out, a widely (though not universally) held hypothesis about the mechanisms causing paranoid behavior. Nor is PERRY a particularly parsimonious model of these mechanisms—it does not produce the surprise we like to receive from scientific theories, of generating much from little. Nevertheless, it does test, as do other simulation models, whether the simple mechanisms it postulates are sufficient to produce behavior of the kind that is observed in humans. Colby has had some sucesss in using a Turing Test to demonstrate this sufficiency (35). Protocols produced by PERRY when interacting with a psychiatrist conducting a diagnostic interview with the program cannot be reliably distinguished by other psychiatrists from protocols produced by paranoid human patients; and psychiatrists can distinguish "mildly paranoid" versions of

PERRY (parameters for affective variables less volatile) from "strongly paranoid" versions (parameters more volatile). Since the capabilities of the present model for understanding natural language are rather unsophisticated, there is reason to believe that the verisimilitude of the simulation could be increased by an improvement of its language-processing component.

THE ELEMENTARY PROCESSOR

Both computer simulation and stochastic models (11, 51, 69) have been constructed to describe cognitive processes. This account is limited to the former. The modeling of cognition in information processing terms has been pursued at two "levels," distinguishable by the nature of the experimental tasks used to test the models. At the higher, more aggregative level has been the modeling of processes in problem-solving, concept-attainment, rule-induction, and language-processing tasks. Most of the preceding pages of this chapter have been devoted to models at this level. At the lower, more detailed level is the modeling of processes in the simpler sorts of tasks that are commonly employed in reaction-time studies. These more detailed models have been especially concerned with the structure and operation of STM and with the interface between cognition and perception. The mechanisms postulated at this more microscopic level are sometimes referred to collectively as the *elementary processor,* and I shall use that term here to denote them.

Until quite recently, most models could be assigned relatively unambiguously to one or the other of these levels, even though the boundary between them is not sharp. Performance of complex tasks depends, quite as much as performance of simple ones, upon the operation of STM and the perceptual apparatus. The data that are observed, however (e.g. thinking-aloud protocols), may not depend much upon the *details* of that apparatus, but only upon some of its gross properties. In that case, it may be (and in fact has been) possible to model the behavior without modeling the details of the elementary processor.

In recent research, however, and especially in the research on semantic memory that has been surveyed above, it has been felt necessary to construct models that depict the elementary mechanisms in some detail, but depict them as organized components of the "whole cognitive person," so that the models will be capable of performing in complex as well as in simple task environments. Models of this genre undertake to stimulate both aggregated and elementary information processes.

The discussion will proceed here first by summarizing the assumptions about the elementary processor that are implicit in models of higher mental processes, and then by examining some examples of models of the elementary processor and the techniques that are used to test their validity.

Aggregative Models

In models of problem solving, concept attainment, or rule induction, the processor is assumed to have both LTM and STM. The LTM is assumed to be associatively organized, to have unlimited capacity, to have a relatively slow storage time (about 8 sec per familiar chunk), and a slightly faster accessing time (of the order of 2 sec). The STM is assumed to have a relatively short storage and access time (a few hundred msec per familiar chunk), but a very limited capacity (perhaps not more than 4 chunks). A relatively rapid recognition process, also requiring no more than a few hundred msec, allows information in LTM to be accessed in the presence of familiar stimuli or stimulus components. [For somewhat more complete characterizations of these models, see (109, 148, 150).] The psychological processes these models postulate generally require a fraction of a second to several seconds for execution.

The assumptions about memory structure in the aggregative models tend to be implicit rather than explicit. The associative character of LTM is automatically provided by writing the simulation programs in list-processing languages in which this feature is already incorporated (9, 109). The slow fixation speed in LTM is reflected in the absence of mechanisms for significant learning during the performance of a task of less than an hour's duration. The limited capacity of STM is reflected in the limited amount of information the system uses in problem-solving search or in selecting new hypotheses for concept-attainment tasks. In models that are written as production systems, limits are generally imposed on the complexity of the conditions that are allowed in any single production. Thus, the aggregative models tend to focus upon the structure of cognitive strategies rather than upon the details of the underlying memory structures and elementary processes that support those strategies.

Models of the Elementary Processor

In contrast, models of the elementary processor make quite explicit many of the assumptions that are left implicit in the aggregative models. On the side of LTM, they incorporate quite definite specifications for the associative structure and for the ways in which stimuli—for example, natural-language sentences—are encoded into the structure (9, Chap. 4–8; 41). On the side of STM, they incorporate definite specifications for capacity or decay rates, for the ordering of symbols in the memory, and for the storage and accessing processes (103, 104, 137, 140).

An example of a model of the elementary processor is Newell's PSG system (104). PSG is a "pure" production system: That is, its explicit LTM consists of a set of productions. The conditions of these productions are tests on the contents of STM, and the actions include introducing symbols into or removing symbols from STM, inputting stimulus symbols into STM, and outputting symbols externally. Since symbols in STM may be compound symbol structures, these structures actually provide a second implicit component of LTM.

To perform in a particular task environment, PSG must be provided with a set of productions that constitutes a strategy for that task. For example, Newell simulates behavior in the S. Sternberg symbol scanning paradigm (159) with a system of 9 productions. One of these productions loads the positive set into STM; another loads the probe digit; two more compare probe digit with the digits of the positive set, and respond "yes" or "no." The remaining 5 productions unpack the positive set in STM so that these symbols can be compared, one by one, with the probe.

This is not the place to discuss the verisimilitude of the model (it does simulate nonterminating search, as the experimental data require). I simply wish to illustrate what constitutes an elementary process in a model of this kind. Two alternative accounts of an elementary strategy for the S. Sternberg paradigm, embedded in the HAM and ACT models of the elementary processor, respectively, are proposed in (9, pp. 373–76) and in (5, pp. 312–13). It can be seen that the behavior observed in the paradigm is compatible with a number of different processing models, and hence cannot be taken by itself as a verification of any one of them.

Flow-Diagram Models

Not all models of the elementary processor take the form of computer programs. In the work of such investigators as Clark (32), Clark, Carpenter & Just (33), Clark & Chase (34), Carpenter & Just (27, 28), R. J. Sternberg (157, 158), and others (59, 116, 122), the models are expressed as flow diagrams whose components are elementary processes. In his theory of analogical reasoning, for example, R. J. Sternberg (158) takes as the component processes encoding, inference, mapping, application, response, and justification. It is not clear in what sense these are intended as, or can be regarded as, "elementary" information processes. Their durations vary widely from one process to another and from one kind of analogy task (people-piece, verbal, or geometric) to another. The application process, for example, ranges from 94 msec to 810 msec in duration over the three types of analogies; the encoding process varies from 556 msec to 2.41 sec. Not only are these processes highly variable in duration, but their durations are quite long, so as to blur the distinction between aggregative models and models of the elementary processor.

R. J. Sternberg's results (157, 158) are not atypical of the findings of reaction-time studies using the additive or subtractive method. Although such studies have produced interesting and plausible process analyses of simple cognitive tasks, they have not yet identified a well-defined set of elementary processes having correspondingly well-defined execution times. Although we get glimpses through such studies of quite rapid processes in the 50 msec range [S. Sternberg's rapid internal scan (159)], and other processes in the 200 msec range (symbol comparison processes), these durations are not sufficiently reproducible among highly similar tasks to give us confidence that they represent a basic cycle time, or a small set of truly basic processes. However, incremental reaction times a fraction of a second in duration have been measured often enough to sustain optimism that a way will be found to describe the elementary processor in terms of component processes that operate in that speed range.

Activation of Memory

On an anecdotal level, most psychologists are aware of "warm-up" phe-nomena in memory that make memory contents more readily available for recall if they have been recalled recently or if closely related memory items have been recalled. Such phenomena suggest the possibility that memory may exist at various levels of activation and that activation level may determine the accessibility of particular memory contents. A number of the memory models that have been proposed in the past few years postulate activation mechanisms of one kind or another (5, 37, 117, 137, 140).

Quillian's semantic network (118) illustrates one kind of activation. Pre-sentation of a stimulus word causes a "wave" of activation to spread out gradually from the node representing that stimulus to adjacent nodes in the network. If two stimuli are presented simultaneously, the two waves of spreading activation will ultimately meet at a common node, thus defining a path between the two stimuli. Hence, each stimulus determines a context for the other, selecting out from the paths radiating from each a preferred path that is relevant to both.

Anderson, in his ACT system (5), proposes to use a spreading activation process of this general kind in lieu of a special STM. In the ACT model, STM is simply that part of LTM which is activated. The system's produc-tions, instead of matching their conditions against the contents of STM, match against the activated contents of LTM.

There has not yet been enough experience with activation mechanisms to make firm judgments about their psychological reality, or to determine clearly what contribution they can make to explaining the control of atten-tion in a cognitive system modeled as a production system.

Automation of Processes

Everyday experience has suggested another idea to modelers of the cogni-tive system. Processes continue to speed up gradually over long periods with practice. At the same time they come to require much less conscious attention and become less accessible to conscious awareness (92). Shiffrin & Schneider have produced considerable evidence, in the context of a simple search and detection task, of a contrast between controlled processing of relatively novel tasks and automated processing of the same tasks after extensive practice (137, 140). On the basis of the size of the effects and the difficulty of reversing them, they argue for a qualitative difference between the two kinds of process.

The UNDERSTAND program (70), described earlier, provides at least one possible mechanism to explicate the distinction between controlled and automatic processing. A computer program written in a higher level language (e.g. FORTRAN, or a list processing language) may be *interpreted* step by step, or it may be *compiled* (translated) into machine language and executed directly in that language. A compiled program typically runs some ten times faster than the corresponding interpreted program. The reason is that the interpreter needs to check repeatedly the situation in which it finds itself in order to determine what to do next, while these decisions have already been made for the compiler. By the same token, the interpreter is more flexible than the compiler—it is better able to adapt its actions to new circumstances than is the compiler, which strives to continue along its preplanned sequence.

When the UNDERSTAND program constructs a legal move operator for a new task environment, the operator is first defined to be executed interpretively. If the interpretive execution is successful, UNDERSTAND is capable of then compiling the program for more rapid execution. It is much easier to construct the program initially in interpretive mode, and this is the reason why UNDERSTAND does not generate the compiled program immediately. Although no direct evidence yet exists to show that the interpret-compile distinction corresponds to the controlled-automatic distinction of Shiffrin & Schroeder (137, 140) and others (92), the former provides at least one possible mechanism for interpreting the observed differences in behavior in information processing terms.

CONCLUSION

This chapter has reviewed the advances since about 1972 in modeling human cognitive processes—with special emphasis upon computer simulation. During this period, models of the problem-solving process, which had reached a considerable level of development for well-structured, puzzle-like tasks, have been extended in several directions. The range of alternative strategies for performing single tasks has been expanded. Beginnings have been made in a theory of expert performance in semantically rich domains.

Models defined in terms of hierarchies of subroutines have been translated into the more flexible, and psychologically more plausible, language of production systems. Natural language processes, including the processes of understanding natural language task instructions, have been modeled successfully.

During the period under review considerable attention has been given to the properties of long-term memory, which is usually modeled as some kind of network of links and nodes, accessed both associatively, along the links, and by direct discrimination and recognition of stimuli. There is still little agreement on the details of these memory models and on the kinds of "schemas," "scripts," "templates," or "frames" that should be used to represent semantic information.

Prior work on modeling rule induction in particular task environments —concept attainment and letter series tasks, for example—has led during the past few years to more general models of inductive, rule-finding processes, which relate these processes to those employed in solving problems. Models of task performance continue to predominate over models of learning and developmental processes, but the past several years have seen some shift in emphasis toward research on learning models, and new mechanisms for realizing learning—especially the mechanism of adaptive production systems—have been proposed and tested with considerable success.

Computer simulation continues to be restricted mainly to the modeling of cognitive processes, and there has been only a little research effort aimed at encompassing motivational and emotional processes in broader models and in exploring the relation of those processes with the cognitive.

Modeling of cognitive processes tends to go on nearly independently at two levels: the level of complex tasks and the level of elementary processes. The processes postulated in models of problem solving or rule induction tend to be too aggregative to be regarded as "elementary." Research on the elementary processor has been pursued vigorously in recent years, and has accumulated an impressive body of experimental data, based in considerable part on reaction-time studies. While several models of the elementary processor have been proposed, it cannot be said that a definitive list of basic cognitive processes or a definitive description of their organization has yet emerged.

If we compare the past 5 or 6 years to the comparable period that preceded them, we see a rapid burgeoning of information processing models of cogniton and of computer simulation of those models. The number of active research scientists working in these directions has probably doubled or tripled during the period. As should be evident from this review, important advances in our knowledge of human cognition have been both the result of, and the cause for, this growth.

Literature Cited

1. Abelson, R. P. 1973. The structure of belief systems. *Computer Models of Thought and Language*, ed. R. C. Schank, K. M. Colby, pp. 287–339. San Francisco: Freeman. 454 pp.
2. Abelson, R. P. 1976. Script processing in attitude formation and decision making. *Cognition and Social Behavior*, ed. J. S. Carroll, J. W. Payne, pp. 33–45. Hillsdale, NJ: Erlbaum. 290 pp.
3. Anderson, J. R. 1974. Retrieval of propositional information from long-term memory. *Cogn. Psychol.* 6:451–74
4. Anderson, J. R. 1974. Verbatim and propositional representations of sentences in immediate and long-term memory. *J. Verb. Learn. Verb. Behav.* 13:149–62
5. Anderson, J. R. 1976. *Language, Memory, and Thought.* Hillsdale, NJ: Erlbaum. 546 pp.
6. Anderson, J. R., Bower, G. H. 1971. On an associative trace for sentence memory. *J. Verb. Learn. Verb. Behav.* 10:673–80
7. Anderson, J. R., Bower, G. H. 1971. Recognition and retrieval processes in free recall. *Psychol. Rev.* 78:97–123
8. Anderson, J. R., Bower, G. H. 1972. Configural properties in sentence memory. *J. Verb. Learn. Verb. Behav.* 11:594–605
9. Anderson, J. R., Bower, G. H. 1973, *Human Associative Memory.* Washington DC: Winston. 524 pp.
10. Anderson, J. R., Hastie, R. 1974. Individuation and reference in memory: Proper names and definite descriptions. *Cogn. Psychol.* 6:495–514
11. Atkinson, R. C., Shiffrin, R. M. 1968. Human memory: A proposed system and its control processes. *The Psychology of Learning and Motivation*, ed. K. W. Spence, J. T. Spence, 2:90–195. New York: Academic. 249 pp.
12. Atwood, M. E., Polson, P. G. 1976. A process model for water jug problems. *Cogn. Psychol.* 8:191–216
13. Bartlett, F. C. 1932. *Remembering.* Cambridge: Cambridge Univ. Press. 317 pp.
14. Bartlett, F. C. 1958. *Thinking.* New York: Basic Books. 203 pp.
15. Baylor, G. W. 1971. *An empirical investigation of visual mental imagery.* PhD thesis. Carnegie-Mellon Univ., Pittsburgh, Pa. 289 pp.
16. Baylor, G. W., Gascon, J. 1974. An information processing theory of aspects of the development of weight seriation in children. *Cogn. Psychol.* 6:1–40
17. Bhaskar, R. 1978. *Problem solving in semantically rich domains.* PhD thesis. Carnegie-Mellon Univ., Pittsburgh, Pa. 196 pp.
18. Bhaskar, R., Simon, H. A. 1977. Problem solving in semantically rich demains: An example from engineering thermodynamics. *Cogn. Sci.* 1:193–215
19. Bloom, L., Rocissano, L., Hood, L. 1976. Adult-child discourse: Developmental interaction between information processing and linguistic knowledge. *Cogn. Psychol.* 8:521–52
20. Bobrow, D. G. 1968. Natural language input for a computer problem-solving system. *Semantic Information Processing*, ed. M. Minsky. pp. 146–226. Cambridge, Mass: MIT Press. 440 pp.
21. Bobrow, D. G., Winograd, T. 1977. An overview of KRL, a knowledge representation language. *Cogn. Sci.* 1:3–46
22. Bower, G. H., Trabasso, T. R. 1964. Concept formation. *Studies in Mathematical Psychology*, ed. R. C. Atkinson, pp. 32–94. Stanford: Stanford Univ. Press. 414 pp.
23. Bransford, J. D., Barclay, J. R., Franks, J. J. 1972. Sentence memory: A constructive versus interpretive approach. *Cogn. Psychol.* 3:193–209
24. Bransford, J. D., Franks, J. J. 1971. The abstraction of linguistic ideas. *Cogn. Psychol.* 2:331–50
25. Brown, J. S., Burton, R. R. 1975. Multiple representations of knowledge for tutorial reasoning. *Representation and Understanding*, ed. D. G. Bobrow, A. M. Collins. pp. 331–50. New York: Academic. 427 pp.
26. Carbonell, J. R., Collins, A. M. 1973. Natural semantics in artificial intelligence. *Int. Joint Conf. Artif. Intell., 3rd,* pp. 344–51. Menlo Park, Calif: Stanford Res. Inst. 703 pp.
27. Carpenter, P. A., Just, M. A. 1975. Sentence comprehension: A psycholinguistic information processing model of verification. *Psychol. Rev.* 82:45–73
28. Carpenter, P. A., Just, M. A. 1976. Models of sentence verification and linguistic comprehension. *Psychol. Rev.* 83:318–22
29. Charniak, E. 1972. *Toward a model of children's story comprehension.* PhD thesis. Massachusetts Inst. Technol., Cambridge, Mass. 63 pp.
30. Chase, W. G., Simon, H. A., 1973. Perception in chess. *Cogn. Psychol.* 4:55–81
31. Chase, W. G., Simon, H. A. 1973. The mind's eye in chess. *Visual Information*

Processing, ed. W. G. Chase, pp. 215–82. New York: Academic. 555 pp.

32. Clark, H. H., 1969. Linguistic processes in deductive reasoning. *Psychol. Rev.* 76:387–404

33. Clark, H. H., Carpenter, P. A., Just, M. A. 1973. On the meeting of semantics and perception. See Ref. 31, pp. 311–82

34. Clark, H. H., Chase, W. G. 1972. On the process of comparing sentences against pictures. *Cogn. Psychol.* 3:472–517

35. Colby, K. M. 1973. Simulations of belief systems. See Ref. 1, pp. 251–86

36. Colby, K. M., Weber, S., Hilf, F. D. 1971. Artificial paranoia. *Artif. Intell.* 2:1–25

37. Collins, A. M., Loftus, E. F. 1975. A spreading-activation theory of semantic processing. *Psychol. Rev.* 82:407–28

38. Collins, A. M., Quillian, M. R. 1969. Retrieval time from semantic memory. *J. Verb. Learn. Verb. Behav.* 9:432–8

39. Collins, A. M., Warnode, E. H., Aiello, N., Miller, M. L. 1975. Reasoning from incomplete knowledge. See Ref. 25, pp. 383–415

40. Cooper, L. A. 1975. Mental rotation of random two-dimensional shapes. *Cogn. Psychol.* 7:20–43

41. Craik, F. I. M., Lockhart, R. S. 1972. Levels of processing: A framework for memory research. *J. Verb. Learn. Verb. Behav.* 11:671–84

42. Davis, J. D., Levine, M. W. 1977. A model for the control of ingestion. *Psychol. Rev.* 84:379–412

43. Davis, R., Buchanan, B. G., Shortliffe, E. H. 1977. Production rules as a representation for a knowledge-based consultation program. *Artif. Intell.* 8:15–46

44. deGroot, A. D. 1946. *Het Denken van den Schaker.* Amsterdam: Noord-Hollandsche. 315 pp.

45. deGroot, A. D. 1965. *Thought and Choice in Chess.* The Hague: Mouton. 463 pp.

46. Dineen, G. P. 1955. Programming pattern recognition. *Proc. 1955 West. Joint Comput. Conf.* 7:94–100

47. Duncker, K. 1945. On problem solving *Psychol. Monogr.* Vol. 58, whole number 270. 113 pp.

48. Egan, D. E. 1973. *The structure of experience acquired while learning to solve a class of problems.* PhD thesis. Univ. Michigan, Ann Arbor, Mich. 100 pp.

49. Egan, D. E., Greeno, J. G. 1974. Theory of rule induction: Knowledge acquired in concept learning, serial pattern learning, and problem solving. *Knowledge and Cognition,* ed. L. W.

Gregg, pp. 43–103. Potomac, Md: Erlbaum. 321 pp.

50. Ericsson, K. A. 1975. *Instructions to Verbalize as a Means to Study Problem-solving Processes with the 8-puzzle: A Preliminary Study.* Stockholm: Univ. Stockholm, Dep. Psychol., 458

51. Estes, W. K. 1976. The cognitive side of probability learning. *Psychol. Rev.* 83:37–64

52. Evans, T. G. 1968. A program for the solution of geometry-analogy intelligence test questions. See Ref. 20, pp. 271–353

53. Farley, A. M. 1974. *VIPS: A visual imagery and perception system: The result of a protocol analysis.* PhD thesis. Carnegie-Mellon Univ., Pittsburgh, Pa. Vol. 1, 158 pp.; Vol. 2, 236 pp.

54. Faught, W. S., Colby, K. M., Parkison, R. C. 1977. Inferences, affects and intentions in a model of paranoia. *Cogn. Psychol.* 9:153–87

55. Feigenbaum, E. A. 1961. The simulation of verbal learning behavior. *Proc. West. Joint Comput. Conf.,* pp. 121–32. Reprinted in *Computers and Thought,* 1963, ed. E. A. Feigenbaum, J. Feldman, pp. 297–309. New York: McGraw-Hill. 535 pp.

56. Feigenbaum, E. A., Buchanan, B. G., Lederberg, J. 1971. On generality and problem solving: A case study using the DENDRAL program. *Machine Intelligence,* ed. B. Meltzer, D. Michie, 6:165–90. New York: American Elsevier. 525 pp.

57. Foss, D. J., Harwood, D. A. 1975. Memory for sentences: Implications for human associative memory. *J. Verb. Learn. Verb. Behav.* 14:1–16

58. Frederiksen, C. H. 1975. Representing logical and semantic structure of knowledge acquired from discourse. *Cogn. Psychol.* 7:371–458

59. Friendly, M. L. 1977. In search of the M-gram: The structure of organization in free recall. *Cogn. Psychol.* 9:188–249

60. Gagné, R. N., Smith, E. C. Jr. 1962. A study of the effects of verbalization on problem solving. *J. Exp. Psychol.* 63:12–18

61. Gerwin, D. 1975. Information processing, data inferences, and scientific generalization. *Behav. Sci.* 19:314–25

62. Gilmartin, K. J., Newell, A., Simon, H. A. 1975. A program modeling short-term memory under strategy control. *The Structure of Human Memory,* ed. C. N. Cofer, pp. 15–30. San Francisco: Freeman. 213 pp.

63. Glucksberg, S., Trabasso, T. R., Wald, J. 1973. Linguistic structures and mental operations. *Cogn. Psychol.* 5:338–70
64. Green, B., Wolf, A. K., Chomsky, C., Laughery, K. 1961. Baseball: An automatic question answerer. See Ref. 55, pp. 219–24. Reprinted in Ref. 55, pp. 207–16
65. Greeno, J. G. 1974. Hobbits and Orcs: Acquisition of a sequential concept. *Cogn. Psychol.* 6:270–92
66. Greeno, J. G. 1976. Indefinite goals in well-structured problems. *Psychol. Rev.* 83:479–91
67. Greeno, J. G. 1977. Process of understanding in problem solving. *Cognitive Theory,* ed. N. J. Castellan Jr., D. B. Pisoni, G. R. Potts, 2:43–84. Hillsdale, NJ: Erlbaum. 342 pp.
68. Greeno, J. G., Simon, H. A. 1974. Processes for sequence production. *Psychol. Rev.* 81:187–98
69. Gregg, L. W., Simon, H. A. 1967. Process models and stochastic theories of simple concept formation. *J. Math. Psychol.* 4:246–76
70. Hayes, J. R., Simon, H. A. 1974. Understanding written problem instructions. See Ref. 49, pp. 167–200
71. Hayes, J. R., Simon, H. A. 1976. Understanding complex task instruction. In *Cognition and Instruction,* ed. D. Klahr, pp. 269–86. Hillsdale, NJ: Erlbaum. 361 pp.
72. Hayes, J. R., Simon, H. A. 1977. Psychological differences among problem isomorphs. See Ref. 67, pp. 21–42
73. Horman, A. M. 1965. GAKU: An artificial student. *Behav. Sci.* 10:88–107
74. Huesmann, L. R., Cheng, C. M. 1973. A theory for the induction of mathematical functions. *Psychol. Rev.* 80:126–38
75. Hunt, E. 1973. The memory we must have. See Ref. 1, pp. 343–71
76. Hunt, E. 1974. Quote the Raven? Nevermore! See Ref. 49, pp. 129–57
77. Jeffries, R., Polson, P. G., Razran, L., Atwood, M. E. 1977. A process model for missionaries-cannibals and other river-crossing problems. *Cogn. Psychol.* 9:412–40
78. Jones, M. R., Zamostny, K. P. 1975. Memory and rule structure in the prediction of serial patterns. *J. Exp. Psychol.: Hum. Mem. Learn.* 104:295–306
79. Just, M. A., Carpenter, P. A. 1976. Eye fixations and cognitive processes. *Cogn. Psychol.* 8:441–80
80. Kintsch, W. 1974. *The Representation of Meaning in Memory.* Hillsdale, NJ: Erlbaum. 279 pp.
81. Kintsch, W., Keenan, J. 1973. Reading rate and retention as a function of the number of propositions in the base structure of sentences. *Cogn. Psychol.* 5:257–74
82. Klahr, D. 1973. A production system for counting, subitizing and adding. See Ref. 31, pp. 527–46
83. Klahr, D. 1973. Quantification processes. See Ref. 31, pp. 3–34
84. Klahr, D., Wallace, J. G. 1972. Class inclusion processes. *Information Processing in Children,* ed. S. Farnham-Diggory, pp. 143–72. New York: Academic. 197 pp.
85. Klahr, D., Wallace, J. G. 1973. The role of quantification operators in the development of conservation of quantity. *Cogn. Psychol.* 4:301–27
86. Klahr, D., Wallace, J. G. 1976. *Cognitive Development: An Information-processing View.* Hillsdale, NJ: Erlbaum. 244 pp.
87. Klein, S., Kuppin. M. A. 1970. *An Intermediate Heuristic Program for Learning Transformational Grammars.* Tech. Rep. No. 97, Comput. Sci. Dep., Univ. Wisconsin, Madison
88. Klix, F. 1971. *Information und Verhalten.* East Berlin: VEB Deutscher Verlag der Wissenschaften. 810 pp.
89. Kosslyn, S. M., Pomerantz, J. R. 1977. Imagery, propositions, and the forms of internal representations. *Cogn. Psychol.* 9:52–76
90. Kosslyn, S. M., Schwartz, S. P. 1977. A simulation of visual imagery. *Cogn. Sci.* 1:265–97
91. Kotovsky, K., Simon, H. A. 1973. Empirical tests of a theory of human acquisition of concepts for sequential patterns. *Cogn. Psychol.* 3:399–424
92. LaBerge, D., Samuels, S. J. 1974. Toward a theory of automatic information processing in reading. *Cogn. Psychol.* 6:293–323
93. Landauer, T. K. 1975. Memory without organization: Properties of a model with random storage and undirected retrieval. *Cogn. Psychol.* 7:495–531
94. Lashley, K. S. 1951. The problem of serial order in behavior. *Cerebral Mechanisms in Behavior: the Hixon Symposium,* ed. L. A. Jeffress, pp. 112–46. New York: Wiley. 311 pp.
95. Lehnert, W. 1977. Human and computational question answering. *Cogn. Sci.* 1:47–73
96. Lindsay, R. 1963. *The reading machine problem.* PhD thesis. Carnegie-Mellon Univ., Pittsburgh, Pa. 93 pp.

97. Mandler, J. M., Johnson, N. S. 1977. Remembrance of things parsed: Story structure and recall. *Cogn. Psychol.* 9:111–51

98. Michon, J. A. 1967. The game of JAM —an isomorph of tic-tac-toe. *Am. J. Psychol.* 80:137–40

99. Minsky, M. 1975. A framework for representing knowledge. *The Psychology of Computer Vision,* ed. P. H. Winston. New York: McGraw-Hill. 282 pp.

100. Moore, J., Newell, A. 1974. How can MERLIN understand? See Ref. 49, pp. 201–52

101. Moran, T. P. 1973. *The symbolic imagery hypothesis: A production system model.* PhD thesis. Carnegie-Mellon Univ., Pittsburgh, Pa. 364 pp.

102. Neves, D. 1977. *A Study of Strategies of the Tower of Hanoi Game.* Presented at Ann. Meet. Midwest. Psychol. Assoc., 49th, Chicago

103. Newell, A. 1973. Artificial intelligence and the concept of mind. See Ref. 1, pp. 1–60

104. Newell, A. 1973. Production systems: Models of control structures. See Ref. 31, pp. 463–526

105. Newell, A. 1973. You can't play 20 Questions with nature and win. See Ref. 31, pp. 283–308

106. Newell, A., Shaw, J. C., Simon, H. A. 1957. Empirical explorations with the Logic Theory Machine. *Proc. West. Joint Comput. Conf.,* 15:218–39. Reprinted in Ref. 55, pp. 109–33

107. Newell, A., Shaw, J. C., Simon, H. A. 1958. Elements of a theory of human problem solving. *Psychol. Rev.* 65:151–66

108. Newell, A., Shaw, J. C., Simon, H. A. 1960. Report on a general problem-solving program for a computer. *Information Processing: Proc. Int. Conf. Inf. Process.,* pp. 256–64. Paris: UNESCO

109. Newell, A., Simon, H. A. 1972. *Human Problem Solving.* Englewood Cliffs, NJ: Prentice-Hall. 920 pp.

110. Nisbett, R. E., Wilson, T. D. 1977. Telling more than we can know: Verbal reports on mental processes. *Psychol. Rev.* 84:231–59

111. Norman, D. A., Rumelhart, D. E., and the LNR Research Group. 1975. *Explorations in Cognition.* San Francisco: Freeman. 430 pp.

112. Novak, G. S. 1977. Representations of knowledge in a program for solving physics problems. *Proc. 5th Int. Joint Conf. Artif. Intell.* 1:286–91

113. Paige, J. M., Simon, H. A. 1966. Cognitive processes in solving algebra word problems. *Problem Solving,* ed. B. Kleinmuntz, pp. 51–119. New York: Wiley. 406 pp.

114. Palmer, S. E. 1977. Hierarchical structure in perceptual representation. *Cogn. Psychol.* 9:441–74

115. Pople, H. 1977. The formation of composite hypotheses in diagnostic problem solving. See Ref. 112, 2:1030–37

116. Posner, M. I., Lewis, J. L., Conrad, C. 1972. Component processes in reading: A performance analysis. *Language by Ear and by Eye,* ed. J. F. Kavanaugh, I. G. Mattingly, pp. 159–92. Cambridge, Mass: MIT Press. 398 pp.

117. Quillian, M. R. 1968. Semantic memory. See Ref. 20, pp. 227–70

118. Quillian, M. R. 1969. The teachable language comprehender: A simulation program and theory of language. *Commun. ACM* 12:459–76

119. Reed, S. K., Ernst, G. W., Banerji, R. 1974. The role of analogy in transfer between similar problem states. *Cogn. Psychol.* 6:436–50

120. Reitman, J. S. 1976. Skilled perception in GO: Deducing memory structures from inter-response times. *Cogn. Psychol.* 8:336–56

121. Reitman, W. R. 1965. *Cognition and Thought: An Information Processing Approach.* New York: Wiley. 312 pp.

122. Resnick, L. B. 1976. Task analysis in instructional design: Some cases from mathematics. See Ref. 71, pp. 51–80

123. Restle, F. 1970. Theory of serial pattern learning: Structural trees. *Psychol. Rev.* 77:481–95

124. Restle, F. 1976. Structural ambiguity in serial pattern learning. *Cogn. Psychol.* 8:357–81

125. Revlis, R. 1975. Two models of syllogistic reasoning: Feature selection and conversion. *J. Verb. Learn. Verb. Behav.* 14:180–95

126. Rieger, C. 1976. An organization of knowledge for problem solving and language comprehension. *Artif. Intell.* 7:89–127

127. Rips, L. J., Shoben, E. J., Smith, E. E. 1973. Semantic distance and the verification of semantic relations. *J. Verb. Learn. Verb. Behav.* 12:1–20

128. Rosenberg, S., Simon, H. A. 1977. Modeling semantic memory: Effects of presenting semantic information in different modalities. *Cogn. Psychol.* 9:293–325

129. Rumelhart, D. E. 1975. Notes on a schema for stories. See Ref. 25, pp. 211–36

130. Rumelhart, D. E., Lindsay, P. H., Norman, D. A. 1972. A process model for long-term memory. *Organization of Memory*, ed. E. Tulving, W. Donaldson, pp. 198–246. New York: Academic. 423 pp.
131. Rumelhart, D. E., Siple, P. 1974. Process of recognizing tachistoscopically presented words. *Psychol. Rev.* 81:99–118
132. Schank, R. C. 1972. Conceptual dependency: A theory of natural language understanding. *Cogn. Psychol.* 3:552–631
133. Schank, R. C. 1973. Identification of conceptualizations underlying natural language. See Ref. 1, pp. 187–248
134. Schank, R. C. 1975. *Conceptual Information Processing*. New York: American Elsevier. 374 pp.
135. Schank, R. C., Abelson, R. P. 1977. *Scripts, Plans, Goals, and Understanding*. Hillsdale, NJ: Erlbaum. 248 pp.
136. Schmidt, C. F. 1976. Understanding human action: Recognizing the plans and motives of other persons. See Ref. 2, pp. 47–67
137. Schneider, W., Shiffrin, R. M. 1977. Controlled and automatic human information processing: I. Detection, search, and attention. *Psychol. Rev.* 84:1–66
138. Selfridge, O. 1955. Pattern recognition and modern computers. See Ref. 46, 7:91–3
139. Selz, O. 1913. *Über die Gesetze des Geordneten Denkverlaufs, I*. Stuttgart: Spemann. 301 pp.
140. Shiffrin, R. M., Schneider, W. 1977. Controlled and automatic human information processing: II. Perceptual learning, automatic attending, and a general theory. *Psychol. Rev.* 84:127–90
141. Shortliffe, E. H. 1976. *MYCIN: Computer-Based Medical Consultation*. New York: American Elsevier. 264 pp.
142. Siegler, R. S. 1976. Three aspects of cognitive development. *Cogn. Psychol.* 8:481–520
143. Siklóssy, L. 1971. A language-learning heuristic program. *Cogn. Psychol.* 2:479–95
144. Simmons, R. F. 1973. Semantic networks: Their computation and use for understanding English sentences. See Ref. 1, pp. 63–113
145. Simon, D. P., Simon, H. A. 1978. Individual differences in solving physics problems. *Children's Thinking: What Develops?* ed. R. S. Siegler. Hillsdale, NJ: Erlbaum. In press
146. Simon, H. A. 1972. Complexity and the representation of patterned sequences of symbols. *Psychol. Rev.* 79:369–82
147. Simon, H. A. 1972. The heuristic compiler. *Representation and Meaning*, ed. H. A. Simon, L. Siklóssy. pp. 9–43. Englewood Cliffs, NJ: Prentice-Hall. 440 pp.
148. Simon, H. A. 1974. How big is a chunk? *Science* 183:482–88
149. Simon, H. A. 1975. The functional equivalence of problem solving skills. *Cogn. Psychol.* 7:268–88
150. Simon, H. A. 1976. The information-storage system called 'human memory.' *Neural Mechanisms of Learning and Memory*, ed. M. R. Rosenzweig, E. L. Bennett, pp. 79–96. Cambridge, Mass: MIT Press. 637 pp.
151. Simon, H. A., Gilmartin, K. 1973. A simulation of memory for chess positions. *Cogn. Psychol.* 5:29–46
152. Simon, H. A., Hayes, J. R. 1976. The understanding process: Problem isomorphs. *Cogn. Psychol.* 8:165–90
153. Simon, H. A., Kotovsky, K. 1963. Human acquisition of concepts for sequential patterns. *Psychol. Rev.* 70:534–46
154. Simon, H. A., Lea, G. 1974. Problem solving and rule induction: A unified view. See Ref. 49, pp. 105–27
155. Simon, H. A., Reed, S. K. 1976. Modeling strategy shifts in a problem-solving task. *Cogn. Psychol.* 8:86–97
156. Smith, E. E., Shoben, E. J., Rips, L. J. 1974. Structure and process in semantic memory: A featural model for semantic decisions. *Psychol. Rev.* 81:214–41
157. Sternberg, R. J. 1977. *Intelligence, Information Processing, and Analogical Reasoning: Componential Analysis of Human Abilities*. Hillsdale, NJ: Erlbaum. 348 pp.
158. Sternberg, R. J. 1977. Component processes in analogical reasoning. *Psychol. Rev.* 84:353–78
159. Sternberg, S. 1966. High speed scanning in human memory. *Science* 153:652–54
160. Sydow, H. 1970. Zur metrischen Erfassung von subjektiven Problemzuständen und zu deren Veränderung im Denkprozers, I and II. *Z. Psychol.* 177:145–98; 178:1–50
161. Thomas, J. C. 1974. An analysis of behavior in the Hobbits-Orcs problem. *Cogn. Psychol.* 6:257–90
162. Thorndyke, P. W. 1977. Cognitive structures in comprehension and memory of narrative discourse. *Cogn. Psychol.* 9:77–110
163. Thorndyke, P. W., Bower, G. H. 1974. Storage and retrieval processes in sen-

tence memory. *Cogn. Psychol.* 6:515–43
164. Uhr, L. 1964. Pattern string learning programs. *Behav. Sci.* 9:258–70
165. Waltz, D. 1975. Machine vision: Understanding line drawings of scenes with shadows. See Ref. 99, pp. 19–91
166. Waterman, D. A. 1970. Generalization learning techniques for automating the learning of heuristics. *Artif. Intell.* 1:121–70
167. Waterman, D. A., Newell, A. 1973. PAS-II: An interactive task-free version of an automatic protocol analysis sys-tem. See Ref. 26, pp. 431–45
168. Watkins, M. J., Tulving, E. 1975. Episodic memory: When recognition fails. *J. Exp. Psychol.: Gen.* 104:5–29
169. Wickens, T. D., Millward, R. B. 1971. Attribute elimination strategies for concept identification with experienced subjects. *J. Math. Psychol.* 8:453–80
170. Young, R. M. 1974. *Children's seriation behavior: A production system analysis.* PhD thesis. Carnegie-Mellon Univ., Pittsburgh, Pa. 316 pp.

Ann. Rev. Psychol. 1979. 30:397–415
Copyright © 1979 by Annual Reviews Inc. All rights reserved

SOCIAL AND CULTURAL INFLUENCES ON PSYCHOPATHOLOGY

♦312

John S. Strauss

Director, Yale Psychiatric Institute, Yale University,
New Haven, Connecticut 06520

CONTENTS

THE TIME OF IMPACT 398
CAUSAL MODELS 399
THE CLASSIFICATION OF PSYCHOPATHOLOGY 399
CULTURAL INFLUENCES ON SYMPTOM TYPE 401
SOCIAL CLASS 403
LABELING 403
SOCIAL SUPPORTS 404
TREATMENT SYSTEMS 405
FAMILY STUDIES 406
LIFE EVENTS 407
THE PSYCHIATRIC HOSPITAL 409
THEORETICAL CONSIDERATIONS 410
CONCLUSIONS 412

There apparently is no Broad Street pump in psychiatry. In the early nineteenth century, John Snow discovered that people who used a particular public pump in London tended to develop cholera. This finding contributed to the control of the disease and to the discovery of its etiology. In understanding social and cultural influences on psychopathology, no analog to the Broad Street pump has been found. The result is a large number of theories and generalizations built around findings that have been difficult to integrate into understanding and treating psychopathology as it occurs in real individual people.

397

0066-4308/79/0201-0397$01.00

Thus, in spite of many findings, some of them replicated, social and cultural factors are largely ignored in much of psychiatric theory and practice (25). Nowhere is this fact so clear as in the basic documents of psychiatric practice, psychiatric records, and case conference reports. Unless these are from a center where social and cultural factors are especially emphasized, it is rare to find the patient's social class, for example, even noted, let alone integrated into understanding the disorder and treatment planning.

The common failure to integrate cultural factors into psychiatry is also demonstrated in the area of diagnosis. The current diagnostic and statistical manual of the American Psychiatric Association (2) does not once mention social or cultural factors. Awareness of this shortcoming, especially of the tendency not to consider subcultural norms in reaching a diagnosis, has led to special workshops to suggest approaches for correcting this problem (12).

One major cause of the failure to integrate sociocultural factors into psychiatric practice is the complexity of the fields involved. But another contributory factor, a treatable one, is the limited number of attempts made to construct specific links between sociocultural phenomena and psychopathology in the individual patient. This report will review recent literature in an attempt to suggest how more links of that kind might be developed.

THE TIME OF IMPACT

A first step in bridging the gap between the psychopathology of the individual and the influence of sociocultural factors is by attempting to determine at what point in a person's life the various sociocultural characteristics have their impact. These points include, for example, the time the parents select each other as mates, infancy, early childhood, the period prior to onset of psychopathology, and the period following onset of disorder. Thus social factors influencing assortative mating (35) between schizophrenic women and sociopathic men would be seen as influencing the offspring's genetic constitution. Deprivation in early childhood might have an impact at that age. Stressful social situations, such as sudden change in community employment levels, might have an impact just prior to onset of disorder, and the community's treatment network and labeling attitudes might influence the period following onset of psychopathology. Attending to these connections between type and time of sociocultural impact is a first step in linking sociocultural factors to psychopathology in the individual.

Ideally, once the time of impact is noted, it should be possible to identify more specifically the roles of such sociocultural influences on psychiatric disorder as social class, life events, labeling processes, the treatment system, presence of protective social supports, and cultural determinants of symptom type. However, as soon as an attempt is made to determine where in the life span each of these factors has its impact, it is impressive how glaringly apparent the areas of ignorance in the field become. This impression is somewhat similar to that generated when an analogous attempt was made to understand the various components of premorbid adjustment (68). These recognitions, although painful, are valuable because they suggest forcefully a basic reality, the complexity that characterizes these areas.

CAUSAL MODELS

A second step in considering the impact of sociocultural factors on psychopathology is to evaluate the type of causal model that might best account for the relationships involved. It is most common to think in terms of simple linear causation. Labeling a patient as being schizophrenic may be viewed as *the cause* of his subsequent chronic course. In many instances, however, complex causal models may be more adequate than linear ones. Interactional models suggest that several variables may combine to cause a disorder. It is also possible that a particular disorder may be the final common pathway for diverse combinations of antecedents. Finally, transactional models of causation may be most suitable in some instances. These view influences on psychopathology as constituting feedback systems (61). The fatigued mother becomes easily irritated by her active child who is hyperresponsive to stimuli. She may withdraw from him, leading to his increased hyperactivity, perhaps followed by her increasing withdrawal, followed by his decompensation. Clearly, if the impact of sociocultural variables on the individual is to be identified, it will be crucial eventually to specify the type of causal model involved.

THE CLASSIFICATION OF PSYCHOPATHOLOGY

A third step in understanding the impact of sociocultural factors on psychiatric disorders is to evaluate the relationship of these factors to various types of psychopathology. For example, most types of psychiatric disorder apparently are not related to social class level. Schizophrenia may be an important exception to this rule.

More complex approaches to classification than conventional diagnosis, however, may be required before it will be possible to relate an individual's disorder to sociocultural factors. There is much to suggest that single-label diagnostic categories such as schizophrenia are only gross approximations of real psychopathologic processes. Because various dysfunctions that define psychopathology may be relatively independent, psychiatric diagnosis is shifting from simple typological models such as those represented by the diagnoses schizophrenia or bipolar affective disorder to a multiaxial diagnostic system. In such a model each patient is given not one but several diagnostic labels, one for each diagnostic axis (22, 52, 60, 66). The next standard *Diagnostic and Statistical Manual for Psychiatric Disorders* will have a multiaxial diagnostic structure (3), probably including as axes the syndrome, personality disorder, physical disability, possible precipitating events, and level of social function.

The value of multiaxial diagnosis has been supported by a number of clinical experiences and systematic studies showing that the major axes have important and somewhat independent treatment, etiologic, and prognostic implications. For example, type of symptom and level of social function are relatively separate characteristics, each having only limited value in predicting the other (67). From findings such as this, it seems possible that the most accurate conception of psychiatric disorders may not be to view them narrowly, as in the infectious disease model of chicken pox or pneumococcal pneumonia, but rather as a confluence of relatively independent processes. Such processes might include, for example, a constitutional vulnerability to cognitive disorganization, low level of social relations function, and a series of life stresses.

In viewing diseases narrowly, social factors—poverty, for example—might be seen in an unspecified way as decreasing the individual's resistance to the disease. In the broader multiaxial approach to diagnosis, the impact of social factors might be clarified more readily. In a multiaxial system, poverty might be seen as increasing a genetically established vulnerability to cognitive disorganization in several ways: by increased life stress, by reducing available resources (such as money to pay for medical bills or car repairs) and also by being associated with social relations dysfunction through limiting the individual's flexibility in learning such functioning (36). If sociocultural factors are to be understood in relation to psychopathology in the individual patient, their impact on the various axes defined above must be established.

Considering the time in the life span that the impact of particular social factors takes place, the types of psychopathology on which the impact occurs, the axes affected, and the most likely causal model involved could provide greatly improved understanding of key social-individual relationships. Clearly, the precision of such a model is hardly a reality at this point in the history of the field. Nevertheless, the ideal must be kept in mind and attempts made to approximate it.

Recognizing this ideal framework, what do recent studies show about how various sociocultural factors influence individual psychopathology? The major variables have been comprehensively reviewed in the previous edition of this publication by King (34). Some of the most important of these characteristics will be mentioned here in an attempt to show how they might be related more to some of the specific considerations described above.

CULTURAL INFLUENCES ON SYMPTOM TYPE

One major issue has been whether general cultural factors determine the type of psychiatric symptoms that are manifested. The relatively simple-appearing issue of finding which types of psychopathology are universal and which are culture-specific has not, in fact, been easy to resolve. Until standardized patient assessment techniques were developed to evaluate key diagnostic criteria across cultural settings, it was only possible with limited evidence to speculate whether diagnostic categories were culture-specific (41). Recently, through the development of structure interviews and operational diagnostic criteria, a series of studies has been carried out to provide more evidence on this question. One investigation (18) showed that diagnostic practices did differ somewhat across cultures, but that similar core patient groups were identified by the same diagnostic labels. In one recent study that included centers from nine different countries (74), it was possible to use similar assessment techniques in the nine different centers and to identify patients in all centers who had symptom characteristics that were associated with the diagnosis of schizophrenia as given by investigators from all centers. This study, together with other research on similar size (23) or smaller groups of subjects (50), indicates that there is a meaningful sense in which schizophrenia can be identified in a wide range of cultures. Studies to determine whether this also holds true for patients with other diagnoses, such as depression, have been carried out (39, 42), showing that in general comparable results are found cross-culturally. Thus, the findings available suggest that cultural relativism, in its extreme form, in regards to schizophrenia and perhaps other major disorders, is invalid.

Although the major types of psychopathology such as schizophrenia appear to be universal, there are some culture-specific syndromes such as amok, koro, latah, and windego (77). There are also important variations within diagnostic groups, both in the relative frequency of particular symptoms such as visual hallucinations (78) and perhaps in prognosis (75).

Perhaps of even greater interest are findings that show certain cultural differences of symptom profiles within a major diagnostic category (42). Important associations between such profiles and local behavior norms have also been demonstrated. Katz & Sanborn (33) studied the relationship among psychopathologic characteristics, specific cultural norms of behavior, the tendency to hospitalize individuals with certain behaviors by a subculture, and change in behaviors of patients from various subcultures once they are hospitalized. A complex interaction among these factors was demonstrated. The findings suggest that although in general there are commonalities of psychopathology across cultures, there are also important differences, especially in terms of symptom profiles and which profiles are considered most pathological by a given culture.

Several questions arise in assessing the value of these findings of cultural universality and variation for working with the individual patient. In certain situations, is the degree to which the patient or the clinician perceives abnormal behavior as some constant deviation from a cultural norm an oversensitive estimate of pathology? Is the sense of being deviant from cultural norms actually a contributor to psychopathology as suggested by personal reports (32)? And conversely, what is the same about schizophrenics across cultures that causes them universally to be seen as disordered? If, as seems likely, the common denominator is a group of symptoms, why does this contrast so much to symptom profiles which tend to be more culture-specific. Expecting answers to these questions is demanding much, but such answers would provide the next step in making cross-cultural findings relevant to determining when the individual person is "really sick."

General cultural patterns may have an impact on prognosis as well as on symptom picture. It has been speculated that industrialization is one major prognostic factor; the more industrialized the society the more guarded is the prognosis (17). Some cross-cultural studies also have implications regarding labeling in relation to prognosis. If there are significant differences (as well as similarities) in behavioral norms and views of abnormality across cultures, it seems likely that certain behaviors will receive a labeling of abnormality in some cultural settings but not others. It might be possible to utilize this difference to help understand the effect of labeling on psychopathology. Townsend (69) and Frias (26) have already shown that attitudes toward a given disorder do vary in different centers and that there is a strong cultural specificity to these attitudes—attitudes shaped by local schools of thought and often shared not only by clinicians, but by patients and their families as well.

There is little evidence so far to indicate at what time point in a person's life specific cultural factors influence psychopathology. It is possible, for example, that cultural influences on symptom characteristics operate early in childhood rather than just prior to the onset of disorder. Investigations could be designed to help clarify this possibility. It is not evident at this point which causal model would be most accurate for reflecting the relationships between cultural factors and psychopathology.

The axis on which the culture appears to operate in these studies is symptoms, but one might also expect to find significant relationships between cultural factors and social functioning or course of disorder. If schizophrenic symptoms in one society evoke different functioning expectations than in another, the effect of these symptoms on patient functioning in the two cultures might be quite different. Understanding these relations more specifically could provide a major tool for learning more about determinants of the relationships between symptoms and social function.

SOCIAL CLASS

Social class has been studied in relation to many aspects of psychopathology, but one finding of particular interest is its association with schizophrenia. A relationship between low social class and increased incidence and prevalence of schizophrenia has been found especially in large cities (14). This association has been attributed either to social drift [schizophrenics do not achieve the educational and occupational levels of their parents (21)] or to the presumed effects of social class. This latter is sometimes explained as the lower-class child's growing up in an environment where flexibility of coping style is not encouraged, where supportive facilities are rare, and where the more frequent stresses experienced are therefore particularly likely to generate catastrophic psychiatric decompensation.

In this instance, proceeding from the general sociocultural finding to the pathologic process in the individual requires a switch to direct study of the constituent hypotheses, for example, to determine if coping styles and their flexibility are related to schizophrenia. It would be important in any such effort to differentiate between the potential etiologic and prognostic roles of such phenomena, since combinations of coping styles, life stress, and support systems influencing course of disorder may well be different from those most important etiologically.

LABELING

There has been a heated dispute whether the society's labeling of the individual as sick actually generates the behavior attributed (28, 62). In this dispute, polarized positions have been generated so that it is sometimes suggested, on the one hand, that labeling causes mental illness or on the other, that it has no effect. Although the illness concept can have a valuable effect for the sick person—permitting the individual the freedom to have problems without being considered a slacker or a criminal—it can also lead to his being treated with contempt or fear. The increased hardship generated by being labeled mentally ill has been described by many individuals (32), but perhaps most poignantly in a recently published letter. In an anonymous letter to *Schizophrenia Bulletin* (4), entitled "On being Diagnosed Schizophrenic," a reader who was so diagnosed and is now pursuing a career in research on schizophrenia writes,

> I had little idea of how dehumanizing and humiliating the hospital would be for me.—My parents were told by my attending physician upon my leaving the hospital that my diagnosis was schizophrenia.—My label seemed to be the focal point of their debasing behavior. I felt that I had partly lost my right to stand among humanity as human—and that for some people I would be forevermore something of a subhuman creature.

The strength and characteristics of the labeling process appear to vary somewhat with the specific culture, epoch, and subcultures, but it seems most likely that the major impact of labeling is on the course of disorder, not as the original cause of disorder. One might speculate that labeling would have its most direct effect on the social relations and occupational functioning axes. Although there has been no systematic study of the specific type of functioning affected, many patients have indicated how difficult it is to return to work or to deal with friends because of shame from their psychiatric problem and the way in which it made them feel different and inferior. Frequently the labeling effect may be increased by other sociocultural factors such as high unemployment rates or cultural belief systems that mitigate against the expsychiatric patient being employed, getting married, or otherwise being accepted in the society as others are.

In considering labeling and the individual, the causal model that might be most appropriate is a complex transactional one in which, for example, the individual's acting somewhat strangely following psychiatric hospitalization leads to his being considered crazy, not being taken seriously, being avoided socially, and unable to find work. This in turn may lead him to withdraw further and perhaps become more symptomatic. Such a transactional causal hypothesis would, of course, need to be evaluated empirically.

SOCIAL SUPPORTS

A major sociocultural factor influencing psychopathology is availability of social supports. As suggested earlier, such supports may help buffer the individual against personal crises. The importance of social supports for a wide range of disorders has been suggested by Cassel (10), and its special implications for psychopathology have been described by many others (9, 15, 43, 64).

When in the person's life would such supports operate? They could have an impact in childhood and adolescence, influencing the development of self-esteem or coping capacities. Probably they also operate after onset of disorder, to provide some limit on what the person is required to manage and some solace and companionship in his attempt to do so. Given the almost certainly major role of social supports—from companionship to assistance in obtaining lodging and employment—in the process of recovering from severe psychopathology, it is amazing how little attention has been paid in the past to providing such facilities as vocational assistance, group homes, cluster apartments, and halfway houses. Perhaps this lack, too, is a reflection of how difficult it has been to integrate sociocultural considerations into the treatment and understanding of the individual patient.

TREATMENT SYSTEMS

The facilities available for treatment are an important component of the broader cultural and social setting and have considerable impact especially on the course of psychiatric disorder. Cultural beliefs are major determinants of what kind of treatment is provided and accepted. To us, this is often more apparent in developing countries than in our own society (31), but undoubtedly it is a major factor in all mental health care systems.

Social systems providing large, impersonal institutions for treating psychiatric patients are likely to generate chronic disability (6). On the other hand, it seems possible that societies with extremely highly developed disability care systems may contribute to chronicity by essentially institutionalizing the expatient in the community and not providing enough incentive for him to function adequately (24). These various considerations have greatly influenced practice and also been the topic of study (37, 48). It is not possible in this context to discuss treatment systems in detail, but some approaches to these problems can be noted. Community mental health centers, of course, are one attempt to provide care that is more generally available and less isolated. Some other methods for avoiding institutionalism in the hospital or the community that have been suggested are the provision of brief, time-limited financial support (47) or the development of systems in which increasing competence is rewarded by decreasing demands, for example, the more a person works in a job, the less he is charged for halfway house rent (59). These are all approaches to treatment that would lend themselves readily to study and need to be investigated further to provide more detailed information about their impact on the patient.

The characteristics described briefly above are some of the major sociocultural factors that have been linked in a general way to psychopathology. Suggestions have been made about more specific studies that might be undertaken to demonstrate the ways these factors relate to the individual patient. But attempting to carry out such studies to lead from the general to the individual is complex, and a somewhat problematic strategy for making such a bridge, since the levels of association between the sociocultural variables described and characteristics of psychiatric disorder are often limited, even when statistically significant. For example, the vast majority of individuals in the lowest social class do not develop major psychopathology.

For these reasons, other approaches for linking sociocultural factors to individual psychopathology must also be explored. One such approach is to study intensively certain topics which in themselves represent a bridge between the individual and the sociocultural. Three areas that have been explored with growing intensity in the last few years could have considerable bridging potential. These areas are: patterns of family interaction, stressful life events, and the psychiatric hospital setting.

FAMILY STUDIES

Since the family represents a major link between the individual and the society, understanding its relationships to the culture on one hand and individual psychopathology on the other could help significantly to bridge the gap between them. Two types of family studies have been particularly impressive in this regard. The first of these involves a series of investigations about the relationship between the family milieu and the likelihood for exacerbation of symptoms in a family member diagnosed schizophrenic. Brown et al (8) and Vaughn & Leff (72) carried out semistructured interviews and detailed ratings to study "expressed emotion" in families in which a discharged schizophrenic was living. Findings showed that high "expressed emotion" (actually hostile feelings and intrusiveness) in families were characteristically reported by relatives of those schizophrenics who most frequently had an exacerbation of symptoms. Although some earlier studies (57) had also suggested that exacerbation of schizophrenic symptoms was most common when a patient was living in a difficult family situation, the Brown et al study was the first in which relatively systematic data collection and analysis demonstrated in detail the nature of the relationship between an aspect of the patient's environment and the likelihood of the disorder's recurrence. Also significantly, Vaughn & Leff noted that the particular family characteristics associated with exacerbation of schizophrenia were not associated with exacerbations in other kinds of psychopathology.

These studies suggest not only that particular milieu factors are associated with exacerbation, but also that these factors have a rather specific interaction with type of psychiatric disorder. Although the studies have been criticized because no direct observations of family interactions were carried out and it is not certain that what family members told the investigators provided an accurate picture of actual communication patterns, still these investigations represent significant progress in methodology and findings suggesting rather specific relationships between the milieu and individual patient characteristics.

A second group of family studies may also have implications for the impact of broader social and cultural factors on individual psychopathology. Reiss (56) and Wynne et al (76), focusing more on form of communication than on content, have suggested that certain formal aspects of communication are found in families of schizophrenic patients. Although the direction of causality has not been shown definitively, it seems likely that certain kinds of communication deviance (76) or a tendency for family members to reach agreement even if reality is distorted in the process (56) might represent a milieu in which individuals are likely to become vulnerable to schizophrenia.

Whether particular kinds of language, thought, or relating characteristics are found more frequently in particular cultural subgroups or settings with higher incidence of psychopathology remains to be determined. However, Miller (44) and Kohn (36) suggest that some aspects of communication tend to be social-class specific. Behrens et al (7), however, have suggested that at least for the model of Wynne et al the communicational patterns found more commonly in certain social classes do not appear to be similar to those identified as related to schizophrenic families. The analogous experiment for the Reiss model has not been performed.

Finding aspects of family systems important to psychopathology may provide a clue to characteristics of broader social structures that also influence psychiatric disorder. If family interaction patterns are related to psychopathology, it can be speculated that analogous patterns in other sociocultural settings may also have an important impact. For example, would a school, work, or friendship setting marked by warmth, nonintrusiveness, communicational clarity, and tendencies not to distort reality for the purpose of reaching consensus provide partial antidotes to possibly harmful communication in the family? On the other hand, interaction characteristics of broader sociocultural structures might add to the possibly pathogenic effects of families.

LIFE EVENTS

A fast-developing area of inquiry that may make important contributions to understanding the impact of sociocultural factors on psychopathology is the study of stressful life events. Stresses or "precipitating events" have for some time been considered as important components of the environment that contribute to psychopathology as well as to other types of disorder. Since the impact and frequency of these events have many sociocultural determinants, they are an important medium between the individual and the culture more generally.

Although the study of these factors at first seemed relatively simple, that has not proved to be the case. The life events scales originally constructed were a considerable improvement over the earlier practice of collecting data on this topic through anecdotal unstructured means. However, these scales and the conceptions on which they were based have been shown to have many shortcomings (54). First, it is difficult with the scales to compensate for the fact that people with certain demographic characteristics (e.g. never married) are less likely to have the same number of stressful life events than others (e.g. married), simply because they are less exposed to several events, such as divorce, loss of a child, or mortgage foreclosure, for example. Second, it has not yet been possible to develop a life events scale to recognize that specific events may be particularly stressful for individuals with certain family backgrounds or personality patterns. It has also been shown that serious reliability and validity problems exist with the life events scales. For example, recall of life events becomes increasingly distorted as each month passes (70).

In spite of the difficulties that have characterized life events research, even the scales already in use have been demonstrated as having some validity across cultural settings (55) and generally across ethnic groups (58). Also, various kinds of life events stress can now be weighted according to the impact of the particular event and its recency (53). With these advances, findings have been generated which, together with clinical judgment, suggest that life events stresses are associated with the occurrence and possibly the exacerbation of most or even all types of psychopathology. Although it had been suggested that measurable life events stress may not be significantly associated with schizophrenia, even this finding has been questioned in a recent study (29).

A phenomenon of particular interest that may represent a specific type or series of life event has been suggested in the rapidly growing literature on "learned helplessness" (63). Although the clinical implications of these studies are still uncertain, the findings reported make a considerable amount of *prima facie* clinical sense. In this area of research, animals and humans are subjected to tasks in which the outcome is independent of the subject's response. The individual becomes aware of this and tends to abandon attempts to master the situation. Such "learned helplessness" behavior may generalize to various modalities and may require specific rigorous training to overcome. This paradigm has been used as the model for the origin of depression, but might also apply to the genesis of schizophrenia where family communication deviance and double binding could have as one result the effect of making it impossible for the individual to understand, let alone manage his environment effectively.

Learned helplessness might also relate to relationships between social class and psychopathology since it seems likely that the lowest social classes have the least resources at their disposal in dealing with a variety of life situations. If this speculation were valid, one might expect to see more depression in lower class persons. This has not been found, however, suggesting that in the form stated here, a learned helplessness/social class/-depression hypothesis is at best speculative.

In general, the learned helplessness model, although appealing as potentially identifying causal factors in psychopathology, must also be accepted with care, since the relationship between learned helplessness and psychopathology has not yet been demonstrated. Nevertheless, learned helplessness may be a valuable concept linking individual psychopathology to environmental conditions, and as such may help form a bridge between individual and sociocultural phenomena.

Although much remains to be learned about the measurement and impact of life events, it seems likely that their influence on psychopathology and health operate throughout the life span. If too severe, they may impair development of important adaptive capacities in childhood, or prior to the onset of disorder. After the onset of disorder, life events may interfere with coping mechanisms and precipitate exacerbations. However, the relationship between life events and psychopathology is not a simple one. For example, it must be remembered that on occasion, severe stressful life events appear to have a positive mobilizing effect—such as in reports of catatonic patients responding appropriately and adequately to fire in a hospital after having been mute and immobile for extended periods of time.

THE PSYCHIATRIC HOSPITAL

Another situation providing a potential for studying the link between individual psychopathology and sociocultural factors is the psychiatric hospital. This setting, as Caudill pointed out (11), is in fact a small society. Although the problems of studying such a society are considerable and care must be used in generalizing findings, much progress has been made in developing the necessary methods to enable this setting to be used to study individual/-sociocultural interaction. The work of Almond (1) and Moos (46) has provided conceptual and methodological advances since the initial pioneering work of Caudill (11), Stanton & Schwartz (65), and Barton (6). Earlier anecdotal data regarding covert power and communication systems and factors promoting "institutionalism" may now be replaced by more systematically collected information providing improved means for generating and testing hypotheses.

Progress in this area has been hindered somewhat as a side effect of the many criticisms of psychiatric hospitals in general and "milieu" treatment in particular. Much of this criticism arises from treatment shortcomings demonstrated in hospital systems previously used and the great expense of the hospital as a treatment modality. In spite of these problems, however, the psychiatric hospital or ward appears to be valuable for certain types of patients and essential for others. At the same time, it provides a setting that can be explored intensively to understand better the relationship between the individual's milieu and the course of his disorder. With the methods now available for studying ward atmosphere and the improved techniques for measuring course of disorder (20), the stage is set for more effective investigations of the psychiatric hospital situation and its implications for understanding relationships between the course of individual psychopathology and the social system.

THEORETICAL CONSIDERATIONS

The literature cited above and the speculations generated from it suggest some approaches for bridging the gap between sociocultural factors and individual psychopathology. Clearly, the difficulties involved and the amount of ignorance still remaining are most impressive. The ideal of defining temporal impact, causal model, and diagnostic axis for the influence of each sociocultural variable as described at the beginning of this paper is far more demanding than any information currently available can achieve. Because it is not possible, or perhaps even desirable, to go about attempting to fill all these gaps randomly, it is worthwhile to suggest some hypotheses arising from available information that may help to guide the priorities for further research.

Three hypotheses not mutually exclusive are of particular interest, given the information now available. The first of these focuses on stimulus level as a key construct. This hypothesis suggests that psychopathology is caused, and chronicity or exacerbations promoted, by extreme levels of stimulation and stress. High levels of stress, whether these be life events such as losses, hostile and intrusive families, or excessive demands, may contribute to psychopathology onset, exacerbations, or chronicity. Insufficient stimulation or expectations of the individual such as one might find, for example, resulting from a labeling system that implied the person would never be able to function again, might lead to withdrawal and flatness and through these to chronicity. This stimulus level hypothesis has been suggested for schizophrenia (73) and may be one important approach for organizing a variety of sociocultural data in relation to other types of psychopathology as well.

The second hypothesis focuses on the presumed importance of the individual's ability to manage stimuli. In a sense, this is the converse of the first hypothesis. Rather than emphasizing environmental stimulus level, however, it focuses on the capacities of the individual to manage the situation in which he finds himself. The extensive literature on coping styles is particularly relevant to this area.

Many authors (e.g. 16, 51) have studied how coping styles and their failure may be related to psychopathology. It seems likely that stressful life events interact in some way with coping styles to determine whether the individual decompensates or not. It is unlikely that the relationship is a simple one, however, since some stresses have been reported clinically to be associated with improvement in psychopathology, not deterioration, and many characteristics, from level of self-esteem (49) to patterns of family function (27), affect the type and adequacy of the individual's coping behaviors. Thus coping styles are not only required to deal with the sociocultural environment, they are also greatly modified by it (5, 38, 45). The ability of an individual to master a situation is determined not only by his basic abilities, but also by the type of problem and the context—including supports, demands, distractions, and other characteristics—in which the problem is embedded.

Understanding the role of coping styles as mediators between the individual, his psychopathology, and the sociocultural environment is not only important theoretically; it is also crucial for rational treatment. For example, Chess (13) has noted that many different factors at successive life stages help to promote coping, adaptation, and growth and can often succeed in this even if a major deficit has arisen at some earlier point. Similarly, considering the availability of alternative ways for the individual to "solve" certain kinds of problems is an important conceptual tool for thinking about treatment and environmental impacts (71). For example, in treating a psychotic person, chlorpromazine, psychotherapy, a therapeutic milieu, or social skills training might all provide useful ways for overcoming particular symptoms and deficits. Even more likely, some combination of these might best meet the needs for stopping the decompensation process and for encouraging return to personal growth. In such a model, sociocultural factors would be seen both as providing a number of adaptational problems to the individual and a variety of ways of helping to overcome them. Using such a model, the analysis of sociocultural factors influencing individual psychopathology could attempt to define these problems or resource functions.

A third hypothesis relevant to sociocultural impacts on individual psychopathology is needed to provide an orientation for considering determinants of type of disorder. Findings from the last few years suggest that the major kinds of psychopathology are found in all cultures. In contrast to what has often been suggested, this does not necessarily indicate that these disorders are mostly biological in origin and relatively unaffected by sociocultural characteristics. It is equally possible that there is a certain range of experiences that are universal to the human condition, for example, perhaps arising out of the need of all infants to be raised by older individuals. But any hypothesis about sociocultural determinants of type of disorder must include the specific as well as the universal factors. In conditions such as latah and windego, specific cultural factors appear to be the predominant determinants of symptomatology, and in all psychiatric disorders symptom profiles and specific content appear to be influenced by local norms and beliefs (40).

One hypothesis that could be used to account for these findings is that several factors exist which determine the degree of impact that specific cultural variables have in determining characteristics of disorder. Isolation of a subculture, limited importance of biologic determinants, personality characteristics of the individual, or the rigidity of family boundaries might all help to determine the degree to which specific cultural factors have an impact on a particular type of psychopathology.

Clearly, the three general hypotheses described above focusing on stimulus level, stimulus management, and ways sociocultural factors influence type of abnormal behavior are not mutually exclusive. They, or hypotheses like them, could be used singly or in combination to suggest a framework for research to set priorities for pursuing the many questions raised earlier in this review. If the stimulus level model were to be explored, for example, a variety of sociocultural influences on that level could be systematically investigated with attention to the time of their impact, the causal model most appropriate, and the specific diagnostic axes involved. It might even be useful to combine the types of hypotheses described above into a concept of vulnerability that could attempt to specify how characteristics like stress, coping abilities, social support systems, and labeling mediate between biologic, psychologic, and sociocultural factors to render the individual likely to develop psychopathology.

CONCLUSIONS

A Broad Street pump has not been found that can simplify the understanding of most psychiatric disorders. In this review, I have tried to describe some of the elements needing consideration in understanding sociocultural influences on psychopathology and some general principles necessary for beginning to organize these data. In a review of literature on premorbid adjustment in schizophrenia, it has been noted that increasing knowledge may highlight the magnitude of our ignorance (68). One must face a similar recognition in reviewing findings about the influence of social and cultural factors on psychopathology. If, as seems likely, there is a relatively specific interaction between the various sociocultural factors and diagnostic characteristics, if, as also seems likely, the causal systems involved are complex, and if psychopathology itself is complex, the few findings that have been isolated seem meager indeed in relation to all that needs to be known. For these reasons, a major need for the next several years is to provide an increasingly valid conceptual structure for organizing and directing investigations concerned with knowledge about how social and cultural factors affect psychiatric disorder in the individual.

Because of the need to generate more specific hypotheses about the complex interactions involved, it might be valuable in research on social and cultural factors to use not only large N or epidemiologic studies, but also to carry out more intensive studies of small numbers of subjects, both cross-culturally and within a community (30). In that way it might be possible to generate more specific hypotheses regarding the major relationships. For example, what are the differences in the individual experience of the discharged schizophrenic from social class 5 in comparison with the experience of a discharged schizophrenic from class 1? How do the differences in stresses, support systems, the need to cope with the welfare bureaucracy or some other type of characteristic influence the disorder in these two kinds of individuals? Although further research on general factors will continue to be valuable, intensive small N research by individuals skilled in both clinical and sociological areas is needed to provide more specific hypotheses and methods to clarify what really is the relationship of social and cultural factors to psychopathology.

Literature Cited

1. Almond, R. 1974. *The Healing Community.* New York: Aronson
2. American Psychiatric Association. 1968. *DSM II.* Washington DC: Am. Psychiatr. Assoc.
3. American Psychiatric Association Task Force on Nomenclature and Statistics. 1968 (draft). *Diagnostic and Statistical Manual of Mental Disorders III*
4. Anonymous. 1977. On being diagnosed schizophrenic. *Schizophr. Bull.* 3:4
5. Argyris, C. 1968. *Understanding Organizational Behavior.* Homewood, Ill: Dorsey
6. Barton, R. 1959. *Institutional Neurosis.* Bristol: Wright
7. Behrens, M. I., Rosenthal, A. T., Chodoff, P. 1968. Communication in lower class families of schizophrenics. *Arch. Gen. Psychiatry* 18:689–96
8. Brown, G. W., Birley, J. L. T., Wing, J. K. 1972. Influence of family life on the course of schizophrenic disorders: A

replication. *Br. J. Psychiatry* 121(562): 241–58
9. Brown, G. W., Bhrolchain, M. N., Harris, T. O. 1975. Social class and psychiatric disturbance among women in an urban population. *Sociology* 9:225–54
10. Cassel, J. 1976. The contribution of the social environment to host resistance. *Am. J. Epidemiol.* 104(2):107–23
11. Caudill, W. 1957. *The Psychiatric Hospital as a Small Society.* Cambridge: Harvard Univ. Press
12. Center for Minority Studies, National Institute of Mental Health. 1977. *Workshop on Minority Research.* Washington DC
13. Chess, S. 1976. *The plasticity of human development: Alternative pathways.* Presented at Ann. Meet. Am. Acad. Child Psychiatry, Toronto
14. Clausen, J. A., Kohn, M. L. 1969. In *Epidemiology of Human Disorder,* pp.

69–94. Am. Assoc. Adv. Sci., Washington DC: A.A.A.S.

15. Cobb, S. 1976. Social support as a moderator of life stress. *Psychosom. Med.* 38(5):300–14

16. Coelho, G. V., Hamburg, D. A., Adams, J. E. 1974. *Coping and Adaptation.* New York: Basic Books

17. Cooper, J., Sartorius, N. 1977. Cultural and temporal variations in schizophrenia: A speculation on the importance of industrialization. *Br. J. Psychiatry* 139:50–55

18. Cooper, J. E., Kendell, R. E., Gurland, B. J., Sharpe, L., Copeland, J. R. M., Simon, R. 1976. *Psychiatric Diagnosis in New York and London.* Oxford Univ. Press

19. DeFries, Z., Grothe, L. 1978. High academic achievement in psychotic students. *Am. J. Psychiatry* 135(2):217–19

20. Docherty, J. P. 1977. *Stages of onset of schizophrenic psychosis.* Presented at Ann. Meet. Am. Psychiatr. Assoc.

21. Dunham, H. W. 1976. Society, culture, and mental disorder. *Arch. Gen. Psychiatry* 33:147–56

22. Essen-Moller, E. 1971. Suggestions for further improvement of the international classification of mental disorders. *Psychol. Med.* 1:308–11

23. Fallik, A., Liron, R. 1976. A follow-up on schizophrenics from various social subgroups seven years after initial hospitalization. *Isr. Ann. Psychiatry Relat. Discip.* 14(3):299–39

24. Fangel, C. 1979. In *New Dimensions in Psychiatry,* ed. S. Arieti, G. Chrzanowski. New York: Wiley. In press

25. Favazza, A. R., Oman, M. 1977. *Anthropological and Cross-Cultural Themes in Mental Health: An Annotated Bibliography, 1925–1974.* Minneapolis: Univ. Minnesota Press

26. Frias, C. A. 1974. A transcultural survey of psychiatric opinion on schizophrenia. *Compr. Psychiatry* 15(3): 225–31

27. Goldstein, M. J., Judd, L., Rodnick, E., Alkire, A., Gould, E. 1968. A method for studying social influence and coping patterns within families of disturbed adolescents. *J. Nerv. Ment. Dis.* 147: 233–51

28. Gove, W., Howell, P. 1974. Individual resources and mental hospitalization: A comparison and evaluation of the societal reaction and psychiatric perspective. *Am. Sociol. Rev.* 39:86–100

29. Harder, D. W., Strauss, J. S., Kokes, R. F., Ritzler, B. A., Gift, T. E. 1977. *Life events and psychopathology among first psychiatric admissions.* Presented at Ann. Meet. Am. Psychol. Assoc.

30. Henry, J. 1965. *Pathways to Madness.* New York: Random House

31. Jegede, R. O. 1977. *Problems encountered in psychotherapy in Nigeria.* Presented at World Congr. Psychiatry, Honolulu

32. Kaplan, B., ed. 1964. *The Inner World of Mental Illness.* New York: Harper & Row

33. Katz, M. M., Sanborn, K. O. 1976. In *International Collaboration in Mental Health,* ed. B. S. Brown, E. F. Torrey. Washington DC: GPO

34. King, L. M. 1978. Social and cultural influences on psychopathology. *Ann. Rev. Psychol.* 29:405–33

35. Kirkegaard-Sorenson, L., Mednick, S. A. 1975. Registered criminality in families with children at high risk for schizophrenia. *J. Abnorm. Psychol.* 84:197–204

36. Kohn, M. 1972. Class, family and schizophrenia: A reformulation. *Soc. Forces* 50(3):295–313

37. Lamb, H. R., Goertzel, V., Mackota, C., Richmond, C., Salkind, I. 1976. *Rehabilitation in Community Mental Health.* San Franciso: Jossey-Bass

38. Lazarus, R. 1966. *Psychological Stress and the Coping Process.* New York: McGraw-Hill

39. Leff, J. P., Fischer, M., Bertelsen, A. 1976. A cross-national epidemiological study of mania. *Br. J. Psychiatry* 129:428–42

40. Leon, C. A. 1975. "El Duende" and other incubi. *Arch. Gen. Psychiatry* 32:155–62

41. Lorion, R. P. 1976. Ethnicity and mental health: An empirical obstacle course. *Int. J. Ment. Health* 5(2):16–25

42. Mezzich, J. E., Raab, E. S. 1977. *Depressive phenomenology across the Americas.* Presented at World Congr. Psychiatry, Honolulu

43. Miller, P., Ingham, J. G. 1976. Friends, confidants and symptoms. *Soc. Psychiatry* 11:51–58

44. Miller, S. M. 1964. In *Mental Health of the Poor,* ed. Reissman, Cohen, Pearl, pp. 139–54. New York: Free Press of Glencoe

45. Mischel, W. 1968. *Personality and Assessment.* New York: Wiley

46. Moos, R. H. 1974. *Evaluating Treatment Environments: A Social Ecological Approach.* New York: Wiley

47. Mosher, L. Personal communication

48. Mosher, L. R., Menn, A. Z. 1976. Dinosaur or astronaut? One-year follow-up

data from the Soteria Project. *Am. J. Psychiatry* 133:919–20

49. Mossman, B. M., Ziller, R. C. 1968. Self-esteem and consistency of social behavior. *J. Abnorm. Psychol.* 73:363–67

50. Murphy, J. M. 1976. Psychiatric labeling in cross-cultural perspective. *Science* 191:1019–28

51. Murphy, L. B., Moriarty, A. E. 1976. *Vulnerability, Coping and Growth from Infancy to Adolescence.* New Haven: Yale Univ. Press

52. Ottosson, J. O., Perris, C. 1973. Multidimensional classification of mental disorders. *Psychol. Med.* 3:238–43

53. Paykel, E. S., McGuiness, B., Gomez, J. 1976. An Anglo-American comparison of the scaling of life events. *Br. J. Med. Psychol.* 49:237–47

54. Rabkin, J. G., Stuening, E. L. 1976. Life events, stress, and illness. *Science* 194:1013–20

55. Rahe, R., Fløistad, I., Bergan, T., Ringdal, R., Gerhardt, R., Gunderson, E., Arthir, R. J. 1974. A model for life changes and illness research: Cross-cultural data from the Norwegian navy. *Arch. Gen. Psychiatry* 31:172–77

56. Reiss, D. 1969. Individual thinking and family interaction. IV. A study of information exchange in families of normals, those with character disorders, and schizophrenics. *J. Nerv. Ment. Dis.* 149:473–90

57. Rin, H., Scholer, C., Caudill, W. 1973. Symptomatology and hospitalization: Culture, social structure and psychopathology in Taiwan and Japan. *J. Nerv. Ment. Dis.* 157(4):296–312

58. Rosenberg, E. J., Dohrenwend, B. S. 1975. Effects of experience and ethnicity on ratings of life events as stressors. *J. Health Soc. Behav.* 16(1):127–241

59. Rothwell, N., Doniger, J. 1966. *The Psychiatric Halfway House.* Springfield, Ill: Thomas

60. Rutter, M., Shaffer, D., Shepherd, M. 1973. An evaluation of the proposal for a multi-axial classification of child psychiatric disorders. *Psychol. Med.* 3:244–50

61. Sameroff, A. 1973. Schizotaxia revisited: Model issues in the etiology of schizophrenia. *Am. J. Orthopsychiatry* 43:744–53

62. Scheff, T. J. 1974. The labelling theory of mental illness. *Am. Sociol. Rev.* 39:444–52

63. Seligman, M. E. P. 1975. *Helplessness.* San Francisco: Freeman

64. Silberfeld, M. 1978. Psychological symptoms and social supports. *Soc. Psychiatry* 13:11–17

65. Stanton, A. H., Schwartz, M. S. 1954. *The Mental Hospital.* New York: Basic Books

66. Strauss, J. S. 1975. A comprehensive approach to psychiatric diagnosis. *Am. J. Psychiatry* 132(11):1193–97

67. Strauss, J. S., Carpenter, W. T. Jr. 1977. Prediction of outcome in schizophrenia. III. Five-year outcome and its predictors. A report from the International Pilot Study of Schizophrenia. *Arch. Gen. Psychiatry* 34:158–63

68. Strauss, J. S., Kokes, R. F., Klorman, R., Sacksteder, J. 1977. Premorbid adjustment in schizophrenia: Concepts, measures and implications. *Schizophr. Bull.* 3(2):182–244

69. Townsend, J. M. 1975. Cultural conceptions and mental illness: A controlled comparison of Germany and America. *J. Nerv. Ment. Dis.* 160(6):409–21

70. Uhlenhuth, E., Balter, M. D., Lipman, R. S., Haberman, S. J. 1977. In *The Origins and Course of Psychopathology,* ed. J. Strauss, H. Babigian, M. Roff. New York: Plenum

71. Vaillant, G. Personal communication

72. Vaughn, C. E., Leff, J. P. 1976. The influence of family and social factors on the course of psychiatric illness: A comparison of schizophrenic and depressed neurotic patients. *Br. J. Psychiatry* 129:125–37

73. Wing, J. K. 1975. In *Life History Research in Psychopathology,* Vol. 4, ed. R. Wirt, G. Winokur, M. Roff. Minneapolis: Univ. Minnesota Press

74. World Health Organization. 1973. *The International Pilot Study of Schizophrenia,* Vol. 1. Geneva: World Health Organ. Press

75. World Health Organization. 1978. *The International Pilot Study of Schizophrenia,* Vol. 2. New York: Wiley

76. Wynne, L. C., Singer, M. T., Toohey, M. L. 1975. *Communication of the adoptive parents of schizophrenics.* Presented at Int. Symp. Psychother. Schizophr., 5th, Oslo

77. Yap, P. M. 1974. *Comparative Psychiatry,* ed, M. P. Lau, A. B. Stokes. Toronto: Univ. Toronto Press

78. Zarroug, E. 1975. The frequency of visual hallucinations in schizophrenic patients in Saudi Arabia. *Br. J. Psychiatry* 127:553–55

Ann. Rev. Psychol. 1979. 30:417–51
Copyright © 1979 by Annual Reviews Inc. All rights reserved

THE PSYCHOLOGY
OF GROUP PROCESSES

♦313

Alvin Zander

Research Center for Group Dynamics, The University of Michigan,
Ann Arbor, Michigan 48109

CONTENTS

THE GROWTH OF A FIELD 418
  The Initial Purposes of Group Psychology 419
  Topics of Research in the Psychology of Groups 420
  Why Particular Topics Have Been Studied 422
  Overlooked Topics in Research 422
  Characteristics of Research on Groups 423
RECENT RESEARCH 424
  Cognitive Behavior in Groups 424
    Decision rules and schemes 425
    Deliberating and deciding 426
    How to improve group decisions 426
  Social Pressures on Group Members 428
    Increasing the effect of social pressures 429
    Deindividuation 431
  Cohesiveness of a Group 433
    Sources of group cohesiveness 433
    Desire to affiliate 436
  Evaluation of Self and Group 438
  Cooperation and Competition 440
  Leadership, Its Nature and Effects 440
    Appraisal of leaders 440
    Leadership and influence 442
    Participation by members in group decisions 443
  Group Size and Density 444
  Group Structure 446
  Summary 447

0066-4308/79/0201-0417$01.00

THE GROWTH OF A FIELD

On a warm September evening in 1942, Kurt Lewin spoke in Washington, D.C. to a dinner meeting of the Society for the Psychological Study of Social Issues. The second World War had just begun and travel was restricted, causing the Society to cancel its annual convention and to substitute this single session for persons in the neighborhood. Everyone was worried in those days about the fate of the country and the future of democracy, thus the audience probably was inclined to welcome the speaker's brave prediction.

> Although the scientific investigations of group work are but a few years old, I don't hesitate to predict that group work—that is, the handling of human beings not as isolated individuals, but in the social setting of groups—will soon be one of the most important theoretical and practical fields. . . . There is no hope for creating a better world without a deeper scientific insight into the function of leadership and culture, and of other essentials of group life (63).

Later he added: "It is easier to affect the personality of ten people if they can be melted into a group than to affect the personality of any one individual separately." After asserting that "all education is group work," he remarked that psychologists who study curves of learning leave the problems of social management in the classroom entirely to practitioners, who accordingly are forced to base their teaching on the primitive method of trial and error or upon a mixture of philosophy and instinct.

He illustrated the kinds of research that could be done in years to come by describing work that he, Lippitt, Bavelas, French, and others had recently conducted into styles of leadership, training of leaders, persuasion of members through group discussion, and group reactions to fearful stimuli. These studies had attracted extraordinary attention from editors in press and radio because the editors were surprised to learn that group members in the experimental laboratory could be induced to show one kind of behavior under one condition (for example, a particular style of leadership) and a contrasting kind under a different condition.

On the whole, Lewin's prediction was correct and he had a major part in making it come true. Earlier, during the period from 1890 until 1940, there had been a gradual growth in the number of published studies on group behavior from one per year to around 30 per year. By the late 1940s this rate had risen to 55 annually and at the end of 1950 to about 150 (41). As far as we can tell, a rate of about 125 per year has persisted through the 60s and 70s on a fairly flat plateau. Although the annual number of publications on research in group processes has not changed much in the last 20 years, the image and content of the work has changed a great deal. Writers on group research in the *Annual Reviews of Psychology* published in 1951,

1953, 1954, and 1956 commented that research on groups was the "most lively and creative" work in social psychology. But by the 1960s the reviewers' remarks were less favorable: research on groups is "badly in need of integration," "it does not amount to much," or "it has come up with nothing new."

In the early 1950s the study of groups received warm public support among ordinary citizens and social scientists alike because it promised to provide answers to problems of the time. This lively interest receded in the 1960s and "group dynamics" became a regular, not especially innovative, course in the catalogs of most campuses. Today its major concern is in developing a body of knowledge, not in solving practical problems. The Research Center for Group Dynamics was founded in 1946 and at one time there were seven similar units around the world, most of which have now disappeared. Members of the Research Center for Group Dynamics nowadays, compared to the 1950s, receive fewer letters asking about the outcomes of their research, fewer requests for speeches about their work or the field, fewer visitors, and they themselves do less research on groups. The number of agencies providing funds for research on groups furthermore has been cut in half.

The amount of research and writing on the psychology of groups in sum developed rapidly, and the field is now a stable and accepted specialty. Will it hold its own or have a new spurt in growth, as some predict? We cannot answer that question, but we can sharpen our understanding of the issue by observing what students of groups have been trying to do, have studied, and have ignored.

The Initial Purposes of Group Psychology

In the late 1940s, after a miserable world-wide economic depression, the rise of dictatorship in Europe, and the development of international aggression there, it had become evident that the democratic nations were more hesitant than the dictorships in planning and initiating action. Many thinkers began to say that we needed a better understanding of how democratic organizations can be made to function more effectively and asked for more research on that problem. Scientists had helped win the war, they said, now research should improve democracy. Scientists, especially social psychologists (a newly arrived specialty), began to conduct studies into group discussion, group productivity, ways of changing attitudes, or problems in leadership, and to test their theories in programs of research. Because testing of theories can best be done through controlled experiments, the number of laboratory investigations (of necessity, on fairly small groups) increased greatly. Many scholars in those days firmly believed that experimental work would soon provide ways of strengthening democratic methods.

A quite different approach also developed in the late 1940s to improve democratic processes. It was based on the notions that leaders needed more skill, that members could improve their own efforts, that organizations could be helped to develop better methods, and that changes within them could be introduced more easily under some conditions than under others. These practical assumptions led "change agents" to a lively commerce in consulting, training, action research, and social engineering. The assumptions furnished basic beliefs for the "human relations" movement during the 1950s and early 1960s. The National Training Laboratory in Group Development, founded in 1947 with the help of the Research Center for Group Dynamics, began to teach about groups in ways the harder sciences had been using for years. The method required that participants examine and discuss events in their own group. The openness of these discussions generated a form of counseling for those who attended a laboratory, and an emphasis on understanding of self eventually displaced the initial interest in groups. Back (5), Marrow (71), and Steiner (97), have described how the followers of such a practical approach developed a special wisdom about the values of sensitive encounters, not based on results of research.

Topics of Research in the Psychology of Groups

Prior to 1920, research into group behavior had been devoted to two simple topics, according to Hare (41): The effect of an audience on the performance of an individual and the contrast between individuals and groups in their ability to solve problems. Murphy, Murphy & Newcomb (77), in their review of social psychology prior to 1937, assert that the topics under study in the 1930s were the willingness of group members to believe (distorted) information (called group suggestibility), causes of laughter in an audience, the effects of competition and rivalry among members, and changes in the motor skills of members while being razzed by friends. Late in the 30s the most notable topics were the effects of varied styles of leadership (109), the reasons that persons become leaders (47), and consequences of social support in an industrial setting (84). In the 1940s, according to Jerome Bruner who wrote the chapter on groups in the 1950 *Annual Review of Psychology*, most research was done on interactions among members of discussion groups and the comparative ability of lectures and group discussions in changing behavior. Fourteen of the 27 volumes in the *Annual Review of Psychology* since 1950 have had chapters on group research. These chapters provide a convenient source for identifying important topics of research as the authors saw them. These areas of research are shown in the following tabulation, along with the years in which each was of lively interest among investigators.

Topic	Years mentioned in *Annual Review of Psychology*
1. Coding the nature of comments by discussants in groups	1950, '51, '53, '58
2. Changing the behavior of individuals through lectures and group discussions	1950
3. The power of a group to determine the behavior of members, social pressures toward uniformity of behavior and belief among members	1951, '52, '53, '55, '56, '57, '58, '60, '67
4. Leadership and management, effects of a leader's style	1951, '52, '58, '73
5. The effect of social networks on communication within groups	1953, '56, '58, '61, '67
6. The conflicted behavior of individuals who observe that the evidence of their own senses contrasts with the (stated) perceptions of others	1954, '73
7. Interpersonal social power and influence, sources and effects	1955, '60, '67, '76
8. The formation of coalitions within larger groups	1955
9. Balance in the social structures of groups	1960, '67
10. Cooperation and competition, prisoner's dilemma, mixed motive games	1967, '73, '76
11. Social facilitation of an observed person's behavior, the effects of mere exposure	1973, '76
12. The "riskiness" of judgments, individuals vs groups, the "risky shift"	1973, '76
13. Cognitive behavior, problem solving, rules of making decisions in groups	1973, '76, '77

Several things are notable about this sample of subjects. First, there are fashions in research, that is, subjects arise, demand attention for awhile, are dropped, and may reappear at a later date. Second, the interest in some topics lasts longer than in other topics. Issues with the longest tenure have been: the power of the group to influence members, communication networks, aspects of leadership, coding the comments of discussants, and interpersonal power. Third, topics that interest many persons do not necessarily retain that interest for a long period of time. Examples are: research on the risky shift, and the "prisoner's dilemma." Although it is not evident in this tabulation, new topics grow out of old ones and are usually stated more precisely than the parent subject. To illustrate: work on the impact of group decisions led into studies of social pressures within groups; demonstrations of leadership style moved into research on social power; research on the risky shift became work on the origins of polarization among members; and investigations of intragroup competition developed into ways of resolving social conflicts.

Why Particular Topics Have Been Studied

A limited set of subjects has thus far been investigated out of the vast array available to scholars. Each area of inquiry in the above tabulation includes a number of investigations, not many in some cases, hundreds in others; research has been deep in a few topics and shallow in a large number. Why were these particular subjects chosen for study? One reason is that a good piece of research by a respected scientist stimulates imitation by others. Leon Festinger's (32) work on social communication and the power of the group over the member inspired other studies at once. The article by Wallach, Kogan & Bem (107) on the "risky shift" instigated an embarrassing number of studies. Zajonc's articles on social facilitation (115), and the writings of Cartwright (13) and also of French & Raven (37) on interpersonal power, aroused wide use of these ideas.

It has been said that some topics in research become interesting because professional practitioners ask researchers for help on them. Perhaps such requests occasionally occur, but I have never seen one. More often problems arise in society (in the media, that is) which suggest subjects worthy of research, as in the failure of neighbors to help Kitty Genovese ward off her attacker, Senator McCarthy's efforts to repress ideas he disliked, "brainwashing" during the Korean war, effects of job stress on mental health, or prejudice against members of minority groups. But it is not possible to say why a given social problem stimulates research while another one does not.

A potent determinant of what is selected to be studied is a researcher's unexpected realization that an already accepted concept or theory in individual psychology is relevant to group life and that the concept can help explain matters in groups that previously had not been understood. The theory of individual need for achievement has been useful, for example, in explaining how and why members choose particular goals for their joint efforts (117). New ideas for research have been suggested by the emergence of new tools such as tape recording machines, TV monitors and cameras, digital computer terminals, or instruments to monitor physiological signs at a distance. Some research methods and designs stimulate use because they are less expensive or complicated than others. The most attractive stimulants to study a given issue are disagreements among researchers about an accepted theory or efforts to expand such a theory in a new direction. These actions allow a scholar to have a legitimate role in the game of research, played for its own sake and not for its relevance to events in natural settings.

Overlooked Topics in Research

Many researchable issues in the psychology of groups have been ignored. Examples of bypassed topics can be put in the form of questions: Why is it so difficult to expel a member from a group? What are the consequences of secrecy within an organization? Why is a manager met with abrasiveness from subordinates? What tools will help committees have more efficient meetings? How do groups react to new regulations laid on them by external agencies? Why do groups select goals that are too difficult? How do members respond to embarrassment about their organization's performance? (120). One can easily think of other subjects that warrant study: changes in the properties of groups over time, why members participate in a group, the sources of conflict between groups, the contrasting effects of centralization and decentralization in a group, the origins of a group's goals, the causes of productivity in a group, or the effects of the social environment on a group.

One reason such subjects have been more or less ignored is that researchers cannot decide how to conceive or measure the events involved in them. Moreover, fund granting agencies may not be willing to support this kind of work and advisers of such agencies may avoid new ideas in favor of ones they already know well. Editors of journals exclude papers on some topics, and federal regulations for treatment of human subjects rule out certain kinds of research or make it too awkward to bother. Problems that once were popular lose their appeal when investigators conclude that the results of their research have not adequately sharpened understanding. A given concept will gradually change its nature as it is used in research and in so doing may become less interesting (e.g. the "risky shift," coalitions within group).

Characteristics of Research on Groups

Over the 30 years since research on groups came into its own, several features have characterized its methods. The majority of studies have been controlled experiments and a good proportion of these have used some simple method, such as the coding of members' behaviors, the use of a specially equipped round table that allows a researcher to open or close channels of communication between members, or the employment of a zero-sum matrix to study cooperation or competition between two persons. Much of the concentration on established and simple procedures is due to the need among graduate students and other underfinanced investigators for inexpensive research results while using a method they are sure will be accepted by their peers. As already implied, there are few well-developed theories about behavior in groups. The theories that do exist, moreover, seldom aid in understanding groups as such, or even the behavior of members in behalf of their groups, because the theories often are based on ideas taken from individual psychology, and these are primarily concerned with the actions of individuals for the good of those individuals. Most researchers into groups, moreover, do not try to explain things that happen to a group as an entity because such investigations require that groups be the units of study which demands too many participants, costs too much, takes too much time, and is too complicated in design and analysis. It is more convenient to study single members than their groups (97).

Researchers in group life are remarkably inventive in creating new names for phenomena that already have a name. A number of synonyms exist, as examples, to denote a member's desire to remain in a group, the functions of a leader, the ends toward which groups strive, the structural properties of groups, and so on. Different terms often have the same definitions, and a given scholar therefore may ignore research done under labels unlike the one he or she prefers even though it is quite relevant to his or her interests.

Commentators about research on groups often say that its findings are not well integrated. Steiner (97) thinks that such integration cannot occur until there is a renewed interest in the study of groups. But varied results from various settings make it difficult to generalize about trends in research so that students in separate disciplines will accept them equally. Also, the basic assumptions of individual psychology, social psychology, sociology, anthropology, and other disciplines do not fit together well because the concepts employed by each field are based on different primitive terms. Can we reasonably hope for a day when similar concepts will be used among all students of group life in all academic fields or professions? That day appears to be far in the future.

RECENT RESEARCH

Cognitive Behavior in Groups

Over the years there have been notably few sound efforts to explain what goes on when groups are making decisions or solving problems. The failure to develop theories in this area is noteworthy because many groups exist to solve or to decide in our society. There are, it is relevant to remind ourselves, thousands of corporations in the United States. When researchers have studied cognitive efforts in groups, they have usually conducted investigations in which they simply describe the steps a typical group follows toward a solution. In the 1960s and 1970s there was an upsurge of interest in cognitive behavior, especially in modes of perceiving and of processing information. Some scholars were stimulated by this upsurge to concentrate on cognitive aspects of interpersonal relations under such topics as cognitive dissonance, attribution theory, game theory, polarization of members' attitudes, social schemas, and the like. Researchers on human interaction under those headings have not been particularly interested in whether these interactions occurred within a group. Indeed, in their chapter on the social psychology of small groups in the 1976 volume of the *Annual Review of Psychology*, Davis, Laughlin & Komarita assert that "small group behavior has come to mean . . . the relatively free interaction of two or more actual persons." Not all students of groups will agree with Davis and his colleagues that group behavior is merely a form of human interaction, but they will probably be impressed by the 503 references cited in their chapter. Most of these citations, however, concern research on the effects of mixed motives among two individuals, and only a few of the references deal with traditional topics in research on groups. In this chapter, our primary emphasis is on the group.

DECISION RULES AND SCHEMES   The bylaws of a deliberative body usually contain a rule about the number of persons who must favor a motion before it can be carried. A two-thirds majority may be needed, for example, or even unanimity. A jury on a criminal case is usually required to reach a unanimous decision about the guilt of an accused person. Would a jury make a different decision if the decision is to be based on a two-thirds majority instead of unanimity? In two laboratory experiments designed to answer that question, it was found that the distribution of guilty and not guilty verdicts was the same regardless of the proportion of jury members who had to concur (21, 79). A replication of this experiment in which the decision now required a mere majority (51 percent or more), versus unanimity, provided a similar result (22). Deliberations within groups that had to attain unanimity, compared to those that had to get agreement among a mere majority, were characterized by more conflict among participants, more shifts of opinion, a longer time to reach a conclusion, and more confidence in the correctness of their verdicts (79). In another study, those groups that had to reach unanimity often failed to reach a decision at all (51). Clearly the attainment of unanimity is harder on the members and is more difficult to complete than is the reaching of a majority.

Laughlin, Kerr, and several colleagues (60, 61) have examined the processes members follow when they solve problems for which the correct answers are known. The authors identified ten social decision schemes such as proportionality (the probability that a group will reach a given decision is equal to the proportion of members advocating it); truth-wins (the right answer, when proposed by a member, is so persuasive that it convinces others); truth-supported wins (the right answer is convincing only if another member supports it); majority wins; majority, if correct, wins; strict equiprobability, etc. Laughlin and colleagues asked: is a group more accurate when it uses one of these schemes than when it uses another?

They observed that groups were more accurate if one member "knew" the correct answer (because the experimenter had given it to him ahead of time) and the group used the truth-wins scheme. The truth-wins scheme was also more effective if all members were highly capable rather than mediocre and if the task demanded insight by members rather than intellectual power. If the group's task required intellectual power (as in jointly solving items on the Otis test for mental ability), a group did better if three or four members had the correct answer and supported one another than if only one person initially had the correct answer. Research is now wanted on the comparative value of such social decisions schemes on an issue for which there is no correct answer. On uncertain tasks it seems unlikely that the truth-wins scheme would be as important to a group as it was above.

DELIBERATING AND DECIDING   As is well known, one of the most venerable methods in studying how groups solve problems is to compare actions by solo individuals and by groups as they work on the same problem. Such an approach allows the researcher to determine if events within a group are due to unique properties of that group or to the way individuals solve problems in any setting. The comparisons are intrapersonal versus interpersonal, private (solo) versus public (group), or minimal social influence versus maximal. Researchers have rung many changes on these themes while observing processes in the solving of problems. The private ideas of members on a given cognitive activity were not different, for example, from the ideas these persons offered during a group discussion (104). The numerical goals members privately chose for their group during a series of trials were the same as the goals that all of the group's membership preferred for it (117). Members of mock juries who were to be publicly accountable for their decisions moved more quickly than members whose decisions would remain private, even though their verdicts did not differ in these two conditions (22).

Often a person attends a meeting as an instructed representative of a group. Wall (105, 106) conducted several experiments in which he examined how the relationship between a representative and his constituents affects his behavior in a meeting where he is acting in behalf of his constituency. Wall reports that the representative is more competitive if he feels his constituents do not trust him, and he receives more pressures to be cooperative from female constituents than from males.

HOW TO IMPROVE GROUP DECISIONS   Social engineers attempt to make cognitive procedures within groups more efficient and accordingly propose methods and tools to improve meetings. Their procedural suggestions are devoted to such things as "shaping" group discussions (70); laying out the best sequence of steps in solving a complex problem, called the Program Evaluation Review Technique (20) and using subgroups to solve conflicts within a larger organization (17). Hardware has also been developed: a terminal for conferencing via computer, a picture-phone for conference calls, an electronic switching device that privately collects and collates information from discussants (92), and so on. These methods and tools warrant more careful evaluation than they have received. Are they really useful or merely ingenious? Such aids for meetings are usually devoted to one of three difficulties in a group's process: overcoming inhibitions among conferees, reducing confusion caused by different backgrounds among members, and making quick decisions when these are urgently needed (120).

How to make a group decision quickly when a crisis demands it has been discussed by several students of these matters. An elaborate model and a review of relevant research are offered by Smart & Vertinsky (93), who assume that the high level of emotional and physical stress during a crisis make deciding and implementing a decision vulnerable to malfunctioning. To prevent this malfunctioning they suggest that members plan how they might meet a sudden disaster, learn how to cope with such an event, and practice doing so. Kupperman, Wilcox & Smith (58) elucidate the difficulties a headquarters staff meets in dealing with a disaster, and Janis & Mann (45) note the steps to be followed in urgent decisions.

Discussions that are stalled because there are sharply contrasting views among the discussants can cause an emergency in a different sense—the problem sits unsolved while deliberators wrangle or refuse to discuss it sensibly. Levi & Benjamin (62) describe a way that such a conflict can be resolved, using an actual conference between Jews and Arabs as their source of data. Deutsch (26) summarizes the results of many laboratory experiments on resolving conflicts. Delbecq, Van de Ven & Gustafson (24) provide a manual containing practical advice for groups composed of persons from different areas of expertise who are working jointly on a problem that affects them all. Their "nominal group technique" is to help these individuals feel comfortable in working together even though each member tends to inhibit the others' participation. The authors also describe the Delphi process, which helps members pool opinions about what might happen, or ought to happen, on a specific issue for which compelling data are not available, such as the content of a curriculum for a high school in a small town. A book on resolving conflict within an organization, written by Likert & Likert (66), places special emphasis on a style of management that may be effective in doing so. An extraordinarily useful overview of research on decision making is included in the volume by Janis & Mann (45). They take a normative approach, describe an ideal process for making a decision, and explain how to attain this ideal. The writers delineate precautions that decision makers must take in order that they not be unhappy with their decision after it is made. The book presents results of research on these methods by solo individuals and groups.

Social Pressures on Group Members

One of the liveliest interests among students of group dynamics is the power of a group to influence the behavior and beliefs of members. Originally, in work on social pressures, researchers assumed these were exerted in order to ensure that the group achieved its objectives or maintained its existence (15). In more recent times, partly because of studies on the riskiness of group decisions, investigators have assumed that social pressures can cause polarization among members. This latter term refers to an increase in the extremity of the average views among sets of participants because persons who believed in idea X prior to a group's discussion become more strongly supportive of X, and those believed in the opposite of X become more supportive of non-X. Eventually the views of those who support X and of those who support the opposite of X move apart and become polarized due to contrasting social pressures.

There is good evidence from research in laboratories and natural settings that polarization often occurs during group discussions. Myers & Lamm (78) have written a fine review of this literature based on 160 articles and books. They consider three explanations for the appearance of polarization. The first is that it is a statistical artifact. The second, that polarization occurs when an individual discovers others share his view more than he had supposed they would. The third, which these authors favor (after rejecting the previous two), is that members learn new arguments during oral interaction which support the opinions they held before the discussion began. Myers and Lamm hold that members' passive receipt of arguments, or awareness of arguments, is not enough to generate this learning; instead the members must take an active part in discussion and thereby rehearse their own as well as others' beliefs. The social confrontation inherent in debate and deliberation, they say, arouses a useful rehearsal procedure, even while participants are contemplating their next remark.

In a neat study as part of an extended program of research supporting the notion of polarization, Burnstein & Vinokur (12) demonstrated that individuals will change their personal beliefs to match those of colleagues if they learn the views of the others and have a chance, in addition, to think about the arguments the others use to support their views (or to hear those arguments presented in a discussion). Participants do not change their beliefs, however, if they merely learn the opinions of others but do not have an opportunity to think about (work with) the arguments in favor of these beliefs. The impact of persuasive arguments, Anderson & Graesser (2) show, is "averaged" by listeners so that they later change their views in a pro or con direction, depending on the relative strength of the favorable or unfavorable arguments they hear, a refreshingly old-fashioned notion.

INCREASING THE EFFECT OF SOCIAL PRESSURES A group's attempts to change the behavior of a member do not always work; thus, students of group life have tried to determine the conditions under which pressures have more predictable effects. A widely accepted rule is that the power of a group over its members is a function of the cohesiveness of that group; or, saying it more precisely, the ability of a group to change the actions of a member depends on how much the latter desires to remain in that group (14). In addition to accepting this rule, Brehm & Mann (11) assume that a member experiences a loss of freedom when he conforms to pressures exerted by his colleagues. The above rule is more often obeyed by a member, they believe, if restriction of his freedom is not important to him, or if he resists the pressures laid on him by his groupmates because he dislikes a loss of freedom. Brehm and Mann found good support for these notions in a laboratory experiment in which the effectiveness of social pressures was reduced if it was important for the member to retain his freedom on the issue at hand, and rejection of the group's influence was also seen by a member to be a way to maintain his freedom.

The attempts by a collection of persons to influence an individual ought to be stronger as that set is larger. In several interesting studies, Wilder (111) has shown that a monolithic whole, regardless of its size, is nowhere near as proficient in inducing conformity among target persons as is a set of separate entities, regardless of their total number. To illustrate, many similar messages from many separate persons had a greater effect than one message from one group composed of many persons. The reasons for this contrast are not fully understood.

When the power of a group is stronger, participants gradually become more uniform in their beliefs. As a result of this similarity, members may not develop wise solutions to problems their group faces, because they believe they already have the best solution and they press one another to be loyal to their established doctrine. Janis (44) labeled this intellectual rigidity "groupthink" and described how actions by several powerful committees in the Federal government were damaged by it, causing unfavorable consequences for the nation. In their recent volume, Janis & Mann (45) more fully explain the origins of such malfunctioning in a group. Flowers (35), a colleague of Janis, conducted an experimental investigation in which groups with either a high or low degree of cohesiveness had a leader who used either an open or a closed style. An open leader welcomed new ideas from members, while a closed leader pressed his own ideas on them. A closed leader, Flowers found, generated more behavior typical of "groupthink" than did an open leader—but variations in cohesiveness were not associated with variations in these behaviors. The weakness of cohesiveness resulted perhaps from her experimental procedure for creating it, which bore little relevance to the definition of cohesiveness. She created groups of low cohesiveness by assembling sets of strangers, and groups of high cohesiveness by assembling sets of persons who had been more or less acquainted with one another. Greater acquaintance among groupmates does not ensure that they will more strongly desire to remain in the group.

The influence a group can have over its members has not been ignored by practitioners, especially those who counsel individuals in how to become more sober, less fat, or more understanding. Many self-help books have been devoted to group work and volumes on T-groups, encounter groups, sensitivity training, and other forms of group "experience" continue to appear. Usually these are based on anecdotes rather than research. Governments of some countries require their citizens to join small groups so they will learn there how to alter society in a "correct" direction. Whyte (110) interviewed hundreds of Chinese refugees who had participated in the small units created to conduct political rituals in China. He describes how pressures toward uniformity were employed in these groups to further movement toward national goals. The small-group political program in China has stimulated imitation in many other lands. Thus, in a conference at the East-West Center in Hawaii, representatives of a dozen Asians nations told of the use of small groups in changing the views and practices of their citizens. These reports are available in a book summarizing the results of that conference (18).

A given group may be pressed to conform to demands originating in a second group. Illustrations of intergroup influences, repeated in many places, are to be seen in the regulations a government agency puts on a business firm, hospital, church, university, city council, or union. Seemingly, additional layers of rules settle each year upon such organizations and every rule or prod requires some change within the target groups. Stone (99) has described special problems of regulating agencies as they enforce regulations that induce changes within organizations. The officers of a target group, moreover, must be wise planners and organizers if they are to help their units respond to external regulations without creating a minor rebellion among their colleagues. There have been no empirical investigations of the conditions that cause these environmental pressures to be effective in changing a group. But sources of a group's resistance to pressures from outside it, the origins of members' tendencies to have their group comply, and how officers go about ensuring conformity to external requirements are discussed by Zander (120). There is reason to believe that the plans of members are more vulnerable to pressures on their group if the changes being pushed on it provide greater benefits for that unit (120). Finally, it is notable that groups are less subject to the effects of social facilitation than individuals are, according to Laughlin & Jaccord (59).

DEINDIVIDUATION   In contrast to the interest in how social pressures change members so that they will act as their group desires, there has been an effort to understand why the effects of a group's pressures have not always been useful to the group or member alike. The parentage of these studies is traceable to a 1952 paper by Festinger, Pepitone & Newcomb (33), who used the graceless term *deindividuation* to describe a psychological state of members who had lost their individualism (their individuatedness) because they had been treated uniformly, not as unique individuals within their group. A characteristic of deindividuated persons, these writers contended, was that the persons became unrestrained and tended to engage in behavior that is disapproved by society. Although this assumption is hardly supported in military squads, football teams, choral groups, or classrooms, it continues to attract the interest of scholars.

Most studies of deindividuation examine the tendency of a group to generate antisocial acts among its members. That groups may have constructive influences on their members is ignored, with the result that these investigations have a one-sided emphasis on what brings out the worst in people. When a child is tempted to steal, as an instance, will the presence of other children encourage him to do so? This was a prime question in an experiment Diener and co-workers (28) conducted with 1300 children who visited private homes to beg for treats on a Halloween evening. Upon their arrival at any of the experimental homes, the children saw a bowl of candy and a bowl of money on a low table. The hostess greeted the young beggars, told them that each could have one piece of candy, said nothing about the money, and disappeared. A hidden observer noted how much candy and money was then taken. Three independent variables were created. The childrens' names and addresses were either requested or not; the children were either in a group, or alone; and among the members in each group, one of them was asked to see that no stealing occurred or not. All three independent variables were effective in determining the amount of stealing. The highest rate of stealing (that is, the most frequent deindividuation) developed when persons were in a group rather than alone and when the identities of members were not known by the hostess. Appointing a theft-preventer was effective in reducing stealing only if that child initially provided a name and address for the hostess. The conditions in this study do not appear to be ones that cause individuation, according to the theory; thus, it is not clear why these researchers say they are studying it.

In a companion study, Diener (27) found, in contrast to the above, that a person displayed less deindividuation in a group than he did alone; indeed, the presence of a group decreased such behavior. In this instance, the deindividuated behaviors were destructive or aggressive actions. The experimenters employed two conditions beyond variations in group membership:

whether the participants were anonymous and whether the subjects had been encouraged by the experimenter to be destructive and aggressive. The presence of anonymity stimulated no more aggressive and destructive behavior than the absence of anonymity. Participants in the experiment showed more aggression and destruction, however, if they earlier had been induced to do so by the experimenter than if they had not. Thus, the more a subject was encouraged by the experimenter to act in an uninhibited manner, the more he showed tendencies to act that way at a later time. Is this deindividuation?

Jorgenson & Dukes (48) conceive of deindividuation as a psychological state characterized by feeling indistinguishable from one's environment, a lowered self-awareness and a lowered evaluation of oneself, as well as a decreased concern about how others evaluate him. All this, they believe, arouses uninhibited behavior. These writers think that deindividuation is more likely to occur in a social aggregate (a set of persons who do not interact with one another) than in a group (a set of persons who do interact, are aware of their common membership, and have a common goal). The larger the aggregate, furthermore, the greater the amount of deindividuation. The writers conducted a natural experiment in a cafeteria, over a period of 30 days, by observing the tendency of customers to take their dirty dishes to a designated place, as requested of all who use that cafeteria. It was noticed that the diners returned their trays less often if the eating hall was crowded than if it was not. But if they were members of a small group seated together at a table, they were more likely to return their trays than if they had eaten alone. In sum, anonymity (or perhaps a crowded room where traffic was slow) among many persons caused them to ignore rules of the house, but membership in a friendly eating group caused them to follow the rules.

Deindividuation and the accompanying loss of inhibition should be less likely to appear in times and places where it is important and necessary for members to pay attention to one another as individuals. Thus, it ought to develop less often in either a cooperative or a competitive group because in such settings a member can profit by paying attention to others and their needs. In an individualistic situation, however, where persons are neither rivals nor collaborators, deindividuation can develop sensibly because neighbors in such a case will neither harm nor benefit a person. These ideas were tested by Hamby (40) in a laboratory experiment and were well supported. Closely related to the things we have been considering is the tendency of an individual to take care of himself versus taking care of others. In an experiment by Dawes, McTavish & Shaklee (23) the participants more often took responsibility during a discussion for helping others instead of themselves, but only if the discussion attempted to determine the members' mutual preferences.

Cohesiveness of a Group

Group cohesiveness, a concept developed in early days at the Research Center for Group Dynamics, is the desire of members to remain as members of a group (14). Current researchers accept this definition, but in the absence of a reliable method for measuring cohesiveness in a natural setting, or a reliable procedure for creating it in the laboratory, one cannot be sure to what phenomena investigators are attending when they examine its origins or effects. Students of groups have for many years concentrated upon the consequences of cohesiveness. During the past few years, however, their interest has shifted to its origins and a good amount of work has been done on that topic.

SOURCES OF GROUP COHESIVENESS   Because cohesiveness is based on the attractiveness of a group for those who participate in it, some current studies attempt to demonstrate that attractiveness becomes stronger as the group is more rewarding. Certain rewards of course serve better than others.

Interracial groups, composed of black and white soldiers born in the southern United States, were used in a study of cohesiveness by Blanchard, Adelman & Cook (9) because such soldiers would not be immediately attracted to one another. All groups were put to work on a cooperative task, the operation of a model railroad. The researchers expected that this activity would generate liking among members, the liking would be stronger if the group was successful than it it was a failure, and would increase more if the participants had much say, rather than little, in running their tiny company. Blanchard and his associates found that interpersonal liking and presumably therefore group cohesiveness increased as the group was more successful. But neither the members' part in decision making nor the racial composition of the group had an effect on the strength of the group's cohesiveness. In a subsequent study, Blanchard & Cook (10) again noted that participants were more attracted to their group if it was more successful. In addition, a participant was more interested in an incompetent member if induced to help the incompetent individual, but not if a groupmate provided that help.

Cohesiveness can be based upon either the interpersonal attraction among members, the performance of the group as a unit (which serves to mediate attainment by individuals), or both. In a study reminiscent of one done by Elizabeth French in 1956 (36), Anderson (1) observed that cohesiveness became greater in task-oriented groups when the groups were more successful, and greater in socially supportive groups when members were more similar in their values. The effect of similarity of members on cohesiveness, on the one hand, and the performance of the group, on the other hand, was also noted in 42 teams of students in an engineering college course on land surveying. The groups were so composed that they varied in the similarity among members' opinions about current events and varied in their average intellectual ability. Each group worked on six projects and each project was given a grade by the professor. Cohesiveness of these groups became greater and grew stronger over time when attitudes of members were more similar. The performance of the group as a unit was better in the groups composed of the better students and was not well correlated with cohesiveness of the group. The authors, Terborg, Castore & DeNinno (100), believed this latter result occurred because all students knew by the end of the third project (halfway through the term) what their grade was likely to be for the course and thus matters other than grades had an opportunity to determine their group's cohesiveness.

In a related study, the amount of time members spent on their assigned tasks versus the time they spent being "gregarious" were measured to see which contributed more to cohesiveness. The groups, four members in each, were observed for 24 hours a day for a week by means of a TV camera, as the men worked, socialized, or rested, inside a deepsea chamber. The number of hours participants spent in performing their duties apparently contributed more to cohesiveness than the amount of time they devoted to friendly interaction, according to Bakeman & Helmreich (7). The measurement of cohesiveness in this instance was how often a person helped a groupmate of his group. Given this way of measuring cohesiveness, the meaning of the reported findings is not entirely clear.

A person who publicly announces that he is a member of a given organization, we may assume, is asserting that the organization is attractive to him and that he will remain within it. Membership in a social unit is typically displayed through colors, buttons, or stickers such as students flaunt to reveal they attend a particular school. Cialdini and five colleagues (19) took it for granted that wearers of these signals are "basking in reflected glory" and that they more often wear such decorations when their organization (or part of it) has been successful than when it has failed. The investigators also expected that students will more often use the pronoun "we" when discussing a victory of their school's team (in which the respondents had no part) than when describing a loss by that team. In a series of ingenious investigations in natural settings on seven college campuses these predictions were supported.

What causes members to be attracted to one another? Insko & Wilson (43) assume, as have others, that individuals become more friendly as they spend more time together; this time must be filled, however, with interpersonal activities such as talking, responding, gesturing, and so on. In a study that allowed each participant to talk separately with each groupmate, and to observe each of his colleagues talking with the others, these assumptions were supported. During the time they spent in conversation, we might add, members sought to discover common interests conducive to harmony between them. Would they have liked one another as well if their interactions had revealed interpersonal differences? Some people like one another less as they interact with one another more.

It is notable that the phenomena most often contained under the term cohesiveness (14) occasionally have been placed under a different label. A case in point is a correlational project by Steers (95), who examined the sources of what he called commitment to an organization. Commitment, he says, is characterized by a member's strong desire to maintain membership in his organization, a willingness to exert effort in its behalf, and an acceptance of its goals and values. This mixture of qualities brings together, under one superterm, three notions that heretofore have been kept separate: cohesiveness, desire for group success (117), and conformity to group standards (15). Steers noted, among employees of a hospital and an engineering firm, that commitment was strongly correlated with desire to remain a member, intent to remain a member, and the actual number of resignations over a period of time. Steers' paper refers to a number of other studies on commitment but to none on cohesiveness, even though articles on cohesiveness exist that are relevant to his results. If commitment and cohesiveness are closely related, it is confusing for separate terms to be used in describing the same events or to amalgamate separate ideas under one heading. Why do researchers create and employ new terms for older ones? That is a question worthy of research.

Other properties of a group beside the quality of its performance and the characteristics of its participants may be precursors of cohesiveness. Three of these are the size of the group, the crowdedness of the space it occupies, and its sexual composition. In a laboratory experiment by Marshal & Heslin (72), the willingness of members to remain in a group they have already occupied for several hours was tested by giving them an opportunity to leave it prior to the last activity in an experimental session. Libo (65) had used this operation for measuring cohesiveness many years earlier. The groups had either 4 or 16 members, were composed of males only, females only, or a mixture, and worked in a room with either ample space or inadequate space. Small groups were more cohesive (kept their members better) than large ones, when all members were of the same gender. But when the groups had members of both sexes, larger groups were more cohesive than smaller ones. This was especially true for the women, and women liked larger groups better if they were more crowded. Crowdedness, in brief, made participants more uncomfortable in a group but not more ready to leave it. Everybody liked mixed groups more than single sex groups, and the males liked mixed groups more than did the females. The size of a group then and density of its physical space have a different instrumental value for different persons under different situations.

Many people believe that a group's cohesiveness will increase if the unit is attacked by external agents. This assumption overlooks the possibility that a group may not meet an attack well and members may thus recognize that their group is not a source of security for them. Or members may believe they are attacked simply because of their group's existence and recognize that attacks on the group will cease only if the group is abandoned or broken up. The proposition that group cohesiveness increases when it is under attack is discussed by Stein (96) in an extensive review of literature from sociology, anthropology, political science, and psychology. Most of the available research seems to support the proposition, but Stein discusses conditions when it does not.

Some groups continue to exist, it appears, because the support they receive from outside their boundaries helps them to prosper and keep their members. No doubt many groups are protected in this way from efforts to eliminate them. In a study of whether old governmental agencies ever die (a question usually raised by the challenger in a political campaign), Kaufman (49) examined the tenure of 175 federal agencies originally established within cabinet-level departments in 1923. By 1973, 148 of these (85 percent) were still going strong. If an agency did die (27 of them did), the function it was created to perform usually stayed alive because it was transferred to a continuing agency. Thus, the groups may die but their functions do not fade away. The survival of these units was probably not due to cohesiveness as defined here, even though that may have contributed to it. The author says the following factors contribute to the survival of an agency: its existence is based on a legal statute, relevant congressional committees need its services and therefore protect it, it is funded each year because its financial needs are small, members of the agency itself fight for its survival, and professional or trade associations support it because it benefits their special interests. Longevity of a group often depends, apparently, on the support it obtains from its environment.

DESIRE TO AFFILIATE   We have been considering thus far the sources of a group's attraction for a person who is already inside it. We need to recognize now that a person who is not in a unit may have more or less desire to join it or more or less interest in it while remaining outside it. What conditions determine whether an outsider feels favorably toward a group before his eyes?

The method originally used by Schachter (86) to study this general issue is still popular today, even though it takes up a rather special situation. Schachter reported that people who are anxious because they are waiting for a stressful event to occur would rather wait for it in the presence of others who are anticipating the same event than wait for it alone. The reason misery likes company, Schachter held, is that in the presence of the others each person can compare his own responses to those of his colleagues and thereby is helped to decide how he "ought" feel in this situation. Schachter observed that first-born children in their families had a stronger tendency to affiliate under such circumstances than did individuals who were later born. Recently, Dembrowski & MacDougall (25) noted that hard-driving, achievement-oriented persons, designated as those of Type A, were more prone to wait with others for a stressful event than were more relaxed (Type B) individuals. The affiliative tendencies of Type A and Type B persons were no different, however, when there was no threat in the offing. When the subjects no longer anticipated stress, because they now were actually engaged in the activity that earlier provoked the anxiety, Type A persons opted to work alone, while Type B persons wanted to work with others. The researchers suggested that Type A persons (more than those of Type B) have a stronger need to control their own fate and to avoid failure in the presence of others, which they can do best while alone.

When individuals are awaiting a stressful situation, do they in fact provide the opportunity for social comparisons that Schachter supposed they do? Morris and seven associates (76) observed the behavior among strangers who were brought into a laboratory room (as in the procedure used by Schachter) while awaiting the beginning of an experimental session. The interactions among persons under three different conditions were compared: fear of an electric shock, embarrassment or anxiety over a forthcoming discussion about sex, and ambiguity, that is, the next event was not known. Talking among members was more frequent, and subjects stood closer to one another while conversing, in the fear condition more than in the other two. Social support seemed to be stronger as the emotional strain was greater.

Individuals in a group may be attracted to membership in a different group, and this intergroup attraction tends to be greater if the separate groups have previously cooperated than if they have competed, according to a report of research by Worchel, Andreoli & Fogler (113). These men combined several small groups to work on a number of tasks and informed participants whether the larger unit had succeeded or failed. Participants were immediately thereafter asked how much they were attracted to membership in the other smaller group. Cooperative work among several groups, and success in their joint actions, increased intergroup attraction, but competition between the groups followed by a failure of the larger unit reduced intergroup attraction.

There are no empirical data available on how separate individuals become attracted to one another so that they form a group, and we know almost nothing about why groups are formed. A rare exception is a study of the purposes of national associations (118). One approach to understanding why individuals create a group is seen in research on the formation of coalitions. A coalition is a subset of persons within a larger group who agree to cooperate so that they can obtain a common reward. Students of coalitions are interested in which persons become inclined to develop a coalition and why. Komarita & Moore (56) presented four theories about the origins of a coalition and conducted an experiment to see which of their four theories was best supported by their data. They concluded that a so-called bargaining theory, which predicts how rewards will be divided among members, worked better than the others.

The dissolution of a larger organization into several smaller ones can be a source of new groups, as in the appearance of a new religious sect within an already established church. Common assumptions in studies of such sects, according to Beckford (8), are that the development of a new movement is an indication all is not well within the parent religion and that the newly formed group is attempting to provide a remedy. Beckford believes these assumptions cannot be tested reliably and suggests that research on the formation of sects might better be devoted to studies of the social structures in the new movements, how they are controlled, how they obtain recruits, or why a new group is more helpful to its members than the old one was.

Members of a group may try to make their unit attractive to persons they would like to recruit into their group. Zander (119) suggests that a given person is more likely to be invited into a unit if his acts or attributes promise to strengthen conditions wanted within that organization. Such outsiders are more desirable to the group if it is more cohesive, their joining of the group will be helpful to them, and the recruiters place strong emphasis on being fair in their recruiting practices. A recruiter will more probably influence the attitudes of a person toward a group if he is attractive than if he is not. This observation has been made by Schlenker (87), who replicated an earlier experiment by Aronson & Mills (4). The experimenter recruited members of a group engaged in a boring discussion. The author believed that the recruiter was effective because he managed to change the unfavorable impression the potential recruit had of the group. Schlenker preferred this view over the one proposed by Aronson and Mills, that a recruiter for a dull group is effective because he offers the outsider a means for reducing cognitive dissonance which arises when he notes that his desire to join the group is dissonant with his knowledge that the group is pretty dull.

Evaluation of Self and Group

In order for a member to decide about his relationship with colleagues in a group, whether, for example, he will remain a member, work in its behalf, conform to its standards, and the like, he may evaluate and compare the group's performance and his own personal output. Generally speaking, we expect a participant will appraise his personal performance favorably if his group does well and unfavorably if his group does poorly. But exceptions have been noted. Members with a peripheral role in a group, compared to those with a central role, are less likely to allow their self evaluations to be influenced by their group's scores. Also, persons with a fear of personal mistakes or a fear of group failure do likewise (117).

Schlenker, Soraci & McCarthy (90) report that members with high self-regard (measured by a paper and pencil test) take personal credit for their group's success but shift the blame to others for their group's failure. However, members with low self-regard feel that the quality of their personal performance is the same as their group's performance regardless of whether the group has done well or poorly. Schlenker thinks the kind of responses made by persons with high self-regard are proof of a self-serving bias among those members. In experiments he conducted with Miller (88, 89), he found that the egocentric bias is stronger if a member believes his view is shared by a majority of his colleagues than if he believes it is shared by only a few.

Even when the tasks of members are ambiguous, as in making estimates based on unreliable data, participants can develop a perception about how well their group is doing. Janssens & Nuttin (46) asked members of groups to judge how many objects they found in a series of pictures. The participants overestimated their success in this task when working in groups but did not overestimate their success when working alone. In a second experiment by the same men, group members interacted with one another before making an estimate of their group's success. Again, members of groups were more likely to overestimate their successes than individuals working alone, and the more they engaged in verbal interaction, the more they perceived their group as successful.

The tendency of members to overvalue their group's product was originally reported some time ago by Ferguson & Kelley (31). In that study, and subsequent ones like it, evaluations of a group were obtained from its members before they knew what scores it had earned in competition with other groups. Worchell, Lind & Kaufman (114) thought that the tendency of members to overestimate their group's performance might be modified if the members knew that their group would (or would not) continue competing, that their group had won (or lost), or that their evaluations of their group would be public (or private). In groups whose members had been told that intergroup competition would continue for a series of trials, members of winning groups were less likely to overevaluate their group if ratings were made in public rather than in private. The experimenters assumed that these results occurred because subjects desired to avoid complacency after a success and despair after a failure. Within groups that were to stop competing, members overrated their group's performance more often in the public condition than in the private one, regardless of whether their group had succeeded or failed. In this latter case the participants apparently wished to reveal to one another that their feelings about their group were favorable.

Cooperation and Competition

The goal structure in a group, whether members are working to help one another achieve the same end or whether they are rivals competing for similar but separate goals, has interested students of groups for a long time. In a recent investigation, Okun & DiVesta (81) created internally cooperative groups and internally competitive ones. Each of these units then cooperated or competed with another. The internally cooperative groups did better than the internally competitive ones, and groups that were competing with one another did better than ones that were cooperating. Goldman, Stockbauer & McAuliffe (39) obtained contrasting results when each member did all the steps in the group's task (as in craft work) or did only one step in the total task (as in an assembly line). In the assembly line procedure, the internally cooperative groups performed better than the internally competitive ones, but in the procedure where each person did all the group's steps on his own, the groups (competitive and cooperative) were not different.

Kuhlman & Wimberley (57) report that persons who are personally disposed to compete perceive that other individuals also prefer to compete. But persons who prefer to cooperate perceive others as either competitors or cooperators, as the true facts of the case may be. These findings agree with results reported earlier by Kelley & Stahelski (50). Thomas & Pondy (102) propose, in a discussion paper on social conflict, that each competitor's views of others' intentions play a crucial role in shaping his reactions to another's hostility. These writers state that their view has been neglected in research and they accordingly offer an "intent" model for studying and managing social conflicts.

Leadership, Its Nature and Effects

APPRAISAL OF LEADERS   Many investigators have noted that persons who talk the most during a group's discussion are chosen to be leaders of a group. Sorrentino & Boutillier (94) review studies of this effect of talkativeness and ask whether frequency of oral participation would be as important if the quality of this participation were known along with its quantity. To study this question, they conducted an experiment in which a paid collaborator (posing as a regular subject) met with a number of four-person groups. The collaborator talked either very much or very little and made either high quality or low quality preplanned comments in each group—in a two-by-two design. After the discussions were completed, members rated each other on a number of characteristics. The authors observed that the quantity of talk was more important than its quality in deciding a group's attitude toward the collaborator as a potential leader. The reason is that sheer quantity, compared to quality, is a clearer indicator that the individual is willing to work in behalf of the unit and therefore is more suitable to be its leader.

Gintner & Lindskold (38) assume, however, that a person who talks a great deal in a group will be chosen as its leader only if he is not an expert in the group's task. If he is an expert, this ability itself causes him to be chosen as leader regardless of how much he occupies the floor during a group's discussion. In an experiment, these scientists again used a collaborator who met with each of a number of groups where he either talked very much or very little and displayed either a high degree of expertness or very little in the group's task (judging the quality of a painting). The researchers observed that the collaborator was more often selected to be leader when he talked more often, but only if he was not an expert. When he was an expert, in contrast, the frequency of his comments did not determine how often he was selected to be leader. In short, anyone who wishes to become leader of a group had better talk more than the others; it also helps a bit if he knows what he is talking about.

When members are satisfied with the way a leader directs their group and want him to continue in that role, they may be said to endorse their leader. Michener & Lawler (74) measured six conditions to see which of them had the greatest effect on the tendency of members to endorse. They found that members more often endorsed their leaders when the group was successful, members got more rewards than the leader, or the leader was not permanently fixed in the office. They neither endorsed the leader nor rejected him if the support he received from members was inconsistent, or if the leader's competence or fairness were inconsistent.

Those who belong to a given group may attribute much or little responsibility for the group's achievements to its chief officer. In a stressful situation, moreover, the leader may be seen as more or less useful in helping the group deal with stress. In a laboratory experiment designed to resemble what might occur if many persons simultaneously tried to escape a building through the same door, Klein (53) noted that more legitimate leaders (who had been elected by their group) were perceived by members to be more responsible for the fate of the group than leaders who were less legitimate. These results occurred when stress was low, but in contrast, when stress was high, the less legitimate leaders were perceived to have more responsibility and competence than the legitimate ones. Thus, a group under stress seemingly prefers a strong leader and places less weight on how much he had been accepted by members.

LEADERSHIP AND INFLUENCE   Different scholars have different conceptions of leadership and the properties of leaders. One widely held notion is that a leader can be effective only if he is able to influence the beliefs and behaviors of his groupmates. It is not surprising then to learn that researchers are studying the sources of social power among individuals who are in positions of authority. Michener & Burt (73), for example, examined what they called the "components" that determine whether a leader obtains compliance to his wishes. They report that the compliance of members is greater when a leader justifies his demands as good for the group, has power to punish persons who do not do as the leader has asked, and has a legitimate right to make demands of subordinates. The success or failure of the group does not affect a leader's ability to influence, nor does approval of him by subordinates.

In quite a different approach to the studying of leadership and social power, Lord (69) identified 12 functions typically performed by a leader. Examples are: developing plans, proposing solutions, and providing resources. He watched to see how often each leader in his sample displayed the 12 functions. In addition, he determined which motive bases the leaders employed in attempts to exert their power, using the bases offered earlier by French & Raven (37). Typical bases are: ability to reward, coerce, or give expert information. Lord then correlated how often each leadership function and basis for social power was used. He found that functional behaviors for completing the work of the group were well related with bases of social power, but functions for socio-emotional relations among members were not correlated with the bases for social power. O'Brien & Harary (80) assumed that a leader may have a given degree of desire to influence members or to be influenced by them. And a leader may have more or less opportunity to satisfy this need because of the position he occupies in his group. These researchers measured the difference between the strength of the desire for power and the opportunity for meeting that desire and observed in several studies that a leader's effectiveness was greater as the size of this discrepancy was smaller.

Several books have discussed leaders and their effects. Kipnis (52) summarized a set of his own and others' studies into the sources and consequences of power among higher status persons—he calls them "powerholders." Argyris (3) wrote a treatise on how to increase the effectiveness of leaders, and Fiedler & Chemers (34) described ways of improving the skill of leaders.

The social power of members in small social units, each composed of a college man and woman who were going steady, was studied by Stewart & Rubin (98). These scholars obtained measures of a disposition called "hope of power." When the male had the stronger hope of power, he anticipated problems in his relationship with the female, and within 2 years that couple was in fact separated. The hope of power among females, however, bore no relationship to interpersonal difficulties or stability of the couple. Finally, an interesting type of data was gathered by Falbo (30), who asked students to write essays on the topic: "How I get my way." They described 16 different strategies. These should be useful in teaching students about the nature and sources of social power.

PARTICIPATION BY MEMBERS IN GROUP DECISIONS   A basic assumption of those who write about proper behavior of managers is that a plan for action by members will be more influential on the members if they have a part in making that plan. This assumption is widely held even though its limits have not been well tested. When members participate in making decisions they are of course being granted some of the leader's power. In order for this grant of power to be used effectively, both the leaders and members must welcome this shift and find it satisfying. There has been some research in the past few years on just that issue.

In a study of attitudes among employees in a small firm, Lischeron & Wall (67) found that the employees desire to be more involved in making decisions. The kind of participation they prefer (whether it be personal, representation, or union) depends upon the nature of the decision to be made. In a separate investigation of the meetings of a planning group containing employees and managers (68), participants felt that conferences were worthwhile even though the meetings did not generate greater satisfaction toward their jobs.

The degree of satisfaction among employees in health and welfare agencies toward their place of work was the focus of a study by Bagley, Hage & Aiken (6). These researchers measured the flow of communication among staff members in formally scheduled meetings as well as in informal contacts of the kind that do much of the work in an organization. The total communication among colleagues was not a notable determinant of satisfaction within the organization. But the direction in the flow of words, whether it was up or down in the hierarchy or among peers at the same level, was well correlated with satisfaction. That is, when most of the informal talk was upward from subordinates to superiors, more unfavorable views of the workplace existed. And when most of the informal messages were directed downward from superiors to subordinates, favorable views of the place were present. When there was ample unscheduled communication among peers, the staff members did not participate actively during formally scheduled meetings.

Several hypotheses concerning causes for greater or lesser participation in decision making among employees in 144 health departments were tested by Mohr (75). His hypotheses are of interest to us largely because they were not well supported even though they appear to be plausible notions. He expected participativeness to be greater if: the organization was less bureaucratized, workers' jobs were more complex, the supervisor was at a higher level in the hierarchy of the organization, the staff had fewer members, and the members wished to participate in decision making. Although the general support for these ideas was not strong, the results were more promising if the supervisor considered himself to be in a higher social class than his subordinates. In such a circumstance he more often initiated opportunities for widely shared and effective decision making among employees. Mohr believes that the social distance between superior and subordinates reduces the interference caused by interpersonal considerations, thus making the manager's decision processes more rational and effective.

Finally, it is of interest to examine how often individuals communicate with one another when there are no requirements on them to talk, they are not members of an established workgroup, they do not depend upon one another to accomplish a task, or they are not regularly assembled in a given place. Wheeler & Nezlek (108) obtained normative data from 58 male and female first-year college students who agreed to keep a daily record of conversations (lasting 10 minutes or more) for two weeks in the fall and two weeks in the spring. The average number of such interactions per person was seven a day. Of these, 48 per cent were with one person, 19 percent with two, 11 percent with 3, and 22 percent with 4 or more. Fifty-six percent were with persons of the same sex and 36 percent with a mixed group. Women reduced their social contacts in the spring because they felt they had wasted too much time on them in the fall. All in all, females socialized less than males.

Group Size and Density

One can sense that a larger group is different in many ways from a smaller one, but students of groups have done little to identify and explain these differences. Most research on the size of social entities has been devoted to comparing large with larger organizations, as in the review of research on group size by Indik (42). Thomas & Fink (101) made a comparable review for small groups years ago.

A consequence of a group's size, not given attention heretofore, is its ability to attract the interest of nonmembers. Larger groups of people ought to be more noticeable than smaller groups, are they also more attractive? Knowles & Bassett (54) studied these questions by positioning sets of students at the entrance to a college library. These social units contained either 2, 4, or 6 members. In addition, the members were either dressed alike or unlike and were either actively talking with one another or silently looking at a spot on the ceiling (designated as groups versus crowds). The behavior of students who passed by these entities when entering the library was photographed. Pedestrians approached the crowd more closely and looked at it for a longer length of time than they did the group. The larger social entities (if 6 persons can be called that) caused more of these differential reactions than did smaller ones, but size of unit and similarity of dress among members had no effect by themselves upon the interest of those passing by. In sum, the activity of a group attracted more attention than did its size, the groups composed of actively conversing persons were more often avoided than were groups of silent persons.

In a later study by Knowles et al (55), a similar design was used to observe the reactions of students, in this case to an empty bench, a solo person, or a group of 2, 3, or 4 persons. These stimulus-entities were placed in a building hallway and the behavior of pedestrians passing by was noted. The pedestrians avoided the groups by a greater distance than they did the individual and avoided the solo person more than the empty bench. The larger a group, the more it was avoided. These findings were replicated in a paper and pencil questionnaire which asked students to indicate what path they would follow past social entities such as these. In an interesting variation on studies of proximity or avoidance, Ryen & Kohen (85) used two triads of persons at a time and observed who sat close to whom. The two triads were in one of the following conditions: coacting, cooperating, or competing. Members in cooperating groups sat near those in their own group and the other group alike. Those in competing groups sat nearer to members of their own group than to others. Those in coacting groups sat randomly. Members of winning teams tried to sit near losers but losers avoided them.

Much research on the effects of group size has reported that a group's performance tends to be poorer on a given task as the group is larger. Chapko & Revers (16), for example, instructed members in units of 6, 12, and 24 members to reach uniformity in the colors each displayed (a member had a choice of two colors to display). Smaller groups did this faster than larger ones. In another study, however, Valenti & Downing (103) compared 6 and 12-member juries in the laboratory under two conditions: either the guilt of the defendant was quite clear or his guilt was uncertain. The size of the jury had no differential effect when the likelihood of guilt was low.

But when the defendant probably was guilty, the 6-person juries made more guilty decisions than did the 12-person juries. The reason for the finding is not evident.

On some kinds of tasks, larger groups do better than smaller ones because bigger units contain more able people. Work by Egerbladh (29) was based on this assumption. He used three sizes of entities—composed of one, two, or three persons—and three ability levels of members—high, middle, or low. The task was an intelligence test to be done under extreme time pressure. Regardless of the size of the unit, there was to be only one answer from it for each item. The larger groups composed of more able members did better than larger units with less capable members and better than smaller units.

The size of a group may effect its performance because larger groups may be more crowded. Paulus et al (82) studied the effects of group size, room size, and interpersonal proximity. Each of these three was found to contribute to a decrement in the group's performance. One of the reasons that a larger group may do less well than a smaller one is that each member in a group may feel less responsible for the group's outcome when his group is larger. Petty and associates (83) gave subjects several cognitive tasks to work on and told the participants that they were the lone participant, one of a group of four, or one of a group of 16 (other members, of course, out of sight). As the group of coworkers was larger, the subjects produced less. It seems probable that these results would not occur if members were collaborating not to do well personally but to have their group be successful as a group.

Group Structure

The structure of a group is composed of its parts (persons, roles, offices, subunits) and the relationships among these. In the past few years, as has always been the case, there has been little research under this broad topic. Three somewhat relevant studies considered how characteristics of members affected their suitability for certain roles.

In one instance, Shaw & Harkey (91) assumed that a group will be more effective if its leader does what is expected of him, and the ability of the leader to do what is expected depends on whether he is suited for the leader's role. In a laboratory experiment, Shaw and Harkey found support for these ideas. Wilson, Aronoff & Messe (112) proposed that the productivity of a group is affected by the fit between the personality of members and the group's social structure. Some persons are more suited to one kind of structure (e.g. autocratic versus egalitarian) and other persons to a different kind. They tested the idea that a hierarchial social structure is more satisfying for an individual who places much emphasis on safety, and an egalitarian structure more satisfying to one who emphasizes self-esteem. These hypotheses were validated in a laboratory experiment.

Finally, Lewis (64) has written a book on the question whether merit determines who gets ahead (moves to higher levels of status) in a university. He asserts that merit cannot determine who scales the ivory tower because only 20 percent of the members in academic disciplines ever publish anything, and ability in teaching cannot be reliably measured. He concludes that a professor who moves upward is one who is best liked by his colleagues. This issue warrants better data and better arguments than Lewis gave to it.

An unusual approach to the study of group structure has developed in research by Zajonc (116) on the consequences of children's birth order. He has found that a child's intellectual ability is affected by the order of his birth among children in his family, the number of children, the space in years between them, and the number of parents. Last-born children appear to do less well than first-born because the last-born does not have as stimulating an environment or as good an opportunity to learn by teaching younger siblings. Although his research is limited to the family group at present, it may provide generalizations that will be useful in other settings devoted to teaching and social support.

Summary

Research into the psychology of groups attracted a quickly increasing number of investigators in the 1940s and 1950s but since the early 1960s the annual rate of publication has remained fairly stable. During the years when the field was rapidly growing, there was a lively interest in group dynamics throughout society. That interest has now calmed down, the study of groups has become a regular part of college curricula, and it has lost its initial resemblance to a social movement as well as its original focus upon practical problems in group life.

In its 30 years of development, research into group behavior has concentrated upon a dozen major topics while many other potentially promising subjects have been ignored. Studies have also more often been focused on the behavior of individuals in group settings than on the properties and outcomes of a group as a unit. Perhaps the major reason the research on group behavior has dealt with only a small number of topics, and concentrated on the individual, is that researchers are attracted by theories, not practical problems, and testing a theory demands a narrow but deep and penetrating examination of a limited intellectual area. Also the study of groups is more expensive and slower than the study of individuals—low cost and quick output are as important to research scholars as to persons in other occupations.

In recent years three familiar topics have attracted greatest interest from students of groups: the origins of group cohesiveness, the nature of social pressures within a group, and the dynamics of making group decisions. An emphasis on the cognitive style used by members of a group has brought a new approach to examining and explaining decision making in groups. Other topics currently winning attention are crowding, density, arrangements among members in physical space, pressures on a group from external agents, and intergroup conflict.

Literature Cited

1. Anderson, A. B. 1975. Combined effects of interpersonal attraction and goal-path clarity on the cohesiveness of task-oriented groups. *J. Pers. Soc. Psychol.* 31:68–75
2. Anderson, N., Graesser, C. 1976. An information analysis of attitude change in group discussion. *J. Pers. Soc. Psychol.* 34:210–22
3. Argyris, C. 1976. *Increasing Leadership Effectiveness.* New York: Wiley Interscience. 286 pp.
4. Aronson, E., Mills, J. 1959. Effect of severity of initiation on liking for group. *J. Abnorm. Soc. Psychol.* 59:177–81
5. Back, K. 1972. *Beyond Words.* New York: Sage. 255 pp.
6. Bagley, C. B., Hage, J., Aiken, M. 1975. Communication and satisfaction in organizations. *Hum. Relat.* 28:611–26
7. Bakeman, R., Helmreich, R. 1975. Cohesiveness and performance: co-variation and causality in an undersea environment. *J. Exp. Soc. Psychol.* 11:478–89
8. Beckford, J. 1977. Explaining religious movements. *Int. Soc. Sci. J.* 22:235–49
9. Blanchard, F. A., Adelman, L., Cook, S. W. 1975. Effect of group success and failure upon interpersonal attraction in cooperating interracial groups. *J. Pers. Soc. Psychol.* 31:1020–30
10. Blanchard, F. A., Cook, S. W. 1976. Effects of helping a less competent member of a cooperating interracial group on the development of interpersonal attraction. *J. Pers. Soc. Psychol.* 34:1245–55
11. Brehm, J., Mann, M. 1975. Effect of importance of freedom and attraction to group members on influence produced by group pressure. *J. Pers. Soc. Psychol.* 31:816–24
12. Burnstein, E., Vinokur, A. 1975. What a person thinks upon learning he has chosen differently from others: nice evidence for the persuasive-arguments explanation of choice shifts. *J. Exp. Soc. Psychol.* 11:412–26
13. Cartwright, D. P., ed. 1959. *Studies in Social Power.* Ann Arbor, Mich: Inst. Soc. Res. 224 pp.
14. Cartwright, D. P. 1968. The nature of group cohesiveness. See Ref. 15, pp. 91–109
15. Cartwright, D. P., Zander, A. F., eds. 1968. *Group Dynamics, Research and Theory.* New York: Harper & Row. 580 pp.
16. Chapko, M. K., Revers, R. R. 1976. Contagion in a crowd: the effects of crowd size and initial discrepancy from unanimity. *J. Pers. Soc. Psychol.* 33:382–86
17. Chevalier, M., Bailey, M., Burns, T. 1975. Toward a framework for large scale problem management. *Hum. Relat.* 27:43–69
18. Chu, G. C., Rahim, S. A., Kincaid, D. L., eds. 1976. *Communication for Group Transformation in Development.* Honolulu: East-West Center. 424 pp.
19. Cialdini, R. B., Borden, R., Thorne, A., Walker, M., Freeman, S. 1976. Basking in reflected glory: three (football) field studies. *J. Pers. Soc. Psychol.* 34:366–75
20. Cook, D. 1966. *Program Evaluation and Review Technique: Application in Education.* Washington DC: US Off. Educ., Coop. Res. Monogr. No. 17. 100 pp.
21. Davis, J. H., Kerr, N., Atkin, R., Holt, R., Meek, D. 1975. The decision process of 6 and 12 person mock juries assigned unanimous and two-third party majority rules. *J. Pers. Soc. Psychol.* 32:1–14
22. Davis, J. H., Stasser, G., Spitzer, C. E., Holt, R. W. 1976. Changes in group members' decision preferences during discussion: an illustration with mock juries. *J. Pers. Soc. Psychol.* 34:1177–87
23. Dawes, R. M., McTavish, J., Shaklee, H. 1977. Behavior, communication, and assumptions about other people's be-

havior in a commons dilemma situation. *J. Pers. Soc. Psychol.* 35:1–11

24. Delbecq, A., Van De Ven, A. H., Gustafson, D. H. 1975. *Group Techniques for Program Planning.* Glenview, Ill: Scott, Foresman. 174 pp.

25. Dembrowski, T. M., MacDougall, J. M. 1978. Stress effects on affiliation preferences among subjects possessing the Type A coronary-prone behavior pattern. *J. Pers. Soc. Psychol.* 36:23–33

26. Deutsch, M. 1973. *The Resolution of Conflict.* New Haven: Yale Univ. Press. 420 pp.

27. Diener, E. 1976. Effects of prior destructive behavior, anonymity, and group presence on deindividuation and aggression. *J. Pers. Soc. Psychol.* 33:497–507

28. Diener, E., Fraser, S. C., Beaman, A. L., Kelem, R. T. 1976. Effects of deindividuation variables on stealing among Halloween trick or treaters. *J. Pers. Soc. Psychol.* 33:178–83

29. Egerbladh, T. 1976. The function of group size and ability level on solving a multidimensional complementary task. *J. Pers. Soc. Psychol.* 34:805–8

30. Falbo, T. 1977. Multidimensional scaling of power strategies. *J. Pers. Soc. Psychol.* 35:537–47

31. Ferguson, C., Kelley, H. H. 1964. Significant factors in overevaluation of own-group's product. *J. Abnorm. Soc. Psychol.* 69:223–27

32. Festinger, L. 1950. Informal social communication. *Psychol. Rev.* 57:271–92

33. Festinger, L., Pepitone, A., Newcomb, T. 1952. Some consequences of deindividuation in a group. *J. Abnorm. Soc. Psychol.* 47:382–89

34. Fiedler, F. E., Chemers, M. 1976. *Improving Leadership Effectiveness: The Leader Match Concept.* New York: Wiley. 219 pp.

35. Flowers, M. L. 1977. A laboratory test of some implications of Janis' groupthink hypothesis. *J. Pers. Soc. Psychol.* 35:888–96

36. French, E. 1956. Motivation as a variable in work partner selection. *J. Abnorm. Soc. Psychol.* 53:96–99

37. French, J. R. P., Raven, B. 1959. The bases of social power. See Ref. 13, pp. 150–67

38. Gintner, G., Lindskold, S. 1975. Rate of participation and expertise as factors influencing leader choice. *J. Pers. Soc. Psychol.* 32:1085–89

39. Goldman, M., Stockbauer, J. W., McAuliffe, T. G. 1977. Intergroup and intragroup competition and cooperation. *J. Exp. Soc. Psychol.* 13:81–88

40. Hamby, R. R. 1976. The effects of motivational orientation on deindividuation. *Hum. Relat.* 29:687–97

41. Hare, P. 1976. *Handbook of Small Group Research.* New York: Free Press. 781 pp.

42. Indik, B. P. 1963. Some effects of organization size on member attitudes and behavior. *Hum. Relat.* 16:369–84

43. Insko, C., Wilson, M. 1977. Interpersonal attraction as a function of social interaction. *J. Pers. Soc. Psychol.* 35:903–11

44. Janis, I. 1972. *Victims of Groupthink.* Boston: Houghton Mifflin. 276 pp.

45. Janis, I., Mann, L. 1977. *Decision Making.* New York: Free Press. 488 pp.

46. Janssens, L., Nuttin, J. R. 1976. Frequency perception of individual and group success as a function of competition, coaction, and isolation. *J. Pers. Soc. Psychol.* 34:830–36

47. Jennings, H. H. 1943. *Leadership and Isolation.* New York: Longmans, Green. 240 pp.

48. Jorgenson, D. O., Dukes, F. O. 1976. Deindividuation as a function of density and group membership. *J. Pers. Soc. Psychol.* 34:24–29

49. Kaufman, H. 1976. *Are Government Organizations Immortal?* Washington DC: Brookings Inst. 79 pp.

50. Kelley, H. H., Stahelski, A. J. 1970. Social interaction basis of cooperators' and competitors' beliefs about others. *J. Pers. Soc. Psychol.* 16:66–91

51. Kerr, N. L., Atkin, R. S., Stasser, G., Meek, D., Holt, R. W., Davis, J. H. 1976. Guilt beyond a reasonable doubt: effects of concept definition and assigned decision rule on the judgments of mock jurors. *J. Pers. Soc. Psychol.* 34:282–94

52. Kipnis, D. 1976. *The Powerholders.* Chicago: Univ. Chicago Press. 227 pp.

53. Klein, A. L. 1976. Changes in leadership appraisal as a function of the stress of a simulated panic situation. *J. Pers. Soc. Psychol.* 34:1143–54

54. Knowles, E. S., Bassett, R. 1976. Groups and crowds as social entities: effects of activity, size, and member similarity on nonmembers. *J. Pers. Soc. Psychol.* 34:837–45

55. Knowles, E. S., Kreuser, B., Haas, S., Hyde, M., Schuchart, G. E. 1976. Group size and the extension of social space boundaries. *J. Pers. Soc. Psychol.* 33:647–54

56. Komorita, S. S., Moore, D. 1976. Theories and processes of coalition formation. *J. Pers. Soc. Psychol.* 33:371–81
57. Kuhlman, D. M., Wimberley, D. L. 1976. Expectations of choice behavior held by cooperators, competitors, and individualists across four classes of experimental game. *J. Pers. Soc. Psychol.* 34:69–81
58. Kupperman, R., Wilcox, R. H., Smith, H. A. 1975. Crisis management: some opportunities. *Science* 187:404–10
59. Laughlin, P. R., Jaccord, J. J. 1975. Social facilitation and observational learning of individuals and cooperative pairs. *J. Pers. Soc. Psychol.* 32:873–79
60. Laughlin, P. R., Kerr, N., Davis, J., Halff, H., Marciniak, K. 1975. Group size, member ability, and social decision schemes on an intellectual task. *J. Pers. Soc. Psychol.* 31:522–35
61. Laughlin, P. R., Kerr, N. L., Munch, M. M., Haggarty, D. A. 1976. Social decision schemes of the same four-person groups on two different intellective tasks. *J. Pers. Soc. Psychol.* 33:80–88
62. Levit, A. M., Benjamin, A. 1976. Jews and Arabs rehearse Geneva: a model of conflict resolution. *Hum. Relat.* 29:1035–44
63. Lewin, K. 1943. Psychology and the process of group living. *Bull. SPSSI, J. Soc. Psychol.* 17:113–31
64. Lewis, L. S. 1975. *Scaling the Ivory Tower.* Baltimore: John Hopkins Press. 238 pp.
65. Libo, L. 1953. *Measuring Group Cohesiveness.* Ann Arbor, Mich: Inst. Soc. Res. 111 pp.
66. Likert, R., Likert, J. 1976. *New Ways of Managing Conflict.* New York: McGraw-Hill. 375 pp.
67. Lischeron, J., Wall, T. D. 1975. Attitudes toward participation among local authority employees. *Hum. Relat.* 28:499–517
68. Lischeron, J., Wall, T. D. 1976. Employee participation: an experimental field study. *Hum. Relat.* 28:863–84
69. Lord, R. G. 1977. Functional leadership behavior: measurement and relation to social power and leadership perceptions. *Adm. Sci. Q.* 22:114–33
70. Maier, N. R. F. 1963. *Problem Solving Discussion and Conferences: Leadership Methods and Skills.* New York: McGraw-Hill. 493 pp.
71. Marrow, A. 1969. *The Practical Theorist.* New York: Basic Books. 351 pp.
72. Marshall, J., Heslin, R. 1975. Boys and girls together: sexual composition and the effect of density and group size on

cohesiveness. *J. Pers. Soc. Psychol.* 31:952–61
73. Michener, H. A., Burt, M. R. 1975. Components of "authority" as determinants of compliance. *J. Pers. Psychol.* 31:606–14
74. Michener, H. A., Lawler, E. J. 1975. Endorsement of formal leaders: an integrative model. *J. Pers. Soc. Psychol.* 31:216–23
75. Mohr, L. B. 1977. Authority and democracy in organizations. *Hum. Relat.* 30:919–47
76. Morris, W., Worchel, S., Bois, J., Pearson, J., Rountree, C., Samaha, G., Wachtler, J., Wright, S. 1976. Collective coping with stress: group reactions to fear, anxiety and ambiguity. *J. Pers. Soc. Psychol.* 33:674–79
77. Murphy, G., Murphy, L., Newcomb, N. 1937. *Experimental Social Psychology.* New York: Harper. 1121 pp.
78. Myers, D. G., Lamm, H. 1976. The group polarization phenomenon. *Psychol. Bull.* 83:602–27
79. Nemeth, C. 1977. Interaction between jurors as a function of majority vs. unanimity decision rules. *J. Appl. Soc. Psychol.* 7:38–56
80. O'Brien, G. E., Harary, F. 1977. Measurement of the interactive effects of leadership style and group structure upon group performance. *Aust. J. Psychol.* 29:59–71
81. Okun, M., DiVesta, F. 1975. Cooperation and competition in coacting groups. *J. Pers. Soc. Psychol.* 31:615–20
82. Paulus, P. B., Annis, A. B., Seta, J. J., Schkade, J. K., Matthews, R. W. 1976. Density does affect task performance. *J. Pers. Soc. Psychol.* 34:248–53
83. Petty, R. E., Harkins, S. G., Williams, K. D., Latané, B. 1977. The effect of group size on cognitive effort and evaluation. *Pers. Soc. Psychol. Bull.* 3:579–82
84. Roethlisberger, F. J., Dickson, W. J. 1939. *Management and the Worker.* Cambridge, Mass: Harvard Univ. Press. 615 pp.
85. Ryen, A. H., Kahn, A. 1975. Effects of intergroup orientation on group attitudes and proxemic behavior. *J. Pers. Soc. Psychol.* 31:302–10
86. Schachter, S. 1959. *The Psychology of Affiliation.* Stanford: Stanford Univ. Press. 141 pp.
87. Schlenker, B. R. 1975. Liking for a group following an initiation: impression management or dissonance reduction? *Sociometry* 38:99–118
88. Schlenker, B. R., Miller, R. S. 1977. Group cohesiveness as a determinant of

egocentric perceptions in cooperative groups. *Hum. Relat.* 30:1039–55

89. Schlenker, B. R., Miller, R. S. 1977. Egocentrism in groups: self serving biases or logical information processing? *J. Pers. Soc. Psychol.* 35:755–64

90. Schlenker, B. R., Soraci, S. Jr., McCarthy, B. 1976. Self-esteem and group performance as determinants of egocentric perceptions in cooperative groups. *Hum. Relat.* 29:1163–76

91. Shaw, M. E., Harkey, B. 1976. Some effects of congruency of member characteristics and group structure upon group behavior. *J. Pers. Soc. Psychol.* 34:412–18

92. Sheridan, T. B. 1975. Community dialog technology. *Proc. Int. Soc. Electr. Eng.* 63:563–75

93. Smart, C., Vertinsky, I. 1977. Designs for crisis decision units. *Adm. Sci. Q.* 22:640–57

94. Sorrentino, R. M., Boutillier, R. G. 1975. The effect of quantity and quality of verbal interaction on ratings of leadership ability. *J. Exp. Soc. Psychol.* 11:403–11

95. Steers, R. M. 1977. Antecedents and outcomes of organizational commitment. *Adm Sci. Q.* 22:46–56

96. Stein, A. 1976. Conflict and cohesion: a review of the literature. *J. Conflict Resolut.* 20:143–72

97. Steiner, I. D. 1974. Whatever happened to the group in social psychology? *J. Exp. Soc. Psychol.* 10:93–108

98. Stewart, A. J., Rubin, Z. 1974. The power motive in the dating couple. *J. Pers. Soc. Psychol.* 34:305–9

99. Stone, C. 1975. *Where the Law Ends.* New York: Harper & Row. 273 pp.

100. Terborg, J. R., Castore, C., DeNinno, J. A. 1976. A longitudinal field investigation of the impact of group composition on group performance and cohesion. *J. Pers. Soc. Psychol.* 34:782–90

101. Thomas, E. J., Fink, C. 1963. Effects of group size. *Psychol. Bull* 60:371–84

102. Thomas, K. W., Pondy, L. R. 1977. Toward an "intent" model of conflict management among principal parties. *Hum. Relat.* 30:1089–1102

103. Valenti, A. C., Downing, L. L. 1975. Differential effects of jury size on verdicts following deliberation as a function of the apparent guilt of a defendant. *J. Pers. Soc. Psychol.* 32:655–63

104. Vinokur, A., Trope, Y., Burnstein, E. 1975. A decision-making analysis of

persuasive argumentation and the choice-shift effect. *J. Exp. Soc. Psychol.* 11:127–48

105. Wall, J. A. 1975. Effects of constituent and representative bargaining orientation on intergroup bargaining. *J. Pers. Soc. Psychol.* 31:1004–12

106. Wall, J. A. 1976. Effects of sex and opposing representative's bargaining orientation on intergroup bargaining. *J. Pers. Soc. Psychol.* 33:55–61

107. Wallach, M. A., Kogan, N., Bem, D. 1962. Group influence on individual risk taking. *J. Abnorm. Soc. Psychol.* 65:75–86

108. Wheeler, L., Nezlek, J. 1977. Sex differences in social participation. *J. Soc. Pers. Psychol.* 35:742–54

109. White, R., Lippitt, R. 1960. *Autocracy and Democracy.* New York: Harper. 330 pp.

110. Whyte, M. K. 1974. *Small Groups and Political Rituals in China.* Berkeley: Univ. California Press. 271 pp.

111. Wilder, D. 1977. Perception of groups, size of opposition, and social influence. *J. Exp. Soc. Psychol.* 13:253–68

112. Wilson, J. P., Aronoff, J., Messe, L. A. 1975. Social structure, member motivation, and group productivity. *J. Pers. Soc. Psychol.* 32:1094–98

113. Worchel, S., Andreoli, V. A., Folger, R. 1977. Intergroup cooperation and intergroup attraction: the effect of previous interaction and outcome of combined effort. *J. Exp. Soc. Psychol.* 13:131–40

114. Worchel, S., Lind, E., Kaufman, H. 1975. Evaluation of group products as a function of expectations of group longevity, outcome of competition, and publicity of evaluations. *J. Pers. Soc. Psychol.* 31:1089–97

115. Zajonc, R. B. 1965. Social facilitation. *Science* 149:269–74

116. Zajonc, R. B. 1976. Family configuration and intelligence. *Science* 192: 227–36

117. Zander, A. F. 1971. *Motives and Goals in Groups.* New York: Academic. 212 pp.

118. Zander, A. F. 1972. The purposes of national associations. *J. Voluntary Action Res.* 1:20–29

119. Zander, A. F. 1976. The psychology of removing group members and recruiting new ones. *Hum. Relat.* 29:969–87

120. Zander, A. F. 1977. *Groups at Work.* San Francisco: Jossey-Bass. 144 pp.

Ann. Rev. Psychol. 1979. 30:453–76
Copyright © 1979 by Annual Reviews Inc. All rights reserved

SMALL GROUP METHODS
OF PERSONAL CHANGE

❖314

John J. Hartman

Department of Psychiatry, University of Michigan, Ann Arbor, Michigan 48109

CONTENTS

INTRODUCTION 453
INDIVIDUAL VERSUS GROUP CONCEPTUAL FRAMEWORK 455
CLINICAL VERSUS STATISTICAL APPROACH TO METHODOLOGY 457
PROCESS VERSUS OUTCOME ORIENTATION 459
    Why these polarities? 459
OUTCOME CONCEPTUALIZATION AND MEASUREMENT 460
    Conceptual Rationale: Definition of Outcome 460
    Conceptual Rationale: Group versus Individual Orientation 461
    Clinical versus Statistical Measurement 462
    Research Strategy 463
    Recent Outcome Literature 463
        Reviews 463
        Negative effects 463
        Other outcome literature 464
                                                                                465
PERSONAL CHANGE PROCESSES 467
    Group versus Individual Orientation 467
    Clinical versus Statistical Methods 468
    Process versus Outcome Orientation 470
    Change Mechanisms 471
TOWARD A SYNTHESIS 472
CONCLUSION 473

INTRODUCTION

This review focuses on the use of small face-to-face groups to produce changes in the attitudes, behaviors, and feelings of individuals. A staggering variety of group techniques to deal with an ever-widening array of problems and populations abound. For this reason alone, systematic research on process and outcome in these groups is urgently needed. Yet there is probably no area in psychology where such research is more difficult and controversial, more fraught with philosophical and methodological conundrums.

453

0066-4308/79/0201-0453$01.00

Choosing the boundaries of what to review is a good case in point. One could restrict such a survey to formal group psychotherapy and behavior change. However, there are sensitivity training, encounter, self-analytic, leaderless, experiential, and self-help group methods being used to change people in classrooms, businesses, churches, and living rooms. A group can meet for "therapy," for "personal growth," for "experiential learning"; it can represent a system of medical repair, a method of learning and skill acquisition, a philosophical outlook on life, or a social movement. Lieberman & Gardner (40) have found that those seeking various experiential groups are similar to those seeking formal psychotherapy in problems, motives, expectations, and goals. Members are looking for techniques to change things in their lives: to feel better, to perform better at work and in relationships with other people. I have chosen, therefore, to broaden this review to include all those efforts to produce personal change in groups. Not only are these groups trying to do the same things with similar kinds of people, but the groups may provide an opportunity for comparative study by their seeming variety of method and outlook.

While widening the landscape of this review I have at the same time chosen to capture it with the broad strokes of a philosophical and critical perspective rather than with the camera lens of extensive literature review. There have been several excellent reviews covering research in this field in the last several years (1, 21, 38, 54, 65, 75). My use of the recent literature is selective and meant to highlight both the past obstacles to and future opportunities for understanding personal change in small groups.

I shall argue in this review that there are a number of dichotomies which have arisen in this field, that while specious, have exerted a very harmful effect on our research efforts and will continue to do so until they are recognized and confronted. The first of these is an individual versus group conceptual framework. Every researcher has to accommodate to the individual-group dialectic in a way similar to that of the group therapist (29). That is, he has to decide when to pay attention to individual, when to dyadic-interactional, and when to group issues. If his background is in clinical psychology, the researcher is apt to neglect factors like peer pressure, group cohesion, and social interaction as relevant variables. If his background is in social psychology, the researcher may downplay factors in the member-leader relationship like transference or transparency. A second dichotomy is a clinical versus statistical approach to methodology. Efforts made by the researcher to concretize variables, to control for factors of change, and otherwise to bring the group situation into line with scientific standards may leave the clinician feeling deprived of the richness, complexity, and, perhaps, the essence of the clinical enterprise. The result of this has been a gulf between the researcher and the clinician, particularly between the social scientist and the group therapist. The third polarity involves a process versus outcome orientation to research. Most group research has focused exclusively on either process or outcome. Systematic studies of process have ignored outcome variables and most outcome studies have relied on pre- and post-test measures with no systematic description of what went on in the groups in between.

Each of these polarities will be discussed with illustrations from the recent literature. Then problems of outcome and process research will be discussed in the light of this analysis. Finally, some research strategies will be presented which move beyond these dichotomies to more integrative approaches. This reviewer concludes that lack of recognition and resolution of these dialectics has caused most research in this area to fall far short of what is needed.

INDIVIDUAL VERSUS GROUP CONCEPTUAL FRAMEWORK

Strupp & Bergin (68) did not include a special section on group therapy in their extensive review of psychotherapy research issues. Their position was that all therapeutic techniques impact on individuals; thus, principles from individual psychotherapy research lay the foundation for effective group methods. The implication is that results are similar in individual and group situations and that the process of change can be reduced to the same common denominators as well. Researchers trained in individual personality theories approach group research questions in this way. Assessment of group performance may be based on data obtained in a dyadic situation and involve behavioral-symptomatic or intrapsychic variables. The group therapeutic process may be viewed as a variant on the same factors inherent in the dyadic situation, whether the group be behavioral or psychoanalytic in approach.

There is a contrary view which perceives group change research from the perspective of group psychology. Here the group situation is all-important in its impact on the individual, and research issues are more likely to involve issues of peer influence, group development, group cohesion, and climate. Individual assessment may even be done in a group situation and involve interpersonal variables. The most extreme example of this line of research is in the area of group development (24). The individual's performance is viewed as embedded in a powerful social matrix.

The practice of group change methods reflects this individual-group polarity as well (60). Some methods focus on the individual exclusively while other members watch and wait their turn. Group processes are downplayed or ignored. Other methods utilize the group-as-a-whole to the point where the group seems to be the patient, not the individuals (48).

What difference does this seeming polarity make to research efforts? It creates a kind of researcher bias in which one perspective on group life is emphasized to the exclusion of another. One way this is manifested is by assuming that factors found to be central to the change process in dyadic therapy are also found fundamental in group therapy as well. This is natural because most group methods began with an individually centered approach to psychopathology.

Gurman & Gustafson (22), however, explored the empirical literature dealing with the relationship between the patient's perception of the therapeutic relationship and outcome in group therapy. Various schools of individual psychotherapy have emphasized the importance of the therapist-patient relationship, and research has generally supported this emphasis at least as a precondition for change. However, their review of the 11 relevant studies applying this hypothesis to group therapy found no such relationship. The authors conclude that group therapy that de-emphasizes the role of leader and emphasizes peer interaction or other group-centered methods may make the therapeutic relationship-outcome connection less salient. They further emphasize that many studies fail to describe adequately the actual techniques of therapeutic intervention, making testing of the hypothesis more difficult. They agree with previous research that found that the ideology of the school of therapy is no indicator of what actually transpires in the group (41).

By emphasizing a therapeutic factor from individual therapy, the researcher may miss a great deal when he turns his attention to groups. Another example deals with self-disclosure (19). The connection between member self-disclosure and outcome is very much dependent on group development. Lieberman, Yalom & Miles (41) found that self-disclosure tended to be ineffective or harmful early in the encounter groups they studied but more beneficial in later stages of group development. The researcher dealing with this variable would have to be familiar with developmental processes in groups to study this variable most usefully.

On the other hand, another study involving self-disclosure shows that a lack of understanding of individual characteristics can have an equally biasing effect. Strassberg, Roback & Anchor (67) studied the self-disclosure of schizophrenics in group therapy in relation to outcome. They found that the more the self-disclosure the worse the outcome. This result is different from the literature on healthier groups of individuals. The authors attribute this result to the inability of the schizophrenic patient to handle affect-arousing self-disclosure.

Strupp & Bergin's conclusion (68) about group methods, however, is not warranted or useful. Group methods may be different in their processes from individual treatments and may include a specific effect, enhanced interpersonal functioning, that has a special place in group work. Truax (72) and Liberman (42) have presented research which supports the notion that group therapy is not merely a complicated version of dyadic therapy, but involves variables unique to the group situation. Yet Strupp and Bergin's reaction is understandable in that there has been a lack of clarification of group methods and how they work.

One is forced to conclude that there is no such thing as a group method of change but group methods, encompassing Alcoholics Anonymous, consciousness-raising groups, groups for schizophrenics in hospitals, and outpatient groups for well-functioning neurotics. Ideologically there are psychoanalytic, behavioral, transactional, and gestalt groups, etc. The goals for change may be quite different in these groups, following the rationale of the particular school or method.

This individual-group bias shows up markedly in assessment techniques and in measures of process. Methods of assessing group members either to predict performance or to measure outcome vary in their emphasis on individual, either intrapsychic or behavioral-symptomatic, or interpersonal, either dyadic or group-wide, dimensions. Clearly the assessment devices a researcher chooses will reflect his or her emphasis on individual or group conceptions of the change process. Likewise, in studying the processes of change in groups, researchers are likely to bias their choices of what to look at. They may focus on the member-leader interactions exclusively or may ignore them in favor of group or interpersonal process variables.

In the group situation, the therapist must always be aware of individual, dyadic, and group forces operating at the same time. By his ideology or clinical sense he may choose to emphasize one over the other, either a great deal or only at certain times. So, too, the researcher emphasizes individual, dyadic, or group forces at the expense of a full understanding of what is going on. In fact, our understanding of group methods from the literature may be skewed in one direction or another by this very kind of bias.

CLINICAL VERSUS STATISTICAL APPROACH TO METHODOLOGY

A similarly specious dichotomy has evolved regarding methods in group research. Meehl (50) has described this as "clinical" versus "statistical" prediction. This same problem has been discussed in more global terms as differences between hedgehogs and foxes after Isaiah Berlin's discussion of Tolstoy (8). Hedgehogs, like most clinicians, aspire to a unifying view, to know "one big thing." Foxes, like empirical scientists, build knowledge on the basis of many little facts, hoping to see a unifying theme emerge. This nomothetic versus idiographic split has haunted personality psychology for years (3). Most of the anecdotal reports that fill the practitioner literature reflect the hedgehog's approach while most of the empirical research exemplifies the fox's methodology.

Group change research highlights this kind of schism in several ways. Efforts made by the researcher to concretize variables, to control for factors in the change process, and otherwise to bring the clinical situation into line with "scientific" standards may leave the clinician feeling deprived of the richness, complexity, and perhaps the essence of the clinical enterprise. He may feel that research has reduced a set of complex human relationships to irrelevant, simplistic variables. He may also believe that prediction about a single, unique case is lost in the nomothetic method.

On the other hand, the researcher in the small group field is appalled by the lack of commitment to look systematically at what is occurring in personal change groups and to subject the enterprise to examination in quantifiable and replicable terms. This involves specificity, precision, quantification, and attempts at uniformity (10). Without such methods, the researcher feels that general statements about the effectiveness of specific groups for specific populations cannot be made.

Again, since people tend to line up on one side of this fence or the other, differences in methodology seem irreconcilable. This produces a gulf between the researcher and the clinician, particularly between the social scientist and the "humanistic" practitioner. There is a difference in goals, values, language, and world view. Attempts to bridge this gulf have been notably unsuccessful (53), and the field proceeds pretty much along these separate paths.

This gulf is best illustrated by the exchange of *ad hominem* arguments about the encounter group study of Lieberman, Yalom & Miles (41). Schutz (61) and Rowan (59) took great exception to the methodology, conclusions, and spirit of this study. These practitioners felt that the researchers were "out to get" the encounter movement and that bias and a lack of understanding of encounter permeated the work. These assertions and the replies (36) serve to highlight the gulf between the researcher and the humanistic practitioner. This exchange is distressing because in actuality Lieberman, Yalom & Miles are able practitioners and Schutz and Rowan former researchers. Yet the study, the most extensive and sophisticated in the group field to date, was experienced as an attack on the fundamental values and world view of encounter.

The clinician-hedgehog proceeds with his world view and may report anecdotal evidence to support it. The foxy researcher may try to employ his methods to produce the "facts" about what is going on. It appears that each is speaking a different language. Understanding change in groups comes down to a test of competing belief systems, and the possibility of using diverse methods of understanding complicated phenomena gets lost in the rhetoric (53).

PROCESS VERSUS OUTCOME ORIENTATION

The third dichotomy which has hampered group change research is the adoption of either a process or an outcome orientation in a particular study (52). Most outcome studies involve primarily pre-test, post-test measures of change. This is a difficult and hazardous undertaking at best and few researchers want to complicate things by introducing process variables. Those doing process studies have tended likewise to ignore outcome. This has seemed a reasonable division of labor.

However, this dichotomy has proved not to be useful. With the lack of conceptual clarity about group change methods, systematic description of intervention methods is crucial. Unless this is done, there is no way to make comparisons between studies and generalizations about methods. Any outcome study should have at least this process dimension. All the controls in the world in the most sophisticated design will not clarify very much if one has to guess about the nature of the treatment the individuals receive (22).

By its very nature, group process research involves the measurement of change. The field of group development illustrates this very well (18, 24). Leader behaviors, feedback, self-disclosure norms may all change with time. The measurement of outcome at the end of treatment or at follow-up is merely tapping into this process at arbitrary times. Any process study would be greatly enhanced by attempts to get some outcome data. *Process and outcome are two sides of the same coin.* Understanding one enhances understanding the other. The process measures utilized by Lieberman, Yalom & Miles (41) clarified their outcome findings in crucial ways. They were able to relate, by virtue of the complexity and sophistication of their design, outcome findings to a variety of process measures. They were able to include leader variables such as styles and interventions, member variables such as role, status, activity, and attraction to group and group variables such as norms, cohesiveness, and climate. To have studied any of these variables, process, or outcome in isolation would have deprived this study of much of its power.

WHY THESE POLARITIES?   It is very hard to say why these polarities have taken root so firmly in the group change field. It seems to this reviewer that this state of affairs itself mirrors well-known group processes which oppose productive integration and work (18). Whatever the cause, these conceptual, methodological, and design polarities have had a deleterious effect, particularly in outcome research where we now focus our attention.

OUTCOME CONCEPTUALIZATION AND MEASUREMENT

Evaluating individual change as a result of group methods is similar to the following: take a group of people who say they feel ill. Randomly administer to them the prescription and nonprescription contents of a drug store. Research finds that some of these people get better, some stay the same, and some die. The researchers are asked to answer the question, does drug therapy work? This approximates the state of outcome research in the group field. Do groups change people for the better? The previously discussed polarities contribute to making this a most puzzling riddle.

Conceptual Rationale: Definition of Outcome

The definition of outcome in personal change groups is dependent on who is doing the assessment and what criteria for success or failure are employed. Patients, therapists, and independent raters do not agree on the success or failure of the therapy. Nor do they employ the same criteria. Strupp & Hadley (69) have offered a tripartite model of outcome which highlights this problem very well. In their view outcome can be assessed on the basis of: 1. personal well-being as judged by the patient, 2. social functioning as judged by significant others in the social environment, and 3. personality integration as assessed by the mental health professional. These judgments may be very different. A similar way to conceptualize this problem is by areas of functioning—symptomatic, interpersonal, and intrapsychic. Each of these areas may be assessed by the client, the practitioner, the independent observer, and significant others. This can be diagrammed as follows:

	CLIENT	PROFESSIONAL		SOCIETY
	Client	Practitioner	Observer	Significant Others
Symptomatic-Behavioral				
Interpersonal				
Intrapsychic-Structural				

In each box may be arrayed the various outcome assessment measures used in the field. The problem is that there is not one outcome; in Strupp's model there may be 9 possibilities, and in mine there may be 12. Any study that measures outcome simply in terms of patient self-report of symptoms is by this standard incomplete.

The definition of outcome is tied closely to the role position of the assessor. It is also closely tied to the philosophical, theoretical, and value position of the assessor as well. For example, the medical repair model of change is vastly different from the human potential growth model of change. These different models dictate differences in outcome criteria and techniques of measurement. Even though Lieberman (40) has found no substantive differences in goals between those attending growth centers and those in psychotherapy, the researcher's model may dictate different definitions of outcome for those in diverse groups. A medical model implies resolution of symptoms, conflicts, and difficulties. A growth model implies the expansion of awareness, and capability of having peak experiences.

Beyond these two general models there are a plethora of different schools of group change, each with its own view of human personality and the mechanisms that change it. This has created a Tower of Babel problem where there are no agreed-upon guidelines for conceptualizing change. Every school has its own. Strupp's model (69) is thus timely and very much needed. Different schools may array themselves differently on his nine criteria but at least some such guidelines could make matters more reasonable. Outcome necessarily involves different aspects of functioning and different observation orientations (47). Unlike the pathologist in the drug store example, the group researcher has no common agreed-upon basic science upon which to conduct studies. We have no table of elements, let alone a biochemistry in which quantitative methods can be applied. Even to those who believe that good therapy is like good symphony we do not have an agreed-upon language of notes and scales with which to compare performances. Such an Esperanto of personality functioning does not seem possible or perhaps even desirable, but this lack of conceptual clarity makes outcome research frustrating and at times meaningless.

Conceptual Rationale: Group versus Individual Orientation

As if this were not enough, group methods present an additional problem in the assessment of outcome. Most conceptualizations of outcome derive from this plethora of schools and ideologies of personality functioning. But these, in turn, give differing weight to the importance of group, social, situational, and interpersonal factors in the development of adult personality functioning. Psychoanalysts and behaviorists may find themselves allied in viewing outcome in individual terms regardless of the individual's social matrix. However, a practitioner with an interactionist point of view may want to assess individual functioning in a group or interpersonal context. Most outcome measures are aimed at the behavioral-symptomatic or intra-psychic spheres of functioning and are administered in a solitary or dyadic situation. Predicting group performance from individually oriented tests is problematic (7, 24, 49). The unique feature of group methods is the use of the interpersonal field for change. Yet our use of group and interpersonal conceptualization of outcome is lacking. By and large, assessment devices developed for individual therapy and personality assessment are used for assessing outcomes in groups as well. There have been some recent attempts to correct this imbalance, however.

Temoshok (70) has developed a video-taped instrument to assess social scripts. The test involves the perception of group vignettes which are used to predict group performance. Hartman (26) has developed a projective film which can be administered in either a dyadic or group form. Responses are coded for interpersonal variables and used to predict group performance on these same variables.

Silbergeld and his associates (63) report an assessment device for evaluating a variety of therapeutic environments, the Group Atmosphere Scale. This process measure can be related to comparative studies of outcome (64).

Clinical versus Statistical Measurement

It naturally follows that these theoretical and philosophical orientations dicate the aspects of functioning assessed and the choice of measuring instruments used. The psychodynamic clinician may be most interested in the intrapsychic-structural dimension and favor global "clinical" ratings and projective tests. The behaviorist may utilize frequency counts of highly specific behaviors as measures of outcome. The encounter-humanist may favor a self-report inventory tapping abstract attitudes about the self. Some clinicians feel that any such mechanistic approach to change assessment is counter-productive and stifling.

These different theoretical approaches to outcome dictate measures that vary considerably in their abstraction. Attempts to anchor complaints and symptoms to specific behavioral indicators is one thing; measuring ego-strength or interpersonal awareness is quite another. Some conceptions of change lend themselves to statistical measurement and some, despite the best ingenuity of researchers, do not.

Another measurement problem has been the idiographic versus nomo-thetic approach. Should outcome be determined by scores on instruments designed to tap universal factors of functioning? Or should outcome be individually tailored to conform to the particular goals and personality of the client? For example, if one were employing a measure of hostility, a shy repressed client might have a positive outcome if her hostility score were increased at the end of a group, whereas an abrasive, violent client might have a positive outcome if his hostility score were reduced. The absolute level of the scale or even of change on that scale may not be as important as the direction and meaning of that change in the individual context.

These issues of measurement, like the issues of conceptualization, indicate that there are no agreed-upon approaches to outcome. Researchers tend not to sample across areas of functioning, not to combine idiographic with nomothetic measurements, and not to ulitize ratings from different sources.

Research Strategy

As mentioned, studies usually involve process or outcome, but rarely both in combination. In outcome studies, there is, therefore, usually a failure to specify the actual intervention techniques utilized, member behaviors in the group itself, and leadership characteristics as well. Even if a sophisticated design involving a randomly assigned control group is employed, a good study is significantly weakened by these failures to specify the process. Something may have happened to produce differences between the groups but one cannot say precisely what. Studies comparing this method with that method often suffer this defect. Because the Lieberman, Yalom & Miles (41) study employed process measures, it was possible to explain the between-group differences with some power.

What has resulted has been a large number of smaller studies which are impossible to compare because of a lack of uniformity and specificity about clients, leaders, group methods, and outcome measures. It has been impossible to build up samples of reliable studies in order to achieve larger and larger numbers of subjects. This has tended to reflect the clinician-researcher and scientist-humanist polarities. Even among systematic researchers there is a tendency to do one's own thing and a failure to build upon previous work. Unlike the earlier drug analogy, there is no FDA to help with guidelines in the post hoc assessment of group modalities.

Recent Outcome Literature

REVIEWS   It is useful to view the group outcome literature in the light of the problems cited above. There have been several recent extensive reviews of outcome studies. Abramowitz (1) reviewed outcome research on children's activity groups, behavior modification, and verbal therapy groups. She found "unconvincing" evidence of their effectiveness. There were an equal number of positive as well as negative results in her sample of studies.

Kilmann & Sotile (32) reviewed 45 studies of outcome for marathon encounter groups and found no substantial evidence for their effectiveness. They found that conclusions were difficult because of the variability of groups with regard to time formats and other variables. The subjects were mostly college student "normals" and the most frequent measure used was the POI, a self-report measure of attitudes. The control group studies used mostly "silent" controls and there were few studies involving follow-up.

Parloff & Dies (54) reviewed the group psychotherapy literature for the period 1966–75. They screened 38 studies which met their inclusion criteria of being group therapy, involving clinical categories of clients and meeting minimal standards of research design. They organized the review around clinical patient categories of schizophrenia, psychoneuroses, crime and delinquency, and addictions. They found no "compelling endorsement" of group therapy for the treatment of any of these populations.

Smith (65) reviewed 100 outcome studies of sensitivity training groups. Each study had to have involved controls, used repeated measures of outcome, and have lasted at least 20 hours. 78% of the studies detected measurable change in the treated as opposed to control group members. Of the 31 studies of follow-up measures of outcome, 21 found significant changes in the treatment group members. The measuring instruments most often used in these studies were self-concept ratings, prejudice scales, FIRO-B, and POI. Self-reports, perceptions of trainees, and organizational behavior were all utilized as outcome measures although rarely in the same study. It is hard to evaluate this "positive" review in the light of the three previous ones. It could be that the criteria of outcome in sensitivity training are different enough from those in "therapeutic" studies to obtain positive results of the type Smith cited (65). The sensitivity outcome measures most often involved self-report measures of attitudes which may be easier to obtain in relatively healthy college populations than symptomatic and behavioral change in clinical populations. All of these findings should be viewed with some caution, because almost all of the studies cited in these reviews suffer from the deficiencies cited earlier in this paper.

NEGATIVE EFFECTS   As if these mixed findings with regard to the efficacy of personal change groups were not enough, there has been increasing attention paid to the negative effects or "casualties" of group experiences (66). Lieberman, Yalom & Miles (41) found that 7.8% of the 206 participants of their encounter group study and 9.1% of those who completed 50% of the group meetings "suffered significant psychological injury." Another 8% were "negative changers" or experienced downward shifts on three or more change measures. Hartley, Roback & Abramowitz (25) thoroughly reviewed the issue more recently. They reviewed nine studies involving encounter group casualties and found proportions of casualties ranging from less than 1% to 47%. They also found differing definitions of casualties depending on the role and training of the evaluator. They suggested member, leader, and group characteristics which seemed to be associated with negative effects.

Cooper (11) also reviewed previous studies of negative outcomes in T-groups and encounter groups. He concluded, however, that these studies have not demonstrated that such groups are psychologically dangerous. He urged more methodologically sophisticated studies and systematic screening procedures to exclude participants with previous psychological disturbances.

The question of negative effects involves the same philosophical and ideological dilemmas discussed earlier with regard to positive change. Even a psychotic break is viewed by some as a growth experience. Still, the criteria for negative effects seem somewhat more explicit than those for positive changes.

OTHER OUTCOME LITERATURE   78 outcome studies which appeared in 1975–76 were surveyed by this reviewer. Thirty-seven of these were simple outcome studies employing no controls or "silent" controls. Of these 78 studies, 9 employed follow-up measures, 2 utilized outcome measures across different observers and levels of functioning, and 9 combined process measures with outcome. To this reviewer, this represents an unsatisfactory quality of research. The gross deficiencies in this literature as a whole make it hard to evaluate the positive or negative findings and, worse yet, impossible to build upon smaller studies to accumulate adequate knowledge in the future.

There are exceptions to this gloomy picture, studies excellent in design and significant in their findings. Malan and his colleagues (48) interviewed 42 randomly selected patients 2 to 14 years after the termination of psychoanalytic group therapy at the Tavistock Clinic. They found that psychodynamic changes in those who stayed less than 6 months were no different than those staying in group therapy 2 years or more. They found that most patients were highly dissatisfied with their treatment. There was a correlation between previous individual therapy and favorable outcome. This study employed a sophisticated design and included specific descriptions of the treatment employed and the clinical ratings used for assessing outcome. This study seems to have made a major impact on the practice of this kind of group therapy in this country (29).

Yalom and his colleagues (76) conducted another study involving follow-up. They studied 33 patients in long-term individual therapy to assess the effect of a weekend group experience on their subsequent individual therapy. The patients were randomly assigned to two gestalt experimental groups and one meditation Tai-Chi control group. A 6 and 12 week follow-up was conducted. At 6 weeks there was improvement in the experimental sample; at 12 weeks this improvement had disappeared. Two patients were felt to have been damaged by the experience. The authors conclude that the arousal of affect per se had no effect on outcome in the subsequent individual therapy. This study also highlights the importance of extended follow-up to assess outcome.

Another study of significance was conducted by Piper and his associates (55, 56). They studied 48 neurotic patients in long-term outpatient therapy. They used a pre-test/post-test control group design by using as controls patients who waited 3 months before receiving therapy. The controls were compared with the experimental group receiving therapy during this same 3 month period. The study conducted in the first year found no significant changes for treated over control patients on 9 of the 10 outcome measures. There was a greater variability for the treated patients with some showing considerable change in the positive direction and some showing considerable change in the negative direction. In the second year treated patients showed slight improvement over controls on 5 outcome criteria. The greatest improvement was in the Interpersonal Behavior Scale developed for this study. The authors describe a strategy for using the same set of criteria, interpersonal functioning, to describe the patient initially, to measure group process, and to measure outcome. This is an intriguing notion and one which should be pursued further. Another important finding of this study was that the Social Desirability Scale of the Personality Research Form correlated significantly with 6 of the first 9 outcome scores. This is consistent with the findings that patients, therapists, and judges rate the same experience quite differently (69). It probably also explains the preponderance of positive findings among simple outcome studies using self-report measures of attitudes. This study is significant in its use of multiple outcome measures sampling interpersonal functioning, psychiatric symptomatology, and patient-specified target symptoms. The generally negative results could have been the result of sampling only 3 months of a long-term therapy. Perhaps if additional follow-up was done at termination, a different picture would emerge.

There are several other recent studies worth noting. Diamond & Shapiro's (13) work on encounter groups offers a solid methodological framework for a research program in this area. Studies attempting to combine process measures with outcome offer a significant beginning to bridging this gap (9, 15, 16, 23, 31, 74). For example, Strassberg and his colleagues (67) found that more self-disclosing schizophrenics made significantly less progress. This finding runs counter to previous studies with nonpsychotics but has important treatment implications. Work by Lipman, Covi & Smith (12, 44) on the comparative effects of drugs and group therapy found imiprimine superior to psychotherapy. Unfortunately, reports of this study do not present the independent effects of group therapy. More research in this area, particularly with depressives, will undoubtedly appear in the years ahead.

Another area which will undoubtedly expand in the future is behavioral approaches to group therapy (42, 58). Behaviorists are able to concretize treatment goals in well-designed experimental paradigms which make for potentially convincing studies. Some behaviorists have shown a willingness to integrate behavioral approaches with small group theory which bodes well for future research.

While the majority of outcome research has been clearly inadequate, a few excellent studies, more willingness to combine process variables with outcome, and behavioral approaches to group give some hope for the future.

PERSONAL CHANGE PROCESSES

The attempt to understand *how* personal change groups work is plagued by some of the same problems as outcome research but to a lesser extent. It is easier to describe what goes on than to evaluate outcome with its philosophical and conceptual complexities. Process research derives from the laboratory tradition of small group work which puts it on a more solid footing as well. Whatever the reason, process research seems to be more sophisticated and of higher quality than outcome research, but it is affected by the polarities of approach described earlier in this paper.

Group versus Individual Orientation

In trying to conceptualize how personal change groups work, the researcher relies on an ideology about personality functioning somewhere on the group-individual continuum. He may conceptualize group processes using dyadic variables like social learning, transference, etc. Thus, the researcher's orientation on the group-individual axis will determine which particular variables he deems relevant to his process study. Schaffer & Galinsky (60), in their study of 11 orientations to personal change groups, point out the group-as-social-system versus therapist-member interpersonal relationship models as one important distinction. Lieberman (37) also has sought to systematize structural characteristics central to the change-induction process. Among the five characteristics he lists is included the extent to which the group as a social microcosm is used as a source of change. It is more important to observe how a group actually operates than to rely on the school or ideology of the leader and, it should be added, of a particular bias of a researcher.

One area where this issue is particularly salient is the relative emphasis of peer versus leader influence. Those groups which derive their ideologies from dyadic approaches place great emphasis on leadership variables or on the member-leader relationship in the change process (2, 20, 30, 62). Aspects of peer or group-as-a-whole influence may be ignored or downplayed. The Lieberman, Yalom & Miles study (41) devoted a good deal of attention to leadership style and outcome. They identified Energizers, Providers, and Social Engineers as well as Impersonals, Laissez-Faire, and Managers. These styles cut across theoretical orientations and each was associated with a level of positive outcome and of risk. The Providers produced the most positive change; the Energizers and Impersonals the most risk.

However, this study also included "leaderless groups" employing tapes, one of which produced one of the highest rates of positive change. In addition, Lieberman, Yalom, and Miles related leader characteristics to social system characteristics like norms, cohesion, member role which they saw as a fuller explanation of the change process than leader characteristics alone. This view seems supported by the increasing research on peer-therapy and self-help groups (4, 34, 39). Although there are no formal studies of the effectiveness of these groups, there is no doubt of their wide appeal. One characteristic of these groups is their anti-leader-as-expert ideology. The influence process is very much peer-oriented.

Dies (14) has thoroughly reviewed theory and research on group therapist transparency or self-disclosure. His conclusion is that the effectiveness of therapist self-disclosure is related to a host of variables unrelated to leadership variables. That is, "when," "where," "to whom," variables involving the social system are crucial to understanding the effectiveness of this single variable.

An individual-group conceptual dichotomy is not useful if it emphasizes leader or therapist-member variables to the exclusion of social system characteristics. A great virtue of comparing the variety of people-changing groups is to see the range of techniques and structures which seem effective. As Gurman & Gustafson (22) suggest in their review of patient perceptions of the therapeutic relationship in psychotherapy, group therapy is different in its therapeutic processes from dyadic therapy. The member's relationship with leader, with peers, and with the group-as-a-whole may all influence the change process. Regardless of his theoretical orientation, the researcher must accept these facts of group life.

To test the relative influence of these various factors, it becomes crucial to have highly specific process measures of member and leader behavior. Ideology does not determine leader behavior and ideology cannot determine the relative influence of leader, peer, group behaviors on outcome.

Clinical versus Statistical Methods

While there has been a great deal of relevant work in the small group field (24, 45, 46), a lack of integration of this work in the clinical setting continues. This state of affairs can be illustrated by the lack of use of content analysis systems of coding interaction process in personal change groups. The coding of leader and member behaviors would seem to be an excellent way of specifying the nature of the intervention and possibly the role of leader and peer influence in the change process.

Such systematic observation techniques have a long history in the small group field beginning with the work of Bales (6). There exist several systems of interaction coding. It is surprising that more use has not been made of these schemes for recording process in clinical settings. Bales' (7) new system is solidly grounded in work with personality variables in self-analytic classrooms. Gibbard & Hartman's (17) scoring system employs categories derived from psychodynamic variables. Hill's (27) system was derived from his work with therapeutic groups. These methods represent attempts to bridge the clinical-statistical gap, but they have rarely been applied to the personal change process. Most studies rely on client self-report measures of the process or sample time periods of the group using ratings on global factors. Even the Lieberman, Yalom & Miles (41) study had no systematic process-recording scheme. They used questionnaires and global rating scales to measure their process variables.

Tresemer (71) has reviewed methods of observing social interaction and makes a case for their utility. Aries (5) applied one such scheme effectively in studying processes in all-male, all-female, and mixed self-analytic groups. O'Day (51) utilized a systematic observation scoring system to derive a typology of leader styles in T-groups. These studies indicate that methods developed in the small group field can be effectively applied to clinical settings.

One problem is that this method is time-consuming and costly. Another problem is that concepts from social psychology may not be compatible with the theoretical outlook of the clinician. The ideal interaction coding system must have categories which are relevant to the clinical situation but broad enough so as to be useful across groups of different intervention ideologies. At this point the choice of process measures mirrors the situation with outcome measures: everyone uses his favorite, making it difficult to compare findings across studies. Again what is needed is some consensus about process measures to allow some accumulation of knowledge across studies.

To this reviewer it seems that process studies would yield more if they were "naturalistic" rather than "experimental" in intent. If the researcher focuses only on leadership or only on self-disclosure, even if these variables are tied to outcome, they are going to be incomplete. Since there is no consensus as to the key variables in the change process, the most reasonable strategy would seem to be a broad multivariate approach. This does not necessarily mean large, expensive studies if comparable methods and instruments are used across studies. Broadly based interaction scoring schemes could be utilized to study leader, member, and group behaviors with multivariate methods.

Process versus Outcome Orientation

Process variables central to change have not usually been integrated with outcome measures. In studies where this has been done, there has often been a failure to specify under what conditions a certain mechanism works and with what kind of people. Process studies tend to focus on a favorite variable to the exclusion of others. This is due to a lack of an integrated conceptualization of the change process and to a lack of a naturalistic approach to assessing group process.

Piper and his colleagues (55, 56) in their excellent outcome study suggest the possibility of using the same set of criteria, interpersonal functioning, to assess the patient, measure group process, and to measure outcome. They suggest using measures from different sources and the use of observer ratings of the group sessions themselves. This is in line with the thrust of this review, as it offers the possibility of integrating process and outcome.

Rose (58), a behaviorist, advocates observation techniques for the monitoring of group interaction data. When such data can be tied to concrete behavioral anchors, they could be used as measures of outcome. He cites an interaction scoring system developed by Linsk and his colleagues (43) as an example of using process measures to chart individual progress in the group.

In a study in progress, Hartman is trying to develop idiographic process measures of outcome for individuals using the Gibbard, Hartman & Mann (18) interaction scoring system. By charting changes in the interpersonal measures in the course of the group itself, it is possible to correlate these change scores with traditional outcome measures sampling symptomatic, interpersonal, and intrapsychic areas of functioning. These interpersonal process measures would be the equivalent of the behaviorally anchored process measures of progress cited by Rose. The integration of assessment, process, and outcome variables seems a promising area for future work.

Yalom's (76) outcome study has some implications for understanding the change process because he systematically sampled group sessions for a process variable like affect arousal. His study suggests that the group arousal of affect per se has no positive effect in subsequent individual therapy. This finding is consistent with the finding of Lieberman, Yalom & Miles (41) that a cognitive framework is necessary for affective learning to take place. Yalom's study is an example of how outcome and process elements of a study can be mutually enriching.

Change Mechanisms

The bottom line for process research is the identification of the mechanisms of the personal change process. There have been two recent contributions which bear on this. Hill (28) combined the change mechanisms found previously by Corsini and Rosenberg, Hill, and Yalom into a single list ranked by degree of consensus among the theorists. Those mechanisms having clear consensus were ventilation, acceptance, spectator therapy, and intellectualization. Of secondary importance were universalization, reality testing, altruism, and socialization. Rohrbaugh & Bartels (57) sought to examine the construct validity of Yalom's original Q-sort of curative factors (75). They concluded that the Lieberman, Yalom & Miles study (41) may have confused conditions for change with mechanisms of change. They assert that members' perceptions of curative events do not necessarily conform to what actually happened or what was causative in the change process.

An understanding of change mechanisms will not come from questionnaire studies of participants nor from the lists of mechanisms we have now. Group cohesion may be a condition of change but not a mechanism. Interpersonal learning (76) is a vague and global term which must have identifiable components. This reviewer feels that there are two future avenues of research into therapeutic mechanisms. The first has been discussed as naturalistic study of group processes through interaction coding design. The second is the comparative systems approach.

By broadening the study of change groups to include nonprofessional indigenous groups like peer-therapy and self-help groups, a perspective on the change process is gained. Levy's (34) study of self-help groups is the best example of this approach. He used a naturalistic observation method to identify four types of self-help groups. His typology includes groups organized for: 1. conduct reorganization, 2. stress reduction, 3. survival against discrimination, and 4. self-actualization. He also identifies 11 processes inherent in these groups. These processes are noteworthy because they bear a resemblance to some of the change mechanisms listed for individual and group psychotherapy. They include four behavioral processes: 1. social reinforcement of egosyntonic behavior and elimination of problems; 2. training, indoctrination, support for self-control behaviors; 3. modeling of methods of changing and coping with stress; 4. an agenda and rationale to change the social environment. He lists seven cognitive processes: 5. rationale for problems and distress and the group's way of dealing with it, demystification, and increasing expectancy for change; 6. provision of normative and instrumental information; 7. expansion of range of alternative perceptions of members' problems and ways to change them; 8. enhancement of discriminative abilities toward stimulus and event contingencies; 9. support for change in attitudes toward self, behavior, and society; 10. reduction or elimination of a sense of isolation or uniqueness regarding problems through social comparisons and consensual validation; 11. development of substitute culture and social system in which members can develop new definitions of identity and new norms on which to base self-esteem. Despite the social-learning language of these processes they bear an interesting resemblance to change mechanisms in the therapy literature.

Antze's (4) study of self-help groups emphasizes the role of ideology in what he calls the persuasive process. He compares the peer-psychotherapy groups he studied with religious groups and Chinese indoctrination programs. These kinds of comparison studies are extremely valuable because they seek to find the commonalities in the large variety of personal change groups past and present. These commonalities cut across the professional ideologies which have made this search so difficult.

TOWARD A SYNTHESIS

This review has not painted a very pretty picture of systematic research on personal change groups. It does seem possible, however, to transcend the specious polarities which have made work in this area so limited. The following proposals are offered as a first step toward a more unified approach to group research.

1. There should be greater use of outcome measures which from past studies have proved reliable and valid. In this way studies can be replicated and built upon. Populations of clients can be defined by scores on reliable measures (like the MMPI) and treatments from different studies compared more easily. This does not mean that new instruments should not be developed for particular studies. New measures should be used in conjunction with established measures of outcome to give such studies a recognizable reference point. Waskow & Parloff's (73) summary of psychotherapy outcome measures is a useful starting point, but it may be necessary to create specific guidelines for group change research.

2. These established outcome measures should include samples from the behavioral-symptomatic, interpersonal, and intrapsychic-structural domains and include variables from client self-report, leader, observer, and significant other ratings. While this would mean a more complex view of outcome, this approach seems more realistic and would allow for greater comparison between studies. It would mean, however, that behaviorists consider including relationship and interaction variables in their group studies (58) and that psychodynamic workers anchor their outcomes to specific and quantifiable behavioral indicators.

3. There should be greater use of individualized measures of outcome such as Goal Attainment Scaling (33). This can be used in conjunction with rating scales for which there are established norms such as the MMPI or SCL-90. This combination of individualized and group norm measures seems superior to either approach by itself and seems to be a possible solution to the idiographic-nomothetic dilemma. Goal Attainment Scaling could also take the form of clinical ratings of more abstract concepts as long as they could be reliably obtained.

4. Greater integration of clinical and statistical outlooks would be useful. More use could be made of social psychological research methods in clinical group settings.

5. Efforts should be made to synthesize group versus individual orientations to research. Outcome measures utilizing samples of group behaviors should be developed and compared with individual measures (26, 64, 70).

6. There should be a greater use of process and outcome variables in the same study. It seems feasible to use interaction measures in the group itself as a measure of outcome (35). There should be greater specificity of treatments, client characteristics, and leadership variables which produce favorable and unfavorable outcomes. Process measurement of intervention techniques seems necessary to provide this specificity.

7. Adequate follow-up after the termination is a necessity. The maintenance of change is an important goal of these groups and without follow-up any results are incomplete at best (48, 76).

8. Process studies should involve systematic ratings which include leader, member, and group variables.

Unless these minimum guidelines are followed, group research in the years ahead will mirror the uncertain results of the past.

CONCLUSION

What kind of studies are likely to maximize our knowledge of personal change groups in the future? It seems to this reviewer that while large multivariate studies with complicated quasi-experimental designs promise a great deal, they are going to be few and far between. They are extremely expensive and time consuming, and in all liklihood resources for such studies will be quite scarce in the future. In addition, such studies ultimately involve many of the same dilemmas of design and execution as smaller studies.

An alternative would be small, tight, replicable studies with multiple measures of outcome and an adequate assessment of process. Such studies could be used as a data base of increasing size which would provide for comparisons across studies of client characteristics, leadership variables, and intervention methods. The interventions would have to be specifically described utilizing a process measure, and both individual and group norm assessments of clients would have to be provided as well. Given this adequate data base with comparable outcome measures, more extensive process studies could be done at a later time or by other researchers. It would also be possible to do experimental case study research (35) or N=1 research (58) using the single group. There would thus be something for the nomothetically inclined as well as for the idiographic researcher. With comparable data, the accumulation of these smaller studies would provide an alternative to the large multivariate studies.

If there could be agreed-upon commonalities for a minimum data base necessary to carry out this kind of approach, comparative studies across diverse methods and populations would be greatly enhanced. Comparative systems research is an exciting approach but will succeed only if a common ground of multiple measurement techniques can be achieved.

The approach offered here can succeed only if there is a consortium of interested researchers who are willing to adhere to a common set of research strategies and measurement techniques. From this unity of purpose will come the basis for comparative systems studies offering us answers about how groups change what people and under what conditions. Without some such approach we are not likely to have these answers in the near future.

Literature Cited

1. Abramowitz, C. V. 1976. The effectiveness of group psychotherapy with children. *Arch. Gen. Psychiatry* 33:320–26
2. Abramowitz, S. I., Schwartz, J. M., Roback, H. B. 1977. Effects of professional discipline and experience on group therapists' clinical reactions. *Int. J. Group Psychother.* 27:165–75
3. Allport, G. W. 1961. *Pattern and Growth in Personality.* New York: Holt, Rinehart & Winston. 593 pp.
4. Antze, P. 1977. The role of ideologies in peer psychotherapy organizations: some theoretical considerations and three case studies. *J. Appl. Behav. Sci.* 12:323–46
5. Aries, E. 1976. Interaction patterns and themes of male, female, and mixed groups. *Small Group Behav.* 7:7–18
6. Bales, R. F. 1950. *Interaction Process Analysis: A Method for the Study of Small Groups.* Reading, Mass: Addison-Wesley. 203 pp.
7. Bales, R. F. 1970. *Personality and Interpersonal Behavior.* New York: Holt. 561 pp.
8. Berlin, I. 1957. *The Hedgehog and the Fox.* New York: Mentor. 128 pp.
9. Cabral, R. J., Best, J., Paton, A. 1975. Patients' and observers' assessments of process and outcome in group therapy: a follow-up study. *Am. J. Psychiatry* 132:1052–54
10. Campbell, D. T., Stanley, J. C. 1966. *Experimental and Quasi-experimental Designs for Research.* Chicago: Rand McNally. 84 pp.
11. Cooper, C. L. 1975. How psychologically dangerous are T-groups and encounter groups? *Hum. Relat.* 28:249–60
12. Covi, L., Lipman, R. S., Derogatis, L. R., Smith, J. E., Pattison, J. H. 1974. Drugs and group psychotherapy in neurotic depression. *Am. J. Psychiatry* 131:191–98
13. Diamond, M. J., Shapiro, J. L. 1975. Method and paradigm in encounter group research. *J. Humanistic Psychol.* 15:59–70
14. Dies, R. R. 1977. Group therapist transparency: a critique of theory and research. *Int. J. Group Psychother.* 27:177–200
15. Flexo, P. A. 1976. *Self-concept change in encounter groups: the effects of verbal-*

ization and feedback. PhD thesis. Calif. Sch. Prof. Psychol., Los Angeles, Calif.

16. Follingstad, D. R., Kilmann, P. R., Robinson, E. A. 1976. Prediction of self-actualization in male participants in a group conducted by female leaders. *J. Clin. Psychol.* 32:706–12

17. Gibbard, G. S., Hartman, J. J. 1973. Relationship patterns in self-analytic groups: a clinical and empirical study. *Behav. Sci.* 18:335–53

18. Gibbard, G. S., Hartman, J. J., Mann, R. D., eds. 1974. *Analysis of Groups.* San Francisco: Jossey-Bass. 444 pp.

19. Goodstein, L. D., Goldstein, J. J., D'Orta, C. V. 1976. Measurement of self-disclosure in encounter groups: a methodological study. *J. Couns. Psychol.* 23:142–46

20. Gruen, W. 1977. The effects of executive and cognitive control of the therapist on the work climate in group therapy. *Int. J. Group Psychother.* 27:139–52

21. Grunebaum, H. 1975. A soft-hearted review of hard-nosed research on groups. *Int. J. Group Psychother.* 25:185–97

22. Gurman, A. S., Gustafson, J. P. 1976. Patients' perceptions of the therapeutic relationship and group therapy outcome. *Am. J. Psychiatry* 133:1290–94

23. Hanson, R. G. 1976. *Reciprocal verbal interaction, personality correlates of participation and leader feedback in sensitivity training groups.* PhD thesis. York University, Toronto, Canada

24. Hare, A. P. 1976. *Handbook of Small Group Research.* New York: Free Press. 781 pp. 2nd ed.

25. Hartley, D., Roback, H. B., Abramowitz, S. I. 1976. Deterioration effects in encounter groups. *Am. Psychol.* 31:247–55

26. Hartman, J. J. 1976. *Hartman Interpersonal Relations Assessment Medium.* Ann Arbor: Univ. Michigan Television Center

27. Hill, W. F. 1966. *Hill Interaction Matrix.* Los Angeles: Youth Studies Center, Univ. South. California

28. Hill, W. F. 1975. Further consideration of therapeutic mechanisms in group therapy. *Small Group Behav.* 6:421–29

29. Horwitz, L. 1977. A group-centered approach to group psychotherapy. *Int. J. Group Psychother.* 27:423–39

30. Hurley, J. R. 1975. 'Some effects of trainers on their T-groups' reconsidered. *J. Appl. Behav. Sci.* 11:190–96

31. Kilmann, P. R., Albert, B. M., Sotile, W. M. 1975. Relationship between lo-

cus of control, structure of therapy, and outcome. *J. Consult. Clin. Psychol.* 43:588

32. Kilmann, P. R., Sotile, W. M. 1976. The marathon encounter group: a review of the outcome literature. *Psychol. Bull.* 83:827–50

33. Kiresuk, T. J., Sherman, R. E. 1968. Goal Attainment Scaling: a general method for evaluating comprehensive community mental health programs. *Commun. Ment. Health J.* 4:443–53

34. Levy, L. H. 1977. Self-help groups: types and psychological processes. *J. Appl. Behav. Sci.* 12:310–22

35. Lewis, P., McCants, J. 1973. Some current issues in group psychotherapy research. *Int. J. Group Psychother.* 23:268–78

36. Lieberman, M. A. 1975. Joy less facts? A response to Schutz, Smith & Rowan. *J. Humanistic Psychol.* 15:49–58

37. Lieberman, M. A. 1975. People-changing groups: the new and not so new. In *The American Handbook of Psychiatry,* ed. S. Arieti, 5:345–66. New York: Basic Books. 1009 pp.

38. Lieberman, M. A. 1976. Change induction in small groups. *Ann. Rev. Psychol.* 27:217–50

39. Lieberman, M. A., Bond, G. R. 1977. The problem of being a woman: a survey of 1700 women in consciousness-raising groups. *J. Appl. Behav. Sci.* 12:363–79

40. Lieberman, M. A., Gardner, J. R. 1976. Institutional alternatives to psychotherapy: a study of growth center users. *Arch. Gen. Psychiatry* 33:157–62

41. Lieberman, M. A., Yalom, I. D., Miles, M. B. 1973. *Encounter Groups: First Facts.* New York: Basic Books. 495 pp.

42. Liberman, R. 1970. A behavioral approach to group dynamics. *Behav. Ther.* 1:141–75

43. Linsk, N., Howe, M. W., Pinkston, E. M. 1975. Behavioral group work in a home for the aged. *Soc. Work* 20:454–63

44. Lipman, R. S., Covi, L., Smith, V. K. 1975. Prediction of response to drug and group psychotherapy in depressed outpatients. *Psychopharmacol. Bull.* 11:38–39

45. Lundgren, D. C. 1975. Interpersonal needs and member attitudes toward trainer and group. *Small Group Behav.* 6:371–88

46. Lundgren, D. C., Schaeffer, C. 1976. Feedback processes in sensitivity training groups. *Hum. Relat.* 29:763–82

47. Malan, D. H. 1973. The outcome problem in psychotherapy research. *Arch. Gen. Psychiatry* 29:719–29

48. Malan, D. H., Balfour, H. G., Hood, V. G., Shooter, A. M. N. 1976. Group therapy: a long-term follow-up study. *Arch. Gen. Psychiatry* 33:1303–15

49. Mann, R. D. 1959. A review of the relationship between personality and performance in small groups. *Psychol. Bull.* 56:241–70

50. Meehl, P. E. 1954. *Clinical Versus Statistical Prediction.* Minneapolis: Univ. Minnesota Press. 149 pp.

51. O'Day, R. 1976. Individual training styles: an empirically derived typology. *Small Group Behav.* 7:147–82

52. Parloff, M. B. 1967. A view from the incompleted bridge: group process and outcome. *Int. J. Group Psychother.* 17:236–42

53. Parloff, M. B. 1970. Assessing the effects of headshrinking and mind-expanding. *Int. J. Group Psychother.* 20:14–24

54. Parloff, M. B., Dies, R. R. 1977. Group psychotherapy outcome research 1966–1975. *Int. J. Group Psychother.* 27:281–319

55. Piper, W. E., Debbane, E. G., Garant, J. 1977. An outcome study of group therapy. *Arch. Gen. Psychiatry* 34:1027–32

56. Piper, W. E., Debbane, E. G., Garant, J. 1977. Group psychotherapy outcome research: problems and prospects of a first-year project. *Int. J. Group Psychother.* 27:321–41

57. Rohrbaugh, M., Bartels, B. D. 1975. Participants' perceptions of curative factors in therapy and growth groups. *Small Group Behav.* 6:430–56

58. Rose, S. D. 1977. *Group Therapy: A Behavioral Approach.* Englewood Cliffs, NJ: Prentice-Hall. 308 pp.

59. Rowan, J. 1975. Encounter group research: no joy? *J. Humanistic Psychol.* 15:19–28

60. Schaffer, J. B. P., Galinsky, M. D. 1974. *Models of Group Therapy and Sensitivity Training.* Englewood Cliffs, NJ: Prentice-Hall. 303 pp.

61. Schutz, W. 1975. Not encounter and certainly not facts. *J. Humanistic Psychol.* 15:7–18

62. Shapiro, R. J., Klein, R. H. 1975. Perceptions of the leaders in an encounter group. *Small Group Behav.* 6:238–48

63. Silbergeld, S., Koenig, G. R., Manderscheid, R. W., Meeker, B. F., Hornung, C. A. 1975. Assessment of environment-therapy systems: the group atmosphere scale. *J. Consult. Clin. Psychol.* 43:460–69

64. Silbergeld, S., Manderscheid, R. W., Koenig, G. R. 1977. The psychosocial environment in group therapy evaluation. *Int. J. Group Psychother.* 27:153–63

65. Smith, P. B. 1975. Controlled studies of the outcome of sensitivity training. *Psychol. Bull.* 82:597–622

66. Smith, P. B. 1975. Are there adverse effects of sensitivity training? *J. Humanistic Psychol.* 15:29–47

67. Strassberg, D. S., Roback, H. B., Anchor, K. N. 1975. Self-disclosure in group therapy with schizophrenics. *Arch. Gen. Psychiatry* 32:1259–61

68. Strupp, H. H., Bergin, A. E. 1969. Some empirical and conceptual bases for co-ordinated research in psychotherapy: a critical review of issues, trends, and evidence. *Int. J. Psychiatry* 7:18–90

69. Strupp, H. H., Hadley, S. W. 1977. A tripartite model of mental health and therapeutic outcomes with special reference to negative effects in psychotherapy. *Am. Psychol.* 32:187–96

70. Temoshok, L. 1976. *The videotaped interpretations of social interactions technique (VISIT): a method to assess social scripts.* PhD thesis. Univ. Michigan, Ann Arbor, Mich. 164 pp.

71. Tresemer, D. 1976. Observing social interaction: methodological models. *Small Group Behav.* 7:47–58

72. Truax, C. B. 1966. Therapist empathy, warmth, and genuineness and patient personality change in group psychotherapy. *J. Clin. Psychol.* 22:225–29

73. Waskow, I. E., Parloff, M. B., eds. 1975. *Psychotherapy Change Measures.* Rockville, Md: N.I.M.H. 327 pp.

74. Weinstein, M. S., Hanson, R. 1975. Leader experience level and patterns of participation in sensitivity training groups. *Small Group Behav.* 6:123–40

75. Yalom, I. D. 1975. *The Theory and Practice of Group Psychotherapy.* New York: Basic Books. 529 pp. 2nd ed.

76. Yalom, I. D., Bond, G., Bloch, S., Zimmerman, E., Friedman, L. 1977. The impact of a weekend group experience on individual therapy. *Arch. Gen. Psychiatry* 34:399–415

Ann. Rev. Psychol. 1979. 30:477–525

PERSONNEL SELECTION AND CLASSIFICATION SYSTEMS

♦315

Marvin D. Dunnette

Department of Psychology, University of Minnesota, Minneapolis, Minnesota 55455 and Personnel Decisions Research Institute, Minneapolis, Minnesota 55402

Walter C. Borman

Personnel Decisions Research Institute, 2415 Foshay Tower, Minneapolis, Minnesota 55402

CONTENTS

THE HISTORICAL CONTEXT OF PERSONNEL SELECTION 478
  Milestones: Personnel Selection Thinking, Research, Technology 478
  The Conservation of Human Talent: 1975–80 481
VALIDITY AND VALIDATION 482
JOB ANALYSIS 484
JOB PERFORMANCE MEASUREMENT 486
  Format Comparisons and Rater Training 486
  Internal Dimensionality and External Validity of Performance Ratings 488
  Individual Differences Correlates of Performance Ratings 489
STATISTICAL CONSIDERATIONS 490
  Validity Estimates and Problems of Shrinkage 490
  Validity Generalization 492
  Utility 493
  Nonlinear Prediction 494
PSYCHOMETRICS OF EQUAL OPPORTUNITY 496
  Differential Validity 496
  Test Fairness 497
LABOR MARKET ISSUES 502
  Labor Markets, Availabilities, and Human Resources Planning 502
SELECTION PRACTICES: RESEARCH RESULTS 504
  The Selection Interview 505
  Biographical Information 509
  Multiple Assessment Procedures 510
  Job Samples 513
  Miscellaneous Other Studies 513
CONTEXT OF THE FUTURE IN PERSONNEL SELECTION 514

0066-4308/79/0201-0477$01.00

THE HISTORICAL CONTEXT OF PERSONNEL SELECTION

Using tests to help make personnel decisions is centuries old, as documented by DuBois (94) and Doyle (93). But the modern era of personnel selection had its beginning on 6 April 1917, when the United States declared war on Germany. That evening, after a hurried meeting, Yerkes, Bingham, and Dodge drafted a letter urging all APA psychologists (N=336) to give whatever professional assistance they could to the war effort. Shortly, two groups of army psychologists were formed. Within less than 2 years, 1,726,966 men were tested (309). In addition, job specifications were written, job knowledge tests (trade tests) invented, officer rating forms devised, and training and psychological counseling programs mounted. All this marked the beginning of large-scale use of tests and other systematic methods to aid personnel decisions in the world of work. Much has happened in personnel selection research and practice in the last 60 years. We believe recent contributions[1] can be most meaningfully interpreted within the context set by significant developments over this span of six decades.

Milestones: Personnel Selection Thinking, Research, Technology

Below we list and briefly discuss the significance of what we believe to be the most important personnel selection milestones over the last 60 years.

1. EARLY DEVELOPMENTS IN SELECTION RESEARCH TECHNOLOGY Early texts (120, 165, 189) specified many selection research procedures and thinking that remain current today. For example, Freyd (120) disavowed blind empiricism, emphasized job analysis, stated the necessity for defining job requirements behaviorally in "universally understood phrases," suggested that cost accounting might well be used to justify doing selection research, specified procedures for inferring psychological constructs from job studies, and discussed the likely usefulness of work samples and simulations for selection.

2. INDIVIDUAL DIAGNOSIS AND VOCATIONAL COUNSELING With publication of *Men, Women, and Jobs* in 1936, Paterson & Darley (242) spelled out how the science and instruments of differential psychology provided the basis for vocational diagnosis and counseling of individuals. Speaking of maladaptive matches between persons and jobs, they stated "Occupational illness can be prevented if guidance ... is made part of

[1]We have reviewed the relevant literature for the period extending from January 1974 through December 1977.

education, of industry, and of community personnel work" (242, p. 135). It is noteworthy that equal billing was given men and women—a fact still widely overlooked by many selection systems and counseling programs.

3. FACTOR ANALYSIS OF HUMAN ATTRIBUTES   Thurstone's contributions were monumental, giving methodological direction to later taxonomic studies of both persons and jobs.

4. LARGE-SCALE PROGRAMS OF INDUSTRIAL SELECTION RESEARCH   Selection research programs were begun by a few corporations (e.g. Sears, P & G, IBM). Thayer (302) recently reviewed selection research done by LIMRA since the program's beginning in 1922.

5. SELECTION TECHNOLOGY IN WORLD WAR II   Selection technology advanced in many ways during the second world war. Criterion development received particular attention. Thorndike's small classic, *Personnel Selection* (303), summarized it all.

6. CRITICAL INCIDENTS METHOD   Flanagan's (117) critical incidents methodology gave operational meaning to the "lip service" of defining jobs behaviorally and led to the later design of behaviorally anchored job performance measurement rating methods (291).

7. GROWTH OF TEST PUBLISHING INDUSTRY   Test publishing has become big business. One reference (63) gives annotated bibliographies for over 3000 measures. Buros's (51) most recent listing classifies and annotates 2467 tests.

8. STANDARDS FOR DEVELOPING AND EVALUATING TESTS   Test standards (5, 6, 90, 177), first published in 1954, have clarified validity concepts and provided professional guidelines for evaluating tests and testing practices.

9. GROWING POLITICAL EMPHASIS ON EQUALITY OF OPPORTUNITY   Concerted efforts began in earnest during the 1950s to pass local, state, and federal legislation against employment discrimination on the basis of race, religion, national origin, and sex. Few psychologists were active in this movement. But, in his Walter Van Dyke Bingham lecture in 1956,[2] Pater-

---

[2]The title of Paterson's address was *The Conservation of Human Talent,* by which he intended to convey processes leading to "the conservation and optimal utilization of our human resources in our total economy" (241, p. 134).

son (241) stated that widespread discrimination against minorities, women, the young, the old, and the handicapped was the primary reason for occupational maladjustment. He called for vocational psychologists to join "the struggle to open up and to maintain nondiscriminatory employment opportunities for everyone in our democratic society" (p. 143), and to help put an end to "the present inexcusable waste of precious human resources."

10. DECISION THEORY IN SELECTION RESEARCH   Though implicit in earlier publications (see 44–46), *utility* received explicit and thorough treatment for the first time by Cronbach & Gleser (76, 77). Utility emphasizes costs and benefits of different selection strategies and focuses attention on *types* of selection errors, their relative incidence, and their associated costs. Decision theory also views selection as a process—a continuing series of decisional steps—instead of a single event. Thus, decision theory in selection also laid the groundwork for sequential selection models and for increased emphasis on adaptive treatment of candidates. [See (54, 169, 175, 265) for recent discussions of utility and decision theory concepts.]

11. NONLINEAR PREDICTION MODELS IN SELECTION RESEARCH Ghiselli's studies (e.g. 123, 125) and issues being discussed in clinical psychology (218) suggested that selection research should be based on more complex psychometric models. Dunnette's (96) *modified selection research model* led to increased research on nonlinear prediction systems in the selection context.

12. SIMULATIONS AND MULTIPLE ASSESSMENT PROCEDURES   Initially developed for evaluating candidates for highly sensitive jobs in the military, multiple assessment procedures were first used more broadly by Bray and his associates in the AT&T Management Progress Study (42). The method has gained wide acceptance in this country and throughout the world and constitutes one of the most extensive *and* expensive practices now being employed for evaluating personnel qualifications.

13. OBJECTIVE METHODS OF JOB ANALYSIS   In no other area of selection research has technology been more greatly influenced by one person than in the area of job analysis. McCormick's first accounts of his work appeared in the late 1950s (213, 216). Comprehensive overviews of research with the *Position Analysis Questionnaire* (PAQ) are contained in two recent handbooks (211, 212). Still his work continues unabated (214, 215). Current methods of content, construct, and job component validation depend heavily on methods growing out of McCormick's task inventory technology.

14. TESTING, SELECTION RESEARCH, AND CIVIL RIGHTS   Finally, a full 100 years after the Civil War, Congress passed the Civil Rights Act (CRA) of 1964 (65). This sweeping act dealt with (*a*) the right to vote, (*b*) desegregation of public facilities, (*c*) desegregation of public education, (*d*) expansion of the powers of the Civil Rights Commission, (*e*) nondiscrimination in federally assisted programs, and (*f*) equal employment opportunity (Title VII). While affirming the right of an employer to "act upon the results of any professionally developed ability test," discrimination in employment on the basis of race, color, religion, sex, or national origin was designated an unlawful employment practice. With this act, selection research became a matter for public and legal concern, and efforts have been made to describe "acceptable" and legally defensible selection research practices in a series of testing guidelines (66, 110, 111, 238). Court decisions involving charges of unfair discrimination have focused much attention on the need to specify circumstances that constitute "unfair" use of tests in selection. Because the psychometric issues are difficult, many employers have apparently dropped testing altogether. Others, responding more constructively, have chosen to support large-scale and carefully planned selection research programs (298).

15. AFFIRMATIVE ACTION PROGRAMS BY EMPLOYERS   In order to assure equal employment opportunity as specified by Title VII of CRA, many employers have adopted programs with ambitious goals for employing and upgrading women and members of minority groups. Such programs have special importance for personnel selection practices because their success depends very much on a broad concern for the best possible utilization and conservation of all human resources. It is important to achieve a balance such that both unfair discrimination and reverse discrimination are avoided. We believe that research on personnel selection and classification systems can aid in developing useful solutions in this difficult area.

The Conservation of Human Talent: 1975–80

Many of the great advances in personnel assessment and utilization over the last 60 years occurred during periods of crisis wrought by severe discontinuities in employment. The greatest need in both world wars was to find people to fill jobs. The greatest need during the Great Depression of the 1930s was to find jobs for people to fill. Both needs required individual diagnosis and vocational decision making and led to rapid growth in the test publishing industry. Civil rights legislation, long overdue, recognized the serious discontinuities of employment caused by years of discrimination against minorities and women. We are at a point now where all persons involved in developing employment policy (lawyers and judges, business executives, government administrators, behavioral scientists, etc) are once again forcefully confronted with the frequent incompatibility between pure selection (*institutional decisions*) and job choice (*individual decisions*). Locating and selecting the most qualified persons for available jobs will almost always yield quite different placement (classification) decisions from locating the most qualified jobs for particular persons.

Conservation of human talent requires that this incompatibility be overcome or substantially reduced. We believe that many of the significant developments of the last 60 years, taken together, can be helpful in doing so.

In contrast with the state of the art even as recently as 1960, today we have improved methods for measuring behavioral components of jobs and of job performance dimensions. We know more about basic structures and taxonomies of human characteristics. Strategies of validation are more sophisticated. Increasing emphasis is being given to *utility* in personnel decisions and to personnel selection and classification as a total system of decision steps instead of just one facet of personnel administration.

Our reading of the personnel selection literature convinces us that such developments have been especially noteworthy during the last four or five years. In fact, we feel a sense of optimism that personnel selection research and practice is now in position to satisfy more fully the needs of *both* organizations and individuals. To be sure, practice still lags far behind research results and thinking. Nonetheless, we look toward the next few years as a time when personnel selection practices can take rapid strides to assure improved matches between persons and jobs for the good of everyone.

We hope the reader may share our optimism after reading the remainder of this review. Our discussion is organized according to the following topics: VALIDITY AND VALIDATION, JOB ANALYSIS, JOB PERFORMANCE MEASUREMENT, STATISTICAL CONSIDERATIONS, PSYCHOMETRICS OF EQUAL OPPORTUNITY, LABOR MARKET ISSUES, and SELECTION PRACTICES: RESEARCH RESULTS.

VALIDITY AND VALIDATION

Much has been written in the last 4 years about test validity and validation strategies. The most significant statements are contained in (*a*) chapters by Guion (141), Campbell (54), and Dunnette (104); (*b*) three "official" documents [APA Standards (6), Division 14 Principles (90), and Proposed Uniform Guidelines (66)]; and (*c*) a series of papers by Guion and others (139, 140, 142–146, 200, 245, 300). Surprisingly little attention is given to validity or to validation by recent textbooks in industrial/organizational psychology (162, 195, 276, 323). One must look to more focused texts (e.g. 7) to find much about validity.

The closest thing to a definition of validity is given by the APA Standards: "Questions of validity are questions of what may properly be inferred from a test score; validity refers to the appropriateness of inferences from test scores or other forms of assessment" (6, p. 25). And, "A thorough understanding of validity may require many investigations . . . processes of gathering and evaluating data are called validation" (6, p. 25). Further, according to the Standards, various validation methods are available, but all require careful designation of what is to be inferred from test scores as well as data showing that the basis for such inferences is acceptable. Unfortunately, in spite of this good beginning, the remaining parts of each of the official documents [APA Standards, Division 14 Principles, Uniform Guidelines] perpetuate a conceptual compartmentalization of "types" of validity—*criterion-related, content,* and *construct.* In our opinion, the implication that validities come in different types leads to confusion and, in the face of confusion, oversimplification.

One serious consequence of oversimplification is that many test users place too much emphasis on deciding what *type* of validity to study instead of specifying exactly *why* they intend to use a test (that is, what inferences they wish to make from it). In fact, the wording of the proposed Guidelines is such as to imply that once one has chosen a type of validation strategy, one is relieved both of further speculation about other kinds of predictor-criterion relationships and of gathering other evidence to increase the wisdom of decisions made in the personnel selection process. Because of this, we urge readers to attend carefully not only to the official documents but to give at least equal time to the chapters mentioned above. Campbell (54, pp. 202–13), in discussing construct validity, provides an excellent overview of the evolution of thinking about validity and of the many types of evidence that may be brought to bear in learning about the meanings that may be attached to scores on a test. Guion (141, pp. 785–806) provides a superb account of the validation process in the context of developing and evaluating rational hypotheses about test scores and their behavioral meanings. As Guion states ". . . hypothesis testing is what validation is all about" (141, p. 803). Dunnette (104, pp. 495–516) refers not at all to "types" of validity but directs attention instead to methods of evaluating degrees of congruence (linkages, levels of job relatedness, etc) between measures of human attributes and measures of work behavior.

Much attention during these 4 years has been devoted to content validity —a concept previously employed much more in educational achievement testing than in personnel selection. Impetus was provided by two Bowling

Green conferences held in late 1974 and mid-1975. Initially Guion (140) expressed cautious optimism that the concept, applied to selection research, would pave the way for new approaches. However, it appears that the effort to consider content validity as a separate entity led almost immediately to confusion (300) and to unwarranted pessimism as shown by Dugan's closing remarks to the second Content Validity Conference. In the years since, Guion (142–146) has clarified several issues concerning the term *content validity*, including that (*a*) *all* validity can be regarded within the general rubric of construct validity, (*b*) *content-oriented test development* better describes the emphasis implied by the term *content validity*, and, (*c*) fairness of procedures developed to sample or portray job content must be subjected to careful scrutiny just as any other type of selection procedure must be. Concerning the latter point, Guion (146) discusses four sources of possible bias in content-oriented test development: (*a*) defining the job content domain; (*b*) individual test items; (*c*) ratings of performance during probationary periods; and (*d*) scoring procedures for content-oriented tests.

In our opinion, the discussions devoted to "content validity" have been important in that increased attention has been directed toward (*a*) improved domain sampling and job analysis procedures, (*b*) better behavior measurement, and (*c*) the role of expert judgment for confirming the fairness of sampling and scoring procedures and for determining degree of overlap between separately derived domains of content.

In sum, we believe it is still best to think of *validation* as a process of learning as much as possible about the behavioral inferences that may properly be made from scores on any selection measure and to recognize that the process is never-ending. Test users should never feel that they know enough about the behavioral meanings of their selection methods—no matter what the APA Standards, the Division 14 Principles, or the government Guidelines say.

JOB ANALYSIS

Legal recognition of the term "job relatedness" (132) came at a time when much of the PAQ work by McCormick and his associates was reaching fruition. Summaries of his overall research program and recent results are given in several reports (211, 212, 214, 215, 286, 287). *Job relatedness* is exactly what McCormick's research and that of several others (37, 48, 106, 114, 245, 246, 306) is all about. The basic assumption underlying these research programs is that jobs can be described objectively with standard checklists and the results used to infer which personal attributes may be most important for doing the jobs. Such knowledge is of obvious use in developing "job-related" selection procedures, and that is how the knowledge has been used by most researchers. However, we believe this knowledge about jobs and inferred attributes can be useful on a much broader scale to help assure improved matches between jobs and people. This can be done by using checklist information to evaluate more objectively each person's previous job experiences, relevant non-job activities and preferences, and to design training and orientation programs which are more directly job related. In fact, we believe that the sophisticated technology now available for developing and scoring job checklists holds great promise for helping to overcome the incompatibility between *institutional* decision making and *individual* decision making. All that is needed is a large and widely used data bank which portrays the parameters of available jobs and the attributes of available persons. Consider for illustrative purposes the following portrayal of an idealized counseling and job placement system: (*a*) Employers cooperate in describing all jobs with standard task checklists which are scorable according to previously derived behavioral and attribute categories. (*b*) "Counselees" (job candidates, students, employees intent on longer term career planning, etc) use similar checklists to record previous work and nonwork experiences, preferences, and estimated capabilities. (*c*) Counselees' responses are scored according to the above job and attribute categories and the scores referred to a data bank for job matching; a preliminary listing of jobs appropriate for each counselee is provided. (*d*) Final steps in the process utilize additional assessment procedures (job samples, job knowledge tests, simulations, aptitude tests) to provide the individualized information necessary for joint decision making.

Obviously no such programmatic capability as this has yet been accomplished, but it does not seem to us to be out of reach. McCormick's data base on jobs is extremely comprehensive, and his research has confirmed the reality of empirical connections between job dimensions and tested attributes of job incumbents. But the PAQ, in its present form, is too difficult (10) and unwieldy for broad use by "counselees," and McCormick's research has not focused directly on either institutional or individual decision making nor upon actual job placement. On the other hand, an approach very similar to what we outlined above has apparently been implemented successfully by Cleff (69, 70). Unfortunately, his data base appears limited according to types of jobs, numbers of persons, and especially, and most unfortunately, published research evidence. Claims are made for rather impressive relationships between job turnover, productivity, supervisory ratings and the magnitude of the "Job Match Index," an index of profile similarity between an incumbent's experience/preference scores on 16 dimensions and scores on the same dimensions derived from description of the incumbent's job. We would like to see the methodology tested more widely and by other investigators. Certainly these first results show promise.

Kuder (193) recently proposed a systematic career matching approach involving person-to-person comparisons of vocational interest inventory responses. He suggests that the approach could easily be extended to the whole range of information available about human beings.

Obviously, several thorny methodological issues still stand in the way of fully realizing what we have outlined above. Some of the most important are: (a) proper sampling of the total job domain; (b) methods for estimating accurately the relative importance, complexity, difficulty, etc of job elements; (c) how to link meaningfully job element estimates of complexity with personal attribute estimates; (d) appropriate statistical criteria for determining job dimensions and relative similarities/differences between jobs; (e) the appropriate role of experts in describing jobs, in judging personal qualifications for those jobs, and in determining the relative degree of congruence between job dimensions and attribute measures (an accumulating amount of evidence does show that most such judgments are made with high interjudge agreement); (f) whether to utilize task-oriented, worker-oriented, or performance-oriented checklists; and (g) how to assure fairness for all persons in the application of job checklist methodology.

All these issues have received attention in a number of recent papers (9, 38, 39, 47, 48, 91, 106, 146, 171, 200, 245, 247, 248, 253). Our reading of them suggests that significant headway is being made, and we look for additional advances and broadened application of this technology in the immediate future.

JOB PERFORMANCE MEASUREMENT

Showing that a selection system is job related requires not only good job analysis but also good job performance measurement. The criterion problem has been with us forever and has received much attention (12, 97, 124, 137, 173, 182, 269, 290, 303, 311). A common theme is that performance measurement, since it rests so heavily on fallible human judgment, can best avoid incompleteness and spuriousness by adopting the conceptual and methodological guidelines of construct validation. Much recent research has studied sources of error in performance ratings, their magnitude, and how to reduce them. Only by reducing such errors can researchers learn more about the behavioral constructs underlying our criterion measures.

Format Comparisons and Rater Training

Smith & Kendall (291) reasoned that rating errors might be reduced substantially by involving job incumbents in choosing and defining job performance rating dimensions via critical incidents methodology. As a result, *behaviorally anchored rating scales* (BARS) have been the subject of many studies to determine whether or not they actually are more "error-free." Results are mixed. Such scales have shown psychometric superiority when used in practice (33, 55, 133, 183), but other studies suggest no consistent advantage when BARS are compared with other types of scales (14, 16, 34, 50, 83, 325). In addition, using behavioral anchors as stimuli in a Guttman-type rating format (i.e. judging whether a given ratee's performance is better than or poorer than that depicted by a behavior statement) has yielded no consistent psychometric superiority (8, 116, 261). Nonetheless, reduced rating errors seem to result when scale development procedures are stringently specified and followed, such as in the "ideal" scale development procedure outlined by Bernardin and his colleagues (17). In fact, Schwab, Heneman & DeCotiis (282) suggest that many of the poor showings made by behaviorally based scales may be due in part to departures from sufficiently careful methodology in developing them.

As mentioned, involvement by job incumbents was seen initially as a cornerstone of the procedure. One study (121) showed that participation was associated with improved quality of ratings but others (17, 183) have failed to do so. Participation can be regarded as one means of training raters to be aware of common sources of error in ratings, and several studies of rater training programs have been done. Latham, Wexley & Pursell (197) designed a workshop to show raters how to avoid several common rating errors. All the errors they emphasized were reduced by the training, and improvement was maintained for at least 6 months. Borman (30) successfully used a brief lecture (5 min) and short group discussion to reduce halo error in a group's ratings; unfortunately, interrater reliability also decreased. Bernardin (15) compared a 5 min training session with a 1 hr session. Halo and leniency errors were decreased immediately after training by both programs (the longer session being more effective), but improvements dissipated over a period of 13 weeks. Most interesting, the degree of error reduction correlated substantially with scores on a test measuring knowledge of rating errors, impressive evidence of good correspondence between internal and external training criteria. Reasoning that systematic behavior observation may be just as important as knowing how to avoid rating errors, Bernardin & Walter (18) asked students to keep diaries of instructors' teaching behavior. This approach, combined with thorough rater training, produced psychometrically superior ratings.

The bright hopes for BARS have not been fully realized. But research on rater training suggests that errors can be reduced when special efforts are taken to help raters do a better job. Conceptually, it seems to us that such training, to be most effective, must be based on behaviorally derived definitions of job performance. Thus, we believe in the basic wisdom of the behavior scaling methodology even though operational use of such scales have frequently yielded disappointing results.

Internal Dimensionality and External Validity of Performance Ratings

Kavanagh, MacKinney & Wolins (182) developed a method for evaluating convergent and discriminant validity of various components of performance ratings. Studies using their strategy have examined supervisory, peer, subordinate, and self ratings (e.g. 50, 121, 279). Results typically yield moderate levels of convergent validity but only limited evidence of discriminant validity. This means that different raters and/or methods tend to rank ratees similarly but that different facets or dimensions of job performance are poorly differentiated. However, studies (87, 133) are suggestive in showing increased discriminant validity when special care is taken in defining the job dimensions to be rated. It is possible that discriminant validity is limited by what Kavanagh et al call "characteristic error"—the inability of raters to go beyond a certain level of precision in making their observations and in recording their ratings. Possible numerical indices of this error are provided by Borman (32).

Studies of the internal psychometric characteristics of performance ratings (e.g. leniency, halo, restriction of range, etc) do not typically evaluate directly the crucial element of *accuracy*—the degree to which ratings are relevant to or correlated with *true criterion scores*. Schwab, Heneman & DeCotiis (282) correctly state that even leniency, halo, and restriction of range errors cannot really be assessed when the real levels of performance are unknown. A few researchers have used external criteria to study ratings. For example, Borman (30) and DeCotiis (83) had raters rate the performance of hypothetical ratees described with vignettes based on previously scaled behavioral examples. In such methodology, since true scale scores are known, accuracy can be evaluated directly. In a similar study, Borman (32) has prepared videotapes of performers who followed scripts written to depict preset levels of performance on several dimensions. Expert ratings confirm that the performers successfully portrayed targeted performance levels. Ratings by persons observing these tapes can, therefore, be evaluated for accuracy and rating errors against the true score ratings. Obviously, these approaches run the risk of seeming to be unrealistic to the raters, and generalization to "real life" rating situations may be limited. Nonetheless, the ability to evaluate ratings against true scores is a great advantage in learning about major determiners of accuracy and error in performance measurement. Another way of examining the external validity of ratings is illustrated in studies where behaviorally oriented ratings have been correlated with important objective measures such as productivity and attendance (196, 198, 254). Cross-validities on samples of loggers are impressively high; such results are reassuring in confirming a degree of external validity for the constructs depicted by performance rating scales.

Individual Differences Correlates of Performance Ratings

Recent emphasis has been given to personal factors that affect the nature of performance ratings. Studies are of three types: (a) rater's organizational level, (b) rater characteristics, and (c) ratee characteristics.

A rater's frame of reference in observing another's job performance may be affected by his or her own organizational level (i.e. superior, peer, subordinate) in relation to that of the ratee. Three studies examined such differing perspectives (29, 153, 187) and found low agreement between raters from different levels. These results agree with the findings of previous research (e.g. 20, 49, 86, 147, 182, 199, 230, 322) in showing that attention must be given to where the rater "is coming from"; raters with different perspectives may frequently record quite different responses on a performance rating scale. Often such lack of agreement is interpreted as evidence of low reliability and, by implication, evidence of low accuracy; in reality, such separate "views" may each be valid according to the different perspectives represented.

Regarding rater characteristics, Schneier (278) found that cognitive complexity of raters is strongly related both to preferences for different kinds of rating scales (behaviorally anchored vs graphic) and to tendencies to make different types of rating errors on particular scales. The more cognitively complex raters tended to prefer behaviorally anchored scales and to make fewer errors in using them. As mentioned, Borman (31) was able to determine rater accuracy (validity) by comparing ratings of videotaped performance with true scores. Sixteen percent of variance in rating accuracy is accounted for by rater differences in such attributes as intelligence, personal adjustment, and detail orientation. Finally, Zedeck & Kafry (324) found no correlates of "rating style" where style was determined by capturing the policy of raters evaluating vignettes of hypothetical ratees. This is an example of a healthy interest in the rating *process* as contrasted with rating *outcomes*. This interest is parallel to the emphasis personality and social psychologists have placed on studying the person perception process, an emphasis that seems to us to be highly fruitful for developing better understanding of accuracy in performance ratings (277, 297).

Studies of possible rater bias due to ratee characteristics such as sex, race, age, etc are difficult to carry out because rating differences may be due to real performance differences, rating biases, or some combination. Either performance across subgroups must be standardized or raters of different sex/race/age are required to observe and rate the same performer. The latter strategy was possible in the large-scale ETS study (78) which showed a modest tendency for black and white supervisors to give elevated ratings to same-race subordinates. The former strategy was employed in two studies by Hamner and his colleagues (22, 150). Actual performance on a repetitive task was standardized at two levels and filmed for black and white, male and female workers. Male and female college student raters tended to give high ratings to same-sex workers. Also, females received significantly higher ratings than males in the *high* performance condition only, and blacks received significantly higher ratings than whites in the *low* performance condition only. Unfortunately, the investigators presented the films in the same order to all subjects; thus order, contrast, fatigue, and memory effects were confounded with sex, race, and performance effects. Other investigators have studied such factors as education and job experience [ratings of police officers were unrelated to both (59)], makeup of work groups [clerical workers with "no basic weaknesses" were given higher ratings and more frequent pay raises when their work groups were comprised of relatively few such workers (131)], and variability of performance [highly variable performance was perceived as connoting high ability and low motivation (285)].

Thus, the rating process and factors affecting ratings are receiving increased attention. Lewin & Zwany (204) suggest a model for understanding the peer rating process which utilizes cognitive process modeling theory (232). Much more research on the performance rating *process* is needed. We believe such research can profitably capitalize on work done in personality and person perception research (e.g. 185, 234, 277, 297), and that major strides toward better understanding of the process are in the offing.

STATISTICAL CONSIDERATIONS

Important advances have been made in several areas of statistical thinking and methodology relevant to the design of personnel selection systems. These include (*a*) improved methods for estimating population validities, (*b*) new approaches to the problem of validity generalization, (*c*) reawakening interest in utility formulations, and (*d*) better understanding of difficulties associated with nonlinear prediction models.

Validity Estimates and Problems of Shrinkage

In tracing the history of multiple regression and its applications, Wherry (318) warns that problems of overfitting and shrinkage are evident in the use of "modern" least squares models such as discriminant analysis, canonical correlation, and multivariate analysis of variance, just as they have been in using multiple regression. For personnel selection researchers, the general problem with overfitting and shrinkage is this: When we use more than one predictor and wish to combine this information optimally to gain maximum accuracy for predicting scores on a single criterion, any weights we select based on sample data (e.g. regression weights) will take advantage of sample-specific configurations of the data, that is, will "overfit" the data; thus, validity obtained in the sample provides an overestimate of the validity to be expected in the long run. The two general approaches for estimating shrinkage, and thereby determining a more realistic validity estimate, have been shrinkage formulae (e.g. 209, 317) and sample-splitting methods for estimating cross-validity (e.g. 227). Two recent Monte Carlo studies have examined some of the issues in employing these approaches.

Campbell (53) studied the accuracy of validity estimates derived from various weighting schemes and one shrinkage formula. He drew successive Monte Carlo generated samples of varying sizes (50–500) from populations of real data, each population containing 10,000 subjects, and used these samples to generate validity estimates. Accuracy of the validity estimates was determined by comparing them with validities obtained when predictor composites with weights derived in the samples were correlated with the population criterion scores. The results obtained within this framework yielded the following observations and recommendations: (a) cross-validity coefficients typically underestimate population validity; (b) zero-order validity weights applied to the total sample provide the best overall estimates of validity; (c) when sample sizes are small (e.g. < 150) and validity is low (e.g. $r < .25$), unit weights provide best estimates; and (d) when samples are large (e.g. > 250) and validity is high (e.g. $r > .60$), multiple regression weights are best, provided the Wherry shrinkage formula is applied (317). But validity weights are optimal for the majority of conditions studied.

A second Monte Carlo Study (273) considered only the multiple regression weighting scheme and compared sample-splitting cross-validity coefficients with shrinkage formulae validity estimates. Under a variety of conditions involving different numbers of predictors, levels of validity, and average predictor intercorrelations, the Lord-Nicholson formula (209, 233) provided excellent estimates of the shrinkage to be expected, with the Darlington formula (79, 295) also yielding accurate but generally more conservative estimates. The averages of the double cross-validation estimates were also quite accurate but their variabilities were large. This is a serious problem because high variability means that a single estimate of cross-validity (or two estimates in the Mosier design) is likely to be in considerable error.

Rosse (259) developed a method to reduce this variability problem. His approach uses a sufficiently large number of sample splits to provide stable cross-validity estimates from the sample's data. The mean or median of the many cross-validity coefficients generated serves as the final cross-validity estimate.

Lessons to be learned from these results are: (a) use of zero-order validity coefficients as weights is an underutilized practice; under a variety of conditions (53) it seems preferable to other approaches; and (b) the shrinkage formulae, especially the Lord-Nicholson, may be more profitably employed than they have been in the past; however, these formula estimates of validity are applicable only to multiple regression model estimates of cross-validity (268), and we know from Campbell's study that other weighting schemes are optimal under many conditions. More needs to be learned about the accuracy and stability of our sample estimates of validity. A greater number of multivariate prediction situations must be studied and a wider variety of prediction schemes should be compared in a single study or series of studies. Studies of the accuracy of various estimation strategies under widely varying but realistic conditions should provide improved guidelines for using strategies. The work reviewed here moves us in the right direction.

Validity Generalization

Considerable variability is observed in validity coefficients obtained from various studies even when jobs and tests used in the studies appear to be similar. This has led to the widespread belief that test validity is highly situation specific. In two important papers, Schmidt and his colleagues (267, 268) offer sound arguments that the belief is erroneous. First (268), they present evidence that the statistical power of most selection studies is low because of small Ns, low criterion reliabilities, and selection-induced range restriction on both predictor and criterion measures. Second (267), they show that the magnitudes of variabilities in validity coefficients across various studies are almost exactly what would be expected, given the typical Ns, reliabilities, and selection ratios encountered in selection research. They conclude that investigators should not rely on results from single studies. Instead, *true validities* for tests and particular job performance measures should be estimated from past studies by using a Bayesian approach. Within such a framework, they argue that if evidence for past validity is strong (i.e. many studies with high validities), a validity study will usually not be necessary. If a study is necessary, the Bayesian approach allows the researcher to use both past validity information and the validity obtained in the study to estimate the true validity of the test for use in similar circumstances.

The most important implication of their work is that *validity generalization* will receive increasing emphasis as more and more selection research is completed by organizations. The approach ties in perfectly with the advances, already discussed, in technology for conducting objective job analyses. Increased knowledge will be available about levels of similarity between jobs, tests, and criteria used in different validation studies. The approach is an ingenious application of Bayesian statistics that promises to shed new light on the long held assumption that validity results are situation specific. In passing, we should also note that several recent articles (128, 172, 179, 274) have appeared discussing multitrait-multimethod techniques, path analytic procedures, and factor analytic strategies as means of developing systematic generalizations about predictor and criterion constructs across different settings.

Utility

Early indices of the usefulness or economic utility of a selection device in personnel selection were the *index of forecasting efficiency*, $1-(1-r^2)^{1/2}$, and the *coefficient of determination*, simply r^2. Taylor & Russell (299) correctly noted that the validity coefficient by itself was not a direct measure of utility when they derived tables (based on validity, selection ratio, and base rate) to estimate the increase in the percentage of successful performers if a selection device was used under specified conditions. The Taylor-Russell approach was based on assuming a dichotomous criterion. Subsequent contributions in utility theory (44, 45, 76, 77) treat job performance more realistically as a continuous variable.

Yet personnel selection research has seldom incorporated formal utility concepts. Despite the considerable advances in utility theory, the question of dollar savings which might be realized by instituting a selection program continues to receive almost no attention. Industrial psychologists may use the Taylor-Russell tables, but sadly, the more precise Cronbach & Gleser treatment of utility gathers dust on many psychologists' bookshelves.

The main reasons for failure to employ utility analyses seem to be ignorance about how to apply the somewhat complicated equations and difficulty in costing some of the elements of these equations, most notably the standard deviation of job performance in dollars (SDe). SDe estimates have been thought to require a careful costing of the dollar value of various levels of performance. This kind of estimate may be possible to develop for certain low-level jobs, but for the vast majority of jobs it has been difficult if not impossible to conceive of a way to make such estimates. It is noteworthy that Cronbach & Gleser (77) could locate only two studies that had made SDe estimates and used their formulae, though these utility formulae had been available for several years.

Recently Hunter & Schmidt (169) suggested two additional reasons for the general disinterest in utility theory concerns: (*a*) psychologists have assumed that utility equations are not appropriate for data that do not fit the linear, homoscedastic model, and (b) as mentioned above, validity has been assumed to be situation-specific, rendering inappropriate the application of utility results to different settings. They advance evidence casting doubt on the validity of these assumptions and present results of a pilot study aimed at evaluating a low-cost method for estimating SDe. They asked supervisors of budget analysts to estimate the value to the organization of the goods and services provided by budget analysts performing at the average level and budget analysts performing at the 85th percentile. To facilitate these judgments, raters were told to imagine how much the goods and services would cost if provided by an outside consulting firm. Acceptable interrater agreement suggested that the magnitude of SDe might be appropriately inferred from the spread of the two mean point estimates. Further successes for this method with other kinds of jobs should spark more interest in and considerably more use of the Cronbach & Gleser equations.

Other papers that touch on utility or decision theory considerations involve (a) a study (202) that applied a utility analysis to a weighted application predictor in order to identify the cutting score providing maximum savings, (b) a presentation of dollar cost savings to be expected from application of a large-scale personnel classification system in the Air Force (1), and (c) a modification of the classic extreme groups design that offers promise for reducing the costs of data collection when this approach is used in personnel selection (3).

We believe the promising results obtained in recent studies warrant much greater emphasis on utility formulations and that utility should become a central concept in personnel selection research. The glaring economic errors possible when cost effective methods are not employed or when cost-in-effective methods are employed argue strongly for such increased emphasis. Later we describe how utility formulations can be incorporated into computerized personnel selection and classification systems for use in developing and monitoring organizations' human resources planning programs.

Nonlinear Prediction

Over 15 years ago, one of the present authors (95) expressed confidence that "subgrouping analysis"[3] would yield greatly increased levels of validity in the years ahead. Unfortunately, these hopes have not materialized. Reviews

---

[3]The term "subgrouping analysis" was used as a general term to refer to a variety of nonlinear prediction methods, including moderated regression, configural scoring, actuarial pattern analysis, quadrant analysis, and sequential prediction systems.

of the poor record of nonlinear methods in selection research appeared in 1971 and 1972. Zedeck (321) noted that such prediction systems when utilized with real data almost never hold up well on cross-validation, and Abrahams & Alf (2) pointed to many methodological difficulties in studies already done and expressed pessimism about their being overcome. Over the last 5 years, researchers' ardor for doing such studies has understandably cooled considerably, though one paper (134) did introduce statistical procedures for evaluating possible moderator effects. Another (249) showed that none of several configural methods was better than a linear method for predicting recidivism among probationers, and Janz (174) showed in a series of Monte Carlo investigations that combinatorial techniques (linear and moderated discriminant functions) gave higher hit rates than configural techniques (pattern analysis and sequential analysis) when applied to samples drawn from populations with several predetermined, complex, parametric characteristics.

In fact, the last mentioned study is remindful of results reported sometime ago by Rorer (255). He generated a number of "populations" by computer in such a way that markedly nonlinear relationships existed between sets of predictors and a criterion. He then used Monte Carlo sampling methods to examine the relative efficiency of simple linear and complex quadratic strategies in "capturing" predicted criterion variance. In all cases, the linear model closely approximated the precision of the nonlinear model. Results were of particular interest in populations where random error had been introduced in order to approximate "real world" data with reliabilities below 1.00. Here the nonlinear model suffered more shrinkage upon cross-validation than the linear model. In yet another striking demonstration of the robustness of the linear model, Dawes & Corrigan (81) showed that linear regression using *randomly assigned weights* outperformed selection judges (who presumably were trying to use nonlinear methods) in five different studies.

Thus it is that nonlinear models have simply not lived up to earlier expectations. In fact, Ghiselli (125) was one of the first to sound a note of caution when he advised against overzealousness in the pursuit of moderator variables. He counseled that time and effort might better be expended on more careful development of predictor and criterion measures. Today we concur wholeheartedly with his admonition. Selection research must devote increased effort toward reducing sources of both variable error (measurement and sampling error) and constant error (e.g. perceptual biases) in the development of instruments and in the design of studies. Nonlinear models may someday once again warrant attention but not until such errors have been reduced sufficiently to overcome the inherently superior robustness of the simple linear model.

PSYCHOMETRICS OF EQUAL OPPORTUNITY

The obligation to avoid unfair discrimination in personnel selection involves a broad array of psychometric and quasi-psychometric issues, including, at least, the following: (a) definitions of validity, (b) statistical power of tests of significance, (c) effects of error and range restriction on correlation, (d) development of improved criterion measures, (e) differential validities according to sex, race, etc, (f) the nature of policy decisions implied by different prediction strategies, (g) utilities associated with selection decision outcomes, and (h) degree of compatibility between institutional decisions and fairness to individuals or groups of individuals. All these matters have been widely discussed over the last 5 years.

Differential Validity

Since validity is defined as the appropriateness of inferences made from scores on a test (6, 90) and since tests in use have for the most part been developed and studied on samples of white, middle-class males, the appropriateness of inferences made from such tests for other subgroups (e.g. minorities) may well be questioned. One aspect of such questioning has taken the form of evaluating whether or not criterion-related validities of tests differ between racial groups (especially whites and blacks). For a time, evidence (67, 113, 130, 186, 208, 260) seemed to indicate that ethnic differences in test validity might indeed be the rule. However, methodological difficulties in many of the studies were pointed out (166, 263, 294). Many investigators had tested each group's validity coefficient separately for significance; and since Ns for blacks were usually smaller than for whites, results tended to show a larger proportion of significant validities for whites than for blacks—an outcome which came to be called *single group validity*. [4] Humphreys (166) declared that the above design was inappropriate for exploring the possibility of *differential validity*—the correct design being to test the significance of the difference between each pair of validities. At the same time, Schmidt, Berner & Hunter (263) attempted to demonstrate that the distribution of all validities obtained in 19 studies was compatible with a statistical model assuming no difference in population validities for blacks and whites. Thus, they concluded that differential validity was an "illusion" and declared it to be a "pseudo-problem." These arguments have not been uniformly accepted, and many additional articles discussing the evidence pro and con have appeared (13, 24, 26, 27, 168, 180, 180a, 237).

---

[4]Strictly speaking, according to Boehm (25), *single group validity* is defined as occurring when only one coefficient is significant and the two coefficients do not differ significantly.

The bulk of evidence suggests now that statistically significant *differential validity* is the exception rather than the rule. Boehm (26) found significant validity differences for only 8 percent of 297 comparisons made in 31 studies she reviewed. In contrast, Katzell & Dyer (180), after deleting comparisons involving "invalid" tests (r's < .20) and examining only independent data sets, found significant validity differences for 23 percent of 90 comparisons derived from the same 31 studies. Of these, validities were greater for whites 11 times and greater for blacks 10 times. They also point out that the likelihood of Type II error is great for almost all the comparisons. In fact, the power of the statistical tests for detecting a true population difference in validities of ±.20 ranged from .09 to .71 with a mean of only .26. This means that the average comparison had only one chance in four of detecting as significant a true population difference as large as .20. As a result, Katzell & Dyer conclude: "The practical implication is obviously to continue to check for evidence of differential validity whenever feasible, as has long been recommended. Failure to do so increases the risk of selection bias" (180, p. 144).

However, Hunter & Schmidt (168) do not agree with this conclusion, criticizing both the Boehm and the Katzell & Dyer studies because of data preselection (that is, deletion of "invalid tests") which they (Hunter & Schmidt) claim produced "massive" biases in favor of concluding that differences exist in the population when in truth they do not. The points stressed by Hunter & Schmidt, in questioning results of these two studies, are not unrelated to their broader views of validity generalization (267), wherein they argue that criterion-related validities have falsely been assumed to be situation-specific when in fact the dispersion of observed sample validities is due to widely varying sample sizes, levels of criterion reliabilities, and amounts of range restriction in measures.

Test Fairness

Regardless of the outcome of the differential validity debate, the issue of test fairness remains. Even when regression slopes are found to be the same across subgroups, regression intercepts frequently differ significantly (251, 266) because subgroups have significantly different means on predictors, criteria, or both. When this occurs with a selection or prediction system, the user is faced with the need to decide upon a strategy that will constitute fair use of the system. Fair use implies in turn that decisions based on the selection system will be equally appropriate regardless of a person's subgroup membership. Many strategies for implementing fair use have been proposed (68, 72, 79a, 109, 205, 206, 305). Each implies a particular ethical position or set of values depending on its proponent's definition of fairness (167). In effect then, different values yield different definitions of fairness resulting in different psychometric models which when used yield different outcomes (that is, differential patterns of accuracy and of error in decisions made). The range of outcomes shown by various models has been the subject of several studies (43, 135, 170, 178). Below we describe several models according to how each defines fairness, what the use of each entails, and how selection decisions based on each would impact on different subgroups.

MODELS OF TEST FAIRNESS   For illustrative purposes, consider that a criterion-related study has been carried out on 200 telephone operators including both females and males. The two validity coefficients are of moderate size and not significantly different. The mean test score for males is one standard deviation lower than the mean test score for females; the mean criterion score for males is one-half standard deviation lower than the mean criterion score for females. Below we discuss different "models" of test fairness according to how this information would be used to make selection decisions, how fairness is defined, and what the results would be if *equal numbers* of males and females apply for employment:

1. *Cleary or Regression Model* (68). TEST USE: Applicants' test scores are interpreted according to separate regression equations for females and males; persons with highest predicted performance are selected. FAIRNESS: Test use is defined as unfair only if consistent non-zero errors of prediction are made for members of one subgroup; the most qualified persons should be selected, regardless of group membership. RESULTS: Average criterion performance of selected persons is high; many fewer males than females are selected (only one or two males out of every ten persons selected); performance of neither males nor females is over or underpredicted, hence incidence of failure is the same for males and females; proportion of potentially successful males rejected is higher than for females.

2. *Einhorn & Bass or Equal Risk Model* (103, 109). TEST USE: Applicants' test scores are interpreted according to separate expectancy charts for females and males; cutting scores are set to yield the same levels of predicted success or failure (risk) for both groups. FAIRNESS: Test use is defined as unfair if expected success and failure rates differ according to subgroup membership; qualified persons are, therefore, identified according to cutting scores established separately by subgroup. RESULTS: Results are essentially the same as with the regression model.

3. *Thorndike or Constant Ratio Model* (305). TEST USE: Points equivalent to one-half standard deviation are added to each male applicant's test score; revised scores are interpreted according to a common regression equation. FAIRNESS: Criterion performance scores define the true poten-

tial' of members of each subgroup; test score distribution is, therefore, modified to be the same as the criterion distribution. RESULTS: Average criterion performance of selected persons is somewhat below that shown by persons selected with the regression model; about three or four males are included among every ten persons selected; performance of males as a group is somewhat overpredicted, hence higher incidence of failure occurs among males than among females; proportion of potentially successful males rejected is somewhat more than for females.

4. *Cole/Darlington Model* (72, 79a). TEST USE: Predictor scores are regressed against criterion scores separately for each group; predictor score distribution is modified (points added to males' scores) to assure that males and females with the same criterion scores also have the same predictor scores; revised scores are interpreted according to common regression equation. FAIRNESS: True performance potential of members of any subgroup is defined according to those who could be successful if selected; thus, test use is defined as unfair if it excludes from selection unequal proportions of potentially successful persons from different subgroups. RESULTS: Average criterion performance of all selected persons is lower than that of persons selected by either the regression or constant ratio models; about four males are included among every ten persons selected; performance of males as a group is considerably overpredicted; hence, much higher incidence of failure occurs among males than among females; proportion of potentially successful males rejected is the same as for females.

5. *Quota Model.* TEST USE: Applicants' test scores are interpreted according to separate regression equations for females and males, but the same selection ratio is used for each group. FAIRNESS: Test use is defined as unfair if different proportions of persons are selected from different subgroups. RESULTS: Average criterion performance of all selected persons is about the same as that for persons selected by the Cole model; equal numbers of males and females are selected; performance of males as a group is considerably overpredicted; hence much higher incidence of failure occurs among males than among females; proportion of potentially successful males rejected is less than for females.

It is apparent that these models give different weight to the benefits and costs associated with different types of selection "hits" and "misses." The regression model maximizes overall criterion performance of selectees and minimizes risks of job failure while denying employment opportunity disproprotionately to potentially successful persons from different subgroups. In contrast, the quota model provides employment opportunity equally to members of all subgroups but at the expense of disproportionate subgroup risks of job failure, decreased mean criterion performance of selectees, and a reversal in the direction of disproportionate subgroup rejection of potentially successful persons. Interestingly, the regression model, with its emphasis on the individual rather than the individual's subgroup, comes closest to satisfying the wording of the Civil Rights Act. But the Cole and quota models are more consistent with the nature of remedies decreed by many courts[5] and with the concern for avoiding adverse impact contained in the proposed Uniform Guidelines.

We must recognize that the circumstances of particular selection situations vary greatly according to group score distributions on both tests and criteria, validities, and the relative seriousness of different types of selection errors. Because of this complexity, we agree with Petersen & Novick (244) that no single model spawned by concepts of culture fairness and group parity should enjoy institutional endorsement. Instead, the complexity is best dealt with by developing and applying utility formulations to define and apply equity in each personnel selection program. Utility formulations have in fact been espoused by Cronbach (75), Petersen & Novick (236, 244), Gross & Su (135), Darlington (80), and most recently, Novick & Ellis (235). The central thrust of utility considerations is that rational judgments by institutional and social policy makers can be quantified and combined with the usual psychometrics of any decision system.

UTILITY AND EQUITY IN SELECTION   One of our major themes in this chapter is that the natural incompatibility between institutional decision making (pure selection) and individual decision making (vocational guidance and job choice) should be overcome. We believe utility models hold most promise for doing so. For example, Darlington's suggestions (80) recognize with great clarity that selection systems should always involve a continuing series of personnel decisions which properly balance the needs of institutions, individuals, and society. He shows how selection systems can be designed to take account of both psychometric and rational input and how computer assistance can be utilized to modify the system's utility matrix as experience with the decisional processes of the system and their results is gained.

Below we portray how utility considerations could be used in designing an organization's total selection and classification system:

1. *Affirmative action policies and labor market constraints.* (*a*) Assume that organizational policies have been stated concerning intentions to move toward certain specified mixes of sex and race subgroups in different job areas; (*b*) labor market availability information specifies likely applicant characteristics according to sex and racial groupings.

---

[5]But at least one court [as reported in (170)] ruled in 1975 that the regression model is the only one that is legally or logically required.

2. *Applicant information.* The organization has available for each applicant: (*a*) demographic information; (*b*) predicted levels on several facets of job performance (e.g. productivity, training time, job tenure, etc) based on test scores, task checklist responses, etc.

3. *Cost/Utility estimates.* Estimates are available for: (*a*) marginal utilities (in dollars) of different levels on the above facets of job performance; (*b*) costs of training according to job tasks and times required; (*c*) recruiting and selection processing costs according to labor force availabilities for various groups.

4. *Policy input.* A panel of organizational and social policy makers provide continuous input [through decision methods such as Delphi or Nominal Group Technique (84)] for deriving consensus judgments and weights for such "intangibles" as accuracy/inaccuracy in individual and institutional decisions, costs for legal defense against discrimination or reverse discrimination charges, welfare payments to unemployed persons of various groups, etc.

5. *Selection processing and system monitoring.* The above information is used to design a selection system with the following features: (*a*) Algorithms are devised and programmed for computer processing for each of the organization's major job areas. (*b*) Applicant information is processed to yield "utility ranks" for all job areas for each applicant. (*c*) The applicant X job area Utility Rank Matrix is processed by the computer in the context of organizational job opportunities and availability rates for both internal and external labor markets and tentative job-applicant matches are listed [this process utilizes classification technology (98, pp. 189–99; 304) so that the initial placement recommendations satisfy optimally the needs of organizations and individuals]. (*d*) With help from employment counselors, applicants interact directly with the computer information system to learn about the jobs recommended (e.g. duties, salary levels, long-term career opportunities, additional training/experience requirements, starting dates, probability of success, etc) and in the process, mutually acceptable job decisions (to both organization and individual) are made. (*e*) Selection, classification, and information systems are monitored and modified continually to take account of changes in utility/cost functions as decisions are made (e.g. marginal utilities, costs associated with recruitment and testing, etc change with each job placement) and to take account over the longer term of job performance and affirmative action outcomes in the organization.

We have portrayed an idealized, computer assisted, interactive personnel selection and classification system. Some readers may think we've strayed too far into the realm of science fiction. We think not. Consider the following factors: first, optimal utilization of human resources demands a complex mix of psychometric and rational input. We have seen that the so-called test fairness models lead to widely varying outcomes when strictly statistical solutions are attempted. In contrast, utility formulations force value judgments to be specified and incorporated into the system explicitly instead of implicitly. Second, and most important, all technology necessary for implementing such personnel selection and classification systems is available; nothing new needs to be invented. In fact, many highly sophisticated computer-assisted occupational information and career guidance systems are already in use in this country; they have recently been described by Super (296). In sum, selection systems should and can be designed to utilize considered, explicit, and consistent information input (both statistical and rational) and implemented as continuous job placement flow processes.

LABOR MARKET ISSUES

Provision 703(j) of Title VII of the 1964 CRA assured employers that Congress did not intend that employers be required to give preferential treatment to individuals just because they belonged to protected classes, no matter what imbalances their current work forces might show. By implication, legal proof of unfair discrimination would require a showing of intent to discriminate against particular individuals. But enforcement of the equal employment opportunity goals of Title VII could not, in practice, rely exclusively on such a difficult burden of proof; thus it is that additional regulations and court interpretations have been promulgated such that the abstraction *equal opportunity* might be defined according to results achieved (*statistical parity*) by an employer's personnel practices. Several authors (28, 127, 136) have recently traced the evolution of events since 1964 marking the transition from "equal opportunity" to "statistical parity." Statistical parity is, of course, related to the concept *adverse impact*. Both involve estimates of the degree of over or under representation of certain groups in an employer's work force, and both obviously depend on knowing something about an employer's labor markets.

Labor Markets, Availabilities, and Human Resources Planning

For any job opening, an employer has two potential sources of candidates: (*a*) available persons already employed in the firm (the internal labor market), and (*b*) available persons not currently employed in the firm (the external labor market). Labor market analyses (particularly the external market) have become increasingly prevalent in Title VII cases (257, 258) in order to compare employers' selection/promotion practices and results (sex/racial mix in various jobs) with availabilities of persons in the labor force. Obviously, the accuracy of conclusions drawn from such comparisons depends on how good the data are and how well defined the methodology is for making the comparisons. Unfortunately, neither the data nor the definitions are much good (219, 220). It has been said (62) that both *data availability* and *availability data* present severe problems. For example, typical data sources (e.g. census information, Department of Labor statistics, etc) suffer from many shortcomings, as detailed by Milkovich (220). Even more serious is the lack of uniformity between government agencies about how they define "availability." In sharp contrast with their recent success in proposing uniform test and selection guidelines, government agencies have apparently made little or no effort to devise uniform methodology describing how to use labor market information for evaluating an employer's work force results (217). Even so, individual agencies have been only too ready to adopt ad hoc methodologies during investigations for violations under Title VII. For example, EEOC's approach has been to define an employer's relevant labor market and available supply according to the entire civilian labor force, *"regardless of qualifications or skills required by jobs, regardless of propensities to move, and regardless of information about job opportunities"* (220, p. 35) [emphasis in original]. Such an approach is absurd because it ignores most of the practical realities associated with systematic procedures of recruitment, personnel selection, and job placement. Labor economists (122, 210, 252) and some psychologists (118, 201) have developed a variety of approaches for examining labor market information to estimate external availabilities more realistically. These include segmentation of standard statistical information according to commuting distances and routes, occupational classifications, area wage rates, and worker qualifications. Traditionally, I/O psychologists have limited their perspective to worker qualifications; we believe the labor economics literature provides a needed broader perspective about issues underlying the determination of adverse impact, and we urge our colleagues to give attention to that literature.

Taking account of all labor market considerations requires careful planning and continuous monitoring by an employer. Milkovich & Mahoney (222) describe the "developing art" of *human resources planning* as a systematic, continuous flow process designed to move an organization from an existing human resources status to an intended future status.[6] The basic approach is to model a firm's internal labor market according to such parameters as growth plans, predicted job vacancies, and availability rates

---

[6]It has not escaped our attention that *human resources planning* apparently is the labor economics analog of the utility based, computerized, continuous flow selection system we have already recommended. However, our labor economist colleagues seem to be ahead of us in developing dynamic models to represent personnel flow as opposed to the static "single time" selection decision models implied so frequently by psychologists.

of various population subgroups in both the internal and external labor markets. The model can be used to determine the feasibility and estimated costs of alternative selection and promotion programs required to accomplish particular affirmative action goals. Utility considerations can, of course, be introduced into the model, and monitoring of results can be done continuously to keep organizational and social policy makers informed of successes and/or difficulties on the road to equal opportunity as defined by results obtained. Examples of such models are appearing with increased frequency in the literature (61, 62, 64, 118, 201, 221). A striking feature of results obtained by all investigators is the long time required (25 to 30 years or more) for firms to achieve anything approximating equal representation of all groups in their work forces—even if complete equivalence in distributions of job qualifications were to be assumed across all groups. This is the case even when lopsided hiring and promotion rates are set (such as 1.5 or 2 times the percentages of available persons in the labor market). Obviously, equal employment opportunity practices will not produce "overnight" success judged from the viewpoint of statistical parity. Nonetheless, equal employment opportunity for individuals is best served by planning, explicit decision making, and continual monitoring of total human resources systems as opposed to the more narrowly based and often haphazard selection practices which have traditionally been utilized.

SELECTION PRACTICES: RESEARCH RESULTS

An assumption underlying use of most devices for vocational diagnosis is that "past behavior is the best predictor of future behavior." Actually, this presumption has been rather hotly debated over the last several years by *situationists* (223, 224, 288) who claim that behavior is mostly a function of cues and rewards peculiar to each situation and *interactionists* (23, 36, 159, 293) who correctly (we believe) point out that many trait concepts have served us well as statements of behavioral probabilities and that the reinforcing properties of situations are, in fact, determined partly by the qualities of persons choosing to interact in them. The controversy is related (albeit remotely) to the distinction drawn by Wernimont & Campbell (315) between *samples* and *signs* and to Dunnette's (100) suggestion that selection methods might well be classified according to whether their job relatedness is justified directly (as with job content *samples*) or indirectly (as with job-relevant constructs or *signs*). The distinction is important to keep in mind because most currently used selection devices contain elements of both samples and signs. The *personal interview* can be conducted to discover previous experiences that sample activities required on the job to be filled, but only rarely is it conducted so wisely. Earlier we suggested that *biographical information* might well consist of responses to a standard task checklist scored objectively according to job-related experiences (samples) as well as being scored according to empirically derived constructs. Standardized simulations (samples) of job content can be devised and incorporated into *multiple assessment procedures;* however, most such exercises are more accurately viewed as methods of eliciting job-relevant behavioral constructs instead of as direct job samples. Finally, *job samples* themselves can be created and used to evaluate a candidate's present proficiency in actually carrying out various tasks involved in the jobs to be filled.

Research on each of these four general methods (interview, biodata, multiple assessments, job samples) has been plentiful during the last 4 years. Below we review this research. But first we should note in passing that the long-awaited *Handbook of Industrial and Organizational Psychology* (105), finally published in 1976, contains several chapters relevant to vocational diagnosis and personnel selection and classification. The reader is referred especially to the chapter by Guion (141) for a general overview of personnel selection issues; to chapters by Campbell (54), Weiss (314), Cook & Campbell (74), and Bouchard (35) for comprehensive accounts of psychometric, experimental, and field research methodologies; to chapters by Dunnette (104), Holland (160), Gough (129), Owens (239), and Finkle (115) for extensive reviews of the current status of several diagnostic and assessment methods; and to chapters by McCormick (212) and Smith (290) on job analysis and criterion development.

The Selection Interview

Schmitt's (270) excellent review of recent research on selection interviewing shows that increased research emphasis is being given to experimental studies of the interview as a decision making process. Though information about the actual validity of an interviewer's selection decisions is still extremely limited, Schmitt does offer eight suggestions for the "practicing personnel interviewer." In a way, the continuing sad state of much of what goes on in actual interviewing practice is reflected in such seemingly obvious suggestions as: (*a*) decide what the purpose of the interview is to be; (*b*) know the job requirements of the job to be filled; (*c*) recognize the public relations implications of the interview; (*d*) allow the applicant time to talk; and (*e*) be aware of the need to avoid bias in interviewing persons of different race, sex, beliefs, etc. For our purposes, it is of greatest use to consider factors that have been shown to affect the outcomes of interviewers' decisions and how interviewing research may be subsumed under the broader area of person perception research.

SEX AND RACE   It is, of course, a truism that no interviewer can remain oblivious to the sex or race of the person being interviewed. How do these factors affect interview decisions? Three studies (60, 71, 229) suggest that interviewers are prone to form sex-role sterotypes; that is, females are seen as more "acceptable" for traditionally female dominated jobs and males as more "acceptable" for traditionally male dominated jobs. Terborg & Ilgen (301) provide an in-depth empirical investigation and a theoretical discussion of sex role stereotyping of females and suggest that attribution theory (184) may be useful in explaining the phenomenon. Their results confirmed findings of a previous study (82) in which females performing at the same level as males on a so-called "masculine" job were seen as "luckier" than their male counterparts. Other studies found sex discrimination in selection decisions to be present, but not of great magnitude (88, 89, 154, 256). With regard to race, no race discrimination was found in a sample of employers who were asked to rate "disadvantaged" hypothetical job candidates (148). Nor was race found to be a factor in assigning Navy personnel to jobs (4). In the Haefner study (148) age (55 versus 25) did affect ratings by employers, with the older persons rated lower. Three studies also investigated physical attractiveness as an independent variable (60, 88, 89). All found that more attractive persons, male or female, are evaluated more favorably, but that the effect is not particularly strong.

Experimental studies such as the ones mentioned are sometimes criticized because subjects are asked to report what they *would do* or how they *would evaluate* hypothetical job candidates. Some of the studies reviewed used quite realistic resume materials, and one even had subjects essentially role playing the decision maker (301). These elaborations reduce the artificiality of the task, but persons who must make the actual selection decisions may be affected differently by some of these factors. The Abrahams, Atwater & Alf (4) study, on the other hand, provided a naturalistic, unobtrusive measure of the extent of racial bias by examining real decisions made over a period of time by Naval classification officers. Studies such as this avoid questions of the generalizability of results. More research is needed which tests experimental results obtained with college student interviewers working in contrived settings for their applicability to the "real world." A hopeful note is sounded, however, in a review paper (19) concluding that college student rating responses in interviewing research are pretty much the same as professional interviewers' responses. Bernstein et al (19) note that student subjects may provide somewhat more lenient ratings but that standard deviations, interrater reliabilities, and other properties of their ratings are similar to those obtained from professional interviewers. Also, conclusions in the Dipboye et al (89) study were the same for student and professional interviewer subjects.

OTHER FACTORS   The effect of *handicapped status* has been studied (192). Results showed that handicapped persons were rated just as high as the nonhandicapped on most criteria and as more qualified in terms of potential loyalty and motivation to perform well. Attention has been given over the years to the relative impact of *positive and negative information* on interviewers' decisions. Two papers (73, 207) refined or elaborated on previous results suggesting that negative information is more salient (292) or that positive information is underweighted (161). Constantin (73) concluded that it is not negative information per se that is salient for interview decisions but deviancy from the norm that such information represents. London & Hakel (207) found that negative information is not so important when the interviewer's expectations are that the applicant is of "high quality." Several studies have addressed issues about the *type of information* available to interviewers. Wiener & Schneiderman (319) report a rather obvious but nonetheless reassuring outcome: when much information is provided about the job, interviewers rely primarily on job-relevant factors in making selection decisions; when they have little information about the job they rely more on factors less relevant to the job.

Study of the *temporal placement* of negative and positive information has continued, Springbett (292) and others having found that when negative information about the interviewee surfaces early in the interview, it has more impact on interview decisions than when it surfaces later. Peters & Terborg (243) also found such a primacy effect but, importantly, the effect was eliminated when considerable information about the job was provided. In a study of interviewers' information processing, Johns (176) discovered that experienced interviewers handled information about an applicant more competently—i.e. they considered more information and could recall more about the applicant—when the data were provided at random rather than allowing the interviewer to control the order in which materials were reviewed. A study with a somewhat similar focus (307) tested a Webster (313) hypothesis that interviewers should not review an application blank before performing the selection interview because this procedure tends to "freeze" the interviewer's perceptions and causes the search for relevant information to be narrowed. Not so, according to this study. Professional interviewers provided with a completed application blank prior to viewing a simulated employment interview recalled more information about the interviewee, even information that was contained *only* in the interview.

Effects of *attitude similarity* between the interviewer and applicant continue to receive attention. In general, an attitude similarity effect is said to exist when applicants with attitudes similar to the interviewer are more likely to receive favorable ratings than are applicants with attitudes different from those of the interviewer. A study mentioned previously (243) revealed a pervasive attitude similarity effect that persisted even when considerable information about the job was provided to undergraduate subjects. Two other studies confirmed the existence of an attitude similarity effect (250, 316) but Frank & Hackman (119) questioned the universality of this effect, particularly when experienced interviewers actually perform interviews (rather than when college student "interviewers" review resumes, for example). They had three college admissions officers interview 29 applicants and found high correlations between similarity in measured attitudes (including background and interests) and interview decisions for only one of the admissions officers. As with everything else, substantial individual differences are likely to exist here.

INTERVIEW VALIDITY AND INTERVIEWING PERCEPTIONS   Two recent studies (155, 194) examined the validity of the interview, one a field study exploring the predictive validity of decisions made by a three-man selection board screening police candidates (194) and the other a laboratory experiment in which college students viewed selection interviews with social worker "applicants" and predicted their performance (155). The former study found low to moderate validities against subsequent performance ratings; the latter study revealed generally low validity coefficients against performance ratings of interviewees actually employed as social workers. Structure of the interview and the availability of biographical data did not appreciably affect validity results in the latter study.

Finally, a recent study turned the tables on the usual focus in interview research and examined the effects of interviewee perceptions of the interviewer on decisions about the company. Schmitt & Coyle (272) found that interviewee perceptions along six factors of interpersonal style and manner of conducting the interview predicted well their decisions about the company, though, as the authors point out, these relationships might provide overestimates because both sets of variables were self-reports. Still, with some check on actual decisions about the company and perhaps certain controls for type of job, this avenue of research appears promising for providing information relevant for the selection and training of interviewers.

INTERVIEWING AND PERSON PERCEPTION RESEARCH   Clearly, the emphasis pioneered by Webster (313) of studying factors related to interview decision making continues to provide valuable information. Studies of the interview *process* should continue. In addition, more should be done on the *validity* of interview decisions, especially studies which seek an understanding of relationships between constructs derived conceptually from job performance criteria and which can be either observed directly or reliably inferred from the interview. This is the position advocated by Guion (141), who states that interviewers should define specific constructs operationally and then evaluate interviewees on those constructs. Such evaluations can in turn be related to conceptually appropriate performance criteria within a multiple criterion framework in a manner suggested by Dunnette (97) and Guion (138).

Research on the selection interview will also profit from continued emphasis within a person perception framework (149). The selection interviewer's job is to develop accurate perceptions of applicants and to evaluate those perceptions in light of job requirements. Learning more about how those perceptions are formed, what affects their development, and what psychological processes best explain their development should receive increased attention. As we have prescribed for research on performance ratings, persons investigating the interview should attend to the person perception literature to aid in developing hypotheses and in understanding results of studies. Attribution theory (184) and personal construct theory (185) offer just two examples of underlying phenomena that may affect person perceptions in the interview. Some of these and other explanatory concepts have been considered to a limited degree by interview researchers (e.g. 301), but more emphasis on *explaining* research results is definitely needed.

Biographical Information

Traditionally, biographical information has suffered a bad reputation among scientific-minded industrial psychologists. The argument has been that weighted application blanks predict job performance quite adequately but they fail to increase our knowledge about predictor-criterion relationships. Recent work by Owens and Schoenfeldt has of course changed this image. Owens (239) outlines the general strategy for use of biographical information. Also, Schoenfeldt has described the assessment-classification model that flows from the strategy (280). Owens views biographical information as providing a picture of where an individual "has been," i.e. a record of a person's life path. He invokes the behavioral consistency notion (315), arguing that a person's past experiences can aid greatly in predicting where he or she is "likely to go" in the future. Owens argues forcefully that "biodata be regarded as providing a postmortem view of the development of the individual" (239).

The major empirical work arising from this philosophy of biodata utilization is a large-scale study of nearly 2000 University of Georgia students who entered that school in 1968. Biographical data were gathered from these students and factor analyses of their responses yielded 13–15 interpretable factors (e.g. warmth of paternal relationship, athletic interest, etc). Students were then subgrouped on the basis of scores on these factors (23 male and 14 female clusters emerged), and some meaningful differences between clusters have been found in such areas as vocational interests, creativity, drug usage, and leadership activities.

SELECTION STUDIES WITH BIOGRAPHICAL DATA   While the Owens-Schoenfeldt approach to using biographical information has received attention recently, studies employing biodata in a more "traditional" manner continue to be conducted. Within the past few years, empirically weighted application blanks have been developed to predict scuba training performance (21), success of men and women in the Israeli Army (231), attrition from the US Army (112), turnover of clerical workers (58), and office equipment sales performance in a number of countries in Europe (158). In a slightly different vein, Tuller & Barrett (308) successfully predicted performance on a sales job by interpreting future-oriented autobiographies written by applicants and scored according to a system developed previously for Peace Corps selection.

Two studies addressed the potential problem of slanted responses to biographical items. Cascio (57) found that a sample of police patrolmen responded very accurately to 17 bio items—median correlation between responses and actual information was .94. And another study (281) suggested that faking responses to bio items may not be a serious problem if applicants are warned of the presence of a lie scale. Finally, Schwab & Oliver (283) cast some doubt on the usefulness of weighted biographical data for predicting tenure. And Pace & Schoenfeldt (240) discuss the problem of some biographical items being discriminatory against minorities. They suggest ensuring that items are selected or developed on rational grounds based on a job analysis and that items also should be examined empirically for evidence of adverse impact. There is little doubt, however, that biographical information can be used effectively to predict success in a variety of jobs. Ghiselli's review of validity studies (126) indicated that biodata was the most successful kind of predictor both for training and for job proficiency criteria, and the results of the studies just reviewed confirm that the method can indeed yield high validities.

Multiple Assessment Procedures

Several reviews of the assessment center method have appeared recently. The reviews vary in purpose, ranging from general overviews of research on the approach (102, 115, 163, 191) to a history and overview of research and practice in one company (42). General descriptions of how the assessment center approach works have also surfaced recently (e.g. 52). With only a few exceptions, reports have been favorable to the assessment center method. The validity of its predictions of managerial effectiveness has been well documented, particularly in the case of the AT&T centers where criterion contamination has been totally controlled (42).

Besides assessment centers for managers, assessment programs have been developed to estimate potential for success in sales (41), leadership in the military (152, 209a, 310), police work at four different levels (107), the pharmacy profession (289), and the stockbroker job (151). Thus, the method is apparently sufficiently flexible to evaluate potential for many occupations. The reliability, dimensionality, and validity of assessment ratings are reviewed elsewhere (99, 115). Here we focus on several studies published recently and suggest avenues of research that appear promising.

INTERNAL ANALYSES AND EXTERNAL VALIDITIES   One study (157) evaluated the "internal consistency" of ratings on different dimensions gathered after different exercises. Results show widely differing reliabilities and might be used to help determine the most useful dimensions to be rated for each exercise. In another study (271) interrater agreement was found to be high both for dimension ratings and for the factor structures of those ratings. Also, dimension ratings contributed much more to overall evaluations than did test scores, suggesting that in making final ratings assessors do rely more heavily on behavioral cues provided by performance in simulations than on test score performance. Finally, Schmitt & Hill (275) studied the impact of sex and race composition in assessee groups on assessment center performance of the group members. In the main, the proportions of males, females, blacks, and whites in the groups did not relate to peer and assessor ratings of the group members. However, ratings of black women seemed to differ somewhat according to the racial and sex mix of the group they were in (they were rated as more forceful when more white females were present, less forceful when more black males were present). Thus, the study alerts us to an important aspect of assessment centers that may profitably be investigated, namely, configurations related to group composition. Size of assessee group, self-perceived reason for attending the center, and factors of similar ilk may contribute to the nature of assessment center ratings and thus are worthy of study.

Two studies have reported validities of managerial assessment ratings for women. One of them showed correlations in the 20s and 30s against a promotion criterion (226), and the other showed even higher correlations for small samples of white and black women against a performance rating criterion (164). Another paper (225) reported relatively high assessment validities when a "salary growth" criterion measure was obtained long after rather than shortly after assessment. A fourth validity study demonstrated the portability of an assessment center for managers (320). A center was developed as a multi-company assessment tool and its concurrent validity in one company was found to be reasonably high. A fifth paper (40) reported modest concurrent validity for in-basket assessment ratings on six dimensions of management functioning that Oldham had developed previously.

POSSIBLE PROBLEMS   The rapid growth in use of assessment methods may be accompanied by sloppy or improper application of assessment procedures. Finkle (115) warned that the assessment center "fad" might lead organizations to "get into assessment" without thinking through the need for it and/or preparing to use the method wisely. Blind acceptance of assessment data without heeding other information on assessees, lack of control of information generated during assessment, failure to evaluate the utility of the assessment program, and use of assessment procedures for purposes other than those for which they were designed are some potential difficulties related to casual application of multiple assessment programs.

A second possible problem with assessment programs was raised recently by Klimoski & Strickland (188), and a related argument has been made by Wallace (312). Klimoski & Strickland suggest that a subtle criterion contamination phenomenon may inflate assessment validities when global ratings or other summary measures of effectiveness (e.g. salary, management level reached, etc) are employed as criteria. This inflation will occur if assessment ratings and the criterion scores contain in common a component not related to true performance, which is instead associated with general halo, likability, or having the "proper" background, appearance, attitude, etc. Regarding advancement as a criterion, for example, assessors may be correctly "capturing the policies" or capturing the *biases* of upper level managers charged with making promotion decisions. One finding that supports this notion is that ratings of overall assessment performance or overall potential for success invariably correlate more highly with criterion performance than do ratings based on individual, presumably more explicitly behavior-based dimensions or composites of these dimension ratings. This raises the possibility that assessors' ratings on the various dimensions are tied closely to actual assessment center performance but that the *overall potential* ratings may reflect an element of bias, either implicitly or explicitly "factored into" the judgments. A wider variety of criteria including more behavior-based ratings and objective measures focused directly on performance (if available) would circumvent this potential difficulty.

CONCLUSION   Lest this section end on a sour note, we should add that the multiple assessment method possesses a number of distinct virtues. The diagnostic information related to performance potential of individuals can be of great help to an organization in making selection or promotion decisions and in helping individuals to learn more about training needs and job opportunities as they plan their longer term careers. Rather than take these virtues for granted however, we should strive to continue to research the method thoroughly and to monitor closely the manner in which multiple assessment procedures are utilized.

Job Samples

Carefully devised work samples have almost always yielded validities superior to those shown for tests. One review (11) concluded that work samples of jobs requiring motor skills showed validities second only to those obtained with biodata. A review (101) of selection studies (both published and unpublished) done on nonexempt jobs in the petroleum industry also showed high mean validities for work samples and job knowledge measures. In specific studies, Campion (56) found much higher concurrent validities for a work sample than for paper-and-pencil tests for the job of maintenance mechanic; Gordon & Kleiman (128a) found that the *predictive* validity for a work sample given to police recruits was better than the validity of an ability test; and, in a "lab" study (228), work samples were better than ability tests in reflecting students' performance levels on the "job" of building things with erector set materials.

The "theory" supporting the use of work samples makes good sense. Asher & Sciarrino (11) suggest guidelines for developing good work samples based on a "point-to-point" model emphasizing matching each work sample element with a corresponding job performance element. Schwartz (284) has outlined a "total strategy" of job analysis and identification of requisite knowledges, skills, and abilities for developing work sample measures. It is apparent, of course, that developing "good" work samples is time consuming and difficult and, as noted by Guion (146), special care must be taken to assure fair scoring procedures. A recent study (264) did, however, show that a job sample test for a machine trade was not only seen as "more fair" by job candidates but that the adverse impact of the test was lower than that of a job knowledge test developed from a content-oriented strategy. Job sample measures merit increased attention. Technology related to their development is not well advanced, but rapid strides are being made.

Miscellaneous Other Studies

Selection studies have been reported for predicting computer programmer training and job success (85), attrition from the Navy (262), and levels of performance in such publicly visible occupations as police officer (203) and firefighter (39). Recent studies of Army generals (92), business executives (190), office clerical personnel (108), and ROTC students (181) confirmed once more the usefulness of peer ratings in predicting later job performance criteria. Finally, Hillery & Fugita (156) found that persons obtained higher scores on both dexterity tests of the GATB when they took the tests in groups instead of individually. The results are especially interesting because mean scores increase in a nearly linear fashion for groups ranging in size from two to nine. Implications of this finding are troublesome in that they suggest that conditions of administration may affect test scores in more subtle ways than had previously been recognized.

CONTEXT OF THE FUTURE IN PERSONNEL SELECTION

The many separate lines of influence and discovery discussed in early pages of this chapter are coming together to form a basis for more effective planning of human resources utilization. Personnel selection and classification systems of the future will be broad in scope and formulated from dynamic models. Significant advances are evident in the technologies of job analysis, criterion measurement, validation, parameter estimation, work sampling, labor market analysis, person-job matching, and personnel flow modeling. Selection research and thinking has profited from increased support growing out of greatly expanded human resources programs established in response to civil rights legislation. Important discussions and exchanges concerning such issues as differential validity, labor market availabilities, and test use fairness have been exceptionally fruitful in leading to new formulations of utility, validity generalization, and Bayesian approaches promising improved use of existing and new research knowledge. We believe the confluence of these several advances renders feasible the design of computer assisted, interactive, personnel selection, classification, and vocational guidance systems to represent and to monitor personnel flow within and between organizations. Paterson's "vision" of a society devoted to, and capable of, conserving human talent seems within reach. The context of the future in personnel selection may well be the eventual actualization of processes leading to an optimal utilization of human resources for the total economy.

Literature Cited

1. Abellera, J. W., Mullins, C. J., Earles, J. A. 1975. *Value of Personnel Classification Information.* Air Force Hum. Res. Lab. Tech. Rep. 75-2, Lackland AFB, Texas
2. Abrahams, N. M., Alf, E. F. 1972. Pratfalls in moderator research. *J. Appl. Psychol.* 56:245–51
3. Abrahams, N. M., Alf, E. F. 1978. Relative costs and statistical power in the extreme groups approach. *Psychometrika.* In press
4. Abrahams, N. M., Atwater, D. C., Alf, E. F. 1977. Unobtrusive measurement of racial bias in job-placement decisions. *J. Appl. Psychol.* 62:116–19
5. American Psychological Association. 1966. *Standards for Educational and Psychological Tests and Manuals.* Washington: Am. Psychol. Assoc. 40 pp.
6. American Psychological Association, AERA, NCME. 1974. *Standards for Educational and Psychological Tests.* Washington: Am. Psychol. Assoc. 76 pp.
7. Anastasi, A. 1976. *Psychological Testing.* New York: MacMillan. 750 pp. 4th ed.
8. Arvey, R. D., Hoyle, J. C. 1974. A Guttman approach to the development of behaviorally based rating scales for systems analysts and programmer analysts. *J. Appl. Psychol.* 59:61–68
9. Arvey, R. D., Mossholder, K. M. 1977. A proposed methodology for determin-

ing similarities and differences among jobs. *Personnel Psychol.* 30:363–74

10. Ash, R. A., Edgell, S. L. 1975. A note on the readability of the Position Analysis Questionnaire. *J. Appl. Psychol.* 60:765–66

11. Asher, J. J., Sciarrino, J. A. 1974. Realistic work sample tests: A review. *Personnel Psychol.* 27:519–33

12. Astin, A. W. 1964. Criterion-centered research. *Educ. Psychol. Meas.* 24: 807–22

13. Bartlett, C. J., Bobko, P., Pine, S. M. 1977. Single-group validity: Fallacy of the facts? *J. Appl. Psychol.* 62:137–45

14. Bernardin, H. J. 1977. Behavioral expectation scales versus summated scales: A fairer comparison. *J. Appl. Psychol.* 62:422–28

15. Bernardin, H. J. 1978. The effects of rater training on leniency and halo errors in student ratings of instructors. *J. Appl. Psychol.* 63:301–8

16. Bernardin, H. J., Alvares, K. M., Cranny, C. J. 1976. A recomparison of behavioral expectation scales to summated scales. *J. Appl. Psychol.* 61: 564–70

17. Bernardin, H. J., LaShells, M. B., Smith, P. C., Alvares, K. M. 1976. Behavioral expectation scales: Effects of developmental procedures and formats. *J. Appl. Psychol.* 61:75–79

18. Bernardin, H. J., Walter, C. S. 1977. Effects of rater training and diary-keeping on psychometric error in ratings. *J. Appl. Psychol.* 62:64–69

19. Bernstein, V., Hakel, M. D., Harlan, A. 1975. The college student as interviewer: A threat to generalizability? *J. Appl. Psychol.* 60:266–68

20. Berry, N. H., Nelson, P. D., McNally, M. S. 1966. A note on supervisor ratings. *Personnel Psychol.* 19:423–26

21. Biersner, R. J., Ryman, D. H. 1974. Prediction of scuba training performance. *J. Appl. Psychol.* 59:519–21

22. Bigoness, W. J. 1976. Effect of applicant's sex, race, and performance on employers' performance ratings: Some additional findings. *J. Appl. Psychol.* 61:80–84

23. Block, J. 1975. *Recognizing the Coherence of Personality.* Presented at Stockholm Conf. Interactional Psychol., Stockholm, Sweden

24. Bobko, P., Bartlett, C. J. 1978. Subgroup validities: Differential definitions and differential prediction. *J. Appl. Psychol.* 63:12–14

25. Boehm, V. R. 1972. Negro-white differences in validity of employment and training selection procedures. *J. Appl. Psychol.* 56:33–39

26. Boehm, V. R. 1977. Differential prediction: A methodological artifact? *J. Appl. Psychol.* 62:146–54

27. Boehm, V. R. 1978. Populations, preselection, and practicalities: A reply to Hunter and Schmidt. *J. Appl. Psychol.* 63:15–18

28. Borgatta, E. F. 1976. The concept of reverse discrimination and equality of opportunity. *Am. Sociol.* 11:62–72

29. Borman, W. C. 1974. The rating of individuals in organizations: An alternate approach. *Organ. Behav. Hum. Perform.* 12:105–214

30. Borman, W. C. 1975. Effects of instructions to avoid halo error on reliability and validity of performance evaluation ratings. *J. Appl. Psychol.* 60:556–60

31. Borman, W. C. 1977. *Some raters are simply better than others at evaluating performance: Individual differences correlates of rating accuracy using behavior scales.* Presented at Ann. Conv. Am. Psychol. Assoc., San Francisco

32. Borman, W. C. 1978. Exploring upper limits of reliability and validity in job performance ratings. *J. Appl. Psychol.* 63:135–44

33. Borman, W. C., Dunnette, M. D. 1975. Behavior based versus trait-oriented performance ratings: An empirical study. *J. Appl. Psychol.* 60:561–65

34. Borman, W. C., Vallon, W. R. 1974. A view of what can happen when behavioral expectation scales are developed in one setting and used in another. *J. Appl. Psychol.* 59:197–201

35. Bouchard, T. J. Jr. 1976. Field research methods: Interviewing, questionnaires, participant observation, systematic observation, unobtrusive measures. See Ref. 105, pp. 363–466

36. Bowers, K. S. 1973. Situationism in psychology: An analysis and critique. *Psychol. Rev.* 80:307–36

37. Bownas, D. A., Heckman, R. W. 1976. *Job Analysis of the Entry Level Firefighter Position.* Minneapolis: Personnel Decisions, Inc.

38. Bownas, D. A., Peterson, N. G. 1978. Skill and task structure and performance acquisition. In *Human Performance and Productivity,* ed. E. I. Fleishman. In press

39. Bownas, D. A., Rosse, R. L., Dunnette, M. D. 1977. *Construct Validation of a Selection Battery for the Entry Level Firefighter Position.* Minneapolis: Personnel Decisions Res. Inst.

40. Brass, D. J., Oldham, G. R. 1976. Validating an in-basket test using an alternative set of leadership scoring dimensions. *J. Appl. Psychol.* 61:652–57
41. Bray, D. W., Campbell, R. J. 1968. Selection of salesmen by means of an assessment center. *J. Appl. Psychol.* 52:36–41
42. Bray, D. W., Campbell, R. J., Grant, D. L. 1974. *Formative Years in Business: A Long-term Study of Managerial Lives.* New York: Wiley
43. Breland, H. M., Ironson, G. H. 1976. *DeFunis* reconsidered: A comparative analysis of alternative admissions strategies. *J. Educ. Meas.* 13:89–99
44. Brogden, H. E. 1946. On the interpretation of the correlation coefficient as a measure of predictive efficiency. *J. Educ. Psychol.* 37:65–76
45. Brogden, H. E. 1949. When testing pays off. *Personnel Psychol.* 2:171–83
46. Brogden, H. E., Taylor, E. K. 1950. The dollar criterion—applying the cost accounting concept to criterion construction. *Personnel Psychol.* 3:133–54
47. Brumback, G. B. 1976. *One method is not enough: An overview of selection oriented job analysis methodology.* Presented at Selection Specialists Symp., Int. Personnel Manage. Assoc., Chicago, Ill.
48. Brumback, G. B., Romashko, T., Hahn, C. P., Fleishman, E. A. 1974. *Model Procedures for Job Analysis, Test Development and Validation.* Washington: Am. Inst. Res.
49. Buckner, D. N. 1959. The predictability of ratings as a function of interrater agreement. *J. Appl. Psychol.* 43:60–64
50. Burnaska, R. F., Hollmann, T. D. 1974. An empirical comparison of the relative effects of rater response biases on three rating scale formats. *J. Appl. Psychol.* 59:307–12
51. Buros, O. K., ed. 1974. *Tests In Print II: An Index to Tests, Test Reviews, and the Literature on Specific Tests.* Highland Park, NJ: Gryphon. 1107 pp.
52. Byham, W. C., Wettengel, C. 1974. Assessment centers for supervisors and managers. An introduction and overview. *Public Personnel Manage.* 3: 352–64
53. Campbell, J. P. 1974. *A Monte Carlo Approach to Some Problems Inherent in Multivariate Prediction: With Special Reference to Multiple Regression.* Tech. Rep. 2002, Personnel Train. Res. Prog. Washington DC: Office of Naval Res.
54. Campbell, J. P. 1976. Psychometric theory. See Ref. 105, pp. 185–222
55. Campbell, J. P., Dunnette, M. D., Arvey, R. D., Hellervik, L. V. 1973. The development and evaluation of behaviorally based rating scales. *J. Appl. Psychol.* 57:15–22
56. Campion, J. E. 1972. Work sampling for personnel selection. *J. Appl. Psychol.* 56:40–44
57. Cascio, W. F. 1975. Accuracy of verifiable biographical information blank responses. *J. Appl. Psychol.* 60:767–69
58. Cascio, W. F. 1976. Turnover, biographical data, and fair employment practice. *J. Appl. Psychol.* 61:576–80
59. Cascio, W. F., Valenzi, E. R. 1977. Behaviorally anchored rating scales: Effects of education and job experience of raters and ratees. *J. Appl. Psychol.* 62:278–82
60. Cash, T. F., Gillen, B., Burns, D. S. 1977. Sexism and "beautyism" in personnel consultant decision making. *J. Appl. Psychol.* 62:301–10
61. Charnes, A. W., Cooper, W. W., Lewis, K. A., Niehaus, R. J. 1975. *A Multiobjective Model for Planning Equal Employment Opportunities.* Springfield, Va: NTIS, Dep. Commerce
62. Chew, W. B., Justice, R. L. 1977. *AAP Modeling for Large Complex Organizations.* Presented at Conf. Affirmative Action Planning. Ithaca, NY: Cornell Univ.
63. Chun, K. T., Cobb, S., French, J. R. P. 1975. *Measures for Psychological Assessment.* Ann Arbor: Inst. Soc. Res.
64. Churchill, N. C., Shank, J. K. 1976. Affirmative action and guilt-edged goals. *Harvard Bus. Rev.* March/April:111–16
65. Civil Rights Act of July 2, 1964, D. L. 88–352, 42 U.S.C., in 64 Ed., effective July 2, 1965, as amended March 24, 1972, D. L. 92–261, 86 Stat 103, Equal Employment Opportunities Act of 1972
66. Civil Service Commission, Equal Employment Opportunity Commission, Department of Justice and Department of Labor. 1977. Uniform Guidelines on Employee Selection Procedures (Proposed Rulemaking). *Fed. Regist.* 42:65542–52
67. Clark, K. B., Plotkin, L. 1963. *The Negro Student at Integrated Colleges.* New York: Natl. Scholarship Serv. and Fund for Negro Students
68. Cleary, T. A. 1968. Test bias: Prediction of grades of Negro and white students in integrated colleges. *J. Educ. Meas.* 5: 115–24
69. Cleff, S. H. 1977. The Cleff Job Matching System: Introduction and review

of developments. In *Personalfuhring, Band VI: Personalinformationssysteme,* ed. G. Reber. Wiesbaden: Gabler Verlag

70. Cleff, S. H., Hect, R. M. 1971. Job/man matching in the 70's. *Datamation,* February

71. Cohen, S. L., Bunker, K. A. 1975. Subtle effects of sex role stereotype on recruiters' hiring decisions. *J. Appl. Psychol.* 60:566–72

72. Cole, N. S. 1973. Bias in selection. *J. Educ. Meas.* 10:237–55

73. Constantin, S. W. 1976. An investigation of information favorability in the employment interview. *J. Appl. Psychol.* 61:743–49

74. Cook, T. D., Campbell, D. T. 1976. The design and conduct of quasi-experiments and true experiments in field settings. See Ref. 105, pp. 223–327

75. Cronbach, L. J. 1976. Equity in selection—where psychometrics and political philosophy meet. *J. Educ. Meas.* 13:31–42

76. Cronbach, L. J., Gleser, G. 1957. *Psychological Tests and Personnel Decisions.* Urbana: Univ. Illinois Press. 1st ed.

77. Cronbach, L. J., Gleser, G. 1965. *Psychological Tests and Personnel Decisions.* Urbana: Univ. Illinois Press. 2nd. ed.

78. Crooks, L. A., ed. 1972. *An Investigation of Sources of Bias in the Prediction of Job Performance: A Six Year Study.* Proc. Inv. Conf. Princeton, NJ: Educ. Test. Serv.

79. Darlington, R. B. 1968. Multiple regression in psychological research and practice. *Psychol. Bull.* 69:161–81

79a. Darlington, R. B. 1971. Another look at "culture fairness." *J. Educ. Meas.* 8:71–82

80. Darlington, R. B. 1976. Defense of "rational" personnel selection and two new methods. *J. Educ. Meas.* 13:43–52

81. Dawes, R. M., Corrigan, B. 1974. Linear models in decision making. *Psychol. Bull.* 81:95–106

82. Deaux, K., Emswiller, T. 1974. Explanations of successful performance on sex-linked tasks: What is skill for the male is luck for the female. *J. Pers. Soc. Psychol.* 29:80–85

83. DeCotiis, T. A. 1977. An analysis of the external validity and applied relevance of three rating formats. *Organ. Behav. Hum. Perform.* 19:247–66

84. Delbecq, A. L., Van de Ven, A. H., Gustafson, D. H. 1975. *Group Techniques for Program Planning: A Guide to Nominal Group and Delphi Processes.* New York: Scott Foresman

85. DeNelsky, G. Y., McKee, M. G. 1974. Prediction of computer programmer training and job performance using the AABP test. *Personnel Psychol.* 27: 129–37

86. Dickinson, T. L., Tice, T. E. 1973. A multitrait-multimethod analysis of scales developed by retranslation. *Organ. Behav. Hum. Perform.* 9:421–38

87. Dickinson, T. L., Tice, T. E. 1977. The discriminant validity of scales developed by retranslation. *Personnel Psychol.* 30:217–28

88. Dipboye, R. L., Arvey, R. D., Terpstra, D. E. 1977. Sex and physical attractiveness of raters and applicants as determinants of resume evaluations. *J. Appl. Psychol.* 62:288–94

89. Dipboye, R. L., Wiback, K., Fromkin, H. L. 1975. Relative importance of applicant sex, attractiveness, and scholastic standing in evaluation of job applicant resumes. *J. Appl. Psychol.* 60:39–43

90. Division of Industrial/Organizational Psychology. 1975. *Principles for the Validation and Use of Personnel Selection Procedures.* Hamilton, Ohio: Hamilton Print. Co.

91. Dowell, B. E., DeNisi, A. S. 1978. Validity of incumbent and expert estimates of job ability requirements. *J. Appl. Psychol.* In press

92. Downey, R. G., Medland, F. F., Yates, L. G. 1976. Evaluation of a peer rating system for predicting subsequent promotion of senior military officers. *J. Appl. Psychol.* 61:206–9

93. Doyle, K. O. 1974. Theory and practice of ability testing in ancient Greece. *J. Hist. Behav. Sci.* 10:202–12

94. DuBois, P. H. 1965. A test-dominated society: China, 1115 B.C.–1905 A.D. *Proc. 1964 Invitational Conf. Test. Probl.* Princeton, NJ: Educ. Test. Serv.

95. Dunnette, M. D. 1962. Personnel management. *Ann. Rev. Psychol.* 13:285–314

96. Dunnette, M. D. 1963. A modified model for test validation and selection research. *J. Appl. Psychol.* 47:317–23

97. Dunnette, M. D. 1963. A note on *the* criterion. *J. Appl. Psychol.* 47:251–54

98. Dunnette, M. D. 1966. *Personnel Selection and Placement.* Belmont, Calif: Wadsworth. 239 pp.

99. Dunnette, M. D. 1971. Multiple assessment procedures in identifying and developing managerial talent. In *Advances in Psychological Assessment,* ed. P. McReynolds, 2:79–108. Palo Alto: Sci. Behav. Books. 395 pp.

100. Dunnette, M. D. 1972. *Strategies for measuring and predicting human work performance.* Presented at Conf. on Use of Psychol. Tests in Employment. Rochester, NY: Univ. Rochester

101. Dunnette, M. D. 1972. *Validity Study Results for Jobs Relevant to the Petroleum Refining Industry.* Washington DC: Am. Petroleum Inst. 51 pp.

102. Dunnette, M. D. 1967. The assessment of managerial talent. In *Measuring Executive Effectiveness,* ed. F. R. Wickert, D. E. McFarland. New York: Appleton-Century-Crofts

103. Dunnette, M. D. 1974. Personnel selection and job placement of disadvantaged and minority persons: Problems, issues, and suggestions. In *Integrating the Organization,* ed. H. L. Fromkin, J. J. Sherwood, 2:55–74. New York: Free Press

104. Dunnette, M. D. 1976. Aptitudes, abilities, and skills. See Ref. 105, pp. 473–520

105. Dunnette, M. D., ed. 1976. *Handbook of Industrial and Organizational Psychology.* Chicago: Rand McNally. 1740 pp.

106. Dunnette, M. D. 1977. *Task and Job Taxonomies as a Basis for Evaluating Employment Qualifications.* Presented at Conf. on Affirmative Action Planning Concepts, Cornell Univ., Ithaca, NY

107. Dunnette, M. D., Motowidlo, S. J. 1975. *Development of a Personnel Selection and Career Assessment System for Police Officers for Patrol, Investigative, Supervisory, and Command Positions.* Minneapolis: Personnel Decisions, Inc.

108. Edwards, R. C. 1977. Personality traits and "success" in schooling and work. *Educ. Psychol. Meas.* 37:125–38

109. Einhorn, H. J., Bass, A. R. 1971. Methodological considerations relevant to discrimination in employment testing. *Psychol. Bull.* 75:261–69

110. Equal Employment Opportunity Commission. 1970. Guidelines on employee selection procedures. *Fed. Regist.* 35: 12333–36

111. Equal Employment Opportunity Commission. 1966. *Guidelines on Employment Testing Procedures.* Washington: Equal Employment Opportunity Commission

112. Erwin, F. W., Herring, J. W. 1977. The feasibility of the use of autobiographical information as a predictor of early Army attrition. US Army Res. Inst. Tech. Rep. TR-77-A6

113. Farr, J. L., O'Leary, B. S., Bartlett, C. J. 1971. Ethnic group membership as a moderator of job performance. *Personnel Psychol.* 24:609–36

114. Fine, S. A., Wiley, W. A. 1970. *An Introduction to Functional Job Analysis.* Kalamazoo, Mich: Upjohn Inst. Employment Res.

115. Finkle, R. B. 1976. Managerial assessment centers. See Ref. 105, pp. 861–88

116. Finley, D. M., Osburn, H. G., Dubin, J. A., Jeanneret, P. R. 1977. Behaviorally based rating scales: Effects of specific anchors and disguised scale continua. *Personnel Psychol.* 30:659–69

117. Flanagan, J. C. 1954. The critical incident technique. *Psychol. Bull.* 51: 327–58

118. Flast, R. H. 1977. Taking the guesswork out of affirmative action planning. *Personnel J.* 56:68–71

119. Frank, L. L., Hackman, J. R. 1975. Effects of interviewer-interviewee similarity on interviewer objectivity in college admissions interviews. *J. Appl. Psychol.* 60:356–60

120. Freyd, M. 1923. Measurement in vocational selection: An outline of research procedure. *J. Personnel Res.* 2:215–49, 268–84, 377–85

121. Friedman, B. A., Cornelius, E. T. III. 1976. Effect of rater participation in scale construction on the psychometric characteristics of two rating scale formats. *J. Appl. Psychol.* 61:210–16

122. Gastwirth, J. L., Haber, S. E. 1976. Defining the labor market for equal employment standards. *Mon. Labor Rev.* 99:32–36

123. Ghiselli, E. E. 1956. Differentiation of individuals in terms of their predictability. *J. Appl. Psychol.* 40:374–77

124. Ghiselli, E. E. 1956. Dimensional problems of criteria. *J. Appl. Psychol.* 40:1–4

125. Ghiselli, E. E. 1963. Moderating effects and differential reliability and validity. *J. Appl. Psychol.* 47:81–86

126. Ghiselli, E. E. 1966. *The Validity of Occupational Aptitude Tests.* New York: Wiley

127. Glazer, N. 1975. *Affirmative Discrimination: Ethnic Inequality and Public Policy.* New York: Basic Books. 248 pp.

128. Golding, S. L., Seidman, E. 1974. Analysis of multitrait-multimethod matrices: A two-step principal components procedure. *Multivar. Behav. Res.* 9:479–96

128a. Gordon, M. E., Kleiman, L. S. 1976. The prediction of trainability using a work sample test and an aptitude test: A direct comparison. *Personnel Psychol.* 29:243–53

129. Gough, H. 1976. Personality and personality assessment. See Ref. 105, pp. 571–607

130. Green, R. L., Farquhar, J. 1965. Negro academic motivation and scholastic achievement. *J. Educ. Psychol.* 56: 241–43

131. Grey, R. J., Kipnis, D. 1976. Untangling the performance appraisal dilemma: The influence of perceived organizational context on evaluative processes. *J. Appl. Psychol.* 61:329–35

132. *Griggs vs. Duke Power Company.* 1971. 401 U.S. 424

133. Groner, D. M. 1974. *Reliability and Susceptibility to Bias of Behavioral and Graphic Rating Scales.* PhD thesis. Univ. Minnesota, Minneapolis, Minn.

134. Gross, A. L., Faggen-Steckler, J., McCarthy, K. 1974. Statistical procedures for evaluating the practical utility of a moderator approach to prediction. *J. Appl. Psychol.* 59:578–82

135. Gross, A. L., Su, W. 1975. Defining a "fair" or "unbiased" selection model: A question of utilities. *J. Appl. Psychol.* 60:345–51

136. Gross, B. R. 1977. *Reverse Discrimination.* Buffalo, NY: Prometheus

137. Guion, R. M. 1961. Criterion measurement and personnel judgments. *Personnel Psychol.* 14:141–49

138. Guion, R. M. 1965. *Personnel Testing.* New York: McGraw-Hill

139. Guion, R. M. 1974. Open a new window: Validities and values in psychological measurement. *Am. Psychol.* 28: 287–96

140. Guion, R. M., ed. 1975. *Content Validity II: Proceedings of Conference on Content Validity in Employee Selection Procedures.* Psychol. Dep., Bowling Green State Univ., Bowling Green, Ohio. 110 pp.

141. Guion, R. M. 1976. Recruiting, selection and job placement. See Ref. 105, pp. 777–828

142. Guion, R. M. 1977. *Content Validity: A Term in Search of a Meaning.* Presented at Content Validity 11.5, Personnel Test. Counc. Conf., Newport Beach, Calif.

143. Guion, R. M. 1977. *"Content Validity" —In Moderation.* Presented at Selection Res. Conf., Univ. Maryland, College Park, Md.

144. Guion, R. M. 1977. Content Validity— the source of my discontent. *Appl. Psychol. Meas.* 1:1–10

145. Guion, R. M. 1977. *Content Validity: Three Years of Talk—What's the Action?* Presented at Int. Personnel Manage. Assoc. Assess. Counc., Kansas City, Mo.

146. Guion, R. M. 1978. Scoring of content domain samples: The problem of fairness. *J. Appl. Psychol.* In press

147. Gunderson, E. K. E., Nelson, P. D. 1966. Criterion measures for extremely isolated groups. *Personnel Psychol.* 19:67–82

148. Haefner, J. E. 1977. Race, age, sex, and competence as factors in employer selection of the disadvantaged. *J. Appl. Psychol.* 62:199–202

149. Hakel, M. D., Dunnette, M. D. 1970. *Checklists for Describing Job Applicants.* Minneapolis: Univ. Minnesota

150. Hamner, W. C., Kim, J. S., Baird, L., Bigoness, W. J. 1974. Race and sex as determinants of ratings by potential employers in a simulated work-sampling task. *J. Appl. Psychol.* 59:705–11

151. Hellervik, L. W., Hunt, A., Silzer, R. F. 1976. *An Assessment Center for Selecting Account Executives.* Minneapolis, Minn: Personnel Decisions, Inc.

152. Helme, W. H., Willemin, L. P., Grafton, F. C. 1974. *Prediction of Office Behavior in a Simulated Combat Situation.* Res. Rep. 1182 AD-779445. Alexandria, Va: US Army Res. Inst.

153. Heneman, H. G. 1974. Comparisons of self and superior ratings of managerial performance. *J. Appl. Psychol.* 59: 638–42

154. Heneman, H. G. 1977. Impact of test information and applicant sex on applicant evaluations in a selection simulation. *J. Appl. Psychol.* 62:524–26

155. Heneman, H. G., Schwab, D. P., Huett, D. L., Ford, J. J. 1975. Interviewer validity as a function of interview structure, biographical data, and interviewee order. *J. Appl. Psychol.* 60:748–53

156. Hillery, J. M., Fugita, S. S. 1975. Group size effects in employment testing. *Educ. Psychol. Meas.* 35:745–50

157. Hinrichs, J. R., Haanpera, S. 1976. Reliability of measurement in situational exercises: An assessment of the assessment center method. *Personnel Psychol.* 29:31–40

158. Hinrichs, J. R., Haanpera, S., Sonkin, L. 1976. Validity of a biographical information blank across national boundaries. *Personnel Psychol.* 29:417–21

159. Hogan, R., DeSoto, C. B., Solano, C. 1977. Traits, tests, and personality research. *Am. Psychol.* 32:255–64

160. Holland, J. L. 1976. Vocational preferences. See Ref. 105, pp. 521–70
161. Hollmann, T. D. 1972. Employment interviewers' errors in processing positive and negative information. *J. Appl. Psychol.* 56:130–34
162. Howell, W. C. 1976. *Essentials of Industrial and Organizational Psychology.* Homewood, Ill: Dorsey. 275 pp.
163. Huck, J. R. 1973. Assessment centers: A review of the external and internal validities. *Personnel Psychol.* 26:191–212
164. Huck, J. R., Bray, D. W. 1976. Management assessment center evaluations and subsequent job performance of white and black females. *Personnel Psychol.* 29:13–30
165. Hull, C. L. 1928. *Aptitude Testing.* Yonkers, NY: World Book. 535 pp.
166. Humphreys, L. G. 1973. Statistical definitions of test validity for minority groups. *J. Appl. Psychol.* 58:1–4
167. Hunter, J. E., Schmidt, F. L. 1976. Critical analysis of the statistical and ethical implications of various definitions of test bias. *Psychol. Bull.* 83:1053–71
168. Hunter, J. E., Schmidt, F. L. 1978. Differential and single-group validity of employment tests by race: A critical analysis of three recent studies. *J. Appl. Psychol.* 63:1–11
169. Hunter, J. E., Schmidt, F. L. 1978. Implications of job assignment strategies for national productivity. In *Human Performance and Productivity,* ed. E. A. Fleishman. In press
170. Hunter, J. E., Schmidt, F. L., Rauschenberger, J. M. 1977. Fairness of psychological tests: Implications of four definitions for selection utility and minority hiring. *J. Appl. Psychol.* 62:245–60
171. Hutchinson, M. F. 1974. *Functional Job Analysis: How To Standardize Task Statements.* Kalamazoo, Mich: Upjohn Inst.
172. Jackson, D. N. 1975. Multimethod factor analysis: a reformulation. *Multivar. Behav. Res.* 10:259–75
173. James, L. R. 1973. Criterion models and construct validity for criteria. *Psychol. Bull.* 80:75–83
174. Janz, J. T. 1976. *Multivariate prediction for employment selection programs: Monte Carlo comparisons of configural and combinatorial techniques.* PhD thesis. Univ. Minnesota, Minneapolis Minn. 154 pp.
175. Janz, J. T., Dunnette, M. D. 1977. An approach to selection decisions: Dollars and sense. In *Perspectives on Behavior in*

Organizations, ed. J. R. Hackman, E. E. Lawler, L. P. Porter, pp. 119–26. New York: McGraw-Hill. 486 pp.
176. Johns, G. 1975. Effects of informational order and frequency of applicant evaluation upon linear information-processing competence of interviewers. *J. Appl. Psychol.* 60:427–33
177. Joint Committee of APA, AERA, NCME. 1954. Technical recommendations for psychological tests and diagnostic techniques. *Psychol. Bull.* 51:201–38
178. Jones, D. P. 1974. *An Examination of Six Fair Selection Models.* Unpublished MA thesis. Bowling Green State Univ. Bowling Green, Ohio
179. Kalleberg, A. L., Kleugel, J. R. 1975. Analysis of the multitrait-multimethod matrix: Some limitations and an alternative. *J. Appl. Psychol.* 60:1–9
180. Katzell, R. A., Dyer, F. J. 1977. Differential validity revived. *J. Appl. Psychol.* 62:137–45
180a. Katzell, R. A., Dyer, F. J. 1978. On differential validity and bias. *J. Appl. Psychol.* 63:19–21
181. Kaufman, G. G., Johnson, J. C. 1974. Scaling peer ratings: An examination of the differential validities of positive and negative nominations. *J. Appl. Psychol.* 59:302–06
182. Kavanagh, M. J., MacKinney, A. C., Wolins, L. 1971. Issues in managerial performances: Multitrait-multimethod analyses of ratings. *Psychol. Bull.* 75:34–49
183. Keaveny, T. J., McGann, A. F. 1975. A comparison of behavioral expectation scales. *J. Appl. Psychol.* 60:695–703
184. Kelley, H. H. 1967. Attribution theory in social psychology. In *Nebraska Symposium on Motivation,* Vol. 15, ed. D. Levine. Lincoln: Univ. Nebraska Press
185. Kelly, G. A. 1955. *The Psychology of Personal Constructs.* New York: Norton
186. Kirkpatrick, J. J., Ewen, R. B., Barrett, R. S., Katzell, R. A. 1968. *Testing and Fair Employment.* New York: New York Univ. Press
187. Klimoski, R. J., London, M. 1974. Role of the rater in performance appraisal. *J. Appl. Psychol.* 59:445–51
188. Klimoski, R. J., Strickland, W. J. 1977. Assessment centers—valid or merely prescient. *Personnel Psychol.* 30:353–61
189. Kornhauser, A. W., Kingsbury, F. A. 1924. *Psychological Tests in Business.* Chicago: Univ. Chicago Press
190. Kraut, A. I. 1975. Prediction of mana-

gerial success by peer and training staff ratings. *J. Appl. Psychol.* 60:14–19

191. Kraut, A. I. 1976. New frontiers for assessment centers. *Personnel* 53:30–38

192. Krefting, L. A., Brief, A. P. 1976. The impact of applicant disability of evaluative judgments in the selection process. *Acad. Manage. J.* 19:675–80

193. Kuder, F. 1977. Career matching. *Personnel Psychol.* 30:1–4

194. Landy, F. J. 1976. The validity of the interview in police officer selection. *J. Appl. Psychol.* 61:193–98

195. Landy, F. J., Trumbo, D. A. 1976. *Psychology of Work Behavior.* Homewood, Ill: Dorsey. 582 pp.

196. Latham, G. P., Wexley, K. N. 1977. Behavioral observation scales for performance appraisal purposes. *Personnel Psychol.* 30:255–68

197. Latham, G. P., Wexley, K. N., Pursell, E. D. 1975. Training managers to minimize rating errors in the observation of behavior. *J. Appl. Psychol.* 60:550–55

198. Latham, G. P., Wexley, K. N., Rand, T. M. 1975. The relevance of behavioral criteria developed from the critical incident technique. *Can. J. Behav. Sci.* 7:349–58

199. Lawler, E. E. III. 1967. The multitrait-multirater approach to measuring managerial job performance. *J. Appl. Psychol.* 51:369–81

200. Lawshe, C. H. 1975. A quantitative approach to content validity. *Personnel Psychol.* 28:563–75

201. Ledvinka, J. L. 1975. Technical implications of equal employment law for manpower planning. *Personnel Psychol.* 28:299–323

202. Lee, R., Booth, J. M. 1974. A utility analysis of a weighted application blank designed to predict turnover for clerical employees. *J. Appl. Psychol.* 59:516–18

203. Lefkowitz, J. 1977. Industrial-organizational psychology and the police. *Am. Psychol.* 32:346–64

204. Lewin, A. Y., Zwany, A. 1976. Peer nominations: A model, literature critique, and a paradigm for research. *Personnel Psychol.* 29:423–47

205. Linn, R. L. 1973. Fair test use in selection. *Rev. Educ. Res.* 43:139–61

206. Linn, R. L. 1976. In search of fair selection procedures. *J. Educ. Meas.* 13:53–58

207. London, M., Hakel, M. D. 1974. Effects of applicant stereotypes, order, and information on interview impressions. *J. Appl. Psychol.* 59:157–62

208. Lopez, F. M. 1966. Current problems in test performance. I. *Personnel Psychol.* 19:10–18

209. Lord, F. M. 1950. *Efficiency of Prediction when a Regression Equation from One Sample is Used in a New Sample.* ETS Res. Bull. 50–40. Princeton, NJ: Educ. Test. Serv.

209a. MacKinnon, D. W. *A Study to Devise Methods for Assessing Air Force Officers for Command and Staff Leadership.* Berkeley, Calif: Inst. Pers. Assess. Res., Univ. California. (Unpublished report, 1957)

210. Marshall, R. F., Carter, A. M., King, A. G. 1976. *Labor and Economics, Wages, Employment and Trade Unionism.* Homewood, Ill: Irwin, 3rd ed.

211. McCormick, E. J. 1974. Job information: Its development and applications. In *ASPA Handbook of Personnel and Industrial Relations,* ed. D. Yoder, H. G. Heneman, 1(4.2):35–83. Washington: Bur. Natl. Affairs. 297 pp.

212. McCormick, E. J. 1976. Job and task analysis. See Ref. 105, pp. 651–96

213. McCormick, E. J., Ammerman, H. L. 1960. *Development of Worker Activity Check Lists for Use in Occupational Analysis.* WADD-TR-60–77. Lackland AFB, Texas: Personnel Lab., Wright Air Dev. Div.

214. McCormick, E. J., DeNisi, A. S., Shaw, J. B. 1977. *Job-derived Selection: Follow-up Report.* West Lafayette, Ind: Dep. Psychol. Sci., Purdue Univ. 53 pp.

215. McCormick, E. J., DeNisi, A. S., Shaw, J. B. 1977. *The Use of the Position Analysis Questionnaire (PAQ) for Establishing Job Component Validity of Tests.* West Lafayette, Ind: Dep. Psychol. Sci., Purdue Univ. 16 pp.

216. McCormick, E. J., Finn, R. H., Scheips, C. D. 1957. Patterns of job requirements. *J. Appl. Psychol.* 41:358–64

217. McGuiness, K. C. 1976. *Government memoranda on affirmative action programs.* Presented at Meet. Equal Employment Advisory Council, Washington DC

218. Meehl, P. E. 1954. *Clinical Versus Statistical Prediction: A Theoretical Analysis and a Review of the Evidence.* Minneapolis: Univ. Minnesota Press

219. Milkovich, G. T. 1976. *A few overlooked research issues on the way to equal opportunity.* Presented at Ann. Meet. Acad. Manage., 36th, Kansas City, Mo.

220. Milkovich, G. T. 1978. An analysis of issues related to availability. In *Perspectives on Availability: A Symposium on Determining Protected Group Representation in Internal and External Labor*

Markets, ed. Equal Employment Advisory Council, Washington D.C. In press

221. Milkovich, G. T., Krzystofiak, F. 1977. *Human resources planning models and affirmative action planning.* Presented at Conf. Affirmative Action Planning, Cornell Univ., Ithaca, NY

222. Milkovich, G. T., Mahoney, T. A. 1976. Human resources planning and personnel and industrial relations policy. In *Handbook of Personnel and Industrial Relations*, ed. D. Yoder, H. Heneman, 4(2.1):1–29. Washington DC: Bur. Natl. Affairs. 198 pp.

223. Mischel, W. 1973. Toward a cognitive social learning reconceptualization of personality. *Psychol. Rev.* 80:252–83

224. Mischel, W. 1977. On the future of personality measurement. *Am. Psychol.* 32:246–54

225. Mitchel, J. O. 1975. Assessment center validity: A longitudinal study. *J. Appl. Psychol.* 60:573–79

226. Moses, J. L., Boehm, V. R. 1975. Relationship of assessment center performance to management progress of women. *J. Appl. Psychol.* 60:527–29

227. Mosier, C. I. 1951. Problems and designs of cross validation. *Educ. Psychol. Meas.* 11:5–11

228. Mount, M. K., Muchinsky, P. M., Hanser, L. M. 1977. The predictive validity of a work sample: A laboratory study. *Personnel Psychol.* 30:637–45

229. Muchinsky, P. M., Harris, S. L. 1977. The effect of applicant sex and scholastic standing on the evaluation of job applicant's resume in sex-typed occupations. *J. Vocat. Behav.* 11:95–108

230. Nealey, S. M., Owen, T. W. 1970. A multitrait-multimethod analysis of predictors and criteria of nursing performance. *Organ. Behav. Hum. Perform.* 5:348–65

231. Nevo, B. 1976. Using biographical information to predict success of men and women in the Army. *J. Appl. Psychol.* 61:106–8

232. Newell, A., Shaw, J. C., Simon, H. A. 1972. *Human Problem Solving.* Englewood Cliffs, NJ: Prentice-Hall

233. Nicholson, G. E. 1960. Prediction in future samples. In *Contributions to Probability and Statistics*, ed. I. Olkin, et al. Stanford, Calif: Stanford Univ. Press

234. Nisbett, R. E., Bellows, N. 1977. Verbal reports about casual influences on social judgments: Private access versus public theories. *J. Pers. Soc. Psychol.* 35:613–24

235. Novick, M. R., Ellis, D. D. 1977. Equal opportunity in educational and employment selection. *Am. Psychol.* 32:306–20

236. Novick, M. R., Petersen, N. S. 1976. Towards equalizing educational and employment opportunity. *J. Educ. Meas.* 13:77–88

237. O'Connor, E. J., Wexley, K. N., Alexander, R. A. 1975. Single group validity: Fact or fallacy? *J. Appl. Psychol.* 60:352–55

238. Office of Federal Contract Compliance. 1968. Validation of employment tests by contractors and subcontractors subject to the provisions of executive order 11246. *Fed. Regist.* 39:2094–96

239. Owens, W. A. 1976. Background data. See Ref. 105, pp. 609–44

240. Pace, L. A., Schoenfeldt, L. F. 1977. Legal concerns in the use of weighted applications. *Personnel Psychol.* 30:159–66

241. Paterson, D. G. 1957. The conservation of human talent. *Am. Psychol.* 12:134–44

242. Paterson, D. G., Darley, J. G. 1936. *Men, Women, and Jobs: A Study in Human Engineering.* Minneapolis: Univ. Minnesota Press. 145 pp.

243. Peters, L. H., Terborg, J. R. 1975. The effects of temporal placement of unfavorable information and of attitude similarity on personnel selection decisions. *Organ. Behav. Hum. Perform.* 13:279–93

244. Petersen, N. S., Novick, M. R. 1976. An evaluation of some models for culture-fair selection. *J. Educ. Meas.* 13:3–29

245. Prien, E. P. 1977. The function of job analysis in content validation. *Personnel Psychol.* 30:167–74

246. Primoff, E. S. 1955. *Test Selection by Job Analysis: The J-Coefficient.* Washington DC: US Civil Serv. Comm.

247. Primoff, E. S. 1972. *Using a Job Element Study for Developing Tests.* Washington DC: US Civil Serv. Comm.

248. Primoff, E. S. 1973. *How to Prepare and Conduct Job Element Examinations.* Washington DC: US Civil Serv. Comm.

249. Pritchard, D. A. 1977. Linear versus configural statistical prediction. *J. Consult. Clin. Psychol.* 45:559–63

250. Rand, T. M., Wexley, K. N. 1975. A demonstration of the Byrne similarity hypothesis in simulated employment interviews. *Psychol. Rep.* 36:535–44

251. Reilly, R. R. 1973. A note on minority group test bias studies. *Psychol. Bull.* 80:130–32

252. Reynolds, L. G. 1975. *Labor Economics and Labor Relations.* Englewood Cliffs, NJ: Prentice Hall. 5th ed.

253. Romashko, T., Hahn, C. P., Brumback, G. B. 1976. *The Prototype Development of Job Related Physical Testing for Philadelphia Policeman Selection.* Washington DC: Am. Inst. Res.

254. Ronan, W. W., Latham, G. P. 1974. The reliability and validity of the critical incident technique: a closer look. *Stud. Personnel Psychol.* 6:53–64

255. Rorer, L. G. 1971. A circuitous route to bootstrapping selection procedures. In *Personality Measurement in Medical Education,* ed. H. B. Haley, A. G. D'Costa, A. M. Schafer. Des Plaines, Ill: Assoc. Am. Med. Coll.

256. Rosen, B., Jerdee, L. H. 1974. Effects of applicant's sex and difficulty of job on evaluations of candidates for managerial positions. *J. Appl. Psychol.* 59: 511–12

257. Rosenblum, M. 1977. *The external measures of labor supply: Recent issues and trends.* Presented at Conf. Affirmative Action Planning, Cornell Univ. Ithaca, NY

258. Rosenblum, M. 1977. The use of labor statistics and analysis in Title VII cases: Rios, Chicago, and beyond. *Ind. Relat. Law J.* 1:685–710

259. Rosse, R. L. 1974. *Estimation of Cross-Validity Through Monte Carlo Sample Splitting: A General Approach.* Minneapolis, Minn: Personnel Decisions Res. Inst.

260. Ruda, E., Albright, L. E. 1968. Racial differences on selection instruments related to subsequent job performance. *Personnel Psychol.* 21:31–41

261. Saal, F. E., Landy, F. J. 1977. The mixed standard rating scale: An evaluation. *Organ. Behav. Hum. Perform.* 18:19–35

262. Sands, W. A. 1978. Enlisted personnel selection for the U. S. Navy. *Personnel Psychol.* 31:63–70

263. Schmidt, F. L., Berner, J. G., Hunter, J. E. 1973. Racial differences in validity of employment tests: Reality or illusion? *J. Appl. Psychol.* 58:5–9

264. Schmidt, F. L., Greenthal, A. L., Hunter, J. E., Berner, J. G., Seaton, F. W. 1977. Job samples versus paper and pencil trades and technical tests: Adverse impact and examinee attitudes. *Personnel Psychol.* 30:187–97

265. Schmidt, F. L., Hoffman, B. 1973. Empirical comparison of three methods of assessing utility of a selection device. *J. Ind. Organ. Psychol.* 1:13–22

266. Schmidt, F. L., Hunter, J. E. 1974. Racial and ethnic bias in psychological tests: Divergent implications of two

definitions of test bias. *Am. Psychol.* 28:1–8

267. Schmidt, F. L., Hunter, J. E. 1977. Development of a general solution to the problem of validity generalization. *J. Appl. Psychol.* 62:529–40

268. Schmidt, F. L., Hunter, J. E., Urry, V. W. 1976. Statistical power in criterion-related validity studies. *J. Appl. Psychol.* 61:473–85

269. Schmidt, F. L., Kaplan, L. B. 1971. Composite versus multiple criteria: A review and resolution of the controversy. *Personnel Psychol.* 24:419–34

270. Schmitt, N. 1976. Social and situational determinants of interview decisions: Implications for the employment interview. *Personnel Psychol.* 29:79–101

271. Schmitt, N. 1977. Interrater agreement in dimensionality and combination of assessment center judgments. *J. Appl. Psychol.* 62:171–76

272. Schmitt, N., Coyle, B. W. 1976. Applicant decisions in the employment interview. *J. Appl. Psychol.* 61:184–92

273. Schmitt, N., Coyle, B. W., Rauschenberger, J. 1977. A Monte Carlo evaluation of three formula estimates of cross-validated multiple correlation. *Psychol. Bull.* 84:751–58

274. Schmitt, N., Coyle, B. W., Saari, B. B. 1977. A review and critique of analyses of multitrait-multimethod matrices. *Multivar. Behav. Res.* 12:447–64

275. Schmitt, N., Hill, T. E. 1977. Sex and race composition of assessment center groups as a determinant of peer and assessor ratings. *J. Appl. Psychol.* 62:261–64

276. Schneider, B. 1976. *Staffing Organizations.* Pacific Palisades, Calif: Goodyear. 257 pp.

277. Schneider, D. J. 1973. Implicit Personality Theory: A review. *Psychol. Bull.* 79:294–309

278. Schneier, C. E. 1977. Operational utility and psychometric characteristics of behavioral expectation scales: A cognitive reinterpretation. *J. Appl. Psychol.* 62: 541–48

279. Schneier, C. E. 1978. *Measuring Human Performance in Organizations: An Empirical Comparison of the Psychometric Properties of Two Types of Criteria Content.* Proc. Nat. Meet. Acad. Manage., San Francisco

280. Schoenfeldt, L. F. 1974. Utilization of manpower: Development and evaluation of an assessment-classification model for matching individuals with jobs. *J. Appl. Psychol.* 59:583–95

281. Schrader, A. D., Osburn, H. G. 1977. Biodata faking: Effects of induced subtlety and position specificity. *Personnel Psychol.* 30:395–404

282. Schwab, D. P., Heneman, H. G., DeCotiis, T. A. 1975. Behaviorally anchored rating scales: A review of the literature. *Personnel Psychol.* 28:549–62

283. Schwab, D. P., Oliver, R. L. 1974. Predicting tenure with biographical data: Exhuming buried evidence. *Personnel Psychol.* 27:125–28

284. Schwartz, D. J. 1977. A job sampling approach to merit system examining. *Personnel Psychol.* 30:175–85

285. Scott, W. E., Hamner, W. C. 1975. The influence of variations in performance profiles on the performance evaluation process: An examination of the validity of the criterion. *Organ. Behav. Hum. Perform.* 14:360–70

286. Shaw, J. B., DeNisi, A. S., McCormick, E. J. 1977. *Cluster Analysis of Jobs Based on a Revised Set of Job Dimensions from the Position Analysis Questionnaire (PAQ).* Report 3. Lafayette, Ind: Dep. Psychol. Sci., Purdue Univ

287. Shaw, J. B., McCormick, E. J. 1976. *The Prediction of Job Ability Requirements Using Attribute Data Based Upon the Position Analysis Questionnaire (PAQ).* Report 1. Lafayette, Ind: Dep. Psychol. Sci., Purdue Univ.

288. Shweder, R. A. 1975. How relevant is an individual difference theory of personality? *J. Pers.* 43:455–84

289. Silzer, R. F. 1978. *Competency assessment: Use of performance rating scales and assessment centers.* Presented at Ann. Conv. APA, Toronto, Ontario, Canada

290. Smith, P. C. 1976. Behaviors, results, and organizational effectiveness: The problem of criteria. See Ref. 105, pp. 745–75

291. Smith, P. C., Kendall, L. M. 1963. Retranslation of expectations: An approach to the construction of unambiguous anchors for rating scales. *J. Appl. Psychol.* 47:149–55

292. Springbett, B. M. 1958. Factors affecting the final decision in the employment interview. *Can. J. Psychol.* 12:13–22

293. Stagner, R. 1973. *Traits are relevant—Logical and empirical analysis.* Presented at Ann. Conv. APA, Montreal, Quebec, Canada

294. Stanley, J. C. 1971. Predicting college success of the educationally disadvantaged. *Science* 171:640–47

295. Stein, C. 1960. Multiple regression. See Ref. 233, p. 24

296. Super, D. E. 1978. From information retrieval through matching to counseling and to career development: Some lessons from the U.S.A. *J. Occup. Psychol.* 51:19–28

297. Tagiuri, R. 1969. Person perception. In *Handbook of Social Psychology,* ed. G. Lindzey, E. Aronson, Vol. 3. Reading, Mass: Addison-Wesley. 2nd ed.

298. Taylor, L. R., Herring, J., Schmidt, F. L., Dawson, R., Dunnette, M. D., Ofsanko, F. J., Sparks, C. P. 1978. *Industry-wide approaches to the study of validity generalizations.* Symp. presented at Ann. Conf. APA, Toronto, Ontario, Canada

299. Taylor, R. C., Russell, J. T. 1939. The relationship of validity coefficients to the practical effectiveness of tests in selection. *J. Appl. Psychol.* 23:565–78

300. Tenopyr, M. L. 1977. Content-construct confusion. *Personnel Psychol.* 30:47–54

301. Terborg, J. R., Ilgen, D. R. 1975. A theoretical approach to sex discrimination in traditionally masculine occupations. *Organ. Behav. Hum. Perform.* 13:352–76

302. Thayer, P. W. 1977. Somethings old, somethings new. *Personnel Psychol.* 30:513–24

303. Thorndike, R. L. 1949. *Personnel Selection: Test and Measurement Techniques.* New York: Wiley. 358 pp.

304. Thorndike, R. L. 1950. The problem of classification of personnel. *Psychometrika* 15:215–35

305. Thorndike, R. L. 1971. Concepts of culture-fairness. *J. Educ. Meas.* 8:63–70

306. Tornow, W. W., Pinto, P. R. 1976. The development of a managerial job taxonomy: A system for describing, classifying, and evaluating executive positions. *J. Appl. Psychol.* 61:410–18

307. Tucker, D. H., Rowe, P. M. 1977. Consulting the application form prior to the interview: An essential step in the selection process? *J. Appl. Psychol.* 62:283–87

308. Tuller, W. L., Barrett, G. V. 1976. The future autobiography as a predictor of sales success. *J. Appl. Psychol.* 61:371–73

309. Uhlaner, J. E. 1977. *The Research Psychologist in the Army—1917 to 1977.* Res. Rep. 1155 (rev.). Alexandria, Va: US Army Res. Inst. 87 pp.

310. Veudry, W. F., Campbell, J. C. 1974. Assessment centers—A new look at leadership evaluation. *Army Mag.* March

311. Wallace, S. R. 1965. Criteria for what? *Am. Psychol.* 20:411–17
312. Wallace, S. R. 1974. How high the validity? *Personnel Psychol.* 27:397–407
313. Webster, E. C. 1964. *Decision Making in the Employment Interview.* Montreal: Eagle
314. Weiss, D. J. 1976. Multivariate procedures. See Ref. 105, pp. 327–62
315. Wernimont, P. F., Campbell, J. P. 1968. Signs, samples, and criteria. *J. Appl. Psychol.* 52:372–76
316. Wexley, K. N., Nemeroff, W. F. 1974. Effects of racial prejudice, race of applicant, and biographical similarity on interviewer evaluations of job applicants. *J. Soc. Behav. Sci.* 20:66–78
317. Wherry, R. J. Sr. 1931. A new formula for predicting the shrinkage of the coefficient of multiple correlation. *Ann. Math. Stat.* 2:440–57
318. Wherry, R. J. Sr. 1975. Underprediction from overfitting: 45 years of shrinkage. *Personnel Psychol.* 28:1–18
319. Wiener, Y., Schneiderman, M. L. 1974. Use of job information as a criterion in employment decisions of interviewers. *J. Appl. Psychol.* 59:699–704
320. Worbois, G. M. 1975. Validation of externally developed assessment procedures for identification of supervisory potential. *Personnel Psychol.* 28:77–91
321. Zedeck, S. 1971. Problems with the use of "moderator" variables. *Psychol. Bull.* 76:295–310
322. Zedeck, S., Baker, H. T. 1972. Nursing performance as measured by behavioral expectation scales: A multitrait-multirater analysis. *Organ. Behav. Hum. Perform.* 7:457–66
323. Zedeck, S., Blood, M. 1974. *Foundations of Behavioral Science Research in Organizations.* Monterey, Calif: Brooks/Cole. 200 pp.
324. Zedeck, S., Kafry, D. 1977. Capturing rater policies for processing evaluation data. *Organ. Behav. Hum. Perform.* 18:269–94
325. Zedeck, S., Kafry, D., Jacobs, R. 1976. Format and scoring variations in behavioral expectation evaluations. *Organ. Behav. Hum. Perform.* 17:171–84

Ann. Rev. Psychol. 1979. 30:527–54

FACIAL EXPRESSIONS
OF EMOTION[1]

❖316

Paul Ekman and Harriet Oster

Department of Psychiatry, University of California,
San Francisco, California 94143

CONTENTS

INTRODUCTION 528
CROSS-CULTURAL STUDIES AND THE ISSUE OF UNIVERSALITY 529
  What Has Been Found 529
  Unanswered or Unasked Questions.. 531
DEVELOPMENTAL STUDIES... 532
  What Has Been Found 533
  Unanswered or Unasked Questions.. 535
FACIAL MEASUREMENT.. 537
  Muscle Tonus Measurement 538
  Measurement of Visible Action 538
    Theory-based selection 538
    Inductively based selection 539
    Anatomically based selection... 539
  Other Facial Measures.. 540
ACCURACY 540
  What Has Been Found 542
  Unanswered or Unasked Questions.. 543
FACIAL FEEDBACK 545
NEURAL CONTROL AND ANS CORRELATES OF FACIAL EXPRESSION .. 547
  Psychophysiological Correlates... 547
  Face and Brain 547
FUTURE DIRECTIONS 548

[1]Because literature references are counted as part of the total number of pages allotted for this chapter, *no* attempt was made to cite most of the studies relevant to each topic discussed. Instead the space allotment was used primarily to discuss issues.

0066-4308/79/0201-0527$01.00

INTRODUCTION

Research on facial expressions of emotion has been episodic. The topic flourished from 1920 to 1940, drawing the attention of well-known psychologists: e.g. Allport, Boring, Goodenough, Guilford, Hunt, Klineberg, Landis, Munn, Titchener, Woodworth. Yet the cumulative knowledge was unimpressive. In the opinion of influential reviewers (15, 76, 127), there were no consistent answers to the most fundamental questions about the accuracy of information provided by facial expressions, their universality and possible innateness, etc. During the next 20 years there were comparatively few studies of facial expression, with the exception of Schlosberg's (112–114) reports that categorical judgments of emotion can be ordered in terms of underlying dimensions. A number of recent trends have contributed to the resurgence of interest in facial expression.

Tomkins (128, 129) provided a theoretical rationale for studying the face as a means of learning about personality and emotion. He (130) also showed that observers can obtain very high agreement in judging emotion if the facial expressions are carefully selected to show what he believes are the innate facial affects. Tomkins greatly influenced both Ekman and Izard, helping each of them to plan their initial cross-cultural studies of facial expression. The resulting evidence that there is universality in facial expression rekindled interest in this topic in psychology and anthropology.

The evidence of universals in facial expression not only fits with Tomkins' theory but also with the newly emerging interest in applying ethological methods and concepts to human behavior. Interested in the biological bases of behavior, human ethologists welcomed evidence of commonalities in social behavior across cultures. Human ethologists provided the first detailed "catalogs" describing naturally occurring facial behavior (10, 13, 66, 93). In recent years developmental psychologists investigating attachment, mother-infant interaction, and the development of emotion have also begun to study facial expression.

Interest in facial expression also reflects the current popularity of nonverbal communication. While most of the research done under this rubric has focused on hand and body movement, gaze direction, or posture, some studies have included a few facial measures or have used a judgment approach to assess the face.

A number of recent reviews have covered the literature on facial expression up to 1970. Ekman, Friesen & Ellsworth (52) reanalyzed many of the experiments conducted from 1914 to 1970. They found, contrary to Bruner & Tagiuri's (15) assessment, that the data yielded consistent, positive answers to fundamental questions about the language used to describe facial expression, the influence of context on judgments of facial expression, the accuracy of judgments, and similarities across cultures. For other reviews of facial expression see: (30) on infants and children; (31, 104) on nonhuman primates; (44) on cross-cultural comparisons; (77) on theories of emotion.

We will focus primarily on studies since these reviews. We will discuss four topics we deem of major importance, either because of their long-standing theoretical significance (cross-cultural, developmental, and accuracy studies) or because of recent methodological advances (facial measurement). We will then more briefly consider research on the influence of facial feedback and on the neural correlates of facial expression. Rather than providing exhaustive coverage of each area, we summarize exemplary findings, point out gaps in empirical knowledge, and delineate questions for future study.

CROSS-CULTURAL STUDIES AND THE ISSUE OF UNIVERSALITY

What Has Been Found

1. *Observers label certain facial expressions of emotion in the same way regardless of culture.* A number of studies (reviewed in 44) attempted to show differences across cultures in the way observers judge isolated facial expressions. In fact, their findings were either ambiguous or showed similarity across cultures. More consistent results have been obtained by investigators who used explicit descriptive criteria (based on theory or empirical results) to select photographs of expressions representative of each emotion. These photographs were shown to observers who selected from a list of emotion terms the one that best described each expression. The majority of observers in each culture interpreted the facial expressions as conveying the same emotions [five literate cultures (43, 55); nine literate cultures (77)]. Similar experiments have obtained comparable results in Malaysia (11) and in two states of the Soviet Union (unpublished report by T. Niit and J. Valsiner).

Two studies investigated judgments of the intensity of emotional expression. Both found high agreement among members of literate cultures (44, 108).

In spite of this evidence, it could still be argued that facial expressions of emotion are culturally variable social signals, and that the commonality in judgments is attributable solely to common learning experience. By this interpretation, exposure to the same mass media representations of emotional expression might have taught people in each culture how to label facial expressions. This explanation was disproved by studies of isolated, preliterate cultures not exposed to the mass media: the South Fore in Papua/New Guinea (47) and the Dani in West Iran [Heider & Heider, reported in (44)]. These people chose the same facial expressions for particular emotions as members of literate cultures.

A limitation of these cross-cultural experiments is that the facial expressions presented were not genuine but posed by subjects instructed to show a particular emotion or to move particular facial muscles. One interpreter of this literature (94) suggested that universality in judgments of facial expression might be limited to just such stereotyped, posed expressions. Two experiments argue against this interpretation. Winkelmayer et al (138) chose motion picture samples from interviews with normal and schizophrenic people to see if emotion judgments by members of different cultures would differ when spontaneous rather than posed expressions were shown. There was no overall difference among American, British, and Mexican observers. However, the Mexican observers were less accurate than the others in judging the facial expressions of normal but not schizophrenic subjects. This difference had not been predicted, may have been due to language and/or culture, and has not been replicated. More clear-cut results were obtained in a study by Ekman (43) in which Japanese and American observers judged whether the facial expressions of Japanese and American subjects were elicited by watching a stressful or neutral film. Observers of both cultures were equally accurate whether they judged members of their own or the other culture. Moreover, persons of either culture who were judged correctly by Americans were also judged correctly by Japanese (correlations above .75). This experiment was replicated with different subjects and observers.

2. *Members of different cultures show the same facial expressions when experiencing the same emotion unless culture-specific display rules interfere.* While many studies have compared judgments of facial expression by observers from different cultures, few studies have compared the facial expressions actually produced by members of different cultures in comparable situations. Without studies measuring actual facial activity, it is not possible to determine which specific aspects of facial expressions are universal, in what social contexts these configurations are shown, nor how cultural norms for managing emotional expression (display rules) operate. Such questions apply both to intended (posed) and spontaneous facial expressions. There has been but one study of each.

Ekman & Friesen (47) found that members of a preliterate New Guinea group showed the same facial movements when posing particular emotions as do members of literate cultures. Ekman (43) and Friesen (61) also found that when Japanese and American subjects sat alone watching either a stress-inducing or neutral film, they showed the same facial actions. However, as predicted by knowledge of display rules in the two cultures, when a person in authority was present, the Japanese subjects smiled more and showed more control of facial expression than did the Americans.

Unanswered or Unasked Questions

1. *How many emotions have a universal facial expression?* Research in literate cultures has found distinctive facial expressions for anger, disgust, happiness, sadness (or distress), fear, and surprise (11, 43, 44, 55, 77, 108). Izard (77) also reported evidence for interest and shame, but inspection of his photographs suggests that head position, not facial expression, may have provided the clues for recognizing these emotions. There have been no other cross-cultural studies of these two emotions. In the preliterate cultures studied, fear and surprise expressions were differentiated from anger, sadness, happiness, and disgust but were confused with each other both in labeling and posing expressions (44). In sum, there is unambiguous evidence of universality only for the expressions of happiness, anger, disgust, sadness, and combined fear/surprise. Further study might reveal universal facial expressions for other emotions.

2. *How many universal expressions are distinguishable for any emotion?* Tomkins (128, 129) hypothesized that each emotion would have both universal and culture-specific expressions, but he did not describe the appearance of the latter in any detail. The cross-cultural studies used only a few examples of each emotional expression and did not analyze observers' judgments to see whether different versions of each expression were judged differently.

3. *How great are the cultural differences in facial expression?* Most accounts of extreme cultural variability in the expression of emotion come from qualitative observations made by single observers who did not control for observer or sampling bias or take display rules into account [Birdwhistell, LaBarre, Leach, Mead, and Montague reviewed in (44, 45)]. One quantitative study of cultural differences is the previously cited finding by Ekman and Friesen (43, 61) that facial expressions in Japanese and American subjects differed in a social situation but not when the same subjects were alone. This fit the authors' hypothesis that socially learned *display rules* for managing facial expression in various contexts are a major source of cultural variation in facial expression. In another study of display rules, Heider (73) confirmed his prediction that one West Irian culture but not another would substitute disgust expressions for anger when asked to portray angry themes. There has been no further cross-cultural study of display rules. A study of yearbook photographs and conversations (116) found evidence for a facial expression "dialect" in patterns of smiling among Southeastern Americans. The origin and interpretation of this dialect remain uncertain.

Ekman (43) postulated that learned triggers for each emotion were another major source of cultural variation, but he hypothesized that these elicitors may have some shared underlying characteristics. Boucher and

Cunningham (unpublished report) found evidence for similarities—but not for the hypothesized differences—in the specific elicitors of certain emotions in quite divergent cultures. In sum, there probably are important cultural differences in facial expression, attributable to learning, but precisely what these are and how they come to be are unknown.

4. *How often do people in natural situations actually show the distinctive, universal patterns of facial expression?* Are these expressions common or relatively rare? Does their occurrence vary with culture, sex, age, or the particular social context? Such questions call for detailed measurement of the facial expressions occurring in specified circumstances in different cultures, as well as knowledge of each culture's display rules. These facts are not available for even one culture.

5. *What are the evolutionary and/or ontogenetic origins of facial expressions?* Why are particular facial muscles activated in particular emotional expressions? For example, why are the lip corners raised in happiness and drawn down in sadness rather than vice versa? The finding of universal facial expressions has been taken as evidence that these expressions are *innate,* prewired, specialized signals (37, 42, 104, 128). Other writers (2, 103) have proposed instead that adult facial expressions derive ontogenetically from species-constant learning and from the biologically adaptive responses of the newborn: movements related to sensory reactions, defensive and orienting responses, crying, sucking, etc.

The crucial data for understanding the origin of facial expressions of emotion—longitudinal study involving detailed measurement of facial movements in infants in a variety of situations and in several unrelated cultures—exist in only piecemeal fashion. Detailed comparison of blind and sighted infants would reveal the importance of visual imitation and the adaptive use of facial movements involved in vision for the development of facial expressions. Studies of cogenitally blind infants (reviewed in 30) have provided the best evidence that direct imitation is unnecessary for the development of smiling, laughter, and crying. However, descriptions of the actual facial movements corresponding to these and other emotions (e.g. surprise, anger) in blind children have been vague and imprecise. Reports that blind infants and children are less facially expressive than sighted children (30, 59) have also lacked detailed description.

DEVELOPMENTAL STUDIES

Most research on facial expression in infants has been concerned with the timetable of emotional development. At what age and in what order do particular emotions emerge? Unfortunately, the behavioral criteria by which various emotional responses have been "recognized" and labeled are often subjective and imprecise, with little attention paid to detailed description of the facial movements themselves. Most early studies also lacked independent, convergent measures for assessing the infant's presumed emotional state. Several recent studies have attempted to deal with these methodological problems (26, 74, 91, 136, 142). Nevertheless, it is still not known when the distinctive, universal facial expressions corresponding to certain emotions first appear, nor how they develop. Part of the problem is that the questions left unanswered by research on infants have not been pursued in studies of toddlers and young children.

What Has Been Found

1. *The facial musculature is fully formed and functional at birth.* Many observers have been struck by the newborn's considerable facial mobility (63, 72). Using a fine-grained measurement system (described below), Oster & Ekman (100) confirmed that all but one of the discrete facial muscle actions visible in the adult can be identified and finely discriminated in full-term and premature newborns. Evidence for organization and temporal patterning in expressive movements such as smiling, brow knitting, and pouting in young infants has also been found by fine-grained analysis (81, 99, 100).

2. *Distinctive facial expressions resembling certain adult expressions are present in early infancy.* Crying, the universal expression of *distress,* is of course present at birth, but there has been little careful description since Darwin of the facial signs of distress and no study of developmental changes, if any, in cry faces. It is not known whether different facial movements correspond to acoustically different cry types or different sources of distress. Newborn infants show expressions resembling adult *disgust* in response to unpleasant tastes (103, 124). These facial responses have been found in anencephalic and hydrocephalic infants, suggesting a brain stem origin (124). The processes by which these facial reactions become associated with a wide range of psychological elicitors are not known. The *startle* reaction can be triggered in the newborn by sudden, intense stimulation and often occurs as a spontaneous discharge in non-REM sleep. There is disagreement about whether startle should be considered an emotional response related to surprise or a physiological reflex (128, 135, 140). The facial response is quite different from surprise and is said not to change throughout life.

Contrary to previous belief, neonatal smiles are neither random nor produced by gas. They occur primarily during REM sleep and seem to reflect periodic, endogenous fluctuations in CNS activity (56, 122, 139). Social smiling, i.e. smiling in an alert, bright-eyed infant who is fixating the caregiver, first occurs around 3 to 4 weeks of age (139). The reliable, full-blown social smile emerges in the third month (56, 139). Smiling in 2- to 3-month-olds has been observed in a variety of experimental situations suggesting that it reflects active cognitive engagement, "mastery," and a sense of efficacy (102, 118, 121, 122, 137). Beginning around the fourth month, smiling becomes increasingly reserved for the infant's primary caregivers (1, 12). With the exception of Wolff's classic study, little is known about developmental changes in the morphology of the smile or about differences—if any—in the appearance of "social," "playful," or "cognitive mastery" smiles (10, 133). Laughter first appears around 4 months. Most studies have focused on changes in the determinants of laughter (121, 122). Insights into the mechanisms underlying smiling and laughter have come from the study of Down's Syndrome infants (32).

3. *Three- to 4-month-olds show differential responses to facial expressions.* Early studies (30) indicated that infants do not begin to discriminate among facial expressions until 5 to 6 months. Several recent studies found differential visual fixation to slides of happy vs neutral or angry faces (84), and surprise vs happy faces (143) in 3- to 4-month-olds. It is not certain which aspect of the faces the infants were responding to, nor whether they perceived the stimuli (other than the smile, perhaps) as meaningful emotional expressions. Measurement of the infant's emotional responses and scan patterns to different facial expressions might help to resolve this question. Three-month-olds typically become "sober" or distressed when the caregiver presents an impassive face, suggesting a sensitivity to the animation and responsiveness of naturally occurring facial behavior (14, 123, 131). Detailed study of infants' responses to the dynamic, temporally patterned, often exaggerated facial expressions used by caregivers (cf 125) might reveal a greater sensitivity to differences in the expressive movements themselves.

4. *Imitation of some facial movements is possible at an early age.* Recent studies suggest that 2- to 3-week-old infants can differentially imitate actions such as mouth opening and tongue or lip protrusion (97), but there is disagreement about the possible mechanism underlying this feat (80, 97). It is not known whether neonates can imitate the principal actions used in emotional expression, nor what role imitation plays in the normal development or "fine-tuning" of facial expression. Such a role is suggested by Kaye & Marcus's recent finding (82) that 6-month-olds gradually accommodate their performance over a series of trials to match the movements modeled (bursts of mouth opening and closing). Many of the specific facial actions found in emotional expression can be imitated by 5 years (105).

5. *Preschool children know what the most common facial expressions look like, what they mean, and what kinds of situations typically elicit them.* The general finding from recognition, discrimination, affective role-taking, and empathy studies is that performance improves from age 3 to 10 (30, 67, 75). The abilities to imitate and voluntarily produce facial expressions to the

satisfaction of adult judges likewise increases with age (30, 70). On both recognition and production tasks the expression of happiness is easiest and fear among the most difficult. Most studies with children have involved cognitive tasks tapping knowledge of emotional expressions rather than measures of spontaneous emotional expression. However, a few empathy studies have shown that preschool children's spontaneous facial expressions reflect the emotions shown by others [(70), review by (75)]. The spontaneous nonverbal expressions of preschool children watching emotion-eliciting slides can be "decoded" by other preschool children, at least in terms of the pleasantness or unpleasantness of the "sender's" reaction (16). But no direct measures of the subject's facial expressions have been made in encoding/decoding studies. The only direct studies of facial behavior in children have come from an ethological perspective, as discussed below.

6. *Facial expression can play a role in the development of social communication.* The young infant is increasingly being viewed as an active individual, equipped with basic signaling capacities that serve to ensure certain kinds of attachment-promoting exchanges between infant and caregivers (1, 12, 14, 92, 131). Facial expression is recognized as a major component of this signaling system.

Ethological studies of natural social interaction in day care or nursery school settings have typically focused on the repertoire of facial and gestural actions associated with agonistic encounters, rough-and-tumble play, and social interaction with adults and peers (10). Ethologists discuss these actions in terms of their presumed motivation and signal function. However, there has been little quantitative documentation that particular expressive movements actually serve the presumed signaling function. Nor have ethologists systematically related the facial movements shown in such actions to emotional expressions. An exception on both scores is a recent ethologically oriented experimental study (28) showing that certain "aggressive" facial configurations used by children defending a desired object predicted both the child's own and his partner's subsequent behavior. The growing social control over emotional expression is suggested by observations that the presence of others can have a facilitative effect on emotional expressions such as crying (10) and humor (29).

Unanswered or Unasked Questions

1. *At what age can emotion be inferred from facial expressions seen in early infancy?* Most psychologists have believed that young infants lack the cognitive prerequisites for the experience of emotion. This belief cuts across the nativist/empiricist spectrum (e.g. 2, 63, 103), though there have been widely differing views on the presumed cognitive prerequisites for experiencing "true emotion," on the age when these attained, and on the ontogenetic mechanisms presumed to be involved. Recent articles

(56, 90, 107, 121) have interpreted expressive movements such as crying and smiling in early infancy as purely passive, reflex-like precursors of later expressions of emotion. There is said to be no "genuine" emotion until the emergence of the first signs of active cognitive processing or "consciousness" around the third month (56, 121), or until the emergence of "self-conscious awareness" around 18 months (90). While not denying the importance of these cognitive achievements, several researchers maintain that emotion is present at birth (79, 128, 129), or suggest a more gradual transition from physiological to psychological causation of emotional expressions (99, 123, 140). This issue cannot be resolved on the basis of available empirical data.

2. *When do adult-like, differentiated facial expressions for the emotions of interest, surprise, sadness, fear, and anger first appear?* "Brightening" of the eyes and face has been noted in alert newborns attending to visual or auditory stimuli. But more detailed study is needed before we could conclude that the expression of interest, as distinct from orienting and attentional responses, is present in early infancy. The typical adult surprise face is infrequently observed in infants less than 1 year old (30, 135), even though infants in the second half year may respond to presumably surprising experimental situations in ways suggesting that they were surprised (38, 74, 135).

We cannot yet specify when discrete negative affect expressions (as distinct from crying) begin to appear on a regular basis, nor in what natural circumstances they are likely to occur. Sadness and distress faces differ in adults, but this distinction has not been made in studies of infants and children. "Wariness" and fear emerge in the second half year of life, as inferred from the onset of hesitant, avoidant, or overtly negative reactions to situations that were not previously distressing, such as heights or the approach of a stranger (27, 38, 56, 120, 121). Anger has been inferred from "tantrum" behaviors and from instrumental acts such as hitting, throwing, and biting (30, 121). But the facial expressions accompanying these emotional responses have not been described in detail. Investigators who coded infants' responses to emotion-arousing situations in terms of specific facial actions (26, 74, 91, 136, 142) have not found differentiated expressions of fear, sadness, or anger, but rather affectively neutral attention and components of pre-cry or distress faces of various intensities. In one of the few studies that tried to elicit several different negative affects (142), the infants' reactions could not be distinguished on the basis of facial expression alone. A finer grain coding system might reveal precursors of adult expressions of anger, sadness, or fear in the cry or pre-cry faces elicited by different events or associated with other behaviors indicative of these affects.

As noted above, 5-year-olds can satisfactorily pose expressions of anger, fear, and sadness. But there has been no systematic study of the actual occurrence of discrete negative affect expressions in natural or laboratory settings. Crying apparently remains the prepotent expression of virtually all strong negative affect throughout early childhood. However, no studies have investigated Tomkins' proposal (129) that different cry vocalizations and cry faces accompany different negative affects. Nor is it clear whether young children cry because they do not yet "use" more discrete facial expressions (which they can, however, produce voluntarily), or because all negative affect is blended with or produces distress at this age.

3. *When—and how—do facial expressions of emotion come under voluntary control?* The development of voluntary control and of culturally defined "display rules" for managing emotional expression remains a virtual *terra incognita*, with only impressionistic observations suggesting a gradual transition from the automatic, uncontrolled expression of emotion in early infancy to the more modulated, subtle, and voluntary expression of emotion seen in older children and adults. The first step is probably the (not fully conscious) instrumental use of crying and smiling, somewhere in the first 2 to 3 months of life—as suggested by subjective impressions of "fake" crying (141); by evidence that both crying and smiling can be brought under the control of social reinforcement (64); and by reports suggesting that during the first half year of life infants begin to acquire a sense of the efficacy of their own signaling behaviors (6). By the end of the first year, one sees what seem to be smiles used as social greetings, deliberate "tantrum" behaviors, and visible efforts to hold back or suppress tears. The specific facial actions used in such behaviors have never been closely examined, however.

As noted above, one form of voluntary control—deliberately imitating or posing facial expressions when the corresponding emotion is (presumably) not felt—is present to some extent in preschool children. One recent study investigating children's verbal knowledge of social display rules (106) found increasing awareness of rules for managing emotional expression from 6 to 10 years. We know of no studies that directly studied children's efforts to control emotional expression or their use of display rules. Despite the general assumption that feedback from others (e.g. "big boys don't cry") plays a crucial role in shaping children's tendencies to manage emotional expression, we know of no objective data on the amount and kind of social feedback that children actually receive in response to their facial expressions, nor the extent to which parents, other adults, and peers serve as direct models.

FACIAL MEASUREMENT

As repeatedly indicated above, many of the central questions in cross-cultural and developmental research require measurement of facial activity itself and cannot be answered solely by reliance upon observers' judgments of emotion. Methods have recently been developed to allow measurement of two different but related aspects of facial activity—muscle tonus changes and visible actions.

Muscle Tonus Measurement

Schwartz and his co-workers (115) have shown that surface electromyographic (EMG) measurements are sensitive to differences among recalled emotions and moods and can distinguish depressive from normal subjects. The EMG leads were placed over facial areas that, according to theory (49, 128, 129), were expected to be differentially active for the emotions studied. While a given placement of leads apparently can differentiate among two or three emotions, it is not certain whether surface EMG procedures could distinguish as many as five or six emotions. A study in progress by Ekman, Schwartz, and Friesen on the relationship between EMG and visible facial activity suggests that the EMG can record muscle tonus changes that are barely visible or totally invisible.

EMG measurement of facial activity may be most applicable when the investigator can specify in advance the emotions of interest, when unobtrusiveness is not crucial, and when the subject will not be likely to move his face. (The leads, paste, and tape tend to inhibit movement and may be torn by strong muscle actions.) EMG should be useful when emotion is aroused by fantasy, recall, listening, viewing a film, etc. EMG is also the only method for studying Birdwhistell's (8) proposal that there are stable individual differences in the pattern of muscular tension maintained when the face is at rest (see 119).

Measurement of Visible Action

The early attempts to measure visible facial action (reviewed in 52, Chap. 16) have been ignored by those who followed. These early methods for measuring facial action did not explain the rationale for their choice of facial measurement units. Yet as Altman commented, "... what stage in our research could be more crucial than this initial choosing of behavioral units. Upon it rests all of our subsequent records of communication interactions and any conclusions we may draw from them ..." (3, p. 501). Selection of behavioral units has been based on theory, inductive observation, or facial anatomy.

THEORY-BASED SELECTION   Ekman, Friesen & Tomkins' (53) Facial Affect Scoring Technique (FAST) specified what they believed—on the basis of previous research—to be the distinctive components of six universal affect expressions. FAST proved useful in studies relating subjects' facial expressions to autonomic responses, experimental conditions, and observers' judgments. FAST is not a general purpose tool, however. It could not be used to determine whether actions other than those specified are relevant to emotion nor to study developmental changes or individual differences in the expression of emotion. The first two criticisms of the inductively derived systems listed below also apply to FAST. Izard's (personal communication) newly developed Facial Expression Scoring Manual, which follows the same general approach as FAST, probably also suffers from the same limitations. Some investigators (e.g. 74; Izard, personal communication) have used theory based systems [e.g. materials developed by Ekman & Friesen (49) for training clinicians, or Izard's FESM] as the basis for scoring emotional expressions or components of those expressions in infants or young children. This approach suffers from the problems outlined above for FAST. There are additional methodological problems inherent in using a theory-based facial measurement system derived from data on adults for research on infants. More serious, such an approach cannot reveal how full-face, adult-like expressions develop and ignores possible early precursors of these expressions.

INDUCTIVELY BASED SELECTION   Several overlapping listings of facial actions have been derived by observing spontaneous behavior in infants (98, 142), children (9, 13, 66, 93), and normal and psychiatric adult patients (66). These systems have been useful in generating "ethograms," or catalogs of the salient behaviors in the communicative repertoire. Blurton Jones' system has been adopted with some variations by a number of developmental psychologists. Yet all suffer from major methodological flaws if considered as general purpose facial measurement systems.

All are incomplete, without explanation of what has been left out or why. All include—without mention—both simple muscle actions and complex movements involving several independent actions. Behavioral units are sometimes given inference-laden names (e.g. "angry frown"), making objective study of the action's meaning difficult. Many units are only vaguely described, so that investigators cannot know if they are coding the same actions. Descriptions of some actions are anatomically incorrect. Finally, individual, racial, or age-related differences in physiognomy may make it difficult to identify certain actions described in terms of static configurations (e.g. "oblong mouth").

ANATOMICALLY BASED SELECTION   Since every facial movement is the result of muscular action, a system for describing facial expression can be comprehensive if the measurement units are based on knowledge of how each muscle acts to change appearance. Any complex facial movement can then be scored analytically in terms of the minimal muscle actions that collectively produce the movement. Three investigators have followed this logic.

Seaford (116) provided an excellent, detailed critique of the hazards involved in theoretically or inductively derived systems. His description of a regional variation in facial expression showed the utility of an anatomical approach. Ermiane & Gregerian (57) have developed a general-purpose, anatomically based facial measurement system. But they do not report reliability data nor mention whether the system can be learned without personal instruction.

Ekman & Friesen's (50, 51) Facial Action Coding System (FACS), also a general-purpose system, was designed to measure all visible facial behavior in any context, not just actions related to emotion. The list of minimal units overlaps considerably with that of Ermiane and Gregarian. However, FACS specifies minimal units not only in terms of anatomically possible actions but also in terms of which actions can be reliably distinguished. Persons who learn the system without personal instruction from the developers have achieved high reliability.

FACS is slow to learn and use, requiring repeated, slow-motion viewing of facial actions. It is thus unsuitable for real-time coding. By its nature, FACS includes more distinctions than may be needed for any particular study, which increases the expense and tedium of measurement. However, once meaningful units of behavior are defined empirically, it is possible in a given study to collapse some of the elementary measurement units or to disregard subtle distinctions. As yet there is no empirical evidence to substantiate which facial actions and combinations, as scored by FACS, correspond to particular emotions.

Other Facial Measures

Perhaps the most popular measure of facial activity has been direction of gaze, yet surprisingly this rarely has been studied in relation to emotion or facial expressions [recent exceptions are (65, 86, 123, 125, 136)]. While pupil dilation has been studied in relation to emotion, we know of no study of associated changes in facial expression. Blood flow, skin temperature, and coloration changes in the face are other measures that so far remain unexplored.

ACCURACY

How are we to determine if the information provided by a person's facial expression is accurate? We must have some criterion—independent of the face itself—for establishing which emotion, if any, was experienced at the moment of facial expression. The problem of independent validation has been the greatest obstacle to research on accuracy. A common approach has been to ask subjects to report their feelings (usually retrospectively) and to see whether their facial expressions differ when reporting emotion A as compared to emotion B. Such self-reports are error-prone, since subjects may fail to remember or to distinguish among the emotions experienced—particularly if several minutes elapse before the report is made. A subject who successively felt anger, disgust, and contempt while watching a film might not recall all three reactions, their exact sequence, or their time of occurrence. This problem can be avoided by limiting self-report to the grosser distinction between pleasant vs unpleasant feelings; but we then cannot determine whether facial expressions convey accurate information about particular unpleasant or pleasant feelings.

A second common approach has been to find out if subjects' facial expressions vary according to the eliciting conditions: e.g. affectively positive vs negative films or slides; anticipation of an electric shock vs a no-shock trial; or hostile vs friendly remarks made by another person. Since it is unlikely that all subjects experience the same, discrete emotion during a particular condition, this approach can usually show only that different facial expressions are used in presumably pleasant and unpleasant situations.

Attempts to pre- or postdict other information about a subject (e.g. whether he has many friends) have also been used to assess accuracy; but this approach implies that facial expressions can provide information about enduring traits in addition to transient states. If particular changes in voice pitch or quality, body movement, or speech were infallible indicators of particular emotions, these could serve as accuracy criteria. Unfortunately, there is no evidence that these channels provide any more accurate information than facial expressions. Similarly, change in autonomic or central nervous system activity could provide a useful criterion if there were evidence that different patterns of neural activity reliably accompany different emotions. The few studies that have explored the neural correlates of facial expression are reviewed in a later section. Since there is no single, infallible way to determine a person's "true" emotional state, it is unfortunate that so few investigators have followed the approach of using multiple convergent measures to gain a more reliable indication of the emotion experienced.

Regardless of the accuracy criterion used, the information provided by facial expression can be studied either indirectly, by observers' judgments (of the emotion experienced, the eliciting conditions, etc), or by direct measurement of facial activity (using any of the techniques described in the previous section). Facial measurement and observer judgments need not yield the same results, even when applied to the same facial expressions. Direct measurement could reveal expressive movements that observers missed in real-time or that they failed to interpret correctly. Conversely, observers could pick up cues that were not among the units measured. Observer judgment studies have far exceeded facial measurement studies, probably because the latter are more expensive and time-consuming than the former.

What Has Been Found

1. *Facial expressions of emotion can provide accurate information about the occurrence of pleasant as compared to unpleasant emotional states.* A reanalysis of studies from 1914 to 1970 (52) concluded that both facial measurement and observers' judgment methods accurately distinguished pleasant from unpleasant states. Since then a number of experiments (cited below) have replicated these findings but have not extended them to possible distinctions among particular positive or negative emotions. There is little information pinpointing the specific facial actions that differentiate between pleasant and unpleasant states. Most investigators have used observers' judgments of facial expression without trying to determine which configurations observers were responding to. Those who directly measured facial expression failed to report the frequency of specific actions or full-face configurations used in the expressions that provided accurate information.

2. *Facial expressions can be disguised to mislead an observer about the emotions experienced.* Among the dozens of recent experiments on interpersonal deceit, only five (48, 71, 88, 95, 145) explicitly instructed subjects to conceal their emotions and also obtained evidence independent of the face that they actually experienced emotion. The results were contradictory, most likely due to variations in the strength or number of emotions aroused, the subjects' motivation to deceive, and their prior practice in perpetrating such deception. However, the experiments also differed in other ways: e.g. whether subjects knew they were being videotaped; whether observers knew that deception might be involved; whether they were trained; whether they heard the deceivers' speech in addition to seeing their faces. Despite the lack of consistency, this seems an important area for further study.

3. *Individuals differ in facial "expressiveness" (encoding ability) and in their ability to judge facial expressions (decoding ability).* In encoding/decoding studies, encoders are videotaped in emotion-arousing situations (while watching slides or undergoing shock); decoders (often the same subjects) then try to infer, from each encoder's facial expressions, the eliciting condition (category of slides or level of shock) or the encoder's rating of his/her own emotional experience. There are marked individual differences in how accurately an individual's facial expressions are judged and in how accurately an individual judges the faces of others (17, 36, 71, 89,

145). This finding is consistent with observations from other experiments that were not specifically looking for individual differences. Attempts to study the relationship between encoding and decoding abilities have produced negative, positive, and insignificant correlations. [See (62) for a careful discussion.] Inconsistent findings have also been obtained in the search for personality correlates of individual differences in encoding and decoding abilities. An exception is the small but consistent superiority of women in both encoding and decoding (68, 69).

These studies are fraught with methodological problems, which may explain some of the inconsistencies. In some studies the subjects must periodically rate their own emotional experience, a task that might affect their facial expressions or the experience itself. Many experiments do not verify which, if any, emotion was experienced by encoders. Exceptions are studies that obtained independent ratings of the emotions aroused by their elicitor (36, 71) or that used psychophysiological measures to indicate arousal, though not which emotion was aroused (88). Most often, the only measure of emotional arousal is the observers' success in inferring the relative pleasantness of the eliciting condition or the subject's subsequent rating of his own feelings (19, 20, 146). Such judgments could be made on the basis of cues having nothing to do with facial expression—e.g. posture, gross body movements—or facial signs of cognitive activity.

Although the search for personality correlates of individual differences in encoding and decoding abilities implies that these differences are stable, there has been no study of test-retest reliability in individual encoding ability or in encoding and decoding abilities in the same subjects. Another problem is that in many decoding tasks observers must judge facial expressions that occurred during speech but with the speech omitted. Only the deaf might have sufficient experience with this condition to develop stable individual differences in decoding such stimuli. Quite a different approach to individual differences is illustrated by Schiffenbauer's (111) finding that the emotional state of the observer influenced the emotion he attributed to a facial expression.

Unanswered or Unasked Questions

1. *Can facial expressions provide accurate information about the distinctions among several negative and positive emotions?* The only evidence that they can is for posed facial expressions.

2. *When can we expect facial expression to provide accurate information about emotion?* Studies showing that the facial expressions of some people are difficult to judge did not determine whether detailed measurement of their facial activity would reveal reliable cues missed by observers, nor

whether those individuals might be more expressive in other social circumstances. Studies showing that people can successfully disguise their facial expressions of emotion did not explore whether this ability is a stable characteristic of the person nor whether measurement of their facial activity would reveal reliable signs (i.e. "leakage") of their actual feelings.

Quite apart from the issues of individual differences and deception—which might limit the accuracy of information provided by facial expression—there is little information about the number and kinds of situations in which facial movement expresses emotion. It has been suggested (45, 46) that most facial activity in social interaction has little to do with emotion, but no empirical studies have compared different types of facial activity in different settings.

3. *How much information does the face, as compared to voice, speech, and body movement, provide about emotion?* A number of studies have compared observers' judgments about an event perceived via different "channels": audiovisual, audio alone, or visual alone. Most experiments found that the face is more accurately judged, produces higher agreement, or correlates better with judgments based on full audiovisual input than do voice or speech (5, 24, 39, 96, 144). A few experiments found that the face was less important than another channel (7, 117) or that channel cue varied with the observer (132). The findings of most "channel" experiments are suspect because the behavior judged was quite contrived. The most extensive series of studies (33) on naturally occurring behavior found that what was said mattered more than the visual input and that knowledge of demographic information produced as much accurate behavioral postdiction as exposure to an audiovisual film.

Another problem in this research is that observers judging the "face" channel are usually shown—without sound—facial expressions that occurred embedded in speech. This could cause misinterpretation of speech-related facial expressions. Moreover, observers who are limited to just the face may get more information than they would ordinarily get from the face when it is viewed in context.

A study in progress by Ekman, Friesen, O'Sullivan, and Scherer found that the relative weight given to facial expression, speech, and body cues depended both upon the judgment task (e.g. rating the stimulus subject's dominance, sociability, or relaxation) and upon the conditions in which the behavior occurred (while subjects frankly described positive reactions to a pleasant film or tried to conceal negative feelings aroused by a stressful film). The correlation between judgments made by observers who saw the face without speech and judgments made by observers who saw the face with speech were quite low on some scales (e.g. calm-agitated) and quite high on other scales (outgoing-withdrawn).

Studies by Bugental et al suggest that the influence of facial expression as compared to other sources depends upon the expressor, the perceiver, the message contained in each channel, and previous experience. Children were less influenced than were adults by a smile shown by an adult female when it was accompanied by negative words and voice tone (21). Some experiential grounds for distrusting mothers' smiles was found in a study showing that smiling in mothers (but not fathers) was not related to the positive vs negative content of the simultaneous speech (22). Also, mothers (but not fathers) of disturbed children produced more discrepant messages (among face, voice, and words) than did parents of nondisturbed children (23).

Although Scherer et al (110) studied judgments of personality rather than emotion, his findings also contradict the simple notion that one channel is better than another. Personality inferences were usually channel specific, some best made from one source, some from another. No one combination of channels (face plus speech, face plus voice, etc) yielded the most accurate judgments. It varied with the trait judged.

The whole question of how much information is conveyed by "separate" channels may inevitably be misleading. There is no evidence that individuals in actual social interaction selectively attend to another person's face, body, voice, or speech or that the information conveyed by these channels is simply additive. The central mechanisms directing behavior cut across channels, so that, for example, certain aspects of face, body, voice, and speech are more spontaneous, while others are more closely monitored and controlled. It might well be that observers selectively attend not to a particular channel but to a particular type of information (e.g. cues to emotion, deception, or cognitive activity), which might be available within several channels. No investigator has explored this possibility or the possibility that different individuals may typically attend to different types of information.

FACIAL FEEDBACK

The next group of studies addresses the long-debated issue of how we know what we feel. Since the demise of the James-Lange theory of emotion—postulating visceral and other somatic feedback as the source of our subjective experience of emotion—cognitive theories have prevailed. These theorists (e.g. Schacter) view emotional arousal as undifferentiated; our experience of a particular emotion, they argue, comes from interpretation of situational cues. By contrast, Tomkins (128, 129) holds that we experience discrete, differentiated emotions via feedback from innately patterned facial expressions.

A variant of the facial feedback hypothesis, set within the framework of self-attribution theory, postulates that we can use information from our own facial (and other) behavior to *infer* how we feel. Laird's (85) study provided a model for later feedback experiments: subjects were instructed to contract particular facial muscles, producing—presumably without their awareness —a "happy" or a "frowning" expression which they held while viewing slides or cartoons. The face manipulation had a significant though small effect (compared with the effect of the slides) on their reported feelings. A subsequent series of experiments found that individual differences on the face manipulation task were related to other indices of an individual's tendency to use "self"- vs "situation"-produced cues (e.g. 41).

A recent experiment (Tourangeau & Ellsworth, unpublished manuscript) failed to confirm the strong version of the facial feedback hypothesis, i.e. that overt facial expression is both necessary and sufficient for the experience of emotion. Facial manipulations had no significant effect on self-reported emotion and only ambiguous effects on physiological responses.

These contradictory findings are difficult to evaluate due to methodological problems inherent in the expression manipulation paradigm: the demand characteristics of the task; the implausibility of the cover stories; and the artificiality of the situation and facial "expressions," which must be held unnaturally long. As Laird (85) cautioned, feedback that is too unnatural could be discounted by the subject (or the CNS), thus working against the hypothesis.

The strongest evidence for a positive link between voluntary facial expression and emotional experience comes from a series of experiments by Lanzetta, Kleck, and colleagues (34, 83, 88) investigating the effect of overt facial expression on the intensity of emotional arousal produced by shock. Attempts to conceal the facial signs of pain consistently led to decreases in both skin conductance and subjective ratings of pain, while posing the expression of intense shock significantly increased both measures of arousal. When subjects were told that they were being observed by another person, they showed less intense facial expressions and correspondingly decreased autonomic responses and subjective ratings of pain—even though they received no instructions to inhibit their responses (83). These findings can be interpreted in various ways (see 88). Before concluding that facial feedback was directly and causally related to the observed changes in arousal, it would be necessary to rule out the possibility that some other strategy used by subjects might have affected both their facial expressions and emotional experience. It is also not clear that the effect is specific to facial vs bodily signs of emotion. Nevertheless, these findings suggest that overt facial expression can affect the intensity of emotional arousal. Evidence that facial feedback can determine *which* emotion we experience is far more ambiguous. It is worth noting that little is known about the nature and quality of feedback from the muscles of facial expression.

NEURAL CONTROL AND ANS CORRELATES OF FACIAL EXPRESSION

Psychophysiological Correlates

Two different approaches have examined the relationship between facial expression and autonomic nervous system responses. In one type of study gross changes in autonomic measures (usually GSR) averaged over some period of time are compared to changes in facial expression (as inferred by observers' judgments of emotion). The other approach has looked for patterning in the moment-to-moment changes in autonomic and facial measures. This approach has produced more consistent results.

Correlational studies of individual differences in ANS responsivity and facial expressiveness (in encoding/decoding studies discussed above) have typically found negative relationships: i.e. subjects whose faces can be accurately judged as anticipating shock (89) or as viewing slides arousing positive vs negative affect show lower GSR responses and vice versa (reviewed in 17). In experimental, within-subject studies, however (e.g. facial feedback and deception studies discussed above), increases in facial expressiveness have been shown to be accompanied by increases in ANS responsivity (88; see other recent studies cited above).

Malmstrom, Ekman & Friesen (147), in a pilot study, found that different patterns of heart rate acceleration and deceleration coincided with facial activity showing elements of disgust vs surprise when subjects viewed a stressful film. Ancoli (4) found that facial expressions of disgust in subjects viewing a stressful film were related to respiration changes (thoracic as compared to abdominal).

In developmental studies of infants' reactions to an approaching stranger, several investigators (e.g. 26; 136, reviewed in 120) have found greater heart rate acceleration in 6- to 10-month-old infants who showed facial signs of "wariness" or distress than in infants who showed neutral or positive expressions. An "open" or affectively neutral, attentive face was typically accompanied by heart rate deceleration. Lewis, Brooks & Haviland (91), while finding a relationship between heart rate deceleration and attentive faces, did not find a significant relationship between heart rate acceleration and negative affect expressions.

Face and Brain

Most knowledge about the neural control of facial expression has come from clinical studies of neurological disorders. The dual control of facial movement is shown by the finding that individuals suffering from complete paralysis of voluntary facial movements (as in pseudobulbar palsy, which affects the corticobulbar tracts) may show spontaneous facial expressions

—often grossly exaggerated—when emotion is aroused (58). Conversely, spontaneous emotional expression but not voluntary movement may be affected by subcortical lesions, postencephalitic Parkinsonism, or "congenital weakness of the facial muscles" (58). The limbic system is known to be important in emotional expression (reviewed in 87), and successive states in the ontogenetic development of spontaneous and volitional facial and vocal expression are probably related to the maturation of specific brain structures and subsystems, though the evidence at present is indirect and often sketchy.

Several converging lines of evidence (brain lesion studies, research on commisurotomized patients, recognition and reaction time experiments with normal subjects) point to a right hemisphere advantage in recognizing faces. This advantage is especially pronounced when the task requires processing in terms of the higher-order, configurational properties of faces, rather than isolated features (25, 40). It is also greater (126) when the faces to be recognized by subjects show emotional expressions than when they are affectively neutral. The ability to use configurational information for recognizing unfamiliar faces does not develop until around 10 years of age. Younger children—like patients with right hemisphere lesions—use piecemeal processing and can be fooled easily by salient paraphernalia such as items of clothing (40). Facial expression was not found to be a source of confusion in children of any age, suggesting that—unlike clothing—it is not normally seen as an isolated cue to identify but rather as linked to the higher-order, configurational properties of faces. This view was confirmed by Campbell's finding (unpublished report) that adults are often misled by facial expression when facial stimuli are projected to the right but not to the left hemisphere (see also 35).

Campbell (25 and unpublished report) used chimeric face stimuli (composites of two half-faces showing different individuals or facial expressions or mirror-reversed expressions) to study lateralization effects in the production and perception of facial expression. Her findings reveal that—in right-handed adults—the perception of facial expression is dominated by the left visual field (i.e. by the viewer's right hemisphere), corresponding to the right side of the face stimuli. At the same time, emotion actually may be expressed more strongly by the left side of the face, controlled by the producer's right hemisphere. Lesion studies (e.g. 18) provide further evidence of a right-hemisphere superiority for emotional expression.

FUTURE DIRECTIONS

The study of facial expression promises to provide new insights into a wide variety of psychological problems. We have already reviewed studies indicating the relevance of facial expression to research in developmental psychology, person perception, theories of emotion, and the neurophysiology of emotion. The relevance of facial expression—and of hypothesized styles of controlling emotional expression (49, 78, 128)—to personality disorders and psychosomatic disease remains unexplored. Unstudied also is the relationship—real or perceived—between facial expression and intelligence, an important issue for the assessment of IQ (72).

In closing we note a number of recent findings that show how the study of facial expressions may help to understand some of the practical aspects of social interaction. An instructor in a learning task delivered less punishment to victims who looked angry rather than joyful (109). Pupils learned more from a teacher who showed positive rather than negative emotional expressions while giving a lesson (60). Children who looked happy rather than sad while watching televised violence subsequently showed more aggressive as compared to altruistic behavior (54). Subjects scoring high on "humanism" smiled more often during conversation than "non-humanist" subjects (134). The type of facial movement used to emphasize speech (46) or to indicate a question (Camras, personal communication) is related to the hypothesized role of those movements in emotional expression; and the differential use of particular facial actions to emphasize speech affects the impressions conveyed to others (101).

Literature Cited

1. Ainsworth, M. 1973. The development of infant-mother attachment. In *Review of Child Development Research,* Vol. 3, pp. 1–94, ed. B. Caldwell, H. Ricciuti. Chicago: Chicago Univ. Press
2. Allport, F. M. 1924. *Social Psychology.* Boston: Houghton Mifflin
3. Altmann, S. 1968. Primates. In *Animal Communication: Techniques and Results of Research,* ed. T. Sebeok, p. 466–522. Bloomington: Indiana Univ. Press
4. Ancoli, S. 1978. *Psychophysiological response patterns to emotions.* PhD thesis. Univ. California, San Francisco, Calif.
5. Argyle, M., Alkema, F., Gilmour, R. 1971. The communication of friendly and hostile attitudes by verbal and non-verbal signals. *Eur. J. Soc. Psychol.* 1(3):385–402
6. Bell, S. M., Ainsworth, M. D. S. 1972. Infant crying and maternal responsiveness. *Child Dev.* 43:1171–90
7. Berman, H. J., Shulman, A. D., Marwit, S. J. 1976. Comparison of multidimensional decoding of affect from audio, video and audiovideo recordings. *Sociometry* 39(1):83–89

8. Birdwhistell, R. L. 1970. *Kinesics and Context.* Philadelphia: Univ. Pennsylvania Press
9. Blurton Jones, N. G. 1971. Criteria for use in describing facial expressions in children. *Hum. Biol.* 41:365–413
10. Blurton Jones, N. G. 1972. Non-verbal communication in children. In *Nonverbal Communication,* ed. R. A. Hinde, pp. 271–96. Cambridge, England: Cambridge Univ. Press
11. Boucher, J. D. 1973. *Facial behavior and the perception of emotion: Studies of Malays and Temuan Orang Asli.* Presented at Conf. Psychol. Related Disciplines, Kuala Lumpur
12. Bowlby, J. 1969. *Attachment and Loss,* Vol. 1. *Attachment.* New York: Basic Books
13. Brannigan, C. R., Humphries, D. A. 1972. Human nonverbal behavior, a means of communication. In *Ethological Studies of Child Behavior,* ed. N. G. Blurton Jones. Cambridge: Cambridge Univ. Press
14. Brazelton, T., Tronick, E., Adamson, L., Als, H., Wise, S. 1975. Early mother-infant reciprocity. *Parent-Infant In-*

550   EKMAN & OSTER

teraction. Amsterdam: Elsevier Exp. Med.

15. Bruner, J. S., Tagiuri, R. 1954. The perception of people. In *Handbook of Social Psychology,* Vol. 2, ed. G. Lindzey. Reading, Mass: Addison-Wesley

16. Buck, R. 1975. Nonverbal communication of affect in children. *J. Pers. Soc. Psychol.* 31:644–53

17. Buck, R. 1977. *Measuring individual differences in the nonverbal communication of affect: The slide viewing paradigm.* Presented at Am. Psychol. Assoc. meet., San Francisco

18. Buck, R., Duffy, R. 1977. *Nonverbal communication of affect in brain-damaged patients.* Presented at Am. Psychol. Assoc. meet., San Francisco

19. Buck, R., Miller, R. E., Caul, W. F. 1974. Sex, personality, and physiological variables in the communication of affect via facial expression. *J. Pers. Soc. Psychol.* 30(4):587–96

20. Buck, R., Savin, V. J., Miller, R. E., Caul, W. F. 1972. Communication of affect through facial expressions in humans. *J. Pers. Soc. Psychol.* 23:362–71

21. Bugental, D., Kaswan, J., Love, L., Fox, M. 1970. Child versus adult perception of evaluative messages in verbal, vocal and visual channels. *Dev. Psychol.* 2(3):367–75

22. Bugental, D., Love, L., Gianetto, R. 1971. Perfidious feminine faces. *J. Pers. Soc. Psychol.* 17(3):314–18

23. Bugental, D., Love, L., Kaswan, J., April, C. 1971. Verbal-nonverbal conflict in parental messages to normal and disturbed children. *J. Abnorm. Psychol.* 77(1):6–10

24. Burns, K. L., Beier, E. G. 1973. Significance of vocal and visual channels in the decoding of emotional meaning. *J. Commun.* 23:118–30

25. Campbell, R. 1978. Asymmetries in interpreting and expressing a posed facial expression. *Cortex.* In press

26. Campos, J. J., Emde, R. N., Gaensbauer, T., Henderson, C. 1975. Cardiac and behavioral interrelationships in the reactions of infants to strangers. *Dev. Psychol.* 11(4):589–601

27. Campos, J. J., Hiatt, S., Ramsay, D., Henderson, C., Svejda, M. 1978. The emergence of fear on the visual cliff. In *The Development of Affect,* ed. M. Lewis, L. Rosenblum, pp. 149–82. New York: Plenum

28. Camras, L. 1977. Facial expressions used by children in a conflict situation. *Child Dev.* 48:1431–35

29. Chapman, A. J., Wright, D. S. 1976. Social enhancement of laughter: An experimental analysis of some companion variables. *J. Exp. Child Psychol.* 21:201–18

30. Charlesworth, W. R., Kreutzer, M. A. 1973. Facial expression of infants and children. In *Darwin and Facial Expression,* ed. P. Ekman, pp. 91–168. New York: Academic

31. Chevalier-Skolnikoff, S. 1973. Facial expression of emotion in non-human primates. See Ref. 30, pp. 11–89

32. Cicchetti, D., Sroufe, L. A. 1978. An organizational view of affect: Illustration from the study of Down's Syndrome infants. See Ref. 27, pp. 309–50

33. Cline, V. B., Atzet, J., Holmes, E. 1972. Assessing the validity of verbal and nonverbal cues in accurately judging others. *Comp. Group Stud.* 3:383–94

34. Colby, C. Z., Lanzetta, J. T., Kleck R. E. 1977. Effects of the expression of pain on autonomic and pain tolerance responses to subject-controlled pain. *Psychophysiology* 14(6):537–40

35. Crouch, W. W. 1976. Dominant direction of conjugate lateral eye movements and responsiveness to facial and verbal cues. *Percept. Mot. Skills* 42:167–74

36. Cunningham, M. R. 1977. Personality and the structure of the nonverbal communication of emotion. *J. Pers.* 45:564–84

37. Darwin, C. 1955. *The Expression of Emotion in Man and Animals.* New York: Philosophical Library (Originally published 1872)

38. Decarie, T. 1978. Affect development and cognition in a Piagetian context. See Ref. 27, pp. 183–204

39. DePaulo, B., Rosenthal, R., Eisenstat, R., Finkelstein, S., Rogers, P. 1978. Decoding discrepant nonverbal cues. *J. Pers. Soc. Psychol.* In press

40. Diamond, R., Carey, S. 1977. Developmental changes in the representation of faces. *J. Exp. Child Psychol.* 23:1–22

41. Duncan, J., Laird, J. D. 1977. Cross-modality consistencies in individual differences in self-attribution. *J. Pers.* 45(2):191–206

42. Eibl-Eibesfeldt, I. 1971. Similarities and differences between cultures in expressive movements. See Ref. 10, pp. 297–312

43. Ekman, P. 1972. Universals and cultural differences in facial expressions of emotion. *Nebr. Symp. Motiv.* 1971, pp. 207–83

44. Ekman, P. 1973. Cross cultural studies

of facial expression. See Ref. 30, pp. 169–229

45. Ekman, P. 1977. Biological and cultural contributions to body and facial movement. In *The Anthropology of the Body*, ed. J. Blacking. London: Academic

46. Ekman, P. 1978. About brows: Emotional and conversational signals. In *Human Ethology*, ed. J. Aschoff, M. von Cranach, K. Foppa, W. Lepenies, D. Ploog. Cambridge: Cambridge Univ. Press. In press

47. Ekman, P., Friesen, W. V. 1971. Constants across cultures in the face and emotion. *J. Pers. Soc. Psychol.* 17: 124–29

48. Ekman, P., Friesen, W. V. 1974. Detecting deception from the body or face. *J. Pers. Soc. Psychol.* 29(3):288–98

49. Ekman, P., Friesen, W. V. 1975. *Unmasking the Face*. Englewood Cliffs, NJ: Prentice-Hall

50. Ekman, P., Friesen, W. V. 1976. Measuring facial movement. *J. Environ. Psychol. Nonverb. Behav.* 1(1):56–75

51. Ekman, P., Friesen, W. V. 1978. *The Facial Action Coding System*. Palo Alto, Calif: Consult. Psychol. Press

52. Ekman, P., Friesen, W. V., Ellsworth, P. 1972. *Emotion in the Human Face*. Elmsford, NY: Pergamon

53. Ekman, P., Friesen, W. V., Tomkins, S. S. 1971. Facial Affect Scoring Technique (FAST): A first validity study. *Semiotica* 3(1):37–38

54. Ekman, P., Liebert, R. M., Friesen, W. V., Harrison, R. A., Zlatchin, C., Malmstrom, E. J., Baron, R. A. 1972. Facial expressions of emotion while watching televised violence as predictors of subsequent aggression. In *Television and Social Behavior Vol. V.: Television's Effects: Further explorations*, ed. G. A. Comstock, E. A. Rubinstein, J. P. Murray. A technical report to the Surgeon General's Scientific Advisory Committee on Television and Social Behavior. Washington, DC: GPO

55. Ekman, P., Sorenson, E. R., Friesen, W. V. 1969. Pan-cultural elements in facial displays of emotion. *Science* 164(3875): 86–88

56. Emde, R. N., Gaensbauer, T. J., Harmon, R. J. 1976. Emotional expression in infancy: A biobehavioral study. *Psychol. Issues Monogr. Ser.* 10, Monogr. 37

57. Ermaine, R., Gregerian, E. 1978. *Atlas of Facial Expressions. Album des expressions du visage*. Paris: La Pensée Universelle

58. Ford, F. R. 1966. *Diseases of the Nervous System in Infancy, Childhood, and Adolescence*. Springfield, Ill: Thomas. 5th ed.

59. Fraiberg, S. 1974. Blind infants and their mothers: An examination of the sign system. See Ref. 92, pp. 215–32

60. Fried, E. 1976. *The impact of nonverbal communication of facial affect on children's learning*. PhD thesis, Rutgers Univ., New Brunswick, NJ

61. Friesen, W. V. 1972. *Cultural differences in facial expressions in a social situation: An experimental test of the concept of display rules*. PhD thesis. Univ. California, San Francisco

62. Fujita, B. 1977. *Encoding and decoding of spontaneous and enacted facial expressions of emotion*. PhD thesis. Univ. Oregon, Portland

63. Gesell, A. 1945. *The Embryology of Behavior*. New York: Harper

64. Gewirtz, J. L., Boyd, E. F. 1976. Mother-infant interaction and its study. *Adv. Child Dev. Behav.* 11: 141–63

65. Graham, J. A., Argyle, M. 1975. The effects of different patterns of gaze combined with different facial expressions, on impression information. *J. Hum. Movement Stud.* 1:178–82

66. Grant, N. G. 1969. Human facial expression. *Man* 4:525–36

67. Greenspan, S., Barenboim, C., Chandler, M. J. 1976. Empathy and pseudoempathy: The affective judgments of first- and third-graders. *J. Genet. Psychol.* 129:77–88

68. Hall, J. 1978. Gender effects in decoding nonverbal cues. *Psychol. Bull.* In press

69. Hall, J. 1978. Gender effects in encoding nonverbal cues. *Psychol. Bull.* In press

70. Hamilton, M. L. 1973. Imitative behavior and expressive ability in facial expression of emotion. *Dev. Psychol.* 8(1): 138

71. Harper, R. G., Wiens, A. N., Fujita, B. 1977. Individual differences in encoding-decoding of emotional expression and emotional dissimulation. Presented at Am. Psychol. Assoc. meet., San Francisco

72. Haviland, J. 1975. Looking smart: The relationship between affect and intelligence in infancy. In *Origins of Infant Intelligence*, ed. M. Lewis. New York: Plenum

73. Heider, K. 1974. *Affect display rules in the Dani*. Presented at Am. Anthropol. Assoc. meet., New Orleans

74. Hiatt, S., Campos, J., Emde, R. 1977. *Fear, surprise, and happiness: The patterning of facial expression in infants*.

Presented at Soc. Res. Child Dev., New Orleans

75. Hoffman, M. L. 1977. Empathy, its development and prosocial implications. *Nebr. Symp. Motiv.* 25: In press

76. Hunt, W. A. 1941. Recent developments in the field of emotion. *Psychol. Bull.* 38(5):249–76

77. Izard, C. 1971. *The Face of Emotion.* New York: Appleton-Century-Crofts

78. Izard, C. 1977. *Human Emotions.* New York, London: Plenum

79. Izard, C. 1978. On the ontogenesis of emotions and emotion-cognition relationships in infancy. See Ref. 27, pp. 389–413

80. Jacobson, S., Kagan, J. 1978. *Released responses in early infancy: Evidence contradicting selective imitation.* Presented at Int. Conf. Infant Stud., Providence, R.I.

81. Josse, D., Leonard, M., Lezine, I., Robinot, F., Rouchouse, J. 1973. Evolution de la communication entre l'enfant de 4 a 9 mois et un adulte. *Enfance* 3(4):175–206

82. Kaye, K., Marcus, J. 1978. Imitation over a series of trials without feedback: Age six months. *Infant Behav. Dev.* 1:141–55

83. Kleck, R. E., Vaughan, R. C., Cartwright-Smith, J., Vaughan, K. B., Colby, C. Z., Lanzetta, J. T. 1976. Effects of being observed on expressive, subjective, and physiological responses to painful stimuli. *J. Pers. Soc. Psychol.* 34:1211–18

84. LaBarbera, J. D., Izard, C., Vietze, P., Parisi, S. A. 1976. Four- and six-month-old infants' visual responses to joy, anger, and neutral expressions. *Child Dev.* 47:535–38

85. Laird, J. D. 1974. Self-attribution of emotion: The effects of expressive behavior on the quality of emotional experience. *J. Pers. Soc. Psychol.* 29(4):475–86

86. Lalljee, M. 1978. The role of gaze in the expression of emotion. *Aust. J. Psychol.* In press

87. Lamendella, J. T. 1977. The limbic system in human communication. In *Studies in Neurolinguistics,* Vol. 3, ed. H. Whitaker, H. A. Whitaker. New York: Academic

88. Lanzetta, J. T., Cartwright-Smith, J., Kleck, R. E. 1976. Effects of nonverbal dissimulation on emotional experience and autonomic arousal. *J. Pers. Soc. Psychol.* 33(3):354–70

89. Lanzetta, J. T., Kleck, R. E. 1970. Encoding and decoding of nonverbal affects in humans. *J. Pers. Soc. Psychol.* 16:12–19

90. Lewis, M., Brooks, J. 1978. Self-knowledge and emotional development. See Ref. 27, pp. 205–26

91. Lewis, M., Brooks, J., Haviland, J. 1978. Hearts and faces: A study in the measurement of emotion. See Ref. 27, pp. 77–124

92. Lewis, M., Rosenblum, L. A., eds. 1974. *The Effect of the Infant on its Caregiver.* New York: Wiley

93. McGrew, W. C. 1972. *An Ethological Study of Children's Behavior.* New York: Academic

94. Mead, M. 1975. Review of *Darwin and Facial Expression,* ed. P. Ekman. *J. Commun.* 25(1):209–13

95. Mehrabian, A. 1971. Nonverbal betrayal of feeling. *J. Exp. Res. Pers.* 5(1):64–73

96. Mehrabian, A., Ferris, S. 1967. Inference of attitudes from nonverbal communication in two channels. *J. Consult. Psychol.* 31(3):248–52

97. Meltzoff, A. N., Moore, M. K. 1977. Imitation of facial and manual gestures by human neonates. *Science* 198:75–78

98. Nystrom, M. 1974. Neonatal facial-postural patterning during sleep: I. Description and reliability of observation. *Psychol. Res. Bull.* 14:7

99. Oster, H. 1978. Facial expression and affect development. See Ref. 27, pp. 43–76

100. Oster, H., Ekman, P. 1978. Facial behavior in child development. *Minn. Symp. Child Psychol.* 11:231–76

101. O'Sullivan, M., Eyman, J. 1978. Signal value of eyebrow movements in conversation. Presented at West. Psychol. Assoc. meet., San Francisco

102. Papousek, H., Papousek, M. 1977. Mothering and the cognitive head-start: psychobiological considerations. In *Studies in Mother-Infant Interaction,* ed. H. R. Schaffer, pp. 63–85. New York: Academic

103. Pieper, A. 1963. *Cerebral Function in Infancy and Childhood.* New York: Consultants Bureau

104. Redican, W. K. 1975. Facial expression in nonhuman primates. In *Primate Behavior Vol. 4,* ed. L. A. Rosenblum. New York: Academic

105. Roper, G. 1977. *The development of voluntary facial imitation in children.* MA thesis. San Francisco State Univ., San Francisco, Calif.

106. Saarni, C. 1978. *Acquisition of display rules for expressive behavior.* Presented

to East. Psychol. Assoc. meet., Washington DC

107. Saarni, C. 1978. Cognitive and communicative features of emotional experience, or do you show what you think you feel? See Ref. 27, pp. 361–76

108. Saha, G. B. 1973. Judgment of facial expression of emotion—a cross-cultural study. *J. Psychol. Res.* 17(2):59–63

109. Savitsky, J. C., Izard, C. E., Kotsch, W. E., Christy, L. 1974. Aggressor's response to the victim's facial expression of emotion. *J. Res. Pers.* 7:346–57

110. Scherer, K. R., Scherer, U., Hall, J. A., Rosenthal, R. 1977. Differential attribution of personality based on multichannel presentation of verbal and nonverbal cues. *Psychol. Res.* 39:221–47

111. Schiffenbauer, A. 1974. Effect of observer's emotional state on judgments of the emotional state of others. *J. Pers. Soc. Psychol.* 30(1):31–35

112. Schlosberg, H. 1941. A scale for the judgment of facial expression. *J. Exp. Psychol.* 29:497–510

113. Schlosberg, H. 1952. The description of facial expressions in terms of two dimensions. *J. Exp. Psychol.* 44:229–37

114. Schlosberg, H. 1954. Three dimensions of emotion. *Psychol. Rev.* 61:81–88

115. Schwartz, G. E., Fair, P. L., Salt, P., Mandel, M. K., Klerman, G. L. 1976. Facial muscle patterning to affective imagery in depressed and non-depressed subjects. *Science* 192(4238):489–91

116. Seaford, H. W. 1976. *Maximizing replicability in describing facial behavior.* Presented at Am. Anthropol. Assoc. meet., Washington DC

117. Shapiro, J. G. 1972. Variability and usefulness of facial and body cues. *Comp. Group Stud.* 3(4):437–42

118. Shultz, T. R., Zigler, E. 1970. Emotional concomitants of visual mastery in infants: The effect of stimulus movement on smiling and vocalizing. *J. Exp. Child Psychol.* 10:390–402

119. Smith, R. P. 1973. Frontalis muscle tension and personality. *Psychophysiology* 10(3):311–12

120. Sroufe, L. A. 1977. Wariness of strangers and the study of infant development. *Child Dev.* 48:731–46

121. Sroufe, L. A. 1978. The ontogenesis of emotion. In *Handbook of Infancy,* ed. J. Osofosky. New York: Wiley. In press

122. Sroufe, L. A., Waters, E. 1976. The ontogenesis of smiling and laughter: A perspective on the organization of development in infancy. *Psychol. Rev.* 83:173–189

123. Stechler, G., Carpenter, G. 1967. A viewpoint on early affect development. In *Exceptional Infant* Vol I.; *The Normal Infant,* ed. J. Hellmuth. New York: Brunner/Mazel

124. Steiner, J. E. 1973. The gustofacial response: Observation on normal and anencephalic newborn infants. In *Fourth Symposium on Oral Sensation and Perception,* ed. J. F. Bosma. Bethesda, Md: US Dep. HEW

125. Stern, D. N., Beebe, B., Jaffe, J., Bennett, S. L. 1978. The infant's stimulus world during social interaction: A study of caregiver behaviours with particular reference to repetition and timing. See Ref. 103, pp. 177–202

126. Suberi, M., McKeever, W. F. 1977. Differential right hemispheric memory storage of emotional and non-emotional faces. *Neuropsychologia* 15:757–68

127. Tagiuri, R. 1968. Person perception. In *The Handbook of Social Psychology,* ed. G. Lindzey, E. Aronson. Reading, Mass: Addison-Wesley

128. Tomkins, S. S. 1962. *Affect, Imagery, Consciousness,* Vol. 1, *The Positive Affects.* New York: Springer

129. Tomkins, S. S. 1963. *Affect, Imagery, Consciousness,* Vol. 2, *The Negative Affects.* New York: Springer

130. Tomkins, S. S., McCarter, R. 1964. What and where are the primary affects? Some evidence for a theory. *Percept. Mot. Skills* 18:119–58

131. Trevarthen, C. 1977. Descriptive analyses of infant communicative behavior. See Ref. 103, pp. 227–70

132. Vande Creek, L., Watkins, J. T. 1972. Responses to incongruent verbal and nonverbal emotional cues. *J. Commun.* 22:311–16

133. van Hooff, J. A. R. A. M. 1972. A comparative approach to the phylogeny of laughter and smiling. See Ref. 10, pp. 209–38

134. Vasquez, J. 1975. *The face and ideology.* PhD thesis. Rutgers Univ., New Brunswick, NJ

135. Vaughn, B. E., Sroufe, L. A. 1976. *The face of surprise in infants.* Presented at Animal Behav. Soc. meet., Boulder, Colo.

136. Waters, E., Matas, L., Sroufe, L. 1975. Infants' reaction to an approaching stranger: Description, validation, and functional significance of wariness. *Child Dev.* 46:348–56

137. Watson, J. S. 1978. Perception of contingency as a determinent of social responsiveness. In *The Origin of the Infant's Social Responsiveness,* ed. E. P.

Thoman. Hillsdale, NJ: Erlbaum. In press

138. Winkelmayer, R., Exline, R. V., Gottheil, E., Paredes, A. 1978. The relative accuracy of U.S., British, and Mexican raters in judging the emotional displays of schizophrenic and normal U.S. women. *J. Clin. Psychol.* In press

139. Wolff, P. H. 1963. Observations on the early development of smiling. In *Determinants of Infant Behavior II,* ed. B. M. Foss. New York: Wiley

140. Wolff, P. H. 1966. The causes, controls, and organization of behavior in the neonate. *Psychol. Issues* 5: Monogr. 17

141. Wolff, P. H. 1969. The natural history of crying and other vocalizations in early infancy. In *Determinants of Infant Behavior IV,* ed. B. M. Foss. London: Methuen

142. Young, G., Decarie, T. G. 1977. An ethology-based catalogue of facial/vocal behaviors in infancy. *Anim. Behav.* 25(1):95–107

143. Young-Browne, G., Rosenfeld, H. M., Horowitz, F. D. 1977. Infant discrimination of facial expressions. *Child Dev.* 48:555–62

144. Zaidel, S., Mehrabian, A. 1969. The ability to communicate and infer positive and negative attitudes facially and vocally. *J. Exp. Res. Pers.* 3:233–41

145. Zuckerman, M., DeFrank, R. S., Hall, J. A., Rosenthal, R. 1978. Nonverbal encoding and decoding of pleasant and unpleasant affects and of honest and deceptive messages. *J. Pers. Soc. Psychol.* In press

146. Zuckerman, M., Hall, J., DeFrank, R. S., Rosenthal, R. 1976. Encoding and decoding of spontaneous and posed facial expressions. *J. Pers. Soc. Psychol.* 34(5):966–77

Added in proof:

147. Malmstrom, E., Ekman, P., Friesen, W. V. 1972. *Autonomic changes with facial displays of surprise and disgust.* Presented at West. Psychol. Assoc. Meet., Portland, Ore.

Ann. Rev. Psychol. 1979. 30:555–602

COUNSELING PSYCHOLOGY ♦317

John D. Krumboltz, Jane F. Becker-Haven, and Kent F. Burnett

School of Education, Stanford University, Stanford, California 94305

CONTENTS

ALTERING MALADAPTIVE RESPONSES... 556
  Social Behavior 556
    School conduct and academic behavior 556
    Aggression.. 558
    Assertiveness 559
    Friendship... 560
    Marital problems.. 561
  Emotional Behavior.. 562
    Sexual disorders 562
    Depression... 563
    Phobias and anxiety... 564
  Health-Related Outcomes 566
    Insomnia 566
    Pain control 567
    Weight control.. 568
    Smoking cessation 570
  Intracounseling Behaviors 570
    Genuineness, warmth, and empathy 571
    Self-disclosure 572
    Social influence.. 574
    Persistence in treatment 576
DEVELOPING SKILL FOR CAREER TRANSITIONS 577
  Decision-Making Skills 577
  Career Maturity.. 581
  Nature and Quality of Vocational Choices... 583
    Nontraditional choices 583
    Career orientation 584
    Realism 584
    Stability 585
    Origins of career choice 585
  Employment Seeking.. 586
  Occupational Adaptation 587
PREVENTING PROBLEMS 588
  Preventing Family Problems 588
  Preventing School Problems.. 589

What do counseling psychologists know better now than they did 4 years ago about helping people solve their problems? In an effort to answer this question, we have surveyed the periodical research literature in the major journals relevant to counseling psychologists during the years 1974 through 1977. With all our biases intact we selected from among some 2500 articles a small fraction for discussion here. Articles were selected either because they were the best and most important, or because they typified a particular line of research or methodological procedure.

In order to make even this fraction more understandable, we attempted to summarize some generalizations that would be useful to counselors. These extrapolations to practice must be interpreted as tentative, but since counseling must proceed in the absence of certain knowledge, educated guesses about trends and directions may prove slightly more helpful than harmful. We informally referred to these summaries as "nuggets of knowledge" and have italicized them throughout the article. The supporting documentation follows each "nugget."

We have organized this review under some selected outcomes that counselors may wish to achieve with their clients. The three major types of outcomes that counseling psychologists are generally responsible for include (a) altering maladaptive responses, (b) helping individuals make more satisfactory career decisions and adjustments, and (c) preventing the occurrence of problems by providing anticipatory educational interventions.

ALTERING MALADAPTIVE RESPONSES

Social Behavior

SCHOOL CONDUCT AND ACADEMIC BEHAVIOR   While the utility of behavior modification procedures in the classroom has been amply demonstrated (220), concern has been expressed over the transfer of training to relevant nontreatment behaviors and settings (294, 322). Counselors have called for treatments that move the client further along the continuum from external toward internal control (154, 293). *In consulting with teachers, counselors may recommend teaching systems in which students are rewarded for cooperative behavior, assume responsibility for self-management of conduct problems, and learn prerequisite cognitive and problem-solving skills.*

Developers of the teams-games-tournament (TGT) program (69) claim that the traditional task and reward systems in classrooms, where individuals compete for a limited number of top grades, interferes with friendship ties between classmates since one child's success decreases the odds that another child will succeed. They have proposed alternative classroom structures for both tasks and rewards. TGT uses cooperative groups and reward structures so that children are encouraged to help their peers learn. Programmatic research on TGT (69, 264) has indicated increases in academic performance in math, reading, and language arts, but not social studies, as well as positive peer interaction in grades three through nine.

Minority students in elementary school made significant gains in academic achievement in an interdependent classroom as compared with a traditional competitive classroom (184). Students must cooperate with each other to learn the course material. Each student learns a piece of the study unit and teaches that portion to the rest of the group. In order to complete the picture, members must share their unique bit of the information puzzle. Important social by-products include improved self-confidence and cross-ethnic peer relations. The model seems particularly well suited to racially tense schools.

When fifth grade students were given major responsibility for structuring the behavior management system, major reductions in conduct problems occurred (24). Rules were requests for positive behavior. Instead of outright refusal of a request, students and teachers had to generate an alternative problem solution. Instead of teacher-imposed penalties for misconduct, students engaged in a self-correction procedure.

A social skills training package has helped withdrawn elementary school students increase their eye contact, loudness of speech, speech duration, and requests for behavior change in others (32). This training regime utilized instructions, feedback, behavioral rehearsal, and modeling in teaching the targeted components of social competency.

Spivack and Shure (261, 269, 270) have identified cognitive mediating skills as the defining factor in the quality of a child's social adjustment. Children taught how to think through and solve interpersonal problems became better adjusted than those who did not learn these skills. Unlike other social skills programs, the curriculum for preschoolers covers prerequisite language and thinking skills before any conflict scenarios are presented. For instance, children learn how to identify emotions in others—happy, sad, or mad—by watching, listening, and asking. The social behavior of preschool and kindergarten children significantly improved after they learned how to generate alternative solutions and to evaluate the consequences of alternative actions. Acting-out children decreased their aggressive behavior, and withdrawn children increased their social interaction. In a 2-year follow-up assessment, changes in interpersonal functioning were maintained at the end of first grade. A similar social problem-solving skill approach has shown promising results within a regular elementary school (1).

AGGRESSION   *To reduce aggressive behavior counselors may teach clients alternative self-instructions to use in the presence of cues which formerly triggered aggressive responses.* Recent work by Camp and her associates points to an ineffective linguistic control system as the common factor in the difficulties experienced by aggressive youngsters in both impersonal and interpersonal problem solving (41, 42). In the interpretation of her massive correlational study, Camp has detected a pattern of cognitive functioning for aggressive boys in which impulsive associative processing predominates. These aggressive young boys seldom use verbal mediation unless specifically requested to do so. Camp's findings would direct intervention strategies toward cueing the use of self-instructions ("now's the time" signals) and focusing self-instructions on relevant content ("cut out distracting garbage" in private monologs.)

Goodwin & Mahoney (100) have extended modeling as a treatment strategy into the area of cognitive processing. They explored a cognitive modeling strategy to improve hyperactive elementary school boys' ability to cope with aggressive verbal attacks from their peers. Subjects participated in a verbal taunting game—seemingly, a version of "verbal dodge ball." Hecklers in a circle tried to make a child in the center "lose his cool" under their jeering and taunting. The first cognitive modeling treatment consisted of watching a 3-minute videotape of the circle game; the boy who was "it" handled the verbal assaults with covert self-instructions, e.g. "I'm not going to let them bug me," "I won't get mad." The second cognitive modeling session added active instruction and rehearsal components.

For these hyperactive boys the vicarious experience of watching another boy cope with verbal aggression from his peers proved not effective enough to change their behavior. Only when a guided practice format was added to the cognitive modeling treatment were these boys able to perform the coping behavior. Whereas vicarious modeling alone might be sufficient for many youngsters in the average elementary school classroom, hyperactive and/or aggressive youngsters seem to require additional directed practice on when and how to use these coping self-instructions.

Novaco has provided a cognitive behavioral treatment of aggression which has been employed successfully with community clients with chronic anger problems (214), hospitalized depressives (215), and law enforcement personnel (216). Novaco's extension of Meichenbaum's (197) stress innoculation program proceeds in three stages: 1. cognitive awareness and preparation, 2. skill acquisition and rehearsal, and 3. practice in "real life."

Novaco utilizes cognitive restructuring, self-instructions and problem-solving techniques in the skills acquisition and rehearsal stage. Since covert language is proposed as the regulatory mechanism over anger and aggression, the counselor helps the client in generating self-instructions for each of the four phases of a conflict situation: 1. preparing for a provocation, 2. impact and confrontation, 3. coping with arousal, and 4. subsequent reflection. He includes in his procedures some of the cleanest examples in the literature of directly modifying self-statements to aid change in overt social behaviors. However, it is important to note that clients must rehearse the overt behaviors at the same time as the covert behaviors to obtain the maximum effectiveness. Teaching new behavior patterns provides an opportune time for coaching new self-statements. Instead of merely teaching new motor behaviors to resolve playground disputes nonviolently, for instance, counselors could teach directly the accompanying private "soundtrack."

ASSERTIVENESS   *To increase assertiveness, counselors should teach clients both the appropriate interpersonal skills and the cognitive self-statements that enable these skills to be used.* Despite widespread use of assertiveness training in various counseling settings, the superiority of any one treatment package has yet to be demonstrated (61, 239). Three factors have been proposed as causes for the development and maintenance of unassertiveness: conditioned anxiety, behavioral response deficiency, and maladaptive cognitions. While treatments based on each of these factors can produce some improvement when compared with no-treatment controls, the comparative merit of all three approaches for various client types awaits a suitable experimental test.

Skills training holds the empirical edge in studies that compare two or more diverse treatments. Twentyman & McFall's (301) benchmark study of female-shy males showed that a treatment consisting of behavioral rehearsal, modeling, and coaching reduced autonomic arousal and self-reported anxiety and improved observer-rated dating performance. Although systematic desensitization proved as successful in alleviating dating anxiety indicators and increasing dating frequency in the short-term as skills training, the subjects in the skills building program performed more skillfully at a 6-month follow-up (62). A similar dating skills training program based on the response acquisition model was found more effective than sensitivity training in reducing dating anxiety and increasing the frequency of actual dates (63). The skill building treatment package used in the last two studies covered the gamut of dating concerns from planning and asking for dates to physical intimacy worries. Methods included information giving, modeling, behavioral rehearsal, coaching, video and group feedback, and in vivo homework assignments (61).

Assertion microtraining (with or without videotape) in which the counselor and client analyzed the response components in actual assertive performance proved superior to insight-oriented therapies on both behavioral measures and self-reported indexes of personal effectiveness and anxiety

(103). Self-referred adults from the community learned and maintained assertive behaviors significantly better in a group treatment using behavioral rehearsal and contingency contracting with a "buddy" program than in a behavioral discussion group treatment; yet both groups claimed equal changes in self-reported assertiveness in a variety of settings (251).

What are the components of the assertive response that prove difficult for a low assertive client? In the initial analysis of assertive response deficits, Schwartz & Gottman (254) found that low assertives reported higher tension, more negative self-statements, and fewer positive self-statements than high or moderate assertives. No differences were found in heart rate or knowledge of appropriately assertive communications. Thus, cognitive mediators of the overt assertive behavior may stand in the way of delivering an assertive communication.

As yet, few studies have focused on these components. When modeling and behavioral rehearsal were augmented by procedures to change self-statements, low assertive women significantly reduced the amount of anxiety experienced while performing an assertive response as compared to women receiving a modeling and behavioral rehearsal only (323).

Changing self-statements of female-shy males increased real-life interaction with females more than response acquisition treatments (92). Although the behavioral response acquisition treatment for dating skills (coaching/modeling/recoaching) did result in better performance during training and role-play assessments, cognitive self-statement treatment produced greater transfer to nontraining situations and greater changes in actual dating behavior.

Junior high students experiencing stress in their interactions with peers, parents, teachers, or siblings increased the comfort they felt in those social interactions through cognitive reappraisal of (a) their view of these social situations as aversive and (b) their ability to perform coping behaviors (246).

These few studies advance the notion that once response acquisition treatments have been completed, cognitive restructuring may aid the actual performance of the skill in other real-life situations.

FRIENDSHIP   *Skills needed for cooperative behavior and friendship can be identified and taught with some expectations of success.* Coaching in friendship skills proved more effective than peer pairing (a "buddy system") in gaining and maintaining higher sociometric ratings and friendship nominations of socially isolated children (218). This friendship skills training method succeeded in maintaining gains in peer status a year after training. The training sequence was as follows: 1. verbal instruction by an adult coach, 2. practice of these skills with a peer during a play period, 3. discussion between coach and child to analyze the peer interaction, and 4. suggestion to use these skills on a daily basis. Participation, cooperation, communication, and validation were emphasized in the training. Prior research has validated those four skill areas as important to peer acceptance (6, 119).

Should an entire group receive consequences because of the behavior of any single member? Hayes (121) has concluded that group contingencies are as effective as individual reward systems in controlling disruptive behavior. When the disruptive behavior is clearly maintained by peer reinforcement, group contingencies are recommended as the method of choice. Cooperative behavior stands out as a positive by-product of group contingencies. However, Hayes warns potential users of this technique to make sure that individuals have the prerequisite skills for performing the target behavior before applying group contingencies.

MARITAL PROBLEMS   *Potentially useful techniques in marriage counseling include the teaching of communication, problem-solving, and contract-negotiation skills.* The limited controlled research points to the utility of behavior change strategies to restructure the interaction patterns of distressed married couples. In the counseling literature, research from a social learning perspective predominates the area of marital adjustment (147). Preliminary normative data indicate that unhappily married couples demonstrate a deficit in problem-solving skills and report significantly more unresolved problems and fewer shared free activities than happily married couples (27).

Couples trained in problem-solving skills and contingency contracting improved their marital relationships as measured by self-observation as well as nonparticipant observation of videotapes (146). The treatment package, following the format suggested by Patterson, Weiss and their associates (227), helped couples learn communication, problem solving, and negotiation strategies based on positive rather than aversive control. Ratings of increased satisfaction with their marriages were maintained at a one-year follow-up.

Ongoing work by Ewart (82) probes systematically the process of change under cognitive-behavioral treatments of marital discord. Using a combination of communication skills training and contingency contracts (105), Ewart is exploring factors in the contracting process. Ewart found contracting to be as effective with middle-aged couples with long histories of marital discord as with the young marrieds. Preliminary analysis showed few outcome differences between types of contracts either in actual changes on day-to-day affectional and verbal behaviors targeted by couples or satisfaction with treatment procedures. Parallel personal goal setting ("I'll keep my end of the bargain regardless of whether you do or not") appeared as powerful in changing behavior as *quid pro quo* contracting ("I'll change if and only if you change").

Emotional Behavior

SEXUAL DISORDERS   *Video desensitization has been helpful in reducing heterosexual anxiety; directed self-masturbation has been effective for female anorgasmia.* Counselors have received little additional guidance from controlled research on sexual problems in the last 4 years. Progress in developing scientifically based treatments is plagued by a preponderance of uncontrolled case studies. Masters & Johnson (190) remains the standard reference in the area.

In the treatment of female sexual dysfunctions, counselors can try directed self-masturbation for anorgasmia and video desensitization for heterosexual anxiety. Barbach (16) and Heiman, LoPiccolo & LoPiccolo (127a) have produced client self-help manuals based on their prior research with behavioral treatments for female orgasmic dysfunction. Both treatments incorporate self-masturbation. Video desensitization reduced heterosexual anxiety in women with essential sexual dysfunction better than standard systematic desensitization. This procedure combined relaxation with a videotaped hierarchy of normal heterosexual behavior. Although the study was intended merely to reduce heterosexual anxiety, one fourth of the nonorgasmic women had become orgasmic by termination of treatment.

When counseling chronic exhibitionists, counselors should consider aversion, covert desensitization, and aversive behavior rehearsal. Chronic exhibitionists benefited in the short term most from aversion, next from self-regulation, and least from relaxation in a study using a balanced, incomplete Latin square design (243a). Unfortunately, after one year more than half of the subjects had reexposed themselves at least once, and 40% of those with prior convictions for exhibitionism had been reconvicted. One study found that covert desensitization combined with the introduction of a malodorous substance at critical times eliminated exposing behavior as well as exhibitionistic fantasies, urges, and dreams (187). Absence of exhibitionism was reported up to one year later. Aversive behavior rehearsal, in which the exhibitionist exposes himself at specific times and places in front of people who know him, has provided relief for a series of chronic exhibitionists (320). No relapses have been reported at follow-ups that range up to 7 years.

The wide variety of sexual disorders and the need for identifying components of effective treatments presents a challenging series of problems for future researchers.

DEPRESSION   *To overcome depression, counselors may effectively use a cognitive approach to substitute data-based for distorted beliefs as well as arranging increased frequencies of positive reinforcement.* Recent research has shown considerable progress in counseling depressed clients, particularly using treatments which follow the recommendations of Beck (22) from the cognitive perspective and Lewinsohn (175) from the behavioral viewpoint. A third formulation, Seligman's (257, 258) "learned helplessness" model, holds promise for future treatment directions. Learned helplessness can be interpreted as a special case of Bandura's (11) self-efficacy model, where the client's efficacy expectation is zero. Seligman proposes that depressed persons have ceased to believe that they can control what happens to them; they have learned that they have no impact on the course of events —good or bad—in their lives. As yet, research based upon this model has been confined to interventions with depressed infrahumans and experimental exercises with college students in the laboratory. Counselors must wait for applied demonstrations of this theoretically tantalizing model.

According to Beck (21, 22), a negative set pervades the cognitions and beliefs of the depressed client. During treatment, the counselor uses both verbal and behavioral techniques to teach the client to "(*a*) recognize the connections between cognition, affect, and behavior, (*b*) monitor his negative thoughts, (*c*) examine the evidence for and against his distorted cognitions, and (*d*) substitute more reality-oriented interpretations for his distorted negative cognitions" (244). In addition, clients learn to recognize and to change their dysfunctional belief systems which act as negatively distorting filters for their experiences. Since many of the specific tactics used to bring about this cognitive restructuring, such as homework assignments, are behavioral in nature, there cannot be as sharp a demarcation between cognitive and behavioral camps as one would be led to believe by the labeling of therapies.

Lewinsohn's (176) conception of depression pinpoints the reduction in the rate of positive reinforcement contingent on responding. Depression is said to result when little or no positive reinforcement occurs or when what reinforcement does occur is not contingent on the person's behavior. Lewinsohn (174) has identified three sets of circumstances in which rates of response-contingent reinforcement may be low: (*a*) events that are contingent on behavior may not prove to be reinforcing; (*b*) events that are reinforcing may not be available; and (*c*) events that are reinforcing are available, but the person may not have the skills needed to secure them. The treatment package based on Lewinsohn's view of depression includes: (*a*) boosting the frequency of pleasant events, (*b*) training in social skills, (*c*) increasing the frequency and comfort of social contacts, (*d*) decreasing negative ruminations, (e) decreasing depression-related verbal behavior, and (f) overcoming sleep difficulties.

Although both Beck's brand of cognitive therapy and the standard tricyclic pharmacotherapy provided significant relief from depression, cognitive therapy surpassed the drug therapy in reducing self-reported and clinically rated symptoms of depression in a community sample (244). Furthermore, almost 80% of the clients in the cognitive treatment achieved marked improvement or complete remission of symptoms over against about 23% of the tricyclic drug clients when absolute scores on the post-treatment measures were examined. Significantly more drug therapy clients terminated prematurely, and early dropout was associated with more severe depression. At a 3-month follow-up, cognitive therapy remained significantly more effective than pharmacotherapy; at 6 months, a trend toward significance in reducing depression persisted in favor of the cognitive therapy.

Beck's cognitive therapy emerged as the clear winner on a controlled comparison of three treatments—cognitive a la Beck, behavioral a la Lewinsohn, and nondirective a la Rogers—as measured against a waiting list control group (260). All treatments were administered in a group format. On both self-report (Beck Depression Inventory) and clinical rating (Hamilton Rating Scale for Depression), the cognitive treatment produced the greatest reductions in depressive symptoms in university students in their late teens to midtwenties.

Another study showed a combination of Beck's cognitive therapy and Lewinsohn's behavior therapy to be more effective in treating depression than either regime alone (285). While all three treatment groups demonstrated improvements compared to the waiting list control, no significant differences showed up between the cognitive and the behavior therapy. The 5-week follow-up fell at midterm examination time for this client group composed of university undergraduates and graduate students. Since treatment gains were maintained or improved even then, these treatments can be viewed as providing coping strategies sufficient to deal with at least one depression-provoking situation.

PHOBIAS AND ANXIETY   *Animal phobias can be conquered rapidly and enduringly through guided participant modeling. Test anxiety can similarly be reduced by a coping model, a cognitive treatment to formulate constructive self-instructions, and a rationale emphasizing self-control.*

Recent work on snake phobia by Bandura focuses on cognitive mediation in behavior change. Bandura (11) contends that a psychological intervention, whatever its format, is successful to the degree that it creates and strengthens clients' belief in their personal efficacy. Once clients have the ability to perform the task and the incentives to do so are present, the clients' perception of their power to accomplish the task is the crucial component in actual performance. In the treatment of extreme snake phobias, participant modeling produced higher ratings of self-efficacy and better performance in snake approach behavior than vicarious modeling (14). Similarly, participant modeling worked better in terms of self-efficacy ratings and performance than desensitization (13).

Charting the process of fear reduction, Schroeder & Rich (253) found that decreases in overt avoidance of the phobic object lagged behind covert avoidance. At a given point in therapy, some clients could not perform the task that they could complete nonanxiously in imagination.

Guided participant modeling proved significantly more effective than covert modeling (288). Under guided participant modeling, almost all clients could reach the highest items on Bandura's behavioral approach hierarchy—allowing the snake to crawl freely over their laps.

Fixed role playing (155) produced swift and lasting changes in both behavioral and subjective measures of snake phobia when compared to videotape modeling (178). College students were instructed to act, think, and feel "as if" they were John/Jane Harris, a fearless snake hobbyist, as they interacted with an imaginary snake in a self-paced approach. While substantial gains were made by fixed role playing subjects in their ability to approach a live boa, few achieved the top item on Bandura's behavioral approach hierarchy.

Research points to the use of in vivo guided participant modeling as the most efficient treatment of small animal phobias. Modeling, whether vicarious or participant, usually is accompanied by a factual, informational narrative. While the superiority of a coping over a mastery model has been shown in the performance of approach behaviors, the analogous coping cognitions have yet to be included in experimental treatments of phobias. Future research might test the effectiveness of adding a coping "self-talk" component to guided participant modeling. Although snakes provide a "phobia of choice" for research on the treatment process (12), it is time for guided participant modeling to tackle a broader range of presenting problems.

Clients best gain control over test anxiety through active coping strategies. Cognitive therapy outdistanced desensitization in Holroyd's (137) group treatment of test anxiety. College students in cognitive therapy experienced less anxiety during an analog testing situation and raised their grade point averages higher than those students who received systematic desensitization, a combined cognitive-desensitization procedure, pseudotherapy, or waiting list controls. Holroyd's cognitive treatment concentrated on eliminating task-irrelevant thoughts that generate anxiety and divert attention from the test. After increasing awareness through self-monitoring and challenging the rational basis for these disruptive thoughts, clients devised coping self-instructions to fight their test anxiety.

When systematic desensitization is recast in a self-control paradigm, as Goldfried (76) has suggested, then test anxiety can be reduced and academic performance enhanced (67, 268). Goldfried recommended presenting the rationale and procedures of desensitization as learning a relaxation skill to cope with anxiety. Compared with clients experiencing a traditional counterconditioning paradigm, clients learning relaxation skills under the self-control paradigm needed fewer and shorter sessions to reduce debilitating test anxiety. Moreover, the self-control clients increased their academic performance in the same and subsequent terms (67).

The utility of modeling coping mechanisms has been supported in a laboratory setting. Sarason (248) found that high test-anxious subjects outperformed their low-anxious counterparts if and only if they were exposed to an experimenter who self-disclosed test anxiety experiences and the successful use of several coping strategies.

Health-Related Outcomes

Counseling and clinical psychologists are becoming more involved in the treatment of health-related problems, teaming with medical personnel when necessary. This involvement has resulted from the growing body of research which has demonstrated the efficacy of behavioral approaches in a wide range of health problems. Clients suffering from chronic insomnia (51), essential hypertension (144), or migraine headache (203) are now finding personal sources of control which are attractive alternatives to pharmacologic measures. Behavioral interventions have also been documented as helpful in weight control (209) and smoking cessation (169), as well as the treatment of diverse disorders such as Raynaud's disease (29), dysmenorrhea (284), chronic low back pain (40), abdominal pain (247), severe tremor (171), and mucous colitis (327).

INSOMNIA   *To reduce insomnia, counselors can teach their clients to arrange sleep-inducing cues in their bedroom and to relax using progressive muscle relaxation, autogenic training, or meditation.*

Pharmacologic measures are by far the most "used and abused" method of relief sought by persons with chronic sleep problems. The heavy reliance on drug treatment, both prescription and over the counter, has been criticized because of "1) tolerance effects, 2) carryover effects, 3) alterations in sleep patterns, 4) rebound effects and 5) attributional effects" (237). It is quite possible, however, that once the "honeymoon period" is over, behavioral scientists will critically examine and find undesirable reactive qualities of behavioral interventions.

Most behavioral treatments for insomnia have focused on teaching clients procedures for managing cognitive and/or somatic anxiety at bedtime. For example, progressive muscle relaxation training (145) has been consistently cited as beneficial in reducing sleep onset times, number of times awakened, and global reports of sleep improvement (123, 124, 177, 212, 326). Other techniques, however, appear to be equally effective: autogenic suggestion (212), meditation training (326), and EMG feedback-assisted relaxation (123). Follow-up data indicate substantial maintenance of treatment gains.

Haynes et al (122) demonstrated a powerful impact of stimulus control procedures in the treatment of insomnia using an ABAB design. All four subjects who were instructed in the modification of the stimulus properties of their bedroom showed improvement; however, two of the subjects failed to demonstrate a reversal during that phase of the program. All subjects maintained treatment gains at a 9-month follow-up. Stimulus control procedures may represent an effective alternative to relaxation therapies in the treatment of insomnia.

These encouraging findings tend to obscure the fact, however, that many individual problem sleepers show moderate or no improvement when treated using these procedures. Further research is required to determine whether "nonresponders" to traditional behavioral treatments for insomnia may benefit from either combined treatments or the development of new approaches such as the elimination of bedtime tension through effective management of daytime stress.

PAIN CONTROL   *Counselors can help clients to control the perception of physical pain by teaching them how to relax and how to use relevant cognitive coping strategies (e.g. imagining pleasant events or insensitivity to pain.)*

Reduction in perception of pain following training in cognitive coping strategies has been demonstrated in a number of studies (48, 173, 266). In a controlled comparison of tolerance for cold pressor pain (hand immersion in ice water), Grimm & Kanfer (109) demonstrated the superiority of specific cognitive coping strategies over (*a*) brief relaxation training, and (*b*) manipulated expectancy. However, the relaxation technique produced the lowest heartrate and the least self-reported pain though actual immersion time was no longer than that of controls. The lack of correspondence between perceived aversiveness and tolerance of pain indicates that further studies of pain control should also incorporate behavioral measures of tolerance (e.g. duration, intensity) as well as subjective discomfort ratings.

It is too soon to conclude, however, that cognitive coping strategies are more effective than relaxation training in the control of pain. Perhaps the discrimination skills needed for effective relaxation simply require more time to learn than the verbal/symbolic activities in cognitive coping strategies. The brief training time required to learn how to use cognitive strategies effectively, however, makes it an attractive therapy in the control of pain. Both externally induced hypnotic suggestion (130) and self-suggested thoughts, ideas, images (e.g. insensitivity to pain) fall within this area. Self-suggestion is currently under investigation and may hold more promise.

Several studies indicate the usefulness of relaxation exercises in the relief of clinical pain such as migraine headache (50, 59, 81, 203). Innovative applications of relaxation exercises include the control of pain associated with dysmennorhea (284) and phantom limb pain (195).

Combined methods may hold the most promise in the control of pain (292), although little research has been done to demonstrate the increased efficacy of such an approach. Mitchell & White (203) used an intensive design over 56 weeks in which a variety of cognitive and behavioral skills were taught to a chronic sufferer of migraine headache pain. At the end of mental and muscular relaxation training, a 64 percent reduction in headaches had occurred. When additional self-management skills were taught, the headaches were reduced by 100 percent. This evidence, although confounded by the passage of time, suggests that combined methods may be more effective. Holroyd et al (138) also used a broad spectrum approach to the treatment of migraine headache pain, teaching a variety of stress-coping skills. Subjects who were taught stress-coping showed considerably more improvement than an EMG biofeedback or control group. Stress-coping skills focused on identifying the antecedents and consequences of tension producing behavior, reappraising attitudes and beliefs about the stressful event, and developing coping self-instructions ("Calm down . . .") or imagery ("Imagine myself for a moment carefree, at the beach").

WEIGHT CONTROL   *Counselors can help obese clients lose weight by teaching a variety of self-management skills for modifying poor eating habits and by helping clients isolate specific situational factors which are associated with personal weight gain.*

Weight control is often cited as an area in which behavioral treatment has been particularly effective (279, 280). In general, however, the treatment effects have been modest for short-term change (2 to 3 months), and reports of long-term change (12 months) are quite infrequent. With one exception (209) there have been no successful replications of the dramatic sustained weight losses demonstrated with obese clients by Stuart (278) in which 80% lost 20 pounds or more and 30% lost 40 pounds or more.

A vast majority of the weight control studies reporting significant results are mere demonstration studies of the efficacy of behavioral approaches for facilitating short-term behavior change. The actual results are usually far from dramatic, averaging slightly over 1 pound weight loss per week over 8–12 weeks of treatment. In these studies, follow-up data indicate that even these modest changes have not been maintained 1 year after therapist contact is ended (4, 113–116, 177, 295). In view of the discouraging data on maintenance, additional short-term change demonstrations seem scarcely justifiable.

The Dietary Rehabilitation Clinic (DRC) at Duke University serves as a model for researchers who wish to apply behavioral principles in intensive settings (209). Major treatment components included three meals per day provided at the clinic dining room (700 calories) and in vivo retraining of eating habits (waiting 1 minute before starting to eat, putting down utensils between mouthfuls, slowing down chewing and increasing total eating time). Cognitive relearning was also stressed, e.g. "unstructured eating" was substituted for the concept of "cheating." In addition to medical supervision, brief consultation (3–5 min) with a psychologist was made available daily to answer questions of concern to clients. Short-term weight loss was 2.3 pounds per week for females (10.4 weeks) and 3.5 pounds per week (8.2 weeks) for males. Musante does not report the number of clients who remained in extended treatment (6–11 months); however, of those who stayed in treatment 84.6% lost 20 pounds or more and 61.5% lost 40 pounds or more. These results are comparable to those obtained by Stuart (278) using similar behavior change techniques.

While intensive treatment seems to be required for behavioral programs to be effective with this complex client problem, Coates & Thoresen (52) provide evidence that not all treatment strategies may be necessary for each individual. A series of single subject research designs was employed to examine the relationships among treatments, eating behaviors, and weight loss in three obese adolescent girls. Detailed self-reports on times, places, and activities associated with eating and exercise were kept by the girls daily over a 3-month period. Objective information on eating behaviors was collected by nonparticipant observers who visited each girl's home at mealtimes on 30 occasions throughout the study.

Weight losses for one girl were highly correlated with storing low caloric food on kitchen shelves and restricting the number of locations in which eating occurred. For another of the girls, weight losses were associated with slowing the rate of eating and reducing the number of second helpings by keeping platters off the table at meals. Individual tailoring of treatment is an obvious benefit of this type of research strategy. Further, these results expand our conceptualization of obesity by suggesting that it is not a unitary client problem but rather a series of learned behaviors which are maintained for each individual by specific situational factors.

SMOKING CESSATION   *Counselors can intervene to help clients abstain from smoking for short periods; however, a broad range maintenance plan including contracts, booster sessions, and group support may be necessary for long-term change.*

Progress in the area of smoking cessation is plagued with many of the same problems that face researchers in weight reduction. A diversity of behavioral techniques (rapid smoking aversion, electric shock aversion, and stimulus control) are quite effective in producing acute behavior change (54, 167, 168, 172, 236); however, demonstrations of maintenance at 6 months or 1 year are unusual. Lando (169) stated that "the point of diminishing returns seems to have been reached in the investigation of one-shot approaches to eliminate chronic cigarette smoking." Only 30% of treated subjects become nonsmokers while about 20% of chronic smokers are able to quit on their own (191).

Lando (169) used rapid smoking aversion therapy (taking a puff every 6 seconds) to virtually eliminate smoking in 34 subjects at the end of 1 week of treatment. He then augmented treatment for half the subjects with a broad range follow-up plan. Subjects in this maintenance condition made contracts with the therapist and friends, attended booster sessions, and participated in supportive group discussions in which effective methods for maintenance were shared by group members. The 6 month abstinence rates were 76% for the maintenance group compared to 35% for the no-contact group. Caution should be exercised, however, in the use of the rapid smoking technique. Reports of numerous potential hazards to cardiovascular health have recently been issued by several investigators (65, 139, 140).

Intracounseling Behaviors

Counseling research has traditionally been divided into process and outcome research. We believe this dichotomous line of reasoning to be logically indefensible. Like a möbius loop, process and outcome are connected and represent different faces of the larger process of client change. In a sense, all client change attributable to counseling begins with new skills, perceptions, or beliefs first learned in the counseling session itself. From this perspective, outcome research is actually the study of the generalization of these changes, begun in the therapeutic context, to everyday behavior. By focusing only on before and after measures, researchers ignore the continuum of client change.

Intensive single subject research designs (291) are an appropriate investigative tool for gaining an initial understanding of this larger process of client change. Intensive data collection procedures (repeated measures) allow process-outcome-process-outcome to be continually assessed. For example, Leitenberg et al (171b) used an intensive design strategy to investigate the role of feedback and therapist praise during the treatment of phobia. After establishing some stability in dependent measures during the baseline phase, praise and therapist feedback were varied systematically and examined in relation to *rate of client improvement*. The results indicated that therapist feedback was important in getting approach behavior underway, but praise plus graduated practice was sufficient to sustain continuing improvement on its own once initial progress had begun. The use of intensive approaches would virtually eliminate the need for a distinction between counseling process and outcome research.

GENUINENESS, WARMTH, AND EMPATHY   *Counselors who wish to be seen as genuine, warm, and empathic should emulate a good model and attempt to gain supervisory feedback on their performance.*

Research efforts to establish a positive link between therapeutic outcome and therapist interpersonal skills resulted in the apparent substantiation of Rogers' triad of therapist genuineness, warmth, and empathy (299). Serious methodological problems, however, have been identified in these studies (102). Chief among these criticisms is the lack of evidence that raters can accurately and reliably measure these dimensions. Low correlations have been found between supervisors' performance ratings and self-report scales (88, 152) as well as other written and verbal measures of counselor facilitativeness (310).

Blass & Heck (28) demonstrated that observers' ratings of therapist empathy were influenced by prior knowledge of the client's problem type and severity. The possible construct contamination becomes more serious when we realize that most studies employ the same observers for repeated measures. Avery and associates (8) have recently questioned the construct validity of Carkhuff's Empathic Understanding Scale. The concept of empathy is rich—richer than any one operational definition of it. We must be careful not to assume that the validation of one scale validates the entire concept (141, 290).

LaCross (166) has shown that client and observer ratings of therapist facilitativeness are highly correlated with ratings of attraction and expertness. These results add support to the position that ratings of facilitativeness actually reflect client perception of a more unified dimension of therapist behavior. This dimension has been identified by LaCross as "charisma" and elsewhere as the "good therapist" quality (97).

Despite these conceptual and measurement problems, reduction in judged empathy level was found to precede client topic change in one methodologically sound study (108). In another well-designed study, reduction in judged empathy level was related to less successful outcome in automated systematic desensitization (205). Further research is needed to determine whether these results are replicable across therapeutic approaches and a diversity of presenting problems.

Some researchers have attempted direct interventions to increase the level of facilitative functioning of counselors and counselor trainees. Modeling has been found to be an effective "high fidelity" method for increasing empathic understanding in a number of studies (111, 243, 272, 275). Specific "how to" instructions appear to be a rather "low fidelity" method, increasing empathic responding in some cases (43, 303) and not in others (275). Supervisory feedback, although less powerful than direct modeling, is also an effective method of training counseling students in empathic responding (43).

SELF-DISCLOSURE   *Counselors can increase client expressiveness and self-disclosure by modeling it, requesting it, sitting moderately close to the client, and arranging a "warm" room. However, the degree to which self-disclosure promotes therapeutic outcomes remains unclear.*

High levels of client expressiveness and intimate self-disclosure have been presented as client process variables predictive of successful outcomes in counseling (36, 238). We were unable, however, to locate any research evidence in the past 4 years to further validate this claim. Wexler & Butler (319) advance the argument based upon clinical experience that the uninvolved client is low in expressiveness and withholds information vital to the success of the therapeutic enterprise. Clients who are actively participating in their own change are more likely, therefore, to be highly expressive and self-disclosing.

On the other hand, serious questions have been put forth regarding these measures. Intimate self-disclosure to a slight acquaintance or person much older or younger was judged as highly inappropriate in a study by Chaikin & Derlega (45). Thus, timing of self-disclosure and situational variables may be very important in assessment. In another study, Derlega & Chaikin (68) demonstrated that self-disclosure is directly related to ratings of female adjustment and inversely related to male adjustment. Gitter & Black (91) presented evidence that intimacy of self-disclosure is related to a tendency to distort the facts: self-disclosure is not always self-revealing. Cultural differences exist in what is judged to be appropriate self-disclosure (180, 281). More precisely, what may be appropriate self-disclosure for one person in a particular situation may not be seen as appropriate for another.

Hence, little solid evidence exists to link high levels of client expressiveness and self-disclosure to more successful therapeutic outcomes. The weight of the evidence suggests a great need for further investigation into the construct validity of these measures. Behavioral investigation has shown that raters tend to have differences in sensitivity to client expressiveness and that interviewers seem to create somewhat idiosyncratic ceiling effects on level of elicited self-disclosure (99, 297).

Valid or not, there is an abundant literature on self-disclosure promoting treatments. Modeling has been shown repeatedly to have a positive effect on client self-disclosure (3, 73, 194, 274, 287, 319). Wexler & Butler (319) utilized an intensive single subject design to show that therapist modeled expressiveness introduced in a single session was directly related to increased ratings of client expressiveness which persisted throughout subsequent sessions. Other studies on modeling have focused on the effects of pretraining volunteer subjects in simulated counseling. One such analog study (46) suggested that "neurotic" individuals respond at a moderate level of self-disclosure regardless of attempts to model the behavior.

Specific instructions to self-disclose were found to be as effective as modeling in increasing self-disclosure (272a). No additive effects were observed in combined treatments. The effect of distance on level of self-disclosure was assessed by Stone & Morden (273). During the initial interview subjects talked longer about personal subjects when seated at an intermediate distance from the interviewer. These results are consistent with earlier work on proximal behavior and self-reported anxiety (71). Future studies may want to examine the durability of these findings over sessions.

It is not surprising that an intimate environment promotes intimacy of self-disclosure. Chaikin et al (47) indicate that intimacy of self-disclosure in counseling analog sessions was increased in an environment featuring pictures on the wall, soft cushioned furniture, a rug, and soft lighting compared to bare cement, block walls, and fluorescent lighting. We expect that environmental variables exert a strong influence over a host of other process-related outcomes. A pioneering study in this regard was conducted by Haase & DiMattia (112) in which they systematically varied room size, distance, and furniture arrangement to assess the impact of environmental manipulation on the conditioning of self-reference statements in counseling analog sessions. Larger room sizes were found to have a positive main effect on the conditioning process.

The theory that client self-disclosure is a function of counselor self-disclosure was given conditional support by Halpern (117). Test-retest data also indicated that a past tendency to self-disclose and the perception of the counselor as warm and empathic were related to a present tendency to self-disclose. Additional evidence that warm, moderately disclosing counselors can help initiate client self-disclosure has been provided in several analog studies (46, 188, 263) as well as by the evidence on counselor modeling of self-disclosure.

SOCIAL INFLUENCE   Social influence factors in counseling process were defined by Strong (276) as counselor credibility (perceived expertness and trustworthiness) and attractiveness. These factors were extrapolated from early social psychological research which linked a communicator's ability to induce behavior change to the listener's perceptions about the communicator (95, 142, 276). The relationship of these factors to client motivation to change has been the subject of much investigation in counseling research.

Attraction   Counselors who want to be seen as attractive should be empathic, warm, and active, should provide information on topics of importance to the client, and should work on both cognitive and behavioral change.
Client attraction to the counselor is a factor believed to account for part of the variance in counselor ability to create an effective therapeutic relationship (276, 277). Recent findings, however, suggest that attraction is not an independent dimension. LaCross (166) demonstrated high correlations between attraction and facilitativeness. Thus, counselors who are perceived as attractive generally are perceived also as genuine, warm, and empathic. In another study, Venzor and associates (305) allowed subjects to choose freely among a large number of adjectives to describe preferred counselor roles. Both client and nonclient subjects most often chose adjectives describing a "nurturant" counselor. We may learn more about preferences if we do not limit subject responses by artificially forcing choices among only a few checklist alternatives.
Analog studies (38, 39, 286) previously have shown more attraction and "relationship centered satisfaction" between client and counselor if they both hold similar attitudes. The validity of these findings for natural settings has been challenged in a study by Cheney (49). Prison inmates, incarcerated for public intoxication, listened to taped therapy sessions and gave higher attraction ratings to therapists who talked about alcohol-related items regardless of the degree of expressed similarity to client attitudes. However, the inmates were not being counseled themselves.
Preferences for an active rather than passive counselor have been demonstrated in college student populations. Dreman (74) found that college students referring themselves for treatment at a university counseling service had preferences for active counselors who worked toward symptom relief of both cognitive and behavioral problems. An analog study of preferred counselor roles by Peoples & Dell (229) also indicated preferences for active versus passive counselors among a college student population of both black and white students. Woods & Zimmer (325) further investigated racial differences in counseling with multiple biracial dyads and found no

differences in client perceptions of attraction as measured by the semantic differential.

Some person variables have been related to counselor preference. Changing trends in women's attitudes reflect a shift toward female preferences for female counselors (262). These findings were obtained in a large sample of women across a broad range of ages and occupations. Physically disabled counselors were seen as more attractive in one study (202). This perception apparently is mediated through the belief that disabled counselors are capable of more understanding and empathy. Finally, and not surprisingly, physically attractive counselors were rated more favorably across a number of dimensions including client attraction to counselor, expertness, and expectancy for positive outcome (44).

Perceived expertness   Counselors who wish to be seen as expert and trustworthy should obtain a PhD degree, display their diplomas, receive a prestigious introduction to clients, and behave in a prepared, confident, and relaxed manner.

Beutler et al (26) clearly demonstrated that client perception of counselor credibility is a crucial determinant of therapeutic outcome. Counselor experience, prestige, verbal and nonverbal behavior have each been shown to mediate this perception.

Contrary to previous findings (252), counselor experience was positively related to perceived expertness in several analog studies (232, 267, 286). In another study (250) conducted with actual clients at a university counseling service, clients of experienced counselors reported better outcomes. The cutoff for "experienced counselors," however, was not amount of experience, but possession of the PhD. Several "inexperienced counselors" had as much or more actual counseling experience. Such an interpretation implies the importance of whatever factors are correlated with possession of a doctoral degree.

Following the suggestion of Strong (276), Heppner & Pew (128) provide additional support for the position that external cues such as diplomas and awards influence client perception of counselor competence. The powerful effect of a prestigious introduction on initial perception of expertness has been demonstrated as well (7, 249). There is no evidence at this point, however, that any of these factors can mask the effects of poor counselor performance over the course of therapy.

Dell & Schmidt (66) investigated the relationship of a variety of factors to client perception of counselor credibility and found that only individual counselor performance is related to perceived expertness in the initial interview situation. Salient behavioral cues included preparedness, gesticulation, use of the client's first name, relaxed posture, and nonmonotonic voice. Sex differences in perceived expertness were not demonstrated in this study or other recent investigations (128, 250).

No one variable has been demonstrated as the main determinant of perceived counselor competence. However, the literature points toward counselor behaviors which project confidence or charisma (166). These behaviors may or may not be related to years of experience or external cues such as diplomas or reputation.

PERSISTENCE IN TREATMENT   *Counselors who want to prevent premature client termination should arrange appointment reminders and convey a sense of involvement, competence, and commitment to helping.*

Saltzman et al (245) conducted an exemplary study which represents both a conceptual and methodological milestone in investigating the formation of an effective therapeutic relationship. Salient process dimensions were studied via self-report forms which both client and counselor filled in immediately following each of the initial ten sessions. Subjects were 91 students referred to a university counseling service for long-term treatment. This intensive data collection procedure allowed the actual "process" of relationship formation to be examined. A wealth of important relationships were identified and changes in these relationships documented across time. Of 14 factors which seemed to predict persistence in counseling through the third session, only the following three specific interaction patterns reliably distinguished those who eventually remained in counseling from those who terminated prematurely: (*a*) In the initial session the anxious client was met by a counselor who conveyed a strong sense of involvement. (*b*) By the third session, the now less anxious client had formed an impression of the counselor as both competent and committed to help. (*c*) In subsequent sessions, a *mutual* sense of being involved in a continuing relationship that both client and counselor think about at times outside of counseling was evident.

Saltzman emphasizes that the results of this study "suggest that it is not only important to know what the client experiences but when he/she experiences it." This study could have been further strengthened had subjects been asked the question: What does the counselor *do* to produce these perceptions?

Fiester & Rudestam (83) conducted a multivariate analysis of the early dropout process and concluded that many clients drop out after the initial interview despite perception of the interview as positive. This conclusion is consistent with the finding of Saltzman that those who drop out after the initial interview are simply low in anxiety and apathetic toward change. Fiester and Rudestam's most important finding was that more disturbed and lower SES clients often were assigned to the lowest level counselors at the two community mental health centers studied and that early termination of treatment was related only to dissatisfaction with services. The authors note that earlier attempts to "conceptualize dropouts as being characteristic of a single type of patient seems to be another unfounded homogeneity myth." In other words, non-YAVIS or HOUND (homely, old, unattractive, nonverbal, dumb) (96) clients, those most in need of an external change agent, are those assigned to the least qualified helpers.

In this regard, caution is advised against the use of the terminator-remainer (TR) battery for predicting early dropouts. Stern, Moore & Gross (271) cite evidence that the TR scale has little predictive validity when social class characteristics are controlled.

In one study, the effects of telephone prompts to *increase* attendance at a community mental health center were examined. Turner & Vernon (300) used a reversal design to show that "no show" rates could be reduced by 20 percent simply by having an administrative staff member deliver a personalized telephone reminder to clients several days before their appointment. This procedure was used for over 1000 clients and the total cost of the procedure was recovered after only six potentially missed appointments were kept.

Prolonging therapy is not a counseling goal, however. The faster client goals are achieved, the better. We should not overlook the possibility that the early terminators efficiently learned exactly what they wanted.

DEVELOPING SKILL FOR CAREER TRANSITIONS

Helping people learn how to make career decisions wisely continues to be one of the major functions of counseling psychologists. Important reviews of the literature on this topic have included those by Osipow (224), Betz (25), Holcomb & Anderson (131) and Super & Hall (282).

How can we tell whether counselors' efforts to help in career decision-making produce any beneficial results? Criterion measures used in the last 4-year period can be grouped conveniently under five major categories: (*a*) improvements in decision-making skills, (*b*) increases in "career maturity," (*c*) changes in the nature or quality of choices, (*d*) improvement in employment seeking skills, and (*e*) improvements in job performance and satisfaction.

Decision-Making Skills

Clients who have developed decision-making skills are those who may have developed one or more of the following skills: the ability to learn about oneself, learn about career opportunities, consider many alternatives, seek information, clarify values, make plans, see oneself in control, engage in exploratory processes with satisfaction, or overcome indecisiveness and its accompanying anxiety.

Measures of career decision-making skill presuppose that those possessing the skill have learned more about occupations, have congruent vocational aspirations, have developed various strategies for coping with decision problems, and can see connections between present actions and future choices.

The measurement of career decision-making ability is difficult and must rest on some inferential processes. One inference is that those who are good at career decision making must have been able to find out more about occupations. Thus, several investigators have developed tests of occupational knowledge (64, 162, 217). Another inference is that those who are good at decision making will show more "congruence" or similarity among their various vocational aspirations, so that more skill can be inferred by noting fewer discrepancies among career goals (132, 133). A third line of reasoning follows Tyler's (302) suggestion that the programs or plans for action that people use to process their experiences would be useful to study. Jepsen (149, 150) attempted to determine how adolescents organize information about themselves, what the structure of their thinking is rather than its content, and then identified 12 strategy types. A structured interview format to measure students' occupational reasoning and knowledge was reported by Perrone & Kyle (230).

Students who are vocationally undecided tend to have lower academic achievement, be more anxiety prone, and have lower self-esteem; however, different types of undecided students may have need for different types of vocational counseling treatment. The problem of vocational indecision seems to plague many young as well as older people. Such indecision could be seen as normal, or even desirable, given the fact that our society provides relatively few opportunities for people to become intelligently informed about the vast array of occupational possibilities. However, the pressures that are put on young people to force early decisions may cause many of them to assume that their indecision is the result of some personal inadequacy on their part. Undecided students tend to have lower grade point averages than the decided students (185, 186), are more anxiety prone (120, 158), and report lower self-esteem (18). Two studies have suggested that vocational indecision may not necessarily be a unitary trait but that there are various types of undecided students who may need different varieties of treatment (135, 225).

High school and college students may go through a variety of exploration and problem-solving strategies as they cope with vocational problems at the various levels of development, but high school students clearly lack information about occupations, perceive the need for help, and report getting very little.

It is small wonder that many students feel inadequate and indecisive about career decision making when we learn how little they actually know about the world of work and what little help they get. In a nationally representative sample of some 32,000 eighth, ninth, and eleventh graders, Noeth, Roth & Prediger (213) found that "less than 50% of the eleventh graders (and only 15% of the eighth graders) correctly answered more than three-quarters of the occupational knowledge items." Approximately 40% of the eleventh graders have never talked with workers on jobs, have never talked with a counselor or teacher about the relationship between jobs and goals, interests, and abilities, and have never read a job description from the guidance office or library. Prediger, Roth & Noeth (234) report that 56% of the eleventh graders receive little or no help with career planning in discussions with counselors, although 84% say that they can usually or almost always see a counselor when they want to. The implication here is that students do not ask for the help they want, do not see the schools as a place to receive it, or do not find counselors willing or able to offer the amount or type of help that seems to be required.

How do decision-making approach skills develop over time? In studying developmental changes through the high school years, Jepsen (151) found that an information search strategy and an elaborate rationale increased in complexity from ninth to twelfth grade and contributed to confident feelings about occupational choices. Baumgardner (20) found university sophomores to be markedly more intuitive than the more analytic freshmen. Those with "soft" majors continued to be intuitive through their senior year whereas those with "hard" majors tended to revert to a more analytical method of thinking about career choice by their senior year.

Counselors may be able to increase scores on various criterion measures of career decision-making ability by administering selected interest inventories, by presenting themselves as "experts," by retaining a high degree of external control, especially with subjects who are low-internal on locus of control, by using computer-based systems, by using modeling and guided practice as in microcounseling, by teaching anxiety management and problem-solving skills, and by teaching appropriately designed workshops.

What can counselors do to help their clients learn career decision-making skills? One study showed some positive effects simply from the administration of an interest inventory. Zytowski (330) found that administering the *Kuder Occupational Interest Survey* to high school students increased self knowledge in comparison to a no-treatment control group. However, other criteria (confidence in or satisfaction with vocational plans, and information seeking) were not affected. Holland's Self-Directed Search (SDS) helped students reduce career indecision (193), select occupations consistent with personality traits (328), and achieve other outcomes equivalent to traditional counseling at one-sixth the cost (163).

But how should counselors present themselves to clients? As "experts"? Or as follow human beings who have suffered through some of the same problems ("referent")? A laboratory study (200) showed that, in general, the subjects of the "expert" interviewers remembered more of the problem-solving processes taught, but the black "expert" and the white "referent" interviewers were most influential in altering both attitude and behavior. However, since only one interviewer occupied each cell in the design, the results may well be due to personality differences associated with the inter-viewers. No differences were associated with subjects categorized as internal or external on locus of control.

However, locus of control did prove to be important in a study reported by Fry (89) for identifying subjects who might learn most from differentially structured occupational exploration activities. The high internal subjects made significant gains in all treatments but learned most when under their own control. The low internal subjects gained significantly more under external control. Fry's analog study suggests a future study with real clients in which the degree of client control over exploratory activities is systemat-ically varied in relation to the clients' locus of control.

The computer beat out the counselor in teaching occupational informa-tion to some occupational work experience students (189). Modeling and guided practice through the microcounseling technique proved superior in teaching decision-making counseling skills to counselor trainees in compari-son with a film or a more traditional didactic method (307), and a model video tape has been shown to increase information seeking (86).

What about all those anxiety-ridden people plagued by vocational indeci-sion? Is there any way to increase their occupational exploratory behavior, help them learn how to solve problems, and make them more aware of career alternatives? According to Mendonca & Siess (199), a treatment combining anxiety management training and problem-solving training was most effective in producing improvements on those criterion measures.

Other workshop formats have produced mixed results when evaluated with various designs: no replication of the treatment (192), a control group selected from a population different than the experimental groups (315), a well-designed study that produced no statistically significant differences (23), and no control group at all (228). A 7-hour values clarification work-shop produced higher "value awareness" scores for both high and low self-esteem participants than for randomly assigned members of a placebo treatment (219). A field trip experience proved informative for kindergart-ners (77).

Perhaps the best designed evaluation study of a vocational workshop was provided by Mencke & Cochran (198). The workshop-treated groups en-gaged in significantly more information seeking, but the expected awareness of more vocational alternatives did not occur. In fact, the control group reported significantly more alternatives than the experimental workshop group. The result can be interpreted as beneficial if the participants wanted to narrow their choices, not expand them. Perhaps the workshop leaders and participants failed to communicate their respective intentions.

Does encouraging all this information-seeking behavior actually help people to make up their mind? A study by Barak, Carney & Archibald (15) suggests that the desired relationship may exist, but just barely. Cross-lagged correlations designed to estimate causal effects provided some scant support for the notion that information-seeking behaviors increase educational and vocational decisiveness.

Career Maturity

Thanks largely to the efforts of people such as Donald Super, John Crites, and Bert Westbrook, the concept of "career maturity" pervades much of the literature on career counseling. Operationally, career maturity is a composite of many of the same criterion measures listed under career decision-making ability. Basically, career maturity consists of activities, knowledge, and attitudes about occupations, planning, and career decision making that tend to show development over the adolescent years. The publication of composite scales of career maturity has made available handy research instruments for evaluating career counseling and for correlating with a wide variety of other measures.

Career maturity measures are substantially interrelated and are positively associated with age, intrinsic work values, higher aspirations and expectations, an internal locus of control, mastery of psychosocial stage crises, congruency, and socioeconomic class. Westbrook (315–317) has done a thorough job of analyzing the various subparts of Crites' Career Maturity Inventory (CMI). In general he finds substantial correlations among the various subparts of the CMI and higher than expected correlations between attitude and competency measures. Hansen (118) has written a thorough review of the CMI, and Crites (60) has further explicated his views on how career development takes place in early adulthood. Support for the notion that various components of career maturity are highly interrelated was provided by Healy (126), who analyzed the Career Development Inventory (CDI) of Super et al (283). In addition, Healy found that certainty about career plans tended to be associated with the amount of thinking and the acquisition of relevant career information, especially so after counseling.

People who score high on career maturity inventories tend to be older (129, 156, 157), to have more specific occupational perceptions (78), to have more intrinsic work values (201, 308), to report higher vocational aspirations and expectations (309), to have a more internal locus of control (90), to have more successfully resolved the first six psychosocial stage crises proposed by Erik Erikson (208), to have more "congruent" vocational interests (311), to be more associated with middle than lower socioeconomic class perspectives (70, 265).

Is there anything that counselors can do to increase career maturity? *Measures of career maturity may be sensitive to counselor interventions such as computer-assisted vocational guidance, group counseling, and educational interventions, though clear-cut cause-effect relationships are often confounded by inadequate experimental designs.* The computerized System of Interactive Guidance Information (SIGI) was evaluated by Cochran in a well-designed experimental study. The only positive results reported were improved skills related to choice of a college major. A study by Pyle & Stripling (235) credited SIGI with improving Career Maturity Inventory attitude scores, but the experimental and control groups were not randomly assigned from the same population, though an attempt was made to equate them statistically. Another computer-based educational and occupational exploration system, ECES, was evaluated by Myers and associates (210) using statistically matched but not randomly assigned experimental and control groups. The computer users showed greater gains from the beginning to the end of the school year on degree of "planfulness" and knowledge and use of resources for career exploration. No differences were found in information about education, occupations, and career decision making. The more time spent on ECES, the greater the gains. Conclusions about the effectiveness of computer-based aids to career maturity await more definitive testing.

A group career counseling experience increased vocational maturity measures in a prison population (84). Similar benefits were reported by Healy (125) for a group counseling experience with junior college students, but only pre-post comparisons were made without any equivalent control group. More encouraging results were obtained in a well-designed study with tenth graders though only 17 experimental subjects were involved (87). The trend of the evidence seems to indicate that some types of counseling experiences can positively affect career maturity measures. Further support for this notion was provided by Graff & Beggs (106), who credited a high school psychology course with improving vocational development even though their control subjects were drawn from a different population. The Career Maturity Inventory was also used to assess outcomes of a career education program among sixth and eighth grade students (223). Some of the subtest scores were higher for students exposed to the career education program, though questions about the equivalence of control and experimental groups remain a serious problem.

Nature and Quality of Vocational Choices

If counselors can increase career maturity or teach better decision-making skills, then it seems reasonable to suppose that the quality of vocational choices made by clients would inevitably improve. How can we tell a "good" vocational choice? Setting aside the ethical dilemma of defining what is good for another person (an issue set aside by most studies in this area), we can examine the criterion measures which have been used in counseling-related studies during the 4 year period under review: the extent to which clients choose occupations inconsistent with conventional sex-role stereotypes; the degree of career orientation (particularly of women); the "realism" of choices; and the stability of choices over time. Some research has also focused on the origin and predictability of vocational choices. *To help clients make "better" choices, counselors may provide appropriate role models, provide occupational and sex-role-myth-destroying information, reinforce "congruent" choices, and give accurate self-knowledge feedback. Recent daydreams and expressed vocational choices are most predictive of future occupations.*

NONTRADITIONAL CHOICES What characterizes women who choose the nontraditional or male-dominated occupations? On the average these "pioneers" tend to have a more internal locus of control (35), higher mathematical ability (94), higher self-esteem (240), more interest in verbal-linguistic occupations (296), less accepting fathers but more father-identification (222), and more cognitive complexity (170).

What steps can counselors take to help females consider a wider range of possible occupations? The presentation of nontraditional role models had no effect on the vocational preferences of kindergarten children (313), but videotaped models plus reinforcement supplied by a male counselor (179) did increase nontraditional choices of college liberal arts women. At the community college level a special curriculum designed to make students aware of the influence of sexism and stereotypic attitudes on their occupational choices failed to have any significant impact (30).

Interest inventories are a possible means for helping people overcome sex role stereotypes. Boyd (34) reconstructed Holland's Self-Directed Search (SDS) to remove all masculine-toned terminology from the items and instructions but found no significant score differences between the reconstructed and standard versions when both were administered to 266 female university students. However, Cooper (55) found that the Vocational Card Sort (VCS) contributed substantially to the career exploration activities of women. The VCS is simply a deck of 90 3X5 cards, each with an occupational title and its corresponding summary of primary job duties as described in the *Dictionary of Occupational Titles.* Subjects are to sort the cards into three piles: "Might Choose," "In Question," and "Would Not Choose." The VCS and some auxiliary information material which informed the female subjects about some common myths and realities of women and men in the world of work increased the number of nontraditional occupations considered as career options.

CAREER ORIENTATION   Many women continue to be troubled by the conflict in roles between a career orientation and a more traditional orientation. Richardson (241) clearly identified two clusters: career-oriented women who valued the career role as primary, and work-oriented women who valued both a career role and marriage and family responsibilities. Sedney & Turner (256) concluded that women's career orientation was due to a high need for achievement which decreases a need for heterosexual affiliation. They rejected the model which implies that a failure in women's heterosexual affiliation leads to a high need achievement which in turn produces a high career orientation. However, the intertwining of sex roles and occupational roles was clearly illustrated by Almquist (2), who found among college men with working wives that the women clearly feared a situation where they might overshadow their husbands. Only 37% of the females would work if they could earn more than their husband, whereas 67% of the males would prefer their wives to work if the wives could earn more.

In a long-term follow-up study of 306 women who had been students at the University of Minnesota during 1933–1936, Wolfson (324) attempted to identify characteristics which distinguished their degree of career orientation. Some 15 of the 29 dependent variables discriminated at the .05 level or better, but none of the significant variables was identifiable at the time the women entered college. However, 5 years after entering college some valid predictions could be made from data accruing during those years. Those with a higher career orientation tended to score lower on the housewife scale of the Strong Vocational Interest Blank, to attend graduate school, and to major more often in vocational than in liberal arts subjects. They also had fewer children and had husbands who earned lower incomes.

REALISM   Counselors would generally concede that they want their clients to make "realistic" decisions. But what is realistic? Thomas (289) showed that both black and white high school males could distinguish between their aspirations and their expectations. Most occupations contain such heterogeneity in personality types and talents (e.g. 134, 233) that it is difficult to define the type of person who ought to enter any given occupation. However, Oliver (221) found that giving positive, verbal reinforcement for making choices congruous with an individual's occupational type as determined by the Vocational Preference Inventory increased career choice realism. In a computer-based vocational exploration system, giving eleventh grade male subjects some feedback about the accuracy of their self knowledge increased the realism ratings of their first occupational choice (231). In this case, realism was defined as a congruence between the measured characteristics of occupational norm groups and the experimental students.

STABILITY   It is usually assumed that vocational choices should become more stable over time, and indeed they do (196). No studies were located in which counselors attempted to produce such stability, but attempts have been made to identify characteristics of more stable choosers. Scott, Fenske & Maxey (255) were unable to find any ability, interest, or family background measures that differentiated vocational choice changers from nonchangers. However, Villwock, Schnitzen & Carbonari (306) confirmed Holland's assertion that stability of vocational choice can be predicted from the congruence of personality with chosen career; and better high school grades predict slightly more stability (161).

ORIGINS OF CAREER CHOICE   The social learning theory of career decision making proposed by Krumboltz, Mitchell & Jones (164) received support for some of its propositions concerning the influence of models and reinforcement. Similarities between parents and their children in occupational choice were noted in three studies. Grandy & Stahmann (107) found that expressed occupational choices of children were similar to the parental occupations in the cases of fathers-sons, fathers-daughters, and mothers-daughters, but not so for mothers-sons. Goodale & Hall (98) identified student perceptions of their parents' interest in their school work and the parents' hopes that their children will attend college as influential mediators for career decisions, but found that the students' own work values were not as influential. For college women, mothers who participated in work and desired a career were more attractive models than mothers who were not career-oriented (19). It seems clear that parental role-modeling and expectations play a large part in students' perceptions of their own career possibilities.

Sex, race, and degree of authoritarianism also seem to be correlated with occupational choices. Males are more likely than females to prefer high prestige occupations (17). Black male inner-city secondary school students more often than a white sample prefer occupations in the artistic, health, and welfare fields (259). The natural sciences such as biology and chemistry tend to be preferred by "authoritarian personalities" more than social sciences and humanities, specifically psychology and philosophy (314).

Can vocational choices be predicted? Methods of making vocational predictions have been examined by Muchinsky & Taylor (207) and Webb,

Hultgen & Craddick (312). Possibly useful predictors include the most recent daydream (298) and expressed vocational choices more than interest inventories (104, 321). Both the Tyler Vocational Card Sort and the Strong Vocational Interest Blank for men predicted occupation held 10 years after original testing with about 50% accuracy (72).

Employment Seeking

Useful training programs for helping clients learn job interviewing and job finding skills are available to counselors, although the effective ingredients of these programs have not yet been identified. How can job interviewing skills best be taught? Hollandsworth, Dressel & Stevens (136) compared a "behavioral group" method with a "discussion group" method. Labels for the two treatment groups, however, are quite misleading since the groups differed not only in method but also in their purpose and content. The "behavioral group" made significant gains in percentage of eye contact maintained during the criterion interview. However, eye contact was one of the five skill areas stressed in that treatment while it was not part of the "discussion group" treatment. The "discussion group" produced superior ratings of ability to present one's own skills and express feelings and personal opinions relevant to the interview. The treatment in the "discussion group" included a professionally developed film strip about the job interview, discussion of a five-page article on the interview, and discussion of a work sheet designed to help participants identify their best skills, weak areas, short-range goals, and long-range ambitions. The so-called "discussion group" treatment might just as well have been labeled "behavioral" because it consisted of a model (the film strip) followed by behavioral rehearsal (the discussion on interview-relevant topics). A more appropriate conclusion from this study would be that college seniors can learn to increase the frequency of whatever behaviors are modeled and rehearsed regardless of the label assigned to the treatment.

For mentally retarded clients, a microcounseling procedure including videotaped feedback with immediate social and monetary reinforcement was most effective at increasing eye contact and encouraging appropriate body posture during simulated job interviews. However, attempts to increase five other verbal and question-asking skill areas did not show significant improvements (110).

But the acid test is not how well simulated job interviews are conducted, it is how successful clients are in obtaining jobs. Parker (226) compared alternative statistical models for predicting employment status for clients of the St. Louis Jewish Employment Vocational Service. He found that the least statistically sophisticated model, the "single best predictor," was the most successful approach. The best predictor turned out to be counselors' and supervisors' ratings of motivation after observing participants' workshop performance for 3 weeks.

Can actual job finding be improved? Perhaps the most encouraging work was reported in a study by Azrin, Flores & Kaplan (9). A job finding club was established in which job seekers helped one another with a "buddy" system and family support to share job leads. Modeling and rehearsal of searching Want Ads, telephoning employers, constructing a resume, and contacting friends were employed. Within 2 months, 90 percent of the counseled group had found jobs, compared with 55% of the noncounseled group, and the starting salary of the counseled group was a third higher.

Bowser, Sherman & Whisler (33) evaluated a treatment consisting of self-analysis, identification of specific industries where abilities could be applied, formulation of a specific and realistic job objective, preparation of a resume and a mailing list of potential employers, role-played telephone interviews, and follow through on actual employer contacts. Interpretation of the results is contaminated by self-selection of the subjects. Eighty-three percent of those completing the training secured employment, but 34% of those who started the project dropped out and no placement data were recorded for them. However, the placement rate for the nonparticipant group was about 7%, consistent with the typical agency record.

Occupational Adaptation

Interest inventories may provide counselors with a useful but imperfect predictor of occupational satisfaction, but no experimental evidence has been uncovered in the last 4 years to show what counselors can do to improve occupational success or satisfaction. The final test of whether any career counseling has been satisfactory must depend upon some measure of how well individuals adapt to the occupations in which they find themselves. That judgment may come from performance measures, job satisfaction ratings, or the ratings of others (supervisors, colleagues, friends, spouses). Some evidence indicates that the two types of ratings are positively correlated (127). A useful review of the literature on job satisfaction from the point of view of expectancy theory has been provided by Mitchell (204). Nelson & Scanlan (211) suggest some 21 basic occupational survival skills rank ordered by urban and rural students and parents. All agree that basic speaking skills are most important.

Most of the studies in this area rely upon self-ratings of job satisfaction rather than external measures. The higher an individual's job satisfaction, the higher the correspondence between the vocational needs of the individual and the rewards of the job (79). Individuals who perceived their job as moderately complex were more satisfied than those who saw it as either high or low in complexity (182). No significant relationship exists between job satisfaction and mental health (242) nor between job satisfaction and degree of father identification among males (143).

The possible use of interest inventories as predictors of later job satisfaction has received some qualified support. The Strong Vocational Interest Blank (SVIB) was significantly related to job satisfaction (165). Subjective ratings of vocational performance were predicted by SVIB Group V scores (206). A correlation of .38 between interest score and job satisfaction was found for females in Israel based on Holland's vocational classification (85). Subjects in occupations consistent with their early interest profiles on the Kuder did not report greater job satisfaction or success but did show greater continuance in their occupational career (329).

Other attempts to predict success and satisfaction produced diverse and inconsistent results. For example, Enderlein (80) found job satisfaction predictable for females but not males. The success of Army officers was best predicted from leadership ratings (37), but the most successful ministers were those who had chosen their career later in life and had earned their own college expenses (304).

Is there anything that counselors can do to help their clients be more successful or more satisfied on the job? If so, no experimental evidence for it was found during the 4-year period surveyed. One might facetiously suggest that counselors could steer their students away from proprietary schools since the nonproprietary programs have been found to produce superior economic gains and expressed satisfaction (153). But even here the self-selection and the wide variation in response would make it impossible to generalize to the individual case.

PREVENTING PROBLEMS

Prevention, unfortunately, continues to occupy last place in the hearts of counseling psychologists, and it is so represented in this review. Studies cannot unambiguously be classified as "preventive" since even obviously remedial procedures may have unanticipated benefits on staff members and nontargeted subjects. In general, preventive work attempts to reduce the frequency or severity of future problems by teaching coping skills or imparting useful knowledge not merely to current sufferers but to persons likely to experience future stress. Only a few illustrative efforts in two areas will be described here.

Preventing Family Problems
Counselors can most effectively prevent family problems by training the whole family in communication skills, problem solving, and contingency contract-

ing. Klein, Alexander & Parsons (160) have compared several interventions with families of delinquents using three criteria: changes within the family interaction pattern, recidivism rates of the identified problem children for 6 to 18 months after treatment, and court referrals of the siblings of identified delinquents for 2½ to 3½ years following treatment. On all three criteria a behaviorally oriented, short-term family treatment outperformed client-centered, eclectic-dynamic, and no-treatment conditions. Most telling were the impacts of the three types of treatments on referral rates for siblings: 20% of the families under the behavioral treatment had sibling referrals compared with 40% of the no-treatment controls, 59% of the client-centered treatment families, and 63% of the eclectic-dynamic treatment families. The behavioral intervention welded the family into a problem-solving unit through communications skills training and contingency contracting that underscored the rights and responsibilities of all members of the family.

Homebuilders, an intensive community counseling service, intercedes with families in crisis to prevent the removal of children to foster homes or residential treatment (159). After defusing the immediate crisis through active listening with individual family members, counselors work with the family for up to 6 weeks on problem solving, using such techniques as behavioral management, fair fighting (10), assertiveness training, and parent effectiveness training (101). Homebuilders boasts a superb track record at keeping high risk clients away from out-of-home placement: 97% of clients counseled in Homebuilders' first 16 months of operation remained at home.

Further recommendation for the preventive aspects of behavioral home intervention comes from the Oregon Research Institute's Social Learning Project for families (5). When parents were taught behavioral management techniques, not only was there a significant reduction in observed deviant behavior in the identified problem child, but also in the siblings. Changes in the behavior of all children were maintained at 6 months' follow-up as reported by nonparticipant observation in the home. Parents seem to have learned generalized parenting skills rather than a stop-gap procedure to use with one problem child.

Preventing School Problems

Some effective and efficient preventive work in schools has relied on weekly support from an adult aide under counselor supervision, but future efforts may capitalize on the teaching of self-guidance methods. The last 4 years have given counselors further installments from the granddaddy of preventive programs in the schools, the Primary Mental Health Project (PMHP), which provides supportive counseling for early identified high risk children. The PMHP has demonstrated that a low cost, low key intervention reduces the frequency and severity of problem behaviors, at least from the perspective of teachers and paraprofessionals working directly with the child (58). In the PMHP, counselors serve as quarterbacks calling the signals for a team of aides who have individual or group contact with troubled children; thus, there is a geometric expansion in the amount of psychological services provided by a single counselor (57).

What the PMHP model has demonstrated amply over the past 20 years is that weekly contact with a supportive adult aide helps moderately troubled primary grade pupils adjust to the school situation. Subsequent ratings by teachers and aides show the treated children much improved in classroom social and task attention skills compared with matched controls. Problem pupils who can make enough progress within a single school year to be terminated from the program appear better adjusted later on than nonterminators (183). This finding underscores the need for development of alternative procedures since nonterminators were rated initially as more maladjusted. The "small is beautiful" phenomenon appeared to be at work: effectiveness deteriorated somewhat when the number of schools served by the project was expanded (56).

While PMHP has provided prime elucidation of the rationale behind a preventive delivery system for psychological services based in the schools, it has not served as a beacon for research in more effective counseling strategies. What seems to be lacking is a clear delineation of the components of that helping process and a focus on generating and evaluating new treatment strategies.

Durlak (75) modified the format of the counseling contact in his adaptation of PMHP. Teachers and college students supplied token reinforcement for targeted social behaviors during group activities with problem children outside the regular classroom. Ratings by teachers and aides showed significant changes for the better in classroom social behavior at both completion of the program and at a 7-month follow-up. Although this project flies a preventive banner, its use of a token economy does not distinguish it from many standard behavior modification projects. Questions of rater bias, in this study as in all the PMHP programs, mask the issue of whether an external control system such as a token economy can have long-term preventive effects. Preventive outcomes would seem better served by internal, self-guidance systems as provided by such interventions as Spivack and Shure's (261, 269, 270) interpersonal cognitive problem-solving program, reviewed elsewhere in this paper. Future preventive efforts may involve both the teaching of self-control techniques and environmental restructuring to make desired behavior easier and more satisfying.

Literature Cited

1. Allen, G. J., Chinsky, J. M., Larcen, S. W., Lochman, J. E., Selinger, H. V. 1976. *Community Psychology and the Schools: A Behaviorally Oriented Multilevel Preventive Approach.* Hillsdale, NJ: Erlbaum
2. Almquist, E. M. 1974. Attitudes of college men toward working wives. *Q. Vocat. Guid.* 23:115–21
3. Annis, L. V., Perry, D. F. 1977. Self-disclosure modeling in same-sex and mixed-sex unsupervised groups. *J. Couns. Psychol.* 24:370–72
4. Aragona, J., Cassady, J., Drabman, R. S. 1975. Treating overweight children through parental training and contingency contracting. *J. Appl. Behav. Anal.* 8:269–78
5. Arnold, J. E., Levine, A. G., Patterson, G. R. 1975. Changes in sibling behavior following family intervention. *J. Consult. Clin. Psychol.* 43:683–88
6. Asher, S. R., Oden, S. L., Gottman, J. M. 1976. "Children's friendships in school settings." In *Current Topics in Early Childhood Education,* Vol. 1, ed. L. G. Katz. Norwood, NJ: Ablex
7. Atkinson, D. R., Carskaddon, G. 1975. A prestigious introduction, psychological jargon, and perceived counselor credibility. *J. Couns. Psychol.* 22:180–86
8. Avery, A. W., D'Augelli, A. R., Danish, S. J. 1976. An empirical investigation of the construct validity of empathic understanding ratings. *Couns. Educ. Superv.* 15:117–83
9. Azrin, N. H., Flores, R., Kaplan, S. J. 1975. Job-find club: A group-assisted program for obtaining employment. *Behav. Res. Ther.* 13:17–27
10. Bach, G. R., Wyden, P. 1968. *The Intimate Enemy.* New York: Morrow
11. Bandura, A. 1977 *Social Learning Theory.* Englewood Cliffs, NJ: Prentice-Hall
12. Bandura, A. 1977. Self-efficacy: Toward a unifying theory of behavioral change. *Psychol. Rev.* 84:191–215
13. Bandura, A., Adams, N. E. 1977. Analysis of self-efficacy theory of behavioral change. *Cogn. Ther. Res.* 1:287–310
14. Bandura, A., Adams, N. E., Beyer, J. 1977. Cognitive processes mediating behavioral change. *J. Pers. Soc. Psychol.* 35:125–39
15. Barak, A., Carney, C. G., Archibald, R. D. 1975. The relationship between vocational information seeking and educational and vocational decidedness. *J. Vocat. Behav.* 7:149–59

16. Barbach, L. G. 1976. *For Yourself: The Fulfillment of Female Sexuality.* Garden City, NY: Doubleday
17. Barnett, R. C. 1975. Sex differences and age trends in occupational preference and occupational prestige. *J. Couns. Psychol.* 22:35–38
18. Barrett, T. C., Tinsely, H. E. A. 1977. Vocational self-concept crystallization and vocational indecision. *J. Couns. Psychol.* 24:301–7
19. Baruch, G. K. 1974. Maternal career-orientation as related to parental identification in college women. *J. Vocat. Behav.* 4:173–80
20. Baumgardner, S. R. 1976. The impact of college experiences on conventional career logic. *J. Couns. Psychol.* 23:40–45
21. Beck, A. T. 1967. *Depression: Clinical, Experimental, and Theoretical Aspects.* New York: Hoeber
22. Beck, A. T. 1976. *Cognitive Therapy and the Emotional Disorders.* New York: Int. Univ. Press
23. Bergland, B. W., Lundquist, G. W. 1975. The vocational exploration group and minority youth: An experimental outcome study. *J. Vocat. Behav.* 7:289–96
24. Besalel-Azrin, V., Azrin, N. H., Armstrong, P. M. 1977. The student-oriented classroom: A method of improving student conduct and satisfaction. *Behav. Ther.* 8:193–204
25. Betz, E. L. 1977. Vocational behavior and career development, 1976: A review. *J. Vocat. Behav.* 11:129–52
26. Beutler, L. E., Johnson, D. T., Neville, C. W. Jr., Elkins, D., Jobe, A. M. 1975. Attitude similarity and therapist credibility as predictors of attitude change and improvement in psychotherapy. *J. Consult. Clin. Psychol.* 43:90–91
27. Birchler, G. R., Webb, L. J. 1977. Discriminating interaction behaviors in happy and unhappy marriages. *J. Consult. Clin. Psychol.* 45:494–95
28. Blaas, C. D., Heck, E. J. 1975. Accuracy of accurate empathy ratings. *J. Couns. Psychol.* 22:243–46
29. Blanchard, E. B., Haynes, M. R. 1975. Biofeedback treatment of a case of Raynaud's disease. *J. Behav. Ther. Exp. Psychiatry* 6:230–34
30. Blimline, C. A. 1976. The effect of a vocational unit on the exploration of nontraditional career options. *J. Vocat. Behav.* 9:209–17
31. Deleted in proof

32. Bornstein, M. R., Bellack, A. S., Hersen, M. 1977. Social skills training for unassertive children: A multiple-baseline analysis. *J. Appl. Behav. Anal.* 10:183–95

33. Bowser, S. E., Sherman, G., Whisler, R. H. 1974. An action-research approach to Central City unemployment. *J. Vocat. Behav.* 4:115–24

34. Boyd, V. S. 1976. Neutralizing sexist titles in Holland's self-directed search: What difference does it make? *J. Vocat. Behav.* 9:191–99

35. Burlin, F. 1976. Locus of control and female occupational aspiration. *J. Couns. Psychol.* 23:126–29

36. Butler, J. M., Rice, L. N., Wagstaff, A. K. 1962. On the naturalistic definition of variables: An analogue of clinical analysis. In *Research in Psychotherapy*, Vol. 2, ed. H. Strupp, L. Luborsky. Washington DC: Am. Psychol. Assoc.

37. Butler, R. P. 1976. Relationships between college performance and success as an army officer. *J. Vocat. Behav.* 9:385–91

38. Byrne, D. 1969. Attitudes and Attraction. *Adv. Exp. Soc. Psychol.*, Vol. 4

39. Byrne, D. 1971. *The Attraction Paradigm.* New York: Academic

40. Cairns, D., Pasino, J. A. 1977. Comparison of verbal reinforcement and feedback in the operant treatment of disability due to chronic low back pain. *Behav. Ther.* 8:621–30

41. Camp, B. W. 1977. Verbal mediation in young aggressive boys. *J. Abnorm. Psychol.* 86:145–53

42. Camp, B. W., Zimet, S. G., Van Doornick, W. J., Dahlem, N. W. 1977. Verbal abilities in young aggressive boys. *J. Educ. Psychol.* 69:129–35

43. Carlson, K. W. 1974. Increasing verbal empathy as a function of feedback and instruction. *Couns. Educ. Superv.*, pp. 208–13

44. Cash, T. F., Begley, P. J., McCown, D. A., Weise, B. C. 1975. When counselors are heard but not seen: Initial impact of physical attractiveness. *J. Couns. Psychol.* 22:273–79

45. Chaikin, A. L., Derlega, V. J. 1974. Variables affecting the appropriateness of self-disclosure. *J. Consult. Clin. Psychol.* 42:588–93

46. Chaikin, A. L., Derlega, V. J., Bayma, B., Shaw, J. 1975. Neuroticism and disclosure reciprocity. *J. Consult. Clin. Psychol.* 43:13–19

47. Chaikin, A. L., Derlega, V. J., Miller, S. J. 1976. Effects of room environment on self-disclosure in a counseling analogue. *J. Couns. Psychol.* 23:479–81

48. Chaves, J. F., Barber, T. X. 1974. Cognitive strategies, experimenter modeling, and expectation in the attenuation of pain. *J. Abnorm. Psychol.* 83:356–63

49. Cheney, T. 1975. Attitude similarity, topic importance, and psychotherapeutic attraction. *J. Couns. Psychol.* 22:2–5

50. Chesney, M. A., Shelton, J. L. 1976. A comparison of muscle relaxation and electromyogram biofeedback treatments for muscle contraction headache. *J. Behav. Ther. Exp. Psychiatry* 7:221–25

51. Coates, T. J., Thoresen, C. E. 1977. *How to Sleep Better.* Englewood Cliffs, NJ: Prentice Hall

52. Coates, T. J., Thoresen, C. E. 1978. Treating obesity in adolescents: A behavioral approach. In *Advances in Behavioral Medicine*, ed. J. M. Ferguson. New York: Academic. In press. Cited in "Why aren't they losing weight?" by R. W. Jeffrey, T. J. Coates. *Behav. Ther.* In press

53. Cochran, D. J., Hoffman, S. D., Strand, K. H., Warren, P. M. 1977. Effects of client/computer interaction on career decision-making processes. *J. Couns. Psychol.* 24:308–12

54. Conway, J. B. 1977. Behavioral self-control of smoking through aversive conditioning and self-management. *J. Consult. Clin. Psychol.* 45:348–57

55. Cooper, J. F. 1976. Comparative impact of the SCII and the vocational card sort on career salience and career exploration of women. *J. Couns. Psychol.* 23:348–52

56. Cowen, E. L., Lorion, R. P., Dorr, D., Clarfield, S. P., Wilson, A. B. 1975. Evaluation of a preventively oriented, school based mental health program. *Psychol. Sch.* 12:161–66

57. Cowen, E. L., Lorion, R. P., Kraus, R. M., Dorr, D. 1974. Geometric expansion of helping services. *J. Sch. Psychol.* 12:288–95

58. Cowen, E. L., Trost, M. A., Lorion, R. P., Dorr, D., Izzo, L. D., Isaacson, R. V. 1975. *New Ways in School Mental Health: Early Detection and Prevention of School Maladaptation.* New York: Behavioral Publ.

59. Cox, D. J., Freundlich, A., Meyer, R. G. 1975. Differential effectiveness of electromyograph feedback, verbal relaxation instructions, and medication placebo with tension headaches. *J. Consult. Clin. Psychol.* 43:892–98

60. Crites, J. O. 1976. A comprehensive model of carrer development in early adulthood. *J. Vocat. Behav.* 9:105–18

61. Curran, J. P. 1977. Skills training as an approach to the treatment of heterosexual-social anxiety: A review. *Psychol. Bull.* 84:140–57

62. Curran, J. P., Gilbert, F. S. 1975. A test of the relative effectiveness of a systematic desensitization program and an interpersonal skills training program with date anxious subjects. *Behav. Ther.* 6:510–21

63. Curran, J. P., Gilbert, F. S., Little, L. M. 1976. A comparison between behavioral replication training and sensitivity training approaches to heterosexual dating anxiety. *J. Couns. Psychol.* 23:190–96

64. Currie, L. E. 1975. An index of vocational awareness. *Q. Vocat. Guid.* 23:347–53

65. Dawley, H. D. Jr., Ellithorpe, D. B., Tretola, R. 1976. Aversive smoking: Carboxyhemoglobin levels before and after rapid smoking. *J. Behav. Ther. Exp. Psychiatry* 7:13–15

66. Dell, D. M., Schmidt, L. D. 1976. Behavioral cues to counselor expertness. *J. Couns. Psychol.* 23:197–201

67. Denney, D. R., Rupert, P. A. 1977. Desensitization and self-control in the treatment of test anxiety. *J. Couns. Psychol.* 24:272–89

68. Derlega, V. J., Chaikin, A. L. 1976. Norms affecting self-disclosure in men and women. *J. Consult. Clin. Psychol.* 44:376–80

69. DeVries, D. L., Slavin, R. E. 1976. *Teams-Games-Tournament: A Final Report on the Research.* Johns Hopkins Univ.

70. Dillard, J. M. 1976. Relationship between career maturity and self-concepts of suburban and urban middle- and urban lower-class preadolescent black males. *J. Vocat. Behav.* 9:311–20

71. Dinges, N., Oetting, E. R. 1972. Interaction distance and anxiety in the counseling dyad. *J. Couns. Psychol.* 19:146–49

72. Dolliver, R. H., Will, J. A. 1977. Ten-year follow-up of the Tyler vocational card sort and the Strong vocational interest blank. *J. Couns. Psychol.* 24:48–54

73. Doster, J. A., Brooks, S. J. 1974. Interviewer disclosure modeling, information revealed, and interviewee verbal behavior. *J. Consult. Clin. Psychol.* 42:420–26

74. Dreman, S. B. 1977. Expectations and preferences of clients for a university student counseling service. *J. Couns. Psychol.* 24:459–62

75. Durlak, J. A. 1977. Description and evaluation of a behaviorally oriented school-based preventive mental health program. *J. Consult. Clin. Psychol.* 45:27–33

76. D'Zurilla, T. J., Goldfriend, M. R. 1971. Problem solving and behavior modification. *J. Abnorm. Psychol.* 78:107–26

77. Edington, E. D. 1976. Evaluation of methods of using resource people in helping kindergarten students become aware of the world of work. *J. Vocat. Behav.* 8:125–31

78. Edwards, K. J., Nafziger, D. H., Holland, J. L. 1974. Differentiation of occupational perceptions among different age groups. *J. Vocat. Behav.* 4:311–18

79. Elizur, D., Tziner, A. 1977. Vocational needs, job rewards, and satisfaction: A canonical analysis. *J. Vocat. Behav.* 10:205–11

80. Enderlein, T. E. 1975. Causal patterns related to post high school employment satisfaction. *J. Vocat. Behav.* 7:67–80

81. Epstein, L. H., Hersen, M., Hemphill, D. P. 1974. Music feedback in the treatment of tension headache: An experimental case study. *J. Behav. Ther. Exp. Psychiatry* 5:59–63

82. Ewart, C. 1978. Behavior contracts in couple therapy: An experimental evaluation of quid pro quo and good faith models. PhD thesis. Stanford Univ., Stanford, Calif.

83. Feister, A. R., Rudestam, K. E. 1975. A multivariate analysis of the early dropout process. *J. Consult. Clin. Psychol.* 43:528–35

84. Feldman, H. S., Marinelli, R. P. 1975. Career planning for prison inmates. *Q. Vocat. Guid.* June:358–62

85. Feldman, S., Meir, E. I. 1976. Measuring women's interests using Holland's vocational classification. *J. Vocat. Behav.* 9:345–53

86. Fisher, T. J., Reardon, R. C., Burck, H. D. 1976. Increasing information-seeking behavior with a model-reinforced videotape. *J. Couns. Psychol.* 23:234–38

87. Flake, M. H., Roach, A. J. Jr., Stenning, W. F. 1975. Effects of short-term counseling on career maturity of tenth-grade students. *J. Vocat. Behav.* 6:73–80

88. Forster, J. R., Hamburg, R. L. 1976. Further exploration of the 16-PF and

Counselor effectiveness. *Couns. Educ. Superv.* 15:184–88

89. Fry, P. S. 1975. Interaction between locus of control, level of inquiry and subject control in the helping process: A laboratory analogue study. *J. Couns. Psychol.* 22:280–87

90. Gable, R. K., Thompson, D. L., Glanstein, P. J. 1976. Perceptions of personal control and conformity of vocational choice as correlates of vocational development. *J. Vocat. Behav.* 8:259–67

91. Gitter, A. G., Black, H. 1976. Is self-disclosure self-revealing? *J. Couns. Psychol.* 23:327–32

92. Glass, C. R., Gottman, J. M., Shmurak, S. H. 1976. Response-acquisition and cognitive self-statement modification approaches to dating-skills training. *J. Couns. Psychol.* 23:520–26

93. Deleted in proof

94. Goldman, R. D., Hewitt, B. N. 1976. The scholastic aptitude test "explains" why college men major in science more often than college women. *J. Couns. Psychol.* 23:50–54

95. Goldstein, A. P., Heller, K., Sechrest, L. B. 1977. *Psychotherapy and the Psychology of Behavior Change.* New York: Wiley

96. Goldstein, A. P., Simonson, N. R. 1971. Social psychological approaches to psychotherapy research. In *Handbook of Psychotherapy and Behavior Change,* ed. A. E. Bergin, S. L. Garfield. New York: Wiley

97. Gomes-Schwartz, B., Hadley, S. W., Strupp, H. H. 1978. Individual psychotherapy and behavior therapy. *Ann. Rev. Psychol.* 29:435–71

98. Goodale, J. G., Hall, D. T. 1976. Inheriting a career: The influence of sex, values, and parents. *J. Vocat. Behav.* 8:19–30

99. Goodstein, L. D., Goldstein, J. J., D'Orta, C. V., Goodman, M. A. 1976. Measurement of self-disclosure in encounter groups: A methodological study. *J. Couns. Psychol.* 23:142–46

100. Goodwin, S. E., Mahoney, M. J. 1975. Modification of aggression through modeling: An experimental probe. *J. Behav. Ther. Exp. Psychiatry* 6:200–2

101. Gordon, T. 1970. *PET: Parent Effectiveness Training.* New York: McKay

102. Gormally, J., Hill, C. E. 1974. Guidelines for research on Carkhuff's training model. *J. Couns. Psychol.* 21:539–47

103. Gormally, J., Hill, C. E., Otis, M., Rainey, L. 1975. A micro-training approach to assertion training. *J. Couns. Psychol.* 22:299–303

104. Gottfredson, G. D., Holland, J. L. 1975. Vocational choices of men and women: A comparison of predictors from the self-directed search. *J. Couns. Psychol.* 22:28–34

105. Gottman, J., Notarius, C., Gonso, J., Markham, H. 1976. *A Couple's Guide to Communication.* Champaign, Ill: Research Press

106. Graff, R. W., Beggs, D. L. 1974. Personal and vocational development in high school students. *J. Sch. Psychol.* 12:17–23

107. Grandy, T. G., Stahmann, R. F. 1974. Types produce types: An examination of personality development using Holland's theory. *J. Vocat. Behav.* 5:231–39

108. Grater, H., Clazton, D. 1976. Counselor's empathy level and client topic changes. *J. Couns. Psychol.* 23:407–8

109. Grimm, L., Kanfer, F. H. 1976. Tolerance of aversive stimulation. *Behav. Ther.* 7:593–601

110. Grinnell, R. M. Jr., Lieberman, A. 1977. Teaching the mentally retarded job interviewing skills. *J. Couns. Psychol.* 24:332–37

111. Gulanick, N., Schmeck, R. R. 1977. Modeling, praise, and criticism in teaching empathic responding. *Couns. Educ. Superv.* June:284–90

112. Haase, R. F., DiMattia, D. J. 1976. Spatial environments and verbal conditioning in a quasi-counseling interview. *J. Couns. Psychol.* 23:414–21

113. Hall, S. M., Borden, B. L., Hall, R. B., Hanson, R. W. 1976. Use of programmed instruction in teaching self-management skills to overweight adults. *Behav. Ther.* 7:366–73

114. Hall, S. M., Hall, R. G., Borden, B. L., Hanson, R. W. 1975. Follow-up strategies in the behavioral treatment of overweight. *Behav. Res. Ther.* 13:167–72

115. Hall, S. M., Hall, R. G., DeBoer, G., O'Kulitch, P. 1977. Self and external management compared with psychotherapy in the control of obesity. *Behav. Res. Ther.* 15:89–95

116. Hall, S. M., Hall, R. G., Hanson, R. W., Borden, B. L. 1974. Permanence of two self-managed treatments of overweight in university and community populations. *J. Consult. Clin. Psychol.* 42: 781–86

117. Halpern, T. P. 1977. Degree of client disclosure as a function of past disclosure, counselor disclosure, and counselor facilitativeness. *J. Couns. Psychol.* 24:41–47

118. Hansen, J. C. 1974. The Career

Maturity Inventory. *J. Couns. Psychol.* 21:168–72

119. Hartup, W. W. 1970. Peer interaction and social organization. In *Carmichael's Manual of Child Psychology*, Vol. 2, ed. P. Mussen. New York: Wiley

120. Hawkins, J. G., Bradley, R. W., White, G. W. 1977. Anxiety and the process of deciding about a major and vocation. *J. Couns. Psychol.* 24:398–403

121. Hayes, L. A. 1976. The use of group contingencies for behavioral control: A review. *Psychol. Bull.* 83:628–48

122. Haynes, S. N., Price, M. G., Simons, J. B. 1975. Stimulus control treatment of insomnia. *J. Behav. Ther. Exp. Psychiatry* 6:279–82

123. Haynes, S. N., Sides, H., Lockwood, G. 1977. Relaxation instructions and frontalis electromyographic feedback intervention with a sleep-onset insomnia. *Behav. Ther.* 8:644–52

124. Haynes, S. N., Woodward, S., Moran, R., Alexander, D. 1974. Relaxation treatment of insomnia. *Behav. Ther.* 5:555–58

125. Healy, C. C. 1974. Evaluation of a replicable group career counseling procedure. *Q. Vocat. Guild.* 23:34–40

126. Healy, C. C. 1974. Interrelationships among indexes of vocational maturity. *Q. Vocat. Guid.* 23:146–51

127. Heath, D. H. 1976. Adolescent and adult predictors of vocational adaptation. *J. Vocat. Behav.* 9:1–19

127a. Heiman, J., LoPiccolo, L., LoPiccolo, J. 1977. *Becoming orgasmic: A sexual growth program for women*. Englewood Cliffs, NJ: Prentice-Hall

128. Heppner, P. P., Pew, S. 1977. Effects of diplomas, awards, and counselor sex on perceived expertness. *J. Couns. Psychol.* 24:147–49

129. Herr, E. L., Enderlein, T. E. 1976. Vocational maturity: The effects of school, grade, curriculum and sex. *J. Vocat. Behav.* 8:227–38

130. Hilgard, E. R., Morgan, A. H., MacDonald, H. 1975. Pain and dissociation in the cold pressor test: A study of hypnotic analgesia with "hidden reports" through automatic key pressing and automatic talking. *J. Abnorm. Psychol.* 84:280–89

131. Holcomb, W. R., Anderson, W. P. 1977. Vocational guidance research: A five-year overview. *J. Vocat. Behavior.* 10:341–46

132. Holland, J. L., Gottfredson, G. D. 1975. Predictive value and psychological meaning of vocational aspirations. *J. Vocat Behav.* 6:349–63

133. Holland, J. L., Gottfredson, G. D., Nafziger, D. H. 1975. Testing the validity of some theoretical signs of vocational decision-making ability. *J. Couns. Psychol.* 22:411–22

134. Holland, J. L., Holland, J. E. 1977. Distributions of personalities within occupations and fields of study. *Q. Vocat. Guid.* 25:226–31

135. Holland, J. L., Holland, J. E. 1977. Vocational indecision: More evidence and speculation. *J. Couns. Psychol.* 24: 404–14

136. Hollandsworth, J. G. Jr., Dressel, M. E., Stevens, J. 1977. Use of behavioral versus traditional procedures for increasing job interview skills. *J. Couns. Psychol.* 24:503–10

137. Holroyd, K. A. 1976. Cognition and desensitization in the group treatment of test anxiety. *J. Consult. Clin. Psychol.* 44:991–1001

138. Holroyd, K. A., Andrasik, F., Westbrook, T. 1977. Cognitive control of tension headache. *Cogn. Ther. Res.* 1:121–33

139. Horan, J. J., Hackett, G., Nicholas, W. C., Linberg, S. E., Stone, C. I., Lukaski, H. C. 1977. Rapid smoking: A cautionary note. *J. Consult. Clin. Psychol.* 45:341–43

140. Horan, J. J., Linberg, S. E., Hackett, G. 1977. Nicotine poisoning and rapid smoking. *J. Consult. Clin. Psychol.* 45:344–47

141. Horwitz, M. B. 1977. A comment on "an empirical investigation of the construct validity of empathic understanding ratings". *Couns. Educ. Superv.* 16:292–95

142. Hovland, C. I., Janis, I. L., Kelley, H. H. 1953. *Communication and Persuasion*. New York: Yale Univ. Press

143. Jackson, R. M., Meara, N. M. 1974. Father identification, achievement, and occupational behavior of rural youth: One year follow-up. *J. Vocat. Behav.* 4:349–56

144. Jacobs, R. G., Kramer, H. C., Agras, W. S. 1977. Relaxation therapy in the treatment of essential hypertension: A review. *Arch. Gen. Psychiatry* 34: 1417–27

145. Jacobson, E. 1938. *You Can Sleep Well. The ABC's of Restful Sleep for the Average Person.* New York: McGraw-Hill

146. Jacobson, N. S. 1977. Problem solving and contingency contracting in the treatment of marital discord. *J. Consult. Clin. Psychol.* 45:92–100

147. Jacobson, N. S., Martin, B. 1976. Be-

havioral marriage therapy: Current status. *Psychol. Bull.* 83:540–56

148. Jason, L. 1975. Rapid improvement in insomnia following self-monitoring. *J. Behav. Ther. Exp. Psychiatry* 6:349–50

149. Jepsen, D. A. 1974. Vocational decision-making patterns among non-college aspiring adolescents. *J. Vocat. Behav.* 4:283–97

150. Jepsen, D. A. 1974. Vocational decision-making strategy-types: An exploratory study. *Q. Vocat. Guid.* 23:17–23

151. Jepsen, D. A. 1975. Occupational decision development over the high school years. *J. Vocat. Behav.* 7:225–37

152. Jones, L. K. 1974. The counselor evaluation rating scale: A valid criterion of counselor effectiveness? *Couns. Educ. Superv.* 14:112–16

153. Jung, S. M., Campbell, V. N., Wolman, J. M. 1976. A comparative study of proprietary and nonproprietary vocational training graduates. *J. Vocat. Behav.* 8:209–25

154. Karoly, P. 1977. Behavioral self-management in children: Concepts, methods, issues, and directions. In *Progress in Behavior Modification,* Vol. 5, ed. M. Hersen, R. M. Eisler, P. M. Miller. New York: Academic

155. Kelly, G. 1955. *The Psychology of Personal Constructs.* New York: Norton. 2 vols.

156. Kelso, G. I. 1975. The influences of stage of leaving school on vocational maturity and realism of vocational choice. *J. Vocat. Behav.* 7:29–39

157. Kelso, G. I. 1977. The relation of school grade to ages and stages in vocational development. *J. Vocat. Behav.* 10:287–301

158. Kimes, H. G., Troth, W. A. 1974. Relationship of trait anxiety to career decisiveness. *J. Couns. Psychol.* 21:277–80

159. Kinney, J. M., Madsen, B., Fleming, T., Haapala, D. A. 1977. Homebuilders: Keeping families together. *J. Consult, Clin. Psychol.* 45:667–73

160. Klein, N. C., Alexander, J. F., Parsons, B. V. 1977. Impact of family systems intervention on recidivism and sibling delinquency: A model of primary prevention and program evaluation. *J. Consult. Clin. Psychol.* 45:469–74

161. Kleinberg, J. L. 1976. Adolescent correlates of occupational stability and change. *J. Vocat. Behav.* 9:219–32

162. Kohen, A. I., Breinich, S. C. 1975. Knowledge of the world of work: A test of occupational information for young men. *J. Vocat. Behav.* 6:133–44

163. Krivatsy, S. E., Magoon, T. M. 1976. Differential effects of three vocational counseling treatments. *J. Couns. Psychol.* 23:112–18

164. Krumboltz, J. D., Mitchell, A. M., Jones, G. B. 1976. A social learning theory of career selection. *Couns. Psychol.* 6:71–81

165. Kunce, J. T., Decker, G. L., Eckelman, C. C. 1976. Strong Vocational Interest Blank basic interest clusters and occupational satisfaction. *J. Vocat. Behav.* 9:355–62

166. LaCross, M. B. 1977. Comparative perceptions of counselor behavior: A replication and extension. *J. Couns. Psychol.* 24:464–71

167. Lando, H. A. 1975. A comparison of excessive and rapid smoking in the modification of chronic smoking behavior. *J. Consult. Clin. Psychol.* 43:350–55

168. Lando, H. A. 1976. Self-pacing in eliminating chronic smoking: Serendipity revisited? *Behav. Ther.* 7:634–40

169. Lando, H. A. 1977. Successful treatment of smokers with a broad-spectrum behavioral approach. *J. Consult. Clin. Psychol.* 45:361–66

170. Lawlis, G. F., Crawford, J. D. 1975. Cognitive differentiation in women and pioneer-traditional vocational choices. *J. Vocat. Behav.* 6:263–67

171. LeBoeuf, A. 1976. The treatment of a severe tremor by electromyogram feedback. *J. Behav. Ther. Exp. Psychiatry* 7:59–61

171a. Deleted in proof

171b. Leitenberg, H., Agras, W. S., Allen, R., Butz, R., Edwards, J. 1975. Feedback and therapist praise during treatment of phobia. *J. Consult. Clin. Psychol.* 43:396–404

172. Levenberg, S. B., Wagner, M. K. 1976. Smoking cessation: Long-term irrelevance of mode of treatment. *Behav. Ther. Exp. Psychiatry* 7:93–95

173. Levendusky, P., Pankratz, L. 1975. Case report and comments: Self-control techniques as an alternative to pain medication. *J. Abnorm. Psychol.* 84:165–68

174. Lewinsohn, P. M. 1974. The behavioral study and treatment of depression. In *Progress in Behavior Modification,* Vol. 1, ed. M. Hersen, R. M. Eisler, P. M. Miller. New York: Academic

175. Lewinsohn, P. M. 1975. Engagement in pleasant activities and depression level. *J. Abnorm. Psychol.* 84:729–31

176. Lewinsohn, P. M., Biglan, A., Zeiss, A. M. 1976. Behavioral treatment of depression. In *The Behavioral Manage-*

ment of Anxiety, Depression, and Pain, ed. P. O. Davidson. New York: Brunner/Mazel

177. Lick, J. R., Heffler, D. 1977. Relaxation training and attention placebo in the treatment of severe insomnia. *J. Consult. Clin. Psychol.* 45:153–61

178. Lira, F. T., Nay, W. R., McCullough, J. P., Etkin, M. W. 1975. Relative effects of modeling and role playing in the treatment of avoidance behaviors. *J. Consult. Clin. Psychol.* 43:608–18

179. Little, D. M., Roach, A. J. 1974. Videotape modeling of interest in nontraditional occupations for women. *J. Vocat. Behav.* 5:133–38

180. Littlefield, R. P. 1974. Self-disclosure among some negro, white, and Mexican-American adolescents. *J. Couns. Psychol.* 21:133–36

181. Deleted in proof

182. London, M., Klimoski, R. J. 1975. Self-esteem and job complexity as moderators of performance and satisfaction. *J. Vocat. Behav.* 6:293–304

183. Lorion, R. P., Caldwell, R. A., Cowen, E. L. 1976. Effects of a school mental health project: A one-year follow-up. *J. Sch. Psychol.* 14:56–63

184. Lucker, G. W., Rosenfield, D., Sikes, J., Aronson, E. 1976. Performance in the interdependent classroom: A field study. *Am. Educ. Res. J.* 13:115–23

185. Lunneborg, P. W. 1975. Interest differentiation in high school and vocational indecision in college. *J. Vocat. Behav.* 7:297–303

186. Lunneborg, P. W. 1976. Vocational indecision in college graduates. *J. Couns. Psychol.* 23:402–4

187. Maletzky, B. M. 1974. "Assisted" covert sensitization in the treatment of exhibitionism. *J. Consult. Clin. Psychol.* 42:34–40

188. Mann, B., Murphy, K. C. 1975. Timing of self-disclosure, reciprocity of self-disclosure, and reactions to an initial interview. *J. Couns. Psychol.* 22:304–8

189. Maola, J., Kane, G. 1976. Comparison of computer-based versus counselor-based occupational information systems with disadvantaged vocational students. *J. Couns. Psychol.* 23:163–65

190. Masters, W., Johnson, V. 1970. *Human Sexual Inadequacy.* Boston: Little, Brown

191. McAlister, A. L., Farquhar, J. W., Thoresen, C. E., Maccoby, N. 1976. Behavioral science applied to cardiovascular health: Progress and research needs in the modification of risk-taking habits

in adult populations. *Health Educ. Monogr.* 4:45–74

192. McCoy, V. R. 1976. Student wives: Lives in limbo. *Q. Vocat. Guid.* 25:35–42

193. McGowan, A. S. 1977. Vocational maturity and anxiety among vocationally undecided and indecisive students. *J. Vocat. Behav.* 10:196–204

194. McGuire, D., Thelen, M. H., Amolsch, T. 1975. Interview self-disclosure as a function of length of modeling and descriptive instructions. *J. Consult. Clin. Psychol.* 43:356–62

195. McKechnie, R. J. 1975. Relief from phantom limb pain by relaxation exercises. *J. Behav. Ther. Exp. Psychiatry* 6:262–63

196. McLaughlin, D. H., Tiedeman, D. V. 1974. Eleven-year career stability and change as reflected in project talent data through the Flanagan, Holland, and Roe occupational classification systems. *J. Vocat. Behav.* 5:177–96

197. Meichenbaum, D. 1975. A self-instructional approach to stress management: A proposal for stress inoculation training. In *Stress and Anxiety,* Vol. 2, ed. C. Spielberger, I. Sarason. New York: Wiley

198. Mencke, R. A., Cochran, D. J. 1974. Impact of a counseling outreach workshop on vocational development. *J. Couns. Psychol.* 21:185–90

199. Mendonca, J. D., Siess, T. F. 1976. Counseling for indecisiveness: Problem-solving and anxiety-management training. *J. Couns. Psychol.* 23:339–47

200. Merluzzi, T. V., Merluzzi, B. H., Kaul, T. J. 1977. Counselor race and power base: Effects on attitudes and behavior. *J. Couns. Psychol.* 24:430–36

201. Miller, M. F. 1974. Relationship of vocational maturity to work values. *J. Vocat. Behav.* 5:367–71

202. Mitchell, D. C., Frederickson, W. A. 1975. Preferences of physically disabled counselors in hypothetical counseling situations. *J. Couns. Psychol.* 22:477–82

203. Mitchell, K. R., White, R. G. 1976. Self-management of tension headaches: A case study. *J. Behav. Ther. Exp. Psychiatry* 7:387–89

204. Mitchell, T. R. 1974. Expectancy models of job satisfaction, occupational preference and effort: A theoretical, methodological, and empirical appraisal. *Psychol. Bull.* 81:1053–77

205. Morris, R. J., Suckerman, K. R. 1974. Therapist warmth as a factor in automated systematic desensitization. *J. Consult. Clin. Psychol.* 42:244–50

206. Muchinsky, P. M., Hoyt, D. P. 1974. Predicting vocational performance of engineers from selected vocational interest, personality, and scholastic aptitude variables. *J. Vocat. Behav.* 5:115–23

207. Muchinsky, P. M., Taylor, M. S. 1976. Intrasubject predictions of occupational preference: The effect of manipulating components of the valence model. *J. Vocat. Behav.* 8:185–96

208. Munley, P. H. 1975. Erik Erikson's theory of psychosocial development and vocational behavior. *J. Couns. Psychol.* 22:314–19

209. Musante, G. J. 1976. The dietary rehabilitation clinic: Evaluative report of a behavioral and dietary treatment of obesity. *Behav. Ther.* 7:198–204

210. Myers, R. A., Lindeman, R. H., Thompson, A. S., Patrick, T. A. 1975. Effects of educational and career exploration system on vocational maturity. *J. Vocat. Behav.* 6:245–54

211. Nelson, R. E., Scanlan, T. 1977. Parents' and students' perceptions of occupational survival skills. *Q. Vocat. Guid.* 25:217–24

212. Nicassio, P., Bootzin, R. 1974. A comparison of progressive relaxation and autogenic training as treatment for insomnia. *J. Abnorm. Psychol.* 83:253–60

213. Noeth, R. J., Roth, J. D., Prediger, D. J. 1975. Student career development: Where do we stand? *Q. Vocat. Guid.* 25:210–18

214. Novaco, R. W. 1975. *Anger Control: The Development and Evaluation of an Experimental Treatment.* Lexington, Mass: Lexington Books

215. Novaco, R. W. 1977. Stress inoculation: A cognitive therapy for anger and its application to a case of depression. *J. Consult. Clin. Psychol.* 45:600–8

216. Novaco, R. W. 1977. A stress inoculation approach to anger management in the training of law enforcement officers. *Am. J. Community Psychol.* 5:327–46

217. Nuckols, T. E., Banducci, R. 1974. Knowledge of occupations—is it important in occupational choice? *J. Couns. Psychol.* 21:191–95

218. Oden, S., Asher, S. R. 1977. Coaching children in social skills for friendship making. *Child Dev.* 48:495–506

219. Ohlde, C. D., Vinitsky, M. H. 1976. Effect of values-clarification workshop on value awareness. *J. Couns. Psychol.* 23:489–91

220. O'Leary, S. G., O'Leary, K. D. 1976. Behavior modification in the school. In *Handbook of Behavior Modification and Behavior Therapy,* ed. H. Leitenberg. Englewood Cliffs, NJ: Prentice-Hall

221. Oliver, L. W. 1974. The effect of verbal reinforcement on career choice realism. *J. Vocat. Behav.* 5:275–84

222. Oliver, L. W. 1975. The relationship of parental attitudes and parent identification to career and homemaking orientation in college women. *J. Vocat. Behav.* 7:1–12

223. Omvig, C. P., Tulloch, R. W., Thomas, E. G. 1975. The effect of career education on career maturity. *J. Vocat. Behav.* 7:265–73

224. Osipow, S. H. 1976. Vocational behavior and career development, 1975: A review. *J. Vocat. Behav.* 9:129–45

225. Osipow, S. H., Carney, C. G., Barak, A. 1976. A scale of educational-vocational undecidedness: A typological approach. *J. Vocat. Behav.* 9:233–43

226. Parker, R. 1974. Methodological pitfalls in predicting counseling success. *J. Vocat. Behav.* 5:31–39

227. Patterson, G. R., Weiss, R. L., Hops, H. 1976. Training of marital skills: Some problems and concepts. In *Handbook of Behavior Modification and Behavior Therapy,* ed. H. Leitenberg. Englewood Cliffs, NJ: Prentice-Hall

228. Patterson, L. W. 1976. Career information: Experience is the best teacher. *Q. Vocat. Guid.* 25:112–18

229. Peoples, V. Y., Dell, D. M. 1975. Black and white student preferences for counselor roles. *J. Couns. Psychol.* 22:529–34

230. Perrone, P. A., Kyle, G. W. 1975. Evaluating the effectiveness of a grade 7–9 career development program. *Q. Vocat. Guid.* 23:317–23

231. Pilato, G. T., Myers, R. A. 1975. The effects of computer-mediated vocational guidance procedures on the appropriateness of vocational preference. *J. Vocat. Behav.* 6:61–72

232. Pope, B., Nudler, S., Vonkorff, M. R., McGhee, J. P. 1974. The experienced professional interviewer versus the complete novice. *J. Consult. Clin. Psychol.* 42:680–90

233. Prediger, D. J., Hanson, G. R. 1976. Holland's theory of careers applied to women and men: Analysis of implicit assumptions. *J. Vocat. Behav.* 8:167–84

234. Prediger, D. J., Roth, J. D., Noeth, R. J. 1974. Career development of youth: A nationwide study. *Personnel Guid. J.* 53:97–104

235. Pyle, K. R., Stripling, R. O. 1976. The counselor, the computer, and career development. *Q. Vocat. Guid.* 25:71–75

236. Relinger, H., Bornstein, P. H., Bugge, I. D., Carmody, T. P. Zohn, C. J. 1977. Utilization of adverse rapid smoking in groups: Efficacy of treatment and maintenance procedures. *J. Consult. Clin. Psychol.* 45:245–49

237. Ribordy, S. C., Denney, D. R. 1977. The behavioral treatment of insomnia: An alternative to drug therapy. *Behav. Res. Ther.* 15:39–50

238. Rice, L. N., Wagstaff, A. K. 1967. Client voice quality and expressive style as indexes of productive psychotherapy. *J. Consult. Psychol.* 31:557–63

239. Rich, A. R., Schroeder, H. E. 1976. Research issues in assertiveness training. *Psychol. Bull.* 83:1081–96

240. Richardson, M. S. 1974. The dimensions of career and work orientation in college women. *J. Vocat. Behav.* 5: 161–72

241. Richardson, M. S. 1975. Self-concepts and role concepts in the career orientation of college women. *J. Couns. Psychol.* 22:122–26

242. Ronan, W. W., Cobb, J. M., Garrett, T. L., Lazarri, J. D., Mosser, D. R., Racine, A. E. 1974. Occupational level and mental health: A note. *J. Vocat. Behav.* 5:157–61

243. Ronnestad, M. H. 1977. The effects of modeling, feedback, and experiential methods on counselor empathy. *Couns. Educ. Superv.* 25:194–201

243a. Rooth, F. G., Marks, I. M. 1974. Persistent exhibitionism: short-term response to self-regulation and relaxation treatment. *Arch. Sex. Behav.* 3:227–48

244. Rush, A. J., Beck, A. T., Kovacs, M., Hollon, S. 1977. Comparative efficacy of cognitive therapy and pharmacotherapy in the treatment of depressed outpatients. *Cogn. Ther. Res.* 1:17–37

245. Saltzman, C., Luetgert, M. J., Roth, C. H., Creaser, J., Howard, L. 1976. Formation of a therapeutic relationship: Experiences during the initial phase of psychotherapy as predictors of treatment duration and outcome. *J. Consult. Clin. Psychol.* 44:546–55

246. Sanchez-Craig, B. M. 1976. Cognitive and behavioral coping strategies in the reappraisal of stressful social situations. *J. Couns. Psychol.* 23:7–12

247. Sank, L. I., Biglan, A. 1974. Operant treatment of a case of recurrent abdominal pain in a 10-year-old boy. *Behav. Ther.* 5:677–81

248. Sarason, I. G. 1975. Test anxiety and the self-disclosing coping model. *J. Consult. Clin. Psychol.* 43:148–53

249. Scheid, A. B. 1976. Clients' perception of the counselor: The influence of counselor introduction and behavior. *J. Couns. Psychol.* 23:503–8

250. Scher, M. 1975. Verbal activity, sex, counselor experience, and success in counseling. *J. Couns. Psychol.* 22:97–101

251. Schinke, S. P., Rose, S. D. 1976. Interpersonal skill training in groups. *J. Couns. Psychol.* 23:442–48

252. Schmidt, L. D., Strong, S. R. 1970. "Expert" and "inexpert" counselors. *J. Couns. Psychol.* 17:115–18

253. Schroeder, H. E., Rich, A. R. 1976. The process of fear reduction through systematic desensitization. *J. Consult. Clin. Psychol.* 44:191–99

254. Schwartz, R. M., Gottman, J. M. 1976. Toward a task analysis of assertive behavior. *J. Consult. Clin. Psychol.* 44:910–20

255. Scott, C. S., Fenske, R. H., Maxey, E. J. 1974. Change in vocational choice as a function of initial career choice, interests, abilities, and sex. *J. Vocat. Behav.* 5:285–92

256. Sedney, M. A., Turner, B. F. 1975. A test of causal sequences in two models for development of career-orientation in women. *J. Vocat. Behav.* 6:281–91

257. Seligman, M. E. P. 1975. *Helplessness.* San Francisco: Freeman

258. Seligman, M. E. P., Klein, D. C., Miller, W. R. 1976. Depression. In *Handbook of Behavior Modification and Behavior Therapy,* ed. H. Leitenberg. Englewood Cliffs, NJ: Prentice-Hall

259. Sewell, T. E., Martin, R. P. 1976. Racial differences in patterns of occupational choice in adolescents. *Psychol. Sch.* 13:326–33

260. Shaw, B. F. 1977. Comparison of cognitive therapy and behavior therapy in the treatment of depression. *J. Consult. Clin. Psychol.* 45:543–51

261. Shure, M. B., Spivack, G. 1978. *Problem-Solving Techniques in Childrearing.* San Francisco: Jossey-Bass

262. Simons, J. A., Helms, J. E. 1976. Influnece of counselors' marital status, sex, and age on college and noncollege women's counselor preferences. *J. Couns. Psychol.* 23:380–86

263. Simonson, N. R. 1976. The impact of therapist disclosure on patient disclosure. *J. Couns. Psychol.* 23:3–6

264. Slavin, R. E. 1977. A student team approach to teaching adolescents with special emotional and behavioral needs. *Psychol. Sch.* 14:77–83

265. Smith, E. J. 1976. Reference group perspectives and the vocational maturity of lower socioeconomic black youth. *J. Vocat. Behav.* 8:321–36

266. Spanos, N. P., Horton, C., Chaves, J. F. 1975. The effects of two cognitive strategies on pain threshold. *J. Abnorm. Psychol.* 84:677–81

267. Spegel, S. B. 1976. Expertness, similarity, and perceived counselor competence. *J. Couns. Psychol.* 23:436–41

268. Spiegler, M. D., Cooley, E. J., Marshall, G. J., Prince, H. T. II, Puckett, S. P., Skenazy, J. A. 1976. A self-control versus a counterconditioning paradigm for systematic desensitization: An experimental comparison. *J. Couns. Psychol.* 23:83–86

269. Spivack, G., Platt, J. J., Shure, M. B. 1976. *The Problem-Solving Approach to Adjustment.* San Francisco: Jossey-Bass.

270. Spivack, G., Shure, M. B. 1974. *Social Adjustment of Young Children.* San Francisco: Jossey-Bass

271. Stern, S. L., Moore, S. F., Gross, S. J. 1975. Confounding of personality and social class characteristics in research on premature termination. *J. Consult. Clin. Psychol.* 43:341–44

272. Stone, G. L. 1975. Effect of simulation on counselor training. *Couns. Educ. Superv.* 23:199–98

272a. Stone, G. L., Gotlib, I. 1975. Effect of instructions and modeling on self-disclosure. *J. Couns. Psychol.* 22:288–93

273. Stone, G. L., Morden, C. J. 1976. Effect of distance on verbal productivity. *J. Couns. Psychol.* 23:486–88

274. Stone, G. L., Stebbins, L. W. 1975. Effect of differential pretraining on client self-disclosure. *J. Couns. Psychol.* 22:17–20

275. Stone, G. L., Vance, A. 1976. Instructions, modeling, and rehearsal: Implications for training. *J. Couns. Psychol.* 23:272–79

276. Strong, S. R. 1968. Counseling: An interpersonal influence process. *J. Couns. Psychol.* 15:215–24

277. Strupp, H. H. 1973. On the basic ingredients of psychotherapy. *J. Consult. Clin. Psychol.* 41:1–8

278. Stuart, R. B. 1967. Behavioral control over eating. *Behav. Res. Ther.* 5:357–65

279. Stuart, R. B., Davis, B. 1971. *Slim Chance in a Fat World: Behavioral Control of Obesity.* Champaign, Ill: Research Press

280. Stunkard, A. J. 1972. New therapies for the eating disorders. *Arch. Gen. Psychiatry* 26:391–98

281. Sue, D. W., Sue, D. 1977. Barriers to effective cross-cultural counseling. *J. Couns. Psychol.* 24:420–29

282. Super, D. E., Hall, D. T. 1978. Career development: Exploration and planning. *Ann. Rev. Psychol.* 29:333–72

283. Super, D. E., Jordaan, J. P., Bohn, M. J., Lindeman, R. H., Forest, D. J., Thompson, A. S. 1971. *Career Development Inventory.* New York: Teachers Coll., Columbia Univ.

284. Tasto, D. L., Chesney, M. A. 1974. Muscle relaxation treatment for primary dysmenorrhea. *Behav. Ther.* 5:668–72

285. Taylor, F. G., Marshall, W. L. 1977. Experimental analysis of a cognitive-behavioral therapy for depression. *Cogn. Ther. Res.* 1:59–72

286. Tessler, R. C. 1975. Clients' reactions to initial interviews: Determinants of relationship-centered and problem-centered satisfaction. *J. Couns. Psychol.* 22:187–91

287. Thase, M., Page, R. A. 1977. Modeling of self-disclosure in laboratory and nonlaboratory interview settings. *J. Couns. Psychol.* 24:35–40

288. Thase, M. E., Moss, M. K. 1976. The relative efficacy of covert modeling procedures and guided participant modeling on the reduction of avoidance behavior. *J. Behav. Ther. Exp. Psychiatry* 7:7–12

289. Thomas, M. J. 1976. Realism and socioeconomic status (SES) of occupational plans of low SES black and white male adolescents. *J. Couns. Psychol.* 23:46–49

290. Thoresen, C. E. 1977. Constructs don't speak for themselves. *Couns. Educ. Superv.* 16:296–303

291. Thoresen, C. E., Anton, J. L. 1974. Intensive experimental research in counseling. *J. Couns. Psychol.* 21:553–59

292. Thoresen, C. E., Coates, T. J. 1978. What does it mean to be a behavior therapist? *Couns. Psychol.* 7:3–21

293. Thoresen, C. E., Kirmil-Gray, K., Crosbie, P. 1977. Processes and procedures of self-control: A working model. *Canadian Counselor* 12:66–75

294. Thoresen, K. E., Thoresen, C. E., Klein, S. B., Wilbur, C. S., Becker-Haven, J. F., Haven, W. G. 1978. Learning house: helping troubled children and their parents change themselves. In *Progress in behavior therapy with delinquents,* Vol. 2, ed. J. S. Stumphauzer. Springfield, Ill: Thomas

295. Thorn, M. E., Boudewyns, P. A. 1976. A behaviorally oriented weight loss pro-

gram for counseling centers. *J. Couns. Psychol.* 23:81–82

296. Tipton, R. M. 1976. Attitudes towards women's roles in society and vocational interests. *J. Vocat. Behav.* 8:155–65

297. Tittler, B. I., Anchor, K. N., Weitz, L. J. 1976. Measuring change in openness: Behavioral assessment techniques and the problem of the examiner. *J. Couns. Psychol.* 23:473–78

298. Touchton, J. G., Magoon, T. M. 1970. Occupational daydreams as predictors of vocational plans of college women. *J. Vocat. Behav.* 10:156–66

299. Truax, C. B., Mitchell, K. M. 1971. Research on certain interpersonal skills in relation to process and outcome. In *Handbook of Psychotherapy and Behavior Change.* ed. A. E. Bergin, S. L. Garfield. New York: Wiley

300. Turner, A. J., Vernon, J. C. 1976. Prompts to increase attendance in a community mental health center. *J. Appl. Behav. Anal.* 9:141–45

301. Twentyman, C. T., McFall, R. M. 1975. Behavioral training of social skills in shy males. *J. Consult. Clin. Psychol.* 43:384–95

302. Tyler, L. E. 1964. Antecedents of two varieties of vocational interests. *Gen. Psychol. Monogr.* 70:177–227

303. Uhlemann, M. R., Lea, G. W., Stone, G. L. 1976. Effect of instructions and modeling on trainees low in interpersonal-communication skills. *J. Couns. Psychol.* 23:509–13

304. Umeda, J. K., Frey, D. H. 1974. Life history correlates of ministerial success. *J. Vocat. Behav.* 4:319–24

305. Venzor, E., Gillis, J. S., Beal, D. G. 1976. Preference for counselor response styles. *J. Couns. Psychol.* 23:538–42

306. Villwock, J. D., Schnitzen, J. P., Carbonari, J. P. 1976. Holland's personality constructs as predictors of stability of choice. *J. Vocat. Behav.* 9:77–85

307. Wallace, W. G., Horan, J. J., Baker, S. B., Hudson, G. R. 1975. Incremental effects of modeling and performance feedback in teaching decision-making counseling. *J. Couns. Psychol.* 22:570–72

308. Walls, R. T., Gulkus, S. P. 1974. Reinforcers, values, and vocational maturity in adults. *J. Vocat. Behav.* 4:325–32

309. Walls, R. T., Gulkus, S. P. 1974. Reinforcers and vocational maturity in occupational aspiration, expectation, and goal deflection. *J. Vocat. Behav.* 5:381–90

310. Wallston, K. A., Weitz, L. J. 1975. Measurement of the core dimensions of helping. *J. Couns. Psychol.* 22:567–69

311. Walsh, W. B., Hanle, N. A. 1975. Consistent occupational preferences, vocational maturity, and academic achievement. *J. Vocat. Behav.* 7:89–97

312. Webb, S. C., Hultgen, D. D., Craddick, R. A. 1977. Predicting occupational choice by clinical and statistical methods. *J. Couns. Psychol.* 24:98–110

313. Weeks, M. O., Thornburg, K. R., Little, L. F. 1977. The impact of exposure to nontraditional vocational role models on the vocational role preferences of five-year-old children. *J. Vocat. Behav.* 10:139–45

314. Weller, L., Nadler, A. 1975. Authoritarianism and job preference. *J. Vocat. Behav.* 6:9–14

315. Westbrook, B. W. 1976. Interrelationship of career choice competencies and career choice attitudes of ninth-grade pupils: Testing hypotheses derived from crites' Model of Career Maturity. *J. Vocat. Behav.* 8:1–12

316. Westbrook, B. W. 1976. The relationship between career choice attitudes and career choice competencies of ninth-grade pupils. *J. Vocat. Behav.* 9:119–25

317. Westbrook, B. W., 1976. Criterion-related and construct validity of the career maturity inventory competence test with ninth-grade pupils. *J. Vocat. Behav.* 9:377–83

318. Deleted in proof

319. Wexler, D. A., Butler, J. M. 1976. Therapist modification of client expressiveness in client-centered therapy. *J. Consult. Clin. Psychol.* 44:261–65

320. Wickramasekera, I. 1976. Aversive behavior rehearsal for sexual exhibitionism. *Behav. Ther.* 7:167–76

321. Wiggins, J. D., Weslander, D. 1977. Expressed vocational choices and later employment compared with vocational preference inventory and Kuder Preference Record-Vocational Scores. *J. Vocat. Behav.* 11:158–65

322. Wildman, R. W. II, Wildman, R. W. 1975. The generalization of behavior modification procedures: A review—with special emphasis on classroom applications. *Psychol. Sch.* 12:432–48

323. Wolfe, J. L., Fodor, I. G. 1977. Modifying assertive behavior in women: A comparison of three approaches. *Behav. Ther.* 8:567–74

324. Wolfson, K. P. 1976. Career development patterns of college women. *J. Couns. Psychol.* 23:119–25

325. Woods, E. Jr., Zimmer, J. M. 1976. Racial effects in counseling-like interviews: An experimental analogue. *J.Couns. Psychol.* 23:527–31

326. Woolfolk, R. L., Carr-Kaffashan, L., McNulty, T. F. 1976. Meditation training as a treatment for insomnia. *Behav. Ther.* 7:359–65

327. Youell, K. J., McCullough, J. P. 1975. Behavioral treatment of mucous colitis. *J. Consult. Clin. Psychol.* 43:740–45

328. Zener, T. B., Schnuelle, L. 1976. Effects of the self-directed search on high school students. *J. Couns. Psychol.* 23:353–59

329. Zytowski, D. G. 1976. Predictive validity of the Kuder Occupational Interest Survey: A 12- to 19-year follow-up. *J. Couns. Psychol.* 23:221–33

330. Zytowski, D. G. 1977. The effects of being interested-inventoried. *J. Vocat. Behav.* 11:153–57

Ann. Rev. Psychol. 1979. 30:603–40

INDIVIDUAL DIFFERENCES IN COGNITIVE ABILITIES[1]

❖318

John B. Carroll

Department of Psychology, University of North Carolina, Chapel Hill, North Carolina 27514

Scott E. Maxwell

Department of Psychology, University of Houston, Houston, Texas 77004

CONTENTS

INTRODUCTION 604
TRAITS, PROCESSES, AND COMPETENCE PHENOMENA IN COGNITIVE
    PSYCHOLOGY 606
STUDIES OF BROAD ABILITY DOMAINS 608
    Standardized Intelligence Tests 608
    Factor-Analytic Studies of Broad Ability Domains 609
    Multifactorial Test Batteries 609
    Factor Models of Cognitive Abilities 610
    Learning-Ability Relationships 611
    Individual Differences Studied in Experimental Cognitive Psychology 611
ABILITIES IN PARTICULAR DOMAINS 613
    Language Abilities and Skills 613
    Creativity and Fluency of Ideation 615
    Thinking, Reasoning, and Problem Solving 616
    Abilities Concerned with Number and Quantity 618
    Perceptual Skills and Processes in Vision and Audition 618
    Memory Skills and Capacities 621
    Cognitive Speed 622

[1]Preparation of this article was supported in part by Contract No. N00014-77-C-0722, NR 150-406 with the Personnel and Training Research Programs, Psychological Sciences Division, Office of Naval Research. The period covered is roughly May 1975 to April 1978, with some attention to important materials that for one reason or another were not mentioned in earlier reviews. This review is highly selective; in numerous instances items mentioned are only illustrative of many similar or related items appearing in the literature.

0066-4308/79/0201-0603$01.00

COGNITION AND PERSONALITY 623
  Field Dependence-Independence 624
CHANGES IN ABILITIES OVER THE LIFE SPAN 624
  Abilities in Infants and Young Children 624
  Abilities in Older Children 625
  Aging and The Question of Declines in Abilities 627
GENETIC AND ENVIRONMENTAL INFLUENCES 629
  Nature-Nurture Issues 629
  Group Differences 631
APPLIED DIFFERENTIAL PSYCHOLOGY 632
  Determinants of School Achievement 632
FINAL REMARKS: THE STATE OF OUR KNOWLEDGE AND ART 633

INTRODUCTION

Traditional topics and issues of differential psychology continue to receive attention in contemporary research. These topics include: the identification and measurement of dimensions of IDs[2]; models of structural relations among these dimensions; the origin, growth, and possible decline of differences in intellectual ability as a function of (a) genetic and maturational factors and (b) environmental factors describable in terms of opportunities for learning, practice, and transfer; and the applications of differential psychology to problems of assessment, selection, guidance, education, and training of individuals.

A discernible new trend, however, is a budding but fitful and hesitant courtship between two traditionally separate disciplines of psychology—psychometrics, on the one hand, and experimental cognitive psychology, on the other. Not clear yet is whether this courtship will eventually lead to anything like a marriage or other basis for cohabitation, but a growing body of literature addresses IDs in cognitive processes identified through experimental investigations, usually carried out in laboratory settings, of performance in various "cognitive" tasks such as comparison of stimuli, "mental rotation" of spatial representations, recognition and recall of series of verbal or figural stimuli, and comprehension of linguistic strings—in short, tasks that in many ways resemble, or are even identical with, those found in conventional tests of aptitudes and abilities (20). Some of this literature purports to be oriented toward the better understanding of the nature of these aptitudes and abilities (77), but some of it is directed toward the use of ID findings in the refinement of psychological theory (42). In either case,

[2]Abbreviations for terms and phrases frequently used in this article are as follows: ETS, Educational Testing Service (Princeton, NJ); FA, factor analysis, factor-analytic; GRE, Graduate Record Examination; ID, individual difference(s); IQ, intelligence quotient; PA, paired-associates; PMA, Primary Mental Abilities (test); RT, reaction time; SAT, SAT-V, Scholastic Aptitude Test (-Verbal); SES, socioeconomic status; SI, structure of intellect; WAIS, Wechsler Adult Intelligence Scale; WISC, Wechsler Intelligence Scale for Children.

it reflects attempts to identify fundamental processes in perception, learning, memory, problem solving, and other mental activities through study of IDs in task performances. Performances either in psychological tests or in laboratory experiments are seen as exemplifying information processing events or sequences thereof; IDs are regarded as residing, at least in part, in the parameters of these events that can be measured or estimated through observations of reaction times, error rates, and other indicants.

In historical perspective, this current trend represents a coming to full circle of tendencies that were evident already around the turn of the century when J. McK. Cattell, Binet, Spearman, and others attempted, with little real success, to measure intelligence through observations of simple processes such as sensory discrimination, choice reaction time, and memory span. What is new is a more precise technology of experimentation and a greatly elaborated approach to the study of mental processes, represented for example in the information processing theories described by Simon in the present volume (see pp. 363–96). The question to be addressed is whether current efforts have any greater promise of success.

We limit this review to consideration of contemporary research and theory in individual (and group) differences in cognitive abilities and performances, including both the work with a primarily psychometric orientation and work being conducted in experimental cognitive psychology. Personality variables are treated only to the extent that they are regarded as indicants of cognitive processes, styles, and strategies of performance.

Partly in response to the intense public concern of recent years about the claimed high heritability of intelligence, the possible involvement of genetic factors in black-white differences in mean IQ, and the decline of scholastic aptitude and achievement among various groups over the past decade (185), there appeared numerous materials addressed to the nature of intelligence, abilities, aptitudes, and achievements. Resnick's (133) collection of conference papers emphasized the above-mentioned possibilities of combining psychometric and experimental approaches in the study of intelligence, but ethological and cultural aspects were also treated. Another set of conference proceedings (57) revealed a continued division of opinion among psychologists as to whether aptitude and achievement variables are distinguishable either theoretically or empirically. In our view, they are, at least in many contexts. Buros (15) brought out a collection of reviews of standardized ability tests and recounted his 50 years of experience in editing test reviews (16). Relevant textbooks included those of Brody & Brody (13) and Buss & Poley (19), the former addressed to the meaning of results from group and individual general intelligence tests, the latter focusing on FA studies of cognitive abilities as well as personality and affective variables. Useful theoretical and historical articles are available (17, 176).

Literature addressed to the general public or to school people included a generally accurate and comprehensive survey of intelligence testing by Fincher (46), a polemic against IQ tests by Fine (47), and a collection of papers generally unfavorable to the use of aptitude tests in schools (71). Psychologists have shown little initiative in providing persuasive answers to the polemic writings.

TRAITS, PROCESSES, AND COMPETENCE PHENOMENA IN COGNITIVE PSYCHOLOGY

Because developments in experimental cognitive psychology and in information processing and similar theories are treated in numerous chapters in this and previous volumes of the *Annual Review of Psychology,* our discussion of relations between cognitive theory and differential psychology can be brief. We must start, however, from the traditional notions of trait, ability, and aptitude that still underlie much work in psychometrics. It is frequently claimed that concepts like intelligence, *"g",* ability factor and the like are statistical abstractions or even artifacts arising from psychometric operations. Some of these concepts may indeed be such artifacts; to a degree, "intelligence" is one such artifact, to the extent that it is measured essentially as a weighted average or composite of a number of more basic traits. But it is not wholly an artifact; it has reality as an underlying dimension that appears in numerous kinds of cognitive tasks. According to at least one type of factor model—the hierarchical model espoused by a number of authorities (24, 69)—factors have different levels of generality, *"g"* being the most general, with *Gf* (fluid intelligence), *Gc* (crystallized intelligence), and possibly *Gv* (visual intelligence) factors having only slightly less generality. At even lower levels of generality, numerous "primary" factors of mental ability have been identified (40). Series of well-designed FA studies have produced solid and generally replicable information on major dimensions of human cognitive ability at various levels of generality, although there is undoubtedly much more to be learned about these dimensions. Interpretations of factors in terms of relative magnitudes of factor loadings and corresponding intuitions or observations concerning the involvement of different kinds of knowledge, skill, and psychological processes have led to generally satisfactory descriptions of the underlying traits. The theory of multi-item tests has achieved much of its success by assuming the operation of "latent traits" in accounting for item and function operating characteristic curves, although test theory has not fully exploited a multifactorial view of item performance, nor have FA studies taken full advantage of test construction procedures suggested by test theory (22, 106).

Studies of cognitive tests in psychometrics have always been inspired at least in part by a process view of mental activity; indeed, Galton, Binet, Spearman, and Thurstone can be regarded as having been among the first cognitive psychologists. There is nothing in the theory of FA that requires that the variables be scores from paper-and-pencil psychometric tests; the variables can equally well be observations (RTs, slope parameters, etc) arising in the study of laboratory tasks. Recent use of FA and other correlational methodologies by the current generation of cognitive psychologists (80, 136) is actually a continuation of a tradition previously established. The use of procedures in which variations in task variables are introduced to generate possible variations in the extent to which a particular ID dimension is revealed in different observed variables represents no real departure. Recent work has not always attended sufficiently to such problems as sample size, avoidance of experimental dependence, and procedures of factor extraction and rotation (21), with the result that some of the results are open to question. Nevertheless, studies employing the new laboratory paradigms have begun to identify several ID dimensions that are not entirely specific to particular cognitive tasks and that show interesting connections with test performances (see below).

Whether ID dimensions are revealed by FA or by several new techniques such as what Sternberg (153) calls componential analysis, the psychological status of such dimensions poses questions. Are these dimensions necessarily linked to actual psychological processes or mental operations? Or do they represent IDs in the contents or capacities of "sensory buffers," "memory stores," or other postulated aspects of "mental architecture"? If they correspond to processes, are these processes of a fundamental and pervasive character, i.e. critical to task performance and generalizable over many types of tasks, or do they reflect particular strategies of task performance that happen to be selected by individual subjects, who can readily use other strategies under appropriate cues? If they represent differences in characteristics of sensory buffers or of memory stores, what does this imply for the nature and organization of the sensorium or of memory?

Further, what is the significance of IDs manifested at a particular point of time in a particular group? Are they reliable and consistent over time? If so, what is the course of their development over the life span? To what extent are they subject to change through maturation, learning, short-term physiological influences, etc?

The posing of such questions may imply particular theories and views of behavior and performance; possibly other kinds of questions would be suggested by theories of behavior that do not depend on information processing views. In any event, there is as yet only very limited information available for answering these questions. Possibly the major virtue in cognitive psychologists' renewed attention to IDs in performance is that it will prompt increased efforts to provide theory and data adequate for answering such questions. Differential psychology may therefore hold promise for encouraging the development of basic psychological theory, with an incidental payoff in the form of better ways of specifying the construct validity of ID dimensions. Notions of trait, ability, and aptitude possibly can be replaced by concepts with a closer nexus with psychological theory.

STUDIES OF BROAD ABILITY DOMAINS

Should we speak of cognitive *ability,* or should we speak of cognitive *abilities?* A persistent tension has existed between those who believe that human cognitive capacities can be well summarized in a single global concept of intelligence and those who prefer to emphasize the multidimensional character of the concept. The bulk of recent research is predicated on a multifactorial view; yet, in the course of providing a 70-year history of the Binet intelligence test, Thorndike (161) questioned the tendency to "fractionate" abilities. He pointed out that as much as 80% of the test variance can be explained by the first principal factor and that the overall IQ score is very stable over time whereas patterns of abilities may be unstable. The issues raised here are complex, but we would point out that even the facts cited by Thorndike are not inconsistent with a multifactorial model that provides for a strong general factor along with group and narrower factors that are differentially subject to genetic and environmental effects.

Standardized Intelligence Tests

Although the period under review apparently produced no new FA studies of the Stanford-Binet intelligence test, the factor composition of several other widely used intelligence tests was often investigated. Studies (149, 184) continued to confirm at least two reliable and interpretable dimensions (verbal and performance) in the WISC and the WAIS; Conger & Conger (28) claimed as many as four or five reliable dimensions in the WISC.

Raven's Progressive Matrices test (in either black-and-white or colored versions) generally has been considered an excellent test of the *g* factor of intelligence. Wiedl & Carlson (183), however, factor-analyzed data from 35 items of the test given to 180 primary-grade children, finding three factors: Concrete and Abstract Reasoning, Continuous and Discrete Pattern Completion, and Pattern Completion Through Closure. Their results implied that the task structure is less differentiated than Raven had suggested, since there was no distinction either between concrete and abstract reasoning items or between continuous and discrete pattern completion. Results must be viewed as tentative, however, because the factors may to some extent be artifacts of item difficulties and age differences. Thissen (158) demonstrated the utility of a multiple category latent trait model for obtaining information about an examinee's overall ability on the Raven test by inspecting specific incorrect responses. For the lower half of the ability range, this approach yielded up to twice as much information as a traditional binary model. The results of these studies might profitably be looked at from the perspective of the information processing model proposed by Hunt (76), who considered what sort of computer program could solve problems presented in Raven's test. Analysis disclosed that a score within the normal adult range on the test could be obtained through the application of either a Gestalt algorithm based on manipulating visual images or a reduced analytic algorithm based on applying formal operations. Hunt noted that a useful diagnostic test or scoring method would differentiate between these two styles of problem solving. The failure of the Raven test to do so thus casts doubt on its use as a measure of general intelligence. Lunneborg (108) found that a battery of information processing task measures could predict only 11% of the variance in Raven test scores, as compared to as much as 36% for vocabulary and the performance scale of the WAIS. Explanations for the relative independence of the information processing tasks and the Raven task remain unclear but deserve further study.

Factor-Analytic Studies of Broad Ability Domains

In recent years there have been few studies that attempted to span a wide range of abilities in a single battery subjected to FA. One investigation of this type, of special interest because it involved brain-damaged patients, is that of Royce et al (138), who administered a battery of 49 measures from 22 brain-damage tests. A FA yielded 6 perceptual factors, 4 conceptual factors, and 3 uninterpretable factors. Correlations of factor scores with presence of damage in 12 neurological categories revealed that about half of the interpretable factors were relatively localized, the remainder being relatively diffuse. Verbal ability was localized in the left hemisphere and spatial orientation in the right hemisphere, in agreement with previous research. In a few cases brain damage was associated with good performance on a factor, a finding that these authors thought might suggest the operation of compensatory functioning.

Multifactorial Test Batteries

A revised version of the well-known ETS Kit of factor reference tests was published (62), primarily to provide better marker tests of 23 distinct factors in research. Oriented toward practical applications in selection and guidance, the Comprehensive Ability Battery (59) offered tests of 20 separate primary factors, along with suggestions concerning scoring to produce measures of group factors. There is marked overlap between these two batteries, both in the factors covered and the types of tests used to identify the factors. Cory (30) developed a computerized battery of tests called the Graphic Information Processing (GRIP) battery. The advantage claimed for this battery is not its potential for adaptive testing, a feature that is not utilized, but the possibly greater verisimilitude of its tasks to real-life tasks; stimuli and test formats are presented at a cathode-ray display terminal. For example, a moving stimulus can be presented, item exposure time can be controlled, measures of tracking performance can be obtained, and response latencies can be recorded. FA and validity studies were claimed to show that the GRIP battery provides valuable information on abilities that is not contained in the operational paper-and-pencil battery used by the Navy for selection and placement. This computerized test battery thus appears to represent a promising development that should be replicated in nonmilitary settings.

Factor Models of Cognitive Abilities

Both Cattell's theory of fluid and crystallized intelligence factors and Guilford's Structure of Intellect (SI) model inspired research during this period. Undheim (166) determined that fluid and crystallized abilities are separable in children but are less differentiated than they are in adults. Hundal & Horn (75) used Tucker's interbattery FA method to relate fluid and crystallized intelligence to performance on 10 learning tasks. Tasks were constructed so as to involve either paired-associates or serial learning, either meaningful or nonsense stimuli, and figural, semantic, or symbolic presentation. Considerable independence between learning and intelligence was found, but the major common variance seemed to represent meaningful associations and learning by such associations, with intelligence involving primary memory to a lesser extent. Fluid and crystallized intelligence were about equally involved in primary memory, but acquisition mediated by meaningful associations was more closely related to crystallized intelligence.

Undheim & Horn (167) criticized the methodology underlying much of Guilford's FA research, arguing that the use of Procrustean rotations and the overextraction of factors may produce misleading results. They emphasized that while Guilford's model has been useful for test construction purposes, there is no compelling support for the model as a description of human behavior. In the context of the SI model, O'Sullivan & Guilford (124) examined social intelligence and obtained evidence for six behavioral cognition factors separate from previously recognized intellectual abilities; these results must be viewed with some caution in the light of Undheim & Horn's criticisms. Favero et al (45) performed an extensive test of the SI model, using one test for each of 76 cells in the model, along with verbal, nonverbal, and composite scores from the Lorge-Thorndike Intelligence Test. Despite a sample size of 34, a FA was performed, the results of which are practically meaningless. Other analyses, however, found that the median correlation between test dissimilar in all the dimensions of the model (operations, contents, products) was substantially greater than zero and did not differ appreciably from the median correlation between tasks similar on a dimension. This finding questions not only the orthogonal structure of the model but also its validity as a model of behavior. If the dimensions of the model have any meaning, it would be expected that tests similar along a dimension would be more highly correlated than dissimilar tests. It is unfortunate that this study, involving an extensive test battery, used so few subjects. This difficulty underscores Undheim and Horn's estimate that a test of the entire SI theory would require at least 96,000 subject hours.

Learning-Ability Relationships

A perennial question has been whether any aspect of measured intelligence predicts ability to learn. Hints of possible relationships were obtained in the study by Hundal & Horn (75) already mentioned. Labouvie-Vief et al (97, 98) met with limited success in a series of experiments investigating the effect of instructional conditions on relations between Raven and digit-span scores and PA learning. The only meaningful result found was that Raven test scores were a better predictor of PA learning when an imagery instruction was employed, while digit-span scores were more predictive when PA items were presented in a speeded condition. These authors concluded that a major source of difficulty in research on learning-ability relationships is the factorial impurity of the ability measures. A study by Hultsch et al (73) provides yet another possible explanation for the general failure of the studies by Labouvie-Vief et al to yield meaningful results. Instead of assuming that learning performance on a task is unidimensional, these authors used Tucker's method of analyzing learning curve data to discover separate components of ability in learning. They found a number of significant learning-ability relations that varied with age and stage of learning, but their study was only partially successful. Relationships between learning performance and ability factors have thus continued to elude meaningful experimental analysis; the studies discussed here illustrate the need to consider both learning performance and ability measures as complex composites of pure components in order to establish interpretable relationships.

Individual Differences Studied in Experimental Cognitive Psychology

In 1973, noting that "modern studies of cognition from an information processing point of view have revealed the existence of a very wide range of individual differences," Hunt, Frost & Lunneborg (79) courageously initiated a program of research designed to develop "theoretically based intelligence tests." Though using relatively small Ns, their pilot studies suggested that parameters of various cognitive tasks had significant relationships with performance on scholastic aptitude tests measuring verbal and quantitative aptitudes. Among the cognitive tasks used were the Atkinson-Shiffrin continuous PA task, the Sternberg STM-search paradigm, the Posner paradigm in which the subject compares alphabet characters either for physical or for name identity, and the Wickens paradigm of release from proactive inhibition in a free-recall task. Later studies (80, 107) tended to confirm the original findings and identified still other relations, using both high-low verbal group comparisons and FA. One of the best confirmed findings is a correlation of about –0.3 between an NI-PI score and verbal ability, the NI-PI score being the increment of mean RT in the Posner task under name-identity instructions over that under physical-identity instructions; this finding has been extended in interesting ways by other investigators (53, 94). Hunt (78) suggests that the magnitude of the relation may be even higher if a sufficiently wide range of ability is considered; he also shows that RT in comprehending negation in the Clark & Chase sentence-picture comparison task is substantially related to verbal ability only when the subject uses a particular strategy in performing the task. Since the appearance of the report by Hunt et al (79), a number of investigators have pursued the possibilities it suggests. Chiang & Atkinson (26) confirmed relations between test scores and the slope parameters of the Sternberg task only when data were analyzed separately by sex; they also established satisfactory day-to-day reliability of these parameters. Snow et al (150) continued to work with these data, introducing further tests and experimental variables, but with somewhat puzzling results. Yen (189) succeeded in finding substantial relations between parameters in two learning tasks and school aptitude and achievement measures in children from fifth to tenth grades. Hogaboam & Pellegrino (65), however, failed to find significant relations between SAT and processing speeds in a semantic judgment task, as Hunt et al's findings might suggest. They propose that Hunt et al's results with the NI-PI variable reflect simply flexibility in meeting the rather unusual requirements of the name-matching task in the Posner paradigm. Nevertheless, these authors' semantic judgment task is not highly similar to the Posner task.

In commenting generally on these highly interesting and provocative endeavors, we would point out that it may be a mistake to use SAT-type measures as indicants of intelligence, such measures being loaded with educational and experiential effects. Some investigators (88, 108, 150) have turned to the use of cognitive ability measures that may be less affected by education, such as Raven's Progressive Matrices test or certain tests from the ETS Kit of Factor Reference Tests. On the other hand, it can be argued that finding information-processing correlates of SAT-type measures could help explain why individuals profit differentially from the learning experiences that to a degree are common to all.

Two other promising theory-based efforts to connect cognitive processing parameters with psychometric variables are those of a group in Canada (90) and the work of Bachelder & Denny (5) in proposing a theory of intelligence based on the complexity or difficulty aspects of memory span performances. In the former case, the investigators reinterpret performances on several types of intelligence and learning tasks in terms of Luria's theory of simultaneous vs successive scanning, but in view of the limited test battery they have assembled they will need to marshal more varied evidence to support their interpretations. Bachelder and Denny offer evidence that many types of conventional intelligence test formats (e.g. arithmetic reasoning tasks involving comprehension of long sentences with numerical details) contain unrecognized span memory components.

ABILITIES IN PARTICULAR DOMAINS

Psychometric studies have identified a substantial number of primary abilities in verbal, fluency, creativity, reasoning, number manipulation, perceptual, spatial, memory, and other domains of cognitive activity. Although the domains themselves are reasonably distinct, in the sense that abilities in different domains are relatively independent, the delineation of separate abilities within domains is generally unclear. This is possibly because the tests used to measure the several abilities in a domain are not sufficiently refined to control the stimulus, process, and response variables that must be controlled to obtain pure ability measurements.

It is not wholly accidental that the tasks that have been studied in recent years by experimental psychologists are frequently tasks that appear in tests of the various primary abilities. Experimental studies hold promise of elucidating the nature and developmental characteristics of these primary abilities, as well as permitting clearer differentiation of these abilities. Here we review selected studies in several important domains. Some studies are cited only because they draw attention to interesting and possibly novel dimensions of IDs, or explore relations of these dimensions to variables like age or social class. Other studies explore covariations of experimental task performances with psychometric measures.

Language Abilities and Skills

It might appear that Hunt (78), in discussing "the mechanics of verbal ability," demonstrates that information processing parameters in several cognitive task performances are related to the well-known "verbal knowledge" factor (V) that is measured particularly well by wide-range vocabulary tests, but since Hunt's results pertain to fairly global measures of verbal aptitude, the relation may have more to do with a higher-order verbal intellectual ability such as Gc as identified by Horn (69) and others. The exact nature of this relation deserves much further examination. Platnick & Richards (129) found no significant relation between tachistoscopic word recognition thresholds and SAT-V scores when word familiarity is controlled.

It may be suspected that many verbal intelligence tests are strongly affected by reading skill, but recent research emphasizes that reading skill is more complicated than it may appear to be. Using a variety of oral reading tasks derived from an information processing analysis, Frederiksen (49) identified five components: grapheme encoding, encoding multiletter units (orthographic patterns with special sound-correspondence features), phonemic translation, automaticity of articulation, and depth of processing of lexical units. In a relatively small sample ($N = 20$ high-school students), individual differences in these components accounted for most of the variance in standardized reading comprehension tests. Studies by a group at the University of Pittsburgh (127, 128), who obtained results in general agreement with Frederiksen's, suggest that speed of word recognition varies widely among high-school students and is a major source of variance in discourse comprehension (by reading) far more important than any differences in strategies specific to understanding discourse as such. Spearritt et al (151) concluded on the basis of an extensive FA study that literal and inferential reading skills are essentially the same. The studies mentioned here would have been more informative if attention had at the same time been given to listening comprehension, i.e. basic knowledge of spoken language apart from reading skill.

In an experimentally oriented study (6) there is a strong suggestion that in tasks involving reading, college-age subjects differ in the extent to which they use or are affected by knowledge of orthographic rules. A priori considerations suggest that these differences might relate to the distinction between "language-bound" and "language-optional" subjects proposed by Day (34), revealed in dichotic-fusion experiments (33), but to our knowledge this possibility has not been investigated.

There is renewed interest in dimensions of speech performance and their correlates in more general cognitive abilities. Studies of children's speech behavior (63, 85) indicate that some aspects, such as syntactical elaboration, are correlated with IQ independent of social class variables; speech styles, however, are related to social class (86). In adults, mean duration of utterance and latency of response to an interviewer are related to verbal IQ (114). In a FA of 46 measures on misarticulating children, clinical judgments of different aspects of speech performance (articulation, auditory processing, reading and spelling, etc) showed good correspondence with psychometric variables (84). One especially interesting aspect of speech performance is the ability to "shadow" speech at short time intervals; Marslen-Wilson (113) found that some individuals can shadow accurately at intervals as short as 0.25 sec. To our knowledge, relations between shadowing ability and other cognitive processing variables have not been investigated from an ID standpoint.

Creativity and Fluency of Ideation

The nature of creative thinking has been further explored in a number of books (156, 177). Stein (152) reviewed procedures for increasing creativity in group and individualized settings; see also experiments by Locurto & Walsh (104) and Meichenbaum (118).

MEASURES OF CREATIVE THINKING   Ward (175) contrasted convergent and divergent measures of creative thinking by administering the Remote Associates Test (in both a recognition and a production format) and Uses and Pattern Meanings tests to children. Convergent and divergent measures shared little variance not also shared with IQ and achievement, both of which tended to correlate more with convergent than with divergent thinking. Gough (56) found that word associations of moderate but not extreme atypicality provided a better prediction of rated creativity than did very rare responses, which may be more indicative of some form of disturbance. An alternate explanation is that the result arose from a statistical artifact, in that measures derived from very rare responses may have had much lower reliability. Gough also obtained tentative support for a hypothesis that stimuli drawn from a specific domain provide better prediction of creative achievement in that domain than would a general word association task. In an approach similar to Gough's, Frederiksen & Ward (50) developed a series of items utilizing complex life-like problems in psychology in order to assess creative potential among undergraduate psychology majors. Following Flanagan's method of obtaining critical incidents in research activities, they composed four types of situational tests: formulating hypotheses, evaluating proposals, solving methodological problems, and measuring constructs. Construct and criterion validity information was obtained from a large sample of persons taking the GRE Advanced Psychology test. The newly developed Tests of Scientific Thinking (TST) were found not to overlap greatly with GRE scores. Students scoring high on the TST tended to engage in more professional activities as first year graduate students, a pattern that was not found for the GRE; thus, the creative thinking tests may provide useful predictive information about graduate student performance.

DIVERGENT THINKING AND COGNITIVE PROCESSES   Sacks & Eysenck (139) related the convergent-divergent thinking distinction to the retention of abstract and concrete sentences. Young adults were classified as convergers or divergers based on an intelligence test and five items of Uses of Objects presented without a time limit. Subjects were then shown six abstract and six concrete sentences and immediately following were given a forced-choice recognition test to measure retention of the sentences. The effect of abstractness-concreteness was highly significant for convergers but not for divergers. Convergers had more difficulty in recognizing abstract sentences. These authors proposed that understanding of abstract sentences requires consideration of more interpretative possibilities than is required for concrete sentences, and that divergers are better than convergers at producing a variety of interpretations.

Thinking, Reasoning, and Problem Solving

Measures of several rather poorly differentiated primary abilities in the reasoning domain are offered in the ETS Kit of factor tests (62): General Reasoning, Logical Reasoning, and Induction. General Reasoning appears to have strong elements of mathematical aptitude. Logical Reasoning seems to represent what was previously called Deduction. Strangely, no test involving analogy items was included in measures of these factors, possibly because tests of analogical reasoning may relate to a higher-order factor such as Gf, and because these tests frequently include an advanced vocabulary component.

Experimental studies, at any rate, have begun to provide detailed analyses of processes in solving several types of reasoning tasks, including inductive, analogical, and deductive reasoning. The most ambitious program is that of Sternberg (153), whose "componential analysis" procedures have already been mentioned. After reviewing earlier theories, Sternberg presents a theory with six information processing components of analogical reasoning that can be operationalized in various experimental settings: encoding, inference, mapping, application, justification, and (as a general control process) preparation-response. Several models concerning the combined operation of these components are tested, some models being better supported by data than others. It is concluded that whatever model is most correct, it is general over subjects, in that there is no evidence of consistent IDs in models used by different subjects. IDs are revealed in the extent to which individuals use any model at all, however, and in their strategies, differentiated by relative amounts of time devoted to the several components—particularly when the discovery of relevant attributes is critical to solution success. Component scores from experimental tasks account for large proportions of variance in reference ability tests, especially in letter-series, reasoning, and vocabulary tests. The preparation-response parameter tends to make the strongest contribution in this. Sternberg claims, with much justice, that his approach represents an information processing analysis of what is ordinarily meant by intelligence. A somewhat related approach, also concerned with analogical reasoning, is that of Whitely (180), but in this case it is addressed particularly to verbal analogy tests. Components classified as short-term and long-term memory processes, control strategies, and response implementation were operationalized in ten tasks representing segments of analogy-item performance; a FA yielded three factors corresponding generally to the three hypothesized types of components. All three factors contributed to the prediction of response time measurements on a complete verbal analogy test. In a further study, Whitely (181) attempted to identify "semantic structures" that govern verbal analogy performance.

At this point it is difficult to align the generally similar results of Sternberg's and Whitely's studies, but these approaches deserve further exploration. Sternberg's analysis seems the more detailed and rigorous, but as Whitely notes, "individual differences in item-solving strategies and the content of memory stores" (180, p. 476) need more attention. Whitely & Dawis (182) have made some progress in exploring effects of cognitive intervention on analogy-item performance.

Effects of cognitive intervention were of central interest in a study (67) of performance on letter-series completion tests, ordinarily regarded as measures of the Induction factor. Following a model provided by a computer simulation, the investigators gave school children explicit training on two out of four hypothesized component processes, the detection of interletter relations, and the discovery of periodicity. Both experimental and control groups made gains (varying somewhat with age); part of the gain could be attributed to practice, but the greater gains in the experimental group indicated that the hypothesized processes are trainable. "Consequently," the authors remark, "this study supported the psychological reality of the identified processes and suggested the potential of instruction in these processes for improving intellectual competence" (67, p. 356).

Possibilities of accounting for and modifying IDs in problem solving ability through cognitive processing analysis have been addressed in several books and monographs (1, 132, 141). Allwood (1) concludes that the analysis of these IDs must take account of the type of problem (a taxonomy is needed!), the individual's knowledge base, and the individual's characteristic solution strategies as they interact with problem type.

The studies and reviews mentioned here have made no explicit attempt to explain or clarify the factorial structure of the abilities in the reasoning domain. In fact, Sternberg's (153) work shows only small evidence of different information processing components as predictors of scores on several psychometric tests that ordinarily have different loadings on verbal, inductive, and deductive factors. It is apparent that much further theoretical and empirical work in coordinating experimental and psychometric findings will be needed.

Abilities Concerned with Number and Quantity

The ETS Kit (62) offers tests of only one factor explicitly concerned with number and quantity, the Number factor, defined by tests of speed in simple arithmetic operations. As mentioned earlier, however, the General Reasoning factor is defined by tests involving reasoning with quantitative concepts. There appears to be little recent work in the experimental analysis of either of these factors. One can continue to assume that the Number factor represents degree of practice and retention of basic arithmetic skills; still largely unknown is whether individuals differ in the extent to which they can develop these skills. Some of the work of Hunt et al (79) found relations between quantitative reasoning aptitude and certain information processing variables, but some of the tasks from which these variables are derived involve numerical operations, as in the Brown-Peterson paradigm where the interference phase of the task requires the subject to count backward by 3s. Persons high on N or quantitative aptitude may incur less interference from this phase.

Taylor et al (155) sought cognitive measures related to high school students' performance in algebra and geometry. Contrary to what might be expected, verbally oriented tasks were more prognostic of success in geometry than they were in algebra. Soviet studies in the mathematical abilities of children have become available through a translation (95) of a work by Krutetskii, who has even used FA, in addition to detailed observations and interviews of individual children solving mathematical problems, in shaping a theory of mathematical giftedness. Some components that help determine giftedness, even though they are of a very general character and not specific to mathematical behavior, are the speed of mental processing, computational skills, good memory for symbols, numbers, and formulas, spatial ability, and the ability to visualize mathematical relationships and dependencies. Krutetskii believes that giftedness in mathematics is furthered by what he calls "inborn inclinations."

Perceptual Skills and Processes in Vision and Audition

Several factors represented by tests in the ETS Kit (62) pertain to abilities in perceiving and manipulating visual forms: Perceptual Speed, Spatial Orientation, Spatial Scanning, Visualization, Flexibility of Closure, and Speed of Closure. Possibly Figural Flexibility and Figural Fluency should also be mentioned in this group as involving the generation of visual forms. The tests of visual perceptual skills included under this group of factors contain many tasks similar to those studied in experimental cognitive psychology. We can discuss only a small sample of the relevant studies.

As pointed out by Ekstrom (40), factor analysts have had continual difficulty in differentiating and interpreting Spatial Orientation and Spatial Visualization factors (131); both of these (as well as some other factors in this domain, such as Perceptual Speed) could be said to involve some kind of mental encoding and representation of spatial configurations along with "mental rotation," operations that have been studied experimentally (125, 146). Let us consider whether experimental studies of visual perceptual tasks might throw light on the structure of abilities in this domain. Because of the paucity of available data, however, much of what we have to say is speculative.

Cooper (29) studied IDs in performing a task in which subjects are first required to mentally rotate a visual shape to a specified position before comparing it as same or different to a probe stimulus that may exhibit any of several degrees of change or perturbation (over and above rotation) from the original. Subjects differed in their mental rotation speeds (during the "preparation" phase); they differed also, somewhat independently of mental rotation speeds, in the manner and extent to which they were affected by the amount of perturbation in the probe stimulus. Type I subjects were fast comparers, unaffected by perturbation; they appeared to make a holistic comparison of mental representation and the probe stimulus. Type II subjects, more plentiful in the small sample tested, were generally slower than Type I subjects on "different" responses, and were much affected by amount of perturbation; they appeared to make analytic, point-by-point comparisons. This difference between Type I and II subjects presents a rough parallel to the contrast between "structural" and "analytic" comparers reported by Hock & Marcus (64), but Cooper points to differences in procedures and results that make this parallelism somewhat suspect. Unfortunately, neither Cooper nor Hock & Marcus administered any spatial ability tests whose correlational patterns with the experimental task parameters might have suggested something about the interpretation of factors underlying the tests. At the same time, the finding of different types of subjects suggests that linear correlational analysis of the data would be problematical, except perhaps by analysis for separate groups. Also, Cooper reported (unpublished information) that to some extent subjects may change strategies when the structure or demands of the task make it appropriate to do so.

One of the few studies to investigate correlations between spatial ability test scores and parameters of experimental tasks in this domain is that by

Egan (39), who adapted Spatial Visualization and Spatial Orientation tests to a format that permitted taking latencies of correct responses. Egan found that number-correct scores on these tests were rather highly correlated, but that they each had negligible correlations with mean latencies of correct responses. He suggested that accuracy scores on Spatial Orientation tests represent "a form of concept verification in which examinees serially check the three spatial dimensions of a figure against their concept of what the figure should be." Visualization tests, on the other hand, "have properties analogous to physically turning an object in space, so that problems requiring a greater number of turns or turns of greater length required more time to solve" (39, p. 24). Putting these results together with the data from Cooper's experiments, we would suggest that the essential element in Spatial Visualization represents IDs in the speed of mental rotation in the preparation phase, while Spatial Orientation taps the ability of the subject to encode a visual form in order to compare it with another. In any case, Egan's results suggest that it is imperative to score spatial ability tests for power or accuracy separately from speed in making correct responses. Further analysis would have to take into account the possibility that subjects can use either of two strategies in making visual comparisons. It is conceivable that these different strategies are reflected in scores in Perceptual Speed tests such as Identical Figures, where figure comparisons are required.

The suggestion that there may be IDs in skill in mental representation and manipulation of spatial forms raises the question of the possible relevance of imagery ability. Ernest (41) identifies three approaches to the measurement of IDs in imagery: self-report questionnaires, spatial ability tests, and performance tasks. Most of the research she reviews on correlates of imagery with learning, memory, perceptual processes, and conceptualization has used self-report questionnaires, but even self-reported imagery appears to be multidimensional. Ernest postulates three dimensions: vividness, habitual use, and control; Cartwright et al (23) specify three dimensions relating to content: figural, symbolic, and mimetic. An elaborate but in some respects questionable FA by Richardson (134) supports relative independence among several dimensions of self-reported imagery, as well as relative independence of self-report dimensions and spatial ability test scores. Nevertheless, Ernest believes that self-report and objective test score dimensions are not wholly independent. If the spatial ability domain could be clarified along the lines suggested above, it might be possible to confirm certain relations with dimensions of imagery identified by self-report procedures.

We briefly note several other intriguing studies in the visual perceptual domain. Duda (38) used an analysis of IDs in the power-law exponents of several subjective magnitude estimation tasks to establish a theoretical interpretation of Stevens's empirical findings in psychophysical judgment. Forsyth & Huber (48) used an ID approach to study stimulus factors in the perception of ambiguous figures as either human or nonhuman. Taylor (157) followed up an early study by Thurstone to identify ID dimensions of susceptibility to visual illusions.

Extensive FA work in auditory abilities is currently being completed (J. L. Horn, personal communication) but has not been published in time for this review.

Memory Skills and Capacities

Theories of cognitive processing assume that memory, in the sense of the acquisition, storage, and retrieval of information, is implicated in practically all performances that could be called cognitive. Eysenck (43) reviews current theory and research on memory, with special attention to relating this work to IDs in intellectual, personality, motivational, and affective variables. He stresses the importance of a process-oriented approach as opposed to a "boxology" that assumes memory storages of different "terms" (short, long, etc). Some of Eysenck's review overlaps considerably with the present review, in fact, except that he pays less attention to FA findings.

However memory is regarded, memory of one kind or another is involved in all the domains and factors of IDs being considered here. For example, the verbal knowledge factor refers to the richness and variety of the individual's memories for words and other linguistic entities; spatial abilities may involve the clarity and persistence of short-term memories for spatial forms. But in FA work, the memory domain has been implicitly defined in terms of abilities that appear to control the individual's success in certain one-time learning tasks such as PA learning and memory span. The latest edition of the ETS Kit (62) offers tests of three factors in this domain: Associative Memory, Memory Span, and Visual Memory, the last of these being a new addition as compared to earlier editions. Ekstrom (40) reviews the empirical support for differentiating these factors.

In an effort to get an interpretation of memory processes that would depend on various assumed attributes of memory contents such as imagery, acoustic, temporal, and affective, Underwood et al (165) performed a FA of 22 variables derived from episodic memory tasks that included standard paradigms in verbal learning research such as PAs, free recall, serial learning, verbal discrimination, and memory span. "Semantic memory" variables such as SAT, vocabulary, and spelling were not included in the factor analysis because they showed no strong or interesting relationships with the episodic memory variables. Five rotated orthogonal factors resulted, all more or less task-specific; roughly they may be identified as Paired-Associate and Serial Learning, Free Recall, Memory Span, Recognition Memory, and Verbal Discrimination. A tentative reanalysis (21) suggests that the first two of these are substantially correlated to form an Associative Memory factor at the second order. These authors failed to find evidence of IDs in the use of memory attributes, explaining this failing as due to the "swamping" of the data by an associative learning factor and to the possibility that subjects are highly flexible in using whatever memory attributes are appropriate in a given task. Thus, although the study confirms and expands previous knowledge about dimensions of memory ability, we come away from it with the feeling that it contributes little to their theoretical explanation. Memory abilities simply exist; they can have considerable generalizability over tasks and conditions (126), but they defy psychological analysis. Even Hundal & Horn's (75) finding of connections between primary and secondary memories and *Gf* and *Gc* abilities, respectively, does little to advance deep understanding of memory abilities.

Jensen's assumption of a distinction between "associative (Level I)" and "conceptual (Level II)" abilities has continued to be questioned by investigators (99, 162) who point out that associative and rote memory tasks can engage higher-order conceptual operations. They find that all types of school success are better predicted by conceptual ability than by associative ability.

As noted above, Bachelder & Denny (5) propose that a general theory of intelligence can be erected on the basis of memory span phenomena. But memory span ability has eluded theoretical analysis as much as associative memory ability. Although it had been suggested (42) that memory span tasks tap individuals' use of mnemonic strategies such as rehearsal, grouping, and chunking, Lyon (109) obtained results that virtually rule out such possibilities. Cohen & Sandberg's (27) data suggest that the connection between IQ and memory span centers in the individual's ability to retain the terminal items of a presented string, but it is not clear from this study what kind of memory store or process is involved. Although they do not note the fact, their results also suggest that there may be other sources of ID variance in memory span performance. Chi (25) suggests that memory span deficits in children may be due to failure to encode the stimuli rapidly and completely.

Cognitive Speed

Cognitive Speed is hardly a distinct domain of abilities; many factors in domains discussed above are characterized by speed elements or contain them to the extent that the tests used to measure them are speeded or administered under a time limit. But perhaps Cognitive Speed *ought* to be considered a separate domain, constituted by reclassifying the speed elements from other domains into this domain. This might be especially desirable in view of the fact that many of the parameters of laboratory tasks refer to rate or speed of performance. It has been noted above that Egan (39) recommended that spatial ability tests should be scored separately for speed and accuracy. The generalizability of a speed element in spatial ability tests to speed elements drawn from other domains is unknown, although earlier studies (e.g. 105) have identified one or more general speed factors. Although cognizant of the problem, Lunneborg (107) might have been more successful in relating reaction time measurements to psychometric variables if his procedures had taken more account of the speed aspects of the latter. It would seem that a desirable strategy in studying relations between laboratory and psychometric tasks would be to insure that speed and accuracy components of performance in each case are separately considered. Such a strategy has seldom been employed in the history of ID research; see also White (179) on this matter.

COGNITION AND PERSONALITY

Factor analysis continues to be a useful tool in the investigation of personality-ability relationships. Messick & French (119) found speed and flexibility of closure factors related to personality variables. Hakstian & Cattell (60) used both Tucker's interbattery FA and canonical correlations to examine relationships between 20 ability variables and 14 personality variables separately for males and females. Relationships between the two domains were tenuous, especially in the case of females. It was suggested that males and females may differ in the extent to which personality and ability measures are related.

Schwartz (145) sought to explain previous findings that arousal during acquisition affects memory sometimes positively and other times negatively. He hypothesized that arousal focuses memory on physical rather than semantic cues, and that its facilitative effect thus depends on the nature of the material to be learned. Results supportive of this hypothesis were obtained for PA learning and clustering in free recall, but the data also permit other explanations.

Turner & Horn (164) used a double cross-validation procedure to examine relationships between the 16 PF (Personality Factors) test and three factors identified in the WAIS. Significant verbal ability-personality relationships were maintained under cross-validation, but there were no such relationships for memory and numerical abilities and only mixed findings for spatial ability. Their methodology emphasizes the need to control for testing the significance of the numerous correlation coefficients in such studies to insure that obtained relationships are not simply spurious results due to Type I errors.

Field Dependence-Independence

The field dependence-independence distinction, regarded as related to both cognition and personality, continued to provoke research during this period, as indicated by an extensive bibliography (186). Witkin et al (188) and Goodenough (54) reviewed implications of field dependence for education and also its relations with learning and memory. Field-dependent and field-independent persons are said to be about equal in learning and memory abilities but different in the strategies they are likely to employ and in the types of material they learn easily. Field-independents tend to make greater use of mediators; field-dependents often either cannot or do not impose structure on material, and thus need an external source of structure.

Writing on the development of field dependence at both the individual and the cultural level, Goodenough & Witkin (55) state that the ontogenetic trend into the midteens is from dependence to independence, but the historical trend in the culture has been in the other direction. Biological, environmental, and cultural factors are invoked to explain these trends. A major restatement of the field dependence theory has also been presented by these authors (187). It now seems that there is no general restructuring ability or style across all domains, because FA studies have revealed that restructuring tendencies in visual and auditory modalities are separable, and such tendencies are related very little if at all across visual and verbal modalities. Further, it is now thought that some individuals are "fixed" in their style while other persons are "mobile," i.e. by adapting their style to a particular situation they can be field-independent and exhibit high interpersonal competence. This reconceptualization would seem to represent a departure from the original value-free notion of the construct, in that now it seems that persons can be classified along a dimension of interpersonal competence as well as along a second (perhaps correlated) dimension of cognitive restructuring, neither of which is value-free.

CHANGES IN ABILITIES OVER THE LIFE SPAN

Recent years have seen increasing emphasis on abilities both in the very young and in the aged. This research has proved useful in broadening our understanding of the nature of abilities, especially of how abilities change with age.

Abilities in Infants and Young Children

The development and measurement of cognition and cognitive abilities in young children has received much attention in books (14, 91, 93, 101, 168). Two noteworthy studies investigated infants' cognitive performance, with emphasis on examining the validity of different measures of intelligence. Lewis & Gallas (102) related scores on the Mental Development Index of the Bayley Scales of Infant Development, the Corman-Escalona Scales of Object Permanence, and measures of habituation and recovery on an attention task for 12-week-old infants. The study is distinctive for its sample size ($N = 189$) and the narrow age range of the children. The highest correlation obtained between any two performance measures was 0.22, suggesting that a developmentally constant, general intelligence factor does not exist in infancy. Miller et al (120), however, found that measures of first fixation habituation ratio obtained from infants between 2 and 4 months old were predictive of performance at age 15 months on scales developed by Užgiris & Hunt (168). It thus appears that although habituation measures do not correlate highly with standardized measures of intelligence in the infant, they may nevertheless possess short-term predictive validity for later cognitive performance.

The Piagetian approach to assessing the development of intelligence in young children has only rather recently been related to psychometric research in IDs in abilities of young children. This research has largely involved correlating performance on Piagetian tasks with performance on psychometric tests. For example, Neimark (122) established a connection between performance on the Embedded Figures Test and development from concrete to formal operational thought in a longitudinal study of several cohorts of children, but it is unclear whether cognitive style per se is important or whether general intelligence is actually responsible for the relationship. Kuhn (96) found that the WISC correlated more highly with Piagetian task performance for children in grades 1–3 than for children in grades 5–7. Kuhn's explanation for this was that a child's general experiences affect performance on Piagetian tasks, whereas specific experiences affect performance on traditional IQ tests. However, other explanations are certainly possible, and indeed the finding itself needs to be replicated with different Piagetian tasks and with one group of same-age young children and another group of same-age older children. Hruza et al (72) concluded from a FA of adult data that Piagetian factors are independent of psychometric factors. Examination of their factor matrix, however, suggests that an oblique structure would disclose a substantial relationship between the two types of factors. Siegler (147, 148) has used a rule assessment methodology in an effective way to discover how children attempt to solve certain Piagetian tasks. Although the focus of this research is on age differences, its methodology would seem useful in investigating individual differences as well.

Abilities in Older Children

Research with older children has been concerned with stability of test scores, relationships between development of different abilities and relationships between age, test scores, and cognitive task performance. Hopkins &

Bracht (68) noted that most previous research on test score stability has concerned individual rather than group IQ tests. Children were administered the California Test of Mental Maturity in grades 1 and 2 and the Lorge-Thorndike Intelligence Test in grades 4, 7, 9, and 11. For verbal IQ, correlations involving measurements at grade 1 or 2 tended to be in the range 0.4 to 0.5, whereas from grade 4 onward, correlations were 0.75 to 0.85. Similar findings occurred for nonverbal IQ, except that stability first became evident at grade 7 rather than at grade 4, and the correlations were overall substantially lower than they were for verbal IQ.

Atkin et al (4) used a multivariate modification of the cross-lagged technique to examine developmental relationships from grade 5 to 11 on 16 cognitive tests. Separate analyses by race and sex revealed that the fifth grade measure of Listening, an aural comprehension test, consistently predicted a composite score from all tests in the eleventh grade better than the composite predicted Listening. No other measure exhibited such cross-lagged differences, a finding that implied that Listening taps sources of later intellectual development more directly than any of the other tests, perhaps because only the Listening test is presented orally and involves no repetition of stimuli, so that it more than any other test demands attention, crucial to development. We suggest an alternative explanation, namely that Listening measures rate of basic language development better than the other tests used, which are affected by extraneous sources of variance due to early differences in the acquisition of reading skills. Atkin et al (3) also examined the differentiation hypothesis using these same data. Several methods of analysis all suggested a small, gradual increase in the number of common factors, expecially for the white groups. Interpretation of any race differences must be very tentative because of small sample sizes for the black groups. Olsson & Bergman (123) used a confirmatory FA model to investigate differentiation in a sample of Swedish children tested at ages 10 and 13. Differentiation occurred in the sense that factors were more separable at age 13, but integration occurred in the sense that unique variances were smaller at the upper age. This finding emphasizes the need to consider not only the particular tests employed and the ages of the subjects but also the definition of differentiation.

The important and pioneering work of Keating & Bobbitt (88), briefly noted above, extends the research methods of Hunt et al (80) into the period of childhood. The basic design included three age levels (grades 3, 7, and 11), two ability levels (classified according to performance on Raven's Progressive Matrices test) and sex of subject. Effects of these factors were examined for variables derived from three cognitive tasks: the Posner letter comparison task, choice reaction time, and the Sternberg memory scanning task. Age and ability main effects were generally significant, but there were no significant sex effects or interactions. Based on a stage analysis of the tasks, results showed that tasks or differences between tasks that had steps in common tended to yield correlations higher that those from tasks with no steps in common. These results supported the validity of the stage analysis and furnished evidence for consistent IDs in the components.

Aging and the Question of Declines in Abilities

The long-standing controversy as to whether any mental abilities decline with age has continued to be debated. Botwinick (10) concludes that both cross-sectional and longitudinal studies show that some declines definitely occur, but that they may begin later in life, may be smaller in magnitude, and may include fewer abilities than previously thought. Horn & Donaldson (70) engaged in a series of spirited debates with Schaie & Baltes (142). These debaters seem to have arrived at a substantial consensus regarding the facts, but their interpretations of the facts and their implications still diverge widely. Horn & Donaldson insisted that the important finding is that aging decline in average intellectual performance is not mythical; there is decline for at least some abilities and some individuals. Schaie & Baltes emphasized, in contrast, that decline does not necessarily occur for the totality of individuals or for all abilities. In any case, future research should examine why some persons show a decline while other persons' abilities remain stable, and there should be further investigation of why different abilities tend to decline at different rates. Schaie & Parham (143) continued the investigation of the relative impacts of cohort and age on ability decline data. With equivalent age and cohort ranges of 7 years, cohort effects were generally larger than age effects until subjects were in their late 60s, at which point age effects began to predominate.

AGING AND MEMORY   Robertson-Tchabo & Arenberg (135) performed a FA of measures of free recall, recognition, forward digit span, dichotic digit pairs, and vigilance for healthy males in three age groups, ages 20–39, 40–59, and 60–80. Data for the pooled groups yielded four factors, interpreted as Speed of Information Processing, Secondary Memory, Attention, and Primary Memory. Factor scores correlated significantly with age (older subjects having lower scores) for all factors except primary memory. These findings tend to corroborate Craik's (31) conclusion that age differences in primary memory are minimal as long as stimuli are fully perceived, no reorganization is required, and attention is not divided, but that if material exceeds the capacity of primary memory and thus engages secondary memory, elderly persons tend to be somewhat deficient. Friedman (51) found a loss of differentiation of memory functions in an elderly group for whom the correlation between digit and word span performances was significantly higher than for younger subjects. This result may provide an example of the similarity between the elderly and children in some respects, since abilities appear to be less differentiated in children than in young adults. Such factors as motivation must, however, be considered as rival or supplementary explanations.

Thomas et al (160) assessed the effects of age on speed of retrieval from long-term memory for healthy males whose ages ranged from 25 to 74. Older subjects were found to have longer picture-naming latencies, but the differences could be minimized by practice or cueing. The fact that the age effect did not interact with word frequency was interpreted as showing that the pattern of results for healthy elderly persons is not the same as that for brain-damaged persons, for whom word frequency has an effect. Walsh & Baldwin (174) investigated age differences in semantic memory, pointing out that most previous research has focused on episodic memory tasks, which may be less interesting to the elderly and also less ecologically valid. Results using the Bransford & Franks paradigm of linguistic abstraction (but is this really semantic memory?) showed that an elderly group did not differ from a group of college students in precision of retained semantic information or in the degree to which linguistic information was integrated into holistic ideas. The elderly group was inferior to the college group on tasks involving secondary memory, as would be expected from previous research. These results suggest that ecologically valid semantic memory functions may not decline with age.

CONTROL OF AGE EFFECTS BY TREATMENTS   Instead of accepting as inevitable a decline of abilities with age, researchers are beginning to investigate other factors that may be responsible for declines as well as to search for treatments that may prevent such a decline. Birkhill & Schaie (7) assessed the effect of differential reinforcement of cautiousness in performance on PMA subtests among elderly subjects averaging 73 years of age. Results showed increased performance on verbal meaning, space, and reasoning subtests when subjects were encouraged to guess answers to questions they might not otherwise answer. Some reported test score declines may thus be artifacts due to overcautiousness. Jordan & Rabbitt (87) examined the effects of increasing practice on the initial disadvantage of elderly subjects in serial choice reaction time to stimuli of varying complexity. When subjects were unpracticed, the magnitude of the repetition effect was greater for the old than for the young subjects, but with moderate practice the magnitude of the effect was the same for both groups. Also, initially there was a complexity-by-age interaction for both number of errors and RT, older subjects being more adversely affected by increased complexity. With practice, however, increased complexity was no longer a problem for the older subjects. This finding indicates the possible importance of practice variables in examining age differences in abilities.

Plemons et al (130) developed a training method to modify fluid intelligence in the elderly. Subjects in the treatment group received a series of eight 1-hour practice sessions on figural relations tasks over a 4 week period. They were found to be superior to subjects in a control group 6 months later on a similar set of figural relations tasks, a result that suggested that the treatment effect was lasting. Comparison on a less similar set of figural relations tasks, however, showed the treatment effect to be significant 1 week after the training but nonsignificant 4 weeks later. This study suggests that tested fluid intelligence may be somewhat modifiable, but at least in this instance generalization of treatment effects was limited.

The limited success up to now of efforts to modify abilities in the elderly should not be taken to signify that greater success cannot be achieved in the future. Further research holds promise of enhancing our understanding of age-ability relationships in a major way.

GENETIC AND ENVIRONMENTAL INFLUENCES

Nature-Nurture Issues

GENETIC INFLUENCES   Because of the availability of recent reviews (35, 36), we need only do some updating and add a few remarks. We very much agree with previous reviewers who point out that "cognitive ability is far too complex to be assessed by a univariate number such as IQ" (36, p. 180). We would insist further that even use of multiple measures of cognitive abilities such as PMA scores does not guarantee that sufficiently well-defined dimensions of cognitive IDs are being employed. The great "IQ controversy" documented by Block & Dworkin (8) and persisting in current debates in the literature (82, 121, 159, 171) is thus doubly flawed, to say nothing of the numerous problems of sampling, study design, statistical models of phenotype-genotype relationships, etc with which research in this area is beset. There is even a question, raised by Roth (137), whether research using cognitive measures attends sufficiently to the "negotiated features of intelligence measurement," i.e. the social and sociolinguistic conditions under which measurements are taken.

At the same time, we also agree with previous reviewers that "a prudent person has no alternative but to reject the hypothesis of zero heritability" of tested cognitive ability (35, p. 501). We can agree with McGuire & Hirsch (116) in denying the "genetic reality" of a general factor of intelligence and in drawing attention to the possible importance of genotype-environment interactions in phenotype-variance equations; on the other hand, on the basis of the considerable evidence on the *relative* unmodifiability of cognitive ability (32, 66) we find it hard to believe that the ranges of genotype reactions over different environments (e.g. teaching methods) can be so large as these authors appear to assume. We believe the accumulated evidence suggests that in representative populations heritability of at least some cognitive abilities can be at least as high as 0.4 or 0.5. It appears, however, that the question of whether cognitive abilities differ in heritability is far from settled.

On matters of the genetics of specific cognitive traits we can mention a review by Vandenberg & Kuse (170) concerned with spatial ability (or abilities?) and Vandenberg's (169) findings suggesting genetic factors in learning abilities manifested in several verbal learning tasks. These latter abilities, however, are perhaps to be identified with the Associative Memory factor identified in FA studies.

ENVIRONMENTAL INFLUENCES   Even if heritability values for cognitive abilities are assumed to range as high as 0.8, there is still play for the operation of environmental variables. There is now impressive evidence for the role of such variables and much interest in modeling relations between such variables and dimensions of cognitive ability (18, 112, 173). Bradley et al (11) found an environmental process measure to be better than SES in predicting IQ at age 3; Trotman (163) obtained similar results for environmental measures as predictors of IQ for both white and black ninth-grade middle-class girls. Kellaghan (89) found relationships between home variables and cognitive measures to be highest for scholastic attainment, somewhat smaller for crystallized intelligence measures, and still smaller for fluid intelligence measures.

Several major studies of environmental intervention appear to show that cognitive abilities can be increased to a certain extent. Through a program of maternal rehabilitation and cognitive stimulation, the Milwaukee Project (52) continues to report success in improving intellectual performance, language development, and behavior styles among young children identified as cultural-familial mental retarded in low SES populations. McKay et al (117) reported that the gap in cognitive ability between "chronically deprived" and privileged children in a Colombian city was significantly narrowed by a treatment program combining nutritional, health, and educational features. The younger the children entered the program, the greater the gains; also, the gains persisted for at least a year after the treatment ended. Interestingly, the study utilized a fair number of differentiated cognitive measures, although the detailed results have yet to be reported.

Zajonc (190) offered further evidence for his "confluence" model of the association between intelligence and family size and birth order, a model that surely implicates environmental influences in the form of teaching and tuition among family members. Crucial tests of this model are apparently as yet unavailable.

Group Differences

SEX   In a comprehensive review of sex differences in motor, spatial, and linguistic abilities, Fairweather (44) suggests that the incidence of reported sex differences is outweighed by qualifications of age, culture, sex of experimenter, etc. He thinks theory development in this area is premature, especially as regards lateralization effects. Nevertheless, proposals are rampant. Believing that maturation rate may be a critical factor, Waber (172) found that among adolescents, early maturers were better at verbal than spatial tasks, the opposite being true for late maturers, regardless of sex. Further analysis showed maturation rate related to spatial ability but not to verbal ability. Late maturers were more lateralized for speech perception. In a study by Welsh & Baucom (178), masculinity-femininity (as defined by self-ratings) was correlated with scores on a nonverbal reasoning test, mean scores on the latter not being significantly different between sexes.

RACE   Research on race differences has continued to focus on black-white differences, although interest in other racial and cultural groups has increased (61, 92, 100). There have been new looks at deficit hypotheses and attempts to investigate factors affecting group differences in test scores. Finding that the notion of a perceptual defect in some black populations is still alive, Mandler & Stein (110) were unable to find solid evidence of such a defect after effects of early experiences and the characteristics of the measures used were discounted. In two studies, Jensen considered the cumulative deficit hypothesis, which he called the "keystone of the rationale for compensatory education" (81, p. 996). In the first study, data from younger and older siblings in black and white families in California showed a small verbal IQ decrement for blacks but none for nonverbal IQ. A second study (83) using data from rural Georgia showed blacks but not whites to have a substantial decrement in both verbal and nonverbal IQ as a linear function of age. Although both heredity and environment could contribute to the decrement, Jensen favors the environmental interpretation because of the superior environment for the California groups.

Bridgman & Buttram (12) found strategy training to reduce race differences in nonverbal reasoning scores, but Humphreys (74) criticized their methodology and the test they used. Samuel (140) investigated effects of test atmosphere, tester expectation, race and sex of tester and of subject, and SES on the performance scale of the WISC. Several complex interactions were obtained, but blacks tended to score below whites across almost all conditions. Samuel concluded that short-term manipulations such as these have little impact on black-white differences in WISC performance scores.

APPLIED DIFFERENTIAL PSYCHOLOGY

Determinants of School Achievement

Relations between abilities and school achievement have been considered in several books. Bloom (9) provided a thorough explication of his theory of school achievement and what he calls "mastery learning," describing relative influences, in interaction with characteristics of instruction, of cognitive and affective "entry characteristics" of students upon learning. He claimed that IDs in aptitudes and achievement can diminish markedly under a proper regimen of teaching, a claim that tends to be supported by his own studies and one by Anderson (2). Cronbach & Snow (32) rekindled interest in aptitude-treatment interaction (ATI) research after a period of discouragement regarding the possibility of finding useful and replicable ATIs had set in.

Marjoribanks (111) used complex regression models allowing for non-linearities and interactions to examine relations among intelligence, creativity, and school achievement. Measures of creativity and of nonverbal reasoning had different relations with achievement, a finding suggesting that creativity measures do not function simply as a second measure of intelligence. There was no support for the view that intelligence is related to achievement up to a threshold point at which creativity overrides intelligence. Instead, at high levels of both dimensions, neither is a good predictor.

Drenth (37) discussed the use of psychological tests in predicting school performance in developing countries.

VALIDITY STUDIES: CHILDHOOD   Stevenson et al (154) studied longitudinally the elementary school learning of reading and arithmetic. Third grade reading and arithmetic achievement were rather highly predictable from scores on an extensive series of cognitive measures taken 4 years earlier; these scores were more predictive than teachers' ratings.

VALIDITY STUDIES: ADOLESCENCE AND ADULTHOOD   Hakstian & Bennet (58) provided evidence of the validity of the Comprehensive Ability Battery (59) for predicting high school grades; this battery was found to compare favorably with the Differential Aptitude Tests. McCall's (115) longitudinal study obtained correlations between IQs taken at different ages with educational and occupational attainment at age 26. Correlations were found to rise until about age 8 after which they remained fairly stable at about 0.5, a finding that McCall explained as due to the onset of formal schooling near age 8. Lin & Humphreys (103) found continued confirmation of their claim that the psychological nature of college achievement changes from freshman to senior year, with intellectual measures relating less to senior grades than freshman grades even when ability is measured in the senior year. Data for undergraduate and postgraduate grades suggest that the first year in a new academic learning situation represents a greater intellectual challenge than subsequent years. It is not clear to what extent this is true because of more stringent course requirements in the first year of a curriculum.

Schmeck et al (144) developed a self-report instrument measuring four types of IDs in learning processes that they found to be related to performance in college under study conditions. The four scales were Synthesis-Analysis, Study Methods, Fact Retention, and Elaboration Processing.

CONCLUDING REMARKS: THE STATE OF OUR KNOWLEDGE AND ART

Twenty-five years ago the senior author wrote the chapter on individual differences for Volume 5 of the *Annual Review of Psychology*. In writing the present epilogue, he hardly dares consult what he wrote earlier, perhaps because he fears that it would be only too painfully evident that in the intervening period ID psychology has not made the substantial progress that he then looked forward to.

If in 1954 he had been able to have a true vision of 1979, he would have been surprised that in 1979 people would still be arguing over what intelligence is and the extent to which it is genetically determined; that by 1979 a number of thoroughly respectable, scientifically based batteries of multifactorial ability tests for different age groups of the population had not been devised; and that in 1979 there would still be a paucity of knowledge about the rate at which different cognitive abilities develop and change over the life span under normal circumstances, or about the extent to which measured abilities are modifiable through experience, training, or instruction.

It would take a lengthy excursion into the intellectual and social history of the intervening period to inquire why differential psychology has not made the kind of progress that might have been possible. There has been some progress, to be sure—certainly in the sophistication of methodologies and to some extent in the accumulation of pertinent knowledge—but it is disturbing to think that even in 1979 psychologists interested in IDs find themselves in a vulnerable position. Their knowledge of many aspects of the nature and determinants of cognitive abilities is still far from satisfying, and they cannot make clear and well-supported statements about the ecological relevance of these abilities or about how they might be susceptible to modification through different social and educational maneuvers.

The fresh wind blowing is that of cognitive psychology and the prospect that its perspectives may be able to reform psychometrics and the theory of IDs in a radical way. Previously in this article we raised the question of whether this new trend, a Phoenix-like revival of directions that were evident 80 years ago, might succeed where the earlier movement had failed. It is not yet possible to answer this question. Our review shows that the real problems and limitations of the new approaches are only beginning to be recognized, promising as they may be. Already it has become clear that there is little hope of being able to replace standard psychometric instruments wholesale with series of reaction-time measurements or the like. But the new directions may prompt ID theorists to reexamine traditional assumptions, and encourage psychometricians to restructure testing instruments and procedures to take account of interactions of psychological processes and mental contents in different individuals under different conditions.

The next 25 years will take differential psychology into the twenty-first century. There is just a faint possibility that some of the things that seemed to be around the corner in 1954 will have come to pass by the year 2004, but if they do, it will surely be in ways that could not have been anticipated then.

Literature Cited

1. Allwood, C. M. 1976. A review of individual differences among problem solvers and attempts to improve problem solving ability. *Göteborgs Psychol. Rep.* 6(11):1–27
2. Anderson, L. W. 1976. An empirical investigation of individual differences in time to learn. *J. Educ. Psychol.* 68:226–33
3. Atkin, R., Bray, R., Davison, M., Herzberger, S., Humphreys, L. G., Selzer, U. 1977. Ability factor differentiation grades 5 through 11. *Appl. Psychol. Meas.* 1:65–76
4. Atkin, R., Bray, R., Davison, M., Herzberger, S., Humphreys, L. G., Selzer, U. 1977. Cross-lagged panel analysis of sixteen cognitive measures at four grade levels. *Child Dev.* 48:944–52
5. Bachelder, B. L., Denny, M. R. 1977. A theory of intelligence: II. The role of span in a variety of intellectual tasks. *Intelligence* 1:237–56
6. Baron, J., Strawson, C. 1976. Use of orthographic and word-specific knowledge in reading words aloud. *J. Exp. Psychol. Hum. Percept. Perform.* 2:386–93
7. Birkhill, W. R., Schaie, K. W. 1975. The effect of differential reinforcement of cautiousness in intellectual performance among the elderly. *J. Gerontol.* 30:578–83

8. Block, N. J., Dworkin, G., eds. 1976. *The IQ Controversy: Critical Readings.* New York: Pantheon. 557 pp.
9. Bloom, B. 1976. *Human Characteristics and School Learning.* New York: McGraw-Hill. 284 pp.
10. Botwinick, J. 1977. Intellectual abilities. In *Handbook of the Psychology of Aging,* ed. J. E. Birren, K. W. Schaie, pp. 580–605. New York: Van Nostrand-Reinhold
11. Bradley, R. H., Caldwell, B. M., Elardo, R. 1977. Home environment, social status and mental test performance. *J. Educ. Psychol.* 69:697–701
12. Bridgman, B., Buttram, J. 1975. Race differences on nonverbal analogy test performance as a function of verbal strategy training. *J. Educ. Psychol.* 67:586–90
13. Brody, E. B., Brody, N. 1976. *Intelligence: Nature, Determinants, and Consequences.* New York: Academic. 241 pp.
14. Broman, S. H., Nichols, P. L., Kennedy, W. A. 1975. *Preschool IQ: Prenatal and Early Developmental Correlates.* Hillsdale, NJ: Erlbaum. 325 pp.
15. Buros, O. K., ed. 1975. *Intelligence Tests and Reviews.* Highland Park, NJ: Gryphon. 1129 pp.
16. Buros, O. K. 1977. Fifty years in testing: Some reminiscences, criticisms,

and suggestions. *Educ. Reschr.* 6(7): 9–15

17. Buss, A. R. 1976. Galton and the birth of differential psychology and eugenics: Social, political and economic forces. *J. Hist. Behav. Sci.* 12:47–58

18. Buss, A. R. 1977. On the relationship between the psychological environment and the development of individual differences in abilities. *Intelligence* 1:192–207

19. Buss, A. R., Poley, W. 1976. *Individual Differences: Traits and Factors.* New York: Gardner. 275 pp.

20. Carroll, J. B. 1976. Psychometric tests as cognitive tasks: A new "Structure of Intellect." See Ref. 133, pp. 27–56

21. Carroll, J. B. 1978. How shall we study individual differences in cognitive abilities?—Methodological and theoretical perspectives. *Intelligence* 2:87–115

22. Carroll, J. B. 1978. On the theory-practice interface in the measurement of intellectual abilities. In *Impact of Research on Education: Some Case Studies,* ed. P. Suppes, pp. 1–105. Washington DC: Natl. Acad. Educ.

23. Cartwright, D. S., Marks, M. E., Durrett, J. H. Jr. 1977. *Definition and Measurement of Three Processes of Imagery Representation: Exploratory Studies of Verbally Stimulated Imagery.* Boulder, Colo: Inst. Study Intellect. Behav., Univ. Colorado. 38 pp.

24. Cattell, R. B. 1971. *Abilities: Their Structure, Growth and Action.* Boston: Houghton-Mifflin. 583 pp.

25. Chi, M. T. H. 1977. Age differences in memory span. *J. Exp. Child Psychol.* 23:266–81

26. Chiang, A., Atkinson, R. C. 1976. Individual differences and interrelationships among a select set of cognitive skills. *Mem. Cognit.* 4:661–72

27. Cohen, R. L., Sandberg, T. 1977. Relation between intelligence and short-term memory. *Cogn. Psychol.* 9:534–54

28. Conger, A. J., Conger, J. C. 1975. Reliable dimensions for WISC profiles. *Educ. Psychol. Meas.* 35:847–63

29. Cooper, L. A. 1976. Individual differences in visual comparison processes. *Percept. Psychophys.* 19:433–44

30. Cory, C. H. 1977. Relative utility of computerized versus paper-and-pencil tests for predicting job performance. *Appl. Psychol. Meas.* 1:551–64

31. Craik, F. I. M. 1977. Age differences in human memory. See Ref. 10, pp. 384–420

32. Cronbach, L. J., Snow, R. E. 1977. *Aptitudes and Instructional Methods: A Handbook for Research on Interactions.* New York: Irvington. 574 pp.

33. Cutting, J. E. 1976. Auditory and linguistic processes in speech perception: Inferences from six fusions in dichotic listening. *Psychol. Rev.* 83:114–40

34. Day, R. S. 1977. Systematic individual differences in information processing. In *Psychology and Life,* ed. P. G. Zimbardo, F. L. Ruch, pp. 5A-5D. Glenview, Ill: Scott, Foresman

35. DeFries, J. C., Plomin, R. 1978. Behavioral genetics. *Ann. Rev. Psychol.* 29:473–515

36. DeFries, J. C., Vandenberg, S. G., McClearn, G. E. 1976. Genetics of specific cognitive abilities. *Ann. Rev. Genet.* 10:179–207

37. Drenth, P. J. 1977. Prediction of school performance in developing countries: School grades or psychological tests? *J. Cross-Cult. Psychol.* 8:49–70

38. Duda, P. D. 1975. Tests of the psychological meaning of the power law. *J. Exp. Psychol. Hum. Percept. Perform.* 1:188–94

39. Egan, D. E. 1976. *Accuracy and Latency Scores as Measures of Spatial Information Processing.* Tech. Rep. 1224, US Naval Aerospace Med. Res. Lab. 27 pp.

40. Ekstrom, R. B. 1973. *Cognitive Factors: Some Recent Literature,* PR-73-30. Princeton, NJ: ETS. 99 pp.

41. Ernest, C. H. 1977. Imagery ability and cognition: A critical review. *J. Ment. Imagery* 1:181–216

42. Estes, W. K. 1974. Learning theory and intelligence. *Am. Psychol.* 29:740–49

43. Eysenck, M. W. 1977. *Human Memory: Theory, Research and Individual Differences.* Oxford: Pergamon. 366 pp.

44. Fairweather, H. 1976. Sex differences in cognition. *Cognition* 4:231–80

45. Favero, J., Dombrower, J., Michael, W. B., Richards, L. 1975. Interrelationships among 76 individually-administered tests intended to represent 76 different structure-of-intellect abilities and a stardardized general intelligence test in a sample of 34 nine-year-old children. *Educ. Psychol. Meas.* 35:993–1004

46. Fincher, J. 1976. *Human Intelligence.* New York: Putnam. 512 pp.

47. Fine, B. 1975. *The Stranglehold of the I. Q.* Garden City: Doubleday. 278 pp.

48. Forsyth, G. A., Huber, R. J. 1976. Selective attention in ambiguous-figure perception: An individual differences analysis. *Bull. Psychon. Soc.* 7:498–500

49. Frederiksen, J. 1978. *A Chronometric Study of Component Skills in Reading.* Cambridge, Mass: Bolt, Beranek & Newman. 24 pp.

50. Frederiksen, N., Ward, W. C. 1978. Measures for the study of creativity in scientific problem-solving. *Appl. Psychol. Meas.* 2:1–24

51. Friedman, H. 1974. Interrelation of two types of immediate memory in the aged. *J. Psychol.* 87:177–81

52. Garber, H. L. 1977. Preventing mental retardation through family rehabilitation. In *Infant Education: A Guide for Helping Handicapped Children in the First Three Years,* ed. B. M. Caldwell, D. M. Stedman, pp. 63–79. New York: Walker

53. Goldberg, R. A., Schwartz, S., Stewart, M. 1977. Individual differences in cognitive processes. *J. Educ. Psychol.* 69:9–14

54. Goodenough, D. R. 1976. The role of individual differences in field dependence as a factor in learning and memory. *Psychol. Bull.* 83:675–94

55. Goodenough, D. R., Witkin, H. A. 1977. *Origins of the Field-Dependent and Field-Independent Cognitive Styles,* RB-77-9. Princeton, NJ: ETS

56. Gough, H. G. 1976. Studying creativity by means of word association tests. *J. Appl. Psychol.* 61:348–53

57. Green, D. R., ed. 1974. *The Aptitude-Achievement Distinction.* Monterey: CTB/McGraw-Hill. 384 pp.

58. Hakstian, A. R., Bennet, R. W. 1977. Validity studies using the Comprehensive Ability Battery (CAB): I. Academic achievement criteria. *Educ. Psychol. Meas.* 37:425–37

59. Hakstian, A. R., Cattell, R. B. 1976. *Comprehensive Ability Battery.* Champaign, Ill: Inst. Pers. Ability Test.

60. Hakstian, A. R., Cattell, R. B. 1978. An examination of inter-domain relationships among some ability and personality traits. *Educ. Psychol. Meas.* 38:275–90

61. Hardy, J. B., Welcher, D. W., Mellits, E. D., Kagan, J. 1976. Pitfalls in the measurement of intelligence: Are standard intelligence tests valid instruments for measuring the intellectual potential of urban children? *J. Psychol.* 94:43–51

62. Harman, H. H., Ekstrom, R. B., French, J. W. 1976. *Kit of Factor Reference Cognitive Tests.* Princeton, NJ: ETS

63. Hass, W. A., Wepman, J. M. 1974. Dimensions of individual difference in the spoken syntax of school children. *J. Speech Hear. Res.* 17:455–69

64. Hock, H. S., Marcus, N. 1976. The effect of familiarity on the processing of fragmented figures. *Percept. Psychophys.* 20:375–79

65. Hogaboam, T. W., Pellegrino, J. W. 1978. Hunting for individual differences in cognitive processes: Verbal ability and semantic processing of pictures and words. *Mem. Cognit.* 6:189–93

66. Hogan, J. C. 1978. *Trainability of Abilities: A Review of Nonspecific Transfer Issues Relevant to Ability Training.* Tech. Rep. Adv. Res. Resour. Organ., Washington DC. 38 pp.

67. Holzman, T. G., Glaser, R., Pellegrino, J. W. 1976. Process training derived from a computer simulation theory. *Mem. Cognit.* 4:349–56

68. Hopkins, K. D., Bracht, G. H. 1975. Ten-year stability of verbal and nonverbal IQ scores. *Am. Educ. Res. J.* 12:469–77

69. Horn, J. L. 1977. Personality and ability theory. In *Handbook of Modern Personality Theory,* ed. R. B. Cattell, R. M. Dreger, pp. 139–65. Washington DC: Hemisphere

70. Horn, J. L., Donaldson, G. 1976. On the myth of intellectual decline in adulthood. *Am. Psychol.* 31:701–19

71. Houts, P. L., ed. 1977. *The Myth of Measurability.* New York: Hart. 398 pp.

72. Hruza, E. A., Kelly, F. J., Hawley, I. B. 1978. Two factor-analytic studies of formal operations and general intelligence among adult males. *Przegl. Psychol.* 21:

73. Hultsch, D. F., Nesselroade, J. R., Plemons, J. K. 1976. Learning-ability relations in adulthood. *Hum. Dev.* 19:234–47

74. Humphreys, L. G. 1976. Strategy training has no significant effect on race differences in nonverbal reasoning. *J. Educ. Psychol.* 68:128–29

75. Hundal, P. S., Horn, J. L. 1977. On the relationships between short-term learning and fluid and crystallized intelligence. *Appl. Psychol. Meas.* 1:11–21

76. Hunt, E. B. 1974. Quote the Raven? Nevermore! In *Knowledge and Cognition,* ed. L. W. Gregg, pp. 129–57. Potomac, Md: Erlbaum

77. Hunt, E. B. 1976. Varieties of cognitive power. See Ref. 133, pp. 237–59

78. Hunt, E. B. 1978. Mechanics of verbal ability. *Psychol. Rev.* 85:109–30

79. Hunt, E. B., Frost, N., Lunneborg, C. E. 1973. Individual differences in cognition: A new approach to intelligence. In

The Psychology of Learning and Motivation: Advances in Research and Theory, ed. G. Bower, 7:87–122. New York: Academic

80. Hunt, E. B., Lunneborg, C. E., Lewis, J. 1975. What does it mean to be high verbal? *Cogn. Psychol.* 7:194–227

81. Jensen, A. R. 1974. Cumulative deficit: A testable hypothesis? *Dev. Psychol.* 10:996–1019

82. Jensen, A. R. 1976. Heritability of IQ. *Science* 194:6–8

83. Jensen, A. R. 1977. Cumulative deficit in IQ of blacks in the rural south. *Dev. Psychol.* 13:184–91

84. Johnson, A. F., Shelton, R. L., Arndt, W. B., Furr, M. L. 1977. Factor analysis of measures of articulation, language, auditory processing, reading-spelling, and maxillofacial structure. *J. Speech Hear. Res.* 20:319–24

85. Johnston, R. P. 1977. Social class and the speech of four year olds: The effect of intelligence. *Lang. Speech* 20:40–47

86. Johnston, R. P., Singleton, C. H. 1977. Social class and communication style: The ability of middle and working class five year olds to encode and decode abstract stimuli. *Br. J. Psychol.* 68:237–44

87. Jordan, T. C., Rabbitt, P. M. A. 1977. Response times to stimuli of increasing complexity as a function of ageing. *Br. J. Psychol.* 68:189–201

88. Keating, D. P., Bobbitt, B. L. 1978. Individual and developmental differences in cognitive processing components of mental ability. *Child Dev.* 49:155–67

89. Kelleghan, T. 1977. Relationships between home environment and scholastic behavior in a disadvantaged population. *J. Educ. Psychol.* 69:754–60

90. Kirby, J. R., Das, J. P. 1978. Information processing and human abilities. *J. Educ. Psychol.* 70:58–66

91. Klahr, D., Wallace, J. G. 1976. *Cognitive Development: An Information-Processing View.* Hillsdale, NJ: Erlbaum. 244 pp.

92. Klein, R. E., Freeman, H. E., Spring, B., Nerlove, S. B., Yarbrough, C. 1976. Cognitive test performance and indigenous conceptions of intelligence. *J. Psychol.* 93:273–79

93. Kogan, N. 1976. *Cognitive Styles in Infancy and Early Childhood.* Hillsdale, NJ: Erlbaum. 146 pp.

94. Kroll, N. E. A., Parks, T. E. 1978. Interference with short-term visual memory produced by concurrent central processing. *J. Exp. Psychol. Hum. Learn. Mem.* 4:111–20

95. Krutetskii, V. A. 1976. *The Psychology of Mathematical Abilities in School Children.* Chicago: Univ. Chicago Press. 417 pp.

96. Kuhn, D. 1976. Relation of two Piagetian stage transitions to IQ. *Dev. Psychol.* 12:157–61

97. Labouvie-Vief, G., Levin, J. R., Hurlbut, N. L., Urberg, K. A. 1977. In pursuit of the elusive relationship between selected cognitive abilities and learning. *Contemp. Educ. Psychol.* 2:239–50

98. Labouvie-Vief, G., Levin, J. R., Urberg, K. A. 1975. The relationship between selected cognitive abilities and learning: A second look. *J. Educ. Psychol.* 67:558–69

99. Lawson, M. J., Jarman, R. F. 1977. A note on Jensen's theory of Level I ability and recent research on human memory. *Br. J. Educ. Psychol.* 47:91–94

100. Lesser, G. S. 1976. Cultural differences in learning and thinking styles. In *Individuality in Learning,* ed. S. Messick, pp. 137–60. San Francisco: Jossey-Bass

101. Lewis, M., ed. 1976. *Origins of Intelligence: Infancy and Early Childhood.* New York: Plenum. 413 pp.

102. Lewis, M., Gallas, H. 1976. *Cognitive Performance in the 12-Week-Old Infant: The Effects of Birth Order, Birth Spacing, Sex, and Social class,* RB-76-23. Princeton, NJ: ETS

103. Lin, P-C., Humphreys, L. G. 1977. Predictions of academic performance in graduate and professional school. *Appl. Psychol. Meas.* 1:249–57

104. Locurto, C. M., Walsh, J. F. 1976. Reinforcement and self-reinforcement: Their effects on originality. *Am. J. Psychol.* 89:281–91

105. Lord, F. M. 1956. A study of speed factors in tests and academic grades. *Psychometrika* 21:31–50

106. Lumsden, J. 1976. Test theory. *Ann. Rev. Psychol.* 27:251–80

107. Lunneborg, C. E. 1977. Choice reaction time: What role in ability measurement? *Appl. Psychol. Meas.* 1:309–30

108. Lunneborg, C. E. 1978. Some information-processing correlates of measures of intelligence. *Multivar. Behav. Res.* 13:153–61

109. Lyon, D. R. 1977. Individual differences in immediate serial recall: A matter of mnemonics? *Cogn. Psychol.* 9:403–11

110. Mandler, J. M., Stein, N. L. 1977. The myth of perceptual defect: Sources and evidence. *Psychol. Bull.* 84:173–92

111. Marjoribanks, K. 1976. Academic achievement, intelligence, and cre-

ativity: A regression surface analysis. *Multivar. Behav. Res.* 11:105–18

112. Marjoribanks, K. 1977. Socioeconomic status and its relation to cognitive performance as mediated through the family environment. In *Genetics, Environment and Intelligence,* ed. A. Oliverio, pp. 385–403. New York: Elsevier/North Holland

113. Marslen-Wilson, W. D. 1973. Linguistic structure and speech shadowing at very short latencies. *Nature* 244:522–23

114. Matarazzo, J. D., Wiens, A. N., Manaugh, T. S. 1975. IQ correlates of speech and silence behavior under three dyadic speaking conditions. *J. Consult. Clin. Psychol.* 43:198–204

115. McCall, R. B. 1977. Childhood IQ's as predictors of adult educational and occupational status. *Science* 197:482–83

116. McGuire, T. R., Hirsch, J. 1977. General intelligence (*g*) and heritability (*H²*, *h²*). In *The Structure of Experience,* ed. I. C. Užgiris, F. Weizmann, pp. 25–72. New York: Plenum

117. McKay, H., Sinisterra, L., McKay, A., Gomez, H., Lloreda, P. 1978. Improving cognitive ability in chronically deprived children. *Science* 200:270–78

118. Meichenbaum, D. 1975. Enhancing creativity by modifying what subjects say to themselves. *Am. Educ. Res. J.* 12:129–45

119. Messick, S., French, J. W. 1975. Dimensions of cognitive closure. *Multivar. Behav. Res.* 10:3–16

120. Miller, D. J., Ryan, E. B., Short, E. J., Ries, P. G., McGuire, M. D., Culler, M. P. 1977. Relationships between early habituation and later cognitive performance in infancy. *Child Dev.* 48:658–61

121. Munsinger, H. 1978. Reply to Kamin. *Psychol. Bull.* 85:202–6

122. Neimark, E. D. 1975. Longitudinal development of formal operations thought. *Genet. Psychol. Monogr.* 91:171–225

123. Olsson, U., Bergman, L. F. 1977. A longitudinal factor model for studying change in ability structure. *Multivar. Behav. Res.* 12:221–41

124. O'Sullivan, M., Guilford, J. P. 1975. Six factors of behavioral cognition: Understanding other people. *J. Educ. Meas.* 12:255–71

125. Paivio, A. 1978. Comparisons of mental clocks. *J. Exp. Psychol. Hum. Percept. Perform.* 4:61–71

126. Peng, S. S., Farr, S. D. 1976. Generalizability of free-recall measurements. *Multivar. Behav. Res.* 11:287–96

127. Perfetti, C. A., Bell, L. C., Hogaboam, T. W., Goldman, S. R. 1977. *Verbal processing speed and reading skill.* Presented at Psychon. Soc., Washington DC

128. Perfetti, C. A., Lesgold, A. M. 1977. Discourse comprehension and sources of individual differences. In *Cognitive Processes and Comprehension,* ed. M. Just, P. Carpenter, pp. 141–84. Hillsdale, NJ: Erlbaum

129. Platnick, D. M., Richards, L. G. 1977. Individual differences related to performance on two word-recognition tasks. *Am. J. Psychol.* 90:133–44

130. Plemons, J. K., Willis, S. L., Baltes, P. B. 1978. Modifiability of fluid intelligence in aging: A short-term longitudinal training approach. *J. Gerontol.* 33:224–31

131. Price, J., Eliot, J. 1975. Convergent and discriminant validities of two sets of measures of spatial orientation and visualization. *Educ. Psychol. Meas.* 35:975–77

132. Raaheim, K. 1974. *Problem Solving and Intelligence.* Bergen, Norway: Universitetsforlaget. 115 pp.

133. Resnick, L. B., ed. 1976. *The Nature of Intelligence.* Hillsdale, NJ: Erlbaum. 364 pp.

134. Richardson, A. 1977. The meaning and measurement of mental imagery. *Br. J. Psychol.* 68:29–43

135. Robertson-Tchabo, E., Arenberg, D. 1976. Age differences in cognition in healthy educated men: A factor analysis of experimental measures. *Exp. Aging Res.* 2:75–89

136. Rose, A. M., Fernandes, K. 1977. *An Information Processing Approach to Performance Assessment: I. Experimental Investigation of an Information Processing Performance Battery.* Tech. Rep. Am. Inst. Res., Washington DC: 85 pp.

137. Roth, D. R. 1974. Intelligence testing as a social activity. In *Language Use and School Performance,* by A. V. Cicourel, K. H. Jennings, S. H. M. Jennings, K. C. W. Leiter, R. MacKay, H. Mehan, D. R. Roth, pp. 143–217. New York: Academic

138. Royce, J. R., Yeudall, L. T., Bock, C. 1976. Factor analytic studies of human brain damage: I. First and second-order factors and their brain correlates. *Multivar. Behav. Res.* 11:381–418

139. Sacks, H. V., Eysenck, M. W. 1977. Convergence-divergence and the learning of concrete and abstract sentences. *Br. J. Psychol.* 68:215–21

140. Samuel, W. 1977. Observed IQ as a function of test atmosphere, tester expectation, and race of tester: A replication for female subjects. *J. Educ. Psychol.* 69:593–604
141. Scandura, J. M. 1977. *Problem Solving: A Structural/Process Approach with Instructional Implications.* New York: Academic. 591 pp.
142. Schaie, K. W., Baltes, P. B. 1977. Some faith helps to see the forest: A final comment on the Horn and Donaldson myth of the Baltes-Schaie position on adult intelligence. *Am. Psychol.* 32:1118–20
143. Schaie, K. W., Parham, I. A. 1977. Cohort-sequential analyses of adult intellectual development. *Dev. Psychol.* 13:649–53
144. Schmeck, R. R., Ribich, F., Ramanaiah, N. 1977. Development of a self-report inventory for assessing individual differences in learning processes. *Appl. Psychol. Meas.* 1:413–31
145. Schwartz, S. 1975. Individual differences in cognition: Some relationships between personality and memory. *J. Res. Pers.* 9:217–25
146. Shepard, R. N. 1978. The mental image. *Am. Psychol.* 33:125–37
147. Siegler, R. S. 1976. Three aspects of cognitive development. *Cogn. Psychol.* 8:481–520
148. Siegler, R. S., Vago, S. 1978. The development of a proportionality concept: Judging relative fullness. *J. Exp. Child Psychol.* 25:371–96
149. Silverstein, A. B. 1977. Alternative factor analytic solutions for the Wechsler Intelligence Scale for Children—Revised. *Educ. Psychol. Meas.* 37:121–24
150. Snow, R. E., Marshalek, B., Lohman, D. F. 1976. *Correlation of Selected Cognitive Abilities and Cognitive Processing Parameters: An Exploratory Study.* Tech. Rep. Stanford Univ. Sch. Educ. 38 pp.
151. Spearritt, D., Spalding, D., Johnston, M. 1977. *Measuring Reading Comprehension in the Upper Primary School.* Canberra: Aust. Gov. Publ. Serv. 148 pp.
152. Stein, M. I. 1974–5. *Stimulating Creativity, Vol. 1: Individual Procedures; Vol. 2: Group Procedures.* New York: Academic. 348, 306 pp.
153. Sternberg, R. J. 1977. *Intelligence, Information Processing, and Analogical Reasoning: The Componential Analysis of Human Abilities.* Hillsdale, NJ: Erlbaum. 348 pp.
154. Stevenson, H. W., Parker, T., Wilkinson, A., Hegion, A., Fish, E. 1976. Lon-
gitudinal study of individual differences in cognitive development and scholastic achievement. *J. Educ. Psychol.* 68:377–400
155. Taylor, C. L., Brown, F. G., Michael, W. B. 1976. The validity of cognitive, affective, and demographic variables in the prediction of achievement in high school algebra and geometry: Implications for the definition of mathematical aptitude. *Educ. Psychol. Meas.* 36:971–82
156. Taylor, I. A., Getzels, J. W., eds. 1975. *Perspectives in Creativity.* Chicago: Aldine. 353 pp.
157. Taylor, T. R. 1976. The factor structure of geometric illusions: A second study. *Psychol. Afr.* 16:177–200
158. Thissen, D. M. 1976. Information in wrong responses to the Raven Progressive Matrices. *J. Educ. Meas.* 13:201–14
159. Thomas, H. 1977. Kinship correlations and scientific nihilism: Reply to Goldberger. *Psychol. Bull.* 84:1245–48
160. Thomas, J. C., Fozard, J. L., Waugh, N. C. 1977. Age-related differences in naming latency. *Am. J. Psychol.* 90:499–509
161. Thorndike, R. L. 1975. Mr. Binet's test 70 years later. *Educ. Reschr.* 4(5):3–7
162. Townsend, M. A. R., Keeling, B. 1976. An investigation of Level I and Level II cognitive processes in the learning and recall of factual and inferential information. *Br. J. Educ. Psychol.* 46:306–17
163. Trotman, F. K. 1977. Race, IQ, and the middle class. *J. Educ. Psychol.* 69:266–73
164. Turner, R. G., Horn, J. M. 1977. Personality scale and item correlates of WAIS abilities. *Intelligence* 1:281–97
165. Underwood, B. J., Boruch, R. F., Malmi, R. A. 1977. *The Composition of Episodic Memory.* Tech. Rep. Northwestern Univ. Dep. Psychol., Evanston Ill: 79 pp.
166. Undheim, J. O. 1976. Ability structure in 10–11-year-old children and the theory of fluid and crystallized intelligence. *J. Educ. Psychol.* 68:411–23
167. Undheim, J. O., Horn, J. L. 1977. Critical evaluation of Guilford's structure-of-intellect theory. *Intelligence* 1:65–81
168. Užgiris, I. Č., Hunt, J. M. 1975. *Assessment in Infancy: Ordinal Scales of Psychological Development.* Urbana: Univ. Ill. Press. 263 pp.
169. Vandenberg, S. G. 1976. Genetic factors in human learning. *Educ. Psychol.* 12:59–63
170. Vandenberg, S. G., Kuse, A. R. 1978. Genetic determinants of spatial ability.

In *Determinants of Sex-Related Differences in Cognitive Functioning*, ed. M. C. Wittig, A. C. Petersen. New York: Academic. In press

171. Vetta, A. 1977. Estimation of heritability from IQ data on twins. *Nature* 266:279

172. Waber, D. P. 1977. Sex differences in mental abilities, hemispheric lateralization, and rate of physical growth at adolescence. *Dev. Psychol.* 13:29–38

173. Walberg, H. J., Marjoribanks, K. 1976. Family environment and cognitive development: Twelve analytic models. *Rev. Educ. Res.* 46:527–51

174. Walsh, D. A., Baldwin, M. 1977. Age differences in integrated semantic memory. *Dev. Psychol.* 13:509–14

175. Ward, W. C. 1975. Convergent and divergent measurement of creativity in children. *Educ. Psychol. Meas.* 35: 87–95

176. Wechsler, D. 1975. Intelligence defined and undefined: A relativistic appraisal. *Am. Psychol.* 30:135–39

177. Welsh, G. S. 1975. *Creativity and Intelligence: A Personality Approach.* Chapel Hill, NC: Inst. Res. Soc. Sci., Univ. North Carolina. 276 pp.

178. Welsh, G. S., Baucom, D. H. 1977. Sex, masculinity-femininity, and intelligence. *Intelligence* 1:218–33

179. White, P. O. 1973. Individual differences in speed, accuracy and persistence: A mathematical model for problem solving. In *The Measurement of Intelligence*, ed. H. J. Eysenck, pp. 246–60. Baltimore: Williams & Wilkins

180. Whitely, S. E. 1977. Information-processing on intelligence test items: Some

response components. *Appl. Psychol. Meas.* 1:465–76

181. Whitely, S. E. 1977. Relationships in analogy items: A semantic component of a psychometric task. *Educ. Psychol. Meas.* 37:725–39

182. Whitely, S. E., Dawis, R. V. 1974. Effects of cognitive intervention on latent ability measured from analogy items. *J. Educ. Psychol.* 66:710–17

183. Wiedl, K. H., Carlson, J. S. 1976. The factorial structure of the Raven Coloured Progressive Matrices Test. *Educ. Psychol. Meas.* 36:409–13

184. Williams, T. H. 1975. The Wechsler scales: Parents and (male) children. *J. Educ. Meas.* 12:119–28

185. Wirtz, W. et al. 1977. *On Further Examination: Report of the Advisory Panel on the Scholastic Aptitude Test Score Decline.* New York: Coll. Ent. Exam. Bd.

186. Witkin, H. A., Cox, P. W., Friedman, F. 1976. *Field-Dependence Independence and Psychological Differentiation, Bibliography with Index, Suppl. No. 2,* RB-76-28. Princeton, NJ: ETS. 127 pp.

187. Witkin, H. A., Goodenough, D. R. 1977. *Field Dependence Revisited,* RB-77-16. Princeton, NJ: ETS. 53 pp.

188. Witkin, H. A., Moore, C. A., Goodenough, D. R., Cox, P. W. 1977. Field-dependent and field-independent cognitive styles and their educational implications. *Rev. Educ. Res.* 47:1–64

189. Yen, W. M. 1978. Measuring individual differences with an information processing model. *J. Educ. Psychol.* 70:72–86

190. Zajonc, R. B. 1976. Family configuration and intelligence. *Science* 192: 227–36

AUTHOR INDEX

A

Abbagnara, L. A., 46, 56
Abbas, P. J., 41, 42, 56
Abdel-Halim, A. A., 247, 272
Abellera, J. W., 494, 514
Abelson, R. P., 65, 98, 376-78, 391
Abrahams, N. M., 494, 495, 506, 514
Abramowitz, C. V., 454, 463, 474
Abramowitz, S. I., 464, 468, 474
Adam, E., 260, 272
Adams, E. F., 248, 272
Adams, J. E., 411, 413
Adams, J. S., 258, 272
Adams, N. E., 565, 591
Adamson, L., 127, 128, 136, 534, 535, 549
Adelman, L., 433, 448
Ader, R., 136
Adesman, P., 72, 98
Adjei, K., 151, 168, 169
Adler, L. L., 145, 169
Adrian, E. D., 285, 318
Agras, W. S., 566, 570, 591
Ahern, G., 316, 318
Ahlskog, J. E., 229, 230, 233
Aiello, N., 369, 378, 391
Aiken, M., 443, 448
Ainsworth, M. D. S., 114, 126, 127, 136, 534, 535, 537, 549
Ajzen, I., 250, 272
Akagi, T., 311, 318
Akert, K., 307, 313, 318
Akiyama, M., 108, 109, 111, 113, 114, 125, 127, 128
Albee, G. W., 104, 136, 174, 182, 183, 187, 193, 195, 204, 205
Albert, B. M., 466, 474
Albert, D. J., 218, 233
Albright, L. E., 496, 514
Albus, J. S., 341, 358
Alderfer, C. P., 252, 272
Alev, N., 318
Alexander, D., 567, 591
Alexander, J. F., 589, 591
Alexander, R. A., 496, 514
Alf, E. F., 494, 495, 506, 514
Alheid, G. F., 217, 218, 229, 233
Alkema, F., 544, 549
Alkire, A., 411, 413
Allen, G. J., 557, 591
Allen, J. D., 222, 233
Allen, L., 184, 189, 201, 205
Allen, R., 570, 591

Allen, W. F., 308, 318
Alley, K. E., 341, 358
Allport, D. A., 75, 98
Allport, F. M., 532, 535, 549
Allport, G. W., 458, 474
Allum, J., 351, 358
Allwood, C. M., 617, 634
Almond, R., 409, 413
Almquist, E. M., 584, 591
Als, H., 127, 128, 136, 534, 535, 549
Altman, J. A., 51, 56
Altmann, S., 538, 549
Alvares, K. M., 270, 272, 487, 514
Amaral, D. G., 230, 233
Amassian, V. E., 307, 318
Ammerman, H. L., 480, 514
Amolsch, T., 573, 591
Anand, B. K., 213, 214, 220, 221, 233
Anastasi, A., 483, 514
Anchor, K. N., 456, 466, 474, 573, 591
Ancoli, S., 547, 549
Anderson, A. B., 433, 448
Anderson, C. R., 246, 272
Anderson, J. R., 65, 66, 79, 81, 87, 92, 97, 98, 366, 370, 371, 376-79, 382, 386-88, 391
Anderson, L. W., 632, 634
Anderson, N., 428, 448
Anderson, R. C., 64, 65, 84, 95, 98
Anderson, W., 318
Anderson, W. P., 577, 591
Andersson, B., 213, 233, 305, 318
Andrasik, F., 568, 591
Andreoli, V. A., 437, 448
Andrisani, P. J., 246, 254, 261, 272
Annis, A. B., 446, 448
Annis, L. V., 573, 591
Antelman, S. M., 212, 233
Anthony, E. J., 198, 205
Anton, J. L., 570, 591
Antonis, B., 75, 98
Antze, P., 468, 472, 474
April, C., 545, 549
Aragona, J., 569, 591
Arazie, R., 222, 233
Arbuckle, T. Y., 77, 98
Archibald, R. D., 581, 591
Ardila, R., 118, 136
Arenberg, D., 627, 634
Argyle, M., 540, 544, 549
Argyris, C., 411, 413, 442, 448
Aries, E., 469, 474
Armstrong, P. M., 557, 591

Arndt, W. B., 615, 634
Arnold, J. E., 589, 591
Aronoff, J., 446, 448
Aronow, H., 48, 56
Aronson, E., 438, 448, 557, 591
Arshavsky, Yu. I., 333, 358
Arthir, R. J., 408, 413
Arvey, R. D., 247, 256, 257, 272, 486, 487, 506, 514
Ash, R. A., 485, 514
Ashe, J. H., 316, 318
Asher, J. J., 513, 514
Asher, S. R., 560, 561, 591
Astin, A. W., 486, 514
Atkin, R., 115, 136, 425, 448, 626, 634
Atkin, R. S., 425, 448
Atkinson, D. R., 575, 591
Atkinson, R. C., 73, 98, 385, 391, 612, 634
Atwater, D. C., 506, 514
Atwood, M. E., 367, 391
Atzet, J., 544, 549
Aubley, P. M., 78, 98
Avery, A. W., 571, 591
Azrin, N. H., 225, 233, 557, 587, 591

B

Baars, B. J., 50, 56
Bach, G. R., 589, 591
Bachelder, B. L., 613, 622, 634
Back, K., 420, 448
Baddeley, A. D., 64-66, 68, 69, 71-74, 77, 81, 98
Badger, E., 127, 136
Badin, I. J., 251, 272
Bagley, C. B., 443, 448
Bailey, C. J., 213, 222, 233
Bailey, M., 426, 448
Baird, L., 490, 514
Baird, L. W., 248, 272
Bakeman, R., 434, 448
Baker, C., 184, 205
Baker, H. T., 489, 514
Baker, L., 85, 86, 98
Baker, S. B., 580, 591
Balagura, S., 213, 216, 221, 227, 230, 231, 233
Baldes, J. J., 255, 272
Baldwin, M., 628, 634
Bales, R. F., 462, 469, 474
Balfour, H. G., 455, 465, 473, 474
Ball, M., 76, 98
Balter, M. D., 408, 413
Baltes, P. B., 627, 629, 634
Banducci, R., 578, 591
Bandura, A., 125, 136, 563-65, 591

Banerji, R., 368, 391
Banks, W. P., 67, 98
Barak, A., 578, 581, 591
Barbach, L. G., 562, 591
Barber, G., 67, 98
Barber, T. X., 567, 591
Barclay, J. R., 377, 391
Bare, J. K., 290, 304, 318
Barenboim, C., 534, 549
Barker, R. G., 200, 205
Barlow, H. B., 130, 131, 136
Barnes, C. A., 112, 136
Barnes, R. H., 225, 233
Barnett, R. C., 585, 591
Baron, J., 614, 634
Baron, R. A., 549
Barr, C. C., 340, 341, 358
Barrett, G. V., 510, 514
Barrett, R. S., 496, 514
Barrett, S. E., 83, 98
Barrett, T. C., 578, 591
Barron, D. H., 285, 318
Barrow, J. C., 263, 269, 272
Barsalou, L. W., 88, 98
Bartels, B. D., 471, 474
Bartlett, C. J., 496, 514
Bartlett, F. C., 365, 376, 391
Bartling, C. A., 88, 98
Bartol, K. M., 270, 272
Barton, R., 405, 409, 413
Bartoshuk, L. M., 292, 302, 303, 318
Bartz, W. H., 82-84, 98
Baruch, G. K., 585, 591
Bass, A. R., 497, 498, 514
Bass, B. M., 266, 272
Bassett, R., 445, 448
Bates, E., 92, 93, 98
Bateson, G., 165, 169
Baucom, D. H., 631, 634
Bauer, B. B., 46, 56
Baulu, J., 230, 231, 233
Baumgardner, S. R., 579, 591
Bayley, N., 201, 205
Baylor, G. W., 378, 381, 391
Bayma, B., 573, 591
Beach, F. A., 106, 107, 120, 136
Beach, L. R., 270, 272
Beal, D. G., 574, 591
Bealer, S. L., 300, 318
Beaman, A. L., 431, 448
Beatty, W. W., 222, 225, 233
Beck, A. T., 563, 564, 591
Becker, B. W., 272
Becker, E. E., 221, 233
BECKER-HAVEN, J. F., 555-602; 556, 591
Beckford, J., 438, 448
Beckwith, L., 126, 136
Beebe, B., 534, 540, 549
Beggs, D. L., 582, 591
Begley, P. J., 575, 591

Behling, O., 255, 272
Behrens, M. I., 407, 413
Beidler, L. M., 291, 301, 318
Beier, E. G., 544, 549
Belendiuk, K., 41, 47, 56
Bell, C., 284, 318
Bell, C. H., 255-57, 262, 272
Bell, L. C., 614, 634
Bell, S. M. V., 114, 126, 136, 537, 549
Bellack, A. S., 557, 591
Bellezza, F. S., 79, 80, 98
Bellman, B. L., 163, 165, 169
Bellows, N., 490, 514
Bellugi, U., 69, 76, 98
Belmont, L., 115, 136
Bem, D., 422, 448
Bem, D. J., 250, 261, 272
Benjamin, A., 427, 448
Benjamin, R. M., 290, 305-8, 313, 316, 318
Bennet, R. W., 632, 634
Bennett, E. L., 131-36
Bennett, M. V. L., 335, 358
Bennett, S. L., 534, 540, 549
Bentley, M., 18, 29
Berg, K., 52, 56
Bergan, T., 408, 413
Berger, C. J., 247, 260, 262, 272
Bergert, B., 48, 49, 52, 56
Bergin, A. E., 455, 456, 474
Bergland, B. W., 580, 591
Bergman, L. F., 626, 634
Berkinblit, M. B., 333, 358
Berland, D. W., 295, 318
Berland, J. C., 168, 169
Berlin, B., 153, 169
Berlin, I., 457, 474
Berliner, J. E., 44, 56
Berman, H. J., 544, 549
Berman, R. F., 117, 136
Bernard, R. A., 292, 298, 300, 311, 318
Bernardin, H. J., 270, 272, 487, 514
Bernardis, L. L., 223-27, 233
Berner, C. N., 220, 233
Berner, J. G., 496, 513, 514
Bernstein, L. A., 116, 136
Bernstein, V., 506, 514
Berntson, G. G., 214, 233
Berry, J. W., 145, 147, 155, 157-59, 169
Berry, N. H., 489, 514
Bertelsen, A., 401, 413
Berthoud, H. R., 223, 233
Besalel-Azrin, V., 557, 591
Best, J., 466, 474
Best, P. J., 212, 233
Betz, E. L., 577, 591
Beutler, L. E., 575, 591
Beyer, J., 565, 591

Bhaskar, R., 367, 369, 374, 391
Bhrolchain, M. N., 404, 413
Biersner, R. J., 510, 514
Biglan, A., 563, 566, 591
Bigoness, W. J., 490, 514
Bilger, R. C., 44, 56
Bilsen, F. A., 36, 38, 54-56
Bindra, D., 226, 229, 231, 233
Birch, H., 194, 195, 205
Birch, H. G., 107, 136
Birchler, G. R., 561, 591
Birdwhistell, R. L., 538, 549
Birkhill, W. R., 628, 634
Birley, J. L. T., 406, 413
Bizzi, E., 341, 351, 358
Bjork, R. A., 81, 83, 98
Bjorklund, A., 229, 233
Blaas, C. D., 571, 591
Black, H., 572, 591
Black, J. B., 65, 93, 94, 98
Black, J. S., 249, 272
Blackburn, R. S., 249, 272
Blackmore, J., 259, 272
Blanchard, E. B., 566, 591
Blanchard, F. A., 433, 448
Blass, E. M., 213, 218, 220, 233
Blehar, M. C., 127, 136
Blimline, C. A., 583, 591
Bloch, S., 465, 470, 471, 473, 474
Block, J., 504, 514
Block, N. J., 629, 634
Blodgett, H. C., 53, 56
Blomquist, A. J., 305, 307, 308, 318
Blood, M., 483, 514
Blood, M. R., 247, 262, 272
Bloom, B., 632, 634
Bloom, L., 378, 391
Bloom, P. J., 46, 56
Blumenthal, A. L., 12, 29
Blundell, J. E., 230, 231, 233
Blurton Jones, N. G., 528, 534, 535, 539, 549
Bobbitt, B. L., 612, 626, 634
Bobko, P., 496, 514
Bobrow, D. G., 65, 96-98, 371, 372, 391
Bock, C., 609, 634
Boehm, V. R., 496, 497, 511, 514
Bohn, M. J., 581, 591
Bois, J., 437, 448
Boling, J. C., 247, 256, 272
Bomazal, R., 249, 272
Bond, G., 465, 470, 471, 473, 474
Bond, G. R., 468, 474
Bons, P. M., 264, 272
Booth, D. A., 224, 233
Booth, J. M., 494, 514
Bootzin, R., 567, 591

Borden, B. L., 569, 591
Borden, D., 264, 272
Borden, R., 434, 448
Borgatta, E. F., 502, 514
Boring, E. G., 10, 12, 13, 18, 24, 29, 284, 318
BORMAN, W.C., 477-525; 487-89, 514
Born, M., 21, 29
Bornstein, M., 153, 169
Bornstein, M. R., 557, 591
Bornstein, P. H., 570, 591
Boruch, R. F., 621, 634
Bosma, J. F., 291, 318
Boston, M., 126, 136
Botwinick, J., 627, 634
Bouchard, T. J. Jr., 271, 272, 505, 514
Boucher, J. D., 529, 531, 549
Boucher, R., 215, 233
Boudewyns, P. A., 569, 591
Boudreau, J. C., 292, 293, 295, 318
Bougon, M. C., 259, 272
Bourne, L. E. Jr., 78, 80, 98
Boutillier, R. G., 440, 448
Bovet, M. C., 150, 151, 168, 169
Bower, G. H., 65, 85, 91, 93, 94, 98, 366, 376, 378, 386, 387, 391
Bower, T. G. R., 127, 136
Bowers, K. S., 504, 514
Bowlby, J., 116, 117, 125, 126, 136, 534, 535, 549
Bownas, D. A., 484, 486, 513, 514
Bowser, S. E., 587, 591
Box, B. M., 214, 233
Boyd, E. F., 537, 549
Boyd, V. S., 583, 591
Boyle, P. C., 221, 233
Bracht, G. H., 626, 634
Bradley, R. H., 110, 113, 115, 136, 630, 634
Bradley, R. W., 578, 591
Braida, L. D., 43-47, 56
Braitman, D. J., 340, 358
Brandt, T., 344, 354, 358
Brannigan, C. R., 528, 539, 549
Bransford, J. D., 78, 80, 96-98, 377, 391
Brass, D. J., 511, 514
Braun, J. J., 316, 318
Braunstein, D. N., 246, 272
Bray, C. W., 286, 318
Bray, D. W., 480, 510, 511, 514
Bray, G. A., 223-25, 233
Bray, R., 115, 136, 626, 634
Brazelton, T. B., 127, 128, 136, 534, 535, 549

Brehm, J., 429, 448
Breinich, S. C., 578, 591
Breisch, S. T., 229-31, 233
Breland, H. M., 498, 514
Brett, G. S., 21, 29
Bridgman, B., 631, 634
Brief, A. P., 506, 514
Brindley, G. S., 341, 355, 356, 358
Brislin, R. W., 145-47, 163, 169
Broadbent, D. E., 88, 89, 98
Broadbent, M. H. P., 88, 89, 98
Broadwell, R. D., 313, 314, 318
Brobeck, J. R., 213, 221, 223, 224, 227, 228, 233
Brodie, D. A., 89, 98
Brodsky, S. L., 181, 205
Brody, E. B., 605, 634
Brody, N., 605, 634
Broedling, L. A., 261, 272
Brogden, H. E., 480, 493, 514
Broman, S. H., 624, 634
Bronowski, J., 19, 29
Bronstein, P. W., 117, 120, 136
Brooks, C. McC., 221-24, 233
Brooks, J., 533, 536, 547, 549
Brooks, S. J., 573, 591
Brooks, V. B., 335, 336, 358
Brookshire, K. H., 117, 136
Brossard, L. M., 113, 136
Brouwer, J. N., 302, 318
Brown, C. A., 249, 272
Brown, F. G., 618, 634
Brown, G. W., 404, 406, 413
Brown, J., 86, 89, 98
Brown, J. S., 367, 369, 391
Brown, R., 65, 95, 98
Brumback, G. B., 484, 486, 514
Bruner, J. S., 528, 549
Buchanan, B. G., 367, 369, 370, 391
Buck, R., 535, 542, 543, 547-49
Buckner, D. N., 489, 514
Bugental, D., 545, 549
Bugge, I. D., 570, 591
Bunker, K. A., 505, 514
Burck, H. D., 580, 591
Burek, L., 226, 233
Burgess, P., 287, 318
Burke, B. W., 245, 272
Burlin, F., 583, 591
Burnaska, R. F., 487, 488, 514
BURNETT, K. F., 555-602
Burns, D. S., 505, 506, 514
Burns, E. M., 38, 56
Burns, H. J., 70, 71, 98
Burns, K. L., 544, 549
Burns, T., 426, 448
Burnstein, E., 426, 428, 448
Buros, O. K., 479, 514, 605, 634
Burt, M. R., 442, 448

Burton, H., 290, 305-8, 313, 318
Burton, M. J., 312, 318
Burton, R. R., 367, 369, 391
Buschke, H., 90, 98
Buschke, M., 90, 98
Buss, A. R., 245, 272, 605, 630, 634
Butcher, L. L., 215, 229, 233
Butler, J. M., 572, 573, 591
Butler, R. A., 41, 47, 56
Butler, R. P., 588, 591
Butter, C. M., 214, 233
Butterfield, D. A., 270, 272
Buttram, J., 631, 634
Butz, R., 570, 591
Buunen, T. J. F., 38, 56
Byham, W. C., 510, 514
Byrne, D., 574, 591

C

Cabanac, M., 304, 318
Cabral, R. J., 466, 474
Cairns, D., 566, 591
Calder, B. J., 262, 268, 269, 272
Caldwell, B. M., 110, 113, 115, 136, 630, 634
Caldwell, R. A., 590, 591
Callaway, J. W., 225, 233
Camp, B. W., 558, 591
Campbell, B. A., 118, 136
Campbell, D. J., 256, 262, 272
Campbell, D. R., 154, 169
Campbell, D. T., 271, 272, 458, 474, 505, 514
Campbell, J. C., 511, 514
Campbell, J. P., 251, 252, 266, 269, 271, 272, 480, 482, 483, 487, 491, 492, 504, 505, 509, 514
Campbell, K. H., 290, 318
Campbell, K. M., 262, 272
Campbell, R., 548, 549
Campbell, R. J., 480, 510, 514
Campbell, V. N., 588, 591
Campion, J. E., 513, 514
Campos, J. J., 127, 136, 533, 536, 539, 547, 549
Camras, L., 535, 549
Cannon, D. S., 117, 136
Cannon, M. W., 45, 56
Car, A., 311, 318
Carbonari, J. P., 585, 591
Carbonell, J. R., 378, 379, 391
Carey, S., 548, 549
Carhart, R., 51, 56
Carlisle, H. J., 223, 233
Carlson, J. S., 608, 634
Carlson, K. W., 572, 591
Carmody, T. P., 570, 591
Carney, C. G., 578, 581, 591

Carpenter, G., 534, 536, 540, 549
Carpenter, P. A., 373, 387, 391
Carpenter, R. G., 224, 226, 233
Carpenter, W. T. Jr., 400, 413
Carr, H., 19, 29
Carrier, S. C., 49, 53, 56
Carr-Kaffashan, L., 567, 591
CARROLL, J. B., 603-40; 604, 606, 607, 622, 634
Carroll, S. J. Jr., 256, 272
Carskaddon, G., 575, 591
Carter, A. M., 503, 514
Carter, D., 220, 233
Carter, S., 356, 358
Cartwright, D. P., 422, 428, 429, 433, 435, 448
Cartwright, D. S., 620, 634
Cartwright-Smith, J., 542, 543, 546, 547, 549
Cascio, W. F., 490, 510, 514
Cash, T. F., 505, 506, 514, 575, 591
Cashman, J. F., 268, 272
Casler, L., 113, 136
Cassady, J., 569, 591
Cassel, J., 404, 413
Castore, C., 434, 448
Cattell, R. B., 132, 136, 606, 609, 623, 632, 634
Caudill, W., 406, 409, 413
Caul, W. F., 543, 549
Ceraso, J., 85, 98
Chabot, R. J., 78, 82, 98
Chadwick-Jones, J. K., 249, 272
Chafin, B. R., 313, 318
Chaikin, A. L., 572, 573, 591
Champoux, J. E., 248, 272
Chandler, M. J., 534, 549
Chapko, M. K., 445, 448
Chapman, A. J., 535, 549
Charlesworth, W. R., 529, 532, 534-36, 549
Charnes, A. W., 504, 514
Charness, N., 72, 78, 98
Charniak, E., 378, 391
Chase, W. G., 367-69, 387, 391
Chaves, J. F., 567, 591
Cheatham, M. A., 41, 56
Cheesman, F. L. II, 80, 98
Chemers, M. M., 264, 272, 442, 448
Cheney, T., 574, 591
Cheng, C. M., 379, 391
Chernenko, G., 130, 136
Chesney, M. A., 566, 568, 591
Chess, S., 194, 195, 205, 411, 413
Chevalier, J. A., 116, 136
Chevalier, M., 426, 448
Chevalier-Skolnikoff, S., 529, 549

Chew, W. B., 503, 504, 514
Chhina, G. S., 214, 220, 221, 233
Chi, M. T. H., 622, 634
Chiang, A., 612, 634
Child, I. L., 112, 136
Childs, C. P., 153, 165, 168, 169
Chinsky, J. M., 557, 591
Chodoff, P., 407, 413
Chomsky, C., 376, 391
Chomsky, N., 108, 136
Chow, K. L., 130, 131, 136
Christiaansen, R. E., 78, 94, 98
Christie, R., 119, 136
Christy, L., 549
Chu, G. C., 430, 448
Chu, J. S., 295, 318
Chun, K. T., 479, 514
Chung, K. H., 261, 272
Churcher, J. H., 347, 358
Churchill, N. C., 504, 514
Cialdini, R. B., 434, 448
Cicchetti, D., 534, 549
Clarfield, S. P., 590, 591
Clark, H. H., 387, 391
Clark, K. B., 496, 514
Clarke, A. D. B., 104, 136
Clarke, A. M., 104, 136
Clarke-Steward, K. A., 113, 136
Clausen, J. A., 403, 413
Clazton, D., 571, 591
Cleary, T. A., 497, 498, 514
Cleff, S. H., 485, 514
Clemente, C. D., 214, 233
Cline, V. B., 544, 549
Clopton, B. M., 131, 136
Clouston, R. A., 215, 216, 233
Coates, T. J., 566, 568, 569, 591
Cobb, J. M., 588, 591
Cobb, S., 404, 413, 479, 514
Cochran, D. J., 580, 591
Coelho, G. V., 411, 413
Coghlan, J. P., 291, 318
Cohen, C., 75, 98
Cohen, L. B., 122, 136
Cohen, M. J., 286, 307, 313, 318
Cohen, R. L., 622, 634
Cohen, S. L., 255, 272, 505, 514
Colburn, H. S., 47, 49, 50, 52-56
Colby, C. Z., 546, 549
Colby, K. M., 383, 384, 391
Cole, J., 165, 169
Cole, M., 145, 153, 155, 159, 160, 163-66, 169
Cole, N. S., 497, 499, 514
Collewijn, H., 343, 344, 358

Collins, A. M., 369, 376, 378, 379, 388, 391
Collins, B. J., 210, 233, 303, 318
Collins, E. H., 213, 214, 233
Coltheart, V., 78, 98
Condon, W. S., 127, 136
Conger, A. J., 608, 634
Conger, J. C., 608, 634
Connolly, T., 253, 272
Connor, P. E., 272
Conrad, B., 335, 336, 358
Conrad, C., 387, 391
Constantin, S. W., 507, 514
Contreras, R. J., 290, 304, 305, 318
Conway, J. B., 570, 591
Conway, M., 268, 272
Cook, D., 426, 448
Cook, S. W., 433, 448
Cook, T. D., 271, 272, 505, 514
Cooley, E. J., 566, 591
Coons, E. E., 213, 233
Cooper, C. L., 465, 474
Cooper, J., 402, 413
Cooper, J. E., 401, 413
Cooper, J. F., 583, 591
Cooper, L. A., 373, 391, 619, 634
Cooper, W. W., 504, 514
Copeland, J. R. M., 401, 413
Corbit, J. D., 225, 233, 302, 318
Cornelius, E. T. III, 487, 488, 514
Corrigan, B., 495, 514
Cory, C. H., 610, 634
Coscina, D. V., 216, 230, 231, 233
Coulter, J. B., 113, 136
Covi, L., 466, 474
Cowen, E. L., 174, 205, 590, 591
Cox, D. J., 568, 591
Cox, J. R. Jr., 41, 56
Cox, P. W., 624, 634
Coyle, B. W., 491, 493, 508, 514
Craddick, R. A., 586, 591
Cragg, B. G., 131, 136
CRAIK, F. I. M., 63-102; 77, 79, 81, 98, 386, 391, 627, 634
Cramer, E. M., 54, 56
Crampon, W. J., 249, 272
Cranny, C. J., 487, 514
Crawford, J. D., 223, 227, 233, 583, 591
Creaser, J., 576, 591
Crites, J. O., 581, 591
Crockett, D. P., 117, 120, 136
Cronbach, L. J., 480, 493, 500, 514, 630, 632, 634

Crooks, L. A., 490, 514
Crosbie, P., 556, 591
Crouch, W. W., 548, 549
Crowder, R. G., 66-68, 77, 83, 87, 89, 98
Cubbage, A., 78, 98
Cudahy, E., 41, 56
Cuddy, D. R., 46, 47, 56
Culler, M. P., 625, 634
Cummings, L. L., 247, 248, 260, 262, 272
Cummings, T. G., 250, 272
Cunningham, M. R., 542, 543, 549
Curran, J. P., 559, 591
Currie, L. E., 578, 591
Cutting, J. E., 614, 634
Cynader, M., 130, 136

D

Dacey, D. M., 214, 233
Dachler, H. P., 271, 272
D'Agostino, P. R., 70, 79, 98
Dahlem, N. W., 558, 591
Dakis, C., 299, 318
Dalezman, R. E., 76, 98
Dallos, P., 40, 41, 56
Daly, M., 136
Daniels, P. D., 338, 358
Danish, S. J., 571, 591
Dansereau, F. Jr., 268, 272
Dark, V. J., 82, 98
Darley, J. G., 478, 479, 514
Darlington, R. B., 491, 497, 499, 500, 514
Darwin, C., 532, 549
Das, J. P., 613, 634
Dasen, P. R., 145, 149, 150, 158, 169
D'Augelli, A. R., 571, 591
Davenport, R. K. Jr., 131, 132, 136
David, J. D., 210, 233
Davidson, A. R., 145, 169
Davies, G., 78, 98
Davies, P., 340, 341, 358
Davis, B., 568, 591
Davis, H., 286, 318
Davis, J. D., 303, 318, 384, 391
Davis, J. H., 425, 426, 448
Davis, M. F., 46, 47, 56
Davis, R., 367, 369, 391
Davis, W. J., 335, 358
Davison, M., 115, 136, 626, 634
Dawes, R. M., 432, 448, 495, 514
Dawis, R. V., 617, 634
Dawley, H. D. Jr., 570, 591
Dawson, R., 481, 514
Day, R. S., 614, 634
Deaux, K., 506, 514

Debbane, E. G., 466, 470, 474
de Boer, E., 36, 38-41, 56
DeBoer, G., 569, 591
Decarie, T. G., 113, 136, 533, 536, 539, 549
Deci, E. L., 262, 272
Decker, G. L., 588, 591
DeCotiis, T. A., 487, 488, 514
DeFrank, R. S., 542, 543, 549
DeFries, J. C., 629, 634
DeFries, Z., 413
deGroot, A. D., 368, 391
DeGroot, J., 214, 233
Delbecq, A. L., 427, 448, 501, 514
De Leo, P. J., 254, 272
Delgado, J. M. R., 215, 233
Deliagina, T. G., 333, 358
Dell, D. M., 574, 575, 591
De Maio, J., 48, 56
Dembrowski, T. M., 437, 448
de Mowbray, J., 79, 98
DeNelsky, G. Y., 513, 514
Denenberg, V. H., 116, 118, 119, 136
DeNinno, J. A., 434, 448
DeNisi, A. S., 480, 484, 486, 514
Denney, D. R., 566, 591
Dennis, M. G., 106, 136
Dennis, W., 106, 107, 136
Denny, M. R., 613, 622, 634
Denton, D. A., 291, 318
DePaulo, B., 544, 549
Derlega, V. J., 572, 573, 591
Derogatis, L. R., 466, 474
Deslauriers, B. C., 260, 272
Desor, J. A., 304, 318
DeSoto, C. B., 504, 514
Dessler, G., 265, 272
Deutsch, M., 427, 448
DeValois, R. L., 287, 318
Devenport, L. D., 221, 227, 233
De Vore, I., 155, 169
DeVries, D. L., 259, 272, 556, 557, 591
Dewhirst, H. D., 247, 256, 257, 272
Dhawan, M., 71, 98
Diamant, H., 302, 318
Diamond, M. C., 133-36
Diamond, M. J., 466, 474
Diamond, R., 548, 549
Diaz, J., 230, 233
Di Cara, L. V., 218, 233, 316, 318
Dichgans, J., 341, 344, 354, 358
Dickinson, T. L., 488, 489, 514
Dickson, W. J., 420, 448
Diener, E., 245, 272, 431, 448
Dies, R. R., 454, 464, 468, 474

Dillard, J. M., 582, 591
Di Lollo, V., 67, 98
DiMattia, D. J., 573, 591
Dineen, G. P., 364, 391
Dinges, N., 573, 591
Dipboye, R. L., 245, 272, 506, 514
DiVesta, F., 440, 448
Docherty, J. P., 410, 413
Doetsch, G. S., 287, 289, 291, 306, 318
Dohrenwend, B. S., 408, 413
Dolliver, R. H., 586, 591
Dombrower, J., 610, 634
Domnitz, R. H., 49, 53, 56
Donald, D. E., 224, 233
Donaldson, G., 627, 634
Doniger, J., 405, 413
Dooling, D. J., 78, 94, 98
Dorr, D., 590, 591
D'Orta, C. V., 456, 474, 573, 591
Dosanjh, D. S., 35, 56
Dossett, D. L., 247, 255-57, 260, 272
Doster, J. A., 573, 591
Doty, R. W., 214, 231, 233
Dowel, W., 152, 169
Dowell, B. E., 486, 514
Downey, H. K., 265, 272
Downey, R. G., 246, 272, 513, 514
Downing, L. L., 445, 448
Doyle, K. O., 478, 514
Drabman, R. S., 569, 591
Drazin, D. H., 344, 358
Dreman, S. B., 574, 591
Drenth, P. J., 632, 634
Dressel, M. E., 586, 591
Dua, S., 214, 220, 221, 233
Dubin, J. A., 487, 514
Dubin, R., 248, 272
DuBois, P. H., 478, 514
Duda, P. D., 620, 634
Duffy, P. J., 246, 272
Duffy, R., 548, 549
Duifhuis, H., 41, 56
Dukes, F. O., 432, 448
Dumas, M., 268, 272
Duncan, J., 546, 549
Duncker, K., 365, 391
Dunham, H. W., 403, 413
Dunham, R. B., 246, 249, 272
Dunn, L. A., 152, 169
DUNNETTE, M. D., 477-525; 244, 252, 272, 480-84, 486, 487, 494, 498, 501, 504, 505, 509-11, 513, 514
Durand, D. E., 270, 272
Durlach, N. I., 36, 43-45, 52, 53, 56
Durlak, J. A., 590, 591
Durrant, J. D., 33, 56

Durrett, J. H. Jr., 620, 634
Dworkin, G., 629, 634
Dworkin, R. H., 245, 272
Dye, R. H., 48, 56
Dyer, E. D., 178, 205
Dyer, F. J., 496, 497, 514
Dyer, L., 248, 253, 254, 261, 272
Dykman, R. A., 116, 136
Dzendolet, E., 300, 318
D'Zurilla, T. J., 566, 591

E

Earles, J. A., 494, 514
Earls, F., 307, 318
Easley, J. A., 150, 169
Easter, S. S., 344, 358
Eckelman, C. C., 588, 591
Eden, D., 269, 272
Edgell, S. L., 485, 514
Edgerton, C., 153, 169
Edington, E. D., 580, 591
Edwards, J., 570, 591
Edwards, K. J., 581, 591
Edwards, R. C., 513, 514
Eells, J. F., 116, 136
Egan, D. E., 378, 379, 391, 620, 623, 634
Egan, J. P., 35, 56
Egerbladh, T., 446, 448
Eggemeier, F. T., 76, 98
Ehman, G. K., 218, 233
Eibl-Eibesfeldt, I., 532, 549
Eich, J. E., 90, 98
Eighmy, B. B., 340, 358
Einhorn, H. J., 497, 498, 514
Eisenstat, R., 544, 549
Eisner, E. J., 261, 272
EKMAN, P., 527-54; 528-31, 533, 538-40, 542, 544, 547, 549
Ekstrom, R. B., 606, 609, 616, 618, 619, 621, 634
Elardo, R., 110, 115, 136, 630, 634
Elberling, C., 35, 56
Eldredge, D. H., 35, 56
Eliot, J., 619, 634
Eliot, T. S., 21, 29
Elizur, D., 587, 591
Elkins, D., 575, 591
Ellis, D. D., 500, 514
Ellison, G., 230, 233
Ellison, G. D., 220, 233
Ellithorpe, D. B., 570, 591
Ellsworth, P., 528, 538, 542, 549
Elmasian, R., 45, 56
Ember, C. R., 148, 169
Emde, R. N., 533, 534, 536, 539, 547, 549
Emerson, P. E., 126, 136

Emerson, R. C., 352, 355, 358
Emmers, R., 305-8, 313, 318
Emswiller, T., 506, 514
Enderlein, T. E., 581, 588, 591
Engen, T., 65, 98, 304, 318
Entingh, D., 231, 233
Epstein, A. N., 213, 220, 223, 227, 229, 233
Epstein, H. T., 124, 136
Epstein, L. H., 568, 591
Erdelyi, M., 90, 98
Erdreich, J., 39, 56
Erez, M., 257, 272
Erickson, R. P., 287, 289, 291, 292, 299, 305, 306, 313, 318
Ericsson, K. A., 374, 391
Erikson, E. H., 125, 136
Erikson, J. M., 200, 205
Erlanger, J., 285, 318
Ermaine, R., 540, 549
Ernest, C. H., 620, 634
Ernits, T., 302, 318
Ernst, G. W., 368, 391
Erskine, J. A., 262, 272
Erwin, F. W., 510, 514
Essen-Moller, E., 400, 413
Estes, W. K., 75, 98, 385, 391, 604, 622, 634
Etkin, M. W., 565, 591
Evans, E. F., 35, 36, 38, 39, 56
Evans, J. D., 82-84, 98
Evans, M. G., 264, 271, 272
Evans, T. G., 379, 391
EVARTS, E. V., 327-62; 335, 336, 358
Everett, P. B., 260, 272
Ewart, C., 561, 591
Ewen, R. B., 496, 514
Exline, R. V., 530, 549
Eyman, J., 549
Eysenck, M. W., 66, 80, 81, 97, 98, 616, 621, 634

F

Faggen-Steckler, J., 495, 514
Fair, P. L., 538, 549
Fairweather, H., 631, 634
Falbo, T., 443, 448
Falender, C., 111, 113, 136
Fallik, A., 401, 413
Fangel, C., 405, 413
Farley, A. M., 378, 391
Farquhar, J., 496, 514
Farquhar, J. W., 570, 591
Farr, J. L., 262, 272, 496, 514
Farr, S. D., 622, 634
Farrow, D. L., 266, 272
Faught, W. S., 383, 391
Faulconer, B. A., 70, 98
Faull, J. R., 302, 318
Favazza, A. R., 398, 413

Favero, J., 610, 634
Feigenbaum, E. A., 364, 365, 368-70, 375, 391
Feister, A. R., 576, 591
Feldman, A. G., 333, 334, 358
Feldman, C. F., 150, 169
Feldman, H. S., 582, 591
Feldman, J., 271, 272
Feldman, S., 588, 591
Feldman, S. M., 214, 233
Fender, D. H., 347, 358
Fenske, R. H., 585, 591
Ferguson, C., 439, 448
Ferguson, J. P., 311, 318
Ferguson, N. B. L., 222, 233
Fernandes, K., 607, 634
Fernandez, C., 338, 358
Ferris, S., 544, 549
Festen, J. M., 38, 56
Festinger, L., 250, 272, 422, 431, 448
Feth, L. L., 38, 44, 56
Fibiger, H. C., 215, 216, 231, 233
Fiedler, F. E., 263, 264, 267, 268, 272, 442, 448
Fincher, J., 606, 634
Fine, B., 606, 634
Fine, S. A., 484, 514
Fink, C., 444, 448
Finkelstein, S., 90, 98, 544, 549
Finkle, R. B., 505, 510-12, 514
Finley, C., 344, 358
Finley, D. M., 487, 514
Finley, G. E., 147, 161, 169
Finn, R. H., 480, 514
Fischer, M., 401, 413
Fischer, S. D., 69, 76, 98
Fish, E., 632, 634
Fisher, A. E., 212, 232, 233
Fisher, T. J., 580, 591
Fitch, F. B., 19, 29
Fitter, M. J., 44, 56
Fjellman, J., 168, 169
Flake, M. H., 582, 591
Flanagan, J. C., 479, 514
Flast, R. H., 503, 504, 514
Flavell, J., 150, 169
Fleishman, E. A., 261, 272, 484, 486, 514
Fleming, T., 589, 591
Flexo, P. A., 466, 474
Flexser, A. J., 84, 85, 88, 89, 97, 98
Floistad, I., 408, 413
Florentine, M., 50, 56
Flores, R., 587, 591
Flowers, M. L., 429, 448
Fodor, E. M., 269, 272
Fodor, I. G., 560, 591
Folger, R., 437, 448
Follingstad, D. R., 466, 474
Fonberg, E., 214, 233

Ford, F. R., 548, 549
Ford, J. D., 267, 272
Ford, J. J., 508, 514
Foreit, K. G., 68, 98
Forest, D. J., 581, 591
Forssberg, H., 329, 358
Forster, J. D., 347, 358
Forster, J. R., 571, 591
Forsyth, G. A., 621, 634
Foshee, D. P., 117, 136
Foss, D. J., 377, 391
Foss, J. A., 230, 233
Foster, L. W., 258, 272
Fourcin, A. J., 54, 56
Fox, F. V., 251, 272
Fox, M., 545, 549
Fozard, J. L., 628, 634
Fraiberg, S., 532, 549
Frake, C. O., 164, 165, 169
FRANK, C., 173-207; 200, 205
Frank, L. L., 507, 514
FRANK, M., 283-325; 288, 290, 292-97, 299, 301, 303, 304, 306, 318
Franklin, K. B., 222, 233
Franks, J. J., 78, 80, 96-98, 377, 391
Fraser, S. C., 431, 448
Frederickson, W. A., 575, 591
Fredericson, E., 123, 136
Frederiksen, C. H., 377, 391
Frederiksen, J., 614, 634
Frederiksen, N., 615, 634
Freeman, H. E., 631, 634
Freeman, S., 434, 448
French, E., 433, 448
French, J. R. P., 422, 442, 448, 479, 514
French, J. W., 609, 616, 618, 621, 623, 634
Freud, S., 112, 115, 119, 136
Freundlich, A., 568, 591
Frey, D. H., 588, 591
Frey, P. W., 72, 98
Frey, R., 355, 358
Freyd, M., 478, 514
Frias, C. A., 402, 413
Fried, E., 549
Friedlander, B. Z., 122, 136
Friedman, A., 78, 80, 98
Friedman, B. A., 487, 488, 514
Friedman, F., 624, 634
Friedman, H., 627, 634
Friedman, L., 465, 470, 471, 473, 474
Friedman, M. I., 223-25, 227, 228, 233
Friendly, M. L., 387, 391
Friesen, W. V., 528-31, 538-40, 542, 547, 549
Frohman, L. A., 223-27, 233
Fromkin, H. L., 506, 514

Fromm, C., 335, 336, 358
Frommer, G. P., 223, 233, 305, 318
Frost, N., 612, 618, 634
Frost, P. J., 256, 272
Fry, P. S., 580, 591
Fuchs, A. F., 338, 341, 347, 350, 358
Fugita, S. S., 513, 514
Fujii, D. S., 270, 272
Fujita, B., 542, 543, 549
Fujiwara, H., 230, 231, 233
Fukson, O. I., 333, 358
Fuller, J. H., 340, 341, 347, 352, 358
Fuller, J. L., 123, 136
Funakoshi, M., 299, 305-7, 312, 318
Furr, M. L., 615, 634
Fuse, S., 215, 233

G

Gable, R. K., 582, 591
Gaensbauer, T. J., 533, 534, 536, 547, 549
Gagné, R. N., 367, 391
Galambos, R., 45, 56, 286, 318
Galbrecht, C. R., 116, 136
Galinsky, M. D., 455, 467, 474
Gallas, H., 624, 634
Ganchrow, D., 291, 318
Ganchrow, J. R., 292, 318
Garant, J., 466, 470, 474
Garattini, S., 230, 233
Garber, H. L., 111, 113, 136, 630, 634
Gardiner, J. M., 76, 98
Gardner, B. T., 108, 136
Gardner, J. R., 454, 461, 474
Gardner, R. A., 108, 136
Garfield, S. L., 178, 180, 205
Garland, H., 251, 272
Garmezy, N., 193, 196, 205
Garrett, T. L., 588, 591
Gary, T. M., 231, 233
Gascon, J., 381, 391
Gasser, H. S., 285, 318
Gaston, M. G., 222, 223, 225, 226, 233
Gastwirth, J. L., 503, 514
Gauron, E., 117, 136
Gauthier, G. M., 340, 358
Gay, J., 155, 164, 169
Gechman, A. S., 250, 272
Geesa, B. H., 53, 56
Geiselman, R. E., 69, 79, 98
Geisler, C. D., 40, 41, 56
Gelfan, S., 356, 358
Gelfand, I. M., 333, 358
Gelman, R., 165, 169
Gentner, D. R., 93, 98
Gerebtzoff, M. A., 308, 318

Gerhardt, R., 408, 413
Gerstein, G. L., 352, 355, 358
Gerwin, D., 379, 391
Gesell, A., 106, 136, 533, 535, 549
Getzels, J. W., 615, 634
Gewirtz, J. L., 537, 549
Ghezzi, D., 230, 233
Ghiselli, E. E., 480, 486, 495, 510, 514
Ghodssi, M., 108, 109, 111, 113, 114, 125, 127, 128
Giachetti, I., 313, 318
Gianetto, R., 545, 549
Gibbard, G. S., 459, 469, 470, 474
Gibbs, G., 79, 98
Gibbs, J., 210, 224, 233
Gibson, E. J., 129, 136
Gift, T. E., 408, 413
Gilbert, F. S., 559, 591
Gillen, B., 505, 506, 514
Gillis, J. S., 574, 591
Gilmartin, K. J., 366, 368, 375, 391
Gilmour, R., 544, 549
Ginsburg, H., 167, 169
Ginsburgh, S., 266, 268, 272
Gintner, G., 441, 448
Gitter, A. G., 572, 591
Gladwin, T., 163, 169
Glanstein, P. J., 582, 591
Glanzer, M., 79, 98
Glaser, R., 617, 634
Glass, A. L., 85, 98
Glass, C. R., 560, 591
Glazer, N., 502, 514
Glenberg, A., 83, 98
Glenny, J., 69, 98
Gleser, G., 480, 493, 514
Glick, J. A., 164, 168, 169
Glick, S. D., 216, 233
Globus, A., 130, 134, 136
Gluck, J. P., 132, 136
Glucksberg, S., 377, 391
Goertzel, V., 405, 413
Goetz, E. T., 64, 65, 98
Gold, R. M., 214, 229, 231, 233
Gold, T., 39, 56
Goldberg, I. A., 43, 56
Goldberg, J. M., 338, 358
Goldberg, J. P., 41, 56
Goldberg, R. A., 612, 634
Goldberg, S., 113, 136
Goldfriend, M. R., 566, 591
Golding, S. L., 493, 514
Goldman, J. K., 223-27, 233
Goldman, M., 440, 448
Goldman, R. D., 583, 591
Goldman, S. R., 74, 78, 82, 98, 614, 634
Goldstein, A. P., 574, 577, 591

Goldstein, J. J., 456, 474, 573, 591
Goldstein, J. L., 33, 36-40, 54, 56
Goldstein, M. J., 411, 413
Goldston, S. E., 174, 176, 205
Gomes-Schwartz, B., 571, 591
Gomez, H., 630, 634
Gomez, J., 408, 413
Gonshor, A., 338, 340, 358
Gonso, J., 561, 591
Gonzales, M. F., 213, 233
Goodale, J. G., 250, 272, 585, 591
Goodenough, D. R., 624, 634
Goodenough, F., 163, 169
Goodman, M. A., 573, 591
Goodman, P. S., 258, 272
Goodnow, J. J., 145, 169
Goodstein, L. D., 456, 474, 573, 591
Goodwin, G. M., 355, 357, 358
Goodwin, S. E., 558, 591
Goody, J., 165, 169
Gopal, V., 302, 318
Gordon, I. J., 188, 192, 205
Gordon, M. E., 513, 514
Gordon, T., 187, 205, 589, 591
Gordon, W., 151, 169
Gormally, J., 560, 571, 591
Gotlib, I., 573, 591
Goto, J., 301, 303, 318
Gottesfeld, H., 174, 205
Gottesman, I. I., 245, 272
Gottfredson, G. D., 178, 205, 578, 586, 591
Gottheil, E., 530, 549
Gottman, J., 561, 591
Gottman, J. M., 560, 561, 591
Gough, H., 245, 272, 505, 514
Gough, H. G., 615, 634
Gould, E., 411, 413
Gove, W., 403, 413
Graen, G., 253, 266, 268, 272
Graesser, A. II., 84, 86, 98
Graesser, C., 428, 448
Graff, H., 222, 228, 233
Graff, R. W., 582, 591
Grafton, F. C., 511, 514
Graham, J. A., 540, 549
Graham Brown, T., 329, 358
Grandall, R., 248, 272
Grandy, T. G., 585, 591
Granit, R., 330, 331, 358
Grant, D. L., 480, 510, 514
Grant, L. D., 230, 231, 233
Grant, N. G., 528, 539, 549
Grantham, D. W., 52, 56
Grater, H., 571, 591
Green, B., 376, 391
Green, C., 83, 98
Green, D. M., 34, 36, 38, 39, 41, 43, 44, 51, 56

Green, D. R., 605, 634
Green, J. D., 214, 233
Green, R. L., 496, 514
Green, S. G., 264, 270, 272
Greenacre, P., 194, 197, 205
Greenberg, D. J., 109, 113, 122, 136
Greenberg, J., 246, 269, 272
Greene, C. N., 266, 272
Greene, L. S., 304, 318
Greenfield, P. M., 149, 151, 153, 165, 168, 169
Greenhaus, J. H., 251, 272
Greeno, J. G., 366, 368, 371, 372, 379, 380, 391
Greenough, W. T., 129, 131-34, 136
Greenspan, S., 534, 549
Greenstein, S., 216, 233
Greenthal, A. L., 513, 514
Greenwood, D. D., 41, 56
Gregerian, E., 540, 549
Gregg, L. W., 365, 378-80, 385, 391
Gregory, R. L., 355, 358
Greller, M. M., 256, 272
Grey, R. J., 490, 514
Griffith, D., 78, 84, 98
Grill, H. J., 314, 315, 318
Grillner, S., 329, 358
Grimm, L., 567, 591
Grinnell, R. M. Jr., 586, 591
Grobstein, P., 130, 131, 136
Groner, D. M., 487, 488, 514
Gross, A. L., 495, 498, 500, 514
Gross, B. R., 502, 514
Gross, S. J., 577, 591
Grossman, L., 215, 217, 220, 230-33
GROSSMAN, S. P., 209-42; 210, 211, 213-15, 217-20, 223-26, 229-33
Grothe, L., 413
Grove, E. K., 76, 98
Gruen, W., 468, 474
Grunebaum, H., 454, 474
Grusec, J. E., 104, 105, 116, 118, 125, 129, 136
Guilford, J. P., 610, 634
Guion, R. M., 482-84, 486, 505, 508, 509, 513, 514
Gulanick, N., 572, 591
Gulkus, S. P., 581, 582, 591
Gunderson, E. K. E., 408, 413, 489, 514
Gurland, B. J., 401, 413
Gurman, A. S., 456, 459, 468, 474
Gurova, R. G., 160, 169
Gustafson, D. H., 427, 448, 501, 514
Gustafson, J. P., 456, 459, 468, 474

H

Haanpera, S., 510, 511, 514
Haapala, D. A., 589, 591
Haas, S., 445, 448
Haase, R. F., 573, 591
Haber, S. E., 503, 514
Haberman, S. J., 408, 413
Habicht, J. P., 168, 169
Hackett, G., 570, 591
Hackman, J. R., 246, 247, 270, 272, 507, 514
Haddad, G., 355, 358
Hadley, S. W., 460, 461, 466, 474, 571, 591
Haefner, J. E., 506, 514
Haessler, H. A., 223, 227, 233
Hafter, E. R., 48, 49, 51, 53, 56
Hage, J., 443, 448
Haggard, E. A., 124, 136
Haggarty, D. A., 425, 448
Hagiwara, S., 286, 318
Hagstrom, E. C., 302, 318
Hahn, C. P., 484, 486, 514
Haith, M. M., 127, 136
Hakel, M. D., 506, 507, 509, 514
Hakstian, A. R., 609, 623, 632, 634
Halaris, A. E., 217, 218, 220, 229-31, 233
Hales, C. N., 223, 226, 227, 233
Halff, H., 425, 448
Hall, D. F., 258, 272
Hall, D. T., 250, 258, 272, 577, 585, 591
Hall, F. S., 258, 272
Hall, J., 246, 272, 543, 549
Hall, J. A., 542, 543, 545, 549
Hall, J. L., 39, 41, 56
Hall, M., 19, 29
Hall, R. B., 569, 591
Hall, R. E., 569, 591
Hall, S. M., 569, 591
Halpern, B. P., 299, 302, 305, 318
Halpern, M., 214, 233, 248, 272
Halpern, T. P., 573, 591
Hamburg, D. A., 411, 413
Hamburg, M. D., 212, 233
Hamburg, R. L., 571, 591
Hamby, R. R., 432, 448
Hamernik, R. P., 35, 56
Hamilton, M. L., 535, 549
Hammond, D. W., 153, 169
Hamner, W. C., 257, 272, 490, 514
Han, P. W., 224, 226, 227, 233
Hand, P. J., 307, 318
Hanle, N. A., 582, 591
Hansen, J. C., 581, 591

Hansen, R. M., 352, 356, 358
Hanser, L. M., 513, 514
Hanson, G. R., 584, 591
Hanson, R. G., 466, 474
Hanson, R. W., 569, 591
Harary, F., 442, 448
Harder, D. W., 408, 413
Hardy, J. B., 631, 634
Hare, A. P., 455, 459, 462, 468, 474
Hare, P., 418, 420, 448
Harkey, B., 265, 272, 446, 448
Harkins, S. G., 446, 448
Harlan, A., 506, 514
Harlow, H. F., 107, 125, 132, 136
Harlow, M. K., 132, 136
Harman, H. H., 609, 616, 618, 621, 634
Harmon, R. J., 533, 534, 536, 549
Harper, K. J., 297, 318
Harper, R. G., 542, 543, 549
Harrington, S., 111, 113, 136
Harris, R., 314, 318
Harris, S., 168, 169
Harris, S. L., 505, 514
Harris, T. O., 404, 413
Harrison, R. A., 549
Hartley, D., 464, 474
Hartman, A., 255, 272
HARTMAN, J. J., 453-76; 459, 462, 469, 470, 473, 474
Hartup, W. W., 561, 591
Harvey, J. A., 216, 233
Harvey, O. J., 199, 205
Harwood, D. A., 377, 391
Hasazi, J. E., 188, 205
Hass, W. A., 614, 634
Hastie, R., 378, 391
Haven, W. G., 556, 591
Haviland, J., 533, 536, 547, 549
Hawkes, C. D., 231, 233
Hawkins, J. G., 578, 591
Hawley, I. B., 625, 634
Hayes, J. R., 367, 371, 372, 389, 391
Hayes, L. A., 561, 591
Haymaker, W., 212, 228, 233
Haynes, M. R., 566, 591
Haynes, S. N., 567, 591
Healy, C. C., 581, 582, 591
Heath, D. H., 587, 591
Hebb, D. O., 105, 121, 132, 136
Heber, F. R., 190, 204, 205
Heber, R., 111, 113, 136
Heberlein, T. A., 249, 272
Hebrank, J., 46, 47, 56
Heck, E. J., 571, 591
Heckman, R. W., 484, 514
Hect, R. M., 485, 514
Heffler, D., 567, 569, 591

Hegion, A., 632, 634
Heider, K., 531, 549
Heier, W. D., 263, 272
Heiman, J., 562, 591
Heimer, L., 313, 318
Heinz, S. P., 84, 98
Hekkanen, J. S., 83, 98
Hellekant, G., 302, 318
Heller, K., 180, 205, 574, 591
Hellervik, L. V., 487, 514
Hellervik, L. W., 511, 514
Hellman, R. P., 45, 56
Hellman, W. S., 45, 56
Hellriegel, D., 246, 272
Helme, W. H., 511, 514
Helmreich, R., 434, 448
Helms, J. E., 575, 591
Helper, M. M., 113, 136
Helson, H., 117, 136
Hemphill, D. P., 568, 591
Henderson, C., 533, 536, 547, 549
Henderson, D., 35, 56
Heneman, H. G., 260, 262, 272, 487-89, 506, 508, 514
Henke, P. G., 225, 233
Henn, V., 344, 358
Henneman, E., 331, 358
Hennessy, J. W., 229, 233
Henning, G. B., 51, 53, 56
Henning, H., 284, 318
Henry, J., 413
Heppner, P. P., 575, 576, 591
Herberg, L. J., 222, 233
Herold, D. M., 269, 272
Heron, A., 152, 169
Heron, W., 131, 136
Herr, E. L., 581, 591
Herrick, J. C., 311, 318
Herring, J., 481, 514
Herring, J. W., 510, 514
Hersen, M., 557, 568, 591
Herzberg, F., 252, 272
Herzberger, S., 115, 136, 626, 634
Heslin, R., 435, 448
Hess, E. H., 120, 136
Hewitt, B. N., 583, 591
Heywood, S., 347, 358
Hiatt, S., 533, 536, 539, 549
Hiji, Y., 302, 318
Hilf, F. D., 383, 384, 391
Hilgard, E. R., 568, 591
Hill, C. E., 560, 571, 591
Hill, T. E., 511, 514
Hill, W. F., 469, 471, 474
Hillery, J. M., 513, 514
Hinrichs, J. R., 510, 511, 514
Hinton, B. L., 269, 272
Hirsch, E., 223, 233
Hirsch, H. V. B., 130, 136
Hirsch, J., 629, 634
Hirsh, I. J., 35, 56
Hirsh, S. K., 35, 56

Hitch, G. J., 73, 77, 98
Ho, E., 87, 98
Hoagland, H., 285, 318
Hoch, E. L., 178, 205
Hock, H. S., 619, 634
Hoebel, B. G., 212, 222, 228-31, 233
Hoffman, B., 480, 514
Hoffman, C., 111, 113, 136
Hoffman, M. L., 534, 535, 549
Hoffman, S. D., 591
Hoffmann, K. P., 130, 136
Hogaboam, T. W., 612, 614, 634
Hogan, J. C., 630, 634
Hogan, R., 504, 514
Holcomb, W. R., 577, 591
Holland, J. E., 578, 584, 591
Holland, J. L., 505, 514, 578, 581, 584, 586, 591
Hollander, E. P., 268, 272
Hollandsworth, J. G. Jr., 586, 591
Hollenback, J. H., 249, 272
Hollmann, T. D., 487, 488, 507, 514
Hollon, S., 563, 564, 591
Holloway, R. L., 134, 136
Holmes, E., 544, 549
Holmes, F. B., 117, 136
Holroyd, K. A., 565, 568, 591
Holt, R. W., 425, 426, 448
Holzman, T. G., 617, 634
Honzik, M. P., 184, 189, 201, 205
Hood, L., 378, 391
Hood, V. G., 455, 465, 473, 474
Hood, W. R., 199, 205
Hooten, T. F., 221, 233
Hopkins, K. D., 626, 634
Hoppe, S. A., 53, 56
Hops, H., 561, 591
Horan, J. J., 570, 580, 591
Horman, A. M., 367, 391
Horn, J. L., 606, 610, 611, 614, 622, 627, 634
Horn, J. M., 623, 634
Hornung, C. A., 462, 474
Horowitz, F. D., 534, 549
Horton, C., 567, 591
Horton, D. L., 84, 98
Horwitz, L., 454, 465, 474
Horwitz, M. B., 571, 591
Hosley, M. A., 295, 318
Houk, J. C., 331, 358
House, R. J., 253, 263-65, 267, 272
Houts, P. L., 606, 634
Houtsma, A. J. M., 37, 56
Hovland, C. I., 19, 29, 574, 591
Howard, L., 576, 591
Howe, M. W., 470, 474

Howell, P., 403, 413
Howell, W. C., 483, 514
Howes, W. L., 45, 56
Hoyle, J. C., 487, 514
Hoyt, D. P., 588, 591
Hruza, E. A., 625, 634
Huang, Y. H., 230, 231, 233
Hubbell, V. R., 188, 205
Hubel, D. H., 130, 136
Huber, R. J., 621, 634
Huck, J. R., 510, 511, 514
Hudson, G. R., 580, 591
Huesmann, L. R., 379, 391
Huett, D. L., 508, 514
Huff, F. W., 117, 136
Huggins, W. H., 54, 56
Hughes, H. C., 214, 233
Hulin, C. L., 247, 248, 272
Hull, C. L., 19, 29, 119, 136, 478, 514
Hultgen, D. D., 586, 591
Hultsch, D. F., 611, 634
Humphreys, L. G., 115, 136, 496, 514, 626, 631, 632, 634
Humphries, D. A., 528, 539, 549
Hundal, P. S., 610, 611, 622, 634
Hunsinger, S., 175, 205
Hunt, A., 511, 514
Hunt, E. B., 379, 380, 391, 604, 607, 609, 612, 613, 618, 626, 634
Hunt, J. B., 266, 272
Hunt, J. G., 266, 268, 272
HUNT, J. McV., 103-43; 104-6, 108-15, 117, 118, 121, 122, 124, 125, 127-29, 131, 136, 624, 625, 634
Hunt, W. A., 528, 549
Hunter, J. E., 480, 492, 493, 496-98, 500, 513, 514
Huntington, D., 186, 205
Hurlbut, N. L., 611, 634
Hurley, J. R., 468, 474
Hurvich, L. M., 287, 318
Hustvedt, B. E., 223, 226, 227, 233
Hutchinson, M. F., 486, 514
Hyde, M., 445, 448

I

Iino, M., 307, 313, 318
Ilgen, D. R., 249, 256, 270, 272, 506, 509, 514
Imhoff, D. L., 84, 98
Imoto, T., 302, 318
Indik, B. P., 444, 448
Ingham, J. G., 404, 413
Inhelder, B., 203, 205
Inoue, S., 224, 233

Insko, C., 434, 448
Ironson, G. H., 498, 514
Irvine, S. R., 356, 358
Isaacson, R. V., 590, 591
Ishibashi, S., 212, 233
Ito, H., 302, 318
Ito, M., 341, 342, 358
Ivancevich, J. M., 254-57, 272
Iversen, S. D., 215, 233
Izard, C. E., 529, 531, 534, 536, 549
Izzo, L. D., 590, 591

J

Jablonsky, S. F., 259, 272
Jaccard, J., 249, 272
Jaccord, J. J., 430, 448
Jackson, D. N., 493, 514
Jackson, R. M., 588, 591
Jacobowitz, D. M., 229, 233
Jacobs, H. L., 223, 233
Jacobs, R., 246, 272, 487, 514
Jacobs, R. G., 566, 591
Jacobson, E., 567, 591
Jacobson, N. S., 561, 591
Jacobson, S., 534, 549
Jacoby, L. L., 82-84, 98
Jacquin, M., 314, 318
Jaffe, J., 534, 540, 549
Jakinovich, W. Jr., 301, 318
James, L. R., 247, 255, 272, 486, 514
James, W., 354, 358
Jameson, D., 287, 318
Janis, I., 427, 429, 448
Janis, I. L., 574, 591
Janssens, L., 439, 448
Janz, J. T., 480, 495, 514
Jarman, R. F., 622, 634
Jason, L., 591
Jaynes, J., 106, 118, 120, 136
Jean, A., 311, 318
Jeanneret, P. R., 487, 514
Jeanrenaud, B., 223, 233
Jeffress, L. A., 39, 47, 49, 50, 53, 55, 56
Jeffries, R., 367, 391
Jegede, R. O., 405, 413
Jencks, C., 111, 186
Jenkins, J. J., 71, 88, 98
Jennings, H. H., 420, 448
Jensen, A. R., 104, 136, 629, 631, 634
Jepsen, D. A., 578, 579, 591
Jerdee, L. H., 506, 514
Jesteadt, W., 39, 41, 44, 56
Jewell, P. A., 305, 318
Jobe, A. M., 575, 591
Joffe, J. M., 187, 195, 204, 205
Joh, T. H., 231, 233
Johns, G., 264, 265, 272, 507, 514

Johnson, A. F., 615, 634
Johnson, D., 190, 205
Johnson, D. T., 575, 591
Johnson, J. C., 513, 514
Johnson, N. S., 65, 91, 94, 98, 378, 391
Johnson, T. W., 265, 272
Johnson, V., 562, 591
Johnson-Laird, P. N., 79, 98
Johnston, M., 614, 634
Johnston, R. P., 614, 634
Johnston, W. A., 84, 98
Johnstone, J. R., 40, 56
Jones, A. P., 231, 233, 247, 255, 272
Jones, D. P., 498, 514
Jones, E. E., 251, 272
Jones, E. G., 337, 358
Jones, G. B., 585, 591
Jones, G. V., 85, 98
Jones, H. E., 109, 136
Jones, L. B., 295, 318
Jones, L. K., 571, 591
Jones, M. R., 380, 391
Jongeward, R. H. Jr., 81, 83, 98
Jordaan, J. P., 581, 591
Jordan, T. C., 628, 634
Jorgenson, D. O., 432, 448
Joseph, S. A., 228, 233
Josse, D., 533, 549
Judd, L., 411, 413
Jules-Rosette, B., 165, 169
Jung, S. M., 588, 591
Juola, J. F., 78, 82, 98
Just, M. A., 373, 387, 391
Justice, R. L., 503, 504, 514
Justis, R. J., 266, 272

K

Kaada, B. R., 215, 233
Kaelber, W. W., 231, 233
Kafry, D., 487, 489, 514
Kagan, J., 147, 161, 169, 534, 549, 631, 634
Kagawa, M., 253, 272
Kahn, A., 445
Kalat, J. W., 316, 318
Kaliszewski, J. M., 295, 318
Kalleberg, A. L., 493, 514
Kallos, T., 352, 355, 358
Kamara, A. I., 150, 169
Kane, G., 580, 591
Kanfer, F. H., 567, 591
Kanner, M., 213, 233
Kantowitz, B., 75, 98
Kapatos, G., 229, 231, 233
Kaplan, B., 402, 403, 413
Kaplan, L. B., 486, 514
Kaplan, S. J., 587, 591
Kappauf, W. E., 49, 56
Karakash, C., 223, 233

Kare, M. R., 291, 318
Karmel, B., 266, 272
Karoly, P., 556, 591
Karten, H. J., 212, 214, 233, 314, 318
Kasahara, Y., 302, 307, 312, 318
Kaswan, J., 545, 549
Katz, M. M., 401, 413
Katz, R., 248, 266, 272
Katz, W. A., 77, 98
Katzell, R. A., 496, 497, 514
Kaufman, G. G., 513, 514
Kaufman, H., 436, 439, 448
Kaufman, N., 220, 233
Kaul, T. J., 580, 591
Kavanagh, M., 259, 272
Kavanagh, M. J., 248, 272, 486, 488, 489, 514
Kawamura, Y., 307, 312, 318
Kay, P., 153, 169
Kaye, K., 534, 549
Keating, D. P., 612, 626, 634
Keaveny, T. J., 487, 514
Keeling, B., 622, 634
Keenan, J., 378, 391
Keenan, J. M., 92, 97, 98
Keesey, R. E., 221, 222, 233
Kejner, M., 250, 272
Kelem, R. T., 431, 448
Kelleghan, T., 630, 634
Keller, E. L., 338, 358
Keller, R. T., 266, 272
Kelley, H. H., 250, 261, 272, 439, 440, 448, 506, 509, 514, 574, 591
Kelley, W. J., 44, 56
Kellogg, W. N., 108, 136
Kelly, F. J., 625, 634
Kelly, G. A., 490, 509, 514, 565, 591
Kelly, J., 217, 218, 233
Kelly, J. B., 192, 198, 205
Kelso, G. I., 581, 591
Kemnitz, J. W., 221, 233
Kemper, T. D., 113, 136
Kenagy, J. G., 297, 318
Kendall, L. M., 479, 486, 514
Kendell, R. E., 401, 413
Kennedy, D., 335, 358
Kennedy, G. C., 223, 226, 227, 233
Kennedy, W. A., 624, 634
Kent, E. W., 217, 218, 233
Kent, M. A., 222, 233
Kerr, N. L., 425, 448
Kerr, S., 263-66, 272
Kessen, W., 304, 318
Kessler, M., 104, 136, 174, 193, 205
Ketkar, I., 45, 56
Kiang, N. Y. S., 40, 43, 56
Kiedel, W. D., 35, 36, 56

Kiefer, S. W., 316, 318
Kijima, H., 301, 318
Kilmann, P. R., 463, 466, 474
Kim, D. O., 41, 56
Kim, J. S., 490, 514
Kimes, H. G., 578, 591
Kimm, J., 223, 233, 338, 358
Kincaid, D. L., 430, 448
King, A. G., 503, 514
King, B. M., 222-26, 233
King, G. W., 249, 272
King, L. M., 400, 413
Kingsbury, F. A., 478, 514
Kinney, J. M., 589, 591
Kintsch, W., 91-94, 98, 369, 378, 391
Kipnis, D., 442, 448, 490, 514
Kirby, J. R., 613, 634
Kiresuk, T. J., 473, 474
Kirk, R. J., 260, 272
Kirkegaard-Sorenson, L., 398, 413
Kirker, W. S., 65, 93, 98
Kirkpatrick, J. J., 496, 514
Kirmil-Gray, K., 556, 591
Kissileff, H. R., 221, 233
Kita, H., 212, 233
Kitsikis, A., 215, 233
Klahr, D., 381, 382, 391, 624, 634
Kleck, R. E., 542, 543, 546, 547, 549
Klee, H., 76, 98
Kleiman, L. S., 513, 514
Klein, A. L., 441, 448
Klein, D. C., 176, 205, 563, 591
Klein, K., 80, 81, 97, 98
Klein, M., 197, 205
Klein, N. C., 589, 591
Klein, R. E., 147, 161, 168, 169, 631, 634
Klein, R. H., 468, 474
Klein, S., 379, 391
Klein, S. B., 556, 591
Kleinberg, J. L., 585, 591
Klerman, G. L., 538, 549
Kleugel, J. R., 493, 514
Klimoski, R. J., 489, 512, 514, 587, 591
Klix, F., 367, 391
Klorman, R., 399, 412, 413
Kluge, L., 222, 223, 233
Knigge, J. M., 228, 233
Knight, J., 291, 318
Knight, J. L. Jr., 75, 98
Knowles, E. S., 445, 448
Koenig, G. R., 462, 473, 474
Koerner, F., 343, 358
Koeze, T. H., 336, 358
Kogan, N., 422, 448, 624, 634
Kohen, A. I., 578, 591
Kohn, M. L., 400, 403, 407, 413

Koikegami, H., 215, 233
Kokes, R. F., 399, 408, 412, 413
Kolb, B., 214, 233
Kolers, P. A., 66, 73, 78, 84, 86, 93, 96-98
Komaki, J., 260, 271, 272
Komorita, S. S., 438, 448
Kopelman, R. E., 253, 254, 259, 272
Koppenaal, L., 79, 98
Korchin, S. J., 116, 136
Korman, A. K., 245, 247, 251, 265, 266, 272
Korman, M., 179, 205
Kornhauser, A. W., 478, 514
Kornmueller, A. E., 355, 358
Kosman, A. J. A., 232, 233
Kosslyn, S. M., 378, 391
Koster, E. P., 291, 318
Kotovsky, K., 365, 378, 379, 391
Kotsch, W. E., 549
Koupernik, C., 198, 205
Kovacs, M., 563, 564, 591
Kozminsky, E., 91, 94, 98
Kraft, R. N., 71, 98
Kraly, F. S., 218, 220, 224, 233
Kramer, H. C., 566, 591
Krantz, D. L., 16, 29
Krasne, F. B., 225, 233
Kraus, R. M., 590, 591
Kraut, A. I., 510, 513, 514
Krech, D., 133, 136
Krefting, L. A., 506, 514
Krettek, J. E., 313, 318
Kreuser, B., 445, 448
Kreutzer, M. A., 529, 532, 534-36, 549
Krieckhaus, E. E., 305, 318
Krivatsy, S. E., 579, 591
Kroll, N. E. A., 612, 634
Kruesi, E., 78, 79, 98
Kruger, S., 292, 293, 295, 318
KRUMBOLTZ, J. D., 555-602; 585, 591
Krutetskii, V. A., 618, 634
Krzystofiak, F., 504, 514
Kucharczyk, J., 220, 233
Kuder, F., 486, 514
Kuhlman, D. M., 440, 448
Kuhn, D., 625, 634
Kuiper, N. A., 65, 93, 98
Kulick, J., 65, 95, 98
Kulikowski, J. J., 355, 358
Kunce, J. T., 588, 591
Kuo, Z. Y., 125, 136
Kupperman, R., 427, 448
Kuppin. M. A., 379, 391
Kurtz, R., 178, 180, 205
Kuse, A. R., 630, 634
Kyle, G. W., 578, 591

L

LaBarbera, J. D., 534, 549
LaBerge, D., 389, 391
LABORATORY OF COMPARATIVE HUMAN COGNITION, 145-72; 165, 169
Labouvie-Vief, G., 611, 634
LaCross, M. B., 571, 574, 576, 591
Ladd, G. T., 21, 29
Laird, J. D., 546, 549
Laker, D. R., 248, 272
Lakey, J. R., 52, 56
Lalljee, M., 540, 549
Lamb, H. R., 405, 413
Lambert, E. F., 221-24, 233
Lambert, R. M., 48, 56
Lamendella, J. T., 548, 549
Lamm, H., 428, 448
Lamoré, P. J. J., 38, 56
Lancy, D. F., 165, 169
Landauer, T. K., 377, 391
Landgren, S., 307, 313, 318
Landin, M. L., 316, 318
Lando, H. A., 566, 570, 591
Landreth, G. E., 344, 358
Landy, F. J., 483, 487, 508, 514
Langelier, P., 215, 233
Langford, T. L., 50, 52, 53, 56
Langlois, J., 187, 188, 205
Lanman, J. M., 351, 358
Lanzetta, J. T., 542, 543, 546, 547, 549
Larcen, S. W., 557, 591
Larkin, R. P., 227, 233
Larson, J. R., 270, 272
Larson, L. L., 266, 268, 272
Larsson, S., 231, 233
Larwood, L., 259, 272
LaShells, M. B., 487, 514
Lashley, K. S., 370, 391
Latané, B., 446, 448
Latham, G. P., 247, 255-57, 260, 272, 487, 489, 514
Laughery, K., 376, 391
Laughlin, P. R., 425, 430, 448
Lave, J., 167, 169
LaVoie, J. C., 113, 136
Lawler, E. E. III, 246, 249, 252, 253, 271, 272, 489, 514
Lawler, E. J., 441, 448
Lawler, W. C., 295, 318
Lawless, H., 65, 98
Lawlis, G. F., 583, 591
Lawshe, C. H., 482, 486, 514
Lawson, M. J., 622, 634
Lazar, I., 188, 205
Lazarri, J. D., 588, 591
Lazarus, R., 411, 413

Lea, G., 379, 391
Lea, G. W., 572, 591
Leblebici, H., 268, 272
LeBoeuf, A., 566, 591
Lederberg, J., 369, 370, 391
Ledvinka, J. L., 503, 504, 514
Lee, C. L., 75, 98
Lee, N. R., 155, 169
Lee, R., 494, 514
Leff, J. P., 401, 406, 413
Lefkowitz, J., 513, 514
Lehnert, W., 378, 391
Leibowitz, S. F., 211, 213, 228, 229, 233
Leighton, D., 355, 358
Leister, A. F., 264, 267, 268, 272
Leitenberg, H., 570, 591
Leksell, L., 331, 358
LeMagnen, J., 291, 318
Le Marchand, Y., 223, 233
Lenneberg, E. H., 108, 136
Leon, C. A., 412, 413
Leonard, C. M., 308, 311, 313, 318
Leonard, D. W., 260, 272
Leonard, M., 533, 549
Lesgold, A. M., 614, 634
Leshowitz, B., 41, 56
Leshowitz, B. H., 39, 40, 56
Lesser, G. S., 631, 634
Leung, T. K., 266, 272
Levak, M., 213, 233
Levenberg, S. B., 570, 591
Levendusky, P., 567, 591
Levenstein, P., 127, 128, 136
Leventhal, G. S., 269, 272
Leviatan, U., 269, 272
Levin, H., 125, 136
Levin, J. R., 611, 634
Levine, A. G., 589, 591
Levine, J., 49, 56
Levine, M. M., 210, 233
Levine, M. S., 220, 233
Levine, M. W., 303, 318, 384, 391
Levine, R., 259, 272
Le Vine, R. A., 145, 169
Levine, S., 116, 118, 136
Levison, M. J., 223, 233
Levit, A. M., 427, 448
Levitt, D. R., 212, 216, 217, 233
Levy, L. H., 468, 471, 474
Lewin, A. Y., 490, 514
Lewin, K., 19, 29, 199, 205, 418, 448
Lewinsohn, P. M., 563, 591
Lewis, E., 163, 169
Lewis, J., 607, 612, 626, 634
Lewis, J. L., 387, 391
Lewis, K. A., 504, 514
Lewis, L. S., 447, 448

Lewis, M. M., 113, 127, 128, 136, 533, 535, 536, 547, 549, 624, 634
Lewis, P., 473, 474
Lewis, V. J., 86, 98
Lezine, I., 533, 549
Liberman, R., 457, 467, 474
Libo, L., 435, 448
Lick, J. R., 567, 569, 591
Licklider, J. C. R., 55, 56
Liebelt, R. A., 224, 233
Lieberman, A., 586, 591
Lieberman, A. F., 127, 136
Lieberman, M. A., 454, 456, 458, 459, 461, 463, 464, 467-71, 474
Liebert, R. M., 549
Lied, T. R., 254, 272
Likert, J., 427, 448
Likert, R., 427, 448
Lim, J. S., 43, 45, 56
Lin, P-C., 632, 634
Linberg, S. E., 570, 591
Lind, E., 439, 448
Lindeman, R. H., 581, 582, 591
Lindholm, B. W., 117, 136
Lindsay, P. H., 376, 391
Lindsay, R., 365, 375, 391
Lindskold, S., 441, 448
Lindvall, O., 229, 233
Linn, C. L., 220, 233
Linn, R. L., 497, 514
Linseman, M. A., 212, 233
Linsk, N., 470, 474
Lipman, R. S., 408, 413, 466, 474
Lippitt, R., 199, 205, 420, 448
Lippman, R. P., 44, 56
Lira, F. T., 565, 591
Liron, R., 401, 413
Lisberger, S. G., 341, 347, 358
Lischeron, J., 443, 448
Little, D. M., 583, 591
Little, L. F., 583, 591
Little, L. M., 559, 591
Littlefield, R. P., 572, 591
Littman, R. A., 117, 136
Liu, A. C., 225, 233
Liu, C. M., 223, 233
Ljungberg, T., 215, 216, 233
Lloreda, P., 630, 634
Lloyd, B. B., 145, 169
Lochman, J. E., 557, 591
Locke, E. A., 248, 251, 255, 258, 260, 272
Lockhart, R. S., 77, 79, 81, 98, 386, 391
Lockwood, G., 567, 591
Locurto, C. M., 615, 634
Lodahl, T., 250, 272
Loftus, E. F., 70, 71, 98, 388, 391
Loftus, G. R., 82, 98

Lohman, D. F., 612, 634
London, M., 248, 256, 257, 272, 489, 507, 514, 587, 591
Long, C. N. H., 213, 221, 228, 233
Lonner, W. J., 145-47, 163, 169
Looft, W. R., 113, 136
Lopez, F. M., 496, 514
LoPiccolo, J., 562, 591
LoPiccolo, L., 562, 591
Lord, F. M., 491, 514, 623, 634
Lord, R. G., 266, 270, 272, 442, 448
Lorden, J., 229, 230, 233
Lorden, J. F., 316, 318
Lorens, S. A., 230, 231, 233
Lorenz, K., 119, 123, 136
Lorion, R. P., 401, 413, 590, 591
Louis-Sylvestre, J., 223, 227, 233
Love, L., 545, 549
Lovo, A., 223, 226, 227, 233
Lovrinic, J. H., 33, 56
Luce, R. D., 43, 44, 56
Lucker, G. W., 557, 591
Ludvigh, E. J., 356, 358
Luetgert, M. J., 576, 591
Lukaski, H. C., 570, 591
Lumsden, J., 606, 634
Lundberg, A., 333, 358
Lundgren, D. C., 468, 474
Lundquist, G. W., 580, 591
Lunneborg, C. E., 607, 609, 612, 618, 623, 626, 634
Lunneborg, P. W., 578, 591
Luria, A. R., 159, 160, 164, 169
Lushei, E. S., 338, 358
Lyon, D. R., 622, 634
Lyon, M., 214, 233
Lytle, L. D., 220, 233

M

Maas, J. W., 230, 231, 233
Maccoby, E. F., 125, 136
Maccoby, N., 570, 591
MacDonald, H., 568, 591
MacDougall, J. M., 437, 448
Macfarlane, J. W., 184, 189, 201, 205
Machinsky, P. M., 253, 254, 272
MacKay, D. M., 356, 358
MacKay, E. M., 225, 233
MacKinney, A. C., 486, 488, 489, 514
MacKinnon, D. W., 511, 514
Mackota, C., 405, 413
MacLean, P. D., 215, 233, 307, 318

MacLeod, P., 291, 313, 318
MacWhinney, B., 92, 97, 98
Madigan, S. A., 90, 98
Madsen, B., 589, 591
Maekawa, K., 341, 358
Magoon, T. M., 579, 586, 591
Maguire, W. M., 67, 68, 98
Mahar, L., 264, 272
Maher, B. A., 245, 272
Mahoney, M. J., 558, 591
Mahoney, R. A., 256, 272
Mahoney, T. A., 503, 514
Maier, N. R. F., 426, 448
Makous, W., 306, 313, 318
Malan, D. H., 455, 461, 465, 473, 474
Maletzky, B. M., 562, 591
Maller, O., 291, 304, 318
Malmi, R. A., 621, 634
Malmstrom, E. J., 547, 549
Malpass, R. S., 145, 157, 169
Maltzman, I., 115, 136
Manaugh, T. S., 614, 634
Mandel, M. K., 538, 549
Mandel, T. S., 91, 94, 98
Manderscheid, R. W., 462, 473, 474
Mandler, G., 78, 83, 84, 86, 88, 89, 98
Mandler, J. M., 65, 71, 91, 94, 98, 119, 136, 378, 391, 631, 634
Mann, B., 573, 591
Mann, L., 427, 429, 448
Mann, M., 429, 448
Mann, R. D., 459, 462, 470, 474
Mannari, H., 249, 272
Manring, S. L., 250, 272
Maola, J., 580, 591
Marciniak, K., 425, 448
Marcus, J., 534, 549
Marcus, N., 619, 634
Margules, D. L., 229, 230, 233
Marinelli, R. P., 582, 591
Marino, R., 307, 318
Marjoribanks, K., 630, 632, 634
Markham, H., 561, 591
Marks, H. E., 222, 233
Marks, I. M., 562, 591
Marks, M. E., 620, 634
Marr, D., 341, 358
Marrazzi, M. A., 213, 214, 233
Marrow, A., 420, 448
Marsden, C. D., 337, 358
Marsh, R. M., 249, 272
Marshalek, B., 612, 634
Marshall, D. A., 287, 289, 318
Marshall, G. J., 566, 591
Marshall, J., 435, 448
Marshall, J. F., 212, 215-17, 224, 233, 314, 317, 318

Marshall, R. F., 503, 514
Marshall, W. L., 564, 591
Marslen-Wilson, W., 78, 98
Marslen-Wilson, W. D., 615, 634
Martin, B., 561, 591
Martin, M., 76, 98
Martin, R. P., 585, 591
Maruyama, G., 259, 272
Marwit, S. J., 544, 549
Marx, M. H., 118, 136
Maslow, A. H., 21, 29, 252, 272
Mason, W. A., 132, 136
Masson, M. E. J., 91, 98
Masters, W., 562, 591
Masuoka, D., 230, 233
Matarazzo, J. D., 614, 634
Matas, L., 533, 536, 540, 547, 549
Mathews, R. C., 79, 98
Matin, E., 356, 358
Matin, L., 356, 358
Matsui, T., 253, 272
Matsunami, K., 335, 336, 358
Matthews, P. B. C., 356-58
Matthews, R. W., 446, 448
Maul, G., 220, 233
Mauser, B., 252, 272
Mawhinney, T. C., 259, 260, 267, 272
Maxey, E. J., 585, 591
MAXWELL, S. E., 603-40
Mayer, J., 223, 233
Mayhew, D., 92, 97, 98
McAlister, A. L., 570, 591
McAuliffe, W. E., 440, 448
McBurney, D. H., 299, 318
McCall, M. W. Jr., 266, 272
McCall, R. B., 632, 634
McCants, K., 473, 474
McCarrell, N., 87, 88, 96-98
McCarter, R., 528, 549
McCarthy, B., 251, 272, 439, 448
McCarthy, D., 108, 136
McCarthy, K., 495, 514
McCay, B. J., 155, 169
McClearn, G. E., 629, 634
McCloskey, D. I., 357, 358
McCormick, E. J., 480, 484, 505, 514
McCown, D. A., 575, 591
McCoy, V. R., 580, 591
McCullough, J. P., 565, 566, 591
McCutcheon, N. B., 300, 318
McDaniel, M. A., 78, 80, 98
McDermott, L. J., 217, 218, 229, 233
McFadden, D., 51, 52, 56
McFall, R. M., 559, 591
McGann, A. F., 487, 514

McGeer, E. G., 215, 216, 233
McGhee, J. P., 575, 591
McGill, W. J., 41, 56
McGowan, A. S., 579, 591
McGrew, W. C., 528, 539, 549
McGuiness, B., 408, 413
McGuiness, K. C., 503, 514
McGuire, D., 573, 591
McGuire, M. D., 625, 634
McGuire, T. R., 629, 634
McIntyre, R. M., 262, 272
McKay, A., 630, 634
McKay, H., 630, 634
McKechnie, R. J., 568, 591
McKee, M. G., 513, 514
McKeever, W. F., 548, 549
McKelvey, B., 250, 272
McKemey, D. R., 254, 255, 272
McLaughlin, D. H., 585, 591
McMahon, J. T., 257, 272
McNally, M. S., 489, 514
McNulty, T. F., 567, 591
McTavish, J., 432, 448
Meacham, J. A., 145, 169
Mead, M., 530, 549
Meara, N. M., 588, 591
Medawar, P., 20, 29
Medin, D., 165, 166, 169
Medland, F. F., 513, 514
Mednick, S. A., 187, 197, 205, 398, 413
Meehl, P. E., 457, 474, 480, 514
Meek, D., 425, 448
Meeker, B. F., 462, 474
Mehrabian, A., 542, 544, 549
Mehrgardt, S., 46, 56
Meichenbaum, D., 558, 591, 615, 634
Meier, G. W., 117, 136
Meile, M. J., 223, 233
Meir, E. I., 588, 591
Meiselman, C. H., 50, 56
Mellert, V., 39, 46, 56
Mellits, E. D., 631, 634
Meltzoff, A. N., 127, 136, 534, 549
Melvill Jones, G., 338, 340, 341, 344, 358
Melzack, R., 287, 318
Mencke, R. A., 580, 591
Mendonca, J. D., 580, 591
Menn, A. Z., 405, 413
Menzel, E. W. Jr., 131, 136
Merluzzi, B. H., 580, 591
Merluzzi, T. V., 580, 591
Merton, P. A., 337, 355, 356, 358
Merzenich, M. M., 41, 56
Messe, L. A., 446, 448
Messick, S., 623, 634
Metcalfe, J., 89, 98
Metzler, J., 130, 136

Meyer, D. R., 231, 233
Meyer, E., 220, 233
Meyer, G. E., 67, 68, 98
Meyer, R. G., 568, 591
Meyer-Lohmann, J., 335, 336, 358
Mezzich, J. E., 401, 413
Micco, D. J., 214, 233
Michael, W. B., 610, 618, 634
Michener, H. A., 441, 442, 448
Michon, J. A., 371, 391
Middlemist, R. D., 259, 272
MILES, F. A., 327-62; 338, 340, 341, 347, 352, 358
Miles, M. B., 456, 458, 459, 463, 464, 468-71, 474
Miles, R. H., 264, 265, 272
Miljus, R. C., 261, 272
Milkovich, G. T., 503, 504, 514
Miller, D. G., 70, 71, 98
Miller, D. J., 625, 634
Miller, D. T., 251, 272
Miller, I. J. Jr., 300, 318
Miller, M., 314, 318
Miller, M. F., 581, 591
Miller, M. L., 369, 378, 391
Miller, N. E., 213, 222, 233
Miller, P., 404, 413
Miller, R. E., 543, 549
Miller, R. S., 439, 448
Miller, S. J., 573, 591
Miller, S. M., 407, 413
Miller, T. J., 78, 82, 98
Miller, W. R., 563, 591
Millhouse, O. E., 212, 233
Mills, A. W., 48, 56
Mills, J., 438, 448
Mills, J. H., 35, 56
Millward, R. B., 378, 391
Milner, P., 290, 318
Milsum, J., 338, 358
Mink, D., 212, 233
Minsky, M., 376, 391
Mintz, E., 214, 233
Mirabella, A., 261, 272
Mirvis, P. H., 249, 272
Mischel, W., 245, 247, 272, 411, 413, 504, 514
Miselis, R., 213, 233
Mistretta, C. M., 299, 318
Mitchel, J. O., 511, 514
Mitchel, J. S., 221, 233
Mitchell, A. M., 585, 591
Mitchell, C. L., 231, 233
Mitchell, D. C., 575, 591
Mitchell, K. M., 571, 591
Mitchell, K. R., 566, 568, 591
MITCHELL, T. R., 243-81; 246, 247, 253-57, 261, 262, 264, 265, 270, 272, 587, 591
Mitchell, V. F., 252, 272
Mittelstaedt, H., 352, 353, 355, 356, 358

Mobley, W. H., 249, 272
Moffit, C. M., 51, 56
Moffitt, W., 265, 272
Mogenson, G. J., 212-14, 220, 223, 226, 227, 233
Mohandessi, K., 108, 109, 111, 113, 114, 125, 127, 128, 136
Mohr, D. J., 132, 136
Mohr, L. B., 444, 448
Moller, A. R., 41, 56
Molnar, C. E., 41, 56
Monahan, J., 180, 205
Monk, A. F., 86, 98
Mook, D. G., 304, 318
Moore, B. C. J., 34, 38, 39, 42, 56
Moore, C. A., 624, 634
Moore, D., 438, 448
Moore, D. N., 104, 136
Moore, J., 370, 391
Moore, M. K., 127, 136, 534, 549
Moore, R. S., 104, 136
Moore, S. F., 577, 591
Moos, R. H., 409, 413
Mora, F., 312, 318
Moran, R., 567, 591
Moran, T. P., 378, 391
Morasso, P., 341, 358
Moray, N., 44, 56
Morden, C. J., 573, 591
Morgan, A. H., 568, 591
Morgan, G. A., 126, 136
Morgane, P. J., 211, 213, 215, 216, 218, 223, 232, 233
Moriarty, A. E., 184, 193, 198, 201, 205, 411, 413
Morita, H., 301, 318
Morley, L., 154, 169
Morolla, F., 115, 136
Morris, C. D., 78, 80, 97, 98
Morris, R. J., 571, 591
Morris, W., 437, 448
Morrison, A. I., 307, 318
Morrison, A. R., 307, 318
Morse, J. R., 312, 318
Morton, H. B., 337, 358
Morton, J., 68, 98
Moses, J. L., 511, 514
Mosher, K. R., 405, 413
Mosier, C. I., 491, 514
Moskowitz, H. R., 291, 304, 318
Moss, M. K., 565, 591
Mosser, D. R., 588, 591
Mossholder, K. M., 486, 514
Mossman, B. M., 411, 413
Motowidlo, S. J., 511, 514
Moudgill, P., 252, 272
Mount, M. K., 513, 514
Mowday, R. T., 246, 272
Mowrer, O. H., 114, 136

Muchinsky, P. M., 262, 272, 505, 513, 514, 585, 588, 591
MUELLER, C. G., 9-29
Mueller, C. W., 86, 98
Mueller, J., 284, 318
Mukanov, M. M., 160, 169
Mullet, G. M., 247, 272
Mullins, C. J., 494, 514
Munch, M. M., 425, 448
Munley, P. H., 582, 591
Munroe, R. H., 145, 169
Munroe, R. L., 145, 169
Munsinger, H., 629, 634
Murdock, B. B. Jr., 75, 89, 98
Murnighan, J. K., 266, 272
Murphy, C., 300, 318
Murphy, C. J., 265, 272
Murphy, G., 14, 29, 193, 205, 420, 448
Murphy, J. M., 401, 413
Murphy, K. C., 573, 591
Murphy, L., 420, 448
MURPHY, L. B., 173-207; 189, 193, 198, 199, 205, 411, 413
Murphy, W. P., 165, 169
Murray, H., 188, 205
Musante, G. J., 566, 568, 569, 591
Musicant, A. D., 50, 56
Myers, D. G., 428, 448
Myers, M., 118, 136
Myers, R. A., 582, 585, 591
Myers, R. D., 213, 233

N

Nachman, M., 225, 233, 290, 304, 316, 318
Nadel, S. F., 165, 169
Nadler, A., 585, 591
Nafe, J. P., 18, 29, 286, 318
Nafziger, D. H., 578, 581, 591
Nagamatsu, J., 253, 272
Nageotte, J., 311, 318
Nakamura, T., 212, 233
Naroll, R., 157, 169
Nauta, W. J. H., 212, 228, 233
Navon, D., 97, 98
Nay, W. R., 565, 591
Naylor, J. C., 119, 136
Nealey, S. M., 489, 514
Nebeker, D. M., 264, 272
Neff, W. D., 35, 36, 56
Neill, D. B., 220, 233
Neimark, E. D., 625, 634
Neisser, U., 20, 29
Nelson, D. L., 70, 71, 79, 98
Nelson, L. M., 305, 318
Nelson, P. D., 489, 514
Nelson, R. E., 587, 591
Nelson, T. E., 293, 318
Nelson, T. O., 78, 81, 82, 98

Nelson, V., 184, 205
Nemeroff, W. F., 507, 514
Nemeth, C., 425, 448
Nerlove, S. B., 168, 169, 631, 634
Nesselroade, J. R., 611, 634
Nestel, G., 246, 254, 272
Neufeld, G. R., 352, 355, 358
Neves, D., 367, 391
Neville, C. W. Jr., 575, 591
Nevo, B., 510, 514
Newcomb, N., 420, 448
Newcomb, T., 431, 448
Newell, A., 364-67, 370, 371, 373, 374, 376, 386, 391, 490, 514
Nezlek, J., 444, 448
Nicassio, P., 567, 591
Nicholas, W. C., 570, 591
Nichols, C. W., 352, 355, 358
Nichols, P. L., 624, 634
Nicholson, G. E., 491, 514
Nicholson, N., 249, 272
Nicolaidis, S., 213, 223, 233
Niehaus, R. J., 504, 514
Nielsen, D. W., 32, 49, 52, 56
Nilsson, H. G., 41, 56
Ninomiya, Y., 299, 305-7, 318
Nisbett, R. E., 365, 391, 490, 514
Nitsch, K. E., 96-98
Nodar, R. H., 45, 56
Noeth, R. J., 579, 591
Noma, A., 301-3, 318
Nonneman, A. J., 214, 233
Nord, S. G., 306, 311, 313, 318
Nord, W. R., 270, 272
Nordmark, J. O., 51, 56
NORGREN, R., 283-325; 228, 233, 305, 307-16, 318
Norman, D. A., 65, 96-98, 376, 377, 391
Northcutt, R. G., 344, 358
Notarius, C., 561, 591
Notz, W. W., 262, 272
Novaco, R. W., 558, 591
Novak, G. S., 369, 372, 391
Novick, M. R., 500, 514
Novin, D., 210, 213, 224, 228, 233
Nowlis, G. H., 296, 299, 304, 316, 318
Nuckols, T. E., 578, 591
Nudler, S., 575, 591
Nuetzel, J. M., 48, 51, 56
Nuttin, J. R., 439, 448
Nystrom, M., 539, 549

O

Oakley, B., 295, 297, 300, 301, 306, 313, 318
O'Brien, G. E., 442, 448
O'Connell, M. J., 248, 272

O'Connor, E. J., 496, 514
O'Day, R., 469, 474
Oden, S. L., 560, 561, 591
Oetting, E. R., 573, 591
Ofsanko, F. J., 481, 514
Ogawa, H., 292, 293, 296-99, 301, 302, 311, 313, 318
Ohlde, C. D., 580, 591
Ohtsuka, Y., 253, 272
Oishi, R., 230, 231, 233
O'Kulitch, P., 569, 591
Okun, M., 440, 448
Oldham, G. R., 246, 247, 253, 254, 256, 257, 267, 272, 511, 514
Olds, J., 212, 213, 233, 290, 295, 318
O'Leary, B. S., 496, 514
O'Leary, J. L., 311, 318
O'Leary, K. D., 556, 591
O'Leary, S. G., 556, 591
Oliver, L. W., 583, 584, 591
Oliver, R. L., 510, 514
Olsson, U., 626, 634
Oltmans, G. A., 216, 229, 230, 233
O'Malley, H., 38, 56
Oman, M., 398, 413
Omvig, C. P., 582, 591
One, T., 212, 233
O'Neill, B. J., 70, 79, 98
O'Neill, M. E., 76, 98
Oomura, Y., 212-14, 233
Ooshima, Y., 307, 313, 318
Opsahl, C. A., 224, 226, 233
Oravec, J., 318
Ore, G., 232, 233
O'Reilly, C. A. III, 246, 266, 272
Organ, D. W., 248, 272
Orlansky, H., 112, 136
Orlovsky, G. N., 333, 334, 358
Ortony, A., 64, 65, 98
Osborn, R. N., 266, 268, 272
Osburn, H. G., 487, 510, 514
Osipow, S. H., 577, 578, 591
Osman, E., 53, 54, 56
OSTER, H., 527-54; 533, 536, 549
O'Sullivan, M., 549, 610, 634
Osumi, Y., 230, 231, 233
Otaala, B., 150, 169
Otis, M., 560, 591
Ottosson, J. O., 400, 413
Owen, T. W., 489, 514
Owens, J., 65, 93, 94, 98
Owens, W. A., 505, 509, 514
Ozeki, M., 300, 318

P

Pace, L. A., 510, 514
Page, R. A., 573, 591
Paige, J. M., 372, 391

Paivio, A., 70, 71, 79, 85, 97, 98, 619, 634
Palef, S. R., 86, 93, 98
Palkovits, M., 229, 233
Palmer, S. E., 378, 391
Pandya, D. N., 337, 358
Pangborn, R. M., 304, 318
Pankratz, L., 567, 591
Panksepp, J., 223, 233
Papousek, H., 127, 128, 136, 534, 549
Papousek, M., 127, 128, 136, 534, 549
Paraskevopoulos, J., 109, 111, 113, 115, 136
Paredes, A., 530, 549
Parham, I. A., 245, 272, 627, 634
Parisi, S. A., 534, 549
Parke, R. D., 114, 126, 136
Parker, D., 253, 254, 261, 272
Parker, R., 586, 591
Parker, S. W., 214, 233
Parker, T., 632, 634
Parkison, R. C., 383, 391
Parks, T. E., 612, 634
Parloff, M. B., 454, 458, 459, 464, 472, 474
Parsons, B. V., 589, 591
Pasanen, E. G., 51, 52, 56
Pasino, J. A., 566, 591
Paterson, D. G., 478-80, 514
Paton, A., 466, 474
Patrick, T. A., 582, 591
Patterson, G. R., 561, 589, 591
Patterson, K. E., 71, 89, 98
Patterson, L. W., 580, 591
Pattison, J. H., 466, 474
Patton, H., 307, 318
Patton, H. D., 307, 318
Paulson, R., 92, 98
Paulus, P. B., 446, 448
Pavlova, G. A., 333, 358
Paxinos, G., 226, 229, 231, 233
Paykel, E. S., 408, 413
Pearce, D. G., 356, 358
Pearce, J. L., 246, 272
Pearce, M. G., 260, 271, 272
Pearson, J., 437, 448
Pearson, K., 329, 358
Peck, J. W., 213, 233
Pedersen, F. A., 111, 113, 114, 136
Peeler, D. F., 117, 136
Pellegrino, J. W., 71, 78, 82, 98, 612, 617, 634
Peng, S. S., 622, 634
Penner, M. J., 41, 56
Peoples, V. Y., 574, 591
Pepitone, A., 431, 448
Pereira, F., 118, 136
Perfetti, C. A., 74, 98, 614, 634
Perkins, D. T., 19, 29
Perl, E. R., 287, 318

Perris, C., 400, 413
Perrone, P. A., 578, 591
Perrott, D. R., 50, 56
Perrotto, R. S., 308, 318
Perry, D. F., 573, 591
Perry, J. H., 233
Peters, J. E., 116, 136
Peters, L. H., 254, 272, 507, 514
Peters, R. H., 222, 233
Petersen, N. S., 500, 514
Peterson, L. R., 75, 98
Peterson, N. G., 486, 514
Peterson, R. B., 259, 272
Pettibone, D., 220, 233
Pettigrew, J. D., 130, 136
Petty, M. M., 264, 265, 272
Petty, R. E., 446, 448
Pew, S., 575, 576, 591
Pezdek, K., 70, 71, 98
Pfaffenberger, C. J., 125, 136
PFAFFMANN, C., 283-325; 117, 136, 285-87, 290-92, 297, 299, 302-6, 308-10, 313, 314, 318
Pfeffer, J., 252, 266, 269, 272
Pfeifer, W. D., 118, 136
Pfeiffer, R. R., 41, 56
Phelps, R. W., 130, 136
Phillips, A. G., 215, 216, 233
Phillips, C. G., 335, 336, 358
Phillips, R. V., 84, 98
PIAGET, J., 1-8; 106, 122, 136, 149, 169, 203, 205
Pichert, J. W., 64, 65, 84, 95, 98
Pickel, V. M., 231, 233
Pieper, A., 532, 533, 535, 549
Pierce, J. L., 246, 272
Pilato, G. T., 585, 591
Pillsbury, W. B., 11, 29
Pinder, C. C., 262, 272
Pine, S. M., 496, 514
Pinkston, E. M., 470, 474
Pinto, P. R., 484, 514
Piper, W. E., 466, 470, 474
Planert, N., 47, 56
Platnick, D. M., 614, 634
Platt, J. J., 557, 590, 591
Plemons, J. K., 611, 629, 634
Plomin, R., 629, 634
Plomp, R., 36, 37, 39, 41, 56
Plotkin, L., 496, 514
Pohlmann, L. D., 54, 56
Poirier, L. J., 215, 233
Polanco, R., 118, 136
Poley, W., 605, 634
Pollack, I., 53, 56
Polson, P. G., 367, 391
Pomerantz, J. R., 378, 391
Pondy, L. R., 440, 448
Poortinga, Y. H., 145, 169
Pope, B., 575, 591
Pople, H., 369, 370, 391

Popper, K. R., 17, 29
Porter, J. H., 222, 233
Porter, L. W., 246, 249, 253, 255, 272
Posner, M. I., 387, 391
Postman, L., 78, 79, 98
Potter, M. C., 70, 98
Powley, T. L., 221, 223-28, 233
Pratt, R. J., 122, 136
Prediger, D. J., 579, 584, 591
Pribram, K. H., 135, 136
Price, J. L., 313, 318
Price, K. H., 251, 272
Price, L., 619, 634
Price, M. G., 567, 591
Price, M. T. C., 231, 233
Price-Williams, D. R., 145, 151, 153, 169
Prien, E. P., 482, 484, 486, 514
Primoff, E. S., 484, 486, 514
Prince, H. T. II, 566, 591
Pritchard, D. A., 495, 514
Pritchard, R. D., 251, 254, 260, 262, 272
Progoff, I., 20, 29
Puckett, S. P., 566, 591
Pumphrey, R. J., 39, 56, 285, 318
Pursell, E. D., 260, 272, 487, 514
Pyle, K. R., 582, 591

Q

Quackenbush, P. M., 229, 233
Quartermain, D., 316, 318
Quay, H. C., 117, 136
Querido, A., 224, 233
Quillian, M. R., 366, 376, 377, 388, 391

R

Raab, D. H., 42, 43, 56
Raab, E. S., 401, 413
Raaheim, K., 617, 634
Raatgever, J., 55, 56
Rabbitt, P. M. A., 628, 634
Rabin, B. M., 224, 233
Rabinowitz, J. C., 88, 89, 98
Rabinowitz, S., 250, 272
Rabinowitz, W. M., 43, 45, 56
Rabkin, J. G., 408, 413
Racine, A. E., 588, 591
Radtke, R. C., 76, 98
Rahe, R., 408, 413
Rahim, S. A., 430, 448
Rainey, L., 560, 591
Ramanaiah, N., 633, 634
Ramirez, M., 151, 169
Ramsay, D., 536, 549
Ramsey, A. O., 120, 136
Rand, T. M., 489, 507, 514
Randall, P. K., 229, 230, 233

Rao, C. R., 202, 205
Rashbass, C., 350, 358
Raskin, D. C., 115, 136
Rauschenberger, J., 491, 514
Rauschenberger, J. M., 498, 500, 514
Raven, B., 422, 442, 448
Rawlings, L., 75, 98
Razran, L., 367, 391
Reardon, R. C., 580, 591
Reddy, B. G., 80, 98
Reder, L. M., 79, 81, 98
Redican, W. K., 529, 532, 549
Redman, G., 76, 98
Redmond, D. E., 230, 231, 233
Reed, S. K., 367, 368, 391
Reeves, A., 307, 318
Reich, M. J., 222, 233
Reichler, M. L., 113, 136
Reilly, R. R., 497, 514
Reinharth, L., 253, 272
Reis, D. J., 231, 233
Reiss, D., 407, 413
Reitman, J. S., 368, 391
Reitman, W. R., 375, 391
Relinger, H., 570, 591
Remley, N. R., 222, 233
Renner, K. E., 119, 136
Resnick, L. B., 164, 165, 169, 387, 391, 605, 634
Resnick, S. B., 44, 56
Restle, F., 378, 380, 391
Reswick, J. B., 347, 358
Revers. R. R., 445, 448
Revlis, R., 378, 391
Reynolds, L. G., 503, 514
Reynolds, P., 75, 98
Reynolds, R. W., 223, 233
Rezak, M., 218, 233
Rezek, M., 224, 233
Rezk, M., 118, 136
Rheingold, H. L., 126, 136
Rhode, J. G., 246, 272
Rhode, W. S., 40, 56
Rhoton, A. L. Jr., 311, 318
Ribble, M. A., 116, 136
Ribich, F., 633, 634
Ribordy, S. C., 566, 591
Ricard, G., 41, 56
Ricciuti, H. N., 126, 136
Rice, L. N., 572, 591
Rich, A. R., 559, 565, 591
Richards, D. L., 79, 98
Richards, L., 610, 634
Richards, L. G., 614, 634
Richardson, A., 620, 634
Richardson, J. S., 215-17, 233, 314, 318
Richardson, M. S., 583, 584, 591
Richmond, C., 405, 413
Richter, C. P., 231, 233, 288, 290, 302, 303, 318
Riegel, K. F., 145, 169

Rieger, C., 369, 391
Ries, P. G., 625, 634
Riesen, A. H., 128-32, 136
Rin, H., 406, 413
Ringdal, R., 408, 413
Rips, L. J., 376, 378, 391
Ritchey, G. H., 71, 98
Ritter, R. C., 213, 229, 233
Ritzler, B. A., 408, 413
Roach, A. J. Jr., 582, 583, 591
Roback, H. B., 456, 464, 466, 468, 474
Roberge, A., 215, 233
Roberts, B. L., 335, 358
Roberts, D. C. S., 231, 233
Roberts, J. M., 168, 169
Roberts, K. H., 247, 266, 272
Roberts, W. W., 212, 233
Robertson-Tchabo, E., 627, 634
Robinot, F., 533, 549
Robinson, C. E., 53, 56
Robinson, D. A., 338, 340, 341, 347, 350, 352, 358
ROBINSON, D. E., 31-61; 52, 53, 56
Robinson, D. L., 335, 358
Robinson, D. N., 13, 29
Robinson, E. A., 466, 474
Robles, L., 40, 56
Rocissano, L., 378, 391
Rodnick, E., 411, 413
Roederer, J. G., 33, 56
Roediger, H. L. III, 75, 86, 98
Roethlisberger, F. J., 420, 448
Rogers, C. M., 131, 132, 136
Rogers, P., 544, 549
Rogers, T. B., 65, 93, 98
Rogoff, B., 147, 161, 168, 169
Rohrbaugh, M., 471, 474
Rolf, J. E., 188, 205
Rolls, B. J., 316, 318
Rolls, E. T., 122, 213, 233, 312, 316, 318
Roman, C., 311, 318
Romashko, T., 484, 486, 514
Ronan, W. W., 489, 514, 588, 591
Ronnestad, M. H., 572, 591
Rooth, F. G., 562, 591
Roper, G., 534, 549
Rorer, L. G., 495, 514
Rosch, E., 153, 154, 169
Rosche, M., 188, 205
Rose, A. M., 607, 634
Rose, S. D., 467, 470, 472, 474, 560, 591
Rosen, B., 506, 514
Rosenberg, E. J., 408, 413
Rosenberg, S., 377, 378, 391
Rosenblum, L. A., 127, 136, 535, 549
Rosenblum, M., 502, 514
Rosenbluth, D., 126, 136
Rosenfeld, H. M., 534, 549

Rosenfield, D., 557, 591
Rosenquist, A. C., 352, 355, 358
Rosenthal, A. T., 407, 413
Rosenthal, R., 542-45, 549
Rosenzweig, M. R., 131-36
Ross, A. C., 178, 205
Ross, J. F., 231, 233
Ross, R., 19, 29
Rosse, R. L., 486, 492, 513, 514
Rossignol, S., 329, 358
Roth, C. H., 576, 591
Roth, D. R., 629, 634
Roth, G. L., 41, 56
Roth, J. D., 579, 591
Roth, S. R., 316, 318
Rothwell, N., 405, 413
Rotundo, R., 118, 136
Rouchouse, J., 533, 549
Rountree, C., 437, 448
Rowan, J., 458, 474
Rowe, E. J., 68, 98
Rowe, P. M., 507, 514
Rowe, W. G., 68, 98
Rowland, K. M., 247, 268, 272
Rowland, N., 223, 233
Rowland, N. E., 212, 233
Royce, J., 188, 205
Royce, J. R., 609, 634
Ruben, R. J., 35, 56
Rubenstein, J. L., 111, 113, 114, 136
Rubin, D. C., 92, 93, 98
Rubin, Z., 443, 448
Ruch, T. C., 307, 318
Ruda, E., 496, 514
Ruderman, M. I., 307, 318
Rudestam, K. E., 576, 591
Ruggero, M. A., 43, 56
Ruh, R. A., 250, 272
Rumelhart, D. E., 64, 65, 84, 91, 93, 98, 376-78, 391
Rundus, D., 83, 98
Rupert, P. A., 566, 591
Rush, A. J., 563, 564, 591
Rush, M. C., 270, 272
Russek, M., 223, 233
Russell, I. J., 335, 358
Russell, J. T., 493, 514
Rutter, M., 400, 413
Ryan, E. B., 625, 634
Ryen, A. H., 445, 448
Ryman, D. H., 510, 514

S

Saal, F. E., 487, 514
Saari, B. B., 493, 514
Saari, L. M., 255, 256, 272
Saarni, C., 536, 537, 549
Sachs, M. B., 41-43, 56
Sacks, H. V., 616, 634
Sacksteder, J., 399, 412, 413

Saha, G. B., 529, 531, 549
Sakitt, B., 67, 98
Saku, C., 302, 318
Sala, L. S., 91, 98
Salama, A. A., 112, 117, 121, 136
Salancik, G. R., 244, 249, 252, 268, 272
Salisbury, R., 223, 233
Salkind, I., 405, 413
Saller, C. F., 230, 231, 233
Salomon, G., 35, 56
Salt, P., 538, 549
Saltz, E., 80, 81, 97, 98
Saltzman, C., 576, 591
Samaha, G., 437, 448
Samanin, R., 230, 233
Sameroff, A., 399, 413
Samuel, W., 631, 634
Samuels, S. J., 389, 391
Sanborn, K. O., 401, 413
Sanchez-Craig, B. M., 560, 591
Sandberg, T., 622, 634
Sandel, T. T., 53, 56
Sander, L. W., 127, 136
Sanderson, J. D., 210, 233
Sands, W. A., 513, 514
Sanford, N., 177, 205
Sank, L. I., 566, 591
Santa, J. L., 85, 86, 98
Sarason, F. G., 245, 272
Sarason, I. G., 566, 591
Sartorius, N., 402, 413
Sato, M., 289, 292, 293, 296-303, 313, 318
Saunders, J., 300, 318
Savin, V. J., 543, 549
Savitsky, J. C., 549
Sawcheko, P. E., 231, 233
Sawin, D., 187, 188, 205
Scally, M. C., 220, 233
Scandura, J. M., 617, 634
Scanlan, T., 587, 591
Schachter, S., 436, 448
Schacknow, P. N., 43, 56
Schaeffer, C., 468, 474
Schaffer, H. R., 126-28, 136
Schaffer, J. B. P., 455, 467, 474
Schaie, K. W., 245, 272, 627, 628, 634
Schallert, D. L., 64, 65, 98
Schank, R. C., 65, 98, 376-78, 391
Scharf, B., 45, 50, 56
Scheff, T. J., 403, 413
Scheid, A. B., 575, 591
Scheips, C. D., 480, 514
Scher, M., 575, 576, 591
Scherer, K. R., 545, 549
Scherer, U., 545, 549
Schickedanz, D., 111, 136
Schiemann, W., 268, 272
Schiff, B. B., 220, 233

Schiffenbauer, A., 543, 549
Schiffman, S. S., 299, 318
Schiller, P. H., 338, 343, 358
Schinke, S. P., 560, 591
Schkade, J. K., 446, 448
Schlenker, B. R., 251, 272, 438, 439, 448
Schlitz, E. A., 132, 136
Schlitz, K. A., 132, 136
Schlosberg, H., 118, 136, 528, 549
Schmeck, R. R., 572, 591, 633, 634
Schmidt, C. F., 383, 391
Schmidt, F. L., 480, 481, 486, 492, 493, 496-98, 500, 513, 514
Schmidt, L. D., 575, 591
Schmitt, N., 491, 493, 505, 508, 511, 514
Schnatz, J. D., 223-27, 233
Schneider, B., 483, 514
Schneider, D., 291, 318
Schneider, D. J., 489, 490, 514
Schneider, W., 73, 74, 97, 98, 386, 388, 389, 391
Schneiderman, M. L., 507, 514
Schneier, C. E., 488, 489, 514
Schnitzen, J. P., 585, 591
Schnuelle, L., 579, 591
Schoenfeldt, L. F., 509, 510, 514
Schoggen, M. F., 115, 136
Scholer, C., 406, 413
Schrader, A. D., 510, 514
Schriesheim, C. A., 255, 263-66, 272
Schroeder, H. E., 559, 565, 591
Schroeder, M. R., 35, 36, 41, 56
Schuchart, G. E., 445, 448
Schuler, R. S., 265, 272
Schultheis, L. W., 340, 341, 358
Schultz, D., 16, 29
Schutz, W., 458, 474
Schwab, D. P., 487, 488, 508, 510, 514
Schwartz, D. J., 513, 514
Schwartz, G. E., 538, 549
Schwartz, J. M., 468, 474
Schwartz, M., 316, 318
Schwartz, M. S., 409, 413
Schwartz, R. M., 560, 591
Schwartz, S., 612, 623, 634
Schwartz, S. P., 378, 391
Schwartzbaum, J. S., 220, 232, 233, 312, 318
Sciarrino, J. A., 513, 514
Sclafani, A., 220, 222, 223, 229, 231, 233
Scott, C. S., 585, 591
Scott, J. H., 116, 136

Scott, J. P., 115, 120, 123, 125, 136
Scott, J. W., 313, 318
Scott, K. D., 247, 272
Scott, T. R., 308, 318
Scott, T. R. Jr., 291, 306, 318
Scott, W. E., 490, 514
Scott, W. E. Jr., 262, 267, 272
Scribner, S., 145, 153, 159, 163-66, 169
Seaford, H. W., 531, 540, 549
Seals, G. W., 248, 272
Searle, C. L., 46, 47, 56
Sears, R. R., 112, 125, 136
Seaton, F. W., 513, 514
Sechrest, L., 146, 169
Sechrest, L. B., 574, 591
Sechzer, J. A., 224, 233
Sedney, M. A., 584, 591
Seidman, E., 493, 514
Sekaran, U., 250, 272
Selfridge, O., 364, 391
Seligman, M. E. P., 408, 413, 563, 591
Selinger, H. V., 557, 591
Selz, O., 365, 391
Selzer, U., 115, 136, 626, 634
Sensenig, L. D., 222, 233
Serpell, R., 145, 155, 158, 168, 169
Seta, J. J., 446, 448
Severin, F. V., 333, 358
Sewell, T. E., 585, 591
Sewell, W. H., 112, 136
Seymore, J. P., 260, 272
Shaffer, D., 400, 413
Shaklee, H., 432, 448
Shakow, D., 193, 195, 205
Shank, J. K., 504, 514
Shapira, Z., 262, 267, 272
Shapiro, J. G., 544, 549
Shapiro, L. J., 466, 474
Shapiro, R. J., 468, 474
Sharp, D. W., 164, 169
Sharpe, L., 401, 413
Shaw, B. F., 564, 591
Shaw, E. A. G., 45, 46, 56
Shaw, J., 573, 591
Shaw, J. B., 480, 484, 514
Shaw, J. C., 364, 391, 490, 514
Shaw, M. E., 265, 272, 446, 448
Shelton, J. L., 568, 591
Shelton, R. L., 615, 634
Shepard, R. N., 619, 634
Shepherd, M., 400, 413
Sheridan, J. D., 336, 358
Sheridan, J. E., 265, 272
Sheridan, T. B., 427, 448
Sherif, C. W., 199, 205
Sherif, M., 199, 205
Sherman, G., 587, 591
Sherman, R. E., 473, 474

Sherman, S. M., 130, 136
Sherrington, C. S., 328-30, 352, 354, 358
Shick, T. R., 299, 318
Shiffrin, R. M., 73-75, 97, 98, 385, 386, 388, 389, 391
Shiflett, S., 246, 272
Shik, M. L., 333, 358
Shimada, I., 301, 318
Shimizu, N., 212, 233
Shiraishi, A., 301, 318
Shmurak, S. H., 560, 591
Shoben, E. J., 376, 378, 391
Shooter, A. M. N., 455, 465, 473, 474
Short, E. J., 625, 634
Shortliffe, E. H., 367, 369, 370, 391
Shulman, A. D., 544, 549
Shultz, T. R., 534, 549
Shure, M. B., 557, 590, 591
Shweder, R. A., 504, 514
Sides, H., 567, 591
Siebeck, R., 355, 358
Siegler, R. S., 165, 169, 382, 391, 625, 634
Siess, T. F., 580, 591
Sikes, J., 557, 591
Siklóssy, L., 379, 382, 391
Silberfeld, M., 404, 413
Silbergeld, S., 462, 473, 474
Silverman, S. R., 35, 56
Silverstein, A. B., 608, 634
Silzer, R. F., 511, 514
Simmons, R. F., 376, 391
Simon, D. P., 367, 369, 391
SIMON, H. A., 363-96; 364-80, 385, 386, 389, 391, 490, 514
Simon, R., 401, 413
Simons, J. A., 575, 591
Simons, J. B., 567, 591
Simonson, N. R., 573, 577, 591
Simpson, J. I., 341, 358
Sims, H. P. Jr., 246, 254, 255, 267, 272
Sims, S. L., 39, 56
Singer, M. T., 407, 413
Singh, B., 214, 233
Singh, D., 222, 225, 226, 231, 233
Singleton, C. H., 614, 634
Sinisterra, L., 630, 634
Sintnicolaas, K., 55, 56
Siple, P., 69, 76, 98, 378, 391
Skavenski, A. A., 338, 341, 352, 355-58
Skeels, H. M., 190, 205
Skenazy, J. A., 566, 591
Skinner, B. F., 259, 272
Skodak, M., 190, 205
Skodak Crissey, M., 190, 205
Skultety, F. M., 231, 233

Slavin, R. E., 556, 557, 591
Slick, T. B., 316, 318
Slocum, J. W., 246, 272
Slocum, J. W. Jr., 265, 272
Small, A. M. Jr., 44, 56
Smart, C., 427, 448
Smith, D. R., 352, 358
Smith, D. V., 299, 300, 306, 311, 318
Smith, E. C. Jr., 367, 391
Smith, E. E., 376, 378, 391
Smith, E. J., 582, 591
Smith, F. J., 247, 249, 272
Smith, G. P., 210, 224, 233
Smith, H. A., 427, 448
Smith, J. C., 291, 318
Smith, J. E., 466, 474
Smith, M. H., 223, 233
Smith, P. B., 454, 464, 474
Smith, P. C., 479, 486, 487, 505, 514
Smith, R. E., 245, 272
Smith, R. P., 538, 549
Smith, S. M., 83, 98
Smith, V. K., 466, 474
Smoorenburg, G. F., 36, 40, 56
Smutz, E. R., 223, 233
Smyser, C. M., 246, 254, 272
Snell, T. L., 292, 303, 318
Snow, R. E., 612, 630, 632, 634
Snyder, D. R., 214, 233
Snyder, R. D., 230, 231, 233
Snyderman, B., 252, 272
Sokolich, W. G., 45, 56
Solano, C., 504, 514
Soloman, T., 246, 272
Solomon, R. J., 266, 272
Solomon, R. L., 118, 121, 136
Sonkin, L., 510, 514
Sontag, L. W., 184, 205
Soraci, S. Jr., 251, 272, 439, 448
Sorensen, J. E., 246, 272
Sorensen, J. P., 230, 231, 233
Sorenson, C. A., 220, 233
Sorenson, E. R., 529, 531, 549
Sorkin, R. D., 54, 56
Sorrentino, R. M., 440, 448
Sotile, W. M., 463, 466, 474
Spalding, D., 614, 634
Spanos, N. P., 567, 591
Sparks, C. P., 481, 514
Sparks, D. L., 221, 233
Spearritt, D., 614, 634
Spegel, S. B., 575, 591
Spencer, D. G., 246, 272
Sperry, R. W., 352, 353, 358
Spiegler, M. D., 566, 591
Spinelli, D. N., 130, 136
Spitz, R. A., 113, 116, 136
Spitzer, C. E., 425, 426, 448
Spivack, G., 557, 590, 591
Spring, B., 631, 634

Springbett, B. M., 507, 514
Spyropoulos, T., 85, 98
Sroufe, L. A., 533, 534, 536, 540, 547, 549
Stagner, R., 504, 514
Stahelski, A. J., 440, 448
Stahmann, R. F., 585, 591
Stamoutsos, B. A., 223, 224, 226, 233
Stancer, H. C., 230, 233
Stanley, J. C., 458, 474, 496, 514
Stanton, A. H., 409, 413
Stark, L., 347, 358
Stasser, G., 425, 426, 448
Staw, B. M., 244, 251, 262, 272
Stayton, D. J., 126, 136
Stebbins, L. W., 573, 591
Stebbins, M. W., 255, 272
Stechler, G., 534, 536, 540, 549
Steers, R. M., 246, 249, 250, 255-57, 272, 435, 448
Steffens, A. B., 223, 226, 227, 233
Steffre, V., 154, 169
Steg, G., 216, 233
Stein, A., 436, 448
Stein, B. S., 78, 80, 98
Stein, C., 491, 514
Stein, M. I., 615, 634
Stein, N. L., 631, 634
Steinbach, M. J., 352, 358
Steinberg, B. M., 152, 169
Steiner, I. D., 420, 424, 448
Steiner, J. E., 304, 315, 318, 533, 549
Steinman, R. M., 355, 358
Stellar, E., 118, 136, 211, 222, 223, 228, 233, 302-4, 318
Stellon, C. C., 86, 98
Stendler, C., 124, 136
Stenning, W. F., 582, 591
Stern, D. N., 534, 540, 549
Stern, S. L., 577, 591
Sternberg, R. J., 90, 98, 387, 391, 607, 616, 617, 634
Sternberg, S., 387, 388, 391
Stevens, J., 586, 591
Stevens, J. K., 352, 355, 358
Stevens, K. V., 64, 65, 98
Stevens, L., 251, 272
Stevens, S. S., 35, 56
Stevenson, H. W., 632, 634
Stevenson, J. A. F., 213, 222, 223, 226, 227, 233
Stewart, A. J., 443, 448
Stewart, C. N., 117, 136
Stewart, M., 612, 634
Stinson, J. E., 265, 272
Stockbauer, J. W., 440, 448
Stogdill, R. M., 263, 264, 272
Stone, C., 430, 448
Stone, C. I., 570, 591

Stone, E. F., 246, 272
Stone, G. L., 572, 573, 591
Stone, J., 130, 136
Storlien, L. H., 218, 233
Strand, K. H., 591
Strassberg, D. S., 456, 466, 474
STRAUSS, J. S., 397-415; 399, 400, 408, 412, 413
Strawson, C., 614, 634
Stricker, E. M., 212, 215, 216, 223, 225, 227, 228, 230-33
Strickland, W. J., 512, 514
Stripling, R. O., 582, 591
Ström, L., 307, 313, 318
Strong, S. R., 574, 575, 591
Strubbe, J. H., 227, 233
Strupp, H. H., 455, 456, 460, 461, 466, 474, 571, 574, 591
Stuart, R. B., 568, 569, 591
Stuening, E. L., 408, 413
Stunkard, A. J., 568, 591
Su, W., 498, 500, 514
Suberi, M., 548, 549
Suckerman, K. R., 571, 591
Sudakov, K., 307, 318
Sue, D., 572, 591
Sue, D. W., 572, 591
Sugimori, M., 212, 233
Sundberg, N. D., 180, 205
Super, D. E., 502, 514, 577, 581, 591
Sutcliffe, J. A., 76, 98
Svejda, M., 536, 549
Switzer, R. C., 313, 318
Sydow, H., 367, 391
Szilagyi, A. D., 246, 254, 255, 266, 272

T

Tagiuri, R., 489, 490, 514, 528, 549
Takagi, S. F., 307, 313, 318
Takatori, S., 230, 231, 233
Tanabe, T., 307, 313, 318
Tanis, D. C., 49, 52, 56
Tanji, J., 335, 336, 358
Tannenbaum, G. A., 226, 233
Taplin, J. R., 180, 205
Tapper, D. N., 299, 318
Tarjan, G., 189, 205
Tarnage, J. J., 262, 272
Tarnecki, R., 307, 318
Tasto, D. L., 566, 568, 591
Taylor, C. L., 618, 634
Taylor, E. K., 480, 514
Taylor, F. G., 564, 591
Taylor, I. A., 615, 634
Taylor, J. R., 481, 514
Taylor, M. S., 585, 591
Taylor, R. C., 493, 514
Taylor, T. R., 621, 634

Teitelbaum, P., 212, 215-17, 222, 223, 233, 313, 314, 316-18
Temoshok, L., 462, 473, 474
Tenopyr, M. L., 482, 484, 514
Tepperman, J., 213, 221, 228, 233
Terborg, J. R., 255, 257, 272, 434, 448, 506, 507, 509, 514
Terhardt, E., 34, 36, 38, 56
Terpstra, D. E., 506, 514
Terzian, H., 232, 233
Tessler, R. C., 574, 575, 591
Thase, M., 573, 591
Thase, M. E., 565, 591
Thayer, P. w., 479, 514
Thelen, M. H., 573, 591
Theriault, R., 248, 272
Thissen, D. M., 609, 634
Thomas, A., 194, 195, 205
Thomas, D. W., 223, 233
Thomas, E. G., 582, 591
Thomas, E. J., 444, 448
Thomas, H., 629, 634
Thomas, J. C., 270, 272, 368, 391, 628, 634
Thomas, K. W., 440, 448
Thomas, M. J., 584, 591
Thompson, A. S., 581, 582, 591
Thompson, C. P., 88, 98
Thompson, D. L., 582, 591
Thompson, D. M., 225, 233
Thompson, H., 106, 136
Thompson, P. H., 254, 272
Thompson, R. F., 287, 318
Thompson, W. R., 104, 105, 116, 118, 125, 129, 131, 136
Thoresen, C. E., 556, 566, 568-71, 591
Thoresen, K. E., 556, 591
Thorn, M. E., 569, 591
Thornburg, K. R., 583, 591
Thorndike, R. L., 479, 486, 497, 498, 501, 514, 608, 634
Thorndike, R. M., 145-47, 163, 169
Thorndyke, P. W., 64, 65, 94, 98, 378, 391
Thorne, A., 434, 448
Thorpe, W. H., 119, 120, 136
Tice, T. E., 488, 489, 514
Tiedeman, D. V., 585, 591
Till, R. E., 92, 98
Tinsely, H. E. A., 578, 591
Tipton, R. M., 583, 591
Titchener, E. B., 18, 29
Tittler, B. I., 573, 591
Tolliver, J., 255, 272
Tomkins, S. S., 528, 531-33, 536-38, 545, 549

Toohey, M. L., 407, 413
Torick, E. L., 46, 56
Tornow, W. W., 484, 514
Tosi, H. L. Jr., 256, 272
Tosi, J. S., 257, 272
Touchton, J. G., 586, 591
Tower, D. B., 35, 56
Townsend, J. M., 402, 413
Townsend, M. A. R., 622, 634
Trabasso, T. R., 377, 378, 391
TRAHIOTIS, C., 31-61; 49, 56
Travers, J. B., 306, 318
Travis, R. P. Jr., 221, 233
Tresemer, D., 469, 474
Tretola, R., 570, 591
Trevarthen, C., 127, 128, 136, 534, 535, 549
Triandis, H. C., 145, 169
Trollip, S. R., 64, 65, 98
Tronick, E., 127, 128, 136, 534, 535, 549
Trope, Y., 426, 448
Trost, M. A., 590, 591
Troth, W. A., 578, 591
Trotman, F. K., 630, 634
Truax, C. B., 457, 474, 571, 591
Trumbo, D. A., 483, 514
Tsuzuki, Y., 301, 318
Tucker, D., 291, 318
Tucker, D. H., 507, 514
Tuller, W. L., 510, 514
Tulloch, R. W., 582, 591
Tulving, E., 76, 77, 80, 84-90, 97, 98, 377, 391
Turner, A. J., 577, 591
Turner, B. F., 584, 591
Turner, B. H., 212, 214, 216, 233, 314, 317, 318
Turner, R., 48, 56, 304, 318
Turner, R. G., 623, 634
Turner, S. G., 224, 233
Turney, J. R., 255, 272
Twentyman, C. T., 559, 591
Tyler, L. E., 180, 205, 578, 591
Tyler, L. K., 78, 98
Tziner, A., 587, 591
Tzuo, H., 54, 56
Tzuo, P. L., 54, 56

U

Uhlaner, J. E., 478, 514
Uhlemann, M. R., 572, 591
Uhlenhuth, E., 408, 413
Uhr, L., 379, 391
Umeda, J. K., 588, 591
Umstot, D. D., 255, 257, 272
Underwood, B. J., 621, 634
Undheim, J. O., 610, 634
Ungerstedt, U., 215, 216, 233
Urberg, K. A., 611, 634

Urry, V. W., 492, 514
Utecht, R. E., 263, 272
Uttal, W. R., 22, 29
Uzgiris, I. C., 108, 109, 111, 113, 115, 122, 127, 128, 136, 624, 625, 634

V

Vago, S., 625, 634
Valenstein, E. S., 212, 233
Valenti, A. C., 445, 448
Valenzi, E. R., 265, 266, 272, 490, 514
Vales, V., 154, 169
Valian, V. V., 70, 98
Vallbo, Å. B., 331, 332, 358
Vallon, W. R., 487, 514
Valzelli, L., 230, 233
van Bekkum, D. W., 224, 233
Van Buskirk, R. L., 311, 313, 318
Vance, A., 572, 591
Vance, E. T., 187, 205
Vance, R. J., 262, 272
Vance, W. B., 223, 233
Vande Creek, L., 544, 549
Vandenberg, S. G., 629, 630, 634
van den Brink, G., 38, 55, 56
Vanderweele, D. A., 210, 224, 233
Van Der Wel, H., 302, 318
Van De Ven, A. H., 427, 448, 501, 514
Van Doornick, W. J., 558, 591
van Hooff, J. A. R. A. M., 534, 549
van Houtte, N., 347, 358
Van Maanen, J., 248, 272
Van Maanen, J. V., 248, 272
van Putten, L. M., 224, 233
van Stam, W. S., 55, 56
Vasquez, J., 549
Vaughan, K. B., 546, 549
Vaughan, R. C., 546, 549
Vaughn, B. E., 533, 536, 549
Vaughn, C. E., 406, 413
Vayda, A. P., 155, 169
Vecchio, R. P., 263, 272
Venzor, E., 574, 591
Verbrugge, R. R., 87, 88, 98
Vernon, J. C., 577, 591
Vertinsky, I., 427, 448
Vetta, A., 629, 634
Veudry, W. F., 511, 514
Vickery, W. D., 261, 272
Viemeister, N. F., 38, 41, 42, 56
Vietze, P., 534, 549
Vilberg, T. R., 225, 233
Villwock, J. D., 585, 591
Vines, C. V., 253, 272

Vinitsky, M. H., 580, 591
Vinokur, A., 426, 428, 448
Viskov, O. V., 51, 56
Vogt, B. A., 337, 358
Volkmar, F. R., 134, 136
von Békésy, G., 287, 288, 318
Von Bergen, C. W. Jr., 254, 260, 272
Von Glinow, M. A., 264, 265, 272
von Helmholtz, H. L. F., 284, 286, 318, 352, 354, 355, 358
von Holst, E., 353, 356, 358
Vonkorff, M. R., 575, 591
von Skramlik, E., 284, 318
Vossius, G., 347, 358
Vroom, V. H., 253, 270, 272
Vygotsky, L. S., 159, 164, 169

W

Waber, D. P., 631, 634
Wachs, T. D., 111, 113, 115, 136
Wachtler, J., 437, 448
Waddell, W. N., 260, 271, 272
Wade, G. N., 230, 233
Wagner, D. A., 162, 169
Wagner, M. K., 570, 591
Wagstaff, A. K., 572, 591
Wahba, M. A., 253, 272
Wakeford, O. S., 53, 56
Walberg, H. J., 630, 634
Wald, J., 377, 391
Waldbillig, R. J., 214, 233
Walker, M., 153, 169, 434, 448
Wall, J. A., 426, 448
Wall, P. D., 287, 318
Wall, T. D., 443, 448
Wallace, J. G., 381, 382, 391, 624, 634
Wallace, S. R., 486, 512, 514
Wallace, W. G., 580, 591
Wallach, M. A., 422, 448
Wallerstein, J. S., 192, 198, 205
Walls, R. T., 581, 582, 591
Wallston, K. A., 571, 591
Walsh, D. A., 628, 634
Walsh, J. F., 615, 634
Walsh, L. L., 219, 220, 231, 233
Walsh, W. B., 582, 591
Walter, C. S., 487, 514
Walters, R. H., 114, 125, 126, 136
Walton, J., 52, 56
Waltz, D., 378, 391
Wampler, R. S., 222, 233
Wang, M. B., 292, 318
Ward, W. C., 615, 634
Warnode, E. H., 369, 378, 391
Warren, M., 145, 169

Warren, P. M., 591
Warren, R. P., 117, 136
Waskow, I. E., 472, 474
Watanabe, H., 215, 233
Watanabe, T., 215, 233
Waterman, D. A., 371, 374, 382, 391
Waters, D. H., 216, 233
Waters, E., 533, 534, 536, 540, 547, 549
Watkins, J. T., 544, 549
Watkins, M. J., 75, 86, 87, 97, 98, 377, 391
Watkins, O. C., 86, 87, 97, 98
Watson, C. S., 35, 44, 56
Watson, J. B., 124, 136
Watson, J. S., 534, 549
Watts, J. C., 111, 113, 115, 125, 128, 136
Waugh, N. C., 628, 634
Way, J. S., 231, 233
Webb, L. J., 561, 591
Webb, S. C., 586, 591
Weber, D. L., 44, 56
Weber, R., 39, 56
Weber, S., 383, 384, 391
Webster, E. C., 507, 508, 514
Webster, F. A., 53, 56
Wechsler, D., 605, 634
Weed, S. E., 246, 254, 265, 272
Weeks, M. O., 583, 591
Weick, K. E., 259, 272
Weick, K. E. Jr., 252, 272
Weiffenbach, J. M., 291, 318
Weinberg, H., 223, 233
Weinberg, J., 118, 136
Weininger, O., 116, 136
Weinstein, M. S., 466, 474
Weise, B. C., 575, 591
Weiss, D. J., 271, 272, 505, 514
Weiss, H. M., 270, 272
Weiss, R. L., 561, 591
Weitz, L. J., 571, 573, 591
Weizmann, F., 122, 136
Welch, B. L., 117, 136
Welcher, D. W., 631, 634
Weldon, L. J., 84, 98
Weller, L., 585, 591
Welsh, G. S., 615, 631, 634
Wenar, C., 113, 136
Wenk, E., 200, 205
Wepman, J. M., 614, 634
Werner, H., 147, 160, 169
Wernimont, P. F., 504, 509, 514
Weslander, D., 586, 591
West, R., 355, 358
Westbrook, B. W., 580, 581, 591
Westbrook, T., 568, 591
Wetherford, M., 122, 136
Wettengel, C., 510, 514
Wever, E. G., 286, 318

Wexler, D. A., 572, 573, 591
Wexley, K. N., 260, 272, 487, 489, 496, 507, 514
Wheaton, G. R., 261, 272
Wheeler, L., 444, 448
Wherry, R. J. Sr., 490, 491, 514
Whisler, R. H., 587, 591
White, B. J., 199, 205
White, B. L., 110, 111, 113, 115, 125, 128, 136, 187, 205
White, G. W., 578, 591
White, J. K., 250, 272
White, N. M., 232, 233
White, P. O., 623, 634
White, R., 420, 448
White, R. G., 566, 568, 591
White, R. R., 199, 205
White, R. W., 128, 136
White, S., 256, 257, 262, 272
White, T. D., 293, 318
Whitely, S. E., 617, 634
Whiting, B., 147, 169
Whitmore, J. K., 54, 56
Whitworth, R. H., 49, 56
Whyte, M. K., 430, 448
Wiback, K., 506, 514
Wickens, D. D., 76, 98
Wickens, T. D., 378, 391
Wickramasekera, I., 562, 591
Wiedl, K. H., 608, 634
Wiener, Y., 507, 514
Wienew, Y., 250, 272
Wiens, A. N., 542, 543, 549, 614, 634
Wier, C. C., 39, 41, 44, 56
Wiesel, T. N., 130, 136
Wiesendanger, M., 335-37, 358
Wiggins, J. D., 586, 591
Wightman, F. L., 34, 37-39, 56
Wilbanks, W. A., 54, 56
Wilbur, C. S., 556, 591
Wilcox, R. H., 216, 233, 427, 448
Wilder, D., 429, 448
Wildman, R. W., 556, 591
Wildman, R. W. II, 556, 591
Wiley, W. A., 484, 514
Wilkinson, A., 632, 634
Will, J. A., 586, 591
Willemin, L. P., 511, 514
Williams, E., 115, 136
Williams, K. D., 446, 448
Williams, T. H., 608, 634
Willis, S. L., 629, 634
Wilpert, B., 271, 272
Wilson, A. B., 590, 591
Wilson, J. P., 35, 36, 38, 40, 56, 446, 448
Wilson, M., 434, 448
Wilson, T. D., 365, 391
Wimberley, D. L., 440, 448

Winder, C. L., 178, 205
Winfield, J. A., 131, 136
Wing, J. K., 406, 410, 413
Winkelmayer, R., 530, 549
Winograd, T., 371, 391
Wirtz, W., 605, 634
Wise, G. W., 112, 136
Wise, S., 127, 128, 136, 534, 535, 549
Wise, S. P., 337, 358
Witkin, H. A., 155, 156, 159, 169, 624, 634
Witkin-Lanoil, G. H., 187, 197, 205
Wittig, B. A., 126, 136
Wittrig, J. J., 117, 136
Wober, M., 145, 169
Wohlwill, J. F., 150, 169
Wolf, A. K., 376, 391
Wolf, G., 218, 233, 305, 307, 313, 316, 318
Wolfe, J. L., 560, 591
Wolff, P. H., 533, 534, 536, 537, 549
Wolfson, K. P., 584, 591
Wolins, L., 486, 488, 489, 514
Wolman, B. B., 177, 205
Wolman, J. M., 588, 591
Wolstenholme, G. E. W., 291, 318
Wood, C. L. III, 53, 56
Wood, D. J., 218, 233
Wood, R. R., 250, 272
Woods, E. Jr., 574, 591
Woodward, A. E. Jr., 81, 83, 98
Woodward, S., 567, 591
Woolfolk, R. L., 567, 591
Worbois, G. M., 511, 514
Worchel, S., 437, 439, 448
Wright, D., 46, 47, 56
Wright, D. S., 535, 549
Wright, S., 437, 448
Wroton, H. W., 44, 56
Wundt, W., 11, 13, 29
Wurtz, R. H., 335, 358
Wyden, P., 589, 591
Wynne, L. C., 407, 413
Wyrwicka, W., 213, 214, 231, 233

Y

Yaksh, T. L., 213, 233
Yalom, I. D., 454, 456, 458, 459, 463-65, 468-71, 473, 474
Yamamoto, T., 307, 318
Yamashita, S., 292, 293, 296-99, 301, 302, 313, 318
Yap, P. M., 401, 413
Yarbrough, C., 168, 169, 631, 634
Yarita, H., 307, 313, 318

Yarrow, L. J., 111, 113, 114, 136
Yasui, S., 347, 358
Yates, L. G., 513, 514
Yen, W. M., 612, 634
Yetton, P. W., 270, 272
Yeudall, L. T., 609, 634
Yin, T. H., 223, 233
Yokoyama, T., 215, 233
York, D. A., 225, 233
Yost, W. A., 32, 48-53, 56
Youell, K. J., 566, 591
Young, G., 533, 536, 539, 549
Young, L. L., 51, 56
Young, L. L. Jr., 49, 56
Young, L. R., 344, 347, 358
Young, R. M., 381, 391
Young, T. K., 225, 233
Young-Browne, G., 534, 549
Yukl, G. A., 247, 255-57, 260, 272
Yunger, L. M., 230, 231, 233
Yunker, G. W., 266, 272

Z

Zahorik, D. M., 120, 136
Zaidel, S., 544, 549
Zajonc, R. B., 422, 447, 448, 630, 634
Zamostny, K. P., 380, 391
ZANDER, A. F., 417-51; 422, 423, 426-28, 430, 435, 438, 439, 448
Zarroug, E., 401, 413
Zarrow, M. X., 118, 136
Zedeck, S., 483, 487, 489, 495, 514
Zeigler, H. P., 212, 214, 233, 314, 318
Zeiss, A. M., 563, 591
Zemlan, F. P., 230, 231, 233
Zener, T. B., 579, 591
Zigler, E., 175, 205, 534, 549
Zigmond, M. J., 212, 215, 216, 232, 233
Ziller, R. C., 411, 413
Zimet, S. G., 558, 591
Zimmer, J. M., 574, 591
Zimmerman, E., 465, 470, 471, 473, 474
Zipser, B., 335, 358
Zis, A. P., 215, 216, 233
Zlatchin, C., 549
Zohn, C. J., 570, 591
Zotterman, Y., 285, 286, 302, 307, 313, 318
Zuckerman, M., 542, 543, 549
Zurek, P. M., 39, 40, 56
Zwaardemaker, H., 284, 318
Zwany, A., 490, 514
Zwicker, E., 36, 38, 43, 45, 56
Zwislocki, J. J., 45, 56
Zytowski, D. G., 579, 588, 591

SUBJECT INDEX

A

Ability
  cognitive
  see Cognitive abilities
  in job motivation studies, 261
Abstract skills
  development of
  and formal schooling, 167
Abstract thought
  and nonliterate people, 160
Acceptance
  as personal change
  mechanism, 471
Acculturation
  in children
  and mental health risk,
  188
  index
  and cognition
  development, 156–58
Acetylcholine
  and rearing condition
  variations, 133
Achievement
  college
  prediction of, 632–33
  and creative thinking
  measures, 615
  maternal expectancies of
  and infant development,
  115
  need for in women
  and career orientation, 584
  in school
  individual determinants of,
  632
Achievement orientation
  and locus of control
  in organizational behavior,
  246
Acidity
  in taste studies, 285, 292–93,
  296–300, 304, 306–7
Acoustic orienting task
  in memory studies, 78
Acoustics
  and auditory psychophysics,
  33
ACT
  computer simulation model
  and semantic memory,
  378, 387–88
Acting-out
  among children
  and social skills training,
  557
Adaptive gain control
  and motor control system
  models, 338–42

Adolescence
  impact of social supports
  during
  and psychopathology, 404
  individual differences in
  validity studies, 632
Adolescents
  and community crime
  prevention programs,
  182
Adrenal responses
  and reduced aversiveness
  in children, 118
Adrenal tumor
  and salt craving
  in taste and behavior
  studies, 290
Affect
  arousal of
  and small group methods,
  446, 470
  role in cognition
  and computer simulated
  models, 383–85
  role in memory encoding,
  92–95
Affective role-taking
  among preschoolers
  and facial expression
  studies, 534–35
Afferent nerves
  in motor organization
  studies, 328–34, 337–38,
  356–57
  and taste neuropsychology,
  285–88, 291, 300, 317
Affirmative action programs
  and personnel selection
  studies, 481, 500
Ageism
  as social-environmental
  stressor, 184
Aggression
  altering through counseling,
  558–59
  and facial expression, 535,
  549
  prevention of
  experimental studies, 199
  and schizophrenia
  vulnerability, 194
Aggressive actions
  and deindividuation
  and group processes,
  431–32
Aging
  individual differences in
  and changes in cognitive
  ability, 624–29
  and memory, 66

Alcoholism
  in children, 175
  and employee emotional
  stress, 181
Altruism
  and facial expression
  during televised violence,
  549
  as personal change
  mechanism, 471
Americans
  and color coding studies,
  154
  facial expression studies of,
  530–31
American Sign Language
  (ASL)
  and memory encoding
  studies, 69
Ammonium chloride
  in taste studies, 294
Amok
  as culture-specific syndrome,
  401
Amygdala
  lesions in
  and motivation studies,
  214–15, 232
  and taste neurophysiology,
  290, 311–12, 314,
  316–17
Anal character
  and early experience studies,
  112
Anger
  as chronic problem
  and cognitive behavioral
  treatment, 558
  facial expression of, 531, 534,
  536
Animal intelligence
  and rearing conditions,
  131–33
Anonymity
  and deindividuation
  and group processes, 432
Anorexia
  see Ingestive behavior
Anthropology
  and facial expression
  universality, 528
Antisocial behavior
  and group pressures, 431
Anxiety
  individual differences in
  and memory, 66
  role in unassertiveness,
  559–60
  and vulnerability to mental
  illness, 197

Aphagia
    and adipsia
    see Ingestive behavior
Apomorphine
    and ingestive behavior
        studies, 215
Applied differential psychology
    and cognitive abilities
        validity studies, 632–33
Aptitude-treatment interaction
        (ATI)
    and applied differential
        psychology, 632
Arabic language
    literacy in
    and cognitive skills,
        166–67
ARGUS
    computer simulation model
    and analogy problems, 375
Arousal
    and biology of motivation,
        209–10, 212–13, 216,
        218, 232–33
    and early experience studies,
        118–19
    emotional
        and facial expression
            studies, 543, 546–47
    and memory, 66
        individual differences in,
            623
Articulatory rehearsal loop
    in short-term memory, 73–74
Aspartame
    and sugar reception studies,
        302
Assassination
    of President Kennedy
    and flashbulb memories, 95
Assertiveness
    altering through counseling,
        559–60
    training
        in family problem
            prevention, 589
Assessment
    of early experience
        of children and infants,
            113–14
    multiple procedures for
        in personnel selection, 480,
            510–12
    of personal change
        and small group methods,
            460–67
    of psychological dysfunction
        and criminal justice
            system, 181–82
Atkinson-Shiffrin PA task
    see Tests and scales
Attachment
    among infants

critical periods for, 123–24
    see also Maternal
Attention set
    and schizophrenia, 197
Attitudes
    change of
        small group methods of,
            453–74
    and personality traits
        in organizational behavior
            studies, 261, 247–51
    self-report measures of
        and sensitivity outcome
            research, 464
    similarity of
        and counselor/client
            attraction, 574
        and personnel selection
            studies, 507–8
    toward schooling
        and cultural cognition, 161
    toward therapists, 574–75
Attraction
    in counseling process, 574–75
    of group members, 434–35
Attractiveness
    and personnel selection, 506
Attributional approach
    to leadership studies, 269–70
Attributions
    of group success or failure
        and self-evaluation, 439
    and job attitudes
        in organizational behavior
            studies, 250–51
Attribution theory
    and sex-role stereotypes, 506
    in personnel selection, 509
Audience
    effect on performance
        and group psychology, 420
Audition
    and cognitive abilities
        individual differences in,
            618–21
    and critical development
        periods, 131
    feature extraction in
        and memory, 68
    neurophysiology of
        and taste studies, 285–87
Auditory experience
    and social responsiveness
        in infants, 114, 126
Auditory memory
    masking and encoding in,
        68–69
Auditory psychophysics, 31–55
    binaural hearing, 45–55
    external ear
        transformations,
            45–46
    lateralization, 48–51

localization, 46–48
    masking, 51–54
    pitch, 54–55
    intensity perception, 41–45
    introduction, 31–32
    nonlinear effects, 39–41
    pitch perception, 36–39
    summary and comments, 55
    textbooks, 32–35
Authoritarianism
    and leadership style, 265
    and occupational choice, 585
Autonomic nervous system
        (ANS)
    and control of facial
        expression, 547–48
Aversion
    conditioned
        and taste neuropsychology,
            299, 315–18
    in smoking cessation, 570
    in treatment of exhibitionism,
            562
Aversive experiences
    and infant development,
            116–18
Avoidance
    and proximity
        in group size studies, 445

B

BASEBALL
    computer program
        and natural-language
            questions, 376
Bayley Scales of Infant
        Development
    see Tests and scales
Beck Depression Inventory
    see Tests and scales
Behavior
    changes in
        small group methods of,
            453–74
    disorders in children
        and mental health risk,
            188–89
    disruptive
        and group contingencies,
            561
    emotional
        see Emotional behavior
    and gustatory stimuli
        neural mechanisms of,
            283–313
    ingestive
        and motivation studies,
            209–33
        see Ingestive behavior
    modification
        in job motivation studies,
            259–61

in leadership, 267
outcome research reviews,
463
in school behavior
changes, 556–57, 590
observation of
and personnel ratings,
287–90
role in homeostasis
and taste studies, 288–89
social
see Social behavior
Behaviorally anchored rating
scales (BARS)
see Tests and scales
Behavioral management
in family problem
prevention, 589
Behavioral process
as personal change
mechanism
in small group studies,
471
Behavioral treatment
of obesity, 568–69
of smoking, 570
Berkeley growth and guidance
studies
see Tests and scales
Bias
age/race/sex
in job performance ratings,
489–90
in personnel selection,
496–502, 505–9,
511–12
in content-oriented tests
and personnel selection,
483–84
cultural
in cross-cultural studies,
147, 150, 163–64
individual vs group
conceptual framework
in small group studies,
455–57, 467–68
Bilingual
mental illness prevention
program
in Houston, 190–91
Bilingualism
and semantic memory
studies, 377–78
Binaural
detection
and pitch perception,
36–37
hearing, 45–55
external ear
transformations,
45–46
lateralization, 48–51
localization, 46–48

masking, 51–54
pitch, 54–55
Biochemical deficiencies
in schizophrenia, 195–97
Biodata
in personnel selection,
509–10
Biological factors
in cognitive development,
149
Biology
and psychology, 1–2
history of, 24–25
Birds
imprinting among
and early experience
studies, 119–23,
135–36
Birth order
and intelligence, 630–31
Birth trauma
and mental illness
vulnerability, 194, 197
Blacks
and occupational choice, 585
see Minorities; Race
Blame
see Attribution
Blind
and sighted infants
facial expression studies of,
532
Bonding
and social responsiveness
in infants, 127
Brain
chemistry
and variable rearing
conditions, 133–35
lesions in
and motivation and
ingestive behavior,
210–33
see also Lesions;
Neurophysiology
organization of
and behavior, 1
Brain-damaged patients
cognitive abilities of
factor analytic studies, 609
Bridge
expert knowledge in playing
and computer cognition
modeling, 368
British people
facial expression studies of,
530–31
Bushman
economic activities of
and cognition
development, 155
Butyryl choline
in taste studies, 293

Butyrylcholinesterase
and rearing condition
variations, 133

C

California Test of Mental
Maturity
see Tests and scales
Career
choice
see Vocational choice
maturity
measures of, 581–82
Career counseling
and skill development,
577–88
career maturity, 581–82
decision-making skills,
577–81
employment seeking,
586–87
occupational adaptation,
587–88
vocational choices, 583–85
Career Development Inventory
(CDI)
see Tests and scales
Career Maturity Inventory
(CMI)
see Tests and scales
Catechol-aminergic projections
and satiety mechanism
in motivation studies, 229,
231–32
Categorization
and cross-cultural universals,
153–54
Cats
eye movement studies
and motor organization,
340
lateralization and binaural
detection, 53
taste neuropsychology of,
285–86, 300, 305, 307,
311, 313
Caudate nucleus
lesions in
and ingestive behavior
studies, 220–21
Cephalic phase hypothesis
and hypothalamic satiety
center, 228
Change
models of
and assessment bias,
460–61
personal processes of, 467–72
change mechanisms,
471–72
clinical vs statistical
methods, 468–70

group vs individual
orientation, 467–68
process vs outcome
orientation, 470–71
Charisma
as leadership quality, 267–68
Chess playing
expert knowledge in
computer modeling of,
366, 368–69
Chess positions
memory for, 72, 78
Child abuse
strategies for prevention, 183
Childhood
social supports during
and psychopathology, 404
Child-rearing
and cognition development
theories, 155, 161
complexity effects of
on neuroanatomy and
neurochemistry,
133–35
on problem-solving and
animal intelligence,
131–33
education of parents in
and mental illness
prevention, 177, 180,
187, 190–92
intervention in
and development, 110–11
Children
activity groups of
and outcome research
reviews, 463
alcoholism in, 175
assessment of early
experience, 113–14
birth order of
and intellectual
development, 447
changing cognitive abilities in
measurement of, 624–27
competence in
and early experience
studies, 113
creative thinking among
testing of, 615
delinquent
and family problem
prevention, 589
dyslexic
and memory studies, 74
emotional disturbance in
and clinical prevention,
173–205
and parents' discrepant
messages, 545
and group process studies,
431
intellect of
psychogenesis of, 2–3

memory tasks for
cross-cultural studies,
161–63
mentally retarded
and Milwaukee Project,
630
neglect of needs of, 175
performance of Piagetian
tasks
and computer simulation
modeling, 381–82
preschool
facial expression studies
among, 534–35, 539
reared in orphanages
and early experience
studies, 107–8, 111,
124–25, 127–28
at risk of mental illness
and prevention, 185–86,
188–92, 196–98, 203,
590
rural Mexican
and conservation tasks,
151–52
school conduct among
altering through
counseling, 556–57
speech performance of
and intelligence testing,
614–15
story recall among, 94
verbatim retention studies of,
93
Chimpanzees
reared in dark
and early experience
studies, 121, 129
China
indoctrination programs in
and small group methods,
430, 472
Chlorpromazine
in psychotic treatment, 411
Choice making
and job motivation, 252–53
Chorda tympani
role in taste neurophysiology,
285–318
Circadian rhythm
breakdown of
and VMH lesions, 221
Classification tasks
in Soviet rural village
and cross-cultural
cognition, 160
Cleary Model
of test fairness, 498
Clinical
vs statistical approach
to small group methods,
457–59, 468–70
Clinical psychology
prevention, 173–205

advocacy role, 174–75
basic understandings in
planning, 193–204
conclusion, 204–5
introduction, 174
local prevention programs,
187–93
national proposals, 182–87
training, 177–82
Cochlea
and auditory psychophysics
electrical activity from, 34
nonlinear effects in, 39–40
Coding
of behavioral interaction
in small group method
studies, 469
Cognition
affect and behavior
in depressives, 563
development of
and mother-infant
relationships, 127–28
among infants and children
and facial expression
studies, 534–35
information processing
models of, 263–90
conclusion, 389–90
elementary processor,
385–89
induction of patterns,
378–80
learning and development,
380–83
motivation and emotion,
383–85
origins of approach,
364–66
problem solving, 366–75
semantic memory, 375–78
maladaptive
altering through
counseling, 556–76
and memory, 66, 73, 96
Cognitive abilities
individual differences in,
603–34
applied differential
psychology, 623–33
broad ability domains,
608–13
changes over life span,
624–29
conclusions, 633–34
genetic and environmental
influences, 629–32
introduction, 604–6
particular domains, 613–23
and personality, 623–24
traits, processes, and
competence, 606–8
Cognitive behavior
in groups, 421, 424–28

Cognitive coping strategies
in pain control, 567–68
Cognitive functioning
and altering aggressive
behavior, 558
Cognitive intervention
among children
and improving intellectual
competence, 617
Cognitive problems
in schizophrenia, 195
Cognitive processes
as personal change
mechanisms
in small group studies,
471
Cognitive-psychological task
analysis
and cross-cultural cognition
studies, 165
Cognitive psychology
cross-cultural, 145–69
basic research approaches,
148
cognitive universals,
148–54
culture and memory,
160–63
ethnographic psychology,
163–67
introduction, 145–48
socialization theories,
154–60
summary, 167–69
experimental
individual differences
studies, 611–13
Cognitive speed
individual differences in,
622–23
Cognitive therapy
for test anxiety, 565–66
Cohesiveness
and group process studies,
421, 429–30, 433–38
of small groups
and personal change
methods, 455, 468
Color
and memory encoding, 76
Color classification
in Soviet rural village, 160
and cross-cultural
cognition, 153–54
Combat stress
and mental health, 184
Commitment
as job attitude
in organizational behavior
studies, 249, 251
Communication
and family studies
role in psychopathology,
407–8

and mother-infant
relationships
and psychological
development, 127–28
nonverbal
and facial expressions,
527–49
and organizational behavior,
244
skills training
and marital counseling,
561–62
tasks
and cross-cultural
cognition, 163
Community activity centers
as prevention, 200–1
Community intervention
family counseling services,
589
and mental illness
prevention, 174, 182
Community mental health
centers
and sociocultural influences
on psychopathology, 405
Compassion
development of
and early experiences,
136
Competence
in children
and early experience
studies, 113–14
in factor analysis studies
of cognitive abilities, 606–8
and mental illness
prevention, 183, 185,
196, 202–3
Competence-performance
in cross-cultural cognition
studies, 150–53, 161
Competition
and cooperation
and group process studies,
421, 440
Comprehensive Ability Battery
see Tests and scales
Computer models
of cognition
see Information processing
Computer programmer training
and selection studies, 513
Computer programming
languages
and cognition models, 363,
365, 389–90
Concept attainment
information processing
models of, 365, 378–80,
386
Conflict resolution
and group process studies,
427

Conformity
and group social pressures,
429, 435
Consciousness
questions about
and origins of psychology,
26
Conservation tasks
and cross-cultural cognition
studies, 151–52
Consideration
as leadership style
and organizational
behavior, 264–66
Consistency theory
of personality and
occupation, 245
Context
and memory encoding, 78,
87–88, 95
Cooperation
and aggression prevention, 199
and competition
and group process studies,
421, 440
Coping behavior
in hyperactive children, 558
among junior high students
and cognitive reappraisal,
560
Coping skills
and mental illness
prevention, 183, 185,
193–94, 198, 201–2,
204–5
in migraine headache
treatment, 568
Coping style
and sociocultural influences
on psychopathology,
403–4, 409, 411
Copulation
among animals
and early experience
studies, 107, 125
Corman-Escalona Scales of
Object Permanence
see Tests and scales
Correction system
and crime prevention work,
182
and environment measuring,
200
and mental illness
prevention, 204
Cost accounting
computer simulation models
of, 367, 369
in personnel selection, 478
Counseling behaviors, 570–77
genuineness, warmth, and
empathy, 571–72
persistence in treatment,
576–77

self-disclosure, 572–74
social influence, 574–76
Counseling psychology, 555–90
altering maladaptive
responses, 556–77
emotional behavior,
562–66
health-related outcomes,
566–70
intracounseling behaviors,
570–77
social behavior, 556–62
developing skill for career
transitions, 577–88
career maturity, 581–83
decision-making skills,
577–81
employment seeking,
586–87
occupational adaptation,
587
vocational choices, 583–86
prevention, 588–90
of family problems, 588–89
of school problems, 589–90
Creativity
and fluency of ideation
and individual differences,
615–16
Crime and delinquency
preventive efforts in, 181–82
Criminal justice system
and clinical psychology,
181–82
see Jury studies
Crisis counseling
of police and prison officers,
182
Critical incidents method
in personnel selection, 479,
486–87
Critical period
and early experience studies,
135–36
Cross-cultural studies
in cognition
see Cognitive psychology
of early parent-infant
interactions, 187
of facial expressions, 528–32,
537
of kinesthetic-vestibular
stimulation
among infants, 114
of life events
and psychopathology,
408
memory tasks, 161–63
of psychopathology, 401–2,
413
Crowdedness
and group cohesiveness, 435,
448

Crying
emotional expression of
and presence of others,
535
see Facial expressions
Cultural
differences
in appropriate
self-disclosure, 572
influences on
psychopathology,
397–413
see also Psychopathology
style
and human ecology, 156
task analysis
and cross-cultural
cognition studies, 165
variability
and cognition studies,
154–60
Culture
and field dependence
development, 624
Cupboard theory
and maternal attachment,
126
Curare
use in motor organization
studies, 333–34, 356
Curiosity
development of
and early experiences,
136
Cybernetics
and psychology, 6–7
Cyclamate
and sugar reception studies,
302

D

Dani
of New Guinea
color categorization
among, 154
of West Iran
facial expression studies of,
529
Dating anxiety
and assertiveness training,
559–60
Day care centers
Milwaukee Project
and early experience
studies, 111
see also Milwaukee Project
in 1930s slums
and fear in children,
117–18
therapeutic
and mental health
prevention, 189, 204

Deaf
Central Institute for the
and audition studies, 35
subjects
and memory encoding, 69
Decerebrates
and taste reactivity, 315
Deci effect
in job motivation studies, 262
Decision making
and career skills, 577–81
in chess playing
and computer simulation
models, 368
in groups, 425–28
and organizational behavior,
244, 270–71
Decision theory
in personnel selection, 480,
494, 501, 505
Dehydration
cellular
and ingestive behavior
studies, 216–18
Deindividuation
and group process studies,
431–32
Delphi decision methods
in organization policy, 501
2-deoxy-D-glucose (2DG)
and metabolism disruption
and motivation studies,
213, 216–17, 219–20,
223, 232
Dependency
on mothers
and later discipline and
aggression, 125
Depression
in children, 175
cognitive behavior treatment
of, 558, 563–64
cultural influences on, 401
and learned helplessness, 408
and loss of spouse
and mental health, 184
Deprivation
in early childhood
and psychopathology, 398
Desensitization
in dating anxiety treatment,
559
in phobia and anxiety
treatment, 565–66
video
as female anorgasmia
treatment, 562
Determination
as balancing strength
and mental illness
prevention, 198
Development
early experience, 103–36

conclusion, 135–36
denial of importance of,
    105–11
effects on problem solving,
neuroanatomy, and
neurochemistry,
    128–35
ethological conceptions,
    119–23
maternal deprivation and
attachment, 124–28
psychoanalytic conceptions,
    112–19
Developmental lag
in children
and psychopathology risk,
    188
Developmental studies
of facial expressions of
emotion, 532–37
Diabetes
in rats
and ingestive behavior
studies, 224
Diagnosis
of psychiatric disorders
and sociocultural
influences, 400, 413
Dichotic listening
and memory studies, 66
Diencephalon
motivational role of, 213–14,
    217
pontine gustatory neurons in,
    311
Differential Aptitude Tests
see Tests and scales
Digit span
in memory studies, 74, 76
Disability
physical
and counselor
attractiveness, 575
Discriminability hypothesis
in auditory memory, 69
Discrimination
in personnel selection, 480,
    496–502, 505–9
Disgust
facial expression of, 531, 537
Display rules
and facial expression studies,
    531, 537
Dissonance theory
and attributions
in organizational behavior
studies, 250–51
Distress
among infants
and inability to
accomodate, 122
facial expression of, 533, 536,
    547

Divorce
children of
and mental disturbance
prevention, 192–93,
    198
Dogs
cage- vs pet-reared
intelligence studies, 131
Dominance
in pitch perception, 37
Dopaminergic pathway (DA)
and lesions
in motivation studies,
    215–19
Down's Syndrome infants
and smiling and laughter
studies, 534
DQ
see Tests and scales
Drive
arousal theory of
and early experience
studies, 118–19
Dulcin
and sugar reception studies,
    302
Dyslexia
in children
and memory studies, 74
Dysmenorrhea
behavioral intervention in,
    566, 568

E

Early childhood
importance of experience in
see Development
social and cultural influences
in
and psychopathology, 398,
    402, 404
Early and Periodic Screening,
Diagnosis, and Treatment
Program (EPSDT)
and mental illness
prevention, 186
ECES
occupational exploration
system
and career maturity,
    582
Echoic memory
traditional studies of, 68
Ecocultural index
and cognition development,
    156–58
Ecology
and behavior
and mental illness
prevention, 200
human
and cultural style, 156

Economic activities
and cognition development
cross-cultural studies, 155
Economics
and psychology, 5
Education
and cognitive performance
and cross-cultural studies,
    156, 158
early experience philosophy
in, 104, 111
field dependence-
independence
and learning and memory,
    624
and goal setting
in job motivation studies,
    256–57
Educational
and cultural transmission
in cognitive development,
    149
Eight-months anxiety
and age level terms, 203
Electrolytic lesions
and motivation
and ingestive behavior,
    211–12, 219–20, 225,
    229, 231
Electromyograph (EMG)
biofeedback
in insomnia treatment, 567
in migraine headache
treatment, 568
in facial expression
measurement, 538
Electronics
expert knowledge in
and computer simulation
modeling, 369
Electrophysiology
in eye movement studies,
    338, 341
and taste neuropsychology,
    285, 287, 290–300, 302,
    305, 308
Embedded figures test
see Tests and scales
Embryonic development
in animals
and early experience
studies, 105
Emotion
expressed
and family studies, 406–7
facial expressions of, 527–49
see Facial expressions
and memory encoding, 93–95
and motivation
in cognitive computer
modeling, 383–85
theories of
and facial expression
studies, 529, 549

Emotional behavior
altering through counseling,
562-66
depression, 563-64
phobias and anxiety,
564-66
sexual disorders, 562
Emotional disturbance
prevention of, 173-205
advocacy role of
psychologists, 174-75
basic understandings in
planning, 193-204
conclusion, 204-5
local prevention programs,
187-93
national proposals, 183-87
training, 177-82
Emotional problems
and employee stress
programs, 181
Empathic Understanding Scale
see Tests and scales
Empathy
and facial expressions,
534-35
of therapists
and outcome studies,
571-72
Employment seeking
and career counseling,
586-87
see Personnel selection
Encoding
and categorization studies
in cross-cultural cognition,
153-54
and decoding
of facial expressions,
542-45, 547
Encoding processes
in human memory, 77-84
alternatives to levels,
79-81
levels of processing, 77-79
rehearsal and repetition,
81-84
see Memory
Encounter groups
casualties of
and outcome research,
464-65
marathon
outcome research on,
463-64
methods of personal change,
458, 466
self-disclosure in
and small group methods,
456
Endocrine glands
and disturbed behavior,
184

dysfunction of
in ingestive behavior
studies, 223
Entorhinal cortex
lesions in
and hyperphagia, 231
Environment
and behavior
and mental illness
prevention, 200
Environmental determinism
and behavior modification
in job motivation studies,
259-61
Environmental influences
in cognitive abilities
and individual differences,
629
EPAM
as cognition model, 364, 368,
370, 375-76, 378
Episodic memory
progress in field, 96-97
Equal opportunity
psychometrics of, 496-502
differential validity, 496-97
test fairness, 497-502
Equilibration factors
in cognitive development, 149
Equilibrium
in infants under stress
and mental illness
prevention, 203, 205
Equity theory
in job motivation studies,
258-59
Ethics
in organizational psychology,
271-72
Ethnic groups
life events studies
and psychopathology, 408
Ethnographic psychology
and cross-cultural cognition
studies, 163-67
Ethology
and early experience studies,
119-24
critical periods, 123-24
imprinting, 119-23
ETS Kit of Factor Reference
Tests
see Tests and scales
Evoked potentials
in taste neurophysiology,
306-8
Evolution
and behavior, 2
Exhibitionism
and aversion treatment, 562
Expectancy theory
in job motivation studies,
253-55

Experience
importance in early
childhood
see Development
role in cognitive development
cross-cultural studies,
151-52
Expert knowledge
and group leadership
appraisal, 441
Extraversion
individual differences in
and memory, 66
Eye contact
and job interviewing skills,
586
and social skills training,
557
Eye movement
and motor control concepts,
337-58
in verbal protocol analysis
and cognition modeling,
373

F

Faces
and memory encoding,
71-72, 87
Faces Scale
see Tests and scales
Facial Action Coding System
(FACS)
see Tests and scales
Facial Affect Scoring
Technique (FAST)
see Tests and scales
Facial expressions
of emotion, 527-49
accuracy, 540-45
cross-cultural studies and
universality, 529-32
developmental studies,
532-37
feedback, 545-47
future directions, 548-49
introduction, 528
measurement, 537-40
neural control and ANS
correlates, 547-48
Facial Expression Scoring
Manual (FESM)
see Tests and scales
Factor analysis
of cognitive abilities
in experimental cognitive
psychology, 611-13
factor models, 610-11
multifactorial test batteries,
609-10
of human attributes
and personnel selection,
479

of individual differences
  in cognitive abilities,
    603–34
Failure
  attribution of
  and organizational
    behavior studies, 251
Family
  problems
    prevention counseling,
      588–89
  and psychopathology studies,
    406–7, 410–11
  size and birth order
    and intelligence, 630–31
Fat metabolism
  disorders in
  and ingestive behavior
    studies, 223, 225, 227
Fear
  conditioning in children
    and child-rearing, 117–18
  facial expression of, 531, 536
Fear response
  maturation of
    and imprinting period,
      121–23
Feature extraction
  and iconic memory studies,
    67–68
Fechner
  and origins of psychology,
    10–11, 24
Feeding frustration
  in infants
    and rapid eating, 118
Feelings
  changes in
    small group methods of,
      453–74
Field dependence-independence
  and cognitive abilities, 624
  and psychological
    differentiation
    and cognition studies, 156
FIRO-B
  see Tests and scales
Fish
  imprinting among, 120
  surgical eye rotation in
    and visuomotor
      coordination, 353
Flashbulb memories
  and memory encoding, 95–96
Flexibility
  as balancing strength
    and mental illness
      prevention, 198
Flocculus
  role in motor organization,
    342, 349, 351
Forgetting
  in memory studies, 75, 91

Formalin
  injections of
  and ingestive behavior
    studies, 219
FORTRAN
  and cognition modeling, 389
Fourier analysis
  of pitch perception, 36–37
Frames
  in cognition models
  and information
    processing, 376, 390
Frequency discrimination
  in auditory psychophysics,
    34, 38–39, 44, 46,
    50–51, 54
Friendship
  in the classroom
  and competition, 556–57
  and cooperative behavior
    skill teaching, 560–61
Fructose
  in taste studies, 294, 301
Functional approach
  to cross-cultural cognition
    studies, 148, 163–67
Functionalism
  and history of psychology, 19

G

Galton's problem
  and cross-cultural testing,
    157
Game theory
  and economics and
    psychology, 5
GATB
  see Tests and scales
Gaze direction
  and facial expression studies,
    528, 540
General Problem Solver (GPS)
  as cognition model, 364,
    366–67, 383
General Rule Inducer (GRI)
  as cognition model, 279–80
Genetic influence
  in cognitive ability
    individual differences
      studies, 629–32
Gesture
  and facial expression studies,
    528, 541, 544
  imitation of
    and infant development,
      108–9
Globus pallidus
  lesions in
    and motivation, 215–16,
      218–19, 221
Glossopharyngeal nerves
  role in taste neuro-

psychology, 295–96,
    308, 317
Glucose
  hypertonic
    and aversiveness studies,
      118
  and metabolism disruption
    in motivation studies,
      213–14, 227
  in taste neuropsychology,
    301, 303
Go
  expert knowledge in playing
    and computer cognition
      modeling, 368
Goal Attainment Scaling
  see Tests and scales
Goal setting
  in job motivation studies,
    255–58
Goldthioglucose
  and VMH disruption, 213
Graphic Information
  Processing battery (GRIP)
  see Tests and scales
Gratification delay
  and schizophrenic
    vulnerability, 196
GRE Advanced Psychology
  test
  see Tests and scales
Gregarious behavior
  and group cohesiveness, 434
Group Atmosphere Scale
  see Tests and scales
Group dynamics
  in organizational behavior,
    244, 270
Group processes, 417–48
  growth of the field, 418–24
  recent research, 424–48
    cognitive behavior in
      groups, 424–28
    cohesiveness of groups,
      433–38
    cooperation and
      competition, 440
    evaluation of self and
      group, 438–40
    group size and density,
      444–46
    group structure, 446
    leadership, 440–44
    social pressures on group
      members, 428–32
    summary, 447–48
Groups
  therapy and self-help
    see Small Groups
Growth hormone
  and VMH lesions
    in ingestive behavior
      studies, 223

Guatemala
  memory studies in, 161–62
Gustatory system
  neural mechanisms of,
    283–318
  see also Ingestive behavior
Gymnemic acid
  and sucrose sensitivity, 302

H

Habituation measures
  in infants, 625
Hallucinations
  as culture-specific syndromes,
    401
Hamilton Rating Scale for
  Depression
  see Tests and scales
HAM model
  and cognition modeling, 387
  and memory studies, 66
Hamsters
  chorda tympani responses of
    in taste studies, 288,
    293–94, 299, 301
Handicapped status
  and personnel selection
    studies, 506–7
Handicaps
  in children
    and mental health risk,
      189
Happiness
  facial expression of, 531,
    534–35, 546
Head Start Program
  and mental illness prevention
    in children, 176, 185
Health
  and counseling psychology,
    566–70
  insomnia, 566–67
  pain control, 567–68
  smoking cessation, 570
  weight control, 568–69
Health care
  and training
    in mental illness
      prevention, 177–80
Hearing
  physiology of
    and history of psychology,
      10
  see Auditory psychophysics
Hebb-Williams mazes
  see Tests and scales
Hedonic processes
  and taste preferences, 302–5
Helmholtz
  and oculomotor studies,
    354–55
  and origins of psychology,
    10, 24, 28

and physiology of taste, 284
and pitch perception, 37, 39
Help
  acceptance of
    and mental illness
      prevention, 198
Heredity vs environment
  in development studies, 110
Heritability
  of intelligence
    and individual differences
      studies, 605, 629–30
History
  of psychology, 9–28
Hospital practice
  of separating mother/infant
    and bonding, 127
Hospitals
  group care in
    and developmental
      retardation, 113
Houston Program
  with bilingual families
    and mental illness
      prevention, 190–91
5-HT
  serotonin
    and ingestive behavior
      studies, 217, 230
Human relations movement
  and group process
    psychology, 420
Human resources planning
  and personnel selection
    studies, 481, 503, 514
Humor
  expression of
    and presence of others,
      535
Hunger
  see Ingestive behavior
Hydrocephalic infants
  facial expression studies of,
    533
6-Hydroxydopamine (6-OHDA)
  and ingestive behavior
    studies, 215–16, 218,
      229–30
Hyperactive
  children
    and coping with
      aggression, 558
Hyperinsulinimia
  and ingestive behavior
    studies, 223, 225–27
Hypermnesia
  and memory studies, 90
Hyperphagia
  and hyperdipsia
    and brain lesions, 212–33
Hypertension
  behavioral treatment of, 566
Hypoglycemia
  insulin induced

and ingestive behavior
  studies, 220, 227, 232
Hypothalamocentric hypothesis
  and motivation studies, 211,
    213–15
Hypothalamus
  lateral
    and motivation biology,
      211–33
    and taste neuropsychology,
      311, 313–17
    and taste neurophysiology,
      290, 312–13
  ventromedial (VMH)
    and motivation studies,
      213, 221–29, 232

I

Ia interneuron
  and motor organization
    concepts, 334–35
Iconic memory
  studies of, 67–68
Identification
  with parent
    and mental illness, 196,
      202
Imagery
  individual differences in
    measurement of, 620–21
Imiprimine
  superior to group therapy,
    466
Imitation
  and communication
    development, 108–9
  and facial expression studies
    in infants and children,
      532, 534–35
  vocal
    and noisy environments,
      115
Imprinting
  and early experience studies,
    119–23
  in human infants
    and sociability, 126
Impulsiveness
  and schizophrenia
    vulnerability, 194, 196
Index of forecasting efficiency
  see Tests and scales
Index of Organizational
  Reactions
  see Tests and scales
Individual
  vs group conceptual method
    in small group studies,
      455–57, 467–68
Individual differences
  and cognition development
    cross-cultural studies,
      155–59

in cognitive abilities, 603–34
  applied differential
    psychology, 632–33
  broad ability domains,
    609–13
  changes over life span,
    624–29
  conclusions, 633–34
  genetic and environmental
    influences, 629–32
  particular domains, 613–23
  and personality, 623–24
  traits, processes, and
    competence, 606–8
in computer cognition
  models, 380
in encoding and decoding
  abilities
  in facial expression studies,
    542–43
in goal setting theory, 258
and job performance ratings,
  489–90
in memory studies, 66
and personality
  in organizational behavior,
    245–47
Indol-aminergic projections
  and satiety mechanism
  in motivation studies,
    231–32
Industrialization
  and psychopathology
    prognosis, 402
Industrial psychology
  see Organizational behavior
Industry
  group psychology in
    and social support, 420
  personnel selection in,
    479
Infancy
  social and cultural influences
    in
    and psychopathology,
      398
Infants
  cognitive abilities in
    measurement of, 624–25
  development of
    and early experience
      studies, 103–36
    negative experiences
      during, 115
  emotional disturbance in
    and clinical prevention,
      173–205
  environment and behavior of,
    200
  facial expression studies of,
    532–37, 539, 547
    review of, 529
  inadequate health care for,
    187–88

psychoanalytic trauma theory
  and development, 115–19
  response to stress
    and mental illness
      prevention, 194, 197,
        204
    at risk of mental illness, 185,
      193–94, 197–98
    tactile stimulation of
      and early experience
        studies, 114, 116
Inflexibility
  and early experience studies,
    112, 125
Influence
  and leadership
    in group process studies,
      442–43
  peer
    and small group methods,
      455, 467–68, 471–72
Information processing models
  of cognition, 263–90
  conclusion, 389–90
  elementary processor,
    385–89
  induction of patterns,
    378–80
  learning and development,
    380–83
  motivation and emotion,
    383–85
  origins of approach,
    364–66
  problem solving, 366–75
  semantic memory, 375–78
Information processing theory
  and individual differences
    in cognitive abilities, 607–8
Ingestive behavior
  computer simulated models
    of, 384
  and motivation studies,
    209–33
  conclusions, 232–33
  hypothalamic satiety
    center, 221
  hypothalamocentric
    hypothesis, 213–14
  introduction, 209
  issues, 210–13
  lateral hypothalamic
    feeding center, 214–21
  and neural mechanisms of
    taste, 283–318
  central anatomy and
    physiology, 305–12
  central involvement in
    complex phenomena,
      312–17
  historical perspectives,
    284–91
  peripheral processes,
    291–305

Initiative
  development of
    and infancy, 125, 136
Insomnia
  behavioral treatment for,
    566–67
Instincts
  as behavior patterns
    and early experience
      studies, 105–9, 111,
        119–24
Institutions
  effects on mental health, 405,
    409
Insulin
  and metabolism disruption
    in motivation studies, 214,
      216–20, 222–26
Intelligence
  of animals
    and rearing conditions,
      131–33
  fluid and crystallized
    and individual differences
      studies, 606, 610, 629
  individual differences in
    and memory, 66
  see Cognitive abilities
Intensity perception
  in auditory psychophysics,
    41–45
Interactionism
  and personnel selection
    practices, 504
Interaction scoring system
  see Tests and scales
Interaural temporal thresholds
  and lateralization, 48–49
Internal capsule (IC)
  surgical knife cuts along
    and ingestive behavior
      studies, 217–18
    and taste neuropsychology,
      311
INTERNIST
  computer simulation model
    in medical diagnosis, 369
Interpersonal Behavior Scale
  see Tests and scales
Intervention
  see Community intervention;
    Small groups
Interview
  and personnel selection
    practices, 504–9
  person perception research,
    508–9
  sex and race, 505–6
  validity, 508
Intoxication
  and state-dependent learning
    studies, 90
Involvement
  in jobs

and organizational
behavior studies, 250
IQ
see Tests and scales
Iran
facial expression studies in,
529–31
Isolation
as rearing condition
and developmental effects,
107, 114, 125, 131–32
Israel
female job satisfaction in,
588
Israeli Army
and biodata selection studies,
510
ISSAC
computer simulation model
and physics problems, 372

J

Japanese
facial expression studies of,
530–31
Job analysis
in personnel selection, 478,
480, 484–86
Job Descriptive Index
see Tests and scales
Job interviewing
and career counseling,
586–87
Job Match Index
see Tests and scales
Job performance measurement
and personnel selection,
486–90
individual differences
correlates, 489
rater training, 486–88
validity of ratings, 488–89
Jokes
memory for, 93
Jury studies
and group decision-making,
425–26, 445–46
Justice
sense of
and job motivation studies,
259

K

Kin terms comprehension
and cross-cultural cognition,
152–53
Koh's blocks
see Tests and scales
Koranic schools
and cognitive skills
development, 166–67

Koro
as culture-specific syndrome,
401
Kpelle
cognition development
among
and economic activities,
155
and intellectual activities,
165
Kuder Occupational Interest
Survey
see Tests and scales

L

Labeling
destructive effects of
and mental illness
prevention, 187, 202
as sociocultural factor
in psychopathology,
398–99, 402–4, 410
Labor
market
and personnel selection,
502–4
sexual division of
and cognition
development, 155
Language
abilities and skills
individual differences in,
613–15
acquisition of
and computer simulation
modeling, 382
comprehension
computer simulation
models of, 378
computer programming
and cognition models, 363,
365, 389
development of
and children's test scores,
626
and early experience
studies, 107–8
and Milwaukee Project,
630
and learning
and origins of psychology,
26
natural
and computer cognition
models, 366–67, 371,
374–77
Language Acquisition Device
(LAD)
and early experience studies,
108
Lashley III maze
see Tests and scales

Latah
as culture-specific syndrome,
401, 412
Lateralization
and auditory psychophysics,
48–51, 53
of cognitive abilities
in brain-damaged patients,
609
and emotional expression
studies, 548
sex differences in, 631
Laughter
development of
and facial expression in
infants, 534
Law enforcement personnel
see Police
Leader Behavior Description
Questionnaire
see Tests and scales
Leadership
assessment of
and personnel selection,
509–11
in group process psychology,
420, 440–44
appraisal of leaders,
440–42
and influence, 442–43
member participation in
groups, 443–44
influence
and small group methods,
468–69
in organizational behavior
studies, 263–71
contingency model, 263–66
new measures, 266–67
new paradigms, 268–70
new theories, 267–68
path-goal theory, 264–65
ratings
and Army officer success,
588
style measures
see Tests and scales
styles of
and group process, 420
Learned helplessness
and depression treatment,
563
and psychopathology, 408–9
Learning
ability relationships
and individual differences
studies, 611
and development
computer cognition
models, 380–83
disabilities
strategies for prevention,
183

questions about
  and origins of psychology,
    26
  rote verbal
    and computer models, 365,
      368
  state-dependent
    and memory studies,
      90–91
Least Preferred Coworker scale
  (LPC)
  see Tests and scales
Lesions
  in brain
    effects on motivation and
      ingestive behavior,
      210–33
    and facial expression studies,
      548
    thalamic and hypothalamic
      and taste neurophysiology,
      306, 313–16
Liberia
  communication and cognition
    studies in, 163
  tailoring and mathematical
    skills in, 167
Life events
  and psychopathology role,
    407–11
Life events scales
  see Tests and scales
Life span
  and cognitive ability changes,
    624–29
    aging and decline, 627–29
    infants and young
      children, 624–25
    older children, 625–27
Light
  experience of
    and critical development
      periods, 123, 129–31,
      134, 136
Limbic system
  and emotional expression
    studies, 548
  and taste neuropsychology,
    312, 316–17
Linear transformations
  in pitch perception, 36–39
Linguistic control
  of aggressive behavior,
    558–59
Linguistic relativity hypothesis
  and categorization, 153
Linguistics
  and psychology, 4–5
LISP
  programming language
    and cognition models, 365
Literacy
  and cognitive skills
    development, 166–67

Localization of sound
  and binaural hearing, 45–48
Locomotion
  among humans
    and early experience
      studies, 107–8
    and motor organization
      concepts, 329–30, 334,
      358
Locus of control
  and career decision-making,
    579–80
  and career maturity
    measures, 582
  and organizational behavior
    studies, 246, 250, 254,
    257
  and women's vocational
    choices, 583
Loggers
  education and goal setting
    among, 256–57
  performance rating of
    and personnel selection
      studies, 489
Logic
  and history of psychology, 19
Logical operations
  and cognitive universals
    in cross-cultural studies,
      148–53, 160
Logico-mathematics
  and psychology, 2–4
Long-term memory (LTM)
  see Memory
Long-term store (LTS)
  in memory studies, 74
Lord-Nicholson formula
  and statistical considerations
    in personnel selection,
      491–92
Lorge-Thorndike Intelligence
  Test
  see Tests and scales
Loss of spouse
  and mental illness
    prevention, 184

M

Macaque monkeys
  chorda tympani of
    and taste studies, 297–98,
      302
Malaysia
  facial expression studies in,
    529
Maltose
  in taste neuropsychology, 303
Mammals
  imprinting among, 120, 123
  sucrose sensitivity in, 301–2
Mapping
  in cognition modeling, 387

Marital problems
  and counseling, 561–62
Masking
  in auditory memory, 68
  binaural
    and auditory
      psychophysics, 51–55
  monaural
    and signal detection
      theory, 35
Maternal deprivation and
  attachment
  and psychological
    development, 124–28,
    136
Mathematical ability
  and individual differences
    studies, 618
Maturation
  developmental role
    and early experience
      studies, 105–6
  rate of
    and spatial ability, 631
Mauritius Project
  and schizophrenia
    prevention, 197, 204
Mayan villages
  and children's memory tasks,
    161
Meaning
  memory encoding of, 92–93
Mechanics
  expert knowledge in
    and computer simulation
      modeling, 369
Medicaid
  and mental illness prevention
    programs, 186
Medical care
  and mental illness
    prevention, 184
Medical diagnosis
  expert knowledge in
    and computer simulation
      models, 369
Memory
  and aging
    and decline of cognitive
      abilities, 627–28
  and culture
    mixed approaches to,
      160–73
  encoding processes, 77–84
    alternatives to levels,
      79–81
    levels of processing, 77–79
    rehearsal and repetition,
      81–84
  future directions, 95–97
  in intensity discrimination,
    44
  among Kpelle, 165
  long-term (LTM)

and computer cognition
    models, 366, 370–71,
    375, 386–90
retrieval processes, 84–91
encoding specificity, 87–88
gaining access to the trace,
    85–87
recall and recognition,
    88–91
semantic
    and computer modeling,
        366, 369–70, 375–78,
        385, 388–90
sensory and representational,
    66–73
    auditory, 68–69
    for chess positions, 72
    faces and scenes, 71–72
    iconic, 67–68
    overview of sensory
        memory, 73
    for pictures and words,
        70–71
    words and gestures, 69
for sentences, stories, and
    discourse, 91–95
    for sentences and
        paragraphs, 92–93
    for stories, 93–95
short-term retention (STM),
    73–77
    characteristics of primary
        memory, 75–76
    and computer cognition
        models, 366–68,
        370–71, 374, 385–88
    recency, 77
    release from proactive
        inhibition, 76
    theoretical developments,
        73–75
skills
    individual differences in,
        621–22
Mental health
    importance of early
        experiences, 104
    and job satisfaction, 248–49
Mental illness
    clinical prevention of,
        173–205
    advocacy role of
        psychologists, 174–75
    basic understandings in
        planning, 193–204
    conclusion, 204–5
    introduction, 174
    local prevention programs,
        187–93
    national proposals, 182–87
    training, 177–82
effects of labeling on, 403–4
see also Psychopathology

Mentally retarded
    and vocational counseling,
        586
    see Milwaukee Project
Mexican-Americans
    community intervention
        programs with, 190–91
Mexicans
    facial expression studies of,
        530
    rural potters and farmers
        and cross-cultural
        cognition studies,
        151–52
Micronesians
    navigational skills of
        and cross-cultural
        cognition studies, 163
Microphysics
    and psychology, 7–8
Migraine headache
    behavioral treatment of, 566,
        568
Military
    leadership in
        and multiple assessment,
            510–11
Milwaukee Project
    and cognitive stimulation, 630
    and early experience studies,
        111
    and mental illness
        prevention, 190, 204
Mind
    questions about
        and origins of psychology,
            25–26
Minnesota Multiphasic
    Personality Inventory
        (MMPI)
    see Tests and scales
Minnesota Satisfaction
    Questionnaire
    see Tests and scales
Minorities
    discrimination against
        in personnel selection,
            480–81, 496–502,
            505–6, 511
    students
        and academic behavior
            changes, 557
Miraculin
    and sugar reception, 302
Mnemonic systems
    textbook on, 66
    see Memory
Modeling
    and career decision-making,
        580
    in coping with aggression,
        558
    and job-seeking skills, 587

in phobia treatment, 564–65
    and self-disclosure in
        therapy, 573
    in social skills training
        and school conduct, 557
Models
    causal
        and sociocultural factors in
            psychopathology, 399,
            404
    of cognition
        information processing,
            363–90
        see also Information
            processing
    factor
        of cognitive abilities,
            610–11
    historical
        of psychology, 15–17
    of motor control systems,
        337–52
        adaptive gain, 338–42
        closed-loop, 342–45
        dynamic errors and
            stability, 345
        open-loop, 337–38
    of test fairness
        and personnel selection,
            498–500
Monkeys
    eye movement studies in
        and motor organization,
            340–42, 347, 350
    lesions in
        and ingestive behavior
            studies, 230–31
    reared in isolation
        and early experience
            studies, 107, 114, 125,
            132
Monte Carlo Study
    and statistical considerations
        in personnel selection,
            491–95
Morocco
    memory studies in, 162
Morrisby shapes
    see Tests and scales
Mössbauer technique
    and basilar membrane
        response
        in auditory psychophysics,
            40
Mother-Child Home Program
    and infant development, 128
Mother-child interaction
    and early experience studies,
        126–28
Mothering behavior
    development of
        and early experience
            studies, 107, 125

and socially responsive
    infants, 114–15
    see also Maternal deprivation
Motivation
    biology of, 209–33
    conclusions, 232–33
    hypothalamic satiety
        center, 221
    hypothalamocentric
        hypothesis, 213–14
    issues, 210–13
    lateral hypothalamic
        feeding center, 214–21
    and emotion
        in cognitive computer
            modeling, 383–85
    intrinsic
        and early experience
            studies, 121–22, 124,
            126
    and job performance
        ratings of handicapped,
        507
    in organizational behavior
        studies, 247, 251–63
    equity theory, 258–59
    expectancy theory,
        253–55
    goal setting, 255–58
    new directions, 261–63
    operant conditioning,
        259–61
Motoneurons
    alpha and gamma
        and motor organization
            studies, 330–37
Motor disturbances
    and lesions
        and motivation studies,
        216, 218–19
Motor organization concepts,
    327–58
    centrally programmed
        movement, 328–37
    alpha-gamma coactivation,
        331–33
    feedback to motor cortex,
        335–37
    proprioception and active
        movement, 330–31
    sensory relay neurons,
        333–35
    control system models,
        337–52
    adaptive gain, 338–42
    closed-loop, 342–45
    dynamic errors and
        stability, 345
    open-loop, 337–38
    efference copy and corollary
        discharge, 352–57
    gamma motoneuron
        discharge, 357–58

perceptual vs motor
    localization, 356
perceptual stability, 354–56
sensations attributable to
    muscle receptors,
    356–57
visuomotor coordination,
    352–54
Mucous colitis
    behavioral treatment of, 566
Multiple Screen Model
    and leadership studies,
    267–68
Muscle relaxation training
    in treating insomnia, 567
    in treating migraine
        headache, 568
Music
    physics and psychophysics
        of, 33
    recognition of
        and pitch perception, 38
MYCIN
    computer simulation model
        in medical diagnosis, 369

N

Natural environments
    memory for, 66, 68
Navigational skills
    of Micronesians
        and cross-cultural
            cognition, 163
Navy
    personnel selection studies in,
        506, 513
    and cognitive ability
        testing, 610
Neglect
    infantile
        and psychopathic
            delinquency, 125
Neonates
    facial expressions of
        and taste preferences,
        304
Nest building
    and early experience studies,
        107
Neural control
    and facial expression of
        emotion, 547–48
Neuroanatomy
    and biology of motivation,
        210–11, 228–32
    and neurochemistry
        effects of early experience
            on, 128, 133–35
Neuromuscular development
    in infants
        and early experience
            studies, 110

Neurons
    alpha and gamma
        and motor organization
            studies, 330–37,
            356–78
    pyramidal tract, 335–37
    sensory relay, 333–35
Neurophysiology
    of emotion, 547–48
    of taste, 283–318
    central anatomy and
        physiology, 305–12
    central involvement in
        complex phenomena,
        312–17
    historical perspectives,
        284–91
    peripheral processes,
        291–305
    see also Motor organization
Neuropsychological functioning
    in schizophrenia, 195–96
Neuropsychology
    and memory, 66
Newborn
    facial expressions of, 532–33
    see Infants
New Guinea
    facial expression studies in,
        529–30
Nigrostriatal projections
    and lesions, 215–16
Noise
    and infant development
        studies, 115
Nominal Group Technique
    decision methods
        in organization policy, 501
Nonlinear effects
    in auditory psychophysics,
        39–41, 55
Non-Western people
    cognitive skills of
        measuring, 163–67
Noradrenergic compounds (NE)
    and lesions
        in motivation studies, 215,
        217–18, 228, 230–31
Norepinephrine
    in brain
        and variable rearing
            conditions, 134
Nursing
    as instinct
        and early experience
            studies, 105–6
Nutrition
    and chemical senses, 291
    and cognitive intervention in
        Colombia, 630
    and mental illness
        prevention, 184, 188,
        198, 204

O

Obesity
  behavioral treatment of, 568–69
  and VMH lesions, 221–26
  see Ingestive behavior
Occupation
  see Organizational behavior;
    Personnel selection
Occupational counseling
  see Career counseling
Oculomotor system
  control systems in, 337–52
Oedipal hypothesis
  and early experience studies,
    113
Olfaction
  and taste neuropsychology,
    285, 291, 304, 312,
    314
Operant conditioning
  in job motivation studies,
    259–61
  in leadership, 267
O phosphorylethanolamine
  in taste studies, 293
Opportunity
  equality of
  and personnel selection,
    479–80, 496–502
Optokinetic system
  and motor organization
    concepts, 337–58
Organization
  concept of
  in memory studies, 90
Organizational behavior,
    243–72
  job attitudes, 247–51
    attributions, 250–51
    commitment, 249
    involvement, 250
    satisfaction, 247–49
  leadership, 263–70
    contingency model, 263–66
    path-goal theory, 264–65
  motivation, 251–63
    equity theory, 258–59
    expectancy theory, 253–55
    goal setting, 255–58
    new directions, 261–63
    operant conditioning,
      259–61
  personality and individual
    differences, 245–47
    main effects, 245–46
    matches and moderators,
      246–47
Orphans
  development among
  and early experience
    studies, 107–8, 111,
    124–25, 127–28

Outcome research
  and intracounseling
    behaviors, 570–77
Outgrowing
  behavior problems
  and mental illness
    prevention, 184, 189,
    202
Overcrowding
  effects on infant
    development, 115
Overstimulation
  and coping
  and mental illness
    prevention, 198, 203

P

Pain
  control of, 566–68
Paired-associates tasks (PA)
  and individual differences
  in cognitive abilities,
    610–12, 621–22
Pakistani gypsies
  socialization practices of
  and cognitive performance,
    168
Parabrachial nuclei
  in taste neuropsychology,
    308, 311–12, 316
Parachloromercuribenzoate
  (PCMB)
  in sugar receptor studies, 301
Paralysis
  of facial movements
  and facial expressions,
    547–48
  and illusory eye movement
  and motor organization
    studies, 355
Paranoia
  computer simulated patient
  and cognition modeling,
    383–85
Paraprofessionals
  in mental health intervention,
    191–92
Parent-child interaction
  and difficult babies
  and mental illness
    prevention, 194–95
Parent effectiveness training
  (PET)
  in family problem
    prevention, 589
  and intervention techniques,
    187
Parenting skills
  training in
  and mental illness
    prevention, 177, 180,
    187, 190–92

Parents
  discrepant messages from
  and children's perceptions,
    545
  similarities with children
  and career choice, 585
Participation
  in group discussions
  and leadership studies,
    440–44
PAS-II
  computer simulation model
  in protocol analysis,
    374–75
Path-goal theory
  in organizational leadership
    studies, 264–65, 267,
    270
Pattern theory
  of taste quality
    discrimination, 286,
    306
Peer influence
  and small group methods,
    455, 467–68, 471–72
Perceived expertness
  of therapist
  and therapeutic outcome,
    575
Perception
  in infants
  and infant-mother
    relationships, 127–28
  of leadership
  and organizational behavior
    studies, 269–70
  of persons
  and personnel selection
    interviews, 508–9
  taste
  neural mechanisms of,
    283–318
  visual
  and motor organization
    concepts, 337–52
  see also Audition; Vision
Perceptual cognitive integration
  loss of
  and schizophrenia
    vulnerability, 194
Perceptual experience
  and imprinting, 121–24
  vs motor experience
  early experience effects,
    128–29
Perceptual skills
  hypothesis
  and cross-cultural
    cognition studies,
    158–59
  individual differences in,
    618–21

PERRY
paranoid patient model
    and cognition studies,
    383–85
Personal change
    small group methods of,
    453–74
    see also Change; Small
    groups
Personality
    authoritarian
        and psychosexual
        development theory,
        112
    and career selection, 579
    and cognition, 623–24
    field dependence-
        independence, 624
    deviant
        and mental illness
        prevention, 193
    and emotion
        and facial expressions, 528
    functioning
        and small group processes,
        467
    and history of psychology,
        19
    and individual differences
        in organizational behavior,
        245–47
    and job leadership, 265–66
    psychopathic
        and child-rearing, 117–18
16 Personality Factors
    see Tests and scales
Personality Research Form
    see Tests and scales
Personal Orientation Inventory
    (POI)
    see Tests and scales
Personnel selection
    and classification systems,
        477–514
    future context, 514
    historical context, 478–82
    job analysis, 484–86
    job performance
        measurement, 486–90
    labor market issues, 502–4
    psychometrics of equal
        opportunity, 496–502
    selection practices, 504–14
    statistical considerations,
        490–96
    validity and validation,
        482–84
Person perception
    and facial expression studies,
    529–32, 549
Phantom limb pain
    relaxation exercise treatment,
    568

Pharmacotherapy
    for depressives, 564
    in insomnia treatment,
        566
Pharmacy profession
    assessment programs for,
        510–11
Phobias
    and anxiety treatments,
        564–66
Phonemic codes
    in memory studies, 77, 80,
        84
Phrenoblysis
    and critical development
        periods, 124
Physics
    computer simulation models
        in, 367, 372
    and psychology, 7–8
    history of, 24
Physiology
    sensory
        and pitch perception,
        36
Piaget
    and universalistic approach
        to cross-cultural cognition
        studies, 148–54
Piagetian task performance
    correlation with cognitive
        testing, 625
    and information processing
        models, 381–82
Pictures
    and memory encoding
        studies, 70–71
Pitch perception
    and auditory psychophysics,
        35–39
    and binaural hearing,
        54–55
Pituitary functions
    and ingestive behavior
        studies, 229, 231
Poisson counting model
    in intensity perception
        studies, 41
Poker
    computer playing
        adaptive production
        system, 382
Polarization
    in group processes, 428
Police
    personnel selection studies of,
        508, 510–11, 513
    treatment of aggression
        among, 558
Political rituals
    in China
        and small group process,
        430, 472

Politics
    and organizational behavior,
        244
Polyethylene glycol
    and dehydration
    and ingestive behavior
        studies, 216, 219
Pontine gustatory neurons
    and taste neuropsychology,
        308, 311, 313
Position Analysis Questionnaire
    (PAQ)
    see Tests and scales
Posner paradigm
    see Tests and scales
Poverty families
    and infant development, 115
    teenage mothers of
        and maternal attachment,
        127
Power
    and organizational behavior,
        244
    social
        and leadership studies,
        442–43
Praxeology
    and economics and
        psychology, 5
Predeterminism
    and preformationism
        in psychological
        development, 104,
        109–12
Premorbid adjustment
    sociocultural factors in, 399,
        412
Preschoolers
    social skills program for, 557
President's Commission on
    Mental Health
    Prevention Task Force,
        182–83
    and National proposals,
        182–87
Prevention
    and counseling, 588–90
    family problems, 588–89
    school problems, 589–90
Prevention planning
    in clinical psychology,
        173–205
    aggression prevention,
        199–200
    antilabelers vs
        diagnosticians, 202–3
    cautions, 203–4
    community activity
        centers, 200–1
    difficult babies, 194–95
    ecology and behavior, 200
    hazards, blinders, and
        reflections, 201

schizophrenia, 195–98
  strengths, 198–99
Primary Mental Abilities Test
  (PMA)
  see Tests and scales
Primary Mental Health Project
  (PMHP)
  and school problem
    prevention, 589–90
Primates
  affectional system in
    development of, 107
  facial expression studies, 529
  problem-solving among
    and rearing conditions,
      131–32
Prisoners
  vocational maturity measures
    among, 582
Privacy
  right to
    in mental-illness
      prevention programs,
      184, 186–87
Proactive inhibition
  release from
    and memory studies, 76
Probationers
  recidivism among
    linear prediction of, 495
Problems
  missionaries and cannibals
    and computer simulation
      models, 367, 371
  number scrabble
    and computer simulation
      modeling, 371
  Prisoner's Dilemma
    and group process studies,
      421
  Tower of Hanoi
    and computer simulation
      models, 367, 371–72
  water jug
    and computer simulation
      models, 367
Problem-solving
  effects of early experience on,
    128–33
  complexity of rearing
    conditions, 131–35
  perceptual vs motor
    experience, 128–29
  variations in sensory
    experience, 129–31
  and group decision making,
    424–27
  Program Evaluation
    Review Technique,
    426
  skills
    and marital problems, 561

theory of
  and information processing
    models, 365–75, 386
  training
    and career
      decision-making, 580
Process theory
  in job motivation studies, 252
Project Head Start
  failure of
    and early experience
      studies, 104
Proprioception
  and active movement
    in motor organization
      studies, 330–31, 352,
      354–55
PSG
  and cognition modeling,
    386–87
Psychiatric hospital
  as sociocultural influence
    in psychopathology,
    409–10
Psychiatric patients
  facial expression
    measurement of, 539
Psychoanalysis
  and conceptions of early
    experience, 112–19
    infantile trauma theory,
      115–19
    psychosexual development
      theory, 112–15
Psychology
  and relations with other
    sciences, 1–8
    biology, 1–2
    cybernetics, 6–7
    economics, 5
    linguistics, 4–5
    logico-mathematical
      disciplines, 2–4
    physics, 7–8
    sociology, 5–6
Psychometric models
  in personnel selection, 480,
    496–502
Psychometrics
  and individual differences
    in cognitive abilities,
      603–34
  see Individual differences
Psychopathic personality
  and child-rearing, 117–18,
    125
Psychopathology
  social and cultural influences
    on, 397–413
    causal models, 399
    classification of
      psychopathology, 399

family studies, 406–7
labeling, 403–4
life events, 407–9
psychiatric hospitals,
  409–10
social class, 403
social supports, 404–5
symptom type, 401–3
theoretical considerations,
  410–12
time of impact, 398
treatment systems, 405–6
Psychosexual development
  and early experience studies,
    112–15
Psychosomatic medicine
  and psychology, 2
Psychotherapy
  and small group methods,
    453–74
  and outcome research,
    464–66, 468
Punishment
  and psychopathic personality
    and child-rearing, 117
Purkinje output cells
  and adaptive gain control
    in motor organization
      studies, 341–42, 347

Q

Q auditory filters
  and pitch perception, 39
Quaranic students
  and memory studies, 162–63
Quinine
  in ingestive behavior studies,
    222–25
  in taste studies, 285, 292–93,
    295–98, 304, 306–7,
    310, 314, 317

R

Race
  differences in cognitive
    abilities, 631–32
  discrimination against
    see Minorities
  and sex
    in children's cognition
      studies, 626
Racial differences
  in counseling, 574–75
Racism
  as social-environmental
    stressor, 184
Raphe nuclei
  and lesions
    and ingestive behavior
      studies, 230–31

Rats
  aphagia and adipsia in,
    214–32
  mothering behavior among,
    107
  tactile contact experiments
    and aversiveness, 116–18
  taste neuropsychology of,
    286, 289–90, 293,
    295–96, 299–301,
    306–11, 313, 317
Raven Progressive Matrices
  see Tests and scales
Raynaud's disease
  behavioral intervention in,
    566
Reaction-time studies
  and cognitive process
    modeling, 385
Reading
  and language abilities, 614
  and working memory theory,
    73–74
Reasoning
  nonverbal
    and achievement, 632
  and problem solving
    individual differences
      studies, 616–18
Recall
  in memory studies, 80,
    82–84, 87–91, 93–94
Receiver Operating
  Characteristic (ROC)
  and signal detection theory,
    35
Recency effect
  in auditory memory studies,
    68, 77
Recognition
  in color coding studies
    and cross-cultural studies,
      154
  in memory encoding, 82–84,
    87–91
  and reaction time
    and facial expression
      studies, 548
Rehearsal
  in memory encoding, 81–84
Reinforcement
  and taste studies, 290, 318
Religious groups
  compared with
    peer-psychotherapy
      groups, 472
Remote Associates Test
  see Tests and scales
Repetition
  and memory encoding, 81–84
Representational memory,
  66–73

auditory, 68–69
for chess positions, 72
faces and scenes, 71–72
iconic, 67–68
overview of sensory
  memory, 73
for pictures and words,
  70–71
words and gestures, 69
Retardation
  and hospital group care, 113
  and maternal deprivation,
    125
  among orphans
    and early experience
      studies, 107–8,
      124–25
Retrieval
  speed of
    effects of aging on, 628
Retrieval processes
  in human memory, 84–91
    encoding specificity, 87–88
    gaining access to the trace,
      85–87
    recall and recognition,
      88–91
Rewards
  intrinsic and extrinsic
    and job motivation studies,
      261–62
Ribonucleic acid (RNA)
  in brain
    and variable rearing
      conditions, 134
Risk
  in group decision making,
    421, 428
  of mental illness
    prediction of, 183–84
Rod and frame test
  see Tests and scales
Rod vision
  and iconic memory, 67
Role theory
  and organizational behavior,
    244
Roller skating
  by infants
    and early experience
      studies, 110, 122
Rooming-in
  and newborn environment,
    200
Rule induction
  computer simulation models
    of, 378, 390

S

Saccadic eye movements
  and adaptive gain control

in motor organization
    studies, 340, 348,
    354–56
Saccharin
  and taste neuropsychology,
    293, 295, 302
Sadness
  facial expression of, 531, 536,
    546
SAD SAM
  computer simulation model
    and genealogies, 375–76
Salt
  in taste studies, 285, 288–90,
    292–93, 296–300, 304–7,
    310, 316
SAPA
  computer simulation model
    in protocol analysis,
      374–75
Satiety
  and motivation studies, 210,
    212, 221–32
Satisfaction
  job
    and career adaptation,
      587–88
    and decision-making
      participation, 443–44
    and organizational
      behavior studies,
      246–49, 257, 264
Schema
  in cognition models
    and information
      processing, 376–77,
      390
  in memory studies, 64–65,
    71–72, 91, 93–94
Schizophrenia
  prevention of
    and children at risk of,
      187–88, 193, 195–98,
      203
  predisposition and
    vulnerability to,
      193–98, 203–5
  sociocultural factors in,
    398–99, 401, 403, 406,
    408, 412
Schizophrenics
  facial expression studies of,
    530
  self-disclosure among
    and small group methods,
      456, 466
Scholastic Aptitude Test (SAT)
  see Tests and scales
School
  achievement determinants
    individual differences, 632
  conduct

altering through
counseling, 556–57
and mental illness prevention
programs
in children, 175, 200
problems
prevention of, 589–90
Schooling
and early experience studies,
104
SCL-90
see Tests and scales
Scratch reflex
in deafferented spinal animals
and motor organization
studies, 328–29, 333,
358
Scripts
in cognition models
and information
processing, 376, 390
Security
loss of
and schizophrenic
vulnerability, 194
Self
evaluation of
and group processes,
438–40
as schema
in memory encoding, 65
Self-analysis
in Soviet rural village
and cross-cultural
cognition, 160
Self-attribution theory
and facial feedback, 545–46
Self-concept ratings
and sensitivity training
groups
outcome studies, 464
Self-confidence
in children
and mental illness
prevention, 198
Self-conscious awareness
and facial expression of
emotion, 536
Self-Directed Search (SDS)
see Tests and scales
Self-disclosure
in counseling
methods to increase,
572–74
and small group methods,
456, 468
Self-efficacy
enhancement of
and phobia treatment,
564–65
Self-esteem
and career anxiety, 578

and group structure, 447
and organizational behavior,
245–46, 254, 257–58
and sociocultural impact on
psychopathology, 404,
411
and women's vocational
choice, 583
Self-help groups
and influence studies, 430,
468, 471–72
Self-report measures
see Tests and scales
Semantic
judgment task
and individual differences
studies, 612
memory
age differences in, 628
and computer modeling,
366, 369–70, 375–78,
385, 388–90
orienting tasks
in memory studies, 65,
77–78, 81
processing
in memory encoding,
79–80, 84, 87, 91
Semantics
sex modification of
and memory encoding, 69
Sense perception theory
and history of psychology, 12
Sensitivity training
and group influence studies,
430
and outcome research, 464
Sensorimotor coordination
and eye movement studies,
337–52
Sensory disturbances
and brain lesions
and motivation studies,
216, 218–19
Sensory experience
effects of variations in
and early experience
studies, 129–31
Sensory memory
see Representational memory
Sentences
memory for, 91–93
Sequence extrapolation
and information processing
models, 365, 378–79
Serotonin (5-HT)
and ingestive behavior
studies, 217, 230
Sex
bias
in leadership rating, 270
in success attribution, 251

discrimination against
and personnel selection
studies, 480–81,
496–502
see also Women
and race
in children's cognition
testing, 626
and semantic modification
in memory encoding, 69
Sex differences
in cognitive abilities
lateralization and spatial
ability, 631
in hope of power
and leadership, 443
in relatedness of personality
and ability, 623
in self-disclosure, 572
in socializing, 444
in success attribution, 251
Sex-role stereotypes
and personnel selection, 506
and vocational choice,
583–86
career orientation, 584
nontraditional choices,
583–84
origins of career choice,
585–86
realism, 584
stability, 585
Sexual
composition of a group
and cohesiveness, 435
disorders
and counseling, 562
division of labor
and cognition
development, 155
Shock
fixitive effects of
and early experience
studies, 112
Short-term memory, 73–77
characteristics of primary
memory, 75–76
recency, 77
release from proactive
inhibition, 76
theoretical developments,
73–75
Signal Detection theory
and auditory psychophysics,
34–35
Signal frequency
in binaural masking, 52–53
Signaling behaviors
among infants
see Facial expressions
Skill
remembering as, 96

Small groups
  and group political pressure,
    430
  methods of personal change,
    453–74
    clinical vs statistical
      approach, 457–59
    individual vs group
      conceptual
      framework, 455–57
    outcome conceptualization
      and measurement,
      460–67
    personal change processes,
      467–72
Smiling
  among infants
    development of, 533–34,
      536–37
  and negative speech
    in facial expression studies,
      545
Smoking cessation
  and counseling, 566, 570
SNOBOL
  programming language
    and cognition modeling,
      365
Social attachment
  among birds and mammals
    critical periods for, 123–24
Social behavior
  altering through counseling,
    556–62
    aggression, 558–59
    assertiveness, 559–60
    friendship, 560–61
    marital problems, 561–62
    school conduct and
      academic behavior,
      556–57
  and facial expressions,
    527–49
Social class
  and schizophrenia, 399–401,
    403, 406, 409
  and speech styles, 614
Social Desirability Scale
  see Tests and scales
Social environment
  and aggression prevention,
    199
Social factors
  in cognitive development,
    149
Social influence
  in counseling, 574–76
    attraction, 574–75
    perceived expertness,
      575–76
  on psychopathology, 397–413
    see Psychopathology

Social intelligence
  and individual differences
    in cognitive abilities,
      610–11
Socialization
  and cross-cultural cognition
    studies, 154–60
    psychological
      differentiation, 155–59
    Soviet cultural-historical
      approach, 159–60
  and maternal attachment and
    deprivation
  and early experience
    studies, 125
Social pressure
  on group members
    and decision making, 421,
      428–32
Social psychology
  group processes, 417–48
    history of the field, 418–24
    recent research, 424–48
Social responsiveness
  among infants
    and auditory and visual
      experience, 114, 136
Social skills training
  of depressives, 563
Socioeconomic status (SES)
  of therapy clients
    and persistence in
      treatment, 576–77
Sociology
  and psychology, 5–6
Sociomedicine
  and origins of psychology,
    25
Sound
  measurement of
    and auditory
      psychophysics, 33
South Fore
  of Papua
    and facial expression
      studies, 529
Soviet cultural-historical
    approach
  to cross-cultural cognition,
    159–60
Soviet Union
  facial expression studies in,
    529
Spatial
  ability
    cognition and personality,
      623
    and genetic influence,
      630
  orientation
    individual differences in,
      619–20

Spectral concept
  in pitch perception studies,
    37–39, 46–47, 54
Speech
  and facial expressions of
    emotion, 544–45, 549
  loss of under stress
    and schizophrenia
      vulnerability, 194
  styles and performance
    and intelligence testing,
      614–15
Spinal cord studies
  and visuomotor coordination,
    357–58
Standardized intelligence tests
  see Tests and scales
Stanford-Binet
  see Tests and scales
State-dependent learning
  and memory studies, 90
Statistics
  in personnel selection
    and nonlinear prediction,
      494–95
Sternberg STM-search
    paradigm
  see Tests and scales
Stevioside
  and sugar reception studies,
    302
Stimulus control
  in insomnia treatment, 567
Stimulus level
  in psychopathology studies,
    410, 412
Stochastic models
  in cognitive process studies,
    385
Stories
  memory for, 93–95
  understanding and telling
    and computer simulation
      models, 378
Stress
  ability to cope with
    and locus of control
      studies, 246
  anticipation of
    and group affiliation,
      436–37
  combat
    and mental health, 184
  emotional and physical
    and group decision making,
      427
  environmental
    and mental illness
      prevention, 183–84,
      187
  and group leadership
    appraisal, 441–42

job
  and emotional problems
    prevention, 181
  and satisfaction, 248, 265
life
  and psychopathology, 400,
    403, 407, 410–11
reactivity to
  and schizophrenic
    vulnerability, 196–97,
    204–5
reduction of
  and self-help groups, 471
Strong Vocational Interest
  Blank
  see Tests and scales
Structuralism
  and history of psychology,
    18
Structure of Intellect model
  (SI)
  and cognitive abilities
    studies, 610–11
STUDENT
  computer simulation model
  and algebra problems, 372
Success
  attribution of
    and organizational
      behavior, 251
  of group
    and cohesiveness, 433–36
Sucrose
  in taste neuropsychology,
    292–93, 295–96, 300–4,
    310, 314–16
Sucrose octaacetate
  and early aversive experience
    in rats, 117
Sugar
  preference
    genesis of, 291
    in taste studies, 285, 290,
      292–93, 295–98, 304,
      306–7
    hedonic processes, 290,
      301–5
Suggestion
  autogenic
    in insomnia treatment, 567
  hypnotic and self-
    in pain control, 568
Suicide
  in children, 175
Surprise
  facial expression of, 531,
    533–34, 536
Swimming
  by infants
    and early experience
      studies, 110
Symbolic communication
  among apes

and language achievement
  theories, 108
Sympathy
  in children
    and overcrowding, 199
Syphilis
  and disturbed behavior, 184
System of Interactive Guidance
  Information (SIGI)
  see Tests and scales

T

Tactile stimulation
  of infants
    and early experience
      studies, 114, 116
Taste
  neurophysiology of
    see Ingestive behavior
  preferences
    and hedonic processes,
      302–5
  unpleasant
    and infant facial
      expression, 533
Taste reactivity test
  see Tests and scales
Teams-games-tournament
  (TGT) program
  and altering school behavior,
    556–57
Teenage mothers
  infants of
    and mental illness
      prevention, 188
Tehran orphanage
  development studies at
    and early experiences,
      107–8, 111, 128
Television
  effects on infant
    development, 115
  violence and behavior
    and facial expression, 549
Temperature
  and taste neurophysiology,
    312–13
Templates
  in cognition models
    and information
      processing, 376, 390
Terminator-remainer battery
  (TR)
  see Tests and scales
Test fairness
  models of, 498–500
Testimony
  in court
    and memory encoding
      studies, 71
Testing
  and civil rights

in personnel selection
  studies, 481
intelligence
  and broad ability domain
    studies, 608–13
  and individual differences,
    605–6
Test publishing industry
  and personnel selection
    history, 479
Tests and scales
  Atkinson-Shiffrin PA task
    and individual differences
      studies, 612
  Bayley Scales of Infant
    Development
    Mental Development
      Index of, 624–25
  Beck Depression Inventory
    and cognitive therapy,
      564
  Behaviorally anchored rating
    scales (BARS)
    in personnel selection, 487
  Berkeley growth and
    guidance studies
    and predetermined
      development, 109
  California Test of Mental
    Maturity
    and test score stability, 626
  Career Development Inventory
    (CDI)
    and career counseling, 581
  Career Maturity Inventory
    (CMI)
    and career counseling,
      581–82
  Comprehensive Ability Battery
    and factor analysis, 609–10
    and predicting high school
      grades, 632
  Corman-Escalona Scales of
    Object Permanence
    and infant cognition, 625
  Differential Aptitude Tests
    and validity studies, 632
  DQ (Developmental Quotient)
    and early experience studies,
      109–11
  Embedded figures test
    and cross-cultural cognition,
      156, 159
    and infant cognition, 625
  Empathic Understanding Scale
    and therapist ratings, 571
  ETS Kit of Factor Reference
    Tests
    and cognitive abilities
      studies, 609, 613, 616,
      618, 621
  Faces Scale
    and job attitudes, 249

Facial Action Coding System (FACS)
and facial expression measurement, 540
Facial Affect Scoring Technique (FAST)
and facial measurement, 538–39
Facial Expression Scoring Manual (FESM)
and facial measurement, 539
fairness models
in personnel selection, 498–500
FIRO-B
and sensitivity training group outcome, 464
GATB
and personnel selection, 513
Goal Attainment Scaling
and small group outcome studies, 473
Graphic Information Processing (GRIP) battery
and cognitive abilities studies, 610
GRE Advanced Psychology test
and creative thinking, 615
Group Atmosphere Scale
and small group methods, 462
Hamilton Rating Scale for Depression
and cognitive therapy, 564
Hebb-Williams mazes
and rearing conditions tests, 132
Index of forecasting efficiency
and personnel selection studies, 493
Index of Organizational Reactions
and job satisfaction, 249
Interaction scoring system
and idiographic process measures, 470
Interpersonal Behavior Scale
and group therapy outcome, 466
IQ (Intelligence Quotient)
black-white differences in, 605, 631–32
and brain maturation spurts, 124
and cognition in young children, 625
criticisms of, 606
and early experience studies, 109, 111

facial expression and intelligence, 549
IQ stability error
and mental illness prevention, 201–2
Job Descriptive Index
and satisfaction, 249
Job Match Index
and personnel selection, 485–86
Koh's blocks
and cross-cultural cognition, 156
Kuder Occupational Interest Survey
and career decision-making, 579
Lashley III maze
and rearing conditions tests, 132
Leader Behavior Description Questionnaire—Form XII
and path-glory theory, 264–65
leadership style measures, 266–67
Least Preferred Coworker (LPC) scale
and leadership effectiveness, 263–64
Life events scales
and psychopathology, 408
Lorge-Thorndike Intelligence Test
and individual differences, 611, 626
Minnesota Multiphasic Personality Inventory (MMPI)
and psychotherapy outcome measures, 472–73
Minnesota Satisfaction Questionnaire
and job attitudes, 249
Morrisby shapes
and cross-cultural cognition, 156
16 Personality Factors
and cognition, 623
Personality Research Form
and group therapy outcome, 466
Personal Orientation Inventory (POI)
and encounter group outcome studies, 464
Position Analysis Questionnaire (PAQ)
and personnel selection studies, 480, 484–85

Posner paradigm
and individual differences studies, 612, 626
Primary Mental Abilities test (PMA)
and aging effects, 628
Raven Progressive Matrices Test
and cognitive ability studies, 608–9, 611–12, 626
and computer cognition modeling, 380
and cross-cultural cognition, 156
Remote Associates Test
and creative thinking, 615
Rod and frame test
and cross-cultural cognition studies, 158
Scholastic Aptitude Test (SAT)
and semantic judgment task, 612
and verbal abilities, 614
SCL-90
and small group outcome studies, 473
Self-Directed Search (SDS)
and career decision-making, 579
removal of masculine terminology from, 583
Self-report measure
of individual differences in learning, 633
Social Desirability Scale
and group therapy outcome, 466
standardized intelligence tests
and broad ability domains, 608–9
Stanford-Binet
and cognitive ability studies, 608
Sternberg STM-search paradigm
and individual differences studies, 612, 626
Strong Vocational Interest Blank
and career counseling, 584, 586
and job satisfaction, 588
System of Interactive Guidance Information (SIGI)
and career maturity, 582
Taste reactivity test
and taste neuropsychology, 314–15
Terminator-remainer battery (TR)
and therapy dropouts, 577

Tests of Scientific Thinking (TST)
and creativity, 615
Turing Test
and computer simulated paranoia, 384
Tyler Vocational Card Sort
and career choice, 586
Uses of Objects
and divergent thinking, 616
Uses and Pattern Meanings test
and creative thinking, 615
Utility Rank Matrix
in equal opportunity assessment, 501
Uzgiris-Hunt scales
and early experience studies, 108–9, 111
verbal analogy tests
and reasoning, 617
Vocational Card Sort (VCS)
and career choice, 583–84, 586
Vocational Preference Inventory
and career counseling, 585
Wechsler Adult Intelligence Scale (WAIS)
and individual differences studies, 608–9, 623
Wechsler Intelligence Scale for Children (WISC)
and individual differences studies, 608, 625, 631
Wickens paradigm
and individual differences studies, 612
T-groups
leader styles in observation and coding of, 469–70
and peer influence studies, 430
Thalamic gustatory relay
and taste neuropsychology, 305–12
Therapist
genuineness and empathy of, 571–72
Therapist-patient relationship
and personal change methods, 456, 468
Therapy
intracounseling behaviors, 570–77
genuineness, warmth, and empathy, 571–72
persistence in treatment, 576–77

self-disclosure, 572–74
social influence, 574–76
Therapy groups
see Small groups; T-groups
Thermodynamics
expert knowledge in and computer simulation modeling, 369
Thinking
creative
measures of, 615–16
reasoning and problem solving
individual differences studies, 616–18
Thirst
see Ingestive behavior
Thought
inferential
and computer simulation modeling, 378
Title VII
of 1964 Civil Rights Amendment
and personnel selection problems, 502–3
Toilet training
and psychosexual development theory, 112
Tone sensation
and binaural hearing, 49–50, 54
and intensity perception, 42–43
and pitch perception, 37–40
Topeka study
of vulnerability, coping, and growth
and mental illness prevention, 193, 198, 201–2
Tower of Hanoi puzzle
see Problems
Trace
in human memory
gaining access to, 85–88, 91, 94, 97
Transactional
models
of psychopathology causation, 399, 404
position
in leadership studies, 268
Transcortical servo hypothesis
in motor organization studies, 335–36
Trauma
infantile
and early experience studies, 115–19
Treatment systems
and sociocultural influences

on psychopathology, 405–6, 409–10
see Counseling
Tremor
behavioral treatment of, 566
Trust
development of
and infancy, 125, 136
Turing Test
see Tests and scales
Twin studies
and early experience effects, 110, 122
Tyler Vocational Card Sort
see Tests and scales
Type A and B persons
and group affiliation under stress, 437

U

UNDERSTAND
computer simulation model
and problem solving, 372, 389
Universality
of facial expression, 529–32
Universals
cognitive
and cross-cultural psychology, 148–54
in memory processes, 161
Urban/rural differences
in short-term memory, 162
Urban stress
and psychopathology, 403
US Administration for Children, Youth, and Families
and services for handicapped, 185
US Army
and personnel selection studies, 510, 513
Uses of Objects test
see Tests and scales
Uses and Pattern Meanings tests
see Tests and scales
Utility
in personnel selection and classification, 493–94
Utility Rank Matrix
see Tests and scales
Uzgiris-Hunt scales
see Tests and scales

V

Vagotomy
and VMH lesions
in ingestive behavior studies, 224, 226

Vai
  literacy in
    and cognitive skills,
      166–67
Validation
  in facial expression
    measurement studies,
      540–45
Validity studies
  in differential psychology,
    632–33
  in personnel selection,
    482–84, 490–92, 496–97
Variability
  cultural
    and cognition theories,
      154–60
Verbal ability
  see Language
Verbal analogy tests
  see Tests and scales
Verbal memory
  interference effects in, 66
Verbal therapy groups
  outcome research reviews of,
    463
Vermont Child Development
    Project
  and psychopathology
    prevention, 188
Vestibulo-ocular reflex (VOR)
  and motor control system
    models, 338–42, 344,
      349–51
Violence
  against children
    and prevention, 175
  televised
    and facial expression
      studies, 549
Vision
  and cognitive abilities
    individual differences in,
      618–21
  critical periods of
    development, 123
  and iconic memory features,
    67–68
  light deprivation effects,
    129–31
  neuroanatomic effects
    and early experiences,
      134–36

neurophysiology of
  and taste studies, 285–87
Visual development
  among infants
    and early experience
      studies, 109–10
    and social responsiveness,
      114, 126
Visual imagery
  and node-link memory
    models, 378
Visual stabilization
  and motor organization
    concepts, 343–44
Visumotor coordination
  and motor organization
    concepts, 352–54,
      357
Vocational Card Sort (VCS)
  see Tests and scales
Vocational choice
  and career counseling,
    583–86
  career orientation, 584
  nontraditional choices,
    583–84
  origins of career choice,
    585–86
  realism, 584
  stability, 585
Vocational counseling
  and personnel selection
    history, 478–79
Vocational Preference
    Inventory
  see Tests and scales
Vocational workshop
  and career decision-making,
    580–81
Völkerpsychologie
  and history of psychology,
    13–14, 24
Vulnerability
  to schizophrenia, 193–98

W

Walking
  and cradling by Hopi
    mothers
    and early experience
      studies, 106

Warmth
  of therapist
    and outcome studies,
      571–72
Weber's Law
  in intensity perception, 42–43
Wechsler Adult Intelligence
    Scale (WAIS)
  see Tests and scales
Wechsler Intelligence Scale for
    Children (WISC)
  see Tests and scales
Weight control
  and counseling, 566, 568–69
Wickens paradigm
  see Tests and scales
Windego
  as culture-specific syndrome,
    401, 412
Withdrawn children
  and social skills training, 557
Women
  attitudes towards counselors,
    575
  discrimination against
    in personnel selection,
      480–81, 496–502,
      505–6, 511
  and facial
    encoding/decoding, 543
  and vocational choice
    and sex-role stereotypes,
      583–85
Words and gestures
  in memory studies, 69–71
Word span
  in memory studies, 75–76
Wundt
  and history of psychology,
    10–17, 21, 23–24, 28

X Y Z

Xylocaine
  and taste neurophysiology
    studies, 308
Yucatan
  memory studies in, 162
Zona incerta (ZI)
  and lesions
    and motivation studies,
      219–20

CUMULATIVE INDEXES

CONTRIBUTING AUTHORS, VOLUMES 26–30

A

Albee, G. W., 26:557–91
Alderfer, C. P., 28:197–223
Alluisi, E. A., 27:305–30
Ash, P., 26:481–507

B

Badin, I. J., 28:175–96
Beck, E. C., 26:233–62
Becker-Haven, J. F., 30:555–602
Bergin, A. E., 26:509–56
Borman, W. C., 30:477–525
Brožek, J., 29:157–77
Burkhart, M. Q., 26:337–66
Burnett, K. F., 30:555–602

C

Campos, J. J., 28:251–93
Carlson, R., 26:393–414
Carroll, J. B., 30:603–40
Cartwright, R. D., 29:223–52
Clark, A. W., 27:405–35
Costa, P. T. Jr., 28:225–49
Cotton, J. W., 27:155–87
Craik, F. I. M., 30:63–102
Cromwell, R. L., 26:593–619

D

Davis, J. H., 27:501–41
deCharms, R., 29:91–113
DeFries, J. C., 29:473–515
Dickinson, A., 29:587–612
Dunnette, M. D., 30:477–525

E

Eagly, A. H., 29:517–54
Ekman, P., 30:527–54
Endicott, J., 26:621–71
Erickson, J. R., 29:61–90
Evarts, E. V., 30:327–62

F

Fischhoff, B., 28:1–39
Fleiss, J. L., 26:621–71
Francès, R., 27:281–304
Frank, C., 30:173–207
Frank, M., 30:283–325

G

Gelman, R., 29:297–332
Ginsburg, H., 27:29–61
Gomes-Schwartz, B., 29:435–71
Greenhaus, J. H., 28:175–96
Gribbin, K., 26:65–96
Grossman, S. P., 30:209–42
Groves, P. M., 27:91–127
Gurland, B., 26:621–71

H

Haber, R. N., 29:31–59
Hadley, S. W., 29:435–71
Haith, M. M., 28:251–93
Hall, D. T., 29:333–72
Hartman, J. J., 30:453–76
Harway-Herman, M., 26:337–66
Heller, F. A., 27:405–35
Helson, R., 29:555–85
Hetherington, E. M., 26:97–136
Hilgard, E. R., 26:19–44
Himmelfarb, S., 29:517–54
Hoffman, M. L., 28:295–321
Horn, J. L., 27:437–85
Hunt, J. McV., 30:103–43
Huston, T. L., 29:115–56

J

Jacobs, G. H., 27:63–89
Jacoby, J., 27:331–58
John, E. R., 29:1–29
Jones, M. R., 29:61–90

K

Kastenbaum, R., 28:225–49
Kelly, J. G., 28:323–61
Kessler, M., 26:557–91
Kiesler, C. A., 26:415–56
Kimmel, M. J., 28:363–92
King, L. M., 29:405–33
Klopfer, W. G., 27:543–67
Komorita, S. S., 27:501–41
Korman, A. K., 28:175–96
Koslowski, B., 27:29–61
Kroeker, L. P., 26:481–507
Krumboltz, J. D., 30:555–602
Kupfermann, I., 26:367–91

L

Laboratory of Comparative Human Cognition, 30:145–72
Lamiell, J. T., 28:113–40
Laughlin, P. R., 27:501–41
Levinger, G., 29:115–56
Lichtenstein, S., 28:1–39
Lieberman, M. A., 27:217–50
Liebert, R. M., 28:141–73
Liebeskind, J. C., 28:41–60
Locke, E. A., 26:457–80
Lott, D. F., 27:129–54
Lumsdaine, A. A., 28:417–59
Lumsden, J., 27:251–80

M

Mackintosh, N. J., 29:587–612
MacLeod, D. I. A., 29:613–45
Mason, W. A., 27:129–54
Maxwell, S. E., 30:603–40
McGlothlin, W. H., 26:45–64
McIntyre, C. W., 26:97–136
Mednick, M. T. S., 26:1–18
Miles, F. A., 30:327–62
Miller, N. E., 29:373–404
Mitchell, T. R., 30:243–81
Mitchell, V., 29:555–85

Morgan, B. B. Jr., 27:305–30
Mueller, C. G., 30:9–29
Muir, M. S., 29:91–113
Muñoz, R. F., 28:323–61
Munson, P. A., 26:415–56
Murphy, L. B., 30:173–207

N

Neimark, E. D., 26:173–205
Norgren, R., 30:283–325

O

Oster, H., 30:527–54

P

Paul, L. A., 28:41–60
Perloff, E., 27:569–94
Perloff, R., 27:569–94
Peterson, L. R., 28:393–415
Pfaffmann, C., 30:283–325
Phares, E. J., 28:113–40
Piaget, J., 30:1–8
Plomin, R., 29:473–515
Plomp, L., 26:207–32
Postman, L., 26:291–335
Pruitt, D. G., 28:363–92

R

Rebec, G. V., 27:91–127
Reitan, R. M., 27:189–216
Reynolds, W. M., 29:
    179–221
Robinson, D. E., 30:31–61
Rusak, B., 26:137–71

S

Salzinger, K., 26:621–71
Santa, J. L., 26:173–205
Schaie, K. W., 26:65–96
Schwartz, E. L., 29:1–29
Schwartzberg, N. S., 28:
    141–73
Schwartzkopff, J., 28:61–84
Sechrest, L., 27:1–27
Simon, H. A., 30:363–96
Slovic, P., 28:1–39
Smith, J. E. K., 27:487–99
Snowden, L. R., 28:323–61;
    29:179–221
Sokolov, E. N., 28:85–112
Spitzer, R. L., 26:621–71
Stokols, D., 29:253–95
Strauss, J. S., 30:397–415

Strupp, H. H., 29:435–71
Suinn, R. M., 26:509–56
Sundberg, N. D., 29:179–221
Super, D. E., 29:333–72
Sussna, E., 27:569–94
Sutton, S., 26:621–71

T

Tapp, J. L., 27:359–404
Taulbee, E. S., 27:543–67
Trahiotis, C., 30:31–61

W

Webb, W. B., 29:223–52
Weintraub, D. J., 26:263–89
Weissman, H. J., 26:1–18
Whiteley, J. M., 26:337–66
Whiteley, R. M., 26:337–66
Winer, B. J., 29:647–81
Wittrock, M. C., 28:417–59

Z

Zander, A., 30:417–51
Zubin, J., 26:621–71
Zucker, L., 26:137–71

CHAPTER TITLES, VOLUMES 26–30

PREFATORY CHAPTER
Relations Between Psychology and Other
  Sciences   J. Piaget   30:1–8
BIOLOGICAL PSYCHOLOGY
Electrophysiology and Behavior   E. C. Beck   26:233–62
Neurophysiology of Learning   I. Kupfermann   26:367–91
Biochemistry and Behavior: Some Central
  Actions of Amphetamine and Antipsychotic
  Drugs   P. M. Groves, G. V. Rebec   27:91–127
Brain Functions: Neuronal Mechanisms of
  Learning and Memory   E. N. Sokolov   28:85–112
The Neurophysiology of Information
  Processing and Cognition   E. R. John, E. L. Schwartz   29:1–29
Nutrition, Malnutrition, and Behavior   J. Brožek   29:157–77
Sleep and Dreams   W. B. Webb, R. C. Cartwright   29:223–52
Behavioral Genetics   J. C. DeFries, R. Plomin   29:473–515
Concepts of Motor Organization   F. A. Miles, E. V. Evarts   30:327–62

CHEMICAL SENSES
See RECEPTOR PROCESSES

CLINICAL PSYCHOLOGY: DIAGNOSIS AND TREATMENT
Individual Psychotherapy and Behavior
  Therapy   A. E. Bergin, R. M. Suinn   26:509–56
Primary Prevention   M. Kessler, G. W. Albee   26:557–91
Assessment of Schizophrenia   R. L. Cromwell   26:593–619
Change Induction in Small Groups   M. A. Lieberman   27:217–50
Projective Tests   W. G. Klopfer, E. S. Taulbee   27:543–67
Social and Community Interventions   J. G. Kelly, L. R. Snowden, R. F.
                                          Munoz   28:323–61
Toward Assessment of Personal Competence
  and Incompetence in Life Situations   N. D. Sundberg, L. R. Snowden,
                                          W. M. Reynolds   29:179–221
Individual Psychotherapy and Behavior
  Therapy   B. Gomes-Schwartz, S. W. Hadley,
                                          H. H. Strupp   29:435–71
Prevention: The Clinical Psychologist   L. B. Murphy, C. Frank   30:173–207
Small Group Methods of Personal Change J. J. Hartman   30:453–76
See also PSYCHOPATHOLOGY

COGNITIVE PROCESSES
Thinking and Concept Attainment   E. D. Neimark, J. L. Santa   26:173–205
Behavioral Decision Theory   P. Slovic, B. Fischhoff, S.
                                          Lichtenstein   28:1–39
Thinking   J. R. Erickson, M. R. Jones   29:61–90
Cognitive Development   R. Gelman   29:297–332
Information Processing Models of Cognition H. A. Simon   30:363–96

COMPARATIVE PSYCHOLOGY, ETHOLOGY, AND ANIMAL BEHAVIOR
Ethology and Comparative Psychology   W. A. Mason, D. F. Lott   27:129–54

COUNSELING
See EDUCATION AND COUNSELING

DEVELOPMENTAL PSYCHOLOGY
Developmental Psychology   E. M. Hetherington, C. W.
                                          McIntyre   26:97–136
Adult Development and Aging   K. W. Schaie, K. Gribbin   26:65–96

Cognitive Development | H. Ginsburg, B. Koslowski | 27:29–61
Human Infancy | M. M. Haith, J. J. Campos | 28:251–93
Personality and Social Development | M. L. Hoffman | 28:295–321
Cognitive Development | R. Gelman | 29:297–332
Psychological Development: Early Experience | J. McV. Hunt | 30:103–43

EDUCATION AND COUNSELING
Counseling and Student Development | J. M. Whiteley, M. Q. Burkhart, M. Harway-Herman, R. M. Whiteley | 26:337–66
Human Abilities: A Review of Research and Theory in the Early 1970s | J. L. Horn | 27:437–85
Instructional Psychology | M. C. Wittrock, A. A. Lumsdaine | 28:417–59
Career Development: Exploration and Planning | D. E. Super, D. T. Hall | 29:333–72
Counseling Psychology | J. D. Krumboltz, J. F. Becker-Haven, K. R. Burnett | 30:555–602

ENVIRONMENTAL PSYCHOLOGY
See SOCIAL PSYCHOLOGY

GENETICS OF BEHAVIOR
See BIOLOGICAL PSYCHOLOGY

GERONTOLOGY (MATURITY AND AGING)
See DEVELOPMENTAL PSYCHOLOGY

HEARING
See RECEPTOR PROCESSES

HYPNOSIS
Hypnosis | E. R. Hilgard | 26:19–44

INDUSTRIAL PSYCHOLOGY
See PERSONNEL-ORGANIZATIONAL PSYCHOLOGY

LEARNING AND MEMORY
Verbal Learning and Memory | L. Postman | 26:291–335
Neurophysiology of Learning | I. Kupfermann | 26:367–91
Models of Learning | J. W. Cotton | 27:155–87
Brain Functions: Neuronal Mechanisms of Learning and Memory | E. N. Sokolov | 28:85–112
Verbal Learning and Memory | L. R. Peterson | 28:393–415
The Neurophysiology of Information Processing and Cognition | E. R. John, E. L. Schwartz | 29:1–29
Biofeedback and Visceral Learning | N. E. Miller | 29:373–404
Classical Conditioning in Animals | A. Dickinson, N. J. Mackintosh | 29:587–612
Human Memory | F. I. M. Craik | 30:63–102

MOTIVATION
Biological Rhythms and Animal Behavior | B. Rusak, I. Zucker | 26:137–71
Motivation: Social Approaches | R. deCharms, M. S. Muir | 29:91–113
The Biology of Motivation | S. P. Grossman | 30:209–42

PERCEPTION
Perception | D. J. Weintraub | 26:363–89
Visual Perception | R. N. Haber | 29:31–59

PERSONALITY
Personality | R. Carlson | 26:393–414
Personality | L. Sechrest | 27:1–27
Personality | E. J. Phares; J. T. Lamiell | 28:113–40
Toward Assessment of Personal Competence and Incompetence in Life Situations | N. D. Sundberg, L. R. Snowden, W. M. Reynolds | 29:179–221
Personality | R. Helson, V. Mitchell | 29:555–85
Individual Differences in Cognitive Abilities | J. B. Carroll, S. E. Maxwell | 30:603–40

PERSONNEL-ORGANIZATIONAL PSYCHOLOGY
Personnel Attitudes and Motivation   E. A. Locke   26:457–80
Personnel Selection, Classification, and
    Placement   P. Ash, L. P. Kroeker   26:481–507
Engineering Psychology and Human
    Performance   E. A. Alluisi, B. B. Morgan Jr.   27:305–30
Consumer Psychology: An Octennium   J. Jacoby   27:331–58
Personnel and Human Resources
    Development   F. A. Heller, A. W. Clark   27:405–35
Personnel Attitudes and Motivation   A. K. Korman, J. H. Greenhaus,
        I. J. Badin   28:175–96
Organization Development   C. P. Alderfer   28:197–223
Organizational Behavior   T. R. Mitchell   30:243–81
Personnel Selection and Classification
    Systems   M. D. Dunnette, W. C. Borman   30:477–525

PSYCHOLINGUISTICS
See COGNITIVE PROCESSES

PSYCHOLOGY IN FRANCE
Psychology in France   R. Francès   27:281–304

PSYCHOPATHOLOGY
Biometric Approach to Psychopathology:
    Abnormal and Clinical Psychology—
    Statistical, Epidemiological, and Diagnostic
    Approaches   J. Zubin, K. Salzinger, J. L. Fleiss,
        B. Gurland, R. L. Spitzer,
        J. Endicott, S. Sutton   26:621–71
Neurological and Physiological Bases of
    Psychopathology   R. M. Reitan   27:189–216
Social and Cultural Influences on
    Psychopathology   L. M. King   29:405–33
Social and Cultural Influences on
    Psychopathology   J. S. Strauss   30:397–415
See also CLINICAL PSYCHOLOGY: DIAGNOSIS AND TREATMENT

PSYCHOPHARMACOLOGY
See BIOLOGICAL PSYCHOLOGY

RECEPTOR PROCESSES
Somesthesis   J. F. Hahn   25:233–46
Auditory Psychophysics   R. Plomp   26:207–32
Color Vision   G. H. Jacobs   27:63–89
Auditory Communication in Lower Animals:
    Role of Auditory Physiology   J. Schwartzkopff   28:61–84
Visual Sensitivity   D. I. A. MacLeod   29:613–45
Auditory Psychophysics   C. Trahiotis, D. E. Robinson   30:31–61
Neural Mechanisms and Behavioral Aspects
    of Taste   C. Pfaffmann, M. Frank,
        R. Norgren   30:283–325

RESEARCH METHODOLOGY
Test Theory   J. Lumsden   27:251–80
Analysis of Qualitative Data   J. E. K. Smith   27:487–99
Statistics and Data Analysis: Trading Bias for
    Reduced Mean Squared Error   B. J. Winer   29:647–81

SLEEP
See BIOLOGICAL PSYCHOLOGY

SOCIAL PSYCHOLOGY
Attitudes and Opinions   C. A. Kiesler, P. A. Munson   26:415–55
The Social Psychology of Small Groups:
    Cooperative and Mixed-Motive Interaction   J. H. Davis, P. R. Laughlin,
        S. S. Komorita   27:501–41

Effects of Mass Media | R. M. Liebert, N. S. Schwartzberg | 28:141–73
Interpersonal Attraction and Relationships | T. L. Huston, G. Levinger | 29:115–56
Environmental Psychology | D. Stokols | 29:253–95
Attitudes and Opinions | A. H. Eagly, S. Himmelfarb | 29:517–54
What's Cultural About Cross-Cultural
Cognitive Psychology? | Laboratory of Comparative Human
Cognition | 30:145–72
The Psychology of Group Processes | A. Zander | 30:417–51

SPECIAL TOPICS

The Psychology of Women—Selected Topics | M. T. S. Mednick, H. J.
Weissman | 26:1–18
Drug Use and Abuse | W. H. McGlothlin | 26:45–64
Psychology and the Law: An Overture | J. L. Tapp | 27:359–404
Program Evaluation | R. Perloff, E. Perloff, E. Sussna | 27:569–94
Psychological and Physiological Mechanisms
of Pain | J. C. Liebeskind, L. A. Paul | 28:41–60
Psychological Perspectives on Death | R. Kastenbaum, P. T. Costa Jr. | 28:225–49
Twenty Years of Experimental Gaming:
Critique, Synthesis, and Suggestions for the
Future | D. G. Pruitt, M. J. Kimmel | 28:363–92
Nutrition, Malnutrition, and Behavior | J. Brožek | 29:157–77
Biofeedback and Visceral Learning | N. E. Miller | 29:373–404
Some Origins of Psychology As Science | C. G. Mueller | 30:9–29
Facial Expressions of Emotion | P. Ekman, H. Oster | 30:527–54

VISION
See RECEPTOR PROCESSES

CHAPTERS PLANNED FOR THE NEXT
ANNUAL REVIEW OF PSYCHOLOGY

Volume 31 (1980)

CHANGES IN CONCEPTS OF CONSCIOUSNESS, *Ernest R. Hilgard*

CHEMISTRY OF MOOD AND EMOTION, *Patrick L. McGeer*

VISION, *Russell DeValois and Karen DeValois*

PERCEPTION, *Gunnar Johansson*

PSYCHOLINGUISTICS, *Sam Glucksberg and Joseph H. Danks*

NEUROCHEMISTRY OF LEARNING AND MEMORY, *Adrian J. Dunn*

ELECTROPHYSIOLOGY AND BEHAVIOR, *Donald B. Lindsley*

SOCIAL MOTIVATION, *Nathan Brody*

COMPARATIVE PSYCHOLOGY, ETHOLOGY, AND ANIMAL BEHAVIOR,
Stephen E. Glickman and Paul W. Sherman

COGNITION AND PERSONALITY, *Walter Mischel and Nancy Cantor*

LIFE-SPAN DEVELOPMENTAL PSYCHOLOGY, *Paul B. Baltes and Gisela
Labouvie-Vief*

PERSONALITY STRUCTURE AND ASSESSMENT, *Douglas N. Jackson and
Sampo V. Paunonen*

BIOLOGICAL PSYCHOPATHOLOGY, *Fini Schulsinger*

SOCIAL AND COMMUNITY INTERVENTIONS, *Bernard L. Bloom*

ATTRIBUTION RESEARCH IN SOCIAL PSYCHOLOGY, *Harold H. Kelley
and John Michela*

PERSONNEL DEVELOPMENT AND TRAINING, *Irwin L. Goldstein*

THE SCHOOL AS A SOCIAL SITUATION, *Paul V. Gump*

MULTIVARIATE ANALYSIS, *Peter M. Bentler*

MULTIDIMENSIONAL SCALING, *J. Douglas Carroll*

EVALUATION RESEARCH, *Gene V. Glass*

SOCIAL DILEMMAS, *Robyn M. Dawes*

Please list on the order blank on the reverse side the volumes you wish to order and
whether you wish a standing order (the latest volume sent to you automatically upon
publication each year). Volumes not yet published will be shipped in month and year
indicated. Prices subject to change without notice. Out of print volumes subject
to special order.

NEW.... to be published in 1980

ANNUAL REVIEW OF PUBLIC HEALTH
$17.00 per copy ($17.50 outside USA)

Volume 1 available May 1980

SPECIAL PUBLICATIONS

ANNUAL REVIEW REPRINTS: CELL MEMBRANES, 1975-1977 (published 1978)
A collection of articles reprinted from recent Annual Review series.
Soft cover $12.00 per copy ($12.50 outside USA)

THE EXCITEMENT AND FASCINATION OF SCIENCE (published 1965)
A collection of autobiographical and philosophical articles by leading scientists.
Clothbound $6.50 per copy ($7.00 outside USA)

THE EXCITEMENT AND FASCINATION OF SCIENCE, VOLUME 2:
Reflections by Eminent Scientists (published 1978)
Hard cover $12.00 per copy ($12.50 outside USA)
Soft cover $10.00 per copy ($10.50 outside USA)

HISTORY OF ENTOMOLOGY (published 1973)
A special supplement to the ANNUAL REVIEW OF ENTOMOLOGY series.
Clothbound $10.00 per copy ($10.50 outside USA)

ANNUAL REVIEW SERIES

Annual Review of ANTHROPOLOGY $17.00 per copy ($17.50 outside USA)
Volumes 1-7 (1972-1978) currently available   Volume 8 available October 1979

Annual Review of ASTRONOMY AND ASTROPHYSICS $17.00 per copy ($17.50 outside USA)
Volumes 1-16 (1963-1978) currently available Volume 17 available September 1979

Annual Review of BIOCHEMISTRY $18.00 per copy ($18.50 outside USA)
Volumes 28-47 (1959-1978) currently available Volume 48 available July 1979

Annual Review of BIOPHYSICS AND BIOENGINEERING $17.00 per copy ($17.50 outside USA)
Volumes 1-7 (1972-1978) currently available   Volume 8 available June 1979

Annual Review of EARTH AND PLANETARY SCIENCES $17.00 per copy ($17.50 outside USA)
Volumes 1-6 (1973-1978) currently available   Volume 7 available May 1979

Annual Review of ECOLOGY AND SYSTEMATICS $17.00 per copy ($17.50 outside USA)
Volumes 1-9 (1970-1978) currently available   Volume 10 available November 1979

Annual Review of ENERGY $17.00 per copy ($17.50 outside USA)
Volumes 1-3 (1976-1978) currently available   Volume 4 available October 1979

Annual Review of ENTOMOLOGY $17.00 per copy ($17.50 outside USA)
Volumes 7-23 (1962-1978) currently available Volume 24 available January 1979

Annual Review of FLUID MECHANICS $17.00 per copy ($17.50 outside USA)
Volumes 1-10 (1969-1978) currently available Volume 11 available January 1979

(continued on reverse side)

Annual Review of GENETICS	$17.00 per copy ($17.50 outside USA)
Volumes 1-12 (1967-1978) currently available	Volume 13 available December 1979
Annual Review of MATERIALS SCIENCE	$17.00 per copy ($17.50 outside USA)
Volumes 1-8 (1971-1978) currently available	Volume 9 available August 1979
Annual Review of MEDICINE: Selected Topics in the Clinical Sciences	$17.00 per copy ($17.50 outside USA)
Volumes 1-3, 5-15, 17-29 (1950-1952, 1954-1964, 1966-1978) currently available	Volume 30 available April 1979
Annual Review of MICROBIOLOGY	$17.00 per copy ($17.50 outside USA)
Volumes 14-32 (1960-1978) currently available	Volume 33 available October 1979
Annual Review of NEUROSCIENCE	$17.00 per copy ($17.50 outside USA)
Volume 1 currently available	Volume 2 available March 1979
Annual Review of NUCLEAR AND PARTICLE SCIENCE	$19.50 per copy ($20.00 outside USA)
Volumes 9-28 (1959-1978) currently available	Volume 29 available December 1979
Annual Review of PHARMACOLOGY AND TOXICOLOGY	$17.00 per copy ($17.50 outside USA)
Volumes 1-3, 5-18 (1961-1963, 1965-1978) currently available	Volume 19 available April 1979
Annual Review of PHYSICAL CHEMISTRY	$17.00 per copy ($17.50 outside USA)
Volumes 9-29 (1958-1978) currently available	Volume 30 available November 1979
Annual Review of PHYSIOLOGY	$17.00 per copy ($17.50 outside USA)
Volumes 19-40 (1957-1978) currently available	Volume 41 available March 1979
Annual Review of PHYTOPATHOLOGY	$17.00 per copy ($17.50 outside USA)
Volumes 1-16 (1963-1978) currently available	Volume 17 available September 1979
Annual Review of PLANT PHYSIOLOGY	$17.00 per copy ($17.50 outside USA)
Volumes 10-29 (1959-1978) currently available	Volume 30 available June 1979
Annual Review of PSYCHOLOGY	$17.00 per copy ($17.50 outside USA)
Volumes 4, 5, 8, 10-29 (1953, 1954, 1957, 1959-1978) currently available	Volume 30 available February 1979
Annual Review of SOCIOLOGY	$17.00 per copy ($17.50 outside USA)
Volumes 1-4 (1975-1978) currently available	Volume 5 available August 1979

To ANNUAL REVIEWS INC., 4139 El Camino Way, Palo Alto, CA 94306 USA (415-493-4400)

Please enter my order for the following publications:
(Standing orders: indicate which volume you wish order to begin with)

_____, Vol(s). _____   Standing order _____

_____, Vol(s). _____   Standing order _____

_____, Vol(s). _____   Standing order _____

_____, Vol(s). _____   Standing order _____

Amount of remittance enclosed $_____   California residents please add sales tax.
Please bill me for the amount $_____   Prices subject to change without notice.

SHIP TO   ·   BILL TO (include institutional purchase order)

Name _____   Name _____

Address _____   Address _____

_____ Postal code ____   _____ Postal code ____

Signed _____ Date _____   Signed _____ Date _____

___ Send free copy of annual Prospectus for current year
___ Send free back contents brochure for Annual Review(s) of _____